DATE DUE

			PRINTED IN U.S.A.

Literature Criticism from 1400 to 1800

Guide to Gale Literary Criticism Series

For criticism on	Consult these Gale series
Authors now living or who died after December 31, 1959	*CONTEMPORARY LITERARY CRITICISM (CLC)*
Authors who died between 1900 and 1959	*TWENTIETH-CENTURY LITERARY CRITICISM (TCLC)*
Authors who died between 1800 and 1899	*NINETEENTH-CENTURY LITERATURE CRITICISM (NCLC)*
Authors who died between 1400 and 1799	*LITERATURE CRITICISM FROM 1400 TO 1800 (LC)* *SHAKESPEAREAN CRITICISM (SC)*
Authors who died before 1400	*CLASSICAL AND MEDIEVAL LITERATURE CRITICISM (CMLC)*
Black writers of the past two hundred years	*BLACK LITERATURE CRITICISM (BLC)*
Authors of books for children and young adults	*CHILDREN'S LITERATURE REVIEW (CLR)*
Dramatists	*DRAMA CRITICISM (DC)*
Hispanic writers of the late nineteenth and twentieth centuries	*HISPANIC LITERATURE CRITICISM (HLC)*
Native North American writers and orators of the eighteenth, nineteenth, and twentieth centuries	*NATIVE NORTH AMERICAN LITERATURE (NNAL)*
Poets	*POETRY CRITICISM (PC)*
Short story writers	*SHORT STORY CRITICISM (SSC)*
Major authors from the Renaissance to the present	*WORLD LITERATURE CRITICISM, 1500 TO THE PRESENT (WLC)*

ISSN 0740-2880

Volume 35

Literature Criticism from 1400 to 1800

Critical Discussion of the Works
of Fifteenth-, Sixteenth-, Seventeenth-, and
Eighteenth-Century Novelists, Poets, Playwrights,
Philosophers, and Other Creative Writers

Jelena O. Krstović, Editor

GALE

DETROIT • NEW YORK • TORONTO • LONDON

STAFF

Jelena O. Krstović, *Editor*

Gerald R. Barterian, *Associate Editor*

Susan M. Trosky, *Managing Editor*

Marlene S. Hurst, *Permissions Manager*
Margaret A. Chamberlain, Maria Franklin, Kimberly F. Smilay, *Permissions Specialists*
Diane Cooper, Edna Hedblad, Michele Lonoconus, Maureen Puhl, Susan Salas, Shalice Shah, *Permissions Associates*
Sarah Chesney, Jeffrey Hermann, *Permissions Assistants*

Victoria B. Cariappa, *Research Manager*
Laura Bissey, Julia C. Daniel, Tammy Nott, Michele Pica, Tracie A. Richardson, Cheryl Warnock, *Research Associates*
Sean Smith, Alfred Gardner, *Research Assistants*

Mary Beth Trimper, *Production Director*
Deborah Milliken, *Production Assistant*

Sherrell Hobbs, *Macintosh Artist*
Pamela A. Hayes, *Photography Coordinator*
Randy Bassett, *Image Database Supervisor*
Mikal Ansari, Robert Duncan, *Scanner Operators*

∞™ This book is printed on acid-free paper that meets the minimum requirements of American National Standard for Information Sciences—Permanence Paper for Printed Library Materials, ANSI Z39.48-1984.

Library of Congress Catalog Card Number 94-29718
ISBN 0-8103-9977-6
ISSN 0740-2880
Printed in the United States of America

10 9 8 7 6 5 4 3 2 1

Contents

Preface   vii

Acknowledgments   xi

Preface

L iterature Criticism from 1400 to 1800 (LC) presents critical discussion of world authors of the fifteenth through eighteenth centuries. The literature of this period reflects a turbulent time of radical change that saw the rise of modern European drama, the birth of the novel and personal essay forms, the emergence of newspapers and periodicals, and major achievements in poetry and philosophy. Many of these historical forces continue to influence modern art and society. *LC,* therefore, provides valuable insight into the art, life, thought, and cultural transformations that took place during these centuries.

Scope of the Series

LC provides an introduction to the great poets, dramatists, novelists, essayists, and philosophers of the fifteenth through eighteenth centuries, and to the most significant interpretations of these authors' works. Because criticism of this literature spans nearly six hundred years, an overwhelming amount of scholarship confronts the student. *LC* organizes this material into volumes addressing specific historical and cultural topics, for example, "Literature of the Spanish Golden Age," or "Literature and the New World." Every attempt is made to reprint the most noteworthy, relevant, and educationally valuable essays available.

Readers should note that there is a separate Gale reference series devoted exclusively to Shakespearean studies. Although belonging properly to the period covered in *LC,* William Shakespeare has inspired such a tremendous and ever-growing corpus of secondary material that the editors have deemed it best to give his works extensive coverage in a separate series, *Shakespearean Criticism.*

Each author entry in *LC* presents a survey of critical response to a topic or an author's oeuvre. Early criticism is offered to indicate initial responses, later selections document any rise or decline in literary reputations, and retrospective analyses provide students with modern views. The size of each author entry is a relative reflection of the scope of criticism available in English. Every attempt has been made to identify and include the seminal essays on each author's work and to include recent commentary providing modern perspectives.

The need for *LC* among students and teachers of literature and history was suggested by the proven usefulness of Gale's *Contemporary Literary Criticism (CLC), Twentieth-Century Literary Criticism (TCLC),* and *Nineteenth-Century Literature Criticism (NCLC),* which excerpt criticism of works by nineteenth- and twentieth-century authors. There is no duplication of critical material in any of these literary criticism series. Major authors may appear more than once in one or more of the series because of the great quantity of critical material available and because of their relevance to a variety of thematic topics.

Thematic Approach

Beginning with Volume 12, the authors in each volume of *LC* are organized around such themes as specific literary or philosophical movements, writings surrounding important political and historical events, the philosophy and art associated with eras of cultural transformation, and the literature of specific social or ethnic groups. Each volume contains a topic entry providing a historical and literary overview, and several author entries which examine major representatives of the featured period.

Organization of the Book

Each entry consists of the following elements: author or thematic heading, introduction, list of principal works, annotated works of criticism (each preceded by a bibliographical citation), and a bibliography of further reading. Also, most author entries contain author portraits and other illustrations.

- The **Author Heading** consists of the author's name (the most commonly used form), followed by birth and death dates. (If an author wrote consistently under a pseudonym, the pseudonym is used in the author heading, with the real name given in parentheses on the first line of the biographical and critical introduction.) Also located here are any name variations under which an author wrote, including transliterated forms for authors whose native languages use nonroman alphabets. Uncertain birth or death dates are indicated by question marks. Topic entries are preceded by a **Thematic Heading,** which simply states the subject of the entry.

- The **Biographical and Critical Introduction** contains background information that concisely introduces the reader to the author or topic.

- Most *LC* author entries include **Portraits** of the author. Many entries also contain illustrations of materials pertinent to an author's career, including author holographs, title pages, letters, or representations of important people, places, and events in an author's life.

- The **List of Principal Works** is ordered chronologically, by date of first book publication, identifying the genre of each work. In the case of foreign authors whose works have been translated into English, the title and date (if available) of the first English-language edition are given in brackets following the foreign-language listing. Unless otherwise indicated, dramas are dated by first performance, not first publication.

- **Criticism** is arranged chronologically in each author entry to provide a useful perspective on changes in critical evaluation over time. For the purpose of easy identification, the critic's name and the date of first composition or publication of the critical work are given at the beginning of each piece of criticism. Unsigned criticism is preceded by the title of the source in which it appeared. All titles by the author featured in the critical entry are printed in boldface type. Publication information (such as publisher names and book prices) and some parenthetical numerical references (such as footnotes or page and line references to specific editions of works) have been occasionally deleted to provide smoother reading of the text.

- Critical essays are prefaced by **Annotations** as an additional aid to students using *LC*. These explanatory notes provide information such as the importance of a work of criticism, the commentator's individual approach to literary criticism, and a brief summary of the reprinted essay. In some cases, these notes cross-reference the work of critics within the entry who agree or disagree with each other.

- A complete **Bibliographical Citation** of the original essay or book precedes each piece of criticism.

■ An annotated bibliography of **Further Reading** appears at the end of each entry and suggests resources for additional study. In some cases, significant essays for which the editors could not obtain reprint rights are included here.

Cumulative Indexes

Each volume of *LC* includes a cumulative **Author Index** listing all the authors that have appeared in the following sources published by Gale: *Contemporary Literary Criticism, Twentieth-Century Literary Criticism, Nineteenth-Century Literature Criticism, Literature Criticism from 1400 to 1800,* and *Classical and Medieval Literature Criticism,* along with cross-references to the Gale series *Short Story Criticism, Poetry Criticism, Children's Literature Review, Authors in the News, Contemporary Authors, Contemporary Authors Autobiography Series, Contemporary Authors Bibliographical Series, Dictionary of Literary Biography, Concise Dictionary of Literary Biography, Something about the Author, Something about the Author Autobiography Series,* and *Yesterday's Authors of Books for Children.* Readers will welcome this cumulative author index as a useful tool for locating an author within the various series. The index, which includes authors' birth and death dates, is particularly valuable for those authors who are identified with a certain period but whose death dates cause them to be placed in another, or for those authors whose careers span two periods. For example, F. Scott Fitzgerald is found in *TCLC,* yet a writer often associated with him, Ernest Hemingway, is found in *CLC.*

Beginning with Volume 12, *LC* includes a cumulative **Topic Index** that lists all literary themes and topics treated in *LC, NCLC, TCLC,* and the *CLC* Yearbook. Each volume of *LC* also includes a cumulative **Nationality Index** in which authors' names are arranged alphabetically under their respective nationalities and followed by the numbers of the volumes in which they appear.

Each volume of *LC* also includes a cumulative **Title Index,** an alphabetical listing of all literary works discussed in the series. Each title listing includes the corresponding volume and page numbers where criticism may be located. Foreign-language titles that have been translated followed by the tiles of the translation—for example, *El ingenioso hidalgo Don Quixote de la Mancha (Don Quixote).* Page numbers following these translated titles refer to all pages on which any form of the titles, either foreign-language or translated, appear. Titles of novels, dramas, nonfiction books, and poetry, short story, or essays collections are printed in italics, while individual poems, short stories, and essays are printed in roman type within quotation marks.

A Note to the Reader

When writing papers, students who quote directly from any volume in the Literary Criticism Series may use the following general format to footnote reprinted criticism. The first example pertains to material drawn from periodicals, the second to material reprinted from books.

T. S. Eliot, "John Donne," *The Nation and the Athenaeum,* 33 (9 June 1923), 321-32; excerpted and reprinted in *Literature Criticism from 1400 to 1800,* Vol. 10, ed. James E. Person, Jr. (Detroit: Gale Research, 1989), pp. 28-9.

Clara G. Stillman, *Samuel Butler: A Mid-Victorian Modern* (Viking Press, 1932); excerpted and reprinted in *Twentieth-Century Literary Criticism,* Vol. 33, ed. Paula Kepos (Detroit: Gale

Research, 1989), pp. 43-5.

Suggestions Are Welcome

Since the series began, features have been added to *LC* in response to various suggestions, including a nationality index, a Literary Criticism Series topic index, and thematic organization of entries.

Readers who wish to suggest new features, themes or authors to appear in future volumes, or who have other suggestions or comments are cordially invited to write to the editor (fax: 313 961-6599).

Acknowledgments

The editors wish to thank the copyright holders of the excerpted criticism included in this volume and the permissions managers of many book and magazine publishing companies for assisting us in securing reproduction rights. We are also grateful to the staffs of the Detroit Public Library, the Library of Congress, the University of Detroit Library, Wayne State University Purdy/Kresge Library Complex, and the University of Michigan Libraries for making their resources available to us. Following is a list of the copyright holders who have granted us permission to reproduce material in this volume of *LC*. Every effort has been made to trace copyright, but if omissions have been made, please let us know.

COPYRIGHTED EXCERPTS IN *LC*, VOLUME 35, WERE REPRODUCED FROM THE FOLLOWING PERIODICALS:

Journal of the History of Ideas, v. XLVIII, January-March, 1987; v. LIV, January, 1993. Copyright 1987, 1993, Journal of the History of Ideas, Inc. Both reproduced by permission of The Johns Hopkins University Press.—*Queen's Quarterly,* v. 95, Spring, 1988 for "Newton and the Scientific Revolution" by Richard S. Westfall. Copyright © 1988 by the author. Reproduced by permission of the Literary Estate of Richard S. Westfall.—*Restoration: Studies in English Literary Culture, 1660-1700,* v. 13, Spring, 1989 for "Isaac Newton's Theological Writings: Problems and Prospects" by Robert Markley. Copyright © 1989 The University of Tennessee, Knoxville. Reproduced by permission of the publisher and the author.—*Ultimate Reality and Meaning,* v. 3, 1980. Reproduced by permission.

COPYRIGHTED EXCERPTS IN *LC*, VOLUME 35, WERE REPRODUCED FROM THE FOLLOWING BOOKS:

Adamson, Donald. From *Blaise Pascal: Mathematician, Physicist and Thinker about God.* St. Martin's Press, 1995. © Donald Adamson 1995. All rights reserved. Reproduced by permission of Macmillan, London and Basingstoke. In the U. S. with permission of St. Martin's Press, Incorporated.—Ayers, Michael. From *Locke Vol. II: Ontology.* Routledge, 1991. © 1991 Michael Ayers. All rights reserved. Reproduced by permission.—Beyssade, Jean-Marie. From "On the Idea of God: Incomprehensibility of Incompatibilities?" translated by Charles Paul, in *Essays on the Philosophy and Science of René Descartes.* Edited by Stephen Voss. Oxford University Press, 1993. Copyright © 1993 by S. Voss. Reproduced by permission of Oxford University Press, Inc.—Burtt, Edwin Arthur. From *The Metaphysical Foundations of Modern Physical Science: A Historical and Critical Essay.* Kegan Paul, Trench, Trubner & Co., Ltd., 1925. Reproduced by permission of the Literary Estate of Edwin Arthur Burtt.—Clarke, Desmond M. From "Descartes' Philosophy of Science and the Scientific Revolution," in *The Cambridge Companion to Descartes.* Edited by John Cottingham. Cambridge University Press, 1992. © Cambridge University Press 1992. Reproduced with the permission of the publisher and the author.—Couturat, Louis. From "On Leibniz's Metaphysics," translated by R. Allison Ryan, in *Leibniz: A Collection of Critical Essays.* Edited by Harry G. Frankfurt. Anchor Books, 1972. Copyright © 1972 by Harry G. Frankfurt. All rights reserved. Used by permission of Doubleday, a division of Bantam Doubleday Dell Publishing Group, Inc.—Debus, Allen G. From *Man and Nature in the Renaissance.* Cambridge University Press, 1978. © Cambridge University Press 1978. Reproduced with the permission of the publisher and the author.—Dobbs, Betty Jo Teeter, and Margaret C. Jacob. From *Newton and the Culture of Newtonianism.* Humanities Press, 1995. © 1995 by Betty Jo Teeter Dobbs and Margaret C. Jacob. All rights reserved. Reproduced by permission of Humanities Press Inc., Atlantic Highlands, NJ 07716.—Garber, Daniel. From "Science and Certainty in Descartes," in *Descartes: Critical and Interpretive Essays.* Edited by Michael Hooker. The Johns Hopkins University Press, 1978. Copyright © 1978 by The Johns Hopkins University Press. All rights reserved. Reproduced by permission.—Home, R. W. From "Force, Electricity, and the Powers of Living Matter in Newton's Mature Philosophy of Nature," in *Religion, Science, and Worldview: Essays in Honor of Richard S. Westfall.* Edited by Margaret J. Osler and Paul Lawrence Farber. Cambridge University Press, 1985. © Cambridge University Press 1985. Reproduced with the permission of the publisher and the author.—Kolakowski, Leszek. From *God Owes Us Nothing: A Brief Remark on Pascal's Religion and on the Spirit of Jansenism.* University of Chicago Press, 1995. © 1995 by The University of Chicago Press. All rights reserved.

Newton, Isaac, painting. The Library of Congress.
Pascal, Blaise, photograph of painting. The Library of Congress.

Renaissance Scientific Movement

INTRODUCTION

Guided by new observations and exciting ideas, and made possible by important discoveries and inventions, the Renaissance scientific movement led Western Europe away from medieval attitudes to the beginnings of the views held by the modern world. Spanning approximately two hundred years, beginning midway into the fifteenth century, the movement saw the university-dominated theological stance begin to yield to the secularization of knowledge.

Particularly important to the spread of knowledge was the invention of the printing press, which allowed for the distribution of standard texts at affordable cost. Coinciding with the means to disseminate ideas was a strong demand for new and more accurate translations and editions of classical texts. Greeks writings that were previously unknown or underutilized were translated into Latin, imparting knowledge and inspiration to the scientists of the Renaissance. Writing in reaction against Aristotelian science made for an atmosphere rich in ideas. In addition, many mystical and occultist writings circulated and these too found a place in the science of the time. Expanded literacy and increased use of vernacular languages gradually ended the exclusivity of knowledge to institutions. In order to apply new discoveries in practical ways, more people became tradesmen and engineers.

Advancements in technology—including the invention of scientific instruments like the microscope, telescope, and the thermometer—contributed to changing the prevailing attitudes toward scientific experimentation. Whereas rationalism, or rationalistic philosophy—whose epistemological and ontological foundations rested solely on *a priori,* or *analytical* reasoning—was the dominant mode of scientific thought, empirical philosophy—whose experimental basis turned to careful observations, or *a posteriori* reasoning—made new inroads. Although both modes of thinking were practiced in varying degrees, the trend was to look outward, not inward, for answers. This spirit of daring is exemplified by Copernicus' radical theory that the earth revolves around the sun and not the sun around the earth; his heliocentric theory removed the earth, and man, from the center of the universe.

OVERVIEWS

Allen G. Debus (essay date 1978)

SOURCE: "Tradition and Reform," in *Man and Nature in the Renaissance,* Cambridge University Press, 1978, pp. 1-15.

[*In the excerpt below, Debus provides an overview of the scientific revolution of the Renaissance, emphasizing the new interest in classical texts, the broader use of vernacular languages, and the expanded roles of observation, mathematics, technology, and mysticism.*]

Few events in world history have been more momentous than the Scientific Revolution. The period between the mid-fifteenth and the end of the eighteenth centuries witnessed the growing cultural and political influence of Western Europe over all other parts of the globe. The new science and technology of the West was a crucial factor in this development, a fact recognized by most scholars at the time. Thus, Francis Bacon (1561-1626) observed in the *Novum organum* (1620) that

> "it is well to observe the force and virtue and consequences of discoveries; and these are to be seen nowhere more conspicuously than in those three which were unknown to the ancients . . . ; namely, printing, gunpowder, and the magnet. For these three have changed the whole face and state of things throughout the world; the first in literature, the second in warfare, the third in navigation; whence have followed innumerable changes; insomuch that no empire, no sect, no star seems to have exerted greater power and influence in human affairs than these mechanical discoveries." [*The Works of Francis Bacon,* ed. James Spedding, Robert Leslie Eillis, and Douglas Dennon Heath (Longmans, 1870)]

For Bacon these discoveries were Western in origin and relatively recent in date. He was neither the first nor the last to make such a statement, but there were few whose works were read more avidly by those who hoped to erect a new science in the seventeenth century.

But if the importance of the Scientific Revolution is readily admitted by all, the more we study its origins, the more unsure we become of its causes. In this volume we shall be concerned primarily with the two centuries from 1450 to 1650, the first date coinciding roughly with the beginning of the new humanistic interest in the classical scientific and medical texts and the second with the years just prior to the general acceptance of the mechanistic science of Descartes (1596-1650), Galileo (1564-1642), Borelli (1608-1679), Boyle (1627-1691), and Newton (1642-1727).

These two centuries present an almost bewildering maze of interests, and only rarely will an individual be found whose scientific methodology would prove to be fully acceptable to a modern scientist. Some of the scholars, whose work contributed to our modern scientific age, found magic, alchemy, and astrology no less stimulating than the new interest in mathematical abstraction, observation, and experiment. Today we find it easy—and necessary—to separate "science" from occult interests, but many then could not. And we cannot relegate this interest in a mystical world view to a few lesser figures forgotten today except by antiquarians. The writings of Isaac Newton and Johannes Kepler (1571-1630) reveal a genuine interest in transmutation and a search for universal harmonies no less than the work of Paracelsus (1493-1541), Robert Fludd (1574-1637), or John Dee (1527-1608). For the most part it has been traditional among historians of science to view their subject by hindsight, that is, to ignore those aspects of an earlier natural philosophy that no longer have a place in our scientific world. However, if we do this we cannot hope to reach any contextual understanding of the period. It will thus be our aim to treat this period in its own terms rather than ours. As we proceed we shall find that controversies over natural magic and the truth of the macrocosm-microcosm analogy were then as important as the better-remembered debates over the acceptance of the heliocentric system or the circulation of the blood.

Renaissance Science and Education

The very words "Renaissance" and "humanism" have been employed with so many connotations that there is little hope of satisfying any two scholars with a single definition. There is no need to try to do so here. To be sure, the Renaissance did involve a kind of "rebirth" of knowledge—no less than it did a rebirth of art and literature. And it was surely the period of the development of a new science. But having granted this, it is necessary to be careful to avoid simplification. The new love of nature expressed by Petrarch (d. c. 1374) and other fourteenth-century humanists had more than one effect. We readily accept that it was instrumental in the rise of a new observational study of natural phenomena, but we also find that Petrarch and later humanists deeply distrusted the traditional scholastic emphasis on philosophy and the sciences. The rhetoric and history they preferred was a conscious reply to the more technical "Aristotelian" studies that had long been the mainstay of the medieval university. The humanists sought the moral improvement of man rather than the logic and scholastic disputations characteristic of traditional higher learning.

Marie Boas comments on the shift from an Aristotelian world view to an empirical one:

One of the most noticeable changes in the period between 1450 and 1630 is the change in attitude towards the ancients. In 1450 men attempted no more than comprehension of what the ancients had discovered, certain that this was the most that could be known; by 1630 things had so changed that the works of the ancients were available in various vernacular translations, and even the barely literate who read these versions were aware that the authority of the Greek and Roman past was under attack. Ancient learning was increasingly old-fashioned; what had been new in 1500 was outmoded by 1600, so relatively rapidly had ideas changed. . . . By 1630 it was obvious that the way was clear for a new physics, as it was for a new cosmology; only Aristotle's zoological work still, precariously, survived.

In 1450 the scientist was either a classical scholar or dangerously close to a magician. By 1630 he was either a new kind of learned man or a technical craftsman. As ancient authority declined and self-confidence in the ability of the moderns grew, the necessity for a classical education grew less, though every scientist was still expected to read and write Latin competently. The sheer success of science and the steady advance of rationalism generally meant the end of the magical tradition. Mathematician no longer meant astrologer; the word chemistry replaced alchemy as a new science was born; the number mysticism Kepler loved gave way to number theory, such as Fermat (1601-65) explored; natural magic was about to be replaced by experimental science and the mechanical philosophy. Science and rationalism were to become synonymous, cemented together by Descartes's *Discourse on Method* (1637).

Marie Boas, in her The Scientific Renaissance: 1450-1630, *Harper & Brothers, 1962.*

These shifting values were to result in a new interest in educational problems. Fourteenth- and fifteenth-century reform programs were to be directed toward elementary education rather than the universities. The humanist educator Vittorino da Feltre (1378-1446) established a new school where students were urged to excel at sports and to learn military exercises. In classrooms they studied rhetoric, music, geography, and history—and, taking their examples from the ancients, they were taught to value both moral principles and political action above the basic principles of the trivium (grammar, rhetoric, and logic) or the study of traditional philosophical and scientific subjects.
Many of the most renowned humanist scholars were to be affected by this movement in educational reform. The result may be clearly seen in the work of Erasmus (1466-1536). He thought it enough for a student to learn of

nature through his normal course of study in the reading of the ancient literary authors. Mathematics was not to him of much importance for an educated man. And Juan Luis Vives (1492-1540), surely the best known of all Renaissance educators, agreed fully when he argued against the study of mathematics that it tended to "withdraw the mind from practical concerns of life" and rendered it "less fit to fuse concrete and mundane realities."

But can we then say that the universities remained the centers of scientific training? For the most part they did, but there was an ever-increasing number of scholars both in medicine and the sciences who rejected the overwhelming conservatism of many—and perhaps most—of the institutions of higher learning. Peter Ramus (1515-1572) recalled his own academic training with despair:

> "After having devoted three years and six months to scholastic philosophy, according to the rules of our university: after having read, discussed, and meditated on the various treatises of the *Organon* (for of all the books of Aristotle those especially which treated of dialectic were read and re-read during the course of three years); even after, I say, having put in all that time, reckoning up the years completely occupied by the study of the scholastic arts, I sought to learn to what end I could, as a consequence, apply the knowledge I had acquired with so much toil and fatigue. I soon perceived that all this dialectic had not rendered me more learned in history and the knowledge of antiquity, nor more skillful in eloquence, nor a better poet, not wiser in anything. Ah, what a stupefaction, what a grief! How did I deplore the misfortune of my destiny, the barrenness of a mind that after so much labor could not gather or even perceive the fruits of that wisdom which was alleged to be found so abundantly in the dialectic of Aristotle!" [*Peter Ramus and the Educational Reformation of the Sixteenth Century,* Frank Pierrepont Graves, 1912]

Ramus was not alone in his frustration—and his complaints were not without grounds. Paris, for example, was acknowledged as a stronghold of Galenic medicine in the sixteenth and seventeenth centuries whereas in England both the Elizabethan statutes for Cambridge (1570) and also the Laudian code for Oxford (1636) maintained the official authority of the ancients. Nor were the early professional societies necessarily better. The London College of Physicians looked on innovation with distrust. Thus, when in 1559 Dr. John Geynes dared to suggest that Galen (129/130-199/200 A.D.) might not be infallible, the reaction was immediate and severe. The good doctor was forced to sign a recantation before being received again into the company of his colleagues.

The conservatism seen in many major universities in the sixteenth and seventeenth centuries may be partially balanced by a critical tradition that had been applied to the ancient scientific texts at Oxford and Paris in the fourteenth century. This work, associated with scholasticism, was to prove particularly beneficial to the study of the physics of motion. As a scholarly tradition it was still in evidence at Padua and other northern Italian universities in the sixteenth century. For many, however, scientific criticism was a curious kind of humanistic game in which the scholar was to be commended for having eliminated the vulgar annotations and emendations of medieval origin that marred the texts of antiquity. His goal was textual purity rather than scientific truth.

In short, the educational climate in the early Renaissance was of questionable value for the development of the sciences. University training in this period may be characterized for the most part as conservative. As for the reform of primary education accomplished in the fourteenth and fifteenth centuries, this was openly antiscientific.

Humanism and Classical Literature

Dedication to the ancients is a familiar characteristic of Renaissance humanism. The search for new classical texts was intense in the fifteenth century, and each new discovery was hailed as a major achievement. No account is better known than that of Jacopo Angelo (fl. c. 1406). His ship sank as he was returning from a voyage to Constantinople made in search of manuscripts, but he managed to save his greatest discovery, a copy of the *Geography* of Ptolemy hitherto unknown in the West. Not long after this, in 1417, Poggio Bracciolini (1380-1459) discovered what was later to be recognized as the only copy of Lucretius's (c. 99-55 B.C.) *De rerum natura* to have survived from antiquity. This was to become a major stimulus for the revived interest in atomism two centuries later. And, just nine years after the recovery of Lucretius, Guarino da Verona (1370-1460) found a manuscript of the encyclopedic treatise on medicine by the second-century author, Celsus. This work, *De medicina,* was to exert a great influence, an influence due perhaps less to its medical content than to its language and style. This was the only major medical work to have survived from the best period of Latin prose and it was to be mined by medical humanists who sought proper Latin terminology and phrasing.

The search for new texts—and new translations—resulted in a new awareness of the importance of Greek. To be sure, Roger Bacon (c. 1214-1294) had already underscored this need in the thirteenth century, but the situation had not materially improved a century later. At that time Petrarch had lamented his own inadequate knowledge of this language. In fact he was not alone. Few Western scholars were able to use Greek until the teacher Manuel Chrysolorus (d. 1415) arrived in Italy with the Byzantine Emperor Manuel Paleologus in 1396. But helpful though Chrysolorus was, much greater enthusiasm was stirred by another Byzantine, Gemistos Plethon, on his arrival at the Council of Florence in 1439. The Greek revival was to affect all scholarly fields in the course of the fifteenth century. In medicine the humanist Thomas Linacre (c. 1460-1524) prepared Latin translations of Proclus (410-485) and of individual works of Galen. Significant though this was, his plans—only partially fulfilled—were actually far more grandiose. He projected a Latin translation of the complete works of Galen—and, with a group of scholars, a Latin translation of the complete works of Aristotle as well. Hardly less industrious was Johannes Guinter of Andernach (1505-1574), whose translations from Galen place him in the front rank of medical humanists. As professor of medicine at Paris, Guinter became one of the most prominent teachers of the young Andreas Vesalius (1514-1564).

This quest for truth in the search for accurate manuscripts was not confined solely to the study of the ancient physicians. Georg von Peuerbach (1423-1461) recognized the need for an accurate manuscript of Ptolemy's *Almagest* while writing his textbook, the *Theoricae novae planetarum*. But Peuerbach died while he was in the process of planning a journey to Italy to accomplish this end. His pupil, Johann Müller (Regiomontanus) (1436-1476) completed his master's journey and published an *Epitome* of the *Almagest*.

But Renaissance humanism cannot simply be reduced to the recovery of a pure Aristotle, Ptolemy, or Galen. No less influential on the development of modern science—and certainly part of the same humanistic movement—was the revival of the neo-Platonic, cabalistic, and Hermetic texts of late antiquity. So important did these seem to be that Cosimo de' Medici insisted that Marsilio Ficino (1433-1499) translate the recently discovered *Corpus hermeticum* (c. 1460) before turning to Plato or Plotinus. These mystical and religious works—to be discussed later in more detail—seemed to justify the pursuit of natural magic, a subject of great popularity among the savants of the sixteenth and seventeenth centuries. Included in this tradition was the call for a new investigation of nature through fresh observational evidence.

Coincidentally, this search for the pure and original texts of antiquity occurred when a new means existed for disseminating this knowledge, the printing press. It is interesting that the earliest printed book from Western Europe dates from 1447, at the very beginning of our period. For the first time it became possible to produce standard texts for scholars at a moderate price. In the scientific and medical fields these incunabula were for the most part printings of the old medieval scholastic texts scorned by the humanists. Thus the first version of Ptolemy's *Almagest* to be printed was the old medieval translation (1515). A new Latin translation appeared next (1528)—and finally the Greek text

(1538), just five years prior to the *De revolutionibus orbium* of Copernicus. Galen and Aristotle were to proceed through the same stages.

The Growth of the Vernacular

Latin and Greek were surely the primary keys to the world of the scholar, but the Renaissance world was also characterized by a rapid growth in the use of the vernacular languages in learned fields. This is seen most strikingly in the religious pamphlets of the Reformation, where the author had an immediate need to reach his audience. But the use of the vernacular also became increasingly important in science and medicine in the course of the sixteenth century. This may be ascribed partially to the conscious nationalistic pride seen in this period. It is a time when authors wrote openly of their love of their native land and of their own language. A second factor was the feeling on the part of many of the need for a decisive break with the past. This seems to be ever more evident after the second quarter of the sixteenth century.

Recent research indicates a rapid increase in the use of the vernacular in the medical texts of the late Middle Ages. This trend intensified in the sixteenth century when a medical pamphlet war divided the Galenists from the Paracelsian medical chemists. This debate had been brought to the university level when Paracelsus lectured on medicine at Basel in his native Swiss-German in 1527. The medical establishment attacked him in force not only for the content of his lectures, but also for his choice of language. The latter was to remain a sore point among his followers for generations to come. Thus, the English Paracelsist Thomas Moffett (1553-1604) admitted—in Latin (1584)—that

"it is true that Paracelsus spoke often in German rather than Latin, but did not Hippocrates speak Greek? And why should they not both speak their native tongues? Is this worthy of reprehension in Paracelsus and to be passed over in Hippocrates, Galen and the other Greeks who spoke in their own language?"

The situation was not appreciably different in mathematics and the physical sciences. Galileo's publications in Italian remain classics of Italian literature today and in England numerous authors presented both popular and technical subjects in Tudor English. Of special interest is John Dee, who took it on himself to compose a preface to the first English translation of the *Elements of Geometry* by Euclid. Here he thought it necessary to explain that such a translation would pose no threat to the universities. Rather, he argued, many common folk might well for the first time be able "to find out, and devise, new workes, straunge Engines, and Instrumentes: for sundry purposes in the Common Wealth or for private pleasure and for the better maintayninge of their owne estate." Similar apologies for the publication of scientific and medical texts in the vernacular are to be found in the other major modern languages from this period.

Observation and Experiment

Any general assessment of Renaissance science must include a discussion of a number of seeming paradoxes. A recurring theme in the sixteenth-century literature is the rejection of antiquity. But, as we have already noted, this rejection most commonly was directed at scholastic translations and commentaries. Some scholars did call for a completely new natural philosophy and medicine, but many adhered to the ancient philosophy—provided that they were assured that their texts were pure and unadulterated. There were those such as William Harvey (1578-1657), who openly praised the Aristotelian heritage. Others—and here Robert Fludd is a good example—attacked the ancients viciously while integrating many ancient concepts in their own work.

Also characteristic of the period was a growing reliance on observation and a gradual move toward our understanding of experiment as a carefully planned—and repeatable—test of theory. Older classics of observational science and method were recognized and praised by Renaissance scholars, who saw in them a model to be emulated. Thus many who rejected Aristotle's physics pointed to his work on animals as a text of major importance. Because of his use of observational evidence, Archimedes (287-212 B.C.) had great weight, whereas among medieval authors Roger Bacon, Peter Perigrinus (of Maricourt) (fl. c. 1270), and Witelo (Theodoric of Freiburg) (thirteenth century) were cited for their "experimental" studies.

Yet even though Roger Bacon and others might speak of a new use of observation as the basis for an understanding of the universe, it was far more customary to rely upon fabulous accounts related by Pliny the Elder (23-79 A.D.) or other ancient encyclopedists. Even the brilliant critique of the ancient physics of motion carried out at Oxford and Paris in the fourteenth century had been based more upon deductive reasoning and the rules of logic than upon the results of any new observational evidence.

The scientists of the sixteenth century did not immediately develop a modern understanding of the use of experiment, but there is evident in their work a more general recourse to observational evidence than existed before. Thus Bernardino Telesio (1509-1588) founded his own academy at Cosenza, which was dedicated to the study of natural philosophy. Rejecting Aristotle, whose work seemed to disagree with both Scripture and experience, he turned instead to the senses as a key to the study of nature. Of equal interest is John Dee, who numbered among his mathematical sciences *Archemastrie*, which "teacheth to bryng to actuall experience sensible, all worthy conclusions by all the Artes Mathematicall purposed. . . . And bycause it procedeth by *Experiences,* and searcheth forth the causes of Conclusions, them selues, in Experience, it is named of some *Scientia Experimentalis.* The *Experimentall Science.*" Here the word "experimental" may best be understood as "observational." The concept of the modern controlled experiment was not part of Dee's methodology.

Mathematics and Natural Phenomena

Surely no less important than the new appreciation of observational evidence was the development of quantification and the increasing reliance on mathematics as a tool. Plato had stressed the importance of mathematics, and the revived interest in his work did influence the sciences in this area. In our period Galileo stands as the key figure in this development. Viewing mathematics as the essential guide for the interpretation of nature, he sought a new description of motion through the use of mathematical abstraction. In doing so Galileo was acutely aware that he was departing from the traditional Aristotelian search for causes.

Combined with the novel use of mathematics in natural philosophy, there were dramatic new developments within mathematics itself. The work of Tartaglia (1500-1557), Cardano (1501-1576), and Viète (1540-1603) in algebra did much to advance that subject in the sixteenth century—and tedious arithmetical calculations were greatly simplified through the invention of logarithms by Napier (1550-1617). And only slightly beyond our period comes the invention of the calculus by the independent efforts of Leibniz (1646-1716) and Newton. All these tools were quickly seized upon by contemporary scientists as aids to their work.

If one were to ask the reasons for this use of mathematics in the sixteenth century, one might arrive at a variety of answers. One would surely be the new availability of the work of Archimedes, the Greek author whose approach most closely approximated that of the new science. His texts had never been completely lost, but there is clear evidence of a new Archimedean influence in the mid-sixteenth century with a series of new editions of his work. Another factor of importance is the persistence of interest in the study of motion initiated by the fourteenth-century scholars at Oxford and Paris. There seems little doubt that Galileo was as a student the beneficiary of this tradition. A third factor was surely the Platonic, neo-Platonic, and Pythagorean revival. This influence often had a mystical flavor, but whatever its form, it was an important stimulus for many scientists of the period. And finally, one might point to the need for practical mathematics associated with the practical arts and technology.

Technology

It is rewarding to pause momentarily to examine this new interest in technology. While the extent of the relationship is open to debate, it is clear that at the very least those interested in warfare required mathematical studies in their use of cannon, and the navigator had to perform calculations to determine his position at sea. This was a period that witnessed impressive advances in instrumentation, ranging from practical astrolabes for the mariner to the massive astronomical instruments built by Tycho Brahe. The telescope, the microscope, the first effective thermometers, and a host of other tools were developed by artisans and scientists alike. Indeed, the scientists were taking an active interest in the work of the tradesmen for the first time. This may be interpreted partially as a revolt against the authority of the ancients, as most ancient and medieval studies of nature were totally divorced from processes employed by workmen. The scholastic student of the medieval university agreed with the ancients and rarely left his libraries and study halls. In the Renaissance, however, we witness a great change. There may be few descriptions of the practical arts in the books of the fifteenth century, but handbooks of mining operations began to appear from the presses as early as 1510 and similar works relating to other fields appeared shortly thereafter.

In contrast to earlier periods the scientists and physicians now acknowledged openly that the scholar would do well to learn from the common man. Paracelsus advised his readers that

> not all things the physician must know are taught in the academies. Now and then he must turn to old women, to Tartars who are called gypsies, to itinerant magicians, to elderly country folk and many others who are frequently held in contempt. From them he will gather his knowledge since these people have more understanding of such things than all the high colleges.

And Galileo candidly began his epoch-making *Discourses and Demonstrations Concerning Two New Sciences* (1638) with the following statement:

> The constant activity which you Venetians display in your famous arsenal suggests to the studious mind a large field for investigation, especially that part of the work which involves mechanics; for in this department all types of instruments and machines are constantly being constructed by many artisans, among whom there must be some who, partly by inherited experience and partly by their own observations, have become highly expert and clever in explanation. [*Dialogues Concerning Two New Sciences*, transl. Henry Crew and Alfonso de Salvio, 1954]

This list could be greatly amplified if we took into account the great mining treatises of Agricola (1494-1555) and Biringuccio (fl. c. 1540), the views of Francis Bacon on the practical purpose of science, and the stated practical goals of the early scientific societies. There is little doubt that some areas of science progressed because the contribution of artisans and scientists fostered the study of practical processes. Johann Rudolph Glauber (1604-1670) was so encouraged by the developments he had witnesses that he forecast the supremacy of Germany over all Western Europe if its rulers would only follow his plan outlined in the *Prosperity of Germany*. And yet, even if we grant this belated recognition of technology by the scientist, there was no appreciable feedback from the small scientific community to technology until well into the eighteenth century.

Mysticism and Science

A fourth ingredient in the formation of the new science—and a most unlikely one from our post-Newtonian vantage point—was the new Renaissance interest in a mystical approach to nature. Much of this may be attributed to the strong revival of interest in the Platonic, neo-Platonic, and Hermetic writings. It is instructive to note this influence first in mathematics and then in the widespread interest in natural magic.

From our point of view Renaissance mathematics had the effect of a double-edged sword. On the one hand, the new interest in mathematics furthered the development of a mathematical approach to nature and the internal development of geometry and algebra; on the other hand, the same interest resulted in occultist investigations of all kinds related to number mysticism. Renaissance cabalistic studies encouraged a mystical numerological investigation of the Scriptures with the hope that far-reaching truths would be found. Similarly magic squares and harmonic ratios seemed to offer insight into nature and divinity. Even in antiquity this tendency was embodied in the Pythagorean tradition prior to the time of Plato. The latter's numerological speculations in the *Timaeus* were to continue to affect the world of learning throughout the Middle Ages, and with the revival of the texts of late antiquity in the fifteenth century the same themes were heard once again.

It is important not to try to separate the "mystical" and the "scientific" when they are both present in the work of a single author. To do so would be to distort the intellectual climate of the period. Of course it is not difficult to point to the mathematical laws governing planetary motions formulated by Kepler or the mathematical description of motion presented by Galileo. These were basic milestones in the development of modern science. But it should not be forgotten that Kepler sought to fit the orbits of the planets within a scheme based upon the regular solids, and Galileo was never to relax his adherence to circular motion for the planets. Both authors reached conclusions that were strongly influenced by their belief in the perfection of the heavens. Today we would call the first examples "scientific," the second not. But to force our distinction upon the seventeenth century is ahistorical.

Robert Fludd offers an excellent example of an Hermetic-chemical approach to mathematics. Few would have insisted more than he that mathematics was essential for any study of the universe. But Fludd would have added that the true mathematician should lift his sights high. His aim should be to show the divine harmonies of nature through the interrelationship of circles, triangles, squares, and other figures. These would clearly indicate the connections of the great world to man. Fludd sought a new approach to nature and, like Kepler and Galileo, he hoped to use mathematics as a key, but for him quantification was something quite different than it was for the others. Fludd believed that the mathematician should use this tool to study the overall design of the universe. He should not—like Galileo—be concerned with lesser phenomena such as the motion of a falling object.

The case of mathematics is of special importance because of the significance of quantification in the rise of modern science, but the occult or mystical influence of late Hellenistic philosophy had a much deeper impact on sixteenth-century thought than this alone Implicit in neo-Platonism and the Christian traditions was the belief in a unity of nature, a unity that encompassed God and the angels at the one extreme and man and the terrestrial world at the other. Along with this was a continued belief in the truth of the macrocosm-microcosm relationship, the belief that man was created in the image of the great world, and that real correspondences do exist between man and the macrocosm.

The general acceptance of the macrocosm and the microcosm along with the great chain of being gave credence to the acceptance of correspondences existing everywhere between the celestial and sublunary worlds. In the ancient world such beliefs seemed to give a solid basis for astrology. It seemed reasonable to assume that stars should influence mankind here on earth. In the Renaissance many agreed, astral influences did indeed affect the earth and man. The Hermetic texts added a new ingredient to this world view. Largely on their basis man was now viewed as a favored link in the great chain of being. Partaking in Divine Grace, he was something more than the passive recipient of starry influences. And, as there is a general sympathy between all parts of the universe, man may affect supernature as well as be affected by it. This concept had immediate value in medicine through the doctrine of signatures. Here it was postulated that the true physician had the power successfully to seek out in the plant and mineral kingdoms those substances that correspond with the celestial bodies, and therefore ultimately with the Creator.

All this is closely related to the basis of Renaissance natural magic. The true physician of the Paracelsus or Ficino type was at the same time a magician who conceived nature to be a vital or magic force. Such a student of nature might learn to acquire natural powers not known to others and thus astonish the populace, even though these powers were known to be God-given and available to all. Indeed, to many this seemed to be one of the most attractive aspects of magic. Thus, late in life, John Dee recalled his student days at Cambridge where he had prepared a mechanical flying scarab for a Trinity College performance of Aristophanes' *Peace,* "whereat was great wondering, and many vaine reportes spread abroad of the meanes how that was effected." Dee's scarab was in the tradition of Hellenistic mechanical marvels, but he was also well aware that true magic meant the observational study of the unexplained or occult forces of nature. Thus in his *Natural Magick* John Baptista Porta (1540-1615) had explained that magic is essentially the search for wisdom and that it seeks nothing else but the "survey of the whole course of nature." Still earlier Heinrich Cornelius Agrippa (c. 1486-1535) called this the most perfect knowledge of all, and Paracelsus equated it with nature itself and spoke of it in terms of a religious quest that would lead the seeker to a greater knowledge of his Creator.

For such men natural magic was far removed from the taint of necromancy. Rather, magic was closely associated with religion through the search for divine truths in created nature. Nevertheless, the scientist who was willing to accept the title of "magician" might well expose himself to danger. Again John Dee will serve as an example. Imprisoned early in life for his active interest in astrology, he was later to have his vast library destroyed by an angry mob. Appealing to his readers for sympathy, he asked whether they could really think him such a fool as "to forsake the light of heauenly Wisedome: and to lurke in the dungeon of the Prince of darknesse?" Despite the accusations that had been made, he held himself to be "innocent, in hand and hart: for trespacing either against the lawe of God, or Man, in any of my Studies of Exercises, Philosophicall, or Mathematicall."

In reality sixteenth-century natural magic was a new attempt to unify nature and religion. For the Hermeticists and the natural magicians the works of Aristotle were flawed by heretical concepts, and they were repeatedly to recall that church councils had condemned many of these Aristotelian errors. This being the case, why should Aristotle and Galen still be the basis of university teaching when there was another interpretation of nature through natural magic and occult philosophy—subjects whose very existence depended upon the sacred Scriptures? How could it be that any Christian should prefer the atheistic Aristotle to this new and pious doctrine? In truth, they argued, knowledge may be acquired by Divine Grace alone; either by some experience such as St. Augustine's divine illumination or else by means of experiment in which the adept might attain his end with the aid of divine revelation. The religious content of early-seventeenth-century Hermeticism is evident in the work of Thomas Tymme (d. 1620), who wrote (1612) that

> the Almighty Creator of the Heavens and the Earth . . . hath set before our eyes two most principal books: the one of nature, the other of his written Word . . . The wisdom of Natures book, men commonly call Natural Philosophy which serveth to allure to the contemplation of that great incomprehensible God, that wee might glorify him in the greatness of his work. For the ruled motions of the Orbes . . . the connection, agreement, force, virtue, and beauty of the Elements . . . are so many sundry natures and creatures in the world, are so many interpreters to teach us, that God is the efficient cause of them and that he is manifested in them, and by them, as their final cause to whom also they tend.

This was written to explain why he had prepared a book devoted to nature, the generation of the elements, and other essentially scientific topics. For an author such as Tymme science and the observation of nature were a form of divine service, a true link with divinity. In a sense natural research was a quest for God.

The student of Renaissance science must thus cope with more than the work of Copernicus and its consequences or the anatomical research leading to the discovery of the circulation of the blood. As for scientific method, the historian must concern himself with the new interest in mathematics and quantification all the while taking care not to divorce it from subjects as alien to modern science as the doctrine of signatures and natural magic. Indeed, our science today owes much to that search for a new synthesis of man, nature, and religion, which characterized the work of many scientists and physicians four centuries ago.

Renaissance science and medicine were deeply influenced by three figures of the sixteenth century and three others from antiquity. The first three were Nicholas Copernicus (1473-1543), Andreas Vesalius, and Philliptus Aureolus Theophrastus Bombastus von Hohenheim, called Paracelsus—the last three Archimedes, Galen, and Ptolemy. All were to register their impact on the learned world at approximately the same time. Indeed, the *De revolutionibus orbium* (Copernicus), *De humani corporis fabrica* (Vesalius), and the first major translation into Latin of the works of Archimedes all appeared in 1543.

The work of Paracelsus began to affect the learned world shortly after his death in 1541 when his scattered manuscripts were collected and published extensively for the first time. It is to his work that we turn next since to a greater extent than the others, Paracelsus may be viewed as a herald of the Scientific Revolution. And yet, though his call for a new approach to nature was coupled with a venomous attack on the followers of the ancients, Paracelsus himself was typical of the Renaissance in his willingness to borrow freely from the very texts and authors he rejected in print. . . .

HISTORICAL BACKGROUND

Bertrand Russell (essay date 1945)

SOURCE: "General Characteristics" and "The Rise of Science," in *A History of Western Philosophy, and Its Connection with Political and Social Circumstances from the Earliest Times to the Present Day*, Simon and Schuster, 1945, pp. 491-95, 525-40.

[*In the following excerpt, Russell puts in perspective both the achievements of Copernicus, Kepler, Galileo, and Newton, and the advances made in astronomy, dynamics, scientific instruments, and mathematics.*]

Almost everything that distinguishes the modern world from earlier centuries is attributable to science, which achieved its most spectacular triumphs in the seventeenth century. The Italian Renaissance, though not medieval, is not modern; it is more akin to the best age of Greece. The sixteenth century, with its absorption in theology, is more medieval than the world of Machiavelli. The modern world, so far as mental outlook is concerned, begins in the seventeenth century. No Italian of the Renaissance would have been unintelligible to Plato or Aristotle; Luther would have horrified Thomas Aquinas, but would not have been difficult for him to understand. With the seventeenth century it is different: Plato and Aristotle, Aquinas and Occam, could not have made head or tail of Newton.

The new conceptions that science introduced profoundly influenced modern philosophy. Descartes, who was in a sense the founder of modern philosophy, was himself one of the creators of seventeenth-century science. Something must be said about the methods and results of astronomy and physics before the mental atmosphere of the time in which modern philosophy began can be understood.

Four great men—Copernicus, Kepler, Galileo, and Newton—are pre-eminent in the creation of science. Of these, Copernicus belongs to the sixteenth century, but in his own time he had little influence.

Copernicus (1473-1543) was a Polish ecclesiastic, of unimpeachable orthodoxy. In his youth he travelled in Italy, and absorbed something of the atmosphere of the Renaissance. In 1500 he had a lectureship or professorship of mathematics in Rome, but in 1503 he returned to his native land, where he was a canon of Frauenburg. Much of his time seems to have been spent in combating the Germans and reforming the currency, but his leisure was devoted to astronomy. He came early to believe that the sun is at the centre of the universe, and that the earth has a twofold motion: a diurnal rotation, and an annual revolution about the sun. Fear of ecclesiastical censure led him to delay publication of his views, though he allowed them to become known. His chief work, *De Revolutionibus Orbium Cælestium,* was published in the year of his death (1543), with a preface by his friend Osiander saying that the heliocentric theory was only put forward as a hypothesis. It is uncertain how far Copernicus sanctioned this statement, but the question is not very important, as he himself made similar statements in the body of the book [See *Three Copernican Treatises,* translated by Edward Rosen, Chicago, 1939]. The book is dedicated to the Pope, and escaped official Catholic condemnation until the time of Galileo. The Church in the lifetime of Copernicus was more liberal than it became after the Council of Trent, the Jesuits, and the revived Inquisition had done their work.

The atmosphere of Copernicus's work is not modern; it might rather be described as Pythagorean. He takes it as axiomatic that all celestial motions must be circular and uniform, and like the Greeks he allows himself to be influenced by æsthetic motives. There are still epicycles in his system, though their centres are at the sun, or, rather, near the sun. The fact that the sun is not exactly in the centre marred the simplicity of his theory. He does not seem to have known of Aristarchus's heliocentric theory, but there is nothing in his speculations that could not have occurred to a Greek astronomer. What was important in his work was the dethronement of the earth from its geometrical pre-eminence. In the long run, this made it difficult to give to man the cosmic importance assigned to him in the Christian theology, but such consequences of his theory would not have been accepted by Copernicus, whose orthodoxy was sincere, and who protested against the view that his theory contradicted the Bible.

There were genuine difficulties in the Copernican theory. The greatest of these was the absence of stellar parallax. If the earth at any one point of its orbit is 186,000,000 miles from the point at which it will be in six months, this ought to cause a shift in the apparent positions of the stars, just as a ship at sea which is due north from one point of the coast will not be due north from another. No parallax was observed, and Copernicus rightly inferred that the fixed stars must be very much more remote than the sun. It was not till the nineteenth century that the technique of measurement became sufficiently precise for stellar parallax to be observed, and then only in the case of a few of the nearest stars.

Another difficulty arose as regards falling bodies. If the earth is continually rotating from west to east, a body dropped from a height ought not to fall to a point vertically below its starting-point, but to a point somewhat further west, since the earth will have slipped away a certain distance during the time of the fall. To this difficulty the answer was found by Galileo's law of inertia, but in the time of Copernicus no answer was forthcoming.

There is an interesting book by E. A. Burtt, called *The Metaphisical Foundations of Modern Physical Science* (1925), which sets forth with much force the many unwarrantable assumptions made by the men who founded modern science. He points out quite truly that there were in the time of Copernicus no known facts which compelled the adoption of his system, and several which militated against it. "Contemporary empiricists, had they lived in the sixteenth century, would have been the first to scoff out of court the new philosophy of the universe." The general purpose of the book is to discredit modern science by suggesting that its discoveries were lucky accidents springing by chance from superstitions as gross as those of the Middle Ages. I think this shows a misconception of the scientific attitude: it is not *what* the man of science believes that distinguishes him, but *how* and *why* he believes it. His beliefs are tentative, not dogmatic; they are based on evidence, not on authority or intuition. Copernicus was right to call his theory a hypothesis; his opponents were wrong in thinking new hypotheses undesirable.

The men who founded modern science had two merits which are not necessarily found together: immense patience in observation, and great boldness in framing hypotheses. The second of these merits had belonged to the earliest Greek philosophers; the first existed, to a considerable degree, in the later astronomers of antiquity. But no one among the ancients, except perhaps Aristarchus, possessed both merits, and no one in the Middle Ages possessed either. Copernicus, like his great successors, possessed both. He knew all that could be known with the instruments existing in his day, about the apparent motions of the heavenly bodies on the celestial sphere, and he perceived that the diurnal rotation of the earth was a more economical hypothesis than the revolution of all the celestial spheres. According to modern views, which regard all motion as relative, simplicity is the only gain resulting from his hypothesis, but this was not his view or that of his contemporaries. As regards the earth's annual revolution, there was again a simplification, but not so notable a one as in the case of the diurnal rotation. Copernicus still needed epicycles, though fewer than were needed in the Ptolemaic system. It was not until Kepler discovered his laws that the new theory acquired its full simplicity.

Apart from the revolutionary effect on cosmic imagination, the great merits of the new astronomy were two: first, the recognition that what had been believed since ancient times might be false; second, that the test of scientific truth is patient collection of facts, combined with bold guessing as to laws binding the facts together. Neither merit is so fully developed in Copernicus as in his successors, but both are already present in a high degree in his work.

Some of the men to whom Copernicus communicated his theory were German Lutherans, but when Luther came to know of it, he was profoundly shocked. "People give ear," he said, "to an upstart astrologer who strove to show that the earth revolves, not the heavens or the firmament, the sun and the moon. Whoever wishes to appear clever must devise some new system, which of all systems is of course the very best. This fool wishes to reverse the entire science of astronomy; but sacred Scripture tells us that Joshua commanded the sun to stand still, and not the earth." Calvin, similarly, demolished Copernicus with the text: "The world also is established, that it cannot be moved" (Ps. XCIII, 1), and exclaimed: "Who will venture to place the authority of Copernicus above that of the Holy Spirit?" Protestant clergy were at least as bigoted as Catholic ecclesiastics; nevertheless there soon came to be much more liberty of speculation in Protestant than in Catholic countries, because in Protestant countries the clergy had less power. The important aspect of Protestantism was schism, not heresy, for schism led to national Churches, and national Churches were not strong enough to control the lay government. This was wholly a gain, for the Churches, everywhere, opposed as long as they could practically every innovation that made for an increase of happiness or knowledge here on earth.

Copernicus was not in a position to give any conclusive evidence in favour of his hypothesis, and for a long time astronomers rejected it. The next astronomer of importance was Tycho Brahe (1546-1601), who adopted an intermediate position: he held that the sun and moon go round the earth, but the planets go round the sun. As regards theory he was not very original. He gave, however, two good reasons against Aristotle's view that everything above the moon is unchanging. One of these was the appearance of a new star in 1572, which was found to have no daily parallax, and must therefore be more distant than the moon. The other reason was derived from observation of comets, which were also found to be distant. The reader will remember Aristotle's doctrine that change and decay

are confined to the sublunary sphere; this, like everything else that Aristotle said on scientific subjects, proved an obstacle to progress.

The importance of Tycho Brahe was not as a theorist, but as an observer, first under the patronage of the king of Denmark, then under the Emperor Rudolf II. He made a star catalogue, and noted the positions of the planets throughout many years. Towards the end of his life Kepler, then a young man, became his assistant. To Kepler his observations were invaluable.

Kepler (1571-1630) is one of the most notable examples of what can be achieved by patience without much in the way of genius. He was the first important astronomer after Copernicus to adopt the heliocentric theory, but Tycho Brahe's data showed that it could not be quite right in the form given to it by Copernicus. He was influenced by Pythagoreanism, and more or less fancifully inclined to sun-worship, though a good Protestant. These motives no doubt gave him a bias in favour of the heliocentric hypothesis. His Pythagoreanism also inclined him to follow Plato's *Timaeus* in supposing that cosmic significance must attach to the five regular solids. He used them to suggest hypotheses to his mind; at last, by good luck, one of these worked.

Kepler's great achievement was the discovery of his three laws of planetary motion. Two of these he published in 1609, and the third in 1619. His first law states: The planets describe elliptic orbits, of which the sun occupies one focus. His second law states: The line joining a planet to the sun sweeps out equal areas in equal times. His third law states: The square of the period of revolution of a planet is proportioned to the cube of its average distance from the sun.

Something must be said in explanation of the importance of these laws.

The first two laws, in Kepler's time, could only be *proved* in the case of Mars; as regards the other planets, the observations were compatible with them, but not such as to establish them definitely. It was not long, however, before decisive confirmation was found.

The discovery of the first law, that the planets move in ellipses, required a greater effort of emancipation from tradition than a modern man can easily realize. The one thing upon which all astronomers, without exception, had been agreed, was that all celestial motions are circular, or compounded of circular motions. Where circles were found inadequate to explain planetary motions, epicycles were used. An epicycle is the curve traced by a point on a circle which rolls on another circle. For example: take a big wheel and fasten it flat on the ground; take a smaller wheel which has a nail through it, and roll the smaller wheel (also flat on the ground) round the big wheel, with the point of the nail touching the ground. Then the mark of the nail in the ground will trace out an epicycle. The orbit of the moon, in relation to the sun, is roughly of this kind: approximately, the earth describes a circle round the sun, and the moon meanwhile describes a circle round the earth. But this is only an approximation. As observation grew more exact, it was found that no system of epicycles would exactly fit the facts. Kepler's hypothesis, he found, was far more closely in accord with the recorded positions of Mars than was that of Ptolemy, or even that of Copernicus.

The substitution of ellipses for circles involved the abandonment of the aesthetic bias which had governed astronomy ever since Pythagoras. The circle was a perfect figure, and the celestial orbs were perfect bodies—originally gods, and even in Plato and Aristotle closely related to gods. It seemed obvious that a perfect body must move in a perfect figure. Moreover, since the heavenly bodies move freely, without being pushed or pulled, their motion must be "natural." Now it was easy to suppose that there is something "natural" about a circle, but not about an ellipse. Thus many deep-seated prejudices had to be discarded before Kepler's first law could be accepted. No ancient, not even Aristarchus of Samos, had anticipated such an hypothesis.

The second law deals with the varying velocity of the planet at different points of its orbit. If S is the sun, and P_1, P_2, P_3, P_4, P_5 are successive positions of the planet at equal intervals of time—say at intervals of a month—then Kepler's law states that the areas P_1SP_2, P_2SP_3, P_3SP_4, P_4SP_5 are all equal. The planet therefore moves fastest when it is nearest to the sun, and slowest when it is farthest from it. This, again, was shocking; a planet ought to be too stately to hurry at one time and dawdle at another.

The third law was important because it compared the movements of different planets, whereas the first two laws dealt with the several planets singly. The third law says: If r is the average distance of a planet from the sun, and T is the length of its year, then r^3 divided by T^2 is the same for all the different planets. This law afforded the proof (as far as the solar system is concerned) of Newton's law of the inverse square for gravitation. But of this we shall speak later.

Galileo (1564-1642) is the greatest of the founders of modern science, with the possible exception of Newton. He was born on about the day on which Michelangelo died, and he died in the year in which Newton was born. I commend these facts to those (if any) who still believe in metempsychosis. He is important as an astronomer, but perhaps even more as the founder of dynamics.

Galileo first discovered the importance of *acceleration* in dynamics. "Acceleration" means change of velocity, whether in magnitude or direction; thus a body moving uniformly in a circle has at all times an acceleration towards the centre of the circle. In the language that had been customary before his time, we might say that he treated uniform motion in a straight line as alone "natural," whether on earth or in the heavens. It had been thought "natural" for heavenly bodies to move in circles, and for terrestrial bodies to move in straight lines; but moving terrestrial bodies, it was thought, would gradually cease to move if they were let alone. Galileo held, as against this view, that every body, if let alone, will continue to move in a straight line with uniform velocity; any change, either in the rapidity or the direction of motion, requires to be explained as due to the action of some "force." This principle was enunciated by Newton as the "first law of motion." It is also called the law of inertia. I shall return to its purport later, but first something must be said as to the detail of Galileo's discoveries.

Galileo was the first to establish the law of falling bodies. This law, given the concept of "acceleration," is of the utmost simplicity. It says that, when a body is falling freely, its acceleration is constant, except in so far as the resistance of the air may interfere; further, the acceleration is the same for all bodies, heavy or light, great or small. The complete proof of this law was not possible until the air pump had been invented, which was about 1654. After this, it was possible to observe bodies falling in what was practically a vacuum, and it was found that feathers fell as fast as lead. What Galileo proved was that there is no measurable difference between large and small lumps of the same substance. Until his time it had been supposed that a large lump of lead would fall much quicker than a small one, but Galileo proved by experiment that this is not the case. Measurement, in his day, was not such an accurate business as it has since become; nevertheless he arrived at the true law of falling bodies. If a body is falling freely in a vacuum, its velocity increases at a constant rate. At the end of the first second, its velocity will be 32 feet per second; at the end of another second, 64 feet per second; at the end of the third, 96 feet per second; and so on. The acceleration, i.e., the rate at which the velocity increases, is always the same; in each second, the increase of velocity is (approximately) 32 feet per second.

Galileo also studied projectiles, a subject of importance to his employer, the duke of Tuscany. It had been thought that a projectile fired horizontally will move horizontally for a while, and then suddenly begin to fall vertically. Galileo showed that, apart from the resistance of the air, the horizontal velocity would remain constant, in accordance with the law of inertia, but a vertical velocity would be added, which would grow according to the law of falling bodies. To find out how the projectile will move during some short time, say a second, after it has been in flight for some time, we proceed as follows: First, if it were not falling, it would cover a certain horizontal distance, equal to that which it covered in the first second of its flight. Second, if it were not moving horizontally, but merely falling, it would fall vertically with a velocity proportional to the time since the flight began. In fact, its change of place is what it would be if it first moved horizontally for a second with the initial velocity, and then fell vertically for a second with a velocity proportional to the time during which it has been in flight. A simple calculation shows that its consequent course is a parabola, and this is confirmed by observation except in so far as the resistance of the air interferes.

The above gives a simple instance of a principle which proved immensely fruitful in dynamics, the principle that, when several forces act simultaneously, the effect is as if each acted in turn. This is part of a more general principle called the parallelogram law. Suppose, for example, that you are on the deck of a moving ship, and you walk across the deck. While you are walking the ship has moved on, so that, in relation to the water, you have moved both forward and across the direction of the ship's motion. If you want to know where you will have got to in relation to the water, you may suppose that first you stood still while the ship moved, and then, for an equal time, the ship stood still while you walked across it. The same principle applies to forces. This makes it possible to work out the total effect of a number of forces, and makes it feasible to analyse physical phenomena, discovering the separate laws of the several forces to which moving bodies are subject. It was Galileo who introduced this immensely fruitful method.

In what I have been saying, I have tried to speak, as nearly as possible, in the language of the seventeenth century. Modern language is different in important respects, but to explain what the seventeenth century achieved it is desirable to adopt its modes of expression for the time being.

The law of inertia explained a puzzle which, before Galileo, the Copernican system had been unable to explain. As observed above, if you drop a stone from the top of a tower, it will fall at the foot of the tower, not somewhat to the west of it; yet, if the earth is rotating, it ought to have slipped away a certain distance during the fall of the stone. The reason this does not happen is that the stone retains the velocity of rotation which, before being dropped, it shared with everything else on the earth's surface. In fact, if the tower were high enough, there would be the opposite effect to that expected by the opponents of Copernicus. The top of the tower, being further from the centre of the earth than the bottom, is moving faster, and therefore the stone should fall slightly to the east of

the foot of the tower. This effect, however, would be too slight to be measurable.

Galileo ardently adopted the heliocentric system; he corresponded with Kepler, and accepted his discoveries. Having heard that a Dutchman had lately invented a telescope, Galileo made one himself, and very quickly discovered a number of important things. He found that the Milky Way consists of a multitude of separate stars. He observed the phases of Venus, which Copernicus knew to be implied by his theory, but which the naked eye was unable to perceive. He discovered the satellites of Jupiter, which, in honour of his employer, he called "sidera medicea." It was found that these satellites obey Kepler's laws. There was, however, a difficulty. There had always been seven heavenly bodies, the five planets and the sun and moon; now seven is a sacred number. Is not the Sabbath the seventh day? Were there not the seven-branched candlesticks and the seven churches of Asia? What, then, could be more appropriate than that there should be seven heavenly bodies? But if we have to add Jupiter's four moons, that makes eleven—a number which has no mystic properties. On this ground the traditionalists denounced the telescope, refused to look through it, and maintained that it revealed only delusions. Galileo wrote to Kepler wishing they could have a good laugh together at the stupidity of "the mob"; the rest of his letter makes it plain that "the mob" consisted of the professors of philosophy, who tried to conjure away Jupiter's moons, using "logic-chopping arguments as though they were magical incantations."

Galileo, as every one knows, was condemned by the Inquisition, first privately in 1616, and then publicly in 1633, on which latter occasion he recanted, and promised never again to maintain that the earth rotates or revolves. The Inquisition was successful in putting an end to science in Italy, which did not revive there for centuries. But it failed to prevent men of science from adopting the heliocentric theory, and did considerable damage to the Church by its stupidity. Fortunately there were Protestant countries, where the clergy, however anxious to do harm to science, were unable to gain control of the State.

Newton (1642-1727) achieved the final and complete triumph for which Copernicus, Kepler, and Galileo had prepared the way. Starting from his three laws of motion—of which the first two are due to Galileo—he proved that Kepler's three laws are equivalent to the proposition that every planet, at every moment, has an acceleration towards the sun which varies inversely as the square of the distance from the sun. He showed that accelerations towards the earth and the sun, following the same formula, explain the moon's motion, and that the acceleration of falling bodies on the earth's surface is again related to that of the moon according to the inverse square law. He defined "force" as the cause of change of motion, i.e., of acceleration. He was thus able to enunciate his law of universal gravitation: "Every body attracts every other with a force directly proportional to the product of their masses and inversely proportional to the square of the distance between them." From this formula he was able to deduce everything in planetary theory: the motions of the planets and their satellites, the orbits of comets, the tides. It appeared later that even the minute departures from elliptical orbits on the part of the planets were deducible from Newton's law. The triumph was so complete that Newton was in danger of becoming another Aristotle, and imposing an insuperable barrier to progress. In England, it was not till a century after his death that men freed themselves from his authority sufficiently to do important original work in the subjects of which he had treated.

The seventeenth century was remarkable, not only in astronomy and dynamics, but in many other ways connected with science.

Take first the question of scientific instruments. [On this subject, see the chapter "Scientific Instruments" in *A History of Science, Technology, and Philosophy in the Sixteenth and Seventeenth Centuries,* by A. Wolf.] The compound microscope was invented just before the seventeenth century, about 1590. The telescope was invented in 1608, by a Dutchman named Lippershey, though it was Galileo who first made serious use of it for scientific purposes. Galileo also invented the thermometer—at least, this seems most probable. His pupil Torricelli invented the barometer. Guericke (1602-86) invented the air pump. Clocks, though not new, were greatly improved in the seventeenth century, largely by the work of Galileo. Owing to these inventions, scientific observation became immensely more exact and more extensive than it had been at any former time.

Next, there was important work in other sciences than astronomy and dynamics. Gilbert (1540-1603) published his great book on the magnet in 1600. Harvey (1578-1657) discovered the circulation of the blood, and published his discovery in 1628. Leeuwenhoek (1632-1723) discovered spermatozoa, though another man, Stephen Hamm, had discovered them, apparently, a few months earlier; Leeuwenhoek also discovered protozoa or unicellular organisms, and even bacteria. Robert Boyle (1627-91) was, as children were taught when I was young, "the father of chemistry and son of the Earl of Cork"; he is now chiefly remembered on account of "Boyle's Law," that in a given quantity of gas at a given temperature, pressure is inversely proportional to volume.

I have hitherto said nothing of the advances in pure mathematics, but these were very great indeed, and were indispensable to much of the work in the physical sciences. Napier published his invention of logarithms in 1614. Co-ordinate geometry resulted from the work of several seventeenth-century mathematicians, among whom the greatest contribution was made by Descartes. The differential and integral calculus was invented independently by Newton and Leibniz; it is the instrument for almost all higher mathematics. These are only the most outstanding achievements in pure mathematics; there were innumerable others of great importance.

The consequence of the scientific work we have been considering was that the outlook of educated men was completely transformed. At the beginning of the century, Sir Thomas Browne took part in trials for witchcraft; at the end, such a thing would have been impossible. In Shakespeare's time, comets were still portents; after the publication of Newton's *Principia* in 1687, it was known that he and Halley had calculated the orbits of certain comets, and that they were as obedient as the planets to the law of gravitation. The reign of law had established its hold on men's imaginations, making such things as magic and sorcery incredible. In 1700 the mental outlook of educated men was completely modern; in 1600, except among a very few, it was still largely medieval.

In the remainder of this chapter I shall try to state briefly the philosophical beliefs which appeared to follow from seventeenth-century science, and some of the respects in which modern science differs from that of Newton.

The first thing to note is the removal of almost all traces of animism from the laws of physics. The Greeks, though they did not say so explicitly, evidently considered the power of movement a sign of life. To common-sense observation it seems that animals move themselves, while dead matter only moves when impelled by an external force. The soul of an animal, in Aristotle, has various functions, and one of them is to move the animal's body. The sun and planets, in Greek thinking, are apt to be gods, or at least regulated and moved by gods. Anaxagoras thought otherwise, but was impious. Democritus thought otherwise, but was neglected, except by the Epicureans, in favour of Plato and Aristotle. Aristotle's forty-seven or fifty-five unmoved movers are divine spirits, and are the ultimate source of all the motion in the universe. Left to itself, any inanimate body would soon become motionless; thus the operation of soul on matter has to be continuous if motion is not to cease.

All this was changed by the first law of motion. Lifeless matter, once set moving, will continue to move for ever unless stopped by some external cause. Moreover the external causes of change of motion turned out to be themselves material, whenever they could be definitely ascertained. The solar system, at any rate, was kept going by its own momentum and its own laws; no outside interference was needed. There might still seem to be need of God to set the mechanism working; the planets, according to Newton, were originally hurled by the hand of God. But when He had done this, and decreed the law of gravitation, everything went on by itself without further need of divine intervention. When Laplace suggested that the same forces which are now operative might have caused the planets to grow out of the sun, God's share in the course of nature was pushed still further back. He might remain as Creator, but even that was doubtful, since it was not clear that the world had a beginning in time. Although most of the men of science were models of piety, the outlook suggested by their work was disturbing to orthodoxy, and the theologians were quite justified in feeling uneasy.

Another thing that resulted from science was a profound change in the conception of man's place in the universe. In the medieval world, the earth was the centre of the heavens, and everything had a purpose concerned with man. In the Newtonian world, the earth was a minor planet of a not specially distinguished star; astronomical distances were so vast that the earth, in comparison, was a mere pin-point. It seemed unlikely that this immense apparatus was all designed for the good of certain small creatures on this pin-point. Moreover purpose, which had since Aristotle formed an intimate part of the conception of science, was now thrust out of scientific procedure. Any one might still believe that the heavens exist to declare the glory of God, but no one could let this belief intervene in an astronomical calculation. The world might have a purpose, but purposes could no longer enter into scientific explanations.

The Copernican theory should have been humbling to human pride, but in fact the contrary effect was produced, for the triumphs of science revived human pride. The dying ancient world had been obsessed with a sense of sin, and had bequeathed this as an oppression to the Middle Ages. To be humble before God was both right and prudent, for God would punish pride. Pestilences, floods, earthquakes, Turks, Tartars, and comets perplexed the gloomy centuries, and it was felt that only greater and greater humility would avert these real or threatened calamities. But it became impossible to remain humble when men were achieving such triumphs:

> Nature and Nature's laws lay hid in night.
> God said "Let Newton be," and all was light.

And as for damnation, surely the Creator of so vast a universe had something better to think about than sending men to hell for minute theological errors. Judas Iscariot might be damned, but not Newton, though he were an Arian.

There were of course many other reasons for self-satisfaction. The Tartars had been confined to Asia, and the Turks were ceasing to be a menace. Comets had been humbled by Halley, and as for earthquakes, though they were still formidable, they were so interesting that men of science could hardly regret them. Western Europeans were growing rapidly richer, and were becoming lords of all the world: they had conquered North and South America, they were powerful in Africa and India, respected in China and feared in Japan. When to all this were added the triumphs of science, it is no wonder that the men of the seventeenth century felt themselves to be fine fellows, not the miserable sinners that they still proclaimed themselves on Sundays.

There are some respects in which the concepts of modern theoretical physics differ from those of the Newtonian system. To begin with, the conception of "force," which is prominent in the seventeenth century, has been found to be superfluous. "Force," in Newton, is the cause of change of motion, whether in magnitude or direction. The notion of cause is regarded as important, and force is conceived imaginatively as the sort of thing that we experience when we push or pull. For this reason it was considered an objection to gravitation that it acted at a distance, and Newton himself conceded that there must be some medium by which it was transmitted. Gradually it was found that all the equations could be written down without bringing in forces. What was observable was a certain relation between acceleration and configuration; to say that this relation was brought about by the intermediacy of "force" was to add nothing to our knowledge. Observation shows that planets have at all times an acceleration towards the sun, which varies inversely as the square of their distance from it. To say that this is due to the "force" of gravitation is merely verbal, like saying that opium makes people sleep because it has a dormitive virtue. The modern physicist, therefore, merely states formulae which determine accelerations, and avoids the word "force" altogether. "Force" was the faint ghost of the vitalist view as to the causes of motions, and gradually the ghost has been exorcized.

Until the coming of quantum mechanics, nothing happened to modify in any degree what is the essential purport of the first two laws of motion, namely this: that the laws of dynamics are to be stated in terms of accelerations. In this respect, Copernicus and Kepler are still to be classed with the ancients; they sought laws stating the shapes of the orbits of the heavenly bodies. Newton made it clear that laws stated in this form could never be more than approximate. The planets do not move in *exact* ellipses, because of the perturbations caused by the attractions of other planets. Nor is the orbit of a planet ever exactly repeated, for the same reason. But the law of gravitation, which deals with accelerations, was very simple, and was thought to be quite exact until two hundred years after Newton's time. When it was emended by Einstein, it still remained a law dealing with accelerations.

It is true that the conservation of energy is a law dealing with velocities, not accelerations. But in calculations which use this law it is still accelerations that have to be employed.

As for the changes introduced by quantum mechanics, they are very profound, but still, to some degree, a matter of controversy and uncertainty.

There is one change from the Newtonian philosophy which must be mentioned now, and that is the abandonment of absolute space and time. The reader will remember a mention of this question in connection with Democritus. Newton believed in a space composed of points, and a time composed of instants, which had an existence independent of the bodies and events that occupied them. As regards space, he had an empirical argument to support his view, namely that physical phenomena enable us to distinguish absolute rotation. If the water in a bucket is rotated, it climbs up the sides and is depressed in the centre; but if the bucket is rotated while the water is not, there is no such effect. Since his day, the experiment of Foucault's pendulum has been devised, giving what has been considered a demonstration of the earth's rotation. Even on the most modern views, the question of absolute rotation presents difficulties. If all motion is relative, the difference between the hypothesis that the earth rotates and the hypothesis that the heavens revolve is purely verbal; it is no more than the difference between "John is the father of James" and "James is the son of John." But if the heavens revolve, the stars move faster than light, which is considered impossible. It cannot be said that the modern answers to this difficulty are completely satisfying, but they are sufficiently satisfying to cause almost all physicists to accept the view that motion and space are purely relative. This, combined with the amalgamation of space and time into space-time, has considerably altered our view of the universe from that which resulted from the work of Galileo and Newton. But of this, as of quantum theory, I will say no more at this time. . . .

John A. Schuster (essay date 1990)

SOURCE: "The Scientific Revolution," in *Companion to the History of Modern Science,* edited by R. C. Olby & others, Routledge, 1990, pp. 217-41.

[In the following essay, Schuster examines the history of the Scientific Revolution and explores the difficulties historians have in reaching agreement concerning matters dealing with the period.]

I. Explaining The Scientific Revolution: Historio-graphical Issues and Problems

The Scientific Revolution is commonly taken to denote the period between 1500 and 1700, during which time the conceptual and institutional foundations of modern science were erected upon the discredited ruins of the Medieval world-view, itself a Christianised elaboration of the scientific and natural philosophical heritage of classical antiquity. The central element in the Scientific Revolution is universally agreed to be the overthrow of Aristotelian natural philosophy, entrenched in the universities, along with its attendant earth-centred Ptolemaic system of astronomy. These were replaced by the Copernican system of astronomy (see art. 14) and the new mechanistic philosophy of nature (see art. 38), championed by René Descartes, Pierre Gassendi, Thomas Hobbes and Robert Boyle. Historians of science agree that by the turn of the eighteenth century, Isaac Newton's scientific and natural philosophical work had subsumed and solidified Copernican astronomy, unified the terrestrial and celestial mechanics deriving respectively from Galileo Galilei and Johannes Kepler, and transformed the mechanical philosophy by adding to it an ontology of immaterial forces and 'ethers' acting on ordinary matter according to mathematically expressed laws. It is also agreed that conceptual breakthroughs in related areas complemented these major transformations: Galileo and Newton laid the foundations for classical mathematical physics; William Harvey established the circulation of the blood, based on the achievements of the sixteenth-century anatomical tradition; and Descartes, Pierre Fermat, Newton and Gottfried Wilhelm Leibniz created the first modern fields of mathematics, coordinate geometry and differential and integral calculus.

The Scientific Revolution is also usually seen as having produced unprecedented changes in the social organisation and social role of natural philosophy and the sciences. The Royal Society of London and the Parisian Académie des Sciences, founded in the 1660s, were the first successful institutions devoted solely to the promotion of the new science of the seventeenth century, and they provided the models for such institutions which proliferated in the eighteenth century. Their organisation and publications did much to shape the scientific community and to create a continuing, stable domain of scientific debate and communication, although this by no means amounted to the sort of professionalisation of science that was to occur in the nineteenth century. (See art. 64.) They also embodied and propagated a triumphant new public rhetoric which praised the usefulness of science, its putative contributions to social and material progress and its objective detachment from the value-laden realms of politics and religion. Although the contributions of science to technological and economic development remained small until the nineteenth century, this public rhetoric, largely derived from the writings of Francis Bacon, did play a role in motivating and legitimating subsequent scientific work. Similarly, despite the fact that the rhetoric of value-neutrality and objectivity was itself an ideology, occluding the values and aims which the new science embodied, this public rhetoric had a significant role in shaping the eighteenth-century Enlightenment, and in promoting liberal and revolutionary social and political causes during the next two centuries.

Richard S. Westfall comments on the scientific revolution:

The scientific revolution was more than a reconstruction of the categories of thought about nature. It was a sociological phenomenon as well, both expressing the ever increasing numbers engaged in the activity of scientific research and spawning a new set of institutions that have played a more and more influential role in modern life. In my opinion, however, the development of ideas following their own internal logic was the central element in the foundation of modern science and, although I have attempted to indicate something of the sociological ramifications of the scientific movement, . . . my conviction [is] that the history of the scientific revolution must concentrate first of all on the history of ideas.

Richard S. Westfall, in his Construction of Modern Science: Mechanisms and Mechanics, *John Wiley & Sons, Inc., 1971.*

Although there is general agreement that such major changes occurred in science and natural philosophy during this period, historians of science have been unable to achieve consensus about any of the historiographical issues central to understanding the Scientific Revolution. They cannot agree on what is to be explained. Was there, for example, a truly revolutionary transformation of the sciences and natural philosophy, and if so, where precisely in the period was this break located—in the work of Newton, or perhaps earlier in the generation of Kepler, Bacon and Harvey? Alternatively, does the period display a slower process of continuous change with developments starting in the Middle Ages and only gradually evolving toward the synthesis of Newton? On a deeper level, no consensus has emerged about what would constitute an adequate explanation of either revolutionary or more continuous change. Much of the discussion of this problem has been bogged down in the debate between internalist and externalist approaches to the history of science. (See art. 3, sects. 2-4.)

To all intents and purposes the canonical statements of the internalist and externalist positions derive from the writings of Alexandre Koyré (1892-1964) and Boris Hessen (1893-1938).[1] Whilst only a few externalists would share Hessen's commitment to a rather crude Marxist economic determinism, his work, contrasted with that of Koyré, defines the boundary between externalism and internalism. This boundary divides those concerned with the intellectual contents of science, with concepts, theories and ideas, on the one hand, and those concerned with the non-cognitive, social, economic and institutional conditions, causes, constraints and (possibly) determinants of scientific theory and practice, on the other hand.

Koyré held that the development of modern science depended upon a revolution in ideas, a shift in intellectual perspective, involving the establishment, within or above scientific thought, of a new metaphysics or set of deep conceptual presuppositions, which in turn shaped thinking, experience and action in the emerging fields of modern science, especially classical mechanics and Copernican astronomy. Galileo's constitutions of classical mechanics within the framework of a loosely 'Platonic' metaphysics was Koyré's exemplary case of the emergence of modern science. According to Koyré, the strategies and practices of scientific research always follow from within one's particular categorical framework, or metaphysics, hence Galileo had no need of the abstract and vague dictates of some presumed correct 'scientific method', which might have provided post-facto legitimatory rhetoric. Galileo succeeded in founding the first version of classical mechanics because he worked, perceived and argued within the correct sort of metaphysical framework, a kind of non-mystical Platonism; a conviction that the basic furniture of the world consists in mathematical objects, moved according to simple and symmetrical mathematical laws. If Galileo had experimented (which Koyré doubted) and if he exploited new 'facts', the experiments and the facts were shaped by cognition and action themselves constrained by this metaphysics. For Koyré such a Platonic metaphysics was the only viable framework for scientific advance, at least in the physical sciences. Other frameworks might have their virtues, but not scientific virtues. For example, Aristotelian natural philosophy and cosmology, themselves coherent as a categorical framework, could never structure experience and reasoning so as to produce modern mathematical physics, since they were too closely enmeshed with the categories of natural language and everyday life.

Hessen's main subject was Newton, and his explanation of the Scientific Revolution depended on showing that Newtonian physics was a response to practical, economically relevant questions raised during the previous century and a half by the development of the fledgling commercial capitalist economy. From the early sixteenth century, capitalist development and the centralisation of states had focused a number of technical problems in areas such as mining, shipbuilding, gunnery, navigation and cartography. In retrospect one sees that in essence these problems pertain to fundamental areas of physics and it is not therefore surprising that at the time they invited solution by the development of Newtonian physics. For Hessen, the content of the new science reduced to (1) provision and use of the correct scientific method, leading to (2) the development of classical physics having clear economic and technological applications.

Hessen granted no essential role to the sort of intellectual factors studied by Koyré, or to merely local social factors, those which could be considered to be contingent in relation to the overriding dynamics of the secular rise of capitalism and the capitalist class. Hessen's detailed argument made this clear. On the one hand he correctly read Newton's *Philosophiae Naturalis Principia Mathematica (Mathematical Principles of Natural Philosophy,* 1687) as a philosophy of nature, rather than as a compendium of piecemeal results in applied physics, because he recognised the theological, philosophical and political resonances of Newton's scientific work. On the other hand, however, he had to view these elements as not essential to Newton's science, but rather as the inevitable but superficial reflections of the immediate historical and social conditions of men of Newton's class; reflections, for example, of the particular political form the 'class war' took at that time, and of the particular legal, religious and political 'superstructures' through which the underlying historical process was reflected in the minds of Newton and his contemporaries. For Koyré such resonances were essential, for they are symptomatic of the metaphysics which shapes more narrow theorising and problem-solving in the sciences. However, Koyré was only interested in these resonances as systems of ideas and not as signs of underlying socio-economic causes of scientific work.

The contrast between the views of Koyré and Hessen begins to suggest the range of disagreement amongst historians of science concerning what needs to be explained in the Scientific Revolution and how it should be explained. Koyré and Hessen focus on different 'sites' of the Scientific Revolution, Galileo versus Newton;[2] they concentrate on different objects of explanation, Galileo's mechanics versus Newton's physics and natural philosophy; and, as noted, they offer widely different sorts of explanations: the triumph of the correct metaphysics versus the technical needs of rising capitalism. Beyond these differences lies a fundamental difference of epistemology and philosophy of science; for Hessen, science is the essentially correct method applied to practical ends, while for Koyré science is essentially correct metaphysics, method being irrelevant, and intellectual comprehension is the main end.

Nevertheless, for all their differences Koyré and Hessen do concur on a critical point—there *was* a revolution in science, a temporally delimited radical transformation of the concepts, aims, techniques and social organisation of science. Hence they fail to provide a measure of the distance separating such (otherwise opposed) advocates of revolution from those who seek

the explanation of the origin of modern science in the gradual and continuous evolution of elements originating in the Middle Ages. For example, advocates of continuity such as Alistair C. Crombie and John Herman Randall see the development and application of scientific method as the central feature of the Scientific Revolution. They trace the slow and continuous development of method from Medieval and Renaissance articulations of Aristotle's methodogical doctrines, down to the heroic methodologists (and founders of modern science) of the seventeenth century, such as Bacon, Descartes, Galileo and Newton, who added to previous ideas about method a better managed dose of experiment, and, above all, more mathematics.[3] Other forms of the continuity thesis stress the debts of Galileo's physics to discussions of difficulties in Aristotle's physics, emanating originally from fourteenth-century Oxford and Paris, or they concentrate on the continuity of Medieval scholastic doctrines of natural law and voluntarist theology (stressing the will and absolute power of God) with those current in the mechanical philosophy of the mid-seventeenth century. Interestingly, for each advocate of continuity pointing to method or natural law as the essence of modern science, there can be found an advocate of revolutionary change concerned with the sudden and dramatic appearance of method or the concept of natural law.[4]

As these examples indicate, the cross-cutting debate amongst internalists and externalists, advocates of continuity and advocates of revolution depends on the assumption that some essence or defining property of modern science, be it method, natural law or Platonic metaphysics can be identified and then used to explain the slow or sudden appearance of that essence. For any given defining property it is possible to find contrasting internalist and externalist explanations of its origin and causes, as well as contrasting revolutionary or continuist interpretations of its historical career. This suggests that the fundamental difficulty with the existing literature is not the unresolved debate between internalists and externalists, and 'revolutionaries' and continuists. Rather, the difficulty and the reason for the continuing lack of resolution of these debates, resides in the universal assumption that modern science has some simply graspable defining feature which, turned into an historical category, invites explanation of the Scientific Revolution through the search for general causes of the appearance, sudden or otherwise, of that feature.

In the last two decades three developments have tended to reduce the plausibility of attempts to grasp the essence of science. In the first place, recent research has highlighted the historical contours and interpretative difficulties of the later periods, making it much more difficult to believe that grasping the putative essence of the Scientific Revolution provides the key to the nature and course of modern science. Secondly, there has been an accelerating accumulation of meticulous but piecemeal studies of seventeenth-century topics, of individual figures and of institutions, schools and traditions. The detail and nuance of much of this literature further weakens the credibility of the traditional search for simple defining features and their equally simplistic causes. Finally, the work of T. S. Kuhn, Paul Feyerabend and Gaston Bachelard has cast doubt on the conviction that science is based on a unique, efficacious and transferable method. Almost all historians of science now question whether the origin and development of modern science can be explained by means of the emergence, refinement and application of 'the scientific method'. Ironically, however, these developments, by dampening enthusiasm for new grand synthetic explanations of the Scientific Revolution, have in effect left in place the older internalist/externalist and revolution/continuity theses. (See art. 1, sect. 10.) They have been challenged and are increasingly seen as irrelevant, but the lack of credible alternatives means that they still influence discussions of the origins of modern science in a subtle way.

In sum, it is no exaggeration to say that the historiography of the Scientific Revolution is in a parlous state. Scholarly debate has been dominated by the clash of simplistic interpretations running along the two axes of internalism-externalism and revolution-continuity. For lack of anything better, such orientations linger, despite rising scepticism about their worth. The major issues in the field, the chief problems of interpretation and the categories available for addressing them have been ossified by the clash, and non-engagement, of contending forms of explanation which now lack credibility. The way out of this impasse lies in adopting perspectives embodied in recent work in the sociology of scientific knowledge and the so-called contextualist historiography of science, both of which have tended to concentrate on nineteenth- and twentieth-century science.

The newer sociology of scientific knowledge (see arts. 5 and 7) has elucidated how scientists within a given field or scientific speciality manufacture knowledge claims, negotiate their status and reinterpret and redeploy them in further cycles of knowledge production. They have observed that this 'social construction' of knowledge is set within the grids of power and cognition characteristic of the community at a given moment, the grids themselves being subject to modification as claims are variously established, extended, reinterpreted or dismantled, and credit is allocated for these accomplishments. Thus social and cognitive issues cannot be separated at the sites where a scientific community manufactures knowledge; instead, scientific knowledge is made in and through social processes that are in turn altered by the changing fabric of knowledge. Contextualist historians of science have reached analogous conclusions; but they have attended more closely to the problem of relating scientific sub-cultures to their larger social, political and economic environments or contexts. They see that although such sub-cultures have their own internal social dynamics and are, to various degrees, insulated from larger social forces, they nevertheless depend for their existence on the configuration of larger forces, which, additionally, can at any time intervene more directly in a sub-culture.

These considerations allow us to see that much of the self-defeating debate between internalists and externalists was due to their exclusive concentration on, respectively, cognitive and social issues. Internalists were inclined to believe that scientific ideas have a special and autonomous cognitive status, and hence that the history of science unfolds through the internal logic and dynamics of ideas alone. They failed to grasp that scientific sub-cultures are relatively autonomous just because they have well-developed social and political micro-structures through which knowledge is produced, and that the micro-structures are variously exposed to, and depend on, the larger factors studied by the externalists. A similar point was missed by the externalists from the other direction. Concentrating on large-scale social and economic factors, they were loath to grant autonomy, and an inner dynamic, to intellectual traditions and sub-cultures. Therefore they, like the internalists, failed to appreciate that intellectual sub-cultures are not merely systems of ideas, but also have 'internal' social structures and political dynamics, partially buffered from the direct impact of larger factors, through which knowledge is manufactured.

The debate between advocates of revolution and continuity can also be defused by adopting this perspective. The sociology of scientific knowledge and contextualist history of science show how, within a given field, scientists struggle to impose significant revisions of the existing conceptual fabric on their peers. This involves bids to reinterpret parts of the existing fabric and often necessitates the importation of conceptual resources from other realms of discourse. Any such process of revision, reinterpretation, negotiation and consensus formation can be variously glossed as involving 'revolutionary' or merely 'continuous' alterations of the conceptual fabric, and this glossing can be done by the scientists who are involved in the struggle, as well as by observing historians and sociologists. In other words, no revisions are inherently and essentially revolutionary or continuous in nature; rather, these are terms deployed by interested parties, historical actors or historians, seeking to explain the process. On the one hand, historians who advocate continuity are simply over-stressing the existence of conceptual borrowing and reinterpretation. They therefore tend to hypostatise a history of *ideas* and their inner, gradually unfolding logic of development. On the other hand, historians who advocate revolutionary displacement of conceptual fabrics are simply overplaying the fact that no revised conceptual framework is exactly like any previous one. A case for 'revolution' can almost always be made out by selectively stressing certain aspects of change at the expense of others.

For an adequate historiography of the Scientific Revolution historians of science must avoid the above pitfalls and instead recognise that natural philosophy and the various sciences constituted sub-cultures: hence the challenge is to describe and explain the processes of change (not necessarily 'progressive') which characterised the systematic natural philosophies and the existing and nascent sciences in the early modern period. This involves forming empirically-based and historically-sensitive conceptions of these sub-cultures as social and cognitive enterprises. It also involves the notion that natural philosophy and the sciences, so conceived, conditioned each other at the same time that they were variously open to, and affected by, the larger social, political and economic contexts in which they were practised or promoted. Finally, this also involves having some working model of the key moments in the process by which these sub-cultures interacted and changed, both amongst themselves and in relation to working models of their (equally historically changeable) contexts. Whether the term 'Scientific Revolution' is retained to denote the period is less important than forming these adequate historical categories and a working description of the processes of change they experienced.

II. APPROPRIATE CATEGORIES: NATURAL PHILOSOPHY, THE SCIENCES AND THE PRACTICAL ARTS.

The Scientific Revolution consisted of a process of change and displacement among and within competing *systems of natural philosophy*. The process involved the erosion and downfall of the dominant Aristotelian philosophy of nature and its replacement during the middle third of the seventeenth century by variants of the newly constructed mechanistic natural philosophy, which, after a period of consolidation and institutionalisation, were modified and partially displaced by the post-mechanist natural philosophies of Leibniz, and especially Newton, setting the stage for the eighteenth century. The erosion of Artistelianism in the sixteenth and early seventeenth centuries was connected with the proliferation of alternative natural philosophies of magical, alchemical and Hermetical colorations, and the mechanical philosophy was as much a response to the social, political and theological threats seemingly posed by these competitors as it was a response to Aristotelianism. Consequently, the crucial moment in this process resides in the first two generations of the seventeenth century, an age of heightened conflict amongst Aristotelianism, its magical/alchemical challengers and nascent mechanism. This in turn suggests that Newtonianism was hardly the teleological goal of the process, but rather a complexly conditioned, contingent (and surprising) modification of the classical mechanism of the mid-seventeenth century.

Viewed in this way, the Scientific Revolution takes on an interesting rhythm as a process of change and transformation of an appropriate 'object'—systematic natural philosophy. There is a preliminary sixteenth-century stage, which will be termed the Scientific Renaissance, characterised by the erosion of Aristotelianism in some quarters, its deepening entrenchment in others and by a ferment of revived alternatives. There follows a 'critical' period (*c.* 1590-1650) of natural philosophical conflict marked by the initial construction of mechanistic philosophies, and then a brief period of relative consensus about, and institutionalisation of, a range of variants of the mechanical philosophy (*c.* 1650-90), punctuated and complicated by the advent of Newtonianism.

In the period of the Scientific Revolution, every system of natural philosophy, whether of a generally Aristotelian, mechanistic or Neo-Platonic magical/alchemical type, purported to describe and explain the entire universe and the relation of that universe to God, however conceived. The enterprise also involved explicitly, a concern with the place of human beings and society in that universe. Each system of natural philosophy rested on four structural elements whose respective contents and systematic relations went a considerable way towards defining the content of that system: (1) a theory of substance (material and immaterial), concerning what the cosmos consists of and what kinds of bodies or entities it contains; (2) a cosmology, an account of the macroscopic organisation of those bodies; (3) a theory of causation, an account of how and why change and motion occur; (4) an epistemology and doctrine of method which purports to show how the discourses under (1), (2) and (3) were arrived at and/or how they can be justified, and how they constitute a 'system'.

At the basis of any system of natural philosophy resided one or more privileged images, metaphors or models, the articulation of which underlay one or more of the elements and/or their modes of systematic interrelation. Such images and metaphors could be drawn from a variety of discursive resources: from common discourse about some phenomenon or craft; from already systematised discourse about politics, society or theology; or from the presumed guiding concepts of some especially valued field of scientific research. Because natural philosophers were selective in their choice of constitutive metaphors and models, the resulting systems embodied and expressed certain values and interests at the expense of others. However, a natural philosophy was not a simple metaphor, but a complex system, the parts of which and their interrelations could be given differential emphases and interpretations. Hence, the values and goals 'belonging' to a given natural philosophy were necessarily open to some variation and reinterpretation, and no system had an unequivocal, single meaning impressed upon it by its inventors or by its audience, hostile or receptive. This explains how natural philosophies could be integrated with political, social or religious systems of thought, and could be used to illustrate and support varied viewpoints about mankind, politics, society and God. They were sensitive to historical changes in their social contexts and helped contribute to them, for they could be focal points in shifts of attitude and interest amongst the educated elite.

It follows that natural philosophies cannot be reduced and explained away as 'reflections' of the social structure of early modern Europe. The construction, modification and purveying of natural philosophies was a rich, *sui generis* social enterprise, to which individuals devoted themselves with seriousness and hard-won skills, just because of the social, intellectual and religious value placed on having the 'correct' view of nature. Natural philosophies were, in short, context-sensitive and context-affecting; but they are not reducible to some simplistic reading of the social context.

Beyond having a workable conception of natural philosophy, the historian of science must also consider those narrow scientific disciplines, or traditions of highly specialised and technical research which either existed or first developed during the Scientific Revolution. Sixteenth-century Europe possessed two sets of mature scientific disciplines. T. S. Kuhn termed the first set the 'classical physical sciences', including geometrical astronomy and optics, statics and mechanics (study of the simple machines), harmonics and geometry itself. To this group of sciences, which were first constituted in classical antiquity, Kuhn added the mathematical treatment of natural change, as it had developed in the Aristotelian schools of the Latin West from the fourteenth century and been enriched in the Renaissance by connection with the statics and hydrostatics of Archimedes, the pseudo-Aristotelian *Mechanical Questions,* and the medieval 'science of weights', thus forming an additional domain of physical inquiry concerned with the quantitative treatment of local motion. these fields shared an essential reliance on mathematical articulation, and they were sufficiently developed in conceptual and technical terms to be able, in principle, to support cumulative traditions of posing and resolving problems about their respective objects of inquiry. Each of them commanded a body of esoteric conceptual material embedded in classical 'textbook' expositions and linked to exemplary sorts of problem situations and solutions.[5]
Similar, though not identical conditions held in the second set of mature sciences, those linked to medical practitioners and medical institutions: human anatomy, physiology and medical theory, the classical medical sciences. These too embodied esoteric, textbook-grounded bodies of material; but they lacked, of course, the mathematical articulation and hence the same degree of specification of problems and modes of solution. However, they did contain outcroppings of a serious and disciplined concern with observation and even in some cases experiment, which played only a minor role in the geometrically-based sciences.

Some enterprises not included in Kuhn's schema may well be added. Astrology was widely considered to be a science because it had a mathematical articulation, a textbook tradition going back to Claudius Ptolemy's *Tetrabiblos* and a long traditional linkage with medicine and with the practitioners of the other mathematically-based sciences. Alchemy should also be included, although its lineage was not so tightly bound to the existing cluster of sciences, and its moral-psychological aspirations and its search for redemption through esoteric knowledge and successful practice, tended to set its adherents apart from other practitioners.

The sciences existed in relation to the enterprise of natural philosophy. Indeed, each science was variously considered to be part of, or conditioned by, one or another system of natural philosophy. In Kuhnian or Koyréan terms the 'metaphysics' of a science was often supplied or enforced by one or another system of natural philosophy. For example, although the elaborate geometrical tools of Ptolemaic astronomy fell outside any plausible realistic interpretation, and hence outside any natural philosophical gloss, the main lines of Ptolemy's astronomy, its 'metaphysics', was clearly shaped by Aristotelian and Platonic natural philosophy: the finite earth-centred cosmos, the distinction between the celestial and terrestrial realms and the primacy of uniform circular motion. When, in the later sixteenth and early seventeenth centuries, Copernican astronomy became a critical issue, it was not as a set of new calculational fictions, but rather as a system with realistic claims implying the need for a framework of non-Aristotelian natural philosophy adequate to justifying its existence and explaining its physical mechanisms.

The shape of a science, its direction of development, and indeed its very legitimacy often depended upon the character of its natural philosophically-enforced metaphysics, which itself might have been the outcome of conflict and debate. So, for example, the mechanical philosophy supplied its spokesmen with metaphysical machinery which could be used either to marginalise scientific enterprises which were subsumed by antagonistic natural philosophies; or to co-opt acceptable portions of otherwise dubious scientific enterprises by reinterpreting them in terms of a mechanistic metaphysics, as was done with portions of the work of such non-mechanists as Harvey, Kepler, William Gilbert and Francis Bacon. Conversely, rapid change in a science and/or a shift in its social evaluation could lead to the constitution, alteration or abandonment of a natural philosophy through the borrowing or rejection of privileged images or models. Paracelsus's 'alchemisation' of natural philosophy comes to mind here, as does the rise of the mechanical philosophy, which was grounded in the concerns of practical mathematicians and devotees of 'mechanics'.

All of this suggests that the Scientific Revolution involved more than a process of change and displacement of natural philosophies. One also needs to attend to the sciences in the period: to their individual patterns of change (which largely conform to the three-stage model); to their relations with the existing natural philosophies; and to the shifting hierarchical patterns imposed on them by the contending systems of nature.

Finally, before the stages in the Scientific Revolution are discussed, one additional category has to be introduced, that of the practical arts, amongst which were numbered at the time navigation, cartography, architecture and fortification, surgery, mining, metallurgy and other chemical arts. In the period of the Scientific Revolution important questions surrounded the social role of the practical arts and the status of their methods, tools and results as 'knowledge'. These questions and the answers they received on the plane of natural philosophical discourse shaped the aims and contents of competing systems of nature and some developments in the individual sciences. The deeper social and economic structures of the age prompted these questions and therefore they affected natural philosophy and the sciences by this mediated pathway.

III. STAGES IN THE PROCESS OT THE SCIENTIFIC REVOLUTION

We can now return to the working periodisation of the process of the Scientific Revolution, articulating it in the light of the discussion of generic natural philosophy, the classical sciences and the practical arts. By concentrating on the so-called critical period as a function of the larger process, we can, on the one hand, prevent misunderstanding such characteristic 'Scientific Renaissance' figures as Nicholas Copernicus and Andreas Vesalius, and, on the other hand, we can avoid conceiving of the Scientific Revolution as a series of events destined to culminate in Newton.

3.1 The Scientific Renaissance: *c.* 1500-1600

The Scientific Renaissance owes its name to the fact that it displays in the realm of the classical sciences as well as that of natural philosophy many of the scholarly aims and practices which already characterised the treatment of classical literature, history and languages in earlier stages of the Renaissance. In the sixteenth century the established humanist practices of textual recovery, editing, translation and commentary were increasingly focused upon the scientific, mathe-matical and natural philosophical heritage of classical antiquity. This late maturation of the scientific phase of the Renaissance was due to several interacting factors. Firstly, there was the increasing penetration of university curricula by humanist studies which partly shifted the foci of intellectual interest and increased the pool of able individuals interested in directing humanist concerns into the sciences, mathematics and natural philosophy. Moreover, increasing numbers of university-educated men, tinged by humanism and possessing practical experience in law, administration, the military and even commerce, came to consider Scholastic Aristotelianism to some degree irrelevant. Such individuals were the instigators of, and audience for, increased attention to non-Artistotelian natural philosophies. Printing also appears to have been a critical factor determining the timing and shaping the outcome. The lure of authorship, authority, prestige, patronage and business made possible by print helped to focus attention on pursuits such as algebra, anatomy, surgery, mechanics and fortification, and natural magic. Ferment in these areas was crucial to some developments in natural philosophy and the sciences. A final factor is the re-evaluation of the status of the practical arts, their products and practitioners, which first began to gain momentum in the sixteenth century, and which catalysed developments in natural philosophy and the sciences.

The sixteenth century was marked by historically high levels of population increase and price inflation, and by an expanding commercial capitalist economy, set against the background of a significant development in the power, and to some degree the size, of state administrations. Overseas trade, and more importantly, internal trade within Europe increased, and the Dutch, followed by the English and hesitantly by the French, began their challenges to the established Spanish and Portuguese overseas empires. The earlier efflorescence of German mining, manufacture and trade continued until it was crippled in the Thirty Years War, and throughout the century the centre of internal European trade began to shift from the Mediterranean basin to the North Sea and Baltic region.

All of this had important consequences for the role and status of the practical arts. The number and diversity of potential patrons and clients for their output increased. At the same time expanded literacy, partly spurred by the Protestant Reformation and partly by access to print on the part of some master practitioners, their cultural allies and patrons, created a domain in which practitioners could compete for recognition and honour, whilst simultaneously contributing to a disparate chorus of claims that the practical arts and artisans deserved higher status, and that their skills and craft knowledge warranted the cultural status of 'science'.

Various groups were touched by this ideological and attitudinal development. There were, for example, leading literate craftsmen and engineers for whom School natural philosophy was irrelevant. Their attitudes could range from bald assertions that facts were better than words and practical action better than verbal disputation, to more sophisticated calls for the reorganisation of education with greater emphasis on the practical arts. The latter demands were sometimes reinforced by educated gentlemen or scholars, including anti-Aristotelian humanists seeking a revised curriculum of 'useful' subjects, ranging from improved rhetoric and dialectic, useful for the diplomat and administrator, to mathematics, useful for the gentleman officer.

Such developments spurred the outcroppings of anti-Aristotelianism which mark the sixteenth century, expressed as piecemeal challenges to traditional pedagogy, as well as adherence to non-Aristotelian natural philosophies. This in turn helps to explain the currency of Platonic themes in the alternative natural philosophies of the sixteenth century. If a practical mathematician, interested gentleman or scholarly humanist had some natural philosophical training and interest, a re-evaluation of the practical arts could support or motivate the advocacy of some philosophical alternative to Aristotle. Here Platonic modes of thought had considerable appeal, because of the great stress which was placed upon mathematics. This also allowed the mathematical arts to be placed in a better light, as, for example, in the work of a figure such as John Dee (1527-1608), for whom magical, neo-Platonic and mystical elements combined with a strong interest in the advocacy of the mathematical arts.

By attending to the sixteenth-century re-evaluation of the practical arts, one can clarify the long-standing question of the status of the classical Marxist explanations of the Scientific Revolution of Hessen, J. D. Bernal and Edgar Zilsel. It becomes clear that the crux of the matter is not how science responded to the technical problems created by nascent commercial capitalism. Rather, the issue becomes one of understanding how this larger development conditioned the re-evaluation of the arts, and how that re-evaluation in turn affected the aspirations, thought and behaviour of natural philosophers and practitioners of the sciences.

Sixteenth-century natural philosophy, which has proved notoriously difficult to analyse, receives some orientation from the notion of a Scientific Renaissance. The recovery, assimilation and publication of natural philosophical systems made available a wide and confusing array of non-Aristotelian approaches. These ranged from neo-Stoicism and Lucretian atomism, through varieties of neo-Platonism, some more or less flavoured with Hermetic influences and variously amalgamated with alchemy, natural and demonic magic and cabala; to more eclectic and idiosyncratic alternatives, derived

from figures such as Bernardino Telesio, Paracelsus, or even Pietro Pompanazzi, an Aristotelian whose natural philosophy was theologically suspect and shared some of the imperatives of natural magic. Nevertheless, it is also crucial to appreciate that throughout the sixteenth century, and frequently well into the seventeenth century as well, Scholastic Aristotelianism was officially entrenched and constituted the central element in the education of virtually all of the men who had any serious concern with natural philosophy. Indeed, the late sixteenth and early seventeenth centuries represented an 'Indian Summer' of Scholastic Aristotelianism, which, having survived the theological fissions of the Reformation, and the onslaughts of humanists and Platonists, found new life in the rapidly rigidifying academic curricula of the Protestant churches and their militant post-Tridentine Catholic opponents. Nor was Aristotelianism yet moribund as a metaphysics for scientific work. It was still a guide to the cosmological foundations of astronomy, while in physiology and anatomy Aristotelian concepts continued to flourish, as in the work of William Harvey.

Aristotelianism was, however, under fire from many directions. The central scientific challenge came from a Copernicanism construed in some very limited quarters as cosmologically true; but this challenge was largely latent until the last generation of the sixteenth century, and only gathered momentum in connection with the career of Galileo after 1609. (See art. 14, sect. 4.) On a more subtle level Aristotelianism was dismissed as irrelevant by elements of the avant-garde literati and by some scientific specialists, as well as by exponents of the practical arts. In seeking to establish the scientific credentials of their fields and their claims to higher status, men as diverse as Giovanni Battista Benedetti and Galileo in mechanics, and Paracelsus in medicine and alchemy had to engage in polemics with the teachings of the Schools. Anti-Aristotelian rhetoric was repeatedly heard outside the universities, in princely courts, print houses and workshops of master artisans; indeed anywhere the practice of a science or art fell outside the scope of Aristotelianism. Such rhetoric, often accompanied by articulation of alternative systems of natural philosophy, indicates that Aristotelianism was losing credibility and relevance within certain social groupings. However, the range of alternatives against Aristotle (and within Aristotelianism) was wide, eclectic and confused. Natural philosophical initiatives subserved a wide variety of social, educational and religious interests and no clear pattern is discernible. Rather than prematurely subsuming these alternatives under simple classifications such as 'the Hermetic tradition' or 'the Chemical philosophy', as some historians do, we should accept this confusion as a complex product of the larger structures of the age.

Turning to the existing classical sciences, one finds a marked increase in their recovery, reconstruction and extension in the Scientific Renaissance. The timing and the pace of recovery, revision and extension differed from field to field. In mathematical astronomy, the Renaissance phase is discernible from the late fifteenth century, whilst in mathematics and geometrical optics the pace of the Renaissance phase only accelerated a century later. Anatomy and medical theory followed more closely upon astronomy, the programme of editing and publishing the body of Galen's works culminating in the 1520s and 30s. In each case there was an initial stage of recovery, improvement and, if necessary, translation of texts. This could lead to positive extension in some cases, even if the advance was imagined to consist in a purification of sources or a return to lost ancient wisdom. The entire process took place amid the catalysing influence of the pedagogical and philosophical assault on Scholastic philosophy; the reassertion of Platonising modes of thought which helped revalue mathematics as the key to knowledge; and the more general trend towards recasting the ideal of knowledge in the image of the ideals of practice, use and progress, rather than contemplation, commentary and conservation.

By the mid- or later-sixteenth century, European scholars were offered a much enriched opportunity for work in each of the classical sciences. In astronomy Copernicus could enter into the highly technical tradition of planetary astronomy, basing himself on the prior labours of Regiomontanus (Johann Müller) and Georg Puerbach, the late-fifteenth-century renovators of the field, who themselves had tried to appropriate and perfect the tradition as it had emerged from the later Middle Ages. In geometry the process of assimilation and purification is even easier to discern, for the century saw not only improved texts and commentaries on Euclid's *Elements,* but the recovery, translation and edition of the texts of higher Greek mathematics.

The work of such Scientific Renaissance figures as Copernicus (1473-1543) and Andreas Vesalius (1514-64) needs to be seen in context and not merely as the first steps towards the 'inevitable' triumphs of Kepler, Harvey and Newton. For example, the work of Vesalius and its standing in the anatomical tradition of the sixteenth century is highly typical of the dynamic of the Scientific Renaissance. Vesalius, like Copernicus, stood roughly in the second generation of the Renaissance of his field. He was heir to, and contributed towards the establishment of, the corpus of Galenic writings. Like Copernicus, he was trying to grapple with newly available or improved classical texts, and in so doing made certain initiatives, all the while claiming that he was clarifying, purifying or recapturing the classical intent and achievement of the field. He stood near the beginning of a critical and cumulative tradition, grounded in the availability of the printed word and the high quality woodcut, and prompted by the rhetoric of the re-evaluation of practice (doing the

surgeon's work oneself). Yet Vesalius and later figures in the tradition remained largely Galenic in physiological theory, and they should not be read as providing steps towards Harvey, nor Whiggishly criticised for failing to reach his results. (See art. 36.)

3.2 The critical period: *c.* 1590-1650

The critical period is characterised by a conjuncture between an unprecedented burst of conceptual transformation in the classical sciences, and a heightened, often desperate, competition amongst systematic natural philosophies (some tied to Utopian and eirenic programmes of religious and social reform) which issued in the construction and initially successful dissemination of the mechanical philosophy. The Renaissance themes of the re-evaluation of practical knowledge and desire for command over nature continued to be sounded, and all of this occurred within a context of apparently heightening political, religious and intellectual turmoil.

The two generations after 1590 saw dramatic developments in mathematical astronomy and the emergence with new urgency of the question of the cosmological status of the Copernican system. The last working years of Tycho Brahe (1546-1601) open the critical period. His attempt to fashion a mathematical and cosmological compromise between Ptolemy and Copernicus raised the issue of cosmology more clearly than had Copernicus, and largely unintentionally did much to undermine the more rigidly Scholastic versions of the Aristotelian basis of the accepted cosmology. Kepler (1571-1630) was certainly the key figure, his active career virtually spanning the period in question. His laws of planetary motion, although not widely recognised during the period, marked the decisive technical break with the tradition of mathematical astronomy and posed the mathematical and physical problem of the motion of the planets in a new light. As he himself recognised, this work marked the birth of a new physico-mathematical field, celestial mechanics, although a sustained tradition of practice did not emerge from it, and Newton's later celestial mechanics was not entirely continuous with it in conceptual terms. More generally, Kepler contributed to the ripening of a cosmological crisis in the minds of early-seventeenth-century thinkers by vigorously asserting, in the light of his overriding philosophy of nature, that empirically determinable simple mathematical harmonies expressed and governed the motions and structure of the heavens and that their existence established the truth of his brand of Copernicanism. The crisis was brought to a head by the telescopic discoveries of Galileo and his polemical agitation starting with his writings of the 1610s.

The critical significance of the period needs little comment in the domain of mechanics and the mathematical study of local motion. With Simon Stevin (1548-1620) and Galileo, the two main trends of sixteenth-century studies of mechanics reached a climax and pointed towards qualitatively different concerns. Through a subtle mixture of practical, theoretical and pedagogical interests, Stevin enriched mechanics with novel insights, for example, a generalised notion of the parallelogram of forces, and a conception of hydrostatic pressure. But his insistence upon strict adherence to Archimedean methods, tied to conditions of equilibrium, led him to deny the possibility of a mathematical science of motion. Galileo's early work also brought him to the point of transcending the sixteenth-century tradition, albeit from a more dynamically-orientated perspective, at least at first, and throughout his career he sought in various ways to exploit geometrical-mechanical exemplars in the formulation of a new mathematical science of local motion. The mathematical account of falling bodies and projectile motion in his *Discorsi (Discourses . . . Concerning Two New Sciences,* 1638) capped the sixteenth-century agitation for a mathematical and anti-Aristotelian science of motion somehow grounded in 'mechanics'. It constituted a radical innovation, the first version of a classical mechanics, which is best seen not as an approximation to or forerunner of Newtonian mechanics, but rather as an initial and *sui generis* species of a new genus.[6]

It can be argued that mathematics revealed the most profound conceptual shifts in the period. With the recovery of the texts of higher Greek mathematics, interest was aroused in the precise manner in which the ancient mathematicians had produced their results. The synthetic and axiomatic style of the extant texts masked the procedures by which the results had first been discovered, although Pappus and other classical writers had hinted at the existence of general methods of discovery for solving problems and finding proofs of theorems. The search for the secret of Greek geometrical analysis became associated with and drew rhetorical force from the broader and very fluid contemporary interest in 'method' as a tool of discovery, proof and teaching, on the part of humanists and Aristotelians alike. In this intellectual environment it was easy for some to construe the hints in Pappus as implying that the Greeks had possessed a method of analysis. The humanist pedagogue and methodologist Petrus Ramus (1515-72) suggested that the traces of this unified analytical method might be found in the problem-solving techniques of the contemporary practical mathematical art of algebra, which itself was profiting from the prevailing re-evaluation of practical pursuits. François Viète (1540-1603) realised this insight, although in fact he drew more inspiration from the revised logistical art of Diophantus than from the procedures of contemporary 'cossic' algebra.

Viète envisioned the extension of his symbolic algebra or 'logistic of species' through the reconstruction of the texts of Greek geometrical analysis and their translation into his improved algebraic syntax. In the early seventeenth century Alexander Anderson, Willebrord

Snel and Marino Ghetaldi, as well as the giants Descartes and Fermat, worked within this tradition, drawing into it more of the resources of algebra, which they simultaneously developed further. With the appearance of Descartes' *Géométrie* (1637) and the mature work of Fermat, the analytical enterprise emerged as a self-conscious new approach to mathematics in which an improved algebra and emergent analytical theory of equations assimilated the field of analysis as previously conceived. New vistas emerged which led, amongst other things, to the invention of calculus later in the century. Greek geometry—synthetic, essentialist and tied to spatial intuition—began to be replaced by an abstract, relational, symbolic and analytical view of mathematics. This was the deepest conceptual transformation of the age, grounded in the attempt to recover and master the classical heritage in an environment coloured by changing views of the aims and bases of mathematical work, as embodied in the up-grading of algebra.

These changes in the classical sciences, included those in optics and physiology which have not been discussed, come closest to looking individually like scientific revolutions and jointly as *the* Scientific Revolution. Yet, even here it is not really fruitful to speak in this manner. One might, for example, try to explicate the expression 'revolution' by invoking a philosophical theory of scientific revolutions, for example Karl Popper's or T. S. Kuhn's. It is far from clear, however, that these would adequately explain the processes of change in each of the domains involved, and it is certainly clear that they would provide no serious rationale for a sense of revolution transcending and embracing all the individual cases. Moreover, one cannot neglect the processes of change in natural philosophy and the relations of those processes to these developments in the classical sciences. It is equally clear that the accelerating transformations of the classical sciences in the period 1590 to 1650 require for their historical comprehension a grasp of the nature of the Scientific Renaissance which they punctuated. This task outstrips the resources of any abstract theory of revolution applicable discipline by discipline. Therefore, these changes have been termed 'radical transformations' or 'significant conceptual shifts' in order to avoid the suggestion that some model of revolution can grasp them in the context of the larger and longer process. That process of the Scientific Revolution is not the sum of these smaller transformations and these transformations require delicate case-by-case treatment in relation to the stages in the larger process, including specific attention to the domain of natural philosophy.

In natural philosophy, the late sixteenth and early seventeenth centuries witnessed a proliferation of and climactic struggle amongst, competing systems. The period is critical, because out of the conflict and confusion of the natural philosophies of the Baroque age, there emerged the mechanical philosophy, which was self-consciously designed and constructed by a handful of innovators, notably Descartes and Pierre Gassendi, who were encouraged by Marin Mersenne, partly inspired by Isaac Beeckman, and followed shortly thereafter by Thomas Hobbes and other early English assimilators of this initially Continental invention, such as Kenelm Digby and Walter Charleton.

In the critical period, the most obvious threat to Aristotelian natural philosophy came from a variety of often Hermetically-tinged, neo-Platonically-based natural philosophies orientated towards alchemy and natural (or even demonic) magic. (See art. 37, sect. 2.) The seventeenth century had opened with the burning in Rome of Giordano Bruno (1548-1600), whose teaching combined appeals to a *prisca theologia* pre-dating Moses, astrology, cabala and magic of the natural and demonic sort. These elements yielded a magical gnosis of distinctly non-Christian temper and misplaced eirenic ambitions. Bruno had not been condemned for his natural philosophy *per se,* of course; nevertheless, his thought marks one extreme point of development of Hermetically- and magically-orientated alternative natural philosophies, and it haunted advanced but orthodox thinkers of the next generation, such as Mersenne and Descartes, who were to forge mechanism. Quite apart from the religious issues raised by the teaching and career of Bruno, cognitively *avant garde* but religiously orthodox thinkers had to contend with the ideological pall which Bruno's work cast upon novelties in natural philosophy, especially those linked to atomism or Copernicanism, or which embodied a high evaluation of mathematics as a key to practical, operative knowledge of nature.

Bruno, however, was only one of a number of challenging alternative figures in natural philosophy who surfaced in the early seventeenth century. Tommaso Campanella advocated a similar brand of general reform mediated by magical and astrological Hermeticism. The Rosicrucian fraternity, in its first incarnation amongst German Lutherans in the 1610s, seemed to be proposing a policy of Protestant reunion, linked to the promise of personal redemption to be achieved through a magical-alchemical science offering medical and spiritual benefits. Although the original wave of agitation was swallowed up in the opening stages of the Thirty Years War, the reputation and aspirations embodied in the Rosicrucian manifestos lived on in the very real persons of Robert Fludd and Michael Maier.

In the early seventeenth century Hermetically-orientated natural philosophies posed a particular challenge to those who stayed abreast of the latest scientific and philosophical currents, and whose commitment to Aristotle was weak or non-existent. Natural philosophies tinctured with Hermeticism were vehicles, but not the exclusive vehicles, of those sixteenth-century currents of opinion which had placed a premium on operative knowledge, on the search for command over the powers of nature. Such systems could marshal powerful sentiments in favour of the combined practical and spiritual value of mathematics. To the extent, which was considerable, that the founders of mechanism resonated similar sentiments, they had to design the mechanical philosophy so that the values were maintained, but the perceived moral, theological and political dangers and associations were held at bay.

The founders of classical mechanism hoped to resolve the conflict of natural philosophies in a way which was cognitively progressive, but religiously and politically conservative; that is, by exploiting and co-opting the achievements of the classical sciences, including the Copernican initiative in astronomy, by amplifying the premium placed upon mathematics and operative knowledge by sections of Renaissance opinion, whilst avoiding the perceived religious, political and moral pitfalls of the alchemical, magical, Hermetic and eclectic atomistic systems then bidding to displace Scholastic Aristotelianism. The mechanical philosophy was constructed so as to embody an arguably orthodox 'voluntarist' vision of God's relation to nature and to mankind, without threatening to collapse the divine into nature and/or to elevate man, as seeker of operative knowledge as well as wisdom, to the level of a 'magus', a status morally and cognitively unacceptable to mainline Catholic and Protestant thought alike. Accordingly, the selection and moulding of conceptual resources to form the mechanistic systems was a nice and dangerous task, firstly because it involved endorsing some values and aims characteristic of magical-alchemical systems, whilst explicitly opposing them as such, and, secondly, because the resulting product was itself intended to displace Aristotelianism in the institutional centres of natural philosophy, a task delayed in the event by one or two generations in virtually all instances.

The rise of mechanism paralleled the final triumph of Copernicanism; indeed an 'elective affinity' existed between the two. Not all realist Copernicans were mechanists; but all mechanists were realist Copernicans. Cause and effect cannot easily be disentangled here. The infinite universe of the mechanists, and the search for a mathematical-mechanical account of order and change, could prompt or reinforce anti-Aristotelianism; or could be selected in order to express such a pre-existing sentiment. On balance it seems that the acceptance of mechanism—for its many perceived cognitive, ethical, political and religious virtues—played a larger role in the widespread acceptance of Copernicanism by the educated public than vice versa.

Several other questions surround the interpretation of the rise of mechanism. Firstly, mechanism was constructed partly with the purpose of co-opting or defeating a certain erudite scepticism current in the early seventeenth century and destructive of dogmatic knowledge claims. But whether one can join some historians in speaking of a 'sceptical crisis' of the time to which the new philosophy proved to be an antidote, is a matter of debate.[7] Similarly, on a still broader contextual plane, the vogue of scepticism and the outbreak of Utopian and eirenic natural philosophies both relate to the religious and political turmoil of the period, notably the tensions within and amongst states leading up to the outbreak of the Thirty Years War in 1618. England can be understood as undergoing a delayed, idiosyncratic version of the process in the generation leading to the outbreak of the Civil Wars of the 1640s. For natural philosophers, systems of nature had valued and significant relations to religious, political and social discourses, and so problems and tensions were viewed through the filter of natural philosophising. This tended to suggest that the problems of the age had some of their basis in the very confusion of competing systems, a view which raised the stakes in finding and enforcing the true philosophy of nature and so fostered the proliferation of competing systems. But, again, whether the disturbed religious, political and social context deserves the title 'crisis' in the sense of a supposed 'general crisis of the seventeenth century' is questionable, as is the role of mechanism as one of the sources of 'resolution' of that crisis.[8]

In order to understand the critical period, it is not sufficient to pay attention only to the victors, the founders of mechanism. For example, Francis Bacon (1561-1626) and Johannes Baptista van Helmont (1579-1644) were major figures filtering and re-ordering the natural philosophical alternatives cast up in the sixteenth century, in order to devise programmes expressive of and responsive to the shifting value-orientations towards operative knowledge and the reform of pedagogy and communication in natural philosophy. Their careers display a driven but idiosyncratic commitment to constructing a novel natural philosophy in a situation viewed as void of credible alternatives.

Van Helmont stood for a transformed and sanitised alchemical natural philosophy, toning down the potential excesses—religious, psychological and political—of Paracelsianism, without sacrificing its stress on 'experience'. He, like certain other reformers of the Paracelsian tradition who exploited Ramus's pedagogical tenets, emphasised a new dispensation of a 'chemical philosophy' under the aegis of sober pedagogy and methodology. One could imagine that had the contextual conditions ultimately favouring mechanism not been present, van Helmont, Fludd and Maier might have been contending for natural philosophical hegemony, rather than Descartes, Gassendi and Hobbes.
Bacon can be seen as a brilliant *bricoleur* of disparate sixteenth-century value re-orientations and natural philosophical attitudes, whose discourse defeats attempts to conjure away his enterprise under the simple

rubrics of Aristotelian, alchemical, Puritan or Ramist 'influence'. He was a filter and refiner of the disparate polemics and attitudinal shifts characteristic of the sixteenth century, addressing on the level of natural philosophical culture the debates over the status of practical knowledge, the aims and method of 'useful' education of gentlemen, and the Protestant stress on cultivating socially useful, secular vocations. Bacon did not construct a system of natural philosophy; rather, he emphasised institutional programmatics, the ethical/valuational position of the natural philosopher, and, of course, method, a crucial but not exhaustive dimension of natural philosophy. An unsystematised and often implicit ontology was present in his work, however, and, like the more systematic and explicit elements of his thought, it was open to selective adoption and re-interpretation by mechanists and a rump of Hermeticists in the succeeding generation.

In sum, all of the major innovators in natural philosophy, whether mechanists or not, were shaped by and responded to the context of the critical stage of the Scientific Revolution. They all aimed to fill a perceived void of natural philosophical authority; they all overtly rejected Scholastic Aristotelianism whilst remaining to varying degrees dependent upon its vocabulary and conceptual resources; they all resonated on the plane of natural philosophical discourse with some positive interpretation of the sixteenth-century revaluation of the practical arts; and they all drew models and exemplars from the accrued catalogue of achievements in the practical arts and classical sciences of that century, although the choice and weighting of privileged items did vary greatly. In addition, most of the innovators stressed proper method and pedagogy as the salient feature of a new natural philosophy. Their strivings grew in all cases from sensitivity to the apparently irreconcilable divisions within religion and natural philosophy. Beyond all this there was the suspicion that natural philosophical dissent was a conditioning cause of the larger political and religious conflicts, which, accordingly, could be wholly or partially cured by the installation of a true philosophy.

3.3. The stage of consensus and consolidation: *c*. 1650-1690

The third stage in the process of the Scientific Revolution is characterised by the dissemination and widespread acceptance of varieties of the mechanical philosophy, and by the progressive melding of mechanism with a doctrine of method, loosely attributable to Bacon, emphasising experimental grounding, tentative theorising, exploitation of instruments and possible technological benefits. A consensus formed around an experimentally-orientated corpuscular-mechanical natural philosophy [hereafter ECM]. It was a loose consensus, to be sure, but none the less real, especially when compared with the conflict of natural philosophies characteristic of the two earlier stages. A further consequence and symptom of the existence of this consensus was the founding of the new permanent scientific societies and the establishment of the newly proclaimed social role and public rhetoric of science (see section I). The Scientific Revolution, conceived as a process emerging from the previous two stages and centred on the career of natural philosophy and the transformation and reordering of the sciences, ends at this stage.

The dominant natural philosophy of the third stage of the Scientific Revolution was not one definitive system, derived, for example, from Gassendi, Descartes, Hobbes, or, in the period itself, from Robert Boyle or Christiaan Huygens. Rather, ECM was a loose template from which were derived specific variants. There was, however, broad agreement about the methodological component of ECM, and it was not at all like the simplistic inductivism sometimes credited to Bacon and later forcefully proclaimed by Newton. In the hands of Boyle, Huygens or Jacques Rohault the methodological discourse of ECM asserted that the fundamental commitment to the metaphysics of corpuscular-mechanism was not, in fact, a metaphysical dogma at all, but rather a modest, albeit highly likely hypothesis. The method further dictated that any particular class of phenomena was to be explained by first devising a specific corpuscular-mechanical model, consistent with, but not deducible from, the deep ontology of 'matter in motion' and the fundamental laws of collision and motion, and then deducing from the model the phenomena in question. Considerations of the range of phenomena explained, the accuracy of the explanations and the absence of any obvious counter-instances, all served as criteria of the heightened probability of the model and explanation. Beyond this, the method stressed, in the manner of Bacon, 'experience' as the outcome of experimentation grounded in the use of instruments, a robust approach to nature promising deeper and more accurate indications of what there was and how it worked, a form of knowledge convertible to power over nature as its test and fruit.

This doctrine of method hardly sufficed to guide the development of ECM or the sciences subordinate to it. Yet, like any such otherwise ineffective and vague method doctrine, it did help to shape the way knowledge claims were assembled, negotiated and entrenched or rejected. It also functioned at the institutional level in providing some of the rhetorical resources for solidifying and delimiting legitimate practitioners and practices, as in the apologetics and programmatic rhetoric of the Royal Society. Under its loose label as 'Baconianism' this method doctrine also helped to solidify the new public rhetoric of science (see section 1).

Experimental corpuscular-mechanism drew great strength from the policy, adopted by the earliest of the mecha-

nists, of co-opting and reinterpreting the scientific triumphs of the critical period, so that they appeared to support or to be derived from the mechanical philosophy and its proclaimed method. Kepler's work was winnowed of its unacceptable neo-Platonism; Harvey was made out to have been a mechanist; and Galileo was, erroneously, turned into a full-blooded systematic mechanical philosopher. Bacon's eclectic ontology and implicit natural philosophy were repressed, and his method, or rather strategic chunks of it, were grafted onto mechanism. Large parts of alchemy, astrology and natural magic were pushed to the periphery of orthodox natural philosophy and culture; yet, in a sanitised form, 'rationalised' by ECM, surprisingly substantial slices of them remained to be pursued.

The impact of ECM upon the existing sciences was correspondingly complex. It would be a mistake simply to assume that the sciences all thoroughly succumbed to the metaphysical determination of ECM; or, in cases where that did happen, to assume that it was necessarily a good thing. Medicine and physiology came rather fully under the sway of ECM, a view which persisted well into the eighteenth century. The body was seen as a machine, both in gross macroscopic terms and on the level of mircro-structure and function. Much was learned in a fairly trivial way about the mechanics of the body; but the really basic problems of biology—those centring on the functional interrelation of the organs and systems and the self-regulation of the body—were systematically occluded by the mechanical model. In celestial mechanics, the domain opened by Kepler's work, the picture was more equivocal. Descartes had attempted a completely mechanistic, if qualitative and verbal, account of the causes of the heavenly motions in the Copernican system. Newton, who, for the time being, solved the main problems of celestial mechanics, had to break with strict mechanism and reintroduce into natural philosophy immaterial forces and agencies of neo-Platonic, Keplerian, or, some argue, Hermetic derivation. And even in the period leading up to the work of Newton, non-mechanical forces had entered the celestial mechanical speculations of Giovanni Alfonso Borelli and Robert Hooke. (See art. 16, sect. 5.)

It is possible, however, to misunderstand the rhythm of the development of modern science by focusing too intently upon Newtonian celestial mechanics. It is arguable that experimental corpuscular-mechanism and its attendant sciences, in their conceptual, institutional and rhetorical garb of the third stage, might have proceeded qualitatively rather undeterred for some considerable time had not something odd and unexpected happened in the form of Isaac Newton (1642-1727). Newton, it is true, redefined the consensus of the third stage whilst building upon it, with his post-mechanical philosophy of nature, reintroducing immaterial forces and powers, and with his dazzling re-working of the existing mathematical sciences—optics, mathematics and celestial and terrestial mechanics—which he unified. But the fact of Newton does not in itself prove that he was the teleological goal of the Scientific Revolution. To see things that way truncates our view of the process leading to the third stage, that of consensus and consolidation. Moreover, historians of science increasingly acknowledge that the eighteenth century was not simply the age of Newton, in natural philosophy, rational mechanics or the emerging fields of experimental science, such as electricity and magnetism, and heat. One can now see, for example, that much of eighteenth-century mechanics and mathematics followed from Continental developments deriving from the work of Huygens, Leibniz, Jakob and Johann Bernoulli, Nicolas Malebranche and others; that early and mid-eighteenth-century natural philosophers often espoused a fairly strict mechanistic ontology, rather than believe in Newtonian forces or ethers; and that the emergent experimental fields of the eighteenth century are not usefully viewed as the straightforward products of some inevitably fruitful Newtonian metaphysics. It is also generally agreed that Newtonianism was institutionalised and popularised in Britain and later on the Continent through institutional, social and political manœuvrings which in turn point up the contingency rather than inevitability of the Newtonian dispensation. (See art. 39.)

Our periodisation of the history of modern European science should take all this into account, starting by seeing the Scientific Revolution in terms of its three stages or moments, punctuated—contingently—by Newton.[9] His work, superimposed upon and partially redefining the third stage of the Scientific Revolution, should then be seen as setting, to a considerable degree, the boundaries of possibility in natural philosophy and the sciences in the eighteenth century, which in turn led to that period of accelerated development of the sciences and their institutional and professional structures between about 1770 and 1830, termed in some quarters 'the second scientific revolution'. (See art. 18, sect. 4.)

Notes

[1] A. Koyré, *Etudes galiléennes* (Paris, 1939); English trans. by J. Mepham, *Galileo studies* (Hassocks, 1978); B. Hessen, 'The social and economic roots of Newton's *Principia*', in *Science at the crossroads*, N. I. Bukharin *et al.* (eds.) (2nd ed., London, 1971), pp. 150-212.

[2] This point is only reinforced by the fact that Koyré's other works locate the revolution elsewhere; e.g. *Newtonian studies* (Chicago, 1965) [Newton, as well as Descartes]; *La révolution astronomique. Copernic, Kepler, Borelli* (Paris, 1961) [Copernicus and especially Kepler].

[3] A. C. Crombie, *Robert Grosseteste and the origins of experimental science: 1100-1700* (Oxford, 1953); J. H. Randall, *The school of Padua and the emergence of modern science* (Padua, 1961).

[4] For example, on natural law cf. M. B. Foster, 'The Christian doctrine of creation and the rise of modern natural science', *Mind,* 43 (1934), 446-68; F. Oakley, 'Christian theology and the Newtonian science', *Church history,* 30 (1961), 433-70 and E. Zilsel, 'The genesis of the concept of physical law', *Philosophical review,* 51 (1942), 245-79. On method cf. Crombie and Randall [note 3] with E. Zilsel, 'The origins of William Gilbert's scientific method', *Journal of the history of ideas,* 2 (1941), 1-32 and any 'internalist' account of the genesis of method in the seventeenth century.

[5] T. S. Kuhn, 'Mathematical versus experimental traditions in the development of physical science', in T. S. Kuhn, *The essential tension. Selected studies in scientific tradition and change* (Chicago, 1977), pp. 31-65.

[6] The fundamental character of Galileo's mechanics is best grasped through an elaboration of Gaston Bachelard's notion of how mathematico-experimental disciplines function, as for example in the work of Maurice Clavelin, *The natural philosophy of Galileo,* trans. A. J. Pomerans (Cambridge, Mass., 1974).

[7] R. H. Popkin, *The history of scepticism from Erasmus to Spinoza* (Berkeley, 1979).

[8] T. K. Rabb, *The struggle for stability in early modern Europe* (Oxford, 1975).

[9] Such a periodisation and conceptualisation of the historical categories in play can provide the basis for a critique of the existing major interpretations of the period as they appear in the works by Koyré, Kuhn, Merton, Yates and Hessen in the Bibliography, and in the works of the crisis theorists [notes 7 and 8].

PHILOSOPHY

Bertrand Russell (lecture date 1914)

SOURCE: A lecture delivered at The Museum on November 18, 1914, in *Scientific Method in Philosophy: The Herbert Spencer Lecture,* Oxford at the Clarendon Press, 1914, pp. 3-30.

[*In the following lecture, Russell summarizes the course of science since Copernicus and asserts that philosophy can progress only by studying, adapting, and applying the methods of science.*]

When we try to ascertain the motives which have led men to the investigation of philosophical questions, we find that, broadly speaking, they can be divided into two groups, often antagonistic, and leading to very divergent systems. These two groups of motives are, on the one hand, those derived from religion and ethics, and, on the other hand, those derived from science. Plato, Spinoza, and Hegel may be taken as typical of the philosophers whose interests are mainly religious and ethical, while Leibniz, Locke, and Hume may be taken as representatives of the scientific wing. In Aristotle, Descartes, Berkeley, and Kant we find both groups of motives strongly present.

Herbert Spencer, in whose honour we are assembled to-day, would naturally be classed among scientific philosophers: it was mainly from science that he drew his data, his formulation of problems, and his conception of method. But his strong religious sense is obvious in much of his writing, and his ethical preoccupations are what make him value the conception of evolution—that conception in which, as a whole generation has believed, science and morals are to be united in fruitful and indissoluble marriage.

It is my belief that the ethical and religious motives, in spite of the splendidly imaginative systems to which they have given rise, have been on the whole a hindrance to the progress of philosophy, and ought now to be consciously thrust aside by those who wish to discover philosophical truth. Science, originally, was entangled in similar motives, and was thereby hindered in its advances. It is, I maintain, from science, rather than from ethics and religion, that philosophy should draw its inspiration.

But there are two different ways in which a philosophy may seek to base itself upon science. It may emphasize the most general *results* of science, and seek to give even greater generality and unity to these results. Or it may study the *methods* of science, and seek to apply these methods, with the necessary adaptations, to its own peculiar province. Much philosophy inspired by science has gone astray through preoccupation with the *results* momentarily supposed to have been achieved. It is not results, but *methods,* that can be transferred with profit from the sphere of the special sciences to the sphere of philosophy. What I wish to bring to your notice is the possibility and importance of applying to philosophical problems certain broad principles of method which have been found successful in the study of scientific questions.

The opposition between a philosophy guided by scientific method and a philosophy dominated by religious and ethical ideas may be illustrated by two notions which are very prevalent in the works of philosophers, namely the notion of *the universe,* and the notion of *good and evil.* A philosopher is expected to tell us something about the nature of the universe as a whole, and to give grounds for either optimism or pessimism.

Both these expectations seem to me mistaken. I believe the conception of 'the universe' to be, as its etymology indicates, a mere relic of pre-Copernican astronomy; and I believe the question of optimism and pessimism to be one which the philosopher will regard as outside his scope, except, possibly, to the extent of maintaining that it is insoluble.

In the days before Copernicus, the conception of the 'universe' was defensible on scientific grounds: the diurnal revolution of the heavenly bodies bound them together as all parts of one system, of which the earth was the centre. Round this apparent scientific fact, many human desires rallied: the wish to believe Man important in the scheme of things, the theoretical desire for a comprehensive understanding of the Whole, the hope that the course of nature might be guided by some sympathy with our wishes. In this way, an ethically inspired system of metaphysics grew up, whose anthropocentrism was apparently warranted by the geocentrism of astronomy. When Copernicus swept away the astronomical basis of this system of thought, it had grown so familiar, and had associated itself so intimately with men's aspirations, that it survived with scarcely diminished force—survived even Kant's 'Copernican revolution', and is still now the unconscious premiss of most metaphysical systems.

The oneness of the world is an almost undiscussed postulate of most metaphysics. 'Reality is not merely one and self-consistent, but is a system of reciprocally determinate parts' [Bosanquet, *Logic,* ii]—such a statement would pass almost unnoticed as a mere truism. Yet I believe that it embodies a failure to effect thoroughly the 'Copernican revolution,' and that the apparent oneness of the world is merely the oneness of what is seen by a single spectator or apprehended by a single mind. The Critical Philosophy, although it intended to emphasize the subjective element in many apparent characteristics of the world, yet, by regarding the world in itself as unknowable, so concentrated attention upon the subjective representation that its subjectivity was soon forgotten. Having recognized the categories as the work of the mind, it was paralysed by its own recognition, and abandoned in despair the attempt to undo the work of subjective falsification. In part, no doubt, its despair was well founded, but not, I think, in any absolute or ultimate sense. Still less was it a ground for rejoicing, or for supposing that the nescience to which it ought to have given rise could be legitimately exchanged for a metaphysical dogmatism.

I

As regards our present question, namely, the question of the unity of the world, the right method, as I think, has been indicated by William James [in *Some Problems of Philosophy*].

"Let us now turn our backs upon ineffable or unintelligible ways of accounting for the world's oneness, and inquire whether, instead of being a principle, the 'oneness' affirmed may not merely be a name like 'substance', descriptive of the fact that certain *specific and verifiable connections* are found among the parts of the experiential flux. . . . We can easily conceive of things that shall have no connection whatever with each other. We may assume them to inhabit different times and spaces, as the dreams of different persons do even now. They may be so unlike and incommensurable, and so inert towards one another, as never to jostle or interfere. Even now there may actually be whole universes so disparate from ours that we who know ours have no means of perceiving that they exist. We conceive their diversity, however; and by that fact the whole lot of them form what is known in logic as 'a universe of discourse'. To form a universe of discourse argues, as this example shows, no further kind of connexion. The importance attached by certain monistic writers to the fact that any chaos may become a universe by being merely named, is to me incomprehensible."

We are thus left with two kinds of unity in the experienced world, the one what we may call the epistemological unity due merely to the fact that my experienced world is what *one* experience selects from the sum total of existence; the other that tentative and partial unity exhibited in the prevalence of scientific laws in those portions of the world which science has hitherto mastered. Now a generalization based upon either of these kinds of unity would be fallacious. That the things which we experience have the common property of being experienced by us is a truism from which obviously nothing of importance can be deducible: it is obviously fallacious to draw from the fact that whatever we experience is experienced the conclusion that therefore everything must be experienced. The generalization of the second kind of unity, namely, that derived from scientific laws, would be equally fallacious, though the fallacy is a trifle less elementary. In order to explain it let us consider for a moment what is called the reign of law. People often speak as though it were a remarkable fact that the physical world is subject to invariable laws. In fact, however, it is not easy to see how such a world could fail to obey general laws. Taking any arbitrary set of points in space, there is a function of the time corresponding to these points, i.e. expressing the motion of a particle which traverses these points: this function may be regarded as a general law to which the behaviour of such a particle is subject. Taking all such functions for all the particles in the universe, there will be theoretically some one formula embracing them all, and this formula may be regarded as the single and supreme law of the spatio-temporal world. Thus what is surprising in physics is not the existence of general laws, but their extreme simplicity. It is not the uniformity of nature that should surprise us, for, by sufficient analytic ingenuity, any

conceivable course of nature might be shown to exhibit uniformity. What should surprise us is the fact that the uniformity is simple enough for us to be able to discover it. But it is just this characteristic of simplicity in the laws of nature hitherto discovered which it would be fallacious to generalize, for it is obvious that simplicity has been a part cause of their discovery, and can, therefore, give no ground for the supposition that other undiscovered laws are equally simple.

The fallacies to which these two kinds of unity have given rise suggest a caution as regards all use in philosophy of general *results* that science is supposed to have achieved. In the first place, in generalizing these results beyond past experience, it is necessary to examine very carefully whether there is not some reason making it more probable that these results should hold of all that has been experienced than that they should hold of things universally. The sum total of what is experienced by mankind is a selection from the sum total of what exists, and any general character exhibited by this selection may be due to the manner of selecting rather than to the general character of that from which experience selects. In the second place, the most general results of science are the least certain and the most liable to be upset by subsequent research. In utilizing these results as the basis of a philosophy, we sacrifice the most valuable and remarkable characteristic of scientific method, namely, that, although almost everything in science is found sooner or later to require some correction, yet this correction is almost always such as to leave untouched, or only slightly modified, the greater part of the results which have been deduced from the premiss subsequently discovered to be faulty. The prudent man of science acquires a certain instinct as to the kind of uses which may be made of present scientific beliefs without incurring the danger of complete and utter refutation from the modifications likely to be introduced by subsequent discoveries. Unfortunately the use of scientific generalizations of a sweeping kind as the basis of philosophy is just that kind of use which an instinct of scientific caution would avoid, since, as a rule, it would only lead to true results if the generalization upon which it is based stood in *no* need of correction.

We may illustrate these general considerations by means of two examples, namely, the conservation of energy and the principle of evolution.

(1) Let us begin with the conservation of energy, or, as Herbert Spencer used to call it, the persistence of force. He says: [in *First Principles,* Part II, beginning of chap. vi.]

> 'Before taking a first step in the rational interpretation of phenomena, it is needful to recognize, not only the facts that Matter is indestructible and Motion continuous, but also the fact that Force persists. An

attempt to ascertain the laws to which manifestations in general and in detail conform, would be absurd if the agency to which they are due could either come into existence or cease to exist. The succession of phenomena would in such case be altogether arbitrary; and Science, equally with Philosophy, would be impossible.'

This paragraph illustrates the kind of way in which the philosopher is tempted to give an air of absoluteness and necessity to empirical generalizations, of which only the approximate truth in the regions hitherto investigated can be guaranteed by the unaided methods of science. It is very often said that the persistence of something or other is a necessary presupposition of all scientific investigation, and this presupposition is then thought to be exemplified in some quantity which physics declares to be constant. There are here, as it seems to me, three distinct errors. First, the detailed scientific investigation of nature does not *presuppose* any such general laws as its results are found to verify. Apart from particular observations, science need presuppose nothing except the general principles of logic, and these principles are not laws of nature, for they are merely hypothetical, and applied not only to the actual world but to whatever is *possible*. The second error consists in the identification of a constant quantity with a persistent entity. Energy is a certain function of a physical system, but is not a thing or substance persisting throughout the changes of the system. The same is true of mass, in spite of the fact that mass has often been defined as *quantity of matter*. The whole conception, of quantity, involving, as it does, numerical measurement based largely upon conventions, is far more artificial, far more an embodiment of mathematical convenience, than is commonly believed by those who philosophize on physics. Thus even if (which I cannot for a moment admit) the persistence of some entity were among the necessary postulates of science, it would be a sheer error to infer from this the constancy of any physical quantity, or the *a priori* necessity of any such constancy which may be empirically discovered. In the third place, it has become more and more evident with the progress of physics that large generalizations, such as the conservation of energy or mass, are far from certain and are very likely only approximate. Mass, which used to be regarded as the most indubitable of physical quantities, is now very generally believed to vary according to velocity, and to be, in fact, a vector quantity which at a given moment is different in different directions. The detailed conclusions deduced from the supposed constancy of mass for such motions as used to be studied in physics will remain very nearly exact, and, therefore, over the field of the older investigations very little modification of the older results is required. But as soon as such a principle as the conservation

of mass or of energy is erected into a universal *a priori* law, the slightest failure in absolute exactness is fatal, and the whole philosophic structure raised upon this foundation is necessarily ruined. The prudent philosopher, therefore, though he may with advantage study the methods of physics, will be very chary of basing anything upon what happen at the moment to be the most general results apparently obtained by those methods.

(2) The philosophy of evolution, which was to be our second example, illustrates the same tendency to hasty generalization, and also another sort, namely, the undue preoccupation with ethical notions. There are two kinds of evolutionist philosophy, of which both Hegel and Spencer represent the older and less radical kind, while Pragmatism and Bergson represent the more modern and revolutionary variety. But both these sorts of evolutionism have in common the emphasis on *progress,* that is, upon a continual change from the worse to the better or from the simpler to the more complex. It would be unfair to attribute to Hegel any scientific motive or foundation, but all the other evolutionists, including Hegel's modern disciples, have derived their impetus very largely from the history of biological development. To a philosophy which derives a law of universal progress from this history there are two objections. First, that the history itself is concerned with a very small selection of facts confined to an infinitesimal fragment of space and time, and even on scientific grounds probably not an average sample of events in the world at large. For we know that decay as well as growth is a normal occurrence in the world. An extra-terrestrial philosopher, who had watched a single youth up to the age of twenty-one and had never come across any other human being, might conclude that it is the nature of human beings to grow continually taller and wiser in an indefinite progress towards perfection; and this generalization would be just as well founded as the generalization which evolutionists base upon the previous history of this planet. Apart, however, from this scientific objection to evolutionism, there is another, derived from the undue admixture of ethical notions in the very idea of progress from which evolutionism derives its charm. Organic life, we are told, has developed gradually from the protozoon to the philosopher, and this development, we are assured, is indubitably an advance. Unfortunately it is the philosopher, not the protozoon, who gives us this assurance, and we can have no security that the impartial outsider would agree with the philosopher's self-complacent assumption. This point has been illustrated by the philosopher Chuang Tz in the following instructive anecdote:

'The Grand Augur, in his ceremonial robes, approached the shambles and thus addressed the pigs: "How can you object to die? I shall fatten you for three months. I shall discipline myself for ten days and fast for three. I shall strew fine grass, and place you bodily upon a carved sacrificial dish. Does not this satisfy you?"

Then, speaking from the pigs' point of view, he continued: "It is better, perhaps, after all, to live on bran and escape the shambles. . . ."

"But then," added he, speaking from his own point of view, "to enjoy honour when alive one would readily die on a war-shield or in the headsman's basket."

So he rejected the pigs' point of view and adopted his own point of view. In what sense, then, was he different from the pigs?'

I much fear that the evolutionists too often resemble the Grand Augur and the pigs.

The ethical element which has been prominent in many of the most famous systems of philosophy is, in my opinion, one of the most serious obstacles to the victory of scientific method in the investigation of philosophical questions. Human ethical notions, as Chuang Tz perceived, are essentially anthropocentric, and involve, when used in metaphysics, an attempt, however veiled, to legislate for the universe on the basis of the present desires of men. In this way they interfere with that receptivity to fact which is the essence of the scientific attitude towards the world. To regard ethical notions as a key to the understanding of the world is essentially pre-Copernican. It is to make man, with the hopes and ideals which he happens to have at the present moment, the centre of the universe and the interpreter of its supposed aims and purposes. Ethical metaphysics is fundamentally an attempt, however disguised, to give legislative force to our own wishes. This may, of course, be questioned, but I think that it is confirmed by a consideration of the way in which ethical notions arise. Ethics is essentially a product of the gregarious instinct, that is to say, of the instinct to co-operate with those who are to form our own group against those who belong to other groups. Those who belong to our own group are good; those who belong to hostile groups are wicked. The ends which are pursued by our own group are desirable ends, the ends pursued by hostile groups are nefarious. The subjectivity of this situation is not apparent to the gregarious animal, which feels that the general principles of justice are on the side of its own herd. When the animal has arrived at the dignity of the metaphysician, it invents ethics as the embodiment of its belief in the justice of its own herd. So the Grand Augur invokes ethics as the justification of Augurs in their conflicts with pigs. But, it may be said, this view of ethics takes no account of such truly ethical notions as that of self-sacrifice. This, however, would be a mistake. The success of

gregarious animals in the struggle for existence depends upon co-operation within the herd, and co-operation requires sacrifice, to some extent, of what would otherwise be the interest of the individual. Hence arises a conflict of desires and instincts, since both self-preservation and the preservation of the herd are biological ends to the individual. Ethics is in origin the art of recommending to others the sacrifices required for co-operation with oneself. Hence, by reflexion, it comes, through the operation of social justice, to recommend sacrifices by oneself, but all ethics, however refined, remains more or less subjective. Even vegetarians do not hesitate, for example, to save the life of a man in a fever, although in doing so they destroy the lives of many millions of microbes. The view of the world taken by the philosophy derived from ethical notions is thus never impartial and therefore never fully scientific. As compared with science, it fails to achieve the imaginative liberation from self which is necessary to such understanding of the world as man can hope to achieve, and the philosophy which it inspires is always more or less parochial, more or less infected with the prejudices of a time and a place.

I do not deny the importance or value, within its own sphere, of the kind of philosophy which is inspired by ethical notions. The ethical work of Spinoza, for example, appears to me of the very highest significance, but what is valuable in such work is not any metaphysical theory as to the nature of the world to which it may give rise, nor indeed anything which can be proved or disproved by argument. What is valuable is the indication of some new way of feeling towards life and the world, some way of feeling by which our own existence can acquire more of the characteristics which we must deeply desire. The value of such work, however immeasurable it is, belongs with practice and not with theory. Such theoretic importance as it may possess is only in relation to human nature, not in relation to the world at large. The scientific philosophy, therefore, which aims only at understanding the world and not directly at any other improvement of human life, cannot take account of ethical notions without being turned aside from that submission to fact which is the essence of the scientific temper.

II

If the notion of the universe and the notion of good and evil are extruded from scientific philosophy, it may be asked what specific problems remain for the philosopher as opposed to the man of science? It would be difficult to give a precise answer to this question, but certain characteristics may be noted as distinguishing the province of philosophy from that of the special sciences.

In the first place a philosophical proposition must be general. It must not deal specially with things on the surface of the earth, or with the solar system, or with any other portion of space and time. It is this need of generality which has led to the belief that philosophy deals with the universe as a whole. I do not believe that this belief is justified, but I do believe that a philosophical proposition must be applicable to everything that exists or may exist. It might be supposed that this admission would be scarcely distinguishable from the view which I wish to reject. This, however, would be an error, and an important one. The traditional view would make the universe itself the subject of various predicates which could not be applied to any particular thing in the universe, and the ascription of such peculiar predicates to the universe would be the special business of philosophy. I maintain, on the contrary, that there are no propositions of which the 'universe' is the subject; in other words, that there is no such thing as the 'universe'. What I do maintain is that there are general propositions which may be asserted of each individual thing, such as the propositions of logic. This does not involve that all the things there are form a whole which could be regarded as another thing and be made the subject of predicates. It involves only the assertion that there are properties which belong to each separate thing, not that there are properties belonging to the whole of things collectively. The philosophy which I wish to advocate may be called logical atomism or absolute pluralism, because while maintaining that there are many things, it denies that there is a whole composed of those things. We shall see, therefore, that philosophical propositions, instead of being concerned with the whole of things collectively, are concerned with all things distributively; and not only must they be concerned with all things, but they must be concerned with such properties of all things as do not depend upon the accidental nature of the things that there happen to be, but are true of any possible world, independently of such facts as can only be discovered by our senses.

This brings us to a second characteristic of philosophical propositions, namely that they must be *a priori*. A philosophical proposition must be such as can be neither proved nor disproved by empirical evidence. Too often we find in philosophical books arguments based upon the course of history, or the convolutions of the brain, or the eyes of shell-fish. Such special and accidental facts are irrelevant to philosophy, which must make only such assertions as would be equally true however the actual world were constituted.

We may sum up these two characteristics of philosophical propositions by saying that *philosophy is the science of the possible*. But this statement unexplained is liable to be misleading, since it may be thought that the possible is something other than the general, whereas in fact the two are indistinguishable.

Philosophy, if what has been said is correct, becomes indistinguishable from logic as that word has now come to be used. The study of logic consists, broadly speaking, of two not very sharply distinguished portions. On the one hand it is concerned with those general statements which can be made concerning everything without mentioning any one thing or predicate or relation, such for example as 'if x is a member of the class a and every member of a is a member of ß, then x is a member of the class ß, whatever x, a and ß may be'. On the other hand, it is concerned with the analysis and enumeration of logical *forms*, i.e. with the kinds of propositions that may occur, with the various types of facts, and with the classification of the constituents of facts. In this way logic provides an inventory of possibilities, a repertory of abstractly tenable hypotheses.

It might be thought that such a study would be too vague and too general to be of any very great importance, and that, if its problems became at any point sufficiently definite, they would be merged in the problems of some special science. It appears, however, that this is not the case. In some problems, for example, the analysis of space and time, the nature of perception, or the theory of judgement, the discovery of the logical form of the facts involved is the hardest part of the work and the part whose performance has been most lacking hitherto. It is chiefly for want of the logical hypothesis that such problems have hitherto been treated in such an unsatisfactory manner, and have given rise to those contradictions or antinomies in which the enemies of reason among philosophers have at all times delighted.

By concentrating attention upon the investigation of logical forms, it becomes possible at last for philosophy to deal with its problems piecemeal, and to obtain, as the sciences do, such partial and probably not wholly correct results as subsequent investigation can utilize even while it supplements and improves them. Most philosophies hitherto have been constructed all in one block, in such a way that, if they were not wholly correct, they were wholly incorrect, and could not be used as a basis for further investigations. It is chiefly owing to this fact that philosophy, unlike science, has hitherto been unprogressive, because each original philosopher has had to begin the work again from the beginning, without being able to accept anything from the work of his predecessors. A scientific philosophy such as I wish to recommend will be piecemeal and tentative like other sciences; above all, it will be able to invent hypotheses which, even if they are not wholly true, will yet remain fruitful after the necessary corrections have been made. This possibility of successive approximations to the truth is, more than anything else, the source of the triumphs of science, and to transfer this possibility to philosophy is to ensure a progress in method whose importance it would be almost impossible to exaggerate.

The essence of philosophy as thus conceived is analysis, not synthesis. To build up systems of the world, like Heine's German professor who knit together fragments of life and made an intelligible system out of them, is not, I believe, any more feasible than the discovery of the philosopher's stone. What is feasible is the understanding of general forms, and the division of traditional problems into a number of separate and less baffling questions. 'Divide and conquer' is the maxim of success here as elsewhere.

Let us illustrate these somewhat general maxims by examining their application to the philosophy of space, for it is only in application that the meaning or importance of a method can be understood. Suppose we are confronted with the problem of space as presented in Kant's Transcendental Aesthetic, and suppose we wish to discover what are the elements of the problem and what hope there is of obtaining a solution of them. It will soon appear that three entirely distinct problems, belonging to different studies, and requiring different methods for their solution, have been confusedly combined in the supposed single problem with which Kant is concerned. There is a problem of logic, a problem of physics, and a problem of theory of knowledge. Of these three, the problem of logic can be solved exactly and perfectly; the problem of physics can probably be solved with as great a degree of certainty and as great an approach to exactness as can be hoped in an empirical region; the problem of epistemology, however, remains very obscure and very difficult to deal with. Let us see how these three problems arise.

(1) The logical problem has arisen through the suggestions of non-Euclidean geometry. Given a body of geometrical propositions, it is not difficult to find a minimum statement of the axioms from which this body of propositions can be deduced. It is also not difficult, by dropping or altering some of these axioms, to obtain a more general or a different geometry, having, from the point of view of pure mathematics, the same logical coherency and the same title to respect as the more familiar Euclidean geometry. The Euclidean geometry itself is true perhaps of actual space (though this is doubtful), but certainly of an infinite number of purely arithmetical systems, each of which, from the point of view of abstract logic, has an equal and indefeasible right to be called a Euclidean space. Thus space as an object of logical or mathematical study loses its uniqueness; not only are there many kinds of spaces, but there are an infinity of examples of each kind, though it is difficult to find any kind of which the space of physics may be an example, and it is impossible to find any kind of which the space of physics is certainly an example. As an illustration of one possible logical system of geometry we may consider all relations of three terms which are analogous in certain formal respects to the relation 'between' as it appears to be in actual space. A space is then defined by means of one such three-term relation. The points of the space are all the terms which have this relation to something

or other, and their order in the space in question is determined by this relation. The points of one space are necessarily also points of other spaces, since there are necessarily other three-term relations having those same points for their field. The space in fact is not determined by the class of its points, but by the ordering three-term relation. When enough abstract logical properties of such relations have been enumerated to determine the resulting kind of geometry, say, for example, Euclidean geometry, it becomes unnecessary for the pure geometer in his abstract capacity to distinguish between the various relations which have all these properties. He considers the whole class of such relations, not any single one among them. Thus in studying a given kind of geometry the pure mathematician is studying a certain class of relations defined by means of certain abstract logical properties which take the place of what used to be called axioms. The nature of geometrical *reasoning* therefore is purely deductive and purely logical; if any special epistemological peculiarities are to be found in geometry, it must not be in the reasoning, but in our knowledge concerning the axioms in some given space.

(2) The physical problem of space is both more interesting and more difficult than the logical problem. The physical problem may be stated as follows:—to find in the physical world, or to construct from physical materials, a space of one of the kinds enumerated by the logical treatment of geometry. This problem derives its difficulty from the attempt to accommodate to the roughness and vagueness of the real world some system possessing the logical clearness and exactitude of pure mathematics. That this can be done with a certain degree of approximation is fairly evident. If I see three people A, B, and C sitting in a row, I become aware of the fact which may be expressed by saying that B is between A and C rather than that A is between B and C, or C is between A and B. This relation of 'between' which is thus perceived to hold has some of the abstract logical properties of those three-term relations which, we saw, give rise to a geometry, but its properties fail to be exact, and are not, as empirically given, amenable to the kind of treatment at which geometry aims. In abstract geometry we deal with points, straight lines, and planes; but the three people A, B, and C whom I see sitting in a row are not exactly points, nor is the row exactly a straight line. Nevertheless physics, which formally assumes a space containing points, straight lines, and planes, is found empirically to give results applicable to the sensible world. It must therefore be possible to find an interpretation of the points, straight lines, and planes of physics in terms of physical data, or at any rate in terms of data together with such hypothetical additions as seem least open to question. Since all data suffer from a lack of mathematical precision through being of a certain size and somewhat vague in outline, it is plain that if such a notion as that of a point is to find any application to

empirical material, the point must be neither a datum nor a hypothetical addition to data, but a *construction* by means of data with their hypothetical additions. It is obvious that any hypothetical filling out of data is less dubious and unsatisfactory when the additions are closely analogous to data than when they are of a radically different sort. To assume, for example, that objects which we see continue, after we have turned away our eyes, to be more or less analogous to what they were while we were looking, is a less violent assumption than to assume that such objects are composed of an infinite number of mathematical points. Hence in the physical study of the geometry of physical space, points must not be assumed *ab initio* as they are in the logical treatment of geometry, but must be constructed as systems composed of data and hypothetical analogues of data. We are thus led naturally to define a physical point as a certain class of those objects which are the ultimate constituents of the physical world. It will be the class of all those objects which, as one would naturally say, *contain* the points. To secure a definition giving this result, without previously assuming that physical objects are composed of points, is an agreeable problem in mathematical logic. The solution of this problem and the perception of its importance are due to my friend Dr. Whitehead. The oddity of regarding a point as a class of physical entities wears off with familiarity, and ought in any case not to be felt by those who maintain, as practically every one does, that points are mathematical fictions. The word 'fiction' is used glibly in such connexions by many men who seem not to feel the necessity of explaining how it can come about that a fiction can be so useful in the study of the actual world as the points of mathematical physics have been found to be. By our definition, which regards a point as a class of physical objects, it is explained both how the use of points can lead to important physical results, and how we can nevertheless avoid the assumption that points are themselves entities in the physical world.

Many of the mathematically convenient properties of abstract logical spaces cannot be either known to belong or known not to belong to the space of physics. Such are all the properties connected with continuity. For to know that actual space has these properties would require an infinite exactness of sense-perception. If actual space is continuous, there are nevertheless many possible non-continuous spaces which will be empirically indistinguishable from it; and, conversely, actual space may be non-continuous and yet empirically indistinguishable from a possible continuous space. Continuity, therefore, though obtainable in the *a priori* region of arithmetic, is not with certainty obtainable in the space or time of the physical world: whether these are continuous or not would seem to be a question not only unanswered but for ever unanswerable. From the point of view of philosophy, however, the discovery that a question is unanswerable is as complete an answer as

any that could possibly be obtained. And from the point of view of physics, where no empirical means of distinction can be found, there can be no empirical objection to the mathematically simplest assumption, which is that of continuity.

The subject of the physical theory of space is a very large one, hitherto little explored. It is associated with a similar theory of time, and both have been forced upon the attention of philosophically minded physicists by the discussions which have raged concerning the theory of relativity.

(3) The problem with which Kant is concerned in the Transcendental Aesthetic is primarily the epistemological problem: 'How do we come to have knowledge of geometry *a priori?*' By the distinction between the logical and physical problems of geometry, the bearing and scope of this question are greatly altered. Our knowledge of pure geometry is *a priori* but is purely logical. Our knowledge of physical geometry is synthetic, but is not *a priori*. Our knowledge of pure geometry is hypothetical, and does not enable us to assert, for example, that the axiom of parallels is true in the physical world. Our knowledge of physical geometry, while it does enable us to assert that this axiom is approximately verified, does not, owing to the inevitable inexactitude of observation, enable us to assert that it is verified *exactly*. Thus, with the separation which we have made between pure geometry and the geometry of physics, the Kantian problem collapses. To the question, 'How is synthetic *a priori* knowledge possible?' we can now reply, 'It is not possible,' at any rate if 'synthetic' means 'not deducible from logic alone'. Our knowledge of geometry, like the rest of our knowledge, is derived partly from logic, partly from sense, and the peculiar position which in Kant's day geometry appeared to occupy is seen now to be a delusion. There are still some philosophers, it is true, who maintain that our knowledge that the axiom of parallels, for example, is true of actual space, is not to be accounted for empirically, but is as Kant maintained derived from an *a priori* intuition. This position is not logically refutable, but I think it loses all plausibility as soon as we realize how complicated and derivative is the notion of physical space. As we have seen, the application of geometry to the physical world in no way demands that there should really be points and straight lines among physical entities. The principle of economy, therefore, demands that we should abstain from assuming the existence of points and straight lines. As soon, however, as we accept the view that points and straight lines are complicated constructions by means of classes of physical entities, the hypothesis that we have an *a priori* intuition enabling us to know what happens to straight lines when they are produced indefinitely becomes extremely strained and harsh; nor do I think that such an hypothesis would ever have arisen in the mind of a philosopher who had grasped the nature of physical space. Kant, under the influence of Newton, adopted, though with some vacillation, the

hypothesis of absolute space, and this hypothesis, though logically unobjectionable, is removed by Occam's razor, since absolute space is an unnecessary entity in the explanation of the physical world. Although, therefore, we cannot refute the Kantian theory of an *a priori* intuition, we can remove its grounds one by one through an analysis of the problem. Thus here, as in many other philosophical questions, the analytic method, while not capable of arriving at a demonstrative result, is nevertheless capable of showing that all the positive grounds in favour of a certain theory are fallacious and that a less unnatural theory is capable of accounting for the facts.

Another question by which the capacity of the analytic method can be shown is the question of realism. Both those who advocate and those who combat realism seem to me to be far from clear as to the nature of the problem which they are discussing. If we ask: 'Are our objects of perception *real* and are they *independent* of the percipient?' it must be supposed that we attach some meaning to the words 'real' and 'independent', and yet, if either side in the controversy of realism is asked to define these two words, their answer is pretty sure to embody confusions such as logical analysis will reveal.

Let us begin with the word 'real'. There certainly are objects of perception, and therefore, if the question whether these objects are real is to be a substantial question, there must be in the world too sorts of objects, namely, the real and the unreal, and yet the unreal is supposed to be essentially what there is not. The question what properties must belong to an object in order to make it real is one to which an adequate answer is seldom if ever forthcoming. There is of course the Hegelian answer, that the real is the self-consistent and that nothing is self-consistent except the Whole, but this answer, true or false, is not relevant in our present discussion, which moves on a lower plane and is concerned with the status of objects of perception among other objects of equal fragmentariness. Objects of perception are contrasted, in the discussions concerning realism, rather with psychical states on the one hand and matter on the other hand than with the all-inclusive whole of things. The question we have therefore to consider is the question as to what can be meant by assigning 'reality' to some but not all of the entities that make up the world. Two elements, I think, make up what is felt rather than thought when the word 'reality' is used in this sense. A thing is real if it persists at times when it is not perceived; or again, a thing is real when it is correlated with other things in a way which experience has led us to expect. It will be seen that reality in either of these senses is by no means necessary to a thing, and that in fact there might be a whole world in which nothing was real in either of these senses. It might turn out that the objects of perception failed of

reality in one or both of these respects, without its being in any way deducible that they are not parts of the external world with which physics deals. Similar remarks will apply to the word 'independent'. Most of the associations of this word are bound up with ideas as to causation which it is not now possible to maintain. *A* is independent of *B* when *B* is not an indispensable part of the *cause* of *A*. But when it is recognized that causation is nothing more than correlation, and that there are correlations of simultaneity as well as of succession, it becomes evident that there is no uniqueness in a series of causal antecedents of a given event, but that, at any point where there is a correlation of simultaneity, we can pass from one line of antecedents to another in order to obtain a new series of causal antecedents. It will be necessary to specify the causal law according to which the antecedents are to be considered. I received a letter the other day from a correspondent who had been puzzled by various philosophical questions. After enumerating them he says: 'These questions led me from Bonn to Strassburg, where I found Professor Simmel.' Now, it would be absured to deny that these questions caused his body to move from Bonn to Strassburg, and yet it must be supposed that a set of purely mechanical antecedents could also be found which would account for this transfer of matter from one place to another. Owing to this plurality of causal series antecedent to a given event, the notion of *the* cause becomes indefinite, and the question of independence becomes correspondingly ambiguous. Thus, instead of asking simply whether *A* is independent of *B*, we ought to ask whether there is a series determined by such and such causal laws leading from *B* to *A*. This point is important in connexion with the particular question of objects of perception. It may be that no objects quite like those which we perceive ever exist unperceived; in this case there will be a causal law according to which objects of perception are not independent of being perceived. But even if this be the case, it may nevertheless also happen that there are purely physical causal laws determining the occurrence of objects which are perceived by means of other objects which perhaps are not perceived. In that case, in regard to such causal laws objects of perception will be independent of being perceived. Thus the question whether objects of perception are independent of being perceived is, as it stands, indeterminate, and the answer will be yes or no according to the method adopted of making it determinate. I believe that this confusion has borne a very large part in prolonging the controversies on this subject, which might well have seemed capable of remaining for ever undecided. The view which I should wish to advocate is that objects of perception do not persist unchanged at times when they are not perceived, although probably objects more or less resembling them do exist at such times; that objects of perception are part, and the only empirically knowable part, of the actual subject-matter of physics, and are themselves properly to be called physical; that purely physical laws exist determining the character and duration of objects of perception without any reference to the fact that they are perceived; and that in the establishment of such laws the propositions of physics do not presuppose any propositions of psychology or even the existence of mind. I do not know whether realists would recognize such a view as realism. All that I should claim for it is, that it avoids difficulties which seem to me to beset both realism and idealism as hitherto advocated, and that it avoids the appeal which they have made to ideas which logical analysis shows to be ambiguous. A further defence and elaboration of the positions which I advocate, but for which time is lacking now, will be found indicated in my book on *Our Knowledge of the External World*.

The adoption of scientific method in philosophy, if I am not mistaken, compels us to abandon the hope of solving many of the more ambitious and humanly interesting problems of traditional philosophy. Some of these it relegates, though with little expectation of a successful solution, to special sciences, others it shows to be such as our capacities are essentially incapable of solving. But there remain a large number of the recognized problems of philosophy in regard to which the method advocated gives all those advantages of division into distinct questions, of tentative, partial, and progressive advance, and of appeal to principles with which, independently of temperament, all competent students must agree. The failure of philosophy hitherto has been due in the main to haste and ambition: patience and modesty, here as in other sciences, will open the road to solid and durable progress.

John Redwood comments on rationality during the "Age of Reason":

The age which has sometimes been loosely characterized as an age of reason was in many ways no more rational than preceding ages. Men have always used reason to make things intelligible for want of anything better, and most people who write prose or who pretend to think about the larger issues of the world and the universe can lay claim to using some form of reason to help guide their thought and construct their arguments. It is difficult to see that Thomas Hobbes was any more reasonable than Thomas Aquinas, impossible to allege that John Locke's reason was necessarily superior to the reason of Duns Scotus. All that can be said is that later seventeenth- and early eighteenth-century thinkers made rather more use of the word 'reason', and heralded it as an agent with which they could construct the new universe, whilst at the same time amongst themselves implicitly if not explicitly they differed fundamentally about the nature of that reason and the impact of its use.

John Redwood, in his Reason, Ridicule and Religion: The Age of Enlightenment in England 1600-1750, *Thames and Hudson, 1976.*

G. H. R. Parkinson (essay date 1993)

SOURCE: An introduction to *The Renaissance and Seventeenth-Century Rationalism,* edited by G. H. R. Parkinson, Routledge, 1993, pp. 1-15.

[*In the following essay, Parkinson provides an overview of philosophy in the Renaissance, focusing on humanism.*]

The philosophy that is discussed in this volume covers a period of some three hundred and fifty years, from roughly the middle of the fourteenth century to the early years of the eighteenth. What is offered, however, is not a comprehensive history of the philosophy of this period. Topics such as the later stages of scholasticism, and the beginnings of British empiricism in the seventeenth century, are not discussed here, but are reserved for other volumes in this series. The substance of the volume is the history of certain important philosophical movements that occurred during this period: namely, Renaissance philosophy and seventeenth-century rationalism. But the volume does not deal with these movements exclusively. If one is to understand Renaissance philosophy, one must also examine the scholastic thought against which it reacted and with which it frequently interacted. Similarly, if one is to understand the seventeenth-century rationalists, one must also understand some of their contemporaries who were not rationalists—men such as Bacon, Gassendi and Hobbes. They therefore find a place here, as do Renaissance scholastics such as Pomponazzi and Cremonini.

The division of the history of philosophy into a number of movements is a procedure that has often been followed, but it has its critics. In recent years, historians of philosophy have emphasized what one might call the individuality, the 'thisness' of philosophers, and have argued that to try to force this or that individual into pre-set categories can lead to distortions. There is indeed a danger of such distortions; on the other hand, it seems fair to say that during certain epochs certain philosophical questions came to the forefront, and that philosophers provided answers which (although different) had some kinship, so that it is possible to speak of a 'movement' in such cases. Such, at any rate, is the assumption made in this volume; whether the assumption is a fruitful one, the volume itself will show.

The term 'Renaissance philosophy' is a controversial one, as indeed is the term 'seventeenth-century rationalism'. It has been argued that the very notion of the Renaissance is a myth,[1] and one may wonder how it can be useful to speak of the philosophy of a myth. But it is important not to exaggerate. Scholars are in general agreement that there was in Western Europe, between roughly 1350 and the first decades of the seventeenth century,[2] a cultural movement which may usefully be called 'the Renaissance', and that a philosophy or group of philosophies formed a part of this movement. What is at issue, when people talk of the myth of the Renaissance, is the making of certain inflated claims on behalf of this movement.

In explaining what is meant here by 'Renaissance philosophy', I will begin by stating a commonplace. This is, that the area covered by the term 'philosophy' has shrunk in the course of the centuries; that, for example, what was once called 'natural philosophy' is now called 'physics', and an important part of what was once called 'mental philosophy' is now called 'psychology'. In the Renaissance, the term 'philosophy' had a very wide sense indeed, covering not only physics and psychology, but also such subjects as rhetoric, poetics and history, and even magic and astrology.[3] However, the term also covered what would now be called 'philosophy'; scholars speak of Renaissance logic and metaphysics, Renaissance theory of knowledge, and Renaissance moral and political philosophy. It is Renaissance philosophy in this sense that will be the concern of the present volume.

I have already implied a distinction between Renaissance philosophy and scholasticism—a movement which, incidentally, continued to exist up to the seventeenth century. This indicates that when 'Renaissance philosophy' is spoken of here the term is not taken to mean every philosophy which existed during the period of the Renaissance. Rather, it means a philosophy which was distinctively Renaissance in character. At this stage, it is necessary to try to be a little clearer about the term 'Renaissance'. I have spoken of the period which the Renaissance is generally agreed to have covered; there is also general agreement that the movement began in Italy and spread to the rest of Western Europe. It was a movement in which (to quote one eminent specialist in the field) 'there was a revival of interest in the literature, styles and forms of classical antiquity'.[4] But this definition generates a problem. I have distinguished Renaissance philosophy from scholasticism; but it is well known that the scholastics, too, derived much inspiration from classical philosophy. The question is, then, what distinguishes Renaissance philosophy from scholasticism. Here, one must first consider what the term 'scholasticism' means. As a philosophical movement, scholasticism reached its peak during the Middle Ages, and for some people the terms 'scholasticism' and 'medieval Christian philosophy' are interchangeable.[5] There is a more precise sense of the term, however. In this sense, scholasticism begins in cathedral schools in the eleventh century, and reaches its peak in the universities of Paris and Oxford during a period that lasted from the early thirteenth to the middle of the fourteenth century. As a guide to the nature of scholasticism, taken in this sense, it is helpful to follow the account given by Dom David Knowles

in his book *The Evolution of Medieval Thought*.[6] Knowles argues that scholasticism was distinguished by its goal, form and technique. Its goal was to provide a preparation for theology and to explain and defend Christian doctrines. In its form, it depended heavily on ancient philosophy, and in particular on Aristotle. Its technique was, *par excellence,* the method of *quaestio, disputatio* and *sententia:* the posing of a problem which was such that authorities differed about the correct answer, arguments concerning the problem, and a solution.[7]

Although Renaissance philosophy did not follow the method of *quaestio, disputatio* and *sententia,* it might be argued that it resembled scholasticism in respect of the fact that it was a book-centred philosophy, deriving its inspiration from the writings of the ancients. It would be granted that Renaissance scholars rediscovered many classical texts, with the result that their knowledge of ancient philosophy was much wider than that which the medievals had. But it may be said that this would not of itself justify one in regarding the Renaissance as a separate movement; it might simply be a movement that did more effectively what the scholastics had tried to do. In order to answer this point, it is necessary to examine more closely the relation between Renaissance writers and classical texts. More specifically, one has to consider that aspect of the culture of the Renaissance which is called 'humanism'. The abstract noun 'humanism', like the term 'the Renaissance', is a nineteenth-century coinage; however, the term 'humanist' is much older. It originated in Italy in the late fifteenth century and was used to refer to a teacher or student of the *studia humanitatis*—the humanities—a term which was used to mean the study of classical texts concerning, in the main, five subjects: grammar, rhetoric, poetics, moral philosophy and history.[8] The deeper knowledge of classical Latin and Greek that the humanists acquired led them to scorn both the scholastics' translations of the classics and their barbarous misuse of the Latin language.[9] Instead of using the cumbrous Latin of the scholastics, the humanists wanted to write about philosophical topics in elegant Latin of the kind that Cicero might have written.

I have said that the philosophy that most concerned the humanists was moral philosophy: that is, a branch of philosophy that concerns human beings and their relations with each other. This concentration of interest upon human beings was emphasized by the Swiss scholar Jakob Burckhardt in his influential book *The Civilisation of the Renaissance in Italy* (1860). Burckhardt saw the Renaissance as an epoch in which man for the first time became a genuine individual; an epoch in which the modern age began. Modern critics are sceptical of Burckhardt's claim, arguing that although the writers and artists of the Renaissance distanced themselves from the Middle Ages, they were in fact more medieval than they realized. When such scholars speak of 'the myth of the Renaissance' it is above all Burck-hardt's picture of the Renaissance that they have in mind.[10]

What, then, was the importance of the Renaissance in the history of Western philosophy? Some scholars point to the way in which late Renaissance philosophy questioned 'all authorities, even the classics'; they also see it as leading to seventeenth-century attempts to establish the unity and coherence of knowledge.[11] To this it may be replied that the philosophers of the Middle Ages were by no means uncritical in their response to the classical philosophers, and that the establishment of the unity of knowledge was surely the aim of the authors of the great medieval *Summae*. That must be granted; but if one is concerned, not with what was new, but rather with what is important about Renaissance philosophy, then what has been said may stand. There is at least one further respect in which the Renaissance did differ from the Middle Ages—though here we are concerned with the Renaissance in general rather than with Renaissance philosophy in particular, and with the sociology of philosophy rather than with philosophy as such. It was during the Renaissance that there began what one may term the laicization of the European culture of the Christian era.[12] Some of the humanists were in holy orders—one may mention Petrarch and Erasmus—but most were not. From the time of the Renaissance onwards, a clerk (in the sense of a scholar) no longer had to be a cleric. In this way, the first moves were made towards loosening the hold that Christian institutions had upon philosophy.

I must emphasize that by the laicization of European culture I do not mean what has been called 'the secularisation of the European mind';[13] that is, the decline in the importance that religious ideas, and more specifically Christian ideas, have had for European thinkers. It is plausible to argue that the two were connected; but they were different from each other. To speak of laicization in this context is to speak of the people who were the bearers of culture, and it is to say that they ceased to be predominantly clerical; it is not to say anything about the content of what such people believed. In fact, what were regarded as Christian concepts and Christian truths continued to be dominant in Renaissance philosophy, just as they had been dominant in the Middle Ages. Humanists might disagree over the answer to the question whether Plato or Aristotle was more compatible with Christianity; but that a sound philosophy should be so compatible was not in dispute. Even the arguments of the ancient sceptics, whose writings became widely available in the sixteenth century, were made to serve religious purposes.[14]

From the Renaissance we move to the beginnings of what may be regarded as modern (as opposed to an-cient, medieval or Renaissance) philosophy. For the majority of contemporary philosophers, the first modern philosopher was Descartes. There are two main reasons for this view. One of the main features of the European philosophy of the eighteenth and nineteenth centuries was the role played in it by one form or other of philosophical idealism, and it is argued that one can trace this idealism back to Descartes's view that the human mind is known before any physical object is known. But even those philosophers for whom idealism is no longer a live issue find that Descartes is relevant to their concerns. When Gilbert Ryle published his influential book *The Concept of Mind* shortly after the end of the Second World War,[15] he presented Descartes as the source of philosophical views about the human mind which were profoundly wrong. However, if one's concerns include science and its philosophy, then there is a case for regarding as the first modern philosopher someone who was born thirty-five years before Descartes. This was Francis Bacon.

Born in 1561, Bacon is sometimes discussed in books on Renaissance philosophy,[16] but it is better to regard him as a modern in whom some traces of the Renaissance remained. Certainly, he agreed with the Renaissance philosophers in his scorn for the scholastics; he agreed, too, with some Renaissance writers in his view that magic was not to be rejected entirely, and his views about the nature of knowledge have a Renaissance ancestry.[17] But he was as dismissive of Renaissance authors as he was of the scholastics, saying of them that their concern was primarily with words.[18] He saw himself as a revolutionary, the provider of a new logic—a 'Novum Organum'—which was to supercede the old 'Organon' of Aristotle. Aristotle's logic had already been attacked by humanist logicians, of whom the most influential in the sixteenth and seventeenth centuries was Ramus (Pierre de la Ramée, 1515-72).[19] But the aims of Bacon and Ramus were quite different. Ramus was concerned with thinking in general, and his aim was to replace the Aristotelian syllogism by a less formal logic, which would correspond more closely to the way in which people actually think.[20] Bacon, on the other hand, was concerned chiefly with scientific thinking.

It has been said of Bacon that he made 'the first serious attempt to formulate and justify the procedure of natural scientists'.[21] For many, this attempt is to be found in Bacon's discussions of induction—that is, of that type of argument in which one reaches universal conclusions from particular instances. His 'Novum Organum', his 'New Instrument', was to be a systematic way of reaching such conclusions. Tables of observations were to be drawn up, and universal laws were to be derived from these by the application of certain rules.[22] Such laws, Bacon thought, were not wholly satisfactory, in that they told us nothing about the fundamental structure of reality; none the less, they were *known,* in that they provided us with rules for the manipulation of nature.[23] This introduces Bacon's distinctive view about the nature of knowledge: namely, that to know is to make. As mentioned earlier, the view has Renaissance antecedents, but Bacon applies it to what we now regard as the beginnings of modern science. It is his emphasis on the fact that the inquirer should not just observe, but should also intervene in nature, that has led him to be called, not the first philosopher of induction, but the first philosopher of experimental science.[24]

Whatever its merits, Bacon's philosophy of science also had serious deficiencies; it is widely recognized that Bacon has no grasp of the importance that mathematics has for the sciences.[25] This cannot be said of the philosophers whose ideas are the concern of over half of this volume: namely, the seventeenth-century rationalists. As mentioned earlier,[26] the term has generated some controversy. It is used to pick out a number of seventeenth-century philosophers, the chief of whom were Descartes, Spinoza and Leibniz, though Malebranche and the Flemish philosopher Geulincx are also included. Now, it must be admitted that none of these ever called himself a rationalist, nor can they be said to have constituted a school, in the sense of a group of people who saw themselves as separated from others by virtue of their adherence to certain shared principles. They seem, indeed, to have been more conscious of their disagreements with each other than with the respects in which they agreed; so, for example, Spinoza criticized Descartes, Malebranche criticized Spinoza, and Leibniz criticized Descartes, Spinoza and Malebranche. Again, those who regard these philosophers as a group often contrast them with the 'British empiricists', namely Locke, Berkeley and Hume. Yet Locke's use of the important term 'idea' owed something to Descartes, and Malebranche influenced both Berkeley and Hume. Despite all this, the philosophers who are commonly called the seventeenth-century rationalists did have a number of basic views in common. All agreed that it is possible to get to know the nature of reality simply by means of *a priori* reasoning; that is, that we can get to know by means of the reason, without any appeal to the senses, truths about reality that are *necessary* truths. It is these points of resemblance, above all, that the term 'rationalist' picks out. In this sense, rationalism is not peculiar to the seventeenth century; the 'dialectic' that is described in Plato's *Republic* (510-11, 532-4) is a rationalist theory. Nor did rationalism come to an end after the death of Leibniz. It continued to exist, not just in the writings of Leibniz's follower Christian Wolff, but also in the form of the 'objective idealism' of Hegel, and perhaps even after that.[27] Our concern, however, is with its seventeenth-century manifestations.

The time-span of the movement is well enough indicated by the name given to it. Its first public manifes-

tation was in Descartes's *Discourse on Method,* published in 1637; it ended in 1716, the year in which Leibniz—still philosophically active—died. Though not as widespread as the Renaissance, it was by no means confined to one country. Descartes worked in France and the Netherlands; Malebranche worked in France; Geulincx and Spinoza worked in the Low Countries, and Leibniz worked mainly in Germany (though one should not overlook a very productive period which he spent in Paris between 1672 and 1676). Seventeenth-century rationalism also spanned the religions. Descartes and Malebranche were Roman Catholics (Malebranche, indeed, was a priest); Geulincx was initially a Catholic but became a convert to Protestantism after being persecuted for Cartesian views; Spinoza was an excommunicated Jew, with friends among some of the smaller Protestant sects.

Like Bacon, the rationalists saw themselves as making a new start. Most of them were contemptuous of Aristotle and the scholastics;[28] indeed, they rejected everything that passed for received wisdom in their time, as long as it did not meet the demands of rational scrutiny. This is very clearly expressed in Descartes's resolve, stated in the first part of his *Meditations,*[29] 'to demolish everything completely and start again right from the foundations'. But no one philosophizes in an intellectual vacuum, and it is important to note that the rise of rationalism in the seventeenth century occurred at the same time as, and was closely associated with, the rise of what one now calls 'modern science'. [H]ere it must be sufficient to say that the old and largely Aristotelian science stressed the qualitative aspect of nature, and was primarily concerned to classify, whereas the new science stressed the quantitative aspect of things, offering explanations that were mathematical in character. Of the seventeenth-century rationalists, some played an important part in the new science. Descartes was philosopher, mathematician and scientist; so, too, was Leibniz. Spinoza and Malebranche, for their part, made no serious contribution to science or mathematics, but were well informed about them. The question is how the seventeenth-century rationalists saw philosophy as related to the natural sciences.[30] For present-day philosophers of science, the sciences stand in no need of justification by philosophy, the business of the philosopher being exclusively one of analysis: the clarification of the nature of scientific propositions and of the methods of science. But it is clear that this was not Descartes's attitude; his search for foundations included a search for the foundations of science,[31] and it is generally held that this is true of the other seventeenth-century rationalists.[32]

For the seventeenth-century rationalists, the foundations that they sought could be discovered only by *a priori* reasoning. Perhaps the clearest arguments for this thesis are provided by Descartes's account of systematic doubt in the *Meditations,* from which it emerges that he regards as known only those propositions whose truth cannot be doubted, and also takes the view that such propositions cannot be empirical. There would be general agreement that there is such knowledge of the truths of logic and of mathematics; but Descartes argued that these truths are only hypothetical, stating that *if*, for example, there is such a figure as a triangle, then its interior angles must equal two right angles.[33] What distinguishes the rationalists is their view that there are existential propositions whose truth can be known *a priori*. Mathematics, although concerned only with hypothetical truths, provided them with methods of procedure.[34] Roughly speaking, what the rationalists tried to do was first of all to obtain *a priori* knowledge of certain basic truths about what exists, and then to derive further truths from these by means of pure reasoning.

As is well known, Descartes stated that the existential truth that he knew first of all was the proposition that he existed as a thinking being, a proposition that he could not doubt as long as he was actually thinking. But it is evident (and it did not escape Descartes's notice) that the truth of this proposition was in a way far from fundamental, in that Descartes's existence depended on that of many other beings. Ultimately, the rationalists argued, it depended on the existence of a supreme being. In a sense, therefore, the fundamental item of knowledge is the knowledge that there must exist such a supreme being, or, as the rationalists said, a 'most perfect' or a 'necessary' being. Belief in the existence of such a being was not peculiar to the rationalists, but their arguments for its existence were distinctive. These arguments had to be *a priori*, and the rationalists based them on the concept of God. One argument offered by Descartes was that this concept was such that only a God could have implanted it in us. Alternatively, Descartes argued that the concept was such that one could not, without self-contradiction, deny that God existed. This was the celebrated 'ontological argument', whose soundness was accepted by Spinoza and Leibniz also.[35]

Given a knowledge of the existence and nature of the supreme being, the task of the rationalist was, as it were, to build on this foundation by deriving the consequences which followed. But there were important differences between the ways in which the seventeenth-century rationalists saw this being. For all of them except Spinoza, the supreme being was a personal deity, creator of the universe, and choosing freely to create it. Spinoza argued that such a concept was incoherent, and that a consistent account of the necessary being must present it as an impersonal being, within which particular things exist, and which cannot rationally be regarded as exercising free will. This was clearly opposed to orthodox Christian doctrine; however, one should not exaggerate Spinoza's role in ending the predominance of Christian ideas in philosophy.[36] His

philosophy, at first bitterly attacked, was later largely forgotten until its revival by the German romantics towards the end of the eighteenth century. A more important factor in the loosening of the ties between Christianity and philosophy was the rise in the seventeenth and eighteenth centuries of deism; that is, of belief in a creative deity, unaccompanied by any belief in a divine revelation. With this, rationalism had little to do.[37]

Today, there is widespread agreement that the seventeenth-century rationalists failed to provide an *a priori* proof of the existence of God, however that God was conceived by them. It would also be agreed that they failed to find, by pure reason, necessary connections between the nature of God and the laws of science.[38] But these failures do not deprive their philosophy of all value. For them, science was not merely something that had to be justified; it was also something that posed problems, and their attempts to solve these problems are still found interesting.

The question whether human beings can strictly speaking be called free had long exercised philosophers. Before the seventeenth century, the problem took a theological form. Philosophers, such as Boethius in the sixth century AD and Lorenzo Valla in the fifteenth, asked how human freedom could be consistent with the foreknowledge and providence of God. These problems continued to be discussed in the seventeenth century, but in that era there was a new problem of freedom. For the new science, all physical events were determined by necessary laws; so the question arose how there could be any human freedom, given that we are (even if only in part) physical objects. Spinoza and Leibniz offered solutions which took the form of what are now called 'compatibilist' theories, arguing, in very different ways, that freedom and determinism can be reconciled.[39]

Science posed another problem for the seventeenth-century rationalist. One of Descartes's best known theses is his view that mind and body are 'really distinct', that is, that each can exist without the other. Behind this, there lay a view about scientific explanation: namely, that bodies are to be understood solely in terms of physical concepts, and minds solely in terms of mental concepts.[40] To explain physical events, therefore, we do not need to postulate the intervention of incorporeal agents (such as, for example, the planetary intelligences). But this raised the philosophical problem of how mind and body could influence each other, and could also constitute one human being. Descartes's solution was notoriously unsatisfactory, and other rationalists took up the problem. Spinoza offered a classical version of the double-aspect theory of mind-matter relations; Malebranche, Geulincx and Leibniz offered various versions of a theory which denied that any created thing strictly speaking acts on any other, and asserted that the apparent interaction was really a divinely produced order that existed between the states of created things—that is, finite minds and bodies.

When Descartes's rationalist successors tried to solve the problem about mind-matter relations that he had bequeathed to them, there were already other solutions in the field. These took the form of saying that there really was no problem, in that mind and matter did not form different kinds of existence. The philosophers who offered these solutions were Gassendi and Hobbes, who were among the contributors to the 'Objections' which were published together with Descartes's *Meditations* in 1641. Neither was a rationalist, but both influenced some of Descartes's rationalist successors,[41] and for this reason their philosophy finds a place in this volume.

Both Gassendi and Hobbes offered materialist theories, though Gassendi was not an out-and-out materialist. A Catholic priest, he resembled the philosophers of the Renaissance in a certain respect, in that he found inspiration in the writings of the ancients. In his case, the inspiration came from the writings of Epicurus; but Gassendi's version of atomism was tailored to fit Christian requirements. In particular, Gassendi shrank from giving a totally materialist account of the human mind, saying that, although the non-rational soul could be explained in materialist terms, such an account could not be given of the rational, immortal soul. In explaining the rational soul and its relation to the human body, Gassendi fell back on the ideas of the scholastics, viewing the soul as the substantial form of the body.

Such Aristotelian ideas were rejected firmly by Hobbes, who offered a materialism of a more radical sort. He was, as his biographer Aubrey put it, 'in love with geometry',[42] and this love was manifested in a theory of method which has undertones of rationalism. Science, Hobbes asserted, is 'the knowledge of consequences, and dependence of one fact on another';[43] what we must do, therefore, is define our terms correctly and argue deductively from them.[44] Like the rationalists, too, Hobbes offered a far-reaching metaphysical system, within the context of which he placed a theory of man and society. But there were also important differences between Hobbes and the rationalists. Although rationalism is not obviously inconsistent with materialism, none of the seventeenth-century rationalists was a materialist; but Hobbes was. A more important difference lies in the field of the theory of knowledge, Hobbes arguing (contrary to the rationalists) that the ultimate source of all our knowledge of what exists is provided by the senses.[45]

The philosophy of Hobbes was found deeply offensive by seventeenth-century divines, who accused him of atheism. If they were right, then we must add the name of Hobbes to the list of those philosophers who began to weaken the links between Christianity and philosophy. But it is not certain that they were right; the subject is one on which scholars still disagree.[46] What is certain is that Hobbes's political philosophy, with its sombre view that a life that satisfies the demands of reason can be lived only under conditions of absolute rule, still fascinates philosophers.[47]

Notes

[1] The arguments for this view have been clearly set out by Peter Burke in his book *The Renaissance* (London, Macmillan, 1987), pp. 1-5. Burke himself does not accept these arguments, saying (p. 5) that the term 'the Renaissance' is 'an organising concept which still has its uses'.

[2] See, for example, C. B. Schmitt and Q. Skinner (eds) *The Cambridge History of Renaissance Philosophy* (Cambridge, Cambridge University Press, 1988: abbreviated, CHRP), p. 5.

[3] CHRP, Introduction, p. 3.

[4] C. B. Schmitt, in R. Sorabji (ed.) *Philoponus and the Rejection of Aristotelian Science* (London, Duckworth, 1988), p. 210.

[5] See, for example, the entries for 'scholasticism' and 'medieval philosophy' in J. O. Urmson and J. Rée (eds), *The Concise Encyclopaedia of Western Philosophy and Philosophers* (London, Unwin Hyman, 1989).

[6] London, Longman, 2nd edn, 1988, pp. 76-82. Dom David's account applies to what one might call the golden age of scholasticism, up to the middle of the fourteenth century; on the new scholasticism of the late sixteenth century, see Stuart Brown in Chapter 2 of this volume, pp. 76, 81-3.

[7] cf. R. W. Southern, *Grosseteste* (Oxford, Claredon, 1986), p. 32.

[8] See, for example, P. O. Kristeller, 'Humanism', in CHRP, pp. 113-37. One should stress the phrase 'in the main'; humanism, like the Renaissance, has a long history, and in the late fifteenth and sixteenth centuries humanists became involved in a range of subjects from logic and science that do not fall within a simple five-part scheme. On this, see the chapters on humanism and science and humanism and philosophy in Jill Kraye (ed.) *The Cambridge Companion to Renaissance Humanism* (Cambridge, Cambridge University Press, forthcoming). See also Anthony Grafton, 'Humanism, Magic and Science', in A. Goodman and A. Mackay (eds) *The Impact of Humanism on Western Europe* (London, Longman, 1990), pp. 99-117.

[9] See especially some remarks of the fifteenth-century Florentine chancellor Leonardo Bruni, quoted by B. P. Copenhaver, CHRP, p. 106.

[10] cf. Burke, op. cit.

[11] Cesare Vasoli, 'The Renaissance Concept of Philosophy', CHRP, p. 73.

[12] See especially J. Stephens, *The Italian Renaissance* (London, Longman, 1990), pp. xvi, 54, 137, 149.

[13] The phrase comes from Owen Chadwick, *The Secularisation of the European Mind in the Nineteenth Century* (Cambridge, Cambridge University Press, 1975).

[14] A Latin translation of Diogenes Laertius' *Life of Pyrrho* was available in the late 1420s; but it was above all the printing of Latin versions of Sextus Empiricus in 1562 and 1569 which stimulated interest in the ancient sceptics. See CHRP, pp. 679-80, and Richard Popkin, *The History of Scepticism from Erasmus to Spinoza* (Berkeley, Calif., University of California Press, 1979), p. 19.

Superficially, the sceptical thesis that one must suspend judgement about everything might seem incompatible with Christian claims to knowledge. In the sixteenth century, however, Catholics employed sceptical arguments against Protestants, arguing that sceptical doubts about the worth of reason meant that it was unsafe to base religion on such a foundation. Religious beliefs must be based on faith, and more specifically on the faith of a community which had endured through the centuries—the Catholic Church. See Popkin, op. cit., pp. 55, 58, 70-3, 78-82, 90, 94-5.

[15] London, Hutchinson, 1949.

[16] E.g. B. P. Copenhaver, 'Astrology and Magic', CHRP, pp. 296-300.

[17] Bacon and the scholastics: *The Advancement of Learning,* Book I, ch. 4 (Everyman's Library Edition, London, Dent, 1973), p. 26. Bacon and magic: Copenhaver, op. cit. Bacon and knowledge: A. Pérez-Ramos, Chapter 4 of this volume, pp. 145-7.

[18] Theirs, said Bacon, was a 'delicate learning', as opposed to the 'fantastical learning' of the scholastics, and they 'began to hunt more after words than matter': *The Advancement of Learning,* Book 1, ch. 4, p. 24.

[19] Bacon knew of Ramus's work, and gave it his (highly qualified) approval (Bacon, op. cit., Book II, ch. 17, p. 144). On Ramus's logic, see for example Lisa Jardine, 'Humanistic Logic', CHRP, pp. 184-6, and Wil-liam and Martha Kneale, *The Development of Logic* (Oxford, Clarendon, revised edn, 1984), pp. 301-6.

[20] CHRP, pp. 185, 673.

[21] W. Kneale, *Probability and Induction* (Oxford, Clarendon, 1949), p. 48.

[22] In this connection, Bacon is praised for having seen the importance of the negative instance—that is, of eliminative induction as opposed to induction by simple enumeration. See Bacon, *Novum Organum,* I, secs 46, 105, and Anthony Quinton, *Francis Bacon* (Oxford, Oxford University Press, 1980), p. 56.

[23] cf. A Pérez-Ramos, Chapter 4 of this volume, p. 151.

[24] Ian Hacking, *Representing and Intervening: Introductory Topics in the Philosophy of Natural Science* (Cambridge, Cambridge University Press, 1983), p. 246.

[25] See, for example, Quinton, op. cit., p. 47.

[26] See p. 2 above.

[27] For an interesting survey of rationalism as a whole, see J. Cottingham, *Rationalism* (London, Paladin, 1984).

[28] Leibniz is an exception: cf. N. Jolley, Chapter 11 of this volume, p. 384.

[29] J. Cottingham, R. Stoothoff and D. Murdoch (eds), *The Philosophical Works of Descartes* (Cambridge, Cambridge University Press, 3, vols, 1985, 1991: abbreviated, CSM), ii, p. 12; cf. *Discourse on Method,* CSM i, pp. 111-19.

[30] The term, incidentally, is to be found in Spinoza, who speaks of believers in miracles as hostile to natural scientists—'iis, qui scientias naturales colunt'. *Tractatus Theologico-Politicus,* ch. 6; Spinoza, *Opera,* ed. C. Gebhardt (Heidelberg, Winter, 4 vols, 1924-6), vol. 3, p. 81.

[31] cf. to Mersenne, 11 October 1638 (CSM iii, p. 124), where Descartes criticizes Galileo on the grounds that 'his building lacks a foundation'. (See also G. Molland, Chapter 3 of this volume, p. 129.)

[32] This view has been challenged, where Spinoza is concerned, by Alan Donagan (*Spinoza,* Brighton, Harvester, 1988, esp. p. 68). Donagan argues that Spinoza did not so much try to justify the principles of the new physics as generalize from them. It has also been argued by Stuart Brown that Leibniz was a foundationalist only during his early years, but later took the view that the philosopher should seek out and explore fruitful hypotheses (Stuart Brown, *Leibniz,* Brighton,

Harvester, 1984). I have discussed this thesis in my paper, 'Leibniz's Philosophical Aims: Foundation-laying or Problem-solving?', in A. Heinekamp, W. Lenzen and M. Schneider (eds) *Mathesis Rationis: Festschrift für Heinrich Schepers* (Münster, Nodus, 1990), pp. 67-78.

[33] *Meditations* V, CSM ii, 45. Compare Leibniz, *Nouveaux Essais,* IV.11.14, on the 'eternal truths' of mathematics.

[34] There were two such methods, traditionally known as 'analysis' and 'synthesis'. These are discussed in this volume in Chapter 3 (pp. 107-9), Chapter 5 (pp. 183-6) and Chapter 8 (pp. 279-80).

[35] Though Leibniz added the qualification that it must first be shown that the concept of God—i.e. of a most perfect or necessary being—is self-consistent. See, for example, Leibniz, *Discourse on Metaphysics,* sec. 23.

[36] cf. p. 4 above.

[37] The main sources of deism were Lord Herbert of Cherbury, *De Veritate* (1624), and Locke, *The Reasonableness of Christianity* (1695). However, they were not the sole sources; as Professor Stuart Brown has pointed out to me, there is reason to believe that the seventeenth-century rationalists had some influence on deistic thought. Deism has a long history, and the term meant different things to different people. (Samuel Clarke, in his *Demonstration of the Being and Attributes of God* (1704-6), recognized no fewer than four types of deism.) What matters here is that many deists believed in a creative deity whose wisdom and power are such as to make it irrational to suppose that he should intervene in the workings of the universe, once he has created it. This position is close to that taken by seventeenth-century rationalists. Pascal declared that he 'could not forgive' Descartes for reducing God's role in the workings of the universe almost to nothing (*Pensées,* Brunschvicg ed., No. 77), and a similar position is implied by what other seventeenth-century rationalists said about miracles. For Spinoza, it was impossible that any miracles should occur; for Leibniz and Malebranche, God's miraculous intervention in the universe was a possibility, but such interventions were very few. See, for example, G. H. R. Parkinson, 'Spinoza on Miracles and Natural Law', *Revue internationale de philosophie* 31 (1977) 145-77, and *Logic and Reality in Leibniz's Metaphysics* (Oxford, Clarendon, 1965), pp. 102, 155-6; Daisie Radner, *Malebranche* (Assen, Van Gorcum, 1978), p. 32.

[38] Descartes tried to derive universal laws of science from the immutability of God. Spinoza seems to have thought that no scientific laws other than those that actually hold are strictly speaking thinkable, though in his attempt to establish such laws he was compelled to

appeal to experience. (See Chapter 8, pp. 289, 298, on Spinoza's 'postulates'. See also Chapter 3, pp. 131-2, for Descartes's view about hypotheses and experience.) Leibniz rejected both these approaches, and argued that scientific laws have to be seen in relation to the wise and good purposes of God.

[39] Spinoza argued that human beings have no free will, since everything in the mind is determined by a cause, and that by another, and so on to infinity (*Ethics,* Pt II, Proposition 48). His way of reconciling determinism and freedom was to say that freedom consists, not in an absence of determination, but in self-determination. Such self-determination occurs when the reason controls the passions, which are in a way outside us. This view—which amounts to saying that to be free is to be master of oneself—is a form of what Isaiah Berlin has called the concept of 'positive freedom' (Berlin, 'Two Concepts of Liberty', *Four Essays on Liberty* (Oxford, Oxford University Press, 1969), pp. 118-72). Leibniz, for his part, discussed both the theological forms of the problem of freedom and the problems posed by the thesis that every event is caused. He accepted this thesis, but argued (contrary to Spinoza) that there is freedom of the will. In essence, his argument was that human actions are indeed necessary, but that they are only *hypothetically* necessary. That is, given that X is, at the moment, my strongest motive, then I must act in accordance with this motive. But I still could have acted otherwise—that is, my will is free—in that my acting in some other way is always *logically* possible.

On Spinoza's views about determinism see (besides Chapter 8, pp. 294-5, and Chapter 9, pp. 323-6) Jonathan Bennett, *A Study of Spinoza's 'Ethics'* (Cambridge, Cambridge University Press, 1984), pp. 315-29; R. J. Delahunty, *Spinoza* (London, Routledge, 1985), pp. 35-48, 155-65; G. H. R. Parkinson, 'Spinoza on the Power and Freedom of Man', in E. Freeman and M. Mandelbaum (eds) *Spinoza: Essays in Interpretation* (La Salle, Ill., Open Court, 1975), pp. 7-33. A general survey of Leibniz's views about human freedom is provided by G. H. R. Parkinson, *Leibniz on Human Freedom* (Wiesbaden, Steiner, 1970). See also, for example, A. Burms and H. de Dijn, 'Freedom and Logical Contingency in Leibniz', *Studia Leibnitiana* 11 (1979) 124-33; Lois Frankel, 'Being Able to do Otherwise: Leibniz on Freedom and Contingency', *Studia Leibnitiana* 16 (1984) 45-59; Pauline Phemister, 'Leibniz, Free Will and Rationality', *Studia Leibnitiana* 23 (1991) 25-39.

[40] In Descartes's terminology, I can have a 'clear and distinct idea' of a mind as a being which is thinking and non-extended, but I have a clear and distinct idea of a body in so far as this is non-thinking and extended. See *Meditations* VI, CSM ii, p. 54, and *Replies to First Objections,* CSM ii, p. 86.

[41] Gassendi's atomism influenced the young Leibniz (see especially K. Moll, *Der junge Leibniz* (Stuttgart, Frommann-Holzboog, 1982), vol 2, who was also influenced by Hobbes (see, for example, J. W. N. Watkins, *Hobbes' System of Ideas* (London, Hutchinson, 2nd edn, 1973), pp. 87-94). Whether Spinoza borrowed from Hobbes is a matter of controversy, but he certainly defined his position by reference to Hobbes. See, for example, A. G. Wernham, *Benedict de Spinoza: The Political Works* (Oxford, Claredon, 1958), pp. 11-36.

[42] John Aubrey, *Brief Lives and Other Selected Writings,* ed. Anthony Powell (London, Cresset Press, 1949), p. 242.

[43] *Leviathan* (Oxford, Blackwell, 1946), ch. 5, p. 29.

[44] ibid.

[45] ibid., ch. 7, p. 40.

[46] For a recent discussion of this issue, see Arrigo Pacchi, 'Hobbes and the Problem of God', in G. A. J. Rogers and Alan Ryan (eds) *Perspectives on Thomas Hobbes* (Oxford, Clarendon, 1988), pp. 171-88.

[47] I am very grateful to Dr Jill Kraye and Professor Stuart Brown for their helpful comments on an earlier draft of this introduction.

METAPHYSICS

Edwin Arthur Burtt (essay date 1924)

SOURCE: An introduction to *The Metaphysical Foundations of Modern Physical Science, revised edition,* Doubleday Anchor Books, 1954, pp. 15-35.

[*In the following excerpt, Burtt traces the development of ideas and changes in terminology concerning man's relation to the world.*]

A. Historical Problem Suggested by the Nature of Modern Thought

How curious, after all, is the way in which we moderns think about our world! And it is all so novel, too. The cosmology underlying our mental processes is but three centuries old—a mere infant in the history of thought—and yet we cling to it with the same embarrassed zeal with which a young father fondles his new-born baby. Like him, we are ignorant enough of its precise nature; like him, we nevertheless take it piously to be ours and allow it a subtly pervasive and unhindered control over our thinking.

The world-view of any age can be discovered in various ways, but one of the best is to note the recurrent problems of its philosophers. Philosophers never succeed in getting quite outside the ideas of their time so as to look at them objectively—this would, indeed, be too much to expect. Neither do maidens who bob their hair and make more obvious their nether bifurcation see themselves through the eyes of an elderly Puritan matron. But philosophers do succeed in glimpsing some of the problems involved in the metaphysical notions of their day and take harmless pleasure in speculating at them in more or less futile fashion. Let us test the modern world-view in this manner. What are the problems whose correct treatment, it has generally been taken for granted, constitute the main business of metaphysical thinkers? Well, most conspicuous of these is the so-called problem of knowledge: the main current of speculative inquiry from Descartes onward has been permeated by the conviction that investigation into the nature and possibility of knowledge forms a necessary preliminary to the successful attack upon other ultimate issues. Now, how did all this come about? What assumptions were people accepting when they plunged themselves into these profound epistemological ponderings? How did these assumptions get into men's thinking? To raise such questions at a time when everybody vigorously believes that philosophy must do this sort of thing, is, of course, inopportune and futile, but now that some contemporary philosophers have made bold to discard epistemology as the study of unreal puzzles, the occasion is ripe to suggest them. Does the problem of knowledge lead thinking into false directions, and nullify its conclusions by unsound premises? What are the premises anyway, how are they related to the other essential features of modern thought, and what was it at bottom that induced people in modern times to think in this fashion? The central place of epistemology in modern philosophy is no accident; it is a most natural corollary of something still more pervasive and significant, a conception of man himself, and especially of his relation to the world around him. Knowledge was not a problem for the ruling philosophy of the Middle Ages; that the whole world which man's mind seeks to understand is intelligible to it was explicitly taken for granted. That people subsequently came to consider knowledge a problem implies that they had been led to accept certain different beliefs about the nature of man and about the things which he tries to understand. What are those beliefs and how did they appear and develop in modern times? In just what way did they urge thinkers into the particular metaphysical attempts which fill the books of modern philosophy? Have these contemporary thinkers who decry espistemology really made this whole process thoroughly objective to themselves? Why, in a word, is the main current of modern thought what it is?

When "the main current of modern thought" is spoken of in this wholesale fashion, a brief word might be injected to show that a certain obvious danger is not blindly fallen into. It may very well be that the truly constructive ideas of modern philosophy are not cosmological ideas at all, but such ethico-social concepts as "progress," "control," and the like. These form a fascinating key to the interpretation of modern thought and give it a quite different contour from that which it assumes when we follow up its metaphysical notions. But with that aspect of modern thinking we are not concerned in the present treatment. In the last analysis it is the ultimate picture which an age forms of the nature of its world that is its most fundamental possession. It is the final controlling factor in all thinking whatever. And that the modern mind clearly has such a picture, as clearly as any previous age that one might wish to select, it will not take us long to see. What are the essential elements in that picture, and how did they come there?

Doubtless it is no mystery why, amid all the genetic studies entered upon with such confidence to-day, the precise nature and assumptions of modern scientific thinking itself have not as yet been made the object of really disinterested, critical research. That this is true is not due merely to the fact, itself important enough, that all of us tend easily to be caught in the point of view of our age and to accept unquestioningly its main presuppositions: it is due also to the associations in our minds between the authoritarian principle and that dominant medieval philosophy from which modern thought broke in successful rebellion. Modern thinkers have been so unanimous and so vigorous in their condemnation of the manner in which large propositions were imposed on innocent minds by external authority that it has been rather easily taken for granted that the propositions themselves were quite untenable, and that the essential assumptions underlying the new principle of freedom, the manner in which knowledge was successfully sought with its support, and the most general implications about the world which seemed to be involved in the process, are thoroughly well grounded. But what business have we to take all this for sound doctrine? Can we justify it? Do we know clearly what it means? Surely here is need for a critical, historical study of the rise of the fundamental assumptions characteristic of modern thinking. At least it will compel us to replace this easy optimism with a more objective insight into our own intellectual postulates and methods.

Let us try to fix in preliminary fashion, although as precisely as we may, the central metaphysical contrast between medieval and modern thought, in respect to their conception of man's relation to his natural environment. For the dominant trend in medieval thought, man occupied a more significant and determinative place in the universe than the realm of physical nature, while for the main current of modern thought, nature holds a more independent, more determinative, and more permanent place than man. It will be helpful to analyse this contrast more specifically. For the Middle Ages man was in every sense the centre of the universe. The whole world of nature was believed to be teleologically subordinate to him and his eternal destiny. Toward this conviction the two great movements which had become united in the medieval synthesis, Greek philosophy and Judeo-Christian theology, had irresistibly led. The prevailing world-view of the period was marked by a deep and persistent assurance that man, with his hopes and ideals, was the all-important, even controlling fact in the universe.

This view underlay medieval physics. The entire world of nature was held not only to exist for man's sake, but to be likewise immediately present and fully intelligible to his mind. Hence the categories in terms of which it was interpreted were not those of time, space, mass, energy, and the like; but substance, essence, matter, form, quality, quantity—categories developed in the attempt to throw into scientific form the facts and relations observed in man's unaided sense-experience of the world and the main uses which he made it serve. Man was believed to be active in his acquisition of knowledge—nature passive. When he observed a distant object, something proceeded from his eye to that object rather than from the object to his eye. And, of course, that which was real about objects was that which could be immediately perceived about them by human senses. Things that appeared different *were* different substances, such as ice, water, and steam. The famous puzzle of the water hot to one hand and cold to the other was a genuine difficulty to medieval physics, because for it heat and cold were distinct substances. How then could the same water possess both heat and cold? Light and heavy, being distinguished by the senses, were held to be distinct qualities, each as real as the other. Similarly on the teleogical side: an explanation in terms of the relation of things to human purpose was accounted just as real as and often more important than an explanation in terms of efficient causality, which expressed their relations to each other. Rain fell because it nourished man's crops as truly as because it was expelled from the clouds. Analogies drawn from purposive activity were freely used. Light bodies, such as fire, tended upward to their proper place; heavy bodies, such as water or earth, tended downward to theirs. Quantitative differences were derived from these teleological distinctions. Inasmuch as a heavier body tends downward more strongly than a lighter, it will reach the earth more quickly when allowed to fall freely. Water in water was believed to have no weight, inasmuch as it was already in its proper place. But we need not multiply instances; these will sufficiently illustrate the many respects in which medieval science testified to its presupposition that man, with his means of knowledge and his needs, was the determinative fact in the world.

Furthermore, it was taken for granted that this terrestrial habitat of man was in the centre of the astronomical realm. With the exception of a few hardy but scattered thinkers, the legitimacy of selecting some other point of reference in astronomy than the earth had never suggested itself to any one. The earth appeared a thing vast, solid, and quiet; the starry heavens seemed like a light, airy, and not too distant sphere moving easily about it; even the keenest scientific investigators of ancient times dared not suggest that the sun was a twentieth of its actual distance from the earth. What more natural than to hold that these regular, shining lights were made to circle round man's dwelling-place, existed in short for his enjoyment, instruction, and use? The whole universe was a small, finite place, and it was man's place. He occupied the centre; his good was the controlling end of the natural creation.

Finally, the visible universe itself was infinitely smaller than the realm of man. The medieval thinker never forgot that his philosophy was a religious philosophy, with a firm persuasion of man's immortal destiny. The Unmoved Mover of Aristotle and the personal Father of the Christian had become one. There was an eternal Reason and Love, at once Creator and End of the whole cosmic scheme, with whom man as a reasoning and loving being was essentially akin. In the religious experience was that kinship revealed, and the religious experience to the medieval philosopher was the crowning scientific fact. Reason had become married to mystic inwardness and entrancement; the crowning moment of the one, that transitory but inexpressibly ravishing vision of God, was likewise the moment in which the whole realm of man's knowledge gained final significance. The world of nature existed that it might be known and enjoyed by man. Man in turn existed that he might "know God and enjoy him forever." In this graciously vouchsafed kinship of man with an eternal Reason and Love, lay, for medieval philosophy, a guarantee that the whole natural world in its present form was but a moment in a great divine drama which reached over countless æons past and present and in which man's place was quite indestructible.

Let us make all this vivid to ourselves by the aid of a few verses from that marvellous poetic product of the philosophy of the Middle Ages, the *Divine Comedy* of Dante. It but puts in sublime form the prevailing conviction of the essentially *human* character of the universe.

> The All-Mover's glory penetrates through the universe, and regloweth in one region more, and less in another.
>
> In that heaven which most receiveth of his light, have I been; and have seen things which whoso descendeth from up there hath nor knowledge nor power to re-tell;
>
> Because, as it draweth nigh to its desire, our intellect sinketh so deep, that memory cannot go back upon the track.

> Nathless, whatever of the holy realm I had the power to treasure in my memory, shall now be matter of my song . . .
>
> Much is granted there which is not granted here to our powers, in virtue of the place made as proper to the human race. . . .
>
> All things whatsoever observe a mutual order; and this the form that maketh the universe like unto God.
>
> Herein the exalted creatures trace the impress of the Eternal Worth, which is the goal whereto was made the norm now spoken of.
>
> In the order of which I speak all things incline, by diverse lots, more near and less unto their principle;
>
> Wherefore they move to diverse ports o'er the great sea of being, and each one with instinct given it to bear it on.
>
> This beareth the fire toward the moon; this is the mover in the hearts of things that die; this doth draw the earth together and unite it.
>
> Nor only the creatures that lack intelligence doth this bow shoot, but those that have both intellect and love . . .
>
> Gazing upon his son with the love which the one and the other eternally breathes forth, the primal and ineffable Worth,
>
> Made whatsoever circleth through mind or space with so great order that whoso looketh on it may not be without some taste of him.
>
> Then, reader, raise with me thy sight to the exalted wheels, directed to that part where the one movement smiteth on the other;
>
> And amorously there begin to gaze upon that Master's art, who within himself so loveth it, that never doth he part his eye from it.
>
> See how thence off brancheth the oblique circle that beareth the planets, to satisfy the world that calleth on them;
>
> And were their pathway not inclined, much virtue in the heaven were in vain, and dead were almost every potency on earth;
>
> And if, from the straight course, or more or less remote were the departure, much were lacking to the cosmic order below and eke above.

From the description of Dante's final mystic union with God:

> O light supreme, who so far dost uplift thee o'er mortal thought, re-lend unto my mind a little of what thou then didst seem,
>
> And give my tongue such power that it may leave only a single spark of thy glory unto the folk to come;
>
> I hold that by the keenness of the living ray which I endured I had been lost, had mine eyes turned aside from it.
>
> And so I was the bolder, as I mind me, so long to

sustain it as to unite my glance with the Worth infinite.

O grace abounding, wherein I presumed to fix my look on the eternal light so long that I consumed my sight thereon!

Within its depths I saw ingathered, bound by love in one volume, the scattered leaves of all the universe;

Substance and accidents and their relations, as though together fused, after such fashion that what I tell of is one simple flame. . . .

This all suspended did my mind gaze fixed, immoveable, intent, ever enkindled by its gazing.

Such at that light doth man become that to turn thence to any other sight could not by possibility be ever yielded.

For the good, which is the object of the will, is therein wholly gathered, and outside it that same thing is defective which therein is perfect. . . .

O Light eternal, who only in thyself abidest, only thyself dost understand, and to thyself, self-understood, self-understanding, turnest love and smiling:

That circling which appeared in thee to be conceived as a reflected light, by mine eyes scanned some little,

In itself, of its own color, seemed to be painted with our effigy and thereat my sight was all committed to it,

As the geometer who all sets himself to measure the circle and who findeth not, think as he may, the principle he lacketh;

Such was I at this new seen spectacle; I would perceive how the image consorteth with the circle, and how it settleth there;

But not for this were my proper wings, save that my mind was smitten by a flash wherein its will came to it.

To the high fantasy here power failed; but already my desire and will were rolled—even as a wheel that moveth equally—

By the Love that moves the sun and the other stars.[1]

Compare with this an excerpt from a representative contemporary philosopher of influence, which embodies a rather extreme statement of the doctrine of man widely current in modern times. After quoting the Mephistophelian account of creation as the performance of a quite heartless and capricious being,[2] he proceeds:

Such, in outline, but even more purposeless, more void of meaning, is the world which Science presents for our belief. Amid such a world, if anywhere, our ideals henceforward must find a home. That man is the product of causes which had no prevision of the end they were achieving; that his origin, his growth, his hopes and fears, his loves and his beliefs, are but the outcome of accidental collocations of atoms; that no fire, no heroism, no intensity of thought and feeling, can preserve an individual life beyond the grave; that all the labours of the ages, all the devotion, all the inspirations, all the noonday brightness of human genius, are destined to extinction in the vast death of the solar system, and that the whole temple of Man's achievement must inevitably be buried beneath the debris of a universe in ruins—all these things, if not quite beyond dispute, are yet so nearly certain, that no philosophy which rejects them can hope to stand. Only within the scaffolding of these truths, only on the firm foundation of unyielding despair, can the soul's habitation henceforth be safely built. . . .

Brief and powerless is Man's life; on him and all his race the slow, sure doom falls pitiless and dark. Blind to good and evil, reckless of destruction, omnipotent matter rolls on its relentless way; for Man, condemned to-day to lose his dearest, to-morrow himself to pass through the gate of darkness, it remains only to cherish, ere yet the blow falls, the lofty thoughts that ennoble his little day; disdaining the coward terrors of the slave of Fate, to worship at the shrine that his own hands have built; undismayed by the empire of chance, to preserve a mind free from the wanton tyranny that rules his outward life; proudly defiant of the irresistible forces that tolerate, for a moment, his knowledge and his condemnation, to sustain alone, a weary but unyielding Atlas, the world that his own ideals have fashioned despite the trampling march of unconscious power.

What a contrast between the audacious philosophy of Dante—reposeful, contemplative, infinitely confident—and this view! To Russell, man is but the chance and temporary product of a blind and purposeless nature, an irrelevant spectator of her doings, almost an alien intruder on her domain.[3] No high place in a cosmic teleology is his; his ideals, his hopes, his mystic raptures, are but the creations of his own errant and enthusiastic imagination, without standing or application to a real world interpreted mechanically in terms of space, time, and unconscious, though eternal, atoms. His mother earth is but a speck in the boundlessness of space, his place even on the earth but insignificant and precarious, in a word, he is at the mercy of brute forces that unknowingly happened to throw him into being, and promise ere long just as unknowingly to snuff out the candle of his little day. Himself and all that is dear to him will in course of time become "buried in a universe of ruins."

This is, of course, an extreme position; at the same time is it not true that the reflective modern man, in his cosmological moods, feels this analysis of the situation thrusting itself upon him with increasing cogency? To be sure, there are always some who try to avoid cosmology; there are likewise a few idealistic philosophers and a much larger number of religious enthusiasts who confidently hold to a different view, but would it not be safe to say that even among their ranks there is much secret fear that something like the above conviction would be found inescapable if the facts were faced with absolute candour? For there is a truth on such matters as on all others. In any case, speculation has clearly been moving in this direction: *just as it was thoroughly natural for medieval thinkers to view nature as subservient to man's knowledge, purpose, and destiny; so now it has become natural to view her as existing and operating in her own self-contained independence, and so far as man's ultimate relation to her is clear at all, to consider his knowledge and purpose somehow produced by her, and his destiny wholly dependent on her.*

B. The Metaphysical Foundations of Modern Science the Key to this Problem

One hardly philosophizes to-day in the true sense of the word unless one understands how it was that this veritable upheaval in the main current of intelligent thought has historically come about. And this is precisely the question we wish to ask. But, and this is now the interesting point, when the question is raised in just this form, one soon realizes that a study of modern philosophy—that is, of the writings of those men whose names fill the histories of modern philosophy—gives one little help in the attempt to answer it. For modern metaphysics, at least beginning with the work of Berkeley and Leibniz, has another and more significant connecting thread than that of its epistemological interest; it is in large part a series of unsuccessful protests against this new view of the relation of man to nature. Berkeley, Hume, Kant, Fichte, Hegel, James, Bergson—all are united in one earnest attempt, the attempt to reinstate man with his high spiritual claims in a place of importance in the cosmic scheme. The constant renewal of these attempts and their constant failure widely and thoroughly to convince men, reveals how powerful a grip the view they were attacking was winning over people's minds, and now, perhaps even more than in any previous generation, we find philosophers who are eager above all things to be intellectually honest, ready to give up the struggle as settled and surrender the field. A philosophy akin to Russell's in the relevant essentials, ventures to-day to call itself by the name "naturalism," implying the assurance that a frank facing of the facts by a normal mind, free from malicious inner distortions, will inevitably lead to acquiescence in his results.

What is the reason for the failure of these attempts? A possible answer to this question is, of course, that they were condemned to be ineffectual from the start, that the modern view of man's relation to his environment, though never acknowledged before in quite this form, is after all the truth. The pathetic characteristic of human nature which enables man easily to think more highly of himself than he ought to think—to swallow gullibly

a flattering notion of his own importance in the drama of the ages—might fairly well explain the fact that in all the dominant currents of thought in almost all previous times and places, even where the theoretic interest had become strong, he was prone to fancy that there was something imbedded in the eternal structure of things more akin to that which was most precious in himself than particles of matter in their changing relations. That the scientific philosophy of the Greeks, with all its sublime passion for the very truth of things, arrived in its turn at an exalted philosophy of man, might be due to the circumstances insisted upon by some historians of thought, that the zenith of Greek metaphysics was attained quite consciously through the extension, to the physical realm, of concepts and methods already found helpful in dealing with personal and social situations. It might be the result of a misapplication, to the universe at large, of a point of view legitimate enough in a certain field, the misapplication being based in the last analysis on the unwarranted assumption that because man, while here, can know and use portions of his world, some ultimate and permanent difference is thereby made in that world.

There might be, however, another possible answer to this question. It is obvious, from a casual observation of the medieval and modern methods of attacking the difficulties of metaphysics, that a radical shift has been made in the fundamental terminology used. Instead of treating things in terms of substance, accident, and causality, essence and idea, matter and form, potentiality and actuality, we now treat them in terms of forces, motions, and laws, changes of mass in space and time, and the like. Pick up the works of any modern philosopher, and note how complete the shift has been. To be sure, works in general philosophy may show little use of such a term as mass, but the other words will abundantly dot their pages as fundamental categories of explanation. In particular it is difficult for the modern mind, accustomed to think so largely in terms of space and time, to realize how unimportant these entities were for scholastic science. Spatial and temporal relations were accidental, not essential characteristics. Instead of spatial connexions of things, men were seeking their logical connexious; instead of the onward march of time, men thought of the eternal passage of potentiality into actuality. But the big puzzles of modern philosophers are all concerned with space and time. Hume wonders how it is possible to know the future, Kant resolves by a *coup de force* the antinomies of space and time, Hegel invents a new logic in order to make the adventures of being a developing romance, James proclaims an empiricism of the "flux," Bergson bids us intuitively plunge into that stream of duration which is itself the essence of reality, and Alexander writes a metaphysical treatise on space, time, and deity. It is evident, in other words, that modern philosophers have been endeavouring to follow the ontological quest in terms of a relatively new background of language and a new undercurrent of ideas. It might be that the reason for the failure of philosophy to assure man something more of that place in the universe which he once so confidently assumed is due to an inability to rethink a correct philosophy of man in the medium of this altered terminology. It might be that under cover of this change of ideas modern philosophy had accepted uncritically certain important presuppositions, either in the form of meanings carried by these new terms or in the form of doctrines about man and his knowledge subtly insinuated with them—presuppositions which by their own nature negatived a successful attempt to reanalyse, through their means, man's true relation to his environing world.

During the last generation these ideas of science have been subjected to vigorous analysis and criticism by a group of keen thinkers, who have asked themselves what modifications in the traditional conceptions would be demanded if we sought to overhaul them in the light of a broader and more consistently interpreted experience. At present this critical investigation has culminated in a rather extensive transformation of the major concepts of scientific thinking, furthered on the one hand by radical physical hypotheses of a gifted student of nature like Einstein, and on the other by the attempted reshaping of scientific methods and points of view by philosophers of science such as Whitehead, Broad, Cassirer.[4] These are the most timely and important happenings in the world of scientific philosophy at the present moment. They are compelling people to ask more fundamental questions than have been asked for generations. They are prodding scientists into an extremely healthy state of scepticism about many of the traditional foundations of their thinking. But the kind of work which these pioneers of thought are eager to see done is only a part of the job that really needs to be done. And that job in its entirety cannot be done merely by confining one's interest to the securing of a consistent conception of method in physical science, nor by a careful analysis of the categories of physics as they reveal their meaning to us in the present era of scientific achievement. Cassirer sins on the first count; Whitehead and Broad on both counts. To follow the remarkably acute German scholar is to gain a magnificent historical perspective but to forget, in the very laboriousness of the effort, the pervasive influence of the movement studied on cosmological thinking among modern intelligent folk generally. To follow the English critics is in addition to take much out of the past for granted which needs just as vigorous prying-into as the contemporary problems to which our inquiring attention has been drawn.[5] We inevitably see our limited problem in terms of inherited notions which ought themselves to form part of a larger problem. The continued uncritical use in the writings of these men of traditional ideas like that of "the external world," the dichotomy assumed between the world of the physicist

and the world of sense, the physiological and psychological postulates taken for granted, as, for example, the distinction between sensation and act of sensing, are a few illustrations of what is meant. Our questions must go deeper, and bring into clear focus a more fundamental and more popularly significant problem than any of these men are glimpsing. And the only way to come to grips with this wider problem and reach a position from which we can decide between such alternatives as the above is to follow critically the early use and development of these scientific terms in modern times, and especially to analyse them as presented in their first precise and, so to say, determinative formulation. Just how did it come about that men began to think about the universe in terms of atoms of matter in space and time instead of the scholastic categories? Just when did teleological explanations, accounts in terms of use and the Good, become definitely abandoned in favour of the notion that true explanations, of man and his mind as well as of other things, must be in terms of their simplest parts? What was happening between the years 1500 and 1700 to accomplish this revolution? And then, what ultimate metaphysical implications were carried over into general philosophy in the course of the transformation? Who stated these implications in the form which gave them currency and conviction? How did they lead men to undertake such inquiries as that of modern epistemology? What effects did they have upon the intelligent modern man's ideas about his world?

When we begin to break up our puzzle into specific questions like these we realize that what we are proposing is a rather neglected type of historical inquiry, that is, an analysis of the philosophy of early modern science, and in particular of the metaphysics of Sir Isaac Newton. Not that much of this has not been written; indeed Professor Cassirer himself has done work on modern epistemology which will long remain a monumental achievement in its field. But a much more radical historical analysis needs to be made. We must grasp the essential contrast between the whole modern world-view and that of previous thought, and use that clearly conceived contrast as a guiding clue to pick out for criticism and evaluation, in the light of their historical development, every one of our significant modern presuppositions. An analysis of this scope and to this purpose has nowhere appeared. Such considerations make it plain, also, why this arduous labour cannot be avoided, as some present-day thinkers fondly hope, by making a large use in our philosophizing of the categories of evolutionary biology. These categories have indeed tended to supplant, in disquisitions about living matter at least, much of the terminology of mechanical physics. But the whole magnificent movement of modern science is essentially of a piece; the later biological and sociological branches took over their basic postulates from the earlier victorious mechanics, especially the all-important postulate that valid explanations must always be in terms of small, elementary units in regularly changing relations. To this has likewise been added, in all but the rarest cases, the postulate that ultimate causality is to be found in the motion of the physical atoms. So far as biology has its own peculiar metaphysical assumptions, they are as yet covered up in the vagueness of its major concepts, "environment," "adaptation," etc., and must be given time to reveal their specific nature. It is the creative period of modern science, then, in the seventeenth century chiefly, to which we must turn for the main answer to our problem. As for pre-Newtonian science, it is one and the same movement with pre-Newtonian philosophy, both in England and on the continent; science was simply natural philosophy, and the influential figures of the periods were both the greatest scientists. It is largely due to Newton himself that a real distinction came to be made between the two; philosophy came to take science, in the main, for granted, and another way to put our central theme is, *did not the problems to which philosophers now devoted themselves arise directly out of that uncritical acceptance?* A brief summary of Newton's work will show that this is very possible.

Since his day, a two-fold importance has generally been ascribed to Newton. Popularly, he has profoundly affected the thinking of the average intelligent man by his outstanding scientific exploits, of which the most striking was his conquest of the heavens in the name of human science by identifying terrestrial gravitation with the centripetal movements of the celestial bodies. Great as is the name of Newton to-day, it is difficult for us to picture the adoration with which he was regarded all over Europe in the eighteenth century. It seemed to men, if we are to trust the voluminous literature of the time, that such achievements as the discovery of the laws of motion and the law of universal gravitation, represented an incomparable, uniquely important victory of mind, which it could fall to the lot of only one man throughout all time to realize—and Newton had been that man. Henry Pemberton, who edited the third edition of the *Principia* for Newton, and who wrote one of the numerous commentaries on it, declared that " . . . my admiration at the surprising inventions of this great man, carries me to conceive of him as a person, who not only must raise the glory of the country which gave him birth, but that he has even done honour to human nature, by having extended the greatest and most noble of our faculties, reason, to subjects which, till he attempted them, appeared to be wholly beyond the reach of our limited capacities."[6] The admiration of other scientific minds is represented by Locke's designation of himself, beside the "incomparable Mr. Newton, an under-labourer, employed in clearing the ground and removing some of the rubbish that lies in the way to knowledge";[7] or by the famous tribute of Laplace who remarked that Newton was not

only the greatest genius that ever had existed, but also the most fortunate; inasmuch as there is but one universe, and it can therefore happen to but one man in the world's history to be the interpreter of its laws. Literary men like Pope found expression for the prevailing veneration of the great scientist in such a famous couplet as:

> Nature and Nature's laws lay hid in night;
> God said, "Let Newton be," and all was light.[8]

while the new authoritarianism that developed under Newton's name, attacked so violently by Berkeley in his *Defence of Free Thinking in Mathematics,* was still deplored twenty years later by eager inquirers such as George Horne:

> The prejudice for Sir Isaac has been so great, that it has destroyed the intent of his undertaking, and his books have been a means of hindering that knowledge they were intended to promote. It is a notion every child imbibes almost with his mother's milk, that Sir Isaac Newton has carried philosophy to the highest pitch it is capable of being carried, and established a system of physics upon the solid basis of mathematical demonstration.[9]

Such representative quotations disclose the creation, under Newton's leadership, of a new background in the minds of Europe's intelligentsia such that all problems must have been viewed afresh because they were seen against it.

A student of the history of physical science will assign to Newton a further importance which the average man can hardly appreciate. He will see in the English genius a leading figure in the invention of certain scientific tools necessary for fruitful further development such as the infinitesimal calculus. He will find in him the first clear statement of that union of the experimental and mathematical methods which has been exemplified in all subsequent discoveries of exact science. He will note the separation in Newton of positive scientific inquiries from questions of ultimate causation. Most important, perhaps, from the point of view of the exact scientist, Newton was the man who took vague terms like force and mass and gave them a precise meaning as quantitative continua, so that by their use the major phenomena of physics became amenable to mathematical treatment. It is because of these remarkable scientific performances that the history of mathematics and mechanics for a hundred years subsequent to Newton appears primarily as a period devoted to the assimilation of his work and the application of his laws to more varied types of phenomena. So far as objects were masses, moving in space and time under the impress of forces as he had defined them, their behavior was now, as a result of his labours, fully explicable in terms of exact mathematics.

It may be, however, that Newton is an exceedingly important figure for still a third reason. He not only found a precise mathematical use for concepts like force, mass, inertia; he gave new meanings to the old terms space, time, and motion, which had hitherto been unimportant but were now becoming the fundamental categories of men's thinking. In his treatment of such ultimate concepts, together with his doctrine of primary and secondary qualities, his notion of the nature of the physical universe and of its relation to human knowledge (in all of which he carried to a more influential position a movement already well advanced)—in a word, in his decisive portrayal of the ultimate postulates of the new science and its successful method as they appeared to him, Newton was constituting himself a philosopher rather than a scientist as we now distinguish them. He was presenting a metaphysical groundwork for the mathematical march of mind which in him had achieved its most notable victories. Imbedded directly and prominently in the *Principia,* Newton's most widely studied work, these metaphysical notions were carried wherever his scientific influence penetrated, and borrowed a possibly unjustified certainty from the clear demonstrability of the gravitational theorems to which they are appended as *Scholia.* Newton was unrivalled as a scientist—it may appear that he is not above criticism as a metaphysician. He tried scrupulosuly, at least in his experimental work, to avoid metaphysics. He disliked hypotheses, by which he meant explanatory propositions which were not immediately deduced from phenomena. At the same time, following his illustrious predecessors, he does give or assume definite answers to such fundamental questions as the nature of space, time, and matter; the relations of man with the objects of his knowledge; and it is just such answers that constitute metaphysics. The fact that his treatment of these great themes—borne as it was over the educated world by the weight of his scientific prestige—was covered over by this cloak of positivism, may have become itself a danger. It may have helped not a little to insinuate a set of uncritically accepted ideas about the world into the common intellectual background of the modern man. What Newton did not distinguish, others were not apt carefully to analyse. The actual achievements of the new science were undeniable; furthermore, the old set of categories, involving, as it appeared, the now discredited medieval physics, was no longer an alternative to any competent thinker. In these circumstances it is easy to understand how modern philosophy might have been led into certain puzzles which were due to the unchallenged presence of these new categories and presuppositions.

Now a penetrating study of post-Newtonian philosophers quickly reveals the fact that they were philosophizing quite definitely in the light of his achievements, and with his metaphysics especially in mind. At the time of his death Leibniz was engaged in a heated debate on the nature of time and space with Newton's theological champion, Samuel Clarke. Berkeley's *Commonplace Book* and *Principles,* still more his lesser works such as *The Analyst, A Defence of Free Thinking in Mathematics,* and *De Motu,* show clearly enough whom he conceived to be his deadly foe.[10] Hume's *Enquiry Concerning Human Understanding and Enquiry Concerning the Principles of Morals* contain frequent references to Newton. The French Encyclopaedists and materialists of the middle of the eighteenth century felt themselves one and all to be more consistent Newtonians than Newton himself. In his early years Kant was an eager student of Newton, and his first works[11] aim mainly at a synthesis of continental philosophy and Newtonian science. Hegel wrote[12] an extended and trenchant criticism of Newton. Of course, these men do not accept Newton as gospel truth—they all criticize some of his conceptions, especially force and space—but none of them subjects the whole system of categories which had come to its clearest expression in the great *Principia* to a critical analysis. It may be that their failure to construct a convincing and encouraging philosophy of man is due in large part to this untested remainder. It may be that many of the terms and assumptions in which their thinking proceeded were in their unanalysed form essentially refractory to any such brilliant achievement.

The only way to bring this issue to the bar of truth is to plunge into the philosophy of early modern science, locating its key assumptions as they appear, and following them out to their classic formulation in the metaphysical paragraphs of Sir Isaac Newton. The present is a brief historical study which aims to meet this need. The analysis will be sufficiently detailed to allow our characters to do much speaking for themselves, and to lay bare as explicitly as possible the real interests and methods revealed in their work At its close the reader will understand more clearly the nature of modern thinking and judge more accurately the validity of the contemporary scientific world-view.

Let us start our inquiry with certain questions suggested by the work of the first great modern astronomer and the founder of a new system of the celestial orbs, Nicholas Copernicus.

Notes

[1] Selections from the *Paradiso,* Cantos I, X, and XXXIII, Temple Classics edition.

[2] Bertrand Russell, *A Free Man's Worship (Mysticism and Logic)* New York, 1918, p. 46, ff.

[3] This author has now adopted a less extreme position on these points. (Revised Edition.)

[4] See especially, A. N. Whitehead, *The Principles of Natural Knowledge,* Cambridge, 1919; *The Concept of Nature,* Cambridge, 1920; *The Principle of Relativity,*

Cambridge, 1923; C. D. Broad, *Perception, Physics, and Reality,* London, 1914; *Scientific Thought,* London, 1923; E. Cassirer, *Das Erkenntniss-problem in der Philosophie und Wissenschaft der neueren Zeit,* 3 vols, Berlin, 1906-20; *Substance and Function and Einstein's Theory of Relativity* (trans. by W. C. and M. C. Swabey), Chicago, 1923; see also the earlier studies of K. Pearson, E. Mach, H. Poincare, and for fuller familiarity with the field the works of Minkowski, Weyl, Robb, Eddington.

[5] This no longer applies to Whitehead. (Revised Edition.)

[6] *A View of Isaac Newton's Philosophy,* London, 1728, Dedication to Sir Robert Walpole.

[7] *Essay Concerning Human Understanding,* Epistle to the Reader.

[8] Epitaph, intended for Newton's tomb in Westminster Abbey, *Poetical Works,* Glasgow, 1785, vol. II, p. 342.

[9] *A Fair, Candid, and Impartial State of the Case between Sir Isaac Newton and Mr. Hutchinson,* Oxford, 1753, p. 72.

[10] The fullest edition of Berkeley's *Works* is that of A. C. Fraser, Oxford, 1871, 4 vols.

[11] See especially his *Thoughts on the True Estimation of Living Forces,* 1746; *General Physiogony and Theory of the Heavens,* 1755; *Monadologia Physica,* 1756; and *Inquiry into the Evidence of the Principles of Natural Theology and Morals,* 1764; in any edition of his works.

[12] Hegel, *Phenomenology of Mind* (Baillie trans.), London, 1910, Vol. I, pp. 124, ff., 233, ff.; *Philosophy of Nature, passim;* and *History of Philosophy* (Haldane trans.), Vol. III, 322, ff.

Ron Millen (essay date 1985)

SOURCE: "The Manifestation of Occult Qualities in the Scientific Revolution," in *Religion, Science, and Worldview: Essays in Honor of Richard S. Westfall,* edited by Margaret J. Osler and Paul Lawrence Farber, Cambridge University Press, 1985, pp. 185-216.

[In the following essay, Millen discusses the evolution of the concept of the occult and its effect, through the Renaissance, on the development of science.]

THE PROBLEM OF OCCULT QUALITIES

"Occult" has become something of a pejorative term among historians of the scientific revolution. According to the dominant view of seventeenth-century science, occult qualities were banished from nature by the new philosophy of mechanism. Even historians of science who have emphasized the hermetic component of the scientific revolution have not really come to grips with the issue of occult qualities in the seventeenth century. The persistence of occult modes of natural action in the writings of prominent virtuosi is viewed as an anomaly, an instance that simply proves that the new science was not altogether new. But the real importance of hidden qualities for the mechanical and experimental philosophers remains unclear.

A recent article "What Happened to Occult Qualities in the Scientific Revolution?" has broken new ground.[1] It presents the thesis that far from banishing these qualities, the new philosophy actually incorporated them into modern science. If the question posed in the title has been too long in the asking, the answer at least does much to clarify contemporary attitudes toward occult qualities. However, the contrast drawn by the author between the views of mechanists and Aristotelians is somewhat misleading; it is indicative of a common tendency to view the scientific revolution in terms of a clash between ancients and moderns. To clarify the issue still further, one must consider the changing attitudes toward occult qualities in the tradition of Renaissance Scholasticism. As the present essay will show, Scholastics in the sixteenth and early seventeenth centuries confronted the problem of how to deal scientifically with the occult, and the methods they developed were not essentially different from those utilized by mechanical philosophers. The philosophical method of explicating causes and the experimental method of investigating effects were the two roads to knowledge of occult virtues, and the approaches of Scholastics as well as mechanists tended in one direction or the other, depending upon which of the two methods had the upper hand. By taking into account the status of occult qualities in the Scholastic tradition, one can get a clearer insight into the attitudes of leading virtuosi and how they incorporated these qualities into the framework of the new philosophy.

To begin, it will be helpful to say something about the meanings associated with the term "occult" in Scholastic philosophy. In the most common sense, the word signified that which was unintelligible. Occult qualities were properties and powers for which one could offer no rational explanation. In the Middle Ages, philosophers attempted to account for corporeal properties in terms of the four elements and their primary qualities: heat, cold, wetness, and dryness. The class of occult or "specific" virtues, as they were called, comprised the powers of bodies that could not be reduced to a certain temperament of the elementary qualities.[2] The source of specific virtues was frequently assigned to the body's immaterial substantial form. For example, some physicians did not regard the power of scammony to purge bile as occult since they believed that the effect could be explained by the drug's particular heat and dryness. Almost everyone, however, admitted that the magnet's capacity to attract iron was occult because magnetic virtue did not result from the specific mixture of the four elements. Obviously, the notion of unintelligibility was somewhat subjective. A property like the purgative virtues of scammony might be treated as a manifest quality by some physicians, as an occult quality by others. Much depended upon one's faith in the ability of reason to comprehend the workings of nature.

A second usage of "occult" emphasized the notion of *insensibility*. A quality was called "occult" or "hidden" if it was not directly perceptible. Unlike the preceding case, there was nothing subjective about this division of corporeal properties into manifest and occult; the demarcation was purely technical. Typical manifest qualities included colors, odors, and tastes, whereas the class of occult qualities contained such entities as the magnetic power of the loadstone, influences emanating from the planets, and the specific virtues of medicines. One finds this technical sense persisting in the seventeenth century even among philosophers who thought that almost all qualities were epistemologically occult. Sennert, for example, wrote:

> Now these Qualities are called Occult, Hidden, Abstruse to distinguish them from the manifest qualities discernable by the external Senses, especially the Feeling; whereas on the contrary these are not perceivable, although their operations are: So we see the attraction made by the Loadstone; but we do not perceive the qualities causing that motion of the Iron.[3]

There was an essential link in medieval philosophy between the connotations of insensibility and unintelligibility. According to Aristotelian epistemology, true scientific knowledge—*scientia*—was derived from sensible images. During sensation, the sensory organs received the forms of manifest qualities abstracted from their subject matter. After the imagination had further abstracted the sensible form, the intellect sifted them, separating the accidental from the essential features until at last it obtained the universal form or essence. According to this sensationalist epistemology, insensible entities were ipso facto unintelligible and therefore outside the domain of true scientific knowledge. One may object that none of the active powers of bodies could be perceived directly by the senses, and yet Scholastics believed that they could give a scientific account for many of them. However, the powers that could be explained were all derived from the primary qualities—heat, cold, wetness, and dryness. In Aristotle's philosophy, these were the principles of all perceptible properties. Thus, Scholastics brought at least some active powers within the scope of natural philos-

ophy by explicating them in terms of the immediately intelligible qualities of nature. Only nonelementary virtues, operating through insensible means, could not be accommodated. As we shall see, the incorporation of occult properties into natural philosophy during the sixteenth and seventeenth centuries depended upon breaking the link between the connotations of insensibility and unintelligibility.

To comprehend more clearly the change in attitude toward occult qualities during this period, it will be helpful to consider briefly their status in medieval natural philosophy and medicine. In general, Peripatetics and Galenists were divided over the reality and importance of occult qualities. Whereas Christian natural philosophers tended to deny that they existed, physicians admitted that certain medicines possessed specific virtues beyond the powers of the elementary qualities. Moreover, an experiential knowledge of these properties was important. In the absence of any detailed study of occult qualities in the Middle Ages, it is not clear to what extent one can pursue the division between philosophers and physicians. However, there are general grounds for believing that the differences were significant, reflecting the combined influence of several factors. Not the least of these was that Aristotle never discussed occult virtues. Whatever his silence implied, it discouraged medieval commentators from taking up the subject. Galen, in contrast, alluded to the powers of specific remedies operating not by contrary qualities but by the similitude of their "total substance." Exactly how he interpreted occult properties is not clear, but the sanction given to them by his authority is evident in the frequent citations of Galen by defenders of occult qualities in the Renaissance.

Peripatetic philosophers had surprising difficulty admitting the existence of insensible entities. Thomas Aquinas denied that there could be animals, or even parts of animals, insensible because of their smallness.[4] The point was of some importance, given the passage in Genesis, where Adam named all the animals at the Creation. Aquinas conceded, as Augustine had earlier, that man's senses may have suffered some loss of acuity as a punishment for the Fall, but the tendency to deny the possibility of insensible material entities seems to have been a common feature of medieval natural philosophy. Aquinas did admit certain insensible natural actions such as magnetic attraction, which he claimed was due to an inexplicable occult virtue. However, he insisted that many similar phenomena that seemed to be natural actually resulted from the supernatural activity of angels and demons.[5] He did not claim that man had absolutely no access to insensible causes since God was the prime example of an occult power, and Aquinas wished to show that man could obtain some natural knowledge of Him. However, he never equated the defective knowledge based on sensed effects with true scientific knowledge of causes derived through the powers of sensation and reason. Thomism, which provided the basis for Christian natural philosophy in the Middle Ages, could not resolve the problem presented by occult qualities, namely, how could a science based upon sensation deal with entities by definition insensible? Before Scholastic philosophers began to discuss occult qualities in the sixteenth century, they had to be prodded by thinkers outside the tradition of Christian Aristotelianism.

Galenists did not manage to solve the problem either. Nevertheless, they included specific virtues within the branch of medicine dealing with materia medica. Traditionally, physicians were less apt to regard their ignorance of the ultimate causes of natural actions as a defect of their knowledge. Sennert noted this when he remarked:

> And therefore those who traduce these Qualities by calling them the Sanctuary of Ignorance are long since worthily refuted by Avicenna . . . when he thus writes: As he that knows fire warms by reason of the heat therein truly knows and is not ignorant, so he that knows the Load-stone draws Iron because it hath a virtue whose nature is to draw Iron without doubt is knowing and not ignorant.[6]

The difference between Avicenna's and Aquinas's attitude toward occult qualities seems to be representative of the greater acceptability of specific virtues within the medical tradition. However, even physicians did little more than note the existence and uses of these powers; there does not seem to have been any attempt to study them methodically.

Occult Qualities in Renaissance Aristotelianism

In the sixteenth and seventeenth centuries, a serious effort was made first by Scholastics and later by proponents of the new science to bring occult qualities within the scope of natural philosophy. Two distinct approaches were taken. Philosophers attacked the thesis that the insensible is unintelligible by attempting to devise causal *explanations* for occult actions. It may seem that by offering rational accounts for marvelous phenomena, they in effect denied the existence of the occult. However, a closer look reveals that philosophers did not challenge the reality of the occult in nature; they challenged the belief that man could not reduce occult properties to intelligible causes. The experimental approach, in contrast, accepted that certain causes could not be explained; nevertheless, they could be brought within the domain of science by investigating their *effects*. Instead of trying to account for the properties of bodies, proponents of the experimenteal method tended to treat every quality as hidden. With the elimination of the epistemological distinction between manifest and occult qualities, the way was open for the incorporation of the latter into an experimental philosophy.

The principal influence prompting Peripatetics in the Renaissance to admit the existence of occult qualities was the rise of natural magic. Proponents of natural magic portrayed it as an occult philosophy of nature capable of explaining in terms of natural causes many marvelous phenomena commonly attributed to angels and demons.[7] Their explanations utilized the activity of insensible—though not necessarily incorporeal—agents. To magicians, insensibility did not carry the connotation of unintelligibility because they emphasized that through special powers of imagination, the adept could grasp the workings of hidden causes. Only common philosophers relying upon the limited faculties of sensation and reason regarded the insensible realm as beyond man's comprehension. Such bold, dogmatic claims presented a challenge to Peripatetic philosophers to come to terms with entities beneath the level of perception. Incorporeal spirits and demons appeared more and more as a refuge of the ignorant.

Christian Aristotelians tended to view natural magic with suspicion. Even though adepts stressed the natural basis of occult actions, they found it difficult to sustain the distinction between natural and supernatural magic. Many opponents followed Giovanni Pico in rejecting natural magic not on the grounds of any inherent implausibility but because it threatened Christianity. However, among Peripatetics of the naturalistic school, conditions were favorable for the incorporation of magical doctrines, including occult qualities, into Aristotelian philosophy. At Padua, the medical rather than the theological faculty exerted the principal influence on the course of studies, and hence the emphasis fell upon Aristotle's scientific writings. The challenge to the Peripatetic view of nature represented by natural magic could not be ignored or put off with superficial arguments; it had to be met head on. In contrast to the confidence with which magicians dealt with occult phenomena, the silence of Scholastic philosophers suddenly seemed embarrassing.

The immediate response of Peripatetics can be seen in one of the influential works of Aristotelian naturalism: Pietro Pomponazzi's *De Naturalium effectuum admirandorum causis et de Incantationibus* (1556).[8] The treatise opened with Pomponazzi's reply to a physician from Mantua who had written concerning the case of two infants, one suffering from erysipelas, the other from burns. It seems that both had been cured by a man who used only words and no other apparent remedies. How, the Mantuan asked, could the Peripatetic philosophy account for such phenomena? Theologians might explain the effect as the result of demons, but Aristotle apparently did not believe in demons. Some might claim that the words used by the man in healing were the instrument of higher powers such as the stars, but it was difficult to see how celestial bodies could have produced such marvels. The physician concluded that Peripatetics must be very embarrassed because they lacked an explanation for such phenomena.

Pomponazzi conceded that it was difficult to indicate what Aristotle actually thought about marvels because he never said anything about them. Perhaps, however, it would be possible to find a satisfactory account of the phenomena in keeping with the *spirit* of Aristotle's philosophy. Pomponazzi never stopped to question the reality of the marvelous cures reported by his correspondent, and throughout the treatise, he continued to display the same uncritical attitude. He tended to take his facts where he could find them, reserving his ingenuity for the task of devising explanations.

Before tackling the case of the two infants, Pomponazzi prepared the ground by setting forth several "Peripatetic hypotheses." The first postulated the existence of invisible, occult powers in natural bodies. The second claimed that the number of occult properties was nearly infinite. In contrast with the reluctance of medieval philosophers to recognize hidden properties, Pomponazzi virtually steeped natural bodies in the occult. His hypotheses represented essentially a magician's view of nature, expressed within the framework of the Peripatetic philosophy.

Lost in the translation was the sense of occult qualities as incorporeal virtues. Traditionally, these powers were associated with substantial forms, not matter. Agrippa described occult qualities as nonelementary virtues originating in the ideas of God and residing in the celestial intelligences.[9] In the process of generation, matter was disposed to receive divine powers, which emanated from the stars to the various stones, herbs, metals, and other bodies in the sunlunar world. Peripatetics divested many occult qualities of their Platonist and Neoplatonist trappings. According to the naturalistic doctrine of the origin of forms, the essential properties of a body resulted from a mixture of the four elementary qualities. Hence, specific virtues could be explained by the body's temperament. Such a theory, in effect, put all corporeal properties on the same plane. One could denominate certain properties as occult, but the term did not mean "unintelligible," simply "not understood." The category of occult qualities grew or shrank depending upon one's faith in the accounts offered for individual effects. In Pomponazzi's writings, the emphasis was upon man's ability to have true scientific knowledge of the occult.

Pomponazzi's conception of the philosopher in *De Incantantationibus* strongly resembled the popular notion of the hermetic adeptus. In one of his hypotheses, he described man as an intermediary being, situated between the realms of corruptible and eternal things.[10] Man did not simply participate in the corruptible realm; he contained it within his human nature and therefore represented a microcosm of the greater world. Through his natural faculties of sensation and reason, man could acquire knowledge of hidden causes. Exactly how one was to obtain sensible images of insensible causes Pomponazzi did not say. Perhaps he believed that man could have only probable knowledge of the occult. In response to the problem posed by the Mantuan physician, he submitted three alternative explanations, as if to say that any one might be true and the philosopher should not seek after certainty. However, skepticism was hardly the theme of the treatise. The portrait of the philosopher drawn by Pomponazzi revealed a man whose powers of cognition extended far above the level of ordinary men, almost to the level of divinity:

> And it follows that there are certain men who have accomplished many prodigies thanks to their science of nature and the stars, which is sometimes attributed to their sanctity or to necromancy, when they are neither saints nor necromancers. It follows also, if it is true as many approved authors have stated, that there are herbs, stones, or other means of this sort which repel hail, rain, winds, and that one is able to find others which have naturally the property of attracting them. Assuming that men are able to know them naturally, it follows that they are able, in applying the active to the passive, to induce hail and rain and to drive them away; as for me, I do not see any impossibility.[11]

How was man to acquire this science? Pomponazzi recommended study and experience, but the real key to his method—if one may call it that—seems to lie in the powers of introspective reason. Occult phenomena in nature corresponded to occult processes in the microcosm of man's psyche, and therefore the hidden causes of things could be discovered by looking within. Despite Pomponazzi's assertions that knowledge required a sensible image, the tendency to elevate philosophers to the level of semidivinities suggested that the true adept could dispense with phantasms and simply intuit the causes of occult actions. Such bold claims were heard again in the seventeenth century from a modern spokesman for the power of introspective reason, René Descartes.

A more solid philosophical approach to the problem of explicating occult qualities can be found in Girolamo Fracastoro's small treatise *De Sympathia et Antipathia Rerum* (1546). Although Fracastoro was Pomponazzi's student, he showed a keener awareness than his teacher that natural philosophy must be based on experience. He also realized that to keep experience from degenerating into fantasy and magic, it must be collected and unified by stable philosophical concepts. Fracastoro found a unifying concept in the Aristotelian notion of cause. According to his analysis, there were three kinds of cause, distinguished according to their proximity to things.[12] He criticized contemporary philosophers and physicians for being preoccupied with universal and remote principles such as matter and form, the four elementary virtues, and the four humors. Although Fracastoro accepted the validity of these ancient concepts, he recognized that they could not be used effectively to order experience. The concern for ultimate principles had left many important topics of physics and medicine unexplored and others not clearly explained.

Fracastoro recommended that philosophers concentrate on the genus of more immediate and particular causes capable of unifying all the phenomena associated with a given subject. The two topics he chose to explore were the nature of contagion and the sympathies and antipathies of things. The subject of contagious diseases was on the minds of many physicians in the early sixteenth century after the pandemic outbreak of syphilis. Galenic remedies had proved to be ineffective in treating the new disease, and the field was left open to empirics. In self-defense, perhaps, Fracastoro encouraged Galenists to pursue a more empirical approach. The selective pattern of the disease's transmission suggested that some occult sympathy was at work, and so the investigation into the causes of contagion required a preliminary inquiry into sympathies and antipathies. By finding causal principles capable of explaining apparent actions at a distance, one would have a foundation upon which to construct the theory of contagious diseases.

Fracastoro warned against pushing the inquiry into the realm of immediate causes since knowledge of these was proper to God and divine intelligences. Man should strive after perfect cognition, but he should remember that anyone who presumed to possess it would only reveal himself as inept and arrogant. Fracastoro's words seemed to be aimed in part at philosophers who attempted to explain occult qualities in terms of a specific proportion of the elements. Since man could not apprehend the internal composition of mixture in bodies, he could not have the kind of perfect scientific knowledge characteristic of higher intelligences. Reason must not go beyond the limits of experience.

In the fifth chapter, Fracastoro took up the question of the principle of motion responsible for attraction between similar things. Included in this class of phenomena were all those that Galenists had described as actions from similitude. Fracastoro rejected the concept of similitude, claiming that if bodies attracted each other in virtue of their similar natures, they should do so no matter what distance separated them. In many cases, however, motion occurred only when the distance was quite small. There was no action, he said, except through the medium of contact. Since similar things attracted toward each other were originally separated, each body had to emit something that touched the other and caused motion. Fracastoro rejected the atomistic theory of an efflux of particles because oc-

casionally the action occurred over distances corpuscles could not reasonably be expected to travel. Since the mechanism of effluvia was not universal, he turned to the theory of spiritual species. He described the species as "simulacra"—tenuous, superficial entities emitted from the crass matter of the body and having the same form. Although the concept of spiritual species was common in Scholastic philosophy, particularly in the theory of optics, their nature was still surrounded with problems. Fracastoro acknowledged that there was some question how a spiritual substance could cause motion in material bodies. He did not pretend to have the answer but suggested a theory in which natural heat operating through spiritual species provided the moving power.

On the whole, Francastoro's treatise appears as a progressive attempt to explicate the causes of occult qualities. There was a recognition that sympathies and antipathies existed and that the basic principles of Aristotelian matter theory were inadequate to account for them. Although the concept of spiritual species gave way to atomistic theories in the seventeenth century, the two theories were very similar. It is not surprising that a confirmed atomist like Walter Charleton praised Fracastoro for his handling of sympathies.[13]

The influence of Fracastoro's ideas can be detected even among his immediate contemporaries. Jerome Cardan took up the subject of the occult in a brief work, *De secretis*.[14] In the beginning, he wrote that although Fracastoro, and even he himself, had written about arcane matters, the "hidden rules of the dialectic" for treating the occult had not yet been found and reduced to order; his book aimed to make clear the method (ratio) for investigating hidden causes.

Cardan's ideas about method reflected his interests in mathematics. On several occasions, he compared the secrets of nature to those of mathematics. In both cases, cognition was based upon causes. However, man had a clearer understanding of the principles of mathematics and hence was able to have greater certainty about mathematical secrets than about occult phenomena. Nevertheless, Cardan believed that one could utilize general principles to explicate certain marvelous natural effects. It was impossible to have perfect cognition; for that depended upon a grasp of the ultimate principles. Only the gods had such knowledge since only they knew the recesses of things. Man's perception was limited to externals. He could know but a few secrets, and those through analogy with mechanical things. Cardan mentioned the example of certain machines and vases in which apparently marvelous effects were produced by the flow of water and steam through the internal parts. He recommended that one follow the example of Hero and Archimedes by utilizing both natural and mathematical principles to give an account of such occult phenomena.

Cardan's suggestions seem reasonable enough, but when we get down to cases, it is clear how little explanatory value his dialectical method actually possessed. He illustrated its application with reference to the paradigm of occult actions: magnetic effects. To explain the phenomena, he set forth certain premises the first two of which were grounded in experience: (1) When the magnet is applied to the end of a bar of iron, it draws the iron toward itself, and (2) when the magnet approaches the bar from the side, it orients the iron so that one end is directed toward the north, the other toward the south. In addition to these empirical premises, Cardan also supposed three general axioms applicable to all natural things: (1) Similar things attract, and contraries repel; (2) if something is not able to draw a like object toward itself, it is drawn toward that object; and (3) anything attached to the attracted object is necessarily drawn along with it. On the basis of this set of five premises, Cardan said, one can explain the causes of all magnetic phenomena. Exactly how was never made clear.

The three figures examined in this section all shared the belief that the Peripatetic philosophy could not ignore the existence of the occult. Some method had to be found to explain marvelous phenomena in terms of natural causes. Although the explanations devised by Scholastic philosophers were swept away by the new philosophy, the attitudes toward the intelligibility of the occult persisted. As long as the effects were produced by natural causes, they fell within the province of the natural philosopher. The mechanical philosophy was marked by a greater skepticism toward the reality of occult effects and by a greater self-assurance in dealing with the occult. It was only in the seventeenth century that occult qualities were fully incorporated into modern science.

OCCULT QUALITIES AND THE MECHANICAL PHILOSOPHY

Almost all historians of the scientific revolution regard occult qualities as a casualty of the mechanical philosophy. It is argued that the modern concept of nature based on the principles of matter and motion banished every kind of occult power. Although there are reasonable grounds for maintaining this position, it tends to misrepresent the attitudes of leading members of the new science. In this section, we shall take a closer look at what might be called the Cartesian method for dealing with occult phenomena. The emphasis was upon explicating these effects by means of particular mechanisms.

Descartes faced a challenge somewhat like the one that had confronted Pomponazzi nearly a century and a half earlier: Given the reality of certain marvelous phenomena in nature, how could one explain them? In the mid-seventeenth century, the challenge came primarily from occult philosophers who boasted that they had

knowledge of the underlying causes of occult effects. For Descartes, to deny the existence of occult qualities altogether would have been to concede that the new philosophy was incapable of handling them. Descartes, of course, made no concessions. On the contrary, he regarded the mechanical philosophy's capacity to account for any and all occult qualities as one of the strong points of the new system. This does not mean that he believed that every marvelous effect described by his opponents was indeed genuine, but for occult properties well documented, he held forth the possibility of a scientific explanation. Aristotelianism had not promised as much. There were many properties of bodies whose derivation from the mixture of the elements Peripatetics did not profess to know. Where Aristotelians hesitated, Descartes plunged ahead. Just after his lengthy mechanical explication of magnetic virtues in the *Principia,* he announced:

> there are no powers in stones or plants so occult, no sympathies or antipathies so miraculous and stupendous, in short, nothing in nature (provided it proceeds from material causes destitute of mind and cognition) that its reason cannot be deduced from these [i.e., mechanical] principles.[15]

Far from denying the existence of occult qualities, Descartes boasted that he had brought them within the province of natural philosophy.

Historians of the scientific revolution commonly point to such passages as this one to support the claim that Descartes rejected the notion of occult qualities. But a closer consideration of the point of Descartes's remarks suggests a different conclusion. The lesson to be learned from the discussion of the loadstone was that one could find explanations for documented cases of occult actions such as magnetic attraction; explanations that did not rely on any other principles besides matter and motion. Having shown how to proceed with the paradigm case of an occult virtue, Descartes pointed to other such properties and told natural philosophers to go and do likewise. To say that he rejected occult qualities is to miss the positive methodological prescription. In the example of the loadstone, he was really setting out a program for the manifestation of the occult.

The celebrated dispute later in the century between Cartesians and Newtonians over universal gravitation illustrates the point. When Cartesians charged that gravity was an occult quality, they were, at bottom, objecting to the way Newtonians treated the property. Newtonians failed to develop an official account of the particular mechanism underlying the observed effects of gravitation; instead, they insisted that it was possible to mathematize the motions of gravity without explaining the causes. Cartesians responded with accusations that their opponents wished to reintroduce occult qualities into physics. Beneath the rhetoric, it is clear that what perturbed the Cartesians was the absence of an explanatory mechanism for the property "gravitas." The Newtonian belief that one could deal scientifically with properties whose causes were unknown ran counter to the whole program of Cartesian physics. What better way to vent one's frustrations than to hurl the epithet "occult" at the enemy? Unfortunately, the use of the term in this way created the impression that Cartesians rejected the existence of these qualities. Neither the Newtonians nor the Cartesians really banished the occult from nature. What the Cartesians prohibited was the notion of an occult quality whose causes were not made manifest. This was the real sin of the Newtonians: They had introduced an occult quality without first explaining it.

Against the interpretation presented here one might object that the Cartesian program undermined the very essence of occult qualities by attempting to make them intelligible. Perhaps if all mechanical philosophers shared Descartes's faith in the powers of human reason, one could make a stronger case for this claim. However, there were many who adopted the Cartesian method yet took a more skeptical attitude toward the possibility of discovering nature's innermost secrets. Walter Charleton spoke for this group in a chapter of his *Physiologia* entitled "Occult Qualities Made Manifest":

> Not that we dare be guilty of such unpardonable Vanity and Arrogance as not most willingly to confess that to *Ourselves all the Operations of Nature are meer Secrets;* that in her ample catalogue of Qualities, we have not met with so much as one which is not really Immanifest and Abstruse when we convert our thoughts either upon its Genuine and Proxime Causes, or upon the Reason and Manner of its perception by that Sense, whose proper Object it is and consequently that as the *Sensibility* of a thing doth no way presuppose its *Intelligibility,* but that many things, which are most obvious and open to the *Sense,* as to their *Effects,* may yet be remote and in the dark to the *Understanding* as to their *Causes.*[16]

Charleton denied that the criterion of sensibility could be used to demarcate qualities into manifest and occult; there was no epistemological ground for the distinction. From a skeptic's vantage point, all qualities in nature, including sensible ones, were really occult.

If so, why did Charleton dislike the word "occult"? He called it an unhappy and discouraging epithet by which a certain class of qualities was set apart from those whose causes were presumed to be known. He described occult qualities—in particular, sympathies and antipathies—as "windy terms" and a "refuge for the idle and ignorant." Again, historians of science have commonly taken such references as evidence of a re-

jection of occult qualities. However, a closer look at the sense of Charleton's words reveals a different attitude:

> For no sooner do we betake ourselves to Either [i.e., occult qualities or sympathies and antipathies] but we openly confess, that all our Learning is at a stand, and our Reason wholly vanquisht, and beaten out of the field by the Difficulty posed. We deny not that most if not All of those Admired Effects of Nature, which even the Gravest Heads have too long thought sufficient Excuses of their Despair of Cognition, do arise from some Sympathy or Antipathy betwixt the Agent and Patient, but for all that have we no reason to concede that Nature doth institute or Cause the Sympathy or Antipathy, or the Effect resulting from either, by any other Lawes, or Means, but what she hath ordained and constantly useth in the production of all other Common and familiar Effects. We acknowledge also that *Sympathy* is a certain *Consent* and *Antipathy* a certain *Dissent* betwixt Two Natures from one or both of which there ariseth some such Effect as may seem to deserve our limited Admiration; but is it therefore reasonable for us to infer that those Natures are not subject unto, not regulated by the General and Ordinary Rules of Action and Passion, whereto Nature hath firmly obliged Herself in the rest of Her Operations?[17]

The passage clearly expresses Charleton's belief that the problem with occult qualities lay not in the qualities themselves but in the attitude of certain "grave philosophers." Instead of taking marvelous effects as a special challenge to man's reason, they gave up the hunt for possible explanations. The class of occult qualities offered a sanctuary to lazy and ignorant minds who lacked the sporting instinct aroused in the mechanist by an occult quality.

Whether one believed that he could actually capture the quality or only surround it with plausible mechanisms, the important thing was that the Cartesian program offered a method for dealing with the marvels of nature scientifically. With the advantage of hindsight, we can see that the value of the method was extremely limited. Devising explanatory models required ingenuity, but when it was done, what did one really have? Hypothetical mechanisms were as fragile as Don Quixote's helmet. The real value of the various fairy-tale-like hypotheses for those who believed in them lay in their capacity to satisfy a fundamental need: the need to know the cause of things. It was the same motive that had prompted Pomponazzi to search for an Aristotelian explanation of the marvels described by the physician of Mantua; and that had prompted Fracastoro to try to explain the causes of sympathies and antipathies. The mechanists' program for dealing with occult qualities was not essentially different from the Aristotelian in the goal of understanding the insensible realm of nature. It was different because mechanical models satisfied the need for clarity better than anything Aristotelians had to offer.

THE PATH OF EXPERIENCE

As the Cartesian program for manifesting occult qualities captured the fancy of intellectuals, it became fashionable to laugh at Scholastics who still talked in terms of powers and faculties. However, Scholastics would be the ones wearing the smiles today; for we no longer require that science provide the kind of ultimate explanations demanded by Descartes. Take, for example, the properties of a familiar drug such as aspirin. It is white; it dissolves in water; but most important, it relieves pain. If we press the investigation into its pain-relieving properties, we find they reside in a so-called "active ingredient." Having isolated this chemical substance, we do not press for a further account of how the molecular structure of the substance produces its effects; it is sufficient to regard the pain-relieving property as something like an occult quality. This does not mean that we have no true scientific knowledge of it; the effects of aspirin on the brain and other parts of the body can be studied experimentally. A great deal can be learned not by attempting to give an account of aspirin's properties, but by studying its effects.

Occult qualities have become part of modern science. We take for granted that we can have true scientific knowledge of them based on an experimental method. However, it was not always so. In the medieval period, the pain-relieving powers of a drug might have been ascribed to an occult virtue known through experience alone. Although physicians valued the knowledge gained by experience, it did not have the status of *scientia,* which demonstrated effects from true causes. In the remainder of the essay, we shall examine a different program for manifesting occult qualities from that developed by Cartesians. The immediate roots of the experimental program lay in the sixteenth-century medical tradition, where one finds the beginnings of a more practical concept of *scientia.*

Jean Fernel, perhaps the greatest physician of the sixteenth century, incorporated occult qualities into the theory of physiology and pathology as part of a program to reform the discipline of medicine. Fernel believed that the medical theory inherited from previous generations was not complete:

> Many tell us that the art of healing, discovered by the labour of our forefathers, and brought to completion by dint of Reason, has now attained its goal. they would have us, who come after, tread in the same footsteps as did the Past. It were a crime, they tell us, to swerve a hair's breadth from the well-established way. But what if our elders, and those who preceded them, had followed simply the path as did those before them? . . . Nay, on the contrary, it seems good for philosophers to move to fresh ways and systems; good for them to allow neither the voice of the detractor, nor the weight of ancient culture, nor the fullness of authority to deter those who would declare their own views. In that way each age produces its own crop of new authors and new arts.[18]

Fernel proceeded to describe the current revival of arts and sciences after twelve centuries of decline. he pointed to many modern achievements but especially to the voyages of discovery, which had given man "a new globe." Were Plato, Aristotle, Ptolemy, and other ancient philosophers who had a knowledge of geography to return today, they would not recognize the world, so much had been discovered. In all of this, we hear the voice of a Humanist scholar embued with the spirit of the Renaissance. Fernel would have set out to reform whatever discipline he took up; as it happened, he chose medicine.

The current theory of medicine was dominated by the ancient doctrine of the elementary qualities and their temperaments. In a word, the doctrine stated that the health of every body consisted in a certain balance of the contrary qualities. Disease was a disturbance of the temperament resulting from the excess or defect of humors. Fernel proposed a new category, diseases of the total substance, in which the idea of an imbalance played no part. In the preface to his influential dialogue *De Abditis Causis* (1548), he related that he had been impressed twenty years earlier with the question in Hippocrates: Is there not in disease something preternatural? Fernel answered that there were certain diseases of an occult nature, namely plague and pestilence. Whereas they were spread by invisible means and were known by various names, they all had one feature in common: Their causes could not be explained by the traditional Galenic theory. Such diseases were not natural in the sense that they resulted from a disturbance in the corporeal humors; instead, they resulted from the weakening of the total substance—the divine substantial form—of the organism. The pathological agents were occult qualities. When Hippocrates asked the question about preternatural diseases, he supposedly had in mind the class of occult diseases.

In the first book of the dialogue, Eudoxus (Fernel's spokesman) established that all natural things consisted of three components: elements, the temperament of elementary qualities, and a divine substance derived from the heavens. The nature of spiritual substance was hidden from man; its powers were called occult because they could not be perceived by the senses and therefore could not be explained by reason. In the second book, Eudoxus applied the general theory of the composition of bodies to human physiology. The result was a radical transformation of the Galenic doctrine of natural faculties. According to orthodox medical theory, the biological functions of the body were performed by varous natural faculties utilizing powers produced through the temperament of elementary qualities. In Fernel's theory, the living body was governed by a spiritual soul whose subordinate faculties consisted of spiritual substances or forms. For some operations, the substantial forms utilized the temperament, and it was possible to account for the effects in terms of elementary qualities. However, the more important operations were above the powers of the elements. These functions required forms acting directly on the body by means of specific virtues or occult qualities. Eudoxus tried to convince his listeners that the doctrine of divine forms was really a Galenist theory. Not only was it not a Galenist theory; it also undermined the foundations of Galenic medicine by introducing a dualism of body and spirit into the theory of biological operations. To Fernel, life was not the activity *of* an organic body—as it was for both Aristotle and Galen—but the activity of a vital principle *within* an organized body. The source of life, the soul, was hidden, and hence, knowledge of biological phenomena could be gained only by observation of living organisms.

Fernel took the reform of medicine seriously. After finishing the *Dialogue,* he began writing the treatises in the *Universa Medicina.* His *Physiology* and *Pathology* broke new ground and established for him a reputation lasting until the eighteenth century. In the preface to the *Therapeutics,* written toward the end of his life, we find a statement of the philosophy underlying the new medicine: "Nothing whatever is discoverable in man which does not obey Nature and Nature's Laws, save and except only man's understanding and man's free-will. Nature throughout is one eternal law, and Medicine is a book written within that law."[19] Belief that the body had its own laws led Fernel to exclude magic from the domain of physiology and medicine. Nothing could be above the necessity governing the operations of the human body except the unique powers belonging to man's immortal soul. It was a bold vision of the living organism. It incorporated the occult at the same time that it subordinated the magical features of occult qualities to the laws of nature.

For all that, Fernel remained a systematizer and not a discoverer of new truths in the discipline of physiology he helped to create. The future of the science lay with those who aimed to explain the processes of life in physical and chemical terms. In the seventeenth century, William Harvey used experimental methods to discover the circulation of the blood, thereby overturning the foundations of Galenic physiology. Although modern physiologists like Harvey turned away from the idea of spiritual faculties, they nevertheless owed an important debt to proponents of these forms. The experimental method of modern science rests upon the assumption that it is possible to gain scientific knowledge of hidden causes by observing their effects. The aim, of course, is to go beyond the level of phenomena and discover causal explanations capable of unifying a variety of effects. Although Fernel did not believe that one could explain the important processes of life, he did believe that one could acquire legitimate scientific knowledge of hidden causes whose effects were observable. More important, he embodied his belief in a systematic treatise presenting physiology for the first time as an integral subject. The work represented a new and more practical idea of *scientiae* than the one found in the Scholastic philosophical tradition. Experience rather than reason provided the basis for a physician's knowledge. However, Fernel realized that mere experience could be deceiving. Eudoxus spoke of the need to observe the effects of medicines under different circumstances and at different times with a view toward obtaining "the perfection, faith, and constancy of experience." Moreover, reason played a part in the process. Eudoxus remarked that the perfect knowledge of experience could not be obtained except by reason.[20] We are not yet at the stage where such prescriptions had coalesced into a working scientific method. But Fernel's words indicate a newly found faith in man's power to chart the terrain of the unexplored world of hidden causes.

The leading Scholastic proponent of hidden qualities in the seventeenth century was Sennert. His ideas were much influenced by Fernel, although Sennert rejected the Neoplatonist theory that forms emanated from the heavens. In the section on occult qualities in the *Hypomnemata physica* (1636), he followed a Scholastic mode of inquiry, asking first what occult qualities are and whether they exist in nature.[21] His definition of occult qualities emphasized the notion of insensibility: "Now these qualities are called occult, hidden, or abstruse to differentiate them from manifest qualities discernable by the external senses, especially touch." The category of manifest properties included primarily the qualities of the four elements and the tangible properties resulting from the particles of bodies such as rarity, density, hardness, softness, roughness, smoothness, and so forth. Other sensible qualities included colors, odors, and tastes, although Sennert seemed hesitant to treat them as manifest. They were sensible, to be sure, but they were derived from nonelemental forms and hence were closely related to the active powers in the class of occult qualities.

In an epistemolgical sense, all qualities were occult. One of the principal themes of Sennert's writings was that forms exceeded man's limited powers of comprehension; not even the simple manifest quality, heat, could be explained. Although such a claim might have been used to undermine the possibility of scientific knowledge, Sennert drew a more positive conclusion: Man could obtain the same degree of certainty about occult qualities as about manifest ones:

Meanwhile all the more learned philosophers and physicians have undertaken to defend the truth and taught that the causes of many things in natural philosophy and medicine depend upon hidden qualities; and that we are frequently glad to fly to the saving sanctuary (as Scaliger calls it in his *Exercit.* 218, sect. 8) of an occult propriety. Although it is called ignorance by some, they rather accuse the weakness of our understanding to dive into the secrets of nature than blame these hidden qualities. For if the true origin of these qualities be sought into (which few have taken care to do) the knowledge thereof will produce as certain science as that of the first qualities. For the natural philosopher knows no more of heat but that it heats and that it flows from and depends upon the form of fire; and this form is as unknown to man as those forms from which the hidden qualities arise.[22]

Sennert chose the example of heat to make a point. If magnetic virtue was the paradigm of an occult quality, heat was the Aristotelian paradigm of a manifest quality. Scholastic philosophers were confident they knew its nature; indeed, if this quality were not known perfectly, none of the other corporeal properties could be known since they were explained in terms of the primary qualities. In the passage above, Sennert undermined Aristotelian efforts to explicate specific virtues by claiming that the very qualities used to manifest the occult were occult qualities themselves.

That occult qualities existed could be proved from two considerations: (1) Many actions in nature were totally different from those of the elements; and (2) the manner in which occult agents acted differed from the elements' mode of operation. Examples of nonelementary actions included magnetic attraction, the dormative effect of opium, the convulsions caused by poisons, and the quieting of convulsions through antidotes. According to Sennert, there were a thousand such actions different from the elementary operations of heating, cooling, humidifying, and drying common to the elements. Regarding the manner of acting, Sennert noted that a sufficient bulk of the elements was required before they could exercise their powers. In addition, it required a period of time for contrary qualities to act upon their opposites. However, extremely small amounts of certain poisons could kill a man almost instantaneously. It did not seem correct to attribute such effects to elementary virtues. The proofs Sennert offered for occult qualities were based on familiar phenomena—at least to physicians—rather than rare and marvelous events. There was certainly something marvelous about the actions described, which is why Sennert chose them, but he might have chosen the action of fire since it was equally occult.

What did it mean, then, to say that one could have scientific knowledge of occult qualities? Sennert maintained that if one investigated their origin, the knowledge acquired was no less certain than the knowledge of sensible properties. He also stated that few had taken the care to make the investigation. Peripatetics had approached the problem with philosophical methods; explaining the origin of a quality meant giving an account based on the primary qualities. Sennert, in contrast, had in mind an empirical investigation. Instead of devising explanations, one should attempt to isolate the material substances in which qualities inhered. The analytical methods of chemistry offered the best means for unlocking natural bodies; indeed, without a knowledge of chemistry, Sennert said, one could not hope to excel in investigating the occult.[23] Sennert's program for the use of empirical methods to discover forms was based on a standard of scientific knowledge closely linked to experience. Experience rather than reason led to the underlying causes of corporeal properties, at least to the extent that man could know them.

Reason had to order experience if one was to obtain genuine knowledge of nature. Since occult qualities could not be explicated, the role of reason was limited to devising ways of classifying the observable effects. The latter half of the chapter on the origin of occult qualities described six classes in which all occult qualities could be arranged. For our purposes, the classes themselves are less important than the general method. Sennert, in effect, approached the subject of occult qualities in the manner of an encyclopedist. The totality of experience was fitted into a tidy systematic schema. It was hoped that by arranging and ordering occult qualities, one could transmit the knowledge of them to future generations. In this way, the investigation into nature's secrets would become a continuing project, drawing upon the work of many naturalists.

HIDDEN QUALITIES IN BACONIAN SCIENCE

Sennert's ideas reflect the contemporary movement to base natural philosophy on the disciplines of natural history. The most well known proponent of the empirical restoration of the sciences was, of course, Francis Bacon. Bacon criticized Scholastics for giving up on the discovery of forms; nevertheless, his ideas owed much to those he criticized. For Bacon, as for Sennert, nature was a realm of occult qualities, and the naturalist's first task was to study their effects. In this section, we shall look more closely at the Baconian approach to the secrets of nature.

References to occult qualities are scattered throughout the *New Organon*. Without exception, they have an unfriendly tone. For example: "Operations by consents and aversions . . . often lie deeply hid. For what are called occult and specific properties, or sympathies and antipathies, are in great part corruptions of philosophy."[24] In another aphorism, Bacon stated:

Now the human understanding is infected by the sight of what takes place in the mechanical arts, in which the alteration of bodies proceeds chiefly by composition or separation, and so imagines that something similar goes on in the universal nature of things. From this source has flowed the fiction of elements, and of their concourse for the formation of natural bodies. Again, when man contemplates nature working freely, he meets with different species of things, of animals, of plants, of minerals, whence he readily passes into the opinion that there are in nature certain primary forms which nature intends to educe, and that the remaining variety proceeds from hindrances and aberrations of nature in the fulfillment of her work, or from the collision of different species and the transplanting of one into another. To the first of these speculations we owe our primary qualities of the elements; to the other our occult properties and specific virtues; and both of them belong to those empty compendia of thought wherein the mind rests, and whereby it is diverted from more solid pursuits.[25]

Such passages give a fairly clear idea of Bacon's complaint against occult qualities. He did not challenge their existence, although he did question many reported instances of magical effects; he was "almost weary of the words sympathy and antipathy on account of the superstitions and vanities associated with them."[26] When one had weeded out the false ascriptions and fables, there remained a small store of genuine sympathies approved by experience, such as those between the magnet and iron, or gold and quicksilver. Chemical experiments involving metals revealed some. But the greatest number were derived from the specific virtues of medicines. For Bacon, the medical tradition constituted the best source of faithful, honest descriptions of occult qualities necessary for a solid, empirical foundation of scientific knowledge.

Scholastic physicians, however, were content merely to describe and catalogue occult virtues. Bacon wanted to do more. His real complaint against Scholastics was that they broke off the investigation into occult qualities too soon; their program resulted in compendia or encyclopedias. Bacon had a grander vision for the reform of science in which compiling natural histories was just the starting point. He hoped to discover the universal laws, the forms, behind occult phenomena. That required *dissecting* both the specific virtues and the configuration of bodies into their simple components. One could not have "much hope of discovering the consents of things before the discovery of forms and simple configurations. For consent is nothing else than the adaptation of forms and configurations to each other."[27]

The key to the discovery of occult virtues was inductive logic. Bacon devoted the entire second book of the *New Organon* to explaining his method of induction. At the conclusion, he boasted that "my logic aims to teach and instruct the understanding, not that it may with the slender tendrils of the mind snatch at and lay hold of abstract notions (as the common logic does), but that it may in very truth dissect nature and discover the virtues and actions of bodies, with their laws as determined in matter."[28] Without logic and true induction, the analysis of bodies was fruitless. Bacon criticized those who relied exclusively on the power of fire to resolve componds; one had to pass from Vulcan to Minerva to discover the true textures and configurations upon which properties depended.

Bacon illustrated the method of investigating forms with the example of heat. As with Sennert, the use of heat contained an implicit lesson. Bacon aimed to show that the form of heat, the prototype of a manifest quality, was more elusive than Scholastics imagined. He drew up three tables of observational data containing instances where the nature of heat was present and absent and where it exhibited variations of degree. Such a collection had to be made in the manner of a natural history "without premature speculation, or any great amount of subtlety." In the next stage, inductive logic entered the picture. Bacon stated that it was necessary to proceed first in a negative way by excluding natures not belonging to the form of heat:

> Then indeed after the rejection and exclusion has been made, there will remain at the bottom, all light opinions vanishing into smoke, a form affirmative, solid, and true and well-defined. This is quickly said; but the way to come at it is winding and intricate.[29]

Before the mind negotiated the maze, it was permitted to take a "first vintage" or "commencement of interpretation." This consisted in a preliminary definition on the basis of the evidence considered. Bacon described the genus of heat as the motion of a body's particles, although he rejected the mechanical doctrine that motion is the universal cause of heat. Rather, the "essence and quiddity" of heat was motion limited by certain specific differences. After discussing four such differences, Bacon finally arrived at the form of heat:

> Heat is a motion, expansive, restrained, and acting in its strife upon the smaller particles of bodies. But the expansion is thus modified; while it expands all ways, it has at the same time an inclination upwards. And the struggle in the particles is modified also; it is not sluggish but hurried and with violence.[30]

All this, one should remember, was just the first vintage. Whatever heat was, after Bacon's subtle mind had finished with it, clearly it was no longer a manifest quality. Its form resided in the midst of a labyrinth, a place traditionally reserved for occult powers.

If discovering the simple nature of heat was so complicated, it is discouraging to imagine the complexity of discovering specific virtues. Nevertheless, Bacon saw his method of induction as a means for acquiring solid scientific knowledge of occult qualities. His method did not explicate them in terms of primary qualities as Peripatetics and mechanists did. Neither did it rest with describing and cataloging. Instead, Bacon aimed to acquire a deeper knowledge by dissecting specific virtues into their simple forms and corporeal structures. The program came to naught because none of his followers knew exactly what to make of the fantastic method outlined in the *New Organon.* However, the idea that experimental philosophy could deal scientifically with occult qualities prevailed. In the later seventeenth century, it was taken up by Robert Boyle, who incorporated the investigation of the forms underlying occult qualities into his own program for experimental science.

Boyle illustrated the experimental philosopher's approach to occult qualities in his *Experiments, Notes, &c. About the Mechanical Origin or Production of Divers Particular Qualities* (1675).[31] He divided all corporeal properties into four classes: (1) "primary qualities" such as heat and cold, (2) sensible qualities such as tastes and odors, (3) secondary or chemical qualities, and (4) occult qualities. The purpose of the treatise was to show that each type could be explained in terms of the mechanical principles, matter and motion. Rather than demonstrate this for a great number of qualities, Boyle chose certain specimens typical of an entire class. For example, occult qualities were represented by magnetism and electricity. Thus, although the treatise dealt with only a few properties, it was universal in scope, "there being scarce one sort of qualities of which there is not an instance given in this small book." Boyle did not regard the class of occult powers as a special case; he placed them on the same plane with sensible qualities. There was no ground for separating the two since both were produced by mechanical means.

Previous mechanists had said the same thing, but Boyle did not advocate the earlier program for explicating occult qualities by devising hypotheses. In the preface, he clearly expressed his attitude toward the business of inventing mechanisms:

> I do not undertake, that all of the following accounts of particular qualities would prove to be the very true ones, nor every explication the best that can be devised. For besides the difficulty of the subject and incompleteness of the history we yet have of qualities, may well deter a man, less diffident of his own abilities than I justly am, from assuming so much to himself, it is not absolutely necessary to my present design.[32]

Boyle's design was to show that the mechanical philosophy could be extended to a wider range of phenomena than many critics of mechanism allowed. He noted that there were many who preferred mechanical explanations but claimed that such accounts applied only to machines and a limited number of natural phenomena. To remove this prejudice, it was not necessary that the explications proposed be the best possible; it was sufficient to treat them as types or models without claiming that they represented the actual modes in which nature operated. Above all, Boyle stressed that he was free to change his mind as the empricial study of qualities progressed:

> I intend not therefore by proposing the theories and conjectures ventured at in the following papers to debar myself of the liberty either of altering them or of substituting others in their place, in case a further progress in the history of qualities shall suggest better hypotheses or explications. . . . my purpose in these notes was rather to shew it was not necessary to betake ourselves to the scholastick or chemical doctrine of qualities, than to act the umpire between the differing hypotheses of the Corpuscularians; and provided I kept myself within the bounds of the mechanical philosophy, my design allowed me a great latitude in making explications of the phaenomena I had occasion to notice.[33]

Given Boyle's attitude toward hypotheses, it is not surprising that the mechanism invented to explain electrical attraction, for example, was rather clumsy. He imagined that viscous effluvia emitted by the electrical body fastened upon the attracted object; when the particles of the electric body were no longer agitated, attraction ceased, and the strings contracted back into the body. Although the hypothesis was crude, it may be said in Boyle's defense that he was not really interested in devising elegant mechanisms; he was primarily concerned with devising experiments to reveal the actions of electrical and magnetic bodies under a variety of conditions. As he noted, the title of the work did not promise discourses, but rather experiments and notes. The two treatises on electricity and magnetism were filled with a numbered series of experiments and observations from which one could infer, in general terms, a mechanical explanation. The form of the treatises contained an implicit statement: Instead of writing theoretical discourses on the origin of qualities, whether occult or manifest, naturalists should try to discover their causes through *experiments*. It was Bacon's program for the discovery of forms incorporated into the general framework of the mechanical philosophy.

Boyle recognized that one could not always, or even generally, obtain clear mechanical accounts for corporeal properties. His only advice was to continue the search. In the following passage, we hear Boyle the natural philosopher speaking:

> The chymists are wont . . . to content themselves to tell us, in what ingredient of a mixt body the quality inquired after does reside, instead of explicating the nature of it, which . . . is as much as if in an inquiry after the cause of salivation, they should think it

enough to tell us, that the several kinds of precipitates of gold and mercury, as likewise of quicksilver and silver . . . do salivate upon the account of the mercury, which though disguised abounds in them; whereas the difficulty is as much to know upon what account mercury it self, rather than other bodies, has that power of working by salivation. Which I say not, as though it were not something (and too often the most we can arrive at) to discover in which of the ingredients of a compounded body the quality, whose nature is sought, resides; but because, though this discovery it self may pass for something, and is oftentimes more than what is taught us about the same subjects in the schools, yet we ought not to think it enough, when more clear and particular accounts are to be had.[34]

Clearly, Boyle did not disdain the effort to locate the proper material subjects of qualities; the kind of program for analyzing bodies recommended by Sennert yielded valuable knowledge. But like Bacon, Boyle felt an urge to go further and discover the principles from which qualities were derived. He was not satisfied to leave them occult, although he was a good enough naturalist and chemist to realize that in most cases, one could not do better. He was fascinated by the siren song promising clear and particular accounts of occult qualities; only a greater desire to observe nature closely prevented him from yielding to the temptation.

In the seventeenth century, John Locke excluded the Cartesian dream of perfect knowledge from the sphere of experimental philosophy. Locke's views, expressed in the *Essay Concerning Human Understanding* (1690), reflect his close association with Boyle and other experimental philosophers as well as his own training as a physician. He accepted the corpuscular doctrine that corporeal properties emanate from the internal constitutions of bodies or, to use Locke's term, their *real essences*. However, forms were hidden from man, and therefore, the particular means by which they produced empirical properties remained occult. If, Locke said, one knew the mechanical affections of the particles in rhubarb, hemlock, and opium in the same way that a watchmaker knows the parts of a watch, he could obtain absolutely certain demonstrations that rhubarb will purge, hemlock will kill, and opium will induce sleep. But man lacked senses acute enough to discover the motions of atoms; hence he had to be content to remain ignorant of the particular causes behind corporeal properties. One could not obtain a degree of certainty about qualities beyond what was warranted by a few experiments. Locke concluded:

And therefore I am apt to doubt that, how far soever human industry may advance useful and *experimental* philosophy in *physical* things, *scientifical* will still be out of our reach: because we want perfect and adequate *ideas* of those very bodies which are nearest to us and most under our command.[35]

To Locke, the quest for absolute certainty was a delu-

sion. He said, "as to a perfect science of natural bodies . . . we are, I think, so far from being capable of any such thing that I conclude it lost labour to seek after it."[36] Clearly, he was not recommending that one abandon the enterprise of science; he was merely stating the limits inherent in the nature of scientific knowledge. Experimental science could gain knowledge of causes only through the study of their sensible effects. Any attempt to discover the forms behind the qualities would seduce man from the rigorous path of experience.

In Locke's epistemology, the distinction between manifest and occult qualities was largely superseded by the doctrine of primary and secondary qualities. All the properties of a body except the size, shape, texture, and motion of the particles belonged in the class of secondary qualities. Only vestiges of the manifest-occult distinction remained in Locke's division of secondary qualities into the sensible powers and the active and passive powers. There were also shades of Galenic faculties in the term "power," by which he described the causes of all secondary qualities, sensible as well as active. He remarked:

> For the colors and taste of *opium* are as well as its soporific or anodyne virtues, mere powers, depending upon its primary qualities, whereby it is fitted to produce different operations upon different parts of our bodies.[37]

In ascribing the soporific virtue of opium to a power, Locke was not intimidated by the Cartesians' ridicule; his epistemology was his reply.

By the end of the seventeenth century, occult qualities not only had been incorporated into modern science; they had become the foundation. Since it is not possible to give an ultimate explanation for corporeal properties, all attempts to account for them must terminate with entities whose properties are, in a sense, occult. This does not mean that they can never be explained; it simply means that the properties of the more fundamental entities are unaccounted for. Today, we take such occult qualities for granted. But prior to the scientific revolution, the existence of unexplained properties constituted an anomaly for natural science, a place where the system broke down. To have scientific knowledge of properties, one had to explain them in terms of perfectly manifest qualities. The program for manifesting occult qualities began with the Aristotelians in the Renaissance and flourished in the writings of mechanical philosophers. Only gradually was an experimental method capable of dealing with occult qualities developed. The first step came with the recognition of their importance—a process in which Scholastic physicians and naturalists played an essential part. As the experimental philosophy came into its own, largely through the work of Boyle, occult qualities were incorporated into a program of research. The difference between them and other types of so-called manifest qualities lost its significance. In the end, occult qualities took their place at the foundations of modern science. That we take them for granted represents one of the triumphs of the scientific revolution.

Notes

[1] Keith Hutchison, "What Happened to Occult Qualities in the Scientific Revolution?" *Isis, 73* (1982), 233-53.

[2] Cf. Thomas Aquinas, "On the Occult Works of Nature" in J. B. McAllister, *The Letter of Saint Thomas Aquinas* (Washington, D.C.: Catholic University Press, 1939), p. 21. See also Lynn Thorndike, *A History of Magic and Experimental Science* (New York: Columbia University Press, 1959), *V*, 550-62, and passim.

[3] Daniel Sennert, *Opera* (Paris: Apud Societatem, 1641), *I*, 142.

[4] Thomas Aquinas, *Commentary on Aristotle's Physics,* trans. R. J. Blackwell et al. (New Haven: Yale University Press, 1963), pp. 33-4.

[5] Aquinas, "Occult Works," pp. 20, 22.

[6] Sennert, *Opera, I,* 142.

[7] D. P. Walker suggests a logical scheme for Renaissance theories of natural magic in *Spiritual and Demonic Magic* (Notre Dame, Ind.: University of Notre Dame Press, 1975), pp. 75-84.

[8] Although the work was first published at Basle in 1556, it was probably written between 1515 and 1520. See the introduction by Henri Busson in his translation, *Les causes des merveilles de la nature ou les enchantements* (Paris: Rieder, 1930).

[9] Cornelius Agrippa, *Three Books of Occult Philosophy or Magic,* ed. and rev. W. Whitehead from 1651 English trans. (London: Aquarian Press, 1975), p. 62.

[10] Pietro Pomponazzi, *Les causes des merveilles* [see note 8], p. 124.

[11] Ibid., p. 133.

[12] Girolamo Fracastoro, *De Sympathia et Antipathia Rerum Liber Unus* (Venetiis, 1546), Introduction.

[13] Walter Charleton, *Physiologia Epicuro-Gassendo-Charltoniana* (London: Thomas Heath, 1654), p. 348.

[14] Jerome Cardan, *Opera Omnia,* facsimile of 1636 Lyons ed. (Stuttgart: Fromann, 1966), *II*, 537-51.

[15] René Descartes, *Oeuvres,* ed. Charles Adam and Paul Tannery (Paris: Vrin, 1969-74), *8*, pt. 2, 314-15.

[16] Charleton, *Physiologia* [see note 13], pp. 341-2.

[17] Ibid., p. 343.

[18] Preface to Book I of *De Abditis Causis,* cited from Charles Sherrington's *The Endeavor of Jean Fernel* (Cambridge: Cambridge University Press, 1946), pp. 16-17.

[19] Cited from Sherrington, *Endeavour,* p. 95; cf. Fernel, *Universalis Therapeutices* in *Universa Medicina* (Genevae: Apud Petrum Chouet, 1638), pp. 1-2.

[20] Fernel, *Universa Medicina,* p. 242.

[21] Sennert, *Opera* [see note 3], *I*, 141-9.

[22] Ibid., 142.

[23] Ibid., 916.

[24] Francis Bacon, *The New Organon* (Indianapolis: Bobbs-Merrill, 1960), p. 261.

[25] Ibid., p. 263.

[26] Ibid.

[27] Ibid., p. 261.

[28] Ibid., p. 265-6.

[29] Ibid., p. 152.

[30] Ibid., p. 162.

[31] Robert Boyle, *Works,* ed. Thomas Birch (London: Andrew Millar, 1744), *III*, 565-652.

[32] Ibid., 569.

[33] Ibid.

[34] Boyle, *works, II,* 41.

[35] John Locke, *An Essay Concerning Human Understanding* (London: Dent, 1961), *II*, 161.

[36] Ibid., 164.

[37] Locke, *Essay, I,* 249.

FURTHER READING

Boas, Marie. "The Organisation and Reorganisation of Science." In her *The Scientific Renaissance: 1450-1630*, pp. 238-64. New York: Harper & Brothers, 1962.

Discusses the evolution of modern scientific thought from Aristotelian and university-dominated to independent and empirical.

Foster, M. B. "The Christian Doctrine of Creation and the Rise of Modern Natural Science." *Mind* XLIII, No. 172 (October 1934): 446-468.

Examines the indebtedness of scientific thought to Christian principles.

Hall, Rupert. "The Scholar and the Craftsman in the Scientific Revolution." In *Critical Problems in the History of Science,* edited by Marshall Clagett, pp. 3-23. Madison: The University of Wisconsin Press, 1959.

Evaluates the role of the tradesman class in the development of science.

Hine, William L. "Marin Mersenne: Renaissance naturalism and Renaissance magic." In *Occult and scientific mentalities in the Renaissance,* edited by Brian Vickers, pp. 165-176. Cambridge: Cambridge University Press, 1984.

Uses the work of Marin Mersenne to discuss the limits of, and differences between, naturalism and magic in the Renaissance.

Loeb, Louis E. "Continental Rationalism and British Empiricism." In his *From Descartes to Hume,* pp. 25-75. Ithaca: Cornell University Press, 1981.

Examines the distinctions between Rationalism and Empiricism and the difficulties in assigning a scientist to one philosophy or the other.

McMullin, Ernan. "Conceptions of science in the Scientific Revolution." In *Reappraisals of the Scientific Revolution,* edited by David C. Lindberg and Robert S. Westman, pp. 27-92. Cambridge: Cambridge University Press, 1990.

Describes and categorizes the methods applied by many of the great Renaissance and post-Renaissance scientists.

McMullin, Ernan. "Empiricism and the Scientific Revolution." In *Art, Science, and History in the Renaissance,* edited by Charles S. Singleton, pp. 331-369. Baltimore: The Johns Hopkins Press, 1967.

Examines the practices of Renaissance scientists and their own understanding of their practices.

McRae, Robert. "The Unity of the Sciences: Bacon, Descartes, Leibniz." In *Roots of Scientific Thought: A Cultural Perspective,* edited by Philip P. Wiener and Aaron Noland, pp. 390-411. New York: Basic Books, 1957.

Examines various organizational plans to create a unity of the sciences.

Popkin, Richard H. "Scepticism, Theology and the Scientific Revolution in the Seventeenth Century." In *Essays on Early Modern Philosophers from Descartes and Hobbes to Newton and Leibniz,* edited by Vere Chappell, pp. 1-28. New York: Garland Publishing, Inc., 1992.

Asserts that the typical understanding of the historic conflict between religion and science in the seventeenth century is too simplistic.

Westfall, Richard S. "The Science of Mechanics." In his *The Construction of Modern Science,* pp. 120-138. New York: John Wiley & Sons, Inc., 1971.

Examines the state of the science of mechanics in the seventeenth century.

Woolhouse, R. S. Introduction to *Descartes, Spinoza, Leibniz: The concept of substance in seventeenth-century metaphysics,* pp. 1-13. London: Routledge, 1993.

Overview of the metaphysical views of Descartes, Spinoza, and Leibniz, particularly concerning "substance."

René Descartes

1596-1650

French philosopher and mathematician.

For additional information on Descartes' life and works, see *LC,* Volume 20.

INTRODUCTION

Descartes is considered the father of modern philosophy and one of the seminal figures of French thought. In his philosophical program, as presented in such important works as *Discourse on Method* and *Meditations on First Philosophy,* he "brought together," as Wilhelm Windelband wrote, "the scientific movement of his time to establish rationalism anew, by filling the scholastic system of conceptions with the rich content of Galilean research." Descartes argued that philosophy must be based on a clear, rational method of inquiry. In order to establish a firm basis for this method, he subjected popularly-held assumptions concerning the nature of the self and the universe to a process of rigorous doubt. Descartes effectively reduced verifiable reality to the thinking self, though he eventually accepted the objective reality of the external world and the existence of God. Critics affirm that the most significant result of Descartes' methodological skepticism was his radical separation of the thinking subject from the physical world, which he viewed in purely scientific, mechanistic terms, suggesting the modern metaphor of the world conceived as an intricate machine.

Biographical Information

Descartes was born in 1596 at La Haye in Touraine. His family belonged to the *noblesse de robe,* or juridical nobility, as attested by his father's position as *councilor* of the *parlement* of Rennes in Brittany. Like his mother, who died of a lung infection a few days after his birth, Descartes suffered from a delicate constitution, and his health was a subject of great concern for his doctors. Nonetheless, in 1604 he was sent to the Jesuit college of La Flèche in Anjou, where he received a largely classical education, but also familiarized himself with new discoveries in optics and astronomy. After graduating from La Flèche in 1612, he studied law at the University of Poitiers until 1616, though he appears never to have practiced. Weary of studying, Descartes finally decided on a military career and served under the banners of Maurice of Nassau and the German emperor Ferdinand during the early phases of the Thirty Years War. During 1618-19 at Breda, Holland,

Descartes became acquainted with the famous mathematician Isaac Beeckman, who encouraged him to return to the study of science and mathematics.

In April, 1619, Descartes began travelling, settling in Neuberg, Germany, where he secluded himself "dans un poêle" ["in a heated room"] for the winter. On November 10, 1619, Descartes experienced a series of extraordinary dreams that led him to believe that he was destined to found a universal science based on mathematics. During the next few years Descartes continued travelling in Europe. He returned to France in 1622, eventually establishing himself in Paris, where he continued to refine his philosophy in the company of mathematicians and scientists. In 1628 Descartes publicly presented his philosophical ideas in a confrontation with the chemist Chandoux, who upheld a probabilistic view of science. Demonstrating to the audience through brilliant argumentation that any philosophical system not grounded in certainty would inevitably fail, Descartes was taken aside after the lecture by Cardinal de Bérulle, who urged him to fully elaborate on his method, explaining that it was God's will for him to do so. Shortly afterward Descartes completed his first substantial work, *Regulae ad directionem ingenii* (1701; *Rules for the Direction of the Mind*), explicating the methodological foundations of the new system.

At the beginning of 1629 Descartes moved to Holland, where he was able to work in an atmosphere of tranquility and intellectual freedom. In 1633 Descartes completed *Le monde de M. Descartes, ou le traité de la lumière* (1644; *The World*), in which he supported the Copernican theory of the earth's movement around the sun. However, he suppressed publication of this work after hearing from his friend Marin Marsenne of Galileo's condemnation by the Roman Catholic church for upholding the same thesis. Four years later, Descartes published *Discours de la méthode de bien conduire sa raison et chercher la vérité dans les sciences; plus la dioptrique; les météores; et la géométrie, qui sont des essais de cette méthode* (1637; *Discourse on the Method of Properly Guiding the Reason in the Search for Truth in the Sciences; also the Dioptric, the Meteors and the Geometry, which are Essays in This Method*). The four-part treatise defined the principles of modern scientific method and applied them to matters of current academic interest. Written in French in order to reach a wider audience, the work caused a critical uproar and was immediately challenged by a number of prominent mathematicians. The years 1641 and 1642 marked the appearance of two editions of the *Meditations: Meditationes de prima philosophia in qua Dei existentia et animae immortalitas demonstratur* (1641; "Meditations on First Philosophy, in which the Existence of God and the Immortality of the Soul are Demonstrated") and *Meditationes de prima philosophia, in quibus Dei existentia et animae humanae a corpore distinctio demonstrantur* (1641-42; *Meditations on First Philosophy, in which the Existence of God and the Distinction between Mind and Body are Demonstrated*), a comprehensive exposition of his epistemological and metaphysical theories. The work did much to augment Descartes' influence in Europe's intellectual circles. However, many of Descartes' positions were attacked by such notable scholars as Pierre Gassendi and Gysbertus Voetius, president of the University of Utrecht, who accused the author of atheism. Throughout the controversy, Descartes was supported by his many friends and admirers, including the refugee Princess Elizabeth of the Palatinate, to whom Descartes dedicated the *Principia philosophia* (1644; *Principles of Philosophy*), a four-part treatise that provided further explanation of the principal ideas of the *Meditations*. Descartes visited Paris in 1647, where he met Blaise Pascal and attended court, securing the promise of a pension from the crown. However, the rebellion of the Fronde in 1648 promptly rendered the promised stipend unavailable, and Descartes again returned to Holland. The following year Queen Christina of Sweden, who decided to found an academy of scholars, requested Descartes to come to Sweden and instruct her in philosophy. After overseeing the publication of *Traité des passions de l'âme* (1649; *The Passions of the Soul*), which sought to explain psychological events in mechanistic terms, Descartes left Amsterdam on September 1, 1649, and reached Stockholm a month later. Descartes was required to tutor the queen in philosophy at five o'clock each morning, a schedule he found extremely taxing. Returning to his lodging one bitter January morning in 1650, he caught pneumonia and died within a fortnight.

Major Works

During the seventeenth century, Descartes was as famous for his scientific treatises as he was for his philosophical works. However, he is known today primarily for the *Discourse on Method* and the *Meditations,* which are numbered among the principal works of modern philosophy. The *Discourse on Method* amplified Descartes' projects for a universal methodology adumbrated in his *Rules for the Direction of the Mind.* The *Discourse on Method* is actually an extended preface to a much larger treatise comprising three separate works—*Dioptrics, Meteors,* and *Geometry,* all of which are technical discussions of scientific subjects.

The *Discourse* itself is divided into six chapters. The first three are primarily autobiographical, touching on Descartes' early education as well as the three dreams of November 10, 1619. Chapter four is concerned with traditional metaphysical questions about the nature of reality and contains the formula *"cogito, ergo sum"* ("I think, therefore I am"). The fifth chapter investigates the subjects of physics and biology, while the final chapter serves as a general conclusion. The six-part *Discourse* is generally upheld as an indispensable introduction to the Cartesian system. Commentators agree that the cornerstone of the work is Descartes' presentation, in Chapter Two, of the four methodological principles that establish the frame for his scientific method. Here Descartes demonstrates that useful knowledge must be founded on clear and distinct judgments which should be as irrefutable as mathematical formulae based on pure intuition and deductive reasoning.

The second edition of the *Meditations of First Philosophy* appeared in 1642 with a compendium of "objections" by such notable thinkers as Thomas Hobbes, Antoine Arnauld, and Pierre Gassendi. Whereas Descartes' previous works were essentially theoretical discussions on methodology, the *Meditations* address specific philosophical issues: skepticism, the nature of God, the metaphysical foundation of truth, and knowledge of the physical world. The work is divided into six separate Meditations, each of which focuses on a particular problem. The First Meditation invokes Descartes' principle of methodological doubt, which he saw as indispensable to creating a positive foundation for knowledge. Beginning with the assumption that all knowledge derives from sensory perception or rational intuition, Descartes purports that sensory perception is questionable. He demonstrates, for example, that in our dreams we perceive objects as clearly as when we are awake. On the other hand, purely intuitive ideas such as those pertaining to mathematics would appear to be irrefutably true, yet Descartes maintains that their relation to objective reality cannot be verified through reason alone. The Second Meditation elaborates on the relation of the thinking subject to objective reality. Descartes maintains that while sensory perceptions and pure intuitions are possibly illusory, the thinking subject cannot be doubted because the "I" accompanies every thought. Therefore, existence must be seen as a predicate of thought, as expressed in the formula "I think, therefore I am." Descartes defines man as a thinking being whose mental operations are separate and distinct from the existence of the external world. In the Third Meditation Descartes attempts to establish formal proof of the existence of God. He reasons that as God is an infinitely perfect being and is not a deceiver, there is no reason to doubt that clear and distinct perceptions correspond to objective reality. In the Fourth and Fifth Meditations, Descartes provides further proofs for the existence of God and contends that the external world can be known with absolute certainly as long as we operate in the realm of clear and distinct ideas. The Sixth Meditation is considered by many critics Descartes' most original contribution to modern philosophy. Here he methodically analyzes the relation between the human soul and the body. Descartes defines the mind (or soul) as a purely volitional and indivisible thinking substance. However, he views the body as a passive object for sensations and says that it is no different than any other physical object, whose essence is extension. Although he later suggests that the mind and body are closely related, he maintains a clear distinction between the two, explaining that he can imagine the mind existing independently of the body. This distinction is seen by many commentators as the starting point of modern philosophy, and is the basis for Cartesian dualism.

Critical Reception

The *Meditations* suggested new ways of conceiving of the rational universe, both physical and spiritual. Although some of his ideas were strongly opposed by contemporary religious thinkers, they were very influential in directing the course of the scientific revolution of the seventeenth century as well as the rationalism of the eighteenth-century French Enlightenment. Descartes' dualism was eventually eclipsed by the monistic systems of Benedictus de Spinoza, Gottfried Wilhelm von Leibniz, and Georg Wilhelm Friedrich Hegel. However, as late-nineteenth-century philosophy turned away from grand systems and focused its atten-

tion on the thinking subject, Descartes' ideas elicited renewed interest among philosophers and scientists. For example, the influence of Cartesian rationalism can be discerned in such important modern schools of thought as phenomenology and structuralism. Cartesian thinking has affected researchers in a variety of fields, including psychology and linguistics, as evidenced by Noam Chomsky's strong emphasis on innate, mental, non-empirical factors operant in the process of language acquisition. So, the *Discourse on Method* and the *Meditations* continue to be central to the Western intellectual tradition.

PRINCIPAL WORKS

Discours de la méthode de bien conduire sa raison et chercher la vérité dans les sciences; plus la dioptrique; les météores; et la géométrie, qui sont des essais de cette méthode (philosophical prose) 1637
[*Discourse on the Method of Properly Guiding the Reason in the Search for Truth in the Sciences; also the Dioptric, the Meteors and the Geometry, which are Essays in This Method,* 1649]
Meditationes de prima philosophia, in quibus Dei ex istentia et animae humanae a corpore distinctio demonstrantur (philosophical prose) 1641-42
[*Meditations on First Philosophy, in which the Exist ence of God and the Distinction between Mind and Body are Demonstrated,* 1680]
Le monde de M. Descartes, ou le traité de la lumière (philosophical prose) 1644
[*The World,* 1979]
Principia philosophia (philosophical prose) 1644
[*Principles of Philosophy,* 1983]
Traité des passions de l'âme (philosophical prose) 1649
[*The Passions of the Soul,* 1650]
Regulae ad directionem ingenii (philosophical prose) 1701
[*Rules for the Direction of the Mind,* 1662]
Oeuvres de Descartes. 13 vols. (philosophical prose) 1897-1913
Philosophical Works of Descartes. 2 vols. (philosoph ical prose) 1955
The Essential Writings of René Descartes (philosoph ical prose) 1977

CRITICISM

Edwin Arthur Burtt (essay date 1925)

SOURCE: "Descartes," in *The Metaphysical Foundations of Modern Physical Science: A Historical and Critical Essay,* Kegan Paul, Trench, Trubner & Co.,

Ltd., 1925, pp. 96-116.

[In the following essay, Burtt examines Descartes' mathematical conception of nature and his motives for proposing a mind-body dualism.]

Descartes' importance in [the] mathematical movement [in science] was twofold; he worked out a comprehensive hypothesis in detail of the mathematical structure and operations of the material universe, with clearer consciousness of the important implications of the new method than had been shown by his predecessors; and he attempted both to justify and atone for the reading of man and his interests out of nature by his famous metaphysical dualism.

While still in his teens, Descartes became absorbed in mathematical study, gradually forsaking every other interest for it, and at the age of twenty-one was in command of all that was then known on the subject. During the next year or two we find him performing simple experiments in mechanics, hydrostatics, and optics, in the attempt to extend mathematical knowledge in these fields. He appears to have followed the more prominent achievements of Kepler and Galileo, though without being seriously affected by any of the details of their scientific philosophy. On the night of November 10th, 1619, he had a remarkable experience which confirmed the trend of his previous thinking and gave the inspiration and the guiding principle for his whole life-work.[1] The experience can be compared only to the ecstatic illumination of the mystic; in it the Angel of Truth appeared to him and seemed to justify, through added supernatural insight, the conviction which had already been deepening in his mind, that mathematics was the sole key needed to unlock the secrets of nature. The vision was so vivid and compelling that Descartes in later years could refer to that precise date as the occasion of the great revelation that marked the decisive point in his career.

(A) *Mathematics as the Key to Knowledge*

The first intensive studies into which he plunged after this unique experience were in the field of geometry, where he was rewarded within a very few months by the signal invention of a new and most fruitful mathematical tool, analytical geometry. This great discovery not only confirmed his vision and spurred him on to further efforts in the same direction, but it was highly important for his physics generally. The existence and successful use of analytical geometry as a tool of mathematical exploitation presupposes an exact one-to-one correspondence between the realm of numbers, *i.e.*, arithmetic and algebra, and the realm of geometry, *i.e.*, space. That they had been related was, of course, a common possession of all mathematical science; that their relation was of this explicit and absolute correspondence was an intuition of Descartes. He perceived

that the very nature of space or extension was such that its relations, however complicated, must always be expressible in algebraic formulae, and, conversely, that numerical truths (within certain powers) can be fully represented spatially. As one not unnatural result of this notable invention, the hope deepened in Descartes' mind that the whole realm of physics might be reducible to geometrical qualities alone. Whatever else the world of nature may be, it is obviously a geometrical world, its objects are extended and figured magnitudes in motion. If we can get rid of all other qualities, or reduce them to these, it is clear that mathematics must be the sole and adequate key to unlock the truths of nature. And it was not a violent leap from the wish to the thought.

During the following ten years, besides his numerous travels, Descartes was engaged in further mathematical studies, which were written down toward the end of this period, and he was also working out a series of specific rules for the application of his all-consuming idea. In these rules we find the conviction expressed that all the sciences form an organic unity,[2] that all must be studied together and by a method that applies to all.[3] This method must be that of mathematics, for all that we know in any science is the order and measurement revealed in its phenomena; now mathematics is just that universal science that deals with order and measurement generally.[4] That is why arithmetic and geometry are the sciences in which sure and indubitable knowledge is possible. They "deal with an object so pure and uncomplicated that they need make no assumptions at all that experience renders uncertain, but wholly consist in the rational deduction of consequences."[5] This does not mean that the objects of mathematics are imaginary entities without existence in the physical world.[6] Whoever denies that objects of pure mathematics exist, must deny that anything geometrical exists, and can hardly maintain that our geometrical ideas have been abstracted from existing things. Of course, there are no substances which have length without breadth or breadth without thickness, because geometrical figures are not substances but boundaries of them. In order for our geometrical ideas to have been abstracted from the world of physical objects, granted that this is a tenable hypothesis, that world would have to be a geometrical world—one fundamental characteristic of it is extension in space. It may turn out that it possesses no characteristics not deducible from this.

Descartes is at pains carefully to illustrate his thesis that exact knowledge in any science is always mathematical knowledge. Every other kind of magnitude must be reduced to mathematical terms to be handled effectively; if it can be reduced to extended magnitude so much the better, because extension can be represented in the imagination as well as dealt with by the intellect. "Though one thing can be said to be more or less white than another, or a sound sharper or flatter, and so on, it is yet impossible to determine exactly whether the greater exceeds the less in the proportion two to one, or three to one, etc., unless we treat the quantity as being in a certain way analogous to the extension of a body possessing figure."[7] Physics, as something different from mathematics, merely determines whether certain parts of mathematics are founded on anything real or not.[8]

What, now, is this mathematical method for Descartes in detail? Faced with a group of natural phenomena, how is the scientist to proceed? Descartes' answer early in the **Rules** is to distinguish two steps in the actual process, *intuition* and *deduction*. "By intuition I understand . . . the conception which an unclouded and attentive mind gives us so readily and distinctly that we are wholly freed from doubt about that which we understand."[9] He illustrates this by citing certain fundamental propositions such as the fact that we exist and think, that a triangle is bounded by three lines only, etc. By deduction he means a chain of necessary inferences from facts intuitively known, the certitude of its conclusion being known by the intuitions and the memory of their necessary connexion in thought.[10] As he proceeds further in the **Rules,** however, he realizes the inadequacy of this propositional method alone to yield a mathematical physics, and introduces the notion of *simple natures,* as discoveries of intuition in addition to these axiomatic propositions.[11] By these simple natures he means such ultimate characteristics of physical objects as extension, figure, motion, which can be regarded as producing the phenomena by quantitative combinations of their units. He notes that figure, magnitude, and impenetrability seem to be necessarily involved in extension, hence the latter and motion appear to be the final and irreducible qualities of things. As he proceeds from this point he is on the verge of most far-reaching discoveries, but his failure to keep his thought from wandering, and his inability to work out the exceedingly pregnant suggestions that occur to him make them barren for both his own later accomplishments and those of science in general. Bodies are extended things in various kinds of motion. We want to treat them mathematically. We intuit these simple natures in terms of which mathematical deductions can be made. Can we formulate this process more exactly, with special reference to the fact that these simple natures must make *extension* and *motion* mathematically reducible? Descartes tries to do so, but at the crucial points his thought wanders, and as a consequence Cartesian physics had to be supplanted by that of the Galileo-Newton tradition. What are those features of extension, he asks, that can aid us in setting out mathematical differences in phenomena? Three he offers, dimension, unity, and figure. The development of this analysis is not clear[12], but apparently a consistent solution of his idea would be that unity is that feature of things which enables simple arithmetic or

geometry to gain a foothold in them, figure that which concerns the order of their parts, while dimension is any feature which it is necessary to add in order that no part of the facts shall have escaped mathematical reduction. "By dimension I understand not precisely the mode and aspect according to which a subject is considered to be measurable. Thus it is not merely the case that length, breadth, and depth are dimensions, but weight also is a dimension in terms of which the heaviness of objects is estimated. So, too, velocity is a dimension of motion, and there are an infinite number of similar instances." This conception of weight, velocity, etc., as further mathematical dimensions akin to length, breadth, and depth, except that they are dimensions of motion rather than of extension, harboured enormous possibilities which were entirely unrealized either in Descartes or in the work of later scientists. Had he succeeded in carrying the thought through, we might to-day think of mass and force as mathematical dimensions rather than physical concepts, and the current distinction between mathematics and the physical sciences might never have been made. It might be taken for granted that *all* exact science is mathematical—that science as a whole is simply a larger mathematics, new concepts being added from time to time in terms of which more qualities of the phenomena become mathematically reducible. In this sense he might have converted the world to his doctrine at the end of the second book of the **Principles**[13], that all the phenomena of nature may be explained by the principles of mathematics and sure demonstrations given of them. There are passages in his later works in which he still seems to be thinking of weight as a dimension of motion. He criticizes Democritus for asserting gravity to be an essential characteristic of bodies, "the existence of which I deny in any body in so far as it is considered by itself, because this is a quality depending on the relationship in respect of situation and motion which bodies bear to one another."[14] In general, however, he tended to forget this significant suggestion, and we find him denying weight as a part of the essence of matter because we regard fire as matter in spite of the fact that it appears to have no weight.[15] It has apparently slipped his mind that he once conceived of such differences as themselves mathematical.

The fact is, Descartes was a soaring speculator as well as a mathematical philosopher, and a comprehensive conception of the astronomico-physical world was now deepening in his mind, in terms of which he found it easy to make a rather brusque disposal of these qualities which Galileo was trying to reduce to exact mathematical treatment, but which could not be so reduced in terms of extension alone. This scheme was in effect to saddle such qualities upon an unoffending ether, or first matter, as Descartes usually calls it, thereby making it possible to view the bodies carried about in this ether as possessing no features not deducible from extension. Descartes' famous vortex theory was the final product of this vigorous, all-embracing speculation. Just how did he reach it?

(B) *Geometrical Conception of the Physical Universe*

We have noted the biographical reasons for Descartes' hope that it would be possible to work out a physics which required no principles for its completion beyond those of pure mathematics; there were also certain logical prejudices operating, such as that *nothing* cannot possess extension, but wherever there is extension there must be some substance.[16] Furthermore, as for motion, Descartes had been able to account for it in a manner which fairly satisfied him; God set the extended things in motion in the beginning, and maintained the same quantity of motion in the universe by his 'general concourse,'[17] which, confirmed by more immediately conceived distinct ideas, meant that motion was just as natural to a body as rest, *i.e.,* the first law of motion. Since the creation then, the world of extended bodies has been nothing but a vast machine. There is no spontaneity at any point; all continues to move in fixed accordance with the principles of extension and motion. This meant that the universe is to be conceived as an extended *plenum,* the motions of whose several parts are communicated to each other by immediate impact. There is no need of calling in the force or attraction of Galileo to account for specific kinds of motion, still less the 'active powers' of Kepler; all happens in accordance with the regularity, precision, inevitability, of a smoothly running machine.

How could the facts of astronomy and of terrestrial gravitation be accounted for in a way which would not do havoc with this beautifully simple hypothesis? Only by regarding the objects of our study as swimming helplessly in an infinite ether, or 'first matter,' to use Descartes' own term, which, being vaguely and not at all mathematically conceived, Descartes was able to picture as taking on forms of motion that rendered the phenomena explicable. This primary matter, forced into a certain quantity of motion divinely bestowed, falls into a series of whirlpools or vortices, in which the visible bodies such as planets and terrestrial objects are carried around or impelled toward certain central points by the laws of vortical motion. Hence the bodies thus carried can be conceived as purely mathematical; they possess no qualities but those deducible from extension and free mobility in the surrounding medium. Verbally, to be sure, Descartes made the same claim for the first matter itself, but it was the world of physical bodies that he was eager to explain, hence in terms of this hypothesis he imagined himself to have realized the great ambition of his life in the achievement of a thoroughly geometrical physics. What he did not appreciate was that this speculative success was bought at the expense of loading upon the primary medium those characteristics which express themselves in gravitation and other variations of velocity—the

characteristics in a word which Galileo was endeavouring to express mathematically, and which Descartes himself in his more exact mathematical mood had conceived as dimensions. This procedure did not at all drive them out of the extended realm but merely hid under cover of vague and general terms the problem of their precise mathematical treatment. To solve that problem, Descartes' work had to be reversed, and the Galilean concepts of force, acceleration, momentum, and the like, reinvoked.

The unfortunate feature of the situation at this time was that thinkers were accepting the notion that *motion* was a mathematical concept, the object of purely geometrical study, whereas with the single exception of Galileo, they had not come to think of it seriously and consistently as *exactly reducible* to mathematical formulae. Galileo had caught this remarkable vision, that there is absolutely nothing in the motion of a physical body which cannot be expressed in mathematical terms, but he had discovered that this can be done only by attributing to bodies certain ultimate qualities beyond the merely geometrical ones, in terms of which this full mathematical handling of their motions can take place. Descartes realized well enough the facts that underlie this necessity—that bodies geometrically equivalent move differently when placed in the same position relative to the same neighbouring bodies—but thinking of motion as a mathematical conception in general and not having caught the full ideal of its exact reduction in a way comparable to his treatment of extension, he failed to work out to a clear issue his earlier suggestion of weight and velocity as dimensions, and turned instead to the highly speculative vortex theory, which concealed the causes of these variations in the vague, invisible medium, and thereby saved the purely geometrical character of the visible bodies.

The vortex theory was, none the less, a most significant achievement historically. It was the first comprehensive attempt to picture the whole external world in a way fundamentally different from the Platonic-Aristotelian-Christian view which, centrally a teleological and spiritual conception of the processes of nature, had controlled men's thinking for a millenium and a half. God had created the world of physical existence, for the purpose that in man, the highest natural end, the whole process might find its way back to God. Now God is relegated to the position of first cause of motion, the happenings of the universe then continuing *in æternum* as incidents in the regular revolutions of a great mathematical machine. Galileo's daring conception is carried out in fuller detail. The world is pictured concretely as material rather than spiritual, as mechanical rather than teleological. The stage is set for the likening of it, in Boyle, Locke, and Leibniz, to a big clock once wound up by the Creator, and since kept in orderly motion by nothing more than his 'general concourse.'

The theory had an important practical value for Descartes as well. In 1633 he had been on the point of publishing his earliest mechanical treatises, but had been frightened by the persecution of Galileo for his advocacy of the motion of the earth in the *Dialogues on the Two Great Systems,* just published. As the impact motion and vortex theory developed in his mind, however, he perceived that place and motion must be regarded as entirely relative conceptions, a doctrine which might also save him in the eyes of the Church. As regards place he had already reached this conviction, defining it in the **Rules** as "a certain relation of the thing said to be in the place toward the parts of the space external to it."[18] This position was reaffirmed more strongly still in the **Analytical Geometry** and the **Dioptrics,** where he states categorically that there is no absolute place, but only relative; place only remains fixed so long as it is defined by our thought or expressed mathematically in terms of a system of arbitrarily chosen co-ordinates[19]. The full consequence of this for a true definition of motion is brought out in the **Principles,** in which, after noting the vulgar conception of motion as the "action by which any body passes from one place to another,"[20] he proceeds to "the truth of the matter," which is that motion is "the transference of one part of matter or one body from the vicinity of those bodies that are in immediate contact with it, and which we regard as in repose, into the vicinity of others."[21] Inasmuch as we can regard any part of matter as in repose that is convenient for the purpose, motion, like place, becomes wholly relative. The immediate practical value of the doctrine was that the earth, being at rest in the surrounding ether, could be said in accordance with this definition to be unmoved, though it, together with the whole vortical medium, must be likewise said to move round the sun. Was this clever Frenchman not justified in remarking that "I deny the movement of the earth more carefully than Copernicus, and more truthfully than Tycho?"[22]

Now during these years in which Descartes was developing the details of his vortex theory and the idea of the extended world as a universal machine, he was occupying himself with still more ultimate metaphysical problems. The conviction that his mathematical physics had its complete counterpart in the structure of nature was being continually confirmed pragmatically, but Descartes was not satisfied with such empirical probabilism. He was eager to get an absolute guarantee that his clear and distinct mathematical ideas *must* be eternally true of the physical world, and he perceived that a new method would be required to solve this ultimate difficulty. A sense of the genuineness and fundamental character of this problem appears definitely in his correspondence early in 1629, and in a letter[23] to Mersenne, April 15, 1630, we learn that he has satisfactorily (to himself) solved it by conceiving the mathematical laws of nature as established by God, the eternal invariableness of whose will is deducible

from his perfection. The details of this metaphysic are presented in the **Discourse,** the **Meditations,** and the **Principles,** where it is reached through the method of universal doubt, the famous *'cogito ergo sum,'* and the causal and ontological proofs of the existence and perfection of God. As regards the subjection of his mental furniture to the method of universal doubt, he had decided ten years earlier, as he tells us in the **Discourse,** to make the attempt as soon as he should be adequately prepared for it; now, however, the main motive that impels him to carry it through is no mere general distrust of his own early beliefs, but a consuming need to get a solution for this specific problem. We shall not follow him through these intricacies, but concentrate our attention upon one famous aspect of his metaphysics, the dualism of two ultimate and mutually independent entities, the *res extensa* and the *res cogitans*.

(C) *'Res extensa' and 'res cogitans'*

In Galileo the union of the mathematical view of nature and the principle of sensible experimentalism had left the status of the senses somewhat ambiguous. It is the sensible world that our philosophy attempts to explain and by the use of the senses our results are to be verified; at the same time when we complete our philosophy we find ourselves forced to view the *real* world as possessed of none but primary or mathematical characteristics, the secondary or unreal qualities being due to the deceitfulness of the senses. Furthermore, in certain cases (as the motion of the earth) the immediate testimony of the senses must be wholly renounced as false, the correct answer being reached by reasoned demonstrations. Just what is, then, the status of the senses, and how are we specifically to dispose of these secondary qualities which are shoved aside as due to the illusiveness of sense? Descartes attempts to answer these questions by renouncing empiricism as a method and by providing a haven for the secondary qualities in an equally real though less important entity, the thinking substance.

For Descartes it is, to be sure, the sensible world about which our philosophizing goes on[24], but the method of correct procedure in philosophy must not rest upon the trustworthiness of sense experience at all. "In truth we perceive no object such as it is by sense alone (but only by our reason exercised upon sensible objects)."[25] "In things regarding which there is no revelation, it is by no means consistent with the character of a philosopher . . . to trust more to the senses, in other words to the inconsiderate judgments of childhood, than to the dictates of mature reason."[26] We are to seek the "certain principles of material things . . . not by the prejudices of the senses, but by the light of reason, and which thus possess so great evidence that we cannot doubt of their truth."[27] Sensations are called 'confused thoughts,'[28] and therefore sense, as also memory and imagination which depend on it, can only be used as aids to the understanding in certain specific and limited ways; sensible experiments can decide between alternative deductions from the clearly conceived first principles; memory and imagination can represent extended corporeality before the mind as a help to the latter's clear conception of it[29]. It is not even necessary, as a basis for a valid philosophy, that we always have the sensible experience to proceed from; reasoning cannot of course alone suffice to give a blind man true ideas of colours, but if a man has once perceived the primary colours without the intermediate tints, it is possible for him to construct the images of the latter[30].

Our method of philosophical discovery, then, is distinctly rational and conceptual; the sensible world is a vague and confused something, *a quo* philosophy proceeds to the achievement of truth. Why, now, are we sure that the primary, geometrical qualities inhere in objects as they really are, while the secondary qualities do not? How is it that "all other things we conceive to be compounded out of figure, extension, motion, etc., which we cognize so clearly and distinctly that they cannot be analysed by the mind into others more distinctly known?"[31] Descartes' own justification for this claim is that these qualities are *more permanent* than the others. In the case of the piece of wax, which he used for illustrative purposes in the second *Meditation,* no qualities remained *constant* but those of extension, flexibility, and mobility, which as he observes, is a fact perceived by the understanding, not by the sense or imagination. Now flexibility is not a property of all bodies, hence extension and mobility alone are left as the constant qualities of all bodies as such; they can by no means be done away with while the bodies still remain. But, we might ask, are not colour and resistance equally constant properties of bodies? Objects change in colour, to be sure, and there are varying degrees of resistance, but does one meet bodies totally without colour or resistance? The fact is and this is of central importance for our whole study, *Descartes' real criterion is not permanence but the possibility of mathematical handling;* in his case, as with Galileo, the whole course of his thought from his adolescent studies on had inured him to the notion that we know objects only in mathematical terms, and the sole type for him of clear and distinct ideas had come to be mathematical ideas, with the addition of certain logical propositions into which he had been led by the need of a firmer metaphysical basis for his achievements, such as the propositions that we exist, that we think, etc. Hence the secondary qualities, when considered as belonging to the objects, like the primary, inevitably appear to his mind obscure and confused[32]; they are not a clear field for mathematical operations. This point cannot be stressed too strongly, though we shall not pause over it now.

But now the addition of such logical propositions as the above to the mathematical definitions and axioms

as illustrations of clear and distinct ideas, is quite important. It occurs as early as the **Rules,** and shows already the beginnings of his metaphysical dualism. No mathematical object is a more cogent item of knowledge than the *'cogito ergo sum';* we can turn our attention inward, and abstracting from the whole extended world, note with absolute assurance the existence of a totally different kind of entity, a thinking substance. Whatever may be the final truth about the realm of geometrical bodies, still we *know* that we doubt, we conceive, we affirm, we will, we imagine, we feel. Hence when Descartes directed his energies toward the construction of a complete metaphysic, this clean-cut dualism was inescapable. On the one hand there is the world of bodies, whose essence is extension; each body is a part of space, a limited spatial magnitude, different from other bodies only by different modes of extension—a geometrical world—knowable only and knowable fully in terms of pure mathematics. The vortex theory provided an easy disposal of the troublesome questions of weight, velocity, and the like; the whole spatial world becomes a vast machine, including even the movements of animal bodies and those processes in human physiology which are independent of conscious attention. This world has no dependence on thought whatever, its whole machinery would continue to exist and operate if there were no human beings in existence at all[33]. On the other hand, there is the inner realm whose essence is thinking, whose modes are such subsidiary processes[34] as perception, willing, feeling, imagining, etc., a realm which is not extended, and is in turn independent of the other, at least as regards our adequate knowledge of it. But Descartes is not much interested in the *res cogitans,* his descriptions of it are brief, and, as if to make the rejection of teleology in the new movement complete, he does not even appeal to final causes to account for what goes on in the realm of mind. Everything there is a mode of the thinking substance.

In which realm, then, shall we place the secondary qualities? The answer given is inevitable. We can conceive the primary qualities to exist in bodies as they really are; not so the secondary. "In truth they can be representative of nothing that exists out of our mind."[35] They are, to be sure, caused by the various effects on our organs of the motions of the small insensible parts of the bodies[36]. We cannot conceive how such motions could give rise to secondary qualities *in the bodies;* we can only attribute to the bodies themselves a disposition of motions, such that, brought into relation with the senses, the secondary qualities are produced. That the results are totally different from the causes need not give us pause:

> The motion merely of a sword cutting a part of our skin causes pain (but does not on that account make us aware of the motion or figure of the sword). And it is certain that this sensation of pain is not less

different from the motion that causes it, or from that of the part of our body that the sword cuts, than are the sensations we have of colour, sound, odour, or taste. [37]

Hence all qualities whatever but the primary can be lumped together and assigned to the second member of the metaphysical wedding. We possess a clear and distinct knowledge of pain, colour, and other things of this sort, when we consider them simply as sensations or thoughts; but

> . . . when they are judged to be certain things subsisting beyond our minds, we are wholly unable to form any conception of them. Indeed, when any one tells us that he sees colour in a body or feels pain in one of his limbs, this is exactly the same as if he said that he there saw or felt something of the nature of which he was entirely ignorant, or that he did not know what he saw or felt.[38]

> We can easily conceive, how the motion of one body can be caused by that of another, and diversified by the size, figure, and situation of its parts, but we are wholly unable to conceive how these same things (size, figure, and motion), can produce something else of a nature entirely different from themselves, as, for example, those substantial forms and real qualities which many philosophers suppose to be in bodies . . . [39]

> But since we know, from the nature of our soul, that the diverse motions of body are sufficient to produce in it all the sensations which it has, and since we learn from experience that several of its sensations are in reality caused by such motions, while we do not discover that anything besides these motions ever passes from the organs of the external senses to the brain, we have reason to conclude that we in no way likewise apprehend that in external objects which we call light, colour, smell, taste, sound, heat, or cold, and the other tactile qualities, or that which we call their substantial forms, unless as the various dispositions of these objects which have the power of moving our nerves in various ways. . . .

Such, then, is Descartes' famous dualism—one world consisting of a huge, mathematical machine, extended in space; and another world consisting of unextended, thinking spirits. And whatever is not mathematical or depends at all on the activity of thinking substance, especially the so-called secondary qualities, belongs with the latter.

(D) *Problem of Mind and Body*

But the Cartesian answer raises an enormous problem, how to account for the interrelation of these diverse entities. If each of the two substances exists in absolute independence of the other, how do motions of extended things produce unextended sensations, and

---

An excerpt from Descartes' *Meditations,* concerning the nature of the human mind:

I will suppose that all I see is false. I will believe that none of those things that my deceitful memory brings before my eyes ever existed. I thus have no senses: body, shape, extension, movement, and place are all figments of my imagination. What then will count as true? Perhaps only this one thing: that nothing is certain.

But on what grounds do I know that there is nothing over and above all those which I have just reviewed, concerning which there is not even the least cause for doubt? Is there not a God (or whatever name I might call him) who instills these thoughts in me? But why should I think that, since perhaps I myself could be the author of these things? Therefore am I not at least something? But I have already denied that I have any senses and any body. Still, I hesitate; for what follows from that? Am I so tied to the body and to the senses that I cannot exist without them? But I have persuaded myself that there is nothing at all in the world: no heaven, no earth, no minds, no bodies. Is it not then true that I do not exist? But certainly I should exist, if I were to persuade myself of something. But there is a deceiver (I know not who he is) powerful and sly in the highest degree, who is always purposely deceiving me. Then there is no doubt that I exist, if he deceives me. And deceive me as he will, he can never bring it about that I am nothing so long as I shall think that I am something. Thus it must be granted that, after weighing everything carefully and sufficiently, one must come to the considered judgment that the statement "I am, I exist" is necessarily true every time it is uttered by me or conceived in my mind.

René Descartes, in his Meditations on First
Philosophy, *1641.*

---

how is it that the clear conceptions or categories of unextended mind are valid of the *res extensa*? How is it that that which is unextended can know, and, knowing, achieve purposes in, an extended universe? Descartes' least objectionable answer to these difficulties is the same answer that Galileo made to a similar though not so clearly formulated problem—the appeal to God. God has made the world of matter such that the pure mathematical concepts intuited by mind are forever applicable to it. This was the answer that the later Cartesians attempted to work out in satisfactory and consistent form. The appeal to God was, however, already beginning to lose caste among the scientific-minded; the positivism of the new movement was above everything else a declaration of independence of theology, specifically of final causality, which seemed to be a mere blanket appeal to a king of answer to scientific questions as would make genuine science impossible. It was an answer to the ultimate *why,* not to the present *how.* Descartes himself had been a powerful figure in just this feature of the new movement. He had categorically declared it impossible for us to know God's purposes.[40] Hence this answer had little weight among any but his metaphysically-minded followers, whose influence lay quite outside the main current of the times; and those passages in which he appeared to offer a more immediate and scientific answer to these overwhelming difficulties, especially when capitalized by such a vigorous thinker as Hobbes, were the ones which proved significant. In these passages Descartes appeared to teach that the obvious relationships between the two entities of the dualism implied after all the real localization of mind, *but it was of the utmost importance for the whole subsequent development of science and philosophy that the place thus reluctantly admitted to the mind was pitifully meagre, never exceeding a varying portion of the body with which it is allied.* Descartes never forswore the main philosophical approach which had led to his outspoken dualism. All the non-geometrical properties are to be shorn from *res extensa* and located in the mind. He asserts in words that the latter "has no relation to extension, nor dimensions,"[41] we cannot "conceive of the space it occupies"; yet, and these were the influential passages, it is "really joined to the whole body and we cannot say that it exists in any one of its parts to the exclusion of the others"; we can affirm that it "exercises its functions" more particularly in the conarion, *"from whence it radiates forth through all the remainder of the body by means of the animal spirits, nerves, and even the blood."* With such statements to turn to in the great philosopher of the new age, is it any wonder that the common run of intelligent people who were falling into line with the scientific current, unmetaphysically minded at best, totally unable to appreciate sympathetically the notion of a non-spatial entity quite independent of the extended world, partly because such an entity was quite unrepresentable to the imagination, partly because of the obvious difficulties involved, and partly because of the powerful influence of Hobbes, *came to think of the mind as something located and wholly confined within the body?* What Descartes had meant was that through a part of the brain a quite unextended substance came into effective relation with the realm of extension. The net result of his attempts on this point for the positive scientific current of thought was that the mind existed in a ventricle of the brain. The universe of matter, conceived as thoroughly geometrical save as to the vagueness of the 'first matter,' extends infinitely throughout all space, needing nothing for its continued and independent existence; the universe of mind, including all experienced qualities that are not mathematically reducible, comes to be pictured as locked up behind the confused and deceitful media of the senses, away from this independent extended realm, in a petty and insignificant series of locations inside of human bodies. This is, of course, the position which had been generally accorded the 'soul' in ancient times, but not at all the 'mind,' except in the case of those philosophers of the sensationalist schools who made no essential distinction between the two.

Of course, the problem of knowledge was not solved by this interpretation of the Cartesian position, but rather tremendously accentuated. How is it possible for such a mind to know anything about such a world? We shall postpone for the present, however, considerations of this sort; all the men with whom we are immediately occupied either failed to see this enormous problem, or else evaded it with the easy theological answer.

Note, however, the tremendous contrast between this view of man and his place in the universe, and that of the medieval tradition. The scholastic scientist looked out upon the world of nature and it appeared to him a quite sociable and human world. It was finite in extent. It was made to serve his needs. It was clearly and fully intelligible, being immediately present to the rational powers of his mind; it was composed fundamentally of, and was intelligible through, those qualities which were most vivid and intense in his own immediate experience—colour, sound, beauty, joy, heat, cold, fragrance, and its plasticity to purpose and ideal. Now the world is an infinite and monotonous mathematical machine. Not only is his high place in a cosmic teleology lost, but all these things which were the very substance of the physical world to the scholastic—the things that made it alive and lovely and spiritual—are lumped together and crowded into the small fluctuating and temporary positions of extension which we call human nervous and circulatory systems. The metaphysically constructive features of the dualism tended to be lost quite out of sight. It was simply an incalculable change in the viewpoint of the world held by intelligent opinion in Europe.

Notes

[1] An admirable account of this event in the light of the available sources, with critical comments on the views of other Cartesian authorities, is given in Milhaud, *Descartes savant,* Paris, 1922, p. 47, ff.

[2] *The Philosophical Works of Descartes,* Haldane and Ross translation, Cambridge, 1911. Vol. I, p. 1, ff., 9.

[3] Vol. I, p. 306.

[4] Vol. I, p. 13.

[5] Vol. I, p. 4, ff.

[6] Vol. II, p. 227.

[7] Vol. I, 56.

[8] Vol. I, 62.

[9] Vol. I, 7.

[10] Vol. I, 8, 45.

[11] Vol. I, 42, ff.

[12] Vol. I, 61, ff.

[13] *Principles of Philosophy,* Part II, Principle 64.

[14] *Principles,* Part IV, Principle 202.

[15] *Principles,* Part II, Principle 11.

[16] *Principles,* Part II Principles 8, 16.

[17] *Principles,* Part II, Principle 36.

[18] *Philosophical Works,* Vol. I, p. 51.

[19] Cf. *Dioptrics,* Discourse 6 (*Oeuvres* Cousin ed., Vol. V, p. 54, ff.).

[20] Part II, Principle 24.

[21] Part II, Principle 25.

[22] *Principles,* Part III, Principles 19-31.

[23] *Oeuvres* (Cousin ed.) VI, 108, ff. Cf. an interesting treatment of this stage in Descartes biography in Liard, *Descartes,* Paris, 1911, p. 93, ff.

[24] *Philosophical Works,* Vol. I. p. 15.

[25] *Principles,* Part I, Principle 73.

[26] *Principles,* Part I. Principle 76. Cf. also Part II, Principles 37, 20.

[27] *Principles,* Part III, Principle I.

[28] *Principles,* Part IV, Principle 197.

[29] *Philosophical Works,* Vol. I, p. 35, 39, ff. *Discourse,* Part V.

[30] Vol. I, p. 54.

[31] Vol. I, p. 41.

[32] *Philosophical Works,* Vol. I, p. 164, ff.

[33] *Oeuvres,* Cousin ed., Paris, 1824, ff., Vol. X, p. 194.

[34] In his *Traité de l'homme* Descartes had asserted that these subsidiary processes can be performed by the body without the soul, the sole function of the latter being to think. Cf. *Oeuvres,* XI, pp. 201, 342: *Dis-*

course (Open Court ed.), p.59, ff.; Kahn, *Metaphysics of the Supernatural,* p. 10, ff. His mature view, however, as expressed in the *Meditations* and *Principles,* is as above stated. Cf., for example, Meditation 11.

[35] *Principles,* Part I, Principles 70, 71.

[36] *Oeuvres* (Cousin), Vol. IV, p. 235, ff.

[37] *Principles,* Part IV, Principle 197.

[38] *Principles,* Part I, Principles 68, ff.

[39] Part IV, Principles 198, 199.

[40] *Principles,* Part III, Principle 2.

[41] *Passions of the Soul,* Articles 30, 31 (*Philosophical Works,* Vol. I, 345, ff.). Italics ours. In his later writings Descartes was much more guarded in his language. Cf. *Oeuvres* (Cousin ed.), X, 96, ff.

Daniel Garber (essay date 1978)

SOURCE: "Science and Certainty in Descartes," in *Descartes: Critical and Interpretive Essays,* edited by Michael Hooker, The Johns Hopkins University Press, 1978, pp. 114-51.

[*In the following essay, Garber traces Descartes' approach to science and scientific practice from the* Regulae *to the* Principia Philosopiae, *contending that Descartes abandoned his early philosophy that science must be deductively certain, instead nearly coming to the conclusion that science relies on hypothetical arguments and experimentation.*]

Descartes's principal project was to build a science of nature about which he could have absolute certainty. From his earliest writings he argues that unless we have absolute certainty about every element of science at every level, we have no genuine science at all. But while the very general sketches Descartes gave for his project were clear, the details of just how he was to build such a science and precisely what it was to look like when he finished were not. The traditional view is that what Descartes had in mind was a science structured somewhat like Euclid's *Elements,* starting with a priori first principles, and deriving "more geometrico" all there is to know about the world. On this view, it is fairly clear why Descartes might have thought that he was building a certain science. A science built more geometrico would seem to be as certain as geometry itself. But among most scholars the traditional view has given way to the realization that observation and experiment play an important role in Descartes's scientific method, both in theory and in practice.[1] There is no question in my own mind that this view of Descartes's science is correct. But this new realization of Descartes the experimenter raises a curious question. If the geometrical model of Cartesian science is not correct, then what of certainty? How could Descartes have thought that he could find certainty in an experimental science? Or for that matter, did Descartes, in the end, think that certainty is possible for science? It is my main goal in this paper to present an alternative to the traditional geometrical model of Cartesian science in which it will be evident why Descartes thought his science both experimental and certain.

But there is an historical dimension to this problem that is often ignored. Descartes's work in natural science falls roughly into two parts. In his earlier works, for the most part those which precede the **Principia Philosophiae** (1644), including the **Regulae ad Directionem Ingenii** (1628?), **Le Monde** (1633), the **Discourse on the Method, Optics,** and **Meteorology** (1637), and the **Meditations** (1641), Descartes is formulating his views on nature and presenting them little by little.[2] In this period, Descartes's work is filled with many promises: programmatic sketches of the science he claims to have formulated, and claims about arguments and deductions he thinks he has found. It is only in his later work, his **Principia Philosophiae,** that he attempts to present his science with any completeness. It is here that we find Descartes's earlier promises kept, and, all too often, broken. If we examine Descartes in this way, we find a noticeable difference between these two periods. In the earlier period Descartes is quite confident that he has found the way to certain knowledge, and it is in this period that the insistence on certainty is strongest. But in the later period, Descartes must come face to face with the extreme difficulty of actually presenting such a science, and his commitment to certainty undergoes interesting changes.

My discussion of certainty in Descartes's science falls into three sections. In the first, I shall discuss the notion of certainty in Descartes's earlier writings and present some of the basic reasons for rejecting the more traditional view of Cartesian science as a deductive system on the model of Euclidean geometry. In the second, main section of this paper, I shall try to replace the geometrical model with a model of the inferential structure of Cartesian science that better reflects Descartes's thinking, at least in the earlier period. I shall present it in such a way that it will be evident how Descartes could think that his science is both experimental and certain. In this section I shall also discuss the status of hypotheses at this point in Descartes's thought. Having seen the outlines of Descartes's early, grand program for the sciences, I shall in section three examine how Descartes's earlier conception fares in the **Principles**. There we shall see strong suggestions that Descartes is moving to give up his earlier conception of certainty in science.
Before I begin this ambitious project, one remark is in

order. I shall not offer any general account of Cartesian method, nor shall I offer any systematic interpretation of the early and problematic **Regulae,** as is common practice in methodological discussions of Descartes's science.[3] Rather, I shall concentrate on the many places in which Descartes talks specifically about the epistemic and inferential structure of his theory of the world. I shall bring in passages from the more general and abstract discussions of method when I feel that their interpretation is sufficiently obvious, and when they bear on the interpretation of some specific point Descartes is making about his conception of science. I make no general claim about the unity of Descartes's methodological thought over and above the specific continuities that I shall point out in the course of this paper.

One last caution before we begin. Though Descartes's goal was certainty, mine is not. In a paper as short as this, I cannot hope to present the case I would like to make in sufficient detail. My only hope is to clear away some of the obscurity surrounding some of the important questions about Descartes's science, and sketch, in broad strokes, one line for reinterpreting his scientific enterprise.

I
Preliminary Remarks on Certainty

Early on in his youthful **Regulae,** Descartes declares:

> *We should be concerned only with those objects regarding which our minds seem capable of obtaining certain and indubitable knowledge [cognitionem].*

> All science [*scientia*] is certain, evident knowledge [*cognitio*], and he who doubts many things is not more learned than he who has never thought about these things. . . . And so, in accordance with this rule, we reject all knowledge [*cognitiones*] which is merely probable [*probabiles*] and judge that only those things should be believed which are perfectly known [*perfecte cognitis*] and about which we can have no doubts.

> [Rule II: AT [Descartes; *Oeuvres de Descartes;* ed. Charles Adam and Paul Tannery; 12 vols.; Paris: Cerf, 1897-1910; reprinted, with new appendices, Paris: Vrin, 1964-] 10:362; HR 1:3]

Certainty was clearly of the greatest importance to Descartes. In this section I would like to explore briefly what he meant by certainty.

In the **Regulae,** Descartes gives us a straightforward account of what he means by certain knowledge, in terms of the cognitive operations that result in certainty, intuition and deduction, "From all these things we conclude . . . that there are no paths to the certain knowledge of truth open to man except evident *intuition* and necessary *deduction*" (Rule XII: AT 10:425; HR 1:45, emphasis added).[4] Certain knowledge, then, is that which can be presented as the product of intuition or deduction.

Descartes explains what he means by intuition in the following passage:

> By intuition I understand . . . the conception of the pure and attentive mind which is so simple and distinct that we can have no further doubt as to what we understand; or, what amounts to the same thing, an indubitable conception of the unclouded and attentive mind which arises from the light of reason alone.
>
> [Rule III: AT 10:368; HR 1:7]

There is much over which one could pause in this account of intuition. For the moment, though, I would merely point out how open this definition is. In this passage of the *Regulae,* the only one in which he attempts a general characterization of intuition, Descartes sets no a priori limits to the domain of intuition. Precisely what knowledge it is that he thinks we can acquire through intuition can be settled only by examining the particular examples of intuition he presents, and cannot be derived from his definition alone. The examples he offers of intuited truths include our own existence, that we think, that a sphere has only one surface, and "other similar things" (AT 10:368; HR 1:7). More generally he associates the domain of intuition with what he calls "absolutes" and "simple natures."[5]

Descartes attempts to characterize deduction in the following passage:

> Many things are known with certainty although they are not evident in themselves for the sole reason that they are *deduced* from true and known [*cognitis*] principles *by a continuous and uninterrupted process of thought, in which each part of the process is clearly intuited.* . . . We can therefore distinguish an intuition of the mind from a deduction which is certain by the fact that in the latter we perceive a movement or a certain [*quaedam*] succession of thought, while we do not in the former.
>
> [Rule III: AT 10:369-70; HR 1:8, emphasis added.][6]

Deduction, then, can be defined in terms of intuition. A deduction is a succession of propositions, ordered in such a way that each one follows from the preceding through an act of intuition.[7] While it is possible to start such a deduction from any premise, Descartes usually limits the applicability of the term "deduction" to those arguments and conclusions which begin with a premise that is derived from intuition, or is the conclusion of another deduction.

As we remarked with respect to intuition, Descartes's conception of deduction is quite loose. A deduction as defined seems to be any argument, whatever its form might be, all of whose steps can be connected by acts of intuition. In the *Regulae,* Descartes is quite clear in disassociating the kind of argument he has in mind from the more formal syllogism:

> But perhaps some will be astonished that . . . we omit all the rules by which the logicians think they regulate human reason. . . . (We) reject those forms of theirs [*istas formas*] as opposed to our teaching, and seek rather all the aids by which our mind may remain alert. . . . And so that it will be more evident that the syllogistic art is of practically no assistance in the search for truth, we should notice that logicians can form no syllogism which reaches a true conclusion unless the heart of the matter is given, that is, unless they previously recognized the very truth which is thus deduced.
>
> [Rule X: AT 10:405-6; HR 1:32]

Obviously, Descartes conceived of deduction as a kind of argument much broader in scope than the syllogism. While nothing important will depend on my rather unorthodox reading, it looks as if he thought that deductive arguments (with intuitive premises, of course) could yield conclusions which are not merely contained in the premises, to criticize the "syllogistic art" the way he does. Precisely what arguments Descartes was willing to accept as deductive, though, cannot be determined by appeal to his definition. As was the case with intuition, to understand what he has in mind we must appeal to the examples of deductive reasoning Descartes gives, and note those arguments that he rejects as yielding uncertain conclusions.

Before I turn to later accounts of certainty in Descartes's writings, a short digression about the relation between certainty and method in the *Regulae* would be in order. The *Regulae* is intended to give us "directions" for finding certainties. Descartes gives a procedure that he thinks will put us in a position so that we can discover intuitive truths, and discover deductive connections. The certain knowledge that is the end product of the *Regulae* is certain, not because it was found using Descartes's method, but because it can be presented as the product of intuition and deduction. This plausible reading of the *Regulae* is supported by two features of that work. First of all, Descartes opens the work with a discussion of what certainty is (Rules I-III) and does not talk at all about the method for finding certainty until Rule IV. When he finally comes to discuss how we find certain truth, he uses a metaphor of finding the road that leads us to the "treasure" (Rule IV: AT 10:371; HR 1:9). This strongly suggests that the method is a way of finding something, like the treasure, whose worth and value lies in something other than the path we take to it. Also, Descartes admits that his method is not the only way of discovering certainty. He recognizes others, but argues that they are more difficult (Rule VI: AT 10:384-87; HR 1:17-19). Thus a given item of knowledge is certain not by virtue of the way we discover it (e.g., by using Cartesian method), but by the way in which we justify it (i.e., by presenting it as the product of intuition and deduction). Consequently, I see no problems in divorcing Descartes's notion of certainty in the *Regulae* from the details of the method offered there.

At the heart of the notion of certainty in the *Regulae* are the notions of intuition and deduction. Descartes's theory of certainty changes, however, in later works, where he adopts a new criterion for certainty, clearness and distinctness. Thus, in the *Discourse on the Method,* Descartes presents the rule that we quoted at the beginning of this section as follows:

> The first rule was never to accept anything as true unless I recognize it to be evidently such: that is, carefully to avoid precipitation and prejudgment [*preuention*], and to include nothing in my conclusions unless it presented itself so clearly and distinctly to my mind that there was no occasion to doubt it.
>
> [AT 6:18; HR 1:92.]

There are a number of anticipations of this somewhat different conception of certainty in the *Regulae*. Descartes often talks about intuition and deduction in terms that involve the notion of distinctness and, occasionally, clearness as well.[8] But the clearness and distinctness account is substantially new in the *Discourse*.

With the introduction of this new vocabulary for discussing certainty come many problems for Descartes and the Cartesian scholar. For Descartes, with the new criterion of certainty comes a new enterprise, that of validating it. For the scholar comes the problem of explicating exactly what Descartes had in mind by clearness and distinctness, and exactly how he thought that his criterion of certainty could be validated (here is where the well-known Cartesian circle enters). In this paper I shall not discuss the criterion of clearness and distinctness or the difficulties raised by Descartes's attempt to validate that criterion. In fact, when discussing certainty I shall avoid the language of clearness and distinctness altogether, and return to the idiom of the *Regulae,* where certainty is characterized in terms of intuition and deduction. My avoidance of foundational problems with regard to certainty can be justified by noting that Descartes himself avoids such questions in his more narrowly scientific work, nor can I see any particularly good reason for raising the foundational problems in that context.[9]

My decision not to use the language of clearness and distinctness also derives from the texts. When talking about scientific questions and the structure of science, Descartes himself seems to avoid the terminology of clearness and distinctness, and falls more naturally into the terminology of intuition (sometimes) and deduction (quite often), as we shall see when we take up such passages in detail. There is thus a certain advantage to following Descartes in this, since it will be thereby easier for us to follow his discussions of certainty in science. The fact that the old way of talking about certainty persists throughout the later writings suggests strongly that Descartes thought that the earlier account could be translated into, or at least justified by, the later account. Just how such a justification, translation, or explication could be given is itself an interpretive problem of major proportions. I assume that everything I say (and Descartes said) about Cartesian science in terms of intuition and deduction can be given a reading *salva veritate* in terms of clearness and distinctness, though I shall not attempt to argue this. There are other problems raised by my choice of the earlier idiom. Most particularly, unlike clearness and distinctness, the characterization of certainty in terms of intuition and deduction gives us no real criteria that can be used for telling when something is certain and when it is not. Consequently we will have to appeal to what Descartes explicitly says is intuitive, deductive, or certain truth, as we noted earlier. But this is a small price to pay for what will turn out to be a major gain in simplicity and naturalness when we talk about Descartes's scientific reasoning.

So my criterion of certainty for Cartesian science will be the following: a body of scientific results will be certain for an individual if and only if that individual could present it as the product of intuition and deduction. The modal 'could' is important here. Descartes does not always have to present his science as derived from intuition and deduction for him to claim that it is certain. What makes it certain for him is that he could present it in that way.[10]

Having outlined Descartes's abstract notion of certainty and the relations it bears to intuition and deduction on the one hand, and clearness and distinctness on the other, I shall close this section with some remarks about the scope of certainty for Descartes.

I pointed out earlier that Descartes's notion of deduction is broader than the notion of deduction in syllogistic logic, and that it seems to allow for arguments that yield conclusions not "contained in" their premises. At this point it might be interesting to draw some consequences from this and bring in some related considerations. In the introduction I noted that the traditional conception of Cartesian science is that of a science more geometrico, conclusions derived logically from a priori first principles. What we noted and conjectured about deduction in Descartes already casts doubt on this picture, but there are other reasons for rejecting it. If that picture is correct, then Cartesian science is limited to a priori certain truth. But it is quite clear that Descartes was willing to admit certainties which can be classed only as a posteriori. For example, in the **Meditations** Descartes offers arguments which he claims meet his criteria for certainty. Yet at least one of these—the argument for the existence of material objects in Meditation VI—is quite definitely not an a priori argument. This argument depends upon a premise (itself apparently intuitive and certain) about the ideas we have of material objects that cannot be a priori on any conception of a priori truth I know of. Thus not everything certain is a priori, and the limitation of science to the certain does not commit Descartes to an a priori science. And furthermore, since the argument I have cited is itself part of Descartes's broadly scientific structure, it is clear that Cartesian science could not be a priori in any modern sense.

But if we are to reject the picture of Cartesian science in which truths of science are logically derived from a priori first principles, what are we to make of the passages in which Descartes compares his enterprise to that of the geometer? Consider the following such passage:

> Those long chains of reasoning, so simple and easy, which enabled the geometricians to reach their most difficult demonstrations, had made me wonder whether all things knowable to men might not follow from one another in the same fashion [*s' entresuiuent en mesme façon*]. If so, we need only to refrain from accepting as true that which is not true, and carefully follow the order necessary to deduce each one from the others, and there cannot be any propositions so abstruse that we cannot prove them, or so recondite that we cannot discover them.
> [*Discourse,* pt. II: AT 6:19; HR 1:92]

From what I said earlier it should be clear that Descartes is *not* looking to build a science like geometry in the sense in which geometry derives theorems from first principles using deductive reasoning taken in the narrowest sense. When he talks about "refraining from accepting as true that which is not true" (intuition?) and carefully following "the order necessary to *deduce* each one from the others," (deduction?) he seems quite consciously to be referring back to his theory of certainty in the **Regulae**. There too he talked about mathematics as a model for natural science, but his explicit conclusion there was that, "In seeking the correct path to truth we should be concerned with nothing about which we cannot have a *certainty equal to that of the demonstrations of arithmetic and geometry*" (Rule II: AT 10:366; HR 1:5, emphasis added).[11] So, if Descartes is to be construed as building a science more geometrico, it is not because he seeks to build a science that is a priori, like geometry, but rather because

for Descartes "more geometrico" means only *more certo*.

The rejection of the naive geometrical model of Cartesian science, and the realization that not everything that is certain is, strictly speaking, a priori constitute an important part of the way toward a proper understanding of the nature of Descartes's science. But even if we understand the true significance of the geometrical model, we must still explain how and why Descartes thought that the science of nature he found was certain. This will be the task of the following section of this paper.

Having noted something that Descartes does not seem to exclude from the possibility of being certain, we should also note briefly something that he does want to exclude from the domain of the certain: probability. While it is traditional to see Descartes's demand for certainty as a response to scepticism, it is no less correct to regard the demand for certainty as a response to those who are willing to make do with probability.

When Descartes says that we must "reject all knowledge which is merely probable," as he does in the passage from the **Regulae** with which this section opened, he meant something somewhat different than we currently do by "probability." The notion of probability he had in mind was largely a notion from dialectic and rhetoric—the theories of debate and public speaking. "Probable" was one way in which the premises and arguments used in such debate were characterized.[12] In that context, "probable" meant something close to "generally accepted."[13]

The rejection of probability is part of Descartes's rejection of the whole rhetorical-dialectical tradition of education so prevalent in the Renaissance university.[14] For the most part, though, Descartes gives little characterization of probability and particular probabilistic modes of argument, except negatively, as things which cannot be (or, maybe, are not) presented either intuitively or deductively. Only one kind of argument is singled out for Descartes's attention, the kind of argument that makes use of conjecture:

> Let us also take heed never to confuse any conjectures [*conjecturas*] with our judgements about the true state of things. Attention to this matter is of no little importance, for there is no stronger reason why contemporary philosophy has found nothing so evident and so certain that it cannot be controverted, than because those eager for knowledge . . . venture to affirm even obscure and unknown things, about which we can make only plausible conjectures [*probabilibus conjecturis*] and then give their whole credence to these, confusing them indiscriminately with the true and evident. Thus they can finally reach no conclusion which does not seem to depend upon some proposition of this sort, and all of their

conclusions are therefore doubtful.
[*Regulae,* Rule III: AT 10:367-68; HR 1:6-7][15]

It is not entirely clear what Descartes means by "conjecture" in this passage. The notion of a conjecture comes up only once again in the *Regulae*. There Descartes gives the following example:

> Persons compose their judgments by conjecture if, for example, considering the fact that water, which is farther from the center of the globe than earth, is also more tenuous, and that air, higher than water, is still more tenuous, they conjecture that above the air there is nothing but a certain very pure ether, and that it is much more tenuous than the air itself, and so on.

[Rule XII: AT 10:424; HR 1:45]

This is something of an argument from analogy. But the earlier characterization of conjecture suggests that conjectures include more than such arguments from analogy. The formula that Descartes uses, talking of those who "venture to affirm even obscure and unknown things . . . and then give their whole credence to these" suggests (though not entirely clearly or unambiguously) that the modern hypothetico-deductive method or method of hypothesis in which we frame hypotheses that best explain experience and hold them until they are falsified would count as one such probabilistic argument by conjecture.[16]

II
Cartesian Science in Theory: The *Discourse*

In the previous section I outlined Descartes's conception of certainty and made some comments about its scope. In the context of the latter discussion, I argued that the picture of science as logically deduced from a priori first principles is not correct. In this section I would like to outline the grand plan for all of science that Descartes presents in the period of the *Discourse*. In so doing, I hope to sketch something of an alternative to the traditional geometrical model of Cartesian science.

In this section I shall organize my discussion around what seems to be the clearest and most explicit statement of the inferential structure of Descartes's science in the earlier writings. I have divided this single passage up into four parts and labeled each. In the discussion that follows I shall refer to each by letter. The passage is the familiar and often quoted one from the *Discourse*:

> A. My own procedure has been the following: I tried to discover the general principles or first causes of all that exists or could exist in the world, without taking any causes into consideration but God as creator, and without using anything save certain

seeds of the truth which we find in our own minds.

> B. After that I examined what were the first and commonest effects which could be deduced from these causes; and it seems to me that by this procedure I discovered skies, stars, and earth, and even, on the earth, water, air, fire, minerals, and several other things which are the commonest of all and the most simple, and in consequence the easiest to understand.

> C. Then, when I wanted to descend to particulars, it seemed to me that there were so many different kinds that I believed it impossible for the human mind to distinguish the forms or species of objects found on earth from an infinity of others which might have been there if God had so willed. Nor, as a consequence, could we make use of things unless we discover causes by their effects, and make use of many experiments. After this, reviewing in my mind all the objects which had ever been presented to my senses, I believe I can say that I have never noticed anything which I could not explain easily enough by the principles I had found. But I must also admit that the powers of nature are so ample and vast, and that these principles are so simple and so general, that I hardly ever observed a particular effect without immediately recognizing several ways in which it could be deduced.

> D. My greatest difficulty usually is to find which of these ways (of deducing the effect) is correct, and to do this I know no other way than to seek several experiments such that their outcomes would be different according to the choice of one or another ways of deducing the effect.

[pt. VI: AT 6:63-65; HR 1:121]

In what follows I shall try to extract the inferential structure of Descartes's science from this and related passages. More precisely, I shall be looking to explicate how Descartes conceived the structure of his science and whether he thought that it could be presented as the product of intuition and deduction. Consequently, we shall appeal to Descartes's scientific practice only insofar as it clarifies his intentions with respect to his theory of science. (I shall point out in the course of this discussion a number of places where Descartes's practice misleads us with respect to his theory.) Because I am interested in eliciting the outline of the whole of Descartes's grand program for science, I shall only give cursory glances at the details behind sections A and B, where the conception seems clearest and seems closest to the Euclidean model. Rather, I shall concentrate on sections C and D where the intentions become foggy, and where he seems, by the introduction of experiment, to diverge most clearly from the Euclidean model.

In A, Descartes discusses his discovery of "general

principles or first causes." It is clear that Descartes has in mind at very least the metaphysical first principles outlined in part IV of the *Discourse* and presented in detail in the *Meditations*. These writings include the proof of his own existence, the proof that God exists, the validation of the criterion of clearness and distinctness, the proof that mind and body are distinct substances, and that the essence of material substance is extension, and the proof that there are material things. The "general principles or first causes" mentioned in A include more than these metaphysical matters, though. Given that B begins with Descartes's cosmology, it is reasonable to suppose that Descartes meant to include in the matters mentioned in A the laws of motion; in the *Discourse* account, these are sandwiched between the metaphysical first principles of part IV and the cosmology taken up at the beginning of part V (AT 6:43; HR 1:107-8).

In section A of his outline of the structure of science, there is relatively little problem with certainty. Though he is not entirely explicit, there is every indication that at this point certainty is maintained, and at least Descartes thought that all arguments referred to in A could be presented in terms of intuition and deduction. In fact, Descartes seemed to regard the metaphysical arguments, at least, as paradigms of proper and certain argumentation. Before going on, though, we might remind ourselves that even at this beginning stage, we have left the a priori, strictly speaking. While all of the arguments Descartes offers for the conclusions cited in this section proceed "without using anything save certain seeds [*semences*] of the truth which we find in our minds," certain of the arguments, like the argument for the existence of material objects, are a posteriori, as we noted earlier in section I.

So much for A. In B, Descartes discusses the first effects "which could be deduced" (*deduire*) from the "general principles or first causes" of A. These effects include the cosmology (sky, stars), the earth, and at least some of the contents of the earth (water, air, fire, minerals, and "several other things").[17] Given that Descartes used the technical term "deduce" (of course, in its French translation) it seems evident that Descartes thought that the effects mentioned in B were, or could be, established with certainty. Though it is not clear just how such a deduction could be given, it seems as if the chain of intuition and deduction is not yet broken, at least in Descartes's own thinking.

One thing should be mentioned at this point. Though in B Descartes talks about "deducing" his cosmology, etc., from first principles, this is not exactly how the argument is presented in the passage of part V of the *Discourse,* where that argument is outlined as it was given in *Le Monde*. There he argues with respect to an imaginary world, not our own, "I therefore resolved to leave this world . . . and to speak only of what would

happen in a new one, if God should now create somewhere in imaginary space enough matter to make one" (AT 6:42; HR 1:107). The "deduction" of cosmology that follows there is thus not for our world, but for this imaginary world, a world that Descartes builds on the basis of certain assumptions. Insofar as the phenomena so deduced resemble our world, Descartes takes his assumptions to be adequate and the explanations correct. Such an argument would not, it seems, particularly in the light of the passage of the *Regulae* about conjecture cited at the end of section I, tell us anything certain about our world. But, given the clear statement in B that cosmology is deduced from the first causes of A, we must suppose here, I think, that Descartes's practice does not reflect his *theory* of science. A number of explanations are possible. It is most likely that in this passage Descartes is describing the route he found he had to take in the early work, *Le Monde,* but in B he is describing a later version of his system, either actual or contemplated, presumably what he hoped would later become his *Principles*. In adopting this explanation, though, I do not mean to ignore the question of how Descartes argued in the part of his scientific practice corresponding to B. I intend only to put that discussion off to a more appropriate place.

In A we saw that the question of intuition, deduction, and the resulting certainty is relatively unproblematic. There can be little question but that certainty is preserved at this point. Section B is somewhat more problematic, since the outlined arguments in the *Discourse* that correspond to that section are given only hypothetically. But in this case it is not implausible to separate the practice of the earlier work (*Le Monde* in this case) from the program that Descartes outlines in B, as I have already suggested. Thus nothing we have seen so far would cause a radical revision of the traditional Euclidean model. While a careful examination of the arguments Descartes has in mind in sections A and B would show us that they are not strictly deductive in the modern sense, as I have argued, the Euclidean model is not a bad fit. But the Euclidean model breaks down completely when we progress to section C. There, where Descartes first explicitly introduces *experiment,* all hope of fitting his conception of science to the Euclidean model seems to end. For that matter, all hope of certainty in science seems to end as well. What, then, is to be made of C? What has happened to deduction and certainty?

Let us examine C carefully. The particulars he has in mind are not entirely obvious. Certainly he intended animals and human beings.[18] Though the text is hardly explicit on this, I would presume that he would include things like magnets (a favorite example in Cartesian science) and other reasonably complex terrestrial phenomena. However, it does not seem tremendously important to specify precisely what belongs under C and what under B. By "descending to particulars" he seems to mean the process of giving an account of what these particulars are, i.e., an account of their natures, their internal structures. Again, though, Descartes is not entirely clear about the kind of account that he has in mind in this passage. If this is what Descartes is talking about here, then what he seems to be claiming is that we cannot give an account of the nature of the particulars in the world without appeal to experiment and reasoning from effect to cause. Furthermore, he also claims that even when we introduce experiments, there are a number of ways in which we can explain any particular on our first principles.

But what precisely does Descartes have in mind when he suggests that we must discover causes through their effects? Though Descartes is not explicit about this here, his scientific practice in two of the three essays (in particular, the **Optics** and the **Meteorology**) for which the **Discourse** serves as an introduction, in the parts of the earlier **Le Monde** that survive, and in the later **Principles,** and his methodological remarks, suggest that Descartes may have in mind some sort of reasoning that makes essential use of hypotheses, perhaps something like the modern hypothetico-deductive method. If we adopt this interpretation of Descartes, then we would reason from effects to causes by making a number of experiments, gathering the results, and framing a hypothesis that would explain those results in terms of our basic principles. If it is the hypothetico-deductive method that Descartes has in mind, then the hypothesis would be supported by virtue of explaining the experiments.[19]

The evidence in favor of the claim that Descartes was seriously committed to hypothetical arguments in science and that this is what he had in mind when he wrote C is substantial. Although I shall later argue against this reading, I shall try to present what seems to be the best evidence for this view. Since we are concerned with Descartes's attitudes and theories before the **Principles,** I shall not consider at this point many of the passages from the later work often cited and discussed in connection with whether or not Descartes adopted a hypothetical mode of argument. Those passages will be discussed in the following section when I discuss deduction and certainty in the **Principles.** And finally, I shall put off the question of certainty until after we present the case for Descartes's endorsement of hypothetical modes of argument.

The evidence that Descartes had some sort of hypothetical mode of argument in mind in this early period comes from both his scientific practice and from his more theoretical writings. I have already pointed out one passage from the **Discourse** where Descartes seems to describe the use of a hypothetical mode of argument in his scientific practice. That passage describes how he argued in **Le Monde** from an imaginary model of our world which in all respects is claimed to agree

with ours at the level of phenomena (AT 6:42-44; HR 1:107-9). The hypothetical mode of argument is used in a different but related way in the **Optics** and the **Meteorology.** At the very beginning of the **Optics** Descartes notes:

> Thus, not having here any other occasion to speak of light than to explain how its rays enter the eye. . . . I need not undertake to explain its true nature. And I believe that it will suffice that I make use of two or three comparisons which help to conceive it in the manner which seems the most convenient to explain [*expliquer*] all of its properties that experience acquaints us with, and to deduce [*deduire*] afterwards all the others which cannot be so easily observed; imitating in this the Astronomers, who although their assumptions [*suppositions*] are almost all false or uncertain, nevertheless, because these assumptions refer [*rapportent*] to different observations which they have made, never cease to draw many very true and well assured conclusions from them.

> [AT 6:83; trans. Olscamp, 66-67]

And later, in the beginning of the **Meteorology,** Descartes notes:

> It is true that since the knowledge [*connaissance*] of these matters depends on general principles of nature which have not yet, to my knowledge, been accurately explained, I shall have to use certain assumptions [*suppositions*] at the outset, as I did in the **Optics.** But I shall try to render them so simple and easy that perhaps you will have no difficulty in accepting them, even though I have not demonstrated [*demonstrées*] them.

> [AT 6:233; trans. Olscamp, 364]

Though these passages seem to support the claim we are examining, a few comments are in order. First of all, the kinds of assumptions that Descartes has in mind here are quite general. In the **Optics** Descartes assumes that light is transmitted instantaneously, in straight paths, and so on, and in the **Meteorology** he assumes that things are made up of corpuscles, that there is no void, and so on.[20] These assumptions clearly correspond to the conclusions discussed in section B, and seem to have little to do with the particulars of C. Consequently, the appeal to these passages may establish little, if anything, about the sort of reasoning that Descartes had in mind in C. But leaving this aside, it is important to recognize that this method of proceeding, while hypothetical, is not strictly hypothetico-deductive. Descartes takes as his starting place certain assumptions, and claims to be able to explain a variety of phenomena on those assumptions. But he makes no claims that the ability to explain the phenomena and deduce new phenomena "which cannot be so easily observed" renders the assumptions in any way true, certain, or even confirmed. In fact, he compares his assumptions with those of astronomy, which he claims are all "false or uncertain." The conception of astronomy he is referring to is one according to which the problem of astronomy is to find hypotheses about the motion of heavenly bodies which will "save the phenomena," while making no claims about the true causes of any of the phenomena.[21] This kind of instrumentalistic conception of theories is often appropriate in astronomy, where for many practical purposes (the construction of calendars, navigation, etc.) it is more important to know when and where in the sky particular bodies will be observed, than why they are there. But such a procedure would seem much less valuable in physics, where we have a greater interest in understanding the phenomena than in saving them. In fact, by the 1630s the traditional instrumentalistic attitude toward astronomical theories had long been given up in favor of a more realistic attitude among the best astronomers, including Copernicus, Tycho Brahe, Kepler, and Galileo.[22] It seems curious that Descartes would recommend that physicists adopt the approach of the astronomers, long after astronomers had given up that approach in favor of the more realistic project of finding the true explanations of things, a project which they borrowed from physics.

Elsewhere, though, Descartes does argue in a more straightforwardly hypothetico-deductive fashion:

> And in all of this, the explanation [*raison*] accords so perfectly with experience [*l'experience*] that I do not believe it possible, after one has studied both carefully, to doubt that the matter is as I have just explained it [*l'expliquer*].
>
> [*Meteorology,* discourse VIII: AT 6:334; trans.
> Olscamp, 338]

Here Descartes is talking about his explanation of the rainbow, a matter much closer to the concerns of section C than is discussed in the earlier passages. Also here, unlike those earlier passages, it does seem as if the explanans gains significant credibility by virtue of its explanatory power. This claim is defended quite explicitly in another passage, one that looks like an unambiguous and theoretical endorsement of the hypothetico-deductive mode of argument, both when we are dealing with particulars, such as rainbows and their nature, and when we are dealing with the sort of general assumptions discussed earlier and compared with astronomical assumptions:

> If some of the matters I deal with at the beginning of *Optics* and *Meteorology* should at first sight appear offensive, because I call them assumptions [*suppositions*] and do not try to prove [*prouver*] them, let the reader have the patience to read all of it with attention, and I hope that he will be satisfied with the result. For it seems to me that the explanations [*raisons*] follow one another in such a way, that just as the last are demonstrated [*demonstrées*] by the first, which are their causes, so these first are demonstrated [*demonstrées*] by the last which are their effects. And

one must not suppose that I have here committed the fallacy which logicians call circular reasoning; for as experience makes most of the effects very certain [*car l'experience rendant la plus part de ces effets tres certains*], the causes from which I deduce [*deduits*] them serve not so much to prove [*prouver*] as to explain them [*expliquer*]; but, on the contrary, the causes are proved by their effects [*ce sont elles qui sont prouuées par eux*].

[*Discourse* VI: AT 6:76; HR 1: 128-29].[23]

This passage, which bears a striking resemblance to modern discussions of hypothetico-deductive method, is echoed in some of the correspondence following the publication of the *Discourse* and the accompanying essays.[24] This passage and the corresponding theoretical comments in the correspondence strike me as the best evidence there is for the claim that Descartes was genuinely committed to the use of hypothetical arguments in science, and that the hypothetico-deductive method is what he has in mind in section C.

Let us review the story up to now. There is considerable evidence that Descartes had in mind some kind of hypothetical mode of argument in the period of the *Discourse*. There are complications, however. For one, it looks as if there are two distinctly different kinds of hypothetical argument in the texts, an astronomical argument, and a hypothetico-deductive argument (it is not clear to me that Descartes distinguished between these two kinds of argument, though). There is a further complication, one that arises when we attempt to argue that this hypothetical argument is what Descartes has in mind in C. Many of the texts supporting Descartes's endorsement of hypothetical modes of argument involve general sorts of assumptions of the sort that arise in B and not in C. These complications hardly seem decisive. However, if this is what Descartes meant by reasoning from effects to causes in C, what of certainty? What of the grand picture of a science grounded in intuition and deduction, as indubitable as geometry?

At this point in the argument there seem to be only two directions in which we can go. We can argue either that Descartes thought (quite mistakenly) that the hypothetical mode of argument yielded certain knowledge, or that by this point, Descartes had abandoned his goal of a science that is certain, having realized that experimental reasoning from effect to cause and certainty are not compatible. One should be somewhat suspicious of both these alternatives. The former seems doubtful, given the remarks concerning assumptions I cited earlier in section I of this paper, and even more doubtful considering Descartes's apparent recognition in C of the multiplicity of causes all of which can explain the same effect. The latter account seems suspicious considering that in part II of the *Discourse* Descartes once again declares his intent to construct a science as certain as mathematics (AT 6:19; HR 1:92-93) and that he reasserts this at the very beginning of his outline of physics in part V: "I have always remained true to the resolution I made . . . not to admit anything as true which did not seem to me clearer and more certain than the demonstrations of the geometricians" (AT 6:40-41; HR 1:106). What then are we to do?

I would like to suggest that a serious mistake has been made in supposing that the hypothetical mode of argument is what Descartes really has in mind in C, and in believing that the hypothetical mode of argument plays a role in Descartes's considered views on reasoning in science, at this stage in his thinking. While we shall find a somewhat different situation when we examine the *Principles,* I shall maintain that in the works we are considering, those written before the *Principles,* Descartes has neither adopted any hypothetical mode of argument, nor has he given up his plan for a certain science, and that, furthermore, this certain science is one in which experiment plays an indispensable role. My argument will be in two parts. I shall first argue that Descartes considered the hypothetical mode of argument only a convenient way of presenting his scientific results without having to present his entire system, and he at least claimed to have in mind a truly deductive argument in cases where he appealed to hypothetical arguments. And secondly, I shall argue for an interpretation of C in which the reasoning Descartes has in mind is both experimental and certain. This will allow us to say that at least before the *Principles,* Descartes had retained the program of building a certain science founded on intuition and deduction.

The hypothetical reasoning that Descartes uses in the *Optics* and the *Meteorology* seems to have been one feature of those works that most disturbed his readers. One of the most revealing insights into Descartes's true intentions in presenting his work in that way comes in a letter to Vatier, where he explains why he chose to argue in a hypothetical mode:

> I cannot prove *a priori* [i.e., from cause to effect] the assumptions I proposed at the beginning of the *Meteorology without expounding my whole physics;* but the phenomena which I have deduced necessarily from them, and which cannot be deduced in the same way from other principles, seem to me to prove them sufficiently *a posteriori* [i.e., from effect to cause]. I foresaw that this manner of writing would shock my readers at first, and I think I could easily have prevented this by refraining from calling these propositions 'assumptions' and by enunciating them only after I had given some reasons to prove them. However, I will tell you candidly that I chose this manner of expounding my thoughts for two reasons. First, *believing that I could deduce them in order from the first principles of my Metaphysics,* I wanted to pay attention to other kinds of proofs; secondly

> I wanted to try whether the simple exposition of truth would be sufficient to carry conviction without any disputation or refutations of contrary opinions.
>
> [AT 1:563; K 48, emphasis added.][25]

Descartes makes two important claims in this passage: that the use of a hypothetical mode of argument is a matter of convenience that allows him to present his findings in a convincing way without revealing the full foundations of his physics; and that for the conclusions presented in those works, he can give complete and certain deductions from first principles.

It is somewhat surprising that Descartes has to go into the question in such detail in the letter quoted and in the two others cited. Both of the points he raises in the letters were mentioned explicitly in the *Discourse*. On the first point, Descartes explicitly notes that in the essays that follow the *Discourse,* he does not intend to divulge fully the principles or the arguments on which his physics rests (pt. VI: AT 6:68-76; HR 1:123-28). In writing the essays he hoped only to:

> choose some topics which would not be too controversial, which would not force me to divulge more of my principles than I wished to, and which would demonstrate clearly enough what I could or could not do in the sciences.
>
> [AT 6:75; HR 1:128]

Furthermore, even in the *Discourse,* the hypothetical mode of argument is defended not as a method of establishing conclusions, either with certainty or without, but as a convenient way of presenting material that is in no way intended to replace a proper deduction from first principles. Immediately following the lengthy and eloquent defense of the hypothetico-deductive mode of argument in the *Discourse* quoted above, Descartes declares:

> And I have called them [i.e., the assumptions at the beginning of the *Optics* and *Meteorology*] assumptions only to let it be known that although *I think I can deduce them from first truths . . .* , I expressly desired not to make the deduction.
>
> [AT 6:76; HR 1:129, emphasis added.][26]

Though these remarks are directed largely at the very general assumptions that Descartes makes at the beginning of the *Optics* and *Meteorology,* some at least can be interpreted as indicating that the hypothetical mode of arguing with respect to assumptions about the nature and inner working of particular things was adopted for similar pragmatic reasons. Elsewhere, Descartes deals more specifically with those kinds of hypothetical arguments. In another letter written shortly after the *Discourse* and essays appeared, Descartes defends argument in the hypothetical mode with regard to the inner make-up of water, given without full demonstrative argument in the *Meteorology* as follows, "But if I had tried to derive all these conclusions like a dialectician, I would have worn out the printers' hands and the readers' eyes with an enormous volume" (AT 1:423-24; K 40).

Though Descartes talks here and elsewhere as if he has all of the deductions worked out, it is probably more accurate to say that he only thought that he could work them out given sufficient time, and in the case of particulars, given a sufficiently large body of experimental data. But even this position, somewhat weaker than the rather stronger claims that Descartes often makes, is quite sufficient for the argument I am making that the hypothetical arguments offered in Descartes's scientific works of this period do not represent a genuine commitment to that method of arguing in science. So, the hypothetical mode of presenting his science, at least in the essays, is intended only to save Descartes the trouble of presenting (or, perhaps, working out) his full system in complete detail, and does not represent a serious commitment to the use of hypothetical arguments in science. Similarly, his apparent defense of hypothetico-deductive method from a theoretical point of view is a defense of it as a method of presentation. In no way does Descartes intend the hypothetical mode of argument to replace strict Cartesian deduction as a way to insure the certainty of our scientific conclusions.[27]

But if the appeal to hypotheses is a matter of expository convenience, what, then, are we to make of section C? What kind of reasoning did Descartes have in mind there? What role does *experiment* play in that reasoning? What role does *certainty* play in that reasoning? In what follows I shall make a conjecture about the kind of argument Descartes may have had in mind in C when he talks about arguing from effects to causes.

Let us look back to C. It is interesting to note that while Descartes claims that when dealing with particulars, he found that he had to argue from effects to causes, and that when doing so, he could always envision a multiplicity of different causes for a given effect, he does not explicitly assert that it is impossible to argue from effects to causes either deductively or with certainty. In fact, after noting that there are often a number of ways of causally explaining a given effect, Descartes tells us just how it is that one can eliminate false causal explanations. The device he has in mind and mentions in D is that of *crucial experiment*. When we have an effect which can be explained by (deduced from) first principles in more than one way, Descartes tells us that we should "seek several experiments such that their outcomes will be different according to the choice" of causal hypothesis. Section D is not the only place in his writings where Descartes brings up crucial experiments in such an explicit way.

In the *Description du Corps Humain* (1648), which is admittedly from a period later than the one we are dealing with, in the context of an argument against Harvey's theory of the heart, Descartes observes:

> And all of this proves nothing but that experiments themselves can on occasion deceive us, when we don't examine well enough all of the causes they can have. . . . But in order to be able to note which of two causes is the true cause, it is necessary to consider other experiments which cannot agree with one another.

[AT 11:242][28]

It is thus clear that Descartes was well aware of the utility of crucial experiments in scientific reasoning.

So, if there is a Cartesian deduction of the nature of particulars outlined in C, it appears that it makes use of crucial experiments. But crucial experiment, by itself, cannot lead to certainty. Even after we eliminate all but one cause using crucial experiments, we still don't know that it is the correct one, since there may be other possible causes that we just have not thought of yet. But, if we can enumerate all possible causes, then it seems as if we can use crucial experiments to eliminate all but one of those causes, and we will know for certain that the one that remains is the true cause. This, in essence, is what I suggest Descartes has in mind in sections C and D.

Before elaborating on this and defending it, let me return to those two sections. What I am claiming is not only that in these sections Descartes is *not* adopting a hypothetical mode of argument with respect to particulars, but that in those passages, Descartes is outlining what a certainty-preserving deduction with respect to particulars would look like. But if this is what is going on in those sections, why does it look so much as if Descartes is giving up deduction and certainty? Two things are in need of explanation. First of all, why, if Descartes claims to have found a way of deducing explanations about particulars, does he declare at the very beginning of C that "it seemed to me that there were so many different kinds [of particulars] that I believed it impossible for the human mind to distinguish the forms or species of objects found on earth from an infinity of others which might have been there if God had so willed"? It seems clear that though he believed that at one time, he later came to believe the contrary, and reports this later in C and D. In a semi-autobiographical account like the *Discourse* we must be careful to distinguish intermediary positions from those that Descartes later adopts. But there is a more serious problem here. If my claim is right, then sections C and D should be enthusiastic reports of a bold new way of reasoning to the nature of particulars with absolute certainty. Why, if certainty is preserved, is the passage so pessimistic? To explain this, we must put the passage into its proper context. Earlier I mentioned that it is more accurate to say that Descartes finds, in principle, no reason for thinking that certainty cannot be attained at every level than it is to say that he has actually found all of the necessary arguments. This is especially true with respect to particulars. Such arguments are especially difficult because they require great numbers of experiments. This seems to be the main point of C and D. Immediately following D in the *Discourse,* not even beginning a new paragraph, Descartes laments the fact that so many experiments are required and that he has so few:

> As for the rest [i.e., those whose true explanation he has not yet been able to find (?)], I have reached the point, it seems to me, where I see clearly enough the direction in which we should go in this research; but I also see that the character and the number of experiments required is such that neither my time nor my resources, were they a thousand times greater than they are, would suffice to do them all. In proportion, therefore, to the opportunity I shall have in the future to do more or fewer of them, I will advance more or less in the understanding of nature. This I expected to convey in my treatise, and I hoped to show clearly how useful my project might be that I would oblige all those who desire human benefit, all those who are truly virtuous and not merely so in affectation or reputation, both to communicate to me the experiments that they have already made and to assist me in the prosecution of what remained to be done.

> [pt. VI: AT 6:65; HR 1:121-22]

So, the despair is not one of having to give up deduction and the certainty that comes with deductive argument when we "descend to particulars." The despair is clearly over the difficulty of providing such arguments.

Let me now set out the argument I have suggested more explicitly. My suggestion is that, for explaining the nature of particulars, Descartes imagined that we would begin with some general principles: metaphysics, the laws of motion, basic facts about the contents of the universe. This, presumably, is the conclusion of sections A and B. We also begin with immediate acquaintance with the phenomena to be explained, the particulars and their properties. This comes from observation and experiment. We then enumerate all of the possible causes that both explain the phenomena, and which are consistent with our general principles. Finally, we perform crucial experiments until we have eliminated all possible explanations except one. This is the true explanation.

There is another way of describing this mode of argument which is equivalent, even though it does not appeal to crucial experiments. On this way of proceeding, we would begin with the same first principles, but with a much wider variety of experimental data, perhaps, the data that we would have gotten if we had performed all of the crucial experiments. Examining the first principles, and the observational data, we would conclude (by intuition or deduction) that there is one and only one explanation of the phenomena consistent with both the phenomena and the first principles.

An example may make this clearer. Suppose that we are trying to find the nature of the magnet. We would begin with our first principles, and with common observations about how magnets behave. We would then, following the first version of this mode of argument, enumerate all possible explanations of the known phenomena that are consistent with our first principles, and eliminate all but one through crucial experiments. Following the second version, we would do the experiments first, and then intuit or deduce the single explanation that satisfies both the phenomena and our assumed first principles.

This form of argument is what I shall call an argument by complete enumeration of explanations, or more simply, argument by enumeration. It should be evident that the two versions of the argument (for convenience I shall call the first version A, and the second version B) are essentially equivalent, differing only in the temporal sequence of steps. In particular, in version B we do not frame any hypotheses until all of the experimental evidence is in, whereas in version A, we frame hypotheses before we have performed all of the experiments. It should be evident that the argument from enumeration is *not* a kind of hypothetico-deductive argument. While the two are very similar, in the argument by enumeration we have a complete enumeration of all possible explanations of phenomena. This is a step lacking in characteristic accounts of hypothetico-deductive argument. Because of this complete enumeration, the argument by enumeration can insure that a particular explanation is true, whereas in a hypothetico-deductive argument the most that can be established is that, since the explanation in question agrees with all observed phenomena, it is plausible to think that it may be true. Thus the argument by enumeration can make a prima facie claim to true and certain knowledge that cannot be made for the hypothetico-deductive argument. With this added power, though, come certain difficulties. It may not always be possible to produce a complete enumeration of possible explanations, nor may it always be possible to eliminate all but one by crucial experiments.[29] But we shall not consider these difficulties.

If the argument by enumeration is what Descartes has in mind, this casts a very interesting perspective on the notion of experiment in Cartesian science. Experiment is required, not as in Bacon or in more modern theories of experimental method to start possible lines of induction, but to close off possible lines of deduction. In the argument by enumeration, experiment eliminates incorrect deductive chains from first principles. It establishes what the facts of the world are that need to be explained, and does so with such finality that, at least in idealization, there is only one possible deductive path for us to follow. It seems curious to us to talk about experiment eliminating incorrect deductions. It would seem as if any deduction from first principles must be true. But in saying that experiment eliminates incorrect deductions, I don't mean to say that these other deductive paths are false, exactly. Rather, these other deductions simply lead to possible effects of our first principles not realized in the specific group of particulars with which we are dealing, which we are trying to explain. The problem experiment solves is the problem of distinguishing the "objects found on earth from the infinity of others which might have been there." Experiment does not eliminate incorrect deductions by showing them false, but by showing them inappropriate to the particular phenomena at hand. Consequently, there is an important sense in which an argument by enumeration is not strictly an argument from effect to cause. The argument is still from previously known causes to their effects, except that experiments tell us which are the "appropriate" effects.

This, then, is the argument that I think Descartes had in mind in sections C and D and in the numerous places where he claimed to be able to give deductive accounts of the nature of particulars. In what follows I shall argue that the argument by enumeration is a deductive argument for Descartes, and that it is the kind of argument that he had in mind in sections C and D.

The best argument for showing that the argument by enumeration is a deductive argument on Descartes's terms is that Descartes uses arguments of exactly the same form in circumstances where it is clear that he intended to give deductive and certain arguments. Most notable of these are the arguments for the existence of God and for the existence of material objects, the latter mentioned earlier as an example of an a posteriori deductive argument. These arguments can be represented schematically as follows:

GOD

1. First principles (assumed)

2. To be explained: I have an idea of God.

3. Possible explanations:

    (a) I caused that idea.

    (b) Nothing caused that idea.

    (c) God caused that idea.

4. Elimination: Further argument convinces me that

only God could have caused that idea.

5. Conclusion: God exists.[30]

MATERIAL OBJECTS

1. First principles (assumed)

2. To be explained: I have ideas of sensible objects.

3. Possible explanations:

    (a) I caused those ideas.

    (b) God caused those ideas.

    (c) Bodies caused those ideas.

4. Elimination: Further argument convinces me that only bodies could have caused those ideas.

5. Conclusion: Material objects exist.[31]

Both of these arguments very clearly have the form of an argument by enumeration. If arguments like the arguments for the existence of God and material bodies lead us to true and certain knowledge of their conclusions, so should all arguments by enumeration.

There is one worry about this reasoning, though, a difference between the arguments I just outlined and arguments by enumeration that may be serious enough to warrant our withholding the certainty from the argument by enumeration that Descartes attributes to the other two arguments. In the two arguments from the *Meditations* that I just outlined, alternative hypotheses are eliminated by reasoning, whereas in the argument by enumeration, it is experience, in the form of crucial experiments, that eliminates alternative hypotheses. Given Descartes's well-known distrust of the senses, might this render the argument uncertain and probable, despite the strong parallels in form between that argument and those other clearly deductive arguments? While I cannot here give a complete defense of the use of experience in a deductive argument of the form of an argument by enumeration, a few remarks are in order. As has been pointed out before, Descartes's distrust of experience has been vastly overemphasized and misinterpreted.[32] Although Descartes does distrust experience *improperly used,* he is equally emphatic about the necessity of using experience *properly* in scientific reasoning.[33] An example of experience properly used is given in the wax example of Meditation II. There, as part of a digression on the utility of experience in gaining knowledge, Descartes discusses the "nature" of a piece of wax. He concludes that the wax is by nature an extended thing, using reasoning strongly suggesting an argument by enumeration. He considers a number of different candidates, color, shape, size, taste, odor, etc., and eliminates all but one by appealing to experience. Though Descartes concludes that "perception [*perceptio*] is not a vision, a touch, nor an imagination . . . but is solely an inspection by the mind [*inspectio mentis*]" (AT 7:31; HR 1:155), this seems too strong a conclusion. In the wax example, it seems as if experience does play a crucial role, that of eliminating incorrect hypotheses. It would be more accurate to say that for Descartes, experience is useless unless properly used by the understanding. And it looks from the wax example as if one of the proper uses of experience is in the context of an argument by enumeration. Thus, the particular use of experience in the argument by enumeration does not render its conclusions uncertain, and it is not a significant difference between the argument by enumeration and the arguments for the existence of God and material bodies that the one appeals to experience where the other appeals to reasoning.

So, the argument by enumeration is a deductive argument. But is it what Descartes had in mind in sections C and D? The evidence that it is is of two kinds. First of all, there is a very strong suggestion of a use of the argument by enumeration in one of the letters where Descartes is defending the claim that he made in the **Meteorology,** that water is made up of oblong, eel-like corpuscles. In the first discourse of the **Meteorology** (AT 6:237-38; trans. Olscamp, 267-68) this claim is presented as one of Descartes's assumptions, and given a hypothetico-deductive defense. But in the correspondence he outlines what he calls there a "proof" (*demonstratio*) (AT 1:422-24; K 39-40). The "proof" involves showing that the account of the make-up of water that Descartes favors is the only one consistent with all the phenomena. This argument closely resembles version B of the argument by enumeration, and thus supports my claim that this is what Descartes had in mind in sections C and D, where he is talking in general terms about such explanations of particulars, even though "water" is placed (misplaced, I think) among the elements in section B.

But there is another reason for thinking that the argument by enumeration is what Descartes had in mind, a reason that is derived more from Descartes's theoretical comments than from his scientific practice.

As I stressed earlier, Descartes does introduce the notion of a crucial experiment in D. Given the context, of course, the only thing that prevents us from saying with complete confidence that Descartes has in mind an argument by enumeration is the fact that Descartes does not explicitly say that we must make a complete enumeration of all possible causal hypotheses. But in the **Discourse,** while discussing the rules of method in science, Descartes adopts the following rule, "The last rule was always to make enumerations [*denombremens*] so complete and reviews so general that I would be

certain that nothing was omitted" (pt. II: AT 6:19; HR 1:92). It seems reasonable to suppose that it is the violation of this rule that Descartes had in mind when, later, in the **Description du Corps Humain** he introduces the brief discussion of crucial experiment by noting that "experiments themselves can on occasion deceive us, when we don't examine well enough *all* of the causes they can have." It thus seems reasonable to suppose in C and D, where crucial experiment comes up as well, that Descartes has followed this rule and made an enumeration of possible explanations "so complete . . . that I would be certain that nothing was omitted," though Descartes did not mention this enumeration explicitly in that passage. So, while the interpretation that Descartes has the argument by enumeration in mind in C and D would involve reading something into that passage, all we have to assume is that Descartes means to follow the very rule that he earlier states, and later appeals to in a corresponding context.[34]

There is considerable further evidence in the **Regulae** that Descartes had an argument like the argument by enumeration in mind.[35] Moreover, I think that my conjectured argument by enumeration is supported by the simple fact that there seems to be no other way to explain how Descartes thought he could unite experiment, deduction, and certainty. But what is most important is that Descartes thought that an experimental argument could be given to establish facts about the nature of particulars with certainty; and that he thought that he could exhibit his entire science, or, at very least, the science presented in the **Optics** and **Meteorology,** as a deductive system. As we have found, this deductive system has a structure considerably different from that of Euclid's **Elements.** At the top are the first principles of metaphysics and the laws of nature, not established a priori in our sense, but established with certainty nevertheless (A). Next come the general principles of Cartesian cosmology, presented hypothetically in **Le Monde,** the **Optics,** and the **Meteorology,** but with deduction (and thus certainty) promised in B. And lastly comes the explanation of particulars. Here the argument gets complex, and we must appeal more and more to experimental arguments. But there is no indication that even at this stage Descartes was prepared to give up the claim to certainty, and much indication that he was not. This is what I propose to replace the traditional geometrical model of Cartesian science. If carried out, it would be a science both experimental and certain.

III
Cartesian Science in Practice: The *Principia*

I shall now turn to the **Principia Philosophiae,** the synoptic and systematic work of Descartes's last period, and examine the extent to which Descartes is able to carry out the program of the earlier period and provide a science based on intuition and deduction. In the earlier period, we found that in certain crucial respects Descartes's theory of science and his scientific practice bear only an indirect relation to one another. Though Descartes believes that his science *can* be presented as the product of intuition and deduction, he makes no serious attempt to do so in the scientific writings. Thus, as I argued, the hypothetical modes of argument used there do not represent an abandonment of the deductive picture of science. In the *Principles* there can be no such gap between theory and practice, insofar as the *Principles* is supposed to fulfill the program that Descartes earlier sketched. Descartes's principal excuse for using hypotheses in the earlier essays was that this mode of argument did not "force me to divulge more of my principles than I wish to" (*Discourse,* pt. VI: AT 6:75, HR 1:128). The fact that in the *Principles* Descartes starts from first principles leaves little doubt that it is there that he intended to fill in all the foundations and complete arguments lacking in the essays, mentioned in the *Discourse,* and promised in the correspondence.[38] But we shall find that, contrary to his earlier promises, Descartes finds that he is unable to present his science deductively, and that, as earlier, he has to appeal to hypotheses. But here he can no longer explain this appeal to hypotheses by claiming that it is not his intention to present the full system and all of the arguments. It is thus in the *Principles* that the necessities of scientific practice force some changes in the Cartesian program for science. I shall argue that in the *Principles,* Descartes makes some important moves away from the earlier program of a certain science founded in intuition and deduction.

Let us begin by examining Descartes's scientific practice in the *Principles*. There is little reason for us to pause over the first two of the four parts into which the *Principles* is divided. It is there that Descartes presents the first principles of metaphysics and the laws of nature described in section A of the programmatic outline in the *Discourse*. There is no question that Descartes was convinced both that the reasoning could be set out with intuitive and deductive certainty, and that he did set it out with certainty there. The arguments of *Principles* I correspond closely to those of the *Meditations* and part IV of the *Discourse,* and have been studied at great length. The arguments of *Principles* II, while less well known, are a direct continuation of the mode of argument of *Principles* I. At no point in these first two parts of the *Principles* is there any indication that Descartes is diverging from the master plan of the *Discourse*.

In *Principles* III Descartes begins the presentation of his cosmology and general theory of the universe. In this part, which corresponds to at least some of the material included in section B of the *Discourse* program, Descartes offers a general theory of matter (the three elements), a theory of the origin of the universe,

and a theory of the nature and behavior of heavenly bodies. In the *Optics* and *Meteorology* he had discussed some of this material hypothetically, as we earlier saw. Descartes framed a certain number of plausible assumptions, and showed how all of the phenomena could be explained by (i.e., deduced from) these assumptions. But the material could be presented deductively, Descartes claimed, assuming nothing but first principles. The *Principles,* and more particularly, this part of the *Principles,* is where he was to have given this deduction. It is interesting to see just how well Descartes succeeds.

Descartes begins *Principles* III with the claim that we must first examine the phenomena, the effects, as a prelude to a proper deduction of effects from causes:

> The principles we have discovered so far [in *Principles* I and II] are so vast and so fertile, that their consequences are far more numerous than the observable contents of the visible universe. . . . For an investigation of causes, I here present a brief account (*historiam*) of the principal phenomena (*phaenomen n*) of nature. *Not that we should use these as grounds (rationibus) for proving anything;* for *our aim is to deduce an account of the effects from the causes,* not to deduce an account of the causes from the effects. It is just a matter of turning our mind to consider some effects rather than others out of an innumerable multitude; all producible, on our view, by a single set of causes.
>
> [III 4: AT 8(1): 81-82: AG 223; emphasis added]

In this passage, highly reminiscent of section C from the *Discourse,* Descartes looks as if he is preparing for an argument by enumeration by setting out the body of data necessary for such an argument. Note at this point, Descartes explicitly says that he intends to give a deduction of effects from first principles.[37]

In the sections that follow, Descartes presents a body of data about the heavenly bodies, the heavens, and so on. The data are not exactly what we would call observational, but they are, by and large, presented in the spirit of facts in need of explanation, and appear to be in preparation for a deductive argument, perhaps an argument by enumeration. (Descartes also presents an astronomical hypothesis, which he compares with those of Copernicus and Tycho. But this seems something of a digression, an anticipation of material to be discussed in greater detail later.)

Having given some data, Descartes seemingly returns to the main thread of his deductive argument in III. 43:

> And certainly, if the only principles we use are such as we see to be most evident, if we infer nothing from them except through mathematical deduction, and if these inferences agree accurately with *all* natural phenomena; then we should, I think, be

wronging God if we were to suspect this discovery of the causes of things to be delusive.

[AT 8(1):99; AG 223-24]

So, Descartes implies that a demonstratively certain argument to the causes of things is possible. (Note how this passage suggests the argument by enumeration.) But, though such an argument is implied, it is not the kind of argument that Descartes intends to give. Rather, in the section following, he declares his intention to argue *hypothetically:*

> However, to avoid the apparent arrogance of asserting that the actual truth has been discovered in such an important subject of speculation, I prefer to waive this point; I will put forward everything I am going to write just as a hypothesis [*hypothesin*]. Even if this be thought to be false, I shall think my achievement is sufficiently worth while if all inferences from it agree with experience [*experimentis*]; for in that case we shall get as much practical benefit from it as we should from the knowledge of the truth.
>
> [AT 8(1):99; AG 224]

And at this point in the argument, Descartes follows the well-worn path he took in the *Optics* and *Meteorology*. He frames a number of hypotheses, some of which he claims to be outright false, and derives "explanations" of the phenomena from these (e.g. III. 45; AT 8(1):99-100; AG 224-25). Given that he has opted to argue hypothetically, the only restriction he places on these hypotheses is that their consequences agree with experience, "We are free to make any assumption we like . . . so long as all the consequences agree with experience" (III. 46: AT 8(1):101; AG 225).

It should be clear that by this point in the *Principles,* Descartes has broken the promise of section B. He has not given us a deduction of his cosmological principles from first principles. Rather, he has used the hypothetical mode of argument he used earlier. Why? He cannot argue, as he did in the *Discourse,* that he did not want to present his first principles and give an exposition of his whole system. The first principles are given in parts I and II, and the purpose of the *Principles* is just to give an exposition of the whole system. Perhaps one should take him at his word, and explain the hypothetical mode of inquiry by saying that Descartes was too modest to assert that he had found the truth about "such an important subject of speculation." But Descartes is hardly modest on other occasions, even earlier in the *Principles* where he doesn't hesitate to declare that he has found the truth about other matters. It is hardly less arrogant to imply that one has found the truth, as he does in III. 43. The natural explanation for the hypothetical mode of argument in this context is that, though he was earlier quite confident that he had a deductive argument for his cosmology, when he came to present it in the *Principles,* he discovered that

it did not work. When it came to actually giving a deduction, he found that he had no deduction to give, even given his broad notion of deduction, and he was forced to return to his hypothetical mode of argument.

Before continuing with the argument, though, an alternative explanation for Descartes's use of hypotheses must be considered. There is a strong suggestion in these texts that Descartes may think he can deduce the hypotheses in question from first principles, but is reluctant to make that claim explicitly or display the deductions for religious reasons. The hypotheses that Descartes frames in *Principles* III. 46 relate to the original state of the universe. Might Descartes have suppressed his deduction and, in fact, even labeled the hypotheses false, in order to avoid a clash with the doctrine of creation in Genesis? This is suggested by considerations raised in *Principles* III. 45 and later in *Principles* IV. 1. But I find it implausible to suppose here that Descartes is purposely hiding a deduction. It is clear that he did not think that he could give a direct, nonexperiential deduction of the sort originally promised in section B, since he does admit with respect to the particles that made up the original state of the universe that "we cannot determine by reason how big these pieces of matter are, how quickly they move, or what circles they describe. God might have arranged these things in countless different ways" (AT 8(1):100-101; AG 225). This leaves open the possibility of a suppressed argument by enumeration, and Descartes suggests just this when he immediately comments that "which way he [God] in fact chose rather than the rest is a thing we must learn from experience." But in order to argue deductively from experience he would have to show that the hypothesis he adopts is the only one consistent with experience. The most he claims about these hypotheses is that he cannot imagine any principles that are "more simple or easier to understand, or indeed more credible [*probabiliora*]" (III. 47: AT 8(1):102; AG 225). Nowhere does he even suggest that the hypotheses in question are the only possible ones. In fact, in *Principles* III. 48 he suggests that a number of different hypotheses, including the assumption of initial chaos, would work just as well. So a suppressed argument by enumeration is also ruled out. The idea that Descartes has a deductive argument in mind will be made still more implausible when we later note the changes in the place of certainty in Descartes's theory of science, changes that he would hardly have made if he really had deduction in question. I would claim that Descartes is not presenting something he can deduce as a hypothesis for religious reasons, but rather, he seems to be appealing to religious considerations to hide the fact that he cannot make the deduction.[38]

Though, as it turns out, Descartes finds in practice that he has to appeal to hypotheses, there is evidence in the *Principles* that this is a move that Descartes strenuously resisted. In *Principles* III. 43, there is still the strong implication that a deduction is possible, even if, as it turned out, Descartes was not able to give one. And in *Principles* III. 4, as we have already seen, Descartes interrupts his deductions to consider some observed phenomena, with the promise that he will return to deduction. There is another notable instance of the earlier deductivism embedded in the account of the magnet given in *Principles* IV. There Descartes claims to have shown how the nature of the magnet follows (*sequentur*) from the principles of nature (*ex principiis Naturae*) (IV. 145; AT 8(1):284). Of course, if the principles of nature include the material of *Principles* II, then the hypothetical mode of reasoning introduced in *Principles* III. 44, makes such a claim obviously false. Another interesting passage is at the very end of *Principles* IV where Descartes is describing the way in which he claims to have found the nature of particulars:

> Starting from the simplest and most familiar principles which are implanted in our understanding by nature, I have considered in general the chief possible differences in size, shape, and position between bodies whose mere minuteness makes them insensible, and the sensible effects of their various interactions. When I have observed similar effects among sensible things, I judged [*existimasse*] that they arose from similar interactions among such bodies, especially since this appeared to be the only possible way of explaining them.

> [IV. 203: AT 8(1):325-26; HR 1:299]

What is notable about this passage, besides the apparent reference to version B of the argument by enumeration, is the fact that, while Descartes was claiming to be describing his practice, there is no mention of any general hypotheses of the sort required in *Principles* III. My conjecture is that these last three passages, *Principles* III. 4, IV. 145, and IV. 203 were all written at an earlier stage in the composition of the *Principles,* when Descartes still thought that it would be possible to iron out the wrinkle in the argument of *Principles* III and before he realized that he would have to appeal to hypotheses. Their presence in the completed *Principles* suggests that it was not until the final stages in the composition of the *Principles* that Descartes finally realized that he had to argue hypothetically. This in turn supports my claim that Descartes attempted to give a wholly deductive argument in the *Principles*, but found in the end that he could not.

The deductive chain is broken in practice, and the argument offered is hypothetical. Starting in *Principles* III. 44, the only standard for correctness Descartes actually uses in practice is that theory should agree with experience. What is particularly interesting is that Descartes did not even have to get as far as section C of our outline from the *Discourse* before deduction

failed. Deduction fails in the material that corresponds to B, where Descartes earlier seemed quite confident of being able to produce deductive arguments without having to appeal to experiment. Insofar as he argues hypothetically about his entire cosmology and his general theory of the world, his explanations of the nature of particulars must fail to have deductive certainty as well. Even if he *could* give deductive arguments with regard to the nature of particulars from his cosmology, they would not be true deductions, because they begin not with certainties, but with hypotheses.

So far we have been talking about Descartes's scientific practice. We have noted that there he makes do with hypothetical arguments. But what of the earlier goal of certainty? For this we must turn back to his program for science. In the earlier works, Descartes could tolerate a great deal of divergence between his theory of science and his scientific practice. But insofar as it was Descartes's seeming intention to realize his program in the *Principles,* such divergence should be an embarrassment. Thus we find that, although Descartes resisted the use of hypothetical reasoning as long as he could, once he finally adopted it his attitude seemed to change. Evidently, if the world will not bend to fit his conception of science, Descartes must bend his conception of science to fit the world. In the *Principles,* hypotheses and hypothetical reasoning seem no longer quite as objectionable as they earlier were in the *Regulae* and in the *Discourse*. Having come to them out of necessity (if my claim is correct) Descartes comes close to embracing them in his theory of science as acceptable modes of reasoning. The first hint of this is in *Principles* III. 44, where Descartes remarks:

> Even if this the hypothesis be thought to be false, I shall think my achievement is sufficiently worth while if all inferences from it agree with observation; for in that case we shall get as much practical benefit from it as we should from the knowledge of the actual truth.

> [AT 8(1):99; AG 224]

Descartes here seems to indicate that it is sufficient for a science to agree with the data of experiment. Truth (not to mention certain truth) seems not to matter.

This position is the one Descartes seems to adopt at the very end of the *Principles*. Descartes admits that, at best, what he has provided is an account of things that agrees with experiment and observation, but which may not give us truth. But, he claims, this is his only goal:

> I believe that *I have done all that is required of me* if the causes I have assigned are such that they *correspond to all the phenomena manifested by nature*. And it will be sufficient for the usages of

life to know such causes, for medicine and mechanics and in general all these arts to which the knowledge of physics subserves, have for their end only those effects which are sensible and which are accordingly to be reckoned among the phenomena of nature.

> [IV. 204: AT 8(1):327; HR 1:300.
> Emphasis added.]

In the course of claiming that all he seeks is an explanation that agrees with the phenomena, Descartes admits that such an account is less than absolutely certain. To put it another way, Descartes admits that this way of proceeding, which he was forced to adopt, yields not true knowledge, or true certainty, but only *moral* certainty:

> *That nevertheless there is a moral certainty that everything is such as I have shown it to be.*

> In fairness to the truth, however, it must be borne in mind that some things are considered as morally certain—certain for all practical purposes—although they are uncertain if we take into account God's absolute power. . . . They who observe how many things regarding the magnet, fire, and the fabric of the whole world are deduced from so few principles *even if they thought my assumption of those principles haphazard and groundless,* would admit that so many things could hardly cohere if they were false.

> [IV. 205: AT 8(1):327-28; HR 1:301.
> Emphasis added.]

So, Descartes claims, the results established in the *Principles,* at least as regards the sensible world, are established with moral certainty. But it should be quite evident that moral certainty is just a species of probability. And this, he argues, is quite sufficient and "all that is required" of him.[39]

The progression in Descartes's thought from the *Regulae,* through the *Discourse* and contemporary writings, ending up in the *Principles,* is quite remarkable. In the *Regulae,* Descartes is quite opposed to all use of probabilities in science, including the use of hypotheses or assumptions. All true scientific reasoning must be able to be formulated in terms of intuition and deduction. The attitude changes somewhat in the *Discourse* and other writings of the same period. There Descartes does make use of hypothetical and consequently nondeductive arguments. However, he consistently insists that such hypothetical arguments do not mean that he has abandoned the search for a deductive science. Rather, he claims to use such arguments as a matter of convenience, so as not to have to give the full argument in all of its deductive glory. He claims, at this point, to be able to give full deductive arguments for everything that he presents hypothetically. But in the *Principles,* it turns out not to be possible to

give the full deductions, though he tries. Although he resists, he finds that he must make use of hypotheses, and in the end, seems finally to give up hope of a certain science grounded in intuition and deduction. In the end the practical difficulties of building a science from intuition and deduction force an important change in his very conception of science: scientific knowledge has become probable knowledge, it seems.

Although I say that in the end, Descartes gave up his earlier program and was willing to make do with moral certainty and probability, this is probably too strong a statement. Though in the passages I quoted from the end of the *Principles* Descartes does give this impression, it is also clear that he is not at all comfortable with this position. Before ending the *Principles,* in the penultimate section he says:

> *That we possess even more than a moral certainty.*

> Moreover there are certain things even among natural objects that we judge to be absolutely and mathematical demonstrations, the knowledge that material objects exist, and all evident reasonings about them. And with these my own assertions may perhaps find a place when it is considered how they have been deduced in an unbroken chain from the simplest primary principles of human knowledge. And the more so if it is sufficiently realized that we can have no sensation of external objects unless they excite some local motion in our nerves, and that the fixed stars, being a vast distance from us, can excite no such motion unless there is also some motion taking place in them and in the whole of the intermediate heavens; for once these facts are admitted, then, at least as regards the general account I have given of the world and the Earth, an alternative to the rest of my explanation appears inconceivable.

> [IV. 206: AT 8(1):328-29; HR 1:301-2]

So, having admitted that probability is all we can have, Descartes makes one last attempt at saving his old program for certainty in science.

Descartes's extreme reluctance to give up his deductive program is also manifest in the introduction he wrote for Abbé Picot's French translation of the *Principles* in 1647, fully three years after the original Latin edition. There Descartes talks quite emphatically about how the proper method in science is to "seek out the first causes and the true principles from which reasons may be deduced for all that we are capable of knowing."[40] This apparent forgetfulness of the difficulties encountered in *Principles* III shows just how tentative Descartes's rejection of deductivism at the end of the *Principles* was, and how uncomfortable he was with that conclusion.

Although Descartes is forced to admit, however unwillingly and tentatively, that natural science cannot be deductive and certain, it is only later in the history of philosophy that deductivism is decisively rejected and natural science is unambiguously associated with the probable. This stop occurs in a philosopher usually counted among Descartes's contraries, but who is in some ways the direct successor to his enterprise, John Locke.[41] For Locke, knowledge is not the only product of the rational faculties. Unlike Descartes, he takes the notion of probability to be an important one for epistemology.[42] Knowledge for Locke is very close to Descartes's conception of certainty, in that the primary ways of attaining knowledge are intuition and deduction.[43] But Locke is aware of the narrow extent to which we have genuine scientific knowledge of material things in the world.[44] This conclusion has caused many to consider Locke a skeptic. But Locke's conclusion is not that we must despair with respect to scientific knowledge, but that where there is no certainty or true knowledge, we must make do with probability. In natural science this means that we must make do with experiment, and whatever can be inferred from experiment by a basically hypothetico-deductive reasoning.[45] It was, then, Locke who took the final step in the retreat from the certainty and deductivism of the *Regulae*. But it was a step that Descartes prepared in his *Principles*.

Notes

[1] The traditional view is too widespread to require citation. On the latter view, see e.g., A. Gewirth, "Experience and the Non-Mathematical in the Cartesian Method," *Journal of the History of Ideas* 2 (1941):183-210; R. M. Blake, "The Role of Experience in Descartes' Theory of Method," in E. H. Madden, ed., *Theories of Scientific Method* (Seattle, 1960); L. J. Beck, *The Method of Descartes* (Oxford, 1952); G. Buchdahl, *Metaphysics and the Philosophy of Science* (Cambridge, Mass., 1969); A. C. Crombie, "Some Aspects of Descartes' Attitude to Hypothesis and Experiment," *Collection des Travaux de l'Academie International d'Histoire des Sciences* 11 (1960):192-201; and the introduction in *Discourse on Method, Optics, Geometry, and Meteorology* trans. P. J. Olscamp (Indianapolis, 1965).

[2] Throughout I have given a reference to an English translation of the passage, when possible to HR [René Descartes; *The Philosophical Works of Descartes;* trans. Elizabeth S. Haldane and G. R. T. Ross; Cambridge: Cambridge University Press, 1911-12; reprinted, with corrections, 1931; reprinted New York: Dover, 1955]. The translations used in the text, though, usually come from other sources, since there are many inaccuracies in HR, particularly in the *Regulae*. I have consulted: AG [Descartes, *Philosophical Writings,* trans. and ed. Elizabeth Anscombe and Peter Thomas Geach, London: Nelson, 1954]; CB [Descartes, *Descartes' Conversation with Burman,* trans. and ed. John Cottingham, Oxford: Clarendon Press, 1976]; K [Descartes,

Philosophical Letters, trans. and ed. Anthony Kenny, Oxford: Clarendon Press, 1970]; *Rules for the Direction of the Mind* (Indianapolis: 1961), and *Discourse on Method and Meditations* (Indianapolis: 1960) both translated by L. J. Lafleur; *Discourse,* trans. Olscamp. When no translation is available in HR, I will refer to the otherwise most available translation.

[3] See Gewirth, "Experience in the Cartesian Method"; Blake, "Role of Experience"; Buchdahl, *Metaphysics;* and Beck, *Method of Descartes.*

[4] Emphasis added. See also AT 10:366, 368 (the text here is disputed), 370, 400; HR 1:5, 7, 8, 28.

[5] Cf. *Regulae,* Rule VI: AT 10:381-83; HR 1:15-16.

[6] Emphasis added. See also AT 10:440; HR 1:55.

[7] Alternatively, a deduction may be a proposition arrived at through such a succession of intuitively made inferential leaps. Descartes recognizes the ambiguity in his use. See *Regulae,* Rule XI: AT 10:407-8; HR 1:33.

[8] See *Regulae:* AT 10:368, 401, 416, 418, 425, 427; HR 1:7, 28, 39, 41, 45, 46.

[9] For a rare exception, see the letter to Regius, 24 May 1640: AT 3:64-65; K 73-74.

[10] Presenting the criterion of certainty in this way leaves out the problems of validation and atheistic science discussed in the letter cited in note 9.

[11] Emphasis added. Cf. AT 5:177; CB 48-49.

[12] See, e.g., Aristotle, *Topics,* 100^{a}18-21 and 100^{b}21-23, and the various Latin translations in *Aristoteles Latinus,* ed. L. Minio-Paluello, 5:1-3 (Leiden, 1969) for the use of the world *probabilis.*

[13] See I. Hacking, *The Emergence of Probability* (Cambridge: 1975), ch. 3. Hacking's account is not entirely accurate in that it emphasizes the use of this archaic notion of probability and ignores quite definite instances of distinctly modern probability concepts in antiquity and the Middle Ages.

[14] Cf. *Regulae:* AT 10:367; HR 1:6; and *Discourse:* AT 6:6, 8, 16, 69, 71; HR 1:84, 85-86, 91, 124, 125. For studies of the rhetorical-dialectical tradition of education in the 16th century see W. S. Howell, *Logic and Rhetoric in England, 1500-1700* (Princeton, 1956); N. W. Gilbert, *Renaissance Concepts of Method* (New York, 1960); and W. J. Ong, *Ramus, Method, and the Decay of Dialectic* (Cambridge, Mass., 1958).

[15] See also AT 10:424 and HR 1:44-45. There is some

dispute about this last text.

[16] There are at least two places in the *Regulae* where Descartes uses hypotheses. Cf. *Regulae,* Rule XII: AT 10:412, 417; HR 1:36, 40. Nothing Descartes says here throws light on the epistemic status of hypotheses.

[17] Precisely what Descartes included here and what he meant to include among the "particulars" of C is not entirely clear. But this will not be an issue.

[18] Cf. *Discourse,* part V: AT 6:45; HR 1:109.

[19] Cf., e.g., introduction in *Discourse,* trans. Olscamp; Buchdahl, *Metaphysics;* and J. Morris, "Descartes and Probable Knowledge," *Journal of the History of Philosophy* 8 (1970):303-12.

[20] Cf. *Optics,* discourse I: AT 6:83-88; trans. Olscamp, 67-70; and *Meteorology,* discourse I: AT 6:233-35; trans. Olscamp, 264-65.

[21] Cf. P. Duhem, *To Save the Phenomena* (Chicago, 1969). Duhem has a definite philosophical ax to grind, but he has presented a very accurate and useful catalogue of historical citations on the question.

[22] See ibid., pp. 61-65, 96-97, 100-104, 108-9.

[23] *Discourse,* part VI: AT 6:76; HR 1:128-29. What precisely Descartes means by "prove" and "explain" in this text are interesting questions, but ones that I shall not enter into.

[24] See AT 2:141-44, 197-99; K 55-56, 57-58.

[25] Emphasis added. See also AT 2:196-200; K 57-59; and AT 3:39; K 70-71.

[26] Emphasis added. Cf. AT 2:200; K 59; and AT 3:39; K 71.

[27] The only passage I know of that is at all difficult to reconcile with this reading is from a letter to Mersenne, 17 May 1638: AT 2:141-44; K 55-56. Read in the context of the other passages cited, though, this letter does not raise any serious problems for my view.

[28] This is a curious thing for Descartes to say, though, given that he thinks that Harvey's theory is inconsistent with the basic principles of his physics.

[29] The difficulty of enumerating possible explanations may not be insuperable, since, given the first principles Descartes is working with, there may be a rather limited set of possible explanations for any given phenomenon. This was pointed out to me by David Kolb.

[30] Cf. *Discourse,* part IV: AT 6:33-35; HR 1:102-3; and Meditation III: AT 7:40-45; HR 1:161-65. My schematic version is closer to the text of the *Discourse.*

[31] Cf. Meditation VI: AT 2:79-80; HR 1:191.

[32] Cf. Gewirth, "Experience in the Cartesian Method," part III.

[33] Contrast *Regulae,* Rule II: AT 10:365; HR 1:4-5, with Rule V: AT 10:380; HR 1:14-15.

[34] "Enumeration" in the *Regulae* seems to have a narrower meaning than later on. There, enumeration is characteristically the process of going through the steps of a deduction in order—cf. Rules VII and XI. However, elsewhere in the *Regulae* it seems to take on a broader meaning; see AT 10:390, 395, 404-5 and HR 1:21, 24, 31. Cf. also Gewirth, "Experience in the Cartesian Method," pp. 200-201, and Beck, *Method of Descartes,* pp. 126-33. In the *Discourse* it clearly has a broader meaning still.

[35] Cf. *Regulae:* AT 10:410, 427, 430-31, 434-35, 439; HR 1:35, 46-47, 49-50, 52, 54-55. The argument suggested in these passages is close to version B of the argument by enumeration. In Gewirth, "Experience in the Cartesian Method," pp. 198-99, a similar interpretation of these passages is suggested.

[36] See, e.g., AT 2:200; K 59.

[37] The claim that he seeks arguments from cause to effect suggests that it is not an argument by enumeration, a kind of argument from effect to cause like that of section C, that Descartes has in mind here, but a more straightforward sort of deduction as described in B. On the other hand, as I noted in section II, above, the argument by enumeration can be considered as a kind of argument from cause to effect.

[38] For Descartes's later remarks on this, see, e.g., AT 4:698; and AT 5:168-69; CB 36-37. In the latter passage, dating from 1648, Descartes tells Burman that he thinks that he *could* give an explanation (a *deductive* explanation?) consistent with Genesis and his first principles. However, he admits both that Genesis is difficult to interpret, and that he has not found a satisfactory account yet.

[39] This is not, by the way, the first time that the notion of moral certainty comes up in Descartes' writings. It is mentioned a few times in the *Discourse,* and in the correspondence—e.g., *Discourse:* AT 6:37, 56, 57; HR 1:104, 116. But it is not until the *Principles* that Descartes even suggests that moral certainty is sufficient in science.

[40] AT 9(2):5; HR 1:206. Cf. AT 9(2):2, 9-11, 12-13;

HR 1:204, 208-9, 210. Note that his account of the role and necessity of experiment in scientific deduction accords perfectly with my account in section II, above. Cf. AT 9(2):20; HR 1:214.

[41] I do not want to suggest that Locke is the only such figure; he is the most influential of those to follow Descartes, and the one responsible for breaking the influence of Cartesian deductivism. Other 17th-century figures did reject deductivism as well; see, e.g., Pierre Gassendi, *Dissertations en forme de Pareadoxes contre les Aristotéliciens* (*Exercitationes Paradoxicae Adversus Aristoteleos*) trans. and ed. Bernard Rochot (Paris, 1959), liber secundus, exercitatio V.

[42] *Essay* IV, ch. 1, 14, 15. All references to Locke are from *An Essay Concerning Human Understanding,* ed. P. H. Nidditch (Oxford, 1975). The references are given in such a way as to be locatable in any currently used edition.

[43] See *Essay* IV, ch. 2. Locke adds sensation to Descartes's account. But his conception of sensation makes it look like a species of Cartesian intuition. *Essay* IV, ch. 11.

[44] See *Essay* IV, ch. 3 (sect. 9-17, 25-26), 4 (sect. 11-12), 6 (sect. 10-15).

[45] Above, notes 42-44, *Essay* IV, ch. 16 (sect. 12).

Charles Larmore (essay date 1980)

SOURCE: "Descartes' Empirical Epistemology," in *Descartes: Philosophy, Mathematics and Physics,* edited by Stephen Gaukroger, The Harvester Press, Sussex, 1980, pp. 6-22.

[*In the essay that follows, Larmore contends that Descartes' epistemology uses experimentation within a framework of* a priori *principles to advance human knowledge.*]

There is something close to a general consensus that Descartes initiated a search for incorrigible foundations of knowledge that deeply shaped modern philosophy and that we have now learned to reject or even ignore. Characteristic of the Cartesian search for certainty, as opposed for example to some tendencies in Greek thought, was that these foundations must be located in individual subjectivity, in our immediate awareness of our own mental states. It implied that unless we could show how our beliefs about the world could be legitimately inferred from this basis, they would have no more rightful claim to being knowledge than would our wildest fantasies.

All the different kinds of errors that lie at the heart of

the foundationalist enterprise do not need rehearsing once again. More directly of interest is the fact that a number of philosophers have taken the demise of this enterprise to mean the end of epistemology itself. What else can epistemology be but the search for the incorrigible foundations of knowledge? If that is so, then epistemology indeed amounts only to a subject with a glorious past. But this is not the proper conclusion to draw. The rejected forms of epistemology proved barren because they restricted themselves to the search for incorrigible truths, untainted by the revisability of the empirical truths they were meant to support. To discard epistemology as a dead subject no longer of interest to living philosophy, for this reason alone, merely continues the original error of believing that the theory of knowledge must be kept pure of all dependence upon the empirical sciences.

There are two areas of inquiry whose pursuit would dissociate epistemology from the ideal of a *prima philosophia.* First of all, we can focus the theory of knowledge upon examples of scientific knowledge in order to formulate criteria of scientific rationality. However, if we are to escape the ideal of a pure epistemology, we must draw out these criteria in a dialectical way from the history of science. Crudely put, we must abstract the criteria from some theories in order both to evaluate other theories in terms of them and to test the criteria against other examples of theories. Otherwise we may find ourselves, as indeed has often been the case in the philosophy of science, stuck with criteria of scientific rationality that no scientific theory has ever met. Obviously, the problems facing this kind of empirical epistemology are immensely difficult. Secondly, we can allow the theory of knowledge to confront what scientific theories imply about the status of our perceptual and experiential image of nature and about the relation between nature and ourselves as knowers. Here the concerns of an empirical epistemology would not be as in the first case methodological, but instead substantive. They would focus upon how we are to understand human knowledge given what we know about the world.

If with these possibilities of an empirical epistemology in mind we look once again at Descartes' theory of knowledge, the traditional picture of Descartes as the founder of *a priori* epistemology begins to appear importantly incomplete. As I shall show in this essay, his search for an incorrigible foundation of empirical knowledge forms but one strand in his theory of knowledge. There are other epistemological problems for whose solution he deliberately resorted to the results of empirical inquiry. First, it might be recalled, in regard to the project of setting out criteria of scientific rationality, that he recommended his idea of scientific method *because* he had found it successful. However, I shall be concerned with the more substantive area of his empirical epistemology, especially as it grows out of his attempt at the mathematization of nature. In the light of these generally ignored aspects of Cartesian philosophy, we will no longer be able to foist upon Descartes the onus of having encouraged the idea that an *a priori* approach is *all* to which epistemology may aspire. Indeed, for the whole of the seventeenth century the theory of knowledge brought together both *a priori* and empirical perspectives. In Descartes, the relation between these strands is governed by a conception of method, whereas in Locke, for example, the character of their relation is far less clear. The origin of the idea that epistemology, as a philosophical discipline, must proceed independently of the sciences belongs to a later time. It arises both with Kantian transcendentalism and with the more recent wish to analyse 'the meaning of the concept of knowledge'. One aim of this essay is to indicate why we need a more complex picture of the origins of modern epistemology in the seventeenth century. But, more directly, the aspects of Descartes' empirical epistemology which I shall treat will be among those that can still interest us today.

It is chiefly in his physiological treatises, such as the **Treatise on Man** and the **Dioptrics,** that we come upon his empirical epistemology. But in order to understand why at a certain point Descartes let his epistemology become empirical, we will first have to look at his conception of scientific method (Part I). In Part II I shall examine the initial physical problem—the mathematization of nature—with which his empirical epistemology begins, then tracing in Part III the broad implications he drew from that for an understanding of the place of knowledge within the natural order.

Part I Descartes' Conception of Scientific Method

Recently it has become increasingly clear just how erroneous was the traditional view that Descartes thought of physical inquiry as a strictly *a priori* concern. We can find no better proof of the untenability of that view than to listen to what Descartes himself had to say in the **Discourse on Method** about the respective roles of the *a priori* and experience:

> I have first tried to discover generally the principles or first causes of everything that is or that can be in the world, without considering anything that might accomplish this end but God Himself. . . . But I must also confess that the power of nature is so ample and vast, and these principles are so simple and general, that I observed hardly any particular effect as to which I could not at once recognize that it might be deduced from the principles in many different ways; and my greatest difficulty is usually to discover in which of these ways the effect does depend on them. As to that, I do not know any other plan but again to try to find experiments of such a nature that their result is not the same if it has to be explained by one of the methods, as it would be if explained by the other.[1]

Thus, according to Descartes, an account of the physical make-up of the world falls into two distinct parts: one we can develop *a priori,* while the other makes essential use of experience. The 'principles or first causes', that cover the most general features of the world, are something that we can attain without appeal to experience or experiment. In this passage Descartes was referring to what he believed he had already accomplished in his earlier treatise **Le Monde.** There, from God's immutability alone, he had derived the three fundamental laws of nature:

1 Every bit of matter continues in the same state until constrained to change by encountering some other object.

2 When one body alters the state of another, it cannot give it any movement which it itself does not lose at the same time.

3 Every body tends to continue to move in a straight line.[2]

The same claim, that the validity of these laws has an *a priori* basis in an understanding of what it means for there to be a God, reappears in the **Discourse** and in the **Principles** as well.[3] These laws of nature can be said to be true *a priori,* of course, only because Descartes thought that he could prove the existence of such a God in a purely *a priori* fashion, and not by means of some natural theology. Both the causal and the ontological proof take as a premise that I do have a concept of something than which nothing greater can be conceived. That I do have the ideas that I believe I do, whatever may be their material truth, is a result guaranteed by the indubitability of the *cogito.* Thus, contrary to what has been sometimes suggested, the *cogito* does play an essential role in the foundation of physical science. It lies at the basis, Descartes believed, of the *a priori* deduction of the three fundamental laws of nature.

It is important to notice how this *a priori* part of Cartesian physics lies on a continuum with *a priori* epistemology. For Descartes, *a priori* epistemology does not issue simply in a prescription for the kinds of propositions that should serve as foundations (that, of course, is the role that more recent phenomenalist epistemologies have taken on). Instead, the *cogito* and the proofs of God's existence imply, so he believed, the fundamental principles of physical science themselves. This continuity between *a priori* epistemology and *a priori* physics should be borne in mind when we come to consider the continuity between physical theory and Descartes' empirical epistemology. It will become clear that it is his conception of scientific method that orders the *a priori* and empirical parts of the theory of knowledge and the theory of nature into a single enterprise. Now this *a priori* physics cannot, as we have seen

Descartes admit, yield a complete picture of the physical world. Only the most general features of the world can be ascertained through deduction from the self-evident first principles. For example, from the three fundamental laws of nature he thought he could deduce the laws of impact among bodies. In *Principles* III, art 46 there occurs a passage where Descartes lists some of the more particular phenomena that we can uncover only through empirical inquiry: the size of the parts into which matter is divided, the speed with which they move, and what circles their movements describe. Clearly, this range of empirical phenomena consists in the numerical values that in any particular case can be given to the variables occuring in the *a priori* laws of motion and their deductive consequences. In the passage cited from the *Discourse* at the beginning of this section, he mentions another area of necessarily empirical inquiry. From the *a priori* laws alone we cannot determine what, in fact, is the mechanical constitution of many of the phenomena we observe. This is the domain of empirical inquiry that will be important in what follows. His empirical epistemology will depend upon understanding the operation of the human eye, for which he will appeal to empirical physiology as well as to a theory of the mechanical nature of light which he found himself forced to justify empirically.

Descartes thus believed that scientific inquiry must begin with an *a priori* demonstration of first principles and then, once the scope of *a priori* physics has been exhausted, it must turn to the construction of empirical hypotheses. Since earlier works like the *Regulae* often suggest a thoroughly aprioristic method, it is with his mature conception of scientific method that I shall henceforth be concerned.[4]

Those explanatory propositions belonging to the empirical part of physical inquiry Descartes himself termed 'hypotheses'. He said that if the consequences of an hypothesis agree with experience and, more particularly, if by way of a crucial experiment they agree with an experimental phenomenon that the deductive consequences of rival hypotheses fail to match, then we have every reason to believe that the hypothesis is true.[5] (It is to be remembered that the Cartesian idea of deduction is broader than the logical concept of deduction—it covers any sequence of propositions where we perceive 'clearly and distinctly' that the conclusion follows from the premises.)

The hypothetico-deductive method, for Descartes, belongs only to the empirical part of physical theory; it does not touch the fundamental laws of nature and their deductive consequences. There is, of course, the famous passage at the close of the *Principles* (IV, art 204) where Descartes refers to the whole of his physical theory as an hypothesis whose truth can be guaranteed only by the match between its deductive consequences and experience. This and similar passages have

sometimes encouraged the view either that toward the end of his life Descartes had begun to doubt his ability to demonstrate any *a priori* physical truths or that, in fact, he had never had that ambition.[6] But this interpretation of the passage is seriously mistaken. At *Principles* IV, art 205, he says that the hypothetico-deductive method can give us only a 'moral certainty' in the truth of an hypothesis; by this he means that when an hypothesis coheres with the phenomena we have no reason to doubt its truth, though of course it could still possibly be false. But in the subsequent section (IV, art 206) he goes on to claim that about a number of propositions we have more than moral certainty, we have in fact 'metaphysical certainty', once we understand that God exists. These propositions are ones that we can deduce from God's existence and include, not only that we can indeed distinguish the true from the false, but also mathematical truths and physical truths that are equally self-evident. These physical truths are, he says, 'the principal and more general ones'—in other words, the three fundamental laws of nature. Thus, Descartes' position at the end of the *Principles* does not differ from what he said in the *Discourse*. His point in the final passages of the *Principles* where he describes the whole of his physical theory as an hypothesis is simply that, *if* we were not able to give an *a priori* demonstration of certain basic physical truths, they too would then have to assume the status of confirmable but ultimately corrigible hypotheses.[7]

Descartes' thesis that propositions lacking an *a priori* demonstration must be treated as hypotheses and tested by means of crucial experiments had an important methodological consequence. If we believe that principles explaining some physical phenomenon can be deduced from other self-evident principles but we do not see yet how the demonstration can be set up, we are not forced to let that part of physical theory lie fallow. Instead, we can admit those principles to the corpus of scientific knowledge if their experimental consequences are borne out. Later, of course, we could return to give them the *a priori* demonstration they deserve. This is, in fact, precisely what Descartes did in the *Dioptrics* and *Meteorology*. Instead of being demonstrated *a priori,* the mechanical nature of light has in these treatises the status of an hypothesis, from which he sought to deduce both the laws of refraction and, along with physiological data, the operation of the human eye.[8] In the *Discourse on Method,* he maintained that in these treatises he has merely withheld the *a priori* demonstration of this hypothesis that he already possesses. But in a more candid letter to Mersenne of 17 May 1638 (shortly after the publication of the *Discourse* and the *Dioptrics*) he confessed that an *a priori* demonstration of the mechanical nature of light is still only a confident hope.[9]

I shall not comment here upon some of the insights about hypothetico-deductive method that Descartes had acquired at this time, such as the importance of consilient confirmations or the way the experimental confirmation of an hypothesis turns on its comparison with competing ones.[10] Of chief concern for our purposes is that we recognize how a combination of *a priori* and empirical elements formed an abiding feature of Descartes' mature conception of scientific method. Naturally, there can be no question that he continually sought to render empirical hypotheses as certain as possible. The two principal ways that he considered for increasing their certainty lay either in giving them, at last, an *a priori* demonstration or in setting up crucial experiments to decide between competing hypotheses. However, he did not believe that every hypothesis could be brought into the first path of certainty. Although he seems never to have ceased hoping for an *a priori* proof of the mechanical nature of light, he never dreamed of finding this sort of demonstration for other hypotheses, such as how the human eye operates. For this kind of phenomenon we could only try, in accordance with the Fourth Rule of Method, for as complete an enumeration as possible of all the relevant hypotheses; then by appropriate experiments we could hopefully narrow the range of hypotheses to one.[11] Clearly, this sort of quest for certainty is one that any rational inquiry must share.

The significant fact, then, about Descartes' mature conception of scientific method is not only that *a priori* demonstration and empirical testing form the means of justifying different parts of physical theory, but also the *a priori* area should be explored as far as possible before empirical investigation begins. Even if the ideal of *a priori* demonstration in physics now seems not just untenable, but perverse, we might still recognize an important truth dimly perceived in Descartes' conception of method. The building of empirical hypotheses should take place within a research programme (like the mechanism expressed in Descartes' *a priori* laws) that sets down some general constraints on permissible modes of explanation, indicates what are the important problems to tackle, and even has something to say about what will count as an acceptable solution—while itself having a far more indirect relation to empirical confirmation. However, instead of pursuing further this somewhat anachronistic line of thought, I shall now examine how, as his physical science shifts from the *a priori* to the empirical, Descartes' theory of knowledge takes up a new set of concerns.

Part II The Mathematization of Nature

As I mentioned at the beginning, there has in recent years been an increasing awareness of the extent to which Descartes meant physical inquiry to be empirical. This is so, even if these new treatments of Cartesian physics have often failed to capture, I believe, just what the role of empirical inquiry was for Descartes. But what has gone unnoticed altogether is that a central area of his empirical science has to do with investigating the character of human knowledge itself and its place in nature. Not only nature, but our knowledge of nature as well comes within the scope of inquiry turned empirical. This is what I shall be calling Descartes' empirical epistemology.

In order to understand how an empirical epistemology can emerge for Descartes, we might picture the Cartesian conception of inquiry as a grand circle. *A priori* epistemology provides the premises for *a priori* physical theory, but since such theory falls far short of giving a complete account of nature it must be supplemented by empirical hypotheses. But these hypotheses in turn can serve to deepen our understanding of the nature of human knowledge, from whose *a priori* insights the whole process set out. The path of inquiry, beginning with the *a priori* truths and then moving into the empirical, doubles back on itself in this way just because—in contrast to much of the philosophy that came after him—Descartes conceived of the theory of nature and the theory of knowledge as lying on a continuum, instead of being wholly different enterprises.

In fact, his empirical epistemology begins precisely at the point at which physical inquiry turns empirical. The character of physical inquiry shifts into a different key with the following questions. Are the qualities attributed to bodies by the *a priori* laws of nature—the mathematical qualities of extension, figure, and motion—the only qualities that physical bodies really have, contrary to what our perceptual experience would indicate? Or does physical theory concern itself only with certain properties of bodies, while abstracting from others? This problem concerns, of course, the mathematization of nature; since the mathematical qualities in question are geometrical ones (to the detriment of Cartesian physics), more exactly it is a geometricization of nature. Descartes' important insight, either overlooked or not pursued by his predecessors, from Cusanus to Galileo, who had espoused the programme of mathematizing nature, was that the development of this programme must proceed in tandem with a theory of perception that shows both that our ideas of nonmathematical properties, such as colour, resemble nothing in nature and that their occurrence is explicable in terms of a mathematical physics. Furthermore, the mathematization of nature was an empirical project. That is so, because he believed that the needed theory of perception must rest upon empirical hypotheses dealing with how the human eye works and what the nature of light is.

To be sure, the hypotheses that Descartes advanced about the structure of our perceptual system, in order to meet the mathematization of nature problem, form part of physiological theory. To what I am calling his empirical theory of knowledge belong, rather, the broad implications he drew from this to describe the relation between our scientific and perceptual images of nature as well as our relation as knowers to the natural order. Perhaps it may be objected that these are not 'philosophical' issues, supposedly because their pursuit must proceed against the backdrop of our knowledge of nature. Definitions of what counts as 'philosophical' are never very fruitful. Their usual intent is to exonerate the philosopher who makes them from having to learn anything about the areas of inquiry they exclude. Problems are a better guide than definitions. If our problem is to understand the relation between scientific knowledge and experience and the place of knowledge in nature, then a philosophical treatment of this problem is one that tries to approach it in the broadest possible way, making use of anything that may be appropriate. This was also Descartes' conception of philosophy, as the use of both *a priori* and empirical approaches to understand mind and nature in a book entitled ***The Principles of Philosophy*** would indicate. In this section, I shall discuss his mathematization of nature and the consequences he drew from it for an understanding of the relation between the scientific and perceptual images of nature. Descartes also exploited his physiological work to describe the place of knowledge within the natural order, and this I shall discuss in the subsequent section.

First, let us see just how the mathematization problem emerges as Cartesian physical inquiry becomes empirical. The three fundamental laws of nature and their deductive consequences are true *a priori* and characterize any possible physical world. That there does indeed exist such a world is something we infer, according to Descartes, from the fact that we experience many of our ideas as something passive, as a mental state caused by external objects, and that we have a divine guarantee that whatever we so clearly and distinctly perceive to be true must be true. Thus, once we see that there is a world of objects and movements, we may then conclude that it falls under the rubric of a 'physical world' governed by such *a priori* laws.[12] Here the mathematization problem first presents itself. Do objects really have only the properties mentioned by these laws?

Significantly, Descartes did not try to establish the mathematization of nature apart from an appeal to empirical considerations, at least in his mature period. He frequently extolled the greater clarity and distinctness enjoyed by perceptions of extension, figure and motion, in contrast to the obscurity affecting perceptions of colour or of hot and cold. But in none of these passages did he make use of this greater clarity to establish the mathematization of nature; it is always some other point that he was concerned to make.[13] In fact, there is a letter that Descartes wrote to Chanut, several years after the publication of the *Principles,* in which he said explicitly that in that work the proof that

ideas such as those of colours are not resemblances comes only at the end of the fourth part, at ***Principles*** IV. arts 189-98, where he refers to the physiological account of perception, given in such previous works as the ***Dioptrics,*** to prove the mathematization thesis.[14] Since these physiological hypotheses belong to the empirical part of physical theory, the mathematization of nature, for Descartes, is an empirical hypothesis.

Thus, it is also clear that for Descartes the mathematization of nature depends upon empirical *scientific* hypotheses about the physiology of perception, and not merely upon everyday observations. This is, in general, an important point just because some philosophers, for example Jonathan Bennett, have claimed that the thesis that colour-ideas do not resemble objective properties of bodies does not require any '*recherché* scientific information'.[15] According to Bennett, reflection upon obvious empirical facts shows that the perception of an object as having some colour does not hang together with the rest of our knowledge in any way so systematically as does our perception of it as having some shape. From this he believes that we may infer that colours do not inhere in the things themselves. But, however poorly entrenched our colour-predicates may be, this argument does not have the force that Bennett thinks it has. At most, it could serve only to render easier the acceptance of the thesis that colour-ideas are not resemblances once that thesis has been independently confirmed on *scientific* grounds. Thus, Descartes was on the right track when he rested his mathematization of nature upon physiological hypotheses.

Before looking at the use that Descartes made of these hypotheses in his empirical epistemology, we must first see just what was the explanation of colour-perception that he presented in the ***Meteorology.*** He traced the perception of different colours to the differing rotational velocities of the light-corpuscles which, interacting with our eye in a mechanically explicable way, cause us to have colour-ideas. We may indeed speak here of the rotational *velocities* of the light-corpuscles, since only in regard to being '*transmitted*' instantaneously can light be but a tendency to movement. This explanation is an empirical one in that both the mechanical nature of light and the account of how the eye reacts to these light-corpuscles and transmits their 'movements' to the brain and then the mind are, according to him, hypotheses that must be confirmed by experience. Now the reason he offers for the causal connection between the rotational velocities of light-corpuscles and ideas of colours is a rather slender one: such velocities form the only remaining degree of freedom for the corpuscles and colour is the only aspect in which our perceptions of light vary.[16]

But whatever the shakiness (not to mention the falsity) of his explanation of colour-perception, Descartes went on to draw from it, and the mathematization of nature it made possible, an important philosophical consequence. This first result in his empirical epistemology is one that even an adequate physiological explanation of colour would inspire. Descartes was not content with claiming merely that our perceptual belief in colours is false. What he did was to set up a *generalized* concept of representation, according to which there are a number of ways our representations may *represent* features of nature besides *resembling* them. The physiological explanation of colour-ideas shows, that, even if they do not resemble actual features of nature, there are nonetheless interconnections among them that represent real relations in nature: the closer to red in the spectrum a colour is, the faster, according to Descartes, the corresponding rotational velocity of the light-corpuscles. Moreover, he might naturally have gone on to speculate about what must be the actual constitution of an object in order for it to reflect light-corpuscles of a certain rotational velocity; then a colour-idea would represent something of the object, though without at all resembling it in that regard. But this was one of the rare cases where Descartes did not seize an opportunity to put forth an hypothesis.

Both in **Le Monde** and the **Dioptrics** this distinction between representation and resemblance is laid out explicitly. There, for example, he compared ideas of colour to scripts or languages that bear a systematic relation to what they represent without resembling it.[17] Descartes needed the generalized concept of representation to make sense of the relation between the scientific and perceptual images of nature. Although his physiological theory shows that certain of our ideas are not resemblances, it also shows how they do, in fact, represent actual properties of nature. In other words, while rejecting our 'natural interpretation' of colour-ideas, what Descartes calls our 'natural belief' that takes them as resemblances, the theory places a new interpretation on them that indicates how they do represent. In this way, only, could he do justice to the fact that our ideas of colour prove useful in guiding our activities in the world. Descartes' general concept of representation expresses a view that we, too, must adopt if we are to understand how modern scientific theory at once characteristically corrects our perceptual image of nature and yet must ultimately be tested against our perceptual experience. As in the case of Descartes' explanation of colour-perception, the scientific theory that refutes our 'natural interpretation' of what we perceive is one that purports to explain why we have the *perceptions* or *ideas* that we do; this explanation we can understand as a new interpretation that tells us how our ideas really do represent. Yet the new interpretation is not tested against sentences expressing the natural interpretation it refutes (an incoherency often used by instrumentalists to discredit the idea that the correcting theory could count as being true). It is tested against an account of what perceptual ideas we do have.

In the past an exclusive concern with Descartes' *a priori* epistemology has portrayed his theory of representation as if it strove chiefly to determine with what right we can come to know that a representation is true or not. Because the empirical dimension of his epistemology was then overlooked, his need to examine the different kinds of representation went unnoticed. Indeed, Descartes considered the generalized concept of representation one of his most important discoveries. To the absence of this concept he traced the failure of the older view that perception occurs through objects transmitting 'intentional species' to the mind; on that view perception could be a matter only of whether an idea resembles an object or not.[18] The generalized concept of representation, explaining how the mathematization of nature is possible, is thus the first key concept of Descartes' empirical epistemology.

Part III The Natural Setting of Human Knowledge

The second set of issues belonging to Descartes' empirical epistemology are ones that have to do with the place of human knowledge within the natural world. This area of his empirical epistemology arose because his physiological theories led inevitably to localizing the mind at a determinate position within the causal order of nature, namely in the vicinity of the pineal gland.[19] Indeed, this conflicted head-on with his *a priori* distinction between mind and body, where spatial location was supposedly a distinctive feature of bodies alone. However, it is not with this conflict between *a priori* and empirical developments and the inadequacies of Cartesian dualism that I intend to deal, but with his empirical epistemology. Before we look at these further aspects of it, we must first take a glance at the theory of ideas that he worked out on *a priori* grounds and that served as the background for how he further exploited his physiological work for epistemological ends.

It is well known that the Cartesian concept of an idea is quite broad in scope, meaning as it does any sort of representation, but chiefly the content of a thought or a perceptual content. Ideas arise from two sources, either from the innate capacities of the mind (these are the *ideae innatae*) or from experience (these are the *ideae adventitae,* or adventitious ideas). When we use any of our ideas to re-interpret or combine other of our ideas, we end up with constructed ideas (or *ideae factae*). As for the nature of ideas themselves, Descartes often, when hurried, treated them as immediate objects of thought or perception, in the sense that they are mental items separate from the acts of thinking or perceiving them. But his more considered view (justifiable, as we shall see, within his physiological theory) was what we might today call an adverbial theory. Then he understood ideas as *features* of the *mental acts* themselves of thinking or perceiving, and not as separate items toward which those mental acts are directed. For example, in this spirit he defined an idea as 'the form of any thought (*cogitatio*) . . . by the immediate awareness of which I am conscious of that said thought', just after he had defined a thought as the mental operation (*operatio*) of thinking, perceiving, or willing.[20] On this view, we are immediately aware of our ideas only because we have immediate reflexive awareness of our thinking, and not because our ideas are separate items uncommonly close to our acts of thinking or perceiving.

Descartes used his physiological work to deepen his account of the character of human knowledge by placing human knowledge in its natural setting. He did this by examining the role of perceptual ideas in our *empirical* knowledge of nature. Remember then on *a priori* grounds Descartes believed that he could prove (in the *Sixth Meditation*) that the causal dependence of perceptual ideas on external objects is just as clear and distinct as our having such ideas at all. What he did in his physiological treatises, the *Treatise on Man* and the *Dioptrics,* was to show just how this causal chain proceeds. In general, he drew a mechanistic picture of how the impingement of the light from the object upon the eye causes certain movements to be transmitted along the optical nerve; these cause movements in the animal spirits of the brain, which in turn induce a particular movement of the pineal gland, which immediately gives rise to a particular idea in the mind.[21] Now, to be sure, knowledge for Descartes consists not simply in having an idea but in the judgement that the idea is true or false. Thus, the causal chain of perception that results in a perceptual idea yields a necessary, but not a sufficient condition for empirical knowledge. The perceptual idea must figure in a judgement for there to be knowledge; and that perceptual idea may also be variously interpreted before a judgement is made. But we can think of Descartes' physiological work as placing empirical knowledge in its natural setting because the possibility and even the scope of such knowledge depends upon the physiology of perception. Furthermore, the mental acts of interpreting and judging, just as much as the ideas upon which they operate, occupy a determinate position in the causal order of nature. They, too, must take place in the vicinity of the pineal gland—contrary to what the distinction between mind and *res extensa* would seem to require.

I shall discuss two ways in which Descartes used his physiological work to fill in the natural setting of empirical knowledge. The first lay in his analysis of the causal link between the pineal movements and the resulting perceptual idea. Of course, he did believe that we cannot come to understand in what, in this case, the causal *operation* consists. But he did say something about the relation between pineal movements

and perceptual ideas that is precisely as sophisticated as we should desire. In the *Dioptrics* he insisted that although the movement of the pineal gland causes the idea in the mind, it is not then the pineal movement that we perceive. The immediate object of perception consists in the content of the idea, while the pineal movements act upon the mind in such a way as to cause the mind to have such an idea.[22] To believe that the pineal gland causes the mind to have a perception by causing the mind to perceive its movements would be to suppose, he wisely pointed out, that the mind itself has an eye to perceive those adjacent movements. Such passages indicate how successfully Descartes was able to integrate the representationalist and physiological components of his theory of perception.

Moreover, the very same kind of argument could have been used to justify his adverbial theory of ideas, the far more acceptable form of representationalism. No more than the mind has an eye to perceive brain-states does it have an eye to perceive ideas as separate mental items. Unfortunately, none of the passages that I have found where Descartes carefully laid out his adverbial theory indicates for what reason he preferred this account. It would not be unreasonable, however, to conjecture that behind this account lay his physiological claims about the relation in perception between brain-states and the mental states they cause.

In this way, Descartes' physiological speculations helped him to fill in his central epistemological thesis that our knowledge of the world takes place by means of our having ideas. Notice that his representationalist theory of empirical knowledge, as put forth on *a priori* grounds alone, was compatible with a range of different accounts. *A priori* introspection yields that adventitious ideas, that lie at the basis of our empirical knowledge, depend causally upon external objects. But this point is compatible with ideas being either the way things themselves look, or 'intentional species' of things transmitted without alteration to the mind.[23] Both of these alternatives were ruled out in virtue of taking mental states as caused by brain-states. But Descartes went on to clarify just what this causal relation means for the character of perceptual ideas. It appears plausible that this clarification led Descartes to his adverbial conception of ideas.

There is a second and more important way in which his physiological work contributed to an empirical account of human knowledge. His physiological investigation of vision showed, not only why our colour-ideas are not resemblances, but also under what conditions even the perception of the mathematical qualities of bodies can go astray. In the *Dioptrics* he showed how the accuracy of distance-perception diminishes when the object is either too near or too far and that bright objects appear closer than they actually are because the intensity of the light causes the same contraction of the pupil that occurs when it is focussed upon nearby objects.[24] Having ascertained the range of accuracy of the eye, he went on in the **Dioptrics** to show how the use of glass lenses, in telescopes or microscopes, could increase our access to the actual mathematical properties of bodies.

The important epistemological consequence that Descartes drew from this aspect of his physiological work lay in his coming to conceive our visual system as simply one kind of optical receptor among others. Our natural organs of perception he treated as lying on a continuum with what he called the 'artificial organs' that can supplement the deficiencies that nature has left us with.[25] He listed four conditions that any optical receptor should meet, and envisaged that sometimes different organs, whether natural or artificial, might satisfy some of these conditions better than others. These four conditions were that the receptor produce images that do not distort features of the object, that these images be detailed, that the light forming the images be strong enough to move the fibres of the optical nerve, and that the images represent at the same time as many different objects as possible. In short, what he was working at was a *generalized* concept of an optical receptor, under which our visual system would fall as simply one among other, 'artificial' ones. This concept formed part of an overall generalizing of our perceptual systems. Descartes' generalized concept of representation, which I discussed in the previous section, was intended to make sense of the fact that much of our perceptual experience represents, without offering resemblances of things. Now, when it comes to those perceptual ideas that can be resemblances—the ideas of the mathematical properties of perceived bodies—we see him generalizing along this axis as well. Artificial organs can, under a great many conditions, yield us resembling images, where our natural organs fail.

This overall generalization is an exceptionally important aspect of Descartes' empirical epistemology. By stressing how in many ways our perceptual image of nature proves inaccurate and how, even where it does offer us resemblances of the way things are, it is far less serviceable than the instruments we can construct, it served to undermine the traditional conception (deriving from both Greek and Christian sources) that God or nature has given us the perceptual organs we have because they naturally display the nature of the world we desire to understand. In short, this aspect of his empirical epistemology served to *de-teleologize* our perceptual system. This is a much-neglected aspect of the break with teleology characteristic of modern physical science, and yet it proved just as significant as the rejection of teleological theories of motion. Its importance lay, not least of all, in recognizing that progress in our knowledge of nature will come, not from the mere observation of nature, but from experimentation. Thus, Descartes thought that the senses should be sub-

servient to the intellect, not simply because in ordinary life we make perceptual errors, but because more fundamentally we must take our perceptual experience as only an indirect access to the actual structure of nature. In the seventeenth century, it was Locke and Robert Hooke who chiefly continued the Cartesian break with the teleology of perception; Hooke recommended that 'The footsteps of Nature are to be trac'd, not only in her *ordinary course,* but when she seems to be put to her shifts, to make many *doublings* and *turnings,* and to use some kind of art in indeavouring to avoid our discovery.'[26] In fact, they went further in this development than Descartes himself. He was willing to de-teleologize our perceptual system probably only because he believed (it seems in contrast to Locke and Hooke) that he had a divine guarantee for the ability of our *intellect* to understand the world.

Since a characteristic feature of modern physical science has been not just its extension, but, in quite fundamental regards, its correction of our perceptual image of nature, physiological theories that de-teleologize perception have played a vital role in its development. In other words, put more generally, the modern theory of nature has required a theory of human knowledge as it exists within the natural setting physical theory describes. To that extent, modern epistemology had to have its empirical dimension, at least as long as it remained in contact with the growth of science. One of Descartes' unsung merits lies in his having perceived so distinctly and so fruitfully the need for an empirical epistemology.

The generalized concept of representation, the relation between perceptual ideas and the brain-states that cause them (as well perhaps as the adverbial theory of ideas), and the generalized concept of an optical receptor are the key features of Descartes' empirical epistemology. It is perhaps not surprising that his empirical epistemology has gone unnoticed for so long. Only recently has the myth been exploded that Cartesian physical science was thoroughly *a priori*. I have sought to show, what has not really been recognized, that for Descartes empirical inquiry was concerned not simply with a deeper understanding of nature, but also with a broader understanding of the nature of our knowledge of nature as well. . . .

Notes

[1] *Discourse on Method,* VI, AT, [*Oeuvres de Descartes,* ed. C. Adam and P. Tannery, 13 vols., Paris: Vrin/ CNRS, 1879-1913], VI, pp. 64-5 (HR, [*The Philosophical Works of Descartes,* trans. Elizabeth S. Haldane and G. R. T. Ross, 2 vols., Cambridge: Cambridge University Press, 1970], I, p. 121).

[2] *Le Monde,* VII, AT, XI, pp. 37-45.

[3] *Discourse on Method,* VI, AT, VI, p. 64 (HR, I, p. 121); *Principles,* II, art 36-42.

[4] In *Regulae,* rule XII (AT, X, p. 427; HR, I, p. 47) Descartes does imply, as in the case of the nature of the magnet, that sometimes we must rest content with hypotheses that are only empirically confirmable; but this passage is surrounded by other comments (AT, X, pp. 419-28; HR, I, pp. 41-7) that imply that all scientific knowledge must be deduced from self-evident 'simple natures'. Since the *Regulae* is so obscure a work, I have chosen to discuss Descartes' conception of scientific method as it emerges with the *Discourse.* In *Le Monde,* four years before the *Discourse,* he boasted that from the three fundamental laws of nature he could deduce *a priori* a complete account of nature (AT, XI, p. 47).

[5] *Discourse on Method,* VI, AT, VI, p. 65 (HR, I, p. 121); *Principles,* III, art 43-4.

[6] For a recent statement of the view that by the end of the *Principles* Descartes had surrendered the idea that any physical truths can be demonstrated *a priori,* see D. Garber, 'Science and Certainty in Descartes', in M. Hooker (ed.) *Descartes: Critical and Interpretative Essays* (Baltimore, 1978, p. 146). Garber takes *Principles,* IV, art 206 to indicate that Descartes was 'uncomfortable' with having just abandoned, in the previous section, the possibility of *a priori* physical truths; in contrast, I take it to express Descartes' simply having finished the thought he began in the previous section—without a knowledge of God all of science would be hypothetical, but we do know God and He lends metaphysical certainty to the basic principles of physical science. For the view that, throughout the whole of his writings, Descartes considered physical science as thoroughly empirical and hypothetical, see A. Gewirth, 'Experience and the Non-Mathematical in the Cartesian Method', *Journal of the History of Ideas,* II (1941), pp. 183 ff.; also E. Cassirer, *Das Erkenntnisproblem,* Vol. I (Wissenschaftliche Buchgesellschaft, 1974; originally 1922), p. 469 ff. R. M. Blake, 'The Role of Experience in Descartes' Theory of Method', in *Theories of Scientific Method,* Seattle, 1960, claims that both *a priori* demonstration and experimental confirmation serve to justify the three fundamental laws of nature. This is an interesting idea, but the passages Blake cites are not convincing. An account generally similar to the one that I have presented may be found in L. J. Beck, *The Method of Descartes* (Oxford, 1952), pp. 239 ff., as well as in L. Laudan, 'The Clock Metaphor and Probabilism', *Annals of Science,* XXII (1966), pp. 73 ff.

[7] Furthermore, Descartes believed that if we did not know the existence of God we would have no right to believe that the experimental confirmation of hypotheses had anything to do with their being true. Thus, in *Principles,* III, art 43, he traces the link between confirmation and truth to a divine guarantee; but in the next section, where no mention is made of God, he begins to hedge on whether hypotheses may be no more than practically useful (as opposed to true).

[8] *Dioptrics,* I, AT, VI, p. 83.

[9] *Discourse on Method,* VI, AT, VI, p. 76 (HR, I, pp. 128-9); To Mersenne, 17 May 1638, AT, II, pp. 134 ff. (PL, pp. 55-6).

[10] For consilience, see To Morin, 13 July 1638, AT, II, pp. 196 ff. (PL, pp. 58-9); for comparative confirmation see *Discourse on Method,* VI, AT, VI, p. 65 (HR, I, p. 121).

[11] In the article cited above, D. Garber claims that at the time of the *Discourse* Descartes believed he could enumerate all possible hypotheses consistent both with the *a priori* principles and with the phenomena to be explained and then, by crucial experiments, he could show with deductive certainty which hypothesis was correct. But none of the passages cited by Garber rules out the interpretation that, according to Descartes, we should try for as complete an enumeration of possible hypotheses as we can; and this (if we leave aside the additional idea that they must be compatible with principles that are *a priori*) would hardly indicate that Descartes did not take the hypothetical method seriously (as, on his interpretation of the passages, Garber maintains). When in *Discourse,* V (AT, VI, pp. 40-1; HR, I, p. 106), Descartes writes that 'I have always remained true to the resolution I made . . . not to admit anything as true which did not seem to me clearer and more certain than the demonstrations of the geometricians', he is referring to *principles* (as the rest of the sentence makes clear), and in particular to the three fundamental laws of nature (as the subsequent sentence makes clear). This passage is used by Garber to support his claim that Descartes believed at this time that he could make the truth of his hypotheses certain.

[12] Although at this point the *a priori* laws of nature are known to apply to the physical world, there remains the problem how they may in fact be applied by us. Descartes' solution would lie in his theory of 'natural geometry' (see Nancy Maull's paper below).

[13] See e.g. *Third Meditation* (AT, IX, p. 34; HR, I, p. 164). Probably as a result of the traditional view of Cartesian physics as thoroughly *a priori* his mathematization of nature is usually seen as *a priori,* not empirical. Cf. e.g., A. J. Kenny, *Descartes* (New York, 1968), p. 207.

[14] To Chanut, 26 February 1649, AT, V. pp. 291-2:

It is necessary to remember, in reading this book [the *Principles*], that although I consider nothing in a body besides the sizes, figures, and movements of their parts, I claim nonetheless to explain there the nature of light, of heat and of all the other sensible qualities; so that I presupposed that these qualities are only in our senses, like tickling or pain, and not in the objects that we perceive, in which there is nothing but certain figures and movements, that cause the perceptions that we call light, heat, etc. This I did not explain and prove until the end of the fourth part. . . .

[my translation].

[15] J. Bennett, *Locke, Berkeley, Hume* (Oxford, 1971), p. 105.

[16] *Meteorology*, VIII, AT, VI, p. 334.

[17] *Le Monde*, AT, XI, pp. 3-4; *Dioptric*, IV, AT, VI, pp. 109-14.

[18] *Dioptric*, IV, AT, VI, p. 112.

[19] See *Treatise of Man*, AT, XI, pp. 131, 143; *Principles*, IV, art 189; *Passions of the Soul*, AT, XI, p. 352 (HR, I, p. 345).

[20] *Reply to Second Objections*, AT, IX, p. 124 (HR, II, p. 52).

[21] At times, Descartes wrote that the perceptual idea occurring at the end of this sequence must be 'innate'; what he meant was that, since the figures and the movements in the sense organs and the brain give rise to ideas that do not resemble them, the mind must have an innate faculty that governs what the content of the perceptual ideas *corresponding* to these figures and movements will be. See *Notes Against a Program*, AT, VIII, pp. 358-9 (HR, I, pp. 442-3). Clearly, Descartes is *not* denying here that the knowledge of the world we gain through perceptual ideas is empirical.

[22] *Dioptric*, VI, AT, VI, p. 130:

Now although this picture, in being so transmitted into our head, always retains some resemblance to the objects from which it proceeds, nevertheless . . . we must not hold that it is by means of this resemblance that the picture causes us to perceive the objects, as if there were yet other eyes in our brain with which we could apprehend it; but rather, that it is the movements of which the picture is composed which, acting immediately on our mind inasmuch as it is united to the body, are so established by nature as to make it have such perceptions.
[Translated by Olscamp, p. 101 in *Discourse on Method, Optics, Geometry, and Meteorology* (Indianapolis, 1965).]

Descartes did not have this insight from the beginning, since in an earlier work like the *Treatise of Man* he suggested that we perceive directly events in the brain; this is because he then thought of the ideas themselves as patterns in the animal spirits of the brain (AT, XI, pp. 176-7). N. K. Smith errs by attributing this earlier position to the whole of Descartes' thought, in his *New Studies In the Philosophy of Descartes* (London, 1952), p. 147.

[23] By rejecting the view that our perceptual ideas are the 'looks' of the things themselves, Descartes' physiological account of perception broke with our everyday understanding of perceptual knowledge. Ordinarily (in the case of vision) we believe that we perceive objects directly. Thus, what we perceive of an object, we think, is how *the object itself* looks in that situation; even if I know that that elliptical shape is actually a circular one, I believe that from this angle the object looks that way. The reason why this view comes so naturally is that in seeing an object we see ourselves seeing it, we see our bodies in a certain position *vis-á-vis* the object. It is this reflexive element that leads us to believe that we can see the object itself as it is causing us to see it. On the everyday view, see J. L. Austin, *Sense and Sensibilia* (Oxford, 1962).

[24] *Dioptric*, VI, AT, VI, p. 144 ff.

[25] For this whole discussion see *Dioptric*, VII, *passim*.

[26] This passage is from the preface to Hooke's *Micrographia* (London, 1665). From Locke, see *Essay Concerning Human Understanding*, Book II, Ch XXIII, 12; there he says that God fitted our senses for our practical welfare, and not for our knowledge of nature (cf., however, *Essay*, Book IV, Ch IV, 4). For the same idea in Descartes, see *Sixth Meditation*, AT, IX, p. 66. Aristotle, as is well known, urged that the theory of nature should remain in harmony with 'ta phainomena'.

Desmond M. Clarke (essay date 1992)

SOURCE: "Descartes' Philosophy of Science and the Scientific Revolution," in *The Cambridge Companion to Descartes*, edited by John Cottingham, Cambridge University Press, 1992, pp. 258-85.

[In the following essay, Clarke examines the epistemological and metaphysical underpinnings of Descartes' philosophy of science, contrasting it with scholasticism.]

Descartes' concept of science can be understood only by paying careful attention to the historical context in which it was constructed. The scientific revolution of the seventeenth century involved two related developments: a change in scientific practice (or, more accurately, a whole series of such changes) which is reflected in the founding of new scientific societies such as the Royal Society and the *Académie royale des sciences,* and a complementary change in how natural philosophers described the kind of knowledge that resulted from the new scientific practices. Descartes contributed to both developments. He shared this distinction with such eminent figures as Galileo Galilei, Francis Bacon, William Harvey, Robert Boyle, Christian Huygens, and Isaac Newton, all of whom were concerned both with improving our knowledge of nature and with clarifying the status of that knowledge.

It would be an obvious oversimplification to classify all the natural philosophers of the seventeenth century as, in some fundamental sense, proposing the same scientific theories. It is equally unsatisfactory to suggest that they all accepted the same theory of science or the same model of scientific knowledge. Yet, despite the pitfalls involved, it may be helpful—at least prior to examining Descartes' texts—to think of many of the most famous natural philosophers of the scientific revolution as sharing a number of new insights about the nature of scientific knowledge and, more importantly, as repudiating certain features of the model of science that was generally accepted in colleges and universities at that time. In fact, there was more agreement about what was being rejected than about what was being proposed in its place. Descartes occupies a pivotal role in the history of this development, in the transition from a widely accepted scholastic concept of science to its complete rejection by practising scientists and the endorsement of some kind of hypothetical, empirically based knowledge of nature. The historical context in which Descartes worked should lead us to expect, therefore, that he struggled with the epistemological and methodological issues involved in this transition. It should also lead us to expect that the transition was neither quick nor clear-cut. In other words, there is a strong likelihood that seventeenth-century natural philosophers continued to accept various features of precisely the model of science which they claimed explicitly to reject, while at the same time adopting elements of the newly developing concept of science that were incompatible with their traditional allegiance.

The traditional concept of science that was almost universally taught in colleges and universities included a number of key features; one was the certainty or necessity of genuine knowledge claims, and their universality. Aristotle says in the *Posterior Analytics:*

> We suppose ourselves to possess unqualified scientific knowledge of a thing, as opposed to knowing it in the accidental way in which the sophist knows, when we think that we know the cause on which the fact depends, as the cause of that fact and of no other, and, further, that the fact could not be other than it

is. . . . Since the object of pure scientific knowledge cannot be other than it is, the truth obtained by demonstrative knowledge will be necessary.

The paradigm of this type of knowledge was pure mathematics. One begins with definitions or first principles which are known with absolute certainty, one proceeds "demonstratively" by deducing other propositions from those already known as certain, and the logical validity of our inferences guarantees the same degree of certainty for our conclusions as was available for the initial premises. The mathematical model of demonstrated knowledge inspired one of the dominant features of the scholastic concept of science that was widely accepted in the early seventeenth century.

Another feature of this concept of science was the claim that our knowledge of physical nature depends ultimately on the reliability of our everyday observations and judgments.[2] This involved two elements. One was the assumption that all our knowledge ultimately depends on sensory evidence and that it includes nothing that was not learned through sensory experience.[3] Secondly, the cognitive faculties with which God has equipped us are completely reliable as long as they are used within the scope of their Creator's design. Thus we know the way the world is, and we can know it with certainty, by consulting the ways in which the world appears to us in sensation.

A further element of the scholastic tradition was the assumption that, if we wish to explain the natural phenomena which appear to us in sensations, we must use the distinction between "matter" and "form."[4] This was a very widely used distinction which varied in meaning from one context to another. It was designed to reflect our common experience of the same type of thing being instantiated in a variety of different ways; for example, dogs may be small or large, their colors can vary, as may many other inessential features, without their ceasing to be dogs. The common, essential features of a dog could be described as the *form* of a dog, while the nonessential, variable features could be described (metaphysically) as the *matter*. What appears in sensation, therefore, is the appearance of an underlying reality (form) which, in turn, is the more fundamental dimension of any reality. This underlying reality, or form, is what explains whatever is necessary or essential in anything. Because the traditional concept of scientific knowledge was limited to knowledge of what is necessarily true, it follows that scholastic *scientia* was directed to acquiring knowledge of forms. Thus a scholastic explanation of a natural phenomenon is a discovery of the forms that underlie the appearances manifest to the human perceiver in reliable sensations.

This very brief summary is almost a caricature of what

scholastics claimed about scientific understanding. However, many of Descartes' contemporaries argued that it was precisely this philosophy that obstructed the consideration of alternative ways of investigating nature. It was this simple-minded model of knowledge that was invoked by those who objected to the new sciences, and that was used as a foil by proponents of the new sciences to show in relief the distinctive features of their own philosophy of science.

HYPOTHESES

Descartes began his account of the natural world in *Le Monde* (c.1632) by discussing the *un*reliability of our sensations as a basis for scientific knowledge.

> In proposing to treat here of light, the first thing I want to make clear to you is that there can be a difference between our sensation of light . . . and what is in the objects that produces that sensation in us . . . For, even though everyone is commonly persuaded that the ideas that are the objects of our thought are wholly like the objects from which they proceed, nevertheless I can see no reasoning that assures us that this is the case. . . . You well know that words bear no resemblance to the things they signify, and yet they do not cease for that reason to cause us to conceive of those things . . . Now if words, which signify nothing except by human convention, suffice to cause us to conceive of things to which they bear no resemblance, why could not nature also have extablished a certain sign that would cause us to have the sensation of light, even though that sign in itself bore no similarity to that sensation?
>
> (AT [*Œuvres de Descartes,* ed. C. Adam and P. Tannery, revised ed., 12 vols., Paris: Vrin/ CNRS, 1964-76] XI 3-4)[5]

Descartes goes on to use the same example as Galileo, to argue that a tickling sensation caused by a feather does not resemble anything in the feather. "One passes a feather lightly over the lips of a child who is falling asleep, and he perceives that someone is tickling him. Do you think the idea of tickling that he conceives resembles anything in this feather?" (AT XI 6)[6] In a similar way, there is no reason to believe "that what is in the objects from which the sensation of light comes to us is any more like that sensation than the actions of a feather . . . are like tickling" (AT XI 6).[7] If we cannot argue validly from a description of our sensation of light to the claim that the light that causes this sensation resembles our experience, then we have a fundamental problem in attempting to base scientific knowledge on our sensations of the world around us. The distinction between our subjective experiences or sensations and their objective causes, between primary and secondary qualities, opens up an epistemic gap that can only be bridged by some other strategy apart from assumptions of resemblance. This strategy is hypothesis, or guesswork. Our guesses may turn out to be very secure, and

there may eventually be many reasons for thinking that they are as certain as one can hope for in the circumstances; but that does not change the fact that we come to have these ideas, in the first place, by guesswork. What should a natural philosopher assume about the physical causes of our perceptions? There are a few reasons why Descartes opts for one assumption rather than another at this crucial juncture, some of which rely on his concept of explanation (which is discussed below). Apart from those reasons, he also presupposes a radical distinction between matter and mind for which he argues in the **Meditations** and the **Principles**. It follows from this that the objective causes of our sensations are material, in some sense. In order to fill in some of the relevant detail, Descartes must engage in elementary physical theory.

The speculations about matter on which Descartes' theory of matter and, subsequently, his concept of science depend include the assumption that the size, shape and motion of small particles of matter would be adequate to explain all their physical effects, including the physical effects on our sensory faculties which stimulate sensations. Some of the reasons for this degree of parsimony in theory construction are mentioned below. In postulating three types of matter in **Le Monde,** Descartes is not very convincing about why he assumes three (rather than more or fewer); however, once they have been introduced, he is quick to take refuge in the construction of a hypothetical world which allows his imagination complete freedom, without having to explain the rationale for each hypothesis as it is made.

> Many other things remain for me to explain here, and I would myself be happy to add here several arguments to make my opinions more plausible. In order, however, to make the length of this discourse less boring for you, I want to wrap part of it in the cloak of a fable, in the course of which I hope that the truth will not fail to come out sufficiently . . .
>
> (AT XI 31)[8]

By the time Descartes wrote the **Principles** twelve years later, he had become more self-conscious about the hypothetical character of his assumptions concerning the size, shape, etc. of particles of matter.

> From what has already been said we have established that all the bodies in the universe are composed of one and the same matter, which is divisible into indefinitely many parts, . . . However, we cannot determine by reason alone how big these pieces of matter are, or how fast they move, or what kinds of circle they describe. Since there are countless different configurations which God might have instituted here, experience alone must teach us which configurations he actually selected in preference to the rest. We are thus free to make any assumption on these matters with the sole proviso that all the consequences of our assumption must agree with our experience.
>
> (AT VIIIA 100-1: CSM [*The Philosophical*

Writings of Descartes; ed. J. G. Cottingham, R. Stoothoff, and D. Murdoch; two vols.; Cambridge University Press, 1985] I 256-7)

Descartes does not claim that we are completely free to assume anything we wish about matter. He argues at great length about the fundamental properties of matter, i.e. their primary qualities, and discusses in detail the need to include or exclude certain primary qualities in a viable theory of nature. He also argues in some detail about the laws of motion or, as he calls them, the laws of nature, which determine the motions of material bodies and the ways in which they may transfer motion from one to another by contact action. However, the relevant point here is that, having decided which variables to attribute to matter, we cannot determine by similar arguments the values of these variables; we cannot decide a priori the number, size, or speed of the various small parts of matter which underpin the whole edifice of Cartesian physics. Nor could we hope to discover by observation which particles there are, what shapes they have or with what speed they move; they are much too small to be perceived directly, even with the use of a microscope. We can do no better than hypothesize answers to these questions, and then subsequently check the plausibility of our guesswork.

Thus the logic of Descartes' theory of sensation and the implications of his theory of matter both suggest that he would have to acknowledge a central place for hypotheses in any coherent account of physical phenomena. The extent to which he recognized this varied from his earlier reflections in the *Regulae* (c.1628), in which there was only a minimal recognition of the role of hypotheses in natural science, to his more mature considerations in the *Discourse* (1637), where the significance of hypotheses and experiments is explicitly acknowledged. The *Discourse* is of paramount importance in this context, because it was composed over a number of years while Descartes was preparing for publication the three major scientific essays for which it serves as a preface. In the "Discourse on the method of rightly conducting one's reason and seeking the truth in the sciences," Part VI, Descartes writes:

> Should anyone be shocked at first by some of the statements I make at the beginning of the *Optics* and the *Meteorology* because I call them 'suppositions' and do not seem to care about proving them, let him have the patience to read the whole book attentively, and I trust that he will be satisfied. For I take my reasonings to be so closely interconnected that just as the last are proved by the first, which are their causes, so the first are proved by the last, which are their effects. . . . For as experience makes most of these effects quite certain, the causes from which I deduce them serve not so much to prove them as to explain them; indeed, quite to the contrary, it is the causes which are proved by the effects.
>
> (AT VI 76: CSM I 150)

This passage raised a number of queries from readers, one of whom was Father Morin. Descartes replied to his concerns in 1638 and answered the objection that hypothetical essays should not be described as demonstrated: "there is a big difference between proving and explaining. To this I add that one can use the word 'demonstrate' to mean one or the other, at least if one understands it according to common usage and not according to the special meaning which philosophers give it" (13 July 1638: AT II 198: CSMK [*The Philosophical Writings of Descartes;* ed. Cottingham, Stoothoff, Murdoch, and Anthony Kenny; Cambridge University Press, 1991] 106). This shows Descartes explicitly breaking with the scholastic tradition, for which the term "demonstrate" had special connotations of deducing a conclusion rigorously from first principles. Instead he invites his readers to understand "demonstration" in a less strict sense in which it can include the reasoning process by which one argues from effects to hypothetical causes or, in the opposite direction, from assumed causes to observed effects.

The relative novelty of this type of demonstration is underlined in a letter to Mersenne in 1638, in which Descartes explains that the types of demonstration available in physics are very different from those which one expects in mathematics:

> You ask if I think that what I wrote about refraction is a demonstration; and I think it is, at least insofar as it is possible to give one in this matter, without having first demonstrated the principles of physics by means of metaphysics . . . and to the extent that any other question of mechanics, optics or astronomy, or any other matter which is not purely geometrical or arithmetical, has ever been demonstrated. But to demand that I give geometrical demonstrations in a matter which depends on physics is to demand the impossible. And if one wishes to call demonstrations only the proofs of geometers, one must then say that Archimedes never demonstrated anything in mechanics, nor Vitello in optics, nor Ptolemy in astronomy, and so on; this, however, is not what is said. For one is satisfied, in these matters, if the authors—having assumed certain things which are not manifestly contrary to experience—write consistently and without making logical mistakes, even if their assumptions are not exactly true. . . . But as regards those who wish to say that they do not believe what I wrote, because I deduced it from a number of assumptions which I did not prove, they do not know what they are asking for, nor what they ought to ask for.[9]

One implication is clear. We cannot expect the same kind of demonstrations in physics as in pure mathematics, and we will have to settle for something else. However, it is not yet clear what this alternative is. Whatever its precise structure and the kind of results which it can deliver, it involves making assumptions about the causes of physical phenomena and then "demonstrating" the plausibility of these assumptions by examining their explanatory role in some comprehensive natural philosophy, a project to which Descartes repeatedly refers in his claim that he could (at least in principle) demonstrate those assumptions from some kind of metaphysical foundation.

THE CONCEPT OF EXPLANATION

Descartes shared with many of his contemporaries the insight that the forms and qualities of the scholastic tradition were, in some fundamental sense, nonexplanatory. If we notice some natural phenomenon such as the effect of a magnet on small pieces of iron, the scholastic tradition tended to explain this by saying that the magnetic stone attracts (or repels) certain bodies because it has a "magnetic form" or a "magnetic quality." There is an obvious sense in which this is true. If any natural object does something, then it must have the capacity to do so! As long as we do not understand what that capacity is or what it consists in, we might name the inscrutable property in question in terms of the effect it produces. Then sleeping pills have a dormitive power, magnets have magnetic powers, and human beings have thinking powers. So far, there is nothing wrong with this; it merely labels what needs to be explained.

However, if one follows the natural tendency of scholastic philosophy and reifies these newly named powers as if they were properties distinct from the natural objects which have them, then two problems emerge. One is a metaphysical one; namely, the multiplication of entities beyond demonstrated necessity. By applying Occam's principle, one would stop short of introducing hundreds of new forms or qualities which overpopulate one's metaphysical space.[10] Descartes adverts to this question about the redundancy of forms in Chapter 2 of **Le Monde,** where he explains how a piece of wood burns and, as it burns, emits light and heat:

> someone else may, if he wishes, imagine the form of 'fire', the quality of 'heat', and the action that 'burns' it to be completely different things in this wood. For my part, afraid of misleading myself if I suppose anything more than what I see must of necessity be there, I am content to conceive there the motion of its parts. . . . provided only that you grant me that there is some power that violently removes the subtler of its parts and separates them from the grosser, I find that that alone will be able to cause in the wood all the same changes that one experiences when it burns.
>
> (AT XI 7-8)[11]

Secondly, the introduction of scholastic forms in this context gave the impression that one had made progress in explaining natural phenomena, and that little else remained to be done. However, the very forms which are assumed as explanatory entities are themselves in need of explanation: "If you find it strange that, in setting out these elements, I do not use the qualities called 'heat', 'cold', 'moistness', and 'dryness', as do the philosophers, I shall say to you that these qualities appear to me to be themselves in need of explanation" (AT XI 25-6).[12]

Thus, for Descartes, scholastic forms are both redundant and pseudo-explanatory. The alternative suggested was to find the material and efficient causes of natural phenomena. Descartes argued that these causes must be described mechanically; in fact, he notoriously argued in a reductionist way that most of the properties that natural phenomena exhibit can be explained ultimately in terms of the size, shape, and motions of the small parts of matter into which, he assumed, physical objects can be analyzed. Therefore to explain any natural phenomenon, in this sense, is equivalent to constructing a model of how small, imperceptible parts of matter can combine to form perceptible bodies, how the properties of bodies result from the properties of their constituent parts, and why we perceive them as we do as a result of the interaction of these bodies with our sensory organs.

It has already been indicated above that Cartesian scientific explanations must be hypothetical, and that one of the reasons for this admission was the unobservability of the particles of matter in terms of which the explanation of natural phenomena must be constructed. But how are we supposed to describe and measure the properties of unobservable particles of matter? Father Morin had this type of objection in mind when, having read the scientific essays of 1637, it seemed to him that Descartes might be attempting to explain what we can readily observe by reference to what we neither observe nor understand: " . . . problems in physics can rarely be resolved by analogies [*comparaisons*]; there is almost always some difference [between the model and reality], or some ambiguity, or some element of the obscure being explained by the more obscure" (12 August 1638: AT II 291). Part of Descartes' reply to this objection includes the claim that there is no way of proceeding in physics except by constructing large-scale models of what is happening at the microscopic level. Thus, for example, we might think of imperceptible particles of light by analogy with wooden spheres the size of billiard balls.

> I claim that they [i.e. models and analogies] are the most appropriate way available to the human mind for explaining the truth about questions in physics; to such an extent that, if one assumes something about nature which cannot be explained by some analogy, I think that I have conclusively shown that it is false.
>
> (12 September 1638: AT II 368: CSMK 122)

This point had already been made in correspondence

with Plempius the previous year: "There is nothing more in keeping with reason than that we judge about those things which we do not perceive, because of their small size, by comparison and contrast with those which we see" (3 October 1637: AT I 421: CSMK 65). Descartes' reply to Father Morin also included the claim that the only relevant features of the model were the size and shape of the spheres, and the direction and speed of their motions, so that the disparity in size could be ignored in constructing an explanation.

> in the analogies I use, I only compare some movements with others, or some shapes with others, etc.; that is to say, I compare those things which because of their small size are not accessible to our senses with those which are, and which do not differ from the former more than a large circle differs from a small one.

(12 September 1638: AT II 367-8: CSMK 122)

Apart from the interesting assumptions about which features of a model are relevant to constructing an explanation, Descartes' comments also raise a question about the extent to which hypotheses must be true in order to be explanatory. In other words, would it help in explaining a physical phenomenon if one constructed a mechanical model of its efficient cause which, in fact, is not true to the reality? Descartes thought so, or at least he argued that a plausible though incorrect model is better than none at all. Besides, it may be the case that we can never discover the values of the variables with which we describe microscopic particles of matter, so that we will have to settle for something less than the ideal understanding which is available to God.

The first concession about false hypotheses is made in a number of places where Descartes wonders about the evolution of the universe from its initial chaos to the highly structured world we see today. Theologians commonly believed in his day, based on a nonmetaphorical reading of *Genesis,* that the world as we see it had been created by God. Descartes comments:

> even if in the beginning God had given the world only the form of a chaos, provided that he established the laws of nature and then lent his concurrence to enable nature to operate as it normally does, we may believe without impugning the miracle of creation that by this means alone all purely material things could in the course of time have come to be just as we now see them. And their nature is much easier to conceive if we see them develop gradually in this way than if we consider them only in their completed form.

(AT VI 45: CSM I 133-4)

This suggests that an explanation of the natural world is better if we imagine the world as gradually evolving from an initial chaos under the control of the laws of

nature, than if we concede to the theologians' belief that God simply made it as it is. The same idea is expressed in the *Principles:*

> There is no doubt that all the world was created with all of its perfection from the very beginning . . . Nevertheless, to understand the nature of plants or of man, it is much better to consider how they can gradually develop from seeds, than to consider how they were created by God at the beginning of the Universe. Thus if we can think of a few very simple and easily known principles from which we can show that the stars and the earth, and everything else we can observe on earth, could have developed as if from seeds—although we know they did not in fact develop in this way—we could explain their nature much better in this way than if we simply described them as they are now, or how we believe they were created.

(AT VIIIA 99-100: CSM I 256)

Thus, Descartes believed for theological reasons that his evolutionary account of the development of natural phenomena was false; he also claimed that, despite being false, it was explanatory.

The second reason for accepting hypotheses which are possibly false was Descartes' pessimism about the feasibility of identifying and accurately measuring relevant variables at the microlevel. There were a number of reasons for this which, in retrospect, would seem to have been well justified and would strike the modern reader as a realistic appraisal of the experimental techniques of the early seventeenth century. If one insisted on withholding hypotheses until all the complexity of the natural world is taken into account, one would make no progress whatsoever. Descartes argued along these lines in response to Mersenne's objections, in 1629, about the interference of the air in measuring the speed of falling bodies.

> However, as regards the interference from the air which you wish me to take into consideration, I claim that it is impossible to cope with it and *it does not fall within the scope of science;* for if it is warm, or cold, or dry, or humid, or clear, or cloudy, or a thousand other circumstances, they can all change the air resistance.[13]

The same justification was offered, almost eighteen years later, for the apparent failure of the impact rules to coincide with our experience of colliding bodies. A number of correspondents objected that the rules proposed by Descartes in the *Principles* (Book II, arts. 46 ff) were contradicted by our experience. Descartes' response was:

> Indeed, it often happens that experience can seem initially to be incompatible with the rules which I have just explained, but the reason for this is

obvious. For the rules presuppose that the two bodies *B* and *C* are perfectly hard and are so separated from all other bodies that there is none other in their vicinity which could either help or hinder their movement. And we see no such situation in this world.

(AT IXB 93)

This was a standard reply to objections about a lack of fit between theory and reality. Cartesian explanations were constructed by analogy with the interactions of macroscopic physical bodies in motion. The underlying reality they purported to explain is microscopic, is inaccessible to human observation, and may involve so many interfering factors that our model is far short of adequately representing it.[14]

Thus a Cartesian explanation is a hypothesis that may be acknowledged to be either false or significantly inadequate to the reality it purports to explain. When we lack the evidence required to identify the actual cause of some phenomenon, "it suffices to imagine a cause which could produce the effect in question, even if it could have been produced by other causes and we do not know which is the true cause" (letter of 5 October 1646: AT IV 516). The suggestion that we settle for the best hypothesis available is reflected in the epistemic status claimed for various explanations in the *Principles*. For example, different astronomical hypotheses are examined, not to decide which one is true, but rather to find out which is more successful as an explanation: "Three different hypotheses, that is suggestions, have been discovered by astronomers, which are considered not as if they were true, but merely as suitable for explaining the phenomena" (AT VIIIA 85: CSM I 250). Descartes' preferred hypothesis is chosen "merely as a hypothesis and not as the truth of the matter" (AT VIIIA 86: CSM I 251).

Evidently it would be better if we could discover the true causes of natural phenomena; but if we cannot, it is still worth while to settle for a possible or plausible cause:

> As far as particular effects are concerned, whenever we lack sufficient experiments to determine their true causes, we should be content to know some causes by which they could have been produced . . .

> I believe that I have done enough if the causes which I have explained are such that all the effects which they could produce are found to be similar to those we see in the world, without inquiring whether they were in fact produced by those or by some other causes.

(AT IXB 185, 322)

The methodology suggested here, of constructing mechanical models as best we can, coincides with Carte-

sian scientific practice. Descartes and his followers in France in the seventeenth century were almost profligate in imagining hypothetical models to explain natural phenomena and, in some cases, to explain what could only be called alleged phenomena; they even constructed explanations of nonevents. It was this widespread and notorious dedication to unrestrained hypothesis construction that helps explain Newton's famous disclaimer: "I do not construct hypotheses."[15]

Yet, despite the fact that the logic of Descartes' philosophy implied that explanations of natural phenomena had to be hypothetical, there are equally clear intimations in his work of a very different methodology. Descartes often referred to the possibility of constructing a natural philosophy based on a metaphysical foundation that would realize the kind of certainty and unrevisability which is apparently at issue in the *Meditations*. This feature of his methodology needs some clarification before inquiring if it is compatible with the story told thus far.

FOUNDATIONS OF SCIENCE

In the Preface to the French edition of the *Principles,* Descartes introduces a metaphor that accurately expresses his views about the relationship of physics to metaphysics. "Thus the whole of philosophy is like a tree. The roots are metaphysics, the trunk is physics, and the branches emerging from the trunk are all the other sciences, which may be reduced to three principal ones, namely medicine, mechanics and morals" (AT IXB 14: CSM I 187). There was nothing unusual in this suggestion. Descartes had maintained for about twenty-five years prior to this that physics, as he understood it, is based on or depends on metaphysics and that any natural philosopher worth his salt had better get his metaphysics in order first, before tackling the explanation of specific natural phenomena. For example, he wrote to Mersenne in 1630 about a short essay on metaphysics he himself had begun to write: "It is there that I have tried to begin my studies; and I can tell you that I would not have been able to discover the foundations of physics if I had not looked for them in this direction" (15 April 1630: AT I 144). This helps explain why he objected to Galileo's methodology. According to Descartes, the Italian natural philosopher had ignored questions about foundations and had applied himself instead directly to explaining particular physical phenomena: "without having considered the first causes of nature, he [Galileo] has merely looked for the explanations of a few particular effects, and he has thereby built without foundations" (to Mersenne, 11 October 1638: AT II 380: CSMK 124). The question arises, therefore, about the kinds of foundations Descartes envisaged for physics, and the connection between those foundations and the various sciences that depend on them.

One way of focusing on this issue is to contrast Descartes' approach with what is standard practice in modern science. Physicists or physiologists of the twentieth century do not begin their research with a study of metaphysics, although they may well make metaphysical assumptions in the course of constructing their theories. Instead, they first develop scientific theories which are tested for viability, and the metaphysical implications of the theories are subsequently read off from the finished scientific product. In this approach there is no independent criterion for the acceptability of ontological commitments, apart from the success or otherwise of a given theory. Descartes held the opposite view. He assumed that we can, and ought, to construct our metaphysics first, and that we should subsequently consider physical theories which are consistent with our metaphysical foundation. Thus there must be available independent criteria for deciding which metaphysics to adopt.

On this issue Descartes is very close to scholastic philosophy. The epistemic foundation of Cartesian metaphysics is reflection on "common sense" or on our everyday experience of the natural world. Rule II of the method proposed in the *Discourse,* which reflects Rule IX of the *Regulae,* was "to begin with the simplest and most easily known objects in order to ascend little by little, . . . to knowledge of the most complex" (AT VI 19: CSM I 120).[16] Where metaphysics is concerned, we begin with such everyday experiences as the experience of thinking, of feeling, of moving, etc. Among these experiences, Descartes favors the most simple, accessible and widely available experiences because he hopes thereby to find indubitable foundations. This strategy was outlined in Part VI of the *Discourse:*

> I also noticed, regarding observations, that the further we advance in our knowledge, the more necessary they become. At the beginning, rather than seeking those which are more unusual and highly contrived, it is better to resort only to those which, presenting themselves spontaneously to our senses, cannot be unknown to us if we reflect even a little. The reason for this is that the more unusual observations are apt to mislead us when we do not yet know the causes of the more common ones, and the factors on which they depend are almost always so special and so minute that it is very difficult to discern them.
>
> (AT VI 63: CSM I 143)

The privileged position of everyday experience coincides with a complementary distrust of sophisticated experiments; the latter are likely to mislead us because they may be poorly executed, their results may be incorrectly interpreted, or they may be compromised by various interfering factors of which we are unaware.[17] Therefore, experimental evidence is too unreliable to provide metaphysical foundations for scientific theories; that can only be done by reflection on ordinary experience.

The central claims of Cartesian metaphysics are summarized in the *Meditations* and in Part I of the *Principles*. While they are discussed elsewhere in this volume, the relevant feature here is the extent to which Descartes relies on a scholastic set of concepts to interpret metaphysically the personal experiences for which he claims indubitability. For example, the distinction between a substance and its modes is central to the Cartesian argument in favor of a radical distinction between things that can think and those that cannot.[18] The same distinction is put to work in defining the essence of matter and in denuding matter of many of the primary qualities other natural philosophers were willing to attribute to it, such as gravity or elasticity. In summary, Descartes' metaphysics is a subtle combination of scholastic categories, metaphysical axioms (e.g., *ex nihilo nihil fit*), and apparently incontrovertible common experience.[19]

Once this foundation is in place, the second stage of theory construction is the formulation of the so-called "laws of nature." Despite the fact that these are said to be "deduced" from a metaphysical foundation, the evidence adduced in favor of the laws, both in *Le Monde* and the *Principles,* is a mixture of metaphysical axioms and everyday observation. For example the first law, to the effect that a material object continues in its condition of rest or motion unless some cause intervenes to change its condition, is partly justified by reference to the general axiom that every event or change requires a cause, and partly by reference to our everyday experience: "our everyday experience of projectiles completely confirms this first rule of ours" (AT VIIIA 63: CSM I 241).[20] The other two laws of nature are confirmed in the same manner, by appealing to metaphysical axioms and to our everyday experience of physical objects that move about in the world (AT VIIIA 64-5: CSM I 242).

Thus the metaphysical foundations Descartes claimed to establish for scientific knowledge included a number of related elements, which relied on the kind of the evidence just discussed: (a) a radical distinction between matter and spirit, and a preliminary identification of the primary qualities of matter. This included an equally confident dismissal of various properties which Descartes claimed matter does not have; (b) a rejection of the scholastic understanding of explanation and, in its place, the substitution of an uncompromising model of mechanical explanation; (c) a sketch of three fundamental laws of nature according to which material particles interact and exchange various quantities of motion.

Once these were in place, the question arose of how Descartes might make progress in constructing the type of mechanical models required by his method. What kind of inference was available to move from general principles to the explanation of specific natural phenomena?

Descartes' actual scientific practice coincided with his description of theory construction in Part VI of the *Discourse*. As he moved further away from general principles and closer to particular phenomena, he found he needed hypotheses and experimental tests:

> First I tried to discover in general the principles or first causes of everything that exists or can exist in the world. . . . Next I examined the first and most ordinary effects deducible from these causes. In this way, it seems to me, I discovered the heavens, the stars, and an earth . . . and other such things which, being the most common of all and the simplest, are consequently the easiest to know. Then, when I sought to descend to more particular things, I encountered such a variety that I did not think the human mind could possibly distinguish the forms or species of bodies that are on the earth from an infinity of others that might be there if it had been God's will to put them there. Consequently I thought the only way . . . was to progress to the causes by way of the effects and to make use of many special observations. . . . I must also admit that the power of nature is so ample and so vast, and these principles so simple and so general, that I notice hardly any particular effect of which I do not know at once that it can be deduced from the principles in many different ways; and my greatest difficulty is usually to discover in which of these ways it depends on them. I know no other means to discover this than by seeking further observations whose outcomes vary according to which of these ways provides the correct explanation.
>
> (AT VI 63-4: CSM I 143-4)

This text is clear in admitting that it is not possible to deduce, in an a priori manner, an explanation of particular natural phenomena from the very general laws of nature Descartes defended, because there is an almost infinite number of alternative paths—all consistent with the laws of nature—by which God might have caused particular natural phenomena. To discover which path he chose, i.e. to discover the mechanism by which natural phenomena are caused by the interaction of particles of matter, one has to have recourse to crucial experiments. And, as has been already acknowledged above, the results which can be gleaned by this method are still hypothetical.

However, Descartes is not consistent in acknowledging that hypothetical initiatives must remain hypothetical, and that they cannot be converted subsequently into something more like the purely formal deductions of mathematics. And, despite the need for experiments to help decide how a natural phenomenon occurs, he sometimes described the results of his scientific method in language which could almost have been taken

directly from the section of Aristotle's *Posterior Analytics* quoted above: "As far as physics is concerned, I believed that I knew nothing at all if I could only say how things may be, without being able to prove that they could not be otherwise" (letter of 11 March 1640: AT III 39: CSMK 145). This raises a question about the kind of certainty Descartes claimed for the results of his scientific method when applied to natural phenomena.

CERTAINTY AND PROBABILITY

Descartes' claims about the relative certainty of scientific explanations are appropriately ambivalent. The ambivalence reflects the comparatively unsophisticated concepts of certainty and uncertainty available to the early seventeenth century. The scholastic tradition was committed to a sharp dichotomy between two kinds of knowledge-claim; one was certain and demonstrated, and the other was dialectical and uncertain. As far as scholastics were concerned, therefore, one had to choose between claiming to have demonstrated, certain knowledge—which was the only kind worth having—or the type of uncertain opinion which hardly deserved further discussion, since it was completely uncorroborated. Descartes' efforts to describe the degree of certainty that resulted from his scientific practice are best understood as a doomed attempt to classify the probability produced by the new scientific method in the language of the scholastics. Thus he sometimes claims that his explanations are certain; he cannot concede that they are uncertain without automatically excluding them as genuine alternatives to the established explanations of the schools. At the same time he recognizes that they are not absolutely certain, that they do not enjoy the type of certainty that can be realized in mathematics, that they are only morally certain or as certain as one could hope to be in this type of enterprise.[21] Another compromise, consistent with the claims about a metaphysical foundation, is the argument that the first principles are certain whereas the explanations of particular natural phenomena are more or less uncertain.

Descartes consistently claims that his first principles, or the more general claims about matter and the laws of nature, are very certain.

> as regards the other things I assumed which cannot be perceived by any sense, they are all so simple and so familiar, and even so few in number, that if you compare them with the diversity and marvellous artifice which is apparent in the structure of visible organs, you will have far more reason to suspect that, rather than include some which are not genuine, I have omitted some which are in fact at work in us. And knowing that nature always operates in the most simple and easy way possible, you will perhaps agree that it is impossible to find more plausible explanations of how it operates than those which are proposed here.
>
> (AT XI 201)

This point was reiterated on a number of occasions; the basic hypotheses of the Cartesian system were said to be simple and relatively few, and at the same time they explained a great variety of disparate natural phenomena. "Simple" had connotations of being easily understood, possibly by analogy with some natural phenomenon with which we are ordinarily familiar. It also implied that a hypothesis was consistent with the limited categories available in Cartesian natural philosophy, such as size, speed, and quantity of motion. In other words, it was possible to imagine or construct a mechanical model of a so-called "simple" hypothesis, whereas the kinds of explanations proposed by others were allegedly difficult to understand, not amenable to simple modeling, and probably expressed in the metaphysical language of the schools. Thus he wrote in Part III of the *Principles:* "I do not think that it is possible to think up any alternative principles for explaining the real world that are simpler, or easier to understand, or even more probable" (AT VIIIA 102: CSM I 257).

Descartes was aware of the objection that one could construct a hypothesis to explain any conceivable phenomenon and that, as a result, hypotheses could be accused of being ad hoc. His answer to this objection included a number of elements. One was that he used only a few hypotheses to explain many different phenomena: "it seems to me that my explanations should be all the more accepted, in proportion as I make them depend on fewer things" (AT VI 239). Given the few principles from which he begins, the variety of phenomena which arc explained provides an extra degree of confirmation.

> In order to come to know the true nature of this visible world, it is not enough to find causes which provide an explanation of what we see far off in the heavens; the selfsame causes must also allow everything which we see right here on earth to be deduced from them. There is, however, no need for us to consider all these terrestrial phenomena in order to determine the causes of more general things. But we shall know that we have determined such causes correctly afterwards, when we notice that they serve to explain not only the effects which we were originally looking at, but all these other phenomena, which we were not thinking of beforehand.
>
> (AT VIIIA 98-9: CSM I 255)

Apart from the points just mentioned, Descartes also argued that the new natural philosophy should be compared, not with some abstract criterion of what counts as a good theory, but with other theories available in the 1630s to explain the same range of phenomena. In that context, Cartesian science was claimed to be the best available. This is clear from a letter to Father Morin of 13 July 1638:

> Finally, you say that there is nothing easier than to fit some cause to any given effect. But although

there are indeed many effects to which it is easy to fit different causes, one to one, it is not so easy to fit a single cause to many different effects, unless it is the true cause which produces them. There are often effects where, in order to prove which is their true cause, it is enough to suggest a cause from which they can all be clearly deduced. And I claim that all the causes which I have discussed are of this type . . . If one compares the assumptions of others with my own, that is, all their real qualities, their substantial forms, their elements and similar things which are almost infinite in number, with this one assumption that all bodies are composed of parts—something which can be observed with the naked eye in some cases and can be proved by an unlimited number of reasons in others . . . and finally, if one compares what I have deduced about vision, salt, winds, clouds, snow, thunder, the rainbow, and so on from my assumptions, with what they have deduced from theirs . . . I hope that would suffice to convince those with an open mind that the effects which I explain have no other causes apart from those from which I deduce them.
>
> (AT II 199-200: CSMK 107)

The conclusion of the *Principles* repeats the same claim; if a few assumptions can explain a wide variety of disparate phenomena, then that argues well for their plausibility:

> Now if people look at all the many properties relating to magnetism, fire and the fabric of the entire world, which I have deduced in this book from just a few principles, then, even if they think that my assumption of these principles was arbitrary and groundless, they will still perhaps acknowledge that it would hardly have been possible for so many items to fit into a coherent pattern if the original principles had been false.
>
> (AT VIIIA 328: CSM I 290)

If we accept the point being made, that a few basic hypotheses are put to work in explaining all the natural phenomena mentioned, what degree of certainty should Descartes claim for his first principles? Not surprisingly, one finds two rather different claims in this context: one of them concedes that the confirmed principles are only more or less probable, whereas the other assumes that they are certain and demonstrated. The more modest claim is found in a letter to an unknown correspondent, written about 1646: "I would not dare claim that those [principles] are the true principles of nature. All I claim is that, by assuming them as principles, I have satisfied myself in all the many things which depend on them. And I see nothing which prevents me from making some progress in the knowledge of the truth" (AT IV 690). The more confident claim about moral and metaphysical certainty comes in the penultimate article of the *Principles:*

> there are some matters, even in relation to the things

in nature, which we regard as absolutely, and more than just morally, certain. . . . This certainty is based on a metaphysical foundation . . . Mathematical demonstrations have this kind of certainty, as does the knowledge that material things exist; and the same goes for all evident reasoning about material things. And perhaps even these results of mine will be allowed into the class of absolute certainties, if people consider how they have been deduced in an unbroken chain from the first and simplest principles of human knowledge. . . . it seems that all the other phenomena, or at least the general features of the universe and the earth which I have described, can hardly be intelligibly explained except in the way I have suggested.

(AT VIIIA 328-9: CSM I 290-1)

The French version of this text is even more explicit on the demonstrative character of the explanations found in Cartesian physics:

I think that one should also recognise that I proved, by a mathematical demonstration, all those things which I wrote, at least the more general things concerning the structure of the heavens and the earth, and in the way in which I wrote them. For I took care to propose as doubtful all those things which I thought were such.

(AT IXB 325)

The problem of classifying the type of certainty Descartes might reasonably have claimed for his principles and hypotheses is best understood historically, by taking account of the lack of a concept of probability in the early part of the seventeenth century and of the assumption of the scholastic tradition that anything less than demonstrated truths was as unreliable as mere opinion or guesswork. In this context, Descartes claimed that his natural philosophy was certain and demonstrated; at the same time, realizing that it could hardly be as certain as the formal proofs of mathematics, he conceded that only the more general assumptions of his system were certain, whereas the explanations of particular natural phenomena were more or less certain.

This point reopens the question about the kind of evidence Descartes thought was appropriate to supporting scientific claims, and the relative importance of metaphysical arguments vis-à-vis experiential evidence. There is no suggestion that Descartes ever reneged on the conviction, so clear in the **Meditations,** that one can realize a degree of certainty which is equivalent to indubitability by reasoning about concepts and axioms. This kind of metaphysical certainty is appropriate to the foundations of our knowledge, whether that knowledge is mathematical, physical, or otherwise.

However, if we wish to make judgments about the physical world, then we cannot assume naively that our sensations reflect the way the world is. Nor can we discover in any detail what kind of natural phenomena occur, nor what mechanisms explain their occurrence, by introspecting our ideas. There has to be some provision, therefore, for beginning with clear and distinct metaphysical concepts and axioms and somehow making the crucial transition to describing and explaining the natural world around us. This can be done only by consulting our experience of the natural world, and this implies that we use our senses in order to gain scientific knowledge.

At the same time, Descartes can be correctly described as a critic of the reliability of empirical evidence. His critique was carefully developed to identify a number of ways in which we might draw erroneous conclusions from our sensory experience. Two of these have already been identified: (a) We might ignore the distinction between primary and secondary qualities and, as a result, assume that our sensations resemble the causes of our sensations; and (b) we might argue too hastily from an experiment to some conclusion without taking account of the many ways in which an experiment can mislead. In general, we are in danger of spontaneously making naive, uncritical judgments about the physical world without questioning the reliability of our sensations or the logic of conclusions drawn from reliable observations. Such spontaneous judgments should be distinguished from other judgments, equally based on sensation, which we make after due deliberation and reflection. Unfortunately for the modern reader, Descartes expressed this distinction in terms of a contrast between experience and reason; what he meant was a contrast between two types of judgment, both equally based on experience. This is made explicit in the following text:

It is clear from this that when we say 'The reliability of the intellect is much greater than that of the senses,' this means merely that when we are grown up the judgments which we make as a result of various new observations are more reliable than those which we formed without any reflection in our early childhood; and this is undoubtedly true.

(Sixth Replies: AT VII 438: CSM II 295)

For this reason, a true philosopher "should never rely on the senses, that is, on the ill-considered judgments of his childhood, in preference to his mature powers of reason" (AT VIIIA 39: CSM I 232).

It is obvious, then, that one cannot avoid the necessity of relying on experientially based evidence. Descartes acknowledges the need for this kind of evidence in natural philosophy and uses it extensively in the scientific experiments which he describes. He says openly, in Part VI of the **Discourse,** "regarding observations, that the further we advance in our knowledge, the more necessary they become" (AT VI 63: CSM I 143). On this point, his scientific practice corresponded with his methodological rule, for he spent much more time doing experiments or reading about those done by others than he ever spent in mere thinking. However, for reasons already mentioned, he had little confidence in experiments he had not checked himself.[22] Hence there were serious limits to the extent to which he could hope to complete a comprehensive explanation of nature; he was likely to be frustrated "by the brevity of life or the lack of observations" (AT VI 62: CSM I 143). For this reason, Descartes decided to devote his life to the pursuit of what he called a "practical philosophy which might replace the speculative philosophy taught in the schools" (AT VI 61: CSM I 142). "I will say only that I have resolved to devote the rest of my life to nothing other than trying to acquire some knowledge of nature from which we may derive rules in medicine which are more reliable than those we have had up till now" (AT VI 78: CSM I 151). This is equivalent to a commitment to doing experiments, the cost of which he often complained of. To attempt to gain this practical knowledge in any other way, apart from experimentally, would be to join those "philosophers who neglect experience and think that the truth will emerge from their own heads as Minerva did from that of Jupiter" (*Regulae* Rule V: AT X 380).

A full account of the contribution of Descartes to the history of philosophies of science would involve examining his work in the light of his successors in the seventeenth century. Without examining this supplementary evidence here—which would include the ways in which Descartes was understood by, for example, La Forge, Malebranche, Rohault, Poisson, Cordemoy and Régis—there is reason to believe that his successors shared a common interpretation of the main features of Descartes' philosophy of science.[23] These common features are best understood in contrast with the scholastic philosophy for which they were proposed as a substitute. For Descartes, the contrast was between the practical and the speculative, the explanatory and the nonexplanatory, the critical and the naively uncritical, the mechanistic and the formal, the mathematical and quantitative versus the qualitative. Despite the favorable contrast with the natural philosophy of the schools, however, Descartes continued to accept the scholastic assumption that we should construct our metaphysics first, on the epistemic basis of reflection on ordinary experience, and that any subsequent explanations of natural phenomena must be consistent with the foundational metaphysics.

Once the foundations were in place, it was accepted that we could never know the way the world is by consulting our sensations and inferring from them that the causes of our sensations must resemble our subjective experiences. Besides, if we assume that physical phenomena are constituted by the interactions of very small particles of matter, then the sheer size of such particles of infinitely divisible matter would put their observation beyond our reach. For these two reasons, we can only come to know how the physical world is by hypothesis.

For Descartes, to explain a natural phenomenon is not to redescribe it in the language of forms and qualities, as was done in the schools. To explain, in this context, is to construct a mechanical model of how the phenomenon in question is caused. This model construction is necessarily hypothetical. So, beginning with the basic laws of nature and the metaphysical foundations established in the *Meditations* or in Book I of the *Principles,* Descartes set out to construct the kind of models his concept of explanation demanded. Although he continued to claim absolute certainty for the foundations, it was clear that he could not be as confident about the more detailed explanations of natural phenomena. These explanations depended on observations, and on performing complex experiments the interpretation of which introduced new reasons for doubt. There was also another reason for caution which emerged at this stage, namely Descartes' skepticism about the possibility of ever identifying the multiplicity of variables involved in any complex natural phenomenon. What begins on "indubitable" foundations, therefore, quickly gets mired in the almost immeasurably complex detail of unobservable particles of matter interacting at unobservable speeds. The crucial experiments which we perform to help choose the most plausible explanation are open to various interpretations. Hence the birth of the well-known Cartesian tradition of simply imagining some mechanism by which small parts of matter in motion might have caused some natural phenomenon which we observe.

To those who objected: this does not result in the kind of demonstrated knowledge prized by the scholastic tradition, Descartes replied that those who demand such demonstrations do not know what they are looking for, nor what they ought to look for. It is not possible to realize the same kind of certainty in physics as in mathematics or metaphysics. We have to settle for less.

This suggests that Descartes' philosophy of science was very much a product of the time in which it was developed. The 1630s and 1640s were a time of transition from the science of forms and qualities to what we describe now as modern science. One finds features of both of these philosophies of science in Descartes. What was significantly new was the commitment to mechanical explanation rather than the "occult powers" of the scholastic tradition, and the recognition that this type of explanation must be hypothetical. But for Descartes, lacking a theory of probability, this seemed compatible with the continued claim that his natural philosophy was not only superior in explanatory power to that of the schools, but that it was just as certain; or at least, that its more fundamental principles were demonstrated.

Notes

1 *Posterior Analytics,* 71b 8-12, 73a 21-2.

2 The extent to which scholastic philosophy influenced the curriculum of colleges and universities in France in the seventeenth century is comprehensively documented in Brockliss, *French Higher Education in the Seventeenth and Eighteenth Centuries.*

3 This was summarized in the axiom: "nihil est in intellectu quod prius non fuit in sensu." French Cartesians in the period immediately after Descartes understood his theory of innate ideas as, in part, a response to what they considered to be a generally accepted scholastic doctrine, that all ideas derive originally from sensation. See, for example, Poisson, *Commentaire ou remarques sur la méthode de M. Descartes,* unpaginated preface, which discusses the "famous principle on which depends some of the dogmas of scholasticism, that nothing enters the mind which does not pass first through the senses." The same doctrine is discussed at some length on pp. 124-38. Cf. Le Grand, *An Entire Body of Philosophy,* p. 4. Among scholastic defenders of the thesis, even after Descartes, see Huet, *Censura Philosophiae Cartesianae,* pp. 51-3.

4 Even dedicated Cartesians, such as Jacques Rohault, continued the tradition of explaining natural phenomena in terms of matter and form. See Rohault, *A System of Natural Philosophy,* translated by J. Clarke, pp. 21-2. The original French text was published in 1671.

5 Mahoney (trans.), *The World,* pp. 1-3.

6 Mahoney, *The World,* p. 5.

7 Mahoney, *The World,* p. 7.

8 Mahoney, *The World,* p. 49.

9 Letter to Mersenne, 27 May 1638 (AT II 141-2, 143-4:CSMK 103). The same use of the word "demonstration" is found in Descartes' letter to Plempius, 3 October 1637 (AT I 420:CSMK 64).

10 The principle of parsimony in metaphysics, that one should not postulate the existence of more distinct entities or types of entity than is necessary, is usually attributed to William of Occam (1280?-1349?). See for example his *Quodlibeta* V, Q.1

11 Mahoney, *The World,* p. 9.

12 Mahoney, *The World,* p. 39.

13 Although the letter was written in French, the italicized phrase was in Latin: *sub scientiam non cadit.* Descartes to Mersenne, 13 November 1629 (AT I 73). See also Descartes to Mersenne, 11 June 1640 (AT III 80); Descartes to Cavendish, 15 May 1646 (AT IV 416-17).

14 Cf. similar responses to Mersenne, 23 February 1643 (AT III 634) and 26 April 1643 (AT III 652).

15 In the original Latin text, "hypotheses non fingo." Isaac Newton, *Mathematical Principles of Natural Philosophy and His System of the World,* ed. Cajori, p. 547.

16 Cf. Rule Nine of the *Regulae:* AT X 400: CSM I 33.

17 Descartes frequently pointed to problems in interpreting experimental results, especially when they seemed to disconfirm his own theories. However, the objections he raised were, in principle, legitimate. See, for example, Descartes to Mersenne, 9 February 1639 (AT II 497-8), 29 January 1640 (AT III 7), 11 June 1640 (AT III 80), 4 January 1643 (AT III 609).

18 Cf. *Principles* Part I, arts. 51-7: AT VIIIA 24-7: CSM I 210-12.

19 In the Third Meditation, Descartes argues that "something cannot arise from nothing" (*nec posse aliquid a nihilo fieri*) (AT VII 40: CSM II 28). In the Second Replies to Objections, he says that the causal principle on which he relied in the Third Meditation was equivalent to "nothing comes from nothing" (*a nihilo nihil fit*) (AT VII 135: CSM II 97).

20 Cf. Mahoney, *The World* pp. 61-76: AT XI 38-47.

21 There was a tradition in scholastic philosophy and theology of distinguishing various degrees of certainty in terms of the kind of evidence required to achieve them and the relative importance of acting on our beliefs in different contexts. "Moral certainty" referred to the certainty required for important human actions, such as marrying one's partner or defending oneself against an aggressor. In this type of case, one does not usually have mathematical certainty about various relevant features of the context, but one is sufficiently certain to act and to be excused of responsibility if, despite taking normal precautions, one is mistaken. Cf. French version of *Principles,* Part IV, art. 205: "moral certainty is certainty which is sufficient to regulate our behaviour, or which measures up to the certainty we have on matters relating to the conduct of life which we never normally doubt, though we know that it is possible, absolutely speaking, that they may be false" (CSM I 289).

22 "I have little trust in experiments which I have not per-

formed myself" (letter to Huygens of 1643: AT III 617).[23] For an analysis of how these authors understood Descartes' philosophy of science, see Clarke *Occult Powers and Hypotheses.*

Jean-Marie Beyssade (essay date 1993)

SOURCE: "On the Idea of God: Incomprehensibility of Incompatibilities?" translated by Charles Paul, in *Essays on the Philosophy and Science of René Descartes,* edited by Stephen Voss, Oxford University Press, 1993, pp. 85-94.

[*In the essay that follows, Beyssade examines the paradoxical claims that form the basis of Descartes' metaphysics: that God is incomprehensible and that, to know anything, one must have a clear and distinct understanding of God.*]

Here I would like to raise the question of the idea of God and its nature, because in the metaphysics of Descartes one thesis remains constant from his lost first draft, written in 1628-29, and because this thesis is paradoxical. The thesis is that the entire methodical structure of scientific knowledge depends on an assured knowledge of God. The paradox is that God is asserted to be incomprehensible.

The totality of Cartesian science is based on metaphysics, and two fundamental principles intersect within this metaphysics or first philosophy: one is called the *cogito* (I think, therefore I am; and I am a thinking substance); the other is called the *divine veracity* (God exists; and he cannot deceive me). To appreciate the function assigned to the idea of God one must understand "in what sense it can be said that, if one is ignorant of God, one cannot have any certain knowledge of any other thing."[1] Any other thing: neither mathematics nor physics nor metaphysics. Mathematics, whose reasoning had provided the model of certainty and evidence before metaphysical reflection, does not suffice to give the atheist geometer a true and certain science; but Descartes believes that he "has found how one can demonstrate metaphysical truths in a manner that is more evident than the demonstrations of geometry,"[2] how one can demonstrate the existence of God "in the same manner" as one demonstrates a property of the triangle, "or in a still more evident manner."[3] Physics, which is the trunk of the Cartesian tree, derives its scientific validity from its metaphysical roots: "this is how I have attempted to begin my studies; and I will tell you that I could not have discovered the foundations of physics if I had not sought them in this way."[4] Here order consists in passing from causes to effects, "without basing my reasons on any other principle than the infinite perfections of God;"[5] for "we will undoubtedly pursue the best method that can be used to discover the truth [*optimam philosophandi viam*] if, from our knowledge of his nature [*ex ipsius Dei cognitione*], we proceed to the explanation of the things he has created, and if we attempt to deduce it from the notions that naturally reside in our souls in such a way that we have a perfect knowledge [*science*] of it, that is, in such a way that we know the effects from the causes [*scientiam perfectissimam, quae est effectuum per causas*]."[6] Finally, in metaphysics—a discipline that is as fundamental for the physics which follows it as for the mathematics that preceded it—if the truth of the *cogito* is the first discovered therein, it appears as derived when retrospectively we connect it to the knowledge of God: "In some manner I had within me the notion of the infinite before [*priorem quodammodo*] I had the notion of the finite, that is, that of God before that of myself."[7] The common root of that triple dependence is to be sought in the general rule of the method: "the very thing that I just now took as a rule [and it matters little whether this *just now* refers to my past as a mathematician or to the *cogito,* which is my first assertion as a metaphysician], namely, that those things which we can very clearly and very distinctly perceive are all true, is guaranteed only because God is or exists, and is a perfect being, and because everything within us derives from him."[8] The evident, that is, the unique criterion of the universal method, namely, clarity and distinctness, therefore hangs on the divine veracity.

Now, by a paradox that is as old as Cartesian metaphysics itself, God is incomprehensible. This thesis appears as early as the letters to Mersenne of spring 1630 on the creation of the eternal truths—the first echo to reach us from the approach adopted in the previous year. "We cannot comprehend [*comprendre*] the greatness of God, even though we know it [*connaissons*]."[9] "Since God is a cause whose power exceeds the limits of human understanding, and since the necessity of these truths (the eternal truths of mathematics) does not exceed our knowledge," one must surmise "that they are something less than this incomprehensible power, and subject to it" (6 May). "I say that I know it, not that I conceive it or comprehend it, because one can know that God is infinite and all-powerful even though our mind, being finite, can neither conceive nor comprehend it" (27 May). Here incomprehensibility is linked to the greatness of God, and in particular to his power. It is, throughout Cartesian metaphysics, the characteristic of the infinite. "The infinite, *qua* infinite, is never truly comprehended, but it is nevertheless understood [*intelligi, entendu*]."[10] "In order to have a true idea of the infinite, it is in no way necessary that one comprehend it, inasmuch as incomprehensibility is itself contained in the formal reason of the infinite."[11] We seem driven to ask whether the method, in requiring divine veracity, may not require a foundation which in its incomprehensibility would violate that very method. In basing the truth of everything that is evident on the divine infinity, the method seems to introduce an element that is irreducible to what is evident, an element perhaps intrinsically obscure and confused. We may go further. If the Cartesian God is not just provisionally misunderstood at the beginning of the process, but if he also reveals himself at the end of it to be definitively incomprehensible, is there not a danger that this avowed incomprehensibility in reality conceals internal contradictions, incompatibilities? "An infinite and incomprehensible being," Descartes had written on 6 May 1630.[12] "An absolutely incomprehensible and contradictory being" is how the atheist critic will translate it, for example Baron d'Holbach in the eighteenth century.[13]

Incomprehensibility or inconsistencies—that is our question concerning the idea of God and the nature of God in the metaphysics of Descartes. The paradox can be extended in various directions. We shall develop only one of those directions. We raise the question how the idea of God is capable of satisfying the requirements of the method. The method is absolutely universal. It requires that every perception (or cognition or idea) without exception be clear and distinct if the corresponding proposition (or judgment or statement) is to be included in science. The idea of God must therefore be clear and distinct, and, if the judgment concerning God is the first one of the true science, this idea must be recognized as "the clearest and most distinct of all those present in my mind."[14] Is there no inconsistency between these two assertions, namely, that the idea of God is incomprehensible and that it is the clearest and most distinct of all ideas?

God, *qua* infinite, is incomprehensible. The idea of God is the clearest and most distinct idea of all. These two theses are both incontestably Cartesian. Are they incompatible? Is there an inconsistency here? We do not think so.

First we need to dig deeper into the correlation between (divine) incomprehensibility and distinctness or differentiation. In fact, from 1630 on, Descartes quite rigorously associates the knowledge of God and the recognition of his inconceivable infinity. The knowledge of God is doubly positive: we know at the same time *that* he exists and, with respect to a certain number of attributes (e.g., omnipotence, immutability, creator of existences and of essences), *what* he is. The recognition of his incomprehensibility is negative at first: the impossibility that we should embrace or encompass or master his nature. If clarity corresponds to presence, then incomprehensibility instead marks an absence, and this is why it seems connected to obscurity and confusion. This contrast is not false, but it is simplistic and one-sided. The truth is that starting with the letters of 1630, the divine incomprehensibility does not only have the neg-

ative function of limiting our knowledge of God by the recognition of something beyond which escapes our grasp. In a positive way it introduces into our idea of God the original and true knowledge of an incommensurable distance. Thanks to it God is not beyond the idea we have of him, like a hidden God, in which case our idea of him would not display him as he is. To the contrary, his greatness is given directly as present, without any possible confusion with our own properties. Incomprehensibility is the positive manner in which the infinite reveals itself to a finite mind as it is, that is to say, as incomparable. By a reversal illustrated in the comparison made between God and a king, what at first seems to be a principle of confusion is shown to be a principle of distinctness.[15] "We cannot comprehend the greatness of God, even though we know it": the phrase "even though," introducing a subordinate clause, contrasts what we know (which is positive, or clear) with what seems negative and obscure (namely, what we cannot comprehend). "But this very fact, that we judge it to be incomprehensible, makes us esteem it the more": the phrase "this very fact" marks the reversal, from a subordinate clause indicating opposition into an explanation indicating assimilation. The failure to reduce (by means of dominating through comprehension) is actually a success; it is the way a finite mind recognizes and esteems the more what in fact can never be esteemed too much, since it is absolute greatness. "Just as a king possesses greater majesty when he is less familiarly known by his subjects": thus distance is a mark of majesty, and to decrease familiarity is not to decrease knowledge, but to disclose to a subject the true knowledge of his unequal relation to his king. On the condition, to be sure, that the distant king is not a king who is hidden or unknown: "provided, however, that this does not make them think that they are without a king, and provided that they know him sufficiently well not to have any doubts about it." The phrase "provided that" leads us back again to the subordinated opposition of the "even though" between knowledge that is sufficient to dispel doubt (presence, or clarity) and noncomprehension (absence, such as distance and distinctness).

This equilibrium is maintained in the great systematic expositions, notably in the Third Meditation.[16] "It is useless to object that I do not comprehend the infinite, or [*vel*] that there are an infinity of other [*alia*] attributes within God that I can neither comprehend nor even perhaps reach by thought in any way at all." Here incomprehensibility seems to function as a barrier between two categories of attributes, the ones that I perceive clearly and distinctly and the rest. The first ones ensure knowledge that is sufficient to dispel doubt: "everything real and true that my mind conceives clearly and distinctly and that contains in itself some perfection is entirely contained and enclosed in that idea." Here clarity of presence extends to conception (the Latin only gives *percipio*), and, it seems at first, to comprehension as well. The other category of attributes ensure distance and majesty. I can neither comprehend them nor perhaps, for certain of them, have any other species of idea of them: this is pure absence or obscurity, which surrounds my knowledge with a black line, like the curtain behind which the king withdraws. "For it is of the nature of infinity that my finite and limited nature cannot comprehend it." The axiom which makes of incomprehensibility the true relation between the infinite and the finite can be counted on to bring us back from opposition (*alia*) to an explanation indicating assimilation.

"And it is sufficient that I conceive this well [*me hoc ipsum intelligere*], and that [*ac*] I judge that all things that I conceive clearly and in which I know there to be some perfection, and perhaps also an infinity of others [*atque etiam forte alia innumera*] of which I am ignorant, are in God formally or eminently, in order for [*ut*] the idea I have of him to be the most true, the most clear, and the most distinct of all those existing in my mind." Two conditions must be met in order that the idea of God attains the maximum of clarity and distinctness. It is sufficient that I perceive thoroughly the link between (positive) infinity and incomprehensibility: *hoc ipsum*, "this very thing," was precisely the reversal of 1630. But this is not the only condition: it is also necessary that I endow God with predicates; and in an attenuated form the *ac* takes up again the phrase "provided that" of 1630. These predicates are of two kinds. One kind are unknown—innumerable *alia* which escape me entirely. The other kind, the first ones named, correspond to perfections recognized and identified by me; they constitute the positive element without which there could be no clarity.

A commentary for the benefit of Clerselier, of 23 April, 1649, fixes the doctrine once and for all. It refers quite specifically to our phrase "and it is sufficient that I understand this very thing well," which I have labeled the *reversal*. Descartes clarifies: "Yes, it is sufficient that I understand this very thing well, namely that God is not comprehended by me, in order that I understand [*intelligam*] God according to the truth of the thing [*juxta rei veritatens*] and such as he is [*qualis est*]."[17] And so incomprehensibility is not an obstacle or a limit to our intellectual understanding of God; on the contrary, it reveals God in his truth, in his real and positive transcendence. This incomprehensibility does not reveal a regrettable and provisional failure of my limited mind, but instead a necessary incommensurability between the infinite and any finite mind, even one more perfect than my own, even the mind of an angel. The truth of my idea is ensured *thanks to* this lack of comprehension, this intellectual understanding of the incomprehensibility, and not *in spite of* it. Must we say, with Alquié, that our intellectual understanding of God consists "sim-

ply in the apprehension of his incomprehensible character"?[18] To do so would be to forget the necessity of the other element, namely, the presence which is required by clarity. The letter to Clerselier restores to it all the amplitude of the subordinate clause; it revives the overly discreet *ac* to its true value, namely, "provided that." "Provided that in addition [*modo praeterea*] I judge that there are in him all the perfections that I know clearly [*clare intelligo*] and moreover [*et insuper*] many others which I cannot comprehend." Incomprehensibility is not devoid of perfections; it is superadded to them: the fact that these two terms are externally related, which is implied by the subordinate phrase (*modo*, "provided that"), is accentuated by *praeterea*, "in addition." And among the required perfections two species are recorded anew: those of which I have a clear intellection and those, much more numerous (*multo plures*), which I cannot comprehend. Does this mean that I comprehend the first kind? One might think so, and assimilate my perception of them to a conception, and even a comprehension. Only the second kind, the *alia*, would then be incomprehensible.

But this would be a mistake. This error must be corrected in order to present Descartes's doctrine in its perfect coherence. The end of the Third Meditation is instructive here. For in fact it discusses, not the divine perfections of which I am ignorant (no doubt there are an infinity of them), but those I know. God exists, therefore, "this same God, I say, the idea of which is within me, that is to say the one who possesses all those exalted perfections [*illas perfectiones*] which I can, as for myself, not comprehend, but in one manner or another [*quocunque modo*] reach [*attingere*] by thought."[19] In the strict sense of the word my thought can never comprehend a single divine perfection. But there are a certain number of them which I can reach and, so to speak, touch by thought, in contrast to an infinity of others of which I am completely ignorant. The perfections to which I can attain are those of which I find marks within myself, such as my knowledge, my free will, my power. I comprehend those perfections within myself from the inside, intimately—even my freedom, which is often said to be infinite.[20] They are like traces which allow me to form the idea of a divine (omniscient) understanding, a divine will, a divine omnipotence.[21] I am able to form a concept or a conception of each of them, and I should then conceive them in God as infinite or as indefinite, the two adjectives, usually contrasted, here being equivalent, not distinct from one another.[22] But we must not allow this legitimate conception to become transformed erroneously into a comprehension, something that would correspond to a drift toward the univocal. It is precisely because all the intelligible perfections are united in God that each of them is, properly speaking, infinite, and none of them can be truly comprehended by me, but only reached by thought or conceived or, still better, understood (*entendu*).

Let us take up the train of thought as the Second Replies explicates it. It is necessary to begin with those "attributes of God of which we recognize some trace within ourselves": we comprehend them within ourselves, and, were no distance or distinctness to be added to their presence and clarity, we would be content to transfer them, in amplified form, into God, which would ensure the strict univocity of the attributes by turning God into a man writ large.[23] "But in addition [*praeterea*] we understand [*intelligimus, concevons*] in God an absolute immensity, simplicity, and unity which embraces and contains all his other attributes, and of which we find no instance either in ourselves or elsewhere."[24] This absolute unity, which is one of the most exalted of the divine perfections, is intelligible but neither comprehensible nor even conceivable. It ensures the absolute inseparability of the divine perfections, which is the same thing as the absolute simplicity of God, or what Spinoza was to call, by contrast with that which is merely infinite in its own kind, the absolutely infinite.[25] This unity, which is not comprehensible by a finite mind, is itself comprehensive. *Non tam capere quam . . . capi:* this divine unity is not comprehended, "grasped together," by finite minds; instead, it grasps them.[26] And— what is a different matter—it grasps or comprehends, embraces, *complectentem,* all the divine attributes.[27] Undoubtedly God comprehends himself; that is, he has an adequate concept of all his properties, both those we know and those of which we are ignorant.[28] But it is different for us. First of all, there are attributes of which we have no idea: these are the *alia,* perhaps innumerable, which are as profoundly unknown as, for Spinoza, all the attributes except for extension and thought are unknown. For Descartes, only revelation is capable eventually of rendering them accessible to us. Then there are attributes of which there are traces within us (e.g., knowledge, will, and power). We may now return to them without risk of univocity.[29] For their union with the other attributes, in other words, their connection with the absolute unity on which they depend, deprives them of any possibility of being comprehended. They are nonetheless conceivable, for their relation to our own perfections precludes our speaking of a simple equivocity. What we have here is analogy in the most traditional sense, since the clarity of presence (which alone leads to identity, to comprehension, to univocity) is qualified by distance as distinctness (which distance alone leads to otherness, to ignorance, to equivocity). The infinite is intelligible for the very reason that it is not comprehensible.

Let us conclude by investigating how the idea of God works in relation to the unique and universal method, whose general rule requires clarity and distinctness. We discover that these characteristics, whose conjunction defines the evident, undergo two successive transformations in the course of the operation carried out by metaphysics. Before that operation, clarity and distinctness had been separated, after the example of mathematics, which had served in the **Rules for the Direction of the Mind** and in Part II of the **Discourse on Method** both as their prototype and as their model. For an object presented to the view of the mind and made subject to its command, clarity signifies presence (the presence of a spectacle to a spectator, *ob-versari,* something which is there to see);[30] and distinctness signifies difference (the difference between two objects next to each other, which are distinguished through *juxta-posing* them, as in the case of a polygon with 1,000 sides next to one with 999 sides).

The procedure of the *cogito* constitutes the first subversion: although the same general rule of evidence, namely, the rule of clarity and distinctness, is derived by reflection on this first truth, the prototype and model has changed, and with it the meaning of the criterion. For a mind which itself makes the discovery of itself, and gradually makes itself better known and more familiar to itself, clarity signifies presence to oneself (the consciousness of a subject which senses and experiences itself, *in se con-versus*);[31] and distinctness signifies exclusion (by means of doubt I make myself distinct, in that I reject through denial everything I face, so that I may grasp myself on each occasion as the subject of that exclusion).[32] Note well that nothing in the rule has changed—either its universality nor its univocity. The new example takes up within itself the previous ones, and deepens them; it leaves the mathematically evident with all of its brilliance, and simply lays claim to being still more evident, on the basis of the very criteria of the older prototype, which is not so much lowered in class as surpassed in class, and whose criteria have not so much changed as they have manifested what remained implicit in them, yet to be perceived.

The same operation is redoubled in the passage from the *cogito* to God. For the infinite, the intellectual grasp of which emerges as soon as I comprehend my finitude, clarity signifies the implicit presence of the being (an immediately given reality, a perfect unity prior to all limitation and fragmentation); and distinctness signifies transcendence (separation by distance, by incomprehensibility, which eliminates all confusion by establishing an insurmountable dissimilarity).

Of course, at each passage it is possible to reject the new model, to reduce rationality to the previous model, to consider the shift in foundation as foreign to the method. But what is characteristic of the Cartesian enterprise is that its methodic procedures remain univocal, and in this sense the idea of God must occupy the first place according to the very order of the true science.[33] That is why this idea must be maximally evident according to the method itself.

It is therefore not sufficient to set in opposition God, who is incomprehensible, and the idea of God, which is clear and distinct. It is not sufficient to distinguish the properties of the idea from those of its object: the idea of red is not red, the idea of a sphere is not spherical, and the idea of obscurity may not be obscure, but clear and distinct.[34] Certainly this difference between the idea and its object is important. In the case under consideration, God is infinite but the idea of God is not infinite: it is, on the contrary, finite and suited to the small capacity of our minds *(finita et ad modulum ingenii nostri accommodata)*.[35] Conversely, if the idea of God is the most clear and the most distinct of all, it would be absurd to speak of God as being clear and distinct: this characteristic pertains to an idea, not to its object. But incomprehensibility, which pertains to the nature of God, or to the nature of the infinite, is also a characteristic of his idea. *Idea . . . infiniti, ut sit vera, nullo modo debet comprehendi:* it is emphatically the idea of God, and not God himself, that is spoken of *(pace* the overzealous translation of Clerselier, not reviewed here by Descartes); and it is this idea which, if it is to be true, must not in any way be comprehended.[36] A characteristic of the object, in this case God or the infinite, which is incomprehensible, is therefore introduced into the idea of the object: this idea, first of all (and then perhaps many other ideas, later on), cannot in any way be comprehended. But it is precisely in the case of this idea that this characteristic is eminently positive. It establishes the true relation—once it is noticed, the difference is incommensurable and impossible to miss—between the Being which it represents on the one hand and any knowable object and my knowing mind on the other hand. It is because God is incomprehensible that the idea of him is also incomprehensible; and it is not *even though* this idea is incomprehensible, but rather *because* it is incomprehensible that it *is* the most clear and the most distinct of all.[37]

Notes

1 *Principles of Philosophy* I, a. 13, developing Meditation III: AT [*Oeuvres de Descartes,* ed. C. Adam and P. Tannery, 13 vols., Paris: Vrin/CNRS, 1879-1913] VII, 36, ll. 28-29; in CSM [*The Philosophical Writings of Descartes;* ed. J. G. Cottingham, R. Stoothoff, and D. Murdoch; two vols.; Cambridge University Press, 1985] II, 25: "for if I do not know this, it seems that I can never be quite certain about anything else."

2 To Mersenne, 15 April 1630: AT I, 144, ll. 14-17; *Descartes: Oeuvres philosophiques,* ed. Ferdinand Alquié, 3 vols. (Paris: Garnier, 1963-73) I, 259 and n. 1 (henceforth abbreviated FA).

3 *Discourse on Method* IV: AT VI, 36, ll. 24 and 27-28, developed in Meditation V: AT VII, 65, ll. 28-29; AT IX, 52; FA II, 472 and n. 2; in HR [*The Philosophical Works of Descartes;* trans. Elizabeth S. Haldane and G.R.T. Ross; Cambridge: Cambridge University Press, 1911-12; reprinted, with corrections, 1931; reprinted New York: Dover, 1955] I, 104: "in the same manner . . . or even more evidently still."

4 To Mersenne, 15 April 1630: AT I, 144, ll. 8-11, developed in the letter to Mersenne of 28 January 1641: AT III, 297-298; FA II, 316-317.

5 *Discourse* V: AT VI, 43, ll. 6-8; FA I, 615 and n. 2; in HR I, 108: "without resting my reasons on any other principle than the infinite perfections of God."

6 *Principles* I, a. 24 (on the difference between the Latin and the French, see FA III, 106, n. 1).

7 Meditation III: AT VII, 45, ll. 27-29; AT IX, 36; in CSM II, 31: "my perception of the infinite, that is God, is in some way prior to my perception of the finite, that is myself."

8 *Discourse* IV: AT VI, 38, ll. 16-21; FA I, 611 and n. 1; in HR I, 105: "that which I have just taken as a rule, that is to say, that all the things that we very clearly and very distinctly conceive of are true, is certain only because God is or exists."

9 To Mersenne, 15 April, 6 May, and 27 May 1630: respectively, AT I, 145, ll. 21-22; 150, ll. 18-22; 152, ll. 9-13; respectively, FA I, 260 and n. 4; 265 and n. 3; 267.

10 First Responses: AT VII, 112, ll. 21-23; AT IX, 89; FA II, 531; in CSM II, 81 (and n. 3): "the infinite, *qua* infinite, can in no way be grasped. But it can still be understood."

11 Fifth Responses: AT VII, 368, ll. 2-4; FA II, 811 and n. 2; in CSM II, 253: "for the idea of the infinite, if it is to be a true idea, cannot be grasped at all, since the impossibility of being grasped is contained in the formal definition of the infinite."

12 To Mersenne, 6 May 1630: AT I, 150, ll. 6-7; FA I, 265.

13 *Le bon sens du Curé J. Meslier,* ch. 40, a work published anonymously in 1772 by d'Holbach, its author.

14 Meditation III: AT VII, 46, ll. 27-28; AT IX, 37; HR I, 166; CSM II, 32.

15 To Mersenne, 15 April 1630: AT I, 145, ll. 21-28; FA I, 260.

[16] Meditation III: AT VII, 46, ll. 16-28; AT IX, 36-37; HR I, 166; CSM II, 32 and n. 1. On the relation between this passage and the end of the Third Meditation: AT VII, 52, ll. 2-6; AT IX, 41; HR I, 171; CSM II, 35, a passage which will be examined later, see J.-L. Marion, "Descartes et l'ontothéologie," *Bulletin de la Societé Française de Philosophie* (24 April 1982), 143; discussed by J.-M. Beyssade in *Bulletin cartésien* XIII, *Archives de Philosophie* 47, no. 3 (July-September 1984): 47; taken up again in *Sur le prisme métaphysique de Descartes* (Presses Universitaires de France: Epimethée, 1986), 119-120 and n. 54. It seems to us that the first passage conjoins *comprehendere* and *attingere* ("*nec* comprehendere *nec* attingere"), while the second one opposes them ("*non* comprehendere *sed* attingere"); but this is because the first passage does not deal with the idea of God in general; it deals only with the *alia,* the unknown perfections ("which I can *neither* comprehend *nor* even reach"), whereas the second one deals with the known perfections ("which I can *certainly* reach in thought *but not* comprehend").

[17] To Clerselier, 23 April 1649: AT V, 356, ll. 22-27; FA III, 924 and n. 2.

[18] F. Alquié, *La découverte métaphysique de l'homme chez Descartes* (Presses Universitaires de France, 1960 and 1966), ch. 10, 216 and n. 2, a formula developed by H. Gouhier in a remarkable commentary to which we owe a great deal, *La pensée métaphysique de Descartes* (Paris: Vrin, 1962), ch. 8, ii, 212 and n. 28.

[19] Meditation III: AT VII, 52, ll. 2-6; AT IX, 41; HR I, 171; in CSM II, 35: "God, a God, I say, the very same being the idea of whom is within me, that is, the possessor of all the perfections which I cannot grasp, but can somehow reach in my thought."

[20] *Principles* I, a. 41: AT VIII, 20, ll. 25, 28-29; HR I, 235.

[21] Second Responses: AT VII, 137; AT IX, 108; FA II, 560 and n. 1; CSM II, 98-99. We comment on this passage later.

[22] *Indefinitae, sive infinitae,* Second Responses: AT VII, 137, ll. 24-25; CSM II, 99, l. 1: "indefinite (or infinite)." Cf. Conversation with Burman: AT V, 154; *Descartes' Conversation with Burman,* ed. John Cottingham (Oxford, 1976), 14-15.

[23] To Regius, 24 May 1640: AT III, 64; FA II, 244 and n. 1.

[24] Second Responses: AT VII, 137: ll. 15-18; AT IX, 108; FA II, 560 and n. 2; CSM II, 98-99; the relevant passage is AT VII, 137, l. 8-138, l. 1.

[25] Meditation III: AT VII, 50, ll. 16-19; AT IX, 40; HR I, 169-170; CSM II, 34.

[26] First Responses: AT VII, 114, l. 7; AT IX, 90; in CSM II, 82: "not so much to take hold of them as to surrender to them."

[27] Second Responses: AT VII, 137, l. 17; AT IX, 108; in CSM II, 98: "which embraces all other attributes."

[28] On adequate concepts, cf. Second, Third (no. 11), and Fifth Responses: respectively, AT VII, 140, ll. 3-4; 189, ll. 17-18; and 365, ll. 3-4. The debate of the Fourth Responses (AT VII, 220) is continued in the Conversation with Burman: AT V, 151-152; *Descartes' Conversation,* 10-11.

[29] *Univoce,* Second Responses: AT VII, 137, l. 22; in CSM II, 98: "in the same sense." On the relation between Cartesianism and analogy, see Gouhier, *La pensée métaphysique,* ch. 8, ii and iii; and J.-L. Marion, *Sur la théologie blanche de Descartes* (Paris: Presses Universitaires de France, 1981).

[30] *Obversari,* Third Meditation: AT VII, 35, ll. 21-22; in HR I, 158: "were presented to my mind"; in CSM II, 24: "appeared before my mind."

[31] *In se conversa,* preface, *Meditations:* AT VII, 7-8; in HR I, 137: "reflecting on itself"; in CSM II, 7: "when directed towards itself."

[32] *Principles* I, 60: AT VIII, 29, l. 2, *excludere;* in HR I, 244: "shut off from itself."

[33] Marion, *Sur le prisme métaphysique de Descartes,* seems to us to be completely right in speaking, not of irrationality, but of "another rationality" (p. 243). But he believes that this metaphysical rationality must be "shielded from the method's domain of application" (p. 242, and again pp. 324-325, n. 29); we are not sure that this is necessary.

[34] Second Responses: AT VII, 147, ll. 18-27; AT IX, 115; FA II, 573 and n. 1; CSM II, 105.

[35] First Response: AT VII, 114, ll. 14-17; AT IX, 90; FA II, 533; in CSM II, 82: "knowledge of the finite kind just described, which corresponds to the small capacity of our minds."

[36] Fifth Responses: AT VII, 368, ll. 2-3; Clerselier's translation in FA II, 811 and n. 2.

[37] I am deeply indebted to Charles Paul and Stephen Voss for many linguistic and philosophical emendations. The remaining mistakes are mine.

FURTHER READING

Cottingham, John. "Cartesian Dualism: Theology, Metaphysics, and Science." In *Reason, Will, and Sensation: Studies in Descartes' Metaphysics,* edited by John Cottingham, pp. 236-57. Oxford: Oxford at the Clarendon Press, 1994.

> Explores Descartes' three approaches to the mind-body distinction—theological, metaphysical, and scientific—and the relations among the different arguments.

Funkenstein, Amos. "Descartes and More." In his *Theology and the Scientific Imagination, from the Middle Ages to the Seventeenth Century,* pp. 72-80. Princeton: Princeton University Press, 1986.

> Discusses some of the problems with Descartes' blending of mathematics, physics, and theology, and the relationship between the philosophies of Descartes and Henry More.

Garber, Daniel. "Descartes' Project." In his *Descartes' Metaphysical Physics,* pp. 30-62. Chicago: University of Chicago Press, 1992.

> Explores the structure of Descartes's scientific program and his emphasis on the interconnectedness of the different branches of knowledge.

Gaukroger, Stephen. "The Sources of Descartes' Procedure of Deductive Demonstration in Metaphysics and Natural Philosophy." In *Reason, Will, and Sensation: Studies in Descartes's Metaphysics,* edited by John Cottingham, pp. 47-60. Oxford: Oxford at the Clarendon Press, 1994.

> Explores Descartes' philosophical method, claiming that it is neither a synthetic nor analytic discovery of truths, but a presentation of accepted truths by "restructur[ing] already developed material in such a way as to draw from it conclusions which may be obscured."

Hacking, Ian. "Proof and Eternal Truths: Descartes and Leibniz." In *Descartes: Philosophy, Mathematics and Physics,* edited by Stephen Gaukroger, pp. 169-80. Sussex: The Harvester Press, 1980.

> Compares Leibniz's more modern opinion that proof is integral to truth to Descartes' disregard of proof as a truth-condition.

Hatfield, Gary. "Reason, Nature, and God in Descartes." In *Essays on the Philosophy and Science of René Descartes,* edited by Stephen Voss, pp. 259-87. New York: Oxford University Press, 1993.

> Considers Descartes' approach to metaphysics to be redefining "the pure intellect as an instrument of cognition" in order to separate science from (Aristotelian) theology, and compares Descartes to such figures as Francisco Suarez.

Hoffman, Paul. "Cartesian Passions and Cartesian Dualism." *Pacific Philosophical Quarterly* LXXI, No. 4 (December 1990): 310-33.

> Considers *Passions of the Soul* to counteract what most commentators consider to be a strict separation of the mental and the physical in Descartes' writings.

Loeb, Louis E. "The Cartesian Circle." In *Reason, Will, and Sensation: Studies in Descartes's Metaphysics,* edited by John Cottingham, pp. 200-35. Oxford: Oxford at the Clarendon Press, 1994.

> Examines different interpretations of the Cartesian circle, arguing in favor of the "psychological interpretation," that indubitable truths are those that are psychologically impossible to doubt.

Popkin, Richard H. "Descartes—Conqueror of Scepticism." In his *The History of Scepticism from Erasmus to Descartes,* pp. 175-96. New York: Humanities Press, 1964.

> Positions Descartes with regard to his pyrrhonian contemporaries, concluding that he failed to counter their skeptical objections.

Rogers, G. A. J. "Descartes and the Method of English Science." *Annals of Science* XXIX, No. 3 (October 1972): 237-55.

> Examines the influence of the Cartesian method on English scientists of the seventeenth century, especially Robert Boyle.

Schuster, John A. "Whatever Should We Do with Cartesian Method?—Reclaiming Descartes for the History of Science." In *Essays on the Philosophy and Science of René Descartes,* edited by Stephen Voss, pp. 195-223. New York: Oxford University Press, 1993.

> Examines the historical significance of Descartes' philosophy of science, rejecting the tendency of modern scholarship to overemphasize his doctrine of method.

Sorell, Tom. "Descartes's Modernity." In *Reason, Will, and Sensation: Studies in Descartes's Metaphysics,* edited by John Cottingham, pp. 29-45. Oxford: Oxford at the Clarendon Press, 1994.

> Defends the notion that Descartes is the father of modern philosophy.

Stout, A. K. "The Basis of Knowledge in Descartes." In *Descartes: A Collection of Critical Essays,* edited by Willis Doney, pp. 169-91. Notre Dame: University of Notre Dame Press, 1967.

> Examines the relationship among the three main grounds of certainty for Descartes: the *cogito,* "clear and distinct" perceptions, and the existence of God.

Additional coverage of Descartes' life and career is contained in the following sources published by Gale Reasearch: *Literature Criticism from 1400 to 1800*, Vol. 20.

Gottfried Wilhelm Leibniz

1646-1716

German philosopher, scientist, and mathematician.

INTRODUCTION

Leibniz was a major force in German intellectual life during the late seventeenth and early eighteenth centuries. His wide-ranging interests included linguistics, jurisprudence, and theology, but he is best remembered for his work in science, metaphysics, and mathematics. Leibniz developed calculus independently of Sir Isaac Newton and his work with binary arithmetic and logic contributed to the development of Boolean algebra and computers. He also contributed to the study of motion and developed a metaphysical system based on the existence of monads, which he described as the basic substance from which all things are composed. Though elements of Leibniz's philosophical teachings were ridiculed by later thinkers—for exapmple, Voltaire in *Candide* (1758)—Leibniz's ideas have influenced a number of seminal philosophers, including Georg Wilhelm Friedrich Hegel and Immanuel Kant.

Biographical Information

Leibniz was born in Leipzig in 1646, into a Protestant family. As a child, he read widely in his father's library and had mastered Latin and Greek by the time he was fourteen. In 1661 he entered the University of Leipzig, where he studied philosophy and law. Leibniz completed his legal studies in 1666 and applied for a doctorate of law, which the university refused to grant because of his age. He subsequently left Leipzig and obtained his degree at the University of Altdorf, which also offered him a professorship. Leibniz declined the offer, however, and took a position as secretary of the Rosicrucian Society in Nuremberg. There, through the influence of the retired statesman Johann Christian von Boyneburg, Leibniz met Johann Philipp von Schönborn, the elector of Mainz, who offered him a position in his court investigating issues of law and politics. From 1672 to 1676 Leibniz lived in Paris, where he furthered his studies in mathematics and science; improved on Blaise Pascal's calculator by adding the ability to perform multiplication and division; and made a number of important friends in the European intellectual community, including Antoine Arnauld, a theologian, and Christian Huygens, the famed Dutch mathematician and astronomer. In 1676 Leibniz left Paris for Hanover, Germany, to serve under Johann Friedrich, the Duke of Hanover. After the death of Johann Friedrich, Leibniz served under Ernst August and later under Georg Ludwig, who was even-

tually crowned George I of England. In 1700 Leibniz persuaded Prince Frederick of Prussia to found the Berlin Society of Sciences, which later became the Prussian Royal Academy. Leibniz's fame as a philosopher and scientist reached its peak in the early 1700s; he was inducted into the Paris Academy of Sciences as a foreign member in 1700, was named president for life of the Berlin Society of Sciences, and was in correspondence with most of the major intellectuals of the period. Leibniz's popularity gradually deteriorated, however, and his death in 1716 passed virtually unnoticed.

Major Works

The philosopher's first work, *Disputatio metaphysica de principio individui* (1663), which he published while a student at the University of Leipzig, concerns the existential nature of the individual, which, Leibniz argued, cannot be explained by form or matter alone, but must be understood as a whole. As a corolary to his arguments, Leibniz suggested that ideas are similar to numbers, in that a complex statement can be derived from simpler statements through a process of combination similar to the multiplication of numbers. In his next major work, *Dissertatio de arte combinatoria* (1666; *On the Art of Combinations*), Leibniz elaborated on this concept and produced a model to explain how complex reasoning is reducible to ordered combinations of simpler elements. This model later became the theoretical ancestor for computers. In his *Meditationes de Cognitione, Veritate, et Ideis* (1684; *Thoughts on Knowledge, Truth, and Ideas*) Leibniz suggested a relationship between the knowledge of God and man. Leibniz published his work on the development of differential calculus in 1684 as *Nova methodus pro maximis et minimis, itemque tangentibus, quae nec fractas, nec irrationales quantitates moratum, et singulare pro illis calculi genus* (*New Method for the Greatest and the Least*). Although Newton had developed similar mathematical concepts as early as 1665, he had not published his findings. The debate over who should have priority as the inventor of calculus became a highly contested subject during the 18th century. *Discours de métaphysique* (1686; *Discourse on Metaphysics*) introduces his doctrine on the relationship between predicates and propositions. According to Leibniz, the predicate—attribute or concept—of any affirmative proposition that is true is contained within the idea of the subject. Leibniz contended that this theory held for both necessary and contingent propositions. (A contingent proposition states what is or is not possible.) In his *Système nouveau de la nature et de la communication des substances, aussi bien que de l'union qu'il ya entre l'âme et le corps* (1695; *New System*) Leibniz examined the relationships between substances and introduced the idea of a pre-established harmony, created by God, between the individual's body and soul, such that the two give meaning to each other. Leibniz published his *Essais de théodicée sur la bonté de Dieu, la liberté de l'homme et l'origine du mal* (*Theodicy: Essays on the Goodness of God, the Freedom of Man, and the Origin of Evil*) in 1710. In this work he expounded his ideas on divine justice and posited that all creatures act according to their nature and in accordance with the universal harmony. Leibniz argued that all creatures with reason are free and that evil is a lack that increases the beauty of the summation of all things. He also argued that God had created the best of all the possible worlds. In his last work, *Principia philosophiae, more geometrico demonstrata* (1714; *The Monadology*), Leibniz synthesized many of the concepts introduced in *Theodicy*.

Critical Reception

Although Leibniz was neglected toward the end of his life and for over a century afterwards, his work has been the object of increasing interest since the mid-nineteenth century to the present. In the 1840s, for instance, the English mathematician George Boole expanded on Leibniz's work on binary arithmetic to develop Boolean algebra. In the area of calculus, Leibniz's system of notation, rather than Newton's, has become the favored method. Much recent work on Leibniz's writings has focused on his metaphysics and his theology. Many of Leibniz's works were published posthumously, and though he never wrote a "grand synthesis" of his philosophy, a number of recent commentators have remarked on the completeness and coherence of Leibniz's philosophical system. Bertrand Russell stated that Leibniz's "greatness is more apparent now than it was at any earlier time. Apart from his eminence as a mathematician and as the inventor of the infinitesimal calculus, he was a pioneer in mathematical logic, of which he perceived the importance when no one else did so. And his philosophical hypotheses, though fantastic, are very clear, and capable of precise expression. Even his monads can still be useful as suggesting possible ways of viewing perception."

PRINCIPAL WORKS

Disputatio metaphysica de principio individui (philosophy) 1663

Dissertatio de arte combinatoria [*On the Art of Combinations*] (nonfiction) 1666

Nova methodus discendae docendaeque jurisprudentine [*New Methods of Teaching and Learning Jurisprudence*] (nonfiction) 1667

Hypothesis physica nova [*New Physical Hypothesis*] (nonfiction) 1671

Meditationes de Cognitione, Veritate, et Ideis [*Thoughts on Knowledge, Truth, and Ideas*] (philosophy) 1684

Nova methodus pro maximis et minimis, itemque tangentibus, quae nec fractas, nec irrationales quantitates moratum, et singulare pro illis calculi genus [*New Method for the Greatest and the Least*] (mathematics) 1684

*Discours de métaphysique [*Discourse on Metaphysics*] (philosophy) 1686

†Systema theologicum [*A System of Theology*] (philosophy) 1686

‡Tentamen anagogicum: Essai anagogique dans la recherche des causes (nonfiction) 1690-95

Système nouveau de la nature et de la communication des substances, aussi bien que de l'union qu'il ya entre l'âme et le corps [*New System*] (philosophy) 1695

§Nouveaux essais sur l'entendement humain [*New Essays Concerning Human Understanding*] (philosophy) 1700-05

Essais de théodicée sur la bonté de Dieu, la liberté de l'homme et l'origine du mal [*Theodicy: Essays on the Goodness of God, the Freedom of Man, and the Origin of Evil*] (philosophy) 1710

#*Principes de la nature et de la grâce fondés en raison* [*Principles of Nature and of Grace*] (philosophy) 1714

***Principia philosophiae, more geometrico demonstrata* [*The Monadology*] (philosophy) 1714

A Collection of Papers, which Passed between the Late Learned Mr. Leibnitz and Dr. Clarke, in the Years 1715 and 1716 (letters) 1717; also published as *The Leibniz-Clarke Correspondence,* 1956

*This work was first published in 1846.
†This work was first published in 1819.
‡This work was first published in 1890.
§This work was first published in 1765.
#This work was first published in 1718 in the journal *L'Europe savant.*
**This work was first published in 1720-21 and is also known as *La monadologie.*

CRITICISM

Bertrand Russell (essay date 1900)

SOURCE: "Leibniz's Premisses" and "Leibniz's Theory of Knowledge," in *A Critical Exposition of the Philosophy of Leibniz,* Cambridge at the University Press, 1900, pp. 1-7, 160-71.

[*In the excerpts below, Russell comments on Leibniz's influences, the major tenets of his philosophy, and his ideas on knowledge. Russell contends that Leibniz's philosophy was an "unusually complete and coherent system."*]

The philosophy of Leibniz, though never presented to the world as a systematic whole, was nevertheless, as a careful examination shows, an unusually complete and coherent system. As the method of studying his views must be largely dependent upon his method of presenting them, it seems essential to say something, however brief, as to his character and circumstances, and as to the ways of estimating how far any given work represents his true opinions.

The reasons why Leibniz did not embody his system in one great work are not to be found in the nature of that system. On the contrary, it would have lent itself far better than Spinoza's philosophy to geometrical deduction from definitions and axioms. It is in the character and circumstances of the man, not of his theories, that the explanation of his way of writing is to be found. For everything that he wrote he seems to have required some immediate stimulus, some near and pressing incentive. To please a prince, to refute a rival philosopher, or to escape the censures of a theologian, he would take any pains. It is to such motives that we owe the *Théodicée,* the *Principles of Nature and of*

Grace,[1] the *New Essays,* and the *Letters to Arnauld.* But for the sole purposes of exposition he seems to have cared little. Few of his works are free from reference to some particular person, and almost all are more concerned to persuade readers than to provide the most valid arguments. This desire for persuasiveness must always be borne in mind in reading Leibniz's works, as it led him to give prominence to popular and pictorial arguments at the expense of the more solid reasons which he buried in obscurer writings. And for this reason we often find the best statement of his view on some point in short papers discovered among his manuscripts, and published for the first time by modern students, such as Erdmann or Gerhardt. In these papers we find, as a rule, far less rhetoric and far more logic than in his public manifestoes, which give a very inadequate conception of his philosophic depth and acumen.

Another cause which contributed to the dissipation of his immense energies was the necessity for giving satisfaction to his princely employers. At an early age, he refused a professorship at the University of Altdorf[2], and deliberately preferred a courtly to an academic career. Although this choice, by leading to his travels in France and England, and making him acquainted with the great men and the great ideas of his age, had certainly a most useful result, it yet led, in the end, to an undue deference for princes and a lamentable waste of time in the endeavour to please them. He seems to have held himself amply compensated for laborious researches into the genealogy of the illustrious House of Hanover by the opportunities which such researches afforded for the society of the great. But the labours and the compensations alike absorbed time, and robbed him of the leisure which might have been devoted to the composition of a *magnum opus.* Thus ambition, versatility, and the desire to influence particular men and women, all combined to prevent Leibniz from doing himself justice in a connected exposition of his system.

By this neglect, the functions of the commentator are rendered at once more arduous and more important than in the case of most philosophers. What is first of all required in a commentator is to attempt a reconstruction of the system which Leibniz should have written—to discover what is the beginning, and what the end, of his chains of reasoning, to exhibit the interconnections of his various opinions, and to fill in from his other writings the bare outlines of such works as the Monadology or the *Discours de Métaphysique.* This unavoidable but somewhat ambitious attempt forms one part—perhaps the chief part—of my purpose in the present work. To fulfil it satisfactorily would be scarcely possible, and its necessity is my only excuse for the attempt. As I wish to exhibit a coherent whole, I have confined myself, as far as possible, to Leibniz's mature views—to the views, that is, which he held, with but slight modifications, from January 1686 till his death in 1716. His earlier views, and the influence of other philosophers, have been considered only in so far as they seemed essential to the comprehension of his final system.

But, in addition to the purely historical purpose, the present work is designed also, if possible, to throw light on the truth or falsity of Leibniz's opinions. Having set forth the opinions which were actually held, we can hardly avoid considering how far they are mutually consistent, and hence—since philosophic error chiefly appears in the shape of inconsistency—how far the views held were true. Indeed, where there is inconsistency, a mere exposition must point it out, since, in general, passages may be found in the author supporting each of two opposing views. Thus unless the inconsistency is pointed out, any view of the philosopher's meaning may be refuted out of his own mouth. Exposition and criticism, therefore, are almost inseparable, and each, I believe, suffers greatly from the attempt at separation.

The philosophy of Leibniz, I shall contend, contains inconsistencies of two kinds. One of these kinds is easily removed, while the other is essential to any philosophy resembling that of the Monadology. The first kind arises solely through the fear of admitting consequences shocking to the prevailing opinions of Leibniz's time—such are the maintenance of sin and of the ontological argument for God's existence. Where such inconsistencies are found, we, who do not depend upon the smiles of princes, may simply draw the consequences which Leibniz shunned. And when we have done this we shall find that Leibniz's philosophy follows almost entirely from a small number of premisses. The proof that his system does follow, correctly and necessarily, from these premisses, is the evidence of Leibniz's philosophical excellence, and the permanent contribution which he made to philosophy. But it is in the course of this deduction that we become aware of the second and greater class of inconsistencies. The premisses themselves, though at first sight compatible, will be found, in the course of argument, to lead to contradictory results. We are therefore forced to hold that one or more of the premisses are false. I shall attempt to prove this from Leibniz's own words, and to give grounds for deciding, in part at least, which of his premisses are erroneous. In this way we may hope, by examining a system so careful and so thorough as his, to establish independent philosophical conclusions which, but for his skill in drawing deductions, might have been very difficult to discover.

The principal premisses of Leibniz's philosophy appear to me to be five. Of these some were by him definitely laid down, while others were so fundamental that he was scarcely conscious of them. I shall now enumerate these premisses, and shall endeavour to show, in subsequent chapters, how the rest of Leibniz follows from them. The premisses in question are as follows:

I. Every proposition has a subject and a predicate.

II. A subject may have predicates which are qualities existing at various times. (Such a subject is called a *substance*.)

III. True propositions not asserting existence at particular times are necessary and analytic, but such as assert existence at particular times are contingent and synthetic. The latter depend upon final causes.

IV. The Ego is a substance.

V. Perception yields knowledge of an external world, *i.e.* of existents other than myself and my states.

The fundamental objection to Leibniz's philosophy will be found to be the inconsistency of the first premiss with the fourth and fifth; and in this inconsistency we shall find a general objection to Monadism.

The course of the present work will be as follows: Chapters II.-V. will discuss the consequences of the first four of the above premisses, and will show that they lead to the whole, or nearly the whole, of the necessary propositions of the system. Chapters VI.-XI. will be concerned with the proof and description of Leibniz's Monadism, in so far as it is independent of final causes and the idea of the good. The remaining chapters will take account of these, and will discuss Soul and Body, the doctrine of God, and Ethics. In these last chapters we shall find that Leibniz no longer shows great originality, but tends, with slight alterations of phraseology, to adopt (without acknowledgment) the views of the decried Spinoza. We shall find also many more minor inconsistencies than in the earlier part of the system, these being due chiefly to the desire to avoid the impieties of the Jewish Atheist, and the still greater impieties to which Leibniz's own logic should have led him. Hence, although the subjects dealt with in the last five chapters occupy a large part of Leibniz's writings, they are less interesting, and will be treated more briefly, than the earlier and more original portions of his reasoning. For this there is the additional reason that the subjects are less fundamental and less difficult than the subjects of the earlier chapters.

The influences which helped to form Leibniz's philosophy are not directly relevant to the purpose of the present work, and have, besides, been far better treated by commentators[3] than the actual exposition of his final system. Nevertheless, a few words on this subject may not be amiss. Four successive schools of philosophy seem to have contributed to his education; in all he found something good, and from each, without being at any time a mere disciple, he derived a part of his views. To this extent, he was an eclectic; but he differed from the usual type of eclectic by his power of transmuting what he borrowed, and of forming, in the end, a singularly harmonious whole. The four successive influences were: Scholasticism, Materialism, Cartesianism, and Spinozism. To these we ought to add a careful study, at a critical period, of some of Plato's Dialogues.

Leibniz was educated in the scholastic tradition, then still unbroken at most of the German universities. He obtained a competent knowledge of the schoolmen, and of the scholastic Aristotle[4], while still a boy; and in his graduation thesis, *De Principio Individui,* written in 1663, he still employs the diction and methods of scholasticism. But he had already, two years before this time (if his later reminiscences are to be trusted), emancipated himself from what he calls the "trivial schools[5]," and thrown himself into the mathematical materialism of the day. Gassendi and Hobbes began to attract him, and continued (it would seem) greatly to influence his speculations until his all-important journey to Paris. In Paris (with two brief visits to England) he lived from 1672 to 1676, and here he became acquainted, more intimately than he could in Germany, with Cartesianism both in mathematics and philosophy—with Malebranche, with Arnauld the Jansenist theologian, with Huygens, with Robert Boyle, and with Oldenburg, the Secretary of the Royal Society. With these men he carried on correspondence, and through Oldenburg some letters (the source of 150 years of controversy[6]) passed between him and Newton. It was during his stay in Paris that he invented the Infinitesimal Calculus, and acquired that breadth of learning, and that acquaintance with the whole republic of letters, which afterwards characterized him. But it was only on his way back from Paris that he learnt to know the greatest man of the older generation. He spent about a month of the year 1676 at the Hague, apparently in constant intercourse with Spinoza; he discussed with him the laws of motion and the proof of the existence of God, and he obtained a sight of part (at any rate) of the *Ethics* in manuscript[7]. When the *Ethics* soon afterwards was posthumously published, Leibniz made notes of it, and undoubtedly bestowed very careful thought upon its demonstrations. Of his thoughts during the years which followed, down to 1684 or even 1686 (since the *Thoughts on Knowledge, Truth and Ideas* deal only with one special subject), only slight traces remain, and it seems probable that, like Kant in the years from 1770 to 1781, he was in too much doubt to be able to write much. He certainly read Plato[8], and he certainly desired to refute Spinoza. At any rate, by the beginning of 1686 he had framed his notion of an individual substance, and had sufficiently perfected his philosophy to send Arnauld what is perhaps the best account he ever wrote of it—I mean the *Discours de*

Métaphysique (G. IV. 427-463). With this and the letters to Arnauld his mature philosophy begins; and not only the temporal, but the logical beginning also is, in my opinion, to be sought here. The argument which forms the logical beginning, and gives the definition of substance, will be found in the four following chapters.

. . . . .

Before I begin an account of Leibniz's theory of knowledge, I may as well point out that what I am going to discuss is not exactly Epistemology, but a subject which belongs in the main to Psychology. The logical discussions of Chapters II.-V. dealt with that part, in what is commonly called Epistemology, which seems to me not psychological. The problem we are now concerned with is of a different kind; it is not the problem: What are the general conditions of truth? or, What is the nature of propositions? It is the entirely subsequent problem, How do we and other people come to know any truth? What is the origin of cognitions as events in time? And this question evidently belongs mainly to Psychology, and, as Leibniz says, is not preliminary in philosophy [G. V. 15 (N. E. 15; D. 95)]. The two questions have been confused—at any rate since Des Cartes—because people have supposed that truth would not be true if no one knew it, but becomes true by being known. Leibniz, as we shall see in discussing God, made this confusion, and Locke might seem to have made it, since he disclaims a merely psychological purpose[1]. But that is no reason for our making it, and in what follows I shall try to avoid it. At the same time Locke is in one sense justified. The problem is not a *purely* psychological one, since it discusses knowledge rather than belief. From the strict standpoint of Psychology, no distinction can be made between true and false belief, between knowledge and error. As a psychical phenomenon, a belief may be distinguished by its content, but not by the truth or falsity of that content. Thus in discussing knowledge, *i.e.* the belief in a true proposition, we presuppose both truth and belief. The inquiry is thus hybrid, and subsequent both to the philosophical discussion of truth, and to the psychological discussion of belief.

I explained briefly in my last chapter the sense in which Leibniz held to innate ideas and truths. They are in the mind always, but only become properly known by becoming conscious objects of apperception. Leibniz only endeavours, in the New Essays, to show the innateness of *necessary* truths, though he is bound to hold, owing to the independence of monads, that all the truths that ever come to be known are innate. He finds it easier, however, to prove the impossibility of learning necessary truths by experience, and trusts, I suppose, that this will afford a presumption against Locke's whole theory of knowledge. He uses the expression *innate truth* in the **New Essays,** to denote a truth in which all the ideas are innate, *i.e.* not derived from sense; but he explains that there is a different use of the word [G. V. 66 (N. E. 70)]. In the sense in which he uses it, "the sweet is not the bitter" is not innate, because *sweet* and *bitter* come from the external senses. But "the square is not the circle" is innate, because *square* and *circle* are ideas furnished by the understanding itself [G. V. 79 (N. E. 84)]. Now the question arises: How does Leibniz distinguish ideas of sense from other ideas? For he cannot hold, as other philosophers might, that ideas of sense are impressed from without. Nor can he hold that they are such as alone are capable of representing external things, for they are one and all confused, and would be absent in a true knowledge of the world [G. V. 77, 109 (N. E. 82, 120)]. Sense-ideas must, therefore, be distinguished by their own nature, and not by a reference to external causes. On this point, Leibniz, so far as I know, says nothing quite definite. The nearest approach to a definite explanation is in the *Discours de Métaphysique* (G. IV. 452). He speaks of the action of objects of sense upon us, he says, in the same way as a Copernican may speak of sunrise. There is a sense in which substances may be said to act upon each other, "and in this same sense it may be said that we receive knowledge from without, by the ministration of the senses, because some external things contain or express more particularly the reasons which determine our soul to certain thoughts." Thus sense-ideas are those in which we are passive in the sense explained in Chapter XII. Again sense-ideas are confused and express the external world. "Distinct ideas are a representation of God, confused ideas are a representation of the universe" [G. V. 99 (N. E. 109)]. He does, as a matter of fact, denote as sense-ideas all those which presuppose extension or spatial externality, though space itself is not an idea of sense. "The ideas which are said to come from more than one sense," he explains, "like those of space, figure, motion, rest, are rather from common-sense, that is from the mind itself, for they are ideas of the pure understanding, but they are related to the external and the senses make us perceive them" [G. V. 116 (N. E. 129)]. Thus the qualities which appear as external are ideas of sense, but all that is involved in externality itself is not sensational. And the qualities that appear as external are confused, since they cannot, as they appear, be states of monads. Ideas derived from reflection, on the contrary, are not necessarily confused (cf. G. II. 265), for if they truly describe our own states of mind, they describe something actual and not a mere phenomenon. Besides this reason, there is also the fact that by reflection we discover the categories (or predicaments, as Leibniz calls them). There is, indeed, much that reminds one of Kant in Leibniz's theory of knowledge. Existence, he says, cannot be found in sensible objects but by the aid of reason, and hence the idea of existence is derived from reflection [G. V. 117 (N. E. 130)]. To the maxim that there is nothing in the intellect but what comes from the senses, Leibniz adds, *except the intellect itself* (G. V. 100;

N. E. 111). "It is very true," he says, "that our perceptions of ideas come either from the external senses, or from the internal sense, which may be called reflection; but this reflection is not limited to the mere operations of the mind, as is stated (by Locke); it extends even to the mind itself, and it is in perceiving the mind that we perceive substance" [G. V. 23 (N. E. 24)]. The soul, he says, is innate to itself, and therefore contains certain ideas essentially [G. III. 479; G. V. 93 (N. E. 100)]. Thus it comprises being, unity, substance, identity, cause, perception, reason, and many other notions which the senses cannot give [G. V. 100 (N. E. 111)]; and these ideas are presupposed in any knowledge that can be derived from the senses. And necessary truths, Leibniz points out, are certainly known, though the senses cannot show them to be necessary [G. V. 77 (N. E. 81)]. It follows that such truths are developed from the nature of the mind. It may be surmised that Leibniz dwelt on necessary truths because, in their case, knowledge cannot be supposed due to a causal action of what is known upon the mind. For what is known, in this case, is not in time, and therefore cannot be the cause of our knowledge. This made it easier to suppose that knowledge is never caused by what is known, but arises independently from the nature of the mind.

The doctrine of innate truths, as developed in the New Essays, is more like Kant's doctrine than it has any right to be. Space and time and the categories are innate, while the qualities which appear in space are not innate. To the general theory that all truths which are known are innate, which Leibniz should have adopted, there is no answer but one which attacks the whole doctrine of monads. But to the theory of the New Essays, which adopts the common-sense view that sense-perceptions are caused by their objects, while innate truths are incapable of such a cause, there are, I think, answers which apply equally against Kant's doctrine that the *à priori* is subjective. The argument for subjectivity seems to be simply this: When what we know is the existence of something now, our knowledge may be supposed caused by that existence, since there is a temporal relation between them. But when what we know is an eternal truth, there can be no such temporal relation. Hence the knowledge is not caused by what is known. But nothing else, it is held, could have caused it unless the knowledge had been already obscurely in the mind. Hence such knowledge must be, in some sense, innate. It is difficult to state this argument in a form which shall be at all convincing. It seems to depend upon the radically vicious disjunction that knowledge must be either caused by what is known or wholly uncaused. In Leibniz, who rejected a causal action of the objects of perception, this argument, as a means of distinguishing different kinds of knowledge, is peculiarly scandalous. But leaving aside this special doctrine, and admitting that objects cause our perceptions, does it follow that necessary truths must be innate? All who hold this view are compelled, like Leibniz, to admit that innate knowledge is only virtual [G. V. 71 (N. E. 76)], while all *conscious* knowledge is acquired, and has its definite causes. Now if the knowledge can be rendered conscious by causes other than what is known, why cannot it be wholly due to such causes? All that we can say is, that the mind must have had a *disposition* towards such knowledge—a vague phrase which explains nothing. Moreover, the same argument applies to sense-perception. If the mind were not capable of sense-knowledge, objects could not cause such knowledge. Sensations of colours, sounds, smells, etc., must be equally innate on this view. There is, in fact, just the same difficulty in admitting *conscious* knowledge of a necessary truth to be caused, as in admitting *any* knowledge of it to be caused. The difficulty, in each case, is manufactured by supposing that knowledge can only be caused by what is known. This supposition would have disappeared if people had asked themselves what really *is* known. It is supposed that in *à priori* knowledge we know a proposition, while in perception we know an existent. This is false. We know a proposition equally in both cases. In perception we know the proposition that something exists. It is evident that we do not merely know the something, whatever it be, for this is equally present in mere imagination. What distinguishes perception is the knowledge that the something exists. And indeed whatever can be known must be true, and must therefore be a proposition. Perception, we may say, is the knowledge of an existential proposition, not consciously inferred from any other proposition, and referring to the same or nearly the same time as that in which the knowledge exists. If this had been duly realized—if people had reflected that what is known is always a proposition—they would have been less ready to suppose that knowledge could be caused by what is known. To say knowledge is caused in perception by what exists, not by the fact that it exists, is at once to admit that such knowledge is not caused by what is known. Thus perception and intellectual knowledge become much more akin than is generally supposed. We must either hold all knowledge to be always in the mind, in which case its emergence into consciousness becomes a problem, or we must admit that all knowledge is acquired, but is never caused by the proposition which is known. What its causes are, in any particular case, becomes a purely empirical problem, which may be left wholly to Psychology.

There is, moreover, a great difficulty as to what Leibniz meant by ideas which are innate. This question is dealt with in the New Essays, at the beginning of Book II [G. V. 99 (N. E. 109)]. "Is it not true," Locke is made to ask, "that the idea is the object of thought?" "I admit it," Leibniz replies, "provided you add that it is an immediate internal object, and that this object is an expression of the nature or the qualities of things. If the idea were the *form* of thought, it would spring up and cease with the actual thoughts which corre-

spond to it; but being the *object*, it may be before and after the thoughts[2]." Thus an idea, though it is in the mind, is neither knowledge nor desire; it is not a thought, but what a thought thinks about. This passage makes it clear that the only reason Leibniz had for saying ideas exist in the mind is that they evidently do not exist outside of it. He seems never to have asked himself why they should be supposed to exist at all, nor to have considered the difficulty in making them merely mental existents. Consider, for example, the idea 2. This is not, Leibniz confesses, my thought of 2, but something which my thought is about. But this something exists in my mind, and is therefore not the same as the 2 which some one else thinks of. Hence we cannot say that there is one definite number 2, which different people think of; there are as many numbers 2 as there are minds. These, it will be said, all have something in common. But this something can be nothing but another idea which will, therefore, in turn, consist of as many different ideas as there are minds. Thus we are led to an endless regress. Not only can no two people think of the *same* idea, but they cannot even think of ideas that have anything in common, unless there are ideas which are not essentially constituents of any mind. With Locke's definition, that an idea is the object of thought, we may agree; but we must not seek to evade the consequence that an idea is not merely something in the mind, nor must we seek to give every idea an existence somewhere else. Precisely the same criticism applies to the statement that knowledge, ideas and truths "are only natural habits, *i.e.* active and passive dispositions and aptitudes" (N. E. 105; G. V. 97).

Sense-knowledge in Leibniz is not properly distinguished from intellectual knowledge by its *genesis*, but by its nature. It differs in that the qualities with which it deals are spatially extended, and are one and all confused. From their confusion it follows that those which seem simple are in reality complex, though we are unable to make the analysis. Thus green, though it appears simple, is, Leibniz thinks, really a mixture of insensible portions of blue and yellow [G. V. 275 (N. E. 320)]. But how blue and yellow would appear, if they were distinctly perceived, he does not inform us. He seems to think, however, as was natural to one who believed in analytic judgments, that the nature of our *evidence* for necessary and for sensational truths is different. The first truth of reason, he says, is the law of contradiction, whilst the first truths of fact are as many as the immediate perceptions. That I think is no *more* immediate than that various things are thought by me, and this is urged as a criticism of Des Cartes' *cogito* [G. IV. 357 (D. 48)]. That is to say, the law of contradiction is the sole ultimate premiss for necessary truths, but for contingent truths there are as many ultimate premisses as there are experiences. Nothing, he says, should be taken as primitive principles, except experiences and the law of identity or contradiction, without which last there would be no difference between truth and falsehood [G. V. 14 (D. 94; N. E. 13)]. Thus many truths of fact have no evidence except self-evidence, but this is only the case, among necessary truths, as regards the law of contradiction. The self-evident truths of fact, however, are all psychological: they concern our own thoughts. To this extent Leibniz is at one with Des Cartes and with Berkeley. Where he is more philosophical than either is in perceiving that truths of fact presuppose necessary truths, and that our own existence is not therefore an ultimate and fundamental premiss for all truths. My own existence is an axiom, he says, in the sense of being indemonstrable, not in the sense of being necessary [G. V. 391 (N. E. 469)]. Like all finite existence, it is contingent, but it is just as *certain* as necessary truths (N. E. 499; G. V. 415). Thus Leibniz agrees with Locke that we have an intuitive knowledge of our own existence, a demonstrative knowledge of God's existence, and a sensitive knowledge of that of other things (*ib.*). But the sensitive knowledge may be doubted, and cannot be accepted without some general ground for the existence of other things [G. V. 117 (N. E. 130)]. In this theory which, in its general outlines, is more or less Cartesian, there are, as I have already pointed out, two distinct advances upon Des Cartes. The first is that my own existence is not taken as the premiss for necessary truths; the second is that the existence of my various thoughts is as certain as the existence of myself. Leibniz did not discover, what seems equally true, that the existence of external things is just as certain and immediate as that of my own thoughts, and thus he was unable, as we saw, to justify his belief in an external world.

I come now to another respect in which Leibniz refined upon Des Cartes, namely in the doctrine known as the quality of ideas. This is developed in the ***Thoughts on Knowledge, Truth and Ideas*** (D. 27-32; G. IV. 422-6) (1684). Des Cartes held that whatever is clearly and distinctly conceived is true. This maxim, Leibniz points out, is useless without criteria of clearness and distinctness [G. IV. 425 (D. 31)]. He therefore lays down the following definitions. Knowledge is either *obscure* or *clear*. Clear knowledge is *confused* or *distinct*. Distinct knowledge is *adequate* or *inadequate,* and is also either *symbolical* or *intuitive*. Perfect knowledge is both adequate and intuitive.

As to the meanings of these terms, a notion is *obscure* when it does not enable me to recognize the thing represented, or distinguish it from other similar things; it is *clear* when it does enable me to recognize the thing represented. Clear knowledge is *confused* when I cannot enumerate separately the *marks* required to distinguish the thing known from other things, although there are such marks. Instances of this are colours and smells, which though we cannot analyze them, are certainly complex, as may be seen by considering their

causes. (We must remember that Leibniz believed perception to have always the same degree of complexity as its object, and since green can be produced by mixing blue and yellow, a green object is complex, and therefore our perception of green is also complex.) Clear knowledge is *distinct,* either when we can separately enumerate the marks of what is known—*i.e.* when there is a nominal definition—or where what is known is indefinable but primitive, *i.e.* an ultimate simple notion. Thus a composite notion, such as gold, is distinct when all its marks are known *clearly;* it is *adequate,* if all the marks are also known *distinctly;* if they are not known *distinctly,* the knowledge is *inadequate.* Leibniz is not certain whether there is any perfect example of adequate knowledge, but Arithmetic, he thinks, approaches it very nearly. Distinct knowledge is also divided according as it is symbolical or intuitive. It is *symbolical* or blind, when we do not perceive the whole nature of the object at one time, but substitute signs or symbols, as in Mathematics, whose meaning we can recall when we will. When we embrace in thought at once all the elementary notions which compose an idea, our thought is *intuitive.* Thus our knowledge of distinct primitive ideas, if we have it, must be intuitive, while our knowledge of complex notions is, in general, only symbolical.

This doctrine has important bearings on definition. A *real* definition, as opposed to one which is merely nominal, shows the possibility of the thing defined, and though this may be done *à posteriori,* by showing the thing actually existing, it may also be done *à priori,* wherever our knowledge is adequate. For in this case, a complete analysis has been effected without discovering any contradiction; and where there is no contradiction, that which is defined is necessarily possible [G. IV. 424-5 (D. 30)]. On definition generally, Leibniz makes many important observations. A definition is only the distinct exposition of an idea [G. V. 92 (N. E. 99)], but it may be either real or nominal. It is nominal when it merely enumerates marks, without showing them to be compatible. It is real when all the marks are shown to be compatible, so that what is defined is possible. The idea defined is then real, even if nothing ever exists of which it can be predicated [G. V. 279 (N. E. 325)]. Simple terms cannot have a nominal definition; but when they are only simple with regard to us, like green, they can have a real definition explaining their cause, as when we say green is a mixture of blue and yellow [G. V. 275 (N. E. 319)]. The continuity of forms gives him some trouble in regard to definition, and compels him to admit that we may be in doubt whether some babies are human or not. But he points out, against Locke, that though we may be unable to decide the question, there always is only one true answer. If the creature is rational, it is human, otherwise it is not human; and it always is either rational or not rational, though we may be in doubt as to the alternative to be chosen [G. V. 290 (N.

E. p. 339)]. There is, however, a real difficulty in all cases of continuity, that an infinitesimal change in the object may make a finite change in the idea; as the loss of one more hair may just make a man bald. In such cases, Leibniz thinks that nature has not precisely determined the notion [G. V. 281 (N. E. 328)]; but this seems an inadequate reply.

Connected with Leibniz's notion of definitions, and of the reduction of all axioms to such as are identical, or immediate consequences of definitions [G. V. 92 (N. E. 99)], is his idea of a *Characteristica Universalis,* or Universal Mathematics. This was an idea which he cherished throughout his life, and on which he already wrote at the age of 20[3]. He seems to have thought that the symbolic method, in which formal rules obviate the necessity of thinking, could produce everywhere the same fruitful results as it has produced in the sciences of number and quantity. "Telescopes and microscopes," he says, "have not been so useful to the eye as this instrument would be in adding to the capacity of thought" (G. VII. 14). "If we had it, we should be able to reason in metaphysics and morals in much the same way as in geometry and analysis" (G. VII. 21). "If controversies were to arise, there would be no more need of disputation between two philosophers than between two accountants. For it would suffice to take their pencils in their hands, to sit down to their slates, and to say to each other (with a friend as witness, if they liked): Let us calculate" (G. VII. 200). By establishing the premises in any *à priori* science, the rest, he thought, could be effected by mere rules of inference; and to establish the right premises, it was only necessary to analyze all the notions employed until simple notions were reached, when all the axioms would at once follow as identical propositions. He urged that this method should be employed in regard to Euclid's axioms, which he held to be capable of proof [G. V. 92 (N. E. 99)]. The Universal Characteristic seems to have been something very like the syllogism. The syllogism, he says, is one of the most fruitful of human inventions, a kind of universal Mathematics [G. V. 460 (N. E. 559)]. What he desired was evidently akin to the modern science of Symbolic Logic[4], which is definitely a branch of Mathematics, and was developed by Boole under the impression that he was dealing with the "Laws of Thought." As a mathematical idea—as a Universal Algebra, embracing Formal Logic, ordinary Algebra, and Geometry as special cases—Leibniz's conception has shown itself in the highest degree useful. But as a method of pursuing philosophy, it had the formalist defect which results from a belief in analytic propositions, and which led Spinoza to employ a geometrical method. For the business of philosophy is just the discovery of those simple notions, and those primitive axioms, upon which any calculus or science must be based. The belief that the primitive axioms are identical leads to an emphasis on *results,* rather than premises, which is radically op-

posed to the true philosophic method. There can be neither difficulty nor interest in the premises, if these are of such a kind as "A is A" or "AB is not non-A." And thus Leibniz supposed that the great requisite was a convenient method of deduction. Whereas, in fact, the problems of philosophy should be anterior to deduction. An idea which can be defined, or a proposition which can be proved, is of only subordinate philosophical interest. The emphasis should be laid on the indefinable and indemonstrable, and here no method is available save intuition. The Universal Characteristic, therefore, though in Mathematics it was an idea of the highest importance, showed, in philosophy, a radical misconception, encouraged by the syllogism, and based upon the belief in the analytic nature of necessary truths[5].

Notes

[1] Accepting Gerhardt's opinion that this work, and not the *Monadology,* was written for Prince Eugene (G. VI. 483).

[2] Guhrauer, *Leibnitz: Eine Biographie,* Vol. 1. p. 44.

[3] See especially Guhrauer, *Leibnitz: Eine Biographie,* Breslau, 1846; Stein, *Leibniz und Spinoza,* Berlin, 1890; Selver, *Entwicklungsgang der Leibnizschen Monadenlehre,* Leipzig, 1885; Tönnies, *Leibniz und Hobbes, Phil. Monatshefte,* Vol. XXIII.; Trendelenburg, *Historische Beiträge,* Vol. II., Berlin, 1855.

[4] Leibniz appears, in spite of the great influence which Aristotle exerted upon him, to have never studied him carefully in the original. See Stein, *op. cit.* p. 163 ff.

[5] Guhrauer, *Leibnitz,* Vol. I. pp. 25, 26; G. III. 606.

[6] These letters were said, by Newton's friends, to have given Leibniz the opportunity for plagiarizing the Calculus—a charge now known to be absolutely groundless.

[7] See Stein, *Leibniz und Spinoza,* Chapter IV.

[8] Cf. Stein, *op. cit.* p. 119.

. . . . .

[1] *Essay,* Introduction, § 2.

[2] Cf. also G. III. 659 (D. 236); IV. 451.

[3] In the *Dissertatio de Arte Combinatoria,* G. IV. 27-102.

[4] Cf. G. VII. 214-15, 230, where several of the rules of the Calculus of Symbolic Logic are given.

[5] For an account of Leibniz's views on this matter see

Guhrauer, *op. cit.* Vol. I. p. 320 ff. For a full treatment, see Couturat, *La Logique de Leibnitz,* Paris, 1900 (in the press).

Louis Couturat (essay date 1902)

SOURCE: "On Leibniz's Metaphysics," translated by R. Allison Ryan, in *Leibniz: A Collection of Critical Essays,* edited by Harry G. Frankfurt, Anchor Books, 1972, pp. 19-45.

[*In the essay below, originally published in French in 1902, Couturat argues the importance of logic and reason in Leibniz's philosophy.*]

In the preface to *La Logique de Leibniz,* we asserted that Leibniz's metaphysics rests entirely on his logic. This thesis is confirmed implicitly in our book and is evident from the texts we had occasion to cite there. Nevertheless, since it is contrary to the classical interpretations and to current opinion, it will be useful to establish it explicitly and in detail. Moreover, although it appears to us to be sufficiently proven by the texts which are already known, we are now able to confirm it by adducing some unpublished documents of unusual value and importance. The most interesting and most significant is a short work of four pages in which Leibniz himself has given a succinct account of his entire metaphysics in deducing it from the Principle of Reason. We cited its essential propositions in our preface and in the course of our book. We [now] want to make the new material available. . . .[1]

This fragment is unfortunately not dated. But, by comparing it to short works and letters of known date, we can conjecture with high probability that it was written about 1686 when Leibniz completed the principles and the essential theses of his system, first in the ***Discours de métaphysique*** and then in his ***Lettres à Arnauld.***[2] In fact, the preceding passage does not contain a single proposition which is not already to be found in one of these works. It is none the less original and valuable, however, in virtue of the order and connection which it establishes among all those known propositions.

In the first place, it formulates precisely the famous principle of reason, of which the classical expression *nihil est sine ratione* is, according to Leibniz, only a popular formula borrowed from common sense.[3] In its exact sense, this principle means that in every true proposition the predicate is contained in the subject; therefore, that every truth can be demonstrated *a priori* by the simple analysis of its terms. In a word, that *every truth is analytic.* This may seem paradoxical and even shocking to us who have read Kant. But it seemed entirely natural and evident to Leibniz's contemporaries who, like him, were trained in the Aristotelian and scholastic tradition. And the proof of this is that Ar-

nauld, who was extremely averse to admitting certain consequences of this principle (in particular, the major thesis that "the individual notion of each person contains definitively all that will ever happen to him"), never dreamed of expressing any reservation or doubt about it. On the contrary, he accepted it without qualification and without discussion.[4]

Why is this principle called the "principle of reason" (of *determining* reason at first and, later, of *sufficient* reason)? It is because it means, in brief, that one can *give the reason* for every truth, that is, demonstrate it by analysis. Thus it was originally called "the principle of giving the reason" (*principium reddendae rationis*).[5] This must not lead one to confuse it with the principle of identity; it is precisely its reciprocal. The principle of identity states: every identity (analytic) proposition is true. The principle of reason affirms, on the contrary: every true proposition is an identity (analytic). Its effect is to subordinate all truths to the principle of identity. One might call it the principle of universal intelligibility, or, if one may venture this barbarism, of universal *demonstrability.*

This is the source of the metaphysical import of the principle, which Leibniz recognized and utilized at an early date.[6] We know how he derived from it the principle of indiscernibles and that other principle, really equivalent to the preceding one, that "there are no purely extrinsic characteristics [*dénominations*]";[7] then, step by step, the notion of the *monad* (though not the name), which includes not only all its past, present, and future states, but also all the successive states of the universe of which it is a mirror or rather a perspective; further, the *pre-established harmony,* which necessarily results from the fact that the monads interact only apparently (*physically*) and not really (*metaphysically*); finally, the ideality of space and time and hence of movement and of bodies, which are reduced to mere "true phenomena," and the immortality not only of souls, but of all substances.[8]

In a word, it is the entire ***Monadology*** which Leibniz thus progressively derives from the principle of reason and which he presents in rational order and in proper perspective. Actually, the ***Monadology*** takes as its point of departure this same notion of the monad which is here the conclusion of a long deduction; it reverses the logical construction of the system in a sense and makes the pyramid rest on its peak. In order to convince oneself that the order followed by the ***Monadology*** is really the inverse of the order that is both logical and genetic, it suffices to notice that one cannot at all see how the principle of reason would follow from the definition of the monad, whereas one understands perfectly how the concept of the monad derives from the principle of reason.[9] The monad is the logical subject elevated to the status of substance; its attributes become the accidents "inherent" in the essence of the substance. It contains in itself the entire sequence of its states (and hence the principle or *law* of their succession), because its essence includes all its past, present, and future accidents. It is a mirror or a perspective of the universe, because its notion implies all the things to which it stands in relation. Now, since there are no purely extrinsic characteristics, every external relation of a substance is expressed by an internal modification, that is, by an accident; and that is why "the monads are windowless." Therefore, every reciprocal action between two monads reduces to the correspondence of their respective perceptions, more distinct in the one which is said to act, more confused in the one which is considered to be passive. And this explains the pre-established harmony. In a word, all the metaphysical properties of the "individual substance" derive, by virtue of the principle of reason, from the logical properties which the "complete and singular" idea possesses.[10]

In the second place, one can no longer fail to recognize the absolutely universal applicability Leibniz attributes to the principle of reason. It holds equally for all kinds of truths, *universal* as well as *singular, necessary* as well as *contingent*. This is rigorously logical, since the principle constitutes the very definition of truth in general and expresses its "nature."[11] With respect to contingent truths in particular, Leibniz affirms their subordination to the principle of reason with a clarity and an insistence which leave no room for doubt.[12] It follows that *contingent truths are not synthetic* to any degree whatsoever, as is generally believed; they are just as analytic as necessary truths are. But then, it will be asked, how do they differ from necessary truths? They differ from them, replies Leibniz, as the infinite differs from the finite, or as irrational and rational numbers differ.[13] Contingent truths are analytic, as are all truths; only the analysis of their terms is *infinite,* so that we cannot demonstrate them by reducing them to propositions of identity. They are no less identities in the eyes of God, who alone can complete this infinite analysis "in a single act of mind." This is how Leibniz believes he can escape the doctrine of universal necessity (to which he was averse for moral and theological reasons) and how he finds the solution to the difficulty in the consideration of mathematical infinity.[14]

Thus the comparison of contingent truths with irrational numbers is not a simple metaphor, but an analogy which Leibniz develops confidently and with a rigorous parallelism; he states many times that contingency is rooted in infinity,[15] and that it is thanks to mathematics (to the infinitesimal calculus) that he has been able to understand and explain the nature of contingent truths. Now, as one readily notices, this difficulty (which, by his own account, had long troubled him) exists only as long as contingent truths are analytic: it is a question of understanding how an analytic proposition can fail to be necessary.[16] As soon as contingent truths are considered to be synthetic, the question disappears and the solution no longer has any sense.

Is the difficulty thus really resolved? We are far from so affirming. But here (as in our book) we are writing as an historian, not as a critic; we are seeking what Leibniz actually thought and not trying to determine whether he was right or wrong to think it. From this point of view, it is interesting to know how he was led to this theory. He states it expressly: what rescued him from (Spinozistic) fatalism was the consideration of the possibles which are not realized and which, indeed, will never be realized.[17] In fact, "nothing is necessary of which the opposite is possible".[18] If there are unrealized possibles, then the realized possibles can only be contingent. (These realized possibles comprise the entire real universe: not only individuals but also the general laws of nature.) By 2 December 1676 (the day after his meeting with Spinoza), Leibniz was denying the Spinozistic thesis—"Everything possible exists"—and he was already opposing to it his own theory that only those compossibles containing the greatest reality exist.[19] The point is that not all possibles are compossibles (otherwise there would be no reason why all possibles should not exist).[20] The only *raison d'être* of the possibles is their quantity of reality or of essence. Each possible tends toward existence in proportion to its degree of "perfection"—that is, of reality. All the possibles struggle among themselves for existence in the Mind of God, which is "the land of the possible realities,"[21] and the outcome of this struggle is the infallible and automatic (not to say necessary) triumph of the system of compossibles which contains the most essence or "perfection." The world is thus the product of a "metaphysical mechanism" and of a "divine mathematics."[22] The creation is the solution to a problem of maximization, and this maximization has a significance much more metaphysical than moral. Such is the logical origin of Leibnizian optimism; and this is why it is a speculative and intellectual optimism rather than a teleological and practical one.

It is apparent what we must think of the synthetic character generally attributed to existential judgments.[23] First of all, existential propositions are not the only contingent propositions. All the laws of nature are equally so, according to Leibniz, and for the same reason—namely, because they include an infinity of elements or of *conditions* [*réquisits*]. Second, they are analytic in the same sense as the other contingent truths. To make of existence an exceptional predicate, whose affirmation would be synthetic, is quite simply to confuse Leibniz with Kant. For Leibniz, existence is nothing more than *l'exigence de l'essence;* it is contained in the essence and can be deduced from it by a simple analysis. *It is wrong,* said Leibniz, to think of existence as having nothing in common with essence; *there is something more* in the concept of what exists than in the concept of what does not exist. And in fact existence consists, *by definition,* in taking part in the most perfect order of things; that is to say, in the system of compossibles which contains the most essence. It is in this sense that existence is a "perfection"—that is, an integrating element of the essence.[24] Such is the reply Leibniz made in advance to the Kantian critique of the ontological argument. Now it is worth noticing that this reply is a logical consequence of the principle of reason: if existence were something other than a requirement of the essence, it would be necessary to seek the reason for existence elsewhere—that is, in another essence.[25] In other words, existence is an attribute which, like every other attribute, must be contained in the subject to which it belongs; otherwise existential judgments would have no "reason." Here as everywhere else, *praedicatum inest subjecto.*

Here an objection arises which we find in a variety of critiques of Leibniz: "Logic has doubtless only to analyze the subjects once they are formulated, but it is metaphysics which formulates them; thus logic is subordinate to metaphysics, all things considered, as is analysis to synthesis." This objection is in a thoroughly modern spirit; Leibniz would not have admitted it, nor perhaps even have understood it. In fact, for him synthesis (like analysis) is a function of logic, of that *Real Logic* which he identified with metaphysics.[26] It is logic, and more specifically *the art of discovery,* which must generate all the possible concepts and which will thus construct the subjects which *the art of judgment* will have to analyze. This inventive and synthetic branch of logic, the most important in his eyes, Leibniz often calls Combination (*la Combinatoire*), because it is the art of combinations which directs the ordered formation of complex concepts by means of the simple and primitive concepts which are the "primary possibles." Human Combination can only imitate and imperfectly reproduce the divine Combination, which gives rise to all the possibles which, as we have seen, struggle for existence. Now by the mere fact that each of these possibles is the combination of a certain number of "primary possibles," it possesses a certain degree of reality. It is this quantity of essence it contains which constitutes its right to existence, and which, if it is realized, will be the "cause" or the "sufficient reason" of its realization. In a word, one can say that its existence is prescribed [*inscrite d'advance*] in its essence, that it is a part of its meaning. Only, in order to extract the existence from the essence, an infinite analysis, indeed an infinitely infinite analysis, would be necessary. It would be necessary to relate this possible to the possible world it implies, and to compare this world with all the other possible worlds. That is why this existence is contingent, inasmuch as it implies an infinity of logical conditions [*réquisits*]. One must not say, accordingly, that logic receives its subjects ready-made from metaphysics; quite the contrary, it is metaphysics which receives its objects (the real beings) from logic and above all from that divine logic which presides at the creation: *Cum Deus calculat. . . , fit mundus.*

. . . . .

It will undoubtedly be objected that the choice among possibles is mechanical only apparently and metaphorically. According to Leibniz's own statements, this choice results from the *free* decrees of God. It depends not on his intelligence, but on his will; not on his wisdom, but on his goodness. Let us therefore examine what Leibniz means by freedom, in man and in God.

We know that he defines freedom as an intelligent or rational spontaneity. Now the spontaneous is that which contains within itself its principle of action.[27] Freedom thus consists in the ability to act or not to act (or to act otherwise), given the same *external* conditions: for action depends on the *internal* dispositions of the agent, and notably on its intelligence. Peter and Paul are *free* because, placed in exactly the same conditions, they will act or react differently. This is not to say that they will act irrationally, nor that their action is undetermined. It has its (logical) reasons in their individual natures; it is contained from all eternity in the notions of "Peterhood" and "Paulhood."[28] Also, God can foresee their action with certainty and infallibility. This freedom has nothing in common with the freedom of indifference, which would be the power to act or not to act, given all the external and *internal* conditions of the action. That, according to Leibniz, is an "impossible chimera," since it is obviously contrary to the principle of reason.[29] He remarks that this conception of freedom was unknown to the ancients and to the great scholastics, and that it originates with the Jesuits (Fonseca and Molina). And to the moderns who reproach him with ignorance of the true idea of free will, Leibniz would undoubtedly reply by asking them if they themselves understand their empty concept of an irrational and undetermined activity, and if they can really think something which violates, by definition, the laws of thought.[30]

Thus freedom, no more than the contingence of which it is but a special case, by no means excludes determinism. On the contrary it implies it, because freedom consists in the determination of action by reason.[31] Spontaneous and intelligent action is *free* only in the sense that it is unpredictable, because it escapes every general law. In this respect, freedom constitutes a higher degree of contingence. For, as we have seen, the laws of nature are already contingent to the same degree as nature itself; but free actions are independent of the laws of nature, not at all because they violate or suspend these laws but because these laws, being *general,* do not suffice to determine the individual action of "intelligent substances." It is in fact intelligence which delivers man from physical determinism, because it complicates *to an infinite degree* the processes which determine his action (namely, attention and reflection) in such a way that one can never predict with certainty which motive will prevail in him. Human actions are, strictly speaking, "incalculable," at least for a finite understanding; but this does not prevent them from being absolutely determined in themselves, nor does it prevent God from knowing them in advance—not through a simple "visual knowledge," which would be nothing but a purely empirical foresight, but through an "intelligent knowledge" which permits him to see its reason and, if necessary, to "give reason to it."[32]

From the psychological point of view, the will is always determined by the apparent good; it tends toward it irresistibly.[33] All differences among individuals, and among their actions, thus derive from the intelligence—that is, from the more or less perfect knowledge of the good. Here again one sees how the intelligence is the condition of freedom. It furnishes the determining motives for action and, through more or less attentive and prolonged reflection, it causes a real good to be preferred over an apparent good; that is, it causes the motive that is rightfully strongest to triumph instead of the one that prevailed at first. It is this operation of reflection which, infinitely complicating the givens of the problem, makes its solution incalculable and unpredictable. The entire difference between the will of man and that of God comes from the difference in their intelligences. The former chooses the apparent good, the latter the real good. Or rather both equally choose the apparent good; only it is clear that what appears good to God is the absolute and real good. It could, in one sense, be said that man is freer than God, for the weakness of man's intelligence gives rise to all sorts of depravities and perversions which make him prefer, under the aspect of apparent goods, evils which are all too real. God, on the other hand, can will only the good; he is in some sense condemned by his infinite wisdom to realize the good unfailingly. This is what the freedom of choice attributed to him comes down to.

But then, it will be said, in what does this "good" or this "better" which God wills and infallibly realizes finally consist? What is the significance of distinguishing his wisdom from his goodness, if his will is entirely determined by his intelligence? From the metaphysical point of view this distinction vanishes, since not only the divine will but *all* will, however perverse, tends essentially toward the good. Moreover, this "good" which is the object of the creating will does not have, nor could it have, any *moral* character. It consists uniquely in metaphysical "perfection"—that is, in the degree of essence or of reality—so that the "principle of perfection" reduces to "God realizes the maximum of essence or of reality," which is a simple consequence of the principle of reason.

. . . . .

There remain one or two apparently insurmountable objections. What becomes, in our interpretation, of the famous distinction between efficient and final causes and of the no less classic distinction between mechanical and metaphysical principles? In order to appreciate the first, one must remember the circumstances in which Leibniz enunciated and adopted it. In 1682 he published his *Unicum opticae, catoptricae et dioptricae principium,*[34] in which he deduced all the laws of the reflection and refraction of light from this single principle: *Lumen a puncto radiante ad punctum illustrandum pervenit via omnium facillima.* [Light travels from the radiating point to the point to be illuminated via the easiest path.] And it is to this memorandum that he repeatedly refers when he maintains (against the Cartesians) the usefulness of studying final causes. Now (without emphasizing what is artificial and paradoxical in considering the "point to be illuminated" as the end toward which the illuminating ray tends, when the rays spread out into space without seeking to illuminate what happens to be there), it suffices to remark that this (apparent) finality translates simply into a problem of maximum and minimum, to which it is difficult to attribute a moral significance. Moreover, the scientific interest in the consideration of finality is not only that the "best" consists in a maximum or a minimum. It is above all that it corresponds to a particular determined instance, mathematically speaking, to a *singularity.* Leibniz recognizes this implicitly in the same passages in which he exalts the "principle of perfection." The forms he calls the "best" are those "which provide a maximum or a minimum"; "nature acts along the shortest paths, or at least along the most determined paths," or again, "God acts in the easiest and the most determined ways." It is apparent that what is essential in this finality that Leibniz investigates is not a quantitative maximum or minimum; it is rather the logical or mathematical *determination* of the problem to be resolved. This is what Leibniz finds the "most beautiful" in the idea.[35] It suffices to say that the *beauty* and *goodness* in question here are entirely rational and metaphysical, having no teleological or moral significance.[36]

Let us go on to the distinction between mechanical and metaphysical principles. What exactly does Leibniz mean when he endlessly repeats that if everything in nature is explained by mechanical laws, then these mechanical laws themselves rest on metaphysical principles? Perhaps one already suspects: these metaphysical principles are the principle of reason and all its corollaries. And if these principles have a *logical* and not a *moral* character, it follows that Leibniz's mechanics is subordinated to his logic and not to his theory of morals or to his theodicy. Moreover, the *finality* Leibniz thinks he has discovered in the laws of mechanics is not of a different nature from that which he recognized in the laws of optics. In all the instances in which he appears to subordinate *mathematical* principles to *metaphysical* principles, he is really subordinating them to the principles of his logic, as is shown by the allusions he makes in those instances to the Universal Characteristic.[37] Indeed, according to him, popular mathematics—the sciences of number and of size (objects of imagination)—depend on a more general science. Sometimes he called this more general science the Combinatory [*la Combinatoire*] or Art of Discovery; sometimes he called it the Universal Mathematics, because it would subordinate to a rigorous calculus even abstract notions which do not depend on the imagination, such as those of metaphysics and mechanics.[38]

This is also evident from certain unpublished texts which date from Leibniz's youth. In the *Consilium de Encyclopaedia nova conscribenda methodo inventoria* (June 1679) he said of mechanics (which he called *scientia de actione et passione, de potentia et motu*): *Haec scientia Physicam Mathematicae connectit. Neque hic agitur quomodo delineanda sint motuum . . . vestigia: id enim pure geometricum est;*[39] *sed quomodo ex corporum conflictu motuum directiones et celeritates immutentur: quod per solam imaginationem consequi non licet, et sublimioris est scientiae.*[40] [This science connects physics with mathematics. And it is not here a question about tracing the paths of motion, for that is a purely geometrical task; rather it is a question of how the direction and speed of motion are changed through the collision of bodies. This cannot be ascertained through the imagination alone and is a question for a more sublime science.] Mechanics does not reduce to geometry nor even to cinematics, because of the mass which intervenes in collisions to modify the movements; it is this element—the mass, revealed by the active force—which escapes the spatial "imagination" and prevents the geometric prediction of the result of the collision, which Descartes thought possible.[41] Mass and active force are what Leibniz invoked when he maintained (against the Cartesians) that the essence of body does not consist in extension. This is indeed the major point on which he breaks with the Cartesian mechanism or rather with its "geometrism." What, then, is this "more sublime science" which will permit the treatment of the problems of mechanics and the penetration of nature? Is it metaphysics? By no means. It is Logic, or Characteristic. Here in fact is what Leibniz wrote in May 1676: *Vera ratiocinandi ars in rebus difficilibus et nonnihil abstrusis, quales sunt physicae, frustra speratur, quamdiu non habetur ars characteristica sive lingua rationalis, quae mirifice in compendium contrahit operationes mentis, et sola praestare potest in Physicis, quod Algebra in Mathematicis.*[42] [The true art of reasoning in difficult and profound matters, such as those of physics, will be sought in vain as long as we do not have an art of characteristic or a rational language, which will wondrously unify mental operations and which alone will be able to serve Physics as Algebra does Mathematics.] And this idea—that the Characteristic is the logic

of physics,[43] and the true experimental method[44]—reappears constantly in the writings of this period. Later he enumerated among the many applications of his universal characteristic the science of cause and effect, of action and passion, i.e., mechanics: "I reduce all mechanics to a single proposition of metaphysics, and I have several important geometrical propositions concerning cause and effect."[45] Now the "metaphysical" principle from which Leibniz deduces all of mechanics is this: "There is always a perfect equation between the full cause and the entire effect."[46] This really means that something remains constant in mechanical phenomena (notably in collisions); and it is this "something" which Leibniz calls "force," as we shall see later. For the moment it is enough to remark that, by virtue of its entirely formal character, this proposition is more a logical than a metaphysical principle, and that in any case it has no teleological significance.[47]

This leads us to explain briefly our position regarding the similarities between Leibniz's metaphysics and his mechanics, similarities which have been peculiarly exaggerated and misrepresented. We do not mean that the studies of mechanics Leibniz pursued from 1678 to 1686 (evident from his unpublished manuscripts[48]) had no influence *whatsoever* on the formation of his system, but rather that they were no more influential than his other scientific studies. Everything considered, his metaphysics inspired his mechanics much more than vice versa; and his metaphysics follows essentially from the logical principles Leibniz adopted at a very early date. We by no means deny that his metaphysics, like all metaphysics worthy of the name, was nourished by critical scientific study, of *all* the sciences (and not merely of one, as is too frequently believed). But this critical study was itself constantly directed by certain *a priori* principles, metaphysical or logical (the name matters little), of the sort we have just mentioned and which Leibniz, far from borrowing from experience, employed to judge and to explain experience.[49]

And now, we must put an end once and for all to that conception of the monad which is still advanced in textbooks and courses and even in certain scientific works,[50] namely, that monads are *forces* (the more scholarly say "centers of force"). To refute this totally, it ought to suffice to recall that *Leibniz never admitted what we call a force in mechanics*. We know how he protested against the hypothesis of attraction, accusing Newton of reinstating the occult qualities of the scholastics, which violate the principle of reason.[51] In the *Tentamen de motuum caelestium causis* (1689), which he proposed in opposition to the Newtonian theory, he excluded all action at a distance and tried to explain the movement of the stars by the pressure of a fluid in which they are immersed.[52] It is a commonplace to oppose Leibniz's *dynamism* to the *mechanism* of Descartes. This distinction does not have the slightest justification. Leibniz is as much a mechanist as Descartes;

even more so, for he is a rigorous determinist. If he modifies the formulas of Cartesian mechanics he none-theless entirely accepts its principle, which is to explain all natural phenomena by collisions or contacts *without the intervention of any force.* What Leibniz calls *force,* and sometimes even *motor force,* is always *active force.*[53]

It seems however that his theory of active force suggested to him his idea of substance, and he himself often presents the latter as a consequence of the former. For example, in the *De causa gravitatis* (1690), after having opposed the *motor force,* which alone is constant, to the quantity of motion, which varies, he concludes: *Unde etiam discimus aliquid aliud in rebus esse quam extensionem et motum.*[54] [Wherefore we say *there is something in things other than extension and motion.*] This idea goes back to 1686, when Leibniz published his *Brevis demonstratio erroris memorabilis Cartesii.*[55] Summarizing this memorandum in the ***Discours de métaphysique,*** § 17, Leibniz draws from it the following conclusion: "The distinction between the force and the quantity of motion is important, among other things, in showing that one must return to meta-physical considerations separate from extension in order to explain bodily phenomena."[56] But this consideration has for him only a negative and polemical value. He used it only to prove, against the Cartesians, that "the essence of body does not consist in extension" (and especially to humiliate them by showing that their master committed gross scientific errors); but it was of no use to him for the discovery and positive determi-nation of this "essence." Moreover, even this negative thesis itself does not originally derive from mechanical considerations, but rather from logico-metaphysical speculations on the nature of substance, which Leibniz summarized in the following way: "If body is a sub-stance and not merely a simple phenomenon like the rainbow nor a being united by accident or through aggregation like a heap of stones, then it cannot con-sist of extension, and one must necessarily conceive something which one calls substantial form and which corresponds in some sense to the soul."[57] Now this thesis proceeds from the remark that, since extension is infinitely divisible, one could not discover any unity in it nor, accordingly, any substantiality.[58] Should one therefore say that Leibniz's metaphysics depends on his geometry? This would indeed be more exact than to make it depend on his mechanics: for he already professed this thesis in his first ***Lettre à Arnauld*** (1672),[59] at a period when he had ideas totally differ-ent from his mechanical theories of the future, and when, on the contrary, he believed he could explain all mechanical phenomena geometrically.[60] Finally, in the ***Discours de métaphysique*** itself, the thesis "that the notions which rely on extension include something imaginary and could not constitute the substance of body" (§ 12) comes well before the considerations regarding active force (§ 18) and is established inde-

pendently of these latter. Let us therefore conclude that the concept of substance owes nothing to Leib-niz's mechanics and proceeds uniquely from his logi-cal and metaphysical principles.

It is the same with the pre-established harmony, which is the keystone of the system. Without doubt, in what he wrote toward the end of his life, Leibniz seems to recognize that this "hypothesis" derives from his me-chanical conceptions. In the ***Theodicy*** (§ 61), after having recalled his law of active force, he says: "If this rule had been known to M. Descartes. . . , I be-lieve that it would have led him straight to the hypoth-esis of the pre-established harmony, to which these same rules have led me."[61] About the same time, he persuaded Christian Wolff to study mathematics rather than philosophy, *praesertim cum ipsa Mathematica potissimum juvent philosophantem, neque ego in Sys-tema Harmonicum incidissem, nisi leges motuum prius constituissem, quae systema causarum occasionalium evertunt,*[62] [chiefly because Mathematics is a very pow-erful aid in philosophy, and I would not have arrived at my System of Harmony unless I had previously known the laws of motion which overthrow the sys-tems of occasional causation]. This is undeniably quite unequivocal. But alas, Leibniz's memory deceived him on this point. This is explained by the fact that discus-sions regarding mechanics had assumed an important role in his battle against the Cartesians and against Malebranche, and thus were inextricably intermingled in his later exposition of his system. For he wrote in 1686: "The hypothesis of concomitance follows from my notion of substance,"[63] and this notion, as we have seen, has a purely logical origin. Moreover, this hy-pothesis is established in § 14 of the ***Discours de métaphysique*** by reasons of a metaphysical nature and independently of any mechanical consideration: "God produces diverse substances according to the different viewpoints he has of the universe, and through the intervention of God the individual nature of each sub-stance ensures that what happens to one corresponds to what happens to the others, without their acting directly upon one another." But there is a yet more decisive proof. It is an unpublished text, dated 1676, in which one finds such statements as these: Every soul perceives the entire universe, but confusedly; these confused perceptions constitute sensations; God creat-ed a multitude of souls in order to have as many dif-ferent perspectives of the world. In this text Leibniz again declares himself an advocate of atoms (and of spherical atoms!), which he tries to reconcile with the plenum by means of the idea of infinitely small parti-cles.[64] Here is, it seems to us, a decisive proof that his essential metaphysical theses are well prior to his mechanical theories, to which they owe absolutely nothing.[65]

Furthermore, if one analyzes these theories themselves one finds nothing in them which could justify either the concept of the monad or, especially, the hypothesis of the pre-established harmony. As Mr. Cassirer has shown perfectly, the law of the conservation of (active) force never had for Leibniz anything but a purely phenomenal value—like motion, mass, and space itself.[66] If Leibniz could for a moment have dreamed of making a substance of the active force (as certain modern thinkers make a substance of energy), that would have brought him to a *monistic* and not to a *monadistic* metaphysics; for the active force of each body varies, and it is only the sum of the active forces which is constant. Shall we then say that the analysis of elastic collision led him to think that every body really is moved only by its own elastic forces which operate, it is true, upon contact with other elastic bodies? But we do not see how this concept would refute the hypothesis of occasionalism, with which it seems perfectly compatible. Actually, it is for purely logical reasons that Leibniz denies all "physical impulse" and all real action of one substance on another, and the phenomenon of elastic collision is nothing for him but a confirmation after the fact, or rather a simple "experimental illustration" of his metaphysical theses. The pre-established harmony is no more a consequence of the laws of mechanics than the monad is an atom or a billiard ball.

Notes

[1] [Translator's note: We indicate by asterisks the omission of the Latin text of the manuscript *Primae Veritates,* which Couturat includes in this paper. This manuscript was discovered by Eduard Bodemann among the non-philosophical manuscripts of Leibniz. See Bodemann, *Die Leibniz-Handschriften* (Hanover, 1895), p. 102. The text is catalogued *Phil.* VIII, 6-7 in L. Couturat, *Opuscules et fragments inédits de Leibniz* (Paris, 1903); there is an English translation in L. Loemker, *Leibniz: Philosophical Papers and Letters* (Chicago, 1956), p. 411. In the footnotes which follow, *Ger. Phil.* designates C. I. Gerhardt, ed., *Philosophische Schriften von G. W. Leibniz,* 7 vols. (Berlin, 1960-61); *Ger. Math.* designates C. I. Gerhardt, ed., *Mathematische Schriften,* 7 vols. (Berlin and Halle, 1849-55). We have revised Couturat's occasional footnote references to the *Primae Veritates* text.]

[2] Let us say, on this point, that the numerous *dated* texts which we have found show that Leibniz's system was much more precocious than has been thought; it was already preformed in the theories of his early youth. See the texts dated 1676 which we will cite later (Couturat, Phil. I, 14, c, 8; VIII, 71).

[3] *Lettre à Arnauld,* 14 July 1686 (*Ger. Phil.* II, 56). *Specimen inventorum* (*Ger. Phil.* VII, 309).

[4] *Letter d' Arnauld,* 28 Sept. 1686: "J'ay sur tout esté frappé de cette raison, que dans toute proposition affirmative véritable, necessaire ou contingente, universelle ou singulière, la notion de l'attribut est comprise en quelque façon dans celle du sujet: *praedicatum inest subjecto.*" [I was especially struck by this reason, that in every true affirmative proposition, necessary or contingent, universal or singular, the notion of the attribute is contained in some fashion in that of the subject: *praedicatum inest subjecto.*] (*Ger. Phil.* II, 64).

[5] "Principium omnis ratiocinationis primarium est, nihil esse aut fieri, quin ration reddi possit, saltem ab omniscio, cur sit potius quam non sit, aut cur sic potius qual aliter; paucis, *omnium rationem reddi posse.*" [The primary principle of every method of reasoning is that nothing is or happens for which it is not possible for the reason to be given, at least from an omniscient point of view, why it is rather than is not or why it is so rather than otherwise; in short, *it is possible for the reason of everything to be given.*] (Couturat, *Phil.* IV, 3, c, 13). "Principium ratiocinandi fundamentale est, *nihil esse sine ratione,* vel . . . nullam esse veritatem, cui ratio non subsit. Ratio autem veritatis consistit in nexu praedicati cum subjecto, seu ut praedicatum subjecto insit . . ." [The fundamental principle of reasoning is that *nothing is without reason,* or that there is no truth for which there is no underlying reason. However, the reason of the truth consists in the connection between the predicate and the subject, whether the predicate is contained in the subject . . .] (Couturat, *Phil.* I, 15). Cf. (*De Synthesi et Analysi universali* (*Ger. Phil.* VII, 296); *Specimen inventorum* (*Ger. Phil.* VII, 309); *Ger. Phil.* VII, 199; Bodemann, p. 115.

[6] Already in November 1677 he wrote, "Principium illud summum: *nihil esse sine ratione,* plerasque metaphysicae controversias finit." [This principle is of the highest importance: *nihil esse sine ratione,* and it will put an end to many of the controversies of metaphysics.] *Scientia media* (Couturat, *Phil.* IV, 3, c, 15). And, in fact, he used it on November 27, 1677, to demonstrate the existence of God in his *Conversatio cum D. Episcopo Stenonio de libertate* (Bodemann, p. 73).

[7] An unpublished fragment begins with this sentence: "Maxime in tota philosophia ipsaque theologia momenti haec consideratio est, nullas esse denominationes pure extrinsecas. . ." [The following consideration is of the utmost importance in all of contemporary philosophy and theology: there are no purely extrinsic characteristics. . .]; and ends with the following remark: "Omnia quae hac et praecedenti pagina diximus oriuntur ex grandi illo principio, quod praedicatum inest subjecto." [Everything which we have said on this and the preceding pages derives from that important principle, the predicate is contained in the subject.] (Couturat, *Phil.* I, 14, c, 7). Now the content of this fragment is entirely metaphysical; it includes in particular a refutation of atomism and a study of the principle of the activity of monads. Elsewhere Leibniz invokes the

principle of reason to exclude from physics occult qualities, such as attraction, and to demonstrate mechanism: "Omnia in corporibus fieri mechanice." [In bodies, everything occurs mechanically.] (Couturat, *Phil.* I, 15).

[8] Compare this deduction with that contained in another unpublished fragment, already cited: Couturat, *Phil.* I, 15.

[9] This reversal of the order of the metaphysical theses in the *Monadology* is explained by the late date of this short work (1714).

[10] Cf. Russell, *A Critical Exposition of the Philosophy of Leibniz,* ch. iv.

[11] "Verum est affirmatum, cujus praedicatum inest subjecto, itaque in omni Propositione vera affirmativa, necessaria vel contingente, universali vel singulari, Notio praedicati aliquo modo continetur in notione subjecti; ita ut qui perfecte intelligeret notionem utramque, quemadmodum eam intelligit Deus, is eo ipso perspiceret praedicatum subjecto inesse." [A statement the predicate of which is in the subject is true, and so in every true affirmative proposition, necessary or contingent, universal or singular, the notion of the predicate is in some way contained in the notion of the subject; and so whoever perfectly understands these notions, in the way that God understands them, thereby perceives that the predicate is in the subject.] (Couturat, *Phil.* IV, 3, a, 1). Cf. the similar passages *De libertate* (L. A. *Foucher de Careil,* 1857, p. 179); *Letter à Arnauld,* 14 July 1686 (Couturat, *Phil.* II, 56), cited in *La Logique de Leibniz,* pp. 208, 209.

[12] "Utrumque (namely: necessarium et contingens) aeque certum seu a Deo *a priori* seu per causas cognitum est. Utrumque vi terminorum verum est, seu praedicatum utrobique inest subjecto, tam in necessariis quam contingentibus." [And both (namely: necessary and contingent truths) are known certainly whether *a priori* by God or through analysis of their reasons. And both are true by virtue of their terms, or the predicate is contained somewhere in the subject, as much in necessary as in contingent truths.] (Couturat, *Phil.* VII, B, 11, 71). Cf. *De libertate:* "Sed in veritatibus contingentibus, etsi praedicatum insit subjecto . . ." [But in contingent truths, although the predicate be in the subject . . .] (*Foucher de Careil,* 1857, p. 182) cited in *La Logique de Leibniz,* p. 211, note 2.

[13] "Origo veritatum contingentium ex processu in infinitum, ad exemplum Proportionum inter quantitates incommensurabiles" (Couturat, *Theol.* VI, 2, f, 11-13.) Cf. *Generales Inquisitiones de Analysi notionum et veritatum,* 1686, § 135 (Couturat, *Phil.* VII, c, 29); Couturat, *Phil.* IV, 3, a, 1, and *Ger. Phil.* VII, 200, 309.

[14] "Tandem nova quaedam atque inexpectata lux oborta est unde minime sperabam: ex considerationibus scilicet mathematicis de natura infiniti." [A new and unanticipated light finally arose from the least expected source: namely, from mathematical considerations concerning the nature of the infinite.] *De libertate* (*Foucher de Careil,* 1857, pp. 179-80).

[15] "Contingentiae radix infinitum." [Contingency is rooted in infinity.] (Bodemann, p. 121). "Ex his apparet radicem contingentiae esse infinitum in rationibus." [From this it appears that the root of contingency is an infinity of reasons.] (Couturat, *Theol.* VI, 2, f, 12).

[16] "Atque ita arcanum aliquod a me evolutum puto, quod me diu perplexum habuit, non intelligentem, quomodo praedicatum subjecto inesse posset, nec tamen propositio fierit necessaria. Sed cognitio rerum geometricarum atque analysis infinitorum hanc mihi lucem accendere, ut intelligerem, etiam notiones in infinitum resolubiles esse." [And so I thought I had formulated some sort of mystery, which puzzled me daily; I could not understand how the predicate could be in the subject without the proposition being necessary. But my knowledge of geometry and analysis of infinites showed me the light so that I understood that these notions are also infinitely analyzable.] (Couturat, *Phil.* IV, 3, a, 1).

[17] Beginning of *De libertate* (*Foucher de Careil,* 1857, p. 178). Leibniz there argues against Descartes's assertion (*Principles of Philosophy* III, 46) that matter must assume successively all possible forms. He maintains, on the contrary, that matter can really be infinitely divisible without thereby realizing all possible divisions (v. *Primae Veritates*). Cf. the *Origo veritatum contingentium:* "Si omne quod fit necessarium esset, sequeretur sola quae aliquando existunt esse possibilia (ut volunt Hobbes et Spinosa) et materiam omnes formas possibiles suscipere (quod volebat Cartesius)." [If everything which exists were necessary, it would follow that only those things are possible which do in fact in some way exist (as Hobbes and Spinoza hold) and matter would assume all possible forms (as the Cartesians claimed)]. (Couturat, *Theol.* VI, 2, f, 11).

[18] *Discours de métaphysique,* § XIII (*Ger. Phil.* IV, 438).

[19] "Principium autem meum est, quicquid existere potest, et aliis compatible est, id existere. . . . Itaque nulla alia ratio determinandi, quam ut existant potiora, quae plurimum involvant realitatis." [However, my principle is that whatever is able to exist, and is compatible with the other things, will exist. . . . And so there is no reason determining existence other than the maximization of reality.] (Couturat, *Phil.* VIII, 71). It is unnecessary to add that this text suffices, in our

opinion, to destory the hypothesis of a lasting and dominating influence exercised by Spinoza on Leibniz.

[20] "Ratio existendi prac omnibus possibilibus non alia ratione limitari debet quam quod non omnia compatibilia." [For there is no reason limiting the existence of everything possible other than the fact that not all possibles are compatible.] (*Ibid.*) This fact, that all possibles are not compatible, is apparently explained by the negation which is necessarily introduced into the complex concepts resulting from the combination of simple concepts. On the contrary, the latter, which Leibniz calls the "primary possibles" and the "absolute attributes of God," are essentially positive and hence compatible. It is thus that the proposition "God is possible" is justified—a proposition which is for Leibniz the indispensable premise of the ontological argument. It is for this reason that he said that his Characteristic had the same basis as the demonstration of the existence of God (*Lettre à la duchesse Sophie* [*Ger. Phil.* IV, 296], cited in *La Logique de Leibniz*, p. 195, note 2). Cf. Couturat, *Phil.* V, 8, f, 25 (April 1679).

[21] *Letter à Arnauld,* 1686 (*Ger. Phil.* II, 55).

[22] *De rerum originatione radicali,* 1697 (*Ger. Phil.* VII, 304).

[23] Mr. Russell maintains that all existential judgments are synthetic for Leibniz, with the exception of the affirmation of the existence of God, which would be analytic. This exception is nowhere indicated, and it is unjustifiable in Leibniz's system.

[24] " . . . Existentia a nobis concipitur tanquam res nihil habens cum Essentia commune, quod tamen fieri nequit, quia oportet plus inesse in conceptu Existentis quam non existentis, seu existentiam esse perfectionem; cum revera nihil aliud sit explicabile in existentia, quam perfectissimam seriem rerum ingredi." [We conceive of Existence as having nothing in common with Essence, which is nevertheless not the case, because it is necessary that there be more in the concept of that which exists than of that which does not exist, if existence is a perfection; for indeed nothing would be explicably in existence except as participating in the most perfect order of things.] (Couturat, *Phil.* I, 14, c, 7 v⁰).

[25] "Si Existentia esset aliud quiddam quam Essentiae exigentia, sequeretur ipsam habere quandam essentiam seu aliquid novum superaddere rebus, de quo rursus quaeri posset an haec essentia existat, et cur ista potius quam alia." [If Existence were something other than the exigency of Essence, it would follow that this itself would have some essence and something new would be added to things about which one again could ask whether this essence existed, or why this one rather

than that.] (*Ger. Phil.* VII, 195, note). [Editor's note: It should be noted that this interpretation requires a rather different reading of the maxim *nihili nullae proprietates sunt* than Benson Mates gives it in his article "Leibniz on Possible Worlds," which is included in the present volume.]

[26] "J'ay reconnu que la vraye Metaphysique n'est guères differente de la vraye Logique, c'est-a-dire de l'art d'inventer en general." [I recognized that the true metaphysics hardly differs from the true logic, that is, from the art of discovery in general.] *Lettre à la duchesse Sophie* (*Ger. Phil.* IV, 292).

[27] Couturat, *Phil.* IV, 3, c, 13.

[28] *Scientia media,* Nov. 1677 (Couturat, *Phil.* IV, 3, c, 15).

[29] Couturat, *Phil.* IV, 3, c, 13.

[30] It is unnecessary to note that the "contingence" he attributes to the laws of nature has nothing in common with what our modern "irrationalists" mean thereby. Leibniz summarized his theory of contingence in this concise formula: "Nulla est in rebus singularibus necessitas, sed omnia sunt contingentia. Vicissim tamen nulla est in rebus indifferentia, sed omina sunt determinata." [There is no necessity in things; everything is contingent . . . on the other hand, however, there is no indifference in things; everything is determined.] (*Ger. Phil.* VII, 108).

[31] This notion of freedom is much closer to Kant's than is generally believed. In fact, the concept of freedom as independence of natural laws is for Kant only a negative concept; freedom consists not in the absence of all determination, but in the determination of the will by reason. Kant explicitly states: "a free will (that is, without law) would be an absurdity." (*Groundwork of the Metaphysics of Morals,* 3rd section). Freedom too has its laws; this is why Kant constantly talks of "causality by freedom." A free will is a will submitted to the moral law; the positive concept of freedom is autonomy.

[32] *Scientia media,* Nov. 1677 (Couturat, *Phil.* IV, 3, c, 15).

[33] "Voluntatis objectum esse bonum apparens, et nihil a nobis appeti nisi sub ratione boni apparentis, dogma est vetustissimum communissimumque." [The object of the will is the apparent good, and we desire nothing except under the form of apparent good. This belief is very old and widespread.] (Couturat, *Phil.* IV, 3, c, 13).

[34] L. Dutens, ed., *God. Guil. Leibnitii . . . Opera omnia.* (Geneva, 1768), III, 145.

[35] V. the *Tentamen Anagogicum,* "où l'on monstre. . .que dans la recherche des Finales il y a des cas où il faut avoir égard au plus simple ou plus determiné, sans distinguer si c'est le plus grand ou le plus petit." [in which one shows. . .that in the study of Finalities there are cases where one must be concerned with the simplest or the most determined, without distinguishing whether it is the largest or the smallest.] (*Ger. Phil.* VII, 270).

[36] Cf. *La Logique de Leibniz,* pp. 230-32.

[37] See especially the end of the *Réponse aux réflexions de M. Bayle* (1702), cited and commented on in *La Logique de Leibniz,* p. 238.

[38] "Constat principia naturae non minus metaphysica quam mathematica esse, vel potius causas rerum latere in metaphysica quadam mathesi quae aestimat perfectiones seu gradus realitatum." [The principles of nature are not less metaphysical than mathematical, or rather the causes of things lie in a certain mathematical metaphysics which calculates the perfections and the degrees of reality.] (*Ger. Phil.* II, 213). This "metaphysical mathematics" is the Characteristic or Combinatory: one sees that its object is to calculate the degree of reality of the *possibles,* and thus to explain the *real* by a simple analysis.

[39] This is the definition of cinematics, which Leibniz (as well as Kant) calls "Phoronomy."

[40] Couturat, *Phil.* V, 7, 4 v⁰.

[41] "Quanti autem momenti sit, recte constitui principia hujus Matheseos vel Physico-Matheseos tam late patentis, quae considerationem virium (rem imaginationi non subditam) addit Geometriae deu scientiae imaginum universali, facile intelligis." [However, as to the quantity of motion, you will easily see that I correctly established the principles of this Mathematics or Physico-Mathematics which is so broadly applicable and which supplements Geometry or the science of universal imagination by consideration of forces (which cannot be subsumed under things of the imagination).] (*Ger. Math.* III, 243).

[42] Couturat, *Phil.* V, 8, g, 30-31.

[43] See, for example, the beginning of the *Pacidius Philalethi* (October 1676), which is published in its entirely in Couturat, *Math.* X, 11, and the end of the *De modo perveniendi ad veram corporum analysin et rerum naturalium causas* (May 1677), in which he says: "Haec autem [the analysis of physical qualities] per definitiones et linguam philosophicam egregie fient." [This however can be achieved splendidly through definitions and a philosophical language.] (*Ger. Phil.* VII, 269).

[44] "Ars characteristica ostendet non tantum quomodo experimentis sit utendum, sed et quaenam experimenta sint sumenda et ad determinandam rei subjectae naturam sufficientia. . ." [The art of Characteristic will show not only how experiments are to be interpreted, but also which experiments are to be undertaken and which are sufficient for determining the nature of the subject in question . . .] (Couturat, *Phil.* V, 8, g, 31).

[45] *Lettre à Arnauld,* 14 July 1686 (*Ger. Phil.* II, 62). Cf. *Lettre à Foucher,* 1687 (*Ger. Phil.* I, 391); *Lettre à Arnauld,* 14 Jan. 1688 (*Ger. Phil.* VII, 199); these texts are cited in *La Logique de Leibniz,* p. 304.

[46] *Ger. Phil.* III, 45. Cf. *Essai de Dynamique (Foucher de Careil,* I, 653).

[47] Just when we finished this article, we received Mr. Cassirer's study, *Leibniz' System in seinen wissenschaftlichen Grundlagen* (Marburg, Elwert, 1902), in which (despite certain divergences in interpretation) we found a valuable confirmation of the thesis we are here holding. Mr. Cassirer states as we do that what Leibniz calls "metaphysical principles" are really logical principles and remarks that he criticized the theological considerations from which Descartes claimed to deduce the *law of conservation* in mechanics (pp. 315-16).

[48] See Bodemann, pp. 301-2, 328-29.

[49] Cf. Cassirer, *op. cit.,* pp. 308 ff., and the texts cited there.

[50] Dühring, *Geschichte der mechanischen Prinzipien,* p. 229 (cited by Cassirer, *op. cit.,* p. 314).

[51] *Antibarbarus physicus pro philosophia reali, contra renovationes qualitatum scholasticarum et intelligentiarum chimaericarum (Ger. Phil.* VII, 337); cf. Couturat, *Phil.* I, 15, Ch. 2.

[52] "Omnia corpora quae in fluido lineam curvam describunt, ab ipsius fluidi motu agi" since bodies can interact only through contact. [All bodies which describe a curve in a fluid are set in motion by that fluid.] (*Ger. Math.* VI, 149, 166).

[53] One must radically distinguish between primitive force (*vis primitiva*), a metaphysical quality which Leibniz attributes to the monads, and derived force (*vis derivativa*), which is a mechanical and *phenomenal* property of bodies (cf. Cassirer, *op. cit.,* p. 315). Here we are speaking only of the latter.

[54] *Ger. Math.* VI, 202. One reads, on the same page: "VIRES MOTRICES, id est, *eas quae conservandae sunt.*" [MOTOR FORCES, they are what are to be conserved.]

[55] *Ger. Math.* VI, 117.

[56] Summary of § 18 of the *Discours de métaphysique* in the *Lettre au landgrave* of 11 Feb. 1686.

[57] Cf. *Lettre à l'étectrice Sophie,* 4 Nov. 1696: "Mes méditations fondamentales roulent sur deux choses, sçavoir sur l'unité et sur l'infini." [My basic meditations concern two topics, namely, unity and infinity.] (*Ger. Phil.* III, 542); cf. *Primae Veritates.*

[58] *Lettre à Arnauld,* 14 July 1686. Cf. *Primae Veritates.*

[59] *Ger. Phil.* I, 72.

[60] See Hannequin, *Quae fuerit prior Leibnitii philosophia . . . ante annum* 1672, p. 110 (Masson, 1893). From 1669 Leibniz made the essence of matter consist in *antitype* or impenetrability (*Lettre à Thomasius, Ger. Phil.* I, 17). In 1670 he made it consist in motion, in *velocity (Hypothesis physica nova),* from which he concluded that mechanics is reducible to geometry.

[61] Cf. *Monadology,* § 80.

[62] *Briefwechsel mit Chr. Wolf,* ed. Gerhardt (1860), p. 51.

[63] *Projet de lettre à Arnauld* (*Ger. Phil.* II, 68); see the development which follows (p. 70).

[64] Couturat, *Phil.* I, 14, c, 8.

[65] Certain texts which seem contrary to our thesis really only confirm it. For example, Leibniz said with respect to his Dynamics: "Vous avez raison, Monsieur, de juger que c'est en bonne partie le fondement de mon système, parce qu'on y apprend la différence entre les verités dont la necessité est brute et géométrique, et entre les verités qui ont leur source dans la convenance et dans les finales." [You are right, Monsieur, to think that it is in large part the basis of my system, because one sees in it the difference between those truths whose necessity is brutish (*brute*) and geometrical and those truths which have their source in purpose (*convenance*) and in finalities.] There follows the classical allusion to the *Phaedo* (*Lettre à Remond,* 22 June 1715; *Ger. Phil.* III, 645). We see in what sense mechanics could be said to serve as the basis of the system: it is not at all that it gives rise to the concept of substance but rather that it confirms the principles of Leibnizian logic. And yet it is able to provide only a confirmation: for we know, from texts *contemporaneous* with the formulation of the system, that the theory of contingent truths was suggested to Leibniz by his infinitesimal calculus. See above, notes 14 and 16.

[66] "Vires quae ex massa et velocitate oriuntur derivativae sunt et ad aggregata seu phaenomena pertinent." [The forces which arise out of mass and velocity are derivative and belong to the aggregate or the phenomena.] *Lettre à de Volder* (*Ger. Phil.* II, 251). "Vires derivativas ad phaenomena relego." [I relegate the derived forces to phenomena.] (*Ger. Phil.* II, 275). . . . [However I of course put corporeal qualities such as corporeal forces among the phenomena.] (*Ger. Phil.* II, 276).

Bertrand Russell (essay date 1945)

SOURCE: "Leibniz," in *A History of Western Philosophy, and Its Connection with Political and Social Circumstances from the Earliest Times to the Present Day,* Simon and Schuster, 1945, pp. 581-96.

[*In the excerpt below, Russell provides an overview of Leibniz's major philosophical tenets.*]

Leibniz (1646-1716) was one of the supreme intellects of all time, but as a human being he was not admirable. He had, it is true, the virtues that one would wish to find mentioned in a testimonial to a prospective employee: he was industrious, frugal, temperate, and financially honest. But he was wholly destitute of those higher philosophic virtues that are so notable in Spinoza. His best thought was not such as would win him popularity, and he left his records of it unpublished in his desk. What he published was designed to win the approbation of princes and princesses. The consequence is that there are two systems of philosophy which may be regarded as representing Leibniz: one, which he proclaimed, was optimistic, orthodox, fantastic, and shallow; the other, which has been slowly unearthed from his manuscripts by fairly recent editors, was profound, coherent, largely Spinozistic, and amazingly logical. It was the popular Leibniz who invented the doctrine that this is the best of all possible worlds (to which F. H. Bradley added the sardonic comment "and everything in it is a necessary evil"); it was this Leibniz whom Voltaire caricatured as Doctor Pangloss. It would be unhistorical to ignore this Leibniz, but the other is of far greater philosophical importance.

Leibniz was born two years before the end of the Thirty Years' War, at Leipzig, where his father was professor of moral philosophy. At the university he studied law, and in 1666 he obtained a Doctor's degree at Altdorf, where he was offered a professorship, which he refused, saying he had "very different things in view." In 1667 he entered the service of the archbishop of Mainz, who, like other West German princes, was oppressed by fear of Louis XIV. With the approval of the archbishop, Leibniz tried to persuade the French king to invade Egypt rather than Germany, but was met with a polite reminder that since the time of Saint

Louis the holy war against the infidel had gone out of fashion. His project remained unknown to the public until it was discovered by Napoleon when he occupied Hanover in 1803, four years after his own abortive Egyptian expedition. In 1672, in connection with this scheme, Leibniz went to Paris, where he spent the greater part of the next four years. His contacts in Paris were of great importance for his intellectual development, for Paris at that time led the world both in philosophy and in mathematics. It was there, in 1675-6, that he invented the infinitesimal calculus, in ignorance of Newton's previous but unpublished work on the same subject. Leibniz's work was first published in 1684, Newton's in 1687. The consequent dispute as to priority was unfortunate, and discreditable to all parties.

Leibniz was somewhat mean about money. When any young lady at the court of Hanover married, he used to give her what he called a "wedding present," consisting of useful maxims, ending up with the advice not to give up washing now that she had secured a husband. History does not record whether the brides were grateful.

In Germany Leibniz had been taught a neo-scholastic Aristotelian philosophy, of which he retained something throughout his later life. But in Paris he came to know Cartesianism and the materialism of Gassendi, both of which influenced him; at this time, he said, he abandoned the "trivial schools," meaning scholasticism. In Paris he came to know Malebranche and Arnauld the Jansenist. The last important influence on his philosophy was that of Spinoza, whom he visited in 1676. He spent a month in frequent discussions with him, and secured part of the *Ethics* in manuscript. In later years he joined in decrying Spinoza, and minimized his contacts with him, saying he had met him once, and Spinoza had told some good anecdotes about politics.

His connection with the House of Hanover, in whose service he remained for the rest of his life, began in 1673. From 1680 onwards he was their librarian at Wolfenbüttel, and was officially employed in writing the history of Brunswick. He had reached the year 1005 when he died. The work was not published till 1843. Some of his time was spent on a project for the reunion of the Churches, but this proved abortive. He travelled to Italy to obtain evidence that the Dukes of Brunswick were connected with the Este family. But in spite of these services he was left behind at Hanover when George I became king of England, the chief reason being that his quarrel with Newton had made England unfriendly to him. However, the Princess of Wales, as he told all his correspondents, sided with him against Newton. In spite of her favour, he died neglected.

Leibniz's popular philosophy may be found in the ***Monadology*** and the ***Principles of Nature and of Grace,*** one of which (it is uncertain which) he wrote for Prince Eugene of Savoy, Marlborough's colleague. The basis of his theological optimism is set forth in the ***Théodicée,*** which he wrote for Queen Charlotte of Prussia. I shall begin with the philosophy expounded in these writings, and then proceed to his more solid work which he left unpublished.

Like Descartes and Spinoza, Leibniz based his philosophy on the notion of substance, but he differed radically from them as regards the relation of mind and matter, and as regards the number of substances. Descartes allowed three substances, God and mind and matter; Spinoza admitted God alone. For Descartes, extension is the essence of matter; for Spinoza, both extension and thought are attributes of God. Leibniz held that extension cannot be an attribute of a substance. His reason was that extension involves plurality, and can therefore only belong to an aggregate of substances; each single substance must be unextended. He believed, consequently, in an infinite number of substances, which he called "monads." Each of these would have some of the properties of a physical point, but only when viewed abstractly; in fact, each monad is a soul. This follows naturally from the rejection of extension as an attribute of substance; the only remaining possible essential attribute seemed to be thought. Thus Leibniz was led to deny the reality of matter, and to substitute an infinite family of souls.

The doctrine that substances cannot interact, which had been developed by Descartes's followers, was retained by Leibniz, and led to curious consequences. No two monads, he held, can ever have any causal relation to each other; when it seems as if they had, appearances are deceptive. Monads, as he expressed it, are "windowless." This led to two difficulties: one in dynamics, where bodies seem to affect each other, especially in impact; the other in relation to perception, which seems to be an effect of the perceived object upon the percipient. We will ignore the dynamical difficulty for the present, and consider only the question of perception. Leibniz held that every monad mirrors the universe, not because the universe affects it, but because God has given it a nature which spontaneously produces this result. There is a "pre-established harmony" between the changes in one monad and those in another, which produces the semblance of interaction. This is obviously an extension of the two clocks, which strike at the same moment because each keeps perfect time. Leibniz has an infinite number of clocks, all arranged by the Creator to strike at the same instant, not because they affect each other, but because each is a perfectly accurate mechanism. To those who thought the pre-established harmony odd, Leibniz pointed out what admirable evidence it afforded of the existence of God.

Monads form a hierarchy, in which some are superior to others in the clearness and distinctness with which they mirror the universe. In all there is some degree of confusion in perception, but the amount of confusion varies according to the dignity of the monad concerned. A human body is entirely composed of monads, each of which is a soul, and each of which is immortal, but there is one dominant monad which is what is called *the* soul of the man of whose body it forms part. This monad is dominant, not only in the sense of having clearer perceptions than the others, but also in another sense. The changes in a human body (in ordinary circumstances) happen for the sake of the dominant monad: when my arm moves, the purpose served by the movement is in the dominant monad, i.e., my mind, not in the monads that compose my arm. This is the truth of what appears to common sense as the control of my will over my arm.

Space, as it appears to the senses, and as it is assumed in physics, is not real, but it has a real counterpart, namely the arrangement of the monads in a three-dimensional order according to the point of view from which they mirror the world. Each monad sees the world in a certain perspective peculiar to itself; in this sense we can speak, somewhat loosely, of the monad as having a spatial position.

Allowing ourselves this way of speaking, we can say that there is no such thing as a vacuum; every possible point of view is filled by one actual monad, and by only one. No two monads are exactly alike; this is Leibniz's principle of the "identity of indiscernibles."

In contrasting himself with Spinoza, Leibniz made much of the free will allowed in his system. He had a "principle of sufficient reason," according to which nothing happens without a reason; but when we are concerned with free agents, the reasons for their actions "incline without necessitating." What a human being does always has a motive, but the sufficient reason of his action has no logical necessity. So, at least, Leibniz says when he is writing popularly, but, as we shall see, he had another doctrine which he kept to himself after finding that Arnauld thought it shocking.

God's actions have the same kind of freedom. He always acts for the best, but He is not under any logical compulsion to do so. Leibniz agrees with Thomas Aquinas that God cannot act contrary to the laws of logic, but He can decree whatever is logically possible, and this leaves Him a great latitude of choice.

Leibniz brought into their final form the metaphysical proofs of God's existence. These had a long history; they begin with Aristotle, or even with Plato; they were formalized by the scholastics, and one of them, the ontological argument, was invented by Saint Anselm. This argument, though rejected by Saint Thomas, was revived by Descartes. Leibniz, whose logical skill was supreme, stated the arguments better than they had ever

been stated before. That is my reason for examining them in connection with him.

Before examining the arguments in detail, it is as well to realize that modern theologians no longer rely upon them. Medieval theology is derivative from the Greek intellect. The God of the Old Testament is a God of power, the God of the New Testament is also a God of love; but the God of the theologians, from Aristotle to Calvin, is one whose appeal is intellectual: His existence solves certain puzzles which otherwise would create argumentative difficulties in the understanding of the universe. This Deity who appears at the end of a piece of reasoning, like the proof of a proposition in geometry, did not satisfy Rousseau, who reverted to a conception of God more akin to that of the Gospels. In the main, modern theologians, especially such as are Protestant, have followed Rousseau in this respect. The philosophers have been more conservative; in Hegel, Lotze, and Bradley arguments of the metaphysical sort persist, in spite of the fact that Kant professed to have demolished such arguments once for all.

Leibniz's arguments for the existence of God are four in number; they are (1) the ontological argument, (2) the cosmological argument, (3) the argument from the eternal truths, (4) the argument from the pre-established harmony, which may be generalized into the argument from design, or the physico-theological argument, as Kant calls it. We will consider these arguments successively.

The ontological argument depends upon the distinction between existence and essence. Any ordinary person or thing, it is held, on the one hand exists, and on the other hand has certain qualities, which make up his or its "essence." Hamlet, though he does not exist, has a certain essence: he is melancholy, undecided, witty, etc. When we describe a person, the question whether he is real or imaginary remains open, however minute our description may be. This is expressed in scholastic language by saying that, in the case of any finite substance, its essence does not imply its existence. But in the case of God, defined as the most perfect Being, Saint Anselm, followed by Descartes, maintains that essence does imply existence, on the ground that a Being who possesses all other perfections is better if He exists than if He does not, from which it follows that if He does not He is not the best possible Being.

Leibniz neither wholly accepts nor wholly rejects this argument; it needs to be supplemented, so he says, by a proof that God, so defined, is possible. He wrote out a proof that the idea of God is possible, which he showed to Spinoza when he saw him at the Hague. This proof defines God as the most perfect Being, i.e., as the subject of all perfections, and a perfection is defined as a "simple quality which is positive and absolute, and expresses without any limits whatever it does express." Leibniz easily proves that no two perfections, as above defined, can be incompatible. He concludes: "There is, therefore, or there can be conceived, a subject of all perfections, or most perfect Being. Whence it follows also that He exists, for existence is among the number of the perfections."

Kant countered this argument by maintaining that "existence" is not a predicate. Another kind of refutation results from my theory of descriptions. The argument does not, to a modern mind, seem very convincing, but it is easier to feel convinced that it must be fallacious than it is to find out precisely where the fallacy lies.

The cosmological argument is more plausible than the ontological argument. It is a form of the First-Cause argument, which is itself derived from Aristotle's argument of the unmoved mover. The First-Cause argument is simple. It points out that everything finite has a cause, which in turn had a cause, and so on. This series of previous causes cannot, it is maintained, be infinite, and the first term in the series must itself be uncaused, since otherwise it would not be the first term. There is therefore an uncaused cause of everything, and this is obviously God.

In Leibniz the argument takes a somewhat different form. He argues that every particular thing in the world is "contingent," that is to say, it would be logically possible for it not to exist; and this is true, not only of each particular thing, but of the whole universe. Even if we suppose the universe to have always existed, there is nothing within the universe to show why it exists. But everything has to have a sufficient reason, according to Leibniz's philosophy; therefore the universe as a whole must have a sufficient reason, which must be outside the universe. This sufficient reason is God.

This argument is better than the straightforward First-Cause argument, and cannot be so easily refuted. The First-Cause argument rests on the assumption that every series must have a first term, which is false; for example, the series of proper fractions has no first term. But Leibniz's argument does not depend upon the view that the universe must have had a beginning in time. The argument is valid so long as we grant Leibniz's principle of sufficient reason, but if this principle is denied it collapses. What exactly Leibniz meant by the principle of sufficient reason is a controversial question. Couturat maintains that it means that every true proposition is "analytic," i.e., such that its contradictory is self-contradictory. But this interpretation (which has support in writings that Leibniz did not publish) belongs, if true, to the esoteric doctrine. In his published works he maintains that there is a difference between necessary and contingent propositions, that only the former follow from the laws of logic, and that all propositions asserting existence are contingent, with

the sole exception of the existence of God. Though God exists necessarily, He was not compelled by logic to create the world; on the contrary, this was a free choice, motivated, but not necessitated, by His goodness.

It is clear that Kant is right in saying that this argument depends upon the ontological argument. If the existence of the world can only be accounted for by the existence of a necessary Being, then there must be a Being whose essence involves existence, for that is what is meant by a necessary Being. But if it is possible that there should be a Being whose essence involves existence, then reason alone, without experience, can define such a Being, whose existence will follow from the ontological argument; for everything that has to do only with essence can be known independently of experience—such at least is Leibniz's view. The apparent greater plausibility of the cosmological as opposed to the ontological argument is therefore deceptive.

The argument from the eternal truths is a little difficult to state precisely. Perhaps we shall do well to state it first in rough outline, and only then proceed to the complete picture. Roughly, the argument is this: Such a statement as "it is raining" is sometimes true and sometimes false, but "two and two are four" is always true. All statements that have only to do with essence, not with existence, are either always true or never true. Those that are always true are called "eternal truths." The gist of the argument is that truths are part of the contents of minds, and that an eternal truth must be part of the content of an eternal mind. There is already an argument not unlike this in Plato, where he deduces immortality from the eternity of the ideas. But in Leibniz the argument is more developed. He holds that the ultimate reason for contingent truths must be found in necessary truths. The argument here is as in the cosmological argument: there must be a reason for the whole contingent world, and this reason cannot itself be contingent, but must be sought among eternal truths. But a reason for what exists must itself exist; therefore eternal truths must, in some sense, exist, and they can only exist as thoughts in the mind of God. This argument is really only another form of the cosmological argument. It is, however, open to the further objection that a truth can hardly be said to "exist" in a mind which apprehends it.

The argument from the pre-established harmony, as Leibniz states it, is only valid for those who accept his windowless monads which all mirror the universe. The argument is that, since all the clocks keep time with each other without any causal interaction, there must have been a single outside Cause that regulated all of them. The difficulty, of course, is the one that besets the whole monadology: if the monads never interact, how does any one of them know that there are any others? What seems like mirroring the universe may be merely a dream. In fact, if Leibniz is right, it *is* merely a dream, but he has ascertained somehow that all the monads have similar dreams at the same time. This, of course, is fantastic, and would never have seemed credible but for the previous history of Cartesianism.

Leibniz's argument, however, can be freed from dependence on his peculiar metaphysic, and transformed into what is called the argument from design. This argument contends that, on a survey of the known world, we find things which cannot plausibly be explained as the product of blind natural forces, but are much more reasonably to be regarded as evidences of a beneficent purpose.

This argument has no formal logical defect; its premisses are empirical, and its conclusion professes to be reached in accordance with the usual canons of empirical inference. The question whether it is to be accepted or not turns, therefore, not on general metaphysical questions, but on comparatively detailed considerations. There is one important difference between this argument and the others, namely, that the God whom (if valid) it demonstrates need not have all the usual metaphysical attributes. He need not be omnipotent or omniscient; He may be only vastly wiser and more powerful than we are. The evils in the world may be due to His limited power. Some modern theologians have made use of these possibilities in forming their conception of God. But such speculations are remote from the philosophy of Leibniz, to which we must now return.

One of the most characteristic features of that philosophy is the doctrine of many possible worlds. A world is "possible" if it does not contradict the laws of logic. There are an infinite number of possible worlds, all of which God contemplated before creating the actual world. Being good, God decided to create the best of the possible worlds, and He considered that one to be the best which had the greatest excess of good over evil. He could have created a world containing no evil, but it would not have been so good as the actual world. That is because some great goods are logically bound up with certain evils. To take a trivial illustration, a drink of cold water when you are very thirsty on a hot day may give you such great pleasure that you think the previous thirst, though painful, was worth enduring, because without it the subsequent enjoyment could not have been so great. For theology, it is not such illustrations that are important, but the connection of sin with free will. Free will is a great good, but it was logically impossible for God to bestow free will and at the same time decree that there should be no sin. God therefore decided to make man free, although he foresaw that Adam would eat the apple, and although sin inevitably brought punishment. The world that resulted, although it contains evil, has a greater surplus of good over evil than any other possible world; it is therefore the best of all possible worlds, and the evil that it contains affords no argument against the goodness of God.

This argument apparently satisfied the queen of Prussia. Her serfs continued to suffer the evil, while she continued to enjoy the good, and it was comforting to be assured by a great philosopher that this was just and right.

Leibniz's solution of the problem of evil, like most of his other popular doctrines, is logically possible, but not very convincing. A Manichæan might retort that this is the worst of all possible worlds, in which the good things that exist serve only to heighten the evils. The world, he might say, was created by a wicked demiurge, who allowed free will, which is good, in order to make sure of sin, which is bad, and of which the evil outweighs the good of free will. The demiurge, he might continue, created some virtuous men, in order that they might be punished by the wicked; for the punishment of the virtuous is so great an evil that it makes the world worse than if no good men existed. I am not advocating this opinion, which I consider fantastic; I am only saying that it is no more fantastic than Leibniz's theory. People wish to think the universe good, and will be lenient to bad arguments proving that it is so, while bad arguments proving that it is bad are closely scanned. In fact, of course, the world is partly good and partly bad, and no "problem of evil" arises unless this obvious fact is denied.

I come now to Leibniz's esoteric philosophy, in which we find reasons for much that seems arbitrary or fantastic in his popular expositions, as well as an interpretation of his doctrines which, if it had become generally known, would have made them much less acceptable. it is a remarkable fact that he so imposed upon subsequent students of philosophy that most of the editors who published selections from the immense mass of his manuscripts preferred what supported the received interpretation of his system, and rejected as unimportant essays which prove him to have been a far more profound thinker than he wished to be thought. Most of the texts upon which we must rely for an understanding of his esoteric doctrine were first published in 1901 or 1903, in two works by Louis Couturat. One of these was even headed by Leibniz with the remark: "Here I have made enormous progress." But in spite of this, no editor thought it worth printing until Leibniz had been dead for nearly two centuries. It is true that his letters to Arnauld, which contain a part of his more profound philosophy, were published in the nineteenth century; but I was the first to notice their importance. Arnauld's reception of these letters was discouraging. He writes: "I find in these thoughts so many things which alarm me, and which almost all men, if I am not mistaken, will find so shocking, that I do not see of what use a writing can be, which apparently all the world will reject." This hostile opinion no doubt led Leibniz, thenceforth, to adopt a policy of secrecy as to his real thoughts on philosophical subjects.

The conception of substance, which is fundamental in the philosophies of Descartes, Spinoza, and Leibniz, is derived from the logical category of subject and predicate. Some words can be either subjects or predicates; e.g., I can say "the sky is blue" and "blue is a colour." Other words—of which proper names are the most obvious instances—can never occur as predicates, but only as subjects, or as one of the terms of a relation. Such words are held to designate *substances*. Substances, in addition to this logical characteristic, persist through time, unless destroyed by God's omnipotence (which, one gathers, never happens). Every true proposition is either general, like "all men are mortal," in which case it states that one predicate implies another, or particular, like "Socrates is mortal," in which case the predicate is contained in the subject, and the quality denoted by the predicate is part of the notion of the substance denoted by the subject. Whatever happens to Socrates can be asserted in a sentence in which "Socrates" is the subject and the words describing the happening in question are the predicate. All these predicates put together make up the "notion" of Socrates. All belong to him necessarily, in this sense, that a substance of which they could not be truly asserted would not be Socrates, but some one else.

Leibniz was a firm believer in the importance of logic, not only in its own sphere, but as the basis of metaphysics. He did work on mathematical logic which would have been enormously important if he had published it; he would, in that case, have been the founder of mathematical logic, which would have become known a century and a half sooner than it did in fact. He abstained from publishing, because he kept on finding evidence that Aristotle's doctrine of the syllogism was wrong on some points; respect for Aristotle made it impossible for him to believe this, so he mistakenly supposed that the errors must be his own. Nevertheless he cherished through his life the hope of discovering a kind of generalized mathematics, which he called *Characteristica Universalis,* by means of which thinking could be replaced by calculation. "If we had it," he says, "we should be able to reason in metaphysics and morals in much the same way as in geometry and analysis." "If controversies were to arise, there would be no more need of disputation between two philosophers than between two accounts. For it would suffice to take their pencils in their hands, to sit down to their slates, and to say to each other (with a friend as witness, if they liked): Let us calculate."

Leibniz based his philosophy upon two logical premisses, the law of contradiction and the law of sufficient reason. Both depend upon the notion of an "analytic" proposition, which is one in which the predicate is contained in the subject—for instance, "all white men are men." The law of contradiction states that all analytic propositions are true. The law of sufficient reason (in the esoteric system only) states that all true propositions are analytic. This applies even to what we should regard as empirical statements about matters of fact. If I make a journey, the notion of me must from all eternity have included the notion of this journey, which is a predicate of me. "We may say that the nature of an individual substance, or complete being, is to have a notion so completed that it suffices to comprehend, and to render deducible from it, all the predicates of the subject to which this notion is attributed. Thus the quality of king, which belongs to Alexander the Great, abstracting from the subject, is not sufficiently determined for an individual, and does not involve other qualities of the same subject, nor all that the notion of this prince contains, whereas God, seeing the individual notion or hecceity of Alexander, sees in it at the same time the foundation and the reason of all the predicates which can be truly attributed to him, as e.g. whether he would conquer Darius and Porus, even to knowing *a priori* (and not by experience) whether he died a natural death or by poison, which we can only know by history."

One of the most definite statements of the basis of his metaphysic occurs in a letter to Arnauld:

> "In consulting the notion which I have of every true proposition, I find that every predicate, necessary or contingent, past, present, or future, is comprised in the notion of the subject, and I ask no more. . . . The proposition in question is of great importance, and deserves to be well established, for it follows that every soul is as a world apart, independent of everything else except God; that it is not only immortal and so to speak impassible, but that it keeps in its substance traces of all that happens to it."

He goes on to explain that substances do not act on each other, but agree through all mirroring the universe, each from its own point of view. There can be no interaction, because all that happens to each substance is part of its own notion, and eternally determined if that substance exists.

This system is evidently just as deterministic as that of Spinoza. Arnauld expresses his horror of the statement (which Leibniz had made): "That the individual notion of each person involves once for all everything that will ever happen to him." Such a view is evidently incompatible with the Christian doctrine of sin and free will. Finding it ill received by Arnauld, Leibniz carefully refrained from making it public.

For human beings, it is true, there is a difference between truths known by logic and truths known by experience. This difference arises in two ways. In the first place, although everything that happens to Adam follows from his notion, *if he exists,* we can only ascertain his existence by experience. In the second place, the notion of any individual substance is infinitely complex, and the analysis required to deduce his predicates is only possible for God. These differences, however, are only due to our ignorance and intellectual limitation; for God, they do not exist. God apprehends the notion of Adam in all its infinite complexity, and can therefore see all true propositions about Adam as analytic. God can also ascertain *a priori* whether Adam exists. For God knows his own goodness, from which it follows that he will create the best possible world; and he also knows whether or not Adam forms part of this world. There is therefore no real escape from determinism through our ignorance.

There is, however, a further point, which is very curious. At most times, Leibniz represents the Creation as a free act of God, requiring the exercise of His will. According to this doctrine, the determination of what actually exists is not effected by observation, but must proceed by way of God's goodness. Apart from God's goodness, which leads Him to create the best possible world, there is no *a priori* reason why one thing should exist rather than another.

But sometimes, in papers not shown to any human being, there is a quite different theory as to why some things exist and others, equally possible, do not. According to this view, everything that does not exist struggles to exist, but not all possibles can exist, because they are not all "compossible." It may be possible that A should exist, and also possible that B should exist, but not possible that both A and B should exist; in that case, A and B are not "compossible." Two or more things are only "compossible" when it is possible for all of them to exist. Leibniz seems to have imagined a sort of war in the Limbo inhabited by essences all trying to exist; in this war, groups of compossibles combine, and the largest group of compossibles wins, like the largest pressure group in a political contest. Leibniz even uses this conception as a way of *defining* existence. He says: "The existent may be defined as that which is compatible with more things than is anything incompatible with itself." That is to say, if A is incompatible with B, while A is compatible with C and D and E, but B is only compatible with F and G, then A, but not B, exists *by definition.* "The existent," he says, "is the being which is compatible with the most things."

In this account, there is no mention of God, and apparently no act of creation. Nor is there need of anything but pure logic for determining what exists. The question whether A and B are compossible is, for Leibniz, a logical question, namely: Does the existence of both

---

An extract from a letter written by Leibniz in 1715 to Samuel Clarke, an English philosopher and disciple of Newton:

It appears that even natural religion is growing very much weaker. Many hold that souls are corporeal; others hold that God himself is corporeal. Mr. Locke and his followers are at any rate doubtful whether souls are not material and naturally perishable. Mr. Newton says that space is the organ which God makes use of to perceive things by. But if he stands in need of any medium whereby to perceive them, they do not then depend entirely on him, and were not produced by him. Mr. Newton and his followers have also an extremely odd opinion of the work of God. According to them God has to wind up his watch from time to time. Otherwise it would cease to go. He lacked sufficient foresight to make it a perpetual motion. This machine of God's is even, on their view, so imperfect that he is obliged to clean it from time to time by an extraordinary concourse, and even to mend it, as a clockmaker might his handiwork; who will be the less skilful a workman, the more often is he obliged to mend and set right his work. According to my view, the same force and vigour goes on existing in the world always, and simply passes from one matter to another, according to the laws of nature and to the beautiful pre-established order. And I hold that, when God performs miracles, it is not to satisfy the needs of nature, but those of grace. To think otherwise would be to have a very low opinion of the wisdom and power of God.

Gottfried Wilhelm Leibniz, in Leibniz: Philosophical Writings, *edited by G. H. R. Parkinson, J. M. Dent & Sons Ltd., 1973.*

A and B involve a contradiction? It follows that, in theory, logic can decide the question what group of compossibles is the largest, and this group consequently will exist.

Perhaps, however, Leibniz did not really mean that the above was a *definition* of existence. If it was merely a criterion, it can be reconciled with his popular views by means of what he calls "metaphysical perfection." Metaphysical perfection, as he uses the term, seems to mean quantity of existence. It is, he says, "nothing but the magnitude of positive reality strictly understood." He always argues that God created as much as possible; this is one of his reasons for rejecting a vacuum. There is a general belief (which I have never understood) that it is better to exist than not to exist; on this ground children are exhorted to be grateful to their parents. Leibniz evidently held this view, and thought it part of God's goodness to create as full a universe as possible. It would follow that the actual world would consist of the largest group of compossibles. It would still be true that logic alone, given a sufficiently able logician, could decide whether a given possible substance would exist or not.

Leibniz, in his private thinking, is the best example of a philosopher who uses logic as a key to metaphysics. This type of philosophy begins with Parmenides, and is carried further in Plato's use of the theory of ideas to prove various extra-logical propositions. Spinoza belongs to the same type, and so does Hegel. But none of these is so clear cut as Leibniz in drawing inferences from syntax to the real world. This kind of argumentation has fallen into disrepute owing to the growth of empiricism. Whether any valid inferences are possible from language to non-linguistic facts is a question as to which I do not care to dogmatize; but certainly the inferences found in Leibniz and other *a priori* philosophers are not valid, since all are due to a defective logic. The subject-predicate logic, which all such philosophers in the past assumed, either ignores relations altogether, or produces fallacious arguments to prove that relations are unreal. Leibniz is guilty of a special inconsistency in combining the subject-predicate logic with pluralism, for the proposition "there are many monads" is not of the subject-predicate form. To be consistent, a philosopher who believes all propositions to be of this form should be a monist, like Spinoza. Leibniz rejected monism largely owing to his interest in dynamics, and to his argument that extension involves repetition, and therefore cannot be an attribute of a single substance.

Leibniz is a dull writer, and his effect on German philosophy was to make it pedantic and arid. His disciple Wolf, who dominated the German universities until the publication of Kant's *Critique of Pure Reason,* left out whatever was most interesting in Leibniz, and produced a dry professorial way of thinking. Outside Germany, Leibniz's philosophy had little influence; his contemporary Locke governed British philosophy, while in France Descartes continued to reign until he was overthrown by Voltaire, who made English empiricism fashionable.

Nevertheless, Leibniz remains a great man, and his greatness is more apparent now than it was at any earlier time. Apart from his eminence as a mathematician and as the inventor of the infinitesimal calculus, he was a pioneer in mathematical logic, of which he perceived the importance when no one else did so. And his philosophical hypotheses, though fantastic, are very clear, and capable of precise expression. Even his monads can still be useful as suggesting possible ways of viewing perception, though they cannot be regarded as windowless. What I, for my part, think best in his theory of monads is his two kinds of space, one subjective, in the perceptions of each monad, and one objective, consisting of the assemblage of points of view of the various monads. This, I believe, is still useful in relating perception to physics.

Margaret D. Wilson (essay date 1966)

SOURCE: "On Leibniz's Explication of 'Necessary Truth'," in *Leibniz: A Collection of Critical Essays,* edited by Harry G. Frankfurt, Anchor Books, 1972, pp. 19-45.

[*In the following essay, originally published in German in 1966, Wilson examines Leibniz's concepts of necessary and contingent truths.*]

Leibniz's remarks on necessity are dominated by two primary themes. The first, of course, is the thesis that a necessary truth may be defined as a proposition which possesses, "implicitly" if not "expressly," a specific logical form. (This is sometimes referred to, in recent works, as the thesis that necessary truths are "analytic.") The second is Leibniz's frequently reiterated contention that while the word "necessary" has application both to voluntary action and in connection with explanations of why the world is as it is, "necessary" as used in these contexts is not equatable with "logically necessary." It is with respect to these contexts that Leibniz speaks of "moral necessity" and "physical necessity," claiming that a distinction must be recognized between different "degrees" or different "species" of necessity.[1]

These two theses can appear incompatible if it is assumed that when Leibniz *defines* a necessary truth as a proposition which possesses a specific logical form he is providing an analysis of his understanding of the meaning of the word "necessary." For if "necessary" simply *means* "analytic," then there cannot be truths which possess a degree of necessity but are not analytic; and there manifestly cannot be different degrees of analyticity.

In the first part of this paper I shall examine the status of Leibniz's unvarying definition of "necessary truth." I shall argue that there are reasonable grounds, independent of his talk of moral and physical necessity, for regarding this definition as something *other* than a purported analysis of the meaning of "necessity." I shall also try to illuminate the important role this definition plays in Leibniz's thought, and very briefly indicate some contrasts with related views on necessary and analytic truth held by Leibniz's predecessors and by more recent philosophers. I shall then briefly consider the question whether the notions of moral and physical necessity, as Leibniz explains them, can in fact be regarded as fundamentally distinct from the notion of logical necessity. (For reasons of space I shall have to ignore here the relevant but involved question of the significance of Leibniz's well-known dictum that for God all truth is somehow conceptual or analytic.) In conclusion I shall make some remarks about Leibniz's handling of a class of truths which seem to have strong claims to "necessity," but which do not seem to fall under the species of necessity that he explicitly recognizes.

I

Leibniz's definition of necessary truth is one of the best known tenets of his philosophy:

> A necessary proposition is one the opposite of which is not possible, or the opposite of which having been assumed, a contradiction is arrived at by resolution.[2]

It is frequently remarked that this definition is "traditional," and it is of course true that the explication of necessary truth in terms of the contradictoriness of the opposite has many antecedents in the writings of scholastic philosophers. Leibniz's definition has, however, special significance because of his strict understanding of the key term "self-contradictory," and must therefore be distinguished from certain previous (as well as later) accounts which superficially resemble his. For philosophers as diverse as Thomas Aquinas and Descartes a self-contradictory assertion is simply a judgment which joins together "mutually opposing" ideas. (*Repugnare, opponere,* and *adversari* are among the verbs used to express this notion.)[3] The recognition of "opposition" among ideas is itself left to intuition stimulated perhaps by a few examples: e.g., "A man is an ass." This position is in fact quite different from that of Leibniz, for whom a self-contradictory proposition is one which *formally entails a denial of (his version of) the principle of non-contradiction:* i.e., a proposition which is either expressly of the form "A is not-A" or "AB is not-A," or can be reduced to a proposition of one of these forms by a series of substitutions of definientia for definienda. (It may be noted that the scholastic chestnut just cited is on this view at best *implicitly* self-contradictory: its contradictoriness remains to be proved through a reduction to the standard form.)

That the opposite or denial of a necessary truth must be self-contradictory in this sense has an important consequence for the form of the necessary truth itself, enabling Leibniz to present a more direct and simple definition of necessity: a necessary truth is an express or implicit "identity," i.e., a proposition which is either expressly or implicitly of the form "A is A," or "AB is A," or may be reduced to one of these forms by the substitution of definitions.[4] Since the principle of identity is treated by Leibniz as merely a part of the complete formulation of the principle of non-contradiction,[5] we may continue to say that necessary truths are founded in or are true by the principle of non-contradiction. Leibniz classes as "contingent" those truths which are not reducible to "identities."

But, we may now ask, precisely what relationship does Leibniz wish to claim between the terms "necessary"—"impossible" on the one hand, and "reducible to identity"—"reducible to contradiction" on the other hand? As I have already noted, it seems natural to assume that the latter pair of expressions are intended as analyses of the meaning of the former terms. If this is Leibniz's position, however, there is an obvious and important objection to it. Adapting G. E. Moore's "open question" argument, we may ask: is it not perfectly intelligible to inquire whether the principle of non-contradiction is itself *necessary?*[6] What this question points up, I think, is that Leibniz's definition, as stated, omits or abstracts from the connotations of inevitability or indispensability normally associated with the word "necessary." To say that a proposition is (implicitly or expressly) identical does not seem to be at all the same as to say that it *has to be true.* Thus, whether having the form of an identity makes a proposition necessary *is* a meaningful or "open" question, as the word "necessary" is ordinarily used. As Bertrand Russell remarks, à propos of Leibniz's definition, "Necessity must *mean* something other than connection with the Law of Contradiction," since "the statement that analytic propositions are necessary is significant." Russell concludes that "it would seem that necessity is ultimate and indefinable."[7]

This line of argument makes it seem desirable to try to find an alternative interpretation of Leibniz's position. It might be suggested that Leibniz intends by his definition to provide, not an analysis of the meaning of "necessary," but only a criterion or mark by which necessary truths are to be distinguished from others. There seems, indeed, to be evidence for the truth of this suggestion in Leibniz's own writings. Consider, for example, the following passages:

> Whatever implies a contradiction is impossible, for this is to say nothing.[8]

> How can faith decree anything, which overthrows a principle without which all creation and affirmation or negation would be vain? It must therefore necessarily be the case [il faut donc necessairement] that two propositions which are true at the same time are not complete contradictories.[9]

> Thus the principle of contradiction is the principle of all truths of reason, and if it is given up [sublato] all reasoning is given up [tollitur]. . . . [10]

The first two of these passages seem sufficient to indicate that Leibniz was not, in the last analysis, inclined to hold that "reducible to identity" is the full meaning of "necessary," nor "reducible to contradiction" of "impossible." For both passages suggest that one can give a reason *why* what is reducible to identity or contradiction *is* (respectively) necessary or impossible: "whatever implies a contradiction is impossible, *for* this is to say nothing"; "it must *therefore necessarily* be the case [that two true propositions are not contradictories]." But if "necessary" *meant* "reducible to identity" (or "impossible," ". . . contradiction"), it would be as absurd to advance reasons why the identical is necessary or the contradictory impossible as to advance reasons why all bachelors are unmarried men. The three passages taken together make it clear that Leibniz is prepared to claim that the principle of non-contradiction is "necessary" on the grounds that it is in some sense an indispensable condition of reasoning or knowledge itself. His position, apparently, is one that goes back to Aristotle: if there is to be meaningful discourse (reasoning), the affirmation of any statement must be taken to exclude the denial.[11]

I do not propose to consider the question whether Leibniz is right in holding the principle of non-contradiction is epistemologically indispensable in this sense, but let us assume for a moment that he is. It might be thought that the "necessity" thus established for the principle could be only a relative necessity—relative, that is, to the conducting of a certain practice, the practice of reasoning. In the same way, it seems, acceptance of the statement "God exists" might be necessary for the practice of worship; however, it is not necessary that we accept this statement, since it is not necessary that we worship. But Leibniz himself expressly indicates in the *Nouveaux essais* that he would not regard this analogy as valid:

> One must distinguish between what is necessary to support our knowledge, and what serves as the foundation of our received doctrines or our practices.[12]

While Leibniz's elaboration of this distinction *in loco* is not very illuminating, the following consideration is perhaps sufficient to suggest that there actually is an important difference between the two cases. An *epistemologically* indispensable truth, as the necessary condition of meaningful affirmation and denial, could not itself be meaningfully denied. In other words, any principle which is a necessary condition of reasoning itself, cannot intelligibly be challenged, since any challenge of the truth of a principle must take place *within the framework* of rational discourse. I think, therefore, that Leibniz may be right in indicating that his argument for the "necessity" of the principle of non-contradiction is more conclusive and less crudely pragmatic than would be the superficially analogous argument for the "necessity" of the proposition "God exists."

Since Leibniz does argue for the "necessity" of the principle of non-contradiction, then, it might seem that "reducibility to identity" should be regarded simply as a characteristic which adequately distinguishes necessary or indispensable truths from others (without standing as an analysis of the meaning of "necessity"). But this interpretation of his definition is not satisfactory either. For in one passage Leibniz expressly indicates that the principle of non-contradiction shares what I have called epistemological indispensability with a *contingent* truth, *quod varia a me percipiantur*.[13] (But if *quod varia a me percipiantur* is epistemologically indispensable, "I exist" should have the same status for Leibniz, since he normally cites this truth too as a "first truth of fact or of experience."[14]) Leibniz's distinction between necessary and contingent truths therefore does not seem to correspond to the distinction between propositions which are epistemologically indispensable and those which are not. But if the definition of necessary truth is neither to be understood as an analysis of the meaning of "necessary," nor as a criterion by which indispensable truths are distinguished from others, how are we to understand it?

I think we must conclude that the sense of "necessary truth" which Leibniz attempts to establish with his definition is a complex and quite strong sense. It is neither independent of considerations of indispensability nor entirely a function of them. For a truth to be necessary in this strict sense it must possess the logical form of an identity, and not all epistemologically indispensable truths do possess this form. Thus Leibniz's definition links up with traditional views of necessity through the notion of the "contradictoriness of the opposite." It also conforms to the traditional tenet that only "eternal" truths may strictly be treated as "necessary"; the principle of non-contradiction, unlike the first truth or truths of experience, can be stated without reference to temporal beings. On the other hand, while all and only non-contingent truths possess the form of identity, their *being necessary* is not merely a matter of their possessing this form. "Necessary truth" is at no point reduced by Leibniz to a bare formal concept, shorn of all connotations of inevitability or indispensability. For these connotations are retained, in the case of logical necessity, by taking into account (or assuming) the epistemological indispensability of the principle of identity itself.

My purpose in examining the notion of epistemological indispensability has been to show that Leibniz's definition of "necessary truth" in terms of identity, far from providing a complete analysis of his understanding of the meaning of "necessary," serves to establish a strict and technical sense of "necessary truth" which is itself partly parasitical upon a broader, nonformal, and perhaps indefinable concept of necessity. This broader concept may, of course, be understood as roughly equivalent to that of indispensability or of inevitability in general. The qualification "epistemological" merely indicates one sort of grounds on which this necessity may be claimed.

Following Leibniz's own usage, we may, when there

is danger of ambiguity, refer to his technical sense of "necessary truth" with the expression "logical necessity."[15] To say that a truth is contingent is to say that it is not *logically* necessary. It does not follow, as we have already seen, that the word "necessary" can have no significant application within the domain of contingent truths. I shall return to this point in a moment. First, however, we must consider one further aspect of the definition of logical necessity.

Leibniz's insistence on the definition of necessary truth by reference to a certain logical form is of course bound up with his methodological position that in scientific thought objective criteria of truth are infinitely to be preferred over "intuition" or psychological incapacity to doubt. He maintains, in particular, that even apparently obvious mathematical and logical propositions must be "proved." The "proof" will consist, precisely, in showing that these propositions are identities.[16] Now the thesis that all of mathematics and logic can in fact be established with formal rigour through employment of definitions and identical axioms alone is an extremely bold and significant one. It is therefore of considerable interest that Leibniz, who throughout his life maintained this thesis with the most absolute conviction, never produced more than meagre substantiation for it. It is true, as Kauppi remarks,[17] that Leibniz "illustrates" his thesis by offering a few sample reductions: e.g., of "2 + 2 = 4,"[18] "equals added to equals yield equals,"[19] and the principle of the syllogism.[20] But these efforts are fragmentary and unsystematic: there is certainly a world of difference between "illustrating" a thesis and establishing it. It is also true that Leibniz expended much effort on developing logical calculi that would make possible the demonstration of logical and mathematical truths. But among the primitives of these calculi one finds not only definitions and identical axioms (in Leibniz's sense of "identical"), but also such non-identical axioms as the principles of permutation and of tautology.[21] Kauppi suggests that the latter principles should be regarded as "hypothetical" axioms—admitted only provisionally until a method of eliminating them might be devised.[22] But one may still wonder why Leibniz persisted in holding so firmly that it is both important and possible ultimately to eliminate all non-identical "axioms." And I think that at least part of the answer to this question must be found in the intimate relation—traditionally and in Leibniz's thinking—between the notion of self-contradictoriness and the concept of a necessary (non-contingent) truth. The enterprise of reducing mathematical and logical truths to a few simple primitives was always regarded by Leibniz as equivalent to establishing their necessity;[23] and one may speculate that the extraordinary faith that he had in the possibility of carrying out this enterprise was partly grounded in the assumption that since these truths are all "necessary" in the same sense they *must* all be reducible to identities, their opposites to contradiction.

It is, therefore, somewhat ironic that the well-known work of the logistic theorists of this century which establishes the immense fruitfulness of Leibniz's reductionistic notions does so precisely at the expense of his conception of logical necessity. Russell, for instance, emphatically denies that the principle of non-contradiction has any "special pre-eminence" over other logical truths; and in the *Principia Mathematica* the law of contradiction. . . is not even treated as a primitive.[24] (It is no doubt significant in this connection that recent discussions of the status of mathematical and logical truths, in relation to the work of the logistic theorists, have tended to concentrate on the newer and less traditional concept of analyticity, rather than the ancient question of necessity.)[25]

II

We may turn now to the contingent truths. These Leibniz customarily divides into two classes: truths about the choices of rational beings ("I am going on a journey"), and truths which assert or describe states of affairs in the physical world ("The sun is shining in the Western Hemisphere"). He wishes to hold that while neither of these two sorts of truths are logically or "absolutely" necessary, they are, respectively, "morally" and "physically" necessary.[26] Leibniz apparently regards these truths as having some claim to "necessity" because he believes that none of them (or, on another level, none of the choices or events, etc. which they assert to occur) is arbitrary or "undetermined": every truth (choice, event) has its determining "reasons."[27] For any event *e* that occurs, it can be said that *e* "had" to occur, on the grounds that sufficient reason for *e*'s occurrence existed at the time *e* occurred. What we must ask is whether there are grounds for claiming that there is a fundamentally different, nonlogical species of necessity involved here.

With respect to physical necessity, the determining conditions for an event are to be sought principally in the hierarchy of increasingly general "laws of nature," together (presumably) with earlier conditions from which *e* follows in accordance with these laws.[28] (This is a somewhat over-simplified account, but good enough for our purposes.) Leibniz believes that while the world is infinitely complex there are a few first or most general laws of nature, which are directly decreed by God.[29] He seems inclined to hold that given the full set of God's initial decrees as premises, the events in the physical world can be deduced with logical rigour.[30] (It is in this way that natural laws provide the "reasons for" an event.) If this is so, the notion of logical necessity is involved in the definition of physical necessity: an event is physically necessary if a proposition affirming the occurrence of the event follows logically from true premises which include statements of the natural laws initially decreed by God. In order to determine whether physical necessity is anything but a special case of logical necessity, we must consider the status of the "premisses"—God's decrees.

These Leibniz emphatically maintains to be contingent: God could have created a world governed by other primary laws.[31] On the other hand, the first decrees are themselves "determined": God had *reasons* for decreeing these laws rather than other possible laws.[32] Thus as Leibniz himself remarks, physical necessity is "grounded in" moral necessity, or the necessity governing choice.[33] That he regards moral necessity as quite distinct from logical necessity seems to be indicated by his frequent contention that the reasons which determine choice "incline without necessitating"[34]—i.e., without yielding logical necessity. Leibniz seems to want to claim that in some sense the chooser "cannot" choose otherwise than he does (hence the expression "moral *necessity*"), and yet that there is no logical contradiction in denying that he makes the choice he does make.

While the complex question of moral necessity cannot exhaustively be dealt with here, we may consider the three most obvious interpretations of Leibniz's position, in order to see what kind of case can be made for a radical distinction between moral and logical necessity. We shall use God's decision to create *this* world as an example.

A. O. Lovejoy, one of the most perceptive American commentators on Leibniz, has asserted that the purported distinction between "inclining" and "necessitating" reasons is "manifestly without logical substance," and that "the fact is so apparent that it is impossible to believe that a thinker of [Leibniz's] powers can have been altogether unaware of it himself."[35] Lovejoy follows up this remark with an interpretation of "moral necessity" according to which this notion, while not strictly identical with logical necessity, may be defined in terms of it. According to Lovejoy, the only position to which Leibniz is entitled is that other worlds besides this one are possible *considered in themselves,* apart from God's choice, but it is not logically possible *that God should create* one of these other worlds. This reading is unavoidable, according to Lovejoy, because both of the following propositions are treated by Leibniz as logically necessary: (1) "God creates the best world," and (2) "This world is the best world."[36] On this view, that our world is the best world *is* the reason which determines God to create it, but the relation between the reason and the choice is, precisely, one of logical necessity. A "morally necessary truth" turns out to be a truth the denial of which is not "in itself" self-contradictory, but gives rise to a contradiction when considered in connection with logically necessary truths about the ground of existence, namely God. (This formula would, of course, have to be modified to provide for the applicability of the concept of moral necessity to the results of human choice.)

While there is much to support Lovejoy's position, it is by no means entirely clear that Leibniz *is* committed to holding as logically necessary the proposition that God creates the best world.[37] We may therefore consider some alternative readings.

In contending that the world, or God's choice of the world, is only morally necessary, Leibniz might mean that God's creation of this world is a logical consequence of certain prior conditions, but these conditions themselves are *not* logically necessary. He indeed seems to lean in this direction when he announces that it was God's first decree always to do what is best.[38] This decree having once been made His creation of this world might be deducible with logical necessity, but the decree is itself contingent.

But this view of the matter does not take us very far towards establishing a distinction between moral and logical necessity. The contingency of the world is traced to the contingency of the first decree, but the manner in which *this decree* was determined has not been elucidated.[39] So far no content has been given to the notion of moral necessity.

In order to give content to this notion, and to preserve its distinctness from logical necessity, it seems requisite to take seriously the distinction which Lovejoy finds nugatory—the distinction between an "inclining" and a "necessitating" reason. Leibniz must be taken to hold that the truths God would present as reasons for His choice, whether themselves logically necessary or merely contingent, do not logically entail that He made that choice. The question is whether any sense can be made of this idea. Does it make any sense to assert both that a decision D was determined or "necessitated" by conditions C, and that the conjunction, "C and not-D," does not imply contradiction?

It is certainly true that in many cases the "reasons" that we give for an action or decision do not logically entail the occurrence of that action or that decision. I might say that the reason I went to the ballgame rather than stay home is that I wanted some fresh air. While this would normally be considered a satisfactory statement of what determined my decision, no one would assert that my "wanting some fresh air" logically entailed that I went to the ballgame. For one thing, there should be other ways to get some fresh air; also, even if this were not true, I might "want some fresh air" yet not go to the ballgame—if, for instance, I considered some other goal (such as finishing a letter) more important.

It might be replied, however, that a reason for an action or decision "determines" one to perform that action or make that decision only under the conditions that (a) no other possible action or decision could fulfill the end stated in the "reason," and (b) there are no conflicting ends to which one attaches equal or greater importance which would provide reasons for a different and incompatible action or decision.[40] These further conditions are *understood* to obtain when the "determining reason" is stated, and together with it do logically entail that the given choice is made.

However, I think it might be open to Leibniz to repudiate this objection in one of the following ways. He might argue either (1) that a choice is correctly said to be determined by the reason for which it is made, and not by the lack of reasons for some other choice; or (2) that it is not in fact the case that the conjunction of relevant reasons for and against making a particular decision normally does *logically entail* that the decision which is in fact made *is* made.

When the issue is stated in this way, it does not seem to me self-evident that Leibniz is wrong and his hypothetical opponent right about the logical relation between reasons and decisions or choices. Neither would I claim that the position here attributed to Leibniz is self-evidently correct. I wish only to suggest that the notion that a choice may be "determined" by reasons without being logically necessitated is *not* "manifestly without logical substance." Despite what Lovejoy says, it is not patently incoherent to speak of determination or "moral necessity" as obtaining where logical necessity does not obtain—at least when the latter notion is given the strict significance that Leibniz in fact accords it. However, I think it must be conceded that the distinction between "inclining" and "necessitating" reasons requires a much fuller explication and vindication than Leibniz ever provides.

III

In conclusion I would like to say a few words about Leibniz's handling of a group of truths, the existence of which has frequently been urged as a decisive objection to an "analytic" definition of necessary truth. This group includes propositions which assert the *difference* of two "ideas," e.g., "white is not red," "yellowness is not sweetness"; and propositions which assert that one attribute either *excludes* another (e.g., "what is white is not black") or necessarily coexists with another (e.g., "what is coloured is extended").[41] These propositions (which are sometimes characterized as "synthetic a priori") seem to be necessary, and they appear at the same time to be completely irreducible to *any* general axiom—including the principle of identity.

It is seldom noticed that in the *Nouveaux essais* Leibniz himself briefly discusses such truths—especially the assertions of the *difference* of two ideas, which he calls "disparates." At no point does he seem to dispute the "necessity" of any of these truths; indeed, he surely does regard them as necessary. How to handle them within his system is, however, clearly a difficult question for him. In Book I of the *Nouveaux*

essais he first says that the disparates are "identities or almost identities," and adds that "the identities or immediates do not receive proof."[42] He does not explain how a proposition can be "almost an identity," but merely offers the highly puzzling "clarification" that these truths involve the application of the "general maxim to particular cases."[43] A little later he seems rather to lean towards the view that the disparates are not primitives, but *are* subject to proof—i.e., to reduction to formal identities.[44] He does not give any indication of how this is to be done. Still another position is adopted in Book IV, where Leibniz classes the disparates as necessary truths and "negative identities," and says that they are primitive, but explicitly contrasts them with the primitive truths which are "contradictories":

> I come now to the negative identities which are either true by the principle of contradiction, or the disparates [*qui sont ou du principe de contradiction, ou des disparates*].[45]

He gives some standard examples of primitive truths which are true by virtue of the principle of contradiction ("An equilateral rectangle cannot be a non-rectangle," etc.) and then proceeds:

> As for the disparates, these are those propositions which say that the object of one idea is not the object of another idea; e.g., that heat is not the same thing as colour, or man and animal are not the same, although every man may be an animal.[46]

These, he says, "can be assured independently of any proof or of the reduction to opposition or to the principle of contradiction. . . ." Although Leibniz does not here explicitly concede that the disparates *cannot* be reduced to identity, but says only that they do not *need* proof, he clearly implies that they are not instances of the principle of non-contradiction. For he contrasts them with truths that *are* instances, and characterizes them as primitives.[47]

At this point one must conclude that Leibniz's "definition" of necessary truth is virtually condemned out of his own mouth by the admission of primitive necessary truths which are not formal identities, unless one can say that the disparates, while "necessary," are not logically necessary. Our previous observations would seem to suggest that the latter move is open to Leibniz. But there is a difficulty. Leibniz holds that all truths which are not *logically* necessary are dependent on the will of God.[48] Can the difference between heat and colour be any more dependent upon the will of God than the sum of three and two?

Notes

[1] Cf. *Théodicée, Préface* (GP VI, pp. 33, 64).—The

following abbreviations are used below: GP = Leibniz, *Die philosophischen Schriften*. Hrsg. C. I. Gerhardt. Bd 1-7. Berlin 1875-90.—*N. E. = Nouveaux essais sur l'entendement humain*. (= Gottfried Wilhelm Leibniz, *Sämtliche Schriften und Briefe*. Hrsg. v. d. Deutschen Akademie der Wissenschaften. R. VI, Bd VI. Berlin 1962.)—C = Leibniz, *Opuscules et fragments inédits*. Ed. Louis Couturat. Paris 1903.

[2] C 374. Translations in this paper are my own unless otherwise indicated.

[3] Cf. e.g., Thomas de Aquino, *Summa theologica,* I, q. 25, a. 3; Descartes, *Oeuvres*. Ed. Ch. Adam and P. Tannery. T. 1-11. Paris 1897-1908. T. VII, p. 152. A similar intuitive, non-formal notion of self-contradiction seems to be present in the writings of various recent philosophers. For instance Alfred Jules Ayer in his *Language, Truth, and Logic*. 2d ed. rev. New York, 1957, maintains that the propositions of logic and mathematics are necessary in that we cannot abandon them "without contradicting ourselves, without sinning against the rules which govern the use of language, and so making our utterances self-stultifying" (p. 77). He also asserts (p. 95) that "the one thing we may not do" is maintain a set of hypotheses which are "incompatible" or mutually self-contradictory. At the same time he vigorously denies (p. 81) that any a priori truth, including the principle of non-contradiction, is prior to others or the grounds of their validity. Thus, while necessity *is* explained with reference to the notion of self-contradiction, this is evidently not the same for Ayer as grounding necessary truth in the *principle of non-contradiction*.

[4] C 371.

[5] Cf. e.g., GP VII, 299.

[6] Cf. George Edward Moore, *Principia Ethica*. Cambridge, England, 1959, pp. 15-16, 21. (The 1st ed. of this work appeared in 1903.)

[7] Bertrand Russell, *A Critical Exposition of the Philosophy of Leibniz*. 2d ed. London 1937, p. 23. (The 1st ed. appeared in 1900.)

[8] From Leibniz's notes on Boyle's *Some Considerations about the Reconcileableness of Reason and Religion,* quoted (in translation) by Leroy Earl Loemker in his article, *Boyle and Leibniz,* In: *Journal of the History of Ideas,* XVI (1955), p. 38.

[9] *N. E.* IV, xviii, § 1.

[10] GP IV, 237.

[11] Cf. Aristotle, *Metaphysics*. iv, 3. 1006a.

[12] *N. E.* IV, xvii, § 19.

[13] Cf. esp. C 183: "Duo illa prima principia: unum rationis: *Identica sunt vera, et contradictionem implicantia sunt falsa,* alterum experientiae: *quod varia a me percipiantur* talia sunt, ut de iis demonstrari possit, primo demonstrationem eorum impossibilem esse; secundo omnes alias propositiones ab ipsis pendere, sive si haec duo principia non sunt vera, nullam omnino veritatem et cognitionem locum habere. Itaque aut admittenda sunt sine difficultate, aut omni inquistioni veritatis renuntiandum est."

[14] Cf. *N. E.* IV, vii, § 7, ix; §§ 3-4.

[15] Cf. e.g., Leibniz's fifth paper in correspondence with Clarke, § 4. Leibniz also uses the terms "absolute necessity," "metaphysical necessity," "geometrical necessity," and "mathematical necessity" as synonymous with "logical necessity."

[16] Cf. *N. E.* I, i, § 5; IV, vii, §§ 1, 8; GP VI, 503-4; GP VII, 296.

[17] Raili Kauppi, *Über die Leibnizsche Logik*. Helsinki 1960. (= *Acta Philosophica Fennica*. Fasc. XII), p. 125.

[18] *N. E.* IV, vii, § 10.

[19] GP III, 258-59.

[20] C 229-30.

[21] See GP VII, 224-47; C 235. Cf. Kauppi, *op. cit.,* p. 160; also, Louis Couturat: *La logique de Leibniz,* Paris 1901, pp. 321, 337, 346, 365.

[22] Kauppi, *op. cit.,* p. 127.

[23] Cf. e.g., *N. E.* IV, xii, 4.

[24] Bertrand Russell, *Introduction to Mathematical Philosophy*. London 1919, p. 203.

[25] Cf. Gottlob Frege, *Die Grundlagen der Arithmetik,* Breslau 1884, § 3; Bertrand Russell, *Introduction to Mathematical Philosophy,* chap. xviii; Morton White, *Toward Reunion in Philosophy,* Cambridge, Mass., 1956, pp. 129-63; Willard Van Orman Quine, *Two Dogmas of Empiricism*. In his: *From a Logical Point of View,* Cambridge, Mass., 1953.

[26] Cf. Leibniz's 5th letter to Clarke, §§ 4-7, 76; *Discours de métaphysique,* xiii; *N. E.* II, xxi, §§ 8-9; *Théodicée, Discours de la conformité de la foi avec la raison,* § 2. In some of these passages Leibniz speaks of "hypothetical necessity" rather than "physical necessity." (There are in fact some subtleties and strange variations in his use of these two expressions which I here disregard.)

[27] See for instance, 5th letter to Clarke, §§ 9, 18-19; *Discours de métaphysique,* xiii.

[28] *Ibid.,* vii; C 19-20.

[29] *Théodicée, loc. cit.;* C 18-29.

[30] *Ibid.* Cf. GP II, 40.

[31] *Discours de métaphysique,* xiii; *Théodicée, loc. cit.*

[32] *Ibid.*

[33] *Ibid.*

[34] See 5th letter to Clarke, § 9; *Théodicée, Remarques sur le livre de M. King,* § 14; C 405.

[35] Arthur Oncken Lovejoy, *The Great Chain of Being,* Cambridge, Mass., 1957, p. 172.

[36] *Ibid.,* p. 173.

[37] See Nicholas Rescher, *Contingence in the Philosophy of Leibniz.* In: *Philosophical Review,* LXI (1952), and below, n. 38.

[38] *Discours de métaphysique,* xiii.

[39] Cf. Russell, *Philosophy of Leibniz,* p. 39n.

[40] In the case of action, we must add the condition that the action is not physically impossible for the agent to perform: in the case of decision, that the end desired is not known by the agent to be unobtainable (or falsely believed to be unobtainable).

[41] See, for instance, Arthur Pap, *Are all Necessary Truths Analytic?* In: *Philosophical Review,* LVIII (1949), where the incompatibles are discussed with some reference to Leibniz's doctrine; also Hao Wang, *Notes on the Analytic-Synthetic Distinction.* In: *Theoria,* XXI (1955); and B. Russell, *Philosophy of Leibniz,* pp. 20-21.

[42] *N. E.* I, i, § 18.

[43] *Ibid.*

[44] *Ibid.*

[45] *N. E.* IV, ii, § 1.

[46] *Ibid.*

[47] For allusions to necessary coexistence and exclusion see *N. E.* IV, vi, § 10.

[48] Cf. *Monadologie,* § 46; *Discours de métaphysique,*

xiii; Leibniz, *Nouvelles lettres et opuscules inédits.* Ed. Alexandre Foucher de Careil, Paris 1857, p. 179.

Nicholas Rescher (essay date 1967)

SOURCE: "God and the Mind of God," in *The Philosophy of Leibniz,* Prentice-Hall, Inc., 1967, pp. 11-21.

[*In the following excerpt, Rescher focuses on Leibniz's concept of substance and explains the centrality of God to Leibniz's philosophy.*]

God

Leibniz, more than any other modern philosopher, took seriously the idea of a *creation* of the universe, giving it a centrally important place in his system. Like the theories of the medievals for whom he had such great respect, his system put God as the *author of creation* at the focal position in metaphysics. The concept of God provides the theoretical foundation upon which the structure of the Leibniz metaphysic is built.

God, for Leibniz, may be defined as "the perfect being."[1] His existence is not a seriously problematic issue; it follows directly from the idea (or essence) of his perfection, by reasonings along the lines of the Ontological Argument of Anselm as refurbished by Descartes, and also by other, related arguments—a topic to which we will return at some length. Indeed, all characteristics of God must inhere in and derive from His attribute as "the perfect being." Three of these characteristics are of primary importance for Leibniz: omniscience, omnipotence, and (omni-) benevolence.[2] These are the operative theological concepts in terms of which the drama of creation unfolds itself.

Substance

In the philosophy of Leibniz, as in that of Descartes and Spinoza, the conception of *substance* plays a fundamental role. Leibniz defines a substance as "a being capable of action."[3] God, of course, is a substance—the primordial substance, the only substance that exists in its own right. All other substances are in the first instance mere possibilities whose actualization hinges upon God, upon the creation. The prime characteristics of Leibniz' *substance* are: 1) a given individual substance is a simple, perduring existent, not in the sense of logical simplicity, but in the absence of spatial parts; 2) a given individual substance is capable of functioning as the subject of propositions, the predicates of true propositions concerning the substance standing for attributes of the substance. One can loosely describe Leibniz' individual substance as a spatio-temporal existent (God apart) without spatial parts, but not without attributes, and with a perduring individuality. One of Leibniz' own characterizations, helpful but incomplete unless interpreted in the context of many variant characterizations, reads as follows:

> There are only *atoms of substance,* that is to say, real unities, that are absolutely devoid of parts, which are the sources of action and the absolute first principles of the composition of all things and, as it were, are the ultimate elements in the analysis of substantial things. One could call them *metaphysical points.* They have something vital, a kind of perception; and mathematical points are their *points of view,* from which they express the universe.[4]

In a cognate passage we read that the individual substances, the monads,

> cannot have shapes, otherwise they would have parts. And consequently a monad, in itself, and at a given moment, cannot be distinguished from another except by its internal qualities and actions which cannot be otherwise than its *perceptions* (i.e., representations of the compound, or of what is outside, in the simple) and its appetitions (i.e., its tendencies to pass from one perception to another), which are the principles of change. . . . It [viz. a monad] is as a center or a point where, simple though it is, an infinity of angles are found made by the lines that come together there.[5]

The identification of the simple (primitive) predicates entering into the defining notions of substances with the simple perfections of God is a point repeatedly insisted upon by Leibniz.[6] This aspect of substances draws together several strands of thought in Leibniz' system, such as his thesis of the varying degrees of perfection (and correlatively their imperfection or finitude), and his penchant for the Ontological Argument for the existence of God. Moreover, it accounts for his conception of the immanence of God in monadic life, a conception which led some writers to class Leibniz among the medieval and Renaissance mystics in whose ideas he displayed great interest.

Against the Cartesian notion of physical substance as pure extension, Leibniz cast three objections of a fundamentally conceptual character: extension cannot comprise the essence of material substance because 1) it is an *incomplete* notion; 2) it is a *complex* and not a simple concept, since it can be analyzed further into plurality, continuity, and coexistence;[7] 3) the very conception of extension is in its genesis imaginary and phenomenal, since size, figure, and so on, are not distinct self-subsisting things, but are relative to our perceptions.[8]

Substance *Sub Ratione Possibilitatis*

Prior to the creation[9] (and we think here not of literal and temporal but of figurative and conceptual priority) all substances aside from God existed, or rather sub-

sisted—since *ex hypothesi* they did not exist—only as ideas in the mind of God:

> in God is found not only the source of existence, but also that of essences, insofar as they are real. In other words, He is the ground of what is real in the possible. For the Understanding of God is the region of the eternal truths and of the ideas on which they depend; and without Him there would be nothing real in the possibilities of things, and not only would there be nothing in existence, but nothing would even be possible.[10]

It should be stressed, however, that although presence in God's thoughts gives to unexistent possibles whatever "existence" they possess, the *nature* of such possibilities is wholly self-determined and in no way subject to God's will.

Since God is omniscient, His concept of the substance is not approximate and incomplete but descends to every detail of its (possible) career, and includes every single one of its properties. With respect to possibles, the principle obtains that alternative "descriptions" of the same thing must, unlike actual existents, be *logically* equivalent. In God's plan for ontological possibilities there is no room for the sort of incompleteness that figures in recipes for cooking or plans of architects ("Take 1 pint of milk." But from which cow? "Use such-and-such a piece of lumber." But from which tree?). Thus every possible substance, not only the ones actually singled out for creation, is represented in the mind of God by what Leibniz calls its *complete individual notion (notio completa seu perfecta substantiae singularis),* in which every detail of the substance at every stage of its (potential) career is fixed.[11] For simplicity and convenience we shall call this complete individual notion of the (possible) substance its *program.* The history of a substance is merely the continuous unfolding of its program with the same inexorable inevitability with which a mathematical series is generated in the successive development of its defining law. This lawfulness comprises the essence of the substance and is the source of its continuing self-identity: "That there is a certain persisting law which involves the future states of that which we conceive as the same—this itself is what I say constitutes the same substance."[12] In view of its specifications through its complete individual notion, every substance "contains in its nature a *law of the continuation of the series* of its own operations and [thus] of everything that has happened or will happen to it."[13] The complete individual notion of a substance is, of course, known only to God, not to mortals:

> The notion of myself, and of any other individual substance, is infinitely more extensive and more difficult to understand than is a generic concept like that of a sphere, which is only incomplete. . . .

Therefore, although it is easy to determine that the number of feet in the diameter is not involved in the concept of a sphere in general, it is not so easy to decide if the journey which I intend to make is involved in my notion; otherwise it would be as easy for us to become prophets as to be Geometers.[14]

The contemplation of substances—not as existent actualities but as subsistent possibilities—forms in God's mind a "realm of possibles" (*pays des possibles*) in which every conceivable substance is presented "under the aspect of possibility" (*sub ratione possibilitatis*).[15] In God's mind we find the entire gamut of cosmological possibilities. (Note here the echo of Nicholas of Cusa's idea of the world as *explicatio dei,* its history being the unfolding of the divine plan, the "reading off" in nature of the book of God.) This part of the contents of the divine mind, the possible worlds, we must study, for it is an essential preliminary to a discussion of Leibniz' theory of creation.

Any actual state of affairs could, conceivably, have been different, for such an assumption involves no contradictory consequences. But if any actual state of affairs were different, then, since it is but the outcome of a natural course of development,[16] the entire universe would have to have a different history of development. In fact, we should have to resort to a world different from ours, involving another possible development of things: our hypothetical investigation would lead us to another, altogether different possible world. Anterior to the existence of our world there was recorded in the divine mind entire infinities of notions of possible individual substances, whose only being at this point is that *sub ratione possibilitatis* in God's mind.

Compossibility and Order

Since the program of a substance involves the specification of literally every facet of its career, it involves all details of the relation of this substance to others. But now suppose that:

1. Possible substance #1 has the property *P* and also has the property that there is no substance having property *Q* to which it (#1) stands in the relationship *R*.

2. Possible substance #2 has the property *Q* and also has the property that every substance having the property *P* stands in the relationship *R* to it (#2).

These two substances are patently incompatible (on logical grounds). God might realize #1 or He might realize #2, but He cannot possibly realize both of them. (It is a fundamental tenet of Leibniz' philosophy that even omnipotence cannot accomplish the impossible.)

Substances which do *not* clash in this way are characterized by Leibniz as *compossible.*

Thus the very concept (i.e., the defining program) of a possible substance marks it as either compossible or incompossible with any other given substance, and the fact that a given substance is compossible with such and such others must be incorporated in its concept. Since each of these possible substances involves one possible history of the development of the universe, only those involving the same history are compatible with each other. Because the actualization of some possibilities is incompatible with that of others, the manifold of possible substances splits into mutually exclusive systems of "compossibles." God's choice of creation is not of selection among individual substances, but among entire possible worlds; His will thus being always general "God never has a *particular will.*"[17]

Possible Worlds

There is an important difference between the *compossibility* of (possible) substances and the *compatibility* of propositions. One proposition can be mutually compatible with each of two others which are, in turn, incompatible with one another. This can happen only when the first proposition is "incomplete," i.e., simply fails to embody any information that commits it one way or another as regards the other two incompatible ones. Since this sort of incompleteness is excluded from the realm of the "complete individual concepts" of possible substances, it follows that whenever one substance is compossible with each of two others, they in turn must be compossible with one another. This is a consequence of the descriptive *completeness* with which every possible substance is identified in terms of its complete individual notion.

By means of this principle the possible substances sort themselves out into *possible worlds*. The possible world of any substance is the totality of all substances compossible with it. Each possible world consists of a family of possible substances, every one of which is compossible with all the rest, and the individual characteristics (and therefore, as we shall see, the mutual relations) of which are determined in every conceivable respect by their individual defining concepts. The substances of each possible world are thus reciprocally adjusted to one another in a thoroughgoing, *total* way. To use one of Leibniz' favorite metaphors, the substances of a possible world "mirror" one another in their mutual accommodation.[18] Since the entire history of each possible world is determined in every possible detail in terms of the complete individual notions of its constituent substances, there is no question of God's direct, immediate intervention in the course of natural events. (The possibility of divine action *within* the course of history is denied by Leibniz, so he rejects on this score both occasionalism and the interventionalism of Newton's divine clock-readjustor. Leibniz does, in the **Theodicy,** admit the possibility of continuous "creation," but this is not a matter of the introduction of new substances but of the temporal *continuation* of existing ones in accordance with a pre-established program.)[19]

Creation and the Actual World

If the concept of creation is to be introduced into the ontological framework just outlined in a viable way, the question of the existence of a possible substance must not be pre-empted by its complete individual notion. Thus Leibniz must either 1) adopt (i.e., anticipate) the Kantian course of denying that existence is a predicate, or else, 2) granting that existence is a predicate, rule existence out from the sphere of predicates that can feasibly enter into the defining notion of individual substances. Although in view of the paucity of evidence one cannot speak very firmly, it does appear that Leibniz took the second course, being willing to regard existence as a predicate,[20] albeit one of a sort that cannot enter into the essence of a substance (other than God), being inevitably consequent upon a pre-specified essence.[21]

The question can be raised: Is there anything to a Leibnizian substance over and above the attributes that belong to it by virtue of the predicates loaded into its complete individual notion? From the human standpoint the answer is *yes*—we actually do not ever know the complete individual notion of a substance, but encounter that substance only in experience (in fact, in confused perception). Even from God's standpoint an affirmative answer must be given, for an existing substance is, *ex hypothesi,* or *existent,* i.e., an entity or a thing, and its existence is never a matter of the attributes overtly guaranteed by its complete individual notion.

Suppose that God, contemplating a conceivable world *sub ratione possibilitatis,* finds it meritorious and chooses to *create* it, i.e., advance it from the status of a *possible* to that of an *actual* substance. Since He is omniscient, He knows the relationship of this substance to all the others that are compossible or incompossible with it. Being beneficent He wishes to *maximize existence,* to create as much as possible,[22] and thus would not choose to actualize a certain possible substance without actualizing other substances compossible with it—i.e., its entire possible world. But which of the possible worlds is God to choose for actualization? Clearly, the answer must be *the best.*[23] But what criterion of merit does God employ to determine whether one possible world is more or less perfect than another?

The Criterion of Goodness

The criterion of goodness for possible worlds is plainly set forth by Leibniz in the following terms:

> God has chosen [to create] that world which is the most perfect, that is to say, which is at the same time the simplest in its hypotheses [i.e., its laws] and the richest in phenomena.[24]

The characteristic properties of each substance change from one juncture to another in accordance with its program. The properties of substance #1 at one juncture may be more or less in accordance with and thus reflected or mirrored in those of substance #2 at this juncture. Out of these mirroring relationships grow the regularities which represent the "hypotheses," the natural laws of the possible worlds. The "best," most perfect possible world is that which exhibits the greatest *variety of its contents* (richness of phenomena) consonant with the greatest *simplicity of its laws.*

Our world—the actual world—is the "best possible world" in this rarified metaphysical sense of *greatest variety of phenomena consonant with greatest simplicity of laws.* Its being the best has (at bottom) little to do with how men (or men and animals) fare in it. The facile optimism of Dr. Pangloss, the butt of Voltaire's parody *Candide—Si c'est ici le meilleur des mondes possibles, que sont donc les autres?*[25]—misses the mark if Leibniz (and not some naive and simple-minded Leibnizian) is intended as its target.

There is, to be sure, a genuine difficulty in the Leibnizian criterion of which he himself was unquestionably aware, but which he did not resolve with the sharpness we might wish for. If merit of a possible world is determined by macro-considerations that operate in the large ("variety," "simplicity"), what assurance is there that the outcome is as we would wish it to be on the basis of micro-considerations that operate in the small (specifically, enumeration of the individual perfections of the several substances that comprise the possible worlds)? Leibniz adduces considerations which may mitigate, but do not wholly remove, doubt:

> The ways of God are those most simple and uniform . . . [being] the most productive in relation to the *simplicity of ways and means.* It is as if one said that a certain house was the best that could have been constructed at the same cost. . . . If the effect were assumed to be greater, but the process less simple, I think one might say when all is said and done, that the effect itself would be less great, taking into account not only the final effect but also the mediate effect. For the wisest mind so acts, as far as is possible, that the *means* are also *ends* of a sort, i.e., are desirable not only on account of what they do, but on account of what they are.[26]

This line of approach glosses over the genuine difficulty of a possibility of conflict between the components of Leibniz' two-factor criterion: What is to be chosen when we confront, for example, a sacrifice in "simplicity of means" for the sake of a greater "variety of phenomena"?

The Monads and God

An existing substance that is a member of the actual, and thus of the best possible, world, Leibniz calls a *monad.* He did not introduce the term monad until relatively late in his career. In the ***Discourse on Metaphysics*** of 1685, the first systematic presentation of his doctrine, he spoke simply of "individual substances." He continued to use this term, sometimes alternating it with *substantial form* and *entelechy,* or (when appropriate in context) *soul* or *spirit.* The term monad first began to be generally used by Leibniz in 1696.[27] Little else can be said about this definition apart from a question that has created something of a flurry of controversy among Leibniz scholars: Is God Himself a monad?

The answer to this must be in the affirmative. God is a monad, but a very special and unique one, for he is the *supreme* and the *prime* monad. The idea that God is a monad was called into question by Bertrand Russell,[28] who proposed to regard those passages where Leibniz explicitly speaks of God as one among the monads[29] as mere "slips." I think it unfortunate to charge an author with more mistakes than absolutely necessary, and see no reason why we must view Leibniz' declarations that God is a monad as errors from the standpoint of his system. That His status is fundamentally similar to that of the monads can be seen from the fact that He, like them, is an existing substance, indeed the supreme substance.[30] Leibniz explicitly assigns God a place in the scale of monads, holding Him to be the highest spirit.[31] Moreover, if God were not a monad it would be a contrastless qualification and senseless redundancy for Leibniz to speak, as he does often, of *created* substances and *created* monads, since God is the only noncreated existent in his ontology. In summary, we may regard it as certain that God has a place in Leibniz' system of monads, although this place is beyond any question a special and pre-eminent one.

Notes

[1] *Un estre absolument parfait. Phil.,* IV, p. 427.

[2] This is explicit in, e.g., the essay *Causa Dei asserta per justitiam ejus cum caeteris ejus perfectionibus. Phil.,* VI, pp. 437 ff. Leibniz follows in the footsteps of the tradition of those who, like St. Thomas Aquinas, hold God to be perfect in being, knowledge, and wisdom. Cf. *Monadology,* § 4.

[3] "Principles of Nature and of Grace," § 1. (This work

is henceforth cited as PNG.)

[4] *Phil.,* IV, pp. 482-83.

[5] *Phil.,* VI, p. 598; PNG, § 2.

[6] See, for example, *Phil.,* V, p. 15 (bottom).

[7] *Phil.,* II, pp. 169-70.

[8] *Discourse on Metaphysics,* § xii. (This essay is henceforth cited as DM.)

[9] *Phil.,* VI, p. 614.

[10] To speak of anything "prior" to the existent universe is to use the term in a purely logical, and by no means temporal, sense; and when one does so, one deals with the necessary being, the necessary truths, and the possible worlds, i.e., one enters the sphere of pure logic. It is hardly possible to find here a place for activity of any sort.

[11] *Monadology,* § 43.

[12] *Phil.,* II, p. 264.

[13] *Phil.,* IV, pp. 432-33; Couturat, *Opuscules,* pp. 403, 520.

[14] *Phil.,* II, p. 45.

[15] This is the key idea of one of Leibniz' ways of establishing the existence of God, since not even possibles would exist without the existence of "a being who could produce the possible" (*Phil.,* III, p. 572).

[16] In Leibniz, one must remember, we are confronted with a strict mechanist.

[17] *Theodicy,* § 206.

[18] It is derived from Nicholas of Cusa, according to whom the entire universe is a mirror of God.

[19] Cf. DM, § xxx: "God in co-operating with our actions ordinarily does no more than to follow the laws He has established, which is to say that He continually preserves and produces our being in such a way that thoughts come to us spontaneously or freely in the order carried in the concept of our individual substance, in which it could have been foreseen through all eternity."

[20] *Phil.,* V, p. 339. Cf. Russell, *Critical Exposition,* pp. 77, 174, 185.

[21] *Phil.,* VII, p. 195.

[22] Leibniz is fundamentally committed to the idea that

existence is preferable to nonexistence.

[23] We return to the topic of creation at greater length in Sec. 4 of Chap. 5.

[24] DM, § 6. Cf. *ibid.,* § 5, and also PNG, § 10; *Theodicy,* 208.

[25] Voltaire, *Candide,* Chap. vi.

[26] *Theodicy,* § 208.

[27] See A. G. Langley (tr.), *G. W. Leibniz: New Essays Concerning Human Understanding* (New York & London: Macmillan Co., 1896), p. 101, notes. Cf. also Gerhardt's observations in *Phil.,* IV, pp. 417-18. Prof. L. E. Loemker informs me, however, that Leibniz employed the term *monas* (pl. *monades*)—albeit in a mathematical sense—as early as the Leipzig period.

[28] Russell, *Critical Exposition,* p. 187.

[29] For example, *Phil.,* III, p. 636; *Phil.,* VIII, p. 502.

[30] *Monadology,* § 40.

[31] *Phil.,* IV, p. 460.

G. H. R. Parkinson (essay date 1972)

SOURCE: An introduction to *Leibniz: Philosophical Writings, revised edition,* edited by G. H. R. Parkinson, translated by Mary Morris and G. H. R. Parkinson, Dent, 1973, pp. vii-xix.

[*In the following excerpt from an essay written in 1972, Parkinson presents an overview of Leibniz's philosophical and scientific theories.*]

Gottfried Wilhelm Leibniz was born in Leipzig on 1 July 1646. The son of a professor of moral philosophy, he studied at the Universities of Leipzig and Jena. Germany had been devastated by the Thirty Years' War, which ended in 1648, and the general cultural backwardness of the country was reflected in the German universities. It may have been this that decided Leibniz to reject the offer of a professorship in 1667, and to enter instead the service of the Baron of Boineburg, who had been a minister of the Elector of Mainz. This proved to be of great, perhaps of decisive importance in Leibniz's career. Whilst in Boineburg's service he was sent on a mission to Paris; this turned into a long stay, lasting from 1672 to 1676. Paris at this time was the intellectual capital of Europe, and Leibniz came into contact with such philosophers as Malebranche and Arnauld; he had access to Pascal's mathematical manuscripts; most important of all, he met the great Dutch physicist Christiaan Huygens, who in ef-

fect introduced him to higher mathematics. Leibniz could never equal Huygens as a physicist, but he was soon to outstrip him in the mathematical field; it was while he was in Paris that he discovered (independently of, but later than Newton) the differential calculus. It was in Paris, too, that he had constructed the first model of his new calculating machine, an improvement on the machine already invented by Pascal.

Boineburg died in 1672, and in 1676 Leibniz accepted a post under the Duke of Hanover. He served three successive dukes until his death in Hanover on 14 November 1716. His duties were various: he was librarian, jurist and official historian. At that time, Hanover was a small town of about 10,000 inhabitants, but Leibniz was far from being provincial in outlook. The first Duke of Hanover to employ him, Johann Friedrich, was a person of wide culture; so, too, was the Duchess Sophia, wife of the next Duke and granddaughter of James I of England. There were journeys to Berlin to visit Sophia's daughter, Sophie Charlotte, Queen of Prussia; there was a long journey to Italy to collect historical material. Further, there was Leibniz's correspondence. During Leibniz's lifetime, learned journals were relatively few, and the private letter was still a major means of communication between scholars. Leibniz's correspondence was vast: the total number of his correspondents exceeds 1,000, and he often corresponded with more than 150 people in a single year.

In his letters, and in a large number of papers, he poured out his ideas on a great range of subjects—on mathematics, logic, science, history, law, theology and philosophy. Relatively little of this was published during his lifetime; it is symptomatic of this that of the works translated in the present volume only the **New System** and **Explanation of the New System** were published before his death. The only philosophical book of any length which he published was the **Theodicy** (1710), a semi-popular and loosely-constructed work which attempted to justify God's ways to man, and in which Leibniz's philosophy is spread somewhat thinly. Nor was any *magnum opus* left behind in his papers; instead, he left behind him a large number of short essays, which reflect his philosophy from various angles, much as (to use one of his favourite illustrations) the same town is differently represented from different points of view. It will be the aim of this introduction to provide a kind of plan of the Leibnizian philosophy, to which the various points of view presented in the papers which follow can be related.

Leibniz's philosophy is usually held to be an example of that philosophical rationalism whose other two great exponents are Descartes and Spinoza. None of the three ever called himself a rationalist, but it is true that, despite great differences, they had much in common, and it is useful to have a common name by which to refer to them. The question is what it is that marks them off from other philosophers. If the term 'rationalism' is taken to mean a philosophy which disregards sense-experience, then neither Descartes, Spinoza nor Leibniz was a rationalist. What they did have in common was the belief that sense-experience is an inferior kind of knowledge, and that genuine knowledge is provided by the reason. More precisely, it is provided by deductive reasoning; knowledge constitutes a deductive system, comparable to a system of geometry. So Descartes could write in Part II of his *Discourse on Method,* published in 1637, that 'Those long chains of reasoning, quite simple and easy, which geometricians use in order to achieve their most difficult demonstrations, had given me occasion to imagine that all things which can be known by man are mutually related in the same way'. Similarly, in his *Of Universal Synthesis and Analysis* of about 1683 Leibniz spoke of his youthful search for categories which would relate, not concepts, but propositions—not realising that what he sought was already provided by geometrical demonstrations.

Leibniz's views about the systematic character of all knowledge are linked with his plans for a universal symbolism, a *Characteristica Universalis*. This was to be a calculus which would cover all thought, and replace controversy by calculation. The ideal now seems absurdly optimistic, but it should be remembered that, in general, the philosophers and scientists of the seventeenth century were not lacking in confidence: Descartes, for example, could claim in his *Principles of Philosophy* (IV, 199) that there was no natural phenomenon not dealt with in the work. What matter here, however, are the implications that this ideal had for Leibniz.

The calculus was to cover all knowledge; it therefore presupposed as a basis an encyclopaedia which would contain, in a non-symbolic form, all that was so far known. Leibniz wrote many sketches of and introductions to such an encyclopaedia, one of which is translated in this volume, but he never completed the undertaking. However, the by-products of the plan were important. Leibniz recognised the essentially co-operative character of the enterprise, and so was led to support the foundation of new academies and of a new learned journal, the *Acta Eruditorum*. But the calculus needed more than an encyclopaedia; it was not only to cover all knowledge, it was also to put it in a systematic form. To show the logical dependence of one proposition on another it was necessary, Leibniz believed, to be able to analyse the concepts which occur in propositions, reducing complex concepts to the simple concepts that are their constituents. It must be stressed that the aim of Leibniz's analysis is not simply the clarification of meaning, nor the solution of puzzles, as in much modern philosophical analysis; the aim is clarification in the service of proof. Further, the termi-

nal points of Leibniz's analysis, his primitive concepts, differ from those of modern philosophers. Leibniz's analysis goes with a metaphysics. This does not, of itself, differentiate it from all modern philosophical analysis; Russell's philosophy of logical atomism involves a metaphysics, and the same can be said of Wittgenstein's. Leibniz's metaphysics, however, differs radically from that of Russell or Wittgenstein. In Leibniz's *Of an Organum or Ars Magna of Thinking* the primitive concepts are said to be of pure being (i.e. God) and of nothing; elsewhere, the primitive concepts are said to be of the attributes of God.

Here, however, a gap opens in Leibniz's analysis, in that the grasping of these primitive concepts is said to be beyond our powers. If we could grasp them, we could show *a priori* how everything follows from God, and this we clearly cannot do. Leibniz therefore has to propose a more modest kind of analysis, which terminates in concepts which are only relatively primitive, primitive for us. He gave various lists of such concepts, one of which can be found in his *Introduction to a Secret Encyclopaedia*. But the limitations on analysis just mentioned must not be exaggerated. What human beings cannot do, Leibniz says, is to show *a priori* how *everything* follows from the attributes of God. It will be seen later, however, that Leibniz thinks that from the concept of God that we have, imperfect as it is, it is possible to deduce something about the nature of the universe. In short, the construction of a deductive metaphysical system is within our power; what is not, is the construction of a metaphysical system which is complete.

First, however, it must be explained why Leibniz should regard the primitive concepts as being of the attributes of God. Here it is necessary to consider the rules of his calculus—that is, the principles of reasoning. Leibniz said many times that reasoning is based on two great principles—that of identity or contradiction, and that of sufficient reason. He did not always make it clear, however, that these principles are, as he once put it, 'contained in the definition of truth and falsity'. This statement occurs in an appendix to the *Theodicy* of 1710 ('Remarks on the book, *On the Origin of Evil*', par. 14), but the relations between the two principles and Leibniz's definition of truth are explored most thoroughly in the *Discourse on Metaphysics* of 1686, and other writings of the same period. Leibniz's view is that every proposition has a subject and a predicate, and a true proposition is one whose predicate is in the subject. So, for example, the proposition 'Every man is rational' is true because rationality is in man, or, as Leibniz would also say, because the concept of rationality is in the concept of man. Leibniz also asserts that every truth is, implicitly or explicitly, an identical proposition. The true proposition 'Every man is rational' is not explicitly identical, but, Leibniz says, it can be reduced to 'A rational animal is rational', which is.

To prove something to be true is to reduce a proposition which is only implicitly identical to one which is explicitly identical; or, it is to show *how* the predicate is in the subject. This is done by the analysis either of the subject, or of the predicate, or of both. All this can now be related to Leibniz's 'two great principles'. Leibniz's definition of truth states that every truth is either an explicitly identical proposition, or is reducible to such. The principle of identity or contradiction says that every identical proposition is true and every self-contradiction is false. The principle of sufficient reason says that every truth can be proved; that is, that every true proposition which is not an explicit identity can be reduced to such a proposition.

The principle of sufficient reason provides Leibniz with an argument for the existence of God, which he expounds in *On the Ultimate Origination of Things* and elsewhere. There are, he says, contingent things, things whose existence is not necessary. These must have a reason, and the reason must lie outside them; for if it lay within them, their existence would be self explanatory. But as long as we seek the reason for a contingent thing in some other contingent thing, so long we are left with something whose existence has in turn to be explained. Therefore the ultimate reason for contingent things must lie in that whose existence is self-explanatory; that is, in a necessary being, or God.

The validity of this argument has been called in question since the time of Kant; the point of mentioning the argument here, however, was to show how Leibniz can say that the primitive concepts are the concepts of the attributes of God. The question remains, how Leibniz viewed the dependence of contingent things on God. Spinoza would have argued that to call things 'contingent' is a mark of ignorance; such things are really modes of the one necessary being. Leibniz disagrees; for him, there is real contingency, in the sense that there are states of affairs which are not logically necessary. As this is so, contingent things cannot be modes of the necessary being, and their dependence must be of another sort. Their dependence is that of creatures on their creator; in other words, the ultimate reason for contingent things is not only a necessary being, but is also a creative deity.

God chooses between various possible states of affairs, various 'possible worlds', and he chooses, and creates, the best possible. This is why Leibniz says that contingent things owe their existence to the 'principle of the best' (e.g. to Clarke, Paper 5, par. 9). The principle of the best is an easy target for the satirist; but Leibniz is no Dr. Pangloss, for whom legs exist in order that we may wear stockings. To an important extent, to say that Leibniz's God acts for the best is to say that he acts in accordance with the principles that the scientist follows in explaining the universe—or, as Leibniz would prefer to say, that scientific explanation

is a kind of copying of the thought-processes of God, a re-tracing of the rational pattern which God follows in creating the universe. 'God', as Leibniz says in *A Specimen of Discoveries,* 'acts like the greatest geometer, who prefers the best constructions of problems'. What this means is that the creation of the best is the production of the maximum effect with the least expenditure, much as a geometer, in constructing a deductive system, prefers that axiom set which is the most economical and from which most consequences can be derived. From this, Leibniz claims to prove a number of scientific and metaphysical propositions, the most important of which is the thesis that there are no atoms and there is no vacuum, but that an infinity of substances exists. Leibniz insists, however, that the principle of the best is not merely quantitative; the substances that God has created also constitute an order which is morally the best.

The principle of the best, which God follows in creating this world in preference to other possible worlds, serves to differentiate the truths of physics from those of mathematics, which are true of all possible worlds. Leibniz also states the distinction between these two sorts of truths by saying that physics, unlike mathematics, requires the principle of sufficient reason (*A Specimen of Discoveries;* cf. to Clarke, Paper 2, par. 1). Here he can hardly mean the principle that every truth can be proved, for this is of universal application, and is presupposed by the mathematician as much as by the physicist. Sometimes he seems to be referring to the principle of the best; sometimes, however, he seems to mean simply that the truths of physics imply a reference to God's choice, and God never chooses without a reason. This principle plays an important part in Leibniz's attack, in his correspondence with Clarke (1715-16), on the Newtonian concept of absolute space, Leibniz's argument being that this concept implies that God must choose something without a reason.

In an earlier paragraph, mention was made of substances. Leibniz's theory of substance contains some of his most characteristic doctrines, and in this theory his views about the nature of truth again play an important part. Aristotle and his followers, Leibniz says, have regarded a substance as a subject to which predicates can truly be ascribed, but which is not in turn a predicate of anything else; and this is true as far as it goes (*Discourse on Metaphysics,* art. 8). However, it fails to make clear what it is for something to be truly ascribed to a subject. The answer has already been given: something is predicated truly of a subject when the concept of that something is contained in the concept of the subject. This means that everything that can truly be said of a substance is contained in the concept of that substance; so, for example, anyone who could grasp fully the concept of Alexander the Great would know *a priori,* and not simply by experience, that he is the conqueror of Darius. Leibniz puts this by saying that every substance has a 'complete' concept.

Leibniz was aware of the fact that he might seem to be abolishing the distinction between contingent and necessary truths, and to be falling into a kind of Spinozism. For example, the concept of the equality of its radii is contained in the concept of a sphere, and the proposition that the radii of a sphere are equal is logically necessary; why, then, is the true proposition that Gottfried Wilhelm Leibniz was born in 1646 not logically necessary? Leibniz's answer is two-fold. First, a logically necessary truth is not to be defined simply as one whose predicate is in its subject; rather, it is a proposition such that the inclusion of its predicate in its subject can be demonstrated in a finite number of steps. In the case of a contingent truth, too, the predicate is in the subject, but here the demonstration of its inclusion would require an infinite number of steps. Second, a contingent truth, unlike a necessary truth, involves a reference to the free decrees of God. God does not decide to make the radii of a sphere equal; that its radii are equal is an eternal truth. God does decide to create a Leibniz who is born in 1646, and the proposition that Leibniz was born in 1646 is therefore a contingent truth.

The idea that a substance has a complete concept involves obvious difficulties for someone who believes that human beings are free, as Leibniz did. In his correspondence with Leibniz, Arnauld pointed out that since, for example, his own complete concept included that of being a bachelor, it seemed to follow that he could not be other than a bachelor. Yet he chose freely to be a bachelor, he *could have* married. Leibniz replied to this and to similar objections by distinguishing between absolute and hypothetical necessity. A proposition is absolutely necessary when it would be self-contradictory to deny it, and in this sense there is no necessity for Arnauld to be a bachelor. However, his being a bachelor is hypothetically necessary; it is necessary given that his being a bachelor is part of the best possible world, and given that there is a God who creates such a world. Against this, it may be argued that all that Leibniz has shown is that when a man chooses something, some other choice is logically possible, and that this is not enough for freedom. The man's choice may, for example, be causally determined, and given the cause, the effect follows necessarily, though (as Hume and Kant showed) it does not follow with logical necessity. Again, in creating Arnauld, in actualising his complete concept, God created an Arnauld who will choose to be a bachelor; how, then, can Arnauld be free in this respect? Leibniz grappled with such problems in many papers, but it cannot be said that he found a satisfactory solution.

Leibniz argues that although determinism is only an apparent consequence of his doctrine of the completeness of the concept of a substance, many important

consequences really follow from it. One of these is the identity of indiscernibles. According to Leibniz the complete concept of a substance, such as Alexander, differs from the concept of an abstraction, such as kingship, in that the former and the former alone is sufficient to identify an individual (*Discourse on Metaphysics,* art. 8). This means that no complete concept of a substance can have more than one instance; that is, there cannot be two substances which are exactly alike, differing in number alone. The point of calling this doctrine the 'identity of indiscernibles' may be brought out by the following example. Suppose that there is a substance called 'Jacob', and suppose that there is a substance called 'Israel'; suppose, also, that what is predicated of each is exactly alike. Then 'Jacob' and 'Israel' do not refer to two substances, but are two names for the same substance. Here it may be objected that although 'Jacob' and 'Israel' are indeed two names for the same person, what is predicated of Jacob and Israel is not exactly alike; for example, one has a name beginning with 'J', the other a name beginning with 'I'. Leibniz would probably reply that in his account of the identity of indiscernibles, predicates that relate to names (as opposed to the predicates of what is named) have to be excluded. This may be part of what he has in mind in his discussion of 'reduplicative' propositions in a paper on the nature of truth (*c.* 1686).

There are other consequences of Leibniz's views about the complete concept of a substance. Such a concept, he has said, includes all that can truly be said about the substance. But all things are interrelated, therefore each substance must 'express' the whole universe. The concept of expression is an important one in Leibniz. One thing expresses another, Leibniz says, when there is a constant and ordered relation between what can be said of the one and of the other (to Arnauld, 9 October 1687); in this sense, an ellipse expresses a circle. In effect, then, to say that A expresses B is to say that the one is what would now be called a function of the other (and in fact Leibniz, in his later mathematical writings, uses the term 'function' in something approaching its modern sense: cf. J. E. Hofmann, in *Leibniz,* ed. Totok and Haase, p. 455, n. 231). To say that each substance 'expresses' the whole universe, therefore, is to say that from the predicates of each substance the predicates of all the others can be inferred. This is what Leibniz means when he says that a substance is a 'mirror' of the universe, and (since it expresses past and future states as well as present ones) is 'big with the future and laden with the past' (*New Essays,* Preface).

Not only is a substance a mirror of the universe; it is also 'like a world apart' (*Discourse on Metaphysics,* art. 14). Leibniz argues that since all the states of a substance are simply the consequences of the complete concept of that substance—since, in other words, all its states are the consequences of its own being, and of that alone—then no other substance in the universe can affect it. Strictly, therefore, no substance (with the exception of God, the creator of all contingent things) acts on any other. From this it follows that, in a sense, all our ideas are innate. In another sense, however, Leibniz asserts that only some ideas are innate, and that others are acquired. This is when he argues in the *New Essays,* against Locke, that a purely empiricist epistemology, according to which all ideas are acquired and none are innate, can account for *a posteriori* but not for *a priori* knowledge.

Though Leibniz has argued that no thing really acts on another, yet it is a fact that people commonly say that they do, that A is cause and B effect, and this has to be explained. Here the notion of expression enters again. Leibniz has said that each substance expresses all others; he adds that it sometimes happens that, for us, substance A expresses substance B 'more distinctly' than B expresses A—that is, it is easier to infer from the states of A to those of B than conversely. When this is the case, we say that A is the cause of changes in B. This leaves the question, how it is that the states of A and B are so correlated that it is possible to infer from the one to the other, even though one does not really act on the other. Leibniz's answer is that they are correlated by God, who 'pre-establishes' a harmony between substances; that is, creates substances which are such that, although independent of each other, they also harmonise. This may seem a metaphysical fantasy; but it is important to realise that Leibniz is making two points which have nothing to do with theism as such, and which are far from fantastic. First, he is saying that when some effect is brought about, no causal agency, no 'influx' is transmitted from one thing to another. Here he agrees with Hume, though he reaches his conclusion by a different route. Second, he is saying in effect that the concept of a cause is a crude one, which (if one wishes to be precise) has to be replaced by the concept of a function—much as Bertrand Russell was to say in 1912 in his essay 'On the Notion of Cause'.

This account of causality provides Leibniz with an answer to the problem of the relations between mind and matter. Descartes had found no problem in the causal connexions between bodies, or within a mind, but he found it hard to understand how such different substances as mind and body could act on each other, as they clearly seemed to do. For Leibniz, the problem of mind-body interaction is no more and no less puzzling than the problem of the action of one body on another. All substances, he argues, harmonise with each other; but what happens in a man's mind corresponds more perfectly to what happens in his body, and it is therefore said that the one acts on the other (*Discourse on Metaphysics,* art. 33; *Monadology,* par. 62). It may be objected that this view (like Descartes' account of

mind and body) destroys the unity of a human being; each of us, it may be said, is one individual and not two. In his correspondence with Arnauld (1686-7) and later in his correspondence with des Bosses (1709-12) Leibniz struggled hard, but not very successfully, to find a reply.

But although Leibniz may not have explained the unity of mind and body, he is insistent that every substance must be one, a unit, a 'monad' (the word for a unit which he applied to substances after 1695). What is not genuinely *one* being, he wrote to Arnauld (30 April 1687), cannot be genuinely one *being;* an aggregate, such as an army, or a machine, is not a substance. Leibniz applies this to the notion of extension. Descartes and Spinoza seemed to regard extension as something indefinable, but Leibniz denies that this is so. To speak of something extended, he says, is to speak of an aggregate; a plurality, continuity and co-existence of parts. It follows from this that no substance can properly be called extended, since 'extended' is a predicate that can be ascribed only to a class, and no substance is a class.

This is part of what Leibniz means when he says that every substance is either a soul or (since not all substances are conscious beings like ourselves) soul-like. But he means more than this. He has said that a substance is 'big with the future' and this, he argues, means that it must have a tendency to other states. He therefore says that a substance has to be viewed in teleological terms; it must have what Aristotle and the Scholastics called a 'form', towards which it strives. The connexion between form and soul is again Aristotelian; for Aristotle, to speak of the human soul is to speak of a form, the form of the human body. Leibniz knew that in rehabilitating forms he was opposing an important thesis of seventeenth-century science. That science was mechanistic, and rejected the idea that nature must be viewed as a kind of organism. Leibniz's view was that to a certain extent it was right in doing so. One may not, he says, use souls or forms to explain particular physical events; such events must be explained in mechanistic terms. He insists, however, that the principles of mechanics themselves cannot be stated adequately without a reference to forms.

What, in conclusion, has Leibniz to offer to the modern reader? Deductive metaphysics of the kind defended in the seventeenth and eighteenth centuries has never recovered from Kant's attacks, and since Kant's time serious criticisms have been brought against Leibniz's philosophy in particular. In *The Philosophy of Leibniz,* Bertrand Russell presented Leibniz as an example of the dangers of over-estimating the importance of subject-predicate propositions and failing to give relational propositions their due. It would generally be agreed that Russell is right on the whole, though he is less than convincing in his thesis that a subject-predicate logic should have led Leibniz to monism. More recently, the theory of monads has been attacked by J. L. Austin, on the grounds that Leibniz makes the mistake of regarding demonstrative expressions (expressions which 'refer') as if they were descriptive (*Philosophical Papers,* Oxford, 1961, p. 90n.). But even if these are errors, they are errors of a deep kind, whose rectification takes one into fundamental issues of philosophy. Again, no one is now likely to defend the theory of the pre-established harmony; yet by regarding the notion of the action of one substance on another as incoherent, Leibniz makes one think about the nature of such action. The idea that all substances are souls or soul-like finds little response today; but the idea that things are essentially dynamic lives on in the Hegelian tradition. As to Leibniz's account of the problem, or rather problems of human freedom, it may fairly be said that despite its shortcomings it belongs to the classical literature on the subject. Finally, something may be said about the relation between Leibniz's metaphysics and his science. Collingwood's thesis that metaphysics is a historical science, the 'science of absolute presuppositions', has not won wide acceptance; nevertheless, it is true that a man's metaphysics shows what he regards as the fundamental constituents of the universe. The principle of the best does not enable Leibniz to establish the timeless truth of certain scientific propositions; but by his use of it he does at any rate show what he regards as the basic concepts and principles of the science of his time.

Robert McRae (essay date 1982)

SOURCE: "Miracles and Laws," in *The Natural Philosophy of Leibniz,* edited by Kathleen Okruhlik and James Robert Brown, D. Reidel Publishing Company, 1985, pp. 171-81.

[*In the essay below, first delivered as a seminar paper in 1982, McRae discusses Leibniz's ideas on the laws governing the natural world and argues that Leibniz categorized miracles as occurrences outside the understanding of human explanation.*]

Leibniz makes the charge, which he constantly renewed, that the laws of nature of the Cartesians and Newton's law of gravitation were really only formulations of perpetual miracles. To make his case he had to define miracle. Because the notion of miracle involves, at least for Leibniz, the notion of law as that to which a miraculous event is an exception, and because accordingly the criteria for miracles become inversely the criteria for laws, the entire polemic throws valuable light on Leibniz's conception of law.

We may, to begin with, observe that there are three types of law for Leibniz. First, there is the law of the whole universe, sometimes also referred to as the concept of the universe. Second, there are certain architectonic principles like the law of continuity and the law of determination by maxima and minima. These laws or principles govern not only the first kind of law, the law of the universe, but also the third kind of law, the laws of nature; for example, the principle of the conservation of force in mechanics, or the principle of the most determined path in optics.

The law which governs the whole universe is the same in kind as the concept of the individual, as for example that of Julius Caesar or Alexander the Great. The concept of the individual is a law analogous to the law of a mathematical series, differing from the latter, however, in that it is a temporal series. Given the law and the starting point of the series it should be possible to deduce all the successive predicates of the subject or, if you like, deduce all the successive events in its history. Leibniz calls this kind of law a "law of order" (G IV, 518; L 493). He says, "When we say that each monad, soul, mind, has received a particular law, we must add that it is only a variation of the general law which rules the universe; and that it is just as a city appears differently according to the different points of view from which we look at it" (G IV, 553-4). The law of the individual is then a perspectival variant of the law of the universe, a law from which every event in the universe can be deduced. The law of the universe, like the laws of its individual members, is a law of order. It will appear moreover that it is logically impossible for the universe not to be subject to order. Section VI of the *Discourse on Metaphysics* is headed, "God does nothing out of order, and it is impossible even to feign events which are not regular." Leibniz explains: "Let us suppose, for example, that someone makes a number of marks on paper quite at random, as do those who practise the ridiculous art of geomancy. I say that it is possible to find a geometrical line, the notion of which is constant and uniform according to a certain rule, such that this line passes through all these points, and in the same order as the hand had marked them. And if someone drew in one stroke a line which was now straight, now circular, now of another nature, it is possible to find a notion or rule, or equation common to all the points of this line, in virtue of which these changes must occur. And there is no face, for example, the outline of which does not form part of a geometrical line and cannot be traced in one stroke by a certain movement according to rule. But when a rule is very complex what conforms to it passes for irregular." Leibniz provides another example in the *Theodicy* of the inescapable nature of order. "One may propose a succession or series of numbers perfectly irregular to all appearance, when the numbers increase and diminish variably without the emergence of any order; and yet he who knows the key to the formula, and who understands the origin and the structure of this succession of numbers, will be able to give a rule which, being properly understood, will show that the series is perfectly regular, and that it even has excellent properties" (par. 242). Up to this point we have the architectonic principle of continuity at work. Now the architectonic principle of determination by maxima and minima comes into play. Leibniz continues in the ***Discourse on Metaphysics,*** "Thus one can say that in whatever way God has created the world, it would always have been regular and in a certain general order. But God has chosen the one that is most perfect, that is to say the one that is at the same time the simplest in hypotheses and the richest in phenomena, as a geometrical line might be, of which the construction was easy and the properties and effects very admirable and of great extent." Or, as he puts it elsewhere "that the maximum effect should be achieved by the minimum outlay." (G VII, 303, L 487).

One may note in passing an anomalous difference in the status of the two principles. That the universe should be without discontinuities is not a matter of divine choice. Discontinuities are simply impossible. That the law of the universe should produce the most by the least is a matter of divine choice and is contingent. Elsewhere Leibniz treats the law of continuity as contingent also. Another thing we may take note of is that when Leibniz speaks of the law of the universe, the universe in question is the total aggregation of monads, spirits and minds. Let us call it the metaphysical universe in order to distinguish it from the universe of natural phenomena. The latter are governed by the laws of motion.

The next section of the ***Discourse on Metaphysics,*** number VII, is headed, "That miracles are in conformity with the general order, although they are counter to subordinate maxims. . . ." He explains: "Now since nothing can be done which is not in order, one can say that miracles are as much in order as natural operations, so called [i.e. natural] because they are in conformity with subordinate maxims. . . . As regards general or particular wills . . . one can say that God does everything according to his most general will, which is in conformity with the most perfect order which he has chosen; but one can also say that he has particular wills which are exceptions to the said subordinate maxims, for the most general of the laws of God which rules the whole sequence of the universe has no exceptions." Section XVII is headed "Example of a subordinate maxim or law of nature. In which it is shown that God always conserves regularly the same force but not the same quantity of motion against the Cartesians and several others." An exception to that law of nature, the conservation of force, would be a miracle. But that same miraculous event would not be an exception to the law of the universe, for exceptions to it, as we have seen, are impossible. From the law of the universe, and for that matter from the law of any individual in it, it would be possible to deduce not only those events in its history which conform to the

laws of nature like the rules of collision, but also exceptions to them, that is to say, those miracles which are necessary for this to be the best of all possible worlds, or as he puts it in the ***Theodicy,*** (par. 248) "God ought not to make choice of another universe, since he has chosen the best and has only made use of miracles necessary thereto."

Leibniz has two related definitions of a miracle and both are continually used in his polemics. First, a miracle is that which exceeds the *power* of creatures, or that which cannot be explained by the *nature* of creatures. "Power" (or "force") and "nature" are equivalent expressions. "The nature inherent, in created things is nothing but the force to act and be acted on" (*De ipsa Natura,* par. 9). Second, a miracle is that which is not conceivable by, or explicable to, the created mind. Although miracles are included in the law of the universe, as well as in the law of each individual in it, and are perfectly intelligible to God who knows his reasons for them, finite minds are incapable of knowing the law of the universe, just as they are incapable of having the complete concept of any individual, and therefore they are incapable of understanding a miracle.

With his two definitions of, or criteria for, a miracle, Leibniz rejects absolutely any mere constant conjunction or uniformity conception of the laws of nature, such as he found in the Cartesians and in Bayle defending them, and also in Clarke's defence of Newton. The issue arises first in connection with the Cartesians' occasionalist account of the relation of mind and body, but it is then almost immediately extended to the occasionalist account of all secondary causes. Bayle in his article on Rorarius remarked, "Furthermore it seems to me that this able man [Leibniz] dislikes the Cartesian system because of a false assumption, for one cannot say that the system of occasional causes makes the action of God intervene by a miracle (*deus ex machina*) in the reciprocal dependence of body and soul. For since God's intervention follows only general laws, he does not therein act in an extraordinary way." In replying to this Leibniz after discussing the mind and body connection goes on to say, "But let us see whether the system of occasional causes does not in fact imply a perpetual miracle. Here it is said that it does not, because God would act only through general laws according to this system. I agree, but in my opinion that does not suffice to remove the miracles. Even if God should do this continuously, they would not cease being miracles, if we take the term not in the popular sense of a rare or wonderful thing, but in the philosophical sense of that which exceeds the powers of created beings. It is not enough to say that God has made a general law, for besides the decree there is also necessary a natural means of carrying it out, that is all that happens must be explained through the nature which God gives to things. The laws of nature are not so arbitrary and indifferent as many people imagine. For example, if God were to decree that all bodies should have a tendency to move in circles and that the radii of the circles should be proportional to the magnitude of the bodies, one would either have to say that there is a method of carrying this out by means of simpler laws, or one would surely have to admit that God must carry it out miraculously, or at least through angels charged expressly with this responsibility. . . . It would be the same if someone said that God had given natural and primitive gravities to bodies by which each tends to the centre of its globe without being pushed by another body, for in my opinion such a system would need a perpetual miracle, or at least the help of angels." (G IV, 520-1; L 494-5). To Arnauld Leibniz writes; "Strictly speaking God performs a miracle whenever he does something that exceeds the forces which he has given to creatures and maintains in them. For instance, if God were to cause a body which had been set in a circular movement, by means of a sling, to continue to move freely in a circle when it had been released from the sling, without being impelled or checked by anything at all, that would be a miracle, for according to the laws of nature it should continue along in a straight line in a tangent; and if God were to decree that that should always occur, he would be performing natural miracles, since this movement is not susceptible of a similar explanation. Likewise one must say that if the continuation of the movement exceeds the force of the bodies, it must be said according to the accepted concept, that the continuation of the movement is a true miracle, whereas I believe that bodily substance has the force to continue its changes according to the laws that God has placed in its nature and maintains there." (G II, 93) Or again, in commenting on the occasionalist Lami's objection to his system: "If God wills that a body tend of itself in a straight line, that will be a law of nature, but if he wills that of itself it goes in a circular or elliptical line that will be a continual miracle." (Rob. 373).

The second criterion of the miraculous is that it is inconceivable to created minds. Thus "A miracle is a divine action which transcends human knowledge; or more strictly which transcends the knowledge of creatures" (C 508). By conceivable or intelligible Leibniz means quite simply that and that only which is susceptible of mechanical explanation. To Lady Masham he writes, "It is well to consider that the ways of God are of two kinds, the ones natural, the others extraordinary or miraculous. Those which are natural are always such as a created mind would be able to conceive . . . but the miraculous ways lie beyond any created mind. Thus the operation of the magnet is natural, being entirely mechanical or explicable, although we are still perhaps not in the position of explaining it perfectly in detail, for want of information; but if anyone maintains that the magnet does not operate mechanically and that it does it all by pure attraction from a distance, without

any intermediary, and without visible or invisible instruments, that would be something inexplicable to any created mind, however penetrating and informed it should be; and in a word it would be something miraculous," (G III, 353) or again in the *New Essays* he says "Matter cannot naturally attract . . . nor of itself proceed in a curved line, because this cannot be explained mechanically, for that which is natural must be capable of being distinctly conceived" (Pref.) Not even God could get us to understand a non-mechanical explanation, as Leibniz points out in a letter to Hartsoeker. "Thus the ancients and moderns, who avow that weight is an occult quality are right if they mean by that that there is a certain mechanism unknown to them, by which bodies are pushed towards the centre of the earth. But if it is their opinion that the thing is done without any mechanism by a simple primitive quality or by a law of God which produces this effect without using any intelligible means, it is an irrational occult quality which is so occult that it is impossible that it can ever become clear, even if an angel, to say nothing of God himself, wanted to explain it" (G III, 519).

With Newton and his spokesman, Clarke, Leibniz came up against a rival conception of the natural and the miraculous, not the less forcefully stated because of the insulting tone in which Leibniz in the opening letter of the exchange with the Englishmen makes the charge that Newton's God has created a world so imperfect that he must resort to miracles to keep the whole machine going, while Leibniz's God with the law of the conservation of force has no need of any such extraordinary interventions. "And I hold," says Leibniz, "that when God works miracles, he does not do so in order to supply the wants of nature, but of grace." (Leibniz, I, 4). From this point on miracles are a major topic throughout the correspondence generating, perhaps, the most heated mutual scorn in the entire exchange.

Clarke's conception of a miracle comes out first in his second letter in which he maintains that the distinction between the natural and the supernatural has no significance in relation to God, but only to human ways of conceiving things. For God nothing is more miraculous than anything else. But for us the natural is the usual or frequent or regular, the supernatural the unusual. Says Clarke, "The raising of a human body out of the dust of the earth, we call a miracle; the generation of a human body in the ordinary way we call natural; for no other reason but because [of] the power of God. . . . The sudden stopping of the sun (or earth,) we call a miracle; the continual motion of the sun (or earth,) we call natural; for the very same reason only, of the one's being usual and the other unusual. Did a man usually arise out of the grave, as corn grows out of seed sown, we should certainly call that also natural; and did the sun (or earth,) constantly stand still, we should then think that to be natural, and its motion at any time would be miraculous" (Clarke, V, 107-109). It is evident that for Clarke it is not the kind of causes involved which determines what is natural or supernatural. "The means by which two bodies attract one another, may be invisible and intangible, and of a different nature from mechanism; and yet, acting regularly and constantly, may well be called natural." (Clarke, IV, 45). To which Leibniz replies: "He might as well have added inexplicable, unintelligible, precarious, groundless and unexampled" (Leibniz, V, 120). Growing tired of being told repeatedly that the natural is that which can be explained by the natures of creatures, Clarke finally protests that "The terms, *nature,* and *powers of nature,* and *course of nature* and the like are empty words; and signify merely that a thing usually or frequently comes about." (Clarke, V, 107-109). As for Leibniz's calling attraction a miracle or an occult quality Clarke finds this most unreasonable "after it has so often been declared,"—and here Clarke quotes several of Newton's disclaimers, which he assumes that Leibniz will have read—"that by that term we do not mean to express the cause of bodies tending towards each other, but barely the effect, or phenomenon itself, and the laws or proportions of that tendency discovered by experience; whatever be or be not the cause of it." (Clarke, V, 110-116). If Leibniz had lived long enough to read these remarks the dispute should have moved away from miracles to the question of the relation of laws and causes, but again there would have been no meeting of minds.

I want now to consider Leibniz's conception of miracles and laws in relation to his celebrated doctrine of possible worlds of which this world is one. To Arnauld (G II, 40) he says, "If this world were only possible, the individual concept of a body in this world, containing certain movements as possibilities, would also contain our laws of motion (which are free decrees of God) but also as mere possibilities. For as there exists an infinite number of possible worlds, there exists also an infinite number of laws, some peculiar to one world, some to another, and each possible individual of any one world contains in the concept of him the laws of his world.". . .

Leibniz has effectively excluded as laws of any possible world such uniformities as the tendency of all bodies of themselves to move in circles, or to tend to the centre of their globes without being pushed there by other bodies, to cite examples with which he responds to Bayle. These would be miracles in all possible worlds according to Leibniz because (a) they are not consequences of the natures which God gives things and (b) they are not conceivable or explicable or intelligible, and these are the criteria of the natural as opposed to the supernatural. Are we then left with any other possible laws of nature for other worlds than those operating in this world? To begin with, can God give bodies natures other than that *vis viva* which he conserves

in this world? It would appear not. Leibniz rejects as occult and unintelligible any other candidates for the nature of a body. In any case if we are talking as Leibniz does to Arnauld about the bodies in different possible worlds, these will all, if they are to be bodies, by definition share the same nature. Given, then, that all possible bodies have this nature, and that only mechanical explanations are intelligible, can there be laws of motion which are possible alternatives for other worlds to those operative in this world? What Leibniz calls "the most universal and inviolable" (G III, 45) law of nature, i.e. the conservation of force, he also regards as "the foundation of the laws of motion," (*De ipsa Natura* par. 4) and indeed claims to "reduce all mechanics" to it (G II, 62). What we are asking, then, is whether there is such a foundational law, other than the conservation of force, peculiar to each of an infinitude of possible worlds and to which all the laws of motion peculiar to each of those worlds can be reduced? The answer would seem clearly to be no, for Leibniz says "I call extraordinary every operation of God demanding something other than the conservation of the nature of things." (A 185). Since the nature of bodies is the same in all possible worlds, i.e. force, an exception to the law of the conservation of force would be a miracle in all possible worlds. It would appear then that Leibniz's conception of the miraculous commits him, contrary, of course, to his deepest intentions, to holding that the laws of motion in this world are the same for all possible worlds, the laws, that is to say, of Leibnizian mechanics. Not only would Euclid's *Elements* be a textbook in all possible worlds, but so also would the elements of Leibnizian mechanics.

As an addendum I should like briefly to consider the relation to possible worlds of another set of laws, those of optics, without reference, however, to the miraculous, but to Leibniz's use of the two architectonic principles, that of order or continuity and that of determination by maxima and minima. In the ***Tentamen Anagogicum*** he combines them to produce the principle of the most determined or unique path for light rays in order to find the laws of reflection or refraction. The unique path is that which has no twin or other path symmetrical with it. All other paths have twins. Implicit in Leibniz's use of this principle is another which he enunciates in his correspondence with Clarke, namely "When two things which cannot both be together, are equally good; and neither by themselves, nor by their combination with other things, has the one any advantage over the other; God will produce neither of them." (Leibniz, IV, 19). God is helpless in choosing between twins; hence if he is to choose at all he must choose the most determined or unique path. The concept of unique determination is purely spatial. If, then, there can be different laws of optics for different worlds, it can only be a consequence of the possibility of different kinds of space for these worlds. Leibniz denies this possibility. "Why," asks Bayle, "has matter precisely three dimensions? Why should not two have sufficed for it? Why has it not four?" To which Leibniz replies, "the ternary number is not determined by reason of the best but by geometrical necessity because geometers have been able to prove that only three straight lines perpendicular to one another can intersect at one and the same point." (*Theodicy,* par. 355). It looks then, as if the laws of optics will join those of motion as applying in all worlds, with, however, this possible qualification. Leibniz indicates to Arnauld that there are bodies and motion in all worlds. Does he believe that there is light in all worlds? By the following speculative steps we must, I think, come to the conclusion that he does. Leibniz says, "For by the individual concept of Adam I mean, to be sure, a perfect representation of a particular Adam who has particular individual conditions and who is thereby distinguished from an infinite number of other possible persons who are very similar but yet different from him "as every ellipse is different from the circle, however much it approximates to it" (G II, 20). In other words the existing Adam is the last term upon which an infinite series of possible Adams converges in the same way as an infinite series of ellipses converges on the circle. If the law of the individual is only a perspectival variant of the law of the universe, there must be a similar series of possible worlds converging on this world. If that is the case for the metaphysical worlds of individuals or monads, it is, perhaps, not too much to suppose that it is the case also for its phenomenal counterpart, the physical world, and consequently there should be ever increasing degrees of illumination in the series of possible worlds converging on this world. If so, Snell's law of refraction must apply in all possible worlds.

Donald Rutherford (essay date 1995)

SOURCE: "Metaphysics and Its Method," in *Leibniz and the Rational Order of Nature,* Cambridge University Press, 1995, pp. 71-98.

[*In the following excerpt, Rutherford examines Leibniz's concept of metaphysics. The critic suggests sources for Leibniz's ideas and focuses on such concepts as substance, cause, and the interpretation of sensory phenomena.*]

Leibniz offers several definitions of the science of metaphysics. In one work he describes it simply as the "science of intelligibles" (C 556).[1] In another he identifies it as the "science which has being, and consequently God, the source of being, for its object" (GP VI 227/H 243-4). In a third he characterizes "real metaphysics" as involving "important general truths based on reason and confirmed by experience, which hold for substances in general" (RB 431). In a fourth, finally, he says that metaphysics is "the science which discusses the causes of things using the principle that

nothing happens without reason."[2] Although there are significant variations among these definitions, they converge on a common conception. In the first place, metaphysics is the science of "intelligibles": concepts that owe nothing to sense but are derived solely from reason or intellect. What is distinctly conceivable by the intellect, however, is "being" or possibility, whose reality Leibniz grounds in the ideas of the divine understanding. Thus, insofar as metaphysics is the science of intelligibles, it is also the science of being and the science of divine understanding. Foremost among the intelligible concepts that form the object of metaphysical knowledge is that of substance, or self-subsistent being; hence, truths about "substances in general" form a central part of metaphysics. Finally, to the extent that metaphysics aims at complete knowledge of the nature of beings, it aims at knowledge that is sufficient to explain why everything is the way it is for such beings. Consequently, metaphysics is intimately connected with the principle of sufficient reason: To engage in metaphysical inquiry is to act on the assumption that the causes of things can in general be understood through knowledge of their natures.

One of the most important sources historically for Leibniz's understanding of metaphysics is Suarez's groundbreaking reinterpretation of Aristotle.[3] In the *Disputationes Metaphysicae* (1597), Suarez defines metaphysics as the science whose proper object is "being inasmuch as it is real being [*ens in quantum ens reale*]" (I, i, 26). Because the defining mark of real being is its intelligibility per se (LIV, 1), or the absence of contradiction (II, iv, 7), metaphysics includes within its purview God and all those finite things (actual or possible) that can be brought into existence through God's power (II, iv, 11-12). Metaphysics thus deals with real being in all its forms: the infinite and the finite, the immaterial and the material, the substantial and the accidental (I, i, 26). In both his understanding of the concept of being, and in his account of the range of beings that constitute the subject matter of metaphysical inquiry, Leibniz closely follows Suarez's lead. In its most basic sense, metaphysics is that science which embraces the totality of real or intelligible being.

Although Suarez defines the broad outlines of Leibniz's conception of metaphysics, there remain significant differences in how they see these outlines as being filled in. Leibniz does not himself, in philosophical style or temperament, incline toward scholasticism. Even if some of his disparagement of the "vague notions and verbal distinctions" (RB 431) of the schools can be dismissed as conventional posing, there is an impatience to his thinking, an eagerness for new discoveries and results, that leaves him fundamentally opposed to the mode of scholastic philosophy. Furthermore, while Leibniz praises Suarez as one of the "deeper scholastics," and claims to have read his writings already as a youth "as easily as the Milesian fables or romances,"[4] it is likely that he experienced the influence of the Spanish philosopher largely indirectly, by way of the tradition of Protestant scholastic philosophy in which he was educated.[5] As such what he received was anything but pure Suarez. Although the Protestant tradition was itself significantly shaped in the seventeenth century through the reception of the *Disputationes Metaphysicae,* Suarez formed only one part of a rich philosophical ferment that included elements of Lutheran and Calvinist theology, Ramism, Lullism, Neoplatonism, the secular Aristotelianism of the Italian universities and, eventually, mechanism. In one way or another, all of these philosophical movements left their stamp on Leibniz's understanding of metaphysics.[6]

Because we are not engaged primarily in a study of the sources of Leibniz's thought, I shall not attempt to tease out these influences in any detail. I suggest, however, that as a result of these other forces Leibniz was led to formulate a conception of metaphysics that extended Suarez's science of real being in two crucial ways. First, under the influence of his Jena teacher Erhard Weigel, he embraces the idea that metaphysics can be given the form of a demonstrative science, whose propositions can in principle be proved with a certainty rivaling that of geometry.[7] Within this framework, the provision of adequate definitions for metaphysical concepts becomes all-important.[8] Not only do such definitions serve as marks of consistency, and hence of real being, but because Leibniz conceives of demonstration itself as founded on the substitution of definitions, the technique of definition also holds the key to the construction of demonstrations in metaphysics. What emerges is a conception of metaphysics as an a priori science every bit as rigorous as the science of geometry. This discipline supplies the basis for what I described at the end of Chapter 3 as a science of divine understanding.

Although primary for Leibniz, this conception of metaphysics as an a priori science does not exhaust its scope. Significantly, there is also a sense for him—and this is the second place at which his position takes a novel turn—in which at least one branch of metaphysics cannot escape the phenomena of the senses. This is because, as the science of being or intelligible reality, metaphysics is concerned not only with being as it is realized within the realm of possibility, the divine understanding, but also as it is realized within the realm of existence or actuality. Yet Leibniz maintains that as finite minds our only means of apprehending existing things is as the objects of sense perception. Consequently, metaphysics must assume the task of attempting to comprehend the reality of existing things *through* the phenomena of our senses. As we shall see in Part III, it is this second branch of metaphysics which offers the hope of a science of divine wisdom: a science

devoted to understanding the harmony of the universe through an application of the intelligible ideas of reason to the facts of experience.

The rest of this chapter explores more fully Leibniz's conception of the method of metaphysics. In the next section, we examine his theory of definition and how it supports the notion of metaphysics as a demonstrative science. We then turn to the distinction he draws between the senses and the intellect as two independent sources of knowledge—one of essence or possibility, the other of existence or actuality. Finally, we look briefly at Leibniz's view of how we come to understand the being of existing things by applying the ideas of the intellect to the interpretation of sense experience.

Metaphysics as a Demonstrative Science

One of Leibniz's most persistent criticisms of past philosophers is that they embarked on exercises of theory building without a sufficient awareness of philosophy's true method. He extends this charge almost without exception: The scholastics, Descartes, Malebranche, Locke, the supporters of materialist and vitalist philosophies of nature—all stumbled in their attempts at theorizing because of their failure to appreciate that philosophical truths are, at bottom, conceptual truths and hence can only be demonstrated once satisfactory definitions of their terms have been established.[9] The tendency of previous philosophers to neglect this point accounts for both the obscurity of metaphysics and the repugnance many feel toward it:

> I find that most people who take pleasure in the mathematical sciences shrink away from metaphysics, because they find light in the former but darkness in the latter. The most important reason for this, I believe, is that the general concepts which are thought to be very well known to everyone have become ambiguous and obscure through the carelessness and changeableness of human thinking and that the definitions commonly given to these concepts are not even nominal definitions and in fact explain nothing. . . . Yet by a sort of necessity men continue to use metaphysical terms and, flattering themselves, believe that they understand the words they have learned to say. It is obvious that the true and fruitful concepts, not only of substance, but of cause, action, relation, similarity, and many other general terms as well, are hidden from popular understanding.
>
> (GP IV 468/L 432)

Leibniz's definitive response to this problem, which he elsewhere condemns as "the abuse of the way of ideas," is found in his short essay *Meditations on Knowledge, Truth, and Ideas* of 1684.[10] In the *Meditations* and later works, he repeatedly stresses the importance of subjecting our ideas or concepts to analysis, with the aim of resolving them into their simpler components.[11] When carried to completion, such an analysis would reveal whether a concept involves any internal contradiction. If it is shown to be consistent, the analysis provides what Leibniz calls a "real definition," or a proof of the possibility of whatever the concept expresses. He contrasts this sort of definition with a merely "nominal" definition, which analyzes a concept into other concepts through which it can be conceived, but does not give a proof of its possibility.[12] Real definitions are crucial for metaphysics, he argues, because only they demonstrate a genuine possibility or, what is equivalent, the essence of a type of being:

> Essence is fundamentally nothing but the possibility of a thing under consideration. Something which is thought possible is expressed by a definition; but if this definition does not at the same time express this possibility then it is merely nominal, since in this case we can wonder whether the definition expresses anything real—that is, possible—until experience comes to our aid by acquainting us *a posteriori* with the reality (when the thing actually occurs in the world).

(NE III, iii, 15; RB 293-4)

Leibniz's insistence on the need for real definitions in metaphysics can only be fully appreciated against the background of a prior assumption he makes about the objects of metaphysical knowledge. With Suarez, he holds that the primary theoretical notion of metaphysics is that of "being" [*ens*], defined as that "whose concept involves something positive or that which can be conceived by us provided that what we conceive is possible or involves no contradiction" (GP VII 319/L 363). As this definition suggests, when we characterize something as a being, we say nothing about its actual existence. To designate something as a being is to say only that it has a distinctly conceivable (or noncontradictory) concept, and that consequently when we comprehend that concept we conceive of something that is possible or that could exist.[13] To the extent that real definitions establish the identity of types of being, or the possibilities of existence, Leibniz regards them as saying something about reality. At the same time, though, he claims that we are only justified in accepting such possibilities as real if they are themselves grounded in some existing thing; for without such a ground it could fairly be objected that "possibilities or essences, whether prior to or abstracted from existence, are imaginary or fictitious" (GP VII 305/L 488). This is an objection that Leibniz firmly rejects; nevertheless, he believes that it can only be successfully turned back, if essences are grounded in the prior reality of the divine understanding:

> [N]either these essences nor the so-called eternal truths about them are fictitious, rather they exist in a certain region of Ideas, if I may so call it, namely in God himself, who is the source of all essence. . . . [T]hrough [God] those possibilities that would otherwise be imaginary are (to use an outlandish but expressive word) realized [*realisentur*].

(GP VII 305/L 488)[14]

The reality of the metaphysically possible is thus closely tied to the notion of a divine understanding: a "region of Ideas," expressing the essence of every possible being. From this region of ideas, God selects those things he brings into existence; and they are created exactly as he conceives them, with a nature identical to that expressed in the corresponding divine idea.[15]

Complementing this assumption about the objects of metaphysical knowledge is a second important claim about how human beings are capable of knowing anything about the reality that metaphysics describes. According to Leibniz, as rational minds, human beings have been granted a significant share in the intelligible reality represented by the divine understanding: "The intelligible world of which the ancients speak so much is in God and in some way also in us" (GP IV 571/L 585). He thus assumes that the human mind possesses ideas that correspond in both structure and content to the divine ideas that ground metaphysical possibility.[16] All metaphysical knowledge is accordingly predicated on our capacity to comprehend the eternal and immutable ideas constitutive of the divine understanding. Because of this capacity we are able to embark on an inquiry aimed at defining those concepts which express the fundamental types and categories of being.[17]

Leibniz's theory of definition leads us naturally to his theory of truth. His basic understanding of truth is articulated in his "predicate in subject principle" (PSP). According to the PSP, a necessary and sufficient condition for the truth of any affirmative, subject-predicate proposition is that the concept expressed by its predicate term be "contained in" the concept expressed by its subject term. This notion of concept containment is best explained in terms of the notion of conceptual analysis. If, as Leibniz believes, the subject and predicate terms of a proposition always express concepts that are in principle analyzable into simpler elements, then a proposition will be true, according to the PSP, just in case the simpler concepts obtained by analyzing its predicate term are among those obtained by analyzing its subject term.[18]

Leibniz's account of truth raises a number of interesting points. It is important, first, to recognize the connection he establishes between this theory and what he describes in the ***Monadology*** as the "two great principles" of his reasoning: the principle of contradiction and the principle of sufficient reason (GP VI 612/P 184). The principle of contradiction (or principle of identity) asserts the fundamental axiom of the logic of truth: Every identical proposition is true and its contradictory false (GP VII 309/P 75).[19] The principle of sufficient reason, on the other hand, is associated with an explanation of the ground or basis (*ratio*) of truth.[20] In its informal expression, the principle of sufficient reason states that "no fact can be real or existing and no proposition can be true unless there is a sufficient reason why it should be thus and not otherwise, even though in most cases these reasons cannot be known to us" (GP VI 612/P 184). In Leibniz's opinion, one of his principal contributions to philosophy is his transformation of this general demand for reason into the PSP, a condition that guarantees a reason for the truth of any proposition in the connection between its subject and predicate terms:

> The fundamental principle of reasoning is *that there is nothing without a reason;* or, to explain the matter more distinctly, there is no truth for which a reason does not subsist. The reason for a truth consists in the connection of the predicate with the subject; that is, the predicate is in the subject.

(C 11/P 172)

Instead of claiming simply that there is a reason why everything is as it is and not otherwise, Leibniz's PSP explains each proposition's being either true or false in terms of the containment or noncontainment of its predicate term in its subject term. In two ways, this represents a significant advance. First, the PSP crystallizes an assumption common to Leibniz and many other metaphysicians about the logical form of reality: In seeking a reason for a given fact or state of affairs, one is, in effect, asking for an account of why a particular predicate is truly asserted of a particular subject. This explanation is provided by the PSP. The second advantage of the PSP is that, in conjunction with the doctrine of real definition, it suggests the means for offering both a complete enumeration and a priori demonstration of every truth assertable of a given subject. This is so because the properties truly predicable of a subject will be just those contained in its concept, which is to say just those which a real definition reveals to be involved in that concept.[21] It is evident from this last point how the PSP supports Leibniz in his deeply held belief in the possibility of a complete rational knowledge of reality. If understanding what any being is, and all that is potentially true of it, can be reduced to an analysis of the essence or defining concept of that being, then we in principle possess the means for comprehending everything there is to know about the world, through our knowledge of the beings that constitute the world.[22]

Leibniz's doctrine of truth draws heavily on the same assumptions as his theory of definition. In one essay, he describes the PSP as requiring that for any true proposition there be "some connection between the notions of the terms, i.e. there should be an objective [*a parte rei*] foundation from which the reason for the proposition can be given, or an *a priori* proof can be found" (C 402/P 93).[23] According to Leibniz, what determines whether a given proposition is objectively true is not that this relation holds among any one person's concepts, or even among any human concepts. An objective ground for truth exists only if there is the appropriate relation among ideas expressed in the intellect of God. The PSP thus asserts that for any true proposition, there is a *real* reason why it is true: an intelligible relation among the divine ideas that are the archetypes of human thought. It follows that the truths we are aware of, insofar as they are truths, are necessarily ones we share with God:

> It would be better to assign truth to the relationships among the objects of ideas, by virtue of which one idea is or is not included within another. That does not depend on languages, and is something that we have in common with God and the angels. And when God displays a truth to us, we come to possess the truth which is in his understanding, for although his ideas are infinitely more perfect and extensive than ours, they still have the same relationship that ours do.

(NE IV, v, 2; RB 397)

We are now in a position to summarize Leibniz's conception of metaphysics as a science, or a system of demonstrative knowledge. We have seen that the ultimate objects of metaphysical knowledge are the essences of beings (actual or possible), which are expressed in the eternal ideas of the divine understanding and in intelligible concepts of the human mind. Combinations of these concepts, in turn, form propositions that assert necessary relations among the essences of different types of being. By a demonstrative *science* of metaphysics, therefore, we mean just this: a system of deductively related propositions that together articulate the conceptual dependence of the principal types of being. Now, it is Leibniz's often repeated belief that metaphysics can in fact be forged into such a demonstrative science, a science that would rival in rigor the paradigmatic science of geometry. This belief has two main sources. First, given his theory of truth, metaphysics has access to a well-defined notion of valid inference. In general, one metaphysical proposition will follow from another if, and only if, the former can be obtained from the latter via a finite number of substitutions of definitionally equivalent terms.[24] There can thus be no objection to the claim that metaphysics can in principle assume the form of a demonstrative science. Second, Leibniz is among the first to recognize that the unparalleled success of sciences like geometry is largely due to their development of suitable forms of symbolic representation, such that valid inferences can be reduced to mechanical procedures in which there is no latitude for errors of reasoning. In his view, there is no reason why the same symbolic method cannot be extended to metaphysics, in which case this science could acquire a certainty equal to that of geometry.[25]

It has recently been argued that this picture of Leibniz as an advocate of a deductivist conception of metaphysics is at odds with the evidence of his best-known writings. In works such as the *New System* and the *Monadology,* it is claimed, we see a Leibniz who is unconcerned with the demonstrative certainty of his doctrines and instead advances his views as hypotheses whose test of adequacy is limited to their capacity to resolve outstanding metaphysical problems.[26] Though consistent with the evidence of most of his published writings, this revisionist reading goes too far in suggesting that Leibniz eventually abandons the view that metaphysics can, and should, take the form of a demonstrative science. Such a reading fails to tally with his own explicit description of such works as the *New System,* as well as unpublished essays including the *Monadology* and the *Principles of Nature and of Grace,* as popular presentations of his doctrines, designed to suit the needs of general audiences.[27] Whether he in fact remained unable to offer convincing demonstrations of his most important metaphysical doctrines, or whether he merely felt it prudent to present them as hypotheses that could easily be withdrawn in the face of hostile criticism, the fact remains that until the end of his life Leibniz continued to express the belief that his central doctrines *could* be advanced in the form of demonstrations.[28]

Throughout Leibniz's career, his underlying conception of metaphysics is that of a *scientia,* or a system of demonstrative knowledge. Metaphysics is a science that potentially yields results possessing the certainty of geometrical theorems. Its truths are demonstrable in exactly the same way, provided that the formal method which has served so well in mathematics can be extended to this higher science. Furthermore, Leibniz clearly takes himself to have had some success in this regard. Writings from the decade leading up to the composition of the *Discourse on Metaphysics* reveal the extent to which he was absorbed with the work of analyzing and defining the concepts required for the demonstration of metaphysical truths.[29] By the time of the *New Essays,* twenty years later, he could confidently report that he hardly needed to think about such matters anymore. With the fundamental notions of metaphysics satisfactorily defined, that science could be rendered as solidly demonstrative as geometry.[30]

Two Sources of Knowledge

The doctrines outlined in the previous section provide the basis for Leibniz's understanding of the science of metaphysics. We must now turn to his efforts to integrate this understanding into a theory of human knowledge. Although epistemological issues are not at the heart of Leibniz's concerns, his account of the cognitive capacity of finite minds is of considerable importance for an appreciation of his metaphysics.

Since Kant, the charge has often been repeated that Leibniz confounds the distinct functions of the senses and the intellect, making the difference between the two merely one of degree rather than of kind. One critic has even claimed that Leibniz, in common with most pre-Kantian philosophers, makes

> the mistake of just overlooking the difference between sense-data and thoughts about sense-data, e.g. between being in a state as though one were seeing something green and, on the other hand, thinking about being in such a state. With that chasm bridged by a sheer failure to notice it, Leibniz can then put the thought of seeming to see something green on a continuum with less directly sense-linked thoughts such as the thought of an active force, or a rational number, or space, or God.[31]

It is beyond the scope of this study to attempt to assess the validity of Kant's critique of Leibniz on the relation of sense and intellect. It will become apparent in what follows that Leibniz is guilty of at least one cardinal Kantian sin: the attempt to offer an analysis of sense experience as an intelligible representation of reality. Granting this point, however, in no way convicts Leibniz of the more facile charge that he simply overlooks the difference between sensation and thought, or between the sensory and the intellectual. As several authors have recently argued, sense perception and intellect are two separate faculties for Leibniz and the sources of two distinct types of knowledge.[32]

For Leibniz, perception is an essential characteristic of all created substances, from the simplest soullike forms, through plant and animal life, up to the rational minds of human beings and higher intelligences.[33] He stresses, though, that it is necessary to distinguish this perception from "awareness" and "reflection":

> [A]t every moment there is in us an infinity of perceptions, unaccompanied by awareness or reflection; that is, of alterations in the soul itself, of which we are unaware because these impressions are either too minute and too numerous, or else too unvarying, so that they are not sufficiently distinctive on their own. But when they are combined with others they do nevertheless have their effect and make themselves felt, at least confusedly, within the whole. This is how we become so accustomed to the motion of a mill or a waterfall, after living beside it for a while, that we pay no heed to it.
> (NE, Preface; RB 53)[34]

As a result of the universal connection of things, all substances at every moment are endowed with an infinity of *petites perceptions*. In the least elevated forms, and in higher souls during periods of sleep or unconsciousness, almost all of these minute perceptions go unregistered. However, even when we are wide-awake and sensitive to our surroundings, "there are countless inconspicuous perceptions, which do not stand out enough for one to be aware of or to remember them but which manifest themselves through their inevitable consequences" (RB 112).[35] In Leibniz's terminology, our perceptions are more or less distinct to the extent that we are aware of differences among them.[36] Consistent with this, he maintains that all sensory perceptions are in some measure confused, for they give us the impression of being homogeneous when in fact they are composed of an infinity of *petites perceptions*.

According to Leibniz, created substances are differentiated from one another on the basis of the relative distinctness of their perceptions: The most elevated minds possess the most distinct perceptions, the lowest soul-like forms the least.[37] In addition to this, however, he indicates a further important difference between the perceptions of animal souls (and all lower forms) and those of intelligent creatures. Even the most distinct perceptions of animals occur without any element of self-awareness, since animals lack a faculty of "reflection" (or "apperception").[38] This does not preclude animals from "noticing" or "paying heed" to varying degrees of detail in their perceptions. Although lacking reflection, animals "have the faculty for awareness of the more conspicuous and outstanding impressions—as when a wild boar is aware of someone who is shouting at it, and goes straight at that person, having previously had only a bare perception of him" (NE II, xxi, 5; RB 173). Nevertheless, only in the case of human beings (and angels) are perceptions "accompanied by the power to reflect, which turns into actual reflection when there are the means for it" (NE II, ix, 13-14; RB 139).

Leibniz describes perceptions that are accompanied by reflection as "thoughts."[39] Thoughts are thus themselves a type of perception, of which we are reflectively aware. By itself, the term "thought" carries no implication of intelligence or understanding. Although only creatures capable of reflection (and hence thought) are capable of understanding, it does not follow that every thought is also an act of understanding:

> We are aware of many things, within ourselves, which we do not understand. . . . "[U]nderstanding" in my sense is what in Latin is called *intellectus,* and the exercise of this faculty is called "intellection," which is a distinct perception combined with a faculty of reflection, which the beasts do not have. Any perception which is combined with this faculty is a thought, and I do not allow thought to beasts any more than I do understanding. So one can say that intellection occurs when the thought is distinct.
>
> (NE II, xxi, 5; RB 173)

For human beings endowed with a faculty of reflection

(but not for animals, which lack this faculty) there can be both confused thoughts and distinct thoughts, depending on the type of perception reflected upon. Intellection presupposes the combination of reflection and distinct perception.

Here, if anywhere, we might seem to find support for the charge that Leibniz confounds the sensory and the intellectual. If intellection is equated with the having of *distinct* perceptions (of which we are reflectively aware), and sensation with the having of *confused* perceptions, then is he not clearly guilty of turning the distinction between the two into a purely formal or logical one? That is, does he not support the position that sensations are just "confused thoughts," and that distinct thoughts differ from confused thoughts in degree rather than in kind? The evidence in favor of this conclusion seems strong. Leibniz himself writes: "It has been believed that confused thoughts differ *toto genere* from distinct ones; in fact, however, they are merely less distinct and less developed, by virtue of their multiplicity" (GP IV 563).[40]

Despite what Leibniz says here, there is reason to believe that sensations and thoughts—both confused and distinct—must differ for him in both origin and kind. Confused perceptions arise as a result of a finite creature's representation of the infinite.[41] As we have seen, what is confused about these perceptions is that they are composed of an infinity of minute perceptions, the totality of which we are unable to discern individually. Some of these perceptions, to be sure, are more distinct than others. A sensation, he says, is a perception that is "distinguished and heightened," and "accompanied by *memory*—a perception, to wit, of which a certain echo long remains to make itself heard on occasion" (GP VI 599/P 196-7). Within the domain of the sensory, then, we can establish a continuous scale of distinctness, based on the degree to which sensations faithfully convey the infinite detail of the universe. Yet even the most distinct sensory perceptions are still inherently confused, since like all representations of the universe they involve infinity.

In minds endowed with the capacity for reflection, sensory perceptions supply the basis for confused thoughts. Yet it would be wrong to see Leibniz as equating the two. Confused thoughts are distinguished from sensations by the fact that they involve reflection on the qualities represented in sensory perceptions.[42] This by itself suggests that confused thoughts cannot be located on the same scale of relative distinctness as sensory perceptions, and that Leibniz is innocent of the charge of simply overlooking the difference between having a sensation and thinking about a sensory quality. A second point to note is that Leibniz recognizes another source of thoughts altogether, over and above those which derive from reflection on sensory qualities. These are distinct intellectual thoughts, which originate in a mind's reflective awareness of its own nature and properties as opposed to its representations of external things.[43] Like sensations, intellectual thoughts are distinct insofar as we are aware of them individually; they are nonetheless categorically different from both sensations and thoughts of sensory qualities in that they are distinct in and of themselves and orginate in a completely different source.

In sum, sensation and intellection can be distinguished on three grounds: (1) Whereas sensation has no necessary connection to reflective awareness, intellection, as a species of thought, requires reflection; (2) all sensory perceptions are in some measure confused, intellectual thoughts are wholly distinct; (3) sensory perceptions (and thoughts of sensory qualities) depend on a mind's representation of the external world; intellectual thoughts, on its reflective awareness of its own nature and properties. Nowhere is there any suggestion by Leibniz that sensations are just confused thoughts, or that distinct thoughts originally arise as the result of analyzing our sensory perceptions. Nor is there any indication that confused thoughts (or sensations) can in principle be rendered wholly distinct through analysis. Between sensations and confused thoughts, on the one hand, and distinct intellectual thoughts, on the other, there is a difference in kind founded on a difference in origin.[44]

This conclusion can be strengthened by examining Leibniz's treatment of ideas. From a cognitive standpoint, ideas are on a par with thoughts in that they both assume a capacity for reflection. Ideas, however, cannot be identified with thoughts, or with the "forms" of thoughts. Since the latter are transitory mental states, when one thought had been replaced by another, the idea would vanish with it. Against this position, Leibniz argues that ideas are enduring mental states, which remain even when we are not aware of them. Ideas, he says, are "the inner objects of thoughts, and as such they can persist" (NE II, 10, 2; RB 140).[45] He expresses his view more fully when he refers to ideas as "dispositions" or "potentialities" for thought, which are realized in actions of the soul: actual thoughts. To have an idea of x is to be disposed to think of x under certain conditions.[46]

The most important division Leibniz marks among our ideas is between those that are "distinct," and those that are "clear" but "confused." In a letter to Thomas Burnett, he describes this difference as follows:

> I call an idea "clear" when it suffices for recognizing a thing, as when I recall a color well enough to recognize it when it is presented to me. But I call an idea "distinct" when I conceive its conditions or requisites, in a word, when I have a definition of it, if it has one.
>
> (GP III 247)

The commonest examples of ideas that are clear but not distinct are those of sensory qualities, such as colors, smells, and tastes. Although we generally have no difficulty in identifying instances of these qualities, it is impossible to explain the content of, or give a definition of, our idea of red or sweetness. Consequently, we are "often obliged to say that it is a *je ne sais quoi* that [we] sense so clearly" (GP III 247).[47] Distinct ideas, by contrast, such as those of mathematics or metaphysics, possess a structure that makes them amenable to analysis. As Leibniz remarks to Burnett, an idea is distinct to the extent that it is conceivable through simpler ideas, its "conditions" or "requisites." As such, a distinct idea is intelligible, or graspable by the mind.[48]

Thus, Leibniz's main principle for the division between distinct and confused ideas is the possibility of analysis: Distinct ideas can be resolved into simpler components, their requisites; confused ideas are those for which we lack an analysis. A second principle, however, is also at work. Leibniz asserts the confused-distinct division as one that is, in addition, based upon the origin of our ideas. Confused ideas are derived from sense perceptions, which are themselves inherently confused. Distinct ideas, by contrast, derive from the intellect alone, independently of the senses.[49] Leibniz thus roundly rejects the empiricist's claim that the soul is a tabula rasa, containing no innate ideas of its own:

> [R]eflection is nothing but attention to what is within us, and the senses do not give us what we carry with us already. In view of this, can it be denied that there is a great deal that is innate in our minds, since we are innate to ourselves, so to speak, and since we include Being, Unity, Substance, Duration, Change, Action, Perception, Pleasure, and hosts of other objects of our intellectual ideas? And since these objects are immediately related to our understanding and always present to it (although our distractions and needs prevent us being always aware of them), is it any wonder that we say that these ideas, along with what depends on them, are innate in us?
>
> (NE, Preface; RB 51-2)[50]

Leibniz's division between distinct and confused ideas on the basis of their origin is again at odds with the charge that he confounds the senses and the intellect. Far from denying the sensory-intellectual distinction, Leibniz heartily affirms it. From sense perception, we derive ideas of sensory qualities. From another source altogether—the mind's reflective awareness of its own nature and properties—we arrive at distinct intellectual ideas, such as *substance, action, one* and *many:*

> [A]cts of reflection . . . make us think of what is called the self, and consider that this or that is within us. And it is thus that in thinking of ourselves, we think of being, of substance, of the simple and the

compound, of the immaterial and of God himself, conceiving that what is limited in us, in him is limitless. And these acts of reflection provide the chief objects of our reasonings.

(Mon § 30; GP VI 612/P 183-4)[51]

In Leibniz's view, there are two independent "sources of our knowledge, the senses and reflection" (NE, Preface; RB 53). And these two sources provide us with two different types of knowledge, that of facts or existence and that of possibility or essence: "There are two sorts of knowledge: that of facts, which is called *perception,* and that of reasons, which is called *intelligence.* Perception is of singular things, intelligence has for its objects universals or eternal truths" (G 583). Through our senses we are apprised of the existence of particular things; through intellection we come to understand the eternal possibilities of existence (the essences of things), and the necessary relations among these possibilities (eternal truths). As we have seen, it is characteristic of intellectual ideas to be distinct in and of themselves, and thus subject to analysis and definition. It is precisely because they can in principle be given a complete analysis and definition that such ideas are expressive of essence, or the possibility of existence: "Essence is fundamentally nothing but the possibility of a thing under consideration. Something which is thought possible is expressed by a definition" (NE III, iii; RB 293-4). This characteristic is not shared by ideas derived from sense perception. Although such ideas "express the power which produces the sensation," Leibniz writes, "they do not fully express it; or at any rate we cannot know that they do" (NE II, xxxi; RB 266). Sensations provide evidence of the existence of particular things, but they do not provide what we need in order to understand *what* those things are—their underlying essence. Only insofar as we rely on distinct ideas derived from the intellect are we guaranteed knowledge of the essences of things. We thus reach the somewhat paradoxical conclusion that we are only able to understand reality, or the objective possibilities of existence, through reflection on our own minds:

> [T]he nature of things and the nature of the mind work together. . . . [Q]uite often a "consideration of the nature of things" is nothing but the knowledge of the nature of our mind and of these innate ideas, and there is no reason to look for them outside oneself.

(NE, Preface; RB 84)[52]

If we were "little Gods," we might be blessed with a life that consisted of nothing but pure thought, a life spent contemplating the essences of things and the eternal truths of reason. Leibniz insists, however, that intellection wholly divorced from sensation is impossible for human beings:

> The situation is that our [specifically human] needs

have forced us to abandon the natural order of ideas, for that order would be common to angels and men and to intelligences in general, and would be the one for us to follow if we had no concern for our own interests. However, we have had to hold fast to the order which was provided by the incidents and accidents to which our species is subject; this order represents the history of our discoveries, as it were, rather than the origin of notions.

(NE II, i, 5; RB 276)[53]

As finite minds, our reflections necessarily begin with thoughts in which the sensory and intellectual are intermingled. We arrive at pure intellectual ideas by abstracting from thought those constants which reflect the mind's own underlying nature and properties. At this point, metaphysics reenters the picture. Distinct ideas of the understanding, expressing the primary types of being, are the subject matter of metaphysics. It is thus the task of this science to extract ideas of substance, unity, cause, and the like from thought, and to subject them to analysis, with the aim of providing adequate definitions of them.[54]

The Analysis of Sensory Phenomena

The account we have so far offered of the method of Leibniz's metaphysics remains in one important respect incomplete. Although Leibniz assigns a secondary status to sensory knowledge, a significant part of his metaphysics is devoted to the project of reinterpreting the phenomena of our senses such that they become intelligible as the appearances of reality. Given his view that we only acquire knowledge of the existence of created things through the evidence of our senses, the need for such a project—one dedicated to revealing the reality underlying sensory appearances—is evident. The results of the last section, however, seem to have raised an obstacle to any inquiry of this kind. If, in Leibniz's view, only distinct intellectual ideas express being or essence, how can we hope to investigate the reality of existing things, beginning with the phenomena of our senses? How can we justify asserting these phenomena as the appearances of reality?

Leibniz's answer to this question begins with the observation that sensory perceptions are never (for human minds, at least) wholly confused, and that insofar as they are distinct they express the essence or reality of existing things: "Before everything in the mind there seems to occur the matter of some positive concept or reality or essence, in which agrees everything at all which is perceived by us. And in this way we call something a being [*ens*], thing [*res*], or subject" (LH IV 7C B1. 105 [V 1300]). Perceived or apparent things qualify as instances of being, Leibniz maintains, provided we can understand them as having an intelligible essence. When we experience the movements and actions of bodies, for example, we identify them as instances of *matter* and ascribe to them certain essential properties. In this case, the mind does not simply isolate the distinct ideas of the intellect from the confused ideas of sense; instead, it applies the former in the interpretation of sense experience in order to identify the intelligible content expressed within it.[55]

We can best illustrate this approach by looking more closely at Leibniz's analysis of corporeal properties. He suggests that the sensible properties of bodies can be divided into two types: the confused and the prima facie distinct or intelligible.[56] "Confused attributes," he writes, "are those which are indeed composite in themselves . . . but are simple to the senses and whose definition therefore cannot be explained" (V 636/L 285). Examples of such attributes are so-called secondary qualities, such as heat, color, and taste. The distinct attributes of body, on the other hand, are those subject to definition, or resolvable into simpler properties, through which they can be understood.[57] These again can be divided into those (like fusability) resolvable only into confused attributes (heat), and those (like rectilinear motion) resolvable into other distinct attributes (distance and time) (V 636/L 285-6).[58] To the last kind of attribute—exemplified by the mechanical properties of size, shape, and motion—Leibniz assigns a special importance. What is unique about mechanical properties is that of all the sensible properties of bodies, they alone are conceivable entirely in terms of distinct ideas: notably, mathematical notions of order and quantity, which are innate to the mind. For this reason, mechanical descriptions offer both a more adequate understanding of material things (an understanding in terms of essence) and one that lends itself more readily to definition and demonstration.[59]

Leibniz is thus in agreement with the main current of seventeenth-century natural philosophy in holding that the phenomena of material things can only be satisfactorily explained in terms of the mechanical properties of size, shape, and motion.[60] Given this commitment, he also confronts the central methodological question for seventeenth-century mechanists: how to give mechanical explanations of phenomena (e.g., evaporation or gravitation) that are initially known to us only in a confused way through sense perception. As we have seen, he denies that we can move directly from confused ideas to distinct ideas via conceptual analysis; in characterizing an idea as "confused" this is precisely what is ruled out. How, then, is an investigation of such phenomena to proceed? Leibniz's answer is the conventional one: by doing experiments that help to suggest distinct ideas that are closely correlated with our confused ideas of a phenomenon and explain its salient features. The success of natural science in understanding the spectrum of colors, for example, depends on our establishing a correlation between our ideas of sensory qualities and ideas graspable by the intellect—those of different wavelengths of light. "This method," he comments, "provides a starting point for analysis" (NE IV, ii, 16; RB 382-3).[61]

Despite this broad ground of agreement with mechanists, Leibniz parts company with their position at a crucial point. Although he accepts their assumption that material phenomena can be adequately explained only in terms of the mechanical properties of size, shape, and motion, he rejects their further conclusion that these notions provide us with an accurate knowledge of reality. His insistence on this point stems from a combination of claims concerning, on the one hand, the infinite complexity of matter and, on the other, the limited cognitive capacity of human minds. Although Leibniz's doctrine of matter falls outside our present concerns, its intimate relation to his account of the possibilities of human knowledge requires that we touch on it briefly. For a variety of reasons connected with his understanding of divine wisdom, Leibniz maintains that all existing matter is divided into parts *in infinitum*.[62] As a consequence, he argues, it is impossible for any finite mind to comprehend fully the character of a particular material thing.[63] In conceiving of a body as a being with a determinate size, shape and motion, we necessarily overlook its infinite complexity and assume precise limits or bounds where none in fact exist: "our senses do not recognize and our understanding conceals an infinity of little inequalities" (GP VII 563). The mechanical properties we assign to material things are thus only prima facie distinct; in common with all properties apprehended through sense, they have something confused about them: "[E]xtension, figure and motion include something imaginary and apparent; and although one conceives of them more distinctly than color or heat, nevertheless when one pushes the analysis as far as I have done, one finds that these notions are still somewhat confused" (GP I 391-2).[64]

Although Leibniz himself does not always highlight it, an important distinction should be noted between the mechanical *properties* of bodies and the distinct *ideas* we employ in conceiving of these properties. We have seen that Leibniz grants rational minds access to a variety of distinct intellectual ideas, among which are the mathematical notions employed in the construction of physical theory.[65] By relying on these concepts we are able to interpret sense experience: We form distinct conceptions of the beings presented in sensation and of the laws governing their effects. In Leibniz's view, however, it is essential that we be clear on the status of these theoretical representations of nature. Mathematical concepts, he says, are merely "ideal." They do not accurately express the true complexity of existing matter (thus the mechanical properties we ascribe to bodies are only prima facie distinct). Mathematical concepts represent finite or limited essences (geometrical figures, determinate quantities), whereas nature is unlimited in its forms:

There are . . . divisions and actual variations in the masses of existing bodies to whatever limits one should go. It is our imperfection and the defect of our senses which make us conceive physical things as mathematical beings, in which there is something undetermined. And one can demonstrate that there is no line or figure in nature which gives exactly and keeps uniformly through the least space and time the properties of a straight line or circle, or anything else whose definition can be comprehended by a finite mind. . . . Nature cannot and divine wisdom does not wish to trace exactly these figures of limited essence which presuppose something undetermined and consequently imperfect in the works of God.

(GP VII 563)

In applying mathematical ideas to the interpretation of nature we necessarily rely on abstractions.[66] And for this reason, mathematical physics can offer no more than an approximate understanding of reality. "The eternal truths founded on limited mathematical ideas" are sufficient in practice, "insofar as it is permissible to abstract from very small inequalities" (GP VII 563); however, they are inadequate as representations of the infinite complexity of matter.

Leibniz thus rejects the claim of mechanists to have provided an accurate picture of reality. He does not, however, rest content with this negative result. Although he is convinced that it is impossible for human minds to comprehend the full complexity of the matter they perceive—what he describes in the *New Essays* as "the jumble of effects of the surrounding infinity" (RB 57)—he nonetheless holds out promise of our making further progress in our understanding of the nature of matter through an analysis of the mechanical laws that govern corporeal phenomena. What is especially significant about this final stage of analysis is that it leads us, in Leibniz's view, from the sensory phenomena of material things to their ground in an intelligible reality of substances:

[I]n the final analysis, it is discovered that physics cannot be isolated from metaphysical principles. For although it can be, or ought to be, reduced to mechanics (this we fully concede to the corpuscular philosophers), there is nevertheless, besides geometry and numbers, something metaphysical in the primary laws of mechanics themselves, concerning cause, effect, power and resistance, change and time, similitude and determination, through which a passage is given from mathematical things to real sub-stances. . . . Rightly, therefore, it must be taught that although all physical things can be reduced to mechanics, the deeper origins and first laws of mechanics can in no way be explained without reference to metaphysical principles and unextended substances.

(C 341-2)[67]

We must leave the details of this final stage of analysis

to a later chapter. Two points, however, should be noted here. First, as suggested in this passage, an analysis of the "primary laws of mechanics" will necessarily implicate such metaphysical concepts as *substance, cause,* and *power.* Consequently, it presupposes that these have been isolated and defined as distinct ideas of the understanding in the manner described earlier. Second, in opposition to Kant's injunction, Leibniz maintains that it is in principle possible to undertake an analysis of the concept of matter that reveals phenomenal things to be grounded in a supersensible reality. Bodies, which appear to the senses as extended objects related in space and time, are understood by the intellect as something quite different: pluralities of unextended soullike substances. With this said, it is important to keep in mind that Leibniz also imposes a significant limitation on our capacity for knowledge. Under no circumstances are we capable of fully comprehending the complexity of any particular material thing. At most, we can aspire to an understanding of the nature of matter in general—one which indirectly demonstrates material things to be very different from what they seem. All in all, then, Leibniz draws both a positive and a negative conclusion concerning the possibilities of human knowledge. Our comprehension of the "general laws of nature" shows that "we have all the distinct ideas that are needed for a knowledge of bodies." Nevertheless, as finite minds we are subject to an irremediable ignorance concerning the infinite complexity of nature: The distinct ideas of our understanding do not provide us with knowledge of the "full detail of the phenomena," and our senses are not "penetrating enough to sort out the confused ideas or comprehensive enough to perceive them all" (NE IV, iii, 27; RB 389).[68] As regards our knowledge of existence, it is this difference that separates us from God:

[O]nly the Supreme Reason, who overlooks nothing, can distinctly grasp the entire infinite and see all the causes and all the results. All we can do with infinities is to know them confusedly and at least to know distinctly that they are there. Otherwise we shall not only judge wrongly as to the beauty and grandeur of the universe, but will be unable to have a sound natural science which explains the nature of things in general, still less a sound pneumatology, comprising knowledge of God, souls and simple substances in general.

(NE, Preface; RB 57)

In the preceding few pages we jumped far ahead in our presentation of Leibniz's philosophy in order to give a full account of his conception of metaphysics. This chapter has uncovered grounds for attributing to Leibniz a twofold understanding of the method of metaphysics. On the one hand, metaphysics is driven by the demand to provide adequate definitions of the intelligible concepts of the understanding: concepts such as *substance* and *cause,* which express the primary categories of being. On the other hand, it is also charged with interpreting sensory phenomena or rendering them intelligible as the apprearances of reality. In this context, it is the method of metaphysics to apply distinct concepts of the understanding in an analysis of the content of sensory experience. Part III looks in detail at the results Leibniz achieves using this latter method. In the next two chapters, we survey his treatment of the concepts of the understanding.

Notes

¹ Cf. C 348.

² *Ad Christophori Stegmanni Metaphysicam Unitariorum,* ca. 1708 (LH IV I 9, Bl. 1-7). The original text is found in Jolley 1975, 179; the translation is quoted from Jolley 1984, 196.

³ Concerning Suarez's accomplishment, see Lohr 1988. For a discussion of some of the subtleties of his doctrine of being, see Doyle 1967. On the relationship of Leibniz to Suarez, see Robinet, 1981.

⁴ RB 431; PG I 4, 168.

⁵ For an example of this indirect influence, see his marginalia to Daniel Stahl's 1655 *Compendium Metaphysicae* (A VI 1, 21-41). On Stahl, see Petersen 1921, 292-3. The impact of Suarez's *Disputationes Metaphysicae* on the development of Protestant scholastic philosophy has been well documented. See Beck (1969, 123, 516-7) and Lohr (1988, 620-38), both of whom give extensive references to the earlier literature.

⁶ On the complexity of the Protestant intellectual background, see Beck 1969, chaps. 6-9; concerning its impact on Leibniz, see Kabitz 1909.

⁷ On the influence of Weigel, see Kabitz 1909, 10-12; Moll 1978; Aiton 1985, 15-16. Cf. *Projet et Essais. . .pour avancer l'art d'inventer:* "There is a very clever professor at Jena named Weigel who has published a fine work entitled *Analysis Euclidea* [*Analysis Aristotelica ex Euclide restituta,* 1658], in which there are many beautiful ideas for perfecting logic and for giving demonstrations in philosophy" (C 179).

⁸ As we shall see in Chapter 5, Leibniz's theory of definition is also importantly influenced by the currents of Ramist and Lullist thinking, which pervade early-seventeenth-century German philosophy.

⁹ See his letter to Bourguet of 22 March 1714: "It is true, Sir, that the excellent modern authors of the *Art of Thinking,* of *The Search After Truth,* and of the *Essay Concerning [Human] Understanding* are not inclined to fix their ideas through definitions; in this they have followed too closely the example of M. Descartes, who scorned the definition of familiar terms which everyone, in his view, understands, and which are indeed ordinarily defined through terms equally obscure. But my method of definition is quite different" (GP III 569).

¹⁰ GP IV 422-6/L 291-5. Cf. "Réflexions sur la secunde Replique de Locke" (A VI 6, 29-30): "However, one must confess that M. Stillingfleet was right to complain of the abuse of the way of ideas. . . . I have also spoken of this abuse, albeit more clearly, in the Leipzig *Acta* of November 1684." See also his letter to Hesse-Rheinfels of 29 December 1684 (A II 1, 544).

¹¹ "In fact, reasoning is nothing other than an analysis of ideas or notions, conceptions, [or] terms, as philosophers called them before the word 'idea' began to be so much used" (GP III 224).

¹² See DM § 24; *On Universal Synthesis and Analysis* (GP VII 293-5/P 12-14); and *A Specimen of Discoveries:* "A real definition is one by which it is established that that which is defined is possible and does not involve a contradiction" (GP VII 310/P 76). Given Leibniz's assertion elsewhere that the human mind is incapable of giving a complete analysis of any concept into its primitive components, it is unclear whether we can actually construct any real definitions, for no matter how far we carry through the analysis of a concept a hidden contradiction might remain. Cf. *On an Organon or Ars Magna of Thinking* (ca. 1679): "Since, however, it is not in our power to demonstrate the possibility of things in a perfectly *a priori* way, . . . it will be sufficient to reduce their immense multitude to a few, whose possibility can either be supposed and postulated, or proved by experience" (C 431/P 3). We return to this point in Chapter 5.

¹³ "I call 'possible' everything which is perfectly conceivable and which consequently has an essence, an idea" (GP VII 573-4).

¹⁴ Cf. *Causa Dei* § 8: "The very *possibility* of things, when they do not actually exist, has a reality grounded in the divine existence: for if God should not exist, there would be no possibility, and possible things are from eternity in the ideas of the divine intellect" (GP VI 440). See also *A Specimen of Discoveries* (GP VII 311/P 77); *Theodicy* § 184.

¹⁵ Cf. *Theodicy* § 52. For a discussion of the work done by the doctrine of divine ideas in the medieval tradition, see Jordan 1984.

¹⁶ "[A]ll the ideas of the intellect have their archetypes in the eternal possibility of things" (NE IV, iv, 5; RB 392). "For ideas are in God from all eternity, and they are in us, too, before we actually think of them" (NE II, iv, 17; RB 300). Leibniz emphasizes here his Neo-

platonic sympathies: "[A]s Plotinus has rightly said, every mind contains a kind of intelligible world within itself. . . . Meanwhile, it can be said that because of the divine concourse which continuously confers upon each creature whatever perfection there is in it, the external object of the soul is God alone, and that in this sense God is to the mind what light is to the eye. This is that divine truth which shines forth in us, about which Augustine says so much and on which Malebranche follows him" (D II 1, 224-5/L 592-3). For more on the Neoplatonic strains in Leibniz's thought, see Politella 1938; Ross 1983; C. Wilson 1989.

[17] Leibniz is seldom careful about such distinctions. At issue are the most general metaphysical concepts, such as *substance, cause,* and *matter,* as well as more specific ones, such as *perception, justice,* and *happiness.* In each case, Leibniz assumes that the concept in question can be given a real definition and that it expresses the essence of a type of being. Thus, *substance* and *cause,* generally understood as categories of being, are also for Leibniz concepts expressing being, since they are distinctly conceivable notions and represent possibilities of existence. We return to his treatment of the categories of being in Chapter 5.

[18] Whether Leibniz can consistently uphold this position, while supporting the contingency of claims about existing things and their properties, is a much debated topic. In the case of necessary or eternal truths, the PSP can be applied straightforwardly. All necessary truths are in effect analytic truths, i.e., they "follow from ideas alone or from definitions of universal ideas" (C 402/P 94). Leibniz, however, maintains that the PSP is also valid for contingent truths, which assert particular matters of fact. If the PSP applies to factual propositions in exactly the same way, it is difficult to avoid the conclusion that all factual propositions are analytic, and hence necessary, although this is a result Leibniz wants to avoid at all costs. During the 1680s, he arrived at a position he believed resolved this problem while upholding the validity of the PSP. For our purposes it is enough to accept the following: Leibniz holds that any necessary or eternal truth can be demonstrated through a finite analysis of its terms. For any contingent truth or particular matter of fact, on the other hand, this is not possible; hence, such a truth cannot be given an a priori demonstration by a human mind. Whether it is coherent to suppose that God is capable of demonstrating such a truth (through an infinite analysis) without its thereby being rendered analytically true—and thus necessary—is a disputed point. Leibniz's considered position seems to be that in the case of contingent truths the validity of the PSP can be maintained without requiring a demonstration of their truth even of God: "[I]n the case of contingent truths, even though the predicate is in the subject, this can never be demonstrated of it, nor can the proposition ever be reduced to an equation of identity. Instead the

analysis proceeds to infinity, God alone seeing—not, indeed, the end of the analysis, since it has no end—but the connection of terms or the inclusion of the predicate in the subject, for he sees whatever is in the series; indeed this very same truth has arisen in part from his own intellect and in part from his will, and expresses in its own way his infinite perfection and the harmony of the whole series of things" (C 211/P 109). Cf. FN 178-85/P 108; C 17-18/P 97-8; C 402/P 94. For further discussion of Leibniz's treatment of contingent truth, see Adams 1977; Blumenfeld 1985; Sleigh 1983, 1990.

[19] At times, Leibniz packs even more than this into what he calls the "principle of contradiction." For example: "*[E]very proposition is either true or false,* That is *false* which is the contradictory of the true; those propositions are *contradictory* which differ only in that one of them is affirmative and the other negative" (C 401/P 93). Cf. GP VII 299/L 225.

[20] Cf. GP VI 413-4/H 419.

[21] Cf. *On Universal Synthesis and Analysis:* "Whatever can be demonstrated from the definition of a thing can be predicted of that thing" (GP VII 294/P 13). Leibniz first develops this theme in his discussion of "inventive logic" in the 1666 essay *On the Art of Combinations* §§ 71-82 (A VI 1, 195-8/PL 5).

[22] This method is closely associated by Leibniz with the project of an encyclopedia, or universal compendium of human knowledge. We examine this project in Chapter 5.

[23] Cf. GP II 56/M 63-4; GP VII 300/L 226.

[24] Cf. Hacking 1973. According to the PSP, a proposition asserting the dependence of two types of being will be true just in case the concept of one is contained in the concept of the other. If so, then any proposition obtained from a true proposition by replacing every instance of a given concept with a definitionally equivalent concept will also be true.

[25] This theme began to appear prominently in Leibniz's correspondence during his Paris period (1672-76), although there were already signs of it in *On the Art of Combinations.* In 1677, he writes to Galloys: "If we had [the characteristic] such as I imagine it, we could reason in metaphysics and in ethics more or less as in geometry and analysis, since the characters would fix our vague and ephemeral thoughts in these matters, in which the imagination offers us no help except by means of characters" (A II 1, 380-1). See also his letters to Tschirnhaus (May 1678; GM IV 461), Foucher (1687; GP I 390-1), and Arnauld (4/14 January 1688; GP II 134/M 168). This idea continued to occupy Leibniz until the end of his life, as is testified by a

letter to Biber from March 1716: "My great historical work prevents me from carrying out the idea I have of displaying philosophy in the form of demonstrations . . . for I see that it is possible to invent a general charecacteristic, which could do in all inquiries capable of certainty what algebra does in mathematics" (BB 15-16). For more on this topic, see Couturat 1901, Chap. 4; Rutherford 1994b.

[26] S. Brown 1984, 63. For a reply to this reading, which follows somewhat different lines from my own, see Parkinson 1990.

[27] In 1704, he writes to Fontenelle: "The true metaphysics or philosophy, if you will, appears to me no less important than geometry, especially if there is a way of also introducing into it demonstrations, which until now have been unduly banished from it, along with the calculus that will be necessary in order to give them all the entry they need. However, it is necessary to prepare readers for this through exoteric writings. The journals have served me until now" (F 234). Following the publication of the *New System* in 1695, Leibniz wrote a number of letters in which he stresses this point. Cf. A I 12, 625-6, 751; A I 13, 554-5, 657; NE II, xxix, 12 (RB 260-1); and his letter to Thomas Burnett of 14 December 1705, quoted in note 30.

[28] Leibniz's hesitation on this point never goes deeper than the cautious remark that "what is not yet ready to be defended by rigorous demonstration will meanwhile commend itself as a hypothesis which is clear and beautifully consistent with itself and with the phenomena" (1699; GP II 168/L 515). During the latter part of his life, his letters are full of complaints about his lack of time due to other burdensome duties—in particular, his work on the history of the House of Brunswick-Lüneberg. Less than two years after the publication of the *New System,* he writes to Gilles Des Billettes: "I still hope to explain demonstratively the nature and properties of substance in general, and in particular of souls. I have already begun to propose something in journals in the form of a hypothesis, but I believe that I have said nothing about it that might not be demonstrated" (A I 13, 657). See also his letters to Bossuet (1694; A I 10, 143), De Volder (1706; GP II 282/L 539), Bourguet (1714; GP III 569), and Remond (1714; GP III 605/L 654). On Leibniz's many time-consuming "distractions," see Couturat 1901, 574-6.

[29] These works are discussed in Chapter 5.

[30] During the composition of the *New Essays,* he remarked to Jacquelot: "You will perhaps be surprised, Sir, to see me write that I have been working on it as if on a work which demands no attention. But this is because I ruled decisively on these general philosophical matters a long time ago, in a way that I believe is

demonstrative or not far from it, with the result that I have hardly any need of new meditations on them" (GP III 474). Cf. his letters to Thomas Burnett of 8/18 May 1697 (GP II 205), and 14 December 1705: "I never write anything in philosophy that I do not treat by definitions and axioms, although I do not always give it that mathematical air which repels people, for it is necessary to speak familiarly in order to be read by ordinary persons. . . . I would even dare to say that I have established sufficiently in all matters of thought what is most fundamental to them, and that I no longer have any need to reason about them. Thus what you wish that I should do was already done a long time ago. I have quite satisfied myself on nearly all general matters of reasoning" (GP III 302-3).

[31] Bennett 1974, 12.

[32] See McRae 1976, 126-9; M. Wilson 1977; Parkinson 1982; C. Wilson 1989, 315-18. I take the main target of Kant's criticism of Leibniz to be the thesis that appearances are confused representations of things in themselves, and that conceptual analysis is sufficient to reveal the grounding of the former in the latter (see *Critique of Pure Reason,* A 264/B 320; A 270-1/B 326-7). As discussed later in this chapter, and at greater length in Chapters 8 and 9, a version of this thesis can be found in Leibniz's writings. This is not to say, however, that he is guilty of every charge brought against him. According to Kant, "The philosophy of Leibniz and Wolff, in . . . treating the difference between the sensible and the intelligible as merely logical, has given a completely wrong direction to all investigations into the nature and origin of our knowledge. . . . [This difference] does not merely concern their form, as being either clear or confused. It concerns their origin and content" (A 44/B 61-2). Although there is, I think, a way of reading this as an accurate diagnosis of Leibniz's "error," some commentators have exaggerated the sense in which there is a merely "logical" or "formal" difference between the sensible and the intelligible, taking this to imply that Leibniz identifies sensations with confused thoughts or concepts (see note 44).

[33] As we saw in Chapter 2, this claim is integral to the doctrine of universal harmony. Given their capacity for perception and activity, Leibniz regards all substances as essentially soullike, although they need not possess either consciousness or rationality.

[34] Cf. NE II, ix, 1 (RB 134); II, xix, 4 (RB 161-2).

[35] Cf. NE II, i, 15 (RB 115-16).

[36] Conversely, "confusion is when several things are present, but there is no way of distinguishing one from another" (C 535/P 146).

[37] "In each created monad only a part [of the universe]

is expressed distinctly which is greater or smaller according to whether the soul is more or less excellent, and all the rest which is infinite is only expressed confusedly" (GP IV 553). Cf. GP IV 546, 548-9; PNG § 13.

[38] The latter term raises difficulties, which are discussed at length in Kulstad 1991. Many have assumed that Leibniz employs the term "apperception" to designate that feature of mentality (consciousness, reflection, reason) which distinguishes human and higher minds from animal souls. Kulstad, however, plausibly suggests that Leibniz may, in fact, distinguish two grades of apperception: one involving only sensory awareness (or awareness of what is without), which is attributable to animal souls, the other involving self-awareness (or awareness of what is within), which is limited to rational minds. I believe that something like this is correct; however, I steer clear of the problem here by avoiding the term "apperception" altogether. In what follows, I assume that "reflection" designates a capacity proper to rational minds.

[39] "It might perhaps be added that beasts have perception, and that they don't necessarily have thought, that is, have reflection or anything which could be the object of it" (NE II, ix, 1; RB 134). Cf. NE II, xxi, 72 (RB 210).

[40] Cf. GP IV 574: "[W]e ordinarily conceive of *confused thoughts* as of a completely different type from *distinct* thoughts. . . . However, at bottom confused thoughts are only a multitude of thoughts, which in themselves are like the distinct ones, but which are so small that each one taken separately does not excite our attention and does not make itself distinguished." Both passages are cited by Parkinson (1982, 3). In light of what I shall argue, these texts must be read in conjunction with NE II, xxi, 72 (RB 210), where Leibniz acknowledges that he himself may sometimes have carelessly confounded the term "thought"—correctly attributed only to minds—with the more general term "perception."

[41] "[I]t is clearly necessary that every simple substance embraces the universe in its confused perceptions or sensations" (GP IV 356).

[42] "The senses provide us with materials for reflections" (NE II, xxi, 73; RB 212). Cf. PNG § 4.

[43] "The mind must at least give itself its thoughts of reflection, since it is the mind which reflects" (NE II, i, 23; RB 119).

[44] Pereboom has argued that Kant's criticism of Leibniz is not simply that he fails to specify different "theoretical tasks" for sensation and intellection, but that he "has a single type of mental representation perform

the function of both concepts and sensations" (1991, 54). So far as I can see, this charge remains unsupported. With the introduction of reflection as the mental faculty definitive of rational minds, Leibniz effectively allows for two different types of representations: sensory perceptions, which are immediate representations of what is outer and are common to all substances (although such perceptions often remain unconscious); and thoughts, which presuppose reflection and are the property of minds alone. That Leibniz refers to both types of mental states as "perceptions" is not a problem; we could in principle take this as a neutral term equivalent to Kant's "representation" (*Vorstellung*), which includes both intuitions and concepts. What is a problem is Leibniz's careless habit of referring to sensory perceptions as "thoughts," thereby seeming to rule out any difference in kind between them (cf. GP IV 574, stressed by Pereboom, and note 40), and his commitment to the view that all created substances can be located on a single scale of relative perfection, with their degrees of perfection being correlated with the degree of distinctness of their perceptions (cf. note 37). It is the confounding of this last notion, which is most appropriately applied to substances' representations of the universe, with the singular capacity of rational minds for purely intellectual thoughts that gets Leibniz into trouble.

[45] "If the idea were the *form* of the thought, it would come into and go out of existence with the actual thoughts which correspond to it, but since it is the *object* of thought it can exist before and after the thoughts" (NE II, i, 1; RB 109). Cf. DM § 26; NE II, xxi, 35 (RB 186).

[46] See NE Preface (RB 52); I, i, 26 (RB 86). We might wonder about the relationship between the claim that ideas are the "inner objects of thought" and the claim that ideas are dispositions to have certain types of thoughts. If Leibniz intended us to see a strict identity here, we would presumably have to say that to entertain an idea of *x* is to be aware of one's disposition to think of *x*. But this cannot be right. In entertaining an idea of *x*, I actualize my disposition to think of *x*. The object of the resulting thought is not the disposition but *x* itself. I conclude that Leibniz is speaking loosely when he refers to ideas as "inner objects of thought," and that what he really means is that certain properties of the soul serve as the objects of lasting dispositions to think of (or reflect on) those properties. Thus, given an innate capacity for reflection, or for the formation of thoughts, it is the soul that serves as "its own immediate inner object" (NE II, i; RB 109). We find this position expressed most fully in the preface to the *New Essays,* in a passage quoted below (RB 51-2). The account I sketch here is in broad agreement with the more careful treatment of Kulstad (1991, chap. 4). For a contrasting view, see Jolley (1990), who argues that Leibniz's descriptions of ideas as both dispositions for

thought and the products of reflection "are in tension—even in contradiction—with each other" (185).

[47] Cf. NE II, xxix, 4 (RB 255-6).

[48] In general, a distinct idea can be defined through an equation relating it to a set of simpler component ideas, which are jointly sufficient conditions for it. Cf. GP III 248: "Whether one says ideas or notions, whether one says distinct ideas or definitions (at least when the idea is not absolutely primitive), it is all the same thing."

[49] See NE I, i, 11 (RB 81); II, i, 23 (RB 119); IV, ii, 16 (RB 382); IV, iv, 5 (RB 382) IV, iv, 5 (RB 392).

[50] Cf. NE II, i, 2 (RB 110-11).

[51] As suggested in note 46, I assume that Leibniz does not defend a "storehouse" model of ideas, whereby the notions of substance, action, etc., are separate objects in the mind, but that instead he regards intellectual ideas as arising from a mind's capacity to reflect on its own properties and actions. We find this position expressed succinctly in a 1706 letter to Burnett: "I have noticed that M. Locke has not investigated deeply enough the origin of necessary truths, which do not depend on the senses, or experience, or facts, but on the consideration of the nature of our soul, which is a being, a substance, having unity, identity, action, passion, duration, etc. One need not be surprised if these ideas and the truths which depend on them are found in us, although reflections may be needed in order to apperceive them and it may sometimes be necessary that experiences excite our reflection or attention, for us to take note of what our nature furnishes us with" (GP III 307-8). Cf. NE, Preface (RB 51-2); I, i, 11 (RB 81); I, i, 23 (RB 85); I, iii, 18 (RB 105).

[52] This is obviously an important claim: Leibniz believes that the nature of our soul is such that we can extract from it knowledge that pertains to all other possibilities of existence, including that of God (cf. Mon § 30). Relevant to understanding this is his view, discussed in Chapter 2, that variety is only realized at a fundamental level through the varying of degrees of perfection, and that the perfections of created things are derived as limitations of the supreme perfections of God. Cf. Jolley 1990, 178.

[53] Cf. NE II, xxi, 73, where Leibniz says that the "analytic order" is not the "usual order in which events prompt us to think of these ideas. The senses provide us with materials for reflections: we could not think even about thought if we did not think about something else, i.e. about the particular facts which the senses provide" (RB 212). See also GP IV 563.

[54] Cf. NE III, v, 3: "What we are concerned with when we separate off the ideal world from the existent world [is the very form or possibility of thoughts]. The real existence of beings which are not necessary is a matter of fact or of history, while the knowledge of possibilities and necessities (the *necessary* being that whose opposite is not *possible*) is what makes up the demonstrative sciences" (RB 301).

[55] In a 1696 letter to Chauvin, Leibniz writes: "I hold that there is thus always something in us that corresponds to the ideas which are in God, and to the phenomena which occur in bodies" (A I 13, 232).

[56] I add the proviso "prima facie" distinct, since it will turn out that these attributes are themselves ultimately the products of confused perception. In an early survey of physical theory, we read: "We shall therefore deal with body and its qualities—both the intelligible, which we conceive distinctly, and the sensible, which we perceive confusedly" (Ge 110).

[57] The same notion of distinctness is at work here as in Leibniz's account of ideas. The mark of a distinct idea or property is the possibility of its definition, or resolution into simpler components.

[58] Thus, as Leibniz notes in DM § 24, "distinct knowledge has degrees, for ordinarily the notions that enter into the defintion are themselves in need of definition and are known only confusedly" (Le 69/AG 56).

[59] Cf. NE II, II, v: "These ideas which are said to come from more than one sense—such as those of space, figure, motion, rest—come rather from the common sense, that is, from the mind itself; for they are ideas of the pure understanding (though ones which relate to the external world and which the senses make us perceive), and so they admit of definitions and of demonstrations" (RB 128).

[60] Cf. V 640/L 288; GP VII 337/AG 312.

[61] Cf. NE II, ii, 1 (RB 120).

[62] Leibniz makes the strong claim that matter is actually infinitely *divided* and not simply infinitely divisible: "I hold that matter is actually fragmented into parts smaller than any given, or that there is no part of matter that is not actually subdivided into others, exercising different motions" (GP II 305). He offers several arguments on behalf of this thesis. Most basically, he appeals directly to divine wisdom, which seeks to maximize both order and variety: "In order to conceive better the actual division of matter to infinity and the exclusion from it of all exact and undetermined continuity, it is necessary to consider that God has already produced as much order and variety as it was possible to introduce so far" (GP VII 562-3). Relatedly, he refers the infinite division of matter to the principle of continuity, which is in turn ascribed to divine wisdom

(NE, Preface; RB 59-60). Finally, Leibniz cites the want of a sufficient reason for actual matter *not* to be divided to infinity (GP III 500, 519-20).

[63] Leibniz contrasts this situation with what would be the case were the world composed of perfectly hard and indivisible Democritean atoms: "If the world were in fact an aggregate of atoms, it could be accurately known through and through by a finite mind that was sufficiently elevated" (GP II 409). In this case, any body could be analyzed into a finite number of atomic parts, each with a determinate position in space and time, and the motion of any body would be a determinate function of the motion of its parts. Cf. RB 289; GP IV 555-6/L 575.

[64] As this passage suggests, to claim that mechanical properties are "somewhat confused" is effectively to claim that they are not real properties of bodies at all, but merely the products of our limited mode of perception: "Far from being constitutive of bodies, figure is not in itself an entirely real and determined quality outside of thought, and one could never assign to a body some precise surface in the way one could if there were atoms. And I can say the same thing of magnitude and motion, namely that these predicates hold of the phenomena like colors and sounds, and although they enclose more distinct knowledge, they can no more sustain the final analysis" (GP II 119/M 152). See also *A Specimen of Discoveries* (GP VII 314/P 81) and the 1683 study *Wonders Concerning the Nature of Corporeal Substance:* "Just like color and sound, so also extension and motion are phenomena rather than true attributes of things which contain some absolute nature independent of us" (V 294).

[65] Cf. NE II, v, quoted in note 59.

[66] "[A]bstractions are necessary for the scientific explanation of things," Leibniz tells De Volder. "It is by means of this abstraction that we can define in phenomena the role to be ascribed to each part of mass and can distinguish and explain the whole rationally" (GP II 252-3/L 531).

[67] For other statements of the claim that the principles of mechanics provide a "passage . . . from mathematical things to real substances," see *Critical Remarks on the General Part of Descartes' Principles,*" ad Article 64 (GP IV 391/L 409); NE IV, iii (RB 378); and his letter to Remond of 10 January 1714 (GP III 606/L 655). We return to this topic in Chapter 9.

[68] Leibniz makes a similar point in this passage concerning our knowledge of the law of justice by which God governs the commonwealth of minds and our ignorance concerning the detailed ways in which he administers the balance of reward and punishment within creation.

Works Cited

Adams, Robert, M. 1977. "Leibniz's Theories of Contingency." *Rice University Studies* 63/4:1-41.

———.1983. "Phenomenalism and Corporeal Substance in Leibniz." *Midwest Studies in Philosophy* 8:217-57.

Aiton, Eric. 1985. *Leibniz: A Biography*. Bristol: Adam Hilger.

Aristotle. 1935. *The Metaphysics, Books I-IX*. Tr. Hugh Tredennick. Cambridge: Harvard University Press.

———.1973. *The Categories*. Tr. Harold P. Cooke. Cambridge: Harvard University Press.

Barber, W. H. 1955. *Leibniz in France, from Arnauld to Voltaire: A Study in French Reactions to Leibnizianism*. Oxford: Oxford University Press.

Bayle, Pierre. 1991. *Historical and Critical Dictionary: Selections*. Tr. Richard H. Popkin. Indianapolis: Hackett.

Becco, Anne. 1978. "Leibniz et François-Mercure van Helmont: Bagatelle pour des Monades." *Studia Leibnitiana,* Sonderheft 7:119-42.

Beck, Lewis White. 1969. *Early German Philosophy: Kant and His Predecessors*. Cambridge, MA: Harvard University Press.

Bennett, Jonathan. 1974. *Kant's Dialectic*. Cambridge: Cambridge University Press.

Bertoloni Meli, Domenico, 1993. *Equivalence and Priority: Newton versus Leibniz*. Oxford: Clarendon Press.

Blumenfeld, David. 1985. "Leibniz on Contingency and Infinite Analysis." *Philosophy and Phenomenological Research* 45:483-514.

———.1988. "Freedom, Contingency, and Things Possible in Themselves." *Philosophy and Phenomenological Research* 49:81-101.

———.1994. "Perfection and Happiness in the Best Possible World." In Jolley, ed., *The Cambridge Companion to Leibniz*.

Boehm, A. 1962. *Le "Vinculum Substantiale" chez Leibniz*. Paris: Vrin.

Bossuet, Jacques-Bénigne. 1912. *Correspondance de Bossuet* (Nouvelle Edition). Ed. C. Urbain and E. Levesque. Paris: Hachette.

Breger, Hebert. 1984. "Elastizität als Strukturprinzip der Materie bei Leibniz." *Studia Leibnitiana,* Sonderheft 13:112-21.

Broad, C. D. 1972. "Leibniz's Predicate-in-Notion Principle and Some of Its Alleged Consequences." In Frankfurt, ed., *Leibniz,* pp. 11-18.

————.1975. *Leibniz: An Introduction.* Ed. C. Lewy. Cambridge: Cambridge University Press.

Brown, Gregory, 1987. "Compossibility, Harmony, and Perfection in Leibniz." *The Philosophical Review* 96:173-203.

————.1988. "Leibniz's Theodicy and the Confluence of Worldly Goods." *Journal of the History of Philosophy* 26:571-91.

Brown, Stuart. 1984. *Leibniz.* Minneapolis: University of Minnesota Press.

Cassirer, Ernst. 1902. *Leibniz' System in seinen wissenschaftlichen Grundlagen.* Darmstadt: Wiss. Buchgesellschaft; repr. Hildesheim: George Olms, 1962.

Cook, Daniel J. 1992. "Understanding the 'Other' Leibniz." *The Philosophical Forum* 23: 198-212.

Costabel, Pierre. 1973. *Leibniz and Dynamics.* Tr. R. E. W. Maddison. Ithaca, NY: Cornell University Press.

Couturat, Louis. 1901. *La Logique de Leibniz, d'après des documents inédits.* Paris: Felix Alcan; repr. Hildesheim: Georg Olms, 1961.

————.1902. "Sur la Métaphysique de Leibniz." *Revue de Métaphysique et de Morale* 10:1-25. ("On Leibniz's Metaphysics," tr. R. Allison Ryan. In Frankfurt, ed., *Leibniz,* pp. 19-45.)

Cover, J. A. 1989. "Relations and Reduction in Leibniz." *Pacific Philosophical Quarterly* 70:185-211.

Doyle, John P. 1967. "Suarez on the Reality of Possibles." *The Modern Schoolman* 45:29-48.

Earman, John. 1977. "Perceptions and Relations in the Monadology." *Studia Leibnitiana* 9:212-30.

————.1979. "Was Leibniz a Relationist?" *Midwest Studies in Philosophy* 4:263-76.

Evans, G. R. 1982. *Augustine on Evil.* Cambridge: Cambridge University Press.

Foucher de Cariel, Alexandre. 1861. *Leibniz: La Philosophie Juive et la Cabale.* Paris: Auguste Durand.

Fouke, Daniel C. 1991. "Spontaneity and the Generation of Rational Beings in Leibniz's Theory of Biological Reproduction." *Journal of the History of Philosophy* 29:33-45.

Frankfurt, Harry G., ed. 1972. *Leibniz: A Collection of Critical Essays.* Notre Dame, IN: University of Notre Dame Press.

Furth, Montgomery. 1967. "Monadology." *The Philosophical Review* 76:169-200.

Gale, George. 1974. "Did Leibniz Have a Practical Philosophy of Science?; or, Does 'Least-Work' Work?" *Studia Leibnitiana,* Supplementa 13:151-60.

————.1976. "On What God Chose: Perfection and God's Freedom." *Studia Leibnitiana* 8:69-87.

Garber, Daniel. 1983. "Mind, Body and the Laws of Nature in Descartes and Leibniz." *Midwest Studies in Philosophy* 8:105-33.

————.1985. "Leibniz and the Foundations of Physics: The Middle Years." In K. Okruhlik and J. R. Brown, eds., *The Natural Philosophy of Leibniz,* pp. 27-130. Dordrecht: D. Reidel.

————.1988. "Does History Have a Future? Some Reflections on Bennett and Doing Philosophy Historically." In P. H. Hare, ed., *Doing Philosophy Historically,* pp. 27-43. Buffalo: Prometheus Books.

————.1992. Review of C. Wilson 1989 and Sleigh 1990. *Journal of Philosophy* 89:151-62.

————.1994. "Leibniz: Physics and Philosophy." In Jolley, ed., *The Cambridge Companion to Leibniz.*

Gilbert, Neal W. 1960. *Renaissance Concepts of Method.* New York: Columbia University Press.

Grua, Gaston. 1953. *Jurisprudence universelle et Théodicée selon Leibniz.* Paris: Presses Universitaires; repr. New York: Garland, 1985.

————.1956. *La Justice humaine selon Leibniz.* Paris: Presses Universitaires: repr. New York: Garland, 1985.

Gueroult, Martial. 1967. *Leibniz: Dynamique et Métaphysique.* Paris: Aubier-Montaigne.

Hacking, I. 1972. "Individual Substance." In Frankfurt, ed., *Leibniz,* pp. 137-53.

————.1973. "Leibniz and Descartes: Proof and Eternal Truths." *Proceedings of the British Academy* 59:1-16.

Hall, A. Rupert. 1990. *Henry More: Magic, Religion*

and Experiment. Oxford: Basil Blackwell.

Hartz, Glenn A. 1992. "Leibniz's Phenomenalisms." *The Philosophical Review* 101:511-49.

Heinekamp, Albert. 1969. *Das Problem des Guten bei Leibniz*. Bonn: H. Bouvier.

Heinekamp, Albert, Wolfgang Lenzen, and Martin Schneider, eds. 1990. *Mathesis Rationis: Festschrift für Heinrich Schepers*. Munster: Nodus Publikationen.

Heinekamp, Albert, and André Robinet, eds. 1992. *Leibniz, le Meilleur des Mondes*. Stuttgart: Steiner.

Hostler, John. 1975. *Leibniz's Moral Philosophy*. London: Duckworth.

Iltis, Carolyn. 1971. "Leibniz and the *Vis Viva* Controversy." *Isis* 62:21-35.

Ishiguro, Hidé. 1990. *Leibniz's Philosophy of Logic and Language*. 2nd ed. Cambridge: Cambridge University Press.

Janke, Wolgang. 1963. *Leibniz: Die Emendation der Metaphysik*. Frankfurt am Main: Klostermann.

Jolley, Nicholas. 1975. "An Unpublished Leibniz MS on Metaphysics." *Studia Leibnitiana* 7:161-89.

————.1984. *Leibniz and Locke: A Study of the New Essays on Human Understanding*. Oxford: Clarendon Press.

————.1986. "Leibniz and Phenomenalism." *Studia Leibnitiana* 18:38-51.

————.1990. *The Light of the Soul: Theories of Ideas in Leibniz, Malebranche, and Descartes*. Oxford: Clarendon Press.

Jolley, Nicholas, ed. 1994. *The Cambridge Companion to Leibniz*. Cambridge: Cambridge University Press.

Jordan, Mark D. 1984. "The Intelligibility of the World and the Divine Ideas in Aquinas." *Review of Metaphysics* 38:17-32.

Kabitz, Willy. 1909. *Die Philosophie des jungen Leibniz*. Heidelberg: Carl Winter's Universitätsbuchhandlung.

————.1932. "Leibniz and Berkeley." *Sitzungsberichte der Preussischen Akademie der Wissenschaften*. Phil. Hist. Klasse (Berlin) 24:623-36.

Kant, I. 1933. *Critique of Pure Reason*. Tr. Norman Kemp Smith. 2nd ed. London: Macmillan.

————.1973. *The Kant-Eberhard Controversy*. Tr. Henry E. Allison. Baltimore: Johns Hopkins University Press.

————.1978. *Lectures on Philosophical Theology*. Tr. Allen W. Wood and Gertrude M. Clark. Ithaca, NY: Cornell University Press.

Kulstad, Mark A. 1977. "Leibniz's Conception of Expression." *Studia Leibnitiana* 9:55-76.

————.1990. "Appetition in the Philosophy of Leibniz." In A. Heinekamp, W. Lenzen, and M. Schneider, eds., *Mathesis Rationis*, pp. 133-51.

————.1991. *Leibniz on Apperception, Consciousness, and Reflection*. Munich: Philosophia Verlag.

Lapidge, Michael. 1978. "Stoic Cosmology." In J. M. Rist, ed., *The Stoics*, pp 161-85. Berkeley: University of California Press.

Leclerc, Ivor, ed. 1973. *The Philosophy of Leibniz and the Modern World*. Nashville, TN: Vanderbilt University Press.

Locke, John. 1975. *An Essay Concerning Human Understanding*. Ed. Peter H. Nidditch. Oxford: Clarendon Press. Originally published 1689.

Loemker, Leroy E. 1961. "Leibniz and the Herborn Encyclopedists." *Journal of the History of Ideas* 22:323-38. Reprinted in Leclerc, ed., *Philosophy of Leibniz*, pp. 276-97.

Lohr, Charles H. 1988. "Metaphysics." In Charles B. Schmitt, ed., *The Cambridge History of Renaissance Philosophy*, pp. 537-638. Cambridge: Cambridge University Press.

McGuire, J. E. 1976. "'Labyrinthus Continui': Leibniz on Substance, Activity and Matter." In P. Machamer and R. Turnball, eds., *Motion and Time, Space and Matter: Interrelations in the History of Philosophy and Science*, pp. 291-326. Columbus: Ohio State University Press.

McLaughlin, Peter. 1993. "Descartes on Mind-Body Interaction and the Conservation of Motion." *The Philosophical Review* 102:155-82.

McMullin, Ernan. 1978. *Newton on Matter and Activity*. Notre Dame, IN: Notre Dame University Press.

McRae, Robert. 1976. *Leibniz: Perception, Apperception, and Thought*. Toronto: University of Toronto Press.

————.1979. "Time and the Monad." *Nature and Sys-*

tem 1:103-9.

Mahnke, Dietrich. 1925. *Leibnizens Synthese von Universalmathematik and Individualmetaphysik.* Halle: Niemeyer.

Martin, Gottfried. 1967. *Leibniz—Logic and Metaphysics.* Tr. K. J. Northcott and P. G. Lucas. New York: Barnes & Noble.

Mates, Benson. 1980. "Nominalism and Evander's Sword." *Studia Leibnitiana,* Supplementa 21:213-35.

————.1986. *The Philosophy of Leibniz: Metaphysics and Language.* New York: Oxford University Press.

Mercer, Christia. In press. *Leibniz's Metaphysics: Its Origins and Development.* Cambridge: Cambridge University Press.

Mercer, Christia, and Robert C. Sleigh, Jr. 1994. "Metaphysics: The Early Period to the *Discourse on Metaphysics.*" In Jolley, ed., *The Cambridge Companion to Leibniz.*

Merchant, Carolyn. 1979. "The Vitalism of Anne Conway: Its Impact on Leibniz's Concept of the Monad." *Journal of the History of Philosophy* 17:255-69.

Meyer, R. W. 1952. *Leibniz and the Seventeenth-Century Revolution.* Cambridge: Bowes & Bowes.

Moll, Konrad. 1978. *Der junge Leibniz I.* Stuttgart-Bad Cannstatt: Frommann-Holzboog.

Mondadori, Fabrizio. 1990a. Review of Mates 1986. *The Philosophical Review* 99:613-29.

————.1990b. "Modalities, Representation and Exemplars: The 'Region of Ideas.'" In A. Heinekamp, W. Lenzen, and M. Scheider, eds., *Mathesis Rationis,* pp. 169-88.

Mugnai, Massimo. 1973. "Der Begriff der Harmonie als metaphysische Grundlage der Logik und Kombinatorik bei Johann Heinrich Bisterfeld und Leibniz." *Studia Leibnitiana* 5:43-73.

————.1990a. "Leibniz's Nominalism and the Reality of Ideas in the Mind of God." In A. Heinekamp, W. Lenzen, and M. Schneider, eds., *Mathesis Rationis,* pp. 153-67.

————.1990b. "A Systematical Approach to Leibniz's Theory of Relations and Relational Sentences." *Topoi* 9:61-81.

————.1992. *Leibniz' Theory of Relations.* Stuttgart: Franz Steiner Verlag.

Müller, Kurt, and Gisela Krönert. 1969. *Leben und Werk von G. W. Leibniz: Eine Chronik.* Frankfurt am Main: Klostermann.

Okruhlik, Kathleen. 1985. "The Status of Scientific Laws in the Leibnizian System." In K. Okruhlik and J. R. Brown, eds., *The Natural Philosophy of Leibniz,* pp. 183-206. Dordrecht: D. Reidel.

Ong, Walter J. 1958a. *Ramus, Method, and the Decay of Dialogue.* Cambridge, MA: Harvard University Press.

————.1958b. *Ramus and Talon Inventory.* Cambridge, MA: Harvard University Press.

Parkinson, G. H. R. 1965. *Logic and Reality in Leibniz's Metaphysics.* Oxford: Oxford University Press.

————.1982. "The 'Intellectualization of Appearances': Aspects of Leibniz's Theory of Sensation and Thought." In M. Hooker, ed., *Leibniz: Critical and Interpretive Essays,* pp. 3-20. Minneapolis: University of Minnesota Press.

————.1990. "Leibniz's Philosophical Aims: Foundation-Laying or Problem-Solving?" In A. Heinekamp, W. Lenzen, and M. Schneider, eds., *Mathesis Rationis,* 67-78.

————.1992. "Introduction." In G. W. Leibniz, *De Summa Rerum: Metaphysical Papers, 1675-1676.* New Haven, CT: Yale University Press.

Pereboom, Derk. 1991. "Kant's Amphiboly." *Archiv für Geschichte der Philosophie* 73:50-70.

Petersen, Peter. 1921. *Geschichte der aristotelischen Philosophie im protestantischen Deutschland.* Leipzig: Felix Meiner.

Politella, Joseph. 1938. *Platonism, Aristotelianism, and Cabalism in the Philosophy of Leibniz.* Ph.D. diss., University of Pennsylvania.

Rescher, Nicholas. 1979. *Leibniz: An Introduction to His Philosophy.* Lanham, MD: University Press of America.

————.1981. *Leibniz's Metaphysics of Nature.* Dordrecht: D. Reidel.

Robinet, André. 1955. *Malebranche et Leibniz: Relations Personelles.* Paris: J. Vrin.

————.1969. "Du nouveau sur la Correspondance Leibniz-Des Bosses." *Studia Leibnitiana* 1:83-103.

————.1981. "Suarez im Werk von Leibniz." *Studia Leibnitiana* 13:76-96.

———.1984. "Dynamique et fondemonts métaphysiques." *Studia Leibnitiana,* Sonderheft 13:1-25.

———.1988. *G. W. Leibniz Iter Italicum.* Firenze: Olschki.

Robinet, André, ed. 1986. *G. W. Leibniz. Principes de la nature et de la grâce fondés en raison. Principes de la philosophie ou Monadologie.* 3rd ed. Paris: Presses Universitaires de France.

Roncaglia, Gino. 1990. "Cum Deus Calculat—God's Evaluation of Possible Worlds and Logical Calculus." *Topoi* 9:83-90.

Ross, George MacDonald. 1983. "Leibniz and Renaissance Neoplatonism." *Studia Leibnitiana,* Supplementa 23:125-34.

Russell, Bertrand. 1903. "Recent Work on the Philosophy of Leibniz." *Mind* n.s. 12:177-201.

———.1937. *A Critical Exposition of the Philosophy of Leibniz.* 2nd ed. London: George Allen & Unwin. Originally published 1900.

Rutherford, Donald. 1988. "Truth, Predication, and the Complete Concept of an Individual Substance." *Studia Leibnitiana,* Sonderheft 15:130-44.

———.1990a. "Leibniz's `Analysis of Multitude and Phenomena into Unities and Reality.'" *Journal of the History of Philosophy* 28:525-52.

———.1990b. "Phenomenalism and the Reality of Body in Leibniz's Later Philosophy." *Studia Leibnitiana* 22:11-38.

———.1992. "Leibniz's Principle of Intelligibility." *History of Philosophy Quarterly* 9:35-49.

———.1993. "Natures, Laws and Miracles: The Roots of Leibniz's Critique of Occasionalism." In S. Nadler, ed., *Causation in Early Modern Philosophy,* pp. 135-58. University Park: Pennsylvania State University Press.

———.1994a. "Leibniz and the Problem of Monadic Aggregation." *Archiv für Geschichte der Philosophie* 76:65-90.

———.1994b. "Philosophy and Language in Leibniz." In Jolley, ed., *The Cambridge Campanion to Leibniz.*

———.1994c. "Metaphysics: The Late Period." In Jolley, ed., *The Cambridge Companion to Leibniz.*

Schepers, Heinrich. 1966. "Leibniz' Arbeiten zu einer Reformation der Kategorien." *Zeitschrift für philosophische Forschung* 20:539-67.

———.1969. "Begriffsanalyse und Kategorialsynthese. Zur Verflechtung von Logik and Metaphysik bei Leibniz." *Studia Leibnitiana,* Supplementa 3:34-49.

Sleigh, Robert C., Jr. 1983. "Leibniz on the Two Great Principles of All Our Reasonings." *Midwest Studies in Philosophy* 8:193-216.

———.1990. *The Leibniz-Arnauld Correspondence.* New Haven, CT: Yale University Press.

Suarez, Francisco. 1965. *Disputationes Metaphysicae.* 2 vols. Hildesheim: Georg Olms. Originally published 1597.

Utermöhlen, Gerda. 1979. "Leibniz' Antwort auf Christian Thomasius' Frage Quid sit substantia?" *Studia Leibnitiana* 11:82-91.

Vieillard-Barton, Jean-Louis. 1979. *Platon et L'Idéalisme Allemand (1770-1830).* Paris: Beauchesne.

Voltaire. 1877. *Oeuvres complètes de Voltaire* (Nouvelle Edition). 52 vols. Paris: Garnier Frères.

Westfall, Richard S. 1971. *Force in Newton's Physics: The Science of Dynamics in the Seventeenth Century.* London: MacDonald.

Wilson, Catherine. 1983. "Leibnizian Optimism." *Journal of Philosophy* 80:765-83.

———.1989. *Leibniz's Metaphysics: A Comparative and Historical Study.* Princeton, NJ: Princeton University Press.

Wilson, Margaret. 1977. "Confused Ideas." *Rice Studies in Philosophy* 63/4:123-37.

Woznicki, Andrew, N. 1990. *Being and Order: The Metaphysics of Thomas Aquinas in Historical Perspective.* New York: Peter Lang.

FURTHER READING

Biography

Aiton, E. J. *Leibniz: A Biography.* Bristol, England: Adam Hilger, 1985, 370 p.

> Places the evolution of Leibniz's philosophical and scientific thought within the intellectual and social context of his lifetime. Aiton draws mainly on printed editions of Leibniz's correspondence, works, and writings.

Criticism

Broad, C. D. *Leibniz: An Introduction,* edited by C. Lewy.

London: Cambridge University Press, 1975, 175 p.
> Text of the late C. D. Broad's lectures given at Cambridge from 1948-50 on the philosophy of Leibniz.

Brown, Gregory. "Compossibility, Harmony, and Perfection in Leibniz." *The Philosophical Review* XCVI, No. 2 (April 1987): 173-203.
> Examines Leibniz's doctrine of concepts and his ideas on perfection.

Chappell, Vere, ed. *Gottfried Wilhelm Leibniz: Part II.* New York: Garland Publishing, 1992, 459 p.
> Reprints essays by prominent scholars in order to give an overview of contemporary thought on Leibniz.

Dascal, Marcelo. *Leibniz: Language, Signs and Thought: A Collection of Essays.* Philadelphia: John Benjamins Publishing Co., 1987, 203 p.
> Examines Leibniz's interest in language and signs and discusses the role his investigations in these areas played in his philosophical system.

Funkenstein, Amos. "God's Omnipresence, God's Body, and Four Ideals of Science." In *Theology and the Scientific Imagination from the Middle Ages to the Seventeenth Century,* pp. 23-116. Princeton, N.J.: Princeton University Press, 1986.
> A section of this chapter is devoted to Leibniz's scientific theories.

Furth, Montgomery. "Monadology." *The Philosophical Review* LXXVI, No. 2 (April 1967): 169-200.
> Examines Leibniz's response to and attempt to resolve the Cartesian mind-body problem.

Hooker, Michael, ed. *Leibniz: Critical and Interpretive Essays.* Minneapolis: University of Minnesota Press, 1982, 373 p.
> Contains sixteen essays covering various aspects of Leibniz's philosophy.

Ishiguro, Hidé. *Leibniz's Philosophy of Logic and Language.* Ithaca, N.Y.: Cornell University Press, 1972, 157 p.
> Analyzes Leibniz's ideas on logic and language, particularly the "philosophical assumptions and consequences of these systems."

Jolley, Nicholas. "Leibniz on Locke and Socinianism." In *Philosophy, Religion and Science in the Seventeenth and Eighteenth Centuries,* edited by John W. Yolton, pp. 170-87. Rochester, N. Y.: University of Rochester Press, 1990.
> Reexamines Leibniz's critique of Locke in light of Leibniz's writings on Socinian metaphysics.

———, ed. *The Cambridge Companion to Leibniz.* Cambridge, England: Cambridge University Press, 1995, 500 p.
> Contains a dozen essays covering various aspects of

Leibniz's philosophy and the historical context in which he wrote.

Loeb, Louis E. "Leibniz's Denial of Causal Interaction between Monads." *From Descartes to Hume: Continental Metaphysics and the Development of Modern Philosophy,* pp. 269-319. Ithaca, N.Y.: Cornell University Press, 1981.
> Analyzes Leibniz's claim that "nothing external acts upon a substance."

McCarthy, John A. "The Philosopher as Essayist: Leibniz and Kant." In *The Philosopher as Writer: The Eighteenth Century,* edited by Robert Ginsberg, pp. 48-74. Cranbury, N.J.: Associated University Presses, 1987.
> Discusses the "place of Leibniz and Kant in the history of the German essay," which McCarthy describes as one of the principal means of expression during the "Age of Reason" and a newly developing literary genre.

Parkinson, G. H. R. *Logic and Reality in Leibniz's Metaphysics.* Oxford: The Clarendon Press, 1965, 196 p.
> Analyzes the "consequences relating to metaphysics which Leibniz derived, or should have derived, from his logic, and [evaluates] that logic and the metaphysics which is related to it."

Rescher, Nicholas. "Monads and Matter: A Note on Leibniz's Metaphysics." *The Modern Schoolman* XXXII, No. 2 (January 1955): 172-75.
> Analyzes Leibniz's concept of *vinculum substantiale,* which explains the fusing of monads into organized structures.

———. "Leibniz's Conception of Quantity, Number, and Infinity." *The Philosophical Review* LXIV, No. 1 (January 1955): 108-14.
> Discusses Leibniz's concept of quantity and number and his rejection of infinite numbers.

———. *Leibniz's Metaphysics of Nature: A Group of Essays.* Dordrecht, Holland: D. Reidel Publishing Company, 1981, 128 p.
> Treats Leibniz's "cosmology of creation and his conception of the real world as one among many equipossible alternatives."

Scheffler, Samuel. "Leibniz on Personal Identity and Moral Personality." *Studia Leibnitiana* VIII, No. 2 (1976): 219-40.
> Examines Leibniz's concepts of personal and moral identity and discusses the role that "memory and other psychological phenomena play in setting the criteria of moral identity."

Wilson, Catherine. *Leibniz's Metaphysics: A Historical and Comparative Study.* Manchester, England: Manchester University Press, 1989, 350 p.
> Provides an overview of Leibniz's system of meta-

physics and attempts to interpret his ideas "in light
of the choices actually open to him, . . . [which] are
defined by his relation to past and present authors."

An Essay Concerning Human Understanding

John Locke

The following entry contains critical discussions of Locke's *An Essay Concerning Human Understanding* published from 1975 through 1994. For further commentary on Locke's career and works, see LC, Volume 7.

INTRODUCTION

An Essay Concerning Human Understanding is one of the most noted and influential works of Locke's career. Concerned with "the origin, certainty, and extent of human knowledge," the *Essay* explores epistemological issues associated with science, as well as Locke's philosophy of language and personal identity. Among the most notable elements of the work is Locke's empiricist rejection of the doctrine of innatism, which held that certain moral "truths" are inborn. Locke rejected this view, arguing that experience—rather than heredity or God—is the primary source of moral, as well as intellectual, ideas. Thus, the position Locke articulated in the *Essay* supports knowledge obtained through scientific methodology (or information perceived through the senses), and implicitly advocates a social philosophy of religious toleration. An important landmark in the history of ideas, the epistemological issues explored in *An Essay Concerning Human Understanding* have continued to be of interest to modern philosophers of the twentieth century.

Biographical Information

Locke composed two drafts of *An Essay Concerning Human Understanding* in 1671, while serving as physician, confidential adviser, and secretary to Lord Ashley, who was a noted and outspoken champion of civil liberty. Locke's projects under Ashley included collaboration on the composition of a constitution for the Carolina colony in America titled Fundamental Constitutions of Carolina. Locke put his Essay aside for several years, but returned to the task in approximately 1678, while he was seeking refuge in Holland from the rising suspicions of the English government associated with his supposed role as a radical. Along with revising drafts of his Essay, Locke wrote a powerful defense of toleration during this time, later published as *Epistola de tolerantia* (1689; *A Letter concerning Toleration*). Following his return to England, Locke published *An Essay Concerning Human Understanding*, which made an immediate and lasting impression on his contemporaries. The remaining years of Locke's career were largely devoted to the prepar-

ation of new editions of the Essay; he produced five editions from 1690 through 1706.

Major Themes

Throughout his career, Locke's philosophy was concerned with four principal issues: politics, education, religion, and knowledge, with the *Essay Concerning Human Understanding* devoted primarily to the fourth of these subjects. Peter Nidditch has commented: "The *Essay* presents, for the first time, a systematic, detailed, reasoned, and wide-ranging philosophy of the mind and cognition whose thrust . . . is empiricist." In the *Essay*, Locke rejects the doctrine of "innate ideas" promoted by Descartes and such Cambridge Platonists as Henry More and Ralph Cudworth, embracing instead an empiricist conception of knowledge as the product of sense perception and experience. In a now-famous metaphor, Locke compares the human mind at birth to a *tabula rasa*—a blank slate—on which morals, values, and beliefs are inscribed by environment and experience rather than heredity; through the accumulation of impressions and experiences, general ideas about the world are formed. Locke believed that absolute truth is difficult or impossible to ascertain through the senses, and his empiricist views are therefore in harmony with his advocation of a social policy of religious toleration. This aspect of his philosophy placed him in direct conflict with the intuitional school of morality which maintained the existence of certain moral axioms as inborn rather than learned through socialization. Although Locke describes knowledge as fundamentally the product of sense perception in the *Essay,* he also suggests that sensation alone does not necessarily constitute knowledge. Knowledge, the *Essay* concludes, is often the result of intuition as well as sense perception: "This part of knowledge," comments Locke, "is irresistible and, like bright sunshine, forces itself immediately to be perceived, as soon as ever the mind turns its view that way; and leaves no room for hesitation, doubt or examination."

Critical Reception

Locke's contemporaries, with the noted exception of the poet Matthew Prior, were virtually unanimous in their praise for *An Essay Concerning Human Understanding.* In a 1695 letter to Locke, for example, John Wynne commented: "[The] truths contained in our book are so clear and evident, the notions so natural and agreeable to reason, that I imagine none that carefully reads and duly considers them, can avoid being enlightened and instructed by them." Nineteenth-century commentators essentially echoed eighteenth-century praise for the work, and emphasized its historical importance to the development of a scientific worldview. John Wilson, for example, credited the *Essay* with subverting the "abstract, speculative, and often obscure doctrine of the scholastic logicians" with the establishment of "surer" scientific principles. Stressing Locke's modernity, twentieth-century critics have also praised Locke for ushering in a new era in the history of ideas. Maurice Cranston has credited Locke with establishing the first modern philosophy of science, while George Santayana has attributed the initiation of two modern disciplines to Locke—the criticism of knowledge and modern psychology. Areas of particular interest for contemporary scholars of Locke include the rhetorical strategy and style of the *Essay* and the tension between the Christian and scientific aspects of Locke's thought. Contemporary critics are perhaps more impressed with the range of Locke's thought in the *Essay* than were Locke's contemporaries. Vere Chappell, for example, has commented: "[Contemporary philosophy is divided into] logic, epistemology, metaphysics, and moral philosophy, and then, by subdividing these, such specializations as the philosophies of language, science, mind, and religion, ethical theory, and political philosophy.

Locke worked actively in nearly all of these areas."

PRINCIPAL WORKS

The Funamental Constitutions of Carolinas [with Anthony Ashley Cooper, and others] (manifesto) 1670

A Letter from a Person of Quality, to His Friend in the Country [with Anthony Ashley Cooper] (essay) 1675

Epistola de tolerantia ad clarissimum virum [*A Letter concerning Toleration, Humbly Submitted*] (essay) 1689

An Essay concerning Humane Understanding (essay) 1690; also published as *An Essay Concerning Human Understanding,* 1726; revised editions, 1694, 1700, and 1705

A Second Letter concerning Toleration to the Author of the Argument of the Letter concerning Toleration [as Philanthropus] (essay) 1690

Two Treatises of Government (essays) 1690

Some Considerations of the Consequences of the Lowering of Interest and Raising the Value of Money (essay) 1690

A Third Letter for Toleration [written as Philanthropus] (essay) 1692

Some Thoughts concerning Education (essay) 1693; revised editions, 1695, 1699, 1705

Further Considerations concerning Raising the Value of Money (essay) 1695

The Reasonableness of Christianity, as Delivered in the Scriptures (essay) 1695

Short Observations on a Printed Paper (essay) 1695

A Vindication of the Reasonableness of Christianity (essay) 1695

A Letter to the Right Reverend Edward Ld Bishop of Worcester, concerning Some Passages Relating to Mr. Locke's Essay of Humane Understanding (essay) 1697

Mr. Locke's Reply to the Right Reverend the Lord Bishop of Worcester's Answer to His Letter, concerning . . . Locke's Essay of Humane Understanding (essay) 1697

Mr. Locke's Reply to the Right Reverend the Lord Bishop of Worcester's Answer to His Second Letter . . . (essay) 1699

Posthumous Works of Mr. John Locke (essays and biography) 1706

CRITICISM

Peter H. Nidditch (essay date 1975)

SOURCE: A foreword to *An Essay Concerning Human Understanding,* by John Locke, edited by Peter H. Nidditch, Oxford at the Clarendon Press, 1975, pp. vii-xxv.

[In the following essay, Nidditch offers an overview of Locke's main objectives in An Essay Concerning Human Understanding *and considers several reasons why the work continues to be actively studied by philosophers.]*

The Ascendancy of the Essay

The *Essay* has long been recognized as one of the great works of English literature of the seventeenth century, and one of the epoch-making works in the history of philosophy. It has been one of the most repeatedly reprinted, widely disseminated and read, and profoundly influential books of the past three centuries, since its initial publication in December 1689. In particular, it has been and continues to be actively studied by philosophers and students of philosophy the world over; the reasons for this are naturally complex, but two focal points may be singled out.

(I) The *Essay* gained for itself a unique standing as the most thorough and plausible formulation of empiricism—a viewpoint that it caused to become an enduring powerful force. Philosophical terms ending in 'ism', e.g. 'empiricism', and their cognates and various other class or type terms are dangerous to apply because they may, and commonly do, conceal historical differences and even divergences; it may therefore be misleading to use them without definite clarification, and it may be impossible to give a satisfactory short account of the meaning of such a term because imprecision may be the price of brief comprehensiveness. The ordinary needs and habits of communication, however, override these difficulties to a great extent. The empiricism of Hobbes (1588-1679), Locke (1632-1704), and Hume (1711-76) should be seen as a compound of several doctrines, not all of them exclusively epistemological. Among them are, as a first approximation: that our natural powers operate in a social and physical environment that we seek to adapt ourselves to, and that the variable functioning of these powers in that environment is the agency by which we get and retain all our ideas, knowledge, and habits of mind; that our capacities of conscious sense-experience and of feeling pleasure or discomfort are primary natural powers; that the abuse of language, especially in scholastic systems and indulgent speculative hypotheses, is a troublesome source of errors and of obstacles to intellectual improvement and moral and social stability; that religious fervour is contemptible and sectarian strife is deplorable; and that although science, which proceeds by reasoning about propositions whose terms represent existent ideas or realities, deserves our respect, its scope for attaining conclusive success is extremely limited at best. A marked difference between Hume's empiricism and Hobbes's and Locke's is his low estimation of the power of reason; Hume's assertion that reason 'can never pretend to any other office than to serve and obey' the passions would have been abhorrent to Hobbes and Locke.

The *Essay* presents, for the first time, a systematic, detailed, reasoned, and wide-ranging philosophy of mind and cognition whose thrust, so far as it is in line with the future rather than the past, is empiricist. It must be acknowledged that it was Hobbes among British philosophers—concurrently with the Frenchman Gassendi (1592-1655)—who first produced in the modern era, especially in his *Leviathan* and *De Corpore,* a philosophy of mind and cognition that built on empiricist principles. A characteristic declaration of Hobbes's empiricism (and nominalism) is:

> No Discourse whatsoever, can End in absolute knowledge of Fact, past, or to come. For, as for the knowledge of Fact, it is originally, Sense; and ever after, Memory. And for the knowledge of Con-sequence, which I have said before is called Science, it is not Absolute, but Conditionall. No man can know by Discourse, that this, or that, is, has been, or will be; which is to know absolutely: but onely, that if This be, That is; if This has been, That has been; if This shall be, That shall be: which is to know conditionally; and that not the consequence of one thing to another; but of one name of a thing, to another name of the same thing.
>
> (*Leviathan,* I. vii).

Nevertheless, that Hobbes was a forerunner does not detract from Locke's achievement and role. Hobbes did not manage to write a book that could begin to match the quickly won and lasting popularity of Locke's major work. His masterpiece, *Leviathan,* differs from the *Essay* in not being chiefly concerned with questions in the philosophy of mind and cognition, and it is these that have been largely dominant since the sixteenth century. Hobbes did not undertake a systematic tracing of our ideas to their empirical origins; this was pioneered by Locke, who deployed in the process an original concept of experience divided into external ('sensation') and internal ('reflection'). Also, in contrast with Locke's emphatic dualism of mind and body, his moderate theism, and his ultimately libertarian account of action, Hobbes's reduction of everything to bodies and motions, his suspected atheism, and his strict determinism were—along with his extreme egoism in ethics—repugnant to his contemporaries and to the next century and beyond; and his theory of matter was soon overtaken by that of Boyle (1627-91), from which Locke's derives. An additional, different sort of reason may be conjectured: Hobbes's name in his own period and in the next century did not, unlike that of the author of the *Essay,* resound with opposition to authoritarianism, with the vindication of toleration (i.e. religious freedom), and with other liberal values, with which the generality of advancing philosophers and educationists associated themselves.

(2) The *Essay* is rich in philosophical matter; this makes

it a much sought-after quarry—both a source and a target. As a glance through the Contents or the book itself reveals, it grapples with fundamental questions in the philosophy of mind and cognition, and with some in the philosophy of language, the philosophy of logic, the philosophy of religion, and moral philosophy; and it touches on numerous other topics. The book is written in a broadly intelligible style, and the gist of its teachings and the outlines of its arguments are tolerably clear. So what it says about, for example, innateness, experience, sense-perception, self-knowledge, qualities, memory, space, time, number, infinity, freedom and necessity, universals, substance, causality, personal identity, truth and falsity, meaning, knowledge, probability, belief, and the role of logical principles, is often found a convenient starting-point for further consideration by practising philosophers. But to the critically minded, even if they find the tenor of his work attractive, Locke's statements, assumptions, and arguments, amidst the rambling rose (and rows) of the *Essay,* are a continual provocation; this comes about especially through his simplicities and conflations, the ambiguities of key terms and hence of key assertions, and inner tensions and clashes in his thought: these sometimes make him resemble Bunyan's Mr. Facing-bothways, Mr. Two-tongues, and the 'Water-man, looking one way, and Rowing another'. On the other hand, the divisions and oppositions in his thought (e.g. between his perceptual idealism and realism, his naturalism and supernaturalism, and his factual claim that 'Number applies it self to . . . every thing' and his nominalist claim that 'Names [are] necessary to Numbers') may well have been creative: without them, he might not have been driven to pursue his problems as persistently and devotedly as he did in preparing the *Essay* over many years—and then, after its publication, recurrently touching it up and writing additions for it—in order to resolve them with full explicitness and coherence. Of course, he did not succeed. But has any other philosopher succeeded better, or been of more widespread service to his fellows?

Locke's Life and Works

Locke's biography, besides its intrinsic interest, affords essential knowledge of the context in which the *Essay* was produced, and of its place among his works.

John Locke (29 August 1632-28 October 1704) was the son of John Locke senior (1606-61), an attorney and small land-owner, and Agnes Locke (*née* Keene) (1597-1654). He was born and brought up in a district of Somerset that was within ten miles of Bristol. One permanently formative part of his upbringing was his induction into his parents' determined Protestant faith; this led him in his manhood to be contemptuous and distrustful of religious enthusiasts, Catholics, and atheists. From the age of fourteen he was educated at Westminster School, which he later described as being a 'very severe schoole' because of the flogging practic-

es there. (In his *Some Thoughts Concerning Education* he counselled strongly against the punishment of children as a means of correcting or guiding them; kind firmness should suffice.) From Westminster, where he received a thorough grounding in Latin and Greek, Locke went in 1652 to Christ Church, Oxford, where, after following the usual Arts course (in Classical studies, grammar, rhetoric, logic, geometry, and moral philosophy) with limited interest and with distaste for the disputatious exercises, he graduated B.A. in 1656. He shortly afterwards became a senior Student of his college and retained this status, with rooms and emoluments, until Charles II (1630-85) personally required his expulsion in 1684, in the wake of Shaftesbury's final fall. It was perhaps in the late 1650s that Locke first read, and was refreshed by, Descartes (1596-1650). About this time or a little later he began to take an interest in physical science, and then in medicine where he became a close associate of Sydenham (1624-89), the distinguished physician with notable empirical learnings. He was acquainted with Boyle, the chemist and physicist (whose liberal views on toleration Locke found persuasive) and probably with other originators of the budding Royal Society, of which he became a Fellow in 1668. He lectured on Greek and rhetoric and performed supervisory duties for his college until 1665, when he left the confines of the academic world, henceforth to mix at home and abroad with persons of rank, affairs, and fortune, and with distinguished virtuosi, physicians, and scholars.

In the winter of 1665-6 he was abroad for the first time, as secretary to Charles II's ambassador to the Elector of Brandenburg at Cleves, where, as he wrote to Boyle, the Calvinists, Lutherans, Catholics, and Anabaptists 'quietly permit one another to choose their way to heaven'. He returned home, his future course still uncertain. He desired to get exemption from the usual obligation of a Student to take holy orders, and to be allowed to remain a layman by qualifying as a physician with a higher degree, and so, without waiting to fulfil the conditions for graduating M.B. first (he obtained this degree in 1675), he made a bid for the degree of Doctor of Medicine; after a failure, he gained his exemption in 1667, but not the degree.

A chance encounter had occurred in 1666 that proved to be the decisive turning-point in Locke's life: he met Lord Ashley (1621-83; created Earl of Shaftesbury, 1672), at that time Chancellor of the Exchequer, who used his influence to get Locke granted the latter's desired exemption from holy orders. Ashley soon invited Locke to take up residence at his London house, where Locke lived, from 1667 to 1675, as confidant and medical adviser. Locke was responsible in 1668 for a life-saving surgical operation on Ashley, who remained duly grateful. He subsequently became Secretary to the Lords Proprietors of Carolina (of whom Ashley was the most important) and to the Council of

Trade and Plantations (of which Ashley was the President), and, during his patron's Lord Chancellorship his Secretary for Presentations. These private and public roles were congenial to him. This was the happy period when the *Essay* was initially engendered, shaped, and developed. Without Ashley, there would have been no *Essay*. Ashley's powerful personality, keen mind, and forward-looking outlook probably did much to strengthen and extend Locke's maturing liberalism, not least by adding an economic dimension to it.

In November 1673 Shaftesbury (as Ashley had become) was dismissed by the King from the Lord Chancellorship; his other offices were then terminated, and the Council of Trade and Plantations was abolished. Locke must have been dismayed by all this; he was a man who (in Sydenham's description) had more than 'naturall tenderness and delicacy of sence', i.e. was hypersensitive. The upset and Locke's resulting fear—those were harsh days of royal retribution—contributed to the return of his asthmatic cough, from which he often suffered till his death.

There was an introverted, valetudinarian component in Locke's nature—which may have aided his self-preservation. He was a careful, cautious man, possessed of a good sense of business and method. Almost until he died he kept, with minute exactness, running accounts of all monies he received, spent, lent, or owed. He shied away from drinking parties and other hectic forms of social life, and from emotionality, high spirits, the dramatic, and even the aesthetic. He never married, and remained, it seems, completely continent; but he liked the attentions of lady admirers. He had many loyal friends, and got on especially well with some of his friends' children. His preference was for undisturbing circumstances and friendly surroundings where he could be active and industrious while maintaining an independence, calmness, self-control, and deliberation in all things; but from time to time unruly events and people unfortunately intruded.

Locke's finances were much improved by an annuity to which Shaftesbury substantially contributed. With Shaftesbury's consent he went abroad, to France (where he had been for a few weeks' holiday in 1672); he stayed there, with bases first at Montpellier and then at Paris, from November 1675 till the end of April 1679, when he returned to England, as it happened promptly on Shaftesbury's resumption of public office. He occupied those years with travel, acting as a tutor-companion, diverse reading, translating (some of the *Essais de morale* of Pierre Nicole (1625-95)), social visits, and numerous scientific, medical, philosophical, and other intellectual interchanges; and with writing up his Journal that he commenced on his departure, filling it with records of books, medical and scientific notes, descriptions of his travels, money accounts, other memoranda, and a variety of philosophical sketches,

many of them substantial and mostly on themes to be found in the *Essay* for which the sketches, after revision, were perhaps designed. It was during this period that he became a friend of the future Earl of Pembroke (1656-1733) to whom the *Essay* is dedicated. (Pembroke achieved a remarkable double: he is also the dedicatee of Berkeley's *Principles of Human Knowledge* (1710).)

When Locke returned from France in 1679, English politics were disturbed, and continued to be so for another ten years, by the consequences of the Catholicism of Charles II's younger brother James (1633-1701), the heir apparent. To many citizens—Locke among them—a papist King meant monarchical despotism, the forced conversion of the nation to a Catholic kingdom, its subservience to foreign powers, and persecution. A number of politicians, with Shaftesbury and his party, the Whigs, in the vanguard, wanted, even desperately, to get James's succession excluded by Act of Parliament. Charles, while an avowed Anglican, had shown that he was not without Catholic sympathies, and on his deathbed he entered the Church of Rome. Further, he saw that a victory for his opponents would affect his own powers. He stood by his brother. The Whigs lost that battle. Shaftesbury, in 1681, now in poor health, was committed to the Tower of London (where he had already spent a year in 1677-8) on a charge of high treason; he had a moment of triumph when he was acquitted by the grand jury, but, fearing revenge for the indignities he had inflicted on the King in recent years, he soon fled to Holland in November 1682 and died in Amsterdam a couple of months later. Locke, who, although he had not returned to Shaftesbury's employment in 1679, had actively continued his association with him, liked and admired him both as a statesman concerned with liberty and toleration and for his personal qualities. Shaftesbury's body was brought back to England for burial; Locke attended the funeral.

We have only sporadic pieces of Locke's philosophical writing during the years 1679-83, when perhaps his principal literary activity was harnessed to politics and toleration. This was interrupted in August 1683. By this time a number of Whigs—peers, publicists, and ordinary followers—had been arrested and Locke, as a known Shaftesburian, planned his removal to Holland (tolerant, and convenient for keeping in touch with friends in England), where he arrived on 7 September into a second exile that was to last longer than his first, French one. It was during his stay in Holland that his decades of reading, thinking, note-making, and drafting leaped towards momentous and manifold authorship. He further drafted and rewrote material for the *Essay,* getting this into final shape; he also made an abridgement of the book which, appearing in French translation in a scholarly periodical in 1688, at once brought international attention to the *Essay*. He wrote his *Epistola de Tolerantia* (*Letter on Toleration*), and possibly worked on the *Two Treatises of Government*. His *Some Thoughts Concerning Education* was mostly composed from letters of this period that he sent to his friend and agent Edward Clarke (*c.* 1650-1710) about the upbringing of the latter's son Edward.

Charles II died in 1685 and James became King, speedily arousing hostility and agitations because some steps and policies of his were markedly Catholic. William of Orange (1650-1702) and his wife Mary (1662-94), who were James's nephew and daughter, and Protestants, became joint King and Queen of England, after James had been compelled by events to withdraw to France in December 1688. William had landed in England in November 1688; Mary, like Locke, waited in Holland until all was settled, when they sailed, in February 1689, in the same yacht to Greenwich.

After his return to England Locke lodged in London, which he continued to visit fairly frequently until 1700 from an estate called Oates, near High Laver (about twenty-five miles from London) in Essex, where from Christmas 1690 he stayed for periods as a paying guest, and then from 1692 settled as a resident in the house of Sir Francis Masham, M.P. (1645-1722) and his second wife, Damaris (1659-1708), a daughter of the Cambridge Platonist, Ralph Cudworth (1617-88): it was probably Damaris who invited Locke to make his home at Oates, and it was she who looked after him in his last days.

Within a week of Locke's arrival in London in 1689 he was offered the post of English ambassador to the Elector of Brandenburg (the future King Frederick I of Prussia). But he resolved, after the dangers, discomforts, and interruptions of so many years, to remain in England; and he never left it again. He declined the King's offer on the grounds of 'that weak and broken constitution of my health which has soe long threatnd my life', his inexperience in diplomatic business, and the disability from his being 'the soberest man in the Kingdom' who knew 'noe such rack in the world to draw out mens thoughts as a well managed Bottle'. The only occupation as a public servant he then accepted was as a Commissioner of Appeals in Excise; later he held the demanding and more important office of a Commissioner of the Board of Trade until 1700. From 1689 he took an active interest in parliamentary affairs and contributed significantly towards the liberation of printing and publishing from the constraints of the Licensing Act.

Locke's refusal of a diplomatic appointment had been motivated not merely by considerations of his health and convenience. He had plans as an author that he was determined to accomplish. He urgently wanted to see the *Essay* and the *Two Treatises of Government* properly in print; the manuscripts of these were in their

almost final state. The completed manuscript of his *Epistola de Tolerantia* had been left behind for printing in the care of his closest Dutch friend van Limborch (1643-1712), a scholar and theologian belonging to the heterodox Remonstrant sect of Dutch Calvinists who believed (as Locke did) that the sovereignty of God is compatible with man's freedom and does not entail predestination; the book was published in Gouda in Spring 1689, and an English translation (by another hand) in London six months later. That Locke's first published book was on toleration and his next to appear, about mid November 1689 (only about a month before the *Essay*), was the *Two Treatises,* with its insistence that the authority of rulers is limited and conditioned by individuals' rights and the sake of 'the Publick Good', is symbolic of Locke's moral priorities, which are largely influential in the *Essay* too. He was already disposed towards the priority of the moral when a young man: his earliest surviving systematic writings, left unpublished, were on questions of toleration, political power, and natural law. He had, in one way or another, been working towards the *Epistola* for nearly thirty years, the *Essay* for nearly twenty years, and the *Two Treatises* for a decade; the results of all these prolonged efforts, made in days of light and shadow, suddenly emerged into public view in 1689, which was indeed Locke's *annus mirabilis*.

The *Essay* bore the author's name, as the already published abridgement had done; the other two books remained anonymous until after his death, when his acknowledgement of their authorship in his last will became known. Whether the anonymity of these and some of his other books was due solely to a wish to appear unegotistically concerned with principles or was in some degree motivated by self-protection against personal attacks by opponents is a matter of conjecture.

Although Locke was approaching sixty, his energy for writing books was far from waning. Two additional pieces on toleration soon followed (1690, 1692; these and other book dates below are those on the title-page of the first printing); three on monetary matters (1692, 1695, 1695); *Some Thoughts Concerning Education* (1693); and *The Reasonableness of Christianity* (1695), and two defences of it (1695, 1697), which represented Christianity, on the historical basis of scripture, in a latitudinarian spirit. Locke was certainly unorthodox; he was also devout.

The last years of the 1690s were taken up with a lot of work relating to the *Essay* again. Locke wrote three successive replies—the first two of moderate length, the third of 120,000 words—to criticisms of the *Essay* made by Edward Stillingfleet, Bishop of Worcester (1635-99). He had carefully revised the *Essay* for the second edition (1694), substantially altering one chapter (II. xxi) and adding another (II. xxvii); he now renewed this task for the fourth edition (1700), and added two more chapters (II. xxxiii and IV. xix). He actively supervised a French translation, and took some interest in the preparation of a Latin translation (1700, 1701, respectively).

Locke's last completed book was the studious ***Paraphrase and Notes on the Epistles of St. Paul;*** this was published posthumously (1705-7), as was a collection of other ***Posthumous Works*** (1706), of which the most substantial item was 'Of the Conduct of the Understanding', edited from an extensive and heavily amended manuscript which Locke had for some years been trying to finalize for incorporating as a very long additional chapter into the ***Essay***.

Objectives of the Essay

During the seventeenth century educated opinion in England—to some extent paralleled on the Continent—drifted from an admiring preoccupation with the history, literature, and language of the ancient world, especially Rome, and from Christian theology and ritual, logical formality, scholastic thought, and authoritarianism, towards, in various degrees of proximity, a confidence in the superiority of modern novelties and modern powers, reasonable religion and secular values, personal expression and plain style, a critical appeal to reason and the rule of sensible evidence, and individualistic, egalitarian freedom of practice, thought, and judgement. The ***Essay*** had this distinction, that in it Locke was a firm spokesman for all these currents at once, in association with an elaborated philosophy of mind and cognition. His progressive predecessors and contemporaries, such as Gilbert (1540-1603), Bacon (1561-1626), Hobbes, Descartes, Spinoza (1632-77), and Bayle (1647-1706), favoured only some of them while opposing others, or did not connect them with a general philosophy suited to propelling them further. The propagation of these currents was a significant part of Locke's purpose in the book, whose prefatory Epistles immediately reveal his attitude in regard to several of them.

Thus, he upheld novelty and the independence of individual judgement by saying that 'The Imputation of Novelty, is a terrible charge amongst those, who judge of Men's Heads, as they do of their Perukes, by the Fashion; and can allow none to be right, but the received Doctrines', and that the quest of the ***Essay*** 'is the Entertainment of those, who let loose their own Thoughts, and follow them in writing'. He stressed the vital role of the search and application of experienced fact in the accumulation and testing of truth; it is 'Trial and Examination must give [Truth] price, and not any antick Fashion'. He returned to these themes repeatedly; and with striking rhetoric near the end of the book he launched attacks on both those who dictate opinions and those who submissively follow them, and de-

rided the suffering of 'the learned Professor' whose 'Authority . . . [is] overturned by an upstart Novelist' ('Novelist' = 'innovator').

He also, influentially, complimented the attainments of the commonwealth of learning of his age, with its 'Master-Builders, whose mighty Designs, in advancing the Sciences, will leave lasting Monuments to the Admiration of Posterity', and blamed the 'learned but frivolous use of uncouth, affected, or unintelligible Terms, introduced into the Sciences' and 'Vague and insignificant Forms of Speech, and Abuse of Language, [which] have so long passed for Mysteries of Science' for the earlier lack of progress. These and other remarks of his soon, and have often since, struck readers as implying that the only profitable intellectual pathway to the knowledge of things is through observational, experimental, and mathematical methods, the only alternative being idle, verbal speculation. And on top of this Locke seemed to boost the branches of learning that use those methods, by describing in very modest terms his philosophical tasks, of analysing the understanding and the pathology and purgation of language, as if they were merely subservient to the smooth advancement of such knowledge. But his turns of phrase here were an ironic masking of his priority of concern with conduct over scientific inquisitiveness. Accordingly, a philosophical inquiry into the nature and grounds of certainty was required above all to determine the application and scope of certainty in the most important cases, namely in religion and ethics.

A passage in the Epistle to the Reader narrates the origin of Locke's engagement with his philosophical tasks: some friends of his at a meeting in his apartment found themselves in difficulties on all sides in the course of their discussion on a subject very remote from that of the understanding; whereupon—Locke now involving himself—'it came into my Thoughts, that we took a wrong course; and that, before we set our selves upon Enquiries of that Nature, it was necessary to examine our own Abilities, and see, what Objects our Understandings were, or were not fitted to deal with'. A partial hint of the subject of the discussion was provided in I. i. 6-7, where after postulating that 'Our Business here is not to know all things, but those which concern our Conduct' . . . a view he shared with Nicole, he went on to explain that 'This was that which gave the first *Rise* to this Essay concerning the Understanding. For I thought that the first Step towards satisfying several Enquiries, the Mind of Man was very apt to run into, was, to take a Survey of our own Understandings, examine our own Powers, and see to what Things they were adapted. Till that was done I suspected we began at the wrong end', this common mistake resulting in the multiplication of irresolvable disputes and in complete scepticism. This throws light on the programme he had just stated: it is 'my *Purpose* to enquire into the Original, Certainty, and Extent of humane Knowledge; together, with the Grounds and Degrees of Belief, Opinion, and Assent . . . It is therefore worth while, to search out the *Bounds* between Opinion and Knowledge; and examine by what Measures, in things, whereof we have no certain Knowledge, we ought to regulate our Assent, and moderate our Perswasions'.

He readily assumed, because of his presupposed identification of what is in the mind and what may be consciously perceived, that an adequate ophthalmology of the eye of the understanding can be discovered by a process of self-examination. But Locke did not regard this as being an *a priori* science that could be completed and made certain once and for all, as Kant (1724-1804) was later to do in respect of his articulation of reason in the first *Critique*. Locke conceded his fallibility, admitting (too much for Kantian and post-Kantian tastes) the limitations and imperfections of his subject—the natural philosophy of mind and cognition, and semantics.

Locke's friend James Tyrrell (1642-1718), whose interests and views regarding politics and toleration were closely similar to Locke's, was present at the original meeting in Locke's apartment; he annotated the passage on the history of the *Essay* in the Epistle to the Reader, and recorded in his copy that the discussion had been about 'the Principles of morality, and reveald Religion'. These were not neglected in the *Essay;* but Locke's version of those principles underlay his text much more than they were his main explicit topics. His direct treatment of those principles here was occasional, and clearer in what it denied than what it affirmed. The innateness of moral principles was controverted in I. iii; the thesis that moral science is capable of demonstration, as well as mathematics is, was adumbrated more than once, although never worked out, despite repeated requests by another friend, the Irishman William Molyneux (1656-98); and an account of moral conditions and relations was included in II. xx-xxi and xxviii. 4-16. These last passages supplied all that Locke wanted to state in the *Essay* about the norms of conduct. The source of the highest of these norms is the divine law, 'whether promulgated to [Men] by the light of Nature, or the voice of Revelation. . . . by comparing them to this Law, it is, that Men judge of the most considerable *Moral Good or Evil* of their Actions; that is, whether as *Duties, or Sins,* they are like to procure them happiness, or misery, from the hands of the ALMIGHTY'. Locke was brief about this supreme matter because he, in part rightly and in part to avoid spoiling his case by the inclusion of controversial details, presumed his readers' awareness of the content of the moral life entailed by his references to 'the light of Nature', i.e. reason, which is 'natural *Revelation*', and to supernatural revelation in the Bible.

Revealed religion was discussed in two chapters (IV. xviii, xix), in which he restricted it, obliquely, to the Christian scriptures by his distrust and contempt of other pretensions to revelation, and rationalistically emphasized that no supposed revealed proposition can contradict our knowledge or reason. There had been anticipations of this distrust, contempt, and rationalism earlier in the Restoration by, amongst others, Joseph Glanvill (1636-80) in his essays on 'The Usefulness of Real Philosophy to Religion', 'The Agreement of Reason and Religion', and 'Anti-fanatical Religion and Free Philosophy'; and prior to the Restoration by Hobbes (*Leviathan,* III. xxxii). Those attitudes and standards prefigured the militant deism and atheism of the eighteenth century, which adopted them against the Christian scriptures too. Locke renewed his inquiry into the principles of revealed religion in his ***Reasonableness of Christianity***. In this, as is clear from its first paragraph, he advocated a historical empiricism, plainness of sense, and the rejection of systems of divinity with their 'learned, artificial, and forced senses' of expressions, in the understanding of the scriptures, which were for him, with his simple faith, designed by God 'for the instruction of the illiterate bulk of Mankind in the way to Salvation; and therefore generally and in necessary points to be understood in the plain direct meaning of the words and phrases, such as they may be supposed to have had in the mouths of the Speakers, who used them according to the Language of that Time and Country wherein they lived'. The considerations adduced here are analogous to or identical with fundamental grounds he utilized in the *Essay*. Locke did not labour to support them: they were what he built on and around.

Human Understanding

It has frequently happened to great philosophers that they have been in the grip of contrastive pairs of fundamental convictions, valuations, or orientations, and hence commonly that what they have constructed is itself riddled with inner clashes and tensions; thus Plato's conceptions of the soul as movement and life, and as allied to the Ideas which are unmoving and lifeless, were scarcely harmonious notions of reality, any more than were his conceptions that each Idea is a supreme reality and that the Ideas are sortally related in a hierarchical way; and underlying Kant's bifurcation of 'the starry heavens above and the moral law within' were his opposing principles about the regulated world of empirical appearances and the free world of spiritual values. Locke likewise was torn or driven in contrary directions. His committed antiscepticism was at odds with his chief epistemological stance, which was agnostic. His restriction of our proper business to knowledge of matters of conduct was, as perhaps he recognized and excused, curious in an author of a large epistemological book that was distinctly reticent, yet not agnostic, about our knowledge of such matters. His perceptual realism pulled against the idealism bound up with ways in which he persistently used the term 'idea' to stand for 'whatsoever is the Object of the

Understanding when a Man thinks', and against his corpuscularian conception of the nature of material things, together with his doctrine of secondary versus primary qualities. His rationalistic canon that 'Reason must be our last Judge and Guide in every Thing' was not readily convergent with his empiricist or his Christian convictions.

These illustrations should be complemented by another observation. In his constructive efforts Locke had to reconcile with one another his repudiation of sophistical speculation and the abuse of language, his wish to be instructive, and his urbane concern that his philosophical output be fit and able to be 'brought into well-bred Company, and polite Conversation' ('polite' = 'civilized'). The latter consideration imparts a new twist to the cause of plain simplicity of utterance advocated a generation or two earlier by preachers and by spokesmen linked with the Royal Society, with the aims—which Locke also shared—of securely effecting moral or scientific improvement. One symptom of his not always successful struggle is that he entitled the book an 'Essay' which suggested a personal, informal, descriptive work catering widely for the ordinary educated reader; and yet within the text he sometimes called it a 'Treatise', which connoted a more ponderous, systematic, and learned book.

One of the consequences of Locke's determination to be informal in the *Essay* was that he did not make clear near the beginning what he meant by the 'human understanding', and it was not until he reached II. vi. 2, after numerous, apparently synonymous references to 'the Mind' and 'the Understanding', that he turned, in passing, to elucidate these terms and the relation between their designations. He distinguished, following tradition, between the 'two great and principal Actions of the Mind', which are perception or thinking, and volition. The understanding—the term corresponded to the Latin *intellectus,* 'intellect'—is the mind's faculty, power, or ability to think; volition is the mind's faculty, power, or ability to will. Locke showed, at II. xxi. that he was aware of some problems about the meaning and use of 'faculty'; but he did not dwell on them. The term 'the Mind' is usually applied in the *Essay* to represent only the understanding. Further, this intellectual faculty is not uniform, but is exercised in a variety of ways, among them contemplating, remembering, distinguishing, comparing, compounding, abstracting, reasoning, judging, knowing, and believing.

With a stab at Descartes's school, Locke excluded the passions, e.g. desire, love, hatred, and anger, from the faculty of volition. He described desire, feeling, and emotion as variants of pleasure or pain, which are states of the understanding. Not surprisingly in view of his medical interests, he assigned an important place in the life of the mind to the passions, especially to what he called uneasiness, 'All pain of the body of what sort soever, and disquiet of the mind'. It is uneasiness alone that determines the will; nevertheless, as Locke insisted in 'Of the Conduct of the Understanding' with Socratic intellectualism, the will 'never fails in its Obedience to the Dictates of the Understanding'. Hence a man's thoughts bear a responsible precedence in him as a cognitive and as an active agent. But neither the understanding nor the will are more than powers: 'it is the Mind that operates, and exerts these Powers; it is the Man that does the Action, . . . or is able to do'.

Why was the title of the *Essay* chosen to refer to 'human understanding'? The epithet 'human' made clear that the book was about man and not about the understanding belonging to God, angelic spirits, or 'intellectual corporeal Beings, infinitely different from those of our little spot of Earth' elsewhere in the universe. The term 'understanding' was more appropriate than 'mind' or 'soul' partly because Locke's inquiry was principally epistemological and partly because it was directly concerned just with conscious perceptions or thoughts, and these are precisely the extension of the understanding; mentality outside the understanding is pertinent only inasmuch as it gives rise to acts or objects of the understanding; e.g. the discussion of the will, liberty, and necessity in II. xxi is relevant to the subject of the understanding inasmuch as the latter has ideas of them.

Locke classified the understanding's acts of perception into three types; only the last two match our usual sense of 'to understand'. There are perceptions of *'Ideas in our Minds'*, of the signification of signs, and of 'the Connexion or Repugnancy, Agreement or Disagreement' between our ideas; he took stock of these three sorts chiefly in Books II, III, and IV, respectively. He first investigated the origin of the ideas in our minds. He maintained that the individual's experience in 'Observation employ'd either about *external, sensible Objects; or about the internal Operations'* of its own *'perceived and reflected on'* by itself is that which supplies it *'with all the materials of thinking'*, a principle he pursued through Book II in reference not only to ideas thus plausibly derived from sense-experience or reflection, but also to ideas, e.g. of space, time, number, infinity, and causality, which were a much sterner test of his hypothesis, this being, he trusted, all the more strongly confirmed by his empirical accounting of them. His assumptions, arguments, and conclusions in this connection were soon disputed, notably by Leibniz (1646-1714), first in personal communications to Locke and then in his long *Nouveaux essais sur l'entendement humain*. Perhaps Leibniz's most effective criticism resulted from deploying his doctrine of subconscious thought, the very possibility of which Locke had repeatedly rejected out of hand. Locke denied that we were born into the world with any completed or incorrigible knowledge, or with any of its conceptual constituents; whether pertaining to the nature of things or to our conduct, an elimination he sought to justify in the main run of chapters of Book I, whose concluding chapter, against innate ideas (as distinct from innate principles, which he had already dealt with), afforded a suitable transition to Book II.

Locke's epistemology is notoriously a 'way of ideas': 'Having *Ideas,* and Perception [are] the same thing'; ''Tis evident, the Mind knows not Things immediately, but only by the intervention of the *Ideas* it has of them'. . . . What exactly these intervening 'ideas' are, and whether experience can be satisfactorily resolved into them or so-called ideas of other sorts, are among Locke's immediate difficulties. Our general knowledge of things has two branches in his account—which runs in two divergent directions. He has a conventionalist (apriorist) view of knowledge regarding our human concepts of the essences of things: 'Truths belonging to Essences of Things, (that is, to abstract *Ideas*) are eternal, and are to be found out by the contemplation only of those Essences'. But he has at the same time an empiricist (aposteriorist) view of other aspects of the knowledge of things. First, the existence of things is to be known only from experience. Secondly, the knowledge of the coexistences of qualities of a (sort of) substance is limited by our mind's inabilities to conceive connections and depends on experience,

> since we neither know the real Constitution of the minute Parts, on which their Qualities do depend; nor, did we know them, could we discover any necessary *connexion* between them, and any of the *secondary Qualities:* which is necessary to be done, before we can certainly know their *necessary co-existence.* . . . Our Knowledge in all these Enquiries, reaches very little farther than our Experience. . . . we are left only to the assistance of our Senses, to make known to us, what Qualities [Substances] contain. For of all the Qualities that are *co-existent* in any Subject, without this dependence and evident connexion of their *Ideas* one with another, we cannot know certainly any two to *co-exist* any farther, than Experience, by our Senses, informs us.

For this and related reasons he maintains that inquiries into the nature of things have exceedingly limited prospects of attaining the status of strict science.

Since Locke, epistemology and the philosophy of science (and the philosophy of mathematics) have strained at the problem of the conflict between conventionalism and empiricism in respect of general knowledge, either by eliminating one of the alternatives—conventionalism at the cost of certainty, or even rational probability; empiricism at the cost of meaningfulness, verifiability, or innovation—or by trying to show how they can be reconciled. This is one of many Lockian problems which have continued to attract philosophers' vigorous, and, happily, increasingly rigorous attention. . . .

John W. Yolton (essay date 1977)

SOURCE: An introduction to *An Essay Concerning Human Understanding,* edited by John W. Yolton, Dent, 1977, pp. ix-xxxi.

[*In the following essay, Yolton discusses the primary philosophical issues and concepts addressed by Locke in Book I of* An Essay Concerning Human Understanding. *He emphasizes Locke's expansive treatment of scientific concepts and problems associated with diverse fields of study including ethics, linguistics, psychology, logic, and theology.*]

In 1671 Locke began to write what became his *Essay concerning Human Understanding,* first published in 1690. During those intervening years the *Essay* went through many drafts, many starts and stops. In letters to friends he discussed some of the problems he confronted during its composition. He himself describes the work as having been 'written by incoherent parcels' ('Epistle to the Reader'). He recognized that what he referred to as, 'This discontinued way of writing may have occasioned, besides others, two faults, viz. that too little and too much be said in it'. He admits that 'possibly it might be reduced to a narrower compass than it is, and that some parts of it might be contracted: the ways it has been writ in, by catches and many long intervals of interruption, being apt to cause some repetitions'. He claimed, however, that he was 'now too lazy, or too busy, to make it shorter'.

When John Wynne, an Oxford tutor, wrote to Locke in 1694 about an abridgment he had begun for his own students, Locke replied in the tones of these remarks from the 'Epistle to the Reader'. He agreed with Wynne that perhaps a shortened version might help to overcome some of the adverse reactions the *Essay* had received. Wynne's published abridgment was essentially a précis, for the most part in Wynne's own words, of what Locke said on various topics and in the different chapters. There were, in the eighteenth and early nineteenth centuries, a number of other abridgments, outlines, synopses of Locke's *Essay,* usually, like Wynne's, designed for the use of students. One interesting book, not purporting to be an abridgment of Locke but one which does come close to being a detailed paraphrase (in many places an almost verbatim reproduction) of Locke's *Essay,* was William Duncan's *The Elements of Logic* (1748). This logic had several reprintings in the century: it was widely read and used.

Duncan's logic, one of a number of indigenous British logics in the eighteenth century, indicates the strength of Locke's influence in that century. These Lockean logics, together with the *Essay* itself, were used by students at Oxford. Jeremy Bentham read Locke while at Oxford. Later, writing to John Lind, Bentham remarked: 'Without Locke I could have known nothing.

But I think I could now take Locke's Essay and write it over again, so as to make it much more precise and apprehensible in half the compass.' [1] Bentham's reaction is probably typical of many readers of Locke. . . .

There is, within the **Essay** itself, a kind of abridgment, an outline or overview. Book I of that work has usually been known for its polemic against innate ideas and principles. But, in fact, that book contains more comment on and appeals to Locke's own positive doctrines than it does negative attacks against innatism. It is a rather cogent foreshadowing of the main doctrines elaborated in the three following books. An examination of those doctrines in the context of Book I can serve as an effective introduction to the study of Locke. Concentrating on what Book I reveals about Locke's views has one other advantage: by placing his own views in the context of those he rejected, we may escape some of the preconceived notions about what he says, which so many of his subsequent readers have brought to their study of Locke.[2] It is often useful, when we seek an understanding of a philosophic text, to pay attention to the doctrines which the author attacks or rejects. What he writes against may be more informative of his own doctrines than are his statements of the alternatives. The first book of Locke's **Essay** is important for just this reason.

1 LOCKE AND INNATISM

While a certain aspect of the theory of innateness has recently been revived by Chomsky, lending perhaps more timeliness to Locke's polemic against innateness in Book I, the doctrine Locke opposed seems to us too naïve to take seriously.[3] The 'established opinion amongst some men' in seventeenth-century Britain was, Locke tells us, 'that there are in the *understanding* certain *innate principles,* some primary notions, . . . characters, as it were, stamped upon the mind of man, which the soul receives in its very first being and brings into the world with it' (1.2.1).[4] Metaphors of 'red letters emblazoned on the heart', of marks on the soul, were, for many of Locke's contemporaries, devices for articulating non-conventional, non-relative moral standards.[5] These metaphors were also ways of referring to maxims from which certain knowledge could be derived. Locke took these metaphors seriously, he pushed the defenders of innatism to justify their claims (e.g. by showing that in fact there are principles universally accepted). He insisted that they clarify whether or not they meant that no experience or reason is necessary for the recognition of the truth of such principles. Locke produced sociological and anthropological evidence to reject the claims of universal acceptance.[6] If the holders of this doctrine of innateness claimed that the principles said to be innate were accepted only after reason or experience had intervened, then, Locke pointed out, a great number—in fact, an indefinite number—of principles and maxims could claim to be innate: all the

truths of mathematics, for example. Locke offered a stronger objection still to innatism, an objection which reveals an important psychological principle of his own. 'To say a notion is imprinted on the mind, and yet at the same time to say that the mind is ignorant of it and never yet took notice of it, is to make this impression nothing' (1.2.5). This psychological truth is almost a conceptual truth: 'it seeming to me near a contradiction to say that there are truths imprinted on the soul which it perceives or understands not'.

This principle, that what is in my mind must be conscious to me, underlies Locke's accounts of awareness and of the nature of ideas. I shall return to it later. It is important here to note that this principle is announced and used in the first book of the **Essay**. By seeing against which alternative account of ideas it is invoked, we can gain some appreciation of the doctrine of ideas in Locke's theory of knowledge. But there are two other aspects of the polemic against innateness which we must examine first.

The particular version of innateness to which Locke objects is of less importance for understanding his own doctrines than are the specific uses to which appeals to innateness were made. There were two specific uses: the one was to provide a basis for morality, in truths common to all mankind; the other was to provide certain primitive notions, basic truths (those Locke called 'speculative principles') which were said to be necessary in accounting for the possibility or actuality of knowledge. To this second use Locke insisted that knowledge is derived from experience, rather than principles.

2 PRINCIPLES OF KNOWLEDGE

Locke was of course aware that in challenging this latter use of innateness he was going against a widely held belief. The way to knowledge was thought to be by means of demonstration from self-evident maxims. The principles Locke mentions (those 'magnified principles of demonstration') are, 'Whatsoever is, is'; 'it is impossible for the same thing to be and not to be'; 'the same is not different'. There were writers who claimed[7] that any identity proposition had to be derived from the general principle of identity, that to know and accept a proposition that, for example (these are Locke's examples), 'green is not red' or that the nurse 'is neither the *cat* it [the child] plays with nor the *blackamoor* it is afraid of', or 'mustard is not an apple', the child must know the general principle that 'it is impossible for the same thing to be and not to be' (1.2.25). We do not acquire our knowledge of the world by working from such general principles. They are 'the language and business of the schools and academies of learned nations, accustomed to that sort of conversation or learning, where disputes are frequent, these maxims being suited to artificial argumentation and useful for conviction, but not much conducing to the discovery of truth or ad· icement of knowledge' (1.2.27).

In Locke's view, we learn all such general propositions after we have acquired specific ideas and understood the meanings of words. As the child acquires his stock of ideas, he learns, without of course formulating it thus, that each idea is what it is and not another idea (1.2.23). Whenever we consider any proposition, 'so as to perceive the two *ideas* signified by the terms and affirmed or denied one of the other, to be the same or different', we are 'presently and infallibly certain of the truth of such a proposition, and this equally whether these propositions be in terms standing for more general *ideas,* or such as are less so, v.g. whether the general *idea* of *being* be affirmed of itself, as in this proposition, *Whatsoever is, is;* or a more particular *idea* be affirmed of itself, as *A man is a man'* (4.7.4). It is the difference of the ideas which, 'as soon as the terms are understood, makes the truth of the proposition presently visible'. The whole of Chapters VII and VIII of Book IV constitutes an extended attack on the scholastic maxim that, 'All reasonings are *ex praecognitis et praeconcessis'* (4.7.8). These chapters are also attacks upon the method of disputation used in the Examination Schools at Oxford, in which syllogisms were freely constructed using general maxims about whole and part, same and difference. No one who is unaware of the pervasive use of this scholastic method of arguing, and of the disdain many people such as Locke had for the frivolity of the disputations at Oxford, can fully appreciate the vehemence of Locke's rejection of the syllogism and such maxims. Knowledge is not, he insisted, acquired by reasoning from general principles, nor is the syllogism a logic of discovery. Against the appeal to maxims, Locke offered his account of the acquisition and understanding of ideas. Against the use of the syllogism, he offered his notion of demonstration as conceptual clarification. His polemic in Book I against innate speculative principles is thus closely related to important doctrines of his own about the nature of knowledge: acquisition of ideas through experience stands in stark opposition to derivation of knowledge from innate (or merely accepted) general principles.

3 MORAL ACTION AND RULES

The other use made of the doctrine of innateness was as a claim for universal moral truths. Locke has an easy time establishing that societies vary in what they accept as moral rules or practices. But a more important objection to innate practical principles is that such principles are not, as are speculative ones, self-evident. Moral principles 'require reasoning and discourse, and some exercise of the mind' (1.3.1). We can always justifiably demand a reason for any moral rule (1.3.4). The truth of moral rules 'plainly depends upon some other, antecedent to them and from which they must be

deduced'. The sort of reasoning and discourse required for moral rules may be demonstration; it is at least a form of conceptual analysis. Before we look more closely at Locke's view of moral reasoning, we need to consider several other aspects of his discussion of innate practical principles.

First of all, we should note that, in one sense of 'practical', Locke recognizes some innate, non-learned principles. A desire for happiness and an aversion to misery are 'innate practical principles which (as practical principles ought) do continue constantly to operate and influence all our actions' (1.3.3). It is 'Nature' that has put into all men these principles, these 'natural tendencies'.[8] Locke even borrows from the innatist's vocabulary and speaks of these tendencies being 'imprinted on the minds of men'. What Locke rejects are 'characters on the mind, which are to be the principles of knowledge, regulating our practice'. The desire for happiness and the aversion to misery are 'principles of action . . . lodged in our appetites'. Not only are they not innate rules, they are not even moral. If 'left to their full swing, they would carry men to the overturning of all morality' (1.3.13). The function of moral laws is to curb and restrain 'these exorbitant desires'.

For Locke, moral action must be rule-following, at least rule-conforming. He makes an important distinction between the *description* of an action as, for example, drunkenness, and the *appraisal* of that action as good, bad, or indifferent. For appraisal, we must refer the description to a rule (2.28.15). Locke recognized that we frequently combine these features (the descriptive or positive feature with the evaluative feature), using the same word to 'express both the mode or action and its moral rectitude or obliquity' (2.28.16). There are three different types of rules to which men refer their actions for appraisal: the divine law, civil law, and the law of opinion or reputation (what he sometimes calls the 'law of fashion or private censure') (2.28.7, 13). He knew that 'virtue' is most commonly taken 'for those actions which according to the different opinions of several countries are accustomed laudable' (1.3.18). Custom is, in fact, 'a greater power than nature' (1.3.25), the principles or rules acquired in our childhood from 'the superstition of a nurse or the authority of an old woman' stay with us and, unless we later become self-critical, these principles become accepted as the standards for action (1.3.22). The force of custom and our fear of discovering that rules we have always taken as sound may have an origin in superstition, lead us to follow the received opinion of our country or party (1.3.25).[9] The difficulties of being critical about rules for our actions are greatly increased if we mistakenly believe our rules to be 'the standard set up by God'.

In these passages of Book I, Locke indicates how it is that 'it comes to pass that *men* worship the idols that have been set up in their minds' (1.3.26). Locke was concerned not only that we mistake as innate, rules which are not innate, but also that we mistake as God's rules those which only have the force of custom behind them. The true ground of morality 'can only be the will and law of a god, who sees men in the dark, has in his hand rewards and punishments, and power enough to call to account the proudest offender' (1.3.6). *'To do as one would be done to'* is 'the great principle of morality' (1.3.7). The principle is described as 'that most unshaken rule of morality and foundation of all social virtue' (1.3.4). Locke makes the general point that 'what duty is cannot be understood without a law, nor a law be known or supposed without a law maker, or without reward and punishment'. It is clear, from numerous passages in Book I and later, that for Locke, the law-maker is God, the reward and punishment is eternal damnation or happiness, and the law against which we should measure all our actions is God's law (see, e.g., 1.3.12, 13). God's law—which he also refers to as the law of nature—is not innate or 'imprinted on our minds in their very originals'. The law of nature is 'something that we, being ignorant of, may attain to the knowledge of, by the use and due application of our natural faculties' (1.3.13).

How can we use our natural faculties to attain the true rule for moral action? In those essays written while Locke was Moral Censor at Christ Church in 1664 (the *Essays on the Law of Nature*) he argues that we at least can, by experience and reason, arrive at 'the notion of the maker of nature'. Once we have this notion, 'the notion of a universal law of nature binding on all men necessarily emerges'. The arguments for a god to which Locke makes reference in these early *Essays* are obviously a variation of the argument from design, an argument derived, as he there says, 'from the matter, motion, and the visible structure and arrangement of this world'. It is, he says, 'surely undisputed that' the beauty, order, and structure of the world 'could not have come together casually and by chance into so regular and in every respect so perfect and ingeniously prepared a structure' (p. 153).[10] We reach the second of the above conclusions—that there is a universal law binding on all men—by an appeal to teleology: God has not created the world 'for nothing and without purpose' (p. 157).[11]

So far, Locke has produced arguments showing how we can reach by reason the conclusion that there is a law-maker who 'intends man to do something'. Can he show, by reason and discourse, how we can discover what it is God intends us to do? Locke's answers are not exactly evasive in these early *Essays,* but he does not produce any specific rules. He thinks, for example, that 'from the end in view for all things', we can discover that, since God is gracious, wise, and perfect, he intends us to glorify God (p. 157). Since man 'is neither made without design nor endowed to no purpose

with these faculties . . . his functions appear to be that which nature has prepared him to perform', that is, to contemplate God's works and his wisdom. Man also 'feels himself not only to be impelled by life's experience and pressing needs to procure and preserve a life in society with other men, but also to be urged to enter into society by a certain propensity of nature, and to be prepared for the maintenance of society by the gift of speech' (p. 157). He makes a few other claims for the law of nature, for example, that it forbids 'us to offend or injure without cause any private person' (p. 163); but he makes no attempt to reason to such specific conclusions. There are many anticipations in these *Essays* of claims and arguments advanced in his later published works, especially in the *Essay* and *Two Treatises*. On the basis of these early *Essays,* the best we can do to establish the nature of moral reasoning is to say, if we accept the argument from design, that reason provides us with what Locke later called the true ground of morality, that is, God as a universal law-maker, who can reward and punish, etc.

There are, in the published works of Locke, various specific rules cited as laws of nature; but his defence of these as laws of nature, not just laws of custom, is not really any stronger than the innatist's defence of his principles. I think that Locke did not much disagree with the sort of moral rules cited by the innatists. What he wanted to do was to attack their claim that these rules are innate. He claimed that the precepts of natural religion are 'plain and very intelligible to all mankind' and that they are seldom controverted (3.9.23), but his claim that we should be able to derive the true measure of right and wrong by going from self-evident propositions to necessary consequences (4.3.18) was never exemplified. It is not entirely clear what he understood by the notion of a demonstrative morality. Did he intend a proper formal deduction of specific rules from some general premise, perhaps from the premise that there is a God? If so, he attempted no such demonstration. He may have thought that such a derivation of moral rules could be made, but perhaps his notion of demonstration would take a different form. There is good evidence in the *Essay* that, by 'demonstrative', Locke (like Descartes) understood a movement of thought much more informal and intuitive.[12] He speaks of ideas placed in an order permitting us to compare them and reach new ideas (1.4.23), of the understanding seeing the agreement or disagreement of ideas when they are so ordered (4.8.3), of the juxtaposition of ideas (4.13.1); and he has a sustained and forceful attack on the formal logic of his day, the syllogism (see, e.g., 4.17.4). If all reasoning proceeds by the understanding's seeing the relation between ideas and then moving through a series, the moral reasoning which he thought essential for all moral rules may have been a species of conceptual analysis, an exposition of the interrelations of our moral concepts. If he was so convinced of what the specific laws of nature were, no other demonstration would have been required.

4 THE DISCOVERY OF TRUTH

We have seen thus far how Locke uses his attack against the innatists as a means of introducing his own alternative claims. Not only are there no innate speculative maxims, knowledge cannot proceed by invoking the standard logical principles of identity and contradiction, or by any other self-evident principle. Knowledge is a product of experience and observation, aided by reason. There are no innate moral rules, moral rules are not self-evident, they can only be reached by reason. There *are* universal rules of action, but they are not universally accepted or acted upon. God is the author of these rules, but he has not stamped them on our minds: he has rather given us the faculties for discovering them. In a parallel fashion, the final chapter of Book I is an attack against the notion of innate *ideas* (the constituents of principles), but it also provides Locke with a forum for some important groundwork on the nature and origin of ideas.

There may be something of the Puritan work ethic in Locke's repeated assurances that God not only intends us to act, but he intends us to use our faculties to discover truth and attain knowledge. He did not have the confidence of a Descartes in the unlimited knowledge available to us. He was convinced that our knowledge is limited, but we can learn all we need for this life. Just as we should not be enticed by the sceptic into giving up the search for knowledge,[13] so we should not seek the easy way by looking for innate knowledge, for which we need expend no energy. Our faculties of knowledge and understanding are more than ample, once we discover where are the limits to human knowledge, and duly apply ourselves to discovering truth. Even the idea of God, the one idea we might think was imprinted on our souls, must be acquired by experience and reason. God has fitted us with faculties to attain this and other ideas; 'It is want of industry and consideration in us and not of bounty in him if we' do not acquire those ideas within our capabilities (1.4.17). His repeated assertion is that *'knowledge depends upon the right use of those powers nature hath bestowed on us';* knowledge does not depend upon innate principles.

How should we employ our faculties in the attainment of truth? Locke's firm answer is: we must not trust authority, even in the area of geometrical truth. We must ourselves examine the demonstrations, we must understand how the conclusion follows from the definitions, axioms, and prior demonstrations. For other truths, truths of the world, we must seek them 'in the fountain, *in the consideration of things themselves'* (1.4.24. Cf. 1.4.21). Each of us must make truth and knowledge his own. Especially in the sciences, 'everyone has so much as he really knows and comprehends: what he believes only and takes upon trust are but

shreds; which, however well in the whole piece, make no considerable addition to his stock who gathers them. Such borrowed wealth, like fairy-money, though it were gold in the hand from which he received it, will be but leaves and dust when it comes to use' (1.4.24). Locke was not so much concerned with the details of methods in science, as he was interested in urging men to attend to and to consider 'the being of things themselves' (1.4.25). He was also concerned (and this was the task he set himself as an under-labourer to the great scientists) to lay the foundations for an account of scientific knowledge. Convinced that there are no innate principles or propositions, it follows that there are no innate ideas, ideas being the constituents of propositions. He had, then, to show how we acquire ideas, and how we form propositions true of the world. He used Descartes' term, 'adventitious truths', to contrast with 'innate' (1.4.23). Book II contains his programme of the acquisition of ideas, but in Book I we find some outlines of that programme. In particular, we find a discussion of the origin of ideas in children: Locke works with a rudimentary genetic psychology.

New-born children do not, Locke thinks, 'bring many *ideas* into the world with them' (1.4.2). They do very likely have experience of hunger, thirst, warmth and perhaps pain in the womb, resulting from their experiences there. Subsequently, other ideas arise from experience and observation. As the range of things with which the child comes into contact increases, so his stock of ideas is enlarged (1.4.13). By retaining ideas in their memories, by learning to 'compound and enlarge them, and several ways put them together', children extend their thoughts.[14] Locke was particularly anxious to point out that the ideas of impossibility and identity are late acquisitions (even some grown men lack them), for these are the ideas necessary for those speculative principles the innatists cited. Moreover, the child learns to distinguish its mother from a stranger well before it learns principles of identity or contradiction (1.4.3). To have an idea of identity would enable us to solve, at least to formulate, some of those puzzles about the sameness of a man which trouble Locke in his long chapter on identity and diversity (2.27). Here, in Book I, he cites some of those puzzles (1.4.4. Cf.2.1.12). At least, if the identity of the same was innate, we would have a clear understanding of how identity is affected if the same soul can inhabit two bodies, and of what would constitute the same man at the resurrection (1.4.5). The idea of identity, then, is not innate or early and easily acquired.[15]

5 TWO CONCEPTS OF IDEAS

One of the more pervasive concepts in the whole of the *Essay* is that of *idea*. Locke was careful to include in Book I several statements about ideas which were most important for his use of that term. These statements were written with the innatist in mind, who worked with a different notion of idea. I have already referred to Locke's remark, in 1.2.5, that to have an idea in the mind but not to be conscious of that idea is impossible. He reverts to this claim in 1.4.2. There, he says that the only way in which there could be ideas in the mind 'which the mind does not actually think on' is if those ideas are in the memory. He formulates his general principle about ideas and awareness as follows: 'Whatever *idea* is in the mind is either an actual perception or else, having been an actual perception, is so in the mind that by the memory it can be made an actual perception again.' This principle, that 'what is not either actually in view, or in the memory, is in the mind no way at all', had for Locke a direct bearing upon a question which the innatists thought important: what is the nature of ideas? The innatists' only possible answer to this question is that ideas are either substances or modes; if substances, then either material or spiritual. One of the earliest attacks against Locke's polemic was written by John Norris, an English follower of the Cartesian Malebranche. For Norris, ideas are real beings, spiritual entities.[16] Locke penned a reply to Norris, the first draft of which has recently been published.[17] In that draft, Locke complains that, 'If you once mention ideas you must be presently called to an account *what kind of things you make these same ideas to be* though perhaps you have no design to consider them any further than as *the immediate objects of perception* or if you have you find they are a sort of sullen things which will only show them what but will not tell you whence they came nor whither they go nor what they are made of.'[18] Two points are worth noting in this remark. First, that Locke only wanted to consider ideas as epistemic objects; secondly, that the ontological consideration of ideas tells us nothing about the important features of ideas: their origin, their make-up, their role in knowledge. Locke's concern was with the second of these points; for that, the consideration of ideas as epistemic objects was sufficient. But there is a more important issue embedded in Locke's remark to Norris: a definite view of the nature of ideas, echoed in many passages in his remarks on Malebranche, in a later draft of his reply to Norris, and in many passages in the ***Essay***. This view was commented upon in an important tract, published anonymously in 1705, *A Philosophick Essay concerning Ideas*.

The author of this tract said that 'Thought and Idea are the same thing', and showed how this account of ideas can be derived from a few definitions, the main two being (1) the definition of 'idea' as 'the Representation of something in the mind' and (2) 'a Representation of something in the mind, and to frame such a Representation of an Object, is to Think'. This author notes that Locke sometimes speaks of ideas as the *objects* of thought, as if ideas are something different from thought; but he takes as Locke's considered statement the passage in 2.1.9, that to have ideas and to perceive are the same. In that passage, Locke gives as the answer, to the question 'at what time does a man first

have any ideas?', 'when he begins to perceive; having *ideas* and perception being the same thing'. In 2.1.5, the ideas of sensible qualities are described as 'all those different perceptions' external objects produce in us. In 2.10.2, he speaks of 'our *ideas* being nothing but actual perceptions in the mind'. The author of this tract considers the definition of ideas as the representation of something to the mind to be a neutral position between the two views of ideas: ideas as 'a Modification of the Mind' or as 'a Distinct Being, or Substance United to the Mind'. The more common view is, he says, the former: ideas 'are not *Real Beings*, but only *Modes of Thinking* upon the several objects presented to the Mind; or if you please, it is the Mind itself operating after *such* and *such* a Manner, just as the Roundness of a Body, and its Motion are nothing but the Body itself figur'd and translated after such and such a Sort'.

This author's recognition of Locke's attempt to use ideas in his theory of knowledge without making them into entities is an indication that he viewed Locke working amid a running battle of some of the Cartesians over the nature of ideas. The insistence that ideas are acts of thought, that to have an idea and to be conscious are the same, was a position taken by Arnauld in his dispute with Malebranche.[19] For Malebranche, ideas were the case of ideas which are resemblances of qualities, for example, size, figure, solidity, he did not think this physiological account explained how perceptions arise out of the motion of animal spirits.[20] He took over the physiology of animal spirits from Descartes and Malebranche, who had given it a detailed analysis. Animal spirits were useful intermediaries between mind and body, for they were less material than solid corpuscles. By means of these spirits we were also thought to move our limbs, although no writer, including Locke, who employed this physiology, professed to understand how we could activate the animal spirits in the brain.

Even though Malebranche used this physiology of animal spirits, he made God the efficient cause of the motion of objects and of our perceptions. Man and external objects are the passive, occasional causes of perceptions: when certain physical motions occur, we have perceptions of a specific sort. Locke believed there was a causal connection between objects and perceptions, just as he believed we have causal power to move our bodies. Thus, when he says that 'the objects of our senses do, many of them, obtrude their particular *ideas* upon our minds whether we will or no', and that the mind in these circumstances 'is merely passive' (2.1.25), he does not mean to make the mind passive in Malebranche's sense, unconnected causally with objects. He used the metaphor of the mind as 'white paper, void of all characters' (2.1.2) as a way of stressing his alternative to innateness. The innate theory located the causal relation between God and our mind, not between objects and our mind. For Locke, we are born into a world 'surrounded with bodies that perpetually and diversely affect' us (2.1.6). Whether 'care be taken about it or no', a variety of ideas 'are imprinted on the minds of children'. Without the relevant sense-object, ideas will not arise; for example, we cannot *fancy* a taste which our palate has never had, nor 'frame the *idea* of a scent' we have never smelt (2.2.2).

In general, then, sense experience provides the necessary conditions for perceptions or ideas. A child's acquisition of more and more ideas is compared with his becoming awake (2.1.22). Once the child has a stock of ideas, he begins to enlarge, compound, and abstract his ideas, and to reason about them. Perception, remembering, considering, reasoning, abstracting, enlarging are just a few of the activities the mind engages in while extending its range of ideas. The mental faculties are a most important ingredient in the metaphorical white paper; waiting for the characters to be imprinted, these faculties soon rush ahead and extend the mind's ideas. Experience for Locke is also internal, in the sense of being directed towards the sensory ideas, as well as the operations of the mind. By attending to our perceiving, recalling, reasoning, we acquire ideas of these activities. By means of some of these operations the mind also acquires more sophisticated ideas, such as those of solidity, space, existence, unity, power, cause. The derivation programme for ideas laid out in Book II is complex and involved, far different from the rather mechanical adding and abstracting which Locke's talk of simple and complex ideas seems to suggest. We should not be misled by his talk of white paper, passivity, imprinting, enlarging.

Locke's account of the formation of the idea of power is not atypical of his derivation programme. In that account, the idea of power emerges after the mind has *taken notice* of the way some things and events cease to be and others begin; has *reflected* on its own change of ideas; has *concluded* that 'like changes will for the future be made in the same things, by like agents, and by the like ways'; and has *considered* 'in one thing the possibility of having any of its simple *ideas* changed, and in another the possibility of making that change' (2.21.1). These mental operations of considering, concluding, reflecting themselves cloak some fundamental assumptions about change and the course of nature, but the account they enable Locke to give of the origin of the idea of power is hardly amenable to the compositionalism frequently credited to Locke, or to the notion of a passive mind commentators sometimes attribute to him.

7 QUALITIES, POWERS AND PARTICLES

In our examination of some of the doctrines of the *Essay,* as they are foreshadowed in Book I, we have come across a number of metaphysical beliefs Locke used: the existence of God; laws of nature established by God for moral action; an orderly, purposive universe; the workings of a specific physiology with its causal antecedents in objects and events; a world around us which activates our perceptual processes (both physiological and psychological). Locke's account of the workings of the mind was based upon what he discovered when he reflected upon his own experience. Convinced that the innatist's account of how the mind discovers moral rules was wrong, that that account was also wrong on how knowledge is or should be obtained, and that the innatist's notion of the contents of the mind as entities was misleading and unnecessary, Locke's alternative account of knowledge and understanding was not divorced from fundamental metaphysical beliefs. He thought that some of these beliefs, for example, of a god, of a purposive universe, of laws of nature, could be reached by reason and experience. Thus, some at least of these beliefs would conform to his general programme for the derivation of ideas. Some other beliefs, for example, in the corpuscular account of matter and in the physiology of perception, he recognized as hypothetical. He very likely thought that Boyle's work in chemistry supported the corpuscular theory of matter.[21] That theory also had general acceptance in the seventeenth century.

The corpuscular theory viewed matter as consisting of insensible particles. The qualities of matter—both in aggregate, sensible states and in particulate, insensible states—were solidity, extension, figure, motion or rest, and number (2.8.9). On this theory, matter also had *powers,* the power to affect and change the constitution of corpuscles in other bits of matter, as fire melts wax or clay, and the power to produce changes in our nerves and brain which in turn give rise to ideas or perceptions (2.8.10). Matter is not, on this theory, coloured, hot, or odoriferous. Some of what we take to be properties of objects—colour, taste, sound, smell—are in fact not properties of objects: they are the result of the powers objects possess to affect our sense organs in specific ways, by the diverse 'motion and figure, bulk and number' of their particles. Locke is not very clear on the status of the powers of matter, but he does talk of powers *belonging* to matter.[22] Presumably, matter has these powers even when it is not manifesting them. Thus, in the absence of sensation, there will be no light or sound, no tastes or smells; but the particular bulk, figure, and motion of the parts of matter would still have the power to cause these sensations in a perceiver (2.8.17). Heat and cold, for example, are 'nothing but the increase or diminution of the motion of the minute parts of our bodies' (the animal spirits); but the difference between the powers of matter and its extension, figure, or motion is that these latter are always present and manifested in matter, while the powers are actualized only when a perceiver is affected by the particles, or when one body is affected by another (2.8.22). Locke's list of the qualities of body (2.8.23) contains both kinds of qualities: those that are always present (the occurrent qualities) and the powers (the dispositional qualities—Locke calls them 'potentialities' in 2.23.7).

The specification of qualities of body to include powers, as well as bulk, figure, number, motion, etc., is meant by Locke as an indication of the nature of matter. He also offers it in the context of his distinction between *qualities* of objects and *ideas* we have of the qualities of objects. We have two sorts of ideas of qualities. The one sort is of the powers of objects. In this case, we normally think our ideas are of qualities, not of powers. That is, we normally think this desk is brown, that cherry sweet. We also of course take the desk to be rectangular and solid, the cherry to be spherical. We have, in short, ideas or perceptions of those qualities which the corpuscular theory says belong to matter always and actually, and those which this theory tells us are only the powers matter has in virtue of the action of its extended, movable, solid particles. Both these sorts of ideas are caused by the same corpuscular and physiological processes. Both kinds of qualities compose the objects around us. Gold, for example, is yellow, but it is also malleable, fusible in fire, and soluble in *aqua regia* (3.6.2). Iron has a certain colour but also the power (in this case, a passive power) of being drawn by a loadstone (2.23.7). Any particular piece of gold or iron of course has also a specific shape and extension; but when we are talking about gold or iron as a *kind* of metal, shape or extension is not relevant at the observable level. The occurrent qualities of gold as gold apply at the insensible level, to the particles composing the micro-structure, the internal constitution of that kind of substance. To identify gold or iron (or any kind of thing), it is the powers of that kind which we use, what Locke calls the secondary qualities (2.23.8. See also the whole of 2.8). The colour we perceive, the solubility or fusibility which occur, are powers of the object, powers of the internal constitution of gold acting on our sense organs and powers of the internal constitution of gold responding to the internal constitution of *aqua regia* and fire. We should guard against considering the secondary qualities as merely colours, sounds, tastes, etc. For Locke, they include as well dispositional properties such as fusibility, malleability, etc. His point is that these latter do not differ from colour, sound, etc., in being powers in the object. Both sorts are powers. That is why he can say that most of the qualities of objects available to us are powers. Not *all* are powers, of course, for we also observe extension, figure, and motion, although not of the particles.

8 THINGS AND KINDS

Locke recognized that our concept of *a thing* is of a collection of properties united together in one substance; but he points out (in Book I) the ambiguity (indeed, the vacuity) of the substance part of this concept. The only content we can give to this notion of a thing, besides the observable qualities, is that of something which supports or is the subject of the qualities. We cannot imagine what the substance is to which the qualities belong (2.21.1-4). We 'cannot conceive how' the qualities which we observe as coexisting 'should subsist alone, nor in one another', so 'we suppose them existing in and supported by some common subject' (2.23.4). As usual, Locke has in mind a specific attempt to supply some content to this notion of a substance or support for qualities. *Substantial forms* were frequently said to be what underlies observed qualities. A form was a kind of matrix, a real type which constitutes gold as gold, iron as iron. But when pressed to explain this notion of a substantial form, all the defenders could say was that it was what made opium soporific, or gold malleable. The attempted explanation merely repeated the qualities for which the substantial form was the supposed cause. Against this traditional way of talking about *a thing* which has specific qualities, Locke insisted first that the 'thing' stood for nothing; secondly, that our ideas of a man, horse, gold, water, etc., were just of coexisting qualities observed and experienced together. Thirdly and most importantly, against the talk of substantial forms, Locke insisted that the corpuscular theory supplies a coherent concept for the internal constitution from which it is supposed the observed qualities flow (2.23.3). Observed qualities (the two sorts of powers) are, as we have seen, a product of the insensible particles of matter.

Substantial forms were supposed to be real kinds in nature, a limited number of types of things that could be. Locke objects to this notion also, on two grounds. First, he did not think there were sharp boundaries in nature, but rather a gradual shading of one type into another. There are no gaps or chasms in the chain of being (3.6.12). Secondly, Locke was convinced that our knowledge did not (and very likely could not) extend to the internal constitution of particles.[23] Nevertheless, the corpuscular theory of matter provided Locke with a theoretic basis to replace the vague one of substantial forms. His philosophy of nature accepted that part of the substantial-form doctrine which saw the forms as the causal basis for observed phenomena. He insisted that what we can *know* is only the coexisting group of qualities which careful observation and experimentation disclose. It is on this observable basis alone that we can classify things and refine our knowledge of nature. Locke uses the term 'nominal essence' to designate the coexisting group of qualities for each kind of thing, as distinguished by us. The 'real essence' 'is the constitution of the insensible parts of that body, on which those qualities and all the other properties of gold depend' (3.6.2).

9 KNOWLEDGE OF THINGS

Were we able to know the real essence, we would have a quite different knowledge of nature from that we in fact have, or are capable of having. In the absence of a knowledge of the internal constitution of matter, our science of nature can only be observational, 'the want of *ideas* of their real *essences* sends us from our own thoughts to the things themselves as they exist. *Experience here must teach me* what reason cannot' (4.12.9. Cf. 4.12.10-13). When, in Book IV, Locke defines knowledge as *'the perception of the connexion and agreement, or disagreement and repugnancy, of any of our ideas'* (4.1.1), he explicitly includes among his list of types of agreement that of *coexistence*. Noting, by observation but also by experimentation, what qualities go with what other qualities was for him, and for many of his fellow members of the Royal Society, the proper task of a scientist. It was an activity which in the seventeenth century was called the making of natural histories of phenomena.

Convinced that God had given us faculties for discovering truths about ourselves and the world, Locke tried to elaborate, in a vocabulary inherited from Cartesian philosophers and from contemporary science, an account of our knowledge of the world. To the extent that we can discover such truths by careful observation and experimentation, Locke accepted the corpuscular account of matter and of perception. Insisting that each one of us must, if we are to avoid borrowed opinions, see truths for ourselves, like Descartes, he placed intuition (cognitive 'seeing', grasping, apprehending) at the head of his list of methods to knowledge. What we intuit are relations between our ideas. That the knowledge relations are features of ideas, not things, is not due to any belief Locke held about the impossibility of knowledge of things. He believed he could precisely specify what we could and could not know about the external world: nominal but not real essence. His definition of knowledge in terms of relations of ideas was a result of (1) the account of the nature of matter which he accepted and (2) his recognition that knowledge relations are not object relations. This account of the nature of matter led him to the conclusion that what we perceive of bodies is for the most part the result of powers that bodies have as matter, not their occurrent qualities. Some of the powers of body are manifested whether we observe them or not; sun melts wax, the loadstone draws iron, one substance dissolves another. Our perception of any of these processes in nature occurs by means of the other sort of powers of bodies, their powers to affect our sense organs and animal spirits, which powers result in ideas and perceptions. We cannot sense or perceive bodies without sensing or perceiving. But perceiving is a cognitive or psychological process. Our awareness of anything is and must be in terms of ideas and perceptions. Otherwise, awareness would not be awareness, would not occur. From this point of view, Locke's definition of knowledge is a truism. The only way we can learn about the world is in terms of awareness. To be aware is to perceive or to have ideas or thoughts.

If ideas are taken as some sort of things, entities (cf. the innatists and Malebranche), then the contents of

awareness are turned into objects, the problems of scepticism begin to affect the theory of knowledge. According to Malebranche's theory, Locke observed, 'we see nothing but God and ideas; and it is impossible for us to know that there is anything else in the universe'.[24] Malebranche had equivocated on the word 'see', restricting the French 'voir' to seeing (that is, apprehending) ideas in the mind of God, and using 'sentiment' and 'apercevoir' for sensation and sensing. But the scepticism Locke notes is inherent in Malebranche's theory of ideas as real beings in the mind of God. Locke, as we have seen, firmly rejected this account of ideas. There has been a long tradition of interpretations of Locke which has found indirectness in his account of knowledge of nature. His talk of some ideas resembling some qualities of body, his frequent talk of ideas as *objects* of the mind when it thinks, even his causal theory of perception have led many readers of Locke to credit him with a representative theory, where ideas as the representatives of things or their qualities stand, as it were, between things and the perceiver. Scepticism is soon discovered at the heart of Locke's account. The very possibility he raised and dismissed in 4.4.3-5 is said to be inescapable. 'If it be true that all knowledge lies only in the perception of the agreement or disagreement of our own *ideas,* the visions of an enthusiast and the reasonings of a sober man will be equally certain. It is no matter how things are: so a man observe but the agreement of his own imaginations and talk conformably, it is all truth, all certainty. Such castles in the air will be as strongholds of truth as the demonstrations of *Euclid'* (4.4.1).

In this Introduction, I cannot extend my suggestion that those who read Locke in this way misread him by overlooking the important distinction between the two concepts of idea which the author of that 1705 tract saw so clearly. I have attempted some elaboration of my suggestion elsewhere,[25] but what is still lacking is a detailed account of the history of the term 'idea' from Descartes to Locke and beyond. What is needed especially is to place Locke in the context of the debate Arnauld had with Malebranche over the nature of ideas, representation, and cognition. Getting clear about these questions of the knowledge of body in Locke will clarify the very nature of his enterprise, for his *Essay* was an attempt at cognitive psychology.

CONCLUSION

Locke's *Essay* is more than an inquiry into the 'original, certainty, and extent of human knowledge, together with the grounds and degrees of belief, opinion, and assent' (1.1.2). There are long discussions of space, time, and infinity (pivotal concepts in the new science); of personal identity and the power of persons in action; of the nature and use of language, especially of the abuse of language through the misuse of words, or the use of words without real meaning. The *Essay* is in fact a mine of concepts, issues, and problems in science, philosophy, ethics, linguistics, psychology, logic, theology. I hope that by working from the contents of Book I, I have succeeded in showing some of those issues and concepts, together with the direction in which Locke approached them.

Notes

[1] Letter of 5 October 1774, in vol. I of *The Correspondence of Jeremy Bentham,* ed. by T. L. S. Sprigge (1968), p. 205.

[2] There is another interesting feature of Book I: between it and the final chapter of the fourth book, there is a symmetry. The first chapter of Book I is an Introduction to the whole of the *Essay.* Each of the three remaining chapters of that book deals in order with Locke's views on logic and knowledge, on action and morality, and on the nature of ideas. This threefold discussion is not unlike the threefold division of the sciences at the very end of the *Essay:* the science of nature, of action, and of signs.

[3] See N. Chomsky, *Cartesian Linguistics* (1966). The central claim of Chomsky's linguistic theory is 'that the general features of grammatical structure are common to all languages and reflect certain fundamental properties of the mind' (p. 59). These grammatical universals set the conditions for language learning; they are not learned themselves but 'provide the organizing principles that make language learning possible, that must exist if data are to lead to knowledge' (pp. 59-60). There are many problems surrounding Chomsky's theory. For two useful recent discussions, in the light of the seventeenth-century doctrine of innateness, see R. Edgley's 'Innate Ideas', in *Knowledge and Necessity,* vol. 3, Royal Institute of Philosophy Lectures, ed. by G. N. A. Vesey (1970), and Jonathan Barnes, 'Mr. Locke's Darling Notion', in *The Philosophical Quarterly,* 22 (1972), pp. 193-214.

[4] All references to Locke are to the Everyman text and are given by these numbers, the numbers representing in order the book, the chapter and the section.

[5] For a detailed discussion of the holders of this doctrine of innateness, see my *John Locke and the Way of Ideas,* Chapter 2 (1956).

[6] See, e.g., *Essay,* 1.3.9-12.

[7] John Sergeant is a good example. See his *Method to Science* (1696). I have a discussion of Locke's method in my *Locke and the Compass of Human Understanding,* Chapter 3 (1970).

[8] His *Some Thoughts concerning Education* (1693) spoke of tendencies, character traits which children have and which the tutor must recognize. See sects. 66, 102, 139, 216).

[9] For similar remarks on the force of custom, see Locke's *Essays on the Law of Nature,* ed. by W. von Leyden (1954) p. 135.

[10] Cf. *Essay,* 1.4.9: 'For the visible marks of extraordinary wisdom and power appear so plainly in all the works of the creation that a rational creature who will but seriously reflect on them cannot miss the discovery of a *deity* . . .'

[11] For other expressions of his belief in a purposive universe, see *Essay,* 2.1.15.

[12] For Descartes' attack on the syllogism, and his less formal notion of demonstration, see his *Regulae,* rules 3, 10, 12, and 13. I have developed the case for an informal logic in Locke, in my *Locke and the Compass of Human Understanding,* pp. 92-103.

[13] See his comment on scepticism in 1.1.5: 'If we will disbelieve everything, because we cannot certainly know all things, we shall do much what as wisely as he who would not use his legs, but sit still and perish because he had no wings to fly.'

[14] For other accounts of the genesis of ideas in children, see 2.1.6, 8, 21, 22; 2.9.5-7. I have given a more detailed account of Locke's genetic psychology in my *John Locke and Education* (1971), Chapter 3.

[15] One idea Locke thinks it would have been useful to have innate is the dea of substance, for this is an important idea but one which is not acquired by experience or reason, 'by *sensation* or *reflection*' (1.4.19). This is an idea, like that of identity, which occupies much of Locke's attention in the rest of the *Essay.* His inclusion of a brief remark about it in Book I can only be understood as part of his expository strategy: in attacking the innatists, he includes as many references as possible to ideas and issues to be discussed in the later books, especially those that constitute some of his more important claims.

[16] John Norris, *Cursory Reflections upon a Book Call'd, An Essay concerning Human Understanding* (1690).

[17] Published by R. Ackworth, in *The Locke Newsletter,* 2 (1971), pp. 7-11.

[18] *Ibid.,* pp. 10-11, unpunctuated, following the manuscript.

[19] Malebranche published his *De la Recherche de la Vérité* in 1674. Arnauld attacked him in *Des Vraies et des Fausses Idées* (1683). A series of exchanges then followed for many years between the two. Monte Cook has recently given a brief but lucid account of Arnauld's doctrine, in his 'Arnauld's Alleged Representationalism', *Journal of the History of Philosophy,* XII

(1974), pp. 53-62.

[20] Cf. *Essay*, 2.8.13 and *Remarks on Norris, Works, X,* sect. 15, pp. 254-5.

[21] See in particular Boyle's *The Origine of Forms and Qualities* (1666). For a good account of Boyle's use of the corpuscular theory, and its distinction between two kinds of qualities, see F. J. O'Toole, 'Qualities and Powers in the Corpuscular Philosophy of Robert Boyle', *Journal of the History of Philosophy,* XII (1974), pp. 295-315.

[22] That he considered powers an important aspect of matter is evidenced by the attention he gives to them when discussing our idea of things in his chapter on substance (2.23.7-10).

[23] The reasons here are complex. He did consider the possibility that the new microscopes might yield some knowledge of the insensible particles, but until we could understand cohesion—why the least particle did not fly apart—he thought we would be unable to understand why and how the observed qualities were caused by the particles (2.23.27).

[24] *Examination of P. Malebranche's Opinion, Works,* IX, sect. 43, p. 239.

[25] In Chapter 5 of my *Locke and the Compass of Human Understanding,* and more recently in 'Ideas and Knowledge in Seventeenth-Century Philosophy', loc. cit.

Robert L. Armstrong (essay date 1980)

SOURCE: "John Locke on Ultimate Reality and Meaning," in *Ultimate Reality and Meaning,* Vol. 3, No. 4, 1980, pp. 264-74.

[*Following a brief overview of Locke's life and writings, Armstrong examines the tension between the Christian and scientific aspects of Locke's thought in an* Essay Concerning Human Understanding. *He argues that Locke's Christian understanding of ultimate reality was balanced by a faith in human reason and experience as significant, although potentially limited, sources of knowledge.*]

1 LIFE AND WRITINGS

John Locke was born at Wrington, England on August 29, 1632. He spent his boyhood in his family's rural home of Beluton near the town of Pensford which is near Bristol. He was the elder of two sons whose mother died during their early childhood. His father was a country attorney who joined the army of Parliament and rose to the rank of captain. The Parliamentary patrons of his father found a place for the boy, when he was

fourteen, at Westminster School where he spent six years. It is possible that he witnessed the death of Charles I in 1649 at Whitehall, marking the culmination of the Puritan revolution.

He was awarded a studentship at Christ Church in 1652 and remained at Oxford for fifteen years. Though Oxford was deeply influenced at that time by Cromwell, the Aristotle of the Schoolmen still determined the content of the curriculum which was uncongenial to Locke, who found it full of obscure terms and useless questions. He preferred facts and persons to abstractions and books. Though discontented with his life at Oxford, he took his B.A. in 1656 and his master's degree in 1658. In 1660, the year of the Restoration, he was a senior student and tutor at Christ Church. At about this time his father died and the small inheritance he received afforded him some degree of independence.

He was strongly influenced by Descartes, the first philosopher he enjoyed reading, but he disclaims any acquaintance with Hobbes' writings and says nothing about Gassendi. He took an interest in the Royal Society and studied medicine. Though he did not take the doctorate in medicine he was familiarly known later in life as 'Doctor Locke'. He had inherited a delicate physical constitution which was unfavourable for the practice of medicine, so he practiced little but was always ready to give friendly medical advice.

His strongest interests at about his 30th year were in questions of social policy such as the constitution of society and the relations of church and state. At this time, he wrote his Essay concerning toleration which anticipates much of his later work. In 1665 he spent several months in diplomatic service as secretary to Sir Walter Vane at the court of the elector of Brandenburg. This introduced him to life outside of England and to the world of commerce and business.

In his thirty-fifth year he met Lord Ashley Cooper, soon after to become the celebrated first Earl of Shaftesbury. In 1667, he exchanged Christ Church for Lord Ashley's Exeter house in London where he remained as physician, and later as secretary, to Lord Ashley for the next sixteen years. He knew both Thomas Sydenham and Robert Boyle very well and was deeply influenced by Sydenham. Though Thomas Hobbes resided in London at this time, there is no evidence that Locke had any intercourse with him.

In the winter of 1670 during a meeting of five or six friends Locke undertook the project which eventually resulted in the ***Essay Concerning Human Understanding***. He undertook the task of clarifying the principles of human understanding, showing that all knowledge comes from sensible experience and not from innate principles. He worked on the ***Essay*** intermittently for most of the next two decades during which time he led an active political life associated with the political fortunes of Lord Ashley. In 1675 Locke retired with Ashley to France where he lived for four years, mostly working on the *Essay*. Returning to London in 1679 he claimed to have completed his work though it was only after another ten years of additions and transformations that it was published in 1690.

During the political turmoil of the 1680's preceding the 'Glorious Revolution of 1688' Locke spent five years in Holland where he was able to put the *Essay* into publishable form. Soon after William of Orange's return to England in 1688 Locke also returned to England. 'The political struggle of half a century was then consummated in the compromise of the Revolution settlement, of which Locke, now rising into popular fame, became the intellectual representative and philosophical defender.' (Locke, 1690a, Prolegomena, xxxvii).

In 1691 Locke, with increasing bodily ailments, retired to the manor house of Oates in Essex, the home of Sir Francis and Lady Masham, who was the very accomplished daughter of Ralph Cudworth. Except for 1696 and the following four years when he served as a Commissioner of the Board of Trade, in London, most of his remaining fourteen years were spent at Oates 'in as much domestic happiness and literary labor as was consistent with declining health, (Locke, 1690a, Prolegomena, xxxix).

The *Essay* rapidly attained a wide popularity which was unprecedented in the case of such an elaborate philosophical treatise. It went through four editions during Locke's lifetime and was translated into both French and Latin. Soon after publication a great many criticisms and some defenses of the Essay appeared in print. Bishop Stillingfleet criticized Locke for not leaving room for the mysteries of the Christian revelation. The *Essay*'s attack on innate ideas and principles shocked many and John Norris strongly criticized Locke for this. Other critics were Thomas Burnet, John Sergeant and Gottfried Leibniz. Locke replied to many of these criticisms, especially those of Bishop Stillingfleet with whom he exchanged a series of letters over a long period of years.

Though much of Locke's time subsequent to the publication of the *Essay* was taken up in the various controversies to which it gave rise, he published a number of other works; *A Third Letter on Toleration* appeared in 1692; *Thoughts Concerning Education* in the following year; and three tracts on *Money, Its Interest and Coinage* in 1691 and 1695. *The Reasonableness of Christianity as Delivered in the Scriptures* was his chief work in 1695. He answered criticism of this work in a *Vindication of the Reasonableness of Christianity* in the same year and in a second *Vindication* in 1697.

After the *Essay*, his other major work is *Two Treatises on Government* which was originally published in 1690. Locke was not satisfied with the several editions of the *Two Treatises* and was engaged in editing it during the last years of his life when he also wrote extensive commentaries on the epistles of St. Paul which were published posthumously.

During the summer of 1704 he continued to decline in health despite the care of Lady Masham. On the 28th of October he died. 'His death was like his life' as Lady Masham was later to say, 'truly pious, yet natural, easy and unaffected; nor can time, I think, ever produce a more eminent example of reason and religion than he was, living and dying' (Bourne, 1876, Vol. 2, p. 560).

2 DEFINITION OF ULTIMATE REALITY

Before attempting to explicate John Locke's conception of *ultimate reality and meaning,* it is necessary to explicate what 'ultimate reality and meaning' *means.* Is there supposed to be one ultimate reality to which everything in the universe is related? And is this relation to ultimate reality what gives *ultimate meaning* to each individual entity or being in the universe? Certainly the metaphysical tradition in philosophy indicates an affirmative answer to these questions. And the literature of this tradition affords a rich variety of answers.

The conception of ultimate reality is relatively easy to grasp. If we begin with a distinction between appearance and reality, it is plausible to ask of any entity, being, or event, whether it is real or mere appearance. In cases where the answer that it is only appearance is given, the further question is generated: If it is mere appearance, then what is real? The real is assumed to be beneath or beyond the appearance. Thus Locke argued that the ideas of perceptions of taste and smell, for example, were secondary qualities which depended upon the peculiarities of the human sensory apparatus (an aspect of *mind*) for their particular character.

Primary qualities, like solidity, extension, figure, motion, and number do not depend upon the human mind but are 'utterly inseparable' from the external material body that is being perceived or is the source of the ideas (perceptions) of both secondary and primary qualities. In general, then, some of the properties of material things are real and some are only appearance.

'Real' means existing as part of the independent external objects. 'Appearance' means wholly or partially dependent upon the peculiar nature of the sensing organism. Thus the characteristic shape of a brick is a primary quality, a *real* quality, since it belongs to the brick itself, an external material object. That shape does not depend upon the sensory apparatus of man. The taste of an orange, on the other hand, does depend upon the sensory apparatus of man. Thus it is a secondary quality, rather an appearance than a reality; and it is conceivable that an orange would have a different quality of taste to some creature other than man.

The meanings of 'reality' and 'appearance' that are defined here are, of course, just one of several meanings that may be found in the rich literature of the metaphysical tradition. The 'real' is that which exists independently of man is best called the 'materialistic definition of reality' and we may note that it was formulated by Democritus in the pre-Socratic era of Greek Philosophy. Any perception that was thought to depend on the mind or senses of man was relegated to the category of appearance—it was *not real* because it did not exist apart from man. In the category of appearance were included all subjective phenomena like dreams, hallucinations, fantasies and anything that was peculiar to man's nature as opposed to the nature of external reality.

Now if this fundamental distinction between appearance and reality is clear we can take another metaphysical step and ask, 'What is the source, or cause or creator of reality?' Now this is certainly not a necessary question to ask, and the question itself according to contemporary views of philosophy may be mired in conceptual confusion or error. However, this question has seemed highly plausible, or even profound, in the metaphysical tradition of the discipline. If independent material things are real—according to the materialistic tradition—then how were they created or what was their origin? This origin or creator could then be conceived as *ultimately* real.

3 ULTIMATE REALITY FOR LOCKE

The popular or orthodox late seventeenth century answer to the question about the nature of ultimate reality was that the Christian God, as the creator of the material universe, is *ultimate reality*. The natural philosophers of John Locke's generation and the generations before and after him (roughly from about 1625 to 1725), men like Isaac Barrow, Samuel Clark, John Keill, Isaac Newton, Thomas Sprat and Colin Maclaurin, to name some of the prominent ones, all embraced the view that the Christian God was the 'author of the natural universe.' These men, as natural philosophers, were impressed with the wonder, intricacy and beauty of the material universe. So was John Locke. They were also devout Christians as was Locke. It was altogether natural for them to believe in the Christian God as the creator of a material universe, the marvelous details of which were almost daily being revealed to them through the successes of the new experimental science and Newtonian natural philosophy.

So John Locke's position regarding ultimate reality was

the orthodox position of his age. The material universe was real and what existed beyond it as ultimate reality was its creator, the Christian Deity. But if John Locke's view of ultimate reality is not remarkable his contribution to the concept of *ultimate meaning* is very much worthy of notice. As *reality* is to be found in the world external to man, meaning must belong to the realm of human experience and knowledge. This is what interested John Locke, as indicated by the title of his major work, ***An Essay Concerning Human Understanding***.

4 THE SOURCE OF MEANING FOR LOCKE

4.1 *The Empiricist vs the Innate Theory of Knowledge*

Locke took a materialistic ontology for granted and focused on the problem of the nature of human understanding. In the tradition of Descartes he wanted to clarify the source and meaning of *certain* knowledge. Descartes, in general, found certainty within human understanding, in 'clear and distinct' ideas, in rational argument. Locke, in contrast, emphasized the external source of ideas as the sole ground for certain or legitimate knowledge. What was given in experience was for him the model for certain knowledge. We are certain of what we sense, of what we see, feel, hear, smell and taste. All ideas derive their legitimacy, validity, authority, and meaning from experience, from their source in the external world. Ideas that were supposed to originate in the mind were suspect since it was difficult or impossible to determine to what extent they were merely subjective.

A perusal of the popular literature of the third quarter of the seventeenth century reveals a wide variety of innate idea doctrines (Yolton, 1956, Chapter 2). Many notions, including the idea of God, logical maxims and a variety of religious beliefs were supposed to be absolutely certain and legitimate because they were *innate* in the mind having been 'imprinted' there by the Author of Nature. The first book of Locke's ***Essay*** was devoted to a polemic against this doctrine of innate ideas. Essentially, he argued that the mind was a 'white paper void of all characters' upon which experience writes. For any notion that Locke regarded as legitimate he provided a persuasive account of its origin from experience. Many of his arguments against innate ideas were less than persuasive, however, as when he argued that if ideas were truly innate they should be found in every human being including infants and the mentally retarded. He went to such lengths in argument because the innate idea doctrine was so attractive to the religious mind. It was reassuring to believe that our most cherished beliefs, the foundations of our understanding (laws of logic, etc.) had their source in God. Locke, of course could not conclusively disprove this doctrine but what he could, and did, do was to provide an alternative account that was plausible and which has some crucial advantages over the innate idea doctrine.

The most basic advantage of the empirical account of the origin of our certain knowledge is that experience is public. That an object has one shape rather than another can be verified by any observer. The notion of the nature and existence of God, on the other hand, was not quite so easily verified. Believers, of course, insisted that this notion was innate to the human mind. But how could a believer convince a non-believer of this? In general, if it was impossible to doubt a proposition, those defending the innate idea doctrine argued that it must be innate. Thus the principle of non-contradiction, a law of logic, could not be doubted so it must be somehow innate to human understanding. This argument is plausible, even convincing, for rules of logic, but some of the other ideas that were supposed to be innate like 'the obscene parts and actions are not to be exposed to public view' (Yolton, 1956, p. 34) are hardly plausible candidates for innateness, at least to twentieth century minds.

What is important to realize at this point in the development of British empirical philosophy is that any doubt as to the explanatory power of the innate idea doctrine forces attention on the question of the actual nature of human understanding. If certain principles, basic notions or cherished beliefs are not the innate furniture of the mind, then what is their actual source? This is the question that Locke asks and thereby advances philosophical thought in the direction of a clear conception of empirical meaning. Thus the rejection of innate ideas was a necessary step in the development of Locke's thought. His basic position is that legitimate meaning in the human mind must have its source in the external world—must be derived from our experience of that world. He presupposes or takes for granted that the external material world *is reality* and that true knowledge must be in the form of conceptions in the mind which are produced by, or caused by, that reality.

We need to be aware that Locke did allow for some legitimate meaning that was not derived from experience. This meaning consists of the 'ideas of reflection' or the rational principles that the mind derives from its own internal operations. Though admitting logical principles, Locke is very careful to insist that this meaning is strictly limited to the operations of the human understanding itself. His intent is to minimize the role of such logical principles and emphasize the importance of the empirical content of thought as the crucial component of legitimate meaning or certain knowledge.

4.2 *Qualities as a Source of Meaning*

Regarding matter, or the real constitution of external things, Locke maintains that there are qualities in matter which correspond to the ideas of sense in the mind.

The chief relation between the idea and the external modification of matter is causation, not similarity. 'Most of the ideas of sensation being in the mind (are) no more the likeness of something without us than the names that stand for them are the likeness of our ideas' (Locke, 1690a, Bk. 2, Chap. 8, par. 7). There is one exception to this dictum, the primary qualities which are 'utterly inseparable from the body' and which mind finds in every 'particle of matter' (Locke, 1690a, Bk. 2, Chapt. 8, par. 9). Thus there is a relation of qualitative similarity between idea and thing regarding the primary qualities which are: *solidity, extension, figure, motion,* and *number*. This relation obtains in addition to the fundamental relation of efficient causation which obtains for all legitimate meaning, 'legitimate' meaning 'causally related to external reality.'

Things in themselves have primary, secondary and tertiary qualities, the secondary qualities consisting in the power to produce the perceptions of colors, sounds, smells and the like in our minds, and the tertiary qualities consisting in a power to produce changes in other material objects. The nature of the real constitution of external things is not indicated by the causal relation itself. Locke can only say that external objects have a power to cause perceptions in us and he admits that the senses do not give us a clear and distinct idea of this power. But he does maintain that the perceptions or ideas of primary qualities are like the real qualities of external things. And these primary qualities are just those qualities that are possessed by material bodies in motion. Thus, though Locke is a materialist regarding the nature of external reality, his real interest is in how the external reality affects the human mind. Essentially, Locke understands 'meaning' as the effect of external reality upon the mind. This definition is certainly not the only sense of the term but it serves to emphasize the connection between *reality* and *meaning* that is central to the philosophy of John Locke.

So it is causality that connects reality and meaning, the world and the human mind, and not likeness or similarity. This position represents a considerable advance in philosophical sophistication over naive empiricism and its faith that what the mind perceives in experience is real. To be sure, Locke is an empiricist and firmly believes that what the mind perceives in experience is real, but it is the perception or idea itself that is real *precisely because it is produced by the external material reality*. As far as meaning and knowledge are concerned the basic reality is the sensible idea of perception. Its reality is derived from its causal relation to external things. Thus, though external objects are also real, in a more fundamental sense, Locke admits sometimes reluctantly and sometimes with alacrity, that they cannot be known in their real constitution. The way is open, then, for doubting the reality of the external world (a path later explored by Berkeley, Hume and Kant). In short, the ultimate outcome of Locke's analysis is that the content of mind, meaning and knowledge, derive their reality from a source which itself cannot be known with certainty. Essentially this is the general position of Immanuel Kant which is anticipated in the third and fourth books of Locke's *Essay*.

It is interesting to compare Locke's position on reality and ideas with that of one of his predecessors in the tradition of British empiricism, Thomas Hobbes. Hobbes maintained that the only reality was material atoms in motion, the external world. He regarded human perceptions and ideas as mere manifestations of external reality. Locke, on the other hand, emphasizes the reality of the ideas of perceptions themselves—because they provide a model of certain knowledge—and treats the external reality as an epistemologically distant source of their reality. It is as if there had been between the thought of Hobbes and Locke a kind of ontological movement of the real from external bodies in motion to the ideas in the mind. We might further remark that this 'ontological movement' continues in the work of Berkeley and Hume who follow Locke in this continuous philosophical analysis (Armstrong, 1970).

Summing up Locke's view of reality and meaning, we have the attitude of naive realism toward the material world combined with the philosophical insight that what we experience as real derives much or most of its character from the structure of our sensory apparatus as 'mind' which is nevertheless causally related to an external, independent reality the character of which cannot be directly known. It can be known, to some extent, however, indirectly by inference or reason. For example, the primary qualities, with the exception of solidity, can be experienced by different senses while the secondary qualities are limited to one sense. Considering how different the ideas of sense are from one another—colors being very different in character from textures that are felt, for example—if a sensible idea like motion can be both seen and felt we may infer, with something less than certainty, of course, that motion is an independent quality. That is, it does not entirely depend upon the peculiar nature of the particular sense, as is the case for colors which are only seen, not felt or heard, and, therefore, most likely derive their nature from our sensory apparatus than external reality. This kind of inductive argument from analogy and disanalogy yields a picture of the external world as variously shaped objects capable of motion in space. They are not *really* colored, noisy, tasty or smelly since these attributes exist only in so far as the external objects interact with the human sensory apparatus or 'mind'.

5 CAUSALITY AND ULTIMATE REALITY

This kind of reasoning has merit—it may even be convincing in the above case--but it is something less than mathematically certain. Locke, however, had great confidence in the power of human reason to reach beyond experience. Thus he claimed that 'from the consideration of ourselves, and what we infallibly find in our own constitutions, our reason leads us to the knowledge of this certain and evident truth,—*that there is an external, most powerful, and most knowing Being*' (Locke, 1690a, Bk. 4, Chap. 10, par. 6). Further, he argued that 'we have a more certain knowledge of the existence of God, than of anything our senses have not immediately discovered to us.' Sensible experience remains as our first criterion of certainty but beyond it, reason can take us considerable distances. Locke felt that 'There is no truth more evident than that something must be from eternity' (Locke, 1690a, Bk. 4, Chap. 10, par. 8). There must be a creator not only of the material universe but, even more imperatively, of human beings who are possessed of reason. Locke held human reason in high esteem and considered it absurd to think that it could be produced from matter alone. *Causality* is the key concept here as it was in the analysis of sense perception. Just as there must be a cause of what we experience by sense perception, external material objects, there must be a further cause of that material universe.

As to the nature of causality Locke believes that our best clue comes from the idea of power. Power is twofold, 'as able to make or able to receive any change. The one may be called *active*, and the other *passive* power' (Locke, 1690a, Bk. 2, Chap. 21, par. 2). Active power, or what initiates change, is the source of causality and Locke maintains that we obtain this idea not from perception or external things but 'from reflection on the operations of our minds' (Locke, 1690a, Bk. 2, Chap. 21, par. 4). Volition, or willing, affords us the clearest understanding of active power. Locke declines to inquire whether or not matter can have active power and this probably indicates that he is aware of a difficulty here. In our experience material objects are 'passive and inert' as Bishop Berkeley is later to argue. How then can matter possess the active power to cause our sensible ideas? Though this is Berkeley's question, it is Locke's analysis of the idea of active power that sets the stage for it.

So, though Locke believed that reality was material, the emphasis he placed on causality, in both his epistemological and his theological arguments, leads us to conclude that he understood *ultimate reality* to be the active power of the creator of the universe. He identified that creator with the Christian deity and devoted much of his energy during the later years of his life to defending the major tenets of Christianity. For example, he accepted Christianity on the authority of Jesus of Nazareth whose authority was established by the miracles he performed. 'To know that any revelation is from God, it is necessary to know that the messenger that delivered it is sent from God, and that cannot be known but by some credential given him by God himself' (Locke, 1695a, *Discourse of Miracles*, p. 80). Thus Locke defended miracles as "the basis on which divine mission is always established, and consequently that foundation on which the believers of any divine revelation must ultimately bottom their faith" (Locke, 1695a, p. 86).

6 CONCLUSION

To sum up John Locke's position regarding ultimate reality and meaning, he found ultimate meaning in both the certainty of knowledge we derive from the simple ideas of sense and the certainty of knowledge we derive from our reason. This ultimate meaning (certainty) is the inner manifestation of external reality and ultimate reality. Reality is the material universe which is the source of human meaning or understanding and ultimate reality is the active power of the creator of that universe.

The key to John Locke's character is that 'he was always in the greatest and in the smallest affairs of human life, as well as in speculative opinions, disposed to follow reason whosoever it were that suggested it; he being ever a faithful servant . . . to Truth; never abandoning her for anything else, and following her, for her own sake, purely' (Lady Masham as quoted by Bourne, 1876, Vol. 2., p. 540). In the *Second Treatise of Civil Government* Locke identifies the "law of nature" which governs the state of nature with *reason* (Locke, 1690b, paragraph 6). So, if we wish to infer what the final horizon or the central idea in terms of which the meaning of human existence is understood according to John Locke, it is reason and Truth. Locke is solidly in the philosophical tradition stemming from Aristotle which holds that the essence of man is *reason* and his purpose in life is to seek the truth about *reality*. Locke's view about the nature of reality is not original but is derived from the materialistic tradition. In his own time the most prominent articulators of this tradition were Thomas Hobbes and Isaac Newton. Essentially Locke accepted the materialistic conception of the nature of external reality and the theories of Newton as to its exact workings and focused his own energies on the problem of the nature of human understanding. Thus his philosophical contribution is in the area of the nature of human meaning rather than reality. As his view of reality was not original neither was his view of ultimate reality. He accepted the power of the Christian God as ultimately real, the source of the material universe and man. And, though for his time he was somewhat daring in his efforts to subject the Christian scriptures to the scrutiny of reason, his findings were hardly radical or original.

As to the question of the meaning of the universe we find little indication in Locke's life or works of an answer to this question. As to the question of the meaning of human existence his answer, eloquently put from both his life and his work, is that it is to be found in the life of reason in the pursuit of Truth. What satisfaction in life that is possible for man is to be found in such a life. Regarding life after death, Locke has little to say, but we may infer from his epistemological doctrine, that human knowledge is always linked to experience of the material world, that he did not believe in a human consciousness after the death of the material body. Bourne's extensive account of the last months of Locke's life contains no reference to a concern or interest on his part in a personal consciousness after death. Locke believed that the meaning of human life was to be found in human society in this earthly life. This, at least, reason assures us is certainly meaningful if we lead a rational life, treat our fellow men with Christian kindness and contribute to the maintenance of human society.

The full consequences of applying reason to the Christian scriptures were not drawn out by Locke. The details of the Christian vision concerning life after death, the attributes of God, the purpose of life, etc., were all soon to be subjected to severe criticism by eighteenth century thinkers like David Hume. We may say that in Britain, at least, Locke started this skeptical line of thought, though he, himself, appears not to have anticipated the depth of skepticism to be reached in only a few generations from his death. Thus Locke's standard of reason and certainty in human knowledge rather soon resulted in a skeptical philosophy which found little merit, or possibility of certain knowledge, in the profound metaphysical questions about the nature of ultimate reality, the meaning of human life or the possibilities of immortal life. In his celebration of reason and its demands for certain and demonstrable evidence Locke stands out in the history of philosophical thought as one who advances the standards of rational and empirical certainty and relegates more ambitious concerns like the nature of ultimate reality, the nature of the universe and the purpose of life to the realm of speculation where rational certainty is impossible.

REFERENCES

Armstrong, R. L. 1970. *Metaphysics and British Empiricism*. Lincoln Nebr.: University of Nebraska Press.

Bourne, H. R. F. 1876. *The Life of John Locke*. 2 volumes. Reprint of the London Edition 1876. Darmstadt: Scientia Verlag Aalen, 1969.

Locke, J. 1690a. *An Essay Concerning Human Understanding*. Collated and annotated, with Prolegomena, Biographical, Critical and Historical, by Alexander Campbell Fraser, 2 volumes. New York: Dover Publications, Inc., 1959.

1690b. *The Second Treatise of Civil Government* and a *Letter Concerning Toleration,* edited with an Introduction by J. W. Gough. Oxford: Basil Blackwell, 1948.

1695. *The Reasonableness of Christianity* with *A Discourse of Miracles* and part of a *Third Letter Con-*

cerning Toleration, edited by I. T. Ramsey, Stanford: Stanford University Press, 1958.

Yolton, J. W. 1956. *John Locke and the Way of Ideas.* London: Oxford University Press.

Locke discusses the epistemological differences between reason and faith:

Reason . . . as contradistinguished to *Faith,* I take to be the discovery of the Certainty or Probability of such Propositions or Truths, which the Mind arrives at by Deductions made from such *Ideas,* which it has got by the use of its natural Faculties, *viz.* by Sensation or Reflection.

Faith, on the other side, is the Assent to any Proposition, not thus made out by the Deductions of Reason; but upon the Credit of the Proposer, as coming from GOD, in some extraordinary way of Communication. This way of discovering Truths to Men we call *Revelation.* . . .

[N]o Proposition can be received for Divine Revelation, or obtain the Assent due to all such, *if it be contradictory to our clear intuitive Knowledge.* Because this would be to subvert the Principles, and Foundations of all Knowledge, Evidence, and Assent whatsoever. . . .

There being many Things, wherein we have very imperfect Notions, or none at all; and other Things, of whose past, present, or future Existence, by the natural Use of our Faculties, we can have no Knowledge at all; these, as being beyond the Discovery of our natural Faculties, and above *Reason,* are, when revealed, *the proper Matter of Faith.*

> *John Locke, in his* Essay Concerning Human Understanding, *1690.*

James Farr (essay date 1987)

SOURCE: "The Way of Hypotheses: Locke on Method," in *Journal of the History of Ideas,* Vol. XLVIII, No. 1, January-March, 1987, pp. 51-72.

[In the following essay, Farr examines two opposing interpretations of Locke's understanding of the functions of scientific hypotheses and proposes an alternative reading of Locke's philosophy in an attempt to reconcile these two positions.]

> "[A]s every ones hypothesis is, soe is his reason disposed to judge . . ."[1]

The specter of empiricism no longer haunts the *Essay Concerning Human Understanding* as once it did. Thanks to historically-minded philosophers and philosophically-minded historians, the interpretation of John Locke's masterwork is at long last being spared the time-honored ritual of reading back into it the concerns of later contrivance. The spell cast by Berkeley and Hume and Russell has largely been broken. The alleged empiricist philosopher of common sense has had restored to him an epistemology devoted to vindicating its theocentric framework[2] and an understanding of the scope and methods of science.[3]

Locke's ideas about science, however, are not so clear and distinct. In the first place "science" carries no unambiguous meaning in the *Essay.* Anticipating modern usage, "science" sometimes means those empirical and theoretical investigations about nature or reality of the sort which "Mr. Newton" undertook when he revealed "new Discoveries of yet unknown Truths."[4] More frequently, however, "science" is equated with demonstrable knowledge as found only in logic or mathematics, an equation which entails that "we are not capable of *scientifical Knowledge*" of natural entities or "the several sorts of Bodies" at all.[5] A consequence of this ambiguity is that the demarcation between science and non-science cannot be drawn sharply. Nor can we readily determine the continuity or discontinuity which Locke thought existed between the various enterprises of the "understanding," say, medicine, natural religion, political knowledge, and the "experimental Philosophy of physical Things."[6] In short the meaning and domain of "science" in Locke's understanding of the "understanding" are not readily fixed.

These ambiguities prefigure another. The *Essay,* taken alone, wavers ambivalently between two competing methods of the understanding: (1) the method of natural history; and (2) the hypothetical method. The first method counsels "Experience, Observation, and natural History," which yield "collections of sensible qualities" perceived to coexist in the world.[7] The second forwards the use of speculations about things which lie beyond "the reach of humane Senses," wherein "we can only guess, and probably conjecture."[8] Even when these two methods assume concrete form in seventeenth century debates in natural philosophy—debates to which Locke was a distant party—his ambivalence appears to persist. On the one hand he invokes "the corpuscularian hypothesis" to explain the ultimate constituents of matter.[9] On the other hand he calls for "improving our knowledge in Substances only by Experience and History," especially where we lack "Microscopical Eyes."[10]

Taking the *Essay* alone, then, Locke's interpreters have ample textual warrant for considering him to be a champion of one or another very different "Lockean" method. R. M. Yost, John W. Yolton, and others take Locke to be a natural historian.[11] Maurice Mandelbaum, Laurens Laudan, and others take Locke to be a proponent of the hypothetical method.[12] The corpuscularian hypothesis figures centrally and intriguingly in this debate, for almost all parties concede that Locke accepted the hypothesis.[13] What remains in dispute is the bearing that Locke's acceptance had on his conception of the method of science and the human understanding. Mandelbaum and Laudan take Locke's acceptance of the corpuscularian hypothesis as consistent with his hypotheticalism, while Yost and Yolton insist that it has no bearing on his general understanding of and prescriptions for the advancement of science. In a postscript to his contribution to this debate, Laudan concludes that a great divide separates the two interpretations of Locke's understanding of science:

> Unfortunately, the interpretative and exegetical divide which separates the Yost-Yolton reading of Locke from the Mandelbaum-Laudan one probably cannot be settled by further citations of "definitive" texts from the *Essay;* taken in isolation, that work provides evidence for both interpretations.[14]

This divide might yet be crossed from two directions. Laudan suggests one direction: "What may help settle the issue is to ask a larger question about where Locke fits into the major intellectual traditions of the seventeenth century."[15] The debate whether Locke is a natural historian of science or a hypotheticalist turns, then, on whether we place him in the tradition of Bacon or in the tradition of Boyle, respectively.

Discussion of "traditions" amidst the incredible novelty and fluidity of seventeenth-century science, however, may impose more order than is to be found. No one then had very steady opinions of the changing ideals of science,[16] and steady interpretations of them are not to be found today. Thus Yolton underscores Boyle's caution about hypotheses and his praise of natural history, while Mandelbaum and Peter Urbach underscore Bacon's commitments to the hypothetical method.[17] Barbara Shapiro notes that "several leading scientists of the pre-Newtonian era suggests how the Baconian research program was forging an alliance with hypothetical reasoning."[18] "The incomparable Mr. Newton"—who shared with Locke his "mystical fansies" and once, in a spell of derangement, even wished him dead[19]—was remarkably ambivalent about the problem of hypotheses versus induction in science, despite *hypotheses non fingo.*[20] In short, the voice of "tradition" is all but inaudible amidst such clamoring of diverse opinion. Locke hardly quiets matters, either, for his praise for Bacon and Boyle and Newton and other scientific lights of his generation makes it all but impossible with any confidence or unanimity to class his ideas with those of any one of his contemporaries. And in the end Locke speaks for himself, whatever Bacon or Boyle or Newton may have said.[21]

In this essay I hope to cross this divide in another way. Setting my sights exclusively on Locke, I engage in a conceptual reconstruction of his views of the human understanding by attending to his explicit invocation of "hypotheses" and "method." In so doing, I shall look beyond the *Essay*—to Locke's other works, to his disputes in print, and to his manuscript on "method." And I shall consider contexts other than those circumscribed by debates over the corpuscularian hypothesis. When this is done—that is, when the range of texts and contexts is enlarged and perused—two general points emerge.

First, Locke recognized the indispensable *use* of "hypotheses" in the advancement of human understanding—not only in what we have come to call physics but also in optics, geology, medicine, natural religion, and politics. Indeed Locke himself advanced and pursued a number of his own hypotheses in these various contexts—all of which or none of which may be considered to be "scientific," depending on Locke's ambiguously different characterizations of "science." Second, Locke outlines a *method* for judging hypotheses. To put it briefly, hypotheses are to be compared and judged competitively, such that one hypothesis is rejected only when another with "greater light" is available to replace it; and this is determined in turn by judging the overall comparative advantage of the "whole systems" from which these competing hypotheses issue. Both points suggest a form of imaginative but disciplined inquiry which Locke could well have called his "way of hypotheses."

Locke's manuscript on "method" helps advance these points in a dramatic way. Despite its publication a century and more ago in Lord Peter King's *Life of John Locke,*[22] this remarkably important and succinct statement has surprisingly failed to figure in the debates over Locke's understanding of science.[23] Given its importance in this context, a more faithful version is introduced and printed below as an appendix. Competing hypotheses, Locke tells us there, provide what little light we have "to finde truth . . . in this our darke and short sighted state."

I. When discussing "the abuse of words" in the *Essay,* Locke complains of the failure of disputants to provide definitions for their words. "If Men would tell, what *Ideas* they made their Words stand for, there could not be half that Obscurity or Wrangling, in the search or support of Truth, that there is."[24] Had Locke followed his own advice by offering a definition or suggesting what Idea it stood for, when, as often, he used the word "hypothesis," perhaps the subsequent history of dispute over his account of science and the human understanding would not have been marked by such "Obscurity or Wrangling" that there has been. But, alas, Locke never defined "hypothesis"; much less did he compose a sustained work on the hypothetical method. He left no Essay, no Treatise, no Letter on the matter. In the absence of a definition or a sustained work, students of Locke's thought must attend carefully and systematically to Locke's uses of the term "hypothesis," for such uses provide the necessary linguistic material out of which Locke's considered views may be reconstructed. This is necessary in order to avoid attributing to Locke certain views or distinctions that he did not hold and to restore the discussion about "hypotheses" to those contexts which he thought the appropriate ones.

There are two principal sorts of these contexts. The second section of this essay will attend to those contexts—which these days we would call philosophical or methodological—in which Locke reflects in very general terms on topics like maxims, probability, bottoming, and explanation. Here he makes a number of references to "hypotheses" from which we may reconstruct his views of the hypothetical method as a whole. The first section attends principally to those contexts—which these days we would call scientific or substantive—in which Locke directs his attention to actual debates over competing hypotheses in physics, geology, natural religion, and politics. Attention to both sorts of contexts takes us far and wide, but the travels are rewarding. At the end we may espy a greater unity than is often seen in Locke's account of the human understanding and the various domains of its inquiry. What he says methodologically about "hypotheses" concords with what he shows substantively about their actual use.

Although Locke provides no explicit definition of "hypotheses," what he states or implies in many contexts, in and out of the *Essay,* suggests what he has in mind. Hypotheses are probable conjectures beyond the facts of observation and experience about things, actions, events, their causes or consequences which issue from some theoretical system serving to explain known phenomena.

Hypotheses, that is, are a species of "conjecture" or "speculation" about empirical matters which attend the inevitable human propensity to "penetrate into the Causes of Things."[25] As such, they are not, strictly speaking, a part of "knowledge" on Locke's reckoning, for knowledge means demonstrable or intuitive certainty such as found only in logic, mathematics, or (as Locke thinks) morality.[26] Rather, hypotheses exist in the "twilight of probability," wherein lies "the greatest part of our Concernment."[27] "Probability," Locke avers, is "to supply the defect of our knowledge, and to guide us where that fails, is always conversant about Propositions, whereof we have no Certainty, but only some inducements to receive them for true."[28] Such inducements to truth as we humans have in this our twilight passage "either concern some . . . matter of fact, which falling under Observation, is capable of humane Testimony; or else concerning Things, which being beyond the testimony of our Senses, are not capable of any such Testimony."[29] Since so very much lies beyond our senses, where "we can only guess, and

probably conjecture," hypotheses are indispensable in the conduct of the human understanding.[30]

Hypotheses, moreover, are seldom isolated conjectures. Rather, they are usually part of "whole systems" of thought. Such systems, as Locke implies in his manuscript on "method" (appended below), are complex structures of propositions and beliefs, whether about matter or thinking, God or political order. These systems establish the relevant cognitive framework for fashioning hypotheses in the first place. Since the human understanding forms a complex and integrated structure of ideas, hypotheses add to and follow from the coherence of our knowledge as a whole. Otherwise they would be but isolated stabs in the dark and of no assistance to "our dim candle, Reason" as it attempts to illuminate the path of "our Pilgrimage."[31]

Despite its reputation as a "philosophical" classic, the *Essay* itself yields numerous references to actually debated and debatable "hypotheses" of the sort here described. Most of these references are of a general nature, and most advise approaching hypotheses warily since many are "false," none "certain," all at best "probable."[32] Especially false, Locke thinks, are those "distinct hypotheses" about "innate practical principles," as well as virtually all the hypotheses held by "the Schoolmen and the Metaphysicians," those "great Mint-Masters" who "coin new words."[33] Indeed it is against the abuse of words of these "Mint-Masters" that Locke's frequently pejorative uses of "hypothesis" may be understood. Animal generation, magnetism, and "intelligent Inhabitants in . . . other Mansions of the vast Universe" are "hypotheses" about which Locke makes no commitments.[34] The "corpuscularian hypothesis," on the other hand, appears to enjoy Locke's full acceptance, for once we conceive of matter as composed of minute corpuscles, "it is thought to go farthest in an intelligible explication of the Qualities of Bodies; and I fear the Weakness of Humane Understanding is scarce able to substitute another."[35]

Weaker still is the human understanding when it hypothesizes about the soul: whether it be an immaterial substance or thinking matter. Warily, Locke calls it a draw:

> He who will give himself leave to consider freely, and look into the dark and intricate part of each Hypothesis, will scarce find his Reason able to determine him fixedly for, or against the Soul's Materiality. Since on which side soever he views it, either as an unextended Substance, or a thinking extended Matter; the difficulty to conceive either, will, whilst either alone is in his Thoughts, still drive him to the contrary side.[36]

Locke does not remain altogether silent, however. For he seizes the opportunity offered by this stalemate of hypotheses to suggest his own, "that GOD can, if he pleases, superadd to Matter a Faculty of Thinking."[37]

For all its references to "hypotheses," the *Essay* understates Locke's use of hypotheses, and his recognition of their indispensability in the conduct of human understanding. Exploring beyond the pages of the *Essay* we discover new worlds of "hypotheses."

"Minute corpuscles" (to begin with the most controversial hypothesis of the *Essay*) emerge again and again as part of the system of mechanical philosophy to explain the ultimate constituents of matter. In the *Conduct of Human Understanding,* in *Elements of Natural Philosophy,* and in *Some Thoughts Concerning Education,* Locke allows, as he puts it in the last mentioned of these works, that "the modern Corpuscularians talk in most Things more intelligibly than the Peripateticks" when they talk the language of "hypotheses."[38] The corpuscularian hypothesis finds another theoretical purpose in explaining perception in the *Examination of P. Malebranche's Opinion.* Against the deficient "hypothesis" of Malebranche that we see all things in God, Locke uses "my hypothesis" to explain "how by material rays of light visible species may be brought into the eye." Given our "animal spirits" (another hypothesis warily advanced in the *Essay*), we perceive "visible species" due to "the motion of particles of matter coming from them and striking on our organs."[39]

But matter—whether it be composed of minute corpuscles or whether it propagates light—does not exhaust Locke's catalogue of physical (much less other) hypotheses. This, indeed, is just the beginning. He accepted the Copernican hypothesis about planetary motions as "the likeliest to be true in itself."[40] He also accepted Newton's hypothesis of gravitational attraction, repeatedly going so far as to think it "demonstrable."[41] And in speculations about the geology of the Biblical Flood, he thought he found something fully as intelligible as gravity.

> And therefore since the Deluge cannot be well explained without admitting something out of the ordinary Course of Nature, I propose it to be considered whether God's altering the Centre in the Earth for a Time (a Thing as intelligible as Gravity itself . . .) will not more easily account for Noah's Flood than any Hypothesis yet made use of to solve it.
>
> This is not a Place for that Argument [Locke goes on] reserving to a fitter Opportunity a fuller Explication of this Hypothesis, and the Application of it to all the Parts of the Deluge, and any Difficulties can be supposed in the History of the Flood, as recorded in the Scripture.[42]

Locke never seized the opportunity he reserved for later. But his correspondents kept alive the topic of "your Hypothesis about the Deluge."[43]

Medicine—the discipline in which Locke was trained—

also abounds with hypotheses, especially "distinct hypotheses concerning distinct species of diseases."[44] In these matters, and often in correspondence with the brothers Molyneux, Locke often rings a tocsin against "speculative hypotheses," praising instead a natural history of disease. Intimations of such complaints against "speculative theorems" and "hypotheses" can be heard as early as 1669 in the manuscript "de Arte Medica."[45] Locke's tone, however, is by no means universally dismissive, as evidenced the very next year in the 1670 fragment on smallpox, where he forthrightly adopts the "hypothesis" that "acute diseases" are inflammations that may be cured in the same way as smallpox.[46] A balanced noted is struck in "Methodus Medendi" (1678).

> Once these ["specific natures" of diseases] are ascertained, then the Rules which dogmatists have built up out of their hypotheses of the humors, plethora, etc., may be very useful in applying the method or remedies, modifying them according to the patient's particular constitution.[47]

Elsewhere Locke speaks even more neutrally of the "ordinary hypothesis" of the humoral theory of disease, a neutrality well-chosen, since he advances an alternative supposition about "the archaeus being enraged," which had even less in its favor than did the ordinary hypothesis.[48] Indeed by 1692 Locke was quite aware that his hypotheses departed from medical orthodoxy. Yet they were no less reasonable on that account, since reason followed hypotheses in such matters. On the occasion of the illness of the young Lord Mordaunt, Locke confessed that

> My notions in physick are soe different from the method which obteins . . . and not being of the [Royal] Colleg [of Physicians] can make noe other figure there but of an Unskilfull empirick, and noe doubt anything I should offer would seeme as strange to his physitians as the way you tell me they take with him seems strange to me. But as every ones hypothesis is, soe is his reason disposd to judge both of disease and medicines.[49]

The battle between hypotheses raged in the heated arenas of natural religion and politics as well. Here too, that is, we find debates over probable conjectures beyond the facts of observation and experience, conjectures which are all the more important because they additionally concern our conduct and the prospects of our right living. Thus, even though Locke thought that we could have demonstrably certain "Knowledge of the Creator and the Knowledge of our Duty,"[50] there was much else only probable and hypothetical and so controversial. Thus his hypothesis that God might superadd thinking to matter did not long remain an innocent metaphysical speculation in the *Essay*. Indeed in John Yolton's intricate telling of the tale of "thinking matter," its obvious flirtation with materialism "raised a storm of protest right through to the last years of the eighteenth century."[51] Sounding suspiciously unitarian (and much else besides) to orthodox ears, Locke's hypothesis helped sustain hundreds of pages of increasingly testy controversy, especially with Thomas Burnet and Edward Stillingfleet, the Bishop of Worcester. In defending more generally what Stillingfleet called his (Locke's) "new hypothesis of reason," Locke stuck to his guns, saying that "it can never be proved that there is a substantial substance in us, because upon that supposition it is possible it may be a material substance that thinks in us."[52] Later still, as replies and recriminations flew back and forth, Locke tried to shift the burden of proof in matters hypothetical, saying to the good Bishop, "I humbly conceive it would be more to your purpose to prove, that the infinite omnipotent Creator of all things out of nothing, cannot, if he pleases, superadd to some parcels of matter . . . a faculty of thinking."[53] Locke's thin veneer of tact with Stillingfleet was wholly absent when debate was not public. In the margins of his copy of Burnet's *Third Remarks Upon an Essay Concerning Human Understanding,* Locke vehemently defends his "hypothesis" against suspicions of deism.

> When you have demonstrated the soule of man to be immaterial your own hypothesis will be clear of these objections against mine, & I shall come over to you & be clear too, if you know more than I can goe beyond probability that it is soe. All my accusations of Philosophical Deisme let the fault of that be what you please fall upon yourself and own hypothesis.[54]

Locke's testiness in these disputes says less about his rancorousness than about the stakes at issue in the debate. Being lumped together with deists, unitarians, and materialists was tantamount to being indicted as an atheist. Indeed two years after Locke's death the "discovery of Atheism" in the *Essay* was explored at considerable length.[55] But Locke was no atheist.[56] And while his theism was a matter of faith, he shored it up with critical engagements by the way of hypotheses. In the context of making more general reflections on "method" (see appendix below), atheism was very much on Locke's mind. Recapitulating the arguments of the *Essay* against the "hypotheses" advanced by "atheists" and "the Men of Matter," Locke explodes the "direct contradictions" of those "who deny a God." These contradictions reveal themselves more clearly than ever in such claims (as Locke reconstructs them) as "thinking things were made out of unthinking things by an unthinking power." Locke brings his attack to a close, saying "these mens hypotheses" are "ridiculous when set up against the supposition of a being that had from eternity more knowledge & power than all matter taken togeather & soe was able to frame it into this orderly state of nature."

In the Preface to the *Two Treatises of Government*

Locke pressed an even more dangerous adversary in the matter of hypotheses. With characteristic finality about political judgments he announced his intentions to strike a final blow against Sir Robert Filmer, for already "the King, and Body of the Nation, have since so thoroughly confuted his Hypothesis."[57] "Sir Robert's Hypothesis" attempted, unsuccessfully in Locke's judgment, to trace all extant political authorities to "Adam's Royal Authority." This was his "whole Hypothesis."[58] But it invoked an entire system of arch-royalist doctrines—patriarchalism, divine-right absolutism, and passive obedience to a *de facto* conqueror—doctrines which Locke wanted publicly renounced and abjured in 1690 in order to settle the nation after the Glorious Revolution.[59]

To all this Locke opposed "my Hypothesis," a hypothesis which invoked, again more generally, his own political system with its doctrines of consent, trust, and natural rights.[60] Locke specified a particularly striking consequence of "this hypothesis" in the closing chapter of the *Second Treatise.*[61] It is the very radical and seditious hypothesis that the people may act legitimately to resist tyrannical sovereigns who have broken their trust. Perhaps it was such sedition which caused Locke to hold his tongue about owning the hypothesis as his, at least until his executors broke the seal on his will.

Lest it be thought that in the above examples Locke uses "hypothesis" indiscriminately or equivocally in too many contexts—or that we might readily distinguish "scientific" from "non-scientific" hypotheses—it should be reemphasized that all of the hypotheses mentioned conform at least rudimentarily to the definition briefly sketched at the outset. Though they may display either speculative or practical functions in everyday life, all are probable conjectures beyond the facts of observation and experience about things, actions, events, their causes or consequences. These conjectures issue from some whole system which serves to explain known phenomena. This is evidently true of hypotheses in natural philosophy or about physical unobservables, like gravity, unextended substance, bodily humors, God's loosing Noah's flood, or His making matter think. It is also true of the hypotheses of natural religion and politics, even though they *additionally* concern human conduct and so invoke still *other* standards for our believing them worthy of acceptance. Locke's pre-Kantian sensibilities allow him to discover or forge continuities between those hypotheses in natural philosophy or about unobservable entities and those hypotheses in natural religion or about political action—even though these latter hypotheses have normative or prescriptive content, as we would put it these days.[62]

Thus, for example, the normative grounds of our obedience and the limits of our prescriptive duties are surely the stakes in the ***Two Treatises***. Nonetheless, Locke's many attacks focus in good part on the causal and empirical claims embedded in "Sir Robert's Hypothesis" of Adam's royal authority. That is, Locke not only found Filmer's hypothesis normatively unacceptable as a morally binding prescription for God's creatures, but he also rejected it for harboring other deficiencies of a non-normative sort, particularly because it was premised on unknowable claims about Adam's lineage and some patently false claims about current rulers. Thus in speaking of the evidence necessary for empirically ascertaining Adam's royal authority after Babel, Locke says facetiously, "If you must find it, pray do, and you will help us to a new piece of History."[63] Of course, Locke thinks no such "new place of History" is to be discovered. So much the worse for Filmer's hypothesis. Thus Locke concludes his indictment of Filmer by observing that "'twas his misfortune to light upon an hypothesis that could not be accommodated to the Nature of things and Human Affairs . . . and therefore must needs often clash with common Sense and Experience."[64]

Locke shores up the non-normative defenses of his own hypothesis by adducing "several examples out of History" about the contractual origins of particular civil societies or of "Men withdrawing themselves . . . and setting up new Governments in other places."[65] Some of these examples are "evident matter of fact"; others "great and apparent Conjectures" of the sort Joseph Acosta had to make in order to account for "many parts of America" in its prehistory.[66] (Beyond his explanatory efforts, Locke is also concerned to refute arguments directed to the consequences of propagating his views. "This hypothesis" does not "lay a ferment for frequent Rebellion," at least "no more than any other Hypothesis."[67] Empirically speaking, "the People" are "not so easily got out of their Old Forms."[68])

The corpuscularian hypothesis, it bears mentioning in this context, is the only hypothesis which at least *sometimes* appears *not* to conform to Locke's account—paradoxical as this might sound given all the attention to this particular hypothesis. For at least occasionally Locke intimates that his "minute particles of Bodies" might be *observable in principle* because already in practice "microscopes plainly discover to us" tiny new things "by thus augmenting the acuteness of our senses." What lies ahead, however, "if Glasses could be found, that yet could magnify them 1000, or 10000 times more, is uncertain."[69] But whatever the final judgment on the direct observability of minute corpuscles, and so of his espousal of the corpuscularian hypothesis, Locke shows himself to be a hypothetical thinker of enormous range and fertility.

Hypotheses, in short, are everywhere evident in Locke's "commonwealth of Learning."[70] They emerge, clearly labelled, in virtually all of his writings—in his major works, in his lesser works, in his published and unpublished disputes, in the seemingly inexhaustible storehouse of reflections preserved in letters, commonplace books, notes for publication, and the margins of books. The intellectual contexts for raising and using hypotheses are as varied as the texts within which they are recorded—in physics, optics, geology, medicine, natural religion, and politics. From minute corpuscles, to thinking matter, to gravity, to the deluge, to humors, to atheism, to Adam's royal authority, to popular resistance, Locke advances or attacks one hypothesis after another. If we fail to appreciate the depth of Locke's commitments to hypotheses, we are in danger of misunderstanding his conception of the speculative and conjectural contours of the human understanding. We may also be in danger of misunderstanding his own scientific and philosophical speculations, advertised to his readers as "hypotheses," "conjectures," and "strange doctrines."[71]

II. If the ***Essay*** intimates but understates Locke's recognition of the *use* of "hypotheses," it likewise intimates but understates his reflections on the hypothetical *method*. To discover his views in full we must turn to his collected writings. But the ***Essay***'s intimations are crucial, for there Locke records the significance he attached to the hypothetical method and the general shape of his thoughts about it.

Hypotheses—at least when "intelligible" and "well made" as the ***Essay*** demands—serve three essential functions for systematic human inquiry. In their "true use" they (1) prove to be "great helps to the Memory"; (2) "direct us to new discoveries"; and (3) help us to "explain any Phenomenon of Nature."[72]

Hypotheses, firstly then, are mnemonic devices. Like stenographers' short-hand or "mathematicians . . . Diagrams and Figures,"[73] such devices bear their histories with them. They compress for ready remembrance the facts they contain, the causal claims they embody, or the occasions under which they were inspired. Without them science would constantly have to retake its first steps and could never proceed to new cases. Medical hypotheses, for example, "are so far useful, as they serve as an art of memory to direct the physician in particular cases."[74]

Besides this use, Locke may have been intimating an even more important insight into science, as well as revealing why memory and discovery make such a natural pair of functions for him. Medicine—like other forms of systematic inquiry—often progresses when facts or symptoms which are already well documented, but otherwise insignificant or apparently irrelevant to the present state of knowledge, suddenly gain theoretical novelty and significance by being connected with other facts, symptoms, or causes of disease. In these cases, as is now being appreciated, long known facts become "novel facts" or new discoveries, despite their pedestrian inheritance.[75] Thus there is an intimate link between memory and discovery, a link made possible by hypotheses.

"The discovery of Truths" comprises the second function of hypotheses, a function denied to syllogisms and "received maxims."[76] Hypotheses "serve as clues to lead us into farther knowledge" when the testimony of our senses fail us, as our senses must with bodies remote or minute, or causes ancient or invisible.[77] This is an obvious function of hypotheses in science, as was noted by Boyle; and Locke, perhaps unfortunately, expends little effort beyond stating the obvious.[78]

In the *Conduct,* in a passage referring to the *Essay,* Locke elaborates upon what he has in mind about the third and most important function of the "true use" of hypotheses.

> True or false, solid or sandy, the mind must have some foundation to rest itself upon, and, as I have remarked in another place, it no sooner entertains any proposition but it frequently hastens to some hypothesis to bottom it on; till then it is unquiet and unsettled. So much do our own very tempers dispose us to a right use of our understandings, if we would follow as we should the inclinations of our nature.[79]

The sections on "fundamental verities" and on "bottoming" remake the same point. Hypotheses, as Locke says there, provide a set of foundational principles or "fundamental truths that lie at the bottom, the basis upon which a great many others rest, and in which they have their consistency." Here our explanations may find a "place of rest and stability."[80]

The gravitational hypothesis—"that admirable discovery of Mr. Newton"—provides Locke with an illustration of this explanatory function of hypotheses.[81] A political hypothesis provides another, one which is especially instructive for understanding Locke's view of explanation as well as reinforcing the observation made in the previous section that Locke saw methodological continuities between hypothetical reasoning in natural philosophy and in matters requiring our political judgments. The more particular question of the grand seigneur's lawful right to appropriate property from his people is to be "bottomed" on the foundational hypothesis whether people are equal or not.[82] In the *Two Treatises* Locke leaves no doubts as to his own assessment of the probable truth of the hypothesis of human equality. He goes on from that hypothesis to explain how men contract to form civil society under a system of laws entrusted to a sovereign body to execute. The violation of this trust—say, by the unlawful appropriation of the people's property—becomes the basis, yet further along the chain of explanations, for explaining popular resistance. Thus, the foundational hypothesis of human equality functions as a bottom for explaining lesser hypotheses, facts, and observations.

Beyond elaborating the three functions of hypotheses, the *Essay* also intimates how hypotheses are produced or generated. In the context of discovery, as we often put it these days, "the best conduct of rational Experiments, and the rise of Hypothesis" follow "a wary Reasoning from Analogy."[83] Analogy, in other words, helps us frame possible theories about things or causes unseen or unknown on the basis of things or causes seen or known. Herein lies a mechanism for educational reinforcement, for he or she who is experienced in producing hypotheses by analogy may "guess righter" in the future.[84]

Method, however, promises and must deliver more than just an account of the "true use" and "rise" of hypotheses. Precisely because our imaginations know no bounds when speculating beyond the testimony of our senses, the human understanding needs a method to *judge*—that is, to justify, retain, modify, or reject—the hypotheses it is compelled to pursue in its search for truth. In this matter the *Essay* must be read with care and eventually with other texts in hand. To appreciate this, consider the very first reference to "hypotheses" in the *Essay:* "But he, that would not deceive himself, ought to build his Hypothesis on matter of fact, and make it out by sensible experience, and not presume on matter of fact, because of his Hypothesis, that is, because he supposes it to be so."[85]

Short work could be made of Locke's conception of method if this oft-quoted remark exhausted his reflections. Taken literally, the admonition "to build . . . Hypothesis on matter of fact and . . . sensory experience" might appear to suggest a method of simple induction or confirmation. But to go by the evidence of the *Essay* alone, Locke cannot have meant it to be taken this way. Hypotheses cannot be built literally on "sensory experience" for they are, by definition, "beyond the testimony of the senses."[86] Moreover, hypotheses and matters of fact form two logically distinct classes of probability claims.

"To build," then, must be taken in a different way, a way which endorses only some sort of empirical basis for our hypotheses. To appreciate what sort, note two important features of Locke's reflections on method. The first is his persistent theme of wariness. Science and the human understanding need a "wary induction of particulars," lest we "cram ourselves with a great load of collections."[87] What is this, Locke asks, but "to make the head a magazine of materials which can hardly be called knowledge; . . . he that makes every thing an observation has the same useless plenty and much more falsehood mixed with it."[88]

The selectiveness of observation, especially to reject falsehood, gives the lie to a simple inductivist reading of Locke's intentions. If anything, Locke's wariness in matters of fact and hypothesis suggests a falsificationist message (to use the idiom of our time). In his earliest speculations in the *Essays on the Law of Nature* Locke criticizes those who do not "suffer [their notions] to be called into question."[89] Later, in the *Conduct,* he speaks more frankly still of the fallacy of "hunting after arguments to make good one side of a question, and wholly to neglect and refuse those which favor the other side."[90] Conversely, he praises those who "freely expose their principles to the test" such that "if there be anything weak and unsound in them, are willing to have it detected."[91]

Hypotheses, in short, are "built" on the facts only insofar as they "freely expose" themselves "to the test." The tests, furthermore, are not simple or easily judged, a point brought out in a second feature of Locke's reflections on method. Only "upon a due ballancing [of] the whole" may we "reject, or receive" an hypothesis, as indeed of any probable proposition.[92] But hypotheses are special probabilities:

> For these and the like coming not within the scrutiny of humane Senses, cannot be examined by them, or attested by any body, and therefore can appear more or less probable, only as they more or less agree to Truths that are established in our Minds, and as they hold proportion to other parts of our Knowledge and Observation.[93]

Thus the rational basis of our hypotheses amounts to their overall "conformity" with what else we know.[94] "Tests" or "observations"—directly or standing alone—neither "build" up nor tear down a hypothesis. "Other parts of our knowledge" also figure as some of the counterweights in our "ballancing" of the whole."

This suggests a rich and complex method for judging hypotheses, one which presses well beyond the boundaries of an imagination hedged round by induction or natural history or even simple falsificationism. But Locke presses further still in the very important manuscript on "method." The full text can be found in the appendix below; only the high points need concern us here. It is worth mentioning that Locke's reflections are strikingly modern in a number of ways, *if* one wishes to read Locke with our own contemporary conceptions ready-to-hand.[95]

Tolerance, tenacity, and an enlarged understanding of alternative hypotheses must guide our "method" along its "way to finde truth." We initially "pursue the hypothesis which seems to us to carry with it the most light and consistency." We come to judge it, however, *only after* tolerating it "as far as it will goe" along a course charted by the "whole system" from which it issues. The system also provides some prima facie reasons for thinking our hypothesis probably true. With its

support we give "what light and strength" we can to our hypothesis, in the face of ostensible inconsistencies or problems.

Although objections to an hypothesis will naturally emerge, they should not be allowed to prove immediately decisive. Tenacity has its advantages. First, the "weakness of our understanding" is such that our hypothesis will always "be liable to some exception beyond our power wholly to cleer it from." (Hypothetical truths are simply like that, given that they cannot, by definition, be produced or defended by reference to direct sensory testimony, much less to "clear demonstrations.") Second, we would "loose all stability" if, upon meeting an objection, we immediately gave up our hypothesis and wildly cast about for another, perhaps eventually thinking it "indifferent" which one we believed. Third, and most importantly, since such objections as we meet are themselves usually grounded in yet other hypotheses, we must "consider upon what foundation they are bottomed, and examine that in all its parts." This examination is particularly important, for as Locke puts it elsewhere, only "when another hypothesis is produced wherein there are not the like difficulties" are we justly tempted to abandon our original hypothesis.[96] To put this other competing hypothesis to the test, however, is to tally its problems and objections, to press it to *its* foundations, and so be led to the "whole system" from which it issues.

Now, at last, we may judge of our original hypothesis.

> To shew which side has the best pretence to truth & followers the two whole systems must be set by one another & considered entirely and then see which is most consistent in all its parts; which least clogd with incoharencies or absurdities & which freest from begd principles and unintelligible notions. This is the fairest way to search after Truth.

The search for truth, in sum, proceeds by the comparative advantage which one competing hypothesis has over another, when the whole systems from which they issue confront one another. This comparative method, as Locke puts it in the parallel paragraph in the *Essay,* prevents the natural inclination of those minds which, finding difficulties with their initial isolated hypothesis, "throw themselves violently into the contrary Hypothesis," even though it too may be "altogether as unintelligible to an unbiassed Understanding."[97] Opponents seize upon this natural inclination, thinking that if they "can finde one weak place" in another's hypothesis, then they have "got the day." But "victory no more certainly always accompanies Truth than it does Right." Truth will out by a more pacific method. In calmly and correctly judging between competing hypotheses, we must lay aside that system which is "liable to most exceptions and labours under the greatest difficulties." The alternative with the "greater light" must guide us.

This is all the light we can ever expect to have "in this our dark and short sighted state." Locke concludes his reflections on "method" not only by condemning the comparative absurdities of "these mens hypotheses" that "denie a God" but by reminding us of our incredible limits when compared with "God's knowledge and power." This is no rhetorical flourish, for God is at the center of Locke's own system. God has prepared us in this our pilgrimage with understanding enough to know ourselves, His existence, and our moral duties. Beyond that we have our senses and a method of hypotheses. Without these our state would be infinitely darker.

Notes

[1] *The Correspondence of John Locke,* ed. E. S. de Beer (Oxford, 1979), in eight volumes, #1501.

[2] See, for example, John Dunn, *Locke* (Oxford, 1984), ch. 3; John Dunn, "From Applied Theology to Social Analysis: The Break Between John Locke and the Scottish Enlightenment," in Istvan Hont and Michael Ignatieff (eds.), *Wealth and Virtue: The Shaping of Political Economy in the Scottish Enlightenment* (Cambridge, 1983), 119-35; David Gauthier, "Why Ought One Obey God? Reflections on Hobbes and Locke," *Canadian Journal of Philosophy,* 7 (1977), 425-46; and Richard Ashcraft, "Faith and Knowledge in Locke's Philosophy," in John W. Yolton (ed.) *John Locke: Problems and Perspectives* (Cambridge, 1969), 194-223.

[3] See, for example, Peter A. Schouls, *The Imposition of Method* (Oxford, 1980); Roger Woolhouse, *Locke's Philosophy of Science and Knowledge* (Oxford, 1971); Gerd Buchdahl, *Metaphysics and the Philosophy of Science* (Oxford, 1969); and the works cited in notes 11, 12, and 23 below.

[4] *Essay,* 4.7.3. This is also the sense of the closing chapter, 4.21.

[5] *Essay,* 4.3.26. Similar views may be found at 4.3.29 and 4.12.10.

[6] *Essay,* 4.3.26.

[7] *Essay,* 4.12.12; 3.6.24.

[8] *Essay,* 4.16.12.
[9] *Essay,* 4.3.16.

[10] *Essay,* 4.12.10; 2.23.12.

[11] R. M. Yost, "Locke's Rejection of Hypotheses about Sub-Microscopic Events," *JHI,* 12 (1951), 111-30; John W. Yolton, *John Locke and the Way of Ideas* (Oxford, 1956); John W. Yolton, *John Locke and the Compass of the Human Understanding* (Cambridge, 1970); and John Losee, *A Historical Introduction to the Philosophy of Science* (Oxford, 1980), ch. 9.

[12] Maurice Mandelbaum, *Philosophy, Science, and Sense Perception* (Baltimore, 1964); and Laurens Laudan, "The Nature and Source of Locke's View of Hypotheses," *JHI,* 28 (1967), 211-23. Buchdahl generally shares this view in *Metaphysics,* 211-15.

[13] See, in particular, Yolton's careful and detailed discussion, in *John Locke and the Compass of Human Understanding,* 64-75. Not all parties appear to make this concession, however. Losee says that Locke "expressed no interest in entertaining hypotheses about atomic structure" in *A Historical Introduction,* 97.

[14] In I. C. Tipton (ed.), *Locke on Human Understanding* (Oxford, 1977), 161.

[15] *Ibid.*

[16] Margaret J. Osler, "John Locke and the Chaning Ideal of Scientific Knowledge," *JHI,* 31 (1970), 3-16.

[17] Yolton, *John Locke and the Compass of Human Understanding,* 57; Mandelbaum, *Philosophy, Science, and Sense Perception,* 51; and Peter Urbach, "Francis Bacon as a Precursor of Popper," *British Journal of the Philosophy of Science,* 33 (1982), 113-32.

[18] Barbara Shapiro, *Probability and Certainty in Seventeenth-Century England* (Princeton, 1983), 49. More generally on early probabilistic reasoning, see Ian Hackig, *The Emergence of Probability* (Cambridge, 1984).

[19] *Correspondence,* ##1357 and 1659.

[20] See, for example, Mandelbaum, *Philosophy, Science, and Sense Perception,* ch. 2; and I. B. Cohen, "Hypotheses in Newton's Philosophy," *Physis,* 8 (1966), 163-84.

[21] Many similarities, of course, may be found. Laudan's case for the filiations between Boyle and Locke is a strong one indeed, as others have also observed. For striking comparisons with Locke in the matter of hypotheses, see Boyle's "MS Notes on a Good and Excellent Hypothesis" in M. A. Stewart (ed.), *Selected Philosophical Papers of Robert Boyle* (Manchester, 1979), 119.

[22] *Life of John Locke, with Extracts from His Correspondence, Journals, and Commonplace Books* (London, 1829). There are also editions from 1858 and 1884.

[23] This situation may finally be changing (to judge by developments which I discovered after finishing this essay). See the brief attention to Locke's manuscript in the essay by David E. Soles's, "Locke's Empiricism and the Postulation of Unobservables," *Journal of the History of Philosophy*, 23 (1985), 365-66. The concluding section of Soles's important essay complements the discussion here.

[24] *Essay*, 3.10.15.

[25] *Essay*, 4.12.13; cf. 4.16.12.

[26] It is a matter of some controversy whether Locke includes sensitive knowledge as a part of genuine knowledge. Nothing discussed here, however, turns on the outcome of that controversy.

[27] *Essay*, 4.14.2.

[28] *Essay*, 4.15.4.

[29] *Essay*, 4.16.5.

[30] *Essay*, 4.16.12.

[31] *Essay*, 4.19.8; 4.14.2.

[32] *Essay*, 4.12.13; 4.16.12; 4.20.11.

[33] *Essay*, 1.3.14; 3.10.2. Also see 3.10.14 and the chapter on "maxims" (4.7).

[34] *Essay*, 4.16.12. Also see the list compiled by Yolton in *John Locke and the Compass of Human Understanding*, 59-60.

[35] *Essay*, 4.3.16.

[36] *Essay*, 4.3.6.

[37] *Essay*, 4.3.6.

[38] *Some Thoughts Concerning Education*, section 193 in *The Works of John Locke* in ten volumes (London, 1812), IX, 185. Also see the explanatory potential of "these small and insensible corpuscles" in *Elements of Natural Philosophy* in *Works*, III, 304.

[39] *orks*, IX, 215-17. Cf. *Essay*, 3.4.10 and *Works*, III, 262-64 where Locke uses the hypothesis of "animal spirits" as the "mechanical cause" to explain certain visions individuals have in the dark.

[40] *Works*, IX, 173.

[41] *Essay*, 4.7.11; *Correspondence*, #1538; *Works*, IX, 186. This is very strong language indeed given Locke's usual strictures on what counts as demonstra-tion.

[42] *Works*, IX, 184-85. Note well here how Locke stands by his hypothesis even against the historical account of the Flood as found in Scripture.

[43] *Correspondence*, #1865. Cf. ##1684 and 2131.

[44] *Correspondence*, #1593. In this letter Locke characterizes "general theories" as "for the most part but a sort of waking dreams."

[45] Quoted in Patrick Romanell, *John Locke and Medicine* (Buffalo, N.Y., 1984), 116.
[46] Quoted in *ibid.*, 71.

[47] Quoted in *ibid.*, 139.

[48] Quoted in *ibid.*, 104.

[49] *Correspondence*, #1501.

[50] *Essay*, 2.23.12.

[51] John W. Yolton, *Thinking Matter* (Minneapolis, 1983), 17. Also see the important essay by M. J. Ayers, "Mechanism, Superaddition, and the Proof of God's Existence in Locke's *Essay*," *Philosophical Review*, 90 (1981).

[52] *Works*, IV, 28-29, 33. Also see discussion of Locke's "hypothesis" about human nature, 74-75.

[53] *Works*, IV, 294.

[54] Quoted in Noah Porter, "Marginalia Lockeana" (1857), reprinted in Peter A. Schouls (ed.), *Remarks upon an Essay Concerning Human Understanding*, (New York, 1984), 49.

[55] William Carroll, *Dissertation upon the Tenth Chapter of the Fourth Book of Mr. Locke's Essay, wherein the author endeavors to establish Spinoza's atheistic hypothesis* (London, 1706), as noted in A. C. Fraser's edition of the *Essay* (New York, 1959), 316 n.

[56] As is well known, Locke went out of his way to exclude atheists (alongside papists) from any act of toleration. See especially the *Letter Concerning Toleration* (New York, 1955), 52. However, in the *Third Letter Concerning Toleration*, Locke proclaimed his position against the "hypothesis for the necessity of force" against atheists in maintaining true Christian religion, as proposed by Jonas Proast. See *Works*, VI, 302. (Incidentally, the *Third Letter* is replete with references to "hypotheses," particualrly chapters 5 and 10).

[57] *Two Treatises of Governmet*, ed. Peter Laslett (New York, 1960), Preface, 171.

[58] *Two Treatises,* 1.32; 1.78.

[59] Locke's radical demands may be found in Bodleian Library MS Locke e. 18, as edited and introduced in James Farr and Clayton Roberts, "John Locke on the Glorious Revolution: A Rediscovered Document," *Historical Journal,* 28 (1985), 385-98.

[60] *Two Treatises,* Preface.

[61] *Two Treatises,* 2.224.

[62] This is a methodological variant of a claim that a number of historians of science have made with regard to Locke's era. For example, M. A. Stewart reminds us in the case of Boyle that "there is no clear line at which the science of nature ends and the theology of nature begins." *Philosophical Papers of Robert Boyle,* xiii. Margaret C. Jacob makes a similar point about Newtonians and Latitudinarians at the end of the seventeenth century. Natural philosophy, natural religion, and political theory all merged. See *The Newtonians and the English Revolution, 1689-720* (Ithaca, 1976).

[63] *Two Treatises,* 1.143; cf. 1.111. The historical or empirical status of Locke's state of nature is less clear. Hans Aarslefffollows Dugald Stewart in holding that it is itself a piece of "conjectural or theoretical history." See "The State of Nature and Human Nature," in Yolton (ed.), *John Locke: Problems and Perspectives,* 103-04. John Dunn denies this in *The Political Thought of John Locke* (Cambridge, 1969), ch. 9. For related discussion, see Richard Ashcraft, "Locke's State of Nature: Historical Fact or Moral Fiction?" *American Political Science Review,* 62 (1968), 898-915.

[64] *Two Treatises,* 1.137.

[65] *Two Treatises,* 2.102; 2.115.

[66] *Two Treatises,* 2.103. Also note the counterfactal language of historical conjecture when Locke discusses early civil societies in the *Third Letter of Toleration:* "Let me ask you, Whether it be not possible that men, to whom the rivers and woods afforded the spontaneous provisions of life, . . . should live in one society . . . under one Chieftain . . . without any municipal laws, judges, or any person with superiority established amongst them. . . ." Cited in Laslett's note to *Two Treatises,* 2.108.

[67] *Two Treatises,* 2.224.

[68] *Two Treatises,* 2.223.

[69] *Essay,* 2.23.11; cf. 4.3.25.

[70] *Essay,* Epistle to the Reader.

[71] A longer study would be required to develop this point in full. But I suspect that there is a much greater degree of coherence between what Locke says in the abstract about science and the human understanding, and what he shows in his own substantive practice than is frequently allowed. As for his self-styled "strange doctrines," see his confessions about medicine (*Correspondence,* #1501); personal identity (*Essay,* 2.27.27; also characterized as a "hypothesis" in *Works,* III, 165); and just-war enslavement excluding the seizure of property (*Two Treatises,* 2.180). For a discussion of the last of these "strange doctrines," see my "'So Vile and Miserable an Estate': The Problem of Slavery in Locke's Political Thought," *Political Theory,* 14 (1986), 263-89.

[72] *Essay,* 4.12.13.

[73] *Essay,* 4.3.19.

[74] *Correspondence,* #1593.

[75] See Elie Zahar's amendment to Imre Lakatos's view of novel facts in "Why Did Einstein's Research Programme Supersede Lorentz's?" *British Journal of the Philosophy of Science,* 24 (1973), 95-123, 223-62.

[76] *Essay,* 4.16.12; 4.7.11; 4.17.6.

[77] *The Conduct of Human Understanding* (Oxford, 1901), 95.

[78] See Boyle's view that an "excellent hypothesis" will "enable a skillful Naturalist to Foretell Future Phaenomena," in Stewart (ed.) *Philosophical Papers of Robert Boyle,* 119. In this connection also see Locke's letter to Boyle in which he hopes for a speedy return to his (Locke's) health so that he may go "trudging up and down in quest of new discoveries." *Correspondence,* #335.

[79] *Conduct,* 17.

[80] *Conduct,* 95-96.

[81] *Conduct,* 95.

[82] *Conduct,* 96.

[83] *Essay,* 4.16.12.

[84] *Essay,* 4.12.10.
[85] *Essay,* 2.1.10.

[86] *Essay,* 4.16.12.

[87] *Conduct,* 37, 45.

[88] *Conduct,* 60.

[89] *Essays on the Law of Nature,* ed. W. von Leyden (Oxford, 1954), 143.

[90] *Conduct,* 38.

[91] *Conduct,* 88.

[92] *Essay,* 4.15.5.

[93] *Essay,* 4.16.12.

[94] *Essay,* 4.15.4.

[95] I have in mind those philosophers of science who suggest the need to compare in a sophisticated and complex way entire research programs or traditions, in particular Imre Lakatos, *The Methodology of Scientific Research Programmes* (Cambridge, 1978); and Larry Laudan, *Progress and Its Problems* (Berkley, 1977).

[96] In Porter, "Marginalia Lockeana," 48.

[97] *Essay,* 4.3.6.

Michael Ayers (essay date 1991)

SOURCE: "Personal Identity before the Essay, in *Locke, Vol. II: Ontology,* Routledge, 1991, pp. 254-59.

[*In the following essay, Ayers discusses Locke's response to questions surrounding the nature of the human mind, soul, and identity in* An Essay Concerning Human Understanding.]

In the first of those few entries in his journals clearly on the subject-matter of the chapter **'Of Identity and Diversity'** (although the word 'identity' does not occur) Locke launched an attack on the doctrine of the natural immortality of the soul. The note begins with a statement of the 'usual physicall proofe' of natural immortality: since matter cannot think, the soul is immaterial; since an immaterial thing is by nature indestructible (because indivisible), the soul is naturally immortal. Materialists, Locke continued, complain that animals have sensation, 'i.e., thinke', so that the same argument would prove that animals too have immortal souls. To this objection immaterialists have three possible responses: to deny (with Descartes) that animals are anything more than 'perfect machins', to allow that they do have immortal souls, or to hold that God arbitrarily annihilates their souls with their bodily deaths. Locke did not say so, but Cudworth, whose book he had just been reading, also identified these three possibilities, preferring the second as being less implausible than the first, and more economical than the third. Cudworth argued that the hypothesis of animal souls is no more disturbing theologically than the accepted principle that any substance, even matter, is naturally indestructible as such, since

division is not annihilation. Locke in effect took up this point, but with a different purpose. The disputants 'perfectly mistake immortality whereby is not meant a state of bare substantiall existence and duration but a state of sensibility'. Even the 'manifestly false' doctrine that the soul thinks essentially, and 'dureing a sound quiet sleep perceives and thinkes but remembers it not', could not save the argument for natural immortality. An eternally existing soul 'with all that sense about it whereof it hath noe consciousness noe memory' simply fails to fulfil the conditions of a morally significant afterlife. To all moral effects and purposes it is dead. Since the consciousness and memory of its states are contingent activities or modifications of the soul, their occurrence at any time 'wholy depends upon the will and good pleasure of the first author': immortality is a state of grace, not the natural state of the soul.[45]

Despite his use of the word 'consciousness', his emphasis on the importance of memory and other anticipations of II.xxvii, Locke's position in this early note was far from that of the second edition. It was a familiar enough point that the Christian life-to-come needs to be more than the survival of a simple immaterial substance or soul. Descartes himself had felt obliged to postulate memory after death: although one type of memory involves the corporeal imagination, the more important type, he claied, is a function of pure intellect.[46] Henry More went further, holding that 'the immediate seat of Memory is the Soul herself': 'All Representations with their circumstances are reserved in her, not in the Spirits . . . nor in any part of the Body.' Indeed, 'Memory is incompetible to Matter.'[47] For More, we shall have better memories out of our bodies than we currently have in them, for embodiment is itself analogous to the diseases known to cause amnesia. It was, then, widely agreed that, as John Tillotson (Archbishop of Canterbury and Locke's friend) put it, 'Immortality, when we acribe it to Men, signifies two things. 1. That the Soul remains after the Body. . . . 2. That it lives [i.e. is active and conscious] in this separate state, and is sensible of Happiness or Misery.' It may reasonably be supposed, Tillotson added, that the souls of animals, in contrast, 'lapse into an insensible condition, and a state of inactivity'.[48]

Perhaps the most original and characteristic thought of that early journal entry is the suggestion that the trite issue of immortality (i.e. whether it is natural or an arbitrary gift to naturally mortal creatures) can be settled in effect quite independently of the issue between materialism and immaterialism. Even if the soul is immaterial and naturally indestructible, immortality properly understood is due to God's special grace. Yet Locke's neutrality on the issue of materialism remained clouded by his readiness to phrase the latter part of his argument in the terms of mind-body dualism. In the following year, however, he turned to the topic of personal identity without explicit reference to immortality, and this time his starting-point seems more favourable to the materialists:

> Identity of persons lies not in haveing the same numericall body made up of the same particles, nor if the minde consists of corporeal spirits in their being the same. But in the memory and knowledge of ones past self and actions (with the same concern one had formerly *deleted*) continued on under the consciousness of being the same person (under the certain knowledge *deleted*) whereby every man ow_nes himself.[49]

This remarkable note seems to be the first extant record of Locke's decision that consciousness of continuity is not just a necessary condition of any continuity's being ethically significant, but actually constitutes such continuity. It is as certain as these things can be that the particular context within which the thought occurred was supplied by the doctrine of the resurrection of the body, the topic of considerable controversy at the time.[50]

The difficulties for a literal interpretation of the doctrine were notorious, in particular the problem set by the possibility that many particles might have been parts of more than one human body during the course of history. On one view, however, the *matter* of the body is unimportant: the same man or person would be resurrected provided only that the soul associated with the new body were the same. The ground generally advanced for this claim was that the soul can constitute the only real link, not only between a natural and a recreated body, but between the body of an infant and the body of an old man. Since the parts of a body are in continual flux, the *principium individuationis* can only lie in the immaterial soul.[51] If this controversy did supply the context of Locke's note, then he was making the following proposal: even if materialism is true, it is the same consciousness rather than the same corporeal substance which unites the natural with the resurrected body. This claim was to be repeated within the much wider argument of the second edition of the *Essay*.[52]

Soon after Locke's note of June 1683, an idea very close to his played a public role in quite another context than the issue of immortality and resurrection, i.e. in the controversy over the doctrine of the Trinity which was later to flare up with particular heat, singeing Locke himself, in the 1690s. In 1685, John Turner, an ex-Fellow of Christ's College, published a work critical of Cudworth which set out to explain 'how it is possible for a plurality of Persons, distinct from one another, to be consistent with a Numerical Identity of Divine Substance'.[53]

The Father, Turner claimed, is the common divine substance or nature, and a person in its own right. The Son is such a union of the divine nature with human nature as constitutes a further distinct person, while the Holy Ghost is a similar union of the divine nature with 'aetherial matter'. As a Cambridge Platonist, if a rebellious one, Turner thought of the omnipresent God as extended, having inseparable parts which are, as he put it, 'all of them acted by the same *Divine Life,* which is one self-consciousness or self-sensation running through the whole, indivisible, inseparable and *tyed* to it self, by a Unity of self-enjoyment'.[54] The thought seems to have been connected, both in content and origin, with Newton's later suggestion that space might be, in effect, the sensorium of God. At the same time, Turner argued, the compound, 'the *human nature of Christ,* vitally and personally *united* to the *Divine* of *God the Father*', possesses a self-consciousness which is logically distinct from the Father's. Father and Son sometimes act and think in concurrence, but at other times the Father 'acts as a Person distinctly by it self'.[55]

An important element in Turner's argument was his analogy with what 'we do all of us every day experience in our selves', namely the 'vital union of an *immaterial* nature to a *material*'.[56] By this familiar union, matter 'is made to *taste* and feel it self, to become the *subject* and *seat,* either of *pleasure* or *pain,* and to concur with [immaterial substance] towards the constituting of a *common Person,* resulting from them both'.[57] There are some occasions, however, in which the immaterial substance withdraws from matter and acts on its own, namely in its purely speculative and intellectual operations. Although Turner seems to have accorded a more fundamental role to the material part of us than Descartes ever did, his account is pretty clearly indebted to Descartes' conception of the intimate, 'substantial' union of soul and body. It is, Turner claimed, even easier to conceive that two immaterial substances should achieve a similar unity-cum-duality: 'for by a *person* nothing else is meant but a *self-conscious nature,* and therefore, where there is in *two personalities* a mutual enjoyment or feeling of each *other's life;* there arises a *compound personality*'.

We know from the journal entry of June 1683 that Locke did not need to read Turner's book before arriving at something like Turner's conception of a person, but that does not establish whether he was there applying to personal continuity an idea already in the air, or whether he was doing something more original. Whichever was the case, his acquaintance William Sherlock published a work in 1690, more incendiary than Turner's, which constituted a definite link between the issue of the Trinity and the doctrines of the *Essay* itself. Sherlock advanced what is essentially Turner's explanation of the Trinity, but without the metaphysical underpinnings. For Sherlock, as for Locke, we are entirely ignorant of essences. Hence 'we know nothing of the unity of the Mind but self-consciousness . . . as far as consciousness reaches, so far the unity of a Spirit extends'. Father, Son and Holy Ghost are distinguished by self-consciousness, but united by mutual consciousness. In these terms we can have an understanding of the Trinity which does not go beyond our own ideas: we need not pretend to know more about the divine essence than that God is an infinite mind.[58] It is interesting in the light of later responses to Locke's theory of personal identity that Sherlock explicitly rejected the 'Sabellian' view that the three divine persons are 'Three Modes of the same infinite God, which is little better than Three Names of One God'.[59] On the contrary, each person is substantial, 'for a Person and an intelligent Substance are reciprocal Terms':[60] a claim which, as we shall see, is open to some question.

Of the two allusions to the problems of identity over time which were present in the first edition of the **Essay,** the less interesting merely claimed that the disputes which have arisen in connection with the flux of matter, with the Neoplatonist doctrine of transmigration and with the doctrine of the resurrection of the body all go to show that, since men do not share a clear and distinct idea of identity, they cannot be supposed to share an innate one.[61] In the rather longer discussion in the central sections of **Essay** II.i, however, the journal thoughts are woven into an extended criticism of the Cartesian doctrine that the soul always thinks. At the heart of this criticism is the Cartesian principle, which Locke of course accepted, that the subject of actual thought must be conscious of its thinking.[62] If the soul were to 'have its Thinking, Enjoyment, and Concerns, its Pleasure and Pain apart' during sleep, then it would constitute a different person (or subject of consciousness) from the waking man 'consisting of Body and Soul': 'For if we take wholly away all Consciousness of our Actions and Sensations, especially of Pleasure and Pain, and the concernment that accompanies it, it will be hard to know wherein to place personal Identity.'[63] Locke added an illustration of this principle which is reminiscent both of Turner's multiplicity of divine persons and of his 'vital union' of soul and body: if two Cartesian body-machines were by turns united with a single Cartesian soul 'which thinks and perceives in one, what the other is never conscious of', then that soul would go to make up, with the bodies, 'two as distinct Persons . . . as Socrates and Plato were'.[64]

Each of the passages from the journals or the first edition so far considered anticipated in some respect the argument of the second edition chapter, 'Of Identity and Diversity', yet none embodied the contention which is central to that later argument, i.e. that the clear distinction between a *person* and a *man* is made possible by the formal analogy between life and consciousness, serving as two distinct principles of unity and continuity. Yet the first edition did foreshadow the man-person distinction in a significant context (discussed in chapter 15, above) when Locke defended the thesis that the real essences 'of the Things moral Words stand for, may be perfectly known' against the objection that the subject-matter of ethical theory comprises substances as well as modes, notably the substance *man*. He distinguished '*Man* in a physical sense' from 'the *moral Man*', defined as 'a corporeal rational Being'. In the latter sense, a rational monkey would be a 'man'. Only its rationality matters, and we know in advance that its other characteristics, including its underlying constitution, are irrelevant to its status as a moral agent subject to law. In the same way a mathematician may reason about 'a Cube or Globe of Gold', although the nature and constitution of the particular body is irrelevant to the reasoning.[65] This last analogy will prove significant, but it is now enough to see that there was already in Locke's mind, without any reference to identity, a distinction between the idea of man as a sort of animal, and the formal idea of a *rational being* which is appropriate to ethics.

These, then, were some of the threads which Locke's theory of personal identity was intended to draw together.

Notes

[45] Locke 1936:121ff (Journal, 20 February 1682). The references to Cudworth's *True Intellectual System* are on 118 (18 February 1682).

[46] Descartes 1964-76:III.143 (to Mersenne, 6 August 1640); III.580 (to Huygens, 10 October 1642).

[47] More 1662:188. Cf. Smith 1660:IV 82ff.

[48] Tillotson 1722:II 128. Cf. Leibniz 1981:236.

[49] Bodleian MS Locke f.7, p.107 (5 June 1683).

[50] Cf. Boyle 1979:192ff ('Some Physico-Theological Considerations about the Possibility of the Resurrection').

[51] Cf. Descartes 1964-76:163-9 (to Mesland 9 February 1645). Some versions of this view, Aristotelian and Neoplatonist, distinguished the animal soul or form responsible for the identity of the living body from the intellectual soul which is immortal in the full sense. Cf. Lee 1702:123; Felton 1725:13.

[52] e.g. at 340,4 (II.xxvii.15) and 344,13 (II.xxvii.23).

[53] Turner 1685:119. I am indebted to the admirable Thiel (1983) for drawing attention to this and other relevant writings.

[54] 128.

[55] 123.

[56] 154.

[57] 152.

[58] Sherlock 1690:68f. Sherlock's book was published six months after the *Essay,* and contains a number of Lockean touches, e.g. the point that 'we know no more, what the substance of Matter, than what the substance of a Spirit is'. Yet he did not question the presumption of a metaphysical spiritual unity and continuity underlying and explaining the phenomenal unity of consciousness, although the latter is the only kind of spiritual unity we can clearly achieve. Very possibly the influence was mutual, since Sherlock's initial account of the various principles of unity was as follows: (i) in the case of an unorganized body, 'whether it be simple or compounded of different kinds of matter, that is One numerical Body, whose Parts hang all together' (cf. Locke 1975:330,14-II.xxvii.3); (ii) in 'organical Bodies' the principle is 'the Union of all Parts, which constitute such an organized Body' (cf. 330,35-II.xxvii.4); (iii) finally, the 'Self-unity of the Spirit', which has 'no Parts and no Extension neither, that we can know of', can be nothing else than 'self-consciousness' (cf. 335,13-II.xxvii.9). That Locke explained 'simple' bodies as atomic rather than homoeomerous and (more significantly) refused to assume an underlying metaphysical simplicity or partlessness of thinking things does not prove that he did not draw on Sherlock's order of exposition here as a model in preparing the new chapter for the second edition. It is at any rate very understandable that Stillingfleet should have associated Locke's theories with unorthodox views of the Trinity.

[59] Sherlock 1690:83.

[60] 69.

[61] Cf. Boyle 1979:194: 'Nor is it by the vulgar only that the notion of *identity* has been uneasy to be penetrated.' The idea that there is a general problem about the concept of identity seems to have been commonplace.

[62] Locke 1975:109,26 (II.i.10).

[63] 110,19 (II.i.11).

[64] 110,34 (II.i.12).

[65] 516,26 (II.xi.16). Leibniz commented on this passage that a finite pure spirit would surely fall into the relevant class. 'Corporeal' would seem a slip, unless Locke had corporeality in mind as a condition of pleasure and pain.

Peter A. Schouls (essay date 1992)

SOURCE: "'Master Builder' and 'Under Labourer'," in *Reasoned Freedom: John Locke and Enlightenment,* Cornell University Press, 1992, pp. 9-29.

[*In the following essay, Schouls argues that the "revolutionary" aspects of Locke's thought are a function of his scientific, as well as political, writings, since both emphasize the primacy of human reason. Schouls places Locke's scientific thought in the revolutionary tradition of Descartes, despite various doctrinal differences.*]

"Master-Builder" and "Under-Labourer"

In the *Essay's* "**Epistle to the Reader**," Locke refers to the "Master-Builders" ("a Boyle, or a Sydenham; . . . the Great—Huygenius, and the incomparable Mr. Newton") and with respect to them pronounces himself to be an "Under-Labourer" whose task consists in "clearing Ground a little, and removing some of the Rubbish, that lies in the way to Knowledge." These "Master-Builders" deal with "nature," with "knowledge" of "substances" and their "qualities" and "relations," with the objects of which we are aware through the senses. They develop sciences like medicine and physics. In this context, Locke's role as "Under-Labourer" includes demonstrating that those who deal with "nature" cannot be armchair scientists because, for example, there is no innate knowledge. It also consists in discussions of ideas such as "substance," "quality," and "relation" in order to demonstrate the limitation of our knowledge in this area. And it involves providing directives[19] for achieving practical certainty or probability (as distinct from theoretical or absolute certainty) in these sciences.

Since there are many studies which deal with Locke's view of "substances," their "qualities" and "relations," and the appropriate way of reasoning about them, there is no urgency for another one.[20] This, however, is not my most important reason for refraining from extensive discussion of Locke on knowledge of "substances." From the relevant parts of the *Essay* as well as from these studies, it is quite clear that, unless we want to designate most of philosophy as "under-labour" to the sciences, Locke was far more than an "Under-Labourer." And when he was an "Under-Labourer" he often was so to himself as "Master-Builder." In addition to procedural directive for disciplines like medicine and physics, he advanced methodological principles for political theory and a hermeneutics for theology. In both these areas he was, no doubt, involved in clearing ground and removing rubbish, in the first by exposing "the well endowed Opinions in Fashion" (4.3.20),[21] and in the second by arguing that there is no place for "Enthusiasm" which "laying by Reason would set up Revelation without it" (4.19.3).[22] But he then proceeded to erect edifices—not the least of which is the *Second Treatise of Government*—which in many ways have dominated the contours of the landscape to our own day.

Of course, the *Essay concerning Human Understanding* is itself an imposing and enduring structure. Two of my major subjects, those of human reason and human freedom, form main parts of it. Reason, or the understanding, is the chief subject throughout, but occupies center stage in Books 1 and 4. In the first of these Locke's interest lies in showing what reason is not (hence this part of the *Essay* might best be seen as the under-labor of removing rubbish) and in the second in what it is. To freedom Locke gave short shrift in the *Essay*'s first edition, but, once the inadequacy of that treatment was pointed out to him, the place in which he dealt with it (2.21) grew to be by far the longest chapter in the course of subsequent editions. Neither the doctrine of reason in Book 4 nor that of freedom in Book 2 has the character of under-labor, or, if they do, they are in the form of the foundations for structures that Locke himself erected on them in his political and theological writings and . . . in his writings on education.

Before I deal with reason as one of these foundations I must first highlight and elaborate on both an important distinction which Locke draws and a restriction which I have placed on myself in terms of that distinction. The distinction is between reasoning and the nature of the results of reasoning concerning, on the one hand, "abstract ideas" (or "general ideas" or "universals") and, on the other hand, physical objects (or "substances"). The restriction is that, when dealing with reasoning, I limit myself almost entirely to the first of these. In preceding paragraphs I referred to medicine and physics as "sciences." Strictly speaking, Locke would not allow that name for such disciplines. In 4.12.10, for example, he writes:

> I deny not, but a Man accustomed to rational and regular Experiments shall be able to see farther into the Nature of Bodies, and guess righter at their yet unknown Properties, than one, that is a Stranger to them: But yet, as I have said, this is but Judgment and Opinion, not Knowledge and Certainty. This way of getting, and improving our Knowledge in Substances only by Experience and History, which is all that the weakness of our Faculties in this State of Mediocrity, which we are in in this World, can attain to, makes me suspect, that natural Philosophy is not capable of being made a Science. We are able, I imagine, to reach very little general Knowledge concerning the Species of Bodies, and their several Properties.

For Locke, scientific knowledge is general knowledge. It is knowledge in which reason is concerned only with necessary connections between or among universals. Hence it is "Knowledge of universal Truths," is characterized by "Certainty" and is the result of "Demonstration" (e.g., 4.3.25-26). Usually Locke is more severe than he is in 4.12.10, where "Experiments" are said to afford "very little general Knowledge." A more typical statement is that of 4.3.26: with respect to the "Bodies, that fall under the Examination of our Senses . . . we are not capable of scientifical Knowledge; nor shall ever be able to discover general, instructive, unquestionable Truths concerning them. Certainty and Demonstration, are Things we must not, in these Matters, pretend to."[23] Thus the distinction Locke draws is that between "general" and "experimental" reasoning, between certainty and probability. It is these two functions and products of reason which we find juxtaposed in a single sentence in the *Essay*'s 4.17.2: "the Mind comes to see, either the certain Agreement or Disagreement of any two Ideas, as in Demonstration, in which it arrives at Knowledge; or their probable connexion, on which it gives or with-holds its Assent, as in Opinion."

Phrases like "we are not capable of" certainty and have "but Judgment and Opinion" in the fields of interest to scientists like Sydenham and Newton should not be read as disparaging comments which would downgrade the importance of either such Master-Builders or their achievements. In these areas, probability is not only all we can hope to attain, it is all we need. If we were to aim at the certainty of general knowledge here, we would be using the wrong method: "He that shall consider, how little general Maxims . . . helped to satisfy the Enquiries of rational Men after real Improvements; How little, I say, the setting out at that end, has for many Ages together advanced Men's Progress towards the Knowledge of natural Philosophy, will think, we have Reason to thank those, who in this latter Age have taken another Course, and have trod out to us . . . a surer way to profitable Knowledge" (4.12.12).

If starting with "general Maxims" does not lead to "real Improvements," does this then imply Locke's disparagement of "general knowledge"? Answering that question affirmatively would be as wrong as it would have been earlier to take Locke as deprecating "probable knowledge." There are two domains in which reason is active: that of universals and that of physical objects. Reason's mode of procedure in the first of these is quite different from that in the second. Whereas in the first it makes abstractions and looks for necessary connections between and among the universals it obtains through this process of abstraction (e.g., 4.12.7), in the second it uses the senses to make observations and conduct experiments. Successful labor in the first of these domains gives us the general knowledge that, once we act on it, engages us in the pursuit of the "*Summum Bonum*" and so holds out the promise of freedom from the fear and bondage entailed by passion and prejudice. Success in the second domain progressively frees us from the drudgery and pain of daily life as the "mechanical sciences" allow us to procure "the Conveniences of Life" and medicine allows us their greater enjoyment through better health and longer life (e.g., 4.12.11-12).

Now that this distinction is in clear focus there remains the matter of why I stress the first and largely disregard the second of these uses of reason. It is not because I take the distinction to be unimportant—quite the contrary, if only because it marks a clear difference between Locke and Descartes. For Descartes, all knowledge is characterized by certainty, one and the same method is to be applied to all areas of knowledge, *and physical nature (including the human body) is one of these areas*. Because it all rests on clear and distinct foundations and is characterized by clarity and distinctness as it is developed on these foundations, all knowledge for Descartes possesses the same attribute of certainty irrespective of what it is about, so that the phrase "probable knowledge" is a contradiction in terms. As we have seen, Locke agrees with Descartes on this characteristic only as long as we limit our discussion to the realm of general knowledge, but he fundamentally disagrees in the realm of knowledge of physical objects.

In his insistence that in the realm of knowledge of nature probability is all we can attain, and all we need for the achievement of mastery, Locke makes himself an object of admiration for eighteenth-century Enlightenment thinkers at precisely the point where Descartes aroused their antagonism. Descartes's insistence that he knew the real essence of matter was, for these thinkers, an instance of the metaphysics which, "vain and ambitious," "wants to search into every mystery" and does not "wisely keep within the bounds prescribed by nature."[24] It was, for them, an example of philosophic "bad taste" when Descartes refused to place "strict limits on the mania for explaining everything" and so disrespected "the wise timidity of modern physics."[25] There was, to them, no vanity in Locke's removing such "rubbish," nothing but good taste in his clearing the ground for the Master-Builders by insisting on the use as well as the limitations of the senses—especially when these limitations in no way stood in the way of the utility that Descartes had foreseen as fruit of the diligent pursuit of the sciences of nature.

Why, then, not focus on the function of reason for which Locke insisted on "wise timidity"? To reiterate: it is not primarily because others have done much work on Locke on substances and our knowledge of substances. It is, rather, that in significant respects the function of reason that deals with universals and gives us the "certainty" of general knowledge has the more crucial place in Locke's works.

There are two main grounds for this claim. First, it is this function of reason which tells us what real essences are, how to obtain knowledge of them,[26] that we are barred from such essences in the realm of "substances" and that consequently we are there dependent on "Experiments" and "Histories." It is this reasoning which juxtaposes the two realms in the words from the headings of the *Essay*'s 4.12.7 and 4.12.9—"The true method of advancing Knowledge, is by considering our abstract Ideas," "But Knowledge of Bodies is to be improved only by Experience"—and which, in the latter paragraph, then insists:

> In our search after the knowledge of Substances, our want of Ideas, that are suitable to such a way of proceeding, obliges us to a quite different method [from that characteristic of this function of reason]. We advance not here, as in the other (where our abstract Ideas are real . . . Essences) by contemplating our Ideas, and considering their Relations and Correspondencies. . . . Here we are to take a quite contrary Course, the want of Ideas of their real Essences sends us from our own Thoughts, to the Things themselves, as they exist. Experience here must teach me, what Reason cannot.

Second, . . . it is this reasoning (rather than that about "substances") whose very process is of prime importance in the destruction of prejudice, thus in the liberation of the reasoner's mind, and in placing the reasoner in the only position from which legitimate mastery may be achieved—whether this be the mastery over self, over nature, or over one's cultural context. Since it is mastery over self that is the first and foremost aim of what Locke takes to be right education, it is this reasoning in which youth (or, for that matter, wrongly educated adults) have to acquire facility to the extent that its exercise becomes habitual for them.

Fundamentally, it is this reasoning on which, for Locke, both human freedom and progress depend. As we can now see, this holds even for progress in the sciences of nature. For without this function of reason directing us here "to take a quite contrary Course . . . from our own Thoughts, to the Things themselves," reason's necessary mode of operation in the realm of universals would, in the realm of physical objects, have become "the source of innumerable errors, as it fills the mind with vague and indeterminate notions, and with words that have no meaning."[27] It is, in short, this function of reason which makes Locke's philosophy revolutionary and which allows for the characterization of Locke as philosopher of mastery.

Locke as a Revolutionary

Especially in view of recent remarks that "the concept of revolution" has "cognitive opacity,"[28] it is necessary first to state the meaning that I attach to "revolution." One way to come to such a statement is by distinguishing "revolutionary" from "reformer."

I take a reformer to be a person who accepts the most important part of an existing set of principles or beliefs and the practices built upon them, but who recognizes that some (perhaps many) of the beliefs of this set may be false and some (perhaps many) of these practices less than good. While accepting much of a particular set of beliefs as true and praising many of the actions based on it, reformers aim to purify both thought and action through identifying some of the beliefs of this set as false and some of its related actions as harmful, and through replacing such beliefs with true beliefs and substituting for such actions those they consider to be salubrious. In their attempts to achieve this aim, reformers are radical because they want to set things straight by returning to the root of the matter: they judge their contemporaries' beliefs and practices by principles that were once accepted but are no longer heeded. In contrast, revolutionaries are more than radical: they mean to uproot all beliefs and practices, and consider themselves free from all of society's present and past principles and from all actions based on them.

Revolutionaries always attempt to start de novo.[29] Their intent is to be, or become, free from all beliefs and practices that their context would impose, free as far as possible from this context itself. They recognize that they must begin their activity somewhere, must start out from some "given." But this given is always kept as minimal as possible and as close to an aspect of (presumed) first-person experience as possible. If Luther is a good example of a reformer, Descartes is a prime example of a revolutionary. All Descartes initially accepts as true is that there is thinking going on. He does not even at first accept this as *his* thinking, that is, as the thinking carried out by the person René Descartes. For this would introduce many other givens, not the least of which are the doctrines of soul and body, the realms of mind and matter. Even the use of "accept" in the statement "he accepts that there is thinking going on" is saying too much if it implies that there is a given. To Descartes, initially nothing is "given" if "to be given" implies a distinction of giver and receiver. Initially, he "gets rid of" all his opinions (and hence all the objects of his opinions) "all at one go" (CSM1, 117; AT6, 13)—as others[30] translate this statement, "he sweeps them completely away"—and then, free from anything his physical or cultural context would impose on him, he starts only with consciousness aware of its own activity.

Elsewhere, I have tried to capture a broad spectrum of statements on the meaning of "revolution" in the definition: "revolution is the introduction of discontinuity, that is, of a radically new situation, order, or condition; the discontinuity is for the sake of obtaining freedom."[31] Given Descartes's position that, at the foundation of one's knowledge, there must be items which are contextless, that is, items which are self-evident or known per se, Descartes is a thinker whom we may call "revolutionary" in this sense of that word. And because of Descartes's influence on him, we may say the same of Locke. But before we go to Locke, it will be helpful to say just a bit more about the revolutionary nature of the Cartesian position. Let me do this by introducing Descartes's criteria of knowledge, "clarity" and "dis-

tinctness" (criteria Locke employed much in the way Descartes did). Descartes stipulates that the criteria of clarity and distinctness must jointly apply to an item if it is legitimately to be called an item of knowledge. He calls "clear" that which "is present and accessible to the attentive mind," and "distinct" that which "is so sharply separated from all other perceptions that it contains within itself only what is clear" (*Principles* I 45: CSM1, 207-8; AT8-1, 21-22). In order therefore for us to be capable of judging anything properly it is not sufficient that we are just fully aware of all of that "thing." That much is compliance only with the first criterion, with "clarity." And such compliance may leave the "thing" intricately enmeshed with many other "things" none of which need themselves be fully understood. "Distinctness" demands that we have before the mind nothing but what pertains to having that item fully before the mind. "Distinctness" therefore requires that, through reductive analysis, we separate that item from all other items that accompany it in our everyday sensous or intellectual experience.

Thus these criteria dictate that we cannot initially accept as knowledge that which is not epistemically completely simple. Even if we are confronted with a complex item which is clear and distinct to others, it cannot be so immediately to us. For, as complex, it is a compound of other items, all of which we must ourselves grasp as clear and distinct. Only then can the relations that hold between and among such items be understood; only then can a complex item be clear and distinct. These criteria therefore demand that at the foundation of knowledge there be utterly simple items, that is, items known apart from any other items, items known per se rather than per aliud. They demand that the materials foundational to knowledge be context-independent in the strongest possible sense: their self-evidence determines them to be context*less*.[32]

That which the senses give us is concrete, enmeshed in its context, and therefore cannot be known immediately. If we call "nature" that which the senses give us, then "nature" cannot be known immediately. It can be understood only once it has been fitted into the rational schemes of a "mechanics," "medicine," or "morals." These "rational schemes" themselves cannot be developed prior to the advancement of the "rational schemes" called "metaphysics" and "physics." These in turn rest on the prior knowledge of certain concepts and principles known per se.

The same holds for what our education or general cultural environment places before us. For neither Euclid's *Elements* nor Aristotle's *Ethics,* neither Aquinas's *Summa Theologica* nor Galileo's *Two New Sciences* show that it derives its conclusions from indubitable principles known per se. None of them even went so far as to attempt to state these principles. Even had they stated them, and even had they derived their conclusions from them by uninterrupted chains of argument, I myself cannot begin at the end, with conclusions. If I am to understand, I must begin where they began to understand, at the level of items known per se. But such items are not "given."

Descartes's epistemology therefore dictates that, whether it is my physical or my cultural context that I am attempting to understand, if I am to understand I must understand for myself, radically so. In the words of the opening paragraph of the *Meditations,* "anything at all in the sciences that" for someone else "was stable and likely to last" is initially of little use to me as a person aspiring to know. For I will not be able to understand it unless I myself "start again right from the foundations." And no foundation is ever given. The foundation is always to be established. Whoever wants to understand will first have to establish his or her own foundation. Moreover, no foundation can be established apart from obeying the reductionistic precepts of the method which Descartes proposes. Thus when in the *Discourse* Descartes writes that "my plan has never gone beyond trying to reform my own thoughts and construct them upon a foundation which is all my own" (CSM1, 118; ΛT6, 15), he speaks for himself and, he believes, for whoever seeks to understand. The need for revolution is dictated by a methodology that goes hand-in-hand with the criteria of clarity and distinctness, as well as with a doctrine of radical epistemic individualism.[33]

Locke, too, is a revolutionary rather than a reformer. He is a revolutionary because he follows Descartes (a statement which must appear contradictory given that I have just said that "revolutionary" involves both contextlessness and individualism; I shall deal with this apparent contradiction in the next section). It is not that Locke follows Descartes in accepting what we would call Cartesian metaphysical doctrines about soul and body, mind and matter; these are among the Cartesian doctrines which he rejects. And out of the rejection of Descartes's doctrine concerning matter there flows the important difference between the two on the kind of *knowledge* of matter or of "nature" that is possible. In spite of all their differences, what accounts for their strong kinship is Locke's adoption of Descartes's method for "general knowledge." When Locke adopts Descartes's methodology, he becomes a revolutionary in the areas covered by "general knowledge." I shall first discuss the phrase "Locke's revolutionary methodology." Discussion of the sentence "Locke accepts the Cartesian revolutionary methodology" will be left for the next section.

It has of course been noted by others that, in the sense in which I use the term, Locke is a revolutionary. The most recent extensive treatment of Locke as revolutionary is Richard Ashcraft's *Revolutionary Politics and Locke's Two Treatises of Government.*[34] Ashcraft, however, divorces Locke's revolutionary stance in politics from his methodological and epistemological doctrines; in this respect, his treatment is retrogressive.[35] For earlier writers did recognize that the revolutionary thrust of Locke's thought is not to be restricted to his political writings. Peter Laslett, for example, has said that "the implications of Locke's theory of knowledge for politics and political thinking were considerable and acted quite independently of the influence of *Two Treatises*." Laslett added that it was the implications of Locke's epistemology which "made men begin to feel that the whole world is new for everyone and we are all absolutely free of what has gone before."[36] As an example of an epistemological tenet with such an influence Laslett points to the doctrine of the tabula rasa. As we shall see at the end of this section, that particular doctrine is not really as fundamentally important as he assumes it to be. More important are the principles of Locke's methodology for development of "general knowledge." They are more important because, in contrast to the doctrine of the tabula rasa, they are unequivocally revolutionary. The aspects of Locke's epistemology which in fact dictate a revolutionary postion are themselves determined by the methodological principles. In these principles Locke transcends the boundaries of what is peculiar to his own position. At bottom, it is these principles that bind him, for example, to his later French *confrères* such as d'Alembert and Condorcet as well as to Descartes. It is these principles that lead to the social and political atomism which Laslett correctly identifies as a direct implication of Locke's theory of knowledge.[37] The application of the principles (about whose nature I will say more in a moment) led to atomism not just in social and political thought. For when others (like Boyle or Hooke or Newton) applied them to "nature" they led to a mechanistic picture of the universe and to theories of an atomistic kind in chemistry and physics. It is Locke's principles that helped bring about the atomism which many have pronounced typical of Enlightenment thought.

This idea of the relation between methodology and atomism, rooted in the seventeenth century and prevalent in the eighteenth, has not infrequently been a topic for comment. Consider Isaiah Berlin, who writes that "the great popularizers of the age . . . headed by Voltaire, Diderot, Holbach, Condorcet, and their followers, whatever their differences," shared the "dominant trend" of "analyzing everything into ultimate, irreducible atomic constituents, whether physical or psychological."[38] It has been widely recognized that such "ultimate components" were not held to be restricted to the realms of the physical or psychological; there were also believed to be epistemic and social or political irreducible constituents. Of the latter, the person of Locke's *Second Treatise of Government* is acknowledged as a prime illustration. The former are the foundational ideas of both Descartes and Locke. Whether, with Descartes, we call these "simple natures" or, with Locke, "simple ideas" or uncompounded "universals," in either case they are characterized by both Descartes and Locke as "clear and distinct" or (to use a word Locke introduces in later editions of the *Essay*) as "determinate." For both Locke and Descartes, a clear and distinct idea is the end product of reason's activity of analysis, or, speaking in terms of methodology, it is the final product of the process of reduction or decomposition. For Locke as for Descartes, it is only from the foundation of these fully known contextless items that theorizing can start, that systematic ("general") knowledge can be achieved. Whether in theory or in practice, to aim for a starting point which is to be characterized as "contextless" is to intend to start de novo. As we have seen, such an intent is typical of the seventeenth- and eighteenth-century revolutionary.

Some of those who connect atomistic doctrines with methodology label these doctrines as revolutionary in import and explicitly attribute them to (among others) Locke. So Charles Taylor writes of "atomist doctrines" which "underly the seventeenth-century revolution in the terms of normative discourse," doctrines "which we associate with the names of Hobbes and Locke," doctrines whose "central . . . tradition" in the domain of political thought "is an affirmation of what we could call the domain of rights."[39] There is thus nothing new in speaking about Locke's ideas as "revolutionary." That is how his ideas appeared to many of his contemporaries—for example, to William Molyneux—as well as to his immediate successors. In spite of the fact that we today find Locke's philosophy "frequently obvious and almost commonplace" (which is "the measure of its influence on us")[40] many recent critics remain struck by its revolutionary character.

Some, like Berlin, without elaboration, summarily refer to Locke's ideas as "genuinely revolutionary."[41] Others attach this label to specific works or to specific themes in them. Among these, John Passmore speaks of the "revolutionary implications" of *Some Thoughts concerning Education*,"[42] John Yolton refers to Locke's "religious views" as "foremost in the ranks of those considered radical and revolutionary,"[43] and Ashcraft calls Locke a "hard-line radical" who published the *Second Treatise* as a "public and solemn statement on . . . the rightness of . . . revolution."[44] What basically accounts for the revolutionary character of Locke's thought is a point on which many of these writers remain imprecise. Most of them, in fact, pass it by altogether. Taylor provides a valuable hint when he relates "revolutionary" and "atomistic." So does Yolton when he writes, "It would be a gross overstatement to claim that Locke was unaware of the implications for religion of many of his epistemological doctrines, for a man so well versed in the controversies of his day could not fail to grasp the revolutionary character of many of these doctrines for religion."[45] Both Taylor and Yolton point in the right

direction: the revolutionary power of Locke's thought is related to the atomism demanded by his epistemology. But neither of them quite reveals the heart of the matter. For the characteristic nature of Locke's epistemology comes about through the adoption of a particular methodological stance and it is, therefore, the revolutionary character of Locke's reductionistic methodology which lends revolutionary force to his epistemology. His methodology and epistemology together, in turn, account for the "revolutionary implications" of his works on politics, on religion, and on education.

Locke himself was quite conscious of the fact that it was from his methodology that revolutionary power emanated into the rest of his writings. This, as we shall see in a moment, is clear enough from his *Essay*. But the point may also be established from other works. Take, as an example, the opening pages of the *Conduct of the Understanding*. Here Locke writes about "the logic, now in use . . . these two or three thousand years" as "not sufficient to guide the understanding." He impugns that "logic" for having "served to confirm and establish errors, rather than to open a way to truth." What is therefore called for, he continues, is "that a better and perfecter use and employment of the mind and understanding should be introduced."[46] "Logic" is here spoken of as "a way," "a use." In other words, logic is to be taken as method. Implied is the revolutionary nature of the new method. The old method debarred us from attaining truth. Its well-entrenched products obstruct our intellectual progress and will have to be expunged. Employment of the new method will lead us totally to abandon the old method and to sweep its products completely away. When we have reached that point we must begin anew in the attempt to develop knowledge. For once we are rid of the old we are still only at the stage where we can "open a way to truth." Truth still has to be won.

A move just made requires, for a moment, interrupting the discussion of Locke as "revolutionary." It is my characterization of Locke's writings on logic as works on method. This identification is plausible if only because of Descartes's influence on Locke, for Descartes writes about his *Discourse on Method* as a work "where I summarized the principal rules of logic."[47] But especially for my discussion of education in later chapters, it is important to establish the legitimacy of this identification more firmly and to demonstrate that Locke himself made it.

The new "logic" is one which Locke took himself to have propounded and used in the *Essay*. That this logic is in fact what (with Descartes and many others) we would call "method" can perhaps be established more easily from that part of the correspondence which passed between Locke and William Molyneux when Locke was preparing his *Some Thoughts concerning Education* for publication.

In a letter of July 16, 1692, Locke thanks Molyneux for "the extraordinary compliment you were pleased to make me in the Epistle Dedicatory" of *Dioptrica Nova. A Treatise of Dioptrics*. This compliment reads as follows:

> But to none do we owe for a greater Advancement in this Part of Philosophy, than to the incomparable Mr. Locke, Who, in his **Essay of Humane Understanding,** has rectified more received Mistakes, and delivered more profound Truths, established on Experience and Observations, for the Direction of Man's Mind in the Prosecution of knowledge, (which I think may be properly term'd *Logick*) than are to be met with in all the Volumes of the Antients.[48]

Throughout the seventeenth and eighteenth centuries works on method were announced as writings on "Truths . . . for the Direction of Man's mind in the Prosecution of knowledge." Molyneux's phrase evokes the titles of Descartes's works on method, the *Discourse on the Method of rightly conducting one's Reason and seeking the Truth in the Sciences,* and the earlier *Rules for the Direction of the Mind* (known to many in manuscript form and first published in Dutch in 1684).[49] His phrase also calls to mind titles and sentences from later works. There is Arnauld's *La logique, ou l'art de penser* (published in 1662, with an explicit acknowledgment that parts of it were taken directly from the manuscript of Descartes's *Rules*),[50] in which the opening sentence of the Introduction begins with the words "Logic is the art of directing reason to a knowledge of things. . . ." And to mention just one of the works written in the eighteenth century, there is Isaac Watts's *Logick: or, the Right Use of Reason in the Enquiry after Truth, with a Variety of Rules to Guard against Error, in the Affairs of Religion and Human Life, as Well as in the Sciences;* the opening chapter begins with the statement "Logick is the Art of using Reason well in our Enquiries after Truth."[51] From the correspondence it is evident that Molyneux sees the basic importance of Locke's *Essay* as lying in the area of "logic" or methodology, and that Locke's great service still to be performed is to republish just these "truths . . . for the direction of man's mind" in a form suitable to be a guide for the education of the young. Locke takes no exception to Molyneux's identification of logic and method: "as to the method of learning," he wrote, "perhaps I may entertain you more at large hereafter."[52] Molyneux then informs Locke that, through a third party, he was told that while exiled in Holland Locke was busy preparing just "such a Work as this I desire" on "the Method of Learning."[53] Locke confirms the correctness of this information, hence explicitly identifying the thrust of the *Essay*'s method with that of the precepts of his major work on education: "The main of what I now publish"—i.e., **Some Thoughts concerning Education**—"is but what was contain'd in several letters to a friend of mine, the greatest part whereof were writ out of Holland."[54] In reply, Molyneux writes that "I can give no better proof of my liking your Book in all these Precepts, than by a strict Observance of them in the Education of My Own. . . . I know no Logick that Deserves to be Named, but the Essay of Humane Understanding."[55]

Locke continues to use "logic" with the sense of "method." And, like Molyneux, he continues to see logic or method as the *Essay*'s epitome: two years after this period of correspondence he tells Molyneux that the third edition of the *Essay* is about to appear and that "what perhaps will seem stranger, and possibly please you better, an abridgment is now making . . . by one of the university of Oxford, for the use of young scholars, in the place of an ordinary system of logick."[56]

These items of correspondence state that the logic of the *Essay* is to be taken as a method for the direction of the mind. They explicitly link the *Essay* and the **Education**. They do not, however, say anything specifically about the main topic of this section, to which I now return: the revolutionary nature of this method. But if we consider some of the *Essay*'s passages in which Locke writes of what he believes the employment of the method will accomplish, then it becomes quite legitimate to say that the designation "revolutionary" is appropriate. Introduction of just a few passages from the first book of the *Essay* will suffice to substantiate this point.

In the third chapter of that first book Locke attempts to explain how it comes about that people "even of good understanding in other matters," in morality and religion "embraced as first and unquestionable" principles and doctrines which, because of "their absurdity, as well as opposition one to another, it is impossible should be true" (1.3.21). He asks, first, what are "the ways, and steps by which it is brought about" that "Doctrines, that have been derived from no better original, than the Superstition of a Nurse, or the Authority of an old Woman" come to "grow up to the dignity of Principles in Religion or Morality"? (1.3.22). Once we have correctly answered this question, we know which wrong ways or methods of thinking and of education we ought to break free from. Second, he asks: how is it possible that in spite of their very wrongness, such methods can be so effective in blinding us to truth? Part of the answer to the first question is that any method is wrong if it does not teach people to be critical of whatever is placed before them. Part of the answer to the second is that a child is very impressionable and has little or no defense against the power of those who dominate its surroundings; it is anything but difficult for adults to impose their principles on the vulnerable child. Parents in particular and educators in general therefore have the task of preventing even the principles dearest to themselves from being impressed on the child's consciousness. The only principle that ought to guide parents is not "to principle" children but to encourage them to develop their power of questioning, of not accepting what may enjoy popular acceptance unless it can withstand criticism, that is, unless the issue in question can be seen by the maturing child to be clear and distinct. Children acquire prejudices whenever they accept as true or good an item which they have not criticized, that is, have not submitted to the criteria of clarity and distinctness. Whether or not the belief accepted is in fact true is not the issue. The point is whether the child adopting it may legitimately adopt it as true. Only when children have themselves recognized, clearly and distinctly, the truth of a belief is their acceptance of that belief legitimate.

Although the question of precisely how the child is to become "critical" must be left for the third part of this book, it is clear that for Locke, the only principle which ought to guide parents is to keep the child from becoming prejudiced. Alas, says Locke, parents and educators generally act quite contrary to this principle.

> For such, who are careful (as they call it) to principle Children well, (and few there be who have not a set of those Principles for them, which they believe in) instil into the unwary, and, as yet, unprejudiced Understanding, (for white Paper receives any Characters) those Doctrines they would have them retain and profess. These being taught them as soon as they have any apprehension; and still as they grow up, confirmed to them, either by the open Profession, or tacit Consent, of all they have to do with; or at least by those, of whose Wisdom, Knowledge, and Piety, they have an Opinion, who never suffer those Propositions to be otherwise mentioned, but as the Basis and Foundation, on which they build their Religion or Manners, come, by these means, to have the reputation of unquestionable, self-evident, and innate Truths.

(1.3.22)

In this way what is really artificial and relative comes to be accepted without question as natural and absolute. That which we should have critically examined we "take . . . upon trust."[57]

Upbringing or education is the greatest culprit but not the only one, for "some, wanting skill and leisure, and others the inclination, and some being taught, that they ought not, to examine; there are few to be found, who are not exposed by their Ignorance, Laziness, Education, or Precipitancy, to take . . . Principles . . . upon trust" (1.3.24). What follows is one of the most revolutionary passages of the *Essay:*

> This is evidently the case of all Children and young Folk; and Custom, a greater power than Nature, seldom failing to make them worship for Divine, what she has inured them to bow their Minds, and submit their Understandings to, it is no wonder, that

grown Men, either perplexed in the necessary affairs of Life, or hot in the pursuit of Pleasures, should not seriously sit down to examine their own Tenets; especially when one of their Principles is, That principles ought not to be questioned. And had Men leisure, parts, and will, Who is there almost, that dare *shake the foundations of all his past Thoughts and Actions,* and endure to bring upon himself, the shame of having been a long time wholly in mistake and error? . . . he will be . . . afraid to *question* those Principles, when he shall think them, as most Men do, *the Standards set up by God in his Mind,* to be *the Rule and Touchstone of all other Opinions.* And what can hinder him from thinking them sacred, when he finds them the earliest of all his own Thoughts, and the most reverenced by others?

(1.3.25, my italics)

For the adult not educated in accordance with the right method one of the "truths . . . for the direction of man's mind in the prosecution of knowledge" is that he must be thoroughly critical of absolutely every belief he happens to hold. For that, he must "shake the foundations of all his past Thoughts and Actions" even if such foundations commonly function as standards and touchstone, even if he himself and those around him believe they have been established by God. Discussion of how this shaking of the foundations is to be accomplished must also be postponed to a later chapter. Suffice it to say here that the principle behind the procedure involved in shaking the foundations is no different from what is present in the upbringing of a young person who is being educated according to the right method. In either case the principle is that of (epistemic) autonomy; in either case it demands the revolutionary's attitude. Nothing believed to be sacred or ultimate by yourself or by society is to be accepted as absolute. All that parents and teachers are allowed to pass on to children is that they must be thoroughly critical of whatever comes before their minds. Thus educators are duty bound to impress upon the pupil not to accept anything as true unless it has withstood criteria imposed by the pupil's own understanding. The criteria in question are those of clarity and distinctness. This manner of educating, according to Locke, is the only way for a new generation to have the best chance of maturing free from prejudice. To be free from prejudice or bias, free from principles whose acceptance one's own reason has not authorized, is the only state in which a person can successfully direct his or her "mind in the prosecution of knowledge." The results then obtained will themselves be free from bias because they carry reason's authoritative stamp.

In the *Essay* Locke does not just advocate this method; he actually uses it. To the extent that he employs it successfully, the *Essay* itself is then a revolutionary document not merely in the method it advocates but also in the manner it deals with its subject matter and in the results it achieves. Book 1 illustrates this well. It introduces a doctrine, that of innatism, which is dear, even sacred, to many of Locke's contemporaries; Locke reduces this doctrine to the obscure ideas and contradictory principles upon which it rests, and then rejects it; and he puts in its place a new doctrine, that of the tabula rasa. The closing paragraphs of Book 1 attest to the fact that Locke was well aware of the revolutionary character of his program. There we read: "What censure, doubting thus of innate Principles, may deserve from Men, who will be apt to call it, pulling up the old foundations of Knowledge and Certainty, I cannot tell." And, it is clear, he does not really care. He continues, "This I am certain, I have not made it my business, either to quit, or follow any Authority in the ensuing Discourse" (1.4.23). What he has made his business is to employ nothing but his own reason on the materials derived from his own experience. As he states in the final sentence of this first book, his business was to present "an unbias'd enquiry after Truth." As we now know, for Locke "unbias'd enquiry" is possible upon disregarding what one's culture would have one accept in the first place. It is necessary to be "indifferent"; hence "I have not made it my business, either to quit, or follow any Authority." It is in the contextlessness created through rejecting the relevance of his culture's authorities that Locke obtains a foundation that he is convinced can stand the test of rational scrutiny: "All that I shall say for the Principles I proceed on, is, that I can only appeal to Mens own unprejudiced Experience, and Observation, whether they be true, or no."

Earlier in this section, I said that when we discuss the revolutionary nature of Locke's position, it will become clear that the doctrine of the tabula rasa does not occupy as fundamental a place as considerations about methodology. We can now see why this is so. The doctrine of the tabula rasa need not have revolutionary implications. For it is not inconceivable for such a doctrine to coexist with one that portrays human beings as social beings, as the kind of beings which are, however, only potentially social. They could then be the kind of beings which cannot come to the realization of their potentiality except through their cultural context, that is, through becoming imbued with the beliefs and attitudes prevalent at the time during which they are in the process of growth and maturation. Such a holistic doctrine is far removed from the atomistic one Locke presents. The one would hold that no beings become fully human unless they come to be imbued with the web of beliefs prevalent in their culture; the other, that they do not become fully human unless they initially reject all prevalent doctrines and opinions and accept only such doctrines as can pass a certain test imposed by each individual's own intellect. Either view might incorporate the doctrine of the tabula rasa. Whether the position is holistic or atomistic, conservatist or revolutionary in implication, the doctrine of the tabula rasa may be used to express the

view that we are not born with some (ineradicable) beliefs. In the one case, a being is to become human through uninhibited exposure to its culture's beliefs and principles, in the other through initial shielding from them. In the one the slate is to be inscribed with the prevalent cultural attitudes at the earliest opportunity, in the other it is to be kept as clean as possible. In the former it might be held that precisely because society can write on the "white paper," new generations of social (hence human) beings can come on the scene. In the latter it might be believed that because minds are like "white paper" people can become ruined for life and never really attain humanhood because of their early upbringing; or that they can be brought up well by being taught to let only their own reason write on the slate; or that they can redeem themselves from the disaster of the wrong kind of upbringing by forcing themselves to erase all marks found on the paper and to let only their reason write on it henceforth.[58] The last two statements are sketches of how Locke sees the emergence of a new truly human being. In both of them the revolutionary implications of the doctrine of the tabula rasa are borrowed from the broader methodological picture in which this doctrine is given its place . . . .

Notes

[19] See, for example, 4.12.9-13. For grounds of such directives see passages such as 4.3.9-14 and 4.6.4-15.

[20] The most impressive and exhaustive of these are Michael Ayers's *Locke, Volume I: Epistemology* and *Locke, Volume II: Ontology* (London, 1991). Some of the more interesting earlier studies are Peter Alexander's *Ideas, Qualities, and Corpuscles* (Cambridge, 1985); the first three chapters of J. L. Mackie's *Problems from Locke* (Oxford, 1976); H. A. S. Schankula's "Locke, Descartes, and the Science of Nature" in Reinhard Brandt, ed., *John Locke: Symposium Wolfenbüttel 1979* (Berlin, 1979); chap. 3 of R. S. Woolhouse's *Locke* (Brighton, 1983); as well as all of the latter's *Locke's Philosophy of Science and Knowledge* (Oxford, 1971); and chap. 6 of his *The Empiricists* (Oxford, 1988).

[21] Locke's anti-Filmer *First Treatise of Government* consists almost entirely of demonstrations that the Royal and Tory view of kingship and the state is nothing but a web of constructing prejudice.

[22] In the *Letters concerning Toleration* following his first one, as well as in the *Vindications* which followed his *Reasonableness of Christianity*, Locke's main concern was the removal of the weeds that threatened to obscure the presence of these two original works, weeds sown by minds which were prejudiced hence predisposed against truth.

[23] The reason for the difference between the two realms is that universals, but not "substances," are made by the thinker; therefore we know the real essence of the first but not of the second. Once we know an entity's "real essence" we know "that Foundation from which all its Properties flow." Because we do not know these essences of physical objects, therefore we cannot know anything about them with certainty, for "general Certainty is never to be found but in our Ideas" and "Whenever we go to seek it elsewhere in Experiment, or Observations without us, our Knowledge goes not beyond particulars," for it is "the contemplation of our own abstract Ideas, that alone is able to afford us general Knowledge" (4.6.16; see also 4.12.9). I have dealt at some length with this making of universals and hence knowledge of essences in chap. 6 of *Imposition of Method*.

[24] These phrases are from Etienne Bonnot de Condillac, *An Essay on the Origin of Human Knowledge*, trans. Thomas Nugent (New York, 1974), p. 2.

[25] Quoted from d'Alembert's *Encyclopedia* entry "Taste" in Nelly S. Hoyt and Thomas Cassirer, *Encyclopedia Selections* (Indianapolis, Ind., 1965), pp. 362-63.

[26] See, again, chap. 6 of *Imposition of Method*.

[27] In this sentence, the first quotation repeats phrases from the passage I have just quoted from the *Essay*'s 4.12.9. The second quotation sounds very Lockean and evokes all sorts of passages from the *Essay* (for example, the last six paragraphs from its "Epistle to the Reader"). It is, however, an immediate continuation of the statement quoted a few paragraphs earlier from Condillac's *An Essay on the Origin of Human Knowledge*.

[28] The phrase is from John Dunn's "Revolution," in *Political Innovation and Conceptual Change*, ed. Terence Ball, James Farr, and Russell Hanson (New York, 1989).

[29] It is unlikely that the term "revolutionary" can be used univocally, so that, for example, the eighteenth-century French and the twentieth-century Russian "revolutions" are essentially similar in all aspects. There may be enough similarities to continue a cautious application of this term to both events. But in the way I develop the term here, it applies better to events and persons in the seventeenth and eighteenth than to those in the nineteenth and twentieth centuries. (The difference is, no doubt, to be accounted for in terms of the advent of Hegel and of historicism.) If there is no strictly univocal use of "revolutionary," then we cannot take any person or event as paradigmatically revolutionary. This holds for Descartes and for any other thinker to whom we might want to apply the term. Again, see Dunn's nuanced treatment of the topic in his "Revolution."

[30] E. S. Haldane and G. R. T. Ross, *The Philosophical Works of Descartes*, 2 vols. (Cambridge, 1911), 1:89.

[31] Critical notice of Richard Ashcraft's *Revolutionary Politics and Locke's Two Treatises of Government*, in *Canadian Journal of Philosophy* 19, no. 1 (1989): 101-16. The definition is on p. 107.

[32] It is reductive analysis that is to lead to clarity and distinctness. This analysis of the Cartesian methodology is therefore quite different from the "analysis" of many of the ancient and medieval philosophers for whom "analysis" did not result in "contextlessness." For them, "contextless items" (if that notion was at all intelligible) would be taken to be unknowable; knowledge of an item involved relating that item to some "universal," to, say, the Good, or God.

[33] With emendations, the five preceding paragraphs are from the article mentioned in note 18 above.

[34] Richard Ashcraft, *Revolutionary Politics and Locke's Two Treatises of Government* (Princeton, 1986).

[35] For my critique of Ashcraft, see the article mentioned in n. 31 above.

[36] Peter Laslett, "Introduction" to *John Locke: Two Treatises of Government* (Cambridge, 1960; rev. 1963; first Mentor printing, 1965). All quotations from the *Second Treatise* are from the Mentor edition. The above quotations are from p. 97.

[37] Laslett does not recognize that, in the end, this atomism is a consequence of Locke's methodology. Hence he (mistakenly) denies the existence of important "connecting links" between the *Second Treatise* and the *Essay*. Cf. *Two Treatises*, pp. 97-105. With respect to this aspect of Laslett's position, Ashcraft's is not as retrogressive as it may at first appear (although he, too, denies the importance of Locke's methodology to his political thought). For an antidote to both Laslett and Ashcraft, see Ruth W. Grant, *John Locke's Liberalism* (Chicago, 1987).

[38] Isaiah Berlin, *The Age of Enlightenment: The Eighteenth Century Philosophers* (Oxford, 1956), p. 20.

[39] Charles Taylor, "Atomism," in *Powers, Possessions and Freedom: Essays in Honour of C. B. Macpherson*, ed. Alkis Kontos (Toronto, 1979), p. 39.

[40] These phrases are Aaron's; *John Locke*, p. 44.

[41] Berlin, *Age of Enlightenment*, p. 31.

[42] John Passmore, "The Malleability of Man," in *Aspects of the Eighteenth Century*, ed. Earl R. Wasserman (Baltimore, 1965), pp. 37-38.

[43] John Yolton, *John Locke and the Way of Ideas* (Ox-

ford, 1956), p. 203.

[44] Ashcraft, *Revolutionary Politics,* p. 600.

[45] Yolton, *Locke and the Way of Ideas,* p. 116.

[46] Para. 1, p. 206-7. Some of these phrases Locke quotes from Bacon's *Novum Organum.*

[47] CSM1, 186; AT9-2, 15.

[48] For both Locke's statement and that of Molyneux, see *The Correspondence of John Locke,* ed. E. S. de Beer, 8 vols. (Oxford, 1976-88), 4:479. No doubt Locke was sincere in calling the compliment "extraordinary." In it, Molyneux spoke of Locke the way Locke had spoken of Newton, so that Locke and Newton now shared the attribute of incomparability. For Locke's compliment to Newton, see the *Essay*'s "Epistle to the Reader," pp. 9-10 of the Nidditch edition. Locke would have been less pleased had he known that, in addition to Newton, he shared this attribute with one of the main targets of his scorn: "that incomparable politician, Sir Robert Filmer." (See Ashcraft, *Revolutionary Politics,* p. 225.)

[49] This Dutch edition was followed by the publication of the original Latin text in 1701.

[50] See the translation of James Dickoff and Patricia James, *The Art of Thinking* (Indianapolis, Ind., 1964), p. 302.

[51] This work, widely read throughout the middle decades of the eighteenth century, both in England and abroad, presents a Lockean epistemology and methodology. Its dedication speaks of "Logick" as "not that noisy Thing that deals in all Dispute and Wrangling, to which former Ages had debased and confined it." Quoted from "The Second Edition, Corrected" (London, 1726); republished (New York 1984), ed. Peter A. Schouls.

[52] 20 January 1693; *Correspondence* 4: 627.

[53] 2 March 1693; *Correspondence* 4: 649.

[54] 28 March 1693; *Correspondence* 4: 665.

[55] 12 August 1693; *Correspondence* 4: 715.

[56] 26 April 1695; *Correspondence* 5: 351.

[57] In his "Governing Conduct" Tully writes: "Principles or ideas and dispositions that are said to be innate are, in fact, the *product* of custom and education. By being called 'innate' or 'divine' and 'first principles' they are insulated from examination and taken on 'trust' . . . This concept of 'trust' is of course the central target of the *Essay*" (pp. 21-22). Locke's anti-trust stance will

surface as crucially important throughout my study. It is a stance dictated by Locke's revolutionary "logic."

[58] In view of the traditional and still influential distinction between empiricism and rationalism, I should stress that my use of reason in these statements is not meant to play down the role of the senses.

Philip Vogt (essay date 1993)

SOURCE: "Seascape with Fog: Metaphor in Locke's *Essay,*" in *Journal of the History of Ideas,* Vol. LIV, No. 1, January, 1993, pp. 1-18.

[*In the following essay Vogt explores the use of metaphor in* An Essay Concerning Human Understanding, *arguing that Locke's imagery and meaning are far more varied, complex, and "probabilistic" than the straightforward empiricism suggested by the famous* tabula rasa *image.*]

No image from John Locke's philosophical work is as widely recognized as that of the white paper, the famous *tabula rasa.* But calls by Dominick LaCapra and other similarly minded theorists of history for a rereading of such "great texts" as **An Essay Concerning Human Understanding** raise the problem of whether this particular metaphor is a suitable synecdoche for Locke's complete philosophy of mind.[1] The same problem emerges both from reappraisals by historians of science of the "experimental method" developed within the Royal Society by an intellectual circle that included Locke, and from reevaluations by cultural historians of the link between symbolism in texts and the symbol systems of the societies in which texts are produced. On close inspection the white paper turns out to be far less revealing and a less integral part of the *Essay* than another Lockean metaphor, that of the ship. The long-standing emphasis on the white paper suits those who reduce Locke's epistemology to a simplistic empiricism, while the more frequently employed ship metaphor confronts us with the probabilistic theory of mind and perception for which Locke is increasingly given credit. The traditional interpretation derives from a nineteenth-century reaction, documented by Hans Aarsleff, against what was perceived to be the shallow materialism of the Enlightenment milieu in which the *Essay* was received so enthusiastically.[2] Jettison that distortion, and Locke's ship arrives at last with its manifest full, not blank.

This is not to say that such a manifest would list none of the empiricism that most have thought was the *Essay*'s sole cargo. To say that Locke's epistemology is probabilistic is to admit instead that contraband rationalism also lies stowed below deck—that study of what the senses report to be the surrounding universe is tempered, for Locke, with acceptance of the possibility that the working of the mind might alone be real and the source of whatever regularity and order we normally accept as existing independently of our perceptions. "[Locke's] empiricism was of a peculiar kind," wrote Maurice Cranston in an early acknowledgment of the *Essay*'s multidimensionality, "for he also entertained several notions which are all characteristic of rationalism"—a "rationalism," however, that "is by definition antithetical to empiricism." According to Cranston, Locke's difficulties began with his borrowing of the Cartesian categories of intuitive, demonstrative, and sensitive knowledge. In the Cartesian schema, the reliability of sensory information falls short of demonstrative certainty, and so Locke (like Descartes) found it necessary to draw a distinction between the "primary" and "secondary" qualities of the objects of perception. Cranston blames Locke for not anticipating Berkeley's conclusion that the so-called "primary" qualities of objects can no more be proven to exist independently of human perception than their mind-dependent "secondary" counterparts.

Cranston insists that had Locke recognized that all knowledge is contingent on perception, he would also have had to acknowledge that all language rests on convention rather than on what we can know to be reliable representations of an external reality. Though Locke launched a critique of imprecise language that Cranston thinks was tending toward this very conclusion, Cranston notes that such vaguely defined terms as "idea" continued to play a central role in the *Essay*. If Gilbert Ryle credited Locke with "adumbrating" but not attaining a version of "scientific probability" that treats words as approximations of what they purport to describe, Cranston is less generous and judges Locke to have been "guilty of the very abuses of language against which he writes so forcefully."[3]

Peter Nidditch, the editor of a recent edition of the *Essay*, differs from Cranston and simply defers to the latter-day consensus in order to sidestep the issue of whether Lockean epistemology is rationalist or empiricist: "The *Essay* presents, for the first time, a systematic, detailed, reasoned, and wide-ranging philosophy of mind and cognition whose thrust, *so far as it is in line with the future rather than the past,* is empiricist."[4] Peter Briggs points out the deliberate linkage between Locke's theory of language and his overall epistemology, refuting Cranston's charge that the two were handled clumsily. Briggs observes that "the fallibilities of language and the failures of man's understanding [in the *Essay*] were related and reciprocal." Nevertheless, he ultimately returns to the familiar shelter to be found in reading the *Essay* as the seminal text of empiricism, which is defined now as the "sanative contact with the real world which differentiates Locke's definition of knowledge from his definition of madness."[5]

David Fate Norton enters the debate by questioning whether Locke is the founder of British Empiricism but not whether he is an empiricist as conventionally defined or whether the epistemology he develops in the *Essay* is accurately represented by the metaphor of the *tabula rasa.* "Locke is presumed to have said that the mind is a mere *tabula rasa,* devoid of innate ideas," Norton writes, adding, "I shall not quarrel with the claim that these are Locke's views."[6] Also accepting the common characterization of the *Essay* as straightforwardly empiricist in its plan, S. H. Clark discovers therein what he imagines to be an embarrassing Platonic element, "a potent residual idealism" that "allows [Locke] . . . vicarious access to an enhancement that his epistemology rigorously excludes." This putative "enhancement" consists of a supersensual realm populated by "spirits," by "angels," and by Locke's beneficent deity. It also includes Locke's "ocular vocabulary," his "vast number of psychic metaphors," and his many "archetypes" and analogies, none of which reproduces the evidence of the senses with the slavish literalism thought appropriate to an empiricist text. Clark appears to be offended by what he perceives to be the sheer intellectual pusillanimity of introducing into the analysis images partially or wholly unsubstantiated by argument, "habitual elisions of terminology," that apologize for the very epistemological limitations that the *Essay* otherwise takes pains to detail. Such devious machinations allegedly follow from Locke's unwillingness to admit the "infinite regress" produced by an honest attempt at turning the faculty of intellectual examination upon itself. The resulting contradiction is said to be felt in Locke's combativeness, his "curious excess of rhetorical energy," and his "uncouthness," while the *Essay*'s broad success in its day is dismissed as merely a "convenient corroboration and codification of popular prejudice and expectation."[7]

Of course, in the eyes of cultural historians, to become "a convenient corroboration and codification of popular prejudice and expectation" is no small thing; and we shall see that Locke's popular success, his use of metaphorical "enhancements," and his disputatiousness were all linked. But first things first: Locke cannot be expected to have demonstrated the courage of simplistic empiricist convictions he never held. If Hans Aarsleff is right about the artificiality of the empiricist-rationalist dichotomy, then the discovery of Platonic elements in the *Essay* is no scandal. Charles Griswold's recent work on the Platonic dialogues illuminates the function of both the "enhancements" and the combativeness identified by Clark. Drawing on Hegel, Griswold argues that disputatiousness follows naturally from a determination to philosophize in the face of an honest admission of Clark's infinite regress. Since the ultimate value of all metaphilosophy, epistemology included, is unprovable, Griswold argues that its practitioners can answer their severest critics only by provoking them into argument; for "to argue *against* philosophy is to engage in it."[8] The disputatiousness in Locke's *Essay* might not appear at first to follow the dialogical form used by Plato (and by Galileo, Hobbes, and Leibniz). Yet on closer examination those passages in which Locke directly addresses his opponents are indeed seen to consist of the point-by-point pattern of assertion and rebuttal that one would find in a formal dialogue. Missing are the dramatic personages who would typically deliver arguments in the form of speeches, but otherwise the method of succinctly recapitulating an opponent's position and the cumulative alternation of opposing arguments is the same.

Nowhere in the *Essay* is this more evident than in the exhaustive attack on innateism in Book I. Not coincidentally, in Book I and the first chapters of Book II Locke's argument generates its richest array of the metaphors, the "elisions of terminology," to which Clark so strenuously objects. If the human mind is not what the proponents of innateism have claimed it to be, it instead resembles an eye (I, i, 1; I, ii, 1; I, ii, 9; I, ii, 25), a candle (I, i, 5), an empty cabinet (I, ii, 15), a beam of light (I, ii, 27, I, iii, 4; I, iii, 13; I, iv, 9), a white paper (I, iii, 22), a siege battery (I, iv, 25), a mirror (II, i, 15; II, i, 25; II, viii, 16), a painting, in general (II, ii, 5; II, ix, 8; II, x, 5), a landscape, in particular (II, i, 7), a clock (II, i, 7), a fountain (II, i, 2), a tomb (II, x, 5), a dark room with windows, suggesting a *camera obscura* (II, xi, 17), and a ship (II, viii, 8; II, xiv, 27). The mind's attempt to know its own operations is like a shipline measuring the depths (I, i, 6) and its shortfalls are like blindness (I, iv, 19; I, iv, 23), while the separation between what can be known and what cannot is likened to a horizon (I, i, 7). Locke also illustrates his more explicit arguments with similes that function as unacknowledged metaphors of mind, as in the case of the chess set invoked to clarify his position on the doctrine of substance (II, viii, 8). These metaphors all serve a purpose in the *Essay* similar to that performed in the Platonic dialogues by myth, functioning as substitutes for the proofs that metaphilosophy simply cannot provide and offering something familiar and seemingly analogous—something persuasive in the absence of proof—instead. As Griswold says, in the absence of anything better, they "reassure us that there are grounds for the hope that philosophy" or in Locke's case, epistemology, "is a worthwhile enterprise."[9]

If some of Locke's metaphors bear a striking resemblance to what may or may not actually be Platonic forerunners—as the dark room and the blindness that would accompany exposure to sensation beyond normal human capacity (II, xxiii, 12) recall the cave that Socrates describes to Glaucon in Book VII of the *Republic*—such parallels for our purposes can be accepted as merely coincidental. The important point here is that Locke's frequent recourse to a style of argument that transcends the evidence of immediate sensory experience indicates that his position cannot simply be forced

into a context of rationalist-empiricist polarization and then summarized as anti-rationalistic (or as bad empiricism, as Clark would have it), regardless of which specific sources might or might not have inspired him.

In addition to the evidence to be inferred from metaphorical usage per se, the same reassurance of the worth of philosophy spoken of by Griswold is explicitly provided by Locke himself at Book IV, Chapter xvi of the *Essay*, "On the Degrees of Assent":

> Concerning the manner of Operation in most parts of the Works of Nature: wherein though we see the sensible effects, yet their causes are unknown, and we perceive not the ways and manner how they are produced. . . . For these and the like coming not within the scrutiny of humane Senses, cannot be examined by them, or be attested by any body, and therefore can appear more or less probable, only as they more or less agree to Truths that are established in our Minds, and as they hold proportion to other parts of our Knowledge and Observation. *Analogy* in these matters is the only help we have, and 'tis from that alone we draw all our grounds of Probability.
>
> (IV, xvi, 12)

Locke says at the outset that since "the *Comprehension* of our Understandings, comes exceedingly short of the vast Extent of Things" we must not "peremptorily, or intemperately require Demonstration, and demand Certainty, where Probability only is to be had, and which is sufficient to govern all our Concernments" (I, i, 5). Now he establishes metaphor, or "analogy," as providing both a means by which probable arguments are constructed and a criterion by which they are judged to the more or less persuasive, "only as they more or less agree to Truths that are established in our Minds, and as they hold proportion to other parts of our Knowledge and Observation." In other words analogical arguments are persuasive to the extent that they invoke some familiar and seemingly relevant image as a substitute for the more compelling proofs that cannot be provided. Such a situation arises, as Griswold said, whenever the issues involved are metaphysical—"coming," in Locke's words, "not within the scrutiny of humane Senses, [when they] cannot be examined by them, or be attested by any body," as happens with either "immaterial Beings" or the "material beings," the "Spirits" and "Angels" that so offended Clark, "which either for their smallness in themselves, or remoteness from us, our Senses cannot take notice of" (IV, xvi, 12; see also II, xv, 11).

Metaphysical proofs in the *Essay* do, therefore, partake of a certain kind of empiricism, but one in which the question of the existence of a physical world independent of human perception has become largely irrelevant and surpassed in importance by Locke's recognition of the inescapably subjective character of the individual human memories to which analogies speak. Those memories are the residue of both empirical (in the sense of universally accessible) and subjective experience— of both the "sensation" and the "reflection" that are first discussed in Book I (I, iv, 18). As Locke says in Book II, "Men . . . come to be furnished with fewer or more simple *Ideas* from without, according as the *Objects,* they converse with, afford greater or less variety; and from the Operation of their Minds within, according as they more or less *reflect* on them" (II, i, 7). Hence, where metaphysics is concerned, it is not an external world existing independently of human perception that is seen to provide the "sanative contact" spoken of by Briggs. The reality against which thought is measured and judged to be either sane or mad is the reality of subjective experience.

Lockean metaphysics employs metaphor for the same reason that Platonic metaphysics employs myth and in the same way, namely, as an appeal to reasonableness—to the admission that proofs are never more than probable—and to the individual reservoir of memory that passes for common sense. The memories to which analogy must make its appeal, the "Truths that are established in our Minds" (IV, xvi, 2-3), vary from person to person. Yet tolerance within debate, not solipsism, is the consequence for philosophy:

> We should do well to commiserate our mutual Ignorance, and endeavor to remove it in all the gentle and fair ways of Information; and not instantly treat others ill, as obstinate and perverse, because they will not renounce their own, and receive our Opinions, or at least those we would force upon them, when 'tis more than probable, that we are no less obstinate in not embracing some of theirs.
>
> (IV, xvi, 4)

As the only form of proof that was entirely independent of the testimony of "fair Witnesses" (IV, xvi, 6), analogy offered an invincibly subjective alternative to the unreflective and factious "enthusiasm" (IV, xix, 3) that characterized much of the philosophical discourse of Locke's day.

Thus, Griswold and Locke agree that a person who argues philosophy engages in philosophy and in so doing accepts a level of meaningfulness that transcends what is strictly demonstrable. Implicit in the recognition of this fact (and Locke's statement that analogical thought is also probabilistic is proof that he recognized it) is the suspension of judgment on the existence of a physical world beyond human perception and the concomitant elevation in importance of mental structures imposed upon that otherwise undefined world that together define rationalism. This is a view intrinsic to both Platonic myth and Lockean metaphor and one that contrast with the dogmatic realist position that the objects of perception actually have existence beyond the mind. The metaphysics of the *Essay* must therefore be seen to be

as much rationalistic as empiricist.

This is not to say that every conception of proof in the Lockean schema is predominantly metaphysical, though none escapes a degree of metaphysical uncertainty to become more than merely probable; nor is it to deny that the nonmetaphysical conceptions are more accurately described by the empiricism traditionally ascribed to the system as a whole. The four "Degrees of Assent" Locke defines in Book IV constitute a hierarchy of probability, with what amount to criteria usually associated with Kant—(rational) necessity *and* (empirical) universality—serving to define the trustworthiness of experience claims. "Analogy" is the least compelling of the four modes. "Assurance" attaches to empirical arguments whose "*probabilities* rise so near to *Certainty,* that they govern our Thoughts as absolutely, and influence all our Actions as fully, as the most evident demonstration." "Confidence" names the degree of probability warranted by an argument "attested by many and undoubted Witnesses." A fourth, unnamed level of empirical proof is marked by the testimony of a lesser number of "Historians of credit" when there is otherwise "nothing for, nor against it" (IV, xvi, 6-9). With its combination of latent empiricism and active rationalism, analogy alone among Locke's proofs is both preeminently metaphysical and entirely independent of objective verification.

So if Peter Alexander is misled into conflating Locke's discussion of metaphysical and nonmetaphysical proofs (even though he, too, recognizes the crucial role played in the *Essay* by the discussion of analogy in Book IV), the culprit once again is the familiar dichotomy of rationalism and empiricism. As a result, the empirical experience against which Lockean analogies are measured appears no different from a simplistically defined empirical experience said to be emerging in the Royal Society as the basis for the experimental method in science. Alexander begins by answering unnamed historians who argue that Locke invented, in Book II of the *Essay,* the very distinction between primary and secondary qualities that Cranston says followed from his uncritical use of Descartes. Like Cranston, Alexander agrees that Locke borrowed the primary-secondary distinction but claims that the source was Robert Boyle and suggests that Locke's use of the primary-secondary distinction, far from being uncritical, was a conscious attempt at transplanting Boyle's experimental mode from science to epistemology.[10] This supposedly entailed nothing less than the discovery, for philosophy, of analogical reasoning itself, based on the example of speculation within the Royal Society into the nature of "primary," microscopic qualities from observations of "secondary," macroscopic phenomena. Alexander's conclusion is that Lockean analogies were part-and-parcel of a Royal Society empiricism that, in its axiomatic acceptance of an independently existing physical world and the radical contingency of human perception, reflects what is commonly read into the *Essay* by traditional Lockean scholarship.[11]

At least as early as the 1950s, however, E. J. Dijksterhuis had pointed out that the distinction between primary and secondary qualities long antedated the works of either Boyle or Descartes. The corollary to Dijksterhuis's observation is that the primary-secondary distinction was borne into the Royal Society on a broader historical current than would make plausible its transmission by any single individual, even a Boyle, to a man of Locke's connections and intellectual stature.[12] Given the breadth of that current, Boyle probably has to be made the agent of transmission if the *Essay* is to be found to partake exclusively of what Alexander calls the intrinsic realism and empiricism of the corpuscularian tradition on which, he claims, the primary-secondary distinction is predicated.[13] Otherwise, the borrowing might be unpredictable and the results not unequivocally those of empiricism. Indeed, a close reading of Book IV of the *Essay* shows that analogical reasoning for Locke was, to say the last, no more empiricist than it was rationalistic: it was largely subjective and, among the four "Degrees of Assent," unique in its freedom from the validation of "fair Witnesses."[14]

A rereading of the *Essay* obviously becomes pertinent at this point to a long-standing debate in the history of science in which the common supposition that Lockean metaphysics are adequately described as empiricist is called into question by disagreement on the relative importance of hypothesis and observation to the so-called experimental method emerging in Locke's day within the Royal Society. Alexander's argument linking Locke to "Boylean corpus-cularianism" has recently been challenged by Margaret Atherton as part of a "contemporary orthodoxy" that aligns Locke with what is imagined to be "the best science of his time," one that treated as real the mechanical hypothesis of physical causality derived from Descartes, in opposition to a "Baconian natural history of [mere] observables." This new "orthodoxy" will apparently concede that Locke, Boyle, and other members of the Royal Society entertained scientific hypotheses, provided that the character of the physical world alone was at issue; any possibility that Society members might have regarded speculation into the invisible causes of visible phenomena as intrinsically heuristic (as, for example, analogy functions within Lockean metaphysics as a heuristic substitute for demonstrative proof) is apparently disallowed. Even the rationalist influence of Cartesian physics is thereby recast in an empiricist mold.[15]

This "orthodoxy" is unable, however, to reconcile occurrences of the mechanical philosophy in the *Essay* with other passages where Locke discounts the possibility of attaining real knowledge of corpuscular processes and structures. Consequently, Atherton suggests that it must have been possible to adopt the corpuscular theory while rejecting the component of "materialist essentialism" that Alexander extracts from Descartes. Instead of establishing that the primary, invisible properties of matter are as real as the secondary properties from which their existence is inferred, Atherton (at points, arguing backwards from Berkeley) takes the discussion of analogy in Book IV of the *Essay* to indicate that Locke regarded corpuscles as perceivable "in principle"—perceivable, that is, through analogy to the commonplace world of macroscopic phenomena—but unknowable in fact. Inasmuch as the existence of corpuscles was required to maintain the optimistic belief that the universe obeys uniform laws even when it eludes observation, Atherton concludes that Alexander errs in imagining that Locke took "the focal question of corpuscular science to be: are the unobservable corpuscles postulated by physics real or are they fictive?" when, as we have noted, Locke considers questions of the physical world's independent existence to be largely irrelevant.

Atherton's analysis is persuasive, as far as it goes, and particularly helpful as a reminder that, far from marking the philosophical debut of analogical reasoning, the arguments in the *Essay* constitute just one instance of what was already a "frequent recourse to analogy" in the seventeenth century. If she stops short of acknowledging the crucial role played by analogy in the totality of Lockean metaphysics, she nevertheless contributes to the placement of Locke's work within an historical context increasingly dominated by the probabilism associated with Newtonianism's disavowal of demonstrative proofs.

Two other recent participants in this debate, Steven Shapin and Simon Schaffer, describe an atmosphere within the Royal Society that, judging by what they say the "fair Witnesses" gathered there really were up to, seems unlikely to account in any way for an analysis of metaphor like that found in the *Essay*'s Book IV. While an important tradition in the history of science has long claimed that the experimental method developed at the Royal Society was inimical to argumentation from hypotheses, Shapin and Schaffer have refined that somewhat embattled commonplace to argue that metaphysical discourse was excluded from the Society's proceedings in the name of a communal unity then emerging among English scientists, taking with it both the metaphors and the disputatiousness that an unbiased reading nevertheless shows to have played an integral role in the *Essay*'s treatment of knowledge and proof. Either Shapin and Schaffer are wrong, or the *Essay* can no longer be taken for granted as product of the Royal Society's intellectual milieu—at least, not as long as that milieu is understood to be, as these historians rather predictably put it, "empiricist and inductivist." Retaining Locke as a central participant in a Royal Society so defined will put historians of science in the dubious position of having to divorce him from his chief philosophical work. Certainly some sort of amputation has to be performed on the Lockean corpus if it is to conform to the conception of probability that Shapin and Schaffer say predominated in the Royal Society, whereby the veracity of any scientific account was considered to be directly proportional to the number of witnesses attesting to it, which is a conception that can cover only the non-analogical definitions of probability given by Locke in the *Essay*'s Book IV.[16]

Shapin and Schaffer's analysis is undoubtedly best taken not as the final statement on what was actually promoted and what might also have been permissible within the Royal Society but as a new and provocative contribution in an ongoing debate. Future installments in that debate cannot count Locke's *Essay* as one of the most important works to come out of the intellectual circle gathered at the Royal Society and at the same time ignore the metaphysical and rationalist character of Locke's discussion of proof in general and of analogy in particular. If they do, then either they will continue to falter when they reach the heavily metaphorical argumentation in Book I and the theoretical statements on metaphor in Book IV, or they will follow what we see is ample precedent and simply ignore the embarrassing portions of the *Essay* altogether. Such, unfortunately, is the approach adopted by Barbara Shapiro, who sets out to reconcile the *Essay* with a by-now familiar picture of the Royal Society, and indeed of the overall English intellectual temper in the late seventeenth century, as inimical to metaphysical discourse. Shapiro is on safe ground in arguing that a scientific consensus toward a "probabilistic empiricism" was emerging in Locke's day from the complex crosscurrents of English intellectual life. Based on what we have seen of the *Essay*'s sophisticated treatment of probabilistic argumentation, she is probably also correct in claiming that Locke "represents *the culmination* of a generation's attempt to devise a new theory of knowledge appropriate to the experimental science of the era." But because such a theory was, as she conceives of it, one from which (after Francis Bacon) "ambiguity and especially metaphor" must have been "utterly excluded," she adopts what an unbiased reading of the *Essay* shows to be an absurd position, joining Locke—for whom she is, of course, unable to cite a single disavowal of metaphor—with Thomas Sprat, John Wilkins, Samuel Parker, Joseph Glanville, William Petty, and Boyle (for whom she is able to produce, if not explicit statements condemning metaphorical discourse, at least approximations thereof) as an opponent of metaphorical usage in scientific discourse.[17]

If the traditional picture of late seventeenth-century English intellectual life as dominated by empiricism and inimical to rationalism is to be retained, then it will have to be without its "culminating" figure. Alternately, important voices in the history of science may continue to force Locke into a mold that a careful reading of his major text reveals to be patently distorting. Of course, neither approach is acceptable: the *Essay* is far too important to be read inaccurately or out of context, and a new reading of the text may well be the beginning of a reappraisal of context (just as interpetations of context must be tested against texts themselves). After all, one premise of cultural history must be that analogical discourse retains a broader meaningfulness than that required merely to rescue it from solipsism. Metaphors within such influential texts as the *Essay* can reasonable be read as cultural exemplars, or as "archetypal analogies," to use the words of M. H. Abrams, whose point that "metaphysical systems . . . are intrinsically metaphorical systems" anticipated Griswold by twenty-five years. But according to Abrams, certain perennially-important metaphors do more than fill the inevitable lacunae in metaphilosophy. Abrams argues that they actually generate the arguments that we normally think of them as merely summarizing after the creative fact. Images of mirrors and of lamps are particularly important, says Abrams, in shaping theories of the mind as either a passive recorder of impressions originating from without or as an active agent in the interpretation of those impressions.[18]

If not the newest version of the dichotomizing tendency that strictly segregates rationalistic thought from empiricism, this nevertheless counts as one of the most sophisticated, in that it acknowledges—indeed, is predicated upon—the heavy reliance on metaphor in the *Essay,* which others who deny its rationalistic element choose (or are forced) to ignore. According to Abrams, the image of the *tabula rasa* does more than provide a fair (if highly abbreviated) synopsis in our own time of Lockean epistemology. The *tabula rasa,* or a metaphor very much like it—the metaphor of the mirror, perhaps, or the *camera obscura,* at any rate, an image suggesting intellectual passivity before nature—embodied in Locke's day what was a then still-dominant empiricist tradition and provided the inspiration for Locke's own supposedly straightforward empiricist theory of mind.[19] What Abrams's argument itself ignores, however, is the array of what would seem to be unequivocally active metaphors of mind in Books I and II of the *Essay*. These include such versions of the lamp metaphor as the candle "that is set up in us, [and] shines bright enough for all our Purposes" (I, i, 5), the "light" that makes certain undeniable propositions seem self-evident (I, iii, 4), and the "light of Nature" by which we overcome ignorance and which is nothing less than the "use and due application of our natural Faculties" (I, iii, 13).

This same metaphor is as useful to Locke in exposing what innateist conceptions of mind lack as it is in illustrating those powers which, in his own conception, the mind actively displays. Locke says that if we possessed innate ideas, they would shine out like "native beams of light" (I, ii, 27) and that innate moral principles, if there were any, would manifest themselves "by their own light" (I, iii, 1). The evidence of metaphorical usage in the *Essay* therefore suggests that if Abrams is correct in saying that the metaphor of the lamp lends itself to dynamic theories of mind, he is nevertheless badly mistaken in assuming that Locke, or by extension seventeenth-century Englishmen in general lacked access to it or formulated conceptions of epistemology that escaped its influence.

What, then, of the passive metaphors, the mirrors that Abrams says should have determined Locke's theory of mind toward that of a "receiver for images presented ready-formed from without"?[20] Explicit reference to mirrors occur twice in the *Essay*'s Book II, first in the immediate aftermath of the attack on innateism at II,i,25, where the metaphor does in fact function as an illustration of the mind's passive receptivity to the "simple ideas" that Locke regards as the essential rudiments (but only the rudiments) of all intellectual activity. Yet in seizing upon this imagery as proof of the essentially empirical quality of Lockean epistemology, Abrams forgets that Locke always couples the "sensation" by which simple ideas are acquired with "reflection," or the capacity for original and independent thought. The "primary" qualities that we infer from our perceptions of "solidity," "extension," "figure," and "mobility" (II, viii, 9) to be inherent in objects themselves are immediately and inevitably accompanied by perceptions of "secondary" phenomena that cannot be separated from the perceptive faculty. For all the philosopher knows, these may be the products of sensation or reflection, though in either case their reliability is uncertain. So it is that the second occurrence of the mirror metaphor invokes intellectual passivity as a reproach to those who indiscriminately attribute qualities to objects alone instead of to the mind (II, viii, 16). Mirrors suggest intellectual passivity in the *Essay* only to the extent that they are used on one occasion to illustrate what is meant by simple ideas; beyond that, they reflect on intellectual passivity in an intentionally derisive way that is a reversal of the meaning that Abrams attributes to them.

As for the *camera obscura,* no specific mention is ever made of it in the *Essay,* though a "dark room" is described whose windows represent both sensation and reflection, suggesting in its layout the *camera obscura* but depicting Lockean epistemology in its entirety and not just in the passive aspects (the realm of sensation) that interest Abrams (II,xi,17). As for that other image of intellectual inertia, the much-touted metaphor of the white paper, Locke has direct recourse to it exactly twice in the *Essay* and makes indirect reference to it exactly four times more. The first mention of the white paper occurs at I, iii, 22, in what may well be Locke's most scathing attack on the same passivity which the metaphor of the mirror was employed against at II, viii,

16 but which traditional Lockean scholarship would have the *tabula rasa* enshrine. The topics are prejudice and the reluctance of most adults critically to examine their own beliefs, which makes them no better than gullible children who hold to "*Doctrines,* that have been derived from no better original, than the Superstition of a Nurse, or the Authority of an old Woman." "White paper receives any characters," Locke offers as an excuse for such children, speaking not about the origin of knowledge, but about moral credulity, and driving home the reproach at I, iii, 21 of "Men even of Good Understanding in other matters, [who] will sooner part with their Lives, and whatever is dearest to them, than suffer themselves to doubt, or others to question, the truth of [their unexamined propositions]." The important point is that the metaphor illustrates here an absence of rationality that is willful rather than intrinsic.

In the second and last explicit occurrence of the white paper metaphor, the image does indeed suggest intellectual passivity but only as the hypothetical precondition for speculation into the origin of knowledge, and not as a final epistemological model: "Let us then suppose the Mind to be, as we say, white Paper, void of all Characters, without any *Ideas;* How comes it to be furnished?" The answer once again incorporates both sensation, or the experience of "*external, sensible Objects,*" which in isolation might be compatible with an empiricist reading of the text, and reflection, or the experience *"about the internal Operations of our Minds, perceived and reflected on by our selves"* that represents the element of intellectual self-sufficiency in Lockean epistemology and of independence from external sensation; and with this the narrwly-empiricist reading is obviously incompatible (II, i, 2).

Thereafter, the imagery of white paper is invoked twice in Book II and twice again in Book IV in purely incidental illustrations of comparatively minor points. Of all our simple ideas, Locke says, none are more distinct than those of number: "For who will undertake [in comparison] to find a difference between the white of this Paper, and that of the next degree to it" (II, xvi, 3)? The simple idea of whiteness, Locke says at II, xxxi, 12, is received from paper, just, as he said earlier at II, xxxi, 2, it is also received from sugar. The immediacy of intuitive knowledge is compared to the eye's instantaneous apprehension of "Whether this Ink, and this Paper be all of a Colour" (IV, ii, 5), and our acceptance of such knowledge without a solid understanding of its origins is likened to the unexamined, commonsensical connection between the paper before us and the descriptor "white" (IV, xi, 2).

So it is that the metaphor of the white paper—the famous image of the *tabula rasa*—functions very differently in Locke's *Essay* from what either intellectual historians or historians of science have traditionally asserted. Its specific role in Lockean epistemology, if minor, is nevertheless integral and not aberrant. The collective contribution made by such metaphors to the elaboration of the argument's metaphysics is technically indispensable, as Locke acknowledges in his treatment of their theoretical status in Book IV. The mere existence of such metaphors calls into question the standard picture in the history of science of what the Scientific Revolution entailed for English thought in general and for the Royal Society in particular. Cultural historians have begun to address this discrepancy, acknowledging that metaphors are, if not the theoretical mainstays of Lockean epistemology, at least factors in shaping both popular and philosophical perceptions of epistemological issues in seventeenth-century England.

The flaw in this approach is in its circumspection, rather than in its misreading of the role of any single metaphor in the **Essay**. Otto Mayr's point that metaphors possess an "inner logic" and exert a "suggestive power" over the arguments that they illustrate is reminiscent of Abrams's thesis that the intellectual function of metaphors is generative. Unlike Abrams's whose "archetypal" metaphors impose meaning on thought and discourse, Mayr seems to concede the point made by Locke in Books II and IV that the resonance produced by any particular metaphor is entirely subjective. The same clock that suggested governmental or technological intrusiveness to the seventeenth-century Englishman in the street embodied a rational and apprehensible cosmos to the member of the Royal Society. This is not to deny that metaphors were just as common within the Society as without, and here at last Robert Boyle becomes more than just a two-dimensional caricature of empiricism. According to Mayr, Boyle's perception of the clock as a metaphor of nature was not fixed. Instead, it underwent a "cautious transition" from the determinism consistent with a narrowly-empirical scientific method to a voluntarism that opened up much wider conceptual possibilities. But if no use of metaphor whatsoever would have been consistent with what Thomas Sprat said were the Society's goals, then Mayr is discriminating enough to know that Sprat was not the whole Society, and Boyle's statements in defense of metaphor, self-conscious, and apologetic though they may have been, are duly noted. An understanding of the Royal Society modified even to this modest degree can accommodate the Locke of the **Essay**'s Books I and II, the polemicist unselfconsciously peppering his arguments with potent analogies. Nowhere, however, does Mary credit Locke with the explicit theoretical appreciation of metaphor that is developed in Book IV. Instead, Mayr's Locke shares in Boyle's embarrassment: "Boyle, who loved metaphors, frequently apologized for this aberration, and John Locke expressed himself against 'figurative speech' and 'ornaments' in philosophy."[21]

No history of the seventeenth century does justice to Locke's approving and richly metaphysical treatment of metaphor. Even the boldest revisions in the often iconoclastic field of cultural history fall short. The explanation for this timidity can lie only in the authoritative weight of a tradition in Lockean scholarship that has succeeded, as Hans Aarsleff says, since the middle of the nineteenth century in reducing the **Essay** to its component empiricism. If, like so many recent commentators on the **Essay** (Cranston, Briggs, Norton, Clark, Alexander, Shapiro, and Abrams) we subscribe to what Aarsleff calls "the pedagogically convenient and ideologically loaded separate-box distinction between rationalism and empiricism" that this same tradition has bequeathed to us—and as indeed we are taught to do by the most common historical periodizations and the most entrenched philosophical categories—then we arrive at the conclusion that Locke's epistemology is empiricist not by critical examination of the text but by predisposition.[22] Given Locke's flamboyant use of metaphor in Book I and his meticulous justification of metaphorical usage in Book IV, it seems probable that the *tabula rasa* has long been extracted from Locke's **Essay** as representing the essence of his epistemology not because it actually functions in the text in the way imagined but instead because the passivity it suggests to readers who have yet to read the book conforms to what they are made to expect to find therein. Before their first encounter in the **Essay** at I, iii, 22, the reader with a basic knowledge of history and philosophy and the metaphor of the white paper are already acquainted.

That is why LaCapra's call for an unconventional reading of "great texts" is so significant. If traditional interpretations of important books are to be reconsidered (which is the same thing as asking if they are to be read afresh or communicated to new audiences via secondary synopses), then the relationships between specific texts and specific contexts must be approached skeptically and perhaps ultimately redefined. But a reading that resists familiar periodizations is one that has at least temporarily cut its moorings and risks drifting into ahistoricity. LaCapra's call for a new and uncanonical approach to a canon of great books and Griswold's defense of dialectical philosophy are both consciously indebted to Heidegger's inconveniently ahistorical notion of the dialogical relationship between reader and text.[23] Rereading Locke's **Essay** and discovering that the metaphors therein function like myths in Platonic dialogues may pose a very interesting challenge to the commonly accepted relationship between this particular text and a context supposedly dominated by a newly ascendant empiricism. But whether or not the revision can provide anything approaching similar detail, coherence, or even historical accuracy is uncertain. If we defy the weight of tradition and say that Locke developed a metaphysics of metaphor, should we not also, like the upholders of the *tabula rasa* whom we would supplant, be able to say that there is a correct metaphor for Lockean metaphysics, a metaphor that is inextricably linked to Locke's particular day and place, even if its influence over the *Essay* is something less than archetypal?

Locke himself answers the question. The metaphor that appears most frequently in the *Essay* is also the one used to illustrate the widest range of arguments. Although the subjectivity of metaphors makes their reception unpredictable, this particular metaphor is also the one whose immediate resonances most reliably convey the probabilism at the center of Locke's theory of mind. The imagery of the ship is used throughout the *Essay* in a complex of explicit and submerged metaphors that invoke the practicality, the ingenuity, and the hazards of seventeenth-century seamanship in order to depict the human intellect operating intrepidly within clearly defined and widely understood limitations. Early in Book I the ship expresses the value of raising epistemological issues even if our weaknesses are thereby exposed: "'Tis of great use to the Sailor to know the length of his Line, though he cannot with it fathom all the depths of the Ocean" (I, i, 6). "But what still remains beyond this [knowledge]," Locke adds in Book II, "we have no more a positive distinct notion of, than a Mariner has of the depth of the Sea, where having let down a large portion of his Sounding-line, he reaches no bottom" (II, xvii, 15).

To demonstrate the futility of wishing that our intellects were keener, Locke later sails the metaphorical ship into the thick of battle: "If our Sense of Hearing were but 1000 times quicker than it is . . . we should in the quietest Retirement, be less able to sleep or meditate, than in the midst of a Sea-fight" (II, xxiii, 12). In Book IV the ship is invoked in an indictment of careless word use, but also more subtly as an encouragement to our confident use of our admittedly imperfect intellectual instrument and perhaps also as a reminder that knowledge is only probabilistic and never certain: "Had Men, in the discoveries of the material, done, as they have in those of the intellectual World, . . . Ships built, and Fleets set out, would never have taught us the way beyond the Line" (IV, iii, 30). We each command, Locke seems to say, a cumbersome and unruly vessel over which we must decisively take charge: "'Til a Man doth this in the primary and original Notions of Things, he builds upon floating and uncertain Principles, and will often find himself at a loss" (II, xiv, 27).

Less pivotal arguments illustrated by the ship metaphor point to the mind's self-reliance in a universe that is ultimately inscrutable. To show that the perception of space is relational, Locke describes chessmen moving across a board, sets the board down stationary within his ship, and then moves the ship along an imaginary coast: "and so both Chess-men, and Board, and Ship, have every one *changed place* in respect of remoter Bodies, which have kept the same distance one with

another" (II, xiii, 8). Locke has only to stop the ship to demonstrate the closely related point that our notion of succession derives merely from the linearity of our own perceptions: "a Man becalmed at Sea, out of sight of Land, in a fair Day, may look on the Sun, or Sea, or Ship, a whole hour together, and perceive no Motion at all in either; though it be certain, that two, and perhaps all of them, have moved, during that time, a great way" (II, xiv, 6). In light of scientific discoveries by which "[t]he Motion of the Sun, which the World used so long, and so confidently for an exact measure of Duration, has . . . been found in its several parts unequal," the perception of time, or "duration," must be seen to be grounded in our own ceaseless "train of ideas": "For if the Motion of the Sun, were as unequal as of a Ship driven by unsteady Winds, sometimes very slow, and at others, irregularly very swift . . . it would not at all help us to measure time, any more than the seeming unequal motion of a Comet does" (II, xiv, 21-22). Finally, to show that the relativity of these perceptions accounts in part for the ambiguity of words, Locke climbs down into the hold: "[t]he Ship has necessary Stores. *Necessary*, and *Stores*, are both relative Words: one having a relation to the accomplishing the Voyage intended, and the other to future use" (II, xxvi, 6). As we began by saying, the stores carried in that hold are both rational and empirical and equally necessary to the probabilistic epistemology that this metaphor represents.

The ship that one sights from time to time in Locke's *Essay* would therefore seem to convey a theory of the mind as adequate to the journey at hand. Such a reading is consistent with what is generally recognized to be the growing confidence of English philosophy in that day. While Frank and Fritzie Manuel found that an opening shipwreck frequently was part of the "stock formula" of sixteenth-century utopias, ships sailing the philosophical literature one hundred years later had apparently become more seaworthy and were successfully attaining more mundane ports of call.[24] If they managed this by sailing cautiously, by hugging empiricism's shore, and by regularly consulting the shiplines of rationalism, they thereby contributed to a new candor in both the rhetoric and the methods of philosophy. As the English expressed this candor through their writings, their Dutch counterparts expressed it through literal renderings of nature in landscapes, or so says Svetlana Alpers.[25] Metaphors, though, are pictures of a sort, and the *Essay* paints a seascape in the meticulous detail of empiricism but with a light wash, a suggestion of fog, reminding us of the irreducible uncertainty acknowledged by a probabilistic epistemology.

Notes

[1] Dominick LaCapra, "Rethinking Intellectual History and Reading Texts," *Modern European Intellectual History: Reappraisals and New Perspectives,* ed. LaCapra and Steven Kaplan (Ithaca, 1982), 49. Fred S.

Michael and Emily Michael, "The Theory of Ideas in Gassendi and Locke," *JHI*, 51 (1990), 392, 398-99, indicate that it was Gassendi who first compared the mind to a *tabula rasa* and Leibniz who first pointed out the similarities between that formulation and elements of Locke's epistemology. They argue convincingly that Gassendi provided the germ for ideas developed later in the *Essay*, but acknowledge that a "full scale study of the relation between Gassendi and Locke" is yet to be undertaken—a deficiency that, I would suggest, can be remedied only after the present reappraisal of Locke's *Essay* is made.

[2] Hans Aarsleff, "Locke's Reputation in Nineteenth-Century England," *From Locke to Saussure: Essays on the Study of Language and Intellectual History* (Minneapolis, 1982), 121.

[3] Maurice Cranston, *John Locke: A Biography* (New York, 1985), 264-78.

[4] Peter H. Nidditch, "Introduction" to John Locke, *An Essay Concerning Human Understanding*, ed. Nidditch (New York, 1975), viii (italics mine). Citations from the *Essay* are from Nidditch's edition.

[5] Peter M. Briggs, "Locke's *Essay* and the Strategies of Eighteenth-Century English Satire," *Studies in Eighteenth-Century Culture*, 10 (1981), 138-39.

[6] David Fate Norton, "The Myth of 'British Empiricism,'" *History of European Ideas*, 1 (1981), 334.

[7] S. H. Clark, "The Philosophical Rhetoric of Locke's 'Essay,'" *The Locke Newsletter*, 17 (1986), 96-99, 102, 109, 112, 115.

[8] Charles L. Griswold, Jr., "Plato's Metaphilosophy: Why Plato Wrote Dialogues," *Platonic Writings, Platonic Readings*, ed. Charles L. Griswold, Jr. (New York, 1988), 154. The unanswerable nature of metaphysical questions is a recurrent theme in the *Essay*, beginning at I, i, 3.

[9] Griswold, "Plato," 159.

[10] Peter Alexander, "Boyle and Locke on Primary and Secondary Qualities," *Locke on Human Understanding: Selected Essays*, ed. I. C. Tipton (New York, 1977), 62-66.

[11] "Locke, in putting forward an empiricist basis for knowledge, was codifying the principles of the experimental natural philosophy which Boyle was championing against speculative natural philosophy." On a separate matter, Alexander blames Locke's lack of clarity of expression for an alleged inconsistency at II, viii, 21, where Locke is thought to be saying that primary qualities could never produce the illusions that secondary qualities sometimes do, which would contradict his argument that (primary) qualities are in objects. If primary qualities never produce illusions, then Alexander seems to be saying that they might just as well be said to be in us as an invariable part of the perceptive faculty. Alexander's solution is that Locke probably meant to say that heat and cold, the examples he chooses, are "merely ideas in us." Since the ideational context is explicit at this point in the *Essay*, Alexander seems to be arguing a non-issue ("Boyle and Locke," 66, 68).

[12] E. J. Dijksterhuis, *The Mechanization of the World Picture*, trans. C. Dikshoorn (New York, 1960), IV, 227, 423. This ancient distinction had gained new and widespread importance earlier in the century in the work of Galileo.

[13] Alexander, "Boyle and Locke," 69.

[14] Alexander's argument notwithstanding, the measure of how handily Locke was able to imbibe corpuscular thought while remaining free of the empiricist metaphysics that its reduction of all physical phenomena to the motions of invisible particles might reasonably (if ahistorically) be thought to entail is found at II, ii, 2, where the division and recombination of ideas in the process of reflection—an entirely mental and "insubstantial" (my term) phenomenon—is described in unmistakably mechanistic terms.

[15] Margaret Atherton, "Corpuscles, Mechanism, and Essentialism in Berkeley and Locke," *Journal of the History of Philosophy*, 29 (1991), 47, 49, 60-61, 66. Atherton responds to a more recent formulation of Alexander's argument incorporating material from the *Ratio* article in his book *Ideas, Qualities and Corpuscles: Locke and Boyle on the External World* (Cambridge, 1985).

[16] Steven Shapin and Simon Schaffer, *Leviathan and the Air Pump: Hobbes, Boyle, and the Experimental Life* (Princeton, 1985), 36, 56.

[17] Barbara J. Shapiro, *Probability and Certainty in Seventeenth-Century England: A Study of the Relationship Between Natural Science, Religion, History, Law and Literature* (Princeton, 1983), 12, 32, 232-45.

[18] M. H. Abrams, *The Mirror and the Lamp: Romantic Theory and the Critical Tradition* (Oxford, 1953), 30-31.

[19] *Ibid.*, 57-58. Abrams does not use the term "empiricism," but his description of Locke's epistemology as "his view of the mind in perception as a passive receiver for images presented ready-formed from without" makes it clear that empiricism is what he means.

[20] *Ibid.*

[21] Otto Mayr, *Authority, Liberty and Automatic Ma-*

chinery in Early Modern Europe (Baltimore, 1986), 30, 61, 82, 94, 217. Though it is presently impossible for me to check the context from which Mayr extracted Locke's statements against figurative speech due to his use of an 1824 edition of the *Essay* that apparently divides chapters with a different notation from that used by Nidditch, the *Essay* is rich in such statements. They are inevitably directed against either the proponents of Innateism or the Scholastics and are not intended as a renunciation of metaphor correctly used.

22 Aarsleff, *From Locke to Saussure,* 9, 139. Also Norton, 331, 333.

23 Dominick LaCapra, *Rethinking Intellectual History: Texts, Contexts, Language* (Ithaca, 1983), 29. Griswold is careful to reject Heidegger's most sweeping attacks on philosophy while accepting that dogmatic metaphilosophical constructs are indefensible (144, 166).

24 Frank E. Manuel and Fritzie P. Manuel, *Utopian Thought in the Western World* (Cambridge, Mass., 1979), 2.

25 Svetlana Alpers, *The Art of Describing: Dutch Art in the Seventeenth Century* (Chicago, 1983), 11.

Roger Woolhouse (essay date 1994)

SOURCE: "Locke's Theory of Knowledge," in *The Cambridge Companion to Locke,* edited by Vere Chappell, Cambridge University Press, 1994, pp. 146-71.

[*In the following essay, Woolhouse examines Locke's view of the relationship between experience, ideas, and knowledge in* An Essay Concerning Human Understanding, *emphasizing Locke's rejection of the innatist conception of the origin of knowledge and "moral truths."*]

In the course of its considerable length the **Essay concerning Human Understanding** deals with many topics; but its main theme and concern is knowledge and the capacity of the human understanding to acquire it. "[M]y *Purpose,*" Locke tells us, is "to enquire into the Original, Certainty, and Extent of humane Knowledge; together, with the Grounds and Degrees of Belief, Opinion, and Assent" (E I.i.2: 43). What is knowledge and how is it acquired? Are there any limits to what we can know and, therefore, things about which we can have only beliefs and things about which we must be ignorant? What, indeed, is the difference between knowledge and belief? As its title indicates, the **Essay** intends these as questions more about the human knower and believer rather than about what is known and believed. What can we, with our minds, know? In setting out to inquire into knowledge Locke is setting out "to take a Survey of our own Understandings, ex-

amine our own Powers, and see to what Things they were adapted" (E I.i.7: 47). [*An Essay Concerning Human Understanding,* edited by Peter H. Nidditch, is abbreviated as E throught this essay.]

In the background to his questions was a contemporary debate that arose from a large number of arguments against the very possibility of knowledge, arguments that were found in an account of early Greek skepticism, *Outlines of Pyrrhonism,* written by Sextus Empiricus (fl. A.D. 200). Pointing out that people disagree, these arguments challenge anyone who thinks the truth can be found to say who is its proper judge or real discoverer. Pointing out that our senses are unreliable and our reasonings often mistaken, they ask by what means truth is to be discovered.

But though Locke is often dealing with questions like this, his ultimate interest is not merely academic. It has to do with the human predicament, or our place in the total scheme of things. A pervading feature of his thought as a whole is a deep concern with how we should lead our lives here and now in this world, as God's creatures and in the light of some expectation of an afterlife in another world. So, since we have been given the ability to reason and think, one aspect of this is how we stand as knowers and believers. His basic aim is to "find out those Measures, whereby a rational Creature put in that State, which Man is in, in this World, may, and ought to govern his Opinions, and Actions depending thereon" (E I.i.6: 46).

There is some disagreement as to how exactly Locke's responses to the challenges of the traditional skeptical arguments relate to those of some of his contemporaries.[1] But there can be no doubt that they, and his underlying interest in how we should arrange our lives and thoughts, are of a piece and form a coherent picture.

His response, as expounded in general terms at the beginning of the **Essay** and confirmed by all of its later detail, is that to an extent the skeptics are right. There are things we do not know, things about which we can only form beliefs and things about which we are ignorant. But some things we do know and our beliefs are often not foundationless. On this earth "we are here," as he records in his journal, "in a state of mediocritie, finite creatures, furnished with powers and facultys very well fited to some purposes, but very disproportionate to the vast and unlimited extent of things" (Journal 1677: Bodleiar library, MS Locke f.2: 126).

The things we do know, furthermore, and the things we justifiably believe, answer to our true needs and real interests. "How short soever . . . [people's] Knowledge may come of an universal, or perfect Comprehension of whatsoever is, it yet secures their great Concernments"

(E I.i.5: 45). In brief, we are not in ignorance of our duties and obligations to each other and to God; we can, that is, know what we need to know for salvation. As to the practicalities of life in this world, we can learn enough for our everyday comfort. People should be "well satisfied with what God hath thought fit for them, since he has . . . put within the reach of their Discovery the comfortable Provision for this Life and the Way that leads to a better" (ibid.).

Not only have we no need to know much of what we do not know, we also are not suited to know it. A skeptical attitude would be avoided if people would recognize "the Horizon . . . between what is, and what is not comprehensible by us" (E I.i.7: 47). If they did they would "not be inclined . . . to . . . Despair of knowing any thing; . . . and disclaim all Knowledge, because some Things are not to be understood" (E I.i.6: 46). It is no wonder that people fall to thinking that the truth as a whole lies beyond their grasp when they concern themselves with matters to which they are not suited. "Men, extending their Enquiries beyond their Capacities, . . . 'tis no Wonder, that they raise Questions . . . which never coming to any clear Resolution, are proper only to . . . confirm them at last in perfect Scepticism" (E I.i.7: 47).

In Locke's picture of things, our capacities and abilities are given us by God. So not only should we thank Him for what we have, also we should be less greedy and "more cautious in meddling with things exceeding [our] Comprehension" (E I.i.4: 45). There is an immodest ungrateful egotism in attempting to know what we are not suited to know, and in complaining that our knowledge has bounds. We should patiently accept our limitations.

When he says that we should not fret at the limitations and bounds to knowledge that are set by the nature of our understandings, Locke does not mean that we should not aim to get what is attainable by us. Rejecting any innateness of knowledge, his view is that what God gave us was not the knowledge that is necessary and useful, but rather the means to acquire it. He speaks of the benefit to mankind of the invention of printing, of the mariner's compass, and of the discovery of quinine, and stresses that he does not "dis-esteem, or *dissuade the Study of nature,*" but only "that we should not be too forwardly possessed with the Opinion, or Expectation of Knowledge, where it is not to be had" (E IV.xii.12: 647).

For substantiation and illustration of this general picture, we must turn to the detail of Locke's inquiry into the origin and extent of human knowledge. In a word, the origin, the "Fountain of Knowledge," is experience: "In that, all our Knowledge is founded; and from that it ultimately derives it self" (E II.i.2: 104). But this view, that knowledge is "founded in" and "ultimately derives from" experience, presupposes a distinction between knowledge as such and the ideas that are "the materials of Knowledge" (E II.i.25: 118).

In a draft version of the *Essay* Locke faces up to an objection, which, he says, he has sometimes met: not all knowledge could have come from experience; some things we know could not have been learned "from our senses." We know that any number is either even or odd. But "we can by noe means be assurd by our senses" of this, "because neither our senses nor thoughts have been conversant about all numbers" (Draft A 43: D I: 74-75).

His answer makes clear that his claim is not that all knowledge is "made out to us by our senses," unassisted and by themselves. This would ignore the fact that human beings have understandings; it would ignore our reason, "which I thinke by a right traceing of those Ideas which it hath received from Sense or Sensation may come to . . . knowledg . . . which our senses could never have discoverd." His claim is, rather, that all ideas, all the materials out of which knowledge is fashioned by our reason, are derived from experience. We do not learn through experience that any number is even or odd. From experience we get the ideas of numbers and of the properties of evenness and oddness; and then, by our reason, we come to know that any number is even or odd. This insistence on the point that the use of reason is in some way involved in the acquisition of knowledge is one thing that shows the need for caution about the common characterization of Locke as an empiricist.

Locke explains that, behind this mistaken objection to his claim that experience is the "Fountain of Knowledge," there lay the view that some of our knowledge is not acquired, does not come from anywhere during our lifetime, but is innate. Book I of the *Essay* is a lengthy attack on this innatist view about the origin of knowledge; and we should look at it before looking at Locke's positive account of the production of ideas by experience and, out of those materials, of knowledge by reason. "It is," he says, "an established Opinion amongst some Men, That there are in the Understanding certain *innate Principles* . . . as it were stamped upon the Mind of Man, which the Soul receives in its very first Being; and brings into the World with it" (E I.ii.1: 48). These supposed innate principles were divided into the "practical," or moral and religious (e.g., the commandment *"Parents preserve and cherish your Children"* [E I.iii.12: 73]), and the "speculative," or theoretical (e.g. *"'Tis impossible for the same thing to be, and not to be"* [E I.ii.4: 49]). The exact identity of those who believed such principles to be "stamped upon the Mind" is not completely clear.[2] Their reasons for the belief are easier to see.

One reason for believing in the innateness of speculative principles has already been mentioned. It is that their innateness explains how we can come by truths which we could not have learned from experience. Even after reading Locke's attacks, this is just how James Lowde defended an innateness of knowledge. He argues that we do have knowledge that in "no ways depends upon Observation" and so concludes that it is innate or "naturally inscribed":

> Our Souls have a native power of finding or framing such Principles or Propositions, the Truth or Knowledge whereof no ways depends upon the evidence of sense or observation: thus knowing what is meant by a whole, and what by a part, hence naturally results the truth of this Proposition [the whole is greater than the parts], without being in any ways oblig'd to sense for it. (Lowde 1694: 53)

Another reason is that the hypothesis of innate knowledge provides a needed explanation why some things should seem obviously true, beyond question, and in no need of support. Some people think, Locke says, that if there are any propositions to which "all Men, even Children, as soon as they hear and understand the Terms, assent," this is "sufficient to prove them innate. For since Men never fail, after they have once understood the Words, to acknowledge them for undoubted Truths, they would inferr, That certainly these Propositions were first lodged in the Understanding . . . without any teaching" (E I.ii.17: 56). Lowde provides an example of this way of thinking too in his reply to Samuel Parker who, along with Locke, was a critic of innatism. According to Parker, there is no need of innate knowledge. Why should God imprint obvious truths on our minds? An obvious truth needs no such artificial support. Lowde's reply makes clear that there is something to explain: "these truths do in great measure, owe their clearness and evidence to their being thus imprinted . . . the needlessness of imprinting such evident Notions cannot be argued from their present clearness; because it is their being thus imprinted or thus connatural to our minds that makes them so" (Lowde 1694: 57).[3]

Since Locke agrees that some propositions (among them those picked out by the innatists) do seem obviously true to all understanding people who consider them, and since he is sure that this is not to be explained by appeal to innate "native Inscription," he is right, despite what Parker says, to acknowledge that he will need to provide an alternative explanation (E I.ii.11: 52-53). Various arguments lie behind his conviction that innateness is not the answer (see Barnes 1972). Innateness will not, or is not the only thing that will, adequately explain what it is meant to explain. It is too liberal: that "white is not black" would be readily accepted, but no one would want so specific a proposition to be innate; and it could be so only if, implausibly, its constituent ideas, "white" and "black" are innate (E I.ii.18-21: 57-60).

Different considerations are brought against the supposed innateness of practical and moral principles. People who accept them do so without question but, unlike speculative principles, they are not accepted by everyone. Anyone who is "but moderately conversant in the History of Mankind" knows this (E I.iii.2: 66). Ready acceptance by those who do accept them cannot, therefore, be explained by innateness. For the same reason, of course, it cannot be explained by the appeal, which Locke himself makes in the case of speculative principles, to some other general feature of the human mind.

What does explain people's unquestioning adherence to their moral principles, Locke thinks, is that as children they took them on trust, and then, due to laziness, lack of time, or timidity, never examined them. Moral principles are "instil[led] into the unwary, and, as yet, unprejudiced Understanding" of infants who, "as they grow up, [have them] confirmed to them, either by the open Profession, or tacit Consent, of all they have to do with" (E I.iii.22: 81), and who, as grown people "perplexed in the necessary affairs of Life, or hot in the pursuit of Pleasures" (E I.iii.25: 82), or afraid to question what is commonly accepted in their society, continue to accept them. The coda to Locke's diagnosis is the ironic twist that people forget how they came by these principles and so suppose them innate!

Though moral principles vary from group to group, and though their being unquestioned means only that they are taken blindly on trust, Locke does not think that there is no moral truth or that we cannot find it. There are moral truths but they are not to be dictated to us. They are, we shall see later, like anything else we come to know, to be worked out by "Reasoning and Discourse, and some Exercise of the Mind" (E I.iii.1: 66).

Having argued that none of our knowledge is innate or has its origin in divine imprinting, Locke turns to give his own positive account. Since knowledge presupposes ideas, which are its materials, he first discusses them.

There is much to be said about "ideas" in seventeenth-century philosophy (see Ashworth 1972, McRae 1965, and Yolton 1975a), and . . . about Locke's own conception of them. Here we need only mention his major points. Having defined an idea as "whatsoever is the Object of the Understanding when a Man thinks" (E I.i.8: 47), Locke follows Descartes and uses "thinking" to cover not just reasoning but also all other mental activities such as sensing, perceiving, remembering, imagining. So ideas not only figure in thinking and the understanding of language, but are also identified with perceptions of objects and their qualities, and with sensations like pain.

We saw earlier that the origin of ideas is, without exception, "experience." So, for example, "*our Senses,* conversant about particular sensible Objects, do *convey into the Mind,* several distinct *Perceptions* of things . . . And thus we come by those *Ideas,* we have of *Yellow, White, Heat, Cold, Soft, Hard, Bitter, Sweet*" (E II.i.3: 105). Prior to experience, the mind is "white Paper, void of all Characters, without any *Ideas*" (E II.i.2: 104). All the content of our thought must, in the end, be derived from experience. "All those sublime Thoughts, which towre above the Clouds, and reach as high as Heaven it self, take their Rise and Footing here" (E II.i.24: 118). This does not necessarily mean that we can have no idea of something of which we have had no experience. But such an idea must be a complex, derived by various mental operations of *"Enlarging, Compounding,* and *Abstracting"* (E II.i.22: 117) on ideas we have had from experience.

How is knowledge produced from such materials? To suppose that knowledge itself, rather than merely ideas, is "made out to us by our senses," unassisted and by themselves is, as noted earlier, "to leave noe roome for reason at all, which I thinke by a right traceing of those Ideas . . . may come to . . . knowledg" (Draft A 43: D I: 75). How, then, does reason produce knowledge from ideas?

Knowledge is defined as *"the perception of the connexion and agreement, or disagreement and repugnancy of any of our Ideas"* (E IV.i.2: 525). The basic thought of this is that some ideas are connected with others, and various truths reflect these connections. Knowledge of these truths consists in the "perception," the recognition by our understanding, of these connections. The angles of a triangle are equal to two right angles; and the idea of this equality is connected with the idea of the triangle's three angles. To know this truth about triangles is to "perceive" the connection between these ideas. Our knowledge consists in the "perception" "that Equality to two right ones, does necessarily agree to, and is inseparable from the three Angles of a Triangle" (ibid.).

Sometimes these connections are direct and immediate, and sometimes indirect, as in the case just now. We have intuitive knowledge when "the Mind perceives the Agreement or Disagreement of two *Ideas* immediately by themselves, without the intervention of any other"; so we can perceive directly "that *Three* are more than *Two,* and equal to *One* and *Two*" (E IV.ii.1: 530-31). This notion of an intuitive grasp of an immediate, direct connection between ideas that were originally derived from experience is, of course, Locke's promised replacement for the doctrine of innate knowledge. It is his explanation of our knowledge of propositions that "the Mind at very first Proposal, immediately closes with, and assents to" (E I.ii.17: 56).

We have demonstrative knowledge when the connection between two ideas is indirect and mediated by oth-

er ideas. "By an immediate view and comparing them" we cannot know that the angles of a triangle are equal to two right angles. A proof is needed. Our mind has to "find out some other Angles, to which the three Angles of a Triangle have an Equality; and finding those equal to two right ones, comes to know their Equality to two right ones" (E IV.ii.2: 532). A straight line across an apex of a triangle and parallel to the opposite side will produce these "other Angles." Of the three angles on that line, which together equal two right angles, one is one of the angles of the triangle, and the others together equal the other two angles of the triangle; and so the triangle's three angles equal two right angles.

Besides the two "degrees" of intuitive and demonstrative knowledge Locke notes a third, sensitive knowledge. This is knowledge of "the existence of particular external Objects, by that perception and Consciousness we have of the actual entrance of *Ideas* from them" (E IV.ii.14: 537-38). Whereas (excepting the intuitive knowledge of our own existence and the demonstrative knowledge of God's) the former concern generalities (such as that triangles have angles adding to two right angles), the latter concerns particularities (such as the reality of what is now going on before my eyes). Another, and connected, difference is that this "degree" of knowledge does not fit Locke's official definition. Sensitive knowledge is not knowledge of some connection between two ideas, but knowledge of the existence now of something in the world corresponding to our present perceptions or ideas. It will be discussed later, when Locke's account of the extent of our knowledge of general truths has been detailed.

These three "degrees" of knowledge cut across a fourfold classification of the agreement or connection between ideas, the perception of which constitutes knowledge, into "sorts" (E IV.i.3: 525): *"Identity, or Diversity"; "Relation"; "Co-existence,* or *necessary connexion";* and *"Real Existence."* The four sorts of proposition these generate are, respectively and roughly, propositions such as that "white is white" or that "three is more than two" (which are intuitively known); general propositions such as those about geometrical figures (which are intuitively or demonstratively known); general propositions about the properties of substances such as gold (about which, as we will see, we have little knowledge); and, leaving aside the intuitively and demonstratively known propositions that we and God really exist, propositions sensitively known. [4]

Now it is plausible to say of our knowledge of the properties of triangles in general that it is not "made out to us by our senses" and is based on our intellectual grasp of connections between ideas. But it is not plausible to say so of our knowledge of silver in general (that, e.g., it dissolves in nitric acid) or of gold (that it does not so dissolve). In these cases there is no discoverable connection between our ideas, and we are "left only to Observation and Experiment" (E IV.iii.28: 558). In these cases it does look as though our knowledge is "made out to us by our senses" and not by our reasoning about ideas. Locke's position on this is, simply, that these are not cases of knowledge. Knowledge is the perception of connections between ideas, so where we do other than perceive such connections we do not have knowledge. What we do have is what he calls "belief" or "opinion" (E IV.xv.3: 655).

In the absence of intuitive or demonstrative knowledge we must exercise judgment about probabilities and what to believe, and Locke devotes a handful of chapters to this investigation of "the Grounds and Degrees of Belief, Opinion, and Assent" (E I.i.2: 43). We do not find in these what hindsight might lead us to expect. In them Locke is not much interested in the extent to which "Observation and Experiment" justify general beliefs and expectations about the properties of material substances that go beyond that observation, nor is he interested in how we decide just which general beliefs we should form on its basis. There is, that is to say, little interest in what became known as Hume's problem of induction, and there is nothing of the kind of the canons of inductive logic later drawn up by John Stuart Mill. He does at one point acknowledge that his experience that this piece of gold is malleable "makes me not certain, that it is so, in all, or any other" similar thing (E IV.xii.9: 644). But his references to "common Experience" and "the ordinary course of Nature" (E IV.xvi.9: 663), and to what "our own and other Men's constant Observation has found always to be after the same manner" (E IV.xvi.6: 661), are not problematic for him in the way they would be for later philosophy. His interest, which he shares with his contemporaries, including the natural philosophers of the Royal Society, is in the rather different matter of the extent to which our own experience, the testimony of others and of written records, lend support to the probability of beliefs about the likelihood of various particular events, both ordinary and miraculous (see Shapiro 1983: Chap. 2).

There is a close relation between Locke's notion of "knowledge" and the more recent one of "a priori" or "conceptual knowledge." He says that "in some of our *Ideas* there are certain Relations, Habitudes, and Connexions, so visibly included in the Nature of the *Ideas* themselves, that we cannot conceive them separable from them, by any Power whatsoever. And in these only, we are capable of certain and universal Knowledge" (E IV.iii.29: 559), and this runs parallel to what is said in this century in explanation of knowledge of the a priori kind such as we have in mathematics and geometry.

There is an equally close relation between Locke's notion of "belief," which is based on "Observation and Exper-

iment" because of "a want of *a discoverable Connection* between those *Ideas* which we have" (E IV.iii.28: 558), and the notion of "a posteriori knowledge" of the kind which we have in a systematic form in empirical sciences such as chemistry. But just as Locke would not call such empirical knowledge "knowledge," but rather "belief," so he would not call chemistry (and other parts of what was then known as "natural philosophy") "a science": a "science" is a body of "knowledge," not one of "belief." So though geometry and arithmetic are sciences for him, and though—so he says—morality could be one, "natural Philosophy is not capable of being made a Science" (E IV.xii.10: 645). These facts—that Locke is not thinking in terms of two kinds of knowledge, and that he sees geometry but not natural philosophy as a science—are symptomatic of differences underlying the similarity between his knowledge-belief distinction and the more recent distinction between a priori and empirical knowledge. These will be reviewed later.

In some cases, then, our understandings grasp necessary connections between our ideas, and in others they do not. In some cases we have "knowledge," and in others we have only "belief" or "opinion." Why is this? The briefest answer is that it is because in some cases our ideas (what Locke calls nominal essences) are ideas of (what Locke calls) real essences, and in others they are not. But this needs explaining.

In claiming that all ideas come from experience, Locke distinguished between simple and complex ideas. At the same time he categorized complex ideas into (among others) substances and modes. . . . They are important for Locke's theory of knowledge, as is evident from the fact that geometrical figures (about which we can have "knowledge") are modes, whereas things such as gold and lead (those things whose properties interest the natural philosopher and about which he has "beliefs") are substances.

The nominal essence of something, mode or substance, is our idea of that thing. So the nominal essence of a triangle or of gold is what we mean by the word "triangle" or "gold," in the sense of being a description or set of characteristics that something must have in order for us to count it as a "triangle" or "gold." It is, Locke says, "nothing but that *abstract* Idea *to which the Name is annexed:* So that every thing contained in that *Idea,* is essential to that Sort" (E III.vi.2: 439). The real essence of something is its "very being . . . whereby it is, what it is" (E III.iii.15: 417); it is that "upon which depends this *nominal Essence,* and all the Properties of that Sort" (E III.vi.2: 439), that "on which all the properties of the *Species* depend, and from which alone they all flow" (E III.v.14: 436-37).

The wonderfully elaborate Strasbourg Cathedral clock provides Locke with a good illustration for this distinction. In Strasbourg on market day, the "gazing Country-man" (E III.vi.3: 440) would be struck by the representation of the moving planets, the lifelike figures that moved on the hours, the mechanical cock that crowed at noon, and other such features of this famous clock. He would doubtless be inclined to accept that there must be something (probably some mechanism of some sort, he would suppose) about the clock that gives rise to all these features by which he recognizes it. But he would know nothing of the complex system of cogs and wheels, which is what the clock would be to the cathedral horologist. In effect, then, the ideas the countryman and the horologist have of the clock, their nominal essences, are importantly different. The countryman's is of some of its observable features and characteristics; the horologist's is of its real essence, of what gives rise to those observable features and characteristics, and so which explains the clock's possession of them.

To allow of something that it has a real essence is to allow that there is something which it fundamentally is and which gives rise to, or explains its having, its characteristic features and properties. If we felt that all there was to it were characteristic features and did not accept that there might be something else about the thing which is basic to it and which produces or explains those characteristics features, then the notion of a real essence would have no place there.

Locke makes a relatively easy application of these thoughts to substances such as lead or gold. On the one hand there are the familiar, observable, and discoverable properties of these things—their particular color, their malleability, their solubility in some acids and not in others. On the other hand, or so it is natural to think, there is something else that lead or gold really is, something on which these properties depend and which can be used to explain why lead and gold have them. Appealing to their latest theories chemists could provide us with detail about what lead or gold is and why these substances have the properties they do. Someone less knowledgeable but not totally ignorant of natural science might well think, somewhat vaguely, in terms of the movements of elementary particles.

Chemical theory has moved on in the three hundred years since Locke, but our thoughts about these things have a basic continuity with his. Specifically, his conception of the real essence of a substance is modeled on the workings of the Strasbourg clock. He supposes that what gold, for instance, basically is, is a collection of minute particles, "insensible Corpuscles" (E IV.iii.25: 555), which only have the so-called primary qualities of solidity, size, shape, and motion. It is in terms of the arrangement and rearrangement of these particles that the observable properties of gold, such as its malleability and solubility in certain acids, are to be explained and understood. The differences in qualities of different substances stem from differences in the shape, size, arrangement, and motion of the insensible corpuscles that make up their corpuscular "real Constitutions" (E III.ix.12: 482).

Though this is the general picture Locke provides of the real essence or inner constitution of substances, he does not think we can fill in the details (in the way chemists now think they can, or as the cathedral horologist could with the Strasbourg clock). God can certainly fill them in and possibly the angels can too (E III.vi.3: 440), but with respect to substances we humans are all "gazing Countrymen." Our nominal essences of substances, our ideas of them, are not ideas of their real essences.

Locke's picture of matter is continuous not only with ours but also with that of the classical Greek atomists, Leucippus, Democritus, and Epicurus. Their theory of the terms in which the phenomena of the material world are to be understood was revived and revitalized in the seventeenth century by Galileo, Gassendi, and Hobbes; and, in its essentials, it was accepted by Locke. But this view of what a substance's "real essence" is like, and how it gives rise to the characteristic qualities of the substance, contrasts with and replaces a quite different view that had some currency in the seventeenth century. As Locke says, "Concerning the real Essences of corporeal Substances, . . . there are . . . two Opinions." His own, the "more rational Opinion," supposes "all natural Things to have a real, but unknown Constitution of their insensible Parts, from which flow those sensible Qualities, which serve us to distinguish them one from another, according as we have Occasion to rank them into sorts, under common Denominations." The other, which he rejects, supposes "a certain number of Forms of Molds, wherein all natural Things, that exist, are cast, and do equally partake" (E III.iii.17: 417-18).

This rejected account of essences belongs to the Aristotelian hylemorphic account of material things. Whereas those in the recently revived atomic tradition thought of a material thing as a collection of corpuscles, the Aristotelians thought of it as a composite of "form" (*morphe*) and "matter" (*hyle*) by analogy with the way a human artifact such as a bronze statue is a composite of bronze matter and of a certain shape or form. It is because some naturally occurring thing has the "form" (or "essence" or "nature") that it does that it is the kind of thing it is and has its characteristic properties. On the face of it there might seem little difference between a corpuscularian real essence and a Scholastic form. After all, they both have the role of explaining and being the source of the characteristic properties of various kinds of thing. But, at least to their opponents, the Scholastics' detailed characterizations of these forms (e.g., "man is a rational animal") seemed like mere verbal definitions, rather than descriptions of what certain things really are, an appearance that was encouraged by there being strict rules for the construction of these definitions. There was a general feeling among the "new philosophers" of the seventeenth century that the Aristotelian hylemorphic theory was useless as a means of understanding the world. It has, as Locke says, "very much perplexed the Knowledge of natural Things" (E III.iii.17: 418). The structure of material things was best seen in the terms of the atomic theory, not in those of Aristotelian hylemorphism.

We saw earlier—to turn now from substances to modes—that the nominal essence of a geometrical figure such as the triangle is our idea of such a thing. Presumably, for most people, something will count as a triangle if it is "a closed figure with three straight sides." What of its real essence? Obviously this cannot be a corpuscular constitution, or arrangement of particles—for the triangle is not a material thing but rather a shape, or way in which material things may be arranged. But it is not immediately obvious what it could be. This may partially explain why some people are less than enthusiastic about the idea of modal real essences.[5] What also may partly explain this is that Locke sometimes speaks of modes as though they were something other than a united whole with a mind-independent coherence—which is, it seems, what something with a real essence should be like. Thus he sometimes speaks of them as though they are simply what we, at our convenience, make them to be: they are, he sometimes says, composed of "scattered and independent *Ideas*" connected only by the mind (E II.xxii.1, 2, 5: 288-89, 290; and E III.v.8, 10: 433, 434). It is a mistake, however, to think that modes do not really have real essences. Locke quite plainly thinks they do, and his theory of knowledge depends on their having them. Moreover considerable sense can be made of the idea.

What is required is room for a distinction between the characteristic properties of some mode, and an essence from which those properties result. Locke plainly and plausibly thinks this requirement can be met for geometrical figures. The real essence of a triangle, he says, is "a Figure including a Space between three Lines." This is "the very *Essentia,* or Being, of the thing it self, that Foundation from which all its Properties flow, and to which they are all inseparably annexed" (E III.iii.18: 418). He intends a parallel between (on the one hand) gold's having certain characteristic properties and their arising from gold's being matter with a certain corpuscular constitution, and (on the other hand) a triangle's having certain characteristic properties and their arising from a triangle's being a closed three-sided figure. The cases are different only in that while we are "gazing Country-men" with respect to gold, ignorant of what precisely its real essence is, we do have knowledge of the real essence of a triangle.

This last fact is what lies behind Locke's remark that "*in* the Species of . . . *Modes,* they [sc. real and nominal essences] *are always the same:* But *in Substances, always quite different*" (ibid.). This remark should not be taken as a definition, a necessary truth about substances and modes. For, as Locke allows, it is possible to be ignorant of the real essence of an ellipse—it has to do with its relation to two points, which are called its foci—and so to have a nominal essence different from it and solely in terms of some of this mode's more obvious properties (E II.xxxi.10-11: 382).

Though considerable sense can be made of the idea of modal real essences there are problems with it. Some people feel it is arbitrary to say that "closed three-sided figure" is a triangle's real essence, what a triangle is, and that having three angles which sum to two right angles is a property that results from that essence. Since all and only closed three-sided figures have angles summing to two right angles, the latter has, they feel, an equal claim to be the real essence. A further problem is that with other modes, such as "procession" (E III.v.13: 436) and "parricide" (E II.xxii.4: 290), it is not obvious how one would even attempt to distinguish between essence and dependent properties.

In summary, then, our ideas (nominal essences) of substances are not of their real essences; our ideas (nominal essences) of modes at least often are. Why does this mean that "natural Philosophy is not capable of being made a Science" (E IV.xii.10: 645), while in geometry we can make systematic deductions? Quite simply, our idea of gold not being of its real essence from which its properties flow, there is no discernible connection between our ideas of gold and of those properties. Quite the contrary would be the case if our idea of gold were of its real essence. On the other hand, our idea of a triangle is of its real essence from which its properties flow, and so those properties are deducible from our idea of a triangle (E II.xxxi.6: 378-80).

So when our ideas are ideas of real essences, we can get "certain and universal Knowledge" (E IV.iii.29: 559) by the a priori methods of intuition and demonstration. This is why Locke says that "*Morality is capable of Demonstration,* as well as *Mathematicks*" (E IV.xii.8: 643). For "the *Ideas* that Ethicks are conversant about" (ibid.) are, he believes, modes whose real essences we do, or could, know. By contrast, however, where, as in natural philosophy, our ideas are not of real essences, we cannot go in for demonstration and acquire real knowledge, but are dependent on beliefs formed in experience.

Substances afford Matter of very little general

Knowledge; and the bare Contemplation of their abstract *Ideas,* will carry us but a very little way in the search of Truth and Certainty. . . . *Experience here must teach me,* what Reason cannot: and 'tis by trying alone, that I can certainly know, what other Qualities co-exist with those of my complex Idea, *v.g.* whether that *yellow, heavy, fusible* Body, I call *Gold,* be *malleable,* or no; which Experience . . . makes me not certain, that it is so, in all, or any other *yellow, heavy, fusible* Bodies, but that which I have tried. . . . Because the other Properties of such Bodies, depending not on these, but on that unknown real Essence, on which these also depend, we cannot by them discover the rest.

(E IV.xii.9: 644)

There is a contemporary context to Locke's view, that the method appropriate to natural philosophy, and to the investigation of the properties of substances, is basically that of observation. A tangible expression of this was the Royal Society of London for the Improving of Natural Knowledge, which was founded in 1660. Besides Locke, it included amongst its fellows various people who figure in histories of the development of modern science, and whom Locke refers to as *"Master-Builders"* of the *"Commonwealth of Learning"* (E Epis: 9): Robert Boyle, Christiaan Huygens, and Isaac Newton. They advocated that natural philosophy must be based on careful observation and the compilation of so-called "natural histories," accounts of observed properties—as in Boyle's *General History of the Air.* Thus Robert Hooke, in his account of things seen under the recently invented microscope, says that what is important in natural philosophy is "the plainness and soundness of Observations on material and obvious things" (Hooke 1665: Preface).

The Royal Society was consciously anti-Scholastic and its recommendation for natural philosophy of what Locke called the "Historical, plain Method" (E I.i.2: 44) was married to its rejection of the ultimately Aristotelian idea of *scientia.* According to this doctrine, *scientia* is knowledge structured in a certain way which gives an understanding of why certain things are necessarily so. One would have "scientific understanding" of something, say gold's being malleable, if one had demonstrated the necessity of its being so by deriving it, from first principles, as the conclusion of certain syllogistic arguments that had to be constructed according to strict canons of form. Among these first principles would be things that, so it was said, have to be known if anything is to be known—"maxims" such as that it is impossible for the same thing to be and not to be. Also among these principles would be a definition, as understood according to the hylemorphic theory, of the "form" or "nature" or "real essence" of the kind of thing whose properties were under investigation. Locke and many of his contemporaries felt that, with the possible exception of geometry, no

"science" as conceived in this way ever had been or could be produced. In particular the strict syllogistic demands placed on the structure of *scientia,* and its association with an unacceptable account of "real essence," did not fit it for use in the study of natural phenomena. It turned attention away from things to words.[6]

We have been brought back, at this point, to the similarities between Locke's distinction between knowledge and belief and the more recent distinction between two kinds of knowledge, a priori or conceptual and a posteriori or empirical. Let us now look at the differences. According to the logical positivists of this century, all a priori knowledge is, in the end, trifling and empty of content. Locke would deny that this is true of all that he calls knowledge (E IV.viii.8: 614).

He would not deny it is true of some. Given an idea of gold as a stuff that is yellow and malleable, there is a necessary connection to be perceived between being gold and being malleable; we can be certain that gold (what we count as gold) is malleable. But, in Locke's view, not all necessary connections between ideas are of this trifling sort. The necessary connection we suppose there is between the real essence or corpuscular constitution of gold and gold's malleability, is not; nor, in his view, is that connection, which we can actually perceive, between the real essence of a triangle as a closed three-sided figure and the property of having angles equal to two right angles. The certainty that a triangle has that property is—in Locke's view—informative. It is to be contrasted with the trifling verbal certainty that three-sided figures have three sides. Whether we think Locke is right depends on how much sympathy we have with his theory of real essence, a theory with which logical positivism shows some impatience.

An antipathy to real essences underlies a further difference between the Lockean and the more recent distinction. The idea that all a priori knowledge is trifling and lacking in content has a natural affinity with the idea that the reason why the properties of substances are not known a priori, the reason why natural philosophy is not (in Locke's terms) a science, lies in the nature of things and not (as for Locke) in the nature of our understandings. To the positivists' way of thinking the natural world is contingent through and through; hence there could be no other way to acquire knowledge of it except by observation and experiment. But to Locke's way of thinking there are necessities in the world; for substances do have real essences from which their characteristic properties flow. Our reliance on observation and experiment is a consequence simply of our ignorance of these essences.

Had we such *Ideas* of Substances, as to know what real Constitutions produce those sensible Qualities we find in them, . . . we could, by the specifick *Ideas* of their real Essences in our own Minds, more certainly find out their Properties . . . than we can now by our Senses: and to know the Properties of *Gold,* it would be no more necessary, that *Gold* should exist, and that we should make Experiments upon it, than it is necessary for the knowing the Properties of a Triangle, that a Triangle should exist in any Matter, the *Idea* in our Minds would serve for the one, as well as the other.

(E IV.vi.11: 585)

Besides looking forward to a more recent distinction, Locke's distinction between knowledge and belief also looks back to an older one: the Aristotelian distinction between "scientific knowledge" and "opinion." Knowledge, as defined and explained in the Aristotelian tradition, has to do with what must be so and cannot be otherwise; and, for Locke too, "knowledge" is "certain and universal" (E IV.iii.29: 559). We have seen, though, that whereas for the Aristotelian knowledge has a structure arising from its development and acquisition on the basis of syllogisms that have maxims and definitions for premises, for Locke it does not. "Science" for him is a body of deductively related knowledge, but he places no particular value on syllogistic methods and abstract maxims.

As for "opinion," it has to do with contingencies on the traditional view, with things that might have been otherwise. As we have seen, however, this is not the case for Locke. It is true that, for him, natural philosophy, that collection of "beliefs" about substances and their properties, is not a science or body of knowledge. But this is because of the nature of our understandings, and not because of the nature of things. So whereas for the Scholastic tradition "opinion" concerns contingencies, for Locke it concerns what to us seem like contingencies, but what in reality may be universal certainties.

A feature of the Scholastic tradition was that the pursuit of *scientia* was the proper use of man's reason. Man is a rational animal, and one thing that was taken to mean is that he is a syllogistic reasoner. Opinion is not worth or even capable of serious and systematic attention. Indeed, talk of "system" is out of place in its connection, for it would imply an arrangement structured by syllogistic demonstrations from first principles. But Locke thinks that "opinion" is worth systematically searching for and having. There can be a body of it, and it is "natural philosophy." Even for him, it is, of course, not a "science"; and to that extent Locke is under some influence from the older tradition. But, as in the activities of many of his colleagues in the Royal Society, it can be systematically pursued; and to that extent, and as witnessed to by his occasionally calling the beliefs of natural philosophy "experimental Knowledge" (E IV.iii.29: 560; E IV.vi.7: 582), he is throwing off that influence.

Now, though we have no knowledge in natural philosophy, geometry and mathematics are not the only areas where we do have it. Commenting that it has indeed "been generally taken for granted, that Mathematicks alone are capable of demonstrative certainty" (E IV.ii.9: 534), Locke says that this assumption is false. Because the relevant ideas are modes, whose real essences we either do or might come to know, he thinks, perhaps surprisingly, that it may be possible to "place *Morality amongst the Sciences capable of Demonstration:* wherein I doubt not, but from self-evident Propositions, by necessary Consequences, as incontestable as those in Mathematicks, the measures of right and wrong might be made out" (E IV.iii.18: 549). This moral science would be based on two ideas. First there would be the idea of God. This idea, of "a supreme Being, infinite in Power, Goodness, and Wisdom" (ibid.), is, of course, not innate but is constructed on the basis of experience (E II.xxiii.33: 314; E IV.x.1: 619). It is a foundation for ethics because moral rules are simply the dictates of such a being: "God has given a Rule whereby Men should govern themselves . . . This is the only true touchstone of *moral Rectitude"* (E II.xxviii.8: 352). The second basic idea would be that of ourselves as beings with understanding and rationality, and who are created by and dependent on God. From this it self-evidently follows both that we can understand God's will and that we should obey it: we "as certainly know that Man is to honour, fear, and obey GOD, as . . . that *Three, Four,* and *Seven,* are less than *Fifteen"* (E IV.xiii.3: 651).

We need to know too, of course, that, beyond our idea of Him, God really does exist; and He Himself has provided us with the means to do so, by creating us with the power of reason and so the ability to demonstrate His existence. Locke says in the *Essay* (E IV.x.7: 622) that the traditional ontological proof should not be used as the only argument for such an important conclusion; later he actually rejected it (Deus: L II: 133-39). His objection is that the existence of something can hardly be proved from a mere idea, but only from the existence of other things. His preferred proof is not open to this objection. Very briefly, starting from our intuitive knowledge of the fact that we exist as intelligent things, he concludes that only an eternal intelligent being could have created us (E IV.x.1-5: 619-21).

Locke recognized that no one had yet produced a demonstrative morality and, despite urging from his friend William Molyneux, did not attempt it himself. But this does not mean to Locke that human reason has failed completely in "its great and proper business of morality" (W VII: 140), for we do have some moral knowledge, acquired in this fashion (E I.iii.1, 4: 65-66, 68; E II.xxviii.8: 352). But, as he makes particularly clear in *The Reasonableness of Christianity,* this process is not easy, and moral knowledge is hard won. There is, however, another source, alternative to our reason and understanding, and one to which those who have neither the time nor the ability may fortunately have recourse. "The Gospel," Locke explains, "contains so perfect a body of Ethics, that reason may be excused from that enquiry" (Letter 2059: *The Correspondence of John Locke,* ed. E. S. de Beer, V: 595). It follows, naturally, that our relation to any moral principles arrived at in this way, from the written revelations of the Gospels and not by our reason and the perception of connections between ideas, can only be one of belief, not of knowledge.

We saw that in the background to what Locke had to say about the origin and extent of knowledge was the debate provoked by Sextus Empiricus. It is there in the background to what he says in particular about the place of reason in the discovery of moral and religious truth, and the importance of the Gospels as a source. For one particular arena where that debate took place was in the religious controversies of the Reformation. The view had been that religious truths were determined by and to be sought in the traditions of the Catholic church, and in the decrees of the pope and of church councils. Martin Luther's challenge was that they were determined by, and to be found in the Scriptures. There is some evidence that it was this specific question about the sources of religious and moral knowledge that initially led to Locke's writing the *Essay*.

In the course of his rejection of innateness Locke inveighs against people who "taking things upon trust, misimploy their power of Assent, by lazily enslaving their Minds, to the Dictates and Dominion of others, in Doctrines, which it is their duty carefully to examine" (E I.iv.22: 99; E IV.xx.17: 718-19). So for him, the possible sources of religious and moral truth come down to two: one's own reason and the Scriptures, "the light of Nature, or the voice of Revelation" (E II.xxviii.8: 352). The central point of his discussion of the relation between these two is that reason has supremacy over revelation. But this does not mean simply that reasoned knowledge is superior to faith, or revelation-based belief. It means also that revelation is answerable to reason.

Some moral truths are discoverable both by reason and by a reading of the Gospels (E IV.xviii.4: 690-91). But the revelations of the latter cannot make us more certain of the discoveries of reason. We need to know we are faced with a genuine revelation, and we cannot be as certain of this as we are of our reason-based knowledge. "The Knowledge, we have, that this *Revelation* came at first from GOD, can never be so sure, as the Knowledge we have from the clear and distinct Perception of the Agreement, or Disagreement of our own *Ideas*" (E IV.xviii.4: 691). Similarly, in the case of

some divergence, we should follow reason rather than the supposed revelation. It "would be to subvert the Principles, and Foundations of all Knowledge . . . if . . . what we certainly know, give way to what we may possibly be mistaken in" (E IV.xviii.5: 692).

But the human understanding does have its limits, and some supposedly revealed truths (e.g., "that the dead shall rise, and live again" [E IV.xviii.7: 694]) are "above Reason" and undiscoverable by it. This still does not mean, however, that reason has no relevance for our acceptance of them. If something is a revelation from God it is bound to be true: "But whether it be a divine Revelation, or no, *Reason* must judge" (E IV.xviii.10: 695).

A further way in which the revelation of truths that are "above Reason" places no restriction on the supremacy of reason is that belief in them is not necessary for salvation. Anything that is necessary for salvation can be reached by our natural faculties. God, Locke says, has "given all Mankind so sufficient a light of Reason, that they to whom this written Word [the Bible] never came, could not (when-ever they set themselves to search) either doubt of the Being of a GOD, or of the Obedience due to Him" (E III.ix.23: 490).

The regulation of revelation by reason distinguishes faith from what was called "enthusiasm"—a religious enthusiast being one who "laying by Reason would set up Revelation without it" (E IV.xix.3: 698). Locke's rejection of enthusiasm, and his allocation of a central role to reason in morality and religion, give him a place in the history of the development of Deism. These are topics of discussion in Chapter 7 of this volume.

Our discussion of the extent of knowledge has so far had as its focus general propositions that have to do with the first three kinds of "connexion and agreement" between ideas—"Identity, or Diversity," "Relation," and "Co-existence, or necessary connexion." Let us turn now to the fourth kind of agreement, and so to our knowledge of particular "Real Existence." We have intuitive knowledge of our own existence and demonstrative knowledge of God's, but what we have of "*the Existence* of any other thing" is sensitive knowledge (E IV.xi.1: 630). The poor fit here with Locke's official definition of knowledge was noted earlier. Sensitive knowledge of some real existence is not knowledge of a connection between two ideas but knowledge of the existence of something in reality corresponding to our perceptions or ideas.

There are, of course, traditional skeptical arguments against the possibility of any such knowledge. Locke rehearses them: though we may be sure that we have an idea in our minds we cannot "thence certainly inferr the existence of any thing without us, which corresponds to that *Idea,* . . . because Men may have such

Ideas in their Minds, when no such Thing exists" (E IV.ii.14: 537). But he is unimpressed. Though he concedes that the certainty he has from "the Testimony of my Eyes" is not so perfect or absolute as that from intuition or demonstration, it yet *"deserves the name of Knowledge"* (E IV.xi.2-3: 631). He appeals to us to acknowledge that the ideas we have in veridical perception just are qualitatively different from those of, for example, memory. The skeptic would feel that this begs the question, for how do we know what veridical perceptions are like when the problem is to know whether we have any veridical perceptions? To say, as Locke does, that "the actual receiving of *Ideas* from without . . . makes us know, that something doth exist at that time without us, which causes that *Idea* in us" (E IV.xi.2: 630) hardly meets the worry. How do we know we are actually receiving ideas "from without" and not dreaming? But Locke's interests and intellectual concerns are quite other than those of the skeptics who put such questions. His response to them fits with what we noted at the outset, namely his concern with how we should live our lives: "no body can, in earnest, be so sceptical, as to be uncertain of the Existence of those Things which he sees and feels" (E IV.xi.3: 631). Meeting the questions with sarcasm and impatience he concludes that "we certainly finding, that Pleasure or Pain follows upon the application of certain Objects to us, whose Existence we perceive, or dream that we perceive, by our Senses, this certainty is as great as our Happiness, or Misery, beyond which, we have no concernment to know, or to be" (E IV.ii.14: 537).

In Locke's view, then, though we are fitted to know some things, we are not fitted to know everything. The most obvious and large-scale limitation is the lack of scientific knowledge in natural philosophy, but there are others that Locke cites—all of them standard and frequently cited problems in seventeenth-century philosophy. We will never know how physical changes in the body produce ideas in the mind, and we will never know how the mind acts on the body to move it— "How any thought should produce a motion in Body is as remote from the nature of our *Ideas,* as how any Body should produce any Thought in the Mind" (E IV.iii.28: 559). We will never know whether an immaterial mind is required for thought or whether thinking could be an ability "given to some Systems of Matter fitly disposed" (E IV.iii.6: 540), and we are quite in the dark as to "how the solid parts of Body are united, or cohere together to make Extension" (E II.xxiii.23: 308).

But we do not just happen to have the faculties and abilities we have. They are those which God chose to give us, and we "have Cause enough to magnify the bountiful Author of our Being, for that Portion and Degree of Knowledge, he has bestowed on us" (E I.i.5: 45). Locke does not explain why there is any need for geometry to be a science, and hence why rules of thumb

such as builders use are not sufficient for practical purposes. But it plainly does not matter to him that natural philosophy will never be one. We have no need of strict knowledge of the properties and characteristics of material substances in order to acquire "whatsoever is necessary for the Conveniences of Life" (ibid.): from "Experiments and Historical Observations . . . we may draw Advantages of Ease and Health, and thereby increase our stock of Conveniences for this Life" (E IV.xii.10: 645).

There is no doubt in Locke's mind that these practical matters are important. He speaks with passion of how benighted the American Indians were who lacked the use of iron (E IV.xii.11: 646). But to want to go beyond such matters of practical importance is to want something that is "of noe solid advantage to us nor help to make our lives the happyer" and is "but the uselesse imployments of idle or over curious brains which amuse them selves about things out of which they can by noe meanes draw any reall benefit" (Journal 1677: Bodleian Library MS Locke f.2: 46).

But our aim here in this world is not merely to live a comfortable life, to have "a quiet prosperous passage through" it. This is secondary to our real concern which is to find our way into the next world. "Heaven being our great businesse and interest the knowledg which may direct us thither is certainly soe too, soe that this is without peradventure the study which ought to take up the first and cheifest place in our thoughts" (Journal 1677: Bodleian Library MS Locke f.2: 92-93). Men have reason to thank God too, then, "that they have Light enough to lead them to the Knowledge of their Maker, and the sight of their own Duties" (E I.i.5: 45). So it is, says Locke, that "I think I may conclude, that *Morality* is *the proper Science, and Business of Mankind in general"* (E IV.xii.11: 646).

Notes

[1] The disagreement concerns whether Locke is to be placed in a tradition of "constructive skepticism" (see Van Leeuwen 1963: 121, 124; Woolhouse 1983: 14, and, in opposition, Ferreira 1986: 211-22).

[2] Two classic discussions of this issue are Gibson 1917: 39-44 and Yolton 1956: 26-71.

[3] Lowde is replying to Parker 1666.

[4] Note that "co-existence" is sometimes taken to refer not only, e.g., to the universal concomitance of the properties of gold in general (about which, we shall see, we have little knowledge), but also to the coinstantiation of those of a particular piece of gold at a particular time (about which, Locke says [E IV.xii.9: 644], we do have "certain," presumably "sensitive" [E

IV.iii.29: 560], knowledge).

[5] See, e.g., Aronson and Lewis 1970: 195-97 and Chapter 5 of this volume. For further references, see Woolhouse 1983: 122-24.

[6] Locke's attack on various parts of this doctrine can be found throughout the *Essay*—see Woolhouse 1983: 65-80. His rejection of innate knowledge can be seen as a facet of it, for, though diverging from Aristotle in this respect, some seventeenth-century defenders of *scientia* thought of "maxims" or "speculative principles" as being innate.

FURTHER READING

Criticism

Ayers, Michael. *Locke: Volume I: Epistemology*. London: Routledge, 1991, 341 p.

> Divides discussion of Locke's epistemology into four sections: "Ideas," "Knowledge and Belief," "Perceptual Knowledge," and "Particulars, Universals and Intuitive Knowledge" with a view to illuminating connections between Locke's thought and the epistemological problems faced by contemporary philosophers.

Fowler, Thomas. "Essay on the Human Understanding." In *Locke*, pp. 127-51. London: Macmillan and Co., 1880.

> Argues that "Locke was the first of modern writers to attempt at once an independent and a complete treatment of the phenomena of the human mind, of their mutual relations, of their causes and limits."

Heyd, Thomas. "Some Remarks on Science, Method and Nationalism in John Locke." *History of European Ideas* 16, Nos. 1-3, (January 1993) 97-102.

> Discusses "first, Locke's relation to science and his method, second, the debt that . . . doctrines supportive of nationalism owe to [Locke's] method and background in science, and, in conclusion, a reason for reassessing Locke's method."

Kraus, John L. *John Locke: Empiricist, Atomist, Conceptualist, and Agnostic*. New York: Philosophical Library, 1968, 202 p.

> Kraus comments: "This present study has a twofold end: its primary end is to examine the theory of universal ideas set forth by John Locke; its secondary end is to show the relation of Locke's theory of universals to the question of a 'science' of physical things." Subjects of discussion include Locke's empiricist perspective con-cerning human knowledge, his "atomic perspective on the real essences of physical things," and his "conceptualistic perspective on universal ideas."

Mackie, J. L. *Problems from Locke*. Oxford: Clarendon Press, 1976, 237 p.

> Examines "a limited number of problems of continuing philosophical interest [associated with the *capacity for human knowledge*] which are raised in Locke's *Essay* Concerning Human Understanding."

O'Connor, D. J. *John Locke*. Melbourne: Penguin Books, 1952, 225 p.

> Includes discussion of Locke's theory of knowledge, his philosophy of language in relation to human thought, and his political theory. O'Connor comments: "[M]y criticism of Locke is inevitably directed by my own philosophical outlook, a moderate empiricism which is not, I hope, too far removed from Locke's own position."

Walmsly, Peter. "Dispute and Conversation: Probability and the Rhetoric of Natural Philosophy in Locke's *Essay*." *The Journal of the History of Ideas* 54, No. 3 (July 1993): 381-94.

> Discusses Locke's objections to "disputation" as a prominent element of university education during his time: "Locke objects [in the *Essay*] that this combative forum stunts intellectual growth."

Wilson, Milton. "Reading Locke and Newton as Literature." *University of Toronto Quarterly* 57, No. 4 (Summer 1988): 471-83.

> Considers Locke's prose style in *An Essay Concerning Human Understanding*: "Locke's Essay is both a perpetually half-revised and an increasingly open-ended book."

Wood, Neal. "*Tabula Rasa*, Social Environmentalism, and the 'English Paradigm'." *The Journal of the History of Ideas* LIII, No. 4 (October-December 1992): 647-68.

> Notes that during the Enlightenment, Locke's empiricism became "a potent intellectual force" that influenced the ideas of diverse thinkers, and argues that "the notion of human malleability was transformed by some English Renaissance thinkers . . . into a 'social psychology' of *tabula rasa*, culminating in Bacon who launched the 'English paradigm' of social discourse."

Woolhouse, R. S. *Locke's Philosophy of Science and Knowledge: A Consideration of Some Aspects of An Essay Concerning Human Understanding*. New York: Barnes & Noble, 1971, 204 p.

> Focuses on "what is beginning to be seen as perhaps Locke's major theme which, amidst his discussion of particular topics, reappears throughout Books II, III, and IV, of the *Essay*: that of natural or scientific laws and our knowledge of them."

Youngren, William. "Founding English Ethics: Locke, Mathematics, and the Innateness Question." *Eighteenth-*

Century Life 16, No. 3 (November 1992): 12-45.
    Discusses Locke's "view that moral knowledge can
attain mathematical certainty" in relation to seventeenth-century moral philosophy.

Additional coverage of Locke's life and career is contained in the following sources published by Gale Research: *Dictionary of Literery Biography*, **Vols. 31, 101;** *Literature Criticism from 1400-1800*, **Vol. 7.**

Isaac Newton

1642-1727

English physicist and mathematician.

INTRODUCTION

Newton's experimental methods and theories in physics, optics, and mathematics crowned the seventeenth century scientific revolution. Building on the work of Galileo Galilei, Johannes Kepler, Nicolaus Copernicus, and others, Newton in his *Philosophiae Principia Naturalis Mathematica,* or *Principia* (1687), explained planetary movement by establishing the three laws of motion and a theory of universal gravitation. The image of the universe as a giant clock set into motion by God but governed by mechanical, rational rules is largely Newton's legacy. His exhaustive experiments using prisms to study light and color led to Newton's devising the reflecting telescope, while his contributions to mathematics included determining the binomial theory and developing differential and integral calculus. Beyond scientific investigation, Newton researched and wrote extensively on alchemy and theology.

Biographical Information

Newton was born on Christmas day at Woolsthorpe, Lincolnshire. His father, an illiterate farmer, had died three months before his son's birth. Hannah Ayscough Newton, Newton's mother, remarried when her son was three, and left with her new husband, a wealthy minister, to rear a second family in neighboring North Witham. Raised by his grandmother, Newton remained separated from his mother until he was eleven, when Hannah, widowed a second time, returned to Woolsthorpe hoping her son would learn to manage her property. Displaying neither the temperament nor ambition for yeomanry, Newton soon returned to grammar school to prepare for university. He graduated from Trinity College, Cambridge, in 1665 with a bachelor degree, but without any record of note. An outbreak of the plague closed the university for the next two years, and Newton returned to Woolsthorpe. In a burst of all-out study and experimentation, Newton realized some of his most ingenious work in astronomy, calculus, optics, and mechanics. When Newton returned to Cambridge in 1667 to complete a master of arts degree, Isaac Barrow, Lucasian chair in mathematics, read some of Newton's privately circulated papers, and immediately championed Newton's intellectual capability. Barrow retired in 1669, and, at his urging, Newton was appointed mathematics professor. By age 27, New-

ton had established a reputation for brilliance. Biographers have speculated, however, that the early years of maternal abandon had deeply scarred his psyche. Throughout his life Newton over-reacted to criticism—lashing out irrationally, and often vindictively, not only at rivals, but often becoming suspicious of his friends, such as John Locke and Samuel Pepys. He was reluctant to share his work with fellow scientists or to give credit to them for their influence upon his work. Unable to withstand the critical scrutiny of his peers, Newton established a pattern of refusing to publish his work until years after its completion. He suffered nervous breakdowns in 1678 and in 1693. In 1696 Newton left Cambridge for London when appointed first warden, and three years later was appointed master of the mint—a post that carried *cache* and paid handsomely. Thought to be incorruptible, Newton proved to be an effective administrator who relentlessly ferreted out counterfeiters during a period of recoinage. In his later years Newton devoted most of his writing to alchemy and theology, subjects that had held his interest all his life. Newton rejected trinitarianism, an orthodox religious doctrine in the seventeenth century, but, mindful of Galileo's fate a generation earlier, did not make his beliefs publicly known. Although by then he had ended most of his scientific experimentation, Newton was regarded as the dean of English science, and elected President of the Royal Society in 1703. His tenure was marred by an enduring feud with astronomer John Flamsteed, which also earned Newton a reputation for autocratic rule. Newton was knighted in 1705 and died in 1727, leaving a considerable estate.

Major Works

Newton published his first paper, "Of Colours," in 1672. Based on a series of lectures he gave in his first three years of teaching, the treatise explained his theories on light and color, and eventually became Book One of *Opticks*. In his experiments with prisms, Newton had broken down white light into a spectrum of primary colors, which led to his theory that light was composed of individual particles or corpuscles. Book Two described experiments Newton conducted with colors of thin films leading to his theory that light could be both reflected and refracted. Book Two was issued along with "Hypothesis Explaining the Properties of Light" (1675), a controversial essay that outlined a new system of nature. The final section of the *Opticks* contains a series of "Queries" posed as hypotheses. Newton refused to publish a completed edition of the *Opticks* until 1704, a year after the death of his nemesis Hooke. Originally published in English, *Opticks* was the most widely read of Newton's books. Later English editions were issued in 1717 and 1721. Latin editions appeared in 1706 and 1719. The theories contained in the *Principia* (1687) had been worked out twenty years prior during the two years Newton lived in Woolsthorpe because of the plague. When astronomer Edmond Halley in 1684 asked Newton if he could describe the orbit of planets, Newton replied that the path was elliptical, and that he had mathematically worked out his theory, but had long since misplaced the computations. After Halley's prodding Newton redid his calculations and sent them to him along with a tract, *De Motu* ("On Motion"). With Halley's encouragement and financial patronage, Newton elaborated and expanded his work, resulting in the *Principia*. Originally published in Latin, an English edition wasn't issued until 1729. Newton added a "General Scholium" to later editions in which he defended his methodologies. Subsequent editions of the *Principia* were issued in 1713 and 1726. Composed of nearly two million words, Newton's theology and alchemy notebooks far surpassed in quantity Newton's scientific papers. Many of the notebooks, however, contain passages Newton recorded from the works of others he was studying. Newton's principal theological writings—*The Chronology of Ancient Kingdoms Amended* (1728) and *Observations upon the Prophecies of Daniel and the Apocalypse of St. John (1733)*—were published after his death. He believed that astronomical computations could be

used to match events in the Bible to a chronology of human history, and estimated the universe to be 5000 years old. Newton did not eliminate God from the universe; rather, God remained as prime mover, poised to intervene to keep the planets in their orbits and the sun, stars, and moon from colliding. Newton's notebooks on alchemy suggest that his experiments were an integral part of his understanding of natural phenomena, rather than mystical or occult excursions.

Critical Reception

Although Newton's first published paper on light was generally well-received, a few scientists responded with skepticism, questioning his departure from the standard scientific method of establishing a hypothesis or exploring alternative theories. Newton's ideas were especially challenged by Hooke and others who subscribed to the Cartesian theory that light was the result of wave-like motions through a material medium. The essay "Hypothesis Concerning the Properties of Light" prompted outrage from Hooke who was convinced that Newton had appropriated his ideas. Although Newton gained international fame after publication of the *Principia,* his paranoid personality dampened the accolades his peers might otherwise have bestowed. Time lapses between work completion and subsequent publication led to disputes with others over who discovered what and when. He engaged in a long-standing feud with Gottfried Wilhelm Leibniz, who felt certain Newton had stolen his ideas on calculus. Many contemporaries believed Newton abused his power as President of the Royal Society, domineering the careers of young scientists while sabotaging rivals. Until this century, Newtonian criticism had been primarily limited to the scientific work, leading to a skewed assessment of his world view. Nineteenth-century Romantics, including William Blake and William Wordsworth, denounced Newton for what they perceived as his ushering in a spiritless, mechanical universe. Newtonian science did create a new paradigm of thought that affected virtually all areas of western culture, and was germane to the Age of Enlightenment and subsequent "revolutions" in history, law, and political-economy. While some of Newton's scientific principles have been supplanted by the theory of relativity and other advances in twentieth-century science, many remain valid. Today much Newtonian scholarship focuses on the increasingly available theological and alchemical manuscripts. Many critics view both Newton's scientific and non-scientific work as essential components for understanding Newton and as the basis for knowing how he comprehended the world.

PRINCIPAL WORKS

Philosophiae Naturalis Principia Mathematica [Mathe-

CRITICISM

David Brewster (essay date 1855)

SOURCE: "Chapter XXIV," in *Memoirs of the Life, Writings, and Discoveries of Sir Isaac Newton, Vol. II,* Thomas Constable and Co., 1855, pp. 313-59.

[*In the excerpt below, Brewster comments in detail on Newton's religious writings, asserting that "if Sir Isaac Newton had not been distinguished as a mathematician and a natural philosopher, he would have enjoyed a high reputation as a theologian."*]

If Sir Isaac Newton had not been distinguished as a mathematician and a natural philosopher, he would have enjoyed a high reputation as a theologian. The occupation of his time, however, with those profound studies, for which his genius was so peculiarly adapted, and in the prosecution of which he was so eminently successful, prevented him from preparing for the press the theological works which he had begun at a very early period of life, and to which he devoted much of his time even when he mixed with the world, and was occupied with the affairs of the Mint. The history of Sir Isaac's theological writings cannot fail to be regarded as an interesting portion of his life, and much anxiety has been expressed for a more precise account than has yet been given of his religious opinions. That the greatest philosopher of which any age can boast was a sincere and humble believer in the leading doctrines of our religion, and lived conformably to its precepts, has been justly regarded as a proud triumph of the Christian faith. Had he exhibited only an outward respect for the forms and duties of religion, or left merely in his dying words an acknowledgment of his belief, his piety might have been regarded as a prudent submission to popular feeling, or as a proof of the decay or the extinction of his transcendent powers;

but he had been a searcher of the Scriptures from his youth, and he found it no abrupt transition to pass from the study of the material universe to an investigation of the profoundest truths, and the most obscure predictions, of holy writ.

The religious opinions of great men,—of those especially who, by force of genius and patient thought, have discovered new and commanding truths, possess an interest of various kinds. The apostle of infidelity cowers beneath the implied rebuke. The timid and the wavering stand firmer in the faith, and the man of the world treats the institutions of religion with more respect and forbearance. Nor are such opinions less influential when they emanate from men who follow truth through her labyrinth, neither impelled by professional ambition, nor alarmed by articles which they have to sign, or creeds which they have to believe. Though often solicited by its highest dignitaries, Newton never thought of entering the Church. He had, therefore, no beacons to dread, and no false lights to mislead him. He was free to range through the volume of inspiration, and to gather from the Sibylline pages of its prophets and apostles, its historians and its poets, the insulated truths which they reveal, and to combine them into a broader faith, and embalm them in a higher toleration.

To the friends and countrymen of Newton, it has been no inconsiderable source of pain that some foreign writers have referred to extraordinary causes his religious opinions and theological writings. While some have ascribed them to the habits of the age in which he lived, and to a desire of promoting civil liberty by turning against the abettors of irresponsible power the sharp weapons which the Scriptures supply, others have endeavoured to show that they were composed at a late period of life when his mind was in its dotage, or had suffered from that supposed mental aberration to which so many acts of his life have been so erroneously ascribed. In answer to such allegations, we may adduce the testimony of one of his most distinguished friends, John Craig, an eminent mathematician, who, in the very year in which Newton died, gave the following account of his theological writings. [Letter to Conduitt, dated 7th April, 1727.]

> I shall not tell you what great improvements he made in geometry and algebra, but it is proper to acquaint you that his great application in his inquiries into nature did not make him unmindful of the Great Author of nature. They were little acquainted with him who imagine that he was so intent upon his studies of geometry and philosophy as to neglect that of religion and other things subservient to it. And this I know, that he was much more solicitous in his inquiries into religion than into natural philosophy, and that the reason of his shewing the errors of Cartes' philosophy was, because he thought it was made on purpose to be the foundation of

infidelity. And Sir Isaac Newton, to make his inquiries into the Christian religion more successful, had read the ancient writers and ecclesiastical historians with great exactness, and had drawn up in writing great collections out of both; and to show how earnest he was in religion, he had written a long explication of remarkable parts of the Old and New Testament, *while his understanding was in its greatest perfection, lest the infidels might pretend that his applying himself to the study of religion was the effect of dotage.* That he would not publish these writings in his own time, because they showed that his thoughts were sometimes different from those which are commonly received, which would engage him in disputes; and this was a thing which he avoided as much as possible. But now it's hoped that the worthy and ingenious Mr. Conduitt will take care that they be published, that the world may see that Sir Isaac Newton was as good a Christian as he was a mathematician and philosopher.

The anxiety to refer the religious writings of Newton to a late period of his life, seems to have been particularly felt by M. Biot, who goes so far as to fix the date of one of his most important works, [*Historical Account of Two Notable Corruptions of the Scriptures,* 50 pp. quarto], and to associate his religious tendencies with the effects of what he calls "the fatal epoch of 1693."

"From the nature of the subject," says he,

> "and from certain indications which Newton seems to give at the beginning of his dissertation, we may conjecture with probability that he composed it at the time when the errors of Whiston and a work of Clarke on the same subject, drew upon them the attacks of all the theologians of England, which would place the date between the years 1712 and 1719. It would then be a prodigy to remark, that a man of from seventy-two to seventy-five years of age was able to compose, *rapidly* as he leads us to believe, so extensive a piece of sacred criticism, of literary history, and even of bibliography, where an erudition the most vast, the most varied, and the most ready, always supports an argument well arranged and powerfully combined. . . . At this epoch of the life of Newton, the reading of religious books had become one of his most habitual occupations, and after he had performed the duties of his office, they formed, along with the conversation of his friends, his only amusement. He had then almost ceased to care for the sciences, and, as we have already remarked, since the fatal epoch of 1693, he gave to the world only three really new scientific productions, of which one had probably been long ready, while the others required from him only a very little time." [The papers here alluded to were one on the Scale of Heat, his Reflecting Sextant, and his Solution of the Problem of Quickest Descent.]

Notwithstanding the prodigy which it involves, M. Biot has adopted 1712-1719 as the date of this critical dis-

sertation;—it is regarded as the composition of a man of seventy-two or seventy-five;—the reading of religious works is stated to have *become* one of his most habitual occupations, and such reading is said to have been his only amusements; and all this is associated with "the fatal epoch of 1693," as if his illness at that time had been the cause of his abandoning science and betaking himself to theology.

The incorrectness of these opinions we are fortunately able to prove. It appears from Mr. Pryme's manuscript, that previous to 1692, when a shade is supposed to have passed over his gifted mind, Newton was well known by the appellation of an "excellent divine,"—a character which could not have been acquired without the devotion of many years to theological researches; but, important as this argument would have been, we are not left to so general a defence. [In a book called "Newton's Waste Book," containing his discoveries in mathematics in the years 1664 and 1665, there are many extracts which prove that he had in these years prosecuted the study of theology.] The correspondence of Newton with Locke, places it beyond a doubt that he had begun his researches respecting the prophecies before the year 1691,—before the forty-ninth year of his age, and before the "fatal epoch of 1693." The following letter shews that he had previously discussed this subject with his friend.

CAMBRIDGE, *Feb.* 7, 1690-1.

SIR,—I am sorry your journey proved to so little purpose, though it delivered you from the trouble of the company the day after. You have obliged me by mentioning me to my friends at London, and I must thank both you and my Lady Masham for your civilities at Oates, and for not thinking that I made a long stay there. I hope we shall meet again in due time, and then I should be glad to have your judgment upon some of my mystical fancies. The Son of Man, (Dan. vii.) I take to be the same with the Word of God upon the White Horse in Heaven, (Apoc. xii.) for both are to rule the nations with a rod of iron; but whence are you certain that the Ancient of Days is Christ? Does Christ anywhere sit upon the throne?—If Sir Francis Masham be at Oates, present, I pray, my service to him, with his lady, Mrs. Cudworth, and Mrs. Masham. Dr. Covel is not in Cambridge.—I am, your affectionate and humble servant,

IS. NEWTON.

Know you the meaning of Dan. x. 21? *There is none that holdeth with me in these things but Mich. your Prince.*

In replying to this letter, Locke does not seem to have distinctly noticed Newton's question, why he thought that Christ was the Ancient of Days, for in another letter [Cambridge, June 30, 1691] addressed to Locke, he says, "Concerning the *Ancient of Days,* Dan. vii., there seems to be a mistake either in my last letter or in yours, because you wrote in your former letter that the Ancient of Days is Christ; and in my last I either did, or should have asked how you knew that. But these discourses may be done with more freedom at our next meeting."

It is obvious, from these facts, that Locke and Newton had corresponded on the prophecies of Daniel so early as 1691, and that these subjects were discussed by them when they met. In replying to some questions of Locke on the subject of miracles, Newton tells him [Cambridge, Feb. 16, 1691-2] that "miracles of good credit continued in the Church for about two or three hundred years. Gregorius Thaumaturgus had his name from them, and was one of the latest who was eminent for that gift, but of their number and frequency I am not able to give you a just account;" and he resumes the subject in the following interesting letter:—

CAMBRIDGE, *May* 3, 1692.

SIR,—Now the churlish weather is almost over, I was thinking within a post or two, to put you in mind of my desire to see you here, where you shall be as welcome as I can make you. I am glad you have prevented me, because I hope now to see you the sooner. You may lodge conveniently either at the Rose Tavern or Queen's Arms Inn. I am glad the edition is stopped, but do not perceive that you had mine, and therefore have sent you a transcript of what concerned miracles, if it come not now too late; for it happens that I have a copy of it by me. Concerning miracles, there is a notable passage or two in Irenæus, L. 22, c. 56, recited by Eusebius, I. 5, c. 17. The miraculous refection of the Roman army by rain, at the prayers of a Christian legion, (thence called fulminatrix,) is mentioned by Ziphilina apud Dionam. in Marco Imp., and by Tertullian, Apolog. c. 5, and ad Scap. c. 4, and by Eusebius, I. 5, c. 5, Hist. Eccl., and in Chronico, and acknowledged by the Emperor Marcus in a letter, as Tertullian mentions. The same Tertullian somewhere challenges the heathens to produce a demoniac, and he shall produce a man who shall cast out the demon. For this was the language of the ancient for curing lunatics. I am told that Sir Henry Yelverton, in a book about the truth of Christianity, has writ well of the ancient miracles, but the book I never saw. Concerning Gregory Thaumaturgus, see Gregory Nystra in ejus vita, and Basil, de Spiritu Sancto, c. 29. My humble service to Sir Francis and his lady. I am, your most humble servant,

IS. NEWTON.

I know of nothing that will call me from home this month.

In the early part of 1703, Locke sent to Newton the manuscript of his Commentary on the Epistles of St. Paul to the Corinthians, which have been published among his posthumous works, and in the following letter he gave him his opinion of the work, with a criticism upon his interpretation of a particular passage.

LONDON, *May* 15, 1703.

SIR,—Upon my first receiving your papers, I read over those concerning the First Epistle of the Corinthians, but by so many intermissions, that I resolved to go over them again, so soon as I could get leisure to do it with more attention. I have now read it over a second time, and gone over also your papers on the Second Epistle. Some faults, which seemed to be faults of the scribe, I mended with my pen as I read the papers; some others I have noted in the enclosed papers. In your paraphrase on 1 Cor. vii. 14, you say, 'the unbelieving husband is sanctified or made a Christian in his wife.' I doubt this interpretation, because the unbelieving is not capable of baptism, as all Christians are. The Jews looked upon themselves as clean, holy, or separate to God, and other nations as unclean, unholy, or common, and accordingly it was unlawful for a man that was a Jew to keep company with, or come unto one of another nation; Acts x. 28. But when the propagation of the gospel made it necessary for the Jews, who preached the gospel, to go unto and keep company with the Gentiles, God showed Peter by a vision, in the case of Cornelius, that he had cleansed those of other nations, so that Peter should not any longer call any man common or unclean, and on that account forbear their company: and thereupon Peter went in unto Cornelius and his companions, who were uncircumcised, and did eat with them; Acts x. 27, 28, and xi. 3. Sanctifying, therefore, and cleansing, signify here, not the making a man a Jew or Christian, but the dispensing with the law whereby the people of God were to avoid the company of the rest of the world as unholy or unclean. And if this sense be applied to St. Paul's words, they will signify, that although believers are a people holy to God, and ought to avoid the company of unbelievers as unholy or unclean, yet this law is dispensed with in some cases, and particularly in the case of marriage. The believing wife must not separate from the unbelieving husband as unholy or unclean, nor the believing husband from the unbelieving wife; for the unbeliever is sanctified or cleansed by marriage with the believer, the law of avoiding the company of unbelievers being, in this case, dispensed with. I should therefore interpret St. Paul's words after the following manner:—

'For the unbelieving husband is sanctified or cleansed by the believing wife, so that it is lawful to keep him company, and the unbelieving wife is sanctified by the husband; else were the children of such parents to be separated from you, and avoided as unclean, but now by nursing and educating them in your families, you allow that they are holy.'

This interpretation I propose as easy and suiting well to the words and design of St. Paul, but submit it wholly to your judgment.

I had thoughts of going to Cambridge this summer, and calling at Oates in my way, but am now uncertain of this journey. Present, I pray, my humble service to Sir Francis Masham and his lady. I think your paraphrase and commentary on these two Epistles is done with very great care and judgment.—I am, your most humble and obedient servant,

IS. NEWTON.

It is obvious from these letters that Newton had carried on his theological studies, and particularly those relating to the Prophecies, long before the epoch of 1693, and there is no reason to believe that any part of his principal theological work on the Prophecies and the Apocalypse was composed after that date. If any farther evidence were required for this fact, it may be derived from his folio **Commonplace Book,** written in his early hand, and containing copious extracts and observations on theological subjects of every kind.

The other work of Newton, entitled **Historical Account of two Notable Corruptions of the Scriptures, in a Letter to a Friend,** is certainly an early production. In 1690, or perhaps earlier, he had corresponded on the subject of it with Locke, who requested a sight of the manuscript. In reply to this request, Newton writes to him, [Cambridge, Sept. 28, 1690], "that he would have answered his letter sooner, but that he stayed to revise and send the papers which he desired; but the consulting of authors proving more tedious than he expected, made him defer sending them till next week." In the following letter to Locke, which accompanies the manuscript, he mentions part of it as something that he "had by him," and it was therefore in all probability written long before 1690:—

November 14, 1690.

SIR,—I send you now by the carrier, Martin, the papers I promised. I fear I have not only made you stay too long for them, but also made them too long by an addition; for, upon the receipt of your letter reviewing what I had by me concerning the text of 1 John v. 7, and examining authors a little further about it, I met with something new concerning that other of 1 Tim. iii. 16, which I thought would be as acceptable to inquisitive men, and might be set down in a little room; but by searching farther into authors to find out the bottom of it, is swelled to the bigness you see. I fear the length of what I say on both texts may occasion you too much trouble, and therefore if at present you get only what concerns

the first done into French, that of the other may stay till we see what success the first will have. I have no entire copy besides that I send you, and therefore would not have it lost, because I may, perhaps, after it has gone abroad long enough in French, put it forth in English. What charge you are at about it (for I am sure it will put you to some) you must let me know, for the trouble alone is enough for you. Pray present my most humble service and thanks to my Lord and Lady Monmouth, for their so kind remembrance of me, for their favour is such that I can never sufficiently acknowledge it. If your voyage hold, I wish you a prosperous one, and happy return. I should be glad of a line from you to know that you have these papers, and how far you have recovered your health, for you told me nothing of that.—I am, Sir, your most faithful and most humble servant,

IS. NEWTON.

When this correspondence was going on, Mr. Locke meditated a journey to Holland, and undertook, in compliance with the wishes of his friend, to have the **Historical Account,** &c., translated into French, and published in Holland. Dreading the intolerance of the divines of his own country, he was anxious to have the opinions of foreign biblical writers before he "put it forth in English." Having abandoned his design of visiting Holland, Locke transmitted the manuscript [1754], in his own handwriting, and without Newton's name, to his friend M. Le Clerc in Holland, with a request to have it translated into French and published. Sir Isaac was not aware of the step that Locke had taken, and knowing that he had not left England, he believed that the manuscript was still in his possession. It had reached M. Le Clerc, however, previous to the 11th April 1691, for, in a letter to Locke of that date, he tells him that he will translate, either into Latin or French, the small **Historical Account,** &c., which deserves to be published. "I believe, however," he adds, "that it would be better if the author had read with care what M. Simon has said on the subject, of which he speaks in his Criticism of the New Testament." In a subsequent letter, Le Clerc tells Locke that he has been prevented, by various occupations, from doing anything with the manuscript, but that he hopes to have an opportunity of publishing it along with some other dissertations, as it is too small to appear alone. In reply to a letter which he had received from Locke, Le Clerc says, "that he will take care to insert in the dissertation on the passage in St. John, the addition which he had sent him, and translate the other, to publish both in Latin."

Locke seems to have intimated the intentions of Le Clerc to Sir Isaac, who lost no time in addressing to him the following letter:—

CAMBRIDGE, *Feb.* 16, 1691-2.

"SIR,—Your former letters came not to my hand, but this I have. I was of opinion my papers had lain still, and am sorry to hear there is news about them. Let me entreat you to stop their translation and impression so soon as you can, for I design to suppress them. If your friend hath been at any pains and charge, I will repay it and gratify him. . . .

Your most affectionate and humble servant,
IS. NEWTON.

From these facts it is obvious that this celebrated treatise, which Biot alleges to have been written between 1712 and 1719, *was actually written in* 1690, or probably much earlier, and was in the hands of Le Clerc on the 11th April 1691, previous to the time of the supposed insanity of its author. Locke lost no time in communicating to his friend the wishes of Newton, and the publication of the **Historical Account** was therefore stopped.

Although we are not acquainted with the reasons which induced Newton to take this step, they may to a certain extent be inferred from Le Clerc's answer to Locke [April 11, 1692]. "It is a pity," he says, "that these two dissertations should be suppressed. I do not think that any person could find out that they were translated, unless it were said so. In a matter of this kind, where I would not fail to seize the meaning of the author, I would have given it an original air which would not have savoured of a translation." And, in another letter, [July 15, 1692], he says, "I will keep carefully the two dissertations, till you tell me what the author wishes me to do with them."

No information concerning these dissertations is contained either in the correspondence of Locke with Newton, or with Le Clerc. We are told by the editor of the edition of 1754, that Le Clerc deposited the manuscript in the Library of the Remonstrants, and that he received, through a friend, the copy of it which he published, under the title of **Two Letters from Sir Isaac Newton to M. Le Clerc, the former containing a Dissertation upon the Reading of the Greek Testament, 1 John v. 7, the latter upon 1 Timothy iii. 16**;—a form which had never been given to it by its author. The copy thus published was a very imperfect one, wanting both the beginning and the end, and erroneous in many places; but Dr. Horsley has published a genuine edition, which has the form of a single letter to a friend, and was copied from a manuscript in Sir Isaac Newton's handwriting, now in the possession of the Reverend Jeffrey Ekins, Rector of Sampford.

Having thus determined, as accurately as possible, the dates of the principal theological writings of Sir Isaac, we shall now proceed to give some account of their contents.

The work entitled **Observations upon the Prophecies** *of Daniel and the Apocalypse of St. John,* is divided into two parts, the first of which treats of the Prophecies of Daniel, and the second of the Apocalypse of St. John. It begins with an account of the different books which compose the Old Testament; and, as the author considers Daniel to be the most distinct in the order of time, and the easiest to be understood, he makes him the key to all the prophetic books in those matters which relate to the "last time." He next considers the figurative language of the prophets, which he regards as taken "from the analogy between the world natural, and an empire or kingdom considered as a world politic;" the heavens, and the things therein, representing thrones and dynasties; the earth, with the things therein, the inferior people; and the lowest parts of the earth the most miserable of the people. The sun is put for the whole race of kings, the moon for the body of the common people, and the stars for subordinate princes and rulers. In the earth, the dry land and the waters are put for the people of several nations. Animals and vegetables are also put for the people of several regions. When a beast or man is put for a kingdom, his parts and qualities are put for the analogous parts and qualities of the kingdom; and when a man is taken in a mystical sense, his qualities are often signified by his actions, and by the circumstances and things about him. In applying these principles he begins with the vision of the image composed of four different metals. This image he considers as representing a body of four great nations which should reign in succession over the earth, viz., the people of Babylonia, the Persians, the Greeks, and the Romans, while the stone cut out without hands is a new kingdom which should arise after the four, conquer all those nations, become very great, and endure to the end of time.

The vision of the four beasts is the prophecy of the four empires repeated, with several new additions. The lion with eagles' wings was the kingdom of Babylon and Media, which overthrew the Assyrian power. The beast like a bear was the Persian empire, and its three ribs were the kingdoms of Sardis, Babylon, and Egypt. The third beast, like a leopard, was the Greek empire, and its four heads and four wings were the kingdoms of Cassander, Lysimachus, Ptolemy, and Seleucus. The fourth beast, with its great iron teeth, was the Roman empire, and its ten horns were the ten kingdoms into which it was broken in the reign of Theodosius the Great.

In the fifth chapter Sir Isaac treats of the kingdoms represented by the feet of the image composed of iron and clay which did not stick to one another, and which were of different strength. These were the Gothic tribes called Ostrogoths, Visigoths, Vandals, Gepidæ, Lombards, Burgundians, Alans, &c., all of whom had the same manners and customs, and spoke the same language, and who, about the year 416 A.C., were all quietly settled in several kingdoms within the empire, not only by conquest, but by grants of the Emperor.

In the sixth chapter he treats of the *ten* kingdoms represented by the ten horns of the fourth beast, into which the Western empire became divided about the time when Rome was besieged and taken by the Goths. These kingdoms were,—

1. The kingdom of the Vandals and Alans in Spain and Africa.
2. The kingdom of Suevians in Spain.
3. The kingdom of the Visigoths.
4. The kingdom of the Alans in Gaul.
5. The kingdom of the Burgundians.
6. The kingdom of the Franks.
7. The kingdom of the Britains.
8. The kingdom of the Huns.
9. The kingdom of the Lombards.
10. The kingdom of Ravenna.

Some of these kingdoms at length fell, and new ones sprung up; but whatever was their subsequent number, they still retain the name of the ten kings from their first number.

The eleventh horn of Daniel's fourth beast is shown in chapter vii. to be the Church of Rome in it triple character of a seer, a prophet, and a king, and its power to change times and laws is copiously illustrated in chapter viii.

In the ninth chapter our author treats of the kingdom represented in Daniel by the ram and he-goat, the ram indicating the kingdom of the Medes and Persians from the beginning of the four empires, and the he-goat the kingdom of the Greeks to the end of them.

The prophecy of the seventy weeks, which had hitherto been restricted to the first coming of our Saviour, is shown to be a prediction of all the main periods relating to the coming of the Messiah, the times of his birth and death, the time of his rejection by the Jews, the duration of the Jewish war, by which he caused the city and sanctuary to be destroyed, and the time of his second coming.

In the eleventh chapter Sir Isaac treats with great sagacity and acuteness of the time of our Saviour's birth and passion,—a subject which had perplexed all preceding commentators.

After explaining in the twelfth chapter the last prophecy of Daniel, namely, that of the scripture of truth, which he considers as a commentary on the vision of the ram and he-goat, he proceeds in the thirteenth chapter to the prophecy of the king who did according to his will, and magnified himself above every god, and honoured Mahuzzims, and regarded not the desire of women. He shows that the Greek empire, after the division of the Roman empire into the Greek and Latin empires, became the king who, in matters of religion, did according to his will, and in legislation exalted and magnified himself above every god.

In the second part of his work, entitled ***Observations on the Apocalypse of St. John,*** consisting of three chapters, Sir Isaac treats in the *first* or introductory chapter, "concerning the time when the Apocalypse was written," which he conceives to have been during John's exile in Patmos, and before the Epistle to the Hebrews and the Epistles of Peter were written, which in his opinion have a reference to the Apocalypse. In the *second* he treats "of the relation which the Apocalypse has to the book of the law of Moses, and to the worship of God in the temple;" and in the *Third,* "of the relation which the prophecy of John hath to those of Daniel, and of the subject of the prophecy."

Sir Isaac regards the prophecies of the Old and New Testament not as given to gratify men's curiosities, by enabling them to foreknow things, but that after they were fulfilled, they might be interpreted by the event, and afford convincing arguments that the world is governed by Providence. He considers that there is so much of this prophecy already fulfilled, as to afford to the diligent student sufficient instances of God's Providence; and he adds, that "amongst the interpreters of the last age, there is scarce one of note who hath not made some discovery worth knowing, and thence it seems one may gather that God is about opening these mysteries. The success of others," he continues, "put me upon considering it, and if I have done anything which may be useful to following writers, I have my design." Such is a brief notice of this ingenious work, which is characterized by great learning, and marked with the sagacity of its distinguished author.

The same qualities of Sir Isaac's mind are equally conspicuous in his ***Historical Account of Two Notable Corruptions of Scripture***. This celebrated treatise relates to two texts in the Epistles of St. John and St. Paul. The first of these is in 1 John v. 7, "For there are three that bear record in heaven, the Father, the Son, and the Holy Ghost, and these three are one." This text he considers as a gross corruption of Scripture, which had its origin among the Latins, who interpreted the Spirit, Water, and Blood, to be the Father, Son, and Holy Ghost, in order to prove them one. With the same view Jerome inserted the Trinity in express words in his version. The Latins marked his variations in the margins of their books; and in the twelfth and following centuries, when the disputations of the schoolmen were at their height, the variation began to creep into the text in transcribing. After the invention of printing, it crept out of the Latin into the printed Greek, contrary to the authority of all the Greek manuscripts and ancient versions; and from the Venetian press it went soon after into Greece. After proving these positions, Sir Isaac gives the following paraphrase of this remarkable passage, which is printed in italics.

> *Who is he that overcometh the world, but he that believeth that Jesus is the Son of God,* that Son spoken of in the Psalms, where he saith, 'thou art my Son; this day have I begotten thee.' *This is he that,* after the Jews had long expected him, *came,* first in a mortal body, *by* baptism of *water, and* then in an immortal one, by shedding his *blood* upon the cross, and rising again from the dead; *not by water only, but by water and blood;* being the Son of God, as well by his resurrection from the dead (Acts xiii. 33) as by his supernatural birth of the virgin, (Luke i. 35.) *And it is the Spirit* also *that,* together with the water and blood, *beareth witness* of the truth of his coming; *because the Spirit is truth;* and so a fit and unexceptionable witness. *For there are three that bear record* of his coming; *the Spirit* which he promised to send, and which was since shed forth upon us in the form of cloven tongues, and in various gifts; *the* baptism of *water,* wherein God testified 'this is my beloved Son;' *and the* shedding of his *blood,* accompanied with his resurrection, whereby he became the most faithful martyr, or witness, of this truth. *And these three,* the spirit, the baptism, and passion of Christ, *agree in* witnessing *one* and the same thing, (namely, that the Son of God is come;) and, therefore, their evidence is strong; for the law requires but two consenting witnesses, and here we have three: *and if we receive the witness of men, the* threefold *witness of God,* which he bare of his Son, by declaring at his baptism, 'this is my beloved Son,' by raising him from the dead, and by pouring out his Spirit on us, *is greater;* and, therefore, ought to be more readily received.

It appears from the introduction to this letter, that Locke, to whom it was addressed, had been reading the "discourses of some *late* writers on the subject," and had expressed to Newton a desire "to know the truth of that text of Scripture concerning the testimony of the three in heaven." Without noticing the views of his predecessors, Sir Isaac contents himself with referring to Luther, Erasmus, Bullinger, and Grotius, and some others, as "the more learned and quick-sighted men, who would not dissemble their knowledge," (of the corruption of this text,) and to "the generality who were fond of the place for its making against heresy." In the last edition of his Bible, published by himself, Luther had expunged the text as spurious, but in deference to popular opinion, it was restored by his followers. Erasmus too, omitted it in his edition of the New Testament, published in 1516 and 1519, but, as Porson informs us, having promised Lee that he would insert the passage in his text if it was found in a single Greek MS., he accordingly inserted it in his edition of 1522, after learning that it existed in a MS. which is now in Trinity College, Dublin. Dr. Clarke came to the conclusion [Clarke's *Works,* vol. iv. p. 121], "that much stress ought not to be laid upon the passage in any question, because the sense of the Epistle was complete without it," and because it was not found in any

MS. before the invention of printing, nor cited by any of the numerous writers in the Arian controversy; and Dr. Bentley read a public lecture to prove that the verse in question was spurious. Gibbon in the third volume of his History, expressed the general opinion of biblical critics upon the subject; and Wetstein and Griesbach adopted the same views. In reply to these authors, Archdeacon Travis entered the field by attacking Gibbon in 1782, and subsequently Newton and Griesbach in 1786 [in letters in the *Gent. Magazine,* re-printed and enlarged in 1784 and 1786]. Michaelis considered it a sufficient answer to the English divine to say, that "he was indisputably half a century behindhand in critical knowledge;" and Porson, indignant at the presumption of his countryman, exposed his ignorance and errors in the celebrated letters which he addressed to him in 1788, 1789, and 1790 [Five of these letters appeared in the *Gent. Magazine* for 1788, and were reprinted with some others, and entitled *"Letters to Mr. Archdeacon Travis,"* &c By R. Porson. Lond. 1790]. In referring to these able letters, Sir Charles Lyell remarks [in *Second Visit to the United States,* vol. 1], that "by them the question was for ever set at rest." Had it been a question in science, it might have been expected that presumptuous error, when once sternly refuted, would not dare to reappear; but theological questions are never set at rest, and the very corruption of the sacred text which Sir Charles characterizes as having been "given up by every one who has the least pretension to scholarship and candour," has been defended in our own day by Dr. Burgess, Bishop of St. David's, and afterwards of Salisbury, with a boldness of assumption, and a severity of intolerance, unworthy of a Christian divine. [*Tracts on the Divinity of Christ.*]

The other notable corruption of Scripture discussed by Sir Isaac, is that which he charges the Greeks with having perpetrated in the text of St. Paul, *Great is the mystery of godliness, God manifest in the flesh.* According to him this reading was effected "by changing . . . whereas all the churches for the first four or five hundred years, and the authors of all the ancient versions, Jerome as well as the rest, read, 'Great is the mystery of godliness which was manifested in the flesh.' For this is the common reading of the Ethiopic, Syriac, and Latin versions to this day, Jerome's manuscripts having given him no occasion to correct the old vulgar Latin in this place."

After showing that the corruption in question took place in the sixth century, Sir Isaac thus sums up his arguments:—"The difference between the Greek and the ancient version puts it past dispute that either the Greeks have corrupted their MSS., or the Latins, Syrians, and Ethiopians their versions; and it is more reasonable to lay the fault upon the Greeks than upon the other three, for these considerations:—It was easier for one nation to do it than for three to conspire,—it was easier to change a letter or two in the Greek than six words in the Latin. In the Greek the sense is obscure,—in the versions clear. It was agreeable to the interest of the Greeks to make the change, but against the interest of other nations to do it, and men are never false to their own interest. The Greek reading was unknown in the times of the Arian controversy, but that of the versions was then in use both among Greeks and Latins. Some Greek MSS. render the Greek reading dubious, but those of the versions, hitherto collated, agree. There are no signs of corruption in the versions, hitherto discovered, but in the Greek we have showed you particularly when, on what occasion, and by whom the text was corrupted."

The view taken of this text by Sir Isaac has been defended by Dr. Clarke, Whiston, Semler, Griesbach, Wetstein, and others. In our own day it has been controverted, with much ability and learning, in an elaborate dissertation by Dr. Henderson, who has not justified its retention as a portion of revealed truth.

As the tendency of the *Historical Account,* &c., was to deprive the defenders of the doctrine of the Trinity of the aid of two leading texts, Sir Isaac Newton has been regarded by the Socinians and Arians, and even by some orthodox divines, as an Antitrinitarian; but this opinion is not warranted by any thing which he has published. "In the Eastern nations," he says, "and for a long time in the Western, the faith subsisted without this text, and it is rather a danger to religion than an advantage to make it now lean upon a bruised reed. There cannot be better service done to the truth than to purge it of things spurious; and, therefore, knowing your prudence and calmness of temper, I am confident I shall not offend you by telling you my mind plainly, especially since it is no article of faith, no point of discipline, nothing but a criticism concerning a text of Scripture, which I am going to write about."

Although it is obvious that, in allowing his Dissertation to be published in Holland, Sir Isaac did not consider himself as supporting the Socinians or the Arians, yet it cannot be doubted that he was afraid of being known as the author of the work, and of holding the opinions which it advocates. The name of the author was never communicated to Le Clerc, but he no doubt learned it from the writings of Whiston, who, after Newton's death, mentioned the Dissertation as his production. After the death of Le Clerc, Wetstein placed Locke's copy of it in the Library of the Remonstrants, and endeavoured in vain to procure, from Newton's heirs, the parts that were deficient in the original.

It does not appear that Newton was charged with being an Arian during his lifetime. Whiston indeed tells us, that he "afterwards found that Sir Isaac Newton was so

hearty for the Baptists, as well as for the Eusebians or Arians, that he sometimes suspected these two were the two witnesses in the Revelations;" and Hopton Haynes, who was employed in the Mint, and who was himself a Humanitarian, mentioned to Richard Baron, that Newton held the same doctrine as himself. In so far as the opinions of Newton, Locke, and Clarke, all of whom were suspected of Arian tendencies, were hostile to the doctrine of the Trinity, they had substantial reasons for keeping them secret. In the Toleration Act passed in 1688, before Newton had sent his Dissertation to Locke, an exception was made of those who wrote against "the doctrine of the blessed Trinity;" and in the Act for the Suppression of Blasphemy and Profaneness, it was provided, that whoever "by printing, teaching, or advisedly speaking, denied any one of the persons of the Holy Trinity to be God," should, "for the first offence, be disabled to have any office or employment, or any profit appertaining thereunto." The expulsion of Whiston from the University of Cambridge in 1711, for holding Arian tenets, though the Queen did not confirm the censure passed by the Convocation, was yet a warning to Antitrinitarians of every class who either held office, or were desirous of holding it, to refrain from the public expression of their opinions; and we have no doubt that Newton was influenced by motives of this kind when he desired Locke "to stop the translation and impression of his papers," and mentioned "his design to suppress them."

Although a traditionary belief has long prevailed that Newton was an Arian, yet the Trinitarians claimed him as a friend, while the Socinians, by republishing his *Historical Account,* &c., under the title of "Sir Isaac Newton on the Trinitarian Corruptions of Scripture," wished it to be believed that he was a supporter of their views. That he was not a Socinian is proved by his avowed belief that our Saviour was the object of "worship among the primitive Christians," and that he was "the Son of God, as well by his Resurrection from the dead, as by his supernatural birth of the Virgin." "He animadverts, indeed," as Dr. Henderson observes, "with great freedom, and sometimes with considerable asperity, on the orthodox; but it does not appear that this arose from any hostility to their views respecting the doctrine of the Trinity, or that it was opposed to any thing beside the unfair mode in which he conceived they had treated one or two passages of Scripture, with a view to the support of that doctrine."

Influenced by similar views, and in the absence of all direct evidence, I had no hesitation when writing the Life of Sir Isaac Newton in 1830, in coming to the conclusion that he was a believer in the Trinity, and in giving this opinion on the creed of so great a man, and so indefatigable a student of Scripture, I was well aware that there are various forms of Trinitarian truth, and various modes of expressing it, which have been received as orthodox in the purest societies of the Christian Church. It may be an ecclesiastical privilege to burrow for heresy among the obscurities of thought, and the ambiguities of language, but in the charity which thinketh no evil, we are bound to believe that our neighbour is not a heretic till the charge against him has been distinctly proved. Truth has no greater enemy than its unwise defenders, and no warmer friends than those who, receiving it in a meek and tolerant spirit, respect the conscientious convictions of others, and seek, in study and in prayer, for the best solution of mysterious and incomprehensible revelations. If the HIGHEST authority has assured us *that no man knoweth the Son but the Father,"* the pretenders to such knowledge impiously presume to be *more than man.*

When I examined in 1836 the manuscripts of Sir Isaac Newton at Hurtsbourne Park, I found various theological papers, some of which were so carefully written, and others so frequently copied, that they must have been intended for publication. We have alrady seen that Craig, the friend of Newton, urged Conduitt to give these writings to the world. His own niece, Mrs. Conduitt, resolved to publish them herself "if God granted her life," but, "as she might be snatched away before she had leisure to undertake so great a work," she made a codicil to her will, charging her executor to submit "them to Dr. Sykes, in hopes that he will prepare them for the press." The manuscripts referred to are—

1. The *Historical Account,* &c., already published.
2. Paradoxical Questions concerning Athanasius.
3. A History of the Creed.
4. A Church History complete.
5. Many Divinity Tracts.

Mr. Conduitt died a few months after the date of this codicil, and Mrs. Conduitt in January 1739, and there is reason to believe that the papers were never put into the hands of Dr. Sykes. After the marriage of Miss Conduitt to Mr. Wallop, afterwards Lord Lymington, the manuscripts went into their possession, and some of them, including the *Historical Account,* were given by Lady Lymington to her executor Mr. Jeffery Ekins, from whom they passed successively into the hands of the Dean of Carlisle, the Rector of Morpeth, and the Rev. Jeffery Ekins, Rector of Sampford, who now possesses them.

The most complete of the manuscripts above enumerated, is the one entitled *Paradoxical Questions concerning the morals and actions of Athanasius and his Followers.* It consists of sixteen questions, and possesses a very considerable interest.

"QUEST. 1. Whether the ignominious death of Arius in a boghouse was not a story feigned and put about by Athanasius above twenty years after his death?"

In answer to this question, Newton shows that though Athanasius pretended to have received this account of Arius's death, and of his dying out of communion, from Macarius, yet he invented it himself and circulated it, "that the miracle of his death being known, it will no longer be doubted whether the Arian heresy be odious to God or not."

"QUEST. 2. Whether the Meletians deserved that ill character which Athanasius gave them?"

The charge against the Meletians that they were excommunicated for crimes, Sir Isaac considers to be a fiction invented by Athanasius in retaliation for his having been tried at the instance of Inschyras, a Meletian presbyter, and condemned by the council of Tyre for having broken the communion cup of Inschyras, demolished his church, and afterwards killed Arsenius, the successor of Meletus.

"QUEST. 3. Whether the council of Tyre and Jerusalem was not an orthodox authentic council bigger than that of Nice?"

Although this council received Arius into communion after he had "disowned the things for which he had been condemned at Nice, and excommunicated Athanasius," Sir Isaac endeavours to show with great ingenuity and force of argument, that it was not an Arian council—that it did not profess Arianism, and that it was a full council, and "as authentic as any Greek council ever was or could be since the Apostles' days, they being in communion with the Church Catholic, and legally convened by the letters of Constantine the Great."

"QUEST. 4. Whether it was a dead man's hand in a bag, or the dead body of Arsenius, which was laid before the council at Tyre to prove that Arsenius was dead?"

"QUEST. 5. Whether it was Arsenius alive, or only his letter which Athanasius produced in the council of Tyre, to prove that he was not dead?"

"QUEST. 6. Whether the story of producing the dead man's hand, and the living Arsenius, in the council of Tyre, was not feigned by Athanasius about twenty-five years after the time of the council?"

In answering these three questions together, Sir Isaac shews that the dead body of Arsenius was, after exhumation, produced before the council of Tyre, to prove that he was murdered by Athanasius, who was found guilty and banished as the murderer. In defence of himself Athanasius invented the story that it was only a dead man's hand that was produced before the council, and that he refuted the charge by producing Arsenius alive.

"QUEST. 7. Whether the letter of Pinnes for proving Arsenius to be alive was not feigned by Athanasius at the same time with the story of the dead man's hand?"

In order to defend Athanasius, a monk confessed that Arsenius had been concealed at Hypseles, and had been sent out of the way to the lower parts of Egypt. Sir Isaac endeavours to show the incorrectness of this story.

"QUEST. 8. Whether the letter of Arsenius was not feigned by Athanasius before the convening of the council of Tyre?"

After an ingenious criticism on Arsenius' letter, Sir Isaac concludes that it is a forgery.

"QUEST. 9. Whether the letter of Inschyras was not feigned by Athanasius?"

This penitential letter, for having prosecuted Athanasius, addressed to the Blessed Pope Athanasius, is suspected on very ingenious grounds, to be a forgery.

"QUEST. 10. Whether the recantation of Valens and Ursatius was not feigned by the friends of Athanasius?"

These recantations are supposed with good reason to be forgeries.

"QUEST. 11. Whether Athanasius was falsely accused, or did falsely accuse Eusebius of adultery before the council of Tyre?"

Athanasius is said to have sent a woman to accuse Eusebius of adultery, in the hope of such a tumult being raised that he might escape being tried. But when Eusebius asked her if she knew the man, she answered that she would not be so senseless as to accuse such men. The friends of Athanasius afterwards inverted this story, as if the woman had been hired by the Eusebians to accuse Athanasius.

"QUEST. 12. Whether Athanasius did sincerely acquit himself of the crime of breaking the communion cup of Inschyras?"

This question is answered in the negative, and Athanasius' ingenious artifice to explain away the charge is well exposed.

"QUEST. 13. Whether Athanasius was not made Bishop of Alexandria by sedition and violence against the Canons of that Church?"

The Bishops who ordained him, after resisting his importunities "for many days together," and having been kept prisoner in a church by a mob of Athanasius's party, were obliged to ordain him. He was only twenty-five years of age, so that "the Meletians used to cry, O wickedness! he a bishop or he a boy?"

"QUEST. 14. Whether Athanasius was not justly deposed by the Council of Tyre?"

The justice of the sentence is proved by seven different arguments.

"QUEST. 15. Whether Athanasius was not seditious?"

This question is answered in the affirmative by an examination of his "Epistle to the Orthodox of all Regions," and a letter entitled "The People of Alexandria to the Catholic Church, which is under Athanasius the most reverend Bishop."

"QUEST. 16. Whether Constantius persecuted the Athanasians for religion, or only punished them for immorality?"

In answering this question, Sir Isaac shows that Constantius and his Bishops, in place of persecuting the Athanasians, treated them with the greatest moderation, and that their martyrs "perished by the sword in resisting the higher powers." He shows that Hilary, who courted martyrdom by insulting Constantius, and was thus guilty of the capital crime of *Læsa Majestas,* was released from banishment by the Emperor, and allowed to return to his own country. After quoting the favourable opinions of the Emperor given by his enemies, he concludes with the following character of him:—"In short, the virtues of this Emperor were so illustrious, that I do not find a better character given of any Prince for clemency, temperance, chastity, contempt of popular fame, affection to Christianity, justice, prudence, princely carriage, and good government, than is given to him even by his very enemies. He kept up the imperial dignity of his person to the height, and yet reigned in the hearts of his people, and swayed the world by their love to him, so that no Prince could be farther from deserving the name of a persecutor."

Among the other theological manuscripts of Sir Isaac, there are none so distinctly written as the *Paradoxical Questions:* but there are so many copies of some of them, that it can scarcely be doubted that they were thus repeatedly corrected for publication. The fact, indeed, of Sir Isaac having, previous to his death, burned many of his letters and papers, and left these theological writings behind him, makes it more than probable that he had no desire to suppress his opinions.

The most remarkable of these MSS. is one entitled *Irenicum, or Ecclesiastical Polity tending to Peace.* It consists of twenty *Positions,* or *Theses,* in which the doctrines of Christianity, the government of the Church, and its relations to the State, are described in a few brief and intelligible paragraphs. As the production of a great and good man who had studied the Scriptures and the history of the Church without any sectarian predilections, it cannot but be interesting to the Christian student.

In a paper of a few pages, entitled *A Short Scheme of the True Religion,* in which religion is described as partly fundamental and immutable, and partly circumstantial and mutable, he treats of *Godliness, Atheism, Idolatry,* and *Humanity,* or our duty to man. "Opposite to godliness," he says, "is Atheism in profession, and idolatry in practice. Atheism is so senseless and odious to mankind, that it never had many professors. Can it be by accident that all birds, beasts, and men have their right side and left side alike shaped, (except in their bowels,) and just two eyes, and no more, on either side of the face; and just two ears on either side the head, and a nose with two holes; and either two fore-legs, or two wings, or two arms on the shoulders, and two legs on the hips, and no more? Whence arises this uniformity in all their outward shapes but from the counsel and contrivance of an Author? Whence is it that the eyes of all sorts of living creatures are transparent to the very bottom, and the only transparent members in the body, having on the outside a hard transparent skin, and within transparent humours, with a crystalline lens in the middle, and a pupil before the lens, all of them so finely shaped and fitted for vision, that no artist can mend them? Did blind chance know that there was light, and what was its refraction, and fit the eyes of all creatures, after the most curious manner, to make use of it? These, and suchlike considerations, always have, and ever will prevail with mankind, to believe that there is a Being who made all things, and has all things in his power, and who is therefore to be feared."

The section on idolatry is concluded with the following summary:—"We are, therefore, to acknowledge one God, infinite, eternal, omnipresent, omniscient, omnipotent, the Creator of all things, most wise, most just, most good, most holy. We must love him, fear him, honour him, trust in him, pray to him, give him thanks, praise him, hallow his name, obey his commandments, and set times apart for his service, as we are directed in the Third and Fourth Commandments, for this is the love of God that we keep his commandments, and his commandments are not grievous, 1 John v. 3. And these things we must do not to any mediators between him and us, but to him alone, that he may give his angels charge over us, who, being our fellow-servants, are pleased with the worship which we give to their God. And this is the first and the principal part of religion. This always was, and always will be the religion of all God's people, from the beginning to the end of the world."

In another manuscript, *On our Religion to God, to Christ, and the Church,* he treats more fully of some of the theses in the *Irenicum,* but his doctrinal opinions are more conspicuous in the following twelve articles, which have no title:—

ART. 1. There is one God the Father, ever living, omnipresent, omniscient, almighty, the maker of heaven and earth, and one Mediator between God and man, the man Christ Jesus.

ART. 2. The Father is the invisible God whom no eye hath seen, or can see. All other beings are sometimes visible.

ART. 3. The Father hath life in himself, and hath given the Son to have life in himself.

ART. 4. The Father is omniscient, and hath all knowledge originally in his own breast, and communicates knowledge of future things to Jesus Christ; and none in heaven or earth, or under the earth, is worthy to receive knowledge of future things immediately from the Father but the Lamb. And, therefore, the testimony of Jesus is the spirit of prophecy, and Jesus is the Word or Prophet of God.

ART. 5. The Father is immovable, no place being capable of becoming emptier or fuller of him than it is by the eternal necessity of nature. All other beings are movable from place to place.

ART. 6. All the worship (whether of prayer, praise, or thanksgiving) which was due to the Father before the coming of Christ, is still due to him. Christ came not to diminish the worship of his Father.

ART. 7. Prayers are most prevalent when directed to the Father in the name of the Son.

ART. 8. We are to return thanks to the Father alone for creating us, and giving us food and raiment and other blessings of this life, and whatsoever we are to thank him for, or desire that he would do for us, we ask of him immediately in the name of Christ.

ART. 9. We need not pray to Christ to intercede for us. If we pray the Father aright he will intercede.

ART. 10. It is not necessary to salvation to direct our prayers to any other than the Father in the name of the Son.

ART. 11. To give the name of God to angels or kings, is not against the First Commandment. To give the worship of the God of the Jews to angels or kings, is against it. The meaning of the commandment is, Thou shalt worship no other God but me.

ART. 12. To us there is but one God, the Father, of whom are all things, and one Lord Jesus Christ, by whom are all things, and we by him.—That is, we are to worship the Father alone as God Almighty, and Jesus alone as the Lord, the Messiah, the Great King, the Lamb of God who was slain, and hath redeemed us with his blood, and made us kings and priests.

On the subject of the Trinitarian controversy, I have found a manuscript of fourteen queries, which may throw some light on the opinions of its author. . . .

Although Sir Isaac, in his observations on the Prophecies of Daniel, has shown how the Church of Rome, as the eleventh horn of the fourth beast, rooted up three of his first horns, the Exarchate of Ravenna, the kingdom of the Lombards, and the dukedom of Rome, and thus rose up as a temporal power, he has not given any account of the steps by which the Bishop of Rome obtained the rank of the Universal Bishop. In a paper of eight queries, containing his views on this subject, he states, that after the death of Constantius in A.D. 341, he began to usurp the universal Bishopric; that the Emperor Constantius abolished Popery in A.D. 361; and that the Emperor Gratian, in 379, restored, by his edict, the universal Bishopric of Rome over all the West.

The tendency of the Church of England to relapse into Romish superstition seems to have shewn itself in the time of Newton, and to have induced him to take steps to counteract it. It is probable that he had been requested by influential persons, both in the Church and in the State, to suggest a legislative measure for correcting an evil which at that time was as dangerous to the State as it was hostile to the articles of the Church and the fundamental truths of Christianity. This proceeding must have taken place at the accession of the House of Hanover in 1714, as will appear from the following draught of an Act of Parliament drawn up by Sir Isaac, and in his own handwriting:—

Whereas of late years, some opinions have been propagated by superstitious men among the Christians of the Church of England, to break all communion and friendship with the Protestant churches abroad, and to return into the communion of the Church of Rome; such as are the opinions, that the Church of Rome is a true church, without allowing her to be a false church in any respect, and that the Protestant churches abroad are false churches, and that they have no baptism, and by consequence are no Christians, and that the Church of England is in danger, meaning, by the succession of the House of Hanover. For preventing the mischiefs which may ensue upon such dangerous, uncharitable, and unchristian principles, be it enacted,—

That the following declaration shall be made and subscribed in open court in the Quarter Sessions next after . . . . . by all persons.

We, whose names are underwritten, do solemnly, and without all equivocation or mental reservation, acknowledge and declare that we do sincerely believe that the Church of Rome is, in doctrine and worship, a false, uncharitable, and idolatrous church, with whom it is not lawful to communicate; and that the churches of the Lutherans and Calvinists abroad are true churches, with whom we may lawfully communicate, and that their baptism is valid and authentic; and that the Church of England is in no danger by the succession of the House of Hanover in the throne of the kingdom of Great Britain."

It is interesting to observe the coincidence of the religious views of Sir Isaac Newton with those of John Locke, his illustrious contemporary and friend. Though, like Newton, he lived in communion with the Church of England, "yet it is obvious," as Lord King says, "from an unpublished reply to a work of Dr. Stillingfleet's, that he entertained a strong opinion that the exclusive doctrines of the Church of England were very objectionable—that he thought them much too narrow and confined, and that he wished for a much larger and easier comprehension of Protestants." In a paper dated 1688, and apparently drawn up for the guidance of a religious society when he was in Holland, we find the following noble article, which Newton would have countersigned, and which, without having adopted the peculiar opinions of these distinguished men, we regard as at once the essence and the bulwark of Protestant truth.

"If any one find any doctrinal parts of Scripture difficult to be understood, we recommend him, 1*st,* The study of the Scriptures in humility and singleness of heart. 2*d,* Prayer to the Father of lights to enlighten him. 3*d,* Obedience to what is already revealed to him, remembering that the practice of what we do know is the surest way to more knowledge; our infallible guide having told us, if any man will do the will of him that sent me [his will,] he shall know of the doctrine, John vii. 17. 4*th,* We leave him to the advice and assistance of those whom he thinks best able to instruct him; no men, or society of men, having any authority to impose their opinions or interpretations on any other, the meanest Christian; since, in matters of religion, every man must know and believe and give an account for himself."

Interesting as any opinion of Newton's must be, on every subject to which he has directed his transcendent powers, there is one prophetic of the future destiny of man which has a peculiar value, and with which we may appropriately close our notice of his theological writings. Although Sir Isaac believed in a plurality of worlds, he has nowhere given it as his opinion that the worlds beyond our own are to be the residence of the blessed. This opinion, however, resting on Scripture and science, and combining what is revealed with what is demonstrated, he has distinctly developed in the following passage:—

> God made and governs the world invisibly, and hath commanded us to love and worship him, and no other God; to honour our parents and masters, and love our neighbours as ourselves; and to be temperate, just, and peaceable, and to be merciful even to brute beasts. And by the same power by which he gave life at first to every species of animals, he is able to revive the dead, and hath revived Jesus Christ our Redeemer, who hath gone into the heavens to receive a kingdom, and prepare a place for us, and is next in dignity to God, and may be worshipped as the Lamb of God, and hath sent the Holy Ghost to comfort us in his absence, and will at length return and reign over us, invisibly to mortals, till he hath raised up and judged all the dead, and then he will give up his kingdom to the Father, and carry the blessed to the place he is now preparing for them, and send the rest to other places suitable to their merits. *For in God's house (which is the universe,) are many mansions, and he governs them by agents which can pass through the heavens from one mansion to another. For if all places to which we have access are filled with living creatures, why should all these immense spaces of the heavens above the clouds be incapable of inhabitants?*

Such is a brief view of the theological manuscripts of Sir Isaac Newton. With the exception of the "Paradoxical Questions concerning Athanasius," none of them were prepared for the press, and there can be no doubt that his representatives, and also Dr. Horsley, exercised a wise discretion in not giving them formally to the world. Had Sir Isaac found leisure to complete the works of which we have but imperfect fragments, they would have displayed his sagacity and varied erudition, and would have exhibited more correctly and fully than the specimens we have given, his opinions on the great questions of Christian doctrine and ecclesiastical polity.

It is scarcely a matter of surprise that sceptical writers should have spoken disrespectfully of the theological writings of a mathematician and philosopher, but it has surprised us that other authors should have regarded the study of the Scriptures as incompatible with scientific research. When Voltaire asserted that Sir Isaac explained the Prophecies in the same manner as those who went before him, he only exhibited his ignorance of what Newton wrote, and of what others had written; and when he stated that Newton composed his Commentaries on the Apocalypse to console mankind for the great superiority which he had over them, he but shewed the emptiness of the consolation to which scepticism aspires.

We have few examples, indeed, of truly great men pursuing simultaneously their own peculiar studies and the critical examination of the Scriptures. The most illustrious have been the ornaments of our own land, and England may well be proud of having had Napier, and Milton, and Locke, and Newton, for the champions both of its faith and its Protestantism. From the study of the material universe—the revelation of God's wisdom, to the study of his holy word—the revelation of his will, the transition is neither difficult nor startling. From the homes of planetary life to the homes of its future destiny the mind passes with a firm and joyous step, and it is only when scepticism or intellectual pride has obstructed the path, that the pilgrim falters in his journey, or faints by the way.

When a philosopher like Newton first directs his energies to the study of the material universe, no indications of order attract his notice, and no proofs of design call forth his admiration. In the starry firmament he sees no bodies of stupendous magnitude, and no distances of immeasurable span. The two great luminaries appear vastly inferior in magnitude to many objects around him, and the greatest distances in the heavens seem even inferior to those which his own eye can embrace on the surface of the earth. The planets, when observed with care, are seen to have a motion among the fixed stars, and to vary in their magnitude and distances, but these changes appear to follow no law. Sometimes they move to the east, sometimes to the west, passing the meridian sometimes near and sometimes far from the horizon, while at other times they are absolutely stationary in their path. No system, in short, appears, and no general law seems to direct their motions. By the observations and inquiries of astronomers, however, during successive ages, a regular system has been recognised in this chaos of moving bodies, and the magnitudes, distances, and revolutions of every planet which composes it have been determined with the most extraordinary accuracy. Minds fitted and prepared for this species of inquiry are capable of appreciating the great variety of evidence by which the truths of the planetary system are established; but thousands of individuals, and many who are highly distinguished in other branches of knowledge, are incapable of understanding such researches, and view with a sceptical eye the great and irrefragable truths of astronomy.

That the sun is stationary in the centre of our system,—that the earth moves round the sun, and round its own axis,—that the diameter of the earth is 8000 miles, and that of the sun *one hundred and ten* times as great; that the earth's orbit is 190 millions of miles in breadth; and that, if this immense space were filled with light, it would appear only like a luminous point at the nearest fixed star,—are positions absolutely unintelligible and incredible to all who have not carefully studied the subject. To millions of our species, then, the Great Book of Nature is absolutely sealed, though it is in the power of all to unfold its pages, and to peruse those glowing passages which proclaim the power and wisdom of its Author.

The Book of Revelation exhibits to us the same peculiarities as that of Nature. To the ordinary eye it presents no immediate indications of its divine origin. Events apparently insignificant—supernatural interferences seemingly unnecessary—doctrines almost contradictory—and prophecies nearly unintelligible, occupy its pages. The history of the fall of man—of the introduction of moral and physical evil—the prediction of a Messiah—the advent of our Saviour—his precepts—his miracles—his death—his resurrection—the gift of tongues—and the subsequent propagation of his religion by the unlettered fishermen of Galilee, are each a stumbling-block to the wisdom of this world. The youthful and vigorous mind, when summoned from its early studies to the perusal of the Scriptures, turns from them with disappointment. It recognises in the sacred page no profound science—no secular wisdom—no disclosures of Nature's secrets—no palpable impress of an Almighty hand. But, though the system of revealed truth which the Scriptures contain is like that of the universe concealed from common observation, yet the labours of centuries have established its divine origin, and developed in all its order and beauty the great plan of human restoration. In the chaos of its incidents, we discover the whole history of our species, whether it is delineated in events that are past, or shadowed forth in those which are to come,—from the creation of man and the origin of evil, to the extinction of his earthly dynasty, and the commencement of his immortal career.

The antiquity and authenticity of the books which compose the sacred canon,—the fulfilment of its prophecies,—the miraculous propagation of the gospel,—have been demonstrated to all who are capable of appreciating the force of historical evidence; and in the poetical and prose compositions of the inspired authors, we discover a system of doctrine, and a code of morality, traced in characters as distinct and legible as the most unerring truths in the material world.—False systems of religion have indeed been deduced from the sacred record,—as false systems of the universe have sprung from the study of the book of nature; but the very prevalence of a false system proves the existence of one that is true; and though the two classes of facts necessarily depend on different kinds of evidence, yet we scruple not to say that the Copernican system is not more demonstrably true than the system of theological truth contained in the Bible. If men of high powers, then, are still found, who are insensible to the evidence which has established the system of the universe, need we wonder that there are others who resist the effulgent evidence which sustains the strongholds of our faith?

If such be the character of Christian truth, we need not be surprised that it was embraced and expounded by such a genius as Sir Isaac Newton. Cherishing its doctrines, and leaning on its promises, he felt it his duty, as it was his delight, to apply to it that intellectual strength which had successfully surmounted the difficulties of the material universe. The fame which that success procured him he could not but feel to be the breath of popular applause, which administered only to his personal feelings; but the investigation of the sacred mysteries, while it prepared his own mind for its final destiny, was calculated to promote the spiritual interests of thousands. This noble impulse he did not hesitate to obey, and by thus uniting philosophy with religion, he dissolved the league which genius had formed with scepticism, and added to the cloud of witnesses the brightest name of ancient or of modern times.

> What wonder then that his devotion swelled
> Responsive to his knowledge! for could he,
> Whose piercing mental eye diffusive saw
> The finished university of things,
> In all its order, magnitude, and parts,
> Forbear incessant to adore that power
> Who fills, sustains, and actuates the whole.
> THOMSON.

Frank E. Manuel (essay date 1968)

SOURCE: "God and the Calling of the New Philosophy," in *A Portrait of Isaac Newton,* Cambridge, Mass.: The Belknap Press of Harvard University Press, 1968, pp. 117-32.

[*In the following essay, Manuel examines the relationship between religion and science in seventeenth-century England, focusing on the psychological underpinnings of Newton's theology.*]

> The World was made to be inhabited by Beasts but studied and contemplated by Man: 'tis the Debt of our Reason we owe unto *God,* and the homage we pay for not being Beasts. . . . The Wisdom of God receives small honour from those vulgar Heads that rudely stare about, and with a gross rusticity admire His works: those highly magnifie Him, whose judicious inquiry into His Acts, and deliberate research into His Creatures, return the duty of a devout and learned admiration.
>
> Thomas Browne, *Religio Medici*

During the three decades of his fervid intellectual activity in Cambridge, an almost incomparable period of protracted effort, Newton was sustained by a consciousness of the direct personal relationship between himself and God his Father, uninterrupted by a mediator. For His glory he labored without surcease, finding his only "divertisement" in moving from one subject to another. In addition to the optics, the calculus, and the great mathematical and physical synthesis upon which his fame rests secure, in the early seventies he amended and published Varenius' world geography,[1] which stood him in good stead in his later chronological researches. Experiments to lay bare the ultimate unity of the chemical elements and perhaps to discover the very elixir of life were conducted in the Cambridge laboratory whose fires he stoked himself, the last trials taking place on the very eve of his departure for London. In a theology, kept secret, he tackled the awesome problems of the Trinity by analyzing every biblical manuscript he could lay hands on—in any language—that touched upon the divine nature of Christ. And he began to pile up historical writings, comprising an interpretation of mythology, a theory of hieroglyphs, a radical revision of ancient chronology founded upon astronomical proofs, an independent reading of the sense of the Bible, and circumstantial demonstrations of prophecy in the historical world.

In all these works Newton was discharging an obligation to God for his being. The sense of owing to progenitors is deep-rooted in man, and a child has various ways of attempting to requite the debt. But the demands of a father whose face has never been seen are indefinable, insatiable. Since Newton's father was unknown to him and he had not received the slightest sign of his affection, he could never be certain that he had pleased or appeased the Almighty Lord with whom this father was assimilated. Many other puritanical scholars, sons of austere, remote elders, experienced similar feelings toward their exigent Master. The God of Abraham, Isaac, and Jacob whom Newton worshiped had been adored in many ways in the long history of Israel and of the church which had renewed the original covenant; it was given to Isaac Newton to bring Him offerings that surpassed the gifts of all other men. Reasoned, philosophical statements of Newton's religious position come late in his life, in the **"Queries"** to the *Opticks,* in the General Scholium to the second edition of the *Principia;* but the enduring, emotive relation of his calling to his God, its sacred character, is attested in writings from the confession of 1662 until the year of his death. Newton's devotion to science as a worship accorded with contemporary beliefs about the connections between science and religion in the collegiate bodies to which he belonged, above all the Royal Society. If he differed from his friends it was in the intensity of his religious quest, not its singularity. Though many scientists tended to de-emphasize the sectarian character of their religious allegiances and Newton was progressing at an even faster pace than his colleagues toward a divorcement of religion from ritual and dogma, his religious convictions were not the less impassioned.

The beginning of the Stuart Restoration, when young Newton came up to Cambridge University, was a revolutionary moment in the scientific and religious life of England less dramatic but as far-reaching in its consequences as the political upheavals of the preced-

ing two Puritan decades. Recent scholarly discussion over whether the original nucleus of the Royal Society was John Wilkins' scientific club at Oxford, or the London group around John Wallis, or Samuel Hartlib and the Puritan pansophists, or informal meetings in Gresham College, is rather parochial—a number of strands were intertwined.[2] Many men of learning on both sides of the barrier had wearied of the religious controversies of the civil war; and though the spirit of zealotry in defense of a particular form of Catholicism, Anglicanism, or Dissent was by no means dead, there was a growing body of irenic opinion and a tendency to embrace latitudinarian solutions. This does not mean that the prelates and scholars ceased to hold firm beliefs; but many of them were prepared to meet in concert with men of divergent religious views for specific intellectual purposes on noncombatant terms.

The original membership of the Royal Society, which in 1662 received a charter from King Charles II, was a heterogeneous religious assemblage that included both practicing Catholics, like the aristocratic Kenelm Digby, and John Wilkins, Cromwell's brother-in-law. It was from the very beginning clearly understood that religious disputations would be banned; nor would the society entertain political questions that might lead the members into labyrinthine civil debates. In his account of the early meetings before a corporate body was established, written in January 1697, John Wallis, one of the oldest members, recollected their decision to be exclusively absorbed with "the New Philosophy . . . precluding matters of Theology & State Affairs."[3] And Newton later reiterated the doctrine that "religion & Philosophy are to be preserved distinct. We are not to introduce divine revelations into Philosophy, nor philosophical opinions into religion."[4] Thus the neutrality of science was formally proclaimed. It was assumed that there existed a sphere of inquiry to which neither the social status of the scientist nor his religious convictions were relevant; an area of knowledge uninvolved with anything but its own concerns was reserved and isolated. This was a comparatively new adventure in Christian Europe, and many members of the Society were at least vaguely aware of its unprecedented character. The French Académie des Sciences was not nearly as free. It may have enjoyed large royal subsidies at an earlier date than the Royal Society, but its spirit was restricted to what an absolute Catholic king could endure. When one recalls that Giordano Bruno was burned in Rome in 1600 and that Galileo recanted before the Inquisition in 1633, the new spirit of English science appears as a unique development, despite recent attempts to prove that post-Trentine Catholicism did not stifle scientific inquiry. Acrimonious debates over matters of fact took place at Royal Society meetings, and there were fights a-plenty in this scientific world but no direct denunciation of another member in the name of God, however sharply one disagreed with him.

The resolution to avoid religious discrimination was, however, not quite as firm as the first members of the Royal Society imagined. At both ends of the spectrum certain religious postures were not countenanced even in England, though there was never any formal debate on the subject within the Society. Enthusiasts, men who spoke with tongues and proclaimed truths by divine inspiration alone, were to be excluded. The members had no intention of listening to Quakers who had suddenly been illuminated or to Dissenters of the Leveller and Digger type who were so uncompromising that as a consequence of direct inspiration from God they would overturn the whole civil and religious establishment of society. An individual member of the Royal Society might still experience direct revelation from God in the secret of his closet, and there is reason to believe that Newton, after arduous efforts, had occasional visitations; but there is no record of anyone's reporting such an event to the Society in defense of a scientific proposition.

The rejection of vulgar prophecies and reports of prodigies and miracles was generally taken for granted. One of the goals that reasonable Anglican divines hoped the Royal Society would realize was a purification of true religion from popular superstition and false prognostics that played on the mob's credulity. The separation of the natural and the lawful from the vapors of the religious fanatic would serve to exalt the supernatural by ridding it of nonsense. During Newton's tenure at Cambridge a great Hebraist, John Spencer, was elected Master of Corpus Christi in 1667 and occupied the post with distinction until his death in 1693. The impress of his studies in comparative religion, and especially his important *De Legibus Hebraeorum,* is marked throughout Newton's manuscript renderings of religious history. Spencer was also his guide in interpreting the nature of prophetic revelation, following the Maimonides tradition, which stresses the rigorous rational and moral preparation of the prophet rather than his wild ecstasy. And Spencer was an enemy of modern prophets and enthusiasts, maintaining that the true gift had probably ceased and deriding them as victims of melancholy and hypochondria. "God would no more be look'd for in the whirlwind of raptures, mystical phrases, and ecstatical Orations, but in the *still voice* of a great humility, a sound mind, and an heart reconciled to himself and all the world. . . . "[5] In manifest form and content Newton's interpretations of prodigies and prophecies and their relation to truth revealed by the scientific study of nature were in the same spirit, hostile to mysticism and enthusiasm and the infatuation of the ignorant with phantoms and ghosts as a derogation of true religion. There is even an anecdote of his upbraiding a crowd of agitated undergraduates possessed with the idea that a house was haunted.[6]
If enthusiasm was not allowed a hearing in the Royal Society, neither was clamorous atheism. Skepticism or a form of deism, which was probably the astronomer Edmond Halley's position, was somehow overlooked as long as it kept its mouth shut in public. Private antireligious jokes were frowned upon by Newton, but at least in Halley's case they did not lead to a complete break in friendship, though there was disapproval and censure. Thomas Hobbes, who surely merited a place in the Royal Society by virtue of his once having been in the entourage of Francis Bacon, secular patron saint of the Society from an earlier generation, and who was engaged in violent controversy with Dr. Wallis over mathematical, not political, questions, was not welcomed to the fellowship, probably because of his reputed materialism and atheism and philosophical immorality.[7] When Newton suffered his psychic crisis in 1693, he thought as the most horrible thing imaginable of his dear friend John Locke that he was a Hobbist. For all their sidestepping of religious issues the men of the Royal Society were Christians, and a writer like Hobbes, who was interpreted as maintaining that religion was a mere artifice of the state to hold power more effectively, could not be invited. Usually the Society also drew the line at dogmatic unitarianism and a denial of the divinity of Christ—again if expressed in public. We now know from his manuscripts that Newton was himself a secret unitarian, but he never spread his opinion abroad.

The quality of religious feeling among the scientists cannot be measured by observance and forbearance alone. A willingness to be in the same room with a person of a different religious persuasion is not to be equated with religious lukewarmness. There were surely more and less devout men among members of the Society. Robert Hooke and Edmond Halley would be illustrious examples of the indifferentists. On the other hand, two of the greatest figures of English science in the second half of the seventeenth century, Boyle and Newton, cannot be put into the category of merely formal believers, and theirs is the predominant attitude. Though both were members of the Anglican Church, there was nothing loose or permissive about their personal behavior, as there was among many aristocratic Anglicans of the Restoration whose cavortings enlivened memoirs of court life. Boyle went through an anguished religious crisis in his youth described in his autobiography, and Newton's shorthand confession in 1662 bears witness to a similar event.

Nineteenth-century histories that depicted the agelong war of "rational" science and "irrational" religion made use of generalizations that had served the polemical purposes of Enlightenment anti-clerical philosophers like Voltaire and Condorcet, nineteenth-century social thinkers like Saint-Simon and Marx, and the Darwinians who were being attacked by fundamentalist clergymen; but their thesis is not applicable to the relationship of science and religion in seventeenth-century England. In our present-day writing interpretive study has moved in another direction. Instead of seeing the history of the world as a combat between benighted, power-lusting medieval priests and embattled scientists, many thinkers have become aware of the deep religious roots of Western science. The Christian view of a Providence who had established a world order was favorable to the scientific outlook and nurtured it in its infancy, particularly during the age of genius. Discovery of the lawfulness of the world did not exclude the miraculous creation or the unknown end.

Since the sociologist Robert Merton's work in 1938, a peculiar symbiotic relationship has been recognized between Puritanism and science, a parallel to the Weber thesis of a harmony between Calvinism and capitalism. The personal qualities extolled by the Puritan divines would serve an assiduous scientific experimenter well: practicality, orderliness, discipline, scrupulosity, a certain literalness that would apply equally to observing nature and interpreting a biblical text, attention to detail, avoidance of debauch and sensate pleasure, asceticism in the world, utter dedication to one's calling. Perhaps the Merton thesis sometimes overreaches itself (as the Weber thesis did). Other religious sects and even philosophical alchemy could foster the same habits for different theological reasons. But the tendency of the Puritan minority to promote scientific endeavor and to engage in it remains statistically convincing. One did not, of course, have to be an actual member of a dissenter Puritan group to be puritanical—Boyle and Newton, though formally Anglican, lived ascetics in the world.

As the intimate relationship between science and theology in the crucial formative period of modern science has come to be appreciated, it has been easier to reconcile the multifarious activities of Newton's life, and to regard all his works as inspired by the same profound religious sentiment—a position set forth with varying emphasis by Edwin Arthur Burtt and G. S. Brett, by Hélène Metzger, and by Koyré, Léon Bloch, and Adolph Judah Snow. Even Vavilov, the Russian biographer of Newton, took a similar position: "Newton doubtless envisaged the whole of his scientific work from a religious viewpoint. Both of his major works, the *Principia* and the *Opticks,* have religious endings which are written with extraordinary pathos."[8]

Despite difficulties in comprehending Newton's religious expressions over the years—and many of them were not philosophically felicitous—some things can be asserted: he never upheld a simple mechanistic view of the universe, nor was he a partisan of plain deistic natural religion. It may be wicked to quote the devil on the God of Isaac Newton when there are so many pious bishops to bear witness, but Voltaire's report, after conversations with Samuel Clarke, has the virtues of clarity and brevity: "Sir Isaac Newton was firmly persuaded of the Existence of a God; by which he understood not only an infinite, omnipotent, and creating being, but moreover a Master who has made a Relation between himself and his Creatures."[9] The world was not eternal. Creation was a specific act in time by a Lord, even though the process of His labors may perhaps have been more complex than the popular impression of the Mosaic account in Genesis might indicate. The planets had to be distributed in a certain manner by an initial act before the principle of gravity could become operative. Comets were phenomena in whose progress God had to intervene from time to time. A repeopling of the earth after major geological or cosmic catastrophes—and there may have been such incidents in the past—required a divine decree. And as the world had a beginning there was likely to be an apocalyptic end. Every discovery of a scientifc principle of matter, every correct reading of a prophetic text, demonstrated the essential goodness and orderliness of the universe that God had created—and what higher praise could be uttered by the religious philosopher, whether Maimonides or Isaac Newton—but this did not signify that He was an absconding Deity. Newton's secret unitarianism was an ardent passion, not the pallid formula of the later Enlightenment.[10]

Newton was not very good at expounding in nonmathematical prose his general ideas about God and the universe, time and space. There was a certain reluctance on his part to philosophize publicly about these ultimate questions, and he usually preferred to let others speak for him on religious subjects, as did Richard Bentley in lectures established by Boyle to combat atheism. Newton was genuinely pleased to have Bentley prove that the world system so marvelously set forth in the *Principia,* far from being inimical to revealed religion, could be used as a mighty bludgeon against atheism. As he said in his famous letter of December 10, 1692: "When I wrote my treatise about our Systeme I had an eye upon such Principles as might work wth considering men for the beleife of a Deity & nothing can rejoyce me more then to find it usefull for that purpose."[11] Newton assured Conduitt that he had written the *Principia* "not with a design of bidding defiance to the Creator but to enforce and demonstrate the power & superintendency of a supreme being."[12] When the Reverend Samuel Clarke defended the Newtonian religious-philosophical views in correspondence with Leibniz and in conversations with Voltaire, he was making explicit what Newton was reticent to say himself, but fervently believed. Newton published nothing significant about God until Clarke's Latin translation of the *Opticks* in 1706, when he carefully worked out his relationship to religion and once and for all refuted the argument that his mechanical philosophy could dispense with an active God.[13] In scientific law he saw His direct and continuous intervention, a traditionalism that separates him sharply from later deist proponents of the mechanical philosophy. Boyle's work *The Christian Virtuoso: shewing that by being addicted to Experimental Philosophy, a man is rather assist-*

ed, than indisposed to be a good Christian (1690, 1691), and other apologiae of science by less prominent men, propagated the same idea—that science was a Te Deum, a laudation, a demonstration of the wonders of God.

There were of course contemporaries who attacked the scientists of the Royal Society on religious grounds, Alexander Ross and Henry Stubbs, for example, themselves not practicing scientists. The arguments of these men—and sometimes Puritan divines like Richard Baxter joined them[14]—were simple and obvious enough, and bore weight. They charged that a concentration of inquiry upon secondary causes, how things worked in the world, would inevitably deflect attention from God as the primary cause. There was a good dose of anti-intellectualism in some of their animadversions against science, reminiscent of one tradition in Christianity that opposed culture and glorified the outpourings of the simple, ignorant, pious heart. A Calvinist could not, after all, maintain that the mysterious gift of grace was more accessible to the learned scientist than to an ordinary man, since it was dependent upon God's arbitrary will. In long terms there was probably some merit to the argument of these mediocre and often venal polemicists against science (Stubbs was paid by the Royal College of Physicians to attack the Royal Society because they feared its competition). But the great seventeenth-century scientists themselves never viewed their activities as a turning away from the love and worship of God.[15] Sir Thomas Browne in the *Religio Medici* (1642/3) had already presented a grand apology for natural philosophy in language that would be repeated with variations for the rest of the century. It was a religious *duty* of the scientist, who was capable of unraveling the wonders of God's creation, to reveal them to mankind. If the scientist failed to acquit himself of this task, he was denying God one form of adoration. Boyle, in the wake of Browne, knew that God would be more gratified by the refined revelations and praise of a sensitive and skillful anatomist than by those of an ignorant butcher. John Ray spent his life unveiling the beauties of the world's flora and fauna that God had made. Even Hooke, perhaps the first to study a flea under a microscope and draw it with intricate detail in his *Micrographia,* pronounced it beautiful in a religious, not an aesthetic, sense.

Seventeenth-century scientists were almost to a man teleologists. They discerned the divine intent in the structure of an animal molar, in the hair of a cheese mite, in the orderly movement of the planets. Everywhere there were traces of divine harmony and perfection. Ray's *Wisdom of God Manifested in the Works of the Creation* and similar justifications of religion reached their epitome in the next generation in the Boyle lectures for 1711 and 1712 on *Physico-Theology: or, a demonstration of the Being and Attributes of God, from his works of creation,* by Newton's friend William Derham, a graduate of Trinity. This work

(which saw twelve editions by 1754) makes the traditional argument from design, but now accoutered with voluminous scientific evidence from aspects of the world animal, vegetable, and mineral, and above all from the idea of gravity. On July 18, 1733, William Derham wrote Conduitt of a "peculiar sort of Proof of God, wch Sr Is: mentioned in some discourse wch he & I had soon after I published my Astro-Theology. He said there were 3 things in the Motions of the Heavenly Bodies, that were plain evidences of Omnipotence & wise Counsel. 1. That the Motion imprest upon those Globes was Lateral, or in a Direction perpendicular to their Radii, not along them or parallel wth them. 2. That the Motions of them tend the same way. 3. That their Orbits have all the same or nearly the same inclination."[16]

At other times scientists could relate their discoveries to mundane activities, to the practicalities of British imperial interests and navigation policy. And perhaps in a broad sense the practice of science and its matter-of-factness were consonant with the interests of the new urban economy and with nascent capitalism. But recognition of the utilitarian ends of science—though it would not be phrased in those portentous words—was by no means at variance with a conception of science as an offering to God and a celebration of His perfection. In the 1670's a scientist could assimilate both ideas.

When Newton was named to the Royal Society in 1672 the discoveries about God's world had already begun to multiply. A monotheistic culture, however, must inevitably become engaged in the search for a unifying principle, and can never remain content with the mere amassing of isolated findings and inventions, astonishing as they may be. Newton represents the fulfillment of that quest for underlying unity. "Without Gravity, the whole Universe . . . would have been a confused Chaos," lectured Bentley.[17] The Newtonian system, with its mathematically described force that applied both to the movements of the heavenly bodies and to things on earth, satisfied a religious as well as a scientific need. In chemistry, where Boyle labored, it was difficult if not impossible to find a single mathematical principle. The naturalists were always on the borderline between science and the mere collecting of prodigies—though the Italian Marcello Malpighi, the greatest of them all, corresponded with the Royal Society and presented it with a theory of embryology.[18] In achieving the great synthesis with a law that showed the interrelationship of all parts of creation, at the very moment when it seemed as if science might remain an agglomeration of curiosities and disparate discoveries, Newton overwhelmed his fellow scientists and became the symbol of science in a Christian society.

The mission of science in the realm of the historical, as contrasted with the physical, world was defined in accordance with how the individual scientist saw the moment in time when he lived in the grand design of God's creation. Despite the Society's formal commitment to the promotion of knowledge, which sounds progressive, the ideal of most members, including Newton, has to be sharply distinguished from late-eighteenth- or nineteenth-century conceptions of human perfectibility. In the seventeenth century there was still a pervasive sense of nature's decay, of a steady corruption or running down of its forces. The function of science would then be to try to arrest decay, to restore nature and man, or to slow the process of degeneration. But any remedies applied by art and science would have their limitations because human capacities were not boundless. Bacon's conception of extending man's power over all things possible does not connote the idea of infinitude. The true spirit of the Baconian ideal can be found in his medical reflections: man in this world walks through a vale of tears and we ought to alleviate his anguish. There is no vision here of a perfected new man. John Wilkins' justification of the mechanical philosophy is equally modest—it will help man to regain some of the capabilities lost through the sinfulness of the Fall. In the introductory material to Dalgarno's *Ars Signorum* (1661), a proposal for a universal sign language, there is an appeal from Charles II to support the author's endeavors in "further repairing the Decayes of Nature, until Art have done its last, or, which is more probable, Nature cease to be, or be Renewed,"[19] a characteristic view that scientific labor is a means of counteracting in some measure the attenuation of nature's force.

The expectation was widespread that ultimately through conflagration or flood, for which the plague and the fire of London were prognostics, the world would be renewed by divine re-creation, or that other worlds would be fashioned.[20] This cyclical conception, which Newton shared with many of his contemporaries, is alien to the canonical eighteenth-century idea of progress. The emotive and intellectual roots of the common seventeenth-century eschatology are to be found in Stoic cyclical theory and in millenarianism, which were united in the conviction that the world was coming to an end. Books on the Second Coming were written by the score during this period, and members of the Royal Society were preoccupied with dating the event. The coming of the Messiah is the subject of a letter from Oldenburg to Manasseh ben Israel, the Amsterdam rabbi, on July 25, 1657.[21] Boyle steadfastly believed that the world would end in annihilation or that it would be totally transformed by a great conflagration which would "destroy the present frame of nature."[22] Newton was convinced that the comet of 1680 had just missed hitting the earth, and in many of his commentaries on Revelations and the Book of Daniel, kept secret during his lifetime, he inclined to the idea that the end of the world in its present form could not be too long delayed, that the times were

about to be fulfilled. But neither Boyle nor Newton went ranting about the imminent destruction of London. It would all happen in due course. Perhaps other worlds would be created thereafter. In the meantime, it was given to them as scientists to lay bare the wonders of God's creation in all its intricacy and all its harmonious simplicity, as they waited for the inevitable drawing to a close.

There were of course men like Joseph Glanvill who had a far more expansive view of the practical possibilities of science and dwelt on its creative role, its shining future in this world, if the achievements of the Royal Society continued to accumulate.

> Me thinks this Age seems resolved to bequeath *posterity* somewhat to remember it: And the glorious Undertakers, wherewith Heaven hath blest our Days, will leave the world better provided then they found it. . . . Should those Heroes go on, as they have happily begun; they'll fill the world with *wonders*. And I doubt not but posterity will find many things, that are now but *Rumors,* verified into practical *Realities*. It may be some Ages hence, a voyage to Southern unknown Tracts, yea possibly the Moon, will not be more strange then one to America. To them, that come after us, it may be as ordinary to buy a *pair* of *wings* to fly into remotest Regions; as now a pair of Boots to ride a Journey. And to conferr at the distance of the Indies by Sympathetick conveyances, may be as usual to future times, as to us in a litterary correspondence. The restauration of gray hairs to Juvenility, and renewing the exhausted marrow, may at length be effected without a *miracle;* And the turning of the now comparatively *desert* world into a Paradise, may not improbably be expected from late Agriculture.[23]

But though Newton early in his Cambridge career read the book in which these marvels of science were predicted, there is no echo of its exultation in any of his writings. The physical transformations science might work upon the earth did not capture his imagination. For most of his life he saw science in an entirely different light and mundane improvements were hardly worthy of his notice. Science for him was a way of knowing his Father, not a means leading to the multiplication of sinful, sensate pleasures. When in the latter part of his career Newton became involved in the relations of science, the government, and the economy, he was serving purposes that in his creative period he would have frowned upon.

The profession of faith which concluded the second edition of the **Principia** and was retained with some emendations in the third—the General Scholium—was a deliberate effort on Newton's part to distinguish his views from those of atheistic atomists and pantheists and to vindicate himself in the face of insinuations that his doctrine might have irreligious connotations. Though Newton's God was ultimately inscrutable and unknowable, He was not to be identified with the heathen Fates, for He was a ruler, and He had left signs of His Providence throughout His creation.

> As a blind man has no idea of colors, so have we no idea of the manner by which the all-wise God perceives and understands all things. He is utterly void of all body and bodily figure, and can therefore neither be seen, nor heard, nor touched; nor ought he to be worshiped under the representation of any corporeal thing. . . . We know him only by his most wise and excellent contrivances of things, and final causes; we admire him for his perfections; but we reverence and adore him on account of his dominion: for we adore him as his servants; and a god without dominion, providence, and final causes, is nothing else but Fate and Nature. Blind metaphysical necessity, which is certainly the same always and everywhere, could produce no variety of things.[24]

What Newton conveyed was a sense of man's puniness before the grandeur and final mystery of God's being, even though men might learn about His governance through the mechanical philosophy, or by resorting to anthropomorphism seek to understand His powers and attributes.

Nothing in the General Scholium represented a novel departure for Newton; he was merely acknowledging publicly the emotions he had experienced throughout his life. God was a lord, a master to be obeyed, not simply a metaphysical entity or a principle arrived at by reasoning. Here lies the powerful and intimate meaning of his exegesis of ordinary religious speech.

> This Being governs all things, not as the soul of the world, but as Lord over all; and on account of his dominion he is wont to be called *Lord God* . . . or *Universal Ruler;* for *God* is a relative word, and has a respect to servants; and *Deity* is the dominion of God not over his own body, as those imagine who fancy God to be the soul of the world, but over servants. The Supreme God is a Being eternal, infinite, absolutely perfect; but a being, however perfect, without dominion, cannot be said to be Lord God; for we say, my God, your God, the God of *Israel,* the God of Gods, and Lord of Lords; but we do not say, my Eternal, your Eternal, the Eternal of *Israel,* the Eternal of Gods; we do not say, my Infinite, or my Perfect: these are titles which have no respect to servants.[25]

If there is support for Newton's assimilation of God with the unknown father to whom it was his duty to submit, before whom he had to become passive, whose yoke he was obliged to bear, it lies in the passionate religious affirmation of the General Scholium. Newton quoted Scripture not only by way of traditional apologetics but to call the witness of mankind to his own feelings. In a passage of the General Scholium introduced into the third edition of the **Principia,** Newton proffered a psychological interpretation of the anthropomorphic images of God in the Bible that, despite his use of the word *allegory* (in this context he means *analogy*), differs from the Stoic tradition and is closer to ideas secretly diffused in Europe through Spinoza. Newton recognized a "similitude" between the ways of men—their ordinary behavior—and their notions of God. "[B]y way of allegory, God is said to see, to speak, to laugh, to love, to hate, to desire, to give, to receive, to rejoice, to be angry, to fight, to frame, to work, to build; for all our notions of God are taken from the ways of mankind by a certain similitude, which, though not perfect, has some likeness, however."[26] Newton is very far from Hume's or Feuerbach's view of God as created by man in his own image, but he has been pondering the nature of religious emotion in himself and in his fellows and has arrived at the conviction that ideas of God are derived from His relationship to man, not alone from the system of the world.

Notes

[1] Bernhard Varenius, *Geographia generalis . . . emendata . . . & illustrata ab Isaaco Newton* (Cambridge, 1672).

[2] See Margery Purver, *The Royal Society: Concept and Creation* (Cambridge, Mass.: Massachusetts Institute of Technology Press, 1967).

[3] Thomas Hearne, *Works* (London, 1810), III, clxi-clxiv, John Wallis to Thomas Smith, January 29, 1697.

[4] Cambridge, King's College Library, Keynes MS. 6, fol. 1r.

[5] John Spencer, *A Discourse concerning Vulgar Prophecies. Wherein the Vanity of receiving them as the certain indications of any future Event is discovered; and some characters of Distinction between true and pretending prophets are laid down* (London, 1665), p. 135.

[6] Abraham de la Pryme, *The Diary of Abraham de la Pryme, the Yorkshire Antiquary,* ed. Charles Jackson (Durham, 1870; Surtees Society Publications, vol. 54), p. 42.

[7] R. S. Westfall, *Science and Religion in the Seventeenth Century* (New Haven: Yale University Press, 1958), p. 20.

[8] S. I. Vavilov, *Isaac Newton,* trans. from the Russian (Berlin: Akademie Verlag, 1951), p. 190. See also Robert H. Hurlbutt III, *Hume, Newton, and the Design Argument* (Lincoln, Neb.: University of Nebraska Press, 1965), chap. i, "Newton's Scientific Theism," and chap. ii, "Other Contemporary Scientists."

[9] Voltaire, *The Metaphysics of Sir Isaac Newton,* trans. David Erskine Baker (London, 1747), p. 3.

[10] Hélène Metzger, *Attraction universelle et religion naturelle chez quelques commentateurs anglais de Newton* (Paris: Hermann et Cie., 1938), part 2, p. 66: "We shall draw the conclusion that Newton's science demands total and passive obedience to suggestions that have been sent to him, that in the first stage he is content to receive, and that then he elaborates with work that is active, no longer passive. We now understand why it can be asserted that Newton's physics was influenced by religious mysticism and Neoplatonism. It is needless to add that once the doctrine was put into the hands of scientists of a completely different upbringing it escaped from the spiritual conditions that gave it birth." See also Gerd Buchdal, *The Image of Newton and Locke in the Age of Reason* (London, New York: Sheed and Ward, 1961), p. 10: "And as we go on we find how the eighteenth-century Enlightenment is steadily squeezing out these spiritual elements—a soul, an immaterial God—and leaving us with a deterministic dance of atoms, as described so powerfully in the popularized versions of these ideas by the celebrated Baron d'Holbach."

[11] Newton, *Correspondence,* III, 233, Newton to Bentley, December 10, 1692; the lectures were published in 1693.

[12] Cambridge, King's College Library, Keynes MS. 130 (6).

[13] In the Latin edition of the *Opticks* (1706) queries of a theological nature appeared among the seven added to the original sixteen, and still others were introduced into the second English edition in 1717/1718.

[14] Richard Baxter, *The Reasons of the Christian Religion* (London, 1667), p. 498.

[15] The position of Newton's friend John Spencer was in thorough accord with that of the scientists. In the preface to his *Discourse concerning Prodigies,* 2nd ed. (London, 1665) he administered a nice rebuff to those who contended that absorption with secondary causes was unchristian: "[T]he noble attempt to satisfie the subtile Phaenomena in Nature from causes natural and immediate, is thought by some to have so much of the Philosopher, that it hath the less of the Christian therein, and seems to make Natural All. As if to shew how many wheels in some great Engine, move in subordination to the production of some great work, were to obscure and eclypse the art of the Artificer."

See also Leibniz on the religious mission of science and the duty of the divinely endowed scientists to answer the call. "It seems to me that the principal goal of the whole of mankind must be the knowledge and development of the wonders of God, and that this is

the reason why God gave him the empire of the globe. And M. Newton, being one of the men on earth who can contribute most to this end it would almost be a crime on his part to allow himself to be distracted by difficulties which are not absolutely insurmountable" (Leibniz, *Die philosophischen Schriften,* ed. C. J. Gerhardt [new ed., Hildesheim, 1960], III, 261: draft of a letter from Leibniz to T. Burnet which was probably not sent; the editor dates it circa 1699-1700).

[16] Keynes MS. 133.

[17] R. Bentley, *Works,* ed. Alexander Dyce (London, 1838), III, 75, fourth Boyle lecture, June 6, 1692.

[18] See Howard B. Adelmann, *Marcello Malpighi and the Evolution of Embryology* (Ithaca: Cornell University Press, 1966).

[19] George Dalgarno, *Ars Signorum, vulgo character universalis et lingua philosophica* (London, 1661), preface.

[20] See David Kubrin, "Newton and the Cyclical Cosmos: Providence and the Mechanical Philosophy," *Journal of the History of Ideas,* XXVIII (1956), 325-346.

[21] Henry Oldenburg, *Correspondence,* ed. and trans. A. Rupert Hall and Marie Boas Hall (Madison and Milwaukee: University of Wisconsin Press, 1965—), I, 123-125, Oldenburg to Manasseh ben Israel, July 25, 1657.

[22] Robert Boyle, *The Excellency of Theology compared with Natural Philosophy (As both are Objects of Men's Study) Discoursed of in a letter to a friend. To which are annexed Some Occasional Thoughts about the Excellency and Grounds of the Mechanical Hypothesis* (1665) (London, 1772), p. 11:

> And as for the duration of the world, which was by the old philosophers held to be interminible, and of which the Stoicks opinion, that the world shall be destroyed by fire, (which they held from the Jews) was physically precarious; theology teaches us expressly from divine revelation, that the present course of nature shall not last always, but that one day this world, or at least, this vortex of ours, shall either be abolished by annihilation, or, which seems far more probable, be innovated, and, as it were transfigured, and that, by the intervention of that fire, which shall dissolve and destroy the present frame of nature: so either way, the present state of things (as well natural as political) shall have an end.

The third of John Ray's *Three Physico-Theological Discourses,* 3rd ed. (London, 1713), concerned the dissolution of the world and its renewal:

As concerning the future Condition of the World after the Conflagration, I find it the general and received Opinion of the ancient Christians, that this World shall not be annihilated or destroyed, but only renewed and purified. . . . [N]ot only all Animals, but all Vegetables too, yea, and their Seeds also, will doubtless be mortified and destroyed by the Violence of the Conflagration; but that the same should be restored, and endued with eternal Life, I know no Reason we have to believe; but rather that there should be new ones produced, either of the same with the former, or of different Kinds, at the Will, and by the Power of the Almighty Creator, and for those Ends and Uses for which He shall design them.

(pp. 324, 415)

[23] Joseph Glanvill, *The Vanity of Dogmatizing* (London, 1661), pp. 181-182.

[24] Newton, *Mathematical Principles of Natural Philosophy* . . . , trans. Andrew Motte, rev. and ed. Florian Cajori (Berkeley, Cal.: University of California Press, 1934), pp. 545-546.

[25] *Ibid.*, p. 544.

[26] *Ibid.*, p. 546.

Richard S. Westfall (lecture date 1982)

SOURCE: "Newton and Alchemy," in *Occult and Scientific Mentalities in the Renaissance,* edited by Brian Vickers, Cambridge University Press, 1984, pp. 315-35.

[*In the essay below, originally delivered as a lecture in 1982, Westfall discusses the proper weight critics should give to the influence of alchemy on Newton's scientific thought, specifically in his work on the concept of force in the natural world.*]

On the whole, Newton preferred not to publicize his involvement in alchemy. Unlike his other major pursuits, nothing of his alchemy, or at least nothing explicitly labeled as alchemy, appeared in print during his lifetime or in the years immediately following his death. A few people did know about it. A fascinating correspondence between Newton and John Locke following the death of Robert Boyle reveals that the three men, possibly the last three men from Restoration England whom one would have expected, only a generation ago, to find so engaged, exchanged alchemical secrets and pledged each other to silence.[1] John Conduitt, the husband of Newton's niece, who gathered material about his life, knew of his experiments in Cambridge and reported that his furnace there remained an item of curiosity shown to visitors. Nevertheless, the adjective Conduitt used was "chymical," not "al-

chymical,"[2] and in a similar manner knowledge of Newton's interest in the art quickly sank from view. When David Brewster found alchemical manuscripts in Newton's own hand among his papers, he was appalled and quickly dismissed them as a curious relic of an earlier age.[3] It waited until the twentieth century for the record to become public, with the auction of the papers still in the hands of the Portsmouth family, and for scholars to come to grips with it. Lord Keynes purchased some of the alchemical papers at the auction and insisted forcefully on their importance,[4] but only in our own generation have scholars ready to take the papers seriously systematically studied the entire corpus, or rather that part—well over 90 percent—of the corpus known to exist that is available to the public. Betty Jo Dobbs and Karin Figala have been the leaders of this investigation.[5] As a result of their outstanding work, we probably know more today about Newton's endeavors in alchemy than anyone, including even his confidants in the art, Locke and Boyle, ever has.

The record is subject, of course, to varying interpretations. Newton was the single most important figure in establishing modern science with its unique view of reality and of the proper procedures to study it. Alchemy was one of the enterprises that modern science put out of business. Indeed, as David Brewster's references to "the most contemptible alchemical poetry," and, in regard to another paper, "the obvious production of a fool and a knave" make manifest, it appears to many as the quintessential embodiment of all that modern science opposes.[6] Not surprisingly then, some scholars, some very considerable scholars, reject the suggestion that alchemy played a significant role in Newton's intellectual life. Despite the manuscripts—and it should be obvious, as they contend, that the existence of the manuscripts does not of itself establish Newton's attitude toward their content—alchemy was in their view an activity peripheral to his central concerns. Those concerns manifested themselves in his **Principia,** his **Opticks,** and his fluxional calculus, the achievements that both shaped the modern scientific tradition and ensured their author's undying fame. Thus Bernard Cohen's recent *Newtonian Revolution* presents an analysis of the development of the **Principia** that focuses on problems internal to the science of dynamics and on Newton's transformation of received concepts of mechanics without saying more than a single word about alchemy. The single word is his emphatic rejection of the argument made by several scholars, including me, that Newton drew the concept of attraction out of the alchemical tradition.[7] Rupert Hall is uneasy that attention to Newton's alchemy will "cloud the clarity of reason and intellectual integrity . . . I would have regarded Newton as a founder of reason; so I think he wished to be regarded (for him reason included God, of course) not as flotsam on the weltering sea of the human unconscious. You must see that if you deny Freud in Manuel, you admit Jung with alchemy. *That* I am sorry about."[8] Cohen and Hall are names to be reckoned with in any discussion of Newton. A consideration of Newton and alchemy that proceeds by ignoring their opinions cannot hope to be taken seriously.

As there are those who reject the contention that alchemy was a central aspect of Newton's career, so there are others who make it the most central aspect. David Castillejo's recent *Expanding Force in Newton's Cosmos* presents the most fully developed expression this position has yet received. Significantly, the ***Principia*** scarcely appears in a work whose title proclaims the exact opposite of universal gravitation, and Newton's achievement in mathematics receives no mention at all. Castillejo opens, rather, with a chapter on alchemy, moves on to a chapter on the prophecies, and primarily from those two topics weaves a fabric that portrays not merely a Newton who let alchemy influence him, but a Newton whose entire intellectual life was thoroughly occult. In Castillejo's opinion, that intellectual life focused always on one investigation of which Newton's various studies were only specific facets, an investigation of two opposing forces, capable both of spiritual and material manifestations, the cyclical pattern of whose contentions has shaped both the universe and human history.[9] Castillejo does not enjoy the renown that Cohen and Half command. Nevertheless, the book rests on very extensive research in the manuscripts, and it is written with insight and conviction. No serious discussion of Newton and alchemy can afford to ignore it any more than Cohen and Hall.

My goal in this chapter is to neglect neither of the two positions, represented by Cohen and Hall on the one hand and by Castillejo on the other, but also to agree with neither. I shall attempt rather to define and defend a position between them, one that asserts the significance of alchemy in Newton's scientific career while it refuses to equate him with the occult.

I begin by taking my stand on three empirically established facts. First, Newton left behind a corpus of papers about alchemy which testify that he took an interest, the nature of which requires definition, in the art. Second, as a natural philosopher Newton introduced a major revision in the prevailing mechanical philosophy by asserting the existence of forces, attractions and repulsions between particles of matter that are not in mutual contact. Third, there was a chronological nexus between the first two points, the interest in alchemy spanning the period that witnessed the revision of natural philosophy. My argument must, of course, include elaborations drawn from the nature of the alchemical papers, but it rests squarely on these three foundation stones and depends directly on their solidity.

As far as I can tell from the surviving manuscripts, alchemy was not among the topics that introduced Newton to natural philosophy while he was still an undergraduate in a university that, like all universities of the age, did not energetically promote anything we would call science. Chemical questions of any sort scarcely figured in his initial reading in natural philosophy. Not long after taking his bachelor's degree, however, Newton did discover chemistry, and according to his custom with any new study, he attempted to systematize what he was learning in a glossary of chemical terms.[10] The distinction between chemistry and alchemy in the seventeenth century, if indeed it is valid to speak of a distinction, is difficult to place with precision, but most people, I think, would incline without hesitation to place the glossary squarely on the side of chemistry. Robert Boyle was his primary authority at this time. His studies did not remain on the chemical side of the line for long, however. His accounts show that on a trip to London in 1669 he purchased *Theatrum chemicum,* the huge collection of alchemical writings in six quarto volumes. He also purchased two furnaces, glass equipment, and chemicals.[11] As we shall see, he quickly learned to put the equipment to work. For the moment note that he also did not allow *Theatrum chemicum* to lie idle. Notes from the essays it contains began to appear among his papers, and a few years later he compiled a list of its most important items.[12] Nor did he confine himself to the *Theatrum.* He ransacked other major collections, such as *Ars aurifera, Musaeum hermeticum,* and *Theatrum chemicum britannicum.* In collections, collected works of single authors, and individual books, he consulted all the major authorities of the long alchemical tradition: Morien, Rosinus, the *Turba philosophorum,* the *Scala,* the *Rosary,* Ripley, Michael Maier, Sendivogius, Eirenaeus Philalethes, and many others it would be pointless to list exhaustively. As he read, he developed criteria of judgment such that, for example, he canceled one passage of notes with a curt dismissal: "I believe that this author is in no way adept."[13] In the opinion of Professor Dobbs, Newton probed "the whole vast literature of the older [i.e., pre-seventeenth-century] alchemy as it has never been probed before and since."[14] A similar assessment of his reading in seventeenth-century alchemists from Sendivogius and Michael Maier to Eirenaeus Philalethes, Theodore Mundanus, and Didier does not seem excessive. Eventually he compiled a massive "Index chemicus," the likes of which alchemy has never seen, to guide him to relevant discussions—over 100 pages crammed with 879 separate headings and approximately 5,000 page references to more than 150 different works.[15] At the same time he began to assemble what must have been one of the great collections, in his day, of alchemical works, so that at his death, nearly thirty years after he had ceased to buy alchemical literature, alchemy still constituted more than 10 percent of his library.[16]

One interesting feature of Newton's alchemical papers,

and one that helps to illuminate his interest in the art, is the appearance among them of copies, in Newton's own hand, of unpublished treatises. Some of them would later see publication. Thus he made extensive notes on Philalethes's *Ripley Reviv'd* about ten years before it appeared in print and copied out a version of his "Exposition upon Sir George Ripley's Epistle to King Edward IV" that differs from the published one.[17] Over a period of nearly thirty years, he appears to have had access to manuscripts that remain unpublished to this day: for example, an anonymous "Sendivogius Explained" and John DeMonte-Snyders's "Metamorphosis of the Planets."[18] A sheaf of unpublished treatises, in at least four different hands, among his papers and his own copies elsewhere of five of the treatises suggest what appears to me as the only plausible interpretation of these papers.[19] Someone lent him the collection to study and copy, and in this case, for reasons we cannot possibly know, he never returned the originals. Similarly, a treatise named "Manna," which is not in his hand, concludes with two pages of variant readings added by Newton together with the information that they were "collected out of a M.S. communicated to Mr F. by W. S. 1670, & by Mr F. to me 1675."[20] I do not see how to account for these copies of unpublished papers without admitting that Newton was in touch with the largely clandestine circle of English alchemists from whom he received manuscripts to copy and to whom, quite possibly, he himself communicated others. In 1683 one Fran. Meheux wrote to him about the progress of some unnamed third man in alchemical experimentation. In 1696, scarcely two weeks before his appointment as warden to oversee His Majesty's coinage in gold and silver, Newton received a visit from a Londoner who was a friend of Boyle and of Dr. Dickinson (a well-known alchemist of the day) who stayed for two days to discuss the work.[21] Mr. F., who lent copies of "Manna," was probably Ezekiel Foxcroft, a fellow of King's College.[22] W. S., Meheux, and the Londoner have all the solidity of shadows at this distance in time, but Newton knew them as sources of information on alchemy.

Newton did more than read. Almost from the beginning he experimented as well. When he moved into the chamber beside the great gate of Trinity in 1673, he set up a laboratory in the garden outside, and there he continued to experiment for more than twenty years.[23] At first glance, nothing could look less alchemical than his laboratory notes. They described severely quantitative experiments with specific substances, even if we cannot always identify the substances Newton's symbols represented; frequently, for example, he systematically varied the amount of a single ingredient (measured by weight) in order to determine the ideal proportions in a given compound.[24] Nevertheless, Professor Dobbs has succeeded in correlating some of the early experiments with the alchemical manuscripts and

has shown that two substances he learned to produce, the star regulus of antimony and the net, were forms of the alchemical hermaphrodite, in which the sulfuric seed of iron (or Mars) was planted in a mercuric matrix, of antimony in the one case, of copper (or Venus) in the other.[25] Hence it appears impossible to avoid the conclusion that the early experiments were alchemical. No one has yet unraveled the later experiments, but it seems suggestive at least that Newton used materials such as the net and the oak, names drawn from the imagery of alchemy that appeared in his alchemical papers, and that he sometimes interrupted his notes with interpretive interjections couched in the imagery of alchemy. "I understood the trident." "I saw sophic sal ammoniac." "I made Jupiter fly on his eagle."[26]

The experimental notes aside, Newton's alchemical papers are sometimes said to consist solely of reading notes. This is simply incorrect. Indeed, the concept of reading notes is itself less clear than one might think. Although some papers are certainly that, others reveal a typically Newtonian effort to organize information, to bind various authorities together into a systematic statement of the art. Thus one early paper drew up a list of forty-seven axioms with references to the authors on whom they were based.[27] He began to correlate the varied imagery he met.

> Concerning Magnesia or the green Lion [he wrote in a list of "Notae" which also treated other terms]. It is called prometheus & the Chameleon. Also Androgyne, and virgin verdant earth in which the Sun has never cast its rays although he is its father and the moon its mother: Also common mercury, dew of heaven which makes the earth fertile, nitre of the wise . . . It is the Saturnine stone.[28]

Some passages of this sort listed as many as fifty different images.[29] In a later paper, Newton distilled the work down to seven aphorisms. "This process," he stated, "I take to be ye work of the best authors, Hermes, Turba, Morien, Artephius, Abraham ye Jew & Flammel, Scala, Ripley, Maier, the great Rosary, Charnock, Trevisan. Philaletha. Despagnet."[30] He collected at least two sets of "Notable Opinions,"[31] and in his most extensive effort at synthesis he set out to compile a treatise in nine "works," for separate parts of which he left in one case seven, in another five, drafts.[32] Newton put these compilations together entirely from the writings of others. Nevertheless, to describe them as mere "reading notes" does not begin to suffice.

And finally, he also composed alchemical treatises himself. Professor Dobbs identified a paper from the late 1670s, entitled **"Clavis,"** as Newton's own composition.[33] Although I find her argument, based on the paper's apparent use of Newton's own experimental results, wholly convincing, the identification has been challenged.[34] No one, I think, could challenge his authorship of another from the same period, entitled **"Separatio elementorum,"** or his latter commentary on the "**Tabula smaragdina**."[35] Both papers are filled with emendations, Newton's typical habit with his own writing but one he never exercised on the writings of others. Undoubtedly his most important composition was an essay he finally called **"Praxis,"** apparently composed in the summer of 1693.[36] It also is undoubtedly his own. We have four successive drafts of it,[37] and it cited Fatio's letter to Newton of May 1693.[38] At its climax, **"Praxis"** described a process that achieved multiplication, the ultimate goal of alchemy, in which the active essence of gold is set free to function.

> Thus you may multiply each stone [alchemical ferment] 4 times & no more for they will then become oyles shining in ye dark and fit for magicall uses. You may ferment it w^{th} . . . [gold] by keeping them in fusion for a day, & then project upon metalls. This is ye multiplication in quality. You may multiply it in quantity by the mercuries of wch you made it at first, amalgaming ye stone wth y^e . . . [mercury] of 3 or more eagles [?] and adding their weight of ye water, & if you designe it for metalls you may melt every time 3 parts of [gold] wth one of ye stone. Every multiplication will encreas it's vertue ten times &, if you use y^e [mercury] of ye 2^d or 3^d rotation w^{th}out ye spirit, perhaps a thousand times. Thus you may multiply to infinity.[39]

When Newton wrote this passage, he was in the state of acute tension that led to his breakdown in September 1693, and we must accordingly use it with caution. On grounds of scientific opinion, I cannot believe that Newton achieved multiplication. Because of his personal state when he wrote it, the passage does not convince me that he thought he had done so. I do accept it as valuable evidence of the extent of his immersion in the world of alchemy.

As another measure of the extent of his immersion, I propose the sheer quantity of the alchemical papers. Indications of their extent have appeared throughout my discussion, but we all know how readily one can contrive to inflate the impression of a small number of papers. Hence it has seemed important to me to arrive at a quantitative measure of these manuscripts by counting pages and words per page. There would be no point in estimating in a similar way the number of words Newton devoted to mathematics or dynamics or even theology, enterprises his commitment to which no one questions. The estimate is, of course, very crude; implicitly it equates the effort devoted to copying a page of a treatise with the effort given to composing a page of his own or to filling a page with experimental notes. Such a count serves only two purposes. It gives substance to the claim that the papers are very extensive, and when it is divided into chronological periods, it gives a rough measure of the intensity of his involvement with alchemy at different times. Restricting

myself for the moment to the first, I note that Newton left behind about 1,200,000 words on alchemy. I see no way to dismiss it as an occasional interest. I think the other evidence I have brought forward indicates beyond reasonable doubt that the interest was sympathetic, the interest of a man who took the art seriously.

Meanwhile, alchemy did not exhaust the whole of Newton's intellectual life. As I suggested, he had found natural philosophy several years earlier. Specifically, about 1664, he had found the new natural philosophy that the seventeenth century called the mechanical philosophy, and in a notebook he recorded his initial contact with it under the heading "**Quaestiones quaedam philosophicae**."[40] For about three years, as his earlier notes indicate, the university had been feeding him on the dry bones of an Aristotelian philosophy desiccated beyond any hope of renewal. The **"Quaestiones quaedam"** recorded a conversion experience, not unlike the revelation we find in the pages of Galileo and Descartes, that natural philosophy could be done in a different way. Under his title Newton later returned to record a slogan: "Amicus Plato amicus Aristoteles magis amica veritas." He had discovered the world of the mechanical philosophy, his new friend Truth, for whom he brusquely abandoned Plato and Aristotle.

If he never returned to the old academic philosophy, he did not long remain entirely happy with his new friend either. About 1668 or 1669 he started a treatise with the title *De gravitatione et equipondio fluidorum.*[41] The Introduction, which was a discussion of the general questions of space, time, body, and motion, together with a couple of propositions, was all he completed. Only four or five years earlier, Descartes had functioned as the guide who led Newton into the new world of the mechanical philosophy. Nevertheless, *De gravitatione* was not merely an anti-Cartesian treatise; it was a violently anti-Cartesian one. The focus of his objection was the charge of atheism. Years later Newton would tell John Craig that "the reason of his showing the errors of Cartes's philosophy, was because he thought it was made on purpose to be the foundation of infidelity."[42] Although Newton showed more sympathy, both in *De gravitatione* and elsewhere, for Gassendi's alternative mechanical system, the weight of his objection to Descartes, that he set up the material world as an autonomous order, did not fall exclusively on the Cartesian version of the mechanical philosophy. Nor did Newton confine himself to hurling the general charge of atheism. The title of the piece suggested a work on fluid mechanics, and his conflict with Descartes took the form of an argument on natural philosophy and on its subtopic, motion. From the time of the composition of *De gravitatione,* Newton regarded the mechanical philosophy with ambiguous feelings. He never made the slightest move to return to academic Aristotelianism, which remained for him as dead as dead could be. At the same time, he never ceased to believe that the mechanical philosophy of nature in its received form required fundamental revision. I do not find it entirely accidental that the composition of *De gravitatione* fell very close to the first recorded manifestations of Newton's interest in alchemy, which embodied a view of nature that gave primacy to spiritual agents.

The ambiguity of his stance appeared in the **"Hypothesis of Light"** which he sent to the Royal Society in 1675.[43] With its universally diffused ether that he employed in mechanistic explanations of the reflection and refraction of light and the descent of heavy bodies toward the earth, the **"Hypothesis"** reads easily as a mechanical system of nature. Other aspects of it fit that mold less readily. Indeed, it has been described as an alchemical cosmology, and one can see why.

> For nature is a perpetuall circulatory worker [Newton asserted], generating fluids out of solids, and solids out of fluids, fixed things out of volatile, & volatile out of fixed, subtile out of gross, & gross out of subtile, Some things to ascend & make the upper terrestriall juices, Rivers and the Atmosphere; & by consequence others to descend for a Requitall to the former.[44]

He ascribed a "principle of motion" to the corpuscles of light, and, in regard to chemical phenomena, he spoke of a "secret principle of unsociablenes," which kept certain substances from mixing together.[45] He specifically denied that the latter could be explained solely by the sizes of particles and pores, as mechanical philosophers tended to do.

About three years later, early in 1679, Newton wrote a long letter to Robert Boyle which was in some ways similar to the **"Hypothesis of Light."**[46] In discussing the cause of solubility, he again introduced his "secret principle in nature by wch liquors are sociable to some things & unsociable to others," and again he denied that the mere sizes of pores and particles could explain it. The question of volatility further drew upon the principle of unsociability, while the tendency of bodies to recede from each other gave the discussion a veneer of mechanical respectability by relating the causes of both phenomena to a universal ether. An unfinished treatise, *De aere et aethere*, from about this time appears to have been an effort to put the content of the letter to Boyle into a systematic form.[47] It began with a consideration of the tendency of air to expand and to avoid bodies, proceeded to note that in general bodies avoid each other, and concluded that air is composed of particles of bodies "torn away from contact, and repelling each other with a certain large force." Once again he apparently set out to explain the repulsion by means of an ether, but he abandoned the effort after only a few lines and never returned to it. Well he might have abandoned it, for his principle of unsocia-

bility and related ideas were moving steadily away from orthodox mechanical philosophy. It cannot have been long after *De aere et aethere* when Newton performed a carefully designed experiment with a pendulum, described in the *Principia,* that encouraged him to abandon belief in the very existence of an ether.[48] An ether, the invisible medium called upon as a causal agent for every apparently nonmechanical phenomenon, was the sine qua non of a workable mechanical philosophy of nature.

When we consider his constant probing of the mechanical philosophy over a period of nearly two decades, we are not surprised that Newton's masterpiece, the *Principia,* based celestial dynamics on a concept no ordinary mechanical philosopher would have considered, a principle of universal attraction. As we now know, Newton intended at one point to go further. In a drafted **"Conclusio,"** he proposed a general revision, based on forces that act at a distance, of all natural philosophy. Nature, he noted, is simple and conformable to itself.

> Whatever reasoning holds for greater motions, should hold for lesser ones as well. The former depend upon the greater attractive forces of larger bodies, and I suspect that the latter depend upon the lesser forces, as yet unobserved, of insensible particles. For, from the forces of gravity, of magnetism and of electricity it is manifest that there are various kinds of natural forces, and that there may be still more kinds is not to be rashly denied. It is very well known that greater bodies act mutually upon each other by those forces, and I do not clearly see why lesser ones should not act on one another by similar forces.[49]

Newton was well aware that he was proposing a major philosophic innovation, and he tried to shield himself from expected criticism. When, in Book I, he came to Section XI and the mutual attraction of bodies, which suggested a more concrete notion of force than earlier abstract propositions had implied, he assured his readers that the demonstrations were purely mathematical. "I here use the word *attraction* in general for any endeavor whatever, made by bodies to approach to each other," he asserted, "whether that endeavor arise from the action of the bodies themselves, as tending to each other or agitating each other by spirits emitted; or whether it arises from the action of the ether or of the air, or of any medium whatever, whether corporeal or incorporeal, in any manner impelling bodies placed therein towards each other."[50] Similarly, some years later, in Query 31, he would declare once more that attractions could be performed by impulses.[51] He went on there to argue for the general necessity of "active Principles" since a purely mechanical universe would run down, and again he attempted to blunt expected objections. "These Principles I consider, not as occult Qualities, supposed to result from the specifick Forms of Things, but as general Laws of Nature, by which the Things themselves are form'd; their Truth appearing to us by Phaenomena, though their Causes be not yet discover'd. For these are manifest Qualities, and their Causes only are occult."[52] Since Book II of the *Principia* had demonstrated both the impossibility that the heavens can be filled with a material medium and the impossibility that a mechanical system can sustain itself without the constant addition of new motion, demonstrations he sought only to strengthen in subsequent editions, Newton had also made it evident to discerning readers that his vision of reality was even farther removed from orthodox mechanical philosophy than the mere concept of action at a distance implied.

Newton was not the only one who recognized that he was proposing a fundamental reordering of natural philosophy. For a generation, mechanical philosophers on the Continent, though they recognized the mathematical power of Newton's demonstrations, refused to have truck with a concept of attraction. Leibniz hinted that it was a return to the "enthusiastic philosophy" of Robert Fludd.[53] He was by no means alone, and more than one mechanical philosopher applied to it the very pejorative, "occult," that Newton had sought to avoid. For their part, Newtonians eventually seized on the concept of forces at a distance as the central characteristic of a new approach to the whole of natural philosophy. Not only British followers, such as Cotes, Pemberton, and McLauren, but early Continental Newtonians, such as Voltaire, `sGravesande, and Algarotti, all grasped attractions and repulsions, not as mathematical abstractions, but as forces that really exist, and treated them as the foundation on which both a different picture of nature and a different form of scientific investigation rested. By the middle of the eighteenth century, there was no one who mattered left to argue with them.

My third premise is the close chronological correlation between the appearance of the Newtonian concept of force and his interest in alchemy. I shall assume that any further discussion of the chronology of the concept of force, which emerged fully with the *Principia,* is unnecessary. Newton's concern with alchemy, however, has not been public knowledge. In describing the papers, I mentioned some dates. Let me be explicit that for most of the papers dating rests solely on the hand in which they were written. Hence a degree of imprecision about their chronology appears unavoidable. The imprecision is less than the uninitiated might think, however. Newton's hand developed through a number of distinctive phases. To me it seems virtually impossible, for example, to confuse the tiny perpendicular hand of the 1660s with the large, sloping, careless hand of the 1690s or the medium-sized but shaky and crabbed hand of the old man. In a number of cases, some of which I mentioned, dates internal to the

manuscripts support evidence drawn from the hand. The laboratory notes are sprinkled with dates that extend from 1678 to 1696. It is relevant to note that Newton performed one set of experiments in the spring of 1686, when the *Principia* was still under composition. Correspondence, such as the letter from Meheux and the exchange with Locke, inevitably carries dates, and Newton dated his memorandum about the Londoner who stayed two days discussing the work. His citation of Fatio's letter of May 1693 establishes the time before which **"Praxis"** could not have been written. In all, I feel complete confidence about the general period as long as one does not insist on precise years. Newton began serious study of alchemy in the late 1660s. I know of nothing that extends it back into his undergraduate career. Once aroused, his interest continued for nearly thirty years, well into the 1690s. Allow me to note that the alchemical papers come from the years of Newton's intellectual maturity, from the very time when, with his capacity as its highest pitch, he produced the book that has made him immortal. There are a few scraps about alchemy on papers associated with his early years at the Mint, but the manuscripts strongly imply that his active involvement with the art ended near the time when he moved to London.

My central question is implicit in the three premises of my argument. Given Newton's interest in alchemy, given his concept of forces that act between particles, and given the fact that the concept of forces appeared during the period when he was immersed in alchemy, can we establish a connection between the two? In my own view, my question is equivalent to asking whether Newton's alchemy was an activity isolated from the rest of his natural philosophy or whether it exerted an influence on his work in physics. Thus the question also implicitly asks if the structure of modern science embodies concepts that trace their lineage in part to alchemy.

In attempting to answer the question, we must plunge into the content of the alchemical papers. One of the earliest of them, a paper of Newton's own composition though it is not a single connected essay, which is known as **"The Vegetation of Metals"** from a phrase in the opening lines, probed the distinction between vegetation and purely mechanical changes. Rearrangements of particles effect mechanical changes; vegetation brings about more profound alterations.

> There is therefore besides ye sensible changes wrough in ye textures of ye grosser matter a more subtile secret & noble way of working in all vegetation which makes its products distinct from all others & ye immediate seate of thes operations is not ye whole bulk of matter, but rather an exceeding subtile & inimaginably small portion of matter diffused through the masse wch if it were seperated there would remain but a dead & inactive earth.[54]

As the concept of the vegetation of metals implies, Newton did not limit vegetation to the realm of plants, but treated it as a process present throughout nature. He sometimes called the principle of vegetable action a spirit, which he described as a "Powerfull agent"; sometimes he referred to it, in the plural, as seeds or seminal virtues, which are nature's "only agents, her fire, her soule, her life."[55] That is, what he found in the world of alchemy was the conviction that nature cannot be reduced to the arrangement of inert particles of matter. Nature contains foci of activity, agents whose spontaneous working produces results that cannot be accounted for by the mechanical philosophy's only category of explanation: particles of matter in motion.

The ultimate active agent of nature is what alchemists called the philosophers' stone, the goal of their search. They applied to it images of all sorts, all of them embodying a concept of activity that contrasted with the passivity of matter in the mechanical philosophy. Flammel called it "a most puissant invincible king"; Philalethes, the "miracle of the world" and "the subject of wonders." The author of *Elucidarius* proclaimed that "it is impossible to express [its] infinite virtues."[56] Sometimes activity took on the form of attraction, which was likened to a magnet. Whereas mechanical philosophers explained magnetic attraction away by imagining whirlpools of invisible particles, alchemists embraced it as a visible image of nature's mode of operation. "They call lead a magnet," Newton learned from Sendivogius, "because its mercury attracts the seed of Antimony as the magnet attracts the Chalybs." He also noted that "our water" is drawn out of lead "by the force of our Chalybs which is found in the belly of Ares [i.e., iron]."[57]

His laboratory experience constantly reinforced the message of the alchemical literature. Thus it is relevant to note the steady appearance of active verbs in his experimental notes. When he added spelter to a solution of aqua fortis and sal ammoniac, "yᵉ menstruum [solvent] wrought upon yᵉ spelter [zinc] continually till it had dissolved it." A solution often "fell a working wᵗʰ a sudden violent fermentation." The spirit, he sometimes noted, "draws" or "extracts" the salts of metals, a usage similar to Sendivogius's magnetic image. When one substance combined with another, it "laid hold" on it; if the two sublimed, one "carried up" the other; if they failed to sublime, one "held" the other "down."[58] It citing these verbs, I seek only to record Newton's immediate perceptions of spontaneous activity in many chemical reactions. The alchemical concept of active agents directly expressed such perceptions. Mechanical philosophers argued that the perceptions were illusions and that the reality behind them consisted solely of inert particles in motion. One cannot infer a choice between two philosophies of nature from the verbs in Newton's experimental notes. They do suggest, however, how he would have been able to understand the images alchemy

employed because he too had witnessed the activity the images expressed.

As he was completing the *Principia* in 1686, Newton composed a **"Conclusio,"** from which I have already quoted, an essay that expanded the message of the book beyond universal gravitation into a manifesto of a new philosophy of nature based on forces that act at a distance. In the end he suppressed the **"Conclusio,"** but twenty years later he expanded it into what we know as Query 31. Newton drew upon a number of sources for his assertion that a wide range of forces exists in nature—phenomena such as the expansion of gases, capillary action, surface tension, and the cohesion of bodies, which had seized his attention already in his undergraduate **"Quaestiones"** and had appeared in later speculations, such as the **"Hypothesis of Light,"** that probed the limits of the mechanical philosophy. Above all, however, he drew upon chemical phenomena.

> Hitherto I have explained the System of this visible world [the **"Conclusio"** began], as far as concerns the greater motions which can easily be detected. There are however innumerable other local motions which on account of the minuteness of the moving particles cannot be detected, such as the motions of the particles in hot bodies, in fermenting bodies, in putrescent bodies, in growing bodies, in the organs of sensation and so forth. If any one shall have the good fortune to discover all these, I might almost say that he will have laid bare the whole nature of bodies so far as the mechanical causes of things are concerned.[59]

The chemical reactions that impressed Newton fell into two general types. Reactions that produce heat formed one of them.

> If spirit of vitriol (which consists of common water and an acid spirit) be mixed with Sal Alkali or with some suitable metallic powder, at once commotion and violent ebullition occur. And a great heat is often generated in such operations. That motion and the heat thence produced argue that there is a vehement rushing together of the acid particles and the other particles, whether metallic or of Sal Alkali; and the rushing together of the particles with violence could not happen unless the particles begin to approach one another before they touch one another . . . So also spirit of nitre (which is composed of water and an acid Spirit) violently unites with salt of tartar; then, although the spirit by itself can be distilled in a gently heated bath, nevertheless it cannot be separated from the salt of tartar except by a vehement fire.

The other type of reaction that he called upon displays selective affinities analogous to his secret principle of sociability and unsociability. Thus he argued that the ability of salt of tartar to precipitate bodies dissolved in acids stems from "the stronger attraction by which the salt of tartar draws those acid spirits from the dissolved bodies to itself. For if the spirit does not suffice to retain them both, it will cohere with that which attracts more strongly."[60]

Newton did not discover the reactions cited here. He could have found them all in the writings of mechanical chemists such as Boyle, with which he was certainly familiar. In Boyle, however, he could not have found the conclusion he derived from them: that particles of matter attract and repel each other. For that matter, he could not have found the conclusion, in the form stated above, in alchemical literature either. What he could have found there, as I have indicated, was a concept of active principles that bears a close resemblance to the manner in which Newton frequently expressed his concept of forces. It is also of some importance to my argument to insist that, without exception, all the chemical phenomena cited in the **"Conclusio"** had appeared in Newton's experimental notes during the previous decade.

It is further relevant to note that Newton composed a paper, **"De natura acidorum,"** in which we can observe the transition from the alchemical concept of active principle to the Newtonian concept of attraction expressed in his own words. In Newton's alchemy, philosophic sulfur, the male principle, was the ultimate causal agent in nature. **"De natura acidorum"** argued that the activity of sulfur, perhaps common sulfur in this case, springs from the acid it conceals. "For what attracts and is attracted strongly, we call acid." Under the images of dragons and serpents that devoured uncounted kings and queens, acids were also active in the world of alchemy. The particles of acids, Newton asserted in a statement that grasps that world in one embrace with his own concept of force, "are endowed with a great attractive force and in this force their activity consists by which they dissolve bodies and affect and stimulate the organs of the senses."[61]

Newton composed **"De natura acidorum"** during the early 1690s, in the years immediately following the *Principia*. It was a period of almost manic intellectual activity in his life. Buoyed by the twin successes of the *Principia* and the Glorious Revolution, in which he had played a significant if minor role, he apparently set out to codify his philosophic legacy. He devoted extensive energy to revising the *Principia*. The book had taken shape, developing and expanding as Newton explored its topic, during a period of about thirty months that began in August 1684. There is every reason to think that he did not regard the form in which it appeared in 1687 as final. We have the manuscripts for important revisions both of the early demonstrations in Book I and of the opening propositions of Book III. The proposed new edition never saw publication in the form then planned, but the surviving manuscripts leave no doubt that Newton worked at it. The same years

saw intense mathematical endeavor, including the composition of a definitive exposition of his fluxional calculus. He began to write his *Opticks,* not the volume he published ten years later, but an *Opticks* in four books, which used optical phenomena to support the Newtonian natural philosophy based on forces between particles. Hence it seems to me a matter of major significance that during this period—in the years, I repeat, immediately following the *Principia*—Newton also invested an enormous effort in alchemy. I suggested before that one use of the quantitative measure of his alchemical papers was the establishment of a rough chronological index of the effort expanded. He wrote about half of the estimated 1,200,000 words on alchemy during the period of seven or eight years that followed the *Principia*. The mere existence of papers from that time cannot, of course, demonstrate a connection between alchemy and the Newtonian concept of force. To me, at least, the papers offer powerful evidence that Newton regarded his alchemical endeavors as a harmonious part of his total philosophical program.

I do not want my argument to be misunderstood. I am seeking the source of the Newtonian concept of forces of attraction and repulsion between particles of matter, the concept that fundamentally altered the prevailing philosophy of nature and ushered in the intellectual world of modern science. I am offering the argument that alchemy, Newton's involvement in which a vast corpus of papers establishes, offered him a stimulus to consider concepts beyond the bare ontology of the mechanical philosophy. It appears to me that the Newtonian concept of force embodies the enduring influence of alchemy upon his scientific thought. As I mentioned, Professor Cohen takes issue with the argument in his recent *Newtonian Revolution*. He presents an analysis of the *Principia*'s development that confines itself to the science of dynamics and its application to orbital motion and treats the concept of attraction as a conclusion that emerged solely from Newton's consideration of such problems. To the suggestion that alchemy influenced Newton, he replies that Newton repeatedly asserted that his success with gravitational attraction led him to consider the possibility of other forces between particles.[62] I wish to say two things in this respect. First, I do not know the assertions to which Professor Cohen alludes. I think he refers primarily to the statement, very similar to the one I quoted above from the **"Conclusio,"** that Newton inserted in the Preface to the *Principia*. What I find in it is an argument from the analogy of nature, not an autobiographical account of his discovery. Second, it appears to me that the technical problems of dynamics, which were of unavoidable importance to Newton's concept of force, can be separated from the conceptual issue with which I have concerned myself in this chapter. Indeed, I believe we have empirical evidence that they were separated in the seventeenth century. Next to Newton, there was no one alive better able to appreciate the technical problems of dynamics than Huygens, Leibniz, and Bernoulli. Each of them studied the *Principia* and appreciated the full extent of its achievement. Even with the book open before him, not one of the three ever admitted the possibility of attractions at a distance. It is my contention that Newton's readiness to consider the possibility derived from the influence of alchemy.

I am not discussing technical dynamics, in which Newton made enormous strides that are obviously related to his concept of force. I am talking rather about a conceptual innovation—an innovation, that is, in relation to the prevailing mechanical philosophy of nature. There are, I insist, strong arguments, summarized in this chapter, for tracing it in part to the influences of alchemy.

J. E. McGuire has recently advanced quite a different argument against the case for alchemy. In a number of articles, McGuire has traced the influence of the Cambridge Platonists on Newton. Why call upon alchemy, he asks, when we have Cambridge Platonism to supply a similar influence?[63] There are also two things I would say in reply to McGuire. First, I see no necessary opposition between us. I do not argue that alchemy exercised the sole influence on Newton. I take McGuire's articles to have demonstrated that Cambridge Platonism, in which one can find a concept of active principles, also influenced Newton. I see no reason why two influences could not operate in the same direction. I say, secondly, that whatever the influence of Cambridge Platonism, the alchemical papers remain. Indeed it is necessary to remark in this respect that for every page in Newton's papers of direct reference to More and Cudworth there are well over a hundred on alchemy. I cannot make those papers disappear.

To say as much is in no way to suggest that Newtonian science—and hence derivatively all of modern science—is a covert form of alchemy. I emphatically reject any attempt to distort my argument in that direction. Hence I must distinguish my position from Castillejo's. No doubt it oversimplifies his book to speak of an equation of Newtonian science with alchemy; but unless I completely misunderstand the work, that statement of his position is far more true than false. With Castillejo's conviction that we need to integrate Newton's alchemical activity into the rest of his intellectual life I am in obvious agreement; beyond that I cannot go. His argument appears to me to neglect the most important aspects of Newton's scientific endeavor—his mathematics, his quantitative science of dynamics, his experimental investigation of light—and to ignore as well the implications of its aftermath—the enormous growth of modern science, three centuries of experimental confirmation, and two centuries of practical confirmation through the successes (and even the

disasters) of scientific technology.

Far from equating Newtonian science with alchemy, I emphasize the extent to which Newton altered what he received. His success in practicing alchemy on alchemy itself may be the ultimate measure of its influence on him. If he derived his concept of force partly from the alchemical active principle, he also transformed it in fundamental ways. Above all, he quantified it, so that it could fit smoothly into the structure of his quantitative dynamics. There is no sense in which I deny the relevance of the technical problems internal to dynamics, which Professor Cohen analyzes so well. Newton may have found an idea of attraction in Sendivogius, but we cannot imagine Sendivogius writing the *Principia*. To that extent Newton transformed what he received.[64]

Hence Newton could see the final result of his work as the perfection of the mechanical philosophy rather than its denial. Physical nature remained for him what it had been for mechanical philosophers: particles of matter in notion. With the quantified concept of force, he called natural philosophy back from its preoccupation with imagining invisible mechanisms and gave decisive demonstration of the power exact mathematical description wields. Perhaps we can best say, using Professor Cohen's approach, that the Newtonian concept of force transformed natural philosophy into modern science. With only modest surprise, I note how close I see myself to Professor Hall for all our surface disagreements. For me also, Newton represents reason; his success in weaving a single fabric from a multiplicity of strands constitutes in my eyes one of the supreme exercises reason has known. We differ, if I understand it correctly, on my readiness to admit that a different standard of rationality in the seventeenth century may have encouraged Newton to open himself to the influence of a tradition that appears to us almost as the antithesis of reason.

Hence also I need to close by pointing as well to the final act in the drama. Newton did in the end turn away from alchemy. Every time I think seriously about Newton and alchemy this final act assumes greater significance. Alchemy formed an integral part of the intense intellectual activity of the early 1690s. The essay **"Praxis,"** composed in the summer of 1693, suggests that the breakdown of that year also had an alchemical dimension. Newton's interest in alchemy did not end suddenly at that moment; there were, for example, dated experimental notes that extended to 1696. Nevertheless, his intense involvement in the art did come to an end about then. A few scraps on alchemy can be dated to his early London years, but only a few. His library contained only three alchemical books published after 1700, two of them by William Y-Worth, presented to him by the author in 1702.[65] Alchemy was the one intellectual pursuit of Newton's Cambridge years that did not follow him to London. Am I wrong then in placing alchemy within the precincts of Newtonian rationality if in the end he turned away from it? **"Praxis,"** with its claim of successful multiplication, does seem to have moved beyond the realm of reason, but 1693 was an extraordinary year for Newton when everything ran over the edge. If that extravagant dream—or nightmare—ended in disillusionment, I suggest that the end of Newton's active involvement in alchemy marked his realization that he had in fact achieved a different success. With his quantified concept of force, he had extracted the essence of the art. Alchemy itself told him to reject the dross as dead and lifeless matter. The seed had found a fertile matrix where it has flourished ever since.

Notes

[1] *The Correspondence of Isaac Newton,* ed. H. W. Turnbull et al., 7 vols. (Cambridge, 1959-77), III, 192-3, 195, 215, 216, 217-19.

[2] Conduitt's memorandum of 31 August 1726; King's College, Cambridge, Keynes MS. 130.10, fol. 3^v.

[3] David Brewster, *Memoirs of the Life, Writings, and Discoveries of Sir Isaac Newton,* 2 vols. (Edinburgh, 1855), II, 371-6.

[4] Lord Keynes, "Newton the Man," in Royal Society, *Newton Tercentenary Celebrations* (Cambridge, 1947), pp. 27-34.

[5] B. J. T. Dobbs, *The Foundations of Newton's Alchemy: The Hunting of the Greene Lyon* (Cambridge, 1975), and "Newton's Copy of *Secrets Reveal'd* and the Regimen of the Work," *Ambix,* 26 (1979), pp. 145-69. Professor Dobbs is presently completing a second book that will extend her study into the alchemical manuscripts that belonged to a later period in Newton's life. As far as I know, Karin Figala's dissertation has, regrettably, not been published; see Karin Figala, "Die 'Kompositionshierarchie' der Materie: Newton's quantitative Theorie und Interpretation der qualitativen Alchemie," unpublished Habilitationsschrift, Technischen Universität, Munich. She presented a brief view of her work in "Newton as Alchemist," *History of Science,* 15 (1977), pp. 102-37, an essay-review of Professor Dobbs's book.

[6] Brewster, II, 375.

[7] I. Bernard Cohen, *The Newtonian Revolution* (Cambridge, 1980). The specific passage to which I refer is on p. 10.

[8] I quote, with Professor Hall's generous permission, from a private letter to me about my recent biography of Newton.

[9] David Castillejo, *The Expanding Force in Newton's Cosmos* (Madrid, 1981).

[10] Bodleian Library, Oxford, MS. Don.b.15.

[11] Accounts in the notebook in the Fitzwilliam Museum, Cambridge.

[12] Manuscript in the Countway Medical Library, Harvard University, item 3, fol. 10^v.

[13] Jewish National and University Library, Yahuda MS. 259, no. 9.

[14] Dobbs, *Foundations,* p. 88.

[15] Keynes MS. 30. See my analysis of its content: "Isaac Newton's Index Chemicus," *Ambix,* 22 (1975), pp. 174-85.

[16] John Harrison, *The Library of Isaac Newton* (Cambridge, 1978).

[17] Keynes MSS. 51 and 52.

[18] Keynes MS. 55 and a manuscript in the Yale Medical Library. Other examples are Keynes MSS. 22, 24, 31, 33, 39, 50, 58 (part only), 62, 65, and 66.

[19] The sheaf is Keynes MS. 67; the notes are Keynes MS. 62.

[20] Keynes MS. 33.

[21] Newton recorded the visit in two largely identical memoranda: Keynes MS. 26 (published in *Correspondence,* IV, 196-8) and MS. 1075-3 in the Joseph Halle Schaffner Collection, University of Chicago Library.

[22] Professor Dobbs so identified him, convincingly: *Foundations,* p. 112.

[23] Early experiments are recorded in Cambridge University Library, Add. MS. 3975, pp. 81-4. Later ones, frequently dated and extending from 1678 to 1696, are found in Add. MSS. 3973 and 3975, pp. 101-58, 267-83. The first examination of Newton's records of his chemical experiments, which remains an indispensable guide to them, is A. R. Hall and Marie Boas [Hall], "Newton's Chemical Experiments," *Archives internationales d'histoire des sciences,* 11 (1958), pp. 113-52.

[24] See, for example, Add. MSS. 3973, fols. 5^v-6, 13-13^v, and 3975, p. 143.

[25] Dobbs, *Foundations,* pp. 146-63.

[26] Add. MSS. 3975, p. 121; 3973, fol. 17; 3975, p. 149.

[27] Countway MS., item 4.

[28] Ibid., item 3, fol. 7.

[29] While similar passages abound, the "Index chemicus" (Keynes MS. 30) is especially rich in them.

[30] Keynes MS. 49, fol. 1.

[31] Keynes MSS. 38 and 56. Keynes MS. 57, which has no title, is a similar compilation.

[32] They are found in Keynes MSS. 40 and 41; Babson College Library, Babson MS. 417; and Dibner Collection, Smithsonian Institution Libraries, Burndy MS. 17.

[33] Dobbs, *Foundations,* pp. 251-5.

[34] Figala, "Newton as Alchemist," p. 107; D. T. Whiteside, "From his Claw the Greene Lyon," *Isis,* 68 (1977), p. 118.

[35] Burndy MS. 10 and Keynes MS. 28.

[36] Babson MS. 420.

[37] The first two, under different names, in Keynes MSS. 21 and 53.

[38] *Correspondence* III, 265-7.

[39] Babson MS. 420, p. 18ᵃ. In the final draft of this passage (p. 17), Newton toned it down somewhat.

[40] Add. MS. 3996, fols. 88-135.

[41] Add. MS. 4003. Published in A. R. Hall and M. B. Hall, *Unpublished Scientific Papers of Isaac Newton* (Cambridge, 1962), pp. 90-121; English trans., pp. 121-56.

[42] Keynes MS. 132.

[43] *Correspondence,* I, 362-86.

[44] Ibid., I, 365-6.

[45] Ibid., I, 368-70.

[46] Ibid., II, 288-95.

[47] Published in Hall and Hall, *Unpublished Papers,* pp. 214-20; English trans., pp. 220-8.

[48] *Principia,* Motte-Cajori trans. (Berkeley, 1934), p. 325. See ed. 1, p. 353, for two important concluding sentences Newton omitted from the second and subsequent editions.

[49] Hall and Hall, *Unpublished Papers,* p. 333.

[50] *Principia,* pp. 164, 192.

[51] *Opticks,* based on 4th ed. (New York, 1952), p. 376.

[52] Ibid., p. 401.

[53] In an "anonymous" review of John Freind's chemical lectures, *Acta eruditorum* (September 1710), p. 412.

[54] Burndy MS. 16, fol. 6ᵛ.

[55] Ibid., fols. 5-5ᵛ.

[56] I cite from Newton's notes: Keynes MSS. 40, fols. 20, 19ᵛ; 41, fol. 15ᵛ; Babson MS. 417, p. 35.

[57] Keynes MS. 19, fols. 1, 3.

[58] Add. MSS. 3973, fol. 42; 3975, pp. 281, 104-5; 3973, fols. 13, 21; 3975, pp. 108-9.

[59] Hall and Hall, *Unpublished Papers,* p. 333.

[60] Ibid., pp. 333-5.

[61] *Correspondence,* III, 209-12.

[62] See the reference above, note 7, and a fuller discussion in an article published after the paper on which this chapter is based was presented: I. B. Cohen, "The *Principia,* Universal Gravitation, and the 'Newtonian Style,' in Relation to the Newtonian Revolution in Science," in *Contemporary Newtonian Research,* ed. Zev Bechler (Dordrecht, 1982), pp. 67-74.

[63] J. E. McGuire, "Neoplatonism and Active Principles: Newton and the *Corpus Hermeticum,*" in Robert S. Westman and J. E. McGuire, *Hermeticism and the Scientific Revolution* (Los Angeles, 1977).

[64] My inability to write this paragraph without Professor Cohen's concept of transformation must be significant.

[65] Harrison, *Library,* items 1138, 1302, 1644.

R. W. Home (essay date 1985)

SOURCE: "Force, Electricity, and the Powers of Living Matter in Newton's Mature Philosophy of Nature," in *Religion, Science, and Worldview: Essays in Honor of Richard S. Westfall,* edited by Margaret J. Osler and Paul Lawrence Farber, Cambridge University Press, 1985, pp. 95-117.

[*In the essay below, Home focuses on the concept of force as a component in Newton's theories of natural phenomena.*]

One of Newton's most widely quoted methodological pronouncements appears in the preface he prepared for the first (1687) edition of his *Principia*. "The whole burden of philosophy seems to consist in this," Newton there wrote: "from the phenomena of motions to investigate the forces of nature, and then from these forces to demonstrate the other phenomena."[1] He made the same point in his other great work, his *Opticks,* towards the end of the long, final Query that he added to the Latin edition published in 1706:

> To tell us that every Species of Things is endow'd with an occult specifick Quality by which it acts and produces manifest Effects, is to tell us nothing: But to derive two or three general Principles of Motion from Phaenomena, and afterwards to tell us how the Properties and Actions of all corporeal Things follow from those manifest Principles, would be a very great step in Philosophy, though the Causes of those Principles were not yet discover'd.[2]

The procedure thus outlined has been seen as encapsulating the very essence of the "Newtonian revolution" in science. Though Newton's world was composed, like that of mechanical philosophers such as Descartes and Gassendi, of material corpuscles in motion, no longer was Newton's science constrained, as the earlier mechanical philosophy had been, to reducing all natural phenomena to empirically inaccessible, and hence merely imagined, motions and impacts of particles. On the contrary, as the passages just quoted reveal, Newton admitted a further explanatory principle into his science, namely force. For Newton, armed as he was with a clearly understood principle of inertia, force became that which changed (or tended to change) the motions of bodies; individual forces came to be measured in terms of the changes of motion they produced; and the chief object of science became the discovery of the various forces acting in the world.[3] As Newton himself demonstrated so convincingly in *Principia* with respect to gravity, such forces were at least in some cases empirically determinable in a way that corpuscular mechanisms were not. Elsewhere in *Principia,* and even more so in *Opticks,* Newton held out the hope that many other kinds of force might eventually become equally as well characterized as gravity now was.

At least as important, in the eyes of many Newtonian scholars, is the fact that, in Newton's hands, "force" became a quantifiable concept. His approach thus held out the prospect of a truly mathematical physics in which various natural effects would be shown to follow in a rigorously demonstrative and quantitatively exact manner from mathematically expressed force laws. This is, of course, what Newton himself achieved in *Principia* in relation to gravity. Though success on a similar scale in other areas of physical inquiry proved elusive, Newton, by focusing on the concept of force,

had dramatically enlarged man's expectations regarding the degree of precision possible in science.

On this much, historians of science are generally agreed. In other respects, however, and especially on the question of what Newton's real attitude was to the various forces he invoked, opinion is divided. Were passages such as those quoted above merely methodological in import, or did they carry with them, as well, an ontological commitment on Newton's part? In other words, when Newton so ostentatiously refrained from offering mechanical explanations of the kind demanded by his critics for the forces of which he wrote, did he in fact do so not only because he believed that such explanations were unnecessary within the context of his inquiry, but also because he believed that these forces had a real existence of their own as true actions at a distance, independent of all mechanical explanation?

Westfall is one of those who has argued most strongly for the latter view. More than this, he has offered a reconstruction of the development of Newton's thought from which such an attitude on Newton's part toward his forces emerges as a natural consequence.[4]

Newton, Westfall has shown, was in his early years profoundly influenced in his thinking about the physical world by the ideas of the seventeenth-century mechanical philosophers—of men such as Descartes, Gassendi, Gassendi's English mouthpiece Walter Charleton, and Robert Boyle.[5] In line with this, we find Newton as an undergraduate embracing (though with a hint of occasional reservations perhaps inspired by Henry More) the fundamental credo of the mechanical philosophy, the reducibility of natural events to the motions and impacts of particles of matter. Similarly, a decade and more later, we find him trying to account for a wide range of natural phenomena in typically mechanistic style in terms of interactions between particles of matter and an all-encompassing material aether (or aethers).[6]

It is now, however, generally recognized that by the early 1680s, Newton had abandoned his former belief in a universal dense aether and had begun to speak instead in what we now see as characteristically "Newtonian" style of forces acting between particles at a distance.[7] Westfall claims to have found an explanation for this change of outlook on Newton's part in the alchemical investigations that engaged so much of Newton's attention at this period. In alchemy, Westfall has argued, Newton found an idea "that refused to be reconciled with the mechanical philosophy. Where that philosophy insisted on the inertness of matter, such that mechanical necessity alone determines its motion, alchemy asserted the existence of active principles in matter as the primary agents of natural phenomena."[8] Westfall finds hints of the idea even in the generally mechanistic **"Hypothesis explaining the Properties** of Light" of 1675, for example in Newton's willingness to ascribe the immiscibility of oil and water to "some secret principle of unsociablenes" between them. However, he dates the full-blown transformation in Newton's thinking to a few years later when, armed with this insight drawn from alchemy, Newton turned anew to the analysis of the planetary motions:

> As it appears to me, Newton's philosophy of nature underwent a profound conversion in 1679-80 under the combined influence of alchemy and the cosmic problem of orbital mechanics, two unlikely partners which made common cause on the issue of action at a distance. . . . Henceforth, the ultimate agent of nature would be for him a force acting between particles rather than a moving particle itself.[9]

Just as widely recognized among Newtonian scholars as the change in Newton's approach in the early 1680s is the fact that, beginning in about 1707 (that is, shortly after the publication of the Latin *Optice*) Newton once more began actively to consider possible causes for many of the forces he had invoked. In particular, Newton, fascinated, it seems, by various electrical experiments devised by Francis Hauksbee, began to explore the notion that many natural powers were manifestations of the activity of a subtle electric spirit that pervaded gross bodies. Hints of these speculations appear in the final paragraph of the "General Scholium" that Newton appended to the second (1713) edition of *Principia,* and in certain passages in the Queries published at the end of the 1717 edition of *Opticks.* They survive in more ample form in extensive unpublished drafts intended for these editions of Newton's two great books. By 1717, however, Newton's thinking had evolved still further, and he now attributed many of the phenomena previously accounted for in terms of the electric spirit to a new form of universal aether, the activity of which might even, he suggested, be sufficient to explain the force of gravity.[10]

Historians such as Westfall and McGuire, who have argued strongly for an ontological rather than a merely methodological commitment to the doctrine of forces on Newton's part in the years after 1680, have found these later vacillations something of an embarrassment. McGuire ignores the many indications that Newton provides that he sees the electric spirit as a material agency, and treats it instead as a generalized force, "an electrical *arche* connecting mind with matter"; and he dismisses the 1717 aether on the ground that it does not conform to his general view of Newton's philosophy of nature:

> it is difficult to suppose that Newton took it seriously. It was subject to obvious conceptual inconsistencies; it was a flagrant example of the sort of intermediate entity which Newton had always tended to reject; and more significantly it repudiated

his basic metaphysics of God in an empty universe.[11]

Westfall, too, treats these later views of Newton's as aberrations, arising, he suggests, from a "growing philosophical caution" that "reflected at once the impact of Hauksbee's electrical experiments on Newton and perhaps also the effect of unrelenting criticism by mechanical philosophers on an aging man no longer able to sustain a revolutionary position in the face of general opposition."[12] He sees Newton's invocation of an electric spirit as a retreat toward a mode of explanation "which at least appeared acceptable to conventional mechanical philosophers," and concludes that "there is no satisfactory explanation of his return to such fluids. . . . It is hard to imagine Newton acquiescing in such a retreat at an earlier, more vigorous age."[13] Consistent with this view, the preparation of the new edition of *Opticks,* with its famous Queries about the aether, is allotted a scant two pages in Westfall's 874-page biography, and these are consigned to a chapter entitled "Years of Decline."[14]

To be sure, there are aspects of the "aether" Queries of the 1717 *Opticks* that give the historian pause. Years before, in composing the concluding sections of Book II of *Principia,* Newton had marshaled overwhelming arguments against the possibility of any dense Cartesian-style aether filling all space. The motions of the planets in accordance with Kepler's laws were, he showed, inconsistent with the existence of such a medium. Hence the new aether of 1717 was, of necessity, of a very different character. It was both exceedingly rare, in order that it might offer no perceptible resistance to the motions of the planets through it, and exceedingly elastic, in order that it might transmit vibrations with the speed required if it were to fulfill the role in the theory of light that Newton wished to ascribe to it. Newton also supposed, however, that it was composed of particles. It followed inevitably, on Newtonian principles, that those particles exerted powerful forces of repulsion upon each other.[15] Hence, even if the 1717 aether offered a satisfactory basis for explaining gravity (and there is some evidence that Newton remained less than fully convinced on this score),[16] it by no means met the fundamental objection leveled by mechanical philosophers against Newton's physics: its reliance on unexplained forces acting at a distance. All the evidence we have suggests that Newton's "aether" Queries do indeed represent a defensive response of an old man to sustained criticism.

There are even indications that Newton subsequently repented their publication. Though historians have often failed to notice the fact, the new Queries were strictly inconsistent with the final paragraph of the concluding General Scholium of the 1713 *Principia,* because various phenomena—the reflection, refraction, inflection, and heating effects of light, and the transmission of sensations through the nerves to the brain and commands of the will from the brain to the muscles—which were there attributed to the action of "a certain most subtle spirit which pervades and lies hid in all gross bodies," were in the 1717 Queries ascribed to a universally disseminated aether. This latter was no mere transmogrification of the earlier subtle spirit, but was a second and quite distinct subtle matter. Even after reintroducing the aether, Newton continued to believe, as well, in the existence of the subtle spirit associated with matter, and to ascribe certain natural effects such as electricity to it;[17] but now he transferred some of the other actions previously ascribed to the subtle matter to the aether. At the very least, therefore, some modification of the General Scholium was called for. In fact, Newton envisaged deleting the entire final paragraph dealing with the subtle spirit from the next edition of *Principia*.[18] When that edition finally saw the light of day, however, in 1726, he did not do so; instead, the subtle matter continued to be invoked to explain the same effects as in 1713. This suggests that, at the very end of his life, Newton may have changed his mind yet again about the aether, and reverted to his previous mode of explanation of the various optical and physiological effects in terms of a subtle spirit associated with bodies.

If we may thus accept Westfall's judgment as to the relative insignificance of the 1717 aether for our general understanding of Newton's thinking about forces, the situation is, I believe, very different with respect to his writings on the subtle spirit. In the various published hints and unpublished drafts on this subject, we surely have before us no last-minute concessions by a declining 74-year-old, as the aether Queries appear to be, but the fruit of at least ten years of speculation and inquiry by a Newton still capable of prodigious feats of intellectual activity. Although much of what he had to say on the matter was consistent with views he had held at an earlier period of his career, these were now given a new lease of life by Hauksbee's remarkable experiments. There is ample evidence of the renewed interest and enthusiasm with which Newton pursued the work.[19] Furthermore, this interest pre-dates the main Continental onslaught on his doctrine of forces, and so cannot be dismissed as a mere defensive response to that criticism. Rather, it should be seen as yet another constructive phase—perhaps, indeed, the last major constructive phase—in his thinking about matter and its powers. If this be accepted, it then becomes of considerable interest to discover precisely what views Newton arrived at concerning the subtle spirit and, more particularly, what implications these views might have for our broader understanding of his philosophy of nature.

I have argued elsewhere that, even at this late period of his life, Newton's ideas regarding the various modes of action of the subtle spirit depended much less than has generally been allowed on his invoking unexplained forces acting at a distance. I have suggested, indeed,

that in many respects his ideas concerning the subtle spirit even then more closely resembled those of that arch-mechanist, Descartes, than they did those of a programmatic "Newtonian," systematically reducing each class of natural phenomena, in turn, to the action of some force or other.

Consider, first of all, the case of electricity, which lies at the heart of Newton's discussions of the subtle spirit. Newton sets out his ideas on this subject at length in a number of surviving documents. One of these is a long, unnumbered draft Query that predates the introduction of the aether hypothesis of 1717. "Do not all bodies abound," Newton here asks rhetorically, "with a very subtil active vibrating spirit by w[ch] . . . the small particles of bodics cohære when contiguous, agitate one another at small distances & regulate almost all their motions amongst themselves as the great bodies of the Universe regulate theirs by the power of gravity?" In particular, Newton believes that diffusion of this subtle matter into the space surrounding a rubbed body such as glass is what brings about electrical attraction, "for electric bodies could not act at a distance without a spirit reaching to that distance." Hauksbee's experiments provide, according to Newton, ample evidence that this diffusion occurs:

> [B]y several experiments shewn by M[r] Hawksksby before y[e] R. Society it appears that a cylindrical rod of glass or hard wax strongly rubbed emitts an electric spirit or vapour w[ch] pushes against the hand or face so as to be felt, & upon application of the finger to y[e] electric body crackles & flashes, & that the electric spirit reaches to y[e] distances of half a foot or a foot from the glass or above . . . ; & that if a globe of glass be nimbly turned round upon an axis & in turning rub upon a man's hand to excite its electric virtue, . . . the glass emitts an electric vapour or spirit w[ch] may be felt by the hand & w[ch] in dashing upon the hand or upon white paper or a handkerchief at the distance of a quarter of an inch or half an inch from the glass or above, illuminates the hand or paper or handkerchief with a white light while the glass continues in motion, the spirit by striking upon those bodies being agitated so as to emit the light. . . . There is therefore an electric spirit by w[ch] bodies are in some cases attracted in others repelled & this spirit is so subtile as to pervade & pass through the solid body of glass very freely . . . , & is capable of contraction & dilatation expanding itself to great distances from the electric body by friction. & thefore [sic] is elastic & susceptible of a vibrating motion like that of air whereby sounds are propagated. & this motion is exceeding quick so that the electric spirit can thereby emit light.[20]

The introduction of the aether hypothesis did not in any way affect Newton's thinking about what lay behind the various phenomena of electricity. This we discover from a passage which Newton at one point numbered "Qu. 18B," intending it to be inserted between two of the early "aether" Queries of the new edition of *Opticks:*

> Do not electric bodies by friction emit a subtile exhalation or spirit by which they perform their attractions? And is not this spirit of a very active nature & capable of emitting light by its agitations? And may not all bodies abound with such a spirit & shine by the agitations of this spirit within them when sufficiently heated? ffor if a long cylindrical piece of Ambar be rubbed nimbly it will shine in the dark & if when it is well rubbed the finger of a man be held neare it so as almost to touch it, the electric spirit will rush out of the Ambar with a soft crackling noise like that of green leaves of trees thrown into a fire, & in rushing out it will also push against the finger so as to be felt like the ends of hairs of a fine brush touching the finger. And the like happens in glass. If a long hollow tube of flint glass about a inch be rubbed nimbly with a paper held in the hand . . . , the electric spirit which is excited by the friction will rush out of the glass with a cracking noise & push against the skin so as to be felt, & in pushing emit light so as to make the skin shine like rotten wood or a glow worm. And if the glass was held neare pieces of leaf brass scattered upon a table the electric spirit wch issued out of the glass would stir them at the distance of 6, 8 or 10 inches or a foot, & put them into various brisk motions, making them sometimes leap towards the glass & stick to it, sometimes leap from it with great force, sometimes move towards it & from it several times with reciprocal motion, sometimes move in lines parall [*sic*] to the tube, sometimes remain suspended in the air, & sometimes move in various curve lines. Which motions shew that this spirit is agitated in various manners like a wind.[21]

The thoroughly mechanistic flavor of these passages is reinforced by yet another draft Query, numbered "Qu. 23" and apparently also intended to accompany the "aether" Queries of the published edition. Whereas in the passages quoted above, Newton focuses chiefly on the new electrical phenomena discovered by Hauksbee, he here discusses, in detail, the cause of the electrical forces of attraction and repulsion:

> Qu. 23. Is not electrical attraction and repuls; performed by an exhalation which is raised out of the electrick body by friction expanded to great distances & variously agitated like a turbulent wind, & wch carries light bodies along with it & agitates them in various manners according to its own motions, making them go sometimes towards the electric body, sometimes from it & sometimes move with various other motions? And when this spirit looses its turbulent motions & begins to be recondensed & by condensation to return into the electrick body doth it not carry light bodies along with it towards the Electrick body & cause them to stick to it without further motion till they drop off?[22]

The import of passages such as these is, in my view, unmistakable. Newton does not regard electricity as a true action at a distance. On the contrary, the various electrical effects are, in his view, brought about in a straightforwardly mechanical way following the agitation, by friction, of subtle spirit residing in the pores of electrifiable bodies such as amber and glass. (As the argument proceeds, Newton in fact concludes that the spirit resides in the pores of all bodies whatsoever.) Set in motion by the friction "like a turbulent wind," the subtle spirit simply sweeps along any light objects it encounters until, as it slows, it recondenses and carries such objects with it towards the electrified body. If it strikes against larger bodies, it may be set vibrating, and it then emits light in just the same way as a vibrating column of air generates sound. This spirit is no generalized immaterial force, but a material agency. To be sure, Newton usually referred to it as a "spirit," but on occasion he called it a "vapour" or "exhalation," terms which in Newton's vocabulary certainly implied materiality. Likewise, the word "spirit" could be used in this way, as he himself made clear in a draft intended for *Principia:*

> Vapours and exhalations on account of their rarity lose almost all perceptible resistance, and in the common acceptance often lose even the name of bodies and are called spirits. And yet they can be called bodies in so far as they are the effluvia of bodies and have a resistance proportional to density.[23]

As I have argued elsewhere, Newton's ideas about electricity, as set out in passages such as those quoted above, were in almost every respect typical of his day. The notion that electrical effects were caused by subtle matter, originally contained in the rubbed body, being excited by the friction, spreading out as effluvia into the surrounding air and sweeping along any light objects lying in the way, had been widely held at least since the time of William Gilbert. It continued to be generally espoused until the 1750s, when it began to be displaced by Benjamin Franklin's notion that the phenomena in question were brought about by static accumulations or "charges" of subtle electric fluid transferred by friction from one body to another.[24] In Newton's day, the main point of contention was not the correctness of the effluvial picture in general terms but the nature of the subtle matter or matters involved. In particular, whereas some maintained that the effluvia were composed of the matter of the rubbed body itself ("the finer parts of the attrahent," as Boyle put it),[25] others, including both Descartes and Newton, held that the stuff involved was a distinct subtle matter—whether the Cartesian "first element" or Newton's "electric and elastic spirit"—common to all bodies. Others again, most notably Niccolò Cabeo and his Jesuit followers, and also Hauksbee, thought that the air, too, was involved in bringing about the attraction.[26]

Magnetism was a power that Newton often cited, together with electricity, as an example of a force known to act in the world. He saw it, however, as a power that was limited in its operation, being confined, so he thought, to iron and some of its ores. Accordingly, only rarely did he mention it in connection with the electric spirit; in particular, magnetism is strikingly absent from the list of effects ascribed in the 1713 General Scholium to the action of this spirit, or in the 1717 "aether" Queries to the action of the aether.[27] For Newton, magnetism seems to have been a separate power, subject to its own laws. Here too, however, such evidence as we have suggests that Newton did not see the magnetic force as a true action at a distance. On the contrary, it appears that, as in the case of electricity, he assumed the existence of an underlying mechanism of unmistakably Cartesian provenance.

Descartes' invention of a mechanism that could account for the archetypically occult power of the magnet had been one of the major early triumphs of the mechanical philosophy. According to his scheme, associated with any magnet were circulating streams of subtle material effluvia of a distinctive kind. These streams passed axially through the magnet, emerging from one pole and returning to the other through the surrounding air before resuming their course. The various known magnetic effects were then explained in terms of interactions between such streams of matter, or between a single stream and pieces of iron that came in its way.

This general picture quickly won wide acceptance and, indeed, remained predominant for a century and more, even though various details propounded by Descartes were challenged and in some cases largely rejected.[28] Newton's early adherence to at least the broad outlines of the theory is clearly displayed in an unpublished manuscript dating from 1666 or 1667, in which he actually sketches the likely patterns of flow of the subtle matter in various circumstances.[29] In another paper, which Westfall dates to the same period, Newton discusses magnetism at greater length than anywhere else. Throughout, he assumes the existence of peculiar "streams" in the vicinity of a magnet; indeed, he assumes (though in terms somewhat different from those used by Descartes) two separate and "unsociable" streams entering a magnet at its two opposite poles and passing through it in opposite directions.[30]

It is tempting to see these papers as characteristic of Newton's youthful flirtation with the mechanical philosophy, and to suppose that he would later have abandoned such unrestrained hypothesizing, as he did in relation to the cause of gravity. The evidence, however, suggests otherwise, for although it is nowhere specific enough to show that Newton remained faithful to the details of his early explanatory scheme, it does unmistakably reveal that even after he had abandoned the search for a mechanical explanation for gravity, he continued to believe that magnetic effects were brought about by the action of subtle effluvia of some kind. Even in the 1690s, at the height of Newton's disillusionment with mechanism, David Gregory recorded, while visiting him, his host's view that the magnetic virtue "seems to be produced by mechanical means."[31] A casual allusion to "magnetick Effluvia" in the first edition of *Opticks,* published ten years later, tells the same story.[32] Finally, from the period with which we are chiefly concerned in this chapter, in one of the "aether" Queries of 1717, Newton uses the existence and activity of the magnetic effluvia, which he again takes as beyond dispute, to justify by analogy assumptions he is making about the nature of the aether: "If any one would ask how a Medium can be so rare," he suggests, "let him tell me . . . how the Effluvia of a Magnet can be so rare and subtile, as to pass through a Plate of Glass without any Resistance or Diminution of their Force, and yet so potent as to turn a magnetick Needle beyond the Glass."[33]

Newton frequently cited electricity and magnetism as other instances, besides gravity, of forces known to act in the world, to support the suggestion that there were many other forces at work as well. Whenever he did so, however, he surrounded the argument with disclaimers, of which the one near the beginning of Query 31 is the most famous:

> How these Attractions may be perform'd, I do not here consider. What I call Attraction may be perform'd by impulse, or by some other means unknown to me. I use that Word here to signify only in general any Force by which Bodies attract one another, and what are the Laws and Properties of the Attraction, before we enquire the Cause by which the Attraction is perform'd.[34]

Historians have tended to place little weight on such remarks, and to dismiss them as little more than symptoms of Newton's habitual caution in expressing his views publicly. In the light of the evidence just presented, however, they take on a new significance. Whatever his attitude toward gravity might have been, Newton, we discover, did not at all suppose that either electricity or magnetism was an irredeemably nonmechanical power. On the contrary, he thought both that there was an underlying mechanism in each case, and that he knew what this was. The disclaimer in the passage just quoted must be taken seriously; Newton believes that some of the attractions of which he speaks *are* "perform'd by impulse." In other words, what is being proposed here is not a general philosophy of nature in which forces have ontological primacy, but rather a methodology only.

According to this methodology, in studying magnetism, for example, one ought above all to try, as Newton did,[35] to discover the mathematical law governing the magnetic force. Such a methodological priority is, however, in no way inconsistent with one's simultaneously having views about the existence and nature of a mechanism that might bring about the attraction in accordance with that law. Nor, for that matter, is having views about the existence of such a mechanism inconsistent with allowing that this may perhaps itself ultimately be found to rest upon the behavior of a fluid the particles of which exert unexplained forces on each other at a distance. Whether that be so, or whether they act on each other only by contact, remains undetermined, in the case of magnetism, at the point reached by Newton's inquiry. In the case of electricity, on the other hand, he seems rather closer to the view that the particles of the subtle matter that provides the mechanism do indeed exert forces on each other at a distance.[36]

Conclusions such as these are further reinforced when we turn to what Newton had to say on another subject, of which the views he expressed have yet to attract systematic study: namely, the powers of living matter. Here, too, Newton's slowness to ascribe an ontological significance to the forces he discovers at work in the world becomes apparent. Once again, he appears much more inclined to assume fairly orthodox mechanistic explanations than one might have expected of a committed "Newtonian" bent on reducing natural events to the actions of independently existing forces. This is not to say, however, that Newton is here bowing to the conceptual constraints imposed by the mechanical philosophy. On the contrary, after reducing a variety of life processes to mechanisms of one kind or another, he eventually concludes that there is associated with living matter a peculiar power for which he offers no hint of an explanation, a power which appears to lie behind the various mechanisms he has described, but which itself appears to be intrinsically nonmechanical.

Newton's best-known statements about living processes comprise, first, anatomical descriptions of the optic system that offer no additional insights into his philosophy of matter[37] and, second, various comments about the operation of the nerves in transmitting sensations from the "organs of sense" to the brain and commands of the will from the brain to the muscles. These latter comments appear in writings from all periods of his career, the best known, however, being his late-in-life remarks in the final paragraph of the 1713 General Scholium and in the last two of the "aether" Queries of 1717 (Queries 23 and 24). In 1713, sensation and the commands of the will were held to be transmitted by vibrations of the subtle electric and elastic spirit "mutually propagated along the solid filaments of the nerves, from the outward organs of sense to the brain, and from the brain into the muscles." By 1717, the vibrations were held to occur not in the subtle spirit but in the newly introduced "Æthereal Medium": In all other

respects, however, the account remained as before.[38] In both cases, the explanations were conceived in wholly mechanistic terms, and bore obvious affinities to the opinion, commonly held at the time, that the nerves functioned as conduits for "animal spirits" flowing between the brain and the various sensory and motor parts of the body.[39] Insofar as they offered scope for characteristically "Newtonian" interpretations, they did so only by admitting the possibility, noted earlier, that the fluid in question might derive the elasticity requisite to sustain the vibrations to which Newton referred, from a repulsive force operating between its particles.[40]

Much more interesting from the point of view of this paper are, first, a manuscript entitled "De vita et morte vegetabile" and, second, sections of some associated draft Queries, prepared by Newton for a new edition of *Opticks* at about the time he composed the concluding General Scholium for the second edition of *Principia,* but never in fact published. In these papers, Newton confronts directly, albeit briefly, the nature of the distinction between living and nonliving matter. In doing so, he reveals yet again the extent to which his physical ideas were in tune with those held more generally in his day. At the same time, the discussion sheds new light on the place of unexplained forces in his mature philosophy of nature.

The passages in question are, in fact, linked with those discussed earlier in which Newton set out at length his ideas on electricity; indeed, the most important of them occur in the very same draft of the Queries from which most of the passages quoted above concerning electricity were drawn. Here as nowhere else in Newton's papers we see revealed the full extent to which his powerful imagination had been captivated by Hauksbee's astonishing experiments. Both the traditional electrical attraction of light objects and the striking new effects studied by Hauksbee arose, Newton had concluded, from the agitation of a very active subtle spirit associated with the particles of bodies. The role of friction in bringing about the phenomena was not, he thought, to generate the "virtue," but only to expand it, the subtle spirit under normal circumstances "reach[ing] not to any sensible distance from the particles."[41] Now, however, he goes on to consider the possibility that there may be other causes, too, by which "the electric vertue is invigorated." One such cause, he says, may be the power of life:

> The vegetable life may also consist in the power of this spirit supposing that this power in substances wch have a vegetable life is stronger then in others & reaches to a greater distance from the particles. ffor as the electric vertue is invigorated by friction so it may be by some other causes. And by being stronger in the particles of living substances then in others it may preserve them from corruption & act upon the nourishment to make it of like form & vertue wth the living particles as a magnet turns iron

to a magnet & fire turns its nourishment to fire & leaven turns past to leaven.[42]

As Newton himself makes plain, he is concerned here not with all properties of living things but only with those that had, since ancient times, been technically distinguished as constituting the vegetative aspects of life. These amounted to the ability of living matter, plant or animal, to maintain its organized form and to organize other matter likewise, whether in the processes of nutrition and growth, whereby existing tissues or organs are renewed or enlarged through the accretion of new matter, or in reproduction, where new living individuals are generated. In these passages, Newton does not discuss the additional powers that distinguish animate from mere vegetative life, or rational animals (i.e., human kind) from the beasts. For Newton, the subtle spirit, the agitation of which through friction gives rise to the phenomenon of electricity, also sustains the organic character of living matter by activity brought about in another way. When, at death, that activity ceases, putrefaction sets in; that is, the organized structures that characterized the matter in question during life now fall into decay.

In order to uphold this general position, Newton in these documents sets out at some length his general views on nutrition, growth, and generation, and contrasts these essentially constructive processes with the destruction and dissolution that constitute putrefaction. The ideas he displays are, in fact, very typical ones for his day.

So far as the reproduction of living forms is concerned, Newton reveals himself as an "ovist," that is, an upholder of that version of the preformation theory that held that the primordium or embryo of the young was present, already formed, in the female egg, and that the role of the male parent was merely to provide an indirect stimulus for its growth.[43] On this view, the process of generation reduces to one of growth of the embryo from suitable nutriment and, at an appropriate stage, a budding off of the embryo from the mother's body. Indeed, Newton draws the analogy with budding explicitly:

> Generation is nothing else then separating a branch from the tree and giving it better nourishment. If a separated branch takes root in the earth or a separated twigg or bud by grafting or inoculation is nourished from ye root of a young stock, it grows into a new tree as big as the tree from which it was separated being better nourished from a young root than from an old one. The seed of a tree has the nature of a branch or twig or bud. While it grows upon ye tree it is a part of the tree: but if separated and set in the earth to be better nourished, the embryo or young tree contained in it takes root & grows into a new tree. [In] like manner the egg of a female wth the embryo formed inside while it

grows in the ovarium is a branch of ye mothers body & partakes of her life, yet the Embryo is as capable of being separated from the mother & growing great by due nourishment as a branch or twigg or bud or seed of a tree is of being separated from the tree & growing into a new tree.[44]

Newton's adherence to the preformation theory, and to the ovist version in particular, is made plain by his reference to "the egg of a female wth the embryo formed inside," growing in the ovarium prior to the intervention of the male parent. This theory was widely held during the last decades of the seventeenth century, though it was being challenged at the end of the period by the animalculist alternative according to which the preformed individual derived not from the female but from the male parent, being present in the spermatozoa newly discovered in the male semen by Leeuwenhoek. Newton does not mention the spermatozoa, which suggests that he adhered to the fairly common opinion that, far from being the essential part of the semen, they were in fact parasites. For him, the male semen played an entirely different role, namely the essentially chemical one of reacting with the female juices to produce the nourishment required by the embryo if it were to grow:

> by the act of generation nothing more is done then to ferment the sperm of the female by ye sperm of ye male that it may thereby become fit nourishment for ye Embryo. ffor ye nourishment of all animals is prepared by ferment & the ferment is taken from animals of the same kind, & makes the nourishment subtile & spiritual. In adult animals the nourishm^t is fermented by the choler and pancreatic juice both wch come from the blood. The Embryo not being able to ferment its own nourishment wch comes from the mothers blood has it fermented by the sperm wch comes from ye fathers blood, & by this nourishment it swells, drops off from ye Ovarium & begins to grow with a life distinct from that of ye mother.[45]

According to this line of thinking, nutrition and growth become *the* fundamental biological phenomena. Nutrition, in turn, was for Newton a two-stage affair. First, a fermentation occurs, brought about by the digestive juices or, in the act of generation, by the male semen. This chemical process breaks down the nutriment into minute, extremely subtle parts:

> Now in all fermentation wch generates spirits, the ferment abounds wth a supprest acid wch being more attracted by the other body forsakes its own to rush upon & dissolve ye other & by the violence of the action breaks both its own particles & the particles of ye other body into smaller particles & these by their great subtilty volatility & continual digestion resolve ye whole mass into as subtile parts as it can be resolved by putrefaction.

Then, these separated parts reassemble under the organizing influence of the body being nourished:

> And when the nourishment is thus prepared by dissolution & subtillation, the particles of the body to be nourished draw to themselves out of the nourishment the particles of the same density & nature wth themselves. ffor particles of one & the same nature draw one another more strongly then particles of different natures do.[46]

Newton alludes at this point to the formation of mineral deposits in the earth as a known instance in which the "like attracts like" principle operates in nature. Yet, such a principle remains insufficient for his purposes because it does not explain that assembling of the new materials into appropriate structures, which manifestly occurs in the nourishment and growth of living creatures. Newton argues that the growth of crystals provides a model here:

> And when many particles of the same kind are drawn together out of ye nourishment they will be apt to coalesce in such textures as the particles wch drew them did before because they are of the same nature as we see in the particles of salts wch if they be of the same kind always crystallize in the same figures.

The analogy is one that was commonly drawn upon by mechanical philosophers. Newton, however, is intellectually rigorous enough to recognize that it remains but an analogy, and does not in any sense constitute an explanation. It is precisely at this point, in order to provide an explanation for the remarkable power that living forms possess of organizing new matter into existing structures, that he invokes the force of electricity:

> And for faciliating [*sic*] this assimilation of ye nourishment & preserving the nourished bodies from corruption it may be presumed that as electric attraction is excited by friction so it may be invigorated also by some other causes & particularly by some agitation caused in the electric spirit by the vegetable life of the particles of living substances: & the ceasing of this vigour upon death may be the reason why ye death of animals is accompanied by putrefaction.[47]

Throughout the different versions of this long draft Query, whenever Newton mentions electricity, he presents it as an effect produced by the agitation of a subtle spirit that pervades the pores of ordinary matter. By contrast, in the document "De vita et morte vegetabile," the electric spirit is not mentioned. Instead, Newton refers repeatedly to the "electrical force" associated with vegetating matter, without any further hint as to its ontological status. It is therefore tempting to date this paper to the period before Hauksbee's spectacular experiments rekindled Newton's belief in the existence of the subtle spirit and his faith in its explanatory possibilities. Other features of the paper seem firmly to link it, however, with the "subtle matter" Queries. Not only are there close parallels between the arguments presented in the two documents, "De vita et morte vegetabile" displays the same striking conviction—which must surely postdate Hauksbee's work—that we find in the "subtle matter" Queries, that electricity is a power universally associated with matter that lies behind many well-known effects not normally thought of as electrical. In this case, the document would stand as a suggestive instance of Newton confining his discussion to forces and offering no explanation for these, even though he actually had an elaborate explanation worked out at the time.

Whether or not this be allowed, however, these discussions by Newton of the vegetative power of living matter are revealing in other ways. In particular, as indicated earlier, they show that here, too, as with (or so I have argued) electricity and magnetism, Newton preferred to adopt a mechanistic (or at least pseudo-mechanistic) theory current in his day, the preformation theory, rather than invoking yet another category of unexplained forces to explain the effects in each case.

Newton, I would suggest, is in fact much more unwilling than has often been supposed to invoke a specific kind of in-principle-inexplicable force to account for each different category of natural event. Unexplained forces remain full of mystery for him; indeed, his conviction that the most famous of them, gravity, brought him close to the activity of God himself is well known,[48] and there is no reason to suppose that others would have had less profound implications.

Prima facie, then, one might expect that Newton would have recourse to entities of this kind only for the most universal of natural powers; and this does, indeed, seem to be the pattern that emerges. Neither the "amber effect"—the drawing of little light objects to rubbed amber or glass—nor the attraction of iron to a magnet, is an effect of sufficient universality; but a force of repulsion acting between the particles of an all-pervading subtle matter and ultimately responsible not just for the macroscopic electrical attraction but for the wide range of natural phenomena listed in the 1713 General Scholium, might be. Similarly, the various specific forces associated with living forms are unlikely to be the end point of the analysis, whereas a very general power of activating the subtle electric spirit even without friction might be what universally distinguishes living from nonliving matter. Something presumably does; and whatever it be, it is likely to be closely linked to the activity of God as the Creator of life and to be irreducibly nonmechanistic in character.

Meanwhile, Newton's scientific method leads him to

invoke forces of all kinds in studying natural processes, and encourages him to focus on discovering the mathematical laws according to which those forces act rather than on explaining their action. In these cases, I believe, as I have indicated above, that we ought to take more seriously than has usually been done Newton's oft-expressed caveat about the causes lying behind the forces of which he spoke. Some of these forces might, he suggested, be "perform'd by impulse."[49] If the interpretation I am suggesting is correct, Newton would in fact have thought that a mechanism was involved in most instances. I have presented evidence, indeed, that he did think so in certain leading cases. He would also not have been surprised, however, if, as these mechanisms were investigated, they were found ultimately to depend upon a small number of irreducibly nonmechanical powers of quasi-universal application. At that point, he would have said—but only at that point—we are indeed approaching a knowledge of the first cause, which is God.

Notes

[1] Isaac Newton, *Mathematical Principles of Natural Philosophy*, trans. Andrew Motte, rev. Florian Cajori (Berkeley: University of California Press, 1934), pp. vii-viii.

[2] Newton, *Opticks, or a Treatise of the Reflections, Refractions, Inflections and Colours of Light* (New York: Dover, 1952), pp. 401-2.

[3] The evolution of the concept of force during the seventeenth century is described in R. S. Westfall, *Force in Newton's Physics: The Science of Dynamics in the Seventeenth Century* (London: MacDonald, 1971).

[4] Richard S. Westfall, *Never at Rest: A Biography of Isaac Newton* (Cambridge: Cambridge University Press, 1980), chaps. 7-9.

[5] Richard S. Westfall, "The Foundations of Newton's Philosophy of Nature," *British Journal for the History of Science, 1* (1962), 171-82; idem, *Never at Rest*, pp. 83-93. Cf. also A. R. Hall, "Sir Isaac Newton's Notebook, 1661-65," *Cambridge Historical Journal, 9* (1948), 239-50; and J. E. McGuire and Martin Tamny, eds., *Certain Philosophical Questions: Newton's Trinity Notebook* (Cambridge: Cambridge University Press, 1983).

[6] Newton, "An Hypothesis explaining the Properties of Light," in H. W. Turnbull et al., eds., *The Correspondence of Isaac Newton* (Cambridge: Cambridge University Press, 1959-77), *1*, 362-86; De Aere et Aethere," in A. R. and M. B. Hall, eds., *Unpublished Scientific Papers of Isaac Newton* (Cambridge: Cambridge University Press, 1962), pp. 214-20 (English trans., pp. 221-8); Newton to Robert Boyle, 28 February 1679, in *Correspondence, II,* 288-95.

[7] Henry Guerlac, "Newton's Optical Aether: His Draft of a Proposed Addition to His *Opticks," Notes and Records of the Royal Society of London,* 22 (1967), 45-57; J. E. McGuire, "Force, Active Principles, and Newton's Invisible Realm," *Ambix,* 15 (1968), 154-208.

[8] Westfall, *Never at Rest,* p. 299.

[9] Ibid., p. 390. Cf. also Westfall, *Force in Newton's Physics,* chap. 7. McGuire has likewise seen a definite ontological commitment in Newton's attitude towards his forces, arguing, indeed, that these become the chief components of the universe as Newton conceived it in the years immediately after the first publication of *Principia:* "Not only did Newton enrich his ontology by including forces, but in the nineties they became essential to his natural philosophy. By 1706, he seemed to consider them, rather than matter, to be the primordials of nature" (McGuire, "Force, Active Principles, and Newton's Invisible Realm," p. 161).

[10] Newton, *Opticks,* Queries 17-24 (pp. 347-54). The "classic" papers on Newton's flirtation with the electric spirit are by Henry Guerlac: "Francis Hauksbee: expérimentateur au profit de Newton," *Archives internationales d'histoire des sciences, 16* (1963), 113-28; "Sir Isaac and the Ingenious Mr. Hauksbee," in I. B. Cohen and R. Taton, eds., *Mélanges Alexandre Koyré* (Paris, 1964), *I*, 228-253; Guerlac, "Newton's Optical Aether" (note 7). See also Joan L. Hawes, "Newton and the 'Electrical Attraction Unexcited.'" *Annuals of Science, 24* (1968), 121-130 and "Newton's Two Electricities," *Annals of Science, 27* (1971), 95-103; and, more recently, R. W. Home, "Newton on Electricity and the Aether," in Z. Bechler, ed., *Contemporary Newtonian Research* (Dordrecht: D. Reidel, 1982), pp. 191-213.

[11] McGuire, "Force, Active Principles, and Newton's Invisible Realm" [see note 7], pp. 176, 187.

[12] Westfall, *Never at Rest,* pp. 644, 793.

[13] Ibid., pp. 793, 747.
[14] Ibid., pp. 792-4.

[15] Newton, *Opticks,* p. 352.

[16] J. T. Desaguliers to Sir Hans Sloane, 4 March 1730/31, quoted by Guerlac, "Newton's Optical Aether" [see note 7], p. 51.

[17] Home, "Newton on Electricity and the Aether" [see note 10], passim.

[18] A. Koyré and I. B. Cohen, eds., *Isaac Newton's Philosophiae Naturalis Principia Mathematica: The Third Edition (1726) with Variant Readings* (Cambridge: Cambridge University Press, 1972), *II,* 764.

[19] Guerlac, "Francis Hauksbee: expérimentateur au profit de Newton" [see note 10], passim.

[20] University Library, Cambridge, Add. MS. 3970, fols. 241ᵛ-241ʳ.

[21] Ibid., fol. 295.

[22] Ibid., fol. 293ᵛ.

[23] University Library Cambridge, Add. MS. 3965. 13, fol. 437ᵛ; quoted by J. E. McGuire, "Body and Void in Newton's De Mundi Systemate: Some New Sources," *Archive for History of Exact Sciences, 3* (1966), 206-48; p. 219 (Latin original, p. 245).

[24] Home, "Newton on Electricity and the Aether" [see note 10], pp. 204-7. Cf. idem, *The Effluvial Theory of Electricity* (New York: Arno Press, 1981), and J. L. Heilbron, *Electricity in the 17th and 18th Centuries: A Study of Early Modern Physics* (Berkeley: University of California Press, 1979).

[25] Robert Boyle, *Experiments and Notes about the Mechanical Origine or Production of Electricity* (London, 1675; reprinted Oxford University Press, 1927), p. 6.

[26] On Hauksbee's ideas, see R. W. Home, "Francis Hauksbee's Theory of Electricity," *Archive for History of Exact Sciences, 4* (1967), 203-17.

[27] On at least one occasion, however, Newton does inexplicably include magnetism in such a list (University Library Cambridge, Add. MS. 3970, fol. 241; quoted by Joan L. Hawes, "Newton's Two Electricities" [see note 10], p. 97). I find it difficult to understand this except as a slip of the pen.

[28] R. W. Home, introduction to *Aepinus's Essay on the Theory of Electricity and Magnetism* (Princeton, N.J.: Princeton University Press, 1979), chap. 4, "Magnetism."

[29] University Library Cambridge, Add. MS. 3974, fols. 1-3.

[30] University Library Cambridge, Add. MS. 3970, fols. 473-4. Cf. Westfall, *Force in Newton's Physics* [note 3], p. 332.

[31] Newton, *Correspondence, III,* 335 (English trans., p. 338). The entry in Gregory's diary is dated 5-7 May 1694.

[32] Newton, *Opticks* (1st ed., 1704), Book II, p. 69. Cf. reprint ed. (New York, 1952), p. 267.

[33] Newton, *Opticks* (reprint ed.), p. 353. For further discussion of Newtonian views on magnetism, see R. W. Home, "'Newtonianism' and the Theory of the Magnet," *History of Science, 15* (1977), 252-66.

[34] *Opticks,* p. 376.

[35] Newton, *Mathematical Principles of Natural Philosophy,* p. 414.

[36] Home, "Newton on Electricity and the Aether" [see note 10], p. 209.

[37] *Opticks,* pp. 15-17. Cf. also three letters of Newton's to William Briggs, 1682-5, in his *Correspondence, II,* 377-8, 381-5, 417-9; and his "Description of the Optic Nerves and their Juncture in the Brain," published in D. Brewster, *Memoirs of the Life, Writings and Discoveries of Sir Isaac Newton* (Edinburgh, 1855), *I,* 432-6.

[38] Newton, *Mathematical Principles of Natural Philosophy,* p. 547; *Opticks,* pp. 353-4.

[39] Cf. René Descartes, *Treatise of Man,* trans. T. S. Hall (Cambridge, Mass.: Harvard University Press, 1972), pp. 21 ff.

[40] In Newton's earliest surviving discussion of the operation of the nerves, in the "Hypothesis explaining the Properties of Light" of 1675, he invokes the additional nonmechanical concepts of sociableness and unsociableness to explain how impulses could be confined to the nerves and how, once arrived at a muscle, they could cause this to contract (Newton, *Correspondence, I,* 368-9).

[41] University Library Cambridge, Add. MS. 3970, fol. 235; quoted by Westfall, *Force in Newton's Physics* [see note 3], p. 394, and Home, "Newton on Electricity and the Aether" [see note 10], p. 197.

[42] University Library Cambridge, Add. MS. 3970, fol. 241; quoted by Home, "Newton on Electricity and the Aether" [see note 10], p. 199. Folios 235 and 241 are the two halves of a single, folded sheet. A long unnumbered Query that begins on fol. 241ᵛ was drafted first. This carries over to fol. 241ʳ and then, briefly, to fol. 235ᵛ. At this stage, however, Newton evidently turned the sheet over and started again on fol. 235ʳ, writing out new Queries which he numbered 24 and 25, intending them to be inserted into the middle of what is now Q. 31 but in the Latin *Optice* of 1706 was Q. 23. A series of dashes in the proposed Q. 25 indi-

cate that the long first paragraph of the unnumbered Query on fol. 241ᵛ is to be taken in at this point. The manuscript headed "De vita et morte vegetabile" is now marked as fol. 237 in the same bundle, with drafts on fols. 238 and 240. It deals with the same subject matter but, as we shall see, in a rather different way. The first few paragraphs and the concluding sentences of this paper have been published by Westfall, *Force in Newton's Physics* (note 3), pp. 417-8.

[43] For a lively account of the preformation theory and its intellectual milieu, see Elizabeth Gasking, *Investigations into Generation: 1651-1828* (London: Hutchinson, 1967), Chapters 2-5. Also see Jacques Roger, *Les sciences de la vie dans la pensée française du XVIIIᵉ siècle* (Paris: Armand Colin, 1963).

[44] University Library Cambridge, Add. MS. 3970, fol. 235.

[45] Ibid.

[46] Ibid., fols. 235-235ᵛ.

[47] Ibid., fol. 235ᵛ.

[48] Westfall, *Force in Newton's Physics* [see note 3], pp. 395ff.

[49] *Opticks*, p. 376.

Richard S. Westfall (essay date 1988)

SOURCE: "Newton and the Scientific Revolution," in Queen's Quarterly, Vol. 95, No. 1, Spring, 1988, pp. 4-18.

[*Below, Westfall discusses Newton's role in the seventeenth-century world of science, noting that "the* Principia *was . . . a synthesis of the major themes of the scientific revolution."*]

Isaac Newton published *Philosophiae naturalis principia mathematica: The Mathematical Principles of Natural Philosophy* in July 1687. Seldom has the significance of a book been more immediately recognized. Indeed, its recognition began even before publication. In the spring of 1687, Fatio de Duillier, a young Swiss mathematician who would play a central role in Newton's life during the following six years, arrived in London. He found the learned community aflutter in expectation of the book which was destined, they told him, to remodel natural philosophy (Fatio 167-69). Similarly the *Philosophical Transactions* of the Royal Society carried a review of the *Principia,* which was in keeping with Fatio's report, shortly before the publication of the book itself. Although it was not signed, the review was composed by Edmund Halley, who knew what he was talking about since he was in fact the publisher. "This incomparable Author having at length been prevailed upon to appear in public," Halley began the review, "has in this Treatise given a most notable instance of the extent of the powers of the Mind; and has at once shown what are the Principles of Natural Philosophy, and so far derived from them their consequences, that he seems to have exhausted his Argument and left little to be done by those that shall succeed him." After summarizing the contents of the book, Halley concluded in the same vein: "it may be justly said, that so many and so valuable Philosophical Truths as are herein discovered and put past Dispute were never yet owing to the capacity and industry of any one man" (review of *Principia*).

It was not long after publication when John Locke, who was then resident in the Netherlands as a political refugee from the regime of James II, heard about the work. Unable to cope with its difficult mathematics, Locke asked Christiaan Huygens whether he could trust the book, and with Huygens's assurance that he could, Locke applied himself to the prose.[1] When he returned to England in the wake of the Glorious Revolution, Locke made it one of his first items of business to form Newton's acquaintance. The learned world in England did not lag behind Locke in acknowledging the *Principia,* so that its author vaulted in one leap from relative obscurity to the position of leadership among English thinkers.

On the Continent the overt indicators of the *Principia*'s reception differed, because continental philosophers had fundamental objections to its concept of attractions. For all that, they did not fail to recognize the power of the book, and they found themselves wholly unable to ignore it. It is indicative of the *Principia*'s impact on the Continent that when the French reorganized the Académie des Sciences in 1698, they made Newton one of the eight original foreign associates (Cohen, "Isaac Newton"). In a word, there has never been a time when the *Principia* was not seen as an epochal work, and there has never been a time since its publication when Newton was not perceived as one of humanity's leading intellects, much more than merely a genius. Although none of the statements I have quoted explicitly say as much, it also seems correct to me to say that there has never been a time when Newton's greatness was not seen to be associated with the fact that he did not stand alone, that he came after Copernicus, Kepler, Galileo, Descartes, Huygens, and numerous others. That is, Newton has always been recognized as the climax of the intellectual movement we call the scientific revolution of the seventeenth century, and that recognition defines the task I have set myself in this paper—to give an account first of the scientific revolution and then of the relation of Newton and his *Principia* to it.

Beyond the ranks of historians of science, in my opinion, the scientific revolution is frequently misunderstood. A vulgarized conception of the scientific method, which one finds in elementary textbooks, a conception which places overwhelming emphasis on the collection of empirical information from which theories presumably emerge spontaneously, has contributed to the misunderstanding, and so has a mistaken notion of the Middle Ages as a period so absorbed in the pursuit of salvation as to have been unable to observe nature. In fact, medieval philosophy asserted that observation is the foundation of all knowledge, and medieval science (which certainly did exist) was a sophisticated systematization of common sense and of the basic observations of the senses. Modern science was born in the sixteenth and seventeenth centuries in the denial of both.

Consider astronomy for example. Nearly everyone takes Copernicus as the beginning of the scientific revolution, and developments in astronomy foreshadowed the course of the scientific revolution as a whole.[2] Medieval astronomy rested on two basic propositions: that the motions observed in the heavens actually take place there, and that we must accept the validity of the basic observation each of us makes every moment, to wit, that we live on a stable earth. Geocentric astronomy followed directly from these premises, a complex system of circles on circles, of deferents, epicycles, and eccentrics, which provided a reasonable account in theory of the observed celestial phenomena.

Early in the sixteenth century, Nicholas Copernicus became dissatisfied with the system. It contained arbitrary elements. For example, in geocentric astronomy the sun was only one planet among seven, and yet the sun was involved in the theories of all the others except the moon. Mercury and Venus never depart far from the sun; they are seen in the west in the evening after sunset, or in the east in the morning before dawn, but never in the midnight sky. In order to make the theories of Mercury and Venus work, the centres of their epicycles had always to lie on the line between the sun and the Earth. Mars, Jupiter, and Saturn, on the other hand, go through their retrogressions when they are in the opposite part of the heavens from the sun; each of them, in the middle of its retrogression, crosses the meridian precisely at midnight. To make their theories correspond to the heavens it was necessary that the radii vectors of their epicycles always be parallel to the line between the sun and the Earth. Why was this so? How was it possible that the sun be merely one planet and yet participate in the theories of the others? Moreover, the geocentric system contained no necessary criteria for orbital size; as long as deferent and epicycle maintained the necessary proportion to each other established by observation, they could be of any size. Hence the planets had no necessary order. The Ptolemaic order was commonly accepted, but only

on the basis of *ad hoc* assumptions that had no intrinsic relation to the system; there was no conclusive argument why Saturn, for example, could not be closer to the Earth than Mercury. And the so-called system did not appear to be a system at all to Copernicus. Consider the order of motions, in the Ptolemaic arrangement, as Copernicus would have known them. The Earth stood motionless in the centre. The moon circled the Earth with a period of one month. Beyond the moon were Mercury, Venus, and the sun, all with periods (for Mercury and Venus, average periods), in the Ptolemaic system, of one year. Then Mars, two years, Jupiter, twelve years, Saturn, thirty years, and beyond all the planets the sphere of the fixed stars with a period of one day in the opposite direction. In Copernicus's eyes, this was not an ordered system, it was chaos.

Copernicus saw that he could remove all of the arbitrary elements and solve all of the problems by the simple expedients of putting the Earth into motion, with both a diurnal rotation and an annual revolution around the sun, and of treating most of the motions in the heavens as mere appearances resulting from the motions of the Earth. All that was necessary was to put the Earth in motion; this was an incredible thought, fundamentally at odds with all experience and with the dictates of common sense. And yet, by accepting that premise, he could arrive at a system that presented a spectacle of mathematical order and harmony not to be found in Ptolemy. For Ptolemaic, geocentric astronomers, each planet was a separate problem. For Copernicus and heliocentric astronomers, system was foremost. In the heliocentric system, the orbits are measurable in terms of the astronomical unit (the distance, not well measured in terrestrial units in Copernicus's age, between the Earth and the sun). Hence they had a necessary order, and that order corresponded to a harmonious system of motions in which periods decreased with distance from the sun, and the fixed stars at the periphery stood motionless. Copernicus threw common sense to the winds in order to pursue the arcane satisfactions of mathematical harmony (Copernicus, *Revolutions*).[3]

Copernicus was only the beginning. If he challenged some of the assumptions of common sense, he was unable to recognize the others to which he still clung. Foremost among these was the conviction that only circular motions can be found in the heavens and thus that astronomy can employ only circles in its account of heavenly phenomena. To the ancient Greeks, the circle had represented the perfect figure, that path in which a body can move forever without altering its relation to the centre, and the perfection of the circle had seemed to correspond to the perfection and immutability of the heavens. Copernicus was as wedded to the notion that the circle was the sole device of astronomical theory as the ancient Greeks, but circles obstructed the pursuit of a mathematically simple and harmonious system. It remained for Johannes Kepler, two generations later, to challenge their role. As Kepler began to propose that the planets move in non-circular orbits, he received a letter of protest from another astronomer who insisted that he was destroying the very foundation of astronomy. In a witty reply, Kepler referred to circles as voluptuous whores enticing astronomers away from the honest maiden Nature (Kepler, "Letter" 205). He knew whereof he spoke, for it had taken Kepler years to escape the attractions of the enchantress. His elliptical orbits, together with his two other quantitative laws of planetary motion, which yielded a system breathtaking in its mathematical simplicity, was another victory of abstract reason over assumptions accepted for centuries as the very embodiment of common sense.[4]

Kepler's three laws did nothing, however, to make the proposition that the Earth is in motion one whit less incredible than it seemed to virtually everyone. Here we confront the phenomena of moving objects, especially falling objects, on an Earth said to be rotating on its axis. The objections raised were by no means silly, and once again they sprang from common sense itself and from the observations all of us constantly make. If the Earth is moving as Copernicans claimed, surely we would perceive the motion. The size of the Earth was known then with sufficient accuracy to make the point. If it is rotating on its axis, we are, at this moment, moving from west to east at approximately a thousand miles per hour. To put the dilemma in twentieth-century terms, which make the problem considerably less difficult than seventeenth-century conditions, we ride in our cars every day, and we never fail to perceive the motion. Is it possible that we are cruising down the cosmic highway at a rate well over ten times the highest speed we ever go in our cars and are yet unaware of the motion? Or drop a stone from the top of a tall building with a flat side. Ballantine Hall on the campus of Indiana University—the twentieth-century example in this case differs from a seventeenth-century one only in the style of the architecture—is nine storeys tall; it takes a stone roughly two and a half seconds to fall from the top to the ground. A thousand miles per hour is equivalent to more than a thousand feet per second. During the time the stone is falling, Ballantine Hall moves more than half a mile to the east. How is it possible that a stone dropped one foot out from the eastern wall of Ballantine falls parallel to its side and lands very nearly one foot from the base of the wall?

The problem of motion on a moving Earth defined the major work of Galileo, who rethought the very conception of motion in order to justify the assertion that the Earth is turning on its axis. Motion, Galileo decided, is not, as Aristotle had thought, a process whereby entities realize their being. Motion is merely a state in which a body finds itself, a state that alters nothing in a body, a state to which a body is indifferent. Hence we are unable to perceive uniform motions in which we participate along with everything around us. When motion is understood in these terms, stones can fall parallel to the vertical walls of buildings when the Earth is in motion as well as they would if the Earth were at rest. Contrary to the central assertion of Aristotle's analysis, uniform motion understood in Galileo's terms requires no cause. As I hold the stone before I drop it from the top of Ballantine Hall, the stone is moving from west to east at the same rate as the building and I. The stone's horizontal motion continues unaffected; the eastern wall of Ballantine does not catch up with the stone. We perceive only the vertical drop in which we do not participate. As Descartes, who shared the new conception, put it, philosophers have been asking the wrong question. They have been asking what keeps a body in motion. The correct question is why does it not continue to move forever (*Oeuvres*). We know the new conception of motion as the principle of inertia. Although Galileo did not use that term, he made the concept the corner-stone of a new science of motion (or mechanics, as physicists call it) which became the central edifice in the whole new complex of modern science, and philosophers of science today agree that the principle of inertia is the basic concept on which the science we know rests.[5]

With Galileo the Copernican universe became believable, but was it true? Or to rephrase the question, what evidence was there in its favour in the early decades of the seventeenth century? As soon as one puts the question in those terms, one is forced to concede that the evidence in its favour was almost precisely the advantage that Copernicus, and Copernicans after him, had pursued, that is, mathematical harmony and simplicity. For the truth is that there was precious little other evidence to support it. Galileo's new science of motion answered the major objection against the system, but it did not count as evidence for it. To be sure, late in 1609 the same Galileo had turned his newly improved telescope on the heavens, but neither Galileo nor anyone else could look through a telescope and see the Earth moving around the sun and rotating on its axis. Galileo did observe the mountainous surface of the moon, the spots on the sun from the motion of which he inferred the rotation of the sun on its axis, and the satellites of Jupiter. These phenomena all fit more smoothly into the Copernican picture of the universe, but they did not demonstrate that it was true. Especially Galileo observed the phases of Venus which did demonstrate that Venus (and by implication Mercury) revolves around the sun and were then logically incompatible with the Ptolemaic system, but the phases of Venus did not demonstrate that the Copernican system is true.[6] One forgets all too easily another observation that Galileo did not make, stellar parallax. If the Earth is moving around the sun in an immense orbit, then if we observe the angle at which some fixed star appears in the middle of the summer and again six months later in the middle of the winter, after the Earth has moved an immense distance, surely the two angular locations will differ. To the naked eye the angles appeared identical. Alas, they also appeared identical through early telescopes. Today we know why: the fixed stars are so far removed that it was well into the nineteenth century before telescopes powerful enough to distinguish the two angles were developed. Such distances were inconceivable to most people in the early seventeenth century. At the least, the failure to observe stellar parallax offset the positive observation of the phases of Venus. Primarily for the ethereal advantages of mathematical harmony and simplicity early scientists asked mankind to surrender the most obvious evidence of the senses and the manifest dictates of common sense. They did not ask in vain. During the seventeenth century a new school of natural philosophers who were ready and indeed eager to accept the invitation appeared until, by the end of the century, none of them could imagine how anyone had ever believed otherwise.

Observe the process that I describe. From Copernicus's question about the order of the universe there spread out an expanding domain of discussion that grew ever broader. It does not appear to me to have been spurred on by issues of practical utility as so much scientific investigation in our age is, but rather by the pursuit of Truth. (I capitalize "truth" as I am convinced sixteenth- and seventeenth-century natural philosophers would have done.) Johannes Kepler, a man without personal resources, who was dependent for his livelihood on the favours of patrons and, conscious as he was of the current patron's mortality, always on the look-out for the next, was willing to live teetering on the brink of oblivion if he could demonstrate the correct pattern of the heavens. Galileo was willing to dare the fury of the Inquisition because it mattered to him whether the universe was geocentric or heliocentric.

The next major step was taken by a Frenchman, René Descartes, to whom such issues also mattered. Instructed in part by Galileo's debacle, he chose to live in exile in the Netherlands in order that he might more freely pursue his thoughts. Descartes universalized the tendencies inherent in the scientific movement. It is not only the heavens that are not as they seem to be, and not only motion. The whole universe is not as it seems to be. We see about us a world of qualities and of life. They are all mere appearances. Reality consists solely of particles of matter in motion. Some of the particles impinge on our senses and produce sensations, but nothing similar to the sensations exists outside ourselves. Reality is quantitative, particles characterized solely by size and shape, and of course motion. The picture of nature that I am describing so briefly was known in the seventeenth century as the mechanical

philosophy; it provided the philosophic framework of the scientific revolution. The world was not like a living being, it was like a great machine. Things such as plants and animals, said to be living—human beings, with their capacity for rational thought were partial exceptions—were only complicated machines. Thus the ultimate implication of the movement Copernicus initiated proved to be much wider than Copernicus had imagined. Humankind was not merely displaced from the centre. It was displaced entirely. Its presence was irrelevant to the universe; the universe was not created for human benefit: it would have been almost entirely the same whether humankind was there or not.[7]

Isaac Newton arrived on the scene after the early stages of the scientific revolution. He was born in 1642, the year Galileo died, twelve years after Kepler died, two years before Descartes published his *Principles of Philosophy*. Everything that I have discussed contributed to his intellectual inheritance. The scientific revolution was a complex movement of many dimensions. For my purposes in this paper, let me summarize it under three major themes, all of crucial importance to Newton. The scientific revolution presented a new picture of the universe, heliocentric rather than geocentric. It presented a new image of nature as inert particles in motion, the mechanical philosophy. And it presented a new vision of reality in terms of quantity rather than quality, so that increasingly science would express itself through mathematical demonstrations. Though implicit in the pursuit of mathematical harmony and simplicity, the third theme has not been explicit in the examples I have cited. To insist on its centrality, let me quote two representative statements. "Geometry," said Kepler, "being part of the divine mind from time immemorial, from before the origin of things, being God Himself (for what is in God that is not God Himself?), has supplied God with the models for the creation of the world and has been transferred to man together with the image of God. Geometry was not received inside through the eyes."[8] The same vision was shared by Galileo, who brought geometry down from the heavens, and building with it on the foundation of his new conception of motion, created what had heretofore appeared to be a contradiction in terms, a mathematical science of terrestrial motion. "Philosophy," said Galileo, "is written in this grand book, the universe, which stands continually open to our gaze. But the book cannot be understood unless one first learns to comprehend the language and read the letters in which it is composed. It is written in the language of mathematics, and its characters are triangles, circles, and other geometric figures without which it is humanly impossible to understand a single word of it . . ." (*Discoveries* 237-8). The new vision of reality, the conviction that the world is structured mathematically, was perhaps more basic to the scientific revolution than anything else.

When Newton enrolled in Cambridge in 1661, none of the early work of the scientific revolution had penetrated the standard curriculum. Despite some superficial changes, the university remained still in its medieval mould, and the philosophy of Aristotle continued to be the focus of the studies it prescribed. Newton was not a docile student, however, and sometime around 1664 he undertook a new programme of study. The record of his reading survives.[9] It contains no suggestion of tutorial guidance; on the contrary, it strongly implies that Newton struck out on his own. First, apparently, he discovered mathematics. In this he may have been influenced by the inaugural lectures of Isaac Barrow in the newly created Lucasian Professorship of Mathematics. Barrow was not Newton's tutor, however, and the two men became close only five years later. The seventeenth century was the most creative period in mathematics since the age of ancient Greece; in the short space of twelve to fifteen months, during what was also his final year as an undergraduate, Newton, by himself, absorbed the entire prior achievement of seventeenth-century mathematics and began to move beyond it towards the calculus. He set down the definitive statement of what he called the fluxional method in October 1666, about one and a half years after he had taken his Bachelor of Arts degree.[10] Mathematics was not all he discovered. He also found the new natural philosophy, especially the writings of Descartes and Pierre Gassendi (whose revival of ancient atomism offered an alternative mechanical philosophy). Within the context of natural philosophy, he came upon the problem of colours. When he was less than a year beyond his BA degree, Newton set down in the same notebook in which he recorded his reading in natural philosophy as a whole the first suggestion of the central concept to which all of his work in optics would be devoted, that light is not homogeneous as everyone had heretofore believed, but a heterogeneous mixture of difform rays that provoke different sensations of colour.[11] During much the same period, Newton also discovered the science of mechanics.[12] One of the best known Newtonian stories, which is drawn from a passage he composed toward the end of his life, claims that he developed the concept of universal gravitation at this time. Newtonian scholars no longer believe that story. Nevertheless, it is clear that he entertained vague thoughts about the dynamics of the heavens at this time, and that he later drew upon and amplified these thoughts (Herivel 183-98).

Later Newton found other interests as well, primarily chemistry/alchemy, and theology, which together largely dominated his time and consciousness from the late 1660s. In August 1684, as even people only vaguely informed about Newton know, he received an unexpected visit from Edmund Halley, who bluntly asked him what would be the shape of the path followed by a body orbiting another that attracted it with a force that varied inversely as the square of the distance. We cannot follow in any depth the psychology of Newton's response to Halley's question. We can only say that somehow the question reawakened earlier interests long dormant, so that late in the same year Newton sent Halley a tract of ten pages, which is known by the title *De motu*.

De motu was a short treatise on orbital dynamics that demonstrated the relation of Kepler's three laws of planetary motion to an inverse square attraction (Herivel 257-92). Although the demonstrations in *De motu* later became part of the *Principia*, they did not rest on a solid foundation in the early tract, for it presented only a primitive and crude science of dynamics. It did not accept the principle of inertia, and it did not state any general force law. Moreover, the defects of *De motu* were not so much the shortcoming of Newton as the limitations of the science of his day. In 1684, no one had constructed a satisfactory science of dynamics that corresponded to the new conception of motion. In Kepler's conclusions about planetary motion and in Galileo's science of uniformly accelerated motion, mechanics had arrived at kinematic laws, but as yet no dynamics to support the kinematics existed. Newton's first task, as he set out to expand and elaborate *De motu*, was to create a workable science of dynamics.

Those papers also survive (Herivel 292-320). They show that during the months following the composition of *De motu* Newton carried out an intense investigation of the fundamental concepts of the science of mechanics. Partly this was a work of definition, and as he proceeded, Newton provisionally defined no less than nineteen different concepts, of which five definitions survived into the *Principia*. From the investigation emerged the three laws of motion that still introduce courses in physics just as they introduced the *Principia* three centuries ago, three laws that constitute a quantitative science of dynamics from which both Galileo's kinematics of uniformly accelerated motion and Kepler's kinematics of planetary motion follow as necessary consequences. Thus Newton's science of dynamics bound celestial mechanics together with terrestrial mechanics, and for this reason people frequently refer to it as the Newtonian synthesis.

As an expression of Newtonian dynamics, the *Principia* was also a synthesis of the major themes of the scientific revolution. It supplied the final justification of the heliocentric system of the universe, in its Keplerian form, by providing its dynamic foundation. It raised the mathematical vision of reality to a new level of intensity. The *Principia* was a book of mathematical science, modelled on Euclid; more than any other work of the scientific revolution, it established the pattern that the whole of modern science has striven to fill in. The third theme that I singled out, the mechanical image of nature, is perhaps less obvious in the *Principia;* nevertheless, the book is unintelligible apart from it. Like every mechanical philosopher in the seventeenth century, Newton looked upon nature as a system of material particles in motion. To the astringent ontology of the prevailing mechanical philosophy, which ascribed to particles only size, shape, and motion, and insisted that all the phenomena of nature are produced by impact alone, Newton added a further category of property—forces of attraction and repulsion—whereby particles and bodies composed of particles act upon other particles and bodies at a distance.[13] The Newtonian conception of attractions also formed an essential dimension of Newton's mathematical view of reality, for the forces were mathematically defined. For example, the gravitational attraction of bodies for each other varied inversely as the square of the distance.

The structure of the *Principia* reflects its dynamic foundation. Book I is all abstract mathematical dynamics of point masses moving without resistance in various force fields. While Newton consistently explored the consequences of different force laws in the problems to which Book I devoted itself, he focussed his attention primarily upon the inverse square attraction and the phenomena of motion it entails. Book II considered the motion of bodies through resisting media and the motions of such media, reaching its climax with the examination of the dynamic conditions of vortical motion. That is, Book II was primarily an attack on the natural philosophy of Descartes and the prevailing mechanical picture of nature he had inspired. Newton demonstrated that vortices are unable to sustain themselves without the constant addition of new energy (or "motion," in the language of the seventeenth century) and are unable to yield Kepler's three planetary laws.

With the alternative system discredited, Book III returned to the demonstrations of Book I, which it applied to the observed phenomena of the universe. Newton's first law states that bodies in motion, undisturbed by any external influence, tend to move in straight lines. Planets move in closed orbits, and in their motions they observe Kepler's second law, the law of areas. For both reasons it follows from Book I that the planets must be attracted toward a point near the centre of their orbits where the sun is located. For the same reasons, the satellites of Jupiter and Saturn must be attracted toward those planets. Moreover, planets travel in ellipses with the sun at one focus, and their lines of apsides (the major axes of the ellipses) remain stable in space. The orbits of the system also obey Kepler's third law. It follows from the demonstrations of Book I that the attraction toward the sun must vary inversely as the square of the distance, and since the satellites of Jupiter conform to Kepler's third law, they too must be attracted by such a force. Furthermore, because the planetary system observes Kepler's third law, the attraction of the sun for each of the planets must be proportional to its quantity of matter. Again, the same holds for the attraction of Jupiter for its satellites, and since the satellites move in orbits that are nearly concentric with Jupiter as it orbits the sun, the attraction of the sun for both Jupiter and its satellites must be proportional to their several quantities of matter.

The Earth also has a satellite, the moon, which constantly accompanies it and does not fly off into space along a straight line; therefore the Earth must attract the moon to hold it in its orbit. Unlike Jupiter, the Earth has only one satellite, and that one with an orbit so highly irregular as not to appear truly elliptical; from such a satellite alone one cannot reason to an inverse square force. However, on the Earth there is a substitute for additional satellites. Heavy bodies fall to its surface where we can experiment with them. Hence the importance of the correlation between the motion of the moon and the measured acceleration of gravity on the surface of the Earth. How far from the Earth is a heavy body we drop—or, to speak in terms of the famous myth, how far is an apple from the Earth? Whether it was an apple or an experimental weight, any body that a seventeenth-century scientist could handle was at most a few feet from the surface of the Earth. Newton's correlation demanded that it must be roughly four thousand miles from the Earth; that is, the crucial distance was not to the surface but to the centre. To put it this way is to insist on the importance of the demonstration at which Newton arrived some time in 1685, that a homogeneous sphere, composed of particles that attract inversely as the square of the distance, itself attracts other bodies, no matter how close they may be, with forces that are inversely proportional to the bodies' distances from the sphere's centre. With the crucial demonstration about spheres, Newton could further demonstrate that the attraction that causes heavy bodies to fall toward the Earth is quantitatively identical to the attraction that holds the moon in its orbit. The critical correlation between the motion of the moon and the acceleration of gravity was the single strand that connected the cosmic attraction, shown to be necessary to hold the solar system together, with terrestrial phenomena, thus allowing him to apply to the attraction the ancient word *gravitas,* heaviness. From the motions of pendulums he could show that heaviness on Earth also varies directly in proportion to the quantity of matter. Thus Newton was brought to state what is perhaps the most famous generalization of modern science, that "there is a power of gravity pertaining to all bodies, proportional to the several quantities of matter which they contain" (*Mathematical Principles* 414).

The principle of universal gravitation, which I have just quoted, appeared early in Book III as Proposition 7, derived from the sharply limited number of phenomena I cited. The rest of the book then applied the principle to a number of other phenomena that had not contributed to its derivation. Recent European expeditions, especially a French expedition to the northern coast of South America, had revealed that the length of a pendulum that completes a swing in one second varies with the latitude. Near the equator a seconds pendulum needs to be shorter than it is in Europe. Newton was able to demonstrate that the shorter length of the pendulum is due to the decrease in the intensity of gravity near the equator because of the oblate shape of the Earth.

He turned from the shape of the Earth to the perturbations of the moon. Over the centuries astronomers had empirically established a number of anomalies in the moon's motion. Newton now showed that all the known perturbations are dynamic effects of the attraction of a third body, the sun. He applied the same analysis of the effects of a third body to the shape of a ring of water treated as a satellite circling the Earth and being perturbed by the combined effects of the moon and the sun, and he arrived at the explanation of the tides. When the "satellite" was the bulge of matter around the equator, the same analysis yielded the conical motion of the Earth's axis known as the precession of the equinoxes. In a final *tour de force,* Newton reversed a tradition as old as astronomy itself and, treating comets as planet-like bodies subject to the same orbital dynamics as planets, he succeeded in describing observed locations of the great comet of 1680-81 in terms of a parabolic orbit.

It would be difficult to overestimate the impact of the ***Principia***. As I insisted, there has never been a time since the day of its publication when it was not perceived as a monumental achievement. Take its treatment of the moon as an example. The ***Principia*** suggested for the first time the cause of the moon's known anomalies, and in so doing inaugurated a wholly new chapter in lunar theory. Much the same can be said of the tides, the precession of the equinoxes, comets, and, of course, the book's central problem, planetary motion. Moreover, all of these phenomena were reduced to a single causal principle, and all was done with a degree of mathematical precision that made it impossible for anyone who understood the mathematics to doubt the theory. In the words of David Gregory, who had just finished reading the ***Principia*** in the late summer of 1687, Newton taught the world "that which I never expected any man should have knwon" (***Correspondence*** 2: 484). In the more recent language of Thomas Kuhn, the ***Principia*** established the paradigm which modern science in its various dimensions has been attempting to emulate ever since.

The ***Principia*** was published three hundred years ago. In comparison to the total population of Europe, it was, to be sure, only a handful who recognized its

significance. Nevertheless, its appearance was the most important event of 1687. I am not exactly an impartial judge, but let me state forthrightly that I am not aware of any event to match its impact on western civilization during the intervening three centuries.

Notes

[1] J. T. Desaguliers stated that he had heard this story from Newton. John Conduitt was also familiar with the story, and we can assume with confidence that he got it from the same source (King's College, Keynes mss. *130.6,* Book 2: *130.5,* Sheet 1). Newton undoubtedly learned it from Locke himself.

[2] For more detailed treatment of the astronomical revolution see Koyré, *Astronomical Revolution* and Kuhn.

[3] For short statements of the system see Copernicus's *Commentariolus* or Rheticus's *Narratio prima* in Copernicus, *Three Treatises.*

[4] See especially Kepler's *Astronomia nova,* the work of 1609 in which he announced his first two laws, and his summary statement of his work in *The Epitome of Copernican Astronomy in the Gesammelte Werke.* Books IV and V of the *Epitome* have been translated into English by C. G. Wallis in vol. 16 of *Great Books.*

[5] For Galileo's discussion of the problem of motion on a moving Earth see primarily the Second Day of his *Dialogue.* For his science of mechanics as a whole, see his *Two New Sciences.* There is an enormous literature on Galileo and his new science of motion. The basic work that shaped our present understanding of Galileo is Koyré, *Galileo Studies.* See also Clavelin.

[6] Galileo's accounts of his observations appear in *The Starry Messenger* (1610), the opening passage of the *Discourse on Bodies in Water* (1612), and the *Letters on Sunspots* (1613). Translations of the first and the third can be found in *Discoveries.* Drake has also edited a seventeenth-century translation of the second, published as a separate volume, and more recently included his own translation of it in Galileo, *Cause.*

[7] See especially Descartes's *Principles* and also the shorter exposition of his natural philosophy in *Le monde.* For discussions of the mechanical philosophy see Hall, Harré, and the relevant chapter of Collingwood.

[8] *Harmonices mundi,* IV, in *Gesammelte Werke,* 6: 223. I quote the translation in Caspar, 271.

[9] See his undergraduate notebook, although it contains the record only of his philosophical studies; the records of his work in mathematics and mechanics are in McGuire and Tamny.

[10] The record of Newton's early studies in mathematics, up to the tract of October 1666, makes up the first volume of *Mathematical Papers*. In the notes to this edition and in other writings, D. T. Whiteside is also the leading commentator on Newton's mathematics.

[11] For Newton's early work in optics see Shapiro and my own article. Shapiro is currently editing a full publication of Newton's optical papers. Volume one, which has appeared, contains the early Lucasion lectures on optics. Volume two will contain the material I am now discussing.

[12] His early notes on mechanics, mostly in another notebook that Newton called the "Waste Book," are published and discussed in Herivel, 121-82.

[13] Scholars argue about whether Newton meant to ascribe forces to bodies or understood that they were caused by some "mechanical" device (in the seventeenth-century meaning of "mechanical") such as a particulate aether. For the view that Newton understood forces as real entities in nature, see McGuire, "Forces," 154-208. For the argument that he understood gravity, for example, to be caused by a material medium, see Cohen, *Newtonian Revolution*. Home, 95-117, vigorously defends the position that Newton never understood electrical and magnetic forces as actions at a distance. I have generally taken the side that Newton did accept forces as real entities in nature, but the argument of this paper does not depend on that position. Whatever Newton thought about the ontological status of forces, the *Principia* proceeded in terms of attractions and repulsions acting at a distance.

WORKS CITED

Caspar, Max. *Kepler*. Trans. C. Doris Hellman. New York: Abelard-Schuman, 1959.

Clavelin, Maurice. *The Natural Philosophy of Galileo*. Trans. A. J. Pomerans. Cambridge, MA: MIT Press, 1974.

Collingwood, R. G. *The Idea of Nature*. Oxford: Clarendon, 1945.

Cohen, I. Bernard. "Isaac Newton, Hans Sloane and the Académie des Sciences." *Mélanges Alexandres Koyré*. 2 vols. Paris: Hermann, 1964. 2:61-116.

_____. *The Newtonian Revolution*. Cambridge and New York: Cambridge UP, 1980.

Copernicus, Nicholas. *On the Revolutions*. Trans. Edward Rosen. Baltimore: Johns Hopkins UP, 1978.

_____. *Three Copernican Treatises*. Trans. Edward Rosen. New York: Dover Publications, 1939.

Desaguliers, J. T. Preface *A Course of Experimental Philosophy*. 2 vols. London, 1734-44.

Descartes, René. *Le monde, ou traité de la lumière*. Trans. Michael Mahoney. New York: Abarus Books, 1979.

_____. *Oeuvres de Descartes*. Ed. Charles Adam and Paul Tannery. 12 vols. Paris: L. Cerf, 1897-1910.

_____. *Principles of Philosophy*. Trans. V. R. and R. P. Miller. Dordrecht: Kluwer, 1983.

Fatio de Duillier, Nicholas. Letter to Christiaan Huygens, 14 June *1687*. Christiaan Huygens. *Oeuvres complètes*. 22 vols. The Hague, 1888-1950. Vol. 9.

Galileo. *Cause, Experiment, and Science*. Trans. Stillman Drake. Chicago: U of Chicago P, 1981.

_____. *Dialogue Concerning the Two Chief World Systems--Ptolemaic and Copernican*. Trans. Stillman Drake. Berkeley: U of California P, 1962.

_____. *Discoveries and Opinions of Galileo*. Trans. Stillman Drake. Garden City, NY: Doubleday, 1957.

_____. *Two New Sciences*. Trans. Stillman Drake. Madison: U of Wisconsin P, 1974.
Great Books of the Western World. Ed. Robert M. Hutchins. 50 vols. Chicago: W. Benton, 1952.

Gregory, David. Letter to Newton. 2 September 1687. Newton, *Correspondence*.

Hall, Marie Boas. "The Establishment of the Mechanical Philosophy." *Osiris* 10 (1952): 412-541.

Harré, Rom. *Matter and Method*. London: Macmillan; New York: St Martin's, 1964.

Herivel, John. *The Background to Newton's* **Principia**. Oxford: Clarendon Press, 1965.

Home, R. W. "Force, Electricity, and the Powers of Living Matter in Newton's Mature Philosophy of Nature." *Religion, Science, and Worldview*. Ed. Margaret J. Osler and Paul L. Farber. Cambridge and New York: Cambridge UP, 1985.

Kepler, Johannes. *Gesammelte Werke*. Ed. Walther von Dyck and Max Caspar. 19 vols. Munich, 1937-83.

_____. Letter to Fabricius. 10 November 1608. *Kepler. Gesammelte Werke*. Vol. 16.

Koyré, Alexandre. *The Astronomical Revolution*. Trans. R. E. W. Maddison. Ithaca: Cornell UP; Paris: Hermann, 1973.

_____. *Galileo Studies*. Trans. John Mepham. Hassocks [Engl.]: Harvester Press, 1978.

Kuhn, Thomas. *The Copernican Revolution*. Cambridge, MA: Harvard UP, 1957.

McGuire, J. E. "Forces, Active Principles, and Newton's Invisible Realm." *Ambix* 15 (1968): 154-208.

McGuire, J. E., and Martin Tamny. *Certain Philosophical Questions: Newton's Trinity Notebook*. Cambridge and New York: Cambridge UP, 1983.

Newton, Isaac. *The Correspondence of Isaac Newton*. Ed. H. W. Turnbull. 7 vols. Cambridge UP, 1959-77.

_____. *The Mathematical Papers of Isaac Newton*. 8 vols. Ed. D. T. Whiteside. Cambridge and New York: Cambridge UP, 1967-81.

_____. *The Optical Papers of Isaac Newton*. Ed. Alan E. Shapiro. 3 (projected) vols. Cambridge and New York: Cambridge UP, 1984.

_____. [*Principia.*] *Sir Isaac Newton's Mathematical Principles of Natural Philosophy and his System of the World*. Ed. Florian Cajori. Trans. Andrew Motte. Berkeley: U of California P, 1934.
Rev. of Principia. Philosophical Transactions of The Royal Society of London 16 (1686-87): 291-97.

Shapiro, Alan E. "The Evolving Structure of Newton's Theory of White Light and Color." *Isis* 71 (1980): 211-35.

Westfall, Richard S. "The Development of Newton's Theory of Colors." *Isis* 53 (1962): 339-58.

Robert Markley (essay date 1989)

SOURCE: "Isaac Newton's Theological Writings: Problems and Prospects," in *Restoration: Studies in English Literary Culture, 1660-1700*, Vol. 13, No. 1, Spring, 1989, pp. 35-48.

[*In the essay below, Markley surveys current scholarship on Newton's theology and notes that critics have used new approaches to his manuscripts to establish the proper relationship between Newton's spiritual inquiries and his scientific work.*]

Over the past fifteen years, studies by Frank Manuel, Richard S. Westfall, and other scholars on the problems posed by Isaac Newton's religious and theological writings have finally put to rest at least some of the hoary myths that had, for over two hundred years, effectively severed Newton the scientist from Newton the alchemist and Newton the supposedly doddering writer on biblical history and prophecy.[1] If the dispersal of Newton's unpublished manuscripts in the 1936 sale to Jerusalem, Wellesley, (Massachusetts), and Cambridge (England) has created logistical problems for scholars interested in Newton's "non-scientific" work, the fact that this vast body of material is now more-or-less accessible has allowed Manuel and Westfall to offer preliminary accounts of what Newton's theological manuscripts contain. I say "preliminary" because both of these noted historians have stopped after a few steps of what promises to be a long journey; they have surveyed the manuscripts, reprinted some, discussed the significance of others, and offered plausible accounts of the basics of Newton's religious beliefs, but they have not investigated in detail the ideological and ideational implications of his theology for our understanding of the scientific work. Although it is now customary for historians of science (and even literary historians) to acknowledge the "significance" of Newton's religious writings, if for no other reason than their sheer bulk, there is still no consensus about what we are supposed to do with this mass of manuscripts: ignore them? study them? edit them? Westfall, who has read through all the available manuscripts, voices a prevalent opinion when he states that if the stuff were not Newton's we would not bother to read it.[2] But a different point of view can be found in James Force's argument that the study of biblical prophecy constitutes an important part of eighteenth-century Newtonianism and, more radically, in the eccentric but at times fascinating account of David Castillejo, who argues that all of Newton's work—theological, alchemical, and mathematical—represents a unified inquiry into God's creation, shot through with numerological symbolism and structured around the dominant symbol of Solomon's Temple.[3]

Admittedly, anyone who has skimmed Newton's posthumously published historical and theological works, *The Chronology of the Ancient Kingdoms Amended* (1728) and *Observations upon the Prophecies of Daniel and the Apocalypse of St. John* (1733), may decide that the problems of Newton's religion are best left to dedicated historians like Manuel and Westfall or confined to "see also" footnotes. But the more scholars plow through the material in Cambridge and Jerusalem, the less likely the questions posed by Newton's theology are to go away. The most obvious of these questions concerns the relation of Newton's theological to his scientific work, but there are others that might provide a necessary—indeed crucial—impetus to our ongoing reinterpretations of Restoration and early eighteenth-century culture.[4] The most basic of these might be for us to ask how "marginal" Newton's theological works really are, and lead us to explore epistemological and methodological relationships between Newton's scientific and theological writing. Another set of questions might seek, like

Force's study and the essays recently collected by Richard Popkin,[5] to re-examine the myths of a progressive "secularization" of science and society in the late seventeenth and early eighteenth centuries. Yet another might encourage us to look more closely at Newton's habits of self-censorship and the resulting differences between public conceptions of his work and his antitrinitarian religious beliefs. In this respect, a shorthand way of reassessing the significance of the specifically literary images of Newtonianism might be to ask what Blake would have made of Newton's legacy had he had access to his predecessor's attacks on the apostasy of trinitarianism. And, to extend the valuable work by M. C. Jacob on Newtonians and radicals in the eighteenth century, we might ask how the sociopolitical and literary implications of Newton's religious views relate to the seemingly contradictory impulses of Newtonian ideology—its justifications of an hierarchically-ordered physical and political universe on the one hand and its insistent, if often muted, questioning of received doctrines and interpretations in both theology and natural philosophy on the other. If nothing else, pondering these kinds of questions might suggest new ways to explain to sceptical audiences of scientists and philosophers why the bulk of the extended correspondence between Newton and Locke concerned alchemical secrets and thinly veiled attacks, particularly by the former, on Athanasius, Jerome, and the doctrine of the Trinity. Obviously, in a brief overview such as this, I do not have time to suggest answers to all or even a few of these questions. My purpose, though, is not to offer a definitive critique of everything written on Newton's religion in the last fifty years but to take stock of where we are and, as my previous questions suggest, to outline some of the ways in which historians of science, intellectual historians, and even literary scholars might go about identifying and tackling the problems posed by the volume and complexity of Newton's non-scientific writing. In my mind, this process also has a heuristic value because it may force us to consider redrawing some of the disciplinary boundaries that have traditionally made the problems of Newton's theology seem trivial or tangential to accounts of his scientific thought.

Any assessment of the problems confronting would-be scholars of Newton's religion must begin with the logistical difficulties of finding the time and money to read his theological manuscripts. Westfall appends a checklist of Newton's known theological manuscripts to his 1982 article: the bulk of these, the Yahuda papers, are in the Jewish National and University Library in Jerusalem; twelve manuscripts . . . are in the Keynes Collection at Cambridge; and still others are in the Bodleian Library, Oxford, the Clark Library in Los Angeles, the Babson College Library in Wellesley, Massachusetts, the Humanities Research Center at the University of Texas, Austin, and the Bodmer Library in Geneva. And we cannot be certain that more manuscripts will not surface in the future; Newton apparently completed a history of the early Church which was extant in the eighteenth century but is now lost. Westfall's list includes one-line descriptions of the contents of each manuscript; however brief, they indicate something of the enormous difficulties facing a scholar who, presumably having piled grant upon grant to travel from Israel to Austin, wishes to analyze Newton's thoughts on even relatively narrow topics. Given Newton's penchant for revision and for drafting new versions of old material, there exist as many as five or six drafts of "treatises" or observations on the same subject. For example, the Clark Library manuscript and Keynes MS. 10 . . . are both devoted to Newton's villifying of Athanasius. But the relationship between the two versions is complex: some passages have been reshaped, others added, and others cut. Although the Keynes manuscript is quite clean, neither it nor the Clark manuscript can be said to represent a final, copytext version of Newton's "intentions." And there are also manuscript notes on Athanasius (Babson MS. 436, in Latin, and Yahuda MS. 5.3 which Westfall describes as "notes on Athanasius [late 1670s]") that have not been examined, as far as I know, in detail.

Westfall makes a similar point about the difficulty of trying to sort out the various manuscript states of Newton's unpublished treatise, *Theologiae gentilis origines philosophicae* (*The Philosophical* [that is, scientific] *Origins of Gentile Theology*), which exists, as he says, "only as a chaos of notes and drafts." To complicate matters, large chunks of various versions of the *Origines* find their way into *The Chronology of Ancient Kingdoms Amended,* which Westfall calls a "sanitized rendition [of Newton's antitrinitarian views] . . . suitable for public consumption."[6] But what Westfall sees as a pallid version of Newton's earlier and more forceful antitrinitarian rhetoric, Kenneth Knoespel argues represents a further refinement—and significant conjunction—of Newton's late scientific and theological thought.[7] To accept either view would require one to formulate, at least embryonically, an account of Newton's habits of composition and an accompanying portrait of him as either a meticulous, even obsessive reviser of his work (Knoespel) or an aging member of the establishment who, late in life, produced an "emasculated embodiment" of his earlier heretical work (Westfall). Regardless of which alternative we choose, we are forced to ask a number of historically and theoretically difficult questions about the processes by which Newton composed, revised, and abandoned the drafts of his work on ancient chronology.

In this regard, Newton's manuscripts seem likely to resist the kind of editorial practice familiar to literary scholars: the establishment of a copytext, the search for variants, the concern with determining the author's intentions. In short, there may not be any easy way to edit Newton, to provide a "clean" version of the *Origines* which might then be compared to the *Chronology*. Although I think it is plausible to assume that the basic tenets of Newton's antitrinitarian theology did not change over the course of his adult life, it seems much more difficult to follow the different transmutations of and tensions within his thought that are represented by the various drafts of his treatises on ancient theology, biblical prophecy, and the politics of the early Church. Westfall argues that when the *Origines* "was composed [in the 1680s], it still only hinted at its own implications," that is, at a far-reaching attack on the basic tenets of Christianity (*"Origines,"* p. 30). This aspect of self-censorship, Newton's compulsive habit of proferring, withdrawing, and recasting interpretations of theological material, underscores the problems inherent in assuming, let alone finding, a definitive "intention" in his work.

The sorts of editorial and ideational problems that I have been discussing point up one of the basic problems for scholars who seek to interpret Newton's work. The disciplinary boundaries of our post-Kantian academic world work against anyone's acquiring the combinations of expertise that would be necessary to navigate the complex currents of his thought. The questions asked by historians of religion generally are not those asked by historians or philosophers of science; nor, for that matter, are the kinds of questions asked by intellectual historians those that trouble literary critics seeking to analyze concepts of language and representation in Newton's England. The efforts by Westfall and Betty Jo Dobbs to demonstrate the importance of alchemy in Newton's thought suggest something of the diligence required to cross disciplinary boundaries.[8] Their studies suggest that when we divide Newton's work among our highly specialized, post-Enlightenment disciplines, we are projecting our ways of seeing, our habits of cultural perception, onto seventeenth-century practices. In effect, when we try to understand what Newton had in mind in his theological writings, we must consciously undo or demystify the conceptions of "science" and "theology" that we have inherited from the eighteenth century. To a great extent the seeming intractability of the *Chronology* and *Observations upon Daniel* results from our lack of a sense of the context in which they were written, although, in this regard, the works of Manuel, Westfall, Force, and Knoespel have made important contributions to our understanding of the place of Newton's non-scientific work in its seventeenth-and eighteenth-century intellectual contexts.

The recent studies of Newton's theological manuscripts have also, then, necessarily complicated our understanding of the relationships between science and religion both in his work and in that of many of his contemporaries. Given the work of Westfall, Castillejo, and Knoespel, we are now in the difficult position of being able neither to assume nor to discount a fundamental coherence among Newton's writings in theology, history, alchemy, and science. We are caught between what scientists would call "weak" and "strong" views of the relationship between Newton's science and his theology. For example, Westfall, while acknowledging the importance of the *Origines* to Newton's thought, downplays its influence on his scientific and mathematical work; at the other extreme, Castillejo maintains that the *Principia* and the *Opticks* reveal myriad mystical connections to the theological manuscripts and semi-direct invocations of the Mosaic science that provides the rationale for all of Newton's scientific, historical, alchemical, and theological projects. Twenty years ago it would have been easy—indeed expected—to dismiss Castillejo as a crackpot who understands nothing about Newton or the history of science. But, as the recent interest among historians in probing the connections between scientific and occult practices in the seventeenth century suggests,[9] the more scholarly work that is done on Newton's theological writings, the less far-fetched Castillejo's admittedly quirky book may seem. Manuel and Westfall, for example, both acknowledge that Newton's scientific projects should be seen within the context of statements like the one that Newton originally intended for the final book of the *Principia* but that remained unpublished until after his death:

> It was the ancient opinion of not a few in the earliest ages of Philosophy, That the fixed Stars stood immoveable in the highest parts of the world; that under the Fixed Stars the Planets were carried about the Sun, that the Earth, as one of the Planets, described an annual course about the Sun, while by a diurnal motion it was in the mean time revolved about its own axe; and that the Sun, as the common Fire which served to warm the Whole, was fixed in the center of the Universe.

> This was the philosophy taught of old by *Philolaus, Aristarchus* of *Samos, Plato* in his riper years, and the whole sect of the *Pythagoreans*. And this was the judgment of *Anaximander*, more ancient than any of them, and that wise king of the *Romans Numa Pompilius. . . .*

> The *Egyptians* were the earliest observers of the heavens. And from them probably this philosophy was spread abroad. For from them it was, and from the nations about them, that the *Greeks,* a people of themselves more addicted to the study of philology than of nature, derived their first as well as their soundest notions of philosophy. And in the vestal ceremonies we may yet trace the spirit of the *Egyptians*. For it was their way to deliver their mysteries, that is, their philosophy of things above the vulgar way of thinking under the veil of religious rites and hieroglyphick symbols.[10]

Given our improved knowledge of Newton's fascination with these ancient "mysteries," it is now ortho-dox, internalist historians of science who are on the defensive in maintaining that his religion and science can and should remain separate areas of scholarly investigation. The traditional spectrum of views on Newton—with, say, Bernard Cohen at one end, West-fall in the middle, and Castillejo at the other, distant extreme—could easily be reimagined as a slippery slope. Once one acknowledges, as Westfall and many others have done, that Newton's theological and sci-entific writings do interpenetrate, it becomes difficult to indicate where one set of interests ends and the other begins, to apply the brakes, in other words, short of endorsing the broad outlines of Castillejo's thesis, if not all of his readings. To try to find a middle ground between, say, Westfall and Castillejo is to risk maintaining that Newton's work is "somewhat" unified or that it gestures towards a quasi-mystical coherence but stops short of a conscious effort to develop a unified, theocentric theory to account for all physical phenomena. In her work on alchemy, Dobbs argues persuasively that Newton was actively seeking in the 1670s and 1680s microcosmic princi-ples in what we would call the atomic world to com-plete his work on the macrocosmic system set forth in the *Principia*. For Newton scholars of the 1990s, then, the surprise might be to find evidence of major ideational ruptures among his theological, historical, experimental, and mathematical writings.

I am not, I should emphasize, arguing for a view of Newton as a latter-day Paracelsian magus. Because his theological manuscripts are not generally accessible, because our understanding of the intellectual substance as well as contexts of seventeenth-century prophetic and mystical writings is still relatively incomplete, any attempts to pigeonhole Newton the historian of reli-gions will, in my mind, prove no more successful than efforts to describe in simple terms his mathematical and experimental achievements. But, at the very least, I would maintain that the mass of his historical, chro-nological, prophetical, and exegetical writings can neither be dismissed nor, what seems more likely, shunted aside as someone else's domain. Although it might well prove a lifetime's undertaking, the ideal for the Newton scholar of, say, the twenty-first century would be to immerse himself or herself in patristic commentaries, Renaissance interpretations of the Old Testament Prophecies and the Book of Revelation, Renaissance histories of the ancient world, commen-taries on the Arian heresies of the third and fourth centuries, sixteenth-and seventeenth-century scholarship on the textual disseminations of various biblical manu-scripts in the middle ages and Renaissance, sixteenth-and seventeenth-century work on chronology and as-tronomy, and various contemporary accounts of Egyp-tian hieroglyphics. In short, the task facing the next generation of Newton scholars may prove to be, in one respect, pulling together the kind of work that is usu-ally done in relative isolation.

This synthesizing process will, by its very nature, cross disciplinary boundaries and require a reassessment of the traditional interpretive languages—historical, theo-logical, philosophical, and scientific—by which New-ton has been understood.[11] The need for scholars to develop (or appropriate) new critical vocabularies to analyze Newton's "non-canonical" works will, I be-lieve, make the impact of new-historicist and postmod-ern approaches to his scientific, alchemical, theologi-cal, and historical writings a crucial issue in Newton studies. In this regard, I would venture the guess that we are at the threshold of an upcoming era of interdis-ciplinary, theoretical, and metacritical commentary on Newton. Although this prospect may initially seem threatening to "internalist" historians of science, it offers the possibility that Newton's scientific and non-scien-tific works will be read and reread from new and po-tentially valuable perspectives—for scientists as well as new-wave historians and theorists. Without claim-ing to offer even a modest blueprint for future studies, I would like to suggest some of the ways in which contemporary literary and psychoanalytical theory might be used to investigate a complex range of issues in Newton's writing. For brevity's sake, I shall confine my discussion to two related areas of cross-disciplin-ary interest—Newton's antitrinitarian theology and its implications for familiar psychological interpretations of his character.

Many, if not most, literary scholars and historians of science have shied away from the problems posed by Newton's religious beliefs because they have tradition-ally been cast in the uncongenial rhetoric of controver-sies about the substance of the Son, the nature of the Holy Spirit, and so on. For many critics, the more detailed the theological archaeology becomes, the less relevant and interesting it seems. A more profitable way to explore Newton's theology, however, might be through an analysis of his tortuous, often contradictory attempts to characterize Christ. My use of the literary term "characterize" here is deliberate; what Newton attempts in many of his theological writings is, in ef-fect, to develop a narrative strategy for dealing with a "Son of Man" who is neither divine nor merely super-fluous to God's ends. At different points in Newton's theological writings, Jesus becomes the last great proph-et, the active agent in God's creation, an earthly inter-mediary for human prayers, a representative of human hope for progress, and an historically-constrained agent whose power extends only so far as the finite creation of this earth which, Newton believed, was but one of an infinite number of possible or potential worlds.[12] Newton's obsession with the status of Jesus is evident in his many tirades against the doctrine of the Trinity, from his **"Letter to a Friend"** on the corruption of Biblical texts (which was almost published in the early 1690s through Locke's agency) to his de facto trials of Athanasius for a variety of historical and historically-embellished crimes, specifically his championing of the doctrine of the Trinity.

As Manuel and Gale Christianson, among others, have demonstrated, Newton's antitrinitarianism cannot be easily divorced from the problems we confront when we try to assess his "character"; the details of Newton's biography at times seem to have been concocted by a conspiratorial clique of orthodox Freudians.[13] Although psychoanalytic interpretations of Newton may tell us more about the ingenuity of his twentieth-century interpreters than about his psychological make-up, they do raise important questions about what we define as constituting historical "evidence," about what we accept as "legitimate" vocabularies of historical investigation and representation. Psychoanalytic interpretations of Newton can easily suspend us between sceptical distrust of their holistic claims and admiration for their narrative consistency and symbolic virtuosity.

Born on Christmas day in 1642, Newton was a posthumous son; his mother remarried when he was three and moved to her new husband's house a mile away, leaving Newton to be raised primarily by his grandmother. It is, then, relatively easy to read in Newton's career a series of attempts to please an always and already absent father; the remoteness of Newton's God may be seen as Manuel argues, as the reinscription of a Freudian conflict in theological terms. But, in this case, his relationship to the Son becomes extremely complicated as the interpretive vocabularies of theology and psychoanalysis are superimposed. In one sense, Newton may see Jesus as a rival for the Father's affection; he may see himself as necessarily having to displace Jesus to (re)gain his Father's approval. In this regard, it is relevant that Newton consistently associates his scientific endeavors with the rediscovery of Mosaic, literally pre-Christian, ancient knowledge.

To displace Jesus, in other words, he must establish his anterior claim to knowledge, to worthiness, to the special status of Son. Jesus also, then, functions as a father-figure who must be displaced to regain the love of the mother who "abandoned" him. Devoted to his mother throughout his adult life, Newton provides a textbook example, at least for Manuel, of a man suffering from repressed homosexual desires; his obsession with Jesus can be interpreted as a form of displaced desire. One might also note, in this regard, how his attacks on Athanasius, the trinitarian villain of much of Newton's theological writing, often slip into fulminations about the lust and depravity of monkish defenders of the Trinity. For Newton, trinitarianism and corruption go hand in hand.

It is easy enough to turn Newton's psychobiography into a caricature of Freudian analysis done at a three-hundred years remove. But my synopsis is not intended to argue for a single, definitive interpretation of Newton's character but to suggest that the implication of Newton's theological beliefs in this psychological history requires a more subtle and flexible vocabulary than the rigorous and nearly self-parodic Oedipal terminology that has so far been applied. Dobbs, for example, in her explication of Newton's alchemy relies on Jung's thesis that alchemy provided a way for would-be adepts to integrate disparate elements of their personalities; alchemy, therefore, becomes a means of psychic healing. But Jung's vocabulary, like that of orthodox Freudians, has been called into question by the re-examination of both psychoanalysis and its analytic vocabularies by a variety of analysts and theorists, including Lacan, Kristeva, Cixous, Bakhtin, and a number of others.[14] Rather than simply imposing prefabricated psychological models on Newton, it seems more worthwhile to ask what kind of psychological assumptions might underlie, inform, or help us account for his theological and historical writings.

The postmodern rereading of psychoanalysis has important implications for how we approach what Derrida calls "the scene of writing." Those critics and theorists who have called into question conventional notions of historical and psychological "truth" and writerly "intention" have also suggested new epistemological approaches to the kinds of difficult questions posed by the intersections of writing, psychology, and, I would argue, even seventeenth-century theological controversies. In their important work on the nature of language, Lev Vygotsky and Mikhail Bakhtin, for example, argue that no difference exists between "inner" psychological "speech" and "outer" sociohistorical discourse; the "internal" language of the individual is itself ideologically constrained because it exists only in the dialogic interaction of the individual word or utterance with the words and utterances of others. For Vygotsky and Bakhtin, there is no pre-existent, pre-linguistic, coherent "self" for us to analyze; there are only the dialogic or double-voiced utterances of the individual that are set against competing utterances within his or her socioeconomic environment. Consequently, a pre-existent, individual "psychology" no longer becomes the primary determinant of behavior; instead, the "self" is historically, ideologically, and materially constituted by and among "internal" and "external" discourses. To develop provisional notions of "style" and "self" along Bahktinian lines, then, is to go beyond narrowly deterministic psychoanalytic accounts of Newton's "character." In this respect, there is no "Newton" who can be authoritatively analyzed as suffering from this or that neurosis, only the writer for whom no clear distinction exists between the external languages of theology and history and the inner discourse of psychological desire and repression. A postmodern reading of Newton would privilege neither psychoanalytic nor theological—nor for that matter scientific—readings of his religious writings. What it would explore is the interplay—the dialogic tension—among the competing discourses that shape his writing.

A postmodern re-envisioning of Newton's theology and psychology would also have important implications for future studies of his prose style and, more broadly, of scientific writing in the seventeenth and eighteenth centuries. In recent years, several critics have challenged simplistic accounts of the "rise" of an objective, scientific prose style under the auspices of the Royal Society in the 1660s and 1670s.[15] However, these much needed efforts to explode the "myth" of a late seventeenth-century change in stylistic practice have stopped short of questioning Newton's status as the pre-eminent figure in the eighteenth century's progress toward a modern, dispassionate, and utilitarian prose style capable of accurately describing natural phenomena. Arakelian, for example, literally makes Newton the hero of this account of stylistic change, arguing that his prose, particularly in the **Opticks,** exhibits the values of orderliness and clarity to a greater extent than the styles of either Addison or Pope. But the more literary critics read Newton's historical, prophetical, and theological writings, the less tenable this traditional view becomes. So, too, I would argue, do assumptions based on schematic views of decorum that suggest Newton wrote one way for scientific audiences and another when he was scribbling about alchemy and hieroglyphics. The privileging of his scientific works over his non-scientific manuscripts ultimately depends on theoretical assumptions about language and on specific assumptions about Newton's style that are, at best, suspect.

At times, particularly in his attacks on Athanasius and the doctrine of the Trinity, Newton's prose is forceful, even strident, and as tightly structured as a legal brief. Each piece of historical or textual evidence is introduced and examined from several vantage points; an interpretation is offered, alternatives considered, and conclusions reached. Allowing for Newton's polemical intentions, this method of investigation is structured in ways that recall his strategies of presentation in his early optical papers presented to the Royal Society. But as Knoespel has demonstrated, the "style" of Newton's **Chronology,** like that of his other theological and historical works, is more complicated and more problematically structured. Also significant is the evidence of Newton's interest over more than half a century in problems of style and representation.[16] These are crucial, I believe, to even a preliminary understanding of his fascination with biblical prophecy.

Newton devotes the second chapter of his **Observations on Daniel** to an "authoritative" account "Of the Prophetic Language"; this chapter is a shortened redaction of a longer manuscript, **"The First Book Concerning the Language of the Prophets"**. . . . The relation between the two versions could itself be the subject of an extended study; in brief, however, it seems that the issues that Newton felt compelled to explore at length in the 1680s are reduced to a series of statements about the exact correspondences of prophetic images to historical and political events. His thesis is that all of the Old Testament prophets "write in one and the same mystical language" that is "certain and definite in its signification" (McLachlan, p. 119). Newton, therefore, sees his work as an attempt to "fix such a signification as agrees best" with all figurative or "mystical" usages in "all the places" in the Bible. This ideal of a stable scheme of representation—an authoritative key to interpreting the scriptures—is founded on his belief that "the language of the Prophets, being Hieroglyphical, had affinity with that of the Egyptian priests and Eastern wise men" and that it operates "by the analogy between the world natural and the world politic" (p. 120).[17] What follows in both the manuscript and published versions is Newton's attempt to "fix" significations by a precise, analogical method: "the heavens and things therein signify thrones and dignities, and those who enjoy them; and the earth, with the things thereon, the inferior people; and the lowest parts of the earth, called *Hades* or Hell, the lowest or most miserable part of them" (**Daniel,** p. 16; and with some changes in the phrasing, McLachlan, pp. 120-21). It does not take a skilled biblical scholar to realize that if one accepts this method of one-to-one correspondence in interpreting the books of prophecy, the analogies of heaven, earth, and hell to the social order of seventeeth- and eighteenth-century England produce a fixed "signification" that equates moral good with the maintenance of the status quo and evil with threats from "below." Yet this sort of schematic structure turns extremely complex, even within the relatively short span of seven pages of the chapter in **Daniel:**[18]

> If the world politic, considered in prophecy, consists of many kingdoms, they are represented by as many parts of the world natural; as the noblest by the celestial frame, and then the Moon and Clouds are put for the common people; the less noble, by the earth, sea, and rivers, and by the animals or vegetables, or buildings therein; and then the greater and more powerful animals and taller trees, are put for Kings, Princes, and Nobles. And because the whole kingdom is the body politic of the King, therefore the Sun, or a Tree, or a Beast, or Bird, or a Man, whereby the King is represented, is put in a large signification for the whole kingdom; and several animals, as a Lion, a Bear, a Leopard, a Goat, according to their qualities, are put for several kingdoms and bodies politic; and sacrificing of beasts, for slaughtering and conquering of kingdoms; and friendship between beasts, for peace between kingdoms. Yet sometimes vegetables and animals are, by certain epithets or circumstances, extended to other significations; as a Tree, when called *the tree of life* or *of knowledge;* and a Beast, when called *the old serpent,* or worshipped.

What Newton ends up describing are interpretive rules

that must be applied contextually, that depend on what are ultimately arbitrary systems of assigning value. In this regard, his efforts to "fix" meanings for the language of prophecy meet a fate reminiscent of the grandiose schemes for "real characters" and "universal languages" proposed by Dalgarno, Wilkins, and others in the 1650s and 1660s. The "certain epithets and circumstances" of the prophetic style force Newton to describe his "system" of fixing meanings relationally. Regardless of his attempts to articulate an ideal scheme of interpretation, the practice of prophetic interpretation becomes, as anyone who has read *Daniel* can testify, increasingly and bewilderingly convoluted.

In an important sense, then, it is ultimately misleading to speak of Newton's "style" of writing. His works display a variety of styles that work against traditional notions of what constitutes "scientific" or "literary" styles. At best, one could offer a few generalizations that might be explored further: Newton's writing is often fragmented into discrete elements conjoined by "and" or ampersands; there is comparatively little logical or rhetorical subordination; and often the complexities of his epistemology depend on what we make of the "ands" and periods that separate clauses and sentences. More radically, however, Newton's "style"—in, for example, the *Chronology*—depends on a complex intersection of different semiotic systems and representational schemes: the historical "narrative" of that work is penetrated by and interacts dialogically with mathematical calculations, genealogical lists, and etymological flights of fancy as Newton seeks to demonstrate that various names for ancient gods and heroes refer to the same historical individual. It is not that Newton's combination of these various epistemological styles is merely idiosyncratic but that his interweaving of them calls into question the very commonplaces about the relationship of style to individuality that figure in most discussions of eighteenth-century literature.[19] The complexities of semiotic systems impinging on each other suggests that we need new sorts of interpretive vocabularies to understand and describe Newton's stylistic experiments as well as his complex theological and polemical agendas.

The advantage of a broadly postmodern approach to Newton's writings is that it can allow us to deploy new interpretive strategies without sacrificing our detailed historical knowledge of his life and scientific works. In fact, I am tempted to claim that it is only through a sophisticated theoretical awareness of the problems of language, narrativity, and referentiality that we can begin to explore the relationships that may exist among Newton's works in science, theology, and history. To take only one example, we might consider the only antitrinitarian tracts that he came close to publishing during his lifetime. In 1690, Newton wrote a third letter to (presumably) Locke, continuing his attacks on the doctrine of the Trinity begun in "*An*

Historical Account of Two Notable Corruptions of Scripture."[20] Ostensibly a discussion of the corruption of 1 John 5.20 (transferring the epithet "true" from God to Jesus) and other "trinitarian" biblical texts, this letter, like its longer predecessor, is concerned to discover the "true," pristine, authoritative, and antitrinitarian text of the Bible. As he does in his other theological manuscripts, Newton demonstrates a vast knowledge of patristic writing and a good deal of rhetorical effectiveness in using his readers' (presumed) anti-Catholic sentiments to undermine their acceptance of the doctrine of the Trinity. Having meticulously detailed specific problems of the transmission of the New Testament text, Newton concludes that there is no scriptural authority for the belief that the Son and the Father are of the same substance:

> By these instances it's manifest that ye scriptures have been very much corrupted in ye first ages & chiefly in the fourth Century in the times of the Arian Controversy. And to ye shame of Christians be it spoken ye Catholicks are here found much more guilty of these corruptions then the hereticks. In ye earliest ages the Gnosticks were much accused of this crime & seem to have been guilty & yet the catholicks were not then wholy innocent. But in the fourth fift & sixt Centuries when the Arians Macedonians Nestorians & Eutychians were much exclaimed against for this crime I cannot find any one instance wherein they were justly accused. The Catholicks ever made ye corruptions (so far as I can yet find) & then to justify & propagate them exclaimed against the Hereticks & old Interpreters, as if the ancient genuine readings & translations had been corrupted. Whoever was the author of the Latin Version wch did insert ye testimony of the three in heaven, he charges the Authors of ye ancient Latin versions with infidelity for leaving it out. . . . And if [the Catholics] have taken this liberty wth ye scriptures, its to be feared they have not spared other authors: So Ruffin (if we may believe Jerome) corrupted Origen's works & pretended that he only purged them from ye corruptions of ye Arians. And such was the liberty of that age that learned men blushed not in translating Authors to correct them at their pleasure & confess openly yt that they did so as if it were a crime to translate them faithfully. All wch I mention out of the great hatred I have to pious frauds, & to shame Christians out of these practices.

(III, 138-139)

Newton's "great hatred," his zeal in attacking the trinitarian corrupters of the Bible, sets his theological works apart from both the scepticism of the deists and from, say, the less passionate defense of religious principles that one finds in Dryden's *Religio Laici*.[21] Newton is, at once, meticulous in documenting his case and ruthless in prosecuting it. The dominant metaphor in Newton's *Letters* on scriptural corruption is legal: the author becomes investigator, prosecutor, and judge determined to eradicate the "crimes" of the "corrupters" and to unveil their false accusations against the Arians. But "corruption" for Newton takes on a complex double meaning: technically, "corruption" refers to those passages that he methodically demonstrates were changed to comply with trinitarian doctrine; morally, it becomes a measure of the depravity of his enemies and the enormities of their "crimes." Newton's claim in his first Letter that his subject is "no article of faith, no point of discipline, nothing but a criticism concerning a text of scripture" (III, 83) belies his sweeping indictment of the "pious frauds of ye Roman Church" and his efforts to "make it part of our religion to detect & renounce all" vestiges of Catholic—and by implication trinitarian—doctrine: "we must acknowledge it," he continues, "a greater crime in us to favor such practices, then in the Papists we so much blame on that account" (III, 83). In this respect, Newton's criticism of the corruption of biblical texts reveals a network of interests: his fervent desire to set aright Church history; his polemical campaign to deny trinitarian doctrines and, in effect, to reconstitute "our religion" along unitarian lines; his obsessive efforts to uncover the origins of the authoritative word of primitive Christianity; and his desire to apply the same kinds of consistent methodological principles to theological controversy that he applies to the investigation and description of natural phenomena. This passage, then, recovered from the manuscript draft of an unpublished treatise, has a great deal to tell us about Newton's habits of thinking, his theological and psychological interests, that would be difficult to glean from his published, self-censored scientific works.

Although any general comments about what we can or will learn by studying Newton's theological writings are necessarily provisional, some tentative claims are probably worth making, if only to serve as targets for others to refute or as initial points from which others may depart. The mass of material that Newton left in incomplete or half-complete form suggests that his writings—scientific, theological, alchemical, and historical—never achieved a grand synthesis or offered a unified theory of nature and that, to the contrary, Newton himself was aware that his was a necessarily incomplete quest to establish an incontrovertible basis for a metaphysical order. His works, in this regard, do not provide the kind of psychological integration that Jung saw as the rationale for alchemical experiments but testify to Newton's struggle to make his own voice heard against a host of competing voices—religious and scientific—that claimed an unquestioning patriarchal and psychopolitical authority. In fact, his theological writings suggest that he saw himself displacing traditional forms of authority—the "voices" of the trinitarian Church, St. Jerome's Bible, and the Athanasian Creed—in his efforts to restore the true, pristine authority of God's word. Newton, then, is not—or not only—the "autocrat of science" attacked by Blake and the Romantics but a dialogician in search of an autho-

rizing Logos.

In this respect, the study of Newton's theological manuscripts may ultimately lead us to reread and revise our understanding of Newtonian science. The allegation that Newton's religion is not important to our understanding of his science because—paradoxically—it tells us the "same" information about the universe may have to be replaced by a recognition that Newton's scientific, alchemical, theological, and historical investigations offer a complex interweaving of different semiotic systems, different "languages," none of which in and of itself is adequate to the complexities of the universe. In this regard, Newton's writings on the prophecies that posit a remote God and a millenarian revelation deferred far into the future, may send us back to Query 31 of the *Opticks* to puzzle out the implications of Newton's questions about the physical nature of creation. A "postmodern" reading of Newton will necessarily transgress the disciplinary boundaries in which his scientific works have been enclosed; if it does nothing else, it will allow for a good deal of debate about what we mean by terms like "Newtonian" and "science." Although such simplifications are risky, it seems worth considering the notion that, for Newton, natural philosophy, like prophecy, can be described only in deliberately heuristic and provisional terms. What Newtonian science would then offer us is not a vision of a coherent system and watertight theories but "systems" and "theories" that resist precisely those definitive formulations which Newton's followers in the early eighteenth century—Whiston, Desaguliers, Martin, 'sGravesande, Derham, Pemberton, and others—abstracted from his work. To conclude, we might find that the piles of scattered theological manuscripts that Newton left behind stand metonymically for the scientific and psychological quests that he undertook but could never complete.

Notes

[1] Manuel, *Isaac Newton, Historian* (Cambridge, Mass: Harvard UP, 1963); *A Portrait of Isaac Newton* (Cambridge, Mass: Harvard UP, 1968); and *The Religion of Isaac Newton* (Oxford; Clarendon, 1974); Richard S. Westfall, *Never at Rest: A Biography of Isaac Newton* (Cambridge: Cambridge UP, 1980); "Newton's Theological Manuscripts," in *Contemporary Newtonian Research*, ed. Zev. Bechler (Dordrecht: Reidel, 1982), pp. 129-43); and "Isaac Newton's *Theologiae Gentilis Origines Philosophicae*," in *The Secular Mind: Transformations of Faith in Modern Europe*, ed. W. Warren Wagar (New York: Holmes & Meier, 1982), pp. 15-34. All of these works contain generous quotations from Newton's unpublished manuscripts that are not otherwise available. H. McLachlan has edited a short collection, *Sir Isaac Newton: Theological Manuscripts* (Liverpool: Liverpool UP, 1950), but as Westfall notes, McLachlan took a number of liberties in his editing

and his versions of the manuscripts must be used with caution. Wherever possible, I have cited published versions of Newton's theological writings.

[2] "Newton's Theological Manuscripts," p. 139. On the same page Westfall makes an important distinction between religious and theological "influences" on Newton's science, although I ultimately disagree with Westfall's claim that "it is difficult if not impossible to demonstrate [a theological] influence on some concrete element of his science" (p. 140). As Westfall argued thirty years ago, invocations of a Supreme Being are legion in seventeenth- and early eighteenth-century scientific texts (*Science and Religion in Seventeenth-Century England* (New Haven: Yale UP, 1958)); "natural philosophy" virtually presupposes the existence of a Judeo-Christian God. But the common vocabulary of religious belief in the period masks profound *theological* disagreements among scientists and allowed men like Newton and Whiston, who were virtual heretics, to conceal their heterodox beliefs within a generalized rhetoric of religious belief. In emphasizing the significance of Newton's theological manuscripts, I am, in effect, arguing that we need to pay more attention to the ways in which ideational tensions and problems within Newton's "non-scientific" writings shaped and were shaped by his scientific work.

[3] Force, *William Whiston, Honest Newtonian* (Cambridge; Cambridge UP, 1985); Castillejo, *The Expanding Force in Newton's Cosmos* (Madrid; Ediciones de Arte y Bibliofilia, 1981).

[4] There have been a number of important reinterpretations of Restoration literary culture in recent years. See, for example, Michael McKeon, *Politics and Poetry in Restoration England: Dryden's "Annus Mirabilis"* (Cambridge: Harvard UP, 1975) and "Marxist Criticism and Marriage à la Mode," *The Eighteenth Century: Theory and Interpretation,* 24 (1983), 141-62; Laura Brown, "The Ideology of Restoration Poetic Form: John Dryden," *PMLA,* 97 (1982), 395-407; J. Douglas Canfield, "The Ideology of Restoration Tragicomedy," *ELH,* 51 (1984), 447-64; J. R. Jacob, *Henry Stubbe: Radical Protestantism and the Early Enlightenment in England* (Cambridge: Cambridge UP, 1983); Nicholas Jose, *Ideas of the Restoration in English Literature 1660-71* (Cambridge, Mass: Harvard UP, 1984); and Susan Staves, *Players' Scepters: Fictions of Authority in the Restoration* (Lincoln: U of Nebraska P, 1979).

[5] *Millenarianism and Messianism in Enlightenment Culture,* ed. Richard Popkin (Berkeley: U of California P, 1987).

[6] Westfall, "Newton's *Origines,*" p. 16. Subsequent quotations will be indicated parenthetically in the text.

[7] Knoespel, "Newton and the School of Time: *The Chronology of Ancient Kingdoms Amended* and the Crisis in Late Seventeenth-Century Historiography," *The Eighteenth Century: Theory and Interpretation,* 29 (1988), forthcoming.

[8] Dobbs, *The Foundations of Newton's Alchemy* (Cambridge: Cambridge UP, 1975), and "Newton's Copy of *Secrets Reveal'd* and the Regimen of the Work, "*Ambix,* 26 (1979), 145-69; Westfall, "The Role of Alchemy in Newton's Career," in *Reason, Experiment, and Mysticism in the Scientific Revolution,* ed. M. L. Righini Bonelli and William R. Shea (New York: Science History Publications, 1975), pp. 189-232, and "Newton and Alchemy," in *Occult and Scientific Mentalities in the Renaissance,* ed. Brian Vickers (Cambridge; Cambridge UP, 1984), pp. 315-35.

[9] On the relationships among the occult, science, and politics see D. P. Walker, *The Decline of Hell* (Chicago: U of Chicago P, 1964); Frances Yates, *The Rosicrucian Enlightenment* (1972; rpt. New York: Routledge and Kegan Paul, 1986); Keith Thomas, *Religion and the Decline of Magic* (London: Weidenfeld, 1971); Margaret C. Jacob, *The Newtonians and the English Revolution, 1689-1720* (Ithaca: Cornell UP, 1976); Christopher Hill, *The World Turned Upside Down: Radical Ideas during the English Revolution* (1971; rpt. Harmondsworth: Penguin, 1975); Brian Easlea, *Witch-Hunting, Magic and the New Philosophy: An Introduction to the Debates of the Scientific Revolution 1450-1750* (Brighton, Sussex: Harvester, 1980); and *Occult and Scientific Mentalities,* ed. Vickers.

[10] Newton, *The System of the World* (London, 1728), pp. 1-2.

[11] For a polemical defense of a "dialogic" analytical language in literary criticism see Don H. Bialostosky, "Dialogics as an Art of Discourse in Literary Criticism," *PMLA,* 101 (1986), 788-97.

[12] Westfall, "Newton's Theological Manuscripts," pp. 137-38.

[13] Christianson, *In the Presence of the Creator: Isaac Newton and His Time* (New York: Free Press, 1984).

[14] See Jacques Lacan, *Ecrits: A Selection,* trans. Alan Sheridan (New York: Norton, 1977); Jane Gallop, *Reading Lacan* (Ithaca: Cornell UP, 1985); Julia Kristeva, *Desire in Language: A Semiotic Approach to Literature and Art,* ed. Leon Roudiez; trans. Alice Jardine, Thomas Gora, and Leon Roudiez (New York: Columbia UP, 1980); Mikhail Bakhtin, *The Dialogic Imagination,* ed. Michael Holquist; trans. Caryl Emerson and Michael Holquist (Austin: U of Texas P, 1981); V. N. Voloshinov [Bakhtin], *Marxism and the Philosophy of Language,* trans. Ladislav Matejka and I. R. Titunik (1973; rpt. Cambridge, Mass.: Harvard UP,

1986); Lev Vygotsky, *Thought and Language,* trans. Alex Kozulin, rev. ed. (Cambridge, Mass.: MIT P, 1986); and the recent special issue of *Critical Inquiry,* edited by Francoise Meltzer, *The Trial(s) of Psychoanalysis,* 13 (1987).

[15] Brian Vickers, "The Royal Society and English Prose Style: A Reassessment," *Rhetoric and the Pursuit of Truth: Language Change in the Seventeenth and Eighteenth Centuries* (Los Angeles: Clark Library, 1985), pp. 1-76; Paul Arakelian, "The Myth of a Restoration Style Shift," *The Eighteenth Century: Theory and Interpretation,* 20 (1979), 227-45.

[16] See Ralph W. V. Elliott, "Isaac Newton's 'Of an Universall Language,'" *MLR,* 52 (1957), 1-18.

[17] Significantly, in *Daniel,* Newton cut all the references to Egyptians, "Eastern expositors," and hieroglyphics, bringing his account of biblical language more in line with traditional interpretations of the prophecies of the sort practiced by Joseph Mede, Henry More, and others in the seventeenth century.

[18] The "First Book" in manuscript runs to over 150 pages; see McLachlan, p. 119.

[19] Drawing on the work of Bakhtin and seventeenth-century writers on language, I have made this argument at greater length in chapters one and two of *Two-Edg'd Weapons: Style and Ideology in the Comedies of Etherege, Wycherley, and Congreve* (Oxford: Clarendon, 1988).

[20] *The Correspondence of Isaac Newton,* seven volumes, ed. H. W. Turnball, et al (Cambridge: Cambridge UP, 1957-1976), III, 83-128; 129-44. For Newton's plans to publish the *"Letter to a friend,"* see pp. 123-24.

[21] See Westfall, *"Origines,"* p. 31 and, on Dryden, Phillip Harth, *Contexts of Dryden's Thought* (Chicago: U of Chicago P., 1968), especially pp. 115-48.

Betty Jo Teeter Dobbs and Margaret C. Jacob (essay date 1995)

SOURCE: "The *Principia:* Composition and Content," in *Newton and the Culture of Newtonianism,* Humanities Press, 1995, pp. 38-46.

[*Below, Dobbs and Jacob briefly outline the origin and content of Newton's* Principia.]

Edmond Halley (1656-1752), Fellow of the Royal Society and later Astronomer-Royal, was a central behind-the-scenes figure in stimulating the writing of Newton's most important work and in seeing it through the press (editing it, correcting proof sheets, drawing

geometric figures, and even funding the publication himself). ***Philosophiae naturalis principia mathematica*** (*The Mathematical Principles of Natural Philosophy*), published in London in 1687 and now usually designated simply by its abbreviated Latin title as ***Principia,*** was the capstone of the Scientific Revolution of the sixteenth and seventeenth centuries and is often said to be the greatest work of science ever published.

The occasion for Newton to write the book arose in the following manner. Halley, Robert Hooke, and Christopher Wren (1632-1723), the great architect responsible for rebuilding many of the churches of London after the Great Fire of 1666, met in London early in 1684 and discussed a problem in celestial mechanics associated with the sun-centered astronomy of Copernicus: what curve would the planets describe if the force of attraction toward the sun varied inversely with the square of the distance of the planets from the sun? The three men reached no firm conclusion, but Halley, having heard that the Lucasian Professor in Cambridge might have some ideas on the subject, traveled to Cambridge in August of 1684 and put the question to Newton. Newton immediately responded that the curve would be an ellipse. When Halley asked Newton how he knew that, Newton responded that he had calculated it. Newton could not find his papers on the subject but promised Halley to do the work again and send the papers to Halley in London. [73; 101]

Whatever Newton might have done before on this matter, it was nothing compared to the power and generality of the work he then produced. By November of 1684 Newton had written and sent to London the first fruits of his new work, a tract on the motion of bodies in orbit. In it he defined centripetal force for the first time: "that by which a body is impelled or attracted towards some point regarded as its centre." He also defined resistance: "that which is the property of a regularly impeding medium," but he hastened to add that for his first several propositions on celestial dynamics "the resistance is nil." Thus by November of 1684 Newton knew the motions of celestial objects were not impeded by the medium through which they moved. [18:130; 73; 101]

If, however, the heavens were filled with the hypothetical aether of the mechanical philosophers, that aether should constitute a resisting medium. Unless the medium is somehow disposed to move with exactly the same variable speed that the planetary body exhibits, the planet should encounter enough resistance from the medium to cause an observed deviation from the mathematical prediction, just as projectiles in the terrestrial atmosphere are observed to deviate from mathematical prediction. [18; 73; 78]

Newton's realization that no form of the hypothetical gravitational aether of the mechanical philosophy could be reconciled with actual celestial motions cleared the deck, so to speak, for the development of his mathematical law of universal gravity, but it must have been rather a shock to him at first. From the time of his introduction to mechanical philosophy in the 1660s until early in the 1680s, he left an extensive record of his aethereal speculations, as we have seen. Even as he modified his schemata from time to time, he seems never to have doubted that the cause of gravity was some sort of material aether. But if the heavens were filled with such an aether, then its presence should produce some notable retardation on the motions of bodies passing through it, and none was in evidence. Newton had had to rethink all his aethereal mechanisms in order to make that statement in the first draft of his small tract on the motion of bodies, and one result of his rethinking is already in evidence in his definition of centripetal force. Whereas in earlier documents Newton had offered explanations of apparent *attractions* in terms of aethereal *impulsions* (impacts or pressure that pushed rather than pulled or attracted in a mysterious fashion), in the new definition he equivocated. Bodies are "impelled or attracted" by a centripetal force, he said. No causal mechanism was suggested nor any preference indicated between the two ways of describing the action of the force, a stance he was soon to adopt in the *Principia* itself. [18:132]

Newton left a great many papers associated with the writing of the *Principia*? He wrote and revised many times as he worked his way through one major conceptual or mathematical or observational difficulty after another. He worked at a very high level of involvement and creativity, by all reports—forgetting to eat, sleeping little. If he started out to go somewhere, a new idea or a fresh solution to an old problem might strike him, in which case he would return to his desk immediately and begin to write again, often even forgetting to sit down. The final work, passing bit by bit through Halley's hands to the press, eventually took the form of three books: the first two were severely mathematical treatments of the motions of bodies and of terrestrial and celestial mechanics, and the last one applied his mathematical discoveries to explicate the system of the world in which we live. It was our own solar system Newton described: the planets (including our earth) move around the sun in elliptical orbits and lesser satellites orbit some of the planets, and the distant stars are understood to be suns similar to our own. The work laid out the grand design of the universe that was accepted by educated people everywhere until modified by Einstein in this century, and it established the basic parameters of classical physics and mechanics. [10; 11; 12; 21; 52; 73; 77; 101]

The problems Newton solved in the *Principia* had become more and more urgent with each stage of development in astronomy and natural philosophy since the sixteenth century. The astronomy of the ancients had been geocentric: that is, with a stable and unmoving earth stood in the center of the cosmic spheres, while the planets and the stars revolved around the earth at constant speeds in circular patterns. It was in the nature of heavenly bodies to move in circles, a perfect and eternal geometric form, the ancients had said; perhaps also, some speculated, the planets and stars were embedded in crystalline spheres that carried them around in their endless circuits, or perhaps they were moved by angels. When Nicholas Copernicus (1473-1543) replaced the central earth with the central sun in 1543, creating a heliocentric (sun-centered) system, the earth was set in motion and became just another planet in orbit around the sun. That was very difficult for people to accept: the earth does not feel to us as if it is in motion; also, traditional Aristotelian physics assumed an immobile earth at the center, so a new physics was required for a moving earth. [10; 52]

Galileo Galilei (1564-1642) supplied the physics for a moving earth, showing how two or more motions could be compounded together, which Aristotle had claimed was impossible. So if the earth moves, everything on the surface of the earth moves with it, as well as having individual motions. Thus a cannonball fired straight up will return to land in the cannon's mouth (wind and other minor irregularities neglected), for the cannonball continues to share the earth's motion even as it ascends and descends. Galileo also found a mathematical law for the accelertion of falling bodies; the distance traveled is proportional to the square of the time the body has been falling from rest, and the constant of proportionality is the acceleration of the body due to gravity. So those that understood it were satisfied that a new physics for a moving earth was possible. But, on the other hand, Galileo's work did not explain much about motions in the heavens. [4; 10; 55]

In the meantime Tycho Brahe (1546-1601), a Danish nobleman, had collected vast new quantities of astronomical data. Utilizing huge observational instruments of his own design, he had obtained the most accurate naked eye (pretelescopic) astronomical data then available, and with Brahe's death in 1601 these data had passed to Johannes Kepler (1571-1630). Kepler, who was a Copernican and the Imperial Mathematician to Emperor Rudolf II in Prague, spent years with the data for Mars, calculating and recalculating in an effort to find a smooth curve that would fit that accurate data. The result was his *Astronomia nova* (*The New Astronomy*), published in 1609, in which he announced his first two laws of planetary motion: (1) planets move around the sun in ellipses (not circles), with the sun at one focus of the ellipse; (2) the area law, that the radius vector (the straight line from the planet to the sun) sweeps out equal areas in equal times. The area law means that when the planet is most distant from the sun in its elliptical orbit (at aphelion) it moves most slowly, whereas when it is closest to the sun (at perihelion) it moves most rapidly. The planet's orbital velocity is not constant, as the ancients had claimed, but varies constantly between the two extremes at aphelion and perihelion. Kepler's third law, the so-called harmonic law, appeared in 1619 in *Harmonice mundi* (*The Harmony of the World*). It tied the entire solar system together mathematically by relating each planet's average distance from the sun to the time that planet takes to complete one orbit around the sun. If one cubes the average distance for any planet and divides that number by the square of the time that same planet takes to go once around the sun (one year in the case of our earth), then the number obtained will be a constant. The same number is obtained for each and every one of the planets in our solar system. Kepler's three laws demonstrated some quite remarkable regularities in the solar system that no one had suspected before, and the third law especially was essential to Newton's discovery of the inverse-square law of gravity. [4; 5; 10; 19; 40; 52; 73; 102; 106; 107]

Kepler's work was fundamental to Newton's, but it was really Kepler's work as much as anything that demanded a new solution to the problem of planetary motion. As long as it was thought that the planets moved at constant speeds in circular patterns because it was the nature of heavenly bodies to move in circles, astronomers had seldom asked what made them move. But with elliptical motion at variable speeds, one could no longer ignore the problem: in the ellipse the planet moves most rapidly when it is closest to the sun (perihelion) and most slowly at the greatest distance from the sun (aphelion), and its speed varies constantly between those two extremes at all the other points in its orbit. What could possibly make an orbiting body behave like that? Kepler had offered a tentative solution—a magnetic force emanating from the sun—but his solution did not work well at all and was not widely accepted. [5; 10]

It fell to Newton to solve the problem and to put the pieces of the puzzle together in a satisfactory way, synthesizing the terrestrial physics of Galileo with the celestial physics of Kepler to found a universal physics based on the law of universal gravity. Gravity is the attractive centripetal force that pulls the planets toward the sun with an acceleration identical to the acceleration of gravity on earth that acts on falling bodies. The tendency of the planet to fall toward the sun is balanced by its other tendency, to continue at every moment to move in a straight line in the direction it was already moving, the force of inertia. That was, of course, the balance of forces Hooke had suggested to Newton in 1679, but Newton carried the solution far beyond Hooke's speculations by powerful mathematical demonstrations and quantitative laws. [10; 73; 77; 101]

There were three axioms, or laws of motion, upon which Newton based this work: (1) every body will continue in its state of rest or uniform motion in a straight line unless it is compelled to change its state by (external) force impressed upon it (the law of inertia); (2) a change of motion is always proportional to the motive force being applied to the body, and the new motion will be in the straight line in which the force is impressed; (3) for every action there is always an equal and opposite reaction. [77]

From that starting point Newton was able to derive mathematically the laws of his predecessors and go on to develop his own law of universal gravity: the force of gravity is always equal to the constant of acceleration times the product of the masses of the two attracting bodies divided by the square of the distance between them. The earth attracts the moon and keeps it in its orbit around the earth: likewise the moon attracts the earth, an effect most noticeable on the watery surfaces of our globe, where it causes the tides. The sun attracts the planets and their satellites; but likewise the planets attract the sun and the other planets, and so forth, the latter effect being noticeable in certain perturbations (disruptions) in the predicted orbits. Since mass is involved in the general equation, Newton was able, once the forces were known, to evaluate the weight of celestial objects far beyond the reach of human scales. One must suppose even Newton himself was a little awed at what he had done; certainly many of his contemporaries and his later followers were. [77; 101]

The *Principia* offered succeeding generations two primary aspects. It synthesized terrestrial and celestial physics in a way that had never been done before, for as we saw above, Aristotle's system was sharply divided at the sphere of the moon and had one set of physical laws below the moon and a different set above the moon. But the *Principia* also had another side. In addition to its grand unified vision of the universe, it provided a rational mechanics for the operations of machines on earth. The artisans who had created the machinery so common in western Europe by the seventeenth century had had handbooks to guide them, and rules of thumb worked out and passed on in craft guilds, but they had never before had definite physical laws to enable them to calculate and predict mechanical forces and rationalize their control. As we will see in Part II, Newton's followers soon spread the new mechanics to sections of the population that could not read the *Principia* for themselves and thus helped facilitate the Industrial Revolution of the eighteenth century.

But for all the importance of his work, Newton no longer had a mechanical explanation for gravity, and that was a serious problem. Continental natural philosophers accused him of reintroducing occult qualities into natural philosophy, meaning that attractive centripetal (center-seeking) force of gravity, because there was no physical, material substrate to explain the action of gravity. Such occult (hidden, secret, nonphysical) qualities and forces were exactly what the seventeenth-century mechanical philosophers had hoped to eliminate with their aethereal explanations, where matter operated on other bits of matter by impact or pressure. Human beings can understand those sorts of contact mechanisms, for it is ever so easy to envision them; we see such contact forces around us every day. But it is impossible to imagine an attractive force of gravity, without physical contact, reaching across millions of miles of empty space to hold a planet in its orbit. So in a sense the Continental philosophers were quite correct in saying that Newton had reintroduced occult qualities into natural philosophy; Newton really was no longer an orthodox mechanical philosopher in the seventeenth-century meaning of the term. Newton had his mathematical laws to explain the action of gravity, and that was all he had. He had no physical explanation of it at all, and that left him very uneasy, for he had previously accepted the argument that all force must be exchanged by some sort of contact mechanism. [18; 101]

FURTHER READING

Bibliography

Wallis, Peter and Ruth Wallis. *Newton and Newtonia, 1672-1975: A Bibliography*. Folkestone, England: Dawson, 1977, 362 p.

    An exhaustive bibliography of works by and about Newton.

Biography

Andrade, E. N. da C. *Isaac Newton*. London: Collins, 1954, 140 p.

    Brief, readable biography containing a lucid description of the *Principia*.

Brewster, David. *Memoirs of the Life, Writings, and Discoveries of Sir Isaac Newton*. 2 vols. Edinburgh: Thomas Constable, 1855.

    A competent, standard life of Newton.

Manuel, Frank E. *A Portrait of Isaac Newton*. Cambridge, Mass.: Harvard University Press, 1968, 478 p.

    Uses Freudian analytical approaches to study Newton's personality.

Westfall, Richard S. *Never at Rest: A Biography of Isaac Newton*. Cambridge: Cambridge University Press, 1980, 328 p.

    A definitive biography using recent scholarship. Contains an extensive bibliographic essay.

Criticism

Burtt, E. A. "The Metaphysics of Newton." In *The Metaphysical Foundations of Modern Physical Science,* pp. 202-99. New York: Harcourt Brace, 1925, 349 p.

    Contains a good essay on Newton's methodology.

Cohen, I. Bernard. *The Newtonian Revolution*. Cambridge and New York: Cambridge University Press, 1980, 404 p.

    Discusses how Newton's work and methods have altered science and history.

Dobbs, Betty Jo Teeter. *The Foundations of Newton's Alchemy; or, "The Hunting of the Greene Lyon"*. Cambridge and New York: Cambridge University Press, 1975, 300 p.

    Thorough introduction to Newton's extensive alchemical work.

Hall, A. R. "Sir Isaac Newton's Note-book, 1661-65." *Cambridge Historical Journal* 9 (1948): 239-50.

    Discussion of Newton's optics using manuscript material.

McMullin, Ernan. "The Significance of Newton's *Principia* for Empiricism." In *Religion, Science, and Worldview: Essays in Honor of Richard S. Westfall*, edited by Margaret J. Osler and Paul Lawrence Farber, pp. 33-59. Cambridge University Press, 1985.

    Examines how Newton's *Principia* challenged classical empiricism and contributed to the development of a modern epistemology.

More, Louis Trenchard. "Argument on the Nature of Light: Newton on Theory and Hypothesis." In *Isaac Newton: A Biography*, pp. 82-121. Charles Scribner's Sons, 1934.

    Discusses Newton's methodology in developing theories on light and color, and traces Newton's rivalry with fellow scientist Robert Hooke.

Strong, E. W. "Newton's 'Mathematical Way'." In *Roots of Scientific Thought: A Cultural Perspective*, edited by Philip P. Wiener and Aaron Noland, pp. 412-32. New York: Basic Books, 1957.

    Explores Newton's use of mathematics in formulating theories on the physical universe.

Turnbull, H. W. *The Mathematical Discoveries of Newton*. London and Glasgow: Blackie & Son, 1945, 68 p.

    Accessible to the non-mathematician.

Blaise Pascal

1623-1662

French scientist, theologian, and philosopher.

INTRODUCTION

Considered one of the most advanced thinkers of his time in the areas of science and mathematics, Pascal is admired today mostly for his spiritual insights, argumentational style and form, and mastery of the French language. His queries into matters both secular and religious involved a uniform methodology—the construction of mathematical proofs—and focused chiefly on the dichotomy between reason and faith. Modern critics and scholars agree that Pascal's influence and participation in some of the most prominent intellectual debates of his time, as well as his writings on such disparate subjects as science and religion, make him an important contributor to the history of ideas.

Biographical Information

Pascal was born to Étienne and Antoinette Begon Pascal, members of the *petite noblesse*, in the provincial town of Clermont en Auvergne in 1623. Pascal's mother died in 1626, leaving his father alone to raise him and his two sisters, Gilberte and Jacqueline. In 1631 the family moved to Paris, where Pascal was schooled solely by his father, a mathematician, who prevented Pascal from studying mathematics until he had first mastered Latin and Greek. A child prodigy, Pascal had secretly taught himself geometry and, by the age of twelve, had demonstrated thirty-two propositions in Euclid's *Elements of Geometry*. Pascal accompanied his father on weekly mathematical lectures organized by Father Marin Mersenne, one of the foremost scholars of that period. In 1638 Pascal's father fled Paris because of disputes over policy issues with Cardinal Richelieu, but was pardoned a year later and appointed royal tax commissioner at Rouen. In 1639 Pascal began writing his first major work, *Essai pour les coniques* (1640). In 1642, he invented the *machine arithmétique*—a device that performed basic mathematical functions—to help his father in his tax work. Pascal also pursued geometry, number theory, and probability theory, and undertook a series of important experiments concerning the behavior of liquids in equilibrium. These experiments in which Pascal attempted to disprove the notion that nature abhors a vacuum, were published in *Expériences nouvelles touchant le vide* (1647). In 1646 the elder Pascal injured his hip in a fall, and for three months was cared for by two men

who were followers of Cornelius Jansen, a Dutch theologian whose ideas about Catholicism were based on the teachings of St. Augustine. Pascal's association with the Jansenists compelled him to practice his own Catholicism more conscientiously. In 1647 Pascal returned to Paris for treatment of chronic headaches, stomach pains, and partial paralysis of the legs. With the death of his father in 1651, Pascal abandoned his religious interests for the Paris social scene. He associated with the freethinking and libertine friends of the Duc de Roannez, his childhood companion, but eventually came to view his social amusements as an impediment to his spiritual progress. On the evening of November 23, 1654, Pascal claimed to have had an experience so profound that he vowed thereafter to devote himself solely to religious activities: he claimed to have been in the presence of the "God of Abraham, God of Isaac, God of Jacob, not of the philosophers and of the learned." Pascal documented this religious experience in a series of notes (called the *Mémorial*) which he had sewn into the lining of his coat and carried around with him to serve as a reminder. In 1655, Pascal made several visits to two Jansenist convents and became acquainted with Antoine Arnauld, a prominent Jansenist accused of heresy by the Jesuits. With the help of Arnauld and Pierre Nicole, Pascal wrote (under the pseudonym Louis dc Montalte) *Lettres provinciales* [1656-57; *Provincial Letters*], a series of eighteen published letters that attacked Jesuit doctrines. By 1659, Pascal's health had deteriorated so much that he was unable to write for extended periods of time. He spent the last years of his life mostly praying, reading the Bible, and helping the poor. Pascal left behind a collection of unfinished fragments at his death—published posthumously as the *Pensées de M. Pascal sur la religion et sur quelques autres sujets* [1670; *Thoughts*]—that was conceived as an *Apologie de la religion chrétienne* [apology for Christianity], which he hoped would dispel the widespread skepticism and hostility toward religion he had witnessed among the upper classes of French society.

Major Works

Pascal's religious writings, especially the *Provincial Letters* and the *Pensées*, enjoy wide readership, and his mathematical and scientific writings continue to interest specialists in these fields. Literary and religious scholars are studying Pascal's mathematical and scientific works to understand not only his concepts of truth and knowledge, but to gain further insight into his religious beliefs. For example, in two of Pascal's most important mathematical works—originally intended as a geometry textbook for the Jansenists schools—*De l'esprit géométrique* and *De l'art de persuader* [*On the Art of Persuasion*], Pascal outlined his epistemology, arguing that certainty in propositions can be logically deduced from simple or first principles. Moreover, Pascal developed many of the ideas concerning the human condition in the *Pensées* that he had previously expressed in the *Provincial Letters*. He explained that shortcomings in man's rational capacities require that these first principles are instinctual or heartfelt. According to Pascal, then, man's dubious understanding of the truth naturally makes him skeptical, but this skepticism can be overcome through divine revelations he receives once he submits to God. Man's limitations and dependence on God are also an important theme of the *Provincial Letters*. These letters assume several different forms: in some, an unnamed observer writes to a friend in the country about the disputes between Jansenist and Jesuit theologians taking place at the Sorbonne; in others, the unnamed observer writes directly to Jesuit theologians; in others, the unnamed observer addresses the Jesuit Père Annat, Louis XIV's confessor. In many of the letters Pascal attempted to disprove the Jesuits' doctrine of *sufficient* grace: the power of humans to either accept or reject God's graces, thereby shaping their own destiny. Rather, Pascal advocated *efficacious* grace: the Jansenist notion that God's graces always ensure salvation, but only for those who

have been predestined for a life of Chrisian virtue. In other letters, Pascal attacked the laxity of the Jesuits' system of moral casuistry, and sought to discredit their moral and theological views by carefully uncovering errors in their reasoning.

Critical Reception

The continuing popularity of the *Provincial Letters* and the *Pensées* derives in large part from their readability. Scholars have consistently remarked on Pascal's literary artistry, praising his various styles and tones; his clever use of imagery, irony, and wit; and his habit of discussing mystical questions in terms of practical problems and consequences. Studies of the *Provincial Letters* and the *Pensées* often focus on Pascal's method of argument—specifically, on how he evidences his analyses of theological doctrines with the construction of mathematical proofs. Pascal's strict separation of reason and faith in both the *Provincial Letters* and the *Pensées* is also a frequent topic of analysis. Books and essays on the *Pensées*, the more widely discussed of the two works, commonly examine Pascal's theories of knowledge as well as correlations between his threefold understanding of reality (corporeal, intellectual, and spiritual) and his three-part system of knowing (sense, mind, and heart). In addition, much critical debate has been stimulated by Pascal's "wager" argument in the *Pensées* which reasons that it is more advantageous to believe than not believe in God. The critical history of the *Pensées* is also in large part a history of its publication. Pascal's planned "apology for Christianity" consisted of approximately one thousand notes of varying lengths, some collected in identifiable units, others not. The first edition of these notes, published in 1670 as the *Pensées*, included only portions of the original manuscript, organized and amended by the editors. It was not until the 1840s that a complete version of the *Pensées* appeared, based on manuscripts in the Bibliothèque Nationale. The 1952 version of the *Pensées* published by one of Pascal's relatives, is believed by scholars to be most accurately representative of the ordering of the notes as Pascal wrote them. This version, compiled by Louis Lafuma, is considered the definitive edition of the work. Critical controversy still exists, however, concerning how the fragments of the *Pensées* should be ordered for purposes of reader accessibility. Some critics argue that they should be arranged according to subject matter, based on informed opinions of what Pascal intended to say. Others contend that Pascal's original ordering should be preserved because it reveals important aspects of his conceptual and compositional process.

PRINCIPAL WORKS

Essai pour les coniques (nonfiction) 1640

Expériences nouvelles touchant le vide (scientific nonfiction) 1647

Lettres provinciales [with Antoine Arnauld and Pierre Nicole under the joint pseudonym of Louis de Montalte] [*Provincial Letters*] (letters) 1656-57

Traité de l'équilibre des liqueurs (treatise) 1663

Traité du triangle arithmétique (treatise) 1665

Pensées de M. Pascal sur la religion et sur quelques autres sujets (nonfiction) 1670

Oeuvres complètes, publiées suivant l'ordre chronologique, avec documents, complémentaires, introductions et notes. 14 vols. (nonfiction) 1904-14

The Physical Treatises of Pascal: The Equilibrium of Liquids and the Weight of the Mass of Air (treatises) 1937

Pensées. The Provincial Letters. (nonfiction/letters) 1941

Great Shorter Works (nonfiction) 1948

Pensées sur la religion et sur quelques autres sujets (nonfiction) 1952

CRITICISM

Isaac Taylor (essay date 1894)

SOURCE: An introduction to *Thoughts on Religion and Philosophy*, by Blaise Pascal, translated by Isaac Taylor, Simpkin, Marshall, Hamilton, Adams, & Co., 1894, pp. iii-lx.

[*In the following excerpt, Taylor argues that the* Pensées *reveal Pascal to be an opponent of, rather than apologist for, Roman Catholicism.*]

Those periodic agitations to which all social systems, whether civil or religious, are liable, carry with them a twofold and opposite influence; the one, and the most direct, tending to give rise to similar movements in neighbouring communities; and the other, operating with hardly less force, to preclude any such convulsions where else they probably would, or certainly must, have taken place. By the very same spectacle of public commotions, minds of a certain class are animated to action, and hurried into the midst of perils; while others are as effectively deterred from giving scope to their rising energies. In this way every revolution which history records may be reckoned at once to have caused, and to have prevented kindred changes.

In no instance has this sort of double influence made itself more apparent than in that of the religious revolution which shook the European system in the sixteenth century; and after having watched the progress of the ecclesiastical renovation of northern Europe, as it spread from land to land, an inquiry, fraught with instruction, might be instituted, concerning that reaction of jealousy, terror, and pious caution, which,

affecting many of the eminent minds of southern Germany, Italy, Spain, and France, smothered those elements of faith and right reason, that, again and again, seemed to be indicating approaching and happy movements.

In Italy, in Austria, in Spain, in France, it was not merely that the dread of reform incited the ecclesiastical and secular authorities to a renewed vigilance, and induced them to have recourse to severities, such as might crush, at the instant, every beginning of change; but much more it was the vague dread of heresy, it was the horror inspired by the mere names of the Reformers, that broke the energy of the very men who, had they been left to the impulse of their own convictions, would, perhaps, themselves, have dared the vengeance of the church, and have led on a reformation. . . .

The writings of Pascal, as well the ***Thoughts*** as the ***Provincial Letters,*** indicate, on almost every page, this latent and indirect influence of the horror of heresy, swaying his mind. The reader, as well in justice to the fame of this great man, as for his own satisfaction, needs to be reminded of the fact now adverted to: and if at any moment he be perplexed by the difficulty of reconciling Pascal's abject and superstitious Romanism with the vigour and clearness of his understanding, and with the simplicity of his piety, he may remember that, beside other causes, not necessary here to specify, this eminent man was well aware that, to give the least indulgence to the impulses of mere reason on certain points of his belief, would involve nothing less than his passing at a leap, or his being forced across the awful gulph that yawned between the paradise of the church, and the gehenna of heresy. A mind like that of Pascal, although it might, in any particular direction, forbid itself to think at all, could never have stayed its own course, midway, had it once started. [A solitary expression, pregnant with meaning, occurs among the *Thoughts,* which should be here pointed out, as indicating Pascal's latent dissatisfaction with the system which he thought it necessary to uphold. So little does the sentiment contained in this passage accord with the general strain of the author's writings, that one is almost inclined to suppose it must have been, as in some other instances is clearly the case, a mere memorandum of an opinion upon which he intended to animadvert.—Il faut avoir une pensée de derière, et juger du tout par-là: en parlant cependant comme le peuple. The full import of this sentence is suggested rather more clearly in the author's own words than in the English; the translator having given the terms an admissible and softened rendering, more in accordance with Pascal's known simplicity and sincerity. Art. cix. p. 198.] And yet it was by submitting to these restraints that he exposed himself to the keen taunts of Voltaire and Condorcet; and it is these bitter sarcasms, read by all the world, that have operated to destroy, almost entirely, the influence he must otherwise have exerted over the minds of his admiring countrymen. What might not have been the issue, for France, had Pascal and his friends held a higher course? But, stooping as they did, before the power that aided the Jesuit in trampling on the Jansenist, they left the field open to the Encyclopedists, who, in the next age, schooled the French people in those lessons of atheism that were to take effect amid the horrors of the revolution.

Putting out of view so much superstition or asceticism as belonged to Pascal's infirm bodily temperament, rather than to his principles as a Romanist, and setting off also, here and there, a phrase in which he does homage to the Romish Church, he may fairly be accounted as one of ourselves—substantially, a protestant: and such in fact he was by his opposition to the spirit and corruptions of that church, as embodied in the society of Jesuits; as well as generally by the position he occupied in common with his friends, as obnoxious to the papacy. Protestants may very properly think of him rather as placed on the same radius with themselves, than as moving in another orbit.

In most instances, when any language meets the reader which reminds him painfully of the writer's enthralment to Rome, the incidental phrase, or the corollary in argument, instead of its standing inseparably connected with the context, as it would have done, had the writer been himself a better papist, hangs loose, and might even be removed without leaving any perceptible hiatus;—nay, such excisions (although not in fact justifiable on the part of an editor or translator) would be like the absorption of flaws from an otherwise spotless surface of marble. On this ground Pascal appears to much advantage when compared with Fenelon, who, although not his inferior in purity and elevation of spirit, had been carried much father from the simplicity of the Christian system by the specious mysticism that has beguiled so many eminent men of the Romish communion. Pascal is no mystic:—his vigorous good sense, although it did not exempt him from some trivial superstitions in his personal conduct, held him back on the brink of that dim gulph wherein secluded speculatists, of every age, have so often been lost. It is thus sometimes that a strong man, who would instantly burst a rope wherewith any might attempt to confine him, yet quietly suffers himself to be held down by a thread. Pascal's French editors, who jeer at his bodily mortifications and his frivolous observances, had not sufficient acquaintance with the history of religion to be conscious of the proof he gave of a substantial force of mind in keeping himself clear of the sophistical pietism by which, on all sides, he was surrounded.

The *Thoughts* of Pascal should never be read without a knowledge of the circumstances that attended their production. . . . In how few instances would an author's loose private notes, and the undigested materials out of

which he had designed to construct what might be intelligible to others, present so much appearance of consistency and order, as, in fact, belong to this collection. Whatever abruptness there may seem in many of the transitions, nevertheless a real and ascertainable unity of purpose pervades the whole. This one purpose, manifestly governing the writer's mind at all times, appears even in those of the *Thoughts* that relate immediately to the mathematics, or to other secular subjects; for it is evident that Pascal was constantly intent upon the great business of establishing sacred truths; and, that, with this view, he laboured so to lay down the principles of reasoning in geometry, or in the physical sciences, as should secure an advantage, more or less direct, for the evidences of Christianity.

It should be said that the confusion in which Pascal's papers were found after his death, and which belonged also to the earlier editions of the *Thoughts,* has been, in great measure, remedied by later editors; and especially by Condorcet, who, little as he relished the principles or the argument of his distinguished countryman, applied to the best purpose, his own eminently perspicacious mind, in disentangling the disordered mass, and in reducing it to some logical consistency. Bossut, adopting, in the main Condorcet's classification, brought it to a higher perfection, and thus, by the labours of these two competent men, the modern reader foregoes, perhaps, but little of the benefit he might have derived from the author's own cares in preparing his thoughts for the public eye. [In some instances, the contrarieties of opinion, between one paragraph and the next, was such, and so alternate, as to make it certain that the author had intended to throw his materials into the form of a dialogue, between a sceptic and himself; and his editors have in some cases, as in chap vii. of the present translation, actually completed what was clearly Pascal's meaning. Unless understood as a dialogue, the whole would be contradictory and unintelligible. It is probable that, in some other places, where the indication is less manifest, a similar distribution of the *Thoughts* was in the author's mind when he committed them to writing.]

Leaving the *Thoughts* in the order to which they have so well been reduced, we shall find a convenience in assuming, for a while, a rather different principle of arrangement, as the ground of the remarks that are to occupy this introductory essay.

With this view, then, we may consider the *Thoughts* as bearing upon—

I. Abstract Philosophy, and the general principles of reasoning.
II. Ethics; and more especially, the Pathology of Human Nature.
III. Devotional Sentiment.
IV. Christian Theology.

V. The argument in behalf, of Religion against Atheists, and of Christianity against Infidels, to which are appended incidental apologies—for Romanism, and for Jansenism; or for the Port Royal party.

In the first place, then, (nor need the merely religious reader think this branch of the subject of no interest to him) something demands to be said of that portion of Pascal's *Thoughts* which relates to Abstract Philosophy, and to the general principles of reasoning.

It does not appear that Pascal had become acquainted with the writings of Lord Bacon, which even so long as forty years after their first publication, had not so commanded the attention of the philosophic world in England or abroad, as to ensure their having been read by all who themselves pretended to take rank among philosophers. His scientific writings, however, afford unquestionable indications of the fact that, along with the great minds of the age, be deeply resented the antiquated tyranny of the pseudo-science, and of the jargon logic which so long had shackled the European intellect. "The true philosophy," says he "is to scout philosophy:" nor was this uttered with a cynical feeling, or in affectation; for in other places he deliberately declares his contempt, both of the Aristotelian logic, and of the method of prosecuting physical inquires, then commonly practised. But although he himself, as in the signal instance of the barometrical experiment, followed as if by instinct, the methods of modern science, (or rather anticipated those methods) and although in the admirable article on "authority in matters of philosophy," he convincingly shows the error of the antiquated system, and points out a better path, yet it does not appear that he had, like Bacon, so digested his notions as to be able to announce a new and hopeful physical logic. On the contrary, his tone in reference to natural philosophy is, altogether, desponding, and he seems so little to have foreseen the happy issue of the revolution which was then actually in its commencement, that he turns towards the mathematics as the only ground on which the (ground of pure faith excepted) any fixed principles, or absolute truth could be met with.

"Every body asks for the means of avoiding error; and the professors of logic pretend to show us the way: but, in fact, the geometrician (mathematician) is the only man who reaches it. Beyond the range of this science, and of what closely follows it, there are no real demonstrations."

This is now true only in a very limited sense; and had Pascal lived to witness, and to take the lead in (as he would had he lived) the conquests of modern science, he would have granted that there *are* conclusions, not mathematical, which it would be most absurd to speak of as at all *less certain* than this—that the three angles of a triangle are equal to two right angles. It can no longer be

admitted, except in a loose and rhetorical style, that, "The sciences touch, at their two extremes—the absolute ignorance of the vulgar, and the conscious ignorance of the greatest and most accomplished minds; who, having learned all that man may know, have found that they know nothing; and who feel themselves to have come home just to that point of universal ignorance whence they started." This mode of speaking, which we still allow the moralists or preacher to use, who vaguely compares the circle of human science, with the infinite and absolute omniscience of the Eternal mind, has actually no meaning, if now applied to any *one* branch of philosophy, as compared with *another*. "What does man know?" exclaims the pensive moralist; and we leave him to reply—"nothing." But if the geometrician were to start up, among his fellows, in the fields of reason, and say "I alone know any thing:—all your pretended sciences are no better than the illusive mists that torment the thirsty traveller on a sandy wilderness:"—we then join issue with this exclusionist; and are prepared to affirm, in behalf of a good portion of all the modern sciences, that they are not a whit less substantial, or less certain, than geometry itself. Pascal, could we now challenge him, would grant as much as this, and would therefore rescind some six or eight of his *Thoughts*.

Mischief arises, in many instances, and especially some damage accrues to the argument in support of Christianity, from the error of confounding the *abstract* certainty or the directness of this or that method of proof, with the certainty of particular propositions, or facts. It would be well if all obscurity were removed from about this very necessary distinction.—Let it be remembered then, that the demonstrations of geometry are, as every one knows, regular, definite, and infallible: while on the other hand, the evidence of testimony is (to speak of it abstractedly) often circuitous, and liable to be fallacious. Be it so; and yet, in fact, there are ten thousand instances in which, not merely is it wise and safe to accept of testimony, as the best sort of proof, under the circumstances, which we can obtain; but in which it would be nothing else but sheer folly to speak of facts, so established, as in any degree *less certain* than are the propositions of Euclid. If seven hundred or seven thousand inhabitants of a town affirm that, last week, or last year, or ten years ago, their market house was burnt down, are we free, sagely to withhold our belief—to shrug the shoulders, and to say—"What you allege may be all very true; but, pardon me, human testimony falls so very far short of mathematical demonstration, that I cannot admit the fact you speak of to be fully established." And what holds good in a comparison of testimony with mathematical proof, holds good also in regard to the physical sciences. The deductions of chemistry, for example, many of them, and even where they involve no mathematical induction, claim to be spoken of as indubitably certain: and so in other departments of philosophy; nor can it be esteemed anything but a foolish and pedantic exaggeration to repeat now, what, in Pascal's time there yet seemed ground to say, namely that—"Out of geometry, man knows nothing." There is indeed a class of persons who, for the sinister purpose of throwing a cloud over the evidence of Christianity, will consent to compromise even the best portions of human knowledge;—the mathematics only excepted. Such persons, knowing well that men will continue to act upon the presumption that the physical sciences are certain, are quite content so long as the sceptical inference of their doctrine is left to attach alone to religion: Pascal himself would have drawn an opposite practical inference from his premises, and have said—"Christianity demands your submission because its truth *is as well* established as that of the physical sciences, on the certainty of which you every day stake your interests, and venture your lives. But we, and especially in the present state of philosophy, are free to deal in another, and a more strenuous manner with pedantic scepticism, and to say— *Many* things are certainly true, besides the propositions of geometry; and among such certainties, are all the principal points of history; and among these, pre-eminently, the facts of the gospel history.

Assuming what we consider as probable, if not absolutely certain, that Pascal had not met with the Novum Organum, or the De Argumentis, it is curious to observe the similarity, or even identity of sentiment, and sometimes of language, which may be traced in those passages where the one and the other speak of the then-existing and ancient philosophy. The scientific reader may with advantage, compare the thoughts referred to in the margin [The reader is referred to the entire chapter, (xxvi), on authority in matters of Philosophy; as well as to the next on Geometry, and to that on the Art of Convincing.] with the preface to the Novum Organum, and with the introductory axioms of the first book. A remarkable coincidence, both of principle and of expression, occurs in the passages in which these two great men state the relative claims of reason and of authority, or of antiquity, as bearing respectively upon the physical sciences, and upon theology: [Compare Pascal's *Thoughts on Authority,* with cap. i. lib. ix, of the De Argumentis, where a remarkable coincidence of thought and expression presents itself. Also aph. 61 and 89, Nov. Organum.] nor can we doubt that, had Pascal lived longer, and directed the main force of his mind to philosophy he would have accelerated its advance, in his own country, at least: and starting forward from the ground where Descartes moved only in a vortex, and where Leibnitz wandered over the wastes of metaphysics, would have opened the road of genuine science;— nay, not improbably he might have snatched from England the glory of a portion of Newton's discoveries.

By no means to be compared with Bacon for grasp of

mind, or for richness, versatility, or boundless faculty of invention, Pascal had more of that caution, justness of intellect, and mathematical simplicity, which belonged to Newton; nor did he want, *intellectually* at least, that high and true independence, and that strong good sense, which impelled the one and the other to break away from the entanglements of the old philosophy. Considering however, his entire constitution, the animal and moral, as well as the intellectual, we may the less regret his having been so soon diverted from scientific pursuits. The reformer, whether in the civil, the ecclesiastical, or the scientific world, should not be merely one of lofty stature in mind, but of a robust moral confirmation. In every age, no doubt, there are minds (accomplishing their course in obscurity) that divine the changes which are to be effected in a future age; but in part the animal force, and in part the opportunity, are wanting to them which are requisite for effectively agitating the inert elements around them. The progress of man has been so slow, not so much because nature generates so few great minds in each age, as because a rare combination of intellectual faculties, of moral qualities, of animal forces, and of external means, are required for enabling any individual to give effect to those improvements which, more than a few in every age, could theoretically have anticipated.

No modern philosophical writer has better than Pascal, marked out the ground occupied by the sciences, and which lies as a middle region between, on the one hand, those elementary principles which are always to be taken for granted, and to be considered as certain, although not capable of being defined or proved;—and, on the other hand—the illimitable space, filled with what is unknown and perhaps inscrutable, but toward which, though never to pervade it, the sciences are continually making incursions, and pushing out their boundaries. Nevertheless the principle of reasoning which he lays down, as universally applicable and sufficient, and which he affirms to be fully carried out in Geometry, namely, to define whatever admits of definition; that is to say everything except our elementary notions; and to prove everything which may be questioned, and which is not self-evident, has in fact only a limited range. This axiom of reasoning, or logical law, applicable as it may be to whatever is *purely abstract,* can subserve no practical purpose or only a very limited one, if brought to bear upon the physical sciences. Pascal cannot be thought to have furnished us with the elements of *Physical Logic,* which still remain to be fully ascertained, and well digested.

To take an example;—what progress could he himself have made in determining the question relative to the alleged weight of the atmosphere, and which he so triumphantly brought to a conclusion by the mere aid of the rules he proposes for deciding between truth and error? We may boldly say, none at all. It is at this point, where heretofore philosophers had come to a stand, that Bacon steps in, and opens wide the path to genuine knowledge, by showing that the methods of *abstract science,* wherein all the entities to be spoken of are creatures of the mind, and therefore fully comprehended and embraced by it—that these methods are totally inapplicable to the *physical sciences,* in relation to which, "man knows absolutely nothing beyond what he may actually have observed." Whether there is in nature, or whether they may be, a perfect vacuum, is a question in deciding which, neither the logic of geometry, nor the logic of metaphysics, can afford us the least assistance: a question like this, involves a knowledge of the most occult properties of matter; and in fact it is a question concerning which, even modern science, is not yet in a position to pronounce with confidence. We well know indeed that it is possible and that it is very easy to exclude, from a certain space, all ponderable or tangible bodies; and we moreover know that the rise of fluids in an exhausted tube is caused by no such "horror of a vacuum," as had been attributed to nature; and that it is as simple a phenomenon as the rise of the scale out of which we have removed the weight that had held the beam in equilibrio. But the fact of a real and absolute vacuum is still a mystery.

There are few portions of the *Thoughts,* if any, that seem to have been more deliberately digested, or that are in fact better condensed, than the entire article "**on the Art of Persuasion,**" [The translator cannot be blamed for rendering—De l' Art de Persuader "on the Art of Persuasion," and yet what Pascal really insists upon in this chapter is not the art of *persuasion,* of which he professes himself no master; but it is the art of *convincing,* or of conducting a purely rational process to a peremptory conclusion.] or what might be termed—the Elements of a true Logic. Pascal, having distinguished between, on the one hand, the methods, various as they may be, which are proper for influencing the minds of men, with all their predilections and personal inclinations, and for bringing them to some given point; and on the other hand, the process of severe reasoning, irrespectively of the condition of the mind to which an argument is addressed; and after professing his inability to offer any system of rules available for the former purpose, proceeds to state the rudiments of the latter method, and which, as stated by him, are substantially those of geometrical demonstration.

"This art, which I call the art of persuasion, and which, properly, is nothing but the management of such proofs as are regular and perfect, consists of three essential parts namely—1. To expound the terms which we intend to employ, by clear definitions;—2. To propound principles or axioms, such as are in themselves evident, for the purpose of establishing the points in question:—3. and then, always to substitute mentally, in the demonstrations, the definitions, in the place of the things defined."

"In adhering to this method," says our author, "we can never fail to produce conviction:" and this may be granted so long as the method itself is applied to those cases only to which it properly attaches. Errors incalculable, and much more than half the logical verbiage, metaphysical, ethical, political, and theological, that encumbers our shelves, has sprung from the practical mistake of forcing the *abstract* method of reasoning upon subjects that are beyond its range:— that is to say which are in whole, or in part, physical. Now it would be easy to show that, while Pascal rejects with scorn the jargon of the Barbara et Baralipton, his own sovereign method is really reducible to the conditions of the syllogistic process:—the substance is the same; the phraseology only being different; for we have but to put in the place of his "self-evident axiom," or principle, the major term of a syllogism; and in the place of the definition, in any particular instance, the minot, and then the "mental substitution" which he speaks of, will stand for the middle term, and involve the conclusion.

In all cases in which the notions, or the things to which a process of reasoning relates, are *the creations of the human mind,* or are, in some other way, thoroughly understood, in their inmost constitution, as, for example, in the several branches of the pure mathematics— in all such cases, what is required in establishing a particular proposition is nothing but to exhibit the relation which a certain quantity or quality bears to some other known quantity or quality. Mathematical reasoning is only the showing forth, or unfolding, of *relations:* and the same may be said of all reasoning which is purely, abstract, or metaphysical. In no such process of reasoning, if scientifically conducted, are we liable to err *by ignorance of the things spoken of;* for these things are notions which the mind penetrates and grasps in the most absolute manner.

But now let it be supposed that some one or more of the things to be defined is an entity, known to the human mind through the senses only, and known in some few of its properties only, or known merely by a limited evidence of testimony; what then becomes of Pascal's "sovereign and infallible method of proof?" it is altogether unavailing. We thoroughly know what we mean by an elliptic curve, generated in such or such a manner; and we may reason concerning its properties with the most entire assurance. But, in the place of a certain curve, abstractedly considered, let it be imagined that we are presuming to predict, irrespectively of experiment, what will be the curve formed by a stream of water, issuing from an aperture in a vessel. In this, as in any similar instance, we find, or soon shall find, that we are "reckoning without our host;" or, in other words, that, in relation to whatever is *physical* there are occult causes at work, all of which must be thoroughly known, before our abstract methods of reasoning can take effect: In physical inquiries, of whatever kind they may be, a vast deal is to be done before we ought to think ourselves in a position, either to define our terms, or to propound our axioms:—so much, in truth, have we to do, that, what remains to be done after this preliminary work has been effected, is a mere form—a verbal winding up, which demands no rules nor any peculiar skill. What pedantry can be more impertinent than that of bringing in the solemnities of the syllogism *after* a course of experiments has so far laid open the constitution of bodies, or their mode of operation one upon another, as that we may safely deduce some general principles concerning them?

All this is now well understood within the circle of the modern physical sciences; and Pascal, had he lived to witness, and to take a part in, what has been effected since his time, would himself have been among the foremost to put in practice modes of reasoning altogether differing from that which he here advances as the one and the only method.

But owing to the indistinctness and imperfection of our notions on subjects connected with morals, religion, and the philosophy of the human mind, and to the vagueness of language, as related to these subjects, the very important distinction between what is purely *abstract,* and what is *physical,* does not here force itself upon our notice, [Bacon in innumerable places of his writings, insists upon the distinction here adverted to, and loudly claims the Philosophy of the mind as belonging to Physics. Universæ illæ (the faculties of the mind) circa quas versartur Scientiæ Logicæ, et Ethicæ; sed in doctrina de anima origines ipsarum tractari debent, idque *physice.* De Aug. Lib. iv, cap. 3. And see particularly the 82d axiom of the Novum Organum, on the inutility of the existing Logic as applied to Physics.] nor, in fact, has it hitherto been much regarded or clearly understood. Hence it has happened that in treating questions of mental and moral philosophy, and of theology too, the logic of *abstract* science has been applied to subjects that are either of a mixed kind, or are perhaps altogether physical. The consequence has been that whatever is the most absurd, and whatever calumniates the Divine nature, or human nature, has been made to appear indubitable, by some process of syllogism. False theories, and errors of reasoning, in relation to the motions of solids and fluids, or to the chemical properties of bodies, are sure after a little while, to meet their refutation by an appeal to facts and experiments; and in such cases we use no ceremony in discarding the logic which has been found to have led us astray. It is otherwise in ethics and theology, wherein errors of a kind to impair the most momentous practical principles, may long maintain themselves, behind the thorny hedges of metaphysical logic. The cessation, in our own times, of theological controversy, and the dead silence that, for some years past, has prevailed within the circle of polemics, may be attributed, as well to other incidental causes, as to a latent feeling that those methods of scholastic disputation which have not as yet been renounced, would, if again put in activity, bring back modes of thinking and opinions, that have been silently consigned to oblivion by the spread of scriptural notions, and by the good sense and better feelings of our times; and especially by the indirect influence of the spirit of Christian zeal and benevolence.

It seemed a proper part of this Introductory Essay to premise a caution concerning that portion of Pascal's *Thoughts* to which, it is manifest, he himself attached a peculiar value; and which perhaps he would have singled out as the most important of them all. Be it remembered then, that, while Pascal's axioms of logic are perfectly sound, when brought to bear upon subjects that already lie wholly within the grasp of the human mind, they can serve us not at all when we approach ground where our knowledge is confessedly partial, and all our notions dim or unfixed. And this assuredly must be admitted in relation to whatever concerns either the Divine Nature, or the constitution of human nature, or the conditions of the unseen world:—on these grounds we may account ourselves qualified to construct syllogisms then, when we have so enlarged our acquaintance with the subjects in question as to be able to define our terms, and to state, without fear of contradiction, our self-evident axioms.

II. We have next to consider Pascal's *Thoughts* as embodying his notions of Ethics, and, more especially, as exhibiting the views he took of the actual condition of human nature, and of its pathology.

It is in the inimitable *Provincial Letters,* rather than in this collection of his *Thoughts,* that Pascal appears to advantage as the firm, acute, and Christian-like moralist. In truth that invigorating excitement at the impulse of which those letters were produced, elevated the writer above himself; or rather, we should say, this extraordinary motive raised him, for a while, to his own real level, beneath which he was too often depressed by the weight of his many bodily infirmities. Not a few of his *Thoughts,* and especially those which convey his notions of human life, are impressions of the mind of Pascal—the valetudinarian, the sufferer, the cœlebs, and the recluse: but when thoroughly roused to come forth as the champion of religion, of morality, and of an oppressed society, he then appears in his proper strength—the strength of his unmatched intellect:—the feeble frame and shattered nerves of the writer have no part in the *Provincial Letters*.

And yet we must acknowledge that, as the antomist of the human heart, and as the keen analyst of its springs of action, the very infirmities of Pascal's animal temperament yielded him an aid. There is, as we well know, a flush and force of full health which is rarely if ever combined with any nice discrimination of character, or with a piercing discernment of the evanescent differences that distinguish man from man. The robust and the happy (the physically happy) are themselves in too much movement to allow of that tranquil subsidence of the thoughts—that refluence of the tide of life, which favours an exact acquaintance with what is latent in human nature. It is not the merry voyagers, who are gaily careering, by favour of wind and tide, upon the sea of life—it is not these that know much of the pebbly bottom, or of the deep grottoes, or gloomy caverns beneath. But Pascal had much to do with the ebbings of animal life; and thus he became familiar with those searching trains of thought that attend superior minds in season of extreme physical depression or exhaustion. When the pulse of life is slow and feeble, the spirit seems to be able to take a nicer hold of minute objects, and to exercise more delicate powers of perception.

Few writers, and perhaps none but the one—his countryman and contemporary, with whom we shall presently find occasion to compare him, have dissected the human heart with a nicer hand than Pascal. His qualification for these difficult intellectual operations appears to have resulted from an uncommon combination of the analytic faculty, proper to the geometrician, with an exquisite moral sense, more often possessed, in this eminent degree, by woman than by man; and very rarely associated with the scientific faculty. Another instance of the sort does not occur to us. He has himself described these two opposite endowments, [Pascal varies a little his phrases in designating these two orders of mind, calling them respectively l'esprit de justesse, and l'esprit de geometrie. The one is force et droiture d'esprit, and the other l'étendue. Again the opposite of l'esprit de geometrie, he names l'esprit de finesse—and what he means is something which, in Scotland, has been called gumption.] and has spoken of them as seldom if ever possessed by the same individual. What he intends in the passage here referred to is, on the one hand, the mathematical power which holds in its grasp a number of principles, with a constant recollection of their various inter-relations, and remote consequences; and on the other, the acute, intuitive perception of minute differences among things which, to common eyes, are undistinguishable; and he affirms that this power and habit of instantaneous discrimination indisposes a mind, so endowed, to give attention to formal methods of proof; while the mathematician, on his part, pays as little respect to perceptions the accuracy of which cannot be methodically proved.

Pascal himself, although he claims no such rare combination of endowments, was at once a proficient in the severest habits of thought, and accustomed to carry the analytic process to its ultimate point; while yet he possessed a penetrating intuition in relation to the commingled elements of our moral nature. So it was that, while mathematical minds, generally, view with contempt, or entirely overlook, whatever cannot be strictly defined, he although pre-eminently mathematical, pursued with as sedulous a curiosity, the occult movements of the human heart, as he did the complex properties of the cycloid.

Certain portions of [Pascal's] *Thoughts* can hardly fail to suggest a comparison of Pascal with Rochefoucauld, his celebrated contemporary; and this involuntary comparison between the religious and the non-religious anatomist of the human heart, brings with it some curious reflections. These two eminent writers were alike remarkable for a justness and perspicacity of understanding which imparted an admirable simplicity and propriety to their style. Both had a great share in fixing the usage of their native language, and in imparting to it that elegance and precision, as well as that thorough transparency, which has become the characteristic and the charm of French philosophical literature. Both, moreover, in their habits of thought, give evidence of their having breathed the atmosphere of a court, where in a peculiar degree, every thing was artificial and false; for although Pascal stood many degrees more remote than the gay Rochefoucauld from the circle of corruption, his rank in society, and his connections, placed him in a position where the court and its manners, were always within his view. With the one therefore, as well as with the other, it is not MAN, who is thought of and described; but the artificial men and women of the French court; and inasmuch as these sophisticated personages were, in an extraordinary degree, cased in the extrinsic and illusory recommendations of rank and luxury—swaddled, like mummies, in perfumed and painted rottenness; and as they needed a great deal of *unwinding,* before the real dimensions and merits of the character could be ascertained, so both these searching spirits acquired a peculiar readiness in performing this stripping operation: when once they set about denuding human nature, they bared it to the very bones.

Those ethical writers whose happy lot it has been to become conversant only, or chiefly, with societies in an unsophisticated state, have usually allowed every thing to pass as really fair and good, which seemed to be so; nor have they often reached any nice discriminations of character. But, on the contrary, those who, like the two writers now spoken of, and others who occupy a similar place in French literature, have known much of the worst specimens of human nature, have lost almost, or altogether, the power of believing any thing at all to be genuine; and have carried the practice of analysis to a point which in reference to human nature, involves an absolute and universal scepticism, and a cheerless contempt of mankind at large.

Rochefoucauld, although himself an amiable man, actually reached this extreme;—and the issue, we have in the "Maxims and Moral Reflections." Pascal was saved from it by his religious sentiments, and by his constant recognition of the original excellence of human nature, and of the immortal dignity opened to man in the Christian system. The one looked no farther than to the degenerate specimens of humanity before him; the other compared these same specimens with an ideal form of absolute moral beauty and perfection. The one views, with cold derision, what the other weeps over. The courtier, in the prospect of wide-spread corruption, indulges his curiosity, undisturbed either by hope or fear:— but the Christian philosopher gazes upon the same field of death, not with unmixed dismay, but with a breathless expectation, waiting until the Spirit from on high shall, in the appointed season, return to reanimate these ghastly forms!

If Rochefoucauld betrays any sort of uneasiness, it is simply that impatience to unmask pretension, and to get every thing valued at its price, and at nothing more, which usually attaches to those who are gifted (or afflicted) with more penetration than their neighbours.— If only every thing can be brought down to its true dimension, if, whatever has hitherto appeared, and is generally accounted noble, can henceforward be thought of as common, or sordid; if only the professors of virtue and honesty can be brought to confess themselves false; if all this can be done, and when whatever has stood high, has been well trodden in the mire, then Rochefoucauld will be content: he has no aspirations, no struggling of a better nature to wrankle in his heart. Not so Pascal, who, himself keenly alive to excellence, mourns to see so many dead to it. This contrast between minds, in some respects, of so analogous a conformation, offers a specimen, the most complete, of two classes of men— the one knowing human nature to consent to it, as it is:—the other, knowing it to sigh and to blush for it, and to attempt its restoration.

A few instances of similarity and of contrast, gathered from the Thoughts, and from the Maxims, may not improperly be adduced to illustrate the comparison we have here instituted, and which is in itself of some significance. In certain passages, as in the one first to be quoted, Pascal seems to have lost hold of that redeeming element which usually distinguishes him from his contemporary, and allows himself to employ the language of exaggeration (against which the reader of the **Thoughts** need be on his guard, as the occasional fault of our author's manner). "Human life is illusion perpetual, and nothing else. All that is passing in the world is a process of deceiving and flattering, one the other. Nobody ever speaks of us to our face, as they speak behind our back. There is no other bond of union among men than this system of mutual deception. Very few friendships would subsist if every one knew what his friend said of him in his absence; although it is there that he speaks sincerely, and dispassionately. Man there-fore is nothing but pretence, falsehood, and hypocrisy, both in himself, and in relation to others; and all these dispositions, so remote from justice and reason, spring naturally from his heart."

How comes there, we may ask, to be any counterfeiting of that which, in fact, has no existence at all? If there really be no sincerity or honesty in the world, what does the word *hypocrisy* mean? How is it that mankind have contrived to form to themselves the notions of falseness, deception, guile, if they have had no means of conceiving of the opposite qualities? If indeed *all* men were liars, would the very designation—liar, ever have been thought of? Had our author never read the Psalmist's confession of his own unwarrantable precipitancy, who had said, "in his haste"—in a fit of splenetic irritation— "all men are liars"? Dismal exaggerations of this sort, although they confute themselves, nevertheless are of very ill consequences, on every side:—They confirm the debauched in their favourite doctrine—That none are better than themselves; and that all virtue is mere pretence;—they dishearten the upright; and they tend to render the presumptuous and pharasaic, who are conscious of some principle, still more arrogant—each thinking himself a phœnix, and believing that truth and goodness will die with him. Let a Rochefoucauld talk in this style; but alas that a Pascal should echo any such cavernous sounds! Ethical and theological over-statements, like bales of heavy goods piled upon deck, make the vessel of religion lurch dangerously, when the wind blows; and many have made shipwreck of faith and virtue in this very way.

Rochefoucauld says as much, in his own manner, as Pascal; but then he gives his dismal report a smart and pleasant turn; and this sparkling of his language serves to moderate what, if nakedly said, must shock our best feelings; as for instance—"How extensive soever may be the discoveries we have made in the country of self-love (or selfishness) there always remains beyond, unknown lands enough,"—which means, in the writer's dialect, that self-love stretches in fact, over the entire surface of human nature:—but then the noisome assertion is politely phrased. In the same spirit this subtle writer, instead of terrifying the reader by too much at once, creeps on, splitting open the virtues, one by one—honesty, chastity, moderation, beneficence, constancy, courage, friendship, and showing you that not one of them contains a kernel, or is any thing more than a husk of selfishness. Such are the maxims of Rochefoucald; various in apparent meaning; but constant and uniform in the one point of proving that there is no virtue in the world, and that hypocrisy apart, all men are absolutely on a level, all equally unprincipled, insincere, selfish, base. But this is said *piecemeal* of the virtues and vices; not bluntly and roundly, as thus:—

"Pride is the same in all men; nor is there any other

difference than that which results from the variety of means resorted to for its indulgence, and the modes of displaying it."

"Sincerity is an opening of the heart, met with in very few and that which one commonly sees is only a refined dissimulation, intended to excite the confidence of others."

"The hatred of falsehood is often only a latent ambition to render our testimony much set by, and to get a religious reverence attached to our words."

"What is true of ghosts, is true of real love—every body talks of both; but very few people have actually seen either."

"What mankind have called friendship, is only a convention, a reciprocal adjustment of interests, an exchange of good offices; in a word, it is only a traffic in which selfishness always goes into the market, in search of gain."

"However rare true love may be, true friendship is yet more rare." [Maximes et Réflexions Morales. How marvellously do philosophers overlook the simplest facts, when intent upon some process of refined analysis! Thus we are told that the emotion which expresses itself in laughter, involves always a feeling of contempt toward the object that immediately excites it, and a comfortable self-gratulation, arising from a secret reference to one's own superiority. Be it so. But an infant of twelve or fifteen months bursts into loud and ecstatic laughter in beholding pussy's freaks and capers, in play with a cork and a string. It might have been thought that here was an instance of laughter *in its unsophisticated and elementary state*—laughter, just such as nature has given it to man. And will then these grave professors of "mental science" make us believe that this babe's mirth springs out of any such sensations of contempt toward poor puss, or of congratulations of itself as her superior? Learned nonsense, like this might indeed generate a sort of laughter such as is supposed by these philosophers. This sort of laughter, however, is not *elementary;* but springs from complicated and artificial emotions: it is not a primitive but a secondary or derived mental state. Now, to come round to our point, the leading fault with Rochefoucauld, and his school, is the taking up of some secondary and artificial instance, of which he gives a very nice analysis, while the primitive element is wholly disregarded. As for example: Rochefoucauld assures us, "That praise is a refined flattery, which one offers to another, first as the purchase-money of his goodwill, and secondly as evidence of his own discrimination, and his candour. All this may be true of sophisticated human nature; but there is, in unsophisticated minds—in the young, and the simple-hearted, and the generous, a pure spontaneous emotion of admiration of what, in any line, is excellent; and there is a *natural impulse,* to express this genuine emotion, and to render to

him who has excited it, the tribute of our pleasureable feelings. Rochefoucauld can never see what is large and obvious, but only what requires a microscope, and the dissecting knife:—hence he has always been a great favourite with *short-sighted* folks.]

All this means much the same as what Pascal roundly affirms—that *every thing* is hollow and false in human nature. How far this miserable doctrine sprung, in the minds of these two eminent writers from their unhappy position, as conversant with little else but the debauchery of the French court, might fairly be determined by turning to a specific instance, in which what is affirmed strikes every one at once as a gross calumny, unless restricted to the most profligate circles or communities. Who that has known any thing of *English* female excellence, or who that has venerated mother, and has lived long enough to see a wife fondly respected by her mature children, can endure to hear it affirmed—"That there are very few women (which, with Rochefoucauld, means none) whose good qualities outlive their beauty." This might be no slander, spoken of the ladies of the court of Louis XIII; but it is abominably false if affirmed of English wives and mothers. And so of the greater part of this writer's sweeping libels upon his fellows. He thoroughly knew men and women of a certain class: not men and women fairly taken as specimens of humanity.

And what we are compelled to say, in the spirit of impartial criticism, of Rochefoucauld, must needs be said too of Pascal; nor would it be ingenious so to yield to a sentiment of deference towards an eminent man, as to omit giving the caution with which his ethical representations ought to be read. Nor is this all; for, as we have already observed, while his personal infirmities, and the general exhaustion of his animal powers, favoured the exercise of that tranquil, penetrating discrimination which belonged to him; the very same constitutional depression manifestly disturbed the notions he entertained of the conditions of human life; and the indulgence of these feelings has exposed him to the jeers of his irreligious editors, Condorcet and Voltaire, who, when he exclaimed—"Quelle chimère est ce donc que l'homme?" exclaim by way of sufficient annotation "Vrai discours du malade!"—"Pascal parle toujours en malade, qui vent que le monde entier souffre."

Pascal says, "I blame alike those who undertake to commend man, and those who set themselves to blame him, and those who endeavour to divert him:" "Ah" says Voltaire, "if you would but yourself have given way a little to amusement, you would have lived longer!" Yes, and if his personal piety had been free from asceticism, and his notions exempt from exaggeration, besides living longer—living to ripen his judgment, to digest his thoughts, and to think and write more, he might, not improbably, have exerted an extensive and lasting influence over the destinies of his country. Voltaire's notes upon Pascal are indeed, for the most part, cold, flippant, and sophistical, like every thing he has written, bearing upon religion; nevertheless, it is but justice to acknowledge that a vein of vigorous good sense runs through them, of which many religious writers might avail themselves, to great advantage.

It is very seldom, except when striving to carry a point, or to give to some important truth the advantage of a violent contrast, that Pascal runs into mysticism: he is not like Fenelon, the mystic always, and by constitution of mind: his statements however are sometimes such as need a little animadversion.—

"The true and only virtue is to hate oneself."—This, by itself, might pass, as meaning only, and by a figure, what our Lord intends when he enjoins his disciples to "hate father, and mother, and their own life also;" but when a phrase of this sort comes to be drawn out, and interpreted literally, by the writer who uses it, it amounts to what is untrue in fact, and unsound in principle.

"There is an injustice in allowing any one to attach himself to us; or to love us; although he may do so freely, and to his own satisfaction . . . We! we, cannot be any one's end; we cannot satisfy any one:—Are we not soon to die, and thus the object of their love will die? We are therefore to be blamed if we allow any fellow-creature to love us; or if we offer ourselves as lovable to any." More to the same purport might be quoted; and Pascal himself carried out this doctrine in his home circle; and affectionate in temper as he was, he assumed a cold and dry manner towards his near and tender relations, with the view of turning them aside, from "the idolatry of loving him." What a contrast is all this to the natural and *man-like* warmth of St. Paul, toward his personal friends! Did not St. Paul love his Lord supremely? and did he not lead others to do so too? yet he well knew that this sovereign motive was likely to take the firmest hold of those very minds that are the most alive to every human affection. Nothing can be more untrue in philosophy, or much more pernicious as a practical doctrine, than the principle, which Pascal appears to have assumed, That love is like a mathematical quantity, from which, if you deduct a part, so much less than the whole remains. If this were the fact, then indeed we should be bound to grudge every atom of affection which was diverted from the Creator, by the creature:—to love any thing but God would be—a fraud!

But how are all such theoretic statements scattered the moment we open the book of divine philosophy! The mystic says—"you must not love the creature, lest you deprive God of his due." The Bible says—"Thou shalt love the Lord thy God with *all* thy heart;" and then *after* this *all* has been bestowed, it adds—"Thou shalt love thy neighbour—not to the exclusion of thyself

but—*as thyself.*" Here indeed is good sense, and sound morality, and true philosophy. Had the amiable and pious Pascal been a father (and how much more useful a writer would he then probably have been) he would have found a practical refutation of his theory of Love, the moment a second child was put, by its mother, into his paternal arms; for at that bright instant, instead of there taking place, in his bosom, a halving of the love of which his first-born had been the object, he would have felt (his heart near bursting at the time) that the very power of loving was now doubled, and more than doubled, so that, instead of loving the two, with a half love, for each; he loved both, and severally, with a double love.—This may not be mathematics; but assuredly it is human nature. And what holds with two, holds with seven, or with ten.

And so in regard to the devout sentiments; it is not the loving a wife and children that precludes our loving God; but the loving them with a love falsely so called, and which, if analysed, would be found to be nothing better than a refined selfishness:—intemperate in its degree, and involving elements of sensuality, pride and vanity; and which re-acts upon others, out of the narrow circle of our affections, in a manner not much differing from hatred. The doating father or mother is very likely to be found a cold-hearted friend, and a surly neighbour; certainly not an eminent Christian. Pascal, although a mathematician, was ordinarily well aware of the absurdity of applying mathematical logic to moral theorems: sometimes however he falls into this error; and on occasions too, in which the inference he so deduces is likely to be mischievous. What havoc has there not been made of simple facts, and plain principles, by dint of irrefragable syllogisms!—By the help of logic, you may make it as clear as the sun at noon day—that there is no sun at noon day; or at least, that nobody has ever yet seen him, or been warmed and cheered by his beams:—as for instance:—

"If there be a God, we should love him only; and not the creatures.—There is a God; let us then take no delight in the creatures. Wherefore, whatever impells us to attach ourselves to the creature is evil, inasmuch as this either prevents our serving God, if we know him, or prevents our inquiring after him, if we know him not. But we are full of concupiscence, therefore full of wickedness, therefore we are bound to hate ourselves, and every thing else which binds us to any thing, but to God alone." [Our author expresses himself with more discretion, and admits what sufficiently refutes the sophism above quoted. This reasoning, if sound at all, is as applicable to Adam in Paradise, as to Adam out of it. How could man have been formed to love himself and to enjoy the creatures innocently, if the being of a God makes it an act of injustice to love any thing but him?]

But in contradiction to this terse and specious logic, we hear God himself declaring that, *"every creature"* of his is "good;" and so far as it may minister to our real well being, to temperate delight, is "not to be refused by them that know the truth." And instead of "hating our-selves," we are to "cherish and nourish," while we keep in subjection, even that part of ourselves which is the seat of concupiscence, namely, "our flesh;" and we are to make this love of ourselves the measure of our love to those around us. What we really are to hate, is, nei-ther our bodies, nor our souls, nor the bodies or souls of our neighbours: but simply the *evil* that dwelleth in ourselves, and in them.

In how different a tone does the same mind express itself, when, softened by the recent death of his vener-ated father, and forgetting at once the mystic, and the logician, Pascal speaks as a man, and a Christian. Let the reader turn from the passages just quoted, to the Thoughts on death, Chap. xxii. Nor is this the only place, far from it, in which this eminent writer gives utterance to the sentiments of a profound, unaffected, and unsophisticated piety. Such passages, and they are many, have rendered the **Thoughts** a favourite book with all persons of kindred temper. But we are approach-ing that part of our subject which we have thought it convenient to separate from the consideration of our author's general views of human nature.

III. We come then to say something further than what has just now been advanced, concerning Pascal's style of Devotional Sentiment. The greater number, no doubt, of those with whom he has been a favourite writer, have regarded him in this point of view, rather than as a rea-soner in behalf of Christianity, on which ground modern writers are more likely to be had recourse to, who deal with the difficulties of the argument in that special form in which they are *now* felt to attach to the subject.

Pascal, as we have already said, stands clear, for the most part, from the entanglements of the illusive mys-ticism which so much disparages many Romanist writ-ers; and he must, in fact, appear to advantage in this respect, if compared with the choicest of them. His pi-ety is straight forward, intelligible, practical; and, in a word, it is the sentiment of an elevated mind, awakened after it had attained its maturity, to a consciousness of spiritual objects; and of one moreover, who, throughout his course, was so hardly and heavily pressed with bodily sufferings, as to keep him free from excessive refine-ments, as well as from dry or airy speculations. Pascal's piety is the strong, yet tranquil working of a soul always held near to reality, by that effective teacher of truth, and that stern mistress, of sobriety—Pain. He had found the need of solid consolation, and had felt, what he express-es, that—"There is *no consolation,* but in Truth;" and this feeling gave him a distaste, not merely of what he might discern to be false, though pleasing, but of what-ever might be, on any account, questioned, or which would not bear the most searching examination. All the powers of his penetrating intellect he employed in sift-

ing those elements, whence he might derive a consola-tion that "maketh not ashamed." Others have put their inventive faculties on the stretch to bring forward some-thing from the depths, or from the heights, wherewith to nourish a dreaming enthusiasm. Pascal found enough, in the simplest and most solemn truths, to engage his heart, and to sustain his fortitude.

Put in comparison with Augustine, as the latter ap-pears in his Confessions, Pascal has not less pathos, nor less genuine elevation; while he avoids altogether those incongruous mixtures of metaphysical specula-tion with devout feeling, which render the Confessions a jumble of piety and subtility, wherein David and Plato, Paul and Aristotle, are heard confusedly talking together. By the side of Ephrem the Syrian, Pascal is more natural: and a brighter evangelic beam shines upon the path he treads; nor is the reader ever discour-aged by the suspicion of an unavowed purpose, beset-ting us in the perusal of the ascetic writers, one and all—that, namely, of holding up, and of glorifying the monkish institution, in the credit of which the interests of its members and chiefs was implicated. Again; if less pithy and ingenious than Macarius, the Egyptian, he exhibits, in such a comparison, the great benefit which even the Romish community had derived from the storms of the reformation, in clearing the church atmosphere of its miasmas. How sincere soever might have been the piety of some of the ascetics, the gar-ments of these good men are strongly scented with the effluvia of the "dead men's bones, and all corruption," that belonged to the sepulchres, not always "whited sepulchres," which they inhabited.

Pascal should not be measured against that ethereal spirit—Thomas à Kempis, who, by a life-long exer-cise in the celestial path, and by the utter renuncia-tion of every object, pursuit, and idea, but that of following "the Shepherd's steps," had become a pro-ficient of the first order, in his class. Yet even here our Pascal possesses an advantage, in as much as the atmosphere he breathed was warmer than that which surrounded the cloistered author of the De Imitatione. If Pascal could but have fairly compared himself with some of the choicest of his own communion, and could have traced the difference, all in his own favour as it was, up to its real source, he must have confessed that, through indirect channels, he owed not a little to the very heretics whose names he is almost afraid to utter;—a debt this which, released long ago from the thraldom of his earthly prejudices, he has had oppor-tunity to acknowledge, in that place of peace, where he has met his brethren in Christ, the leaders of the Reformation.

What is it, we might ask, that has made the vast and striking difference which presents itself in turning from the devotional pages of Pascal, to those, for example, of St. Bernard, where, along with impressive, elevated, and Christian-like strains of piety, the reader is repulsed by shocking superstitions, by indications of a disguised ecclesiastical ambition, and by the smothered pride of the ascetic? Why does not Pascal, like the Abbot of Clairvaux, [How lamentably do some of our modern restorers of "ancient catholicism" fall short of the thorough-going piety of St. Bernard! Hear him—In te (Maria) enim angeli lætitiam, justi gratiam, *peccatores veniam,* inveniunt in æternum! and again: In periculis, in angustis, in rebus dubiis, Mariam cogita, *Mariam invoca.* Non recedat ab ore; non recedat à corde! Whole pages equally edifying, or more so, might easily be quoted. But alas for St. Bernard! how feebly do even the most "catholic" among us tread in his steps!] spend his ingenuity, and recommend his eloquence, in dressing up tawdry garlands for the "Queen of Heaven"? or why does he not, in the empassioned tone of a lover, and in the extravagant phrases of a courtier, invoke "Mary, the virgin princess of Angels and Archangels!" If Pascal did nothing of this sort, it was not because his church had taught him better; or had, as a church, admitted any kind of reform, or had disowned and condemned these enormities of her middle-ages saints; for, on the contrary, she had striven hard to keep them agoing, after the world had cried shame of them. But in fact, in the times of Pascal, all sincere and sane minds, within the Romish pale—all but the spiritually debauched, had tacitly admitted a certain element of the reformation, which, while it allowed them to remain within that communion, wrought in them an abhorrence, and an avoidance of its worst corruptions. And what might not have been effected within the morass of popery by the occult operation of this same under current, had the streams continued to flow with a cleansing force and clearness. But the waters of the Reformation, almost immediately becoming turbid, ceased, after the first gush, to carry health at large, to the nations.

But how acceptable soever Pascal's profound devotional sentiments may be to the pious reader, he will probably feel as if still a something were wanting to bring these sentiments intimately home to his *protestant* notions of evangelical piety. Let this be granted; and when it is granted, let the significant fact be adverted to—That, as often as we move from the narrow ground of our own times and community, as often as we, so to speak, change climate in Christianity, and put ourselves under another aspect of the heavens, we become conscious of a difference, which at the first, at least, we pronounce to be a difference for the worse. The temperature of the foreign region is not what our spiritual sensations accord with: the conventional style is not the same:—it is the same gospel we are looking at, but seen at a different angle.

With most pious persons it happens, when they may have chanced thus to set foot upon a foreign soil of Christianity, that they hasten homeward, tightened rather than loosened in their predilections, Be it so;—the many, we must allow, are more safe in a strict adherence to the religious usages of their minds, than they could be in admitting any, even the slightest modifications of them. But it should be otherwise with those, and surely they are more than a few, whose habit it is to think and compare, and who dare to bring every principle they hold and every practice they conform to, under scrutiny. Such then will be forward to confess that the Christianity of their particular times, and country, and communion, is at the best—only a particular style of the universal Truth:—a phase of the absolute brightness—a mode of the unchanging perfection. The Christianity of the New Testament is one; but has the Christianity of *any* body of men, since the apostolic times, been *that one,* and neither more nor less? Christianity, look for it where or when we may, is a something more, and a something less than the simple truth, embodied in the apostolic writings.

There are those who, while they would be shocked to affirm of any individual Christian, that he held, and held forth, and realized, the Truth, without alloy or defect, yet cherish a silent persuasion, concerning the particular form of it to which they are attached, that it is (or is within a *very little* of being) the absolutely True; and their persuasion goes someway beyond the sober belief that *among* various styles of Christianity, their own, taken as a whole, is to be preferred. Now one of the consequences of harbouring any such fond supposition, is not simply the fostering an exclusive temper, likely to degenerate into sheer uncharitableness, but the shutting ourselves out from the signal benefits to be derived from a free communion with the pious—the true church, of all times and countries. The Christian, enfeebled by this sort of sensibility of the spiritual appetite, can eat of no loaf that has not been baked in his own oven:—the slightest peculiarity of flavour, even in the most wholesome food, gives him a suspicion of poison, and a nausea; and his spiritual condition is precisely analagous to that of some pitiable hypochondriacs, who can never travel without the attendance of their own cook, without a supply of water from their own spring, or without their own bed and linen—in a word, a caravan equipment.

But can we wish, for ourselves, to be trained in this sort of hyper-delicacy? If not, and the more effectually to get rid of it, we should (to return to our figure) use ourselves to as much travelling as we can afford; that is to say, in plain terms, make ourselves conversant with the piety of the Christians of other times and countries. Even if it were true that we may always be supplied from our home circle with enough of what is edifying; and with more than hitherto we have made good use of, still are we not exempted from the obligation (if we would be substantially wise) of looking wider for our spiritual nourishment; and if indeed the ailment be intrinsically wholesome, the farther it has come, in reaching us, the better.

The benefits are great of thus going abroad for our religious reading. At the first, we distaste the foreign article, but after awhile we confess the good it has done us. Those who think themselves to be gifted, or who in fact are gifted, with the requisite intelligence and discretion, and are not so unstable in mind as to be liable to be presently moved from their firmest convictions, will not fail to derive a marked invigoration of their religious feelings, as well as a happy expansion of their Christian sympathies, from the practice of going far and wide in their devotional and theological reading. How small soever may be the portion of time which can be allotted, daily, to such means of improvement, let the rule be to spend it, not in the company of the writers of our own age, country, and sect; but rather with such as may come to hand from remote times and places, and from other communions.

In compliance with this rule (if it be a good one) many of the Romanist devotional writers may be read with advantage; and if we would wish for one to lead the way in this field, Pascal is the very writer in whose company we shall feel the least strange: and who in the easiest manner, will introduce us to the circle of his associates. Are we afraid of popery?—those only need admit this fear whose minds are already in a thraldon which is essentially popish.

IV. Pascal does not, in this collection of his *Thoughts,* present himself, formally, in the character of a theologian. The *Thoughts,* many of them, are argumentative; but few of them polemical. It may however be useful to the reader to prepare him to see, in a true light, that aspect of Christian theology, in which Pascal, and a host of excellent writers besides, out of the pale of the Lutheran reformation, have regarded the scheme of salvation.

Nothing less than a habit of extensive reading, or we should better say, of reading *in all directions,* will make it easy for us to place ourselves in a position whence we may candidly and correctly estimate the doctrinal principles of writers, either anterior to the Lutheran reformation, or not participating in its spirit. A certain phraseology, a certain intentness and explicitness, in reference to a single point of Christian belief; a peculiar animation, the product of a momentous and eager controversy, have attached, more or less to all protestant divines, and especially to those among ourselves who rank with what is termed, the evangelical school. Now it must be granted that, whatever importance we may attribute either to the doctrine maintained by the reformers against Rome, or to the particular phrases which have been authenticated as the best for conveying that doctrine, it is one thing to have opposed a particular truth, when directly affirmed in our hearing; and another thing not to fall in with the terms of it, because we have not come into collision with the argument concerning it. Thus, to take another instance, the rule and the test of orthodoxy, in regard to the doctrine of the Trinity, which we may apply to writers contemporary with the Arian controversy, ought not, in equity, to be applied to the ante-nicene Fathers.—Certain points however, important they were found to be, on inquiry, not having been formally argued, the modes of expression current, were more vague and far more susceptible of an ambiguous rendering. It is controversy that fixes the usage of theological language; as well as actually compels them, individually, to wheel to the right, or left, and to choose their party.

Now our Pascal speaks of salvation by Christ, not precisely as Luther, Calvin, Knox, and Jewel, have taught Protestants to speak of it, and which mode or style, is not so altogether simple and spontaneous, as it is polemical. Nevertheless he speaks of it—of redemption, and of the Redeemer, and of the mode of our reconciliation with God, just as we find the same momentous truths expressed by the Greek Christian writers, one and all, from Polycarp to Chrysostom. Did these good men allow it to be supposed that there was salvation in any other name than in that of Christ? or did they scruple to affirm that this salvation was effected by his offering himself up, "the just for the unjust?" Is the name of the Saviour, as the only hope of guilty man, and as the gracious Shepherd of souls, seldom on their lips? By no means. But they none of them use (nor does Pascal) that precise controversial style in speaking of justification, or observe that *polemical precision,* which has come to be considered in certain quarters as the criterion of soundness in the faith.

And yet, could but the most jealous stickler for evangelical accuracy read the "Thoughts on death," particularly the passages referred to in the margin, or the "Prayer for grace in Sickness," not knowing whence they came, and uninformed of the fatal circumstance, that these breathings issued from papistical lips;—could such a reader doubt the spirituality of the author? This we must assume to be impossible; and if so, then we also assume it as certain that there are more styles than one of that piety which is conveyed to the hearts of men by "one and the same Spirit:"—It must then be an impiety to disallow any of the species or varieties of the grace so imparted; nor is it anything less than to limit the divine operations.

"Justification by faith," to quote an excellent writer, "or that free forgiveness which is offered, without our deservings, through the righteousness of Christ, has, we all know, been styled by a great authority, the articulus stantis vel cadentis ecclesiæ. But, profoundly important and absolutely essential as this great doctrine is, still, it may be questioned whether its rank, comparatively with other doctrines, is not higher in the scale of Protestantism, than in that of the scripture revelation generally; whether in other words, it does not occupy a more prominent part in the system of Christianity as opposed to popery, than in the system of Christianity considered in itself." [Woodward's Thoughts, Essays, and Sermons.]

It does not appear that Pascal had, in any instance, directed the forces of his mind toward theological questions, as such:—he took things as he found them among the better class of Romanist divines. It is thus that he states in rather crude terms, the doctrine of original sin; and if he affirms nothing more than what might be made good by quotations from Augustine or from some modern writers, he surely goes beyond what can be sustained by fair usage of Scripture. But then, again, he perplexes the partisans of any school; for if on one page, he falls in with the Westminster Confession, on the next, perhaps he is found no better than a sheer Arminian. Nevertheless, whether Calvinist, or Arminian, or neither, he speaks as one who has been "taught from above," and who knows how to build on "the sure foundation." The time, let it be hoped, is coming on, in which less solicitude will be felt concerning the theological dialect of parties, or of individuals; and when far more importance will be attached to what are the unquestionable and the palpable evidences of spirituality. It was thus in the primitive age, when, whoever lived a Christian life, and was faithful to the death, was accounted a Christian; but it ceased to be so after the time when all minds had been thoroughly heated and distorted by furious and wordy controversies.

V. We have, in the last place, to speak of Pascal's *Thoughts* as embodying an argument for Religion in general; and for Christianity, as well as for Jansenism, and for Romanism.

Looking simply at the relative bulk of the several parts of this collection, the argumentative portion is the larger, or at least it amounts to a full half of the whole. Those of the *Thoughts* which, in the present translation, stand foremost, constitute a regular, although it may seem a broken chain of reasoning, in the course of which a gradual development of consecutive propositions is effected, such as might be imagined actually to have been elicited by an intelligent and candid mind, honestly inquiring for truth, and starting from principles questioned by few. These *Thoughts* offer a sort of ratiocinative soliloquy, sometimes running into the form of a dialogue, and (a fact which the reader should be apprised of, and should bear in mind) sometimes propounding, without notice, the probable objections of an opponent, which are to meet their reply in the next paragraph. A very unfair advantage has been taken, by some of Pascal commentators, of this mode of presenting his argument; and which, no doubt, he

would have set clear of any possible ambiguity, had he lived to digest his materials.

The utility and merit of treatises in defence of religion generally, or specifically of Christianity, must be held to hinge on the previous question—To what class of persons is the argument addressed?—to *Assailants,* who are to be driven from their ground; or to *Inquirers,* who desire to be informed and confirmed. It would have been well if these very distinct purposes, which demand to be pursued each in the mode and spirit proper to it, had always been kept apart by Christian apologists. There seems some reason to believe that the slight, and often ambiguous effect produced by the ablest works of this kind, upon the minds of the persons for whose benefit they are intended, is to be accounted for mainly on this ground—that a mixture of incongruous arguments has been admitted into them; the writers, on one page, encountering the perverse, obdurate, and flippant *disbeliever,* and on the next, addressing himself to those who ask for nothing but to have the question fairly and calmly set forth, and cleared of the difficulties which, in their view, surround it. An argument may be such that, while it fails to confound the scoffer, it may be so much more than enough for simply informing the inquirer, that it rather alarms and perplexes him. Meantime those just and calm representations which, though not severely conclusive, would satisfy and gladden a candid temper, furnish only occasions of triumph to the virulent sophist, who is not to be silenced but by the most severe and condensed reasoning.

In fact there are hardly to be found two classes of minds more dissimilar in their intellectual and moral characteristics, than the two, now referred to, and which have often been treated as one and the same, by those who have undertaken to deal with infidelity. The ill consequences of this want of discrimination, on the part of many of our apologists, has perhaps been of small account in relation to those whose infidelity, springing from impulses not at all connected with reason, is not to be removed by argument. Such persons may be silenced for an hour; but they are never convinced by that which is enough to convince them. But as to those who, in fact, should be chiefly if not exclusively kept in view by Christian apologists, these, conscious as they are of a willingness—nay perhaps, an intense anxiety to be relieved of their doubts, and yet finding themselves treated as opponents, if not enemies, have either mournfully turned away from their unfriendly guide, or have given indulgence to a reciprocal feeling of resentment, of which in the end, the Christian system itself, and all its professors, have come to be the objects.

Pascal's strain of argument for religion, and for Christianity, ought, in the main, to be considered as addressed to minds of the last named class; that is to say, to persons occupying the position in which he himself had stood, when, having been profoundly affected by religious considerations, he had looked about for *reasons, corroborative* of the principles which already, though vaguely apprehended, had obtained a decisive influence over him. The author seems, in fact, to be retracing his own path, and to be formally stating the considerations or the general proofs, which had presented themselves to his own mind in working his way onward toward a full and cordial acceptance of the hope of the gospel; and to persons in a like state of mind, these *Thoughts* can hardly fail to be highly acceptable.

The Christian revelation, while, as to its external form, it is a communication of facts previously unknown, is, as to its *substance,* a fresh conveyance to mankind of the lost elements of moral and spiritual well-being. Now, while mere reasoning may suffice to put beyond all reasonable doubt the *facts* affirmed in the Scriptures, much more than any process of reasoning can supply, is needed to bring any human mind into the position in which the *substance* of the Christian revelation can be apprehended: and yet it is alone from such an apprehension of these moral and spiritual rudiments, that an efficacious or steady belief even of the facts of Christianity can arise. A belief in these facts is an opinion, coming and going, like the gleams of a showery day; but not beaming with any power, upon the character or conduct:—nothing is ripened by any such variable influence.

But the belief that attends, or that springs from a perception of the moral and spiritual elements of the gospel scheme—a belief animated by a discernment of the divine perfection of our Lord's character, constitutes altogether another sort of mental condition, and is as unlike the other, as our waking impressions are unlike our dreams. The seeming paradox is therefore substantially true, that the Christian system must already have been admitted, as real and divine, before the main part of its evidence, or the more convincing portion of it, can have been understood.

The most irreligious minds have, at all times, dimly discerned the moral splendour of the gospel; just as we are conscious of the presence of the sun above the horizon, in a cloudy day; and such minds, moreover, have admitted the wisdom and excellence of single points of the Christian ethics; just as the blind are pleased when, from a collection of rare and beautiful objects, this and that article, a stalactite, a nautilus, a gem, is put into their hands: "Ah, how fine is this," say they; but what know they of the wonders of the museum, as it offers its ten thousand specimens to those who have eyes?

A genuine history of conversions from infidelity would, we believe, confirm our principle, that, in all such cases, a vital change, by whatever means effected, has first put the intellect in a new position; as

well as altered the temperament of the soul; and that then, the argumentative evidence, which never disappoints those who ingenuously give it their attention, has made them rationally, as well as spiritually, believers. It is well that there should be treatises (concise and dense always) to which, when occasion demands, infidels may be referred, and which they may be boldly challenged to refute. But we want works of a very different sort to meet the case of those who are to be treated as having already taken their position on the side of truth.

Pascal's *Thoughts* (the portion now spoken of) come under the latter, rather than the former description. Had they been of the kind to stop the mouth of the gainsayer, or to chastise his arrogance and flippancy, neither Voltaire nor Condorcet, we may be assured, would have given them to the world with their annotations. The reader, then, should look only for what he will actually find—namely, *considerations,* not condensed proofs. In our own sifting times the Christian evidences have been analysed, and brought into a state of argumentative perfection, which leaves Pascal's mode of treating them in the rear; that is to say, if we are in quest of irrefragable logic. Yet it is true that minds seeking rather for general views of the subject, than for the severity of proof, may, with peculiar advantage, take him as their guide.

A general scheme of the author's argument in behalf of Christianity, as sketched by himself in a long conversation with his friends, and of which notes were taken soon afterwards, has been prefixed to the Thoughts by the French editors. But a concise statement, to the same purport, constitutes the 11th chapter of the present edition, and to this the reader is referred, as being, in fact, a proper introduction to the whole of the *argumentative* portion of the *Thoughts.* The intelligent reader will not need more than he there finds, for opening to him the plan which the author would have fully developed, had he lived to prepare his *Thoughts* for the press.

If, once and again, the English reader thinks that he recognises in these pages certain views of the evidences, not new to him, and which he may even remember to have seen more fully expounded elsewhere; he should, in mere justice to our author, be reminded, that Pascal was in fact the first modern writer to suggest some very striking and convincing considerations, which others, and especially those of our own country, have caught up, elaborated, and presented in a still more advantageous manner. Pascal has set in a new light, or was the first to discern, some of those nicer characteristics of historical and moral truth which the acumen, and the fine moral feeling of the modern European mind fits it to appreciate. The early Christian apologists have indeed anticipated most of the prominent proofs of the truth of Christianity; but there are other proofs, not at all less conclusive, although of a refined and occult kind, which it required the intelligence of later times to discover. Neither Porphyry, nor Celsus, nor their contemporaries, could have been made to comprehend, even if Origen himself had perceived them, those delicate, yet infallible marks of genuineness in the gospel history, and in the Epistles, which, to modern minds, constitute the irrefragable part of the argument.

One might take, as an instance, a thought propounded in a very broken manner by Pascal, but which has been adopted, and much insisted upon, by later writers. What we mean is the indirect argument in proof of the reality of our Lord's statements concerning the invisible world, and the vast movements of the Divine government, resulting from the ease, simplicity, and nativeness (naïvete) of his manner, when touching upon these superhuman subjects. "An artisan or labourer who speaks of the wealth he has never touched or seen, a lawyer who talks of battles, or a private man who describes the state of kings, is wont to speak in terms of exaggeration, or of wonder, or of constraint; whereas the wealthy talk of the disposal of large sums, with indifference, and in a common style; the general describes a siege coolly and simply; and a king enters upon the interests of an empire, just as a private person does upon the most ordinary affairs. And thus it is that Jesus Christ speaks of the things of God, and of eternity. To feel the full force of this argument, or consideration, one should be well aware of the style of those, whether Jewish prophets, or Grecian sages, who, heretofore, had taken up kindred topics. Our Lord's manner, in every such instance, was precisely what was *natural,* and what became him who, having, "been with the Father from before the foundation of the world," had lately descended to hold converse with man, concerning the things which he had seen and known.

In meeting then, in Pascal, with thoughts of this sort, some of them perhaps, hastily and incompletely expressed, let not the reader think slightingly of them, as having found the same better stated elsewhere; but rather remember that Pascal's *Thoughts* have now, for a hundred years and more, been carried hither and thither; and that the collection has been a seed-book, which has stocked the fields of our English Christian literature with fruitfulness and beauty.

Moreover, some few of the *Thoughts,* in this portion of the work, may, at the first, startle the reader, who perhaps will be ready to reject them as paradoxical, exaggerated, or absolutely false. But in most such instances, if what is roughly thrown out in one place, be collated with analogous passages elsewhere occurring, a clue will be furnished for discovering those modifications, or connecting statements, which were present to the writer's mind, and apart from which he would never have given such passages to the world.

Many things also are advanced peremptorily, which must be received with limitations or exceptions, as thus—"Charity is the one and only thing aimed at in Scripture; and whatsoever therein found does not tend directly to this end, is to be accounted figurative; for inasmuch as there is but one (ultimate) end or intention, all that, in plain terms, does not point that way, is figure." This may be true, roundly stated, or very generally understood; but if assumed as *a rule of interpretation,* it would carry us as far from sober truth as the Rabbins, or as Origen and some of the Fathers have gone, in allegory; and would turn the history of real events—the story of battles and conspiracies, into something as airy as Bunyan's Holy War.

Pascal, as we have already said, although perfectly sincere in his profession of Romanism, took a position in relation to those corruptions that are properly popish, such as places him *toward* protestantism; and, a few incidental phrases excepted, it might not be easily guessed that he was not such in fact. It is only as occasion offers that he comes forward, as the apologist of the Romish church; and it is due to him—to his friends of Port Royal, and to many of the best of men who have lived and died within its pale, to place ourselves, for a moment, in that point of view whence they were accustomed to look abroad over Christendom. It is not difficult to gather either, from the explicit arguments, or from the casual phrases employed by writers of the class to which Pascal belonged, the general principles or axioms, which, when once admitted as unquestionable, secured their submission to the church, notwithstanding their knowledge of her flagrant corruptions and gross superstitions.

Resting chiefly upon the purport of our Lord's last conversations with his disciples, as recorded by St. John, and which may fairly be assumed as intended, in a peculiar manner, to embody the first principles of the institute he was then consigning to their hands, the good men now referred to, gathered what they might well consider as the prime and constant characteristics of the true church, namely, union, uniformity of worship, agreement in opinion, and continuity, or a perpetuated, unbroken transmission, from age to age, of the doctrine and the institutions of the gospel.

Now although it may be very easy to invalidate, in detail, the claims advanced by the Church of Rome to these characteristics, and to show, that her boasted union has been that only of a civil despotism—that her uniformity, so far as it has been maintained, has been the product of terror and cruelty; and that the scheme of religion she has transmitted has been, not the apostolic doctrine, and worship, but a mass of later inventions;—notwithstanding these just exceptions, which we protestants take against the pretensions of Rome; yet it must be granted that she possesses—or that at least she can make a show of possessing, what, in some tolerable degree, answers to the above named characteristics. Of whatever sort it may have been, and by whatever unholy means secured, the Church of Rome has actually held up, before the world, the imposing spectacle of a widely extended polity, united under one head—adhering, in all lands to the same worship, and to the same ecclesiastical constitution, and flowing down, from age to age, without any such violent or conspicuous interruptions, as could be held to destroy the identity of the system. The Romanist could always say, "*We* are one church: we have one head, one faith, and the same sacraments; and what we are now, is what those were from whom we derived one spiritual existence: *we* have not innovated, *we* have not revolted."

This view of their position, even considered by itself, could not but strongly influence serious minds: and then, with what was it contrasted? The first and broad characteristic of the Reformation—the mark which it carried with it into every country, was—not ecclesiastical revolt merely, in relation to Rome, but internal variance—disunion, and innovation, or novelty. But were not these the very tokens of error—the symbols of antichrist? Could it be necessary to inquire any further concerning the pretension of those who were seen to be waging a bitter and fierce warfare among themselves? Thus Pascal, and Fenelon, and many others, have looked at the question between the Romish Church, and her assailants: and although they ought to have gone more deeply into this question, and to have reached its real merits, they felt, as men fearing God, satisfied that they stood on the *safer side* of the great modern schism; and that even if the Church might cover some abuses, she was THE CHURCH still; and the sole mistress or dispensatrix of eternal life.

Not only have views, such as these, retained good and enlightened men of the past age in allegiance to Rome; but they still produce the same effects, and must continue to secure for her the vitalizing support of many conscientious persons, throughout Europe, until protestantism, or, let us rather say, until the Christianity of the New Testament, shall have approved itself to the world by exhibiting the genuine characteristics of union, uniformity, or unanimity, and perpetuity. Then shall all men flock toward the church, when they know, without a question, where to find it!

A very useful lesson may be gathered in following a mind, like Pascal's on those particular occasions when, overruled, or, we might say, overawed, by an assumed axiom, it comes to regard the plainest matters of fact altogether in a false light. We may be ready to wonder that one so well informed as was Pascal, and so clear-sighted, could have blinded himself to the true state of the case regarding the Romish auricular confession.

"Can one imagine," says he, "anything more kind, more tender than the practice of the church (in directing us to unburden our consciences to the priest, and to him alone)? Nevertheless, such is the depravity of the human mind, that it thinks even this benign law hard; and in fact, this has been one of the principal reasons of the revolt of a great part of Europe against the church."

Pascal, who was conversant with the ecclesiastical history of Spain—to say no more, had he not come to the knowledge of the unutterable abominations connected with the confessional in that country? or could he think that these abuses, everywhere prevalent, as they were, and in some countries reaching the extreme point of atrocity, could he think them incidental only, or that the evils inseparable from the practice were yet outweighed by its benefical consequences? No:—he could not have made good any one of these suppositions; but, at all events, auricular confession was an inseparable part of the Romish system; and to question its expediency would have been to stand out, declared, as a heretic. He scorned to shelter himself in mere silence; and therefore breaks through every check of reason, not to say of truth, boldly to defend what, although indefensible, could not be disclaimed.

As a matter of history, every one knows, that it was not confession, but the confessional;—not the abstract usage, or principle; but the universal and invariable abuse of it, that roused the indignation of northern Europe, and put into the hands of the Reformers one of the most efficacious of those weapons with which they demolished the papal edifice, in their several countries.

It would be easy to dispose, in a similar manner, of all those passages wherein Pascal explicitly vindicates the practices of the Romish Church; but it cannot be necessary to do so: his personal adherence to that church is a matter, as of no perplexity, so of no general importance; he advances nothing in behalf of its errors that is new, or that has not been, a hundred times, met by irrefragable argument; mean time, as we have said, the main stress of his mind presses *against* the *spirit* of the Romish Church; nor is he a writer whom modern Romanists can be fond of adducing, as an authority on their side. Take this specimen of Pascal's *feeling* in relation to the sacramental question, a question which, in fact, condenses within itself the elements of the great and ancient controversy between superstition and Christianity: and, which in its modern form, is the pivot of the polemics of our day.

"The Jews were of two parties—the one having the sentiments only of the heathen world:—the other possessing the feelings of Christians (essentially so). The Messiah, according to the carnal Jews, was to be a great secular prince; and according to the carnal Christians he has come to release us from the obligation of loving God, and to bestow upon us sacraments, which work every thing for us, apart from our concurrence. But neither was the one true Judaism, nor is the other true Christianity. The real Jews, and the real Christians, have acknowledged a Messiah, who should make them love God; and by the means of this love, triumph over their enemies."

This passage expresses as well, and as concisely perhaps, as it could be expressed, the vital distinction which, in all ages, has divided the professedly Christian world. Whoever takes his part with the secular minded Jew, attaches himself to a system obsolete, corruptible, and evanescent. But concerning those who "hold to the spirit," we need hardly ask whether, in, and by the world, they be called papists or protestants; for they are of that kingdom that "shall not be shaken," and they are those who, in the end, shall be knit together as members of the true church.

Firm in this great and first principle, Pascal too readily admitted some positions which his acute and logical mind must instantly have rejected, had he chosen to bring them under examination. Thus, for instance, he so lays down the conditions of an authentic miracle, as shall save ample space for all the lying wonders of the Romish romancers—"When a miracle," says he, "is witnessed, one ought either to yield to it (admit its reality) or be able to adduce extraordinary reasons to the contrary:—one should ask, whether he who performs it denies the being of a God, denies Jesus Christ, or denies the Church?" Now we might be very content to let this rule pass without comment, if only a due care were always given to the determination of the previous, and very pertinent question—Is such or such an alleged miracle, a miracle indeed? The exercise of this necessary and reasonable discretion would, in fact, supersede Pascal's rule, inasmuch as the few instances, remaining, after such a scrutiny has been made, would, all of them, be on the side of truth, and would all range around the apostolic history. But Pascal had, as a Romanist, to look to innumerable miracles beside those wrought in the first age of the church; and among the number, to that of the "Holy Thorn."

Were there not an inference of practical importance—an inference touching our own times, derivable from the fact, one should willingly draw a veil over the extreme credulity of so great a man: (we will not now speak of the cure itself in whatever way effected) we mean his credulity in regard to this boasted relic of Port Royal. Did he then know so little of the wholesale manufacture of, not "holy thorns" merely, but of true crosses—veritable nails—genuine rags, reeds, hammers, spikes, as well as of leg-bones, arm-bones, finger-joints, and what not? Did he know so little of this monkish craft, as to believe, without inquiry, in the genuineness of the Port Royal "holy thorn?" And must we yield an indulgence to Pascal, the geometrician, of the 17th century, which we do not grant, without reluctance, to the benighted St. Louis of the 13th century? One might have thought that the author of the tract on the properties of the cycloid, would have left "holy thorns" to be the play-things of the debauched and debilitated understandings of monks! But it is not so; meantime who shall calculate the damage thus done to the religious sentiments of mankind, by the like insanities of powerful minds? It has been thus that the entire influence of Pascal's religious writings in France has been turned aside, and his powerful thrust at impiety successfully parried by a contemptuous reference, on the part of his infidel commentators, to the childish superstitions to which he was accustomed to surrender himself. For example. Condorcet, in putting forward a foolish paper of abbreviated notes of Pascal's daily religious observances, and which was constantly worn by him as a sort of amulet, stitched in his dress, insultingly exclaims—"What an interval between this paper and the treatise on the cycloid? Nothing, in fact, can better serve to explain how all the thoughts contained in this collection could have come from the same brain.—The author of the treatise on the cycloid wrote some; and the rest are the work of the author of the amulet."

So it is, and it must be confessed with some appearance of reason, however inequitably, that the whole weight of Pascal's testimony in favour of religion, is thrown out of the scale, and placed to the account of that infirmity of temper to which he gave way. Let good and eminent men be as absurd as they please in things which the world can never hear of; but let them remember that every absurdity of theirs which comes to be talked of, costs nothing less than the well-being of hundreds, or of thousands of souls! Expensive recreations truly, are the religious freaks and follies—the superstitions and the extravagancies, of the wise and good.

There are those around us, even now, who might derive a caution or two, of another kind, from this great man's example. Pascal—right in a general principle, but deplorably wrong in the application of it, believed himself compelled to deliver over to hopeless perdition, one and all, the very men whose memory we protestants love and honour, as the restorers of Christianity, and the emancipators of Europe. "The body can no more live," says he, "without the head, than the head without the body. Whoever then separates himself from the one, or the other, no longer belongs to the body, and has nothing more to do with Jesus Christ. Neither all the virtues, nor martyrdom, nor any austerities, nor any good works, can be of the least utility *out of the pale of the Church,* and apart from the communion of the head of the Church, that is to say—the Pope."

How sad the consequences, as affecting his own charity

and comfort as a Christian—how sad as affecting his influence in after times, was that artificial blindness which excluded from his view the unquestionable piety of many of the reformers, and of thousands of their followers? What has so often—nay in every age hitherto, of the Christian history, turned the best heads, and chilled the best hearts, has been the placing reliance upon that flimsy ecclesiastical logic which has made it appear that the great realities, for the very sake of which the Christian dispensation was given to men, namely—the active love of God, and of our neighbour, are of no account, apart from certain conditions, attaching to the medium of conveying this dispensation from hand to hand. As if, in visiting a people full-grown, fair, and ruddy, whom one found to subsist on the "finest of the wheat," one should sourly turn upon them, and say—'you delude yourselves, altogether, in fancying yourselves robust and happy:—these appearances of health are utterly fallacious:—you are, in fact, although you think it not, you are emaciated, squallid, and feeble—You *must* be so, for the seed-corn wherewith, at the first, your fields were sown, was surreptitiously obtained from the royal granaries, and therefore *could not* produce a wholesome crop—nay, it is all virulent poison.'

Such is the language that has been held by narrow minds to whoever has stood outside of their little enclosure! The ecclesiastical virulence of one age differs extremely little from that of another: All is the same, saving a phrase or two. "Except ye be circumcised, and keep the law of Moses, ye cannot be saved." So spake the staunch men of the apostolic age. "Out of the church, that is to say, not in allegiance to the Pope; there is no salvation." So have spoken the successors and representatives of the Jewish zealots, from Gregory I, to the present day. "Deprived of Christ's sacraments, there can be no life in you; but Christ's sacraments are in the hands of Christ's ministers, and of none else; and his ministers are they whose canonical descent from the apostles, in the line of episcopal ordination, can be unequivocally traced:—the merest shadow of uncertainty in the matter, of ecclesiastical genealogy, is fatal to the pretensions of the holiest of men, or of any who may seem holy; for them, and the communities under their care, the abyss of perdition yawns wide." Thus, even now, is one half of the protestant world talked to by the other half!

But what must we think if, in the fine net-work of reasoning on which these anathemas hang, there should be some flaw!—some rotten thread! what if, in the historical materials out of which it is spun, some facts have been too hastily assumed!—What? why then these adventurous logicians have been coolly outraging Christian charity, they have been maligning thousands of Christ's faithful people, they have been poisoning the hearts of their followers, they have been heaping calumnies upon the gospel itself, and so have turned

multitudes of souls out of the path of truth, and all this has been done on the strength of a chain of syllogisms, which alas! happens, in some part of it, to want a link!

Many there are, unthought of by these zealots, who, with some honest anxiety, desiring to inform themselves concerning Christianity, stumble at the threshold, when they find that those of its adherents who stand the highest in rank and office, and who claim to be the only authorized interpreters of its mysteries, are inflamed by the spirit of cursing and bitterness, and that arrogance and jealousy are the characteristics of their temper! The vague and suppressed feeling excited in thousands of ordinary minds, on such occasions, gets utterance through the lips of the crafty and politic enemies of all religion. We are unwilling here to quote Voltaire, at length; yet it might be useful (to some at least) to read and take home to themselves, the keen and just, although in the main sophistical comment, which he attaches to that passage of the *Thoughts* in which Pascal sums up his argument for Christianity; an argument irrefragable, if the gospel be looked at abstractedly; or if the noiseless story of its genuine followers in every age, be regarded; but miserably contradicted by the general current of what is called church history;—the history of ecclesiastical arrogance.

Pascal's better nature triumphs, once and again, over his faulty church logic, when happily, he forgets Rome, and the heretics. In the passage referred to in the margin, he lays down a great principle—a principle clear and inexpressibly momentous, and which in substance is this— That the manifest operation and indwelling of the Holy Spirit, producing the Christian graces in the hearts of men, must, *in all cases,* be acknowledged and allowed to authenticate, substantially, the institutions through which the Spirit has thus deigned to operate. To reject or to scorn the work of God, in renovating the souls of men, is, if not to commit the sin against the Holy Ghost, at least to limit him, and to arrogate to ourselves the disposal of his sovereign favours!

Nearly all that relates, in this collection, to the Jansenist and Port Royal controversies, is comprised in the passages referred to beneath; nor do these passages demand any special remark;—they are *out* of the author's ordinary style—less calm, less logical, and such as, by themselves, would leave the reader in suspense, as to the merits of the controversy between the Jesuits and the Jansenists; or rather, would give him the impression that this controversy, like so many, evenly divided faults and merits. Yet this was not the fact, and a perusal of the story of the Port Royalists may almost be spoken of as an act of justice, due to those oppressed witnesses for the truth in France.

In England, Pascal's writings, and his *Thoughts* especially, have always been in favour among meditative and intelligent religious readers. But with us, whose religious literature is so ample and various, this single writer presents himself as one in a crowd:—we converse with him delighted, for an hour, and turn to another. In France, which can hardly be said to possess a native religious literature, or at best a very limited classical indigenous divinity, Pascal is read much rather as an authenticated model of style, and as an acute and eloquent dialectician, than properly as a religious writer: there are not religious readers enough to maintain his celebrity in that character. His mind and his language are admired:—his principles utterly disregarded; at least it is generally so. Nor indeed can it be thought likely that, as a *religious* writer, he should regain his influence at home. The controversy in which he acquired his chief celebrity, was special and temporary; and if ever the Gallican church shall be anew agitated by theological debate, the questions then to be mooted will be of quite another sort; neither St. Cyran, nor Jansen, nor St. Agustin will give their names to the quarrel. And as to the ***Thoughts,*** the greater portion of them, relating to the Christian evidences, are likely to be superseded (if ever the general subject awakens the French mind) by works produced at the spur of the occasion, adapted to modern modes of thinking, and squared by more exact and erudite methods of argumentation.

May that day of religious agitation in France soon come on! Nor must it be said that there are *no* indications of its near approach. We do not here allude to the silent diffusion of the Scriptures, which, it may be hoped, will produce at length, a happy effect upon the middle and lower classes. Nor should we care to enquire particularly into the internal condition and prospects of the Reformed and Lutheran communions; inasmuch as many reasons, not now to be set forth, seem to render it highly improbable that the religious renovation of France (if it is ever to take place) should burst out from the dying embers of protestantism.—The French people, we may be sure, will not take their religion from those who appear themselves to have so little to spare; or in fact from the decandants and representatives of the Hugunots.

There are, however, facts which warrant the belief that a stirring of life is even now taking place in the heart of the Gallican church:—inquiry is awake, and sedulous studies are pursued, such as must, or probably will, bring with them some change of the ecclesiastical position of the church, and some reforms. The French clergy of the present day, very unlike, as a body, the creatures of the revolution, and of Napoleon's church government, are reported to be men who will not leave themselves to be contemned, like their immediate predecessors, as the dregs of the people—persons who, for a morsel of bread, would do the dirty work of the state, in carrying forward the mummeries of the government

superstition. Such, too generally, were the Bonaparte clergy; but such are not, if report speak truly of them, the clergy of the Gallican church at the present moment.

Feeling their destitution of a native theological literature, the clergy (as it appears) are eagerly demanding that of other countries, even not exclusive of some of our protestant commentaries. But especially are they recurring to the Greek and Latin Fathers—the accredited literature of the Romish church. The lately revived demand for the Fathers in *this* country, had already added a thirty per cent, to the commercial value of the best editions; and now, a not less vivid anxiety, on the part of the French clergy, to possess them, has still further enhanced that value. Until of late, the tide of ecclesiastical literature set steadily from France and Germany, towards England, where a ready sale was obtained for the importations which drained the foreign shops and libraries. But at length this tide has turned, and many ponderous works—the Benedictine editions, and the like, after having seen the day and "taken the air," during a few years' sojourn in England, are finding their way again across the channel, and to Paris, where they meet purchasers, eager to possess them at a price which leaves a handsome profit in the hands of all who have been concerned in pushing them round in this circuit.

Nor is this all; for at a time when no such enterprise would be ventured upon in London, the Parisian press is issuing costly editions of the most voluminous of the Fathers—Chrysostom, and Augustin:—reprints of the noble abours of the congregation of St. Maur!

But it will be said, disdainfully or despondingly, "What of this? What will be the probable issue of a revived study of the Fathers in France, except it be to rivet popery anew upon the minds of the clergy? What are the Fathers but the authors and patrons of popery?" We look for a different and happier result of this return of ecclesiastical erudition. Taught by the course of controversies elsewhere, and of which they cannot be ignorant, to look out, as they read, for the distinction between the Romish superstitions and ancient Christianity, this distinction will meet them at every turn: it will (with all its important consequences) be forced upon their notice; and even if, for a while, they are confirmed in their respect for so much of popery as belongs to ancient Christianity, they can hardly fail, in the end, to resent, with a fresh indignation (as the Gallican church has in fact heretofore resented) those impositions and corruptions which are attributable, not to the Fathers, but to the Bishops of Rome, and in which popery—if we use the designation with any pertinence, really consists.

Our times are times of irresistible progression, in every path on which movement takes place at all. Ecclesiastical research, once set on foot (in France or elsewhere), once gone into with eagerness, and undertaken by men who are commencing their professional career, will not, as we venture to predict, come to a stand at any point of arbitrary limitation; but will go as far as it can go:—it will reach the real or natural boundary of the ground within which it is carried on. French science, French historical learning, are not now sleepy, inert, or superstitiously timid; but are bold, persevering, and exact. French ecclesiastical learning, reared in the same schools, will partake of the same spirit, and will hold a similar course:—it will pursue its objects, and will overtake them. And while, in this country, we are going round about, feeling our way in the dark, a very few competent to take their part in any such inquiries, and more deprecating them as pernicious or idle;—while, in England, we are very likely to reap only new embarrassments from our inadequate researches into Christian antiquity, it may be predicted, as a not improbable event, that the French ecclesiastical scholars, less encumbered in fact than ourselves, less *beset,* and not distracted by the foresight of secular and political consequences, attached to these pursuits, may get fairly ahead of us, and become our masters. The Germans, as every body knows, have long since done so in whatever is purely erudite and critical—in whatever relates to the historical interpretation of the sacred text; and as, in times gone by, we have looked to the French ecclesiastical compilers and historians, as to the only men who were thoroughly conversant with the subject, so may we again have to go to our neighbours for the result of their independent and scholastic inquiries concerning the doctrine and polity of the early church.

To themselves, these inquiries, as they are not likely to be cut short, can hardly fail to be in the highest degree beneficial; and the probable consequences it might not be very difficult to anticipate. This, however, is a subject we must not here pursue. We might perhaps wish something else for the clergy of France than that they should give themselves to the painful perusal of the Greek and Latin divines. But He who "leadeth the blind, often, in a way that they know not," toward the fulness of truth, may be preparing, even now, happy changes for France, in this very path. Or should nothing further or better be the result, what protestant would not heartily rejoice to know that the superstitions of Gregory I, of Gregory VII, and of Gregory IX, were giving way, among our neighbours, to the superstititious Christianity, albeit, of Chrysostom, Cyprian, and Tertullian?

In connection with the topic here adverted to, a consideration is suggested by Pascal's usage (common to Romanist writers) and which he adheres to, as well in his ***Thoughts***, as in the ***Provincial Letters,*** of making all his quotations from Scripture in the Latin of the Vulgate. Be it remembered that, when stating his reasons for adopting a lively and popular style, in the

Provincial Letters, he plainly avows that he wished to gain the ear of the people at large;—of the unlearned and of women; and he felt that he should have failed in this object, had he written gravely and scholastically. We have his own confession then, that he wrote for all. But now to have allowed the *people,* through the medium of his pages, to have heard our Lord and his apostles speaking of salvation in the vernacular dialect, would have been tantamount to heresy: it would have been to countenance the abominations of Wickliffe, Luther, Calvin, Tindal. Pascal did not forget that the intention of that stupendous miracle which first declared the promised presence of the Spirit with the apostles, was to allow every man to hear "the words of life in the tongue in which he was born." But the Romish church had thought fit to contravene the Holy Ghost, and to reverse, by her decrees, the will of the ascended Saviour. The church therefore, not the Lord, the Pope, not the Holy Ghost, man, not God, was to be obeyed; and here is one of the most enlightened and pious of Romanists yielding obedience to the impious restrictions, and giving the sign of his approbation of the Romish practice of denying the Scriptures to the people. Let it be so. Pascal and his contemporaries have long ago fulfilled their course. But how is this main article of the Romish despotism likely to be thought of in the present day, and when it comes to be seen broadly opposed to the authority and opinion of the Fathers, one and all? Men of vigorous minds, breathing the atmosphere of intellectual independence, when they come, in the course of their daily studies, to meet with proofs, fresh and pointed, of the *recentness,* as well as of the deliberate wickedness of the papal innovations, are surely not unlikely to conceive and to cherish a burning resentment against the usurpation altogether. May they not—we mean the intelligent and erudite French clergy, come to say, 'We will betake ourselves to ancient Christianity, and rid ourselves of the puerile superstitions, and the degrading ordinances of the middle ages?'

While, on the one hand, the Scriptures, whether the clergy will it or not, are creeping on in Frauce, and are coming into all hands, they themselves are finding, on the pages of the authorized doctors of their church, the most strenuous exhortations, addressed to the people— to men and to women, to peruse the inspired writings. A volume of such passages might soon be gathered from those of the Fathers whom Rome herself has canonized. Or let the French clergy confine themselves, in this particular, to their own Hiliary of Poictiers, who, in an age as enlightened and as pure surely as that of Innocent III and St. Dominic, lost no occasion on which to urge upon all the diligent study of Scripture. But should it once come to this, that the clergy grant that, what the Fathers, one and all, allow and recommend, and what the spirit of the times calls for, is no longer rightfully to be refused; our neighbours may then think and say what they please of the English and German Reformers; so that they do but read the Bible themselves, and promote its circulation among their people.

Pascal himself, in a tract to which we have not as yet referred—"a comparison between the Christians of the early ages, and those of the present times;" indicates the sense he had of the greatness of the changes that had come upon the professedly Christian world; and as, in relation to physical science, he held a clue which, if he had pursued it, would have brought him soon upon the solid ground, and the open field of modern philosophy, so in this tract, and elsewhere, he incidentally throws out a hint which, had he followed it up, would have set him clear of the errors of the papacy. France, if her Pascal did not, has trod even steps with England on the walks of science: may she soon do so, although he did not, on the path of heavenly truth!

Jean Mesnard (essay date 1952)

SOURCE: A conclusion to *Pascal: His Life and Works*, translated by G. S. Fraser, Harvill Press, 1952, pp. 179-201.

[*Below, Mesnard examines Pascal's life and career as a scientist, thinker, theologian, and artist.*]

I. *The Man*

"Pascal, not the writer, but the man": with this phrase the Swiss moral philosopher, Vinet, drawing his inspiration from one of the most famous of the *Pensées,* headed one of the chapters of his *Etudes sur Pascal*. It is, indeed, one of the most notable facts about Pascal's astonishing personality that, however great his genius as a mere writer may appear to us to be, it is Pascal the man, in the end, whom we really wish to grasp; even more than Pascal's thought, it is the soul of Pascal that criticism seeks to revive for us. Let us, in our turn, seek to lay bare his secret.

Though there have been numerous reactions against the romantic critics, modern criticism is on the whole still obsessed with their picture of Pascal as himself a romantic, first brilliantly sketched by Chateaubriand, more methodically worked out by Victor Cousin, and finished off in several different styles by the various Pascal enthusiasts of the last century. This romantic picture is that of a man tending in all directions towards excess; using up his strength in the pursuit of science, flinging himself madly into the fashionable world, and then suddenly won over by a kind of fanaticism and wasting himself away in austerities. Full of anguish when confronted with the silence of the world and the mystery of God's grace, this romantic Pascal is thought of as having been assailed by doubt and

having rescued himself from misery by rushing headlong into belief. Finally, this romantic Pascal is thought of as above all a sick man, a "sublime madman", in the phrase of Voltaire which Chateaubriand repeated; as a man owing his genius to his excessively neurotic temperament, to the hallucinatory vividness of his imagination; as a man writing in pain and fever.

Such a picture of Pascal bears too obviously the marks of the age which conceived it to remain a really authoritative one. A biographical study, like our own, which aims at precision is obliged to tone down these glaring colourings and to depict the inner life of Pascal and its development with a more delicate balance of light and shade. What critics have taken as Pascal's personal anguish is, after all, only the anguish of humanity deprived of God, as it is described at the outset of the *Apology*. The famous cry, "The everlasting silence of these infinite spaces frightens me," ought to be placed, as Tourneur has shown, in the mouth of the unbeliever whose plight Pascal is considering; or even if it was a cry from Pascal's own heart, it could only be considered as expressing a transitional moment in a process of thought soon to conclude in triumphant certainty. In a word, it is futile to seek to explain Pascal by his illness. Nobody, in fact, has been able to say exactly what the nature of this illness was. In a recent work, Dr. Onfray diagnoses it as ophthalmic migraine; an attractive hypothesis, and valid up to a point, but one which does not appear to us to take account of the whole range of documented facts about the illness. While we are still waiting for really decisive medical researches on Pascal, let us confine ourselves to asking a single question: what is it, in Pascal's life and his work, that betrays the sick man? It must be admitted that, in their answers to this question, critics have been rather lax in their notions of what constitutes evidence and also rather simple-minded. How many facts have been attributed to Pascal's illness for which there is a much simpler explanation if one consults the relevant documents or even places oneself in the climate of Pascal's age! Here is an example: Pascal's handwriting, which is, we are told, "shaken by fever". Let us compare it, however, with other typical handwritings of the time. It is a thin, regular handwriting, very similar to other seventeenth-century cursive scripts, much more legible than that of many Parliamentary records and many legal documents. Is it generally known that Pascal's will, written by the hand of his attorney, Guineau, is much harder to decipher than the manuscript of the *Pensées?* Finally, we ought once more to make a close study of contemporary descriptions of Pascal's illness, notably those of Boulliau. It is obvious from these that physical suffering, far from producing a sort of nervous exaltation in Pascal, crushed and overwhelmed him and made him incapable of any sort of work—and less capable, if possible, of intellectual work than of any other kind. Such descriptions appear to us to have a symbolic value: Pascal's life and work were, in fact, the fruit of a constant victorious struggle *against* his illness. Pascal's genius is not to be explained by his illness; on the contrary it was able to expand and achieve itself *in spite* of his illness.

It is starting, therefore, from other premises that we shall sketch out the broad lines of our portrait of this extraordinarily striking figure.

Incontestably, Pascal was in the first place a *violent* man. This violence, however, was not that of a neurotic, but the violence proper to that tough and vigorous generation of the first half of the seventeenth century in France; his was the violence which one also discovers in his father and in Jacqueline—in this, truly the female counterpart of her brother—in the Arnaulds, and in the men of the Fronde. Basically, this violence is an ardent zest for life. We are wrong to think of Pascal as always shut up within the four walls of a study, a literary drawing-room, a cell. He was a traveller; he travelled from Clermont to Paris and from Paris to Rouen more often than has been generally noticed; we find him at Poitiers and at Fontenay-le-Comte, taking the waters at Bourbon, certainly also at Dieppe and possibly at Lyons, visiting his friend Desargues. He had the temperament of a man of action, a love for grandiose undertakings; he carried out spectacular experiments, tried to exploit his calculating machine commercially, had a share in the project for draining the Poitou marshes, formed a project of his own for the education of a prince, established in Paris a carriage service at a fare of five sols. This ardent zest for life, moreover, was often transformed in Pascal into a dominating pride. Conscious of his own supreme genius, Pascal as a scientist could brook no contradiction and showed himself merciless to such adversaries as Father Noël or Father Lalouère. Pascal the convert was never able, moreover, wholly to root out and destroy this natural arrogance; in a moment of anger he could terrify Singlin, whose inadequacies on the intellectual plane could not escape him; he humiliated Arnauld and Nicole when he made it clear that he thought their conduct pusillanimous. This need to dominate over other souls, though much purified by Pascal's conversion, explains, no doubt, his violence and impetuosity as a religious apologist. But this violence and impetuosity can also be considered as a kind of passion. There is, in Pascal, a passion for truth in all its shapes; this is seen as clearly, in spite of the reservations we have occasionally thought fit to make, in Pascal's investigations into the nature of a vacuum as in his controversies about the formula. Even more, there is in Pascal a passion for the infinite; thanks to that, transcending the rather elementary common sense with which average minds content themselves, he was able to pave the way for the discovery of the infinitesimal calculus, to denounce the vanity of every kind of merely human social organization, and to define

one of the highest forms of the religious ideal.

This fundamental violence was linked, however, in Pascal's nature to a profound *sensibility*. This sensibility, however, found hardly any satisfaction in the outer natural world. Intellectually, Pascal was able to appreciate the picturesque aspects of nature, but he got no profound enjoyment out of them. The social sentiments were far more deeply rooted in him. We know the tenderness of his feelings for his family, a tenderness sometimes a little exclusive and self-centred, which led to his at first opposing Jacqueline's entry into Port-Royal; but a tenderness all the more moving because the seventeenth century offers us hardly any other famous examples of such united families. Pascal's tender feelings towards friends were hardly less strong. Gilberte Périer bears witness to this, and it is proved also by the attachment which Pascal always showed towards the Duc de Roannez and his sister; we should be in a better position to appreciate this tenderness if the greater part of Pascal's correspondence were not lost.

But a sensibility so profound could only, in the end, be satisfied by an infinite object: it could reach its real flowering only in the attitude of the mystic. Nature, which in itself did not touch Pascal's feelings, nevertheless nourished this mysticism of his to the degree in which it is itself only a "forest of symbols", a *figurative* representation of the Infinite that has created it. "Invisible things" are represented in "the visible". God hides himself under the veil of sensible appearances. But the chief source of Pascal's profounder emotions lay in the sense of communication with God, with the living God of the Bible. The ***Mémorial*** is an impulse of love reaching out towards the God of Abraham, of Isaac and of Jacob; in ***The Mystery of Jesus*** the note of exaltation becomes so deep that the crucified Christ is caught up in a dialogue with the penitent human soul.

It is from this unique and individual sensibility that all the sublimity of the Pascalian sense of disquiet arises. It is the expression, by a man of genius, of a more general Christian disquiet. There is a sense of disquiet about one's own salvation: who can be certain of persevering in the ways of grace, and who does not feel in himself the fountainhead of these evil desires that cause divine grace to be lost? Ought Pascal not to be all the more fearful, in that he had already fallen? However, on this point, he remained strongly confident. What troubled him much more was disquiet about the salvation of others; when he put himself, in fancy, in the place of the unbeliever, Pascal felt a kind of shudder; the moment when he appreciated the position of the unbeliever from his own believer's point of view was also the moment in which a sense of the tragedy of human fate gripped him with a kind of anguish. Here and there this disquiet already lends feeling to ***The Provincial Letters;*** and it is what gives the ***Pensées*** their gripping note.

But Pascal would not be a true contemporary of Corneille, of the author of *Cinna* and *Polyeucte,* if this inner violence and this profound sensibility of his were not linked to a great *self-mastery*. This violent man is not a man who acts on his instincts; this "man of feeling" reflects on his emotions. Pascal's natural impetuosity very rarely carries him beyond the boundaries which it has fixed for itself; at the moment of the most intense ecstasy, the lucidity of reason does not lose its rights. Pascal dominates both his own life and his own work through the strength of his will and the clarity of his intelligence.

It would not be surprising if such a man, in his youth, had been strongly influenced by Stoicism: when Jacqueline in her *Stances contre l'Amour* exalts the power of reason over the passions, it is very probable that she is expressing an ideal she shared with her brother. In the *salons,* those who preached the ideal of the *honnête homme* tended to intellectualize the emotions and demanded from their disciples first submission to others, and then self-control and self-transcendence. After his second conversion, Pascal sought to check and tame a sensibility which he knew to be sometimes excessive and an inner violence which kept him at a distance from Christian humility. If he did succeed in the end in becoming "as simple as a child", it was at the price of patient effort and not without numerous fallings by the way. It was the strength of his will that enabled him to attain the state in which he had, as it were, stripped himself of worldliness.

This self-mastery is to be found also in Pascal's literary work, which is wholly and in every part governed by his intelligence. In this connection, the unfinished state of the **Pensées** ought not to deceive us. There can be no longer any question of considering these as a "shapeless heap of materials". The **Pensées** were methodically prepared, and even methodically grouped, by a genius who had a complete mastery of his own gifts and was extremely conscious of the effects he sought to obtain. Pascal was never tempted to equate sincerity with spontaneity or art with self-abandonment to instinct. If he hastens towards truth with a sort of violent passion, he nevertheless conducts his investigations into what may be truth with an extremely acute critical spirit and shows himself as strict as can be in his weighing of evidence. If his thinking aspires towards an infinite God, it remains none the less the thinking of a man who is a scientist as well as a mystic, and it also tends to express itself in an artistically perfect form. The completed **Pensées** would have had all the finish of **The Provincial Letters;** the violence of the feeling would have been wedded to a subtle elaboration of form.

From Pascal's whole personality there emanates a kind of imperious attraction. He attracted by imposing himself. We know what an ascendancy he gained over the Duc de Roannez, how this great nobleman made himself Pascal's humble disciple and retained all his life a touching fidelity to his master. We know also, through many witnesses, how Pascal's spoken words remained, as it were, engraved in the memories of those who heard him. Having moved his contemporaries so strongly, he could not fail to exercise a strong fascination over posterity.

II. *The Thinker*

But Pascal does not attract us only by the vigour of his personality; he possesses in addition the prestige which properly belongs to every powerful and original thinker. Not that he was, strictly speaking, a philosopher; he did not organize his notions into a complete and coherent system. But his work carries a "message", if one understands by that certain great ideas which Pascal grasped profoundly and to which he gave a lasting life; exciting enthusiasm on the one hand, and arousing violent opposition on the other.

One primary aspect of this message can be defined as *the primacy of experience and the experimental method.* This is already, in his purely scientific work, one of the chief lessons he has to teach us. "Experiments are the only basis of physical science." In opposition to Descartes, for whom physical science rests on mathematical deductions from purely rational principles, and for whom experiments merely confirm these deductions, Pascal claims that the explanation of phenomena must rest on experiments only, and not on any system of thought that may claim priority to experience; we must not assert anything more than our experiments allow us to. In all this, Pascal made a much more important contribution than Descartes to the separation of physics from metaphysics and towards laying the foundations of modern science.

The habit of mind of Pascal, the man of science, can also be discovered in Pascal, the theologian. Just as he disallows purely deductive reasoning in physics, so he disallows it in theology. The theologian confines himself to acquiring knowledge of *the facts* contained in Revelation and Tradition. Experience is the basis of human science, revelation of divine science; in both cases, reason, as such, has a limited part to play. Revelation and experience thus, taken together, define two classes of facts which are totally independent of each other and between which, therefore, no contradiction is possible. Nothing which is accessible to experience has been revealed: that is the basis of the attitude of Pascal and his friends on "the question of fact". But the theologian may have to take simultaneous cognizance of these two classes of facts, experiential and revealed. Thus no theologian's theory of the nature of the moral act may contradict psychological realities; every system of casuistry must be based at once on a scrupulous fidelity to Tradition and on an exact knowledge of human nature. Pascal reproaches the Jesuits not only with forgetting the lessons of the Christian

Fathers, but also with being ignorant of man's real nature.

In a word, Pascal's religious apologetic is based on the principle: God is accessible to us through facts and not through reasonings. This does not mean that Pascal denies any value at all to human reason; he merely takes note of the fact that, in the world as we find it, it is not reasonings that convince men; if the reign of true justice should commence on earth, men would still oppose that justice; and though the argument from the orderliness of the universe may really prove the existence of a God, it does so in vain, since men do not believe any more firmly in God because of that proof. The facts of the case, on the other hand, are of a nature to constrain any mind that is not made blind by concupiscence. Thus the whole dialectic of the *Apology* rests on two facts: the fact of man and the fact of history. What is it that experience reveals to us about man? It is essentially his dual nature, his wretchedness and his greatness. Only one system can explain this fact of man's dual nature, and that system is Christianity. What does the examination of history reveal to us? The fulfilment of Biblical prophecies, the perpetuity of a religion opposed to the passions of man, and therefore the presence of a miracle, of the divine, in the world. And this note of the divine is attached to the Christian religion alone, under its two forms, which an analysis of the documents shows to be identical with each other: the Jewish form, and the strictly Christian form. In all this argument of Pascal's there has been no place anywhere for abstract deduction.

But if we pass from the methodological realm of discourse to that of philosophy, the primacy of experience can be equated with the primacy of *existence*. As has often been noticed, Pascal is in effect a precursor of contemporary existentialism. Like the existentialists, he takes his stance in concrete living, he strives to consider the situation of man with fresh eyes, to get back to the primitive feeling of existence: and in fact he manages to make us feel astonished that we *do* exist. We discover in the *Pensées* one of the most cherished topics of existentialism: the absurdity of the human condition, expressed by Pascal in terms like "contrariness" or "disproportion"; the anguish that results from this absurdity; even M. Sartre's "nausea" to which Pascal's "weariness" (*ennui*), taken in the strong, seventeenth-century sense, corresponds; we discover also the necessity of choice, of commitment, of "the wager". Pascal's Christianity can also be called an existential Christianity. It is through reflecting on his own existence that man discovers the necessity of God, who is alone capable of filling the emptiness which man feels in himself: a living, incarnate God, who lives in each of us, members of His Mystical Body. Nevertheless, Pascal's existentialism is a very original existentialism. It widely tran-

scends the limits of modern types of existentialism, even if only through its concern for the universal. The existentialist attitude is nearly always combined with a profound pessimism, as the themes touched on above have already made clear. In fact, a second aspect of Pascal's message may be expressed in the words: *the wretchedness of man without God*. Among all his writings, it may be that the pages devoted to the description of this wretchedness have awakened the profoundest echo.

But in the *Pensées* this idea is brought forward in a very original and precise shape. The essence of man's wretchedness lies in his *powerlessness*. And man's wretchedness, also is caused by his greatness. Man resembles the animals, and these are not wretched; but he finds himself in a far loftier station than they and the vague memory which he retains of his first state makes his present condition unbearable to him. The wretchedness of man comes from the contradiction between the reality of what he is and the ideal to which he aspires. He aspires to truth and finds only error; he aspires towards real justice and finds only false justice; he aspires towards the infinite and finds only the finite. Man is therefore a divided being; his life is a perpetual drama.

Pascal is, however, at the opposite pole to Kierkegaard in that he never gives the impression that man is necessarily crushed under the weight of his destiny, necessarily condemned to a perpetual painful anxiety. His description of man's wretchedness is an invitation to man to transcend himself, to discover that infinite towards which he aspires. Thus even the most pessimistic pages at the outset of the *Apology* contain an appeal to the heroic element in human nature, an appeal to man to turn towards God. Man's wretchedness is merely the wretchedness of man "without God". Everything evil comes from man, everything good from God; to be delivered from his wretchedness, man must renounce himself.

Pascal's dramatic vision of humanity awakens a deep echo in all unsatisfied souls, particularly in "times of troubles", when man becomes tragically aware of his own destiny. But it is also this part of his argument that arouses the most lively opposition. There are two groups of thinkers who react against the harshness, the naked heroism, of his portrait of human nature; on the one hand, those who uphold a kind of optimistic rationalism; and on the other, the partisans of "the pursuit of happiness", and, in general, those who assign to man no other end, or aim, than himself.

The best representative of the first group, the upholders of an optimistic rationalism, is obviously Voltaire. His famous "observations" on Pascal, contained in the twenty-fifth of his *Letters Philosophiques,* are familiar to most readers, at least in France. To Pascal's assertion that man is wretched, Voltaire opposes the assertion that human happiness is a reality; and he appears to himself to be stating a plain fact. Our impulses, according to Voltaire, are in themselves good; nothing, for instance, is healthier than that human self-esteem, or self-love, which Pascal hated. Rational self-love is the foundation of social life, of, indeed, every form of human activity; it alone really makes us exist. There is nothing, again, for Voltaire, disquieting about human destiny; our destiny is marked out for us by our place in the great chain of being, a little above the animals, a little below pure spirits like the angels. There is nothing that we need worry and torment ourselves about in the riddle of the universe; why not simply trust ourselves to a benevolent Providence? Voltaire's optimistic rationalism issues, therefore, in a kind of exaggerated Molinism. These criticisms have been repeated, since Voltaire's time, in a hundred different styles; some of them have been brilliantly restated in our own day by the early Aldous Huxley.

In our second group, that of the humanist opponents of Pascal, we include those thinkers who are less concerned to attack Pascal's picture of the wretchedness of man than to refute the moral he draws from it. They substitute for Pascal's ideal of human self-transcendence a new ideal of human completeness or fulfilment. Life for them is like the elaboration of a work of art, which must draw as near as it can to perfection, but to a perfection that will always remain finite. This is the common note of Nietzsche who, putting forward the ideal of the superman, comes sharply up against Pascal, whose sheer power nevertheless overawes him, and of Gide, who refuses to "work out his salvation with fear and trembling", and who, without failing to recognize the element of illusion in it, nevertheless rehabilitates the notion of "diversion", of amusement or distraction, in its forms of sport or art. These, in spite of everything, do enable man to fulfil himself.

These are the two principal lines of opposition to Pascal. There is no place here for a discussion of the validity of these criticisms. Let us repeat, merely, an observation that has often been made before; in the end, the thinker who really raises man up to the highest level, who sets before him the highest aim, is the very thinker who insists most strongly on man's "lowly" and "wretched" condition; the thinker who shows the greatest humanity, the greatest understanding of man, in that he refuses to betray, by denying, man's secret suffering, is the very thinker who demands that man should die to himself.

While the adversaries of Pascal have always concentrated on the problem of man's wretchedness, it is Pascal's strictly religious message which has gained him his warmest adherents. If the reading of the **Pensées** occasionally leads to religious conversions, it is less because it disquiets the soul than because it offers to the reli-

gious need and impulse in man the highest conceivable ideal. For the third aspect of Pascal's message is: "There is no religion without love". Without love, which is to say, without charity or love of God. In that are summed up "all the law and the Prophets".

The principle of the love of God plays an essential part in Pascal's apologetic. True religion can consist only of the love of God. "If there is a single principle underlying everything, a single end set for everything, then everything exists through that principle and everything exists for the sake of it. It is therefore necessary that true religion should teach us to adore nothing but this principle, to love only it." Every religion which does not put the love of God in the first place is false, since it is incapable of satisfying that need for the infinite which our intellect and our emotions both experience: love, in fact, is precisely this human gift or capacity for the infinite. That is why, for instance, the religion of Mahomet appears to Pascal "absurd". But, somewhere between the true religions and the false ones, there exists, problematically, the religion of the Jews. Can we halt, in our religious development, at the letter of the Law and of the ceremonies of the Old Testament? One cannot, in fact, say about these that they had charity as their sole aim; and therefore the religion of the Jews would be, according to Pascal's criterion, a false one. But an exact interpretation of the Biblical texts enables Pascal to reach this conclusion: "Everything (in the Bible) that does not make for charity is figurative." All the precepts of the Mosaic Law are only various expressions of the central precept of charity. "The one end at which Holy Scripture aims is charity." In its basis, therefore, the Jewish religion is true; it is identical with the Christian religion.

But let us leave the plane of apologetic for that of the moral life. How can we define in terms of psychology the presence of the love of God in a soul? As we have already said, the love of God for Pascal is primarily and essentially a good direction of the will: a faithfulness in man to the call which he has heard leading him towards something higher than himself, his response to his "vocation".

Thus it is love which conducts the infidel towards faith. It is love which leads us to undertake that quest for the truly Good which is nothing other than the quest for God Himself. Whoever feels his own wretchedness and has a deeply-rooted desire to cure it; whoever feels that he cannot find any real consolation in created things; such a man in the end will find his "Liberator". It is not the evidence for the truth of Christianity that by itself convinces the unbeliever; the love of God must clarify his reasoning faculty before he will be able to perceive the truth of the evidence.

In the same way, with the believer, it is only love that

gives religious practice life. That is the real lesson of *The Provincial Letters*. It was by no means Pascal's intention merely to substitute an austere religious formalism for the lax religious formalism of the Jesuits; he repudiates formalism in all its shapes. Nothing is really at a more opposite pole than Jansenism to that middle-class Puritanism of seventeenth-century Protestant countries with which historians too often tend to confuse it. For Jansenism, the sacraments, if they are really going to be the instruments of grace, must be received with a purified heart; for absolution to be valid, the penitent must manifest a sincere goodwill in relation to his future conduct. In order to act morally, we must be ready to respond to the stirrings of a conscience which we have taken care to orientate towards the quest for truth, and to make more scrupulous by the practice of putting ourselves under spiritual direction. This is the lesson which Pascal repeats at the end of his *Apology,* in the chapter called **"Christian Morals"**, where he allots their respective shares to external practice and the inner life in the conduct of the Christian. The leading image in this chapter is that of the Mystical Body. The limbs, the members, live only through the body as a whole; man lives only through God. If I wish to attain to the true life of the spirit, "I must love only God and hate only myself."

Though Pascal puts this ideal forward to all men, it is an ideal which is likely to be realized only by an *élite*. This fact does not diminish the sympathy which many Protestants feel for Pascal, but it does worry some Roman Catholics. It worries them because it tends to lessen the importance of external rites and ceremonies, because it bases religion on a personal link between man and God, and because it demands of the believer that he should seek to be perfect. Thus Pascal has aroused a certain mistrust, which has been formulated now more, and now less, clearly, among those who prefer, to a reflective Christianity, or a Christianity of the inner man, the faith of the simple, a popular piety, even if that has to be mingled with a certain amount of superstition. It has excited distrust also among those who think of the Church as a kind of sacred army, regulated, like an army, by the law of unquestioning obedience; and finally by those who fear that, by demanding too much, Pascal will discourage the weaker brethren. With these reservations, we have to admit that Roman Catholic opinion in general has always considered Pascal as one of the masters of the spiritual life and has always considered his apologetic as a model.

III. *The Artist*

However many opponents the thought of Pascal may have encountered, his art as a writer has been universally admired. However, this powerful and subtle art of his does not lend itself easily to analysis; it is extremely spontaneous and yet it has been carefully thought out; it is the art of a man who possessed in the highest degree the two essential gifts of a writer, richness of invention and sureness of taste. These two qualities are united in Pascal, balancing each other in a way that is extremely rare in literary history. He is always the master of his inspiration even when it surges forth most strongly; the innumerable corrections in the manuscript of the *Pensées* never destroy the freshness of the original vision. Thus, if the literary art of Pascal is based on a few grand and general aesthetic principles, it none the less expresses also the man himself in the very essence of his soul.

Certain theoretical writings help us to grasp some aspects of the ideal which Pascal, as a typical man of good taste of his century, had accepted for himself. We have already shown, in analysing *L'Art de Persuader,* what is the philosophical foundation of what has been called Pascal's "rhetoric". Some of the *Pensées* define the practical consequences of these rhetorical theories. Two ideas are outlined with particular sharpness and clarity: that of "order", as an element of good style, and that of "naturalness".

In arranging his papers with his *Apology* in mind, Pascal had formed a first chapter called **"Order"**, in which he grouped together all his reflections about the disposition of the material in his intended work. But, in repeating the word "order" so often, Pascal had not in any sense in mind the trite idea that a work of literature ought to be clearly and solidly composed. On the contrary, he thought the rigorous divisions of topics which he discovered in scholastic treatises artificial and therefore to be condemned. Order for him was not an abstraction, not something independent of the idea to be expressed. A thought, for Pascal, could not receive a faithful expression, nor attain the purpose which the writer had in mind in expressing it, unless a certain "order" had been imposed on it. "The same words differently arranged convey different meanings, and the same meanings differently arranged have different effects on the reader." In the same way, a chapter, or a work taken as a whole, ought to develop itself in an orderly fashion, in harmony with the subject treated, or the leading idea to be emphasized. Thus, wishing to speak of Pyrrhonism, Pascal warns his reader: "I shall put down my thoughts here without any order, and yet perhaps not in mere purposeless confusion; this is the proper order, which, by its very disorder, indicates my theme." Apparent disorder is also a kind of order; in this sense disorder can be not only a source of beauty, as Boileau had already seen, but also of truth. It is therefore in the search for a proper order that a thinker's labours achieve their purpose; it is in its order that the real originality of a work of literature lies. "Let nobody say that I have said nothing new. The arrangement of the material is new."

Thus "order" in writing, though primarily intended to convey the author's idea faithfully, in the end also expresses his personality. And to find the right order for what one has to say is to achieve "naturalness". Here we have the formulation of Pascal's grand aesthetic principle. All useless ornaments ought to be lopped away; the writer must eschew "false beauties", "mock windows put in for the sake of symmetry". He must also eschew everything that smacks of specialization. "We must be able to say of a writer neither that he is a mathematician, nor a preacher, nor an able orator, but that he is an honest man. Only that universal quality pleases me." Finally "the author" must give way to "the man". No doubt he must seek to please, but it is only naturalness that really pleases. "We need both what is pleasant and what is solid, but what is pleasant must be itself based on truth." Pointed sentences and brilliant antitheses excite only an artificial and transitory pleasure. On the contrary, the writer who paints the passions in their natural colours makes his readers recognize, in their own inner selves, the truth of his observations; he pleases in the real sense of the phrase, he makes himself loved. All these ideas, partly inspired perhaps by the Chevalier de Méré, show that Pascal belonged completely to the seventeenth-century French classical tradition.

In his actual writing, moreover, Pascal was able to put his theories of composition magnificently into practice. If there is order and naturalness in everything he writes, the reason is that in his writing he is always profoundly himself. In Pascal's literary art, we find Pascal the man completely expressed; the temperament of a scientist blended with that of a poet.

The scientific habit of Pascal's mind can be traced in his eagerness to define his terms strictly, an eagerness which we see demonstrated at the beginning of the fourth "Provincial Letter", or in the mathematical precision of some of his formulas. We shall attempt to draw attention, especially, to the influence of this scientific habit of mind on Pascal's methods of composition. The method of the physicist explains the development of a fragment, like that in the **Pensées** on the subject of "diversion", of amusement or distraction. Pascal begins by noting facts, which, taken together, permit him to assert that men suffer from a kind of restlessness which is not linked to any coherent sense of need or purpose. Then he postulates a hypothesis to explain this restlessness; man is seeking to forget his wretched condition. The hypothesis is then demonstrated in an extreme and crucial case; that of a king, who, though the most favoured of mortals, must nevertheless seek distraction like other men to avoid unhappiness. Finally, the demonstration of this hypothesis is followed by a return to the facts which Pascal started with. But a new light has been shed on these; every kind of human activity can be explained by the great principle of man's need for distraction. A similar movement of thought can often be discovered in Montaigne, but it lacks in him this scientific character. The same method appears in other fragments of the **Pensées,** like that on imagination. Other passages make us think less of the experimental method of natural science than of that of pure mathematics. In the fragment on the two

kinds of infinity, we see the universe working outwards or inwards in concentric circles; it is the geometrical method which is our model. Elsewhere, we have indicated the sources in geometry of Pascal's idea of the three orders of greatness. The presentation of the idea, however, has its model in an arithmethical symbolism, the sum in proportion: as flesh is to spirit, so is spirit to charity. The whole development of the thought consists in the postulation of the equality of these relations in eight different fashions. (The problem is made more complex, of course, by the fact that these relations, unlike those in a sum in proportion, are relationships between infinite values.) We can see that Pascal's thought has a natural tendency to shape itself in a scientific mould.

It might be feared that methods of exposition borrowed from the sciences would entail a certain dryness. But as the fragment on the three orders wonderfully proves, the method has an opposite result. Pascal's prose acquires through his scientific approach a purity and nakedness of line which brings out the whole substance of his thought and feeling. The strictness of the approach assists, rather than hinders, the lyrical impetus.

In fact Pascal was primarily a poet, He was a poet above all through his gift for creating images. But these images, in his case, are never used merely to adorn an abstract idea, or even to make it clearer by a concrete example; the image in Pascal, is of one flesh with the idea, it is summoned by the idea. It is the warmth of the argument that gives birth to the vision; it is the emotion excited by the idea that begets the image. In his genius for the powerful and original metaphor, Pascal is closely related to the great French romantics.

What is the nature of these images? Some of them reveal a gift of penetrating observation, an observation turned on outward nature, on the pictorial aspects of the world, as much as on the moral attitudes of men. In his descriptions of the "human comedy", Pascal's minute realism sometimes even verges on triviality— though not to the extent which certain blundering editors of the romantic period might make us believe, who read "trognes d'armées" (high-coloured faces of armies, flushed as if with drink) where Pascal had merely written "troupes d'armées" and "foisons de religions" (heaps of religions) where he had merely written "faiseurs de religions". But there *are* descriptions like those of the magistrates with "their red robes, their ermines, in which they swaddle themselves like cats in their fur"; or there is the spectacle of the dance, one of the best means man has of forgetting his condition: "You have to think carefully where you put your feet." More often, however, external reality is transcended. Pascal's imagination is superior even to his gift of observation, and starting with some concrete detail we reach up towards an infinity which is, as it were, made palpable to us: the "atomic tininess" which we reach in dissecting as thoroughly as we can the body of an alimentary parasite suddenly expands into an "infinity of universes".

How are these images fitted into the general pattern of the development of Pascal's thought? Usually, the metaphor is rapidly sketched in. Pascal asks himself whether our reason is abused by our imagination. "Ridiculous reason that the wind shifts, and shifts in every direction!" The spectacle of the search for distraction extorts from him the cry: "How hollow the heart of man is, and how full of filth!" Sometimes the metaphor is expressed through a violent foreshortening and thus becomes all the more striking. Compared to the infinity of celestial space this familiar universe of ours is only "a prison cell". Finally, in certain images which he has allowed himself to develop with more elaboration, Pascal touches the height of his powers: "We drift on a vast scene, always uncertain and floating, thrust from one goal towards another. If there is some boundary to which we think we can hold on and there assert ourselves, it shakes us off and leaves us and, if we follow it, it escapes our grasp, glides away from us and flees with an eternal flight."

Pascal is a poet, also, through his acute sense of rhythm. If we read the sentence just quoted, in French, we find ourselves in the presence of what is really a strophe, beginning with two octosyllables, "Nous voguons sur un milieu vaste, toujours incertains et flottants", and the various climaxes of this fantastic voyage, as Tourneur has remarked, are evoked by "the balance of the sentence, its jolts, its prolonged development, its cadences and the sounds of the individual words". There are very many passages of the *Pensées* and also of *The Provincial Letters* which, if arranged on the page in "free verse" form, would at once reveal their cunning management of sound and rhythm. The French alexandrine itself is often "in ambush" in this poetic prose. Here is an example, a line of piercing harmony, which concludes a discussion of reality and dreams: *Car la vie est un songe un peu moins inconstant.* (This also comes naturally over into an English heroic line: *Life is a slightly less inconstant dream.*) Pascal, therefore, is a poet not only through his visionary power but because he makes use of the poet's actual techniques.

But Pascal is a poet, above all, through the emotional power which animates his sentences. The *Pensées* are one huge poem in the lyrical mode. We can distinguish in them two different kinds of lyricism, differing according to the nature of the underlying emotion. In the first part of the *Apology,* we have the lyricism of man's wretchedness. By a kind of act of poetic substitution, Pascal identifies himself with that humanity deprived of God, whose distress he lives through. Elsewhere, there is a *mystical* lyricism, nourished by an ardent love for the person of Christ, humble and poor throughout His life, in the end pouring out His Blood on the

Cross for the salvation of sinners. Pascal reaches his emotional heights when he most completely strips himself.

Thus Pascal is very profoundly a literary artist in the classical tradition: classical in the theoretical principles of his art, classical in his concern for perfection of form, classical in that he considers reflection inseparable from the creative task. But through the sheer power of his genius he so infinitely transcends all the groups and schools of his time that the romantics, later, were able to claim him as one of themselves.

One lesson, we believe, emerges from this study: that there is a profound unity between Pascal's life and his work. All critical efforts to divide Pascal from himself have ended in failure. We cannot radically oppose the scientist to the man of the world, or the scientist or the man of the world to the Christian; Pascal, was always, in various fashions, a scientist, a man of the world, *and* a Christian. It is futile to try to set the doctrine of *The Provincial Letters* against that of the *Pensées,* or to try to set the dying Pascal against the living Pascal. The foregoing examination of Pascal's life and writings has shown, on the contrary, that the same doctrines, the same topics, the same habits of mind are found throughout his works and link them together. Pascal's art cannot be explained without considering his science, nor his efforts as a Christian apologist without considering his polemics and his theology. In the unity of his personality and his work, Pascal, like Corneille, expresses in a very original fashion the trends and the aspirations of the age, in France, of Louis XIII and the minority of Louis XIV. He expresses the spirit of that ardent and sturdy generation, proud and independent, setting out like explorers towards the discovery of the physical and moral worlds; a generation with a passion for concrete reality and yet an idealistic generation, men who disciplined their natural impetuosity by accepting the authority of reason, who were eager for distinction and in love with fine manners, but eager also for, and in love with, heroism and sanctity.

Jan Miel (essay date 1969)

SOURCE: "Pascal and Theology," in *Blaise Pascal,* edited by Harold Bloom, Chelsea House Publishers, 1989, pp. 115-22.

[*In the following essay, which originally appeared in* Pascal and Theology *in 1969, Miel emphasizes the historical nature of Pascal's vision of humanity as well as his theological basis for nearly all his thought.*]

The historicity of man's condition is certainly one of the most difficult of all theological principles to discuss and keep firmly in mind. Rational thought is by its nature opposed to historical truth, aiming as it does at a truth that transcends historical vicissitudes. Yet, as we have seen [elsewhere], every important element of Pascal's analysis of man must be defined historically. There is no human nature separable from the story of a mankind that was created sane, just, and free, and which lost those attributes through Adam's Fall. The attempt to define a nonhistorical human nature is the worm in the apple of Thomism which the Jesuits swallowed whole and brought forth as the viper's tangle of casuistry and the new morality. And the attempt to interpret the *Pensées* as a description of such a permanent human nature leads to the idea of the "sublime misanthrope" or the anguished preromantic, or other mistaken views of their author.

It may seem untoward to insist so on the historical nature of Pascal's thought when one of his most distinguished modern critics has taken him to task exactly for lacking a sense of history. The question raised by M. Béguin [in *Pascal par lui-même*] is in fact several questions which we must try to keep distinct. There is the first and fundamental question as to whether the unfolding of time plays an essential role in his thought, or whether Pascal's vision is classical, timeless, nonhistorical. Here, it seems to me, we must insist most strongly on the essentially historical nature of his vision. In an age of philosophical systems, and a physical mechanism that transcended and destroyed time, Pascal more than anyone in his age and society—even among his Augustinian friends—upheld the Augustinian vision, not only against the Jesuits, but against Thomists and Cartesians, scientists and mathematicians: "Dieu d'Abraham, Dieu d'Isaac, Dieu de Jacob, non des Philosophes et des savants" (*Mémorial*). The revelation of Christianity is essentially a Sacred History, and the events of that history from the Creation and the Fall of Adam to the Incarnation and the awaited Second Coming are, for Pascal, more important and more enlightening than any philosophical system known or possible; philosophical systems are in fact shown to be themselves mere temporal manifestations and are seen in the light of an historical development that transcends them. It is hardly necessary to emphasize the role of this "theology of history" in Pascal's thought: it was to play an enormous part in the Apology, and the ramifications of it fill only slightly less than half of the total pages of the *Pensées*. And one of the main points of the rest of the Apology was to show that man is a "monstre incompréhensible" as long as he tries to understand himself in purely philosophical terms without reference to his historical situation. But this is of course always with reference to Sacred History; Béguin's criticism is rather that Pascal's thought seems to have no place in it for secular history, or rather to describe secular history as pure vanity—an enormous waste motivated by concupiscence and doomed to damnation.

Once again a distinction must be made between two questions: the first would concern the individual's attitude toward secular life, i.e., to what extent the Christian is called to participate in the society of his time and in the better aims of that society; we shall return to this question shortly. The other question is the intellectual question of how we conceive secular history, particularly in its relation to the History of Salvation. Here, as Béguin recognizes, we are outside the scope of the Apology and consequently need not expect to find very many helpful texts, but there are nonetheless indications of Pascal's position. As Béguin says, there is none of the meditation on the density and mystery of historical becoming that characterizes some thinkers since the nineteenth century, and also perhaps certain passages of St. Augustine. But the elements of the Augustinian view are all there: the emphasis on the Mystical Body and the insistence on the invisibility of election, which we saw developed in the *Ecrits sur la grâce* as an essential difference between Jansenists and Calvinists; this doctrine sees God's intentions as hidden and mysterious until the end of time: a doctrine which in fact puts considerable weight on an historical development which cannot exclude secular history, since it cannot really distinguish it from the History of Salvation. And finally there is the generosity and justice of God toward all men (not just the elect) and the desire of Christ for the salvation of all.

This last position, involving the fifth condemned proposition of Jansenius, has led some commentators to see Pascal as abandoning the Jansenist position on this point. However, this is difficult to maintain: the position in the texts in the *Pensées* is exactly that of the *Ecrits sur la grâce* and of the *Abrégé de la vie de Jésus Christ,* namely, that the statement "Christ died for all men" can be understood in two ways depending on whether you are considering Christ as a man or Christ as God. This is merely a matter of common sense; Pascal goes further, however, and finds fault with those who emphasize the fact that his death did not benefit all men, rather than the fact that it was offered for all. It is possible that he has in mind some of his Jansenist friends, but possible also that, as in the *Ecrits sur la grâce,* he means the Calvinists, and wishes to preserve the Augustinian doctrine from the gloomy air they seem to give it. In any case, it is clear that although all humanity will not finally be saved, only God's judgment will discern, at the end of time, the Elect from the damned. So, what Henri Marrou says of the Augustinian doctrine could also express the conception of Pascal: "Nous possédons le sens de l'histoire, mais par la Foi, c'est-à-dire d'une connaissance qui demeure partiellement obscure. C'est le sens global de l'histoire qui nous est révélé; non le détail, les modalités de sa réalisation." Although the unbeliever must be made to see the vanity of the ideals of secular society, the Christian, enlightened as to the ultimate direction of history, will look for the hand of God at work even through the vanity of men, drawing good out of evil. Pascal was more concerned to lead the unbeliever to the point where he could receive this vision than to produce meditations upon it which might please the mind but leave the heart untouched. For a philosophy of history remains always a philosophy and therefore is itself ahistorical; but an apology that rejects philosophy and attempts rather to move its readers into a religion that is in its very essence historical hardly deserves the reproach of lacking a sense of history. In the History of Salvation, Pascal is undoubtedly more interested in the salvation than in the history, but the one cannot exist without the other, and Pascal was one of the very few in an age of philosophy and science to see this clearly and to base all his thinking on it.

Finally, concerning the question as to what extent the Christian is called to participate in the society of his time and in general to contribute to the better aims of society, it seems incredible that anyone familiar with Pascal's life could suppose that he somehow rejected society or life in the world. It is true of course that he admired and encouraged those who chose to withdraw for the sake of the religious life—his sister Jacqueline and Charlotte de Roannez are notable examples. But his attitude on the question of the signature also made it clear that he did not consider even the religious as exempt from the cares and obligations of other Christians, and indeed in the seventeenth century they were not. In any case, although Pascal must have considered the religious life for himself, he not only rejected such a withdrawal but seems to have accepted his worldly condition with an equanimity bordering on lightheartedness.

Nor do the *Pensées* anywhere contradict such an attitude. On the contrary, near the end of the wager he reminds his interlocutor of the advantages of choosing God and losing oneself: "Vous serez fidèle, honnête, humble, reconnaissant, bien faisant, ami sincère, véritable." And elsewhere he says, "Nul n'est heureux comme un vrai chrétien, ni raisonnable, ni vertueux, ni aimable." The import of these statements is clearly that the Christian convert does not withdraw from human society, but becomes more truly human. He has of course undergone a change of heart: his activity is no longer mere diversion or distraction, motivated by concupiscence and egoism—although these are never in this life entirely absent; his motivation is now primarily charitable, done not for his own gain or glory, but for others, and so for God. Conversion, for Pascal, was never a refusal of society or history, of the world as our scene of operations, our very condition of life. It was rather a reentry into human society with purified motives, an entry into history with a fuller understanding and acceptance of its process. And to return to our old question of freedom, the true Christian's activity in the world will actually be freer. Because,

although it is always possible for him to fall from grace, he is yet free from the anxiety of having to merit his salvation. His most characteristic virtue is hope, a virtue that presupposes existence in time and precludes both a fatalistic attitude and also a Pelagian one, for, as Pascal notes, if we could truly earn our salvation, "le juste ne devrait donc plus espérer en Dieu, car il ne doit pas espérer, mais s'efforcer d'obtenir ce qu'il demande!"

The very real contrast between the outlook of Pascal and that of the "humanisme dévot" of the sixteenth and seventeenth centuries has led too many to suppose that Pascal is a sort of antihumanist. The following passage [from the *Pensées*], besides giving us a clear picture of Pascal's goal as apologist, also shows much about his assessment of man.

> Contrariétés. Après avoir montré la bassesse et la grandeur de l'homme.—*Que l'homme maintenant s'estime son prix. Qu'il s'aime, car il y a en lui une nature capable de bien; mais qu'il n'aime pas pour cela les bassesses qui y sont. Qu'il se méprise, parce que cette capacité est vide; mais qu'il ne méprise pas pour cela cette capacité naturelle. Qu'il se haïsse, qu'il s'aime: il a en lui la capacité de connaître la vérité et d'être heureux; mais il n'a point de vérité, ou constante, ou satisfaisante.*

> *Je voudrais donc porter l'homme à désirer d'en trouver, à être prêt, et dégagé des passions, pour la suivre où il la trouvera, sachant combien sa connaissance s'est obscurcie par les passions; je voudrais bien qu'il haït en soi la concupiscence qui le détermine d'elle-même, afin qu'elle ne l'aveuglât point pour faire son choix, et qu'elle ne l'arrêtât point quand il aura choisi.*

This passage summarizes much of what I have tried to bring out already: man's true nature as a "capacité vide," the need to both love and hate oneself, and so forth. It also shows the precise limits of Pascal's ambition, not just for his Apology, but for self-knowledge and the efforts of human reason. It has been said that Pascal's vision is essentially discontinuous, there being no communication between the three orders of body, mind, and heart; and that there exists likewise an unbridgeable abyss between man and God. One author says that Pascal wished to "couper les ponts de l'homme à Dieu sans renoncer à les faire exister l'un pour l'autre." Such a notion, however, presupposes that outlook, characteristic of Renaissance Humanism, in which man sets out to reach God and can do so only by deeds of valor or towers of intellect. The ideal of a St. Ignatius, at least in the early stages of his conversion, was totally that of the heroic deeds to be done to reach God, and the ideal of the chivalrous saints does not seem so far from that of the chevalier of metaphysics, Descartes. The bridges built in the name of an all too human rationalism and "gloire" had to be destroyed. Yet Pascal did not accept the total lack of communication that seems to be characteristic of both Calvinism and the fideism of Montaigne; they are accused of fostering despair or a "nonchalance du salut." The true way to God, then, was not through building great edifices, which could only be towers of Babel, nor in despairing of all communication, but, as the above passage says, in being ready and alert and wanting to find the bridge that God built to man. So the "humanisme dévot" of the Renaissance depended on a notion of man as fundamentally independent of God but with the power to reach God through his efforts. Pascal, on the other hand, notes that "l'homme n'est ni ange ni bête, et le malheur veut que qui veut faire l'ange fait la bête." Man's efforts to scale the heights are doomed, but once he recognizes his radical dependency on God and accepts God's efforts to reach him through Jesus Christ, he is more truly human in this life and destined for a glory greater than that of the angels. Pascal's humanism thus lies more in his hope for humanity than in his confidence in man's powers; but his descriptions of the spiritual life of the true Christian show far more than a narrow theologism. Hatred for self is counterbalanced by a new self-acceptance, and, as one no longer feels endangered by other Egos, one's relations to others are also transformed in the direction of self-effacement and generosity. And even one's relation to nature is affected; as one learns to abandon the "esprit de système" and live in the present, nature is no longer merely an object to be subjected to laws, but speaks directly to the heart in a relation that approaches intersubjectivity. There is no doubt a dimension that is properly mystical involved here, though this is a debated point; the relation to a recognized Christian mystical tradition is not so clear. But there are points in Pascal that suggest closer parallels may be found in oriental mystical doctrines, in particular that of Zen Buddhism with its emphasis on an immediate and mindless relation to the world, however different may be the paths that lead to this new awareness.

Theology, as I have tried to show throughout [*Pascal and Theology*], played a far more important role in the development of Pascal's thought than is usually supposed. His interest in theology and his efforts to acquire a serious understanding of its implications date from the time of his first conversion (1646), and his interest, his study and meditation of the Bible, and even the presumption that he understood some aspects of theology better than the professionals: all can be traced to this early period. Further, there is no reason to suppose that this interest was lost even in the so-called mundane period; and there is no justification at all for supposing that when he came to the writing of the **Letters provinciales** he was still theologically naïve and had to have his theology dictated to him by Arnauld and Nicole.

As to what his theology was, there is not the slightest doubt that it was the Augustinian theology as interpreted by Jansenius and Saint-Cyran and their followers. Difficulties over Pascal's Jansenism invariably arise out of the habit of regarding Jansenism as some sort of bugbear, a pernicious and monolithic heresy that taints all associted with it. A sensible historical perspective reveals that it is merely a label given to a group of defenders of the Augustinian doctrine of grace as that doctrine was undermined and threatened with extinction in the Renaissance. Nor is this to say that the Jansenists were right and the Molinists wrong: both groups can claim their ancient authorities—the Molinists echoed not only Pelagius but also the almost unanimous sentiment of the pre-Augustinian Fathers. And if the Jansenists can claim the weight of Conciliar support, Molinists nevertheless represented something like a new mind of the Church struggling against Augustinian conservatism.

Pascal claims to have looked at both sides of these questions and opted most decisively for the Augustinian view, for reasons that may originally have had more to do with the question of reason and revelation than with questions concerning grace and free will; our knowledge of Pascal's early thought is too sparse to allow any definite conclusions on that point. In any case he clearly never abandoned the basic Augustinian doctrines but rather proceeded to elaborate on them in his own way with a view, perhaps again dating from soon after the first conversion, to the writing of an Apology for Christianity. In both the projected Apology and in the **Lettres provinciales** the Augustinian (or Jansenist) theology is not only very much present, but supplies the real intellectual basis for both works, being at the source of all the apparently diverse discussions and attacks in the **Provinciales,** and supplying the framework for understanding the whole anthropology of the **Pensées**. Even the tactics of the Apology presuppose a Jansenist view of man, and not only as regards the role of reason. For example, Pascal offers us no vision of damnation such as we find in a Dante or a Bernanos, and the reason is that fear was not considered, in the Jansenist theory of "delectatio," to be an adequate motive force to turn the heart toward God.

But in looking at Pascal's own attempts to write real theology—the so-called **Ecrits sur la grâce**—we discover that although the doctrine is Jansenist, the style is not. Here Pascal shows not just a clarity and conciseness which contrast strongly with the style of an Arnauld, but as always an originality of approach. His emphasis on linguistic analysis is virtually unique in theological writing before the twentieth century. It is not at all the same sort of thing that occupied the Scholastics, who were concerned with precision of concepts; Pascal was keenly aware that theological statements, even those of a Pope or a Council, were made by men who meant something by them in a particular historical, intellectual context; so although their truth is *not* therefore relative, their meaning is.

And this characteristic of his theological writing carries over into all his writing, especially into the *Pensées*. It is an almost unparalleled ability to rethink man's problems entirely from within the limitations of our condition. So when writing against the vanity even of philosophers, who are after all only seeking their own glory, Pascal adds, "Et ceux qui écrivent contre veulent avoir la gloire d'avoir bien écrit; et ceux qui les lisent veulent avoir la gloire de les avoir lus; et moi, qui écris ceci, ai peut-être cette envie; et peut-être que ceux qui le liront." Denouncing "amour-propre" does not make one exempt from it; quite the contrary. Of course, as a thinker who saw that a fly could disrupt a metaphysical proof, that a pretty face or a kidney stone could change the course of history, and who considered a sneeze to be as worthy of philosophical reflection as deeds of valor, Pascal was not so original; the example of Montaigne was always before him. But Pascal refused the Montaignian shrug of the shoulders ("que sais-je?") and sought always to get as near to the truth as the condition of our language and our reason allow. Questions such as that of the existence of God and of the immortality of the soul are real questions of vital importance to every man; but philosophical answers are not real answers, because philosophers assume they can be answered in the abstract, out of time, free from the passions which animate us, ignoring the role of the questioner. This, then, is the primary characteristic of that strange argument, the wager, which has enticed but often repelled philosophers: that it tries to give the best answer possible to these questions without attempting to rise above the conditions of human existence to do it. So much of what seems to be paradoxical in the *Pensées* arises out of the same point of view. It is not, as M. Goldmann would have it, a refusal of the world from within the world: it is rather a total acceptance of the world in the knowledge that all our aspirations are other-worldly; it is the application to our intellectual life of the mystery of the Incarnation.

Yet this also echoes, and for Pascal probably arises out of meditation on the Augustinian doctrine of grace. For man's will is free, but he cannot freely will his salvation unless predestined to do so, and God's predestination is entirely beyond our grasp. In fact it was the aspiration toward freedom as independence that lost us our freedom in the Garden of Eden, and which still distorts our notions of freedom so that we cannot abide grace. For even grace does not restore the absolute freedom Adam enjoyed, but only a present sense of radical dependency on God's will which enables one to reason in good faith, to live in hope, and to act in charity. We become, at best, free as the birds are free, that is, in harmony with a nature that is the always actual expression of God's will.

The Augustinian theology would seem to me then the only basis for a consistent interpretation of Pascal's thought, for that thought is largely theological in its origins and in its continued inspiration. It is a theology which, in Pascal's version, leaves a large place to observation, because events are direct expressions of the will of God and because "les choses corporelles ne sont qu'une image des spirituelles." Behind the observations of human nature and society in the *Pensées,* however, there is almost always a theological understanding which alone supplies their coherence. And it is because of this underlying unity of his thought that Pascal never feared to stretch his ideas to their limits, for in doing so he felt neither contradiction nor anguish but only the omnipresence of a central and substantial Truth.

David Wetsel (essay date 1994)

SOURCE: "Catechesis and Conversion in the *Pensées*," in *Pascal and Disbelief: Catechesis and Conversion in the "Pensees,"* The Catholic University of America Press, 1994, pp. 327-86.

[*In the following excerpt, Wetsel seeks to determine the person(s) to whom the* Pensées *are principally addressed, largely basing his conclusions on Pascal's portrayal and analysis of atheists and agnostics in fragments 427 and 429.*]

Many sections of the *Pensées* must remain enigmatic until we are able to reconstruct more completely the mental universe of Pascal's potential convert. But . . . who is he? The *Pensées* give us a number of quite dissimilar portraits of disbelief. Is Pascal's potential interlocutor the hardened skeptic of fragment 427? [References to fragment numbers of the *Pensées* are to Louis Lafuma's edition of *Pascal: Oeuvres complètes* (Paris: Seuil, 1963).] Or is he the troubled agnostic of fragment 429? The question is crucial to an understanding of the scope of Pascal's unfinished Apology. First, let us take the hypothesis that the Apology would have been addressed to the hardened atheist portrayed in fragment 427. If this is the case, we must explain how this hardened skeptic will be transformed into the unhappy agnostic sketched in fragment 429. We could, of course, try to argue that the first half of the Apology is designed to shock the hardened atheist into the uncertainty of agnosticism. However, to do so would mean having to ignore the important theological dimensions inherent in Pascal's apologetic strategy.

From a theological perspective, the distance between

the unhappy unbeliever portrayed in fragment 429 and the *chercheur* of fragment 198 is not all that great. It can be bridged by the process of Christian catechesis. From the same perspective, however, the distance between the hardened disbelief of fragment 427 and the unhappy disbelief of fragment 429 is tantamount to a yawning abyss. Hardened disbelief, in Pascal's view, is more or less immune to the effects of apologetics or catechesis. No human remedy can reverse a blindness which is supernatural in origin. Only the workings of Grace might serve to convert those who are truly sunk in disbelief. "Il n'y a rien à leur dire non par mépris, mais parce qu'ils n'ont pas le sens commun. Il faut que Dieu les touche" ("That shows that there is nothing to be said to them, not out of contempt, but because they have no common sense. God must touch them.") (821/432-4).

Much modern commentary on the **Pensées** seems to accept as a given that the itinerary traced by the first half of the Apology will so shake the hardened unbeliever that he will somehow be transformed into the *chercheur* who suddenly emerges in the *liasse* [chapter] **"Transition"** (XV). However, given Pascal's neo-Augustinian theories of Grace and conversion, is such a transformation really possible? Let us one last time review the evidence as contained in Pascal's texts on the subject of disbelief.

In the *liasses* of 1658, Pascal draws a clear distinction between his more strident opponents (the hardened atheists, the *impies,* and the *libertins de profession*) and those whom apologetic discourse may possibly convert. The distinction is Pascal's own, reiterated three times in the *liasse* **"Commencement"** (XII):

Plaindre les athées qui cherchent. Car ne sont-ils pas assez malheureux? Invectiver contre ceux qui en font vanité.

Pity the atheists who seek, for are they not unhappy enough? Inveigh against those who boast about it. (156)

Il n'y a que trois sortes de personnes: les uns qui servent Dieu l'ayant trouvé, les autres qui s'emploient à le chercher ne l'ayant pas trouvé, les autres qui vivent sans le chercher ni l'avoir trouvé. Les premiers sont raisonnables et heureux, les derniers sont fous et malheureux, ceux du milieu sont malheureux et raisonnables.

There are only three sorts of people: those who have found God and serve him; those who are busy seeking him and have not found him; those who live without either seeking or finding him. The first are reasonable and happy, the last are foolish and unhappy, those in the middle are [un]happy and

reasonable. (160)

Commencer par plaindre les incrédules. Ils sont assez malheureux par leur condition. Il ne les faudrait injurier qu'au cas que cela servît. Mais cela leur nuit.

Begin by pitying the unbelievers; their condition makes them unhappy enough.

They ought not to be abused unless it does them good, but in fact it does them harm. (162)

In these texts, Pascal's distinction between two categories of unbelievers very much reflects the conflicting portraits of disbelief presented in fragments 429 and 427. The potential *chercheur* pictured in fragment 429 clearly falls into the category of "les athées qui cherchent" ("the atheists who seek") (156). Like that class of people who seek God for the very reason that they have not yet found Him (160), the agnostic of fragment 429 is unhappy yet reasonable. He can be numbered among those "incrédules" ("unbelievers") who, "assez malheureux par leur condition" ("very unhappy because of their state"), should not be abused because it will only do them harm (162). The hardened skeptic of fragment 427, on the other hand, obviously figures among those who are blind to their true "condition." They are not just "malheureux" ("unhappy"); they are "fous" ("insane") (160). They have neither found God nor taken the trouble to seek Him. They merit, not compassion, but the most harsh criticism: "Invectiver contre ceux qui en font vanité" ("Inveigh against those who boast about it") (156).

Clarifying Pascal's fundamentally different attitudes toward what he sees as two distinct categories of disbelief helps to give us a new perspective on the entire Apology. Pascal's projected work had several objectives. In the first place, it was to be a defense of Christianity's claim to be the one revealed Truth. At the same time, it was written as a refutation of disbelief's claim to be based upon rational principles. Superimposed upon these two objectives—and at times not yet perfectly integrated into them—is a third process: a call to inner conversion issued to those among the unbelievers whose hearts have not yet been completely hardened against the Truth. It seems fairly clear that the finished Apology would not have contained a series of point by point refutations of the historical and philosophical objections to Christianity outlined by the *libertins érudits*. However, this is not to say that Pascal is not vitally concerned with refuting the premise that disbelief is an intellectually tenable position. Indeed, Pascal's critique of the hardened skeptic in fragment 427 is designed to demonstrate that disbelief is not only profoundly unreasonable but contrary to common sense and, in the final analysis, tantamount to insanity.

Pascal's ultimate objective in neutralizing disbelief is to shield his potential *chercheur* from what has been a poisonous influence. But it does not necessarily follow that those hardened atheists already sunk deep in unbelief will somehow be transformed into "ceux qui cherchent en gémissant" ("those who seek with groans") (405). For Pascal, hardened atheism and unhappy agnosticism are not simply greater and lesser degrees of some abstract construct called disbelief. Rather, they are mutually exclusive categories. The hardened skeptic who brags that he has transcended the desire for a life beyond this one is, for Pascal, fundamentally different from the unhappy agnostic who declares, "Rien ne me serait trop cher pour l'éternité" ("No price would be too high for me to pay for eternity") (429).

In order to understand disbelief as a fundamental context in the *Pensées* properly, we must reconstruct not one, but two, mentalities. But upon what texts shall we draw? The theoretical concept of two very different categories of disbelief is clearly enunciated in the *liasse* **"Commencement."** However, elsewhere in the dossiers of 1658 the unbelievers are rarely allowed to speak their minds. When they do, it is far from easy to decide to which category they belong. The unbelievers cited in the following fragments could well be hardened skeptics. But, on the other hand, might they not just as well be seekers legitimately struggling with their doubts? One can imagine the fragments which follow spoken either in a cynical tone by a hardened skeptic or in a sincere and disquieted manner by a *chercheur*:

> "Ne voyons-nous pas," disent-ils, "mourir et vivre les bêtes comme les hommes, et les Turcs comme les chrétiens; ils ont leurs cérémonies, leurs prophètes, leurs docteurs, leurs saints, leurs religieux comme nous, etc."

> "Do we not see," they say, "animals live and die like men, Turks like Christians? They have their ceremonies, their prophets, their doctors, their saints, their religious like us, etc." (150)

> "S'il avait voulu que je l'adorasse il m'aurait laissé des signes de sa volonté."

> "If he had wanted me to worship him, he would have left me some signs of his will." (158)

> "Si j'avais vu un miracle," disent-ils, "je me convertirais."

> "If I had seen a miracle," they say, "I would be converted." (378)

Pascal identifies the unbelievers cited in the first of these three fragments as "les impies qui font profession de suivre la raison" ("the ungodly who propose to follow reason") (150). One might suppose that these "impies" are hardened disbelievers. Their argument, which

could have been lifted almost verbatim from La Mothe le Vayer's *Parallèles historiques,*[54] sound like one formulated by the more erudite *libertins*. However, Pascal appears unsure whether the "impies" are hardened skeptics or potential *chercheurs*. When he addresses them directly, he seems prepared to give them the benefit of the doubt:

> Si vous ne vous souciez guère de savoir la vérité, en voilà assez pour vous laisser en repos. Mais si vous désirez de tout votre coeur de la connaître ce n'est pas assez regardé au détail. C'en serait assez pour une question de philosophie, mais ici où il va de tout. . . . Et cependant après une réflexion légère de cette sorte on s'amusera, etc.

> If you hardly care about knowing the truth, that is enough to leave you in peace, but if you desire with all your heart to know it, you have not looked closely enough at the details. This would do for a philosophical question, but here where everything is at stake. . . . And yet, after superficial reflection of this kind we amuse ourselves, etc.(150)

As in fragment 427, Pascal makes a fundamental distinction between those whose skepticism has seduced them into a fatal "repos" ("state of rest") and those who are bent upon knowing the truth. Those who cannot be bothered to seek the truth will treat Christianity's claims to possess the one revealed truth as some mere philosophical matter. As a result, they will be blinded by the superficial resemblances between Christianity and other religions. Likewise, because their reason is illuminated only by the false lights of nature, they will erroneously conclude that the ultimate fate of human beings does not differ from that of the other animals. "Après une réflexion légère de cette sorte" ("after superficial reflection of this kind"), they will turn back to *divertissement* in an attempt to divert their thoughts from the sorry spectacle of their own mortality.

Those whose hearts are fixed upon knowing the truth will instinctively realize that the question of the mortality or immortality of the soul is far more than a mere academic or philosophical question: "Ici . . . il va de tout"[55] ("Here . . . everything is at stake"). Those who truly seek will be persuaded to examine in detail ("au détail") the false premise that Christianity is like every other religion. They can be made to understand the warning of Scripture that Revelation has been hidden from those who are wise by the standards of this world. "Cela est-il contraire à l'Ecriture, ne dit-elle pas tout cela?" ("Is that contrary to Scripture? Does it not say all that?") (150). Indeed, Christianity teaches the existence of that very "obscurité" which has so deceived the philosophers and skeptics. "Qu'on s'informe de cetter religion, même si elle ne rend pas raison de cette obscurité, peut-être qu'elle nous l'apprendra" ("Let us inquire of this religion; even if it does not explain the obscurity away, perhaps it will teach us about it" (150).

Those "impies" cited in fragment 150 may well turn out to number among the hardened skeptics whom Pascal analyzes in fragment 427, where he enters into a detailed analysis of their "négligence en une affaire où il s'agit d'eux-mêmes, de leur éternité, de leur tout" ("negligence in a matter where they themselves, their eternity, their all are at stake") (427). The unbeliever with whom Pascal imagines a brief exchange in fragment 158, on the other hand, more closely resembles the potential *chercheur* of fragment 429. Pascal warns the unbeliever who speaks in fragment 158, "Vous devez vous mettre en peine de rechercher la vérité, car si vous mourez sans adorer le vrai principe vous êtes perdu" ("You must take the trouble to seek the truth, for if you die without worshipping the true principle you are lost"). The unbeliever's reply is significant: "Mais . . . s'il avait voulu que je l'adorasse il m'aurait laissé des signes de sa volonté" ("But . . . if he had wanted me to worship him, he would have left me some signs of his will"). Pascal seems to think that this unbeliever is on the right track. Some innate instinct prompts him to postulate the possible existence of a God who reaches out to humankind. In this instance, encouragement, not invective, is in order. The unbeliever complains that God has not shown him "des signes de sa volonté" ("signs of his will"). Pascal is then able to reply: "Aussi a(-t-)il fait, mais vous les négligez. *Cherchez-les;* cela le vaut bien" ("So he did, but you pay no heed. *Look for them* then; it is well worth it") (158, italics mine).

It is difficult to know which category of disbelief best suits the unbelievers cited in fragment 378. Once again, they protest that they have been denied divine illumination: "'Si j'avais vu un miracle,' disent-ils, 'je me convertirais'" ("'If I had seen a miracle,' they say, 'I should be converted'"). This time, however, their complaint merits, not the sympathy, but rather the invective of the apologist: "Comment assurent-ils qu'ils feraient ce qu'ils ignorent . . ." ("How can they be positive they would do what they know nothing about . . ."). (378) "Les miracles ne servent pas à convertir mais à condamner." ("Miracles do not serve to convert but to condemn.") (379)

[W]e have . . . to account for why . . . an exchange [with Pascal's theory of conversion] occurs in the final chapter (**"Conclusion"**) of the Apology envisaged by the *liasses* of 1658. Surely Jean Mesnard is correct when he asserts that Pascal's interlocutor is considered to be almost converted by the time the Apology reaches this final chapter.[57] Yet is it not odd that the unbelievers cited in this chapter are still speaking about conversion in such a hypothetical way? Indeed, they protest that it would take a miracle to convert them. The answer must be that the *chercheur* whose spiritual evolution we have tried to trace no longer figures among their number. After all, their protestation about requiring a miracle to convert them is precisely the kind of "réflexion légère" ("superficial reflection") which Pascal so severely censures in fragment 150.

Perhaps Pascal cites this flippant "réflexion légère" as a kind of warning to the *chercheur* who stands on the threshold of conversion. The *chercheur* must not be tempted to suppose that his intellectual assent to Christianity means that his conversion is complete. True conversion is inner conversion, conversion of the heart. "Qu'il y a loin de la connaissance de Dieu à l'aimer" ("What a long way it is between knowing God and loving him!") (377). "La conversion véritable consiste à s'anéantir devant cet être universel . . . à reconnaître qu'on ne peut rien sans lui et qu'on n'a rien mérité de lui que sa disgrâce" ("True conversion consists in self-annihilation before the universal being . . . in recognizing that we can do nothing without him and that we have deserved nothing but his disfavor") (378).

While always keeping in mind that Pascal believes that only Grace can effect a conversion of the heart, we should not underestimate the role of intellectual assent to Christianity in Pascal's theory of conversion. Pascal views the *chercheur*'s very ability to recognize the truth of Revelation when it is presented to him in the course of the apologist's historical demonstrations as a sign that his conversion is possible. To be sure, the intellectual assent of the *chercheur* is no guarantee that he will come to be numbered among the elect. The ways of Grace are inscrutable. But it is as a result of his acceptance of the historical truth of Christianity that the *chercheur* will make the conscious decision to return to the practice of the Christian faith.

The emergence of the *Pensées* as a literary text has often served to obscure the centrality of Pascal's historical demonstrations both in his apologetic schema and in his theory of conversion. R. E. Lacombe speaks for most modern readers of the *Pensées* when he concludes, "Ce qui fait l'originalité de l'apologétique pascalienne, c'est d'abord la place qu'y occupe la peinture de la misère humaine"[58] ("The great originality of Pascal's apologetics is constituted first of all by the place he gives to the depiction of the human condition"). In Lacombe's estimation, nearly all the most celebrated fragments of the *Pensées*—"ceux qui font la gloire de Pascal et sont susceptibles de toucher l'incrédule" ("those for which Pascal is so celebrated and which may really come to influence the unbeliever")—belong to the first part of the Apology.[59]

Lacombe's assessment goes to the heart of the modern conception of what the *Pensées* are about. Those who have experienced the *Pensées* primarily as a literary text will not easily be persuaded that the most significant meaning of Pascal's projected Apology lies outside those fragments which Lacombe qualifies as most celebrated. When we think of disbelief, we almost automatically think of that modern disbelief inspired by the revelations of science. We do not easily conceive of an agnostic's being convinced by Pascal's historical demonstrations. We are far more drawn to Pascal's attempt to unsettle disbelief than we are to his exposition of the historical truth of Christianity. Yet, if we really desire to avoid projecting our own preconceptions into the mental universe of the author of the **Pensées,** then we must make an honest attempt to grasp Pascal's own conception of the ultimate goal of his apologetic discourse.

Fragment 12 (**"Ordre"**), I believe, begins to make a good deal more sense in light of our attempt to elaborate Pascal's twin theories of conversion and catechesis:

> Les hommes ont mépris pour la religion. Ils en ont haine et peur qu'elle soit vraie. Pour guérir cela il faut commencer par montrer que la religion n'est point contraire à la raison. Vénérable, en donner respect.
>
> La rendre ensuite aimable, faire souhaiter aux bons qu'elle fût vraie et puis montrer qu'elle est vraie.
>
> Vénérable parce qu'elle a bien connu l'homme.
>
> Aimable parce qu'elle promet le vrai bien.
>
> Men despise religion. They hate it and are afraid it may be true. The cure for this is first to show that religion is not contrary to reason, but worthy of reverence and respect.
>
> Next make it attractive, make good men wish it were true, and then show that it is.
>
> Worthy of reverence because it really understands human nature.
>
> Attractive because it promises true good.(12)

In the Apology anticipated by the *liasses* of 1658, Pascal sets out to demonstrate that Christianity is "vénérable" if only because it is the only system of thought which has taken into account humankind's fallen condition ("misère"). Christianity cannot be shown to be contrary to reason ("contraire à la raison"), because reason itself can be shown to be an inadequate vehicle for the perception of truth. The unbelievers, who profess to make a cult of reason, hate Christianity. They do, not because they truly believe it to be false, but because they are unconsciously afraid that it is true. Pascal's ultimate mission is to separate those who can be made to wish that Christianity were true from the company of the hardened unbelievers. "Faire souhaiter *aux bons* qu'elle fût vraie" ("Make *good men*

wish it were true") (12, italics mine). The demonstration which will follow ("montrer qu'elle est vraie" ["show that it is true"]) will be addressed, not to the mass of unbelievers, but only to those whose hearts can be made to burn to know the truth. "*Faire souhaiter* aux bons qu'elle fût vraie" ("*Make* good men *wish* it were true") (12, italics mine). Once again, we find Pascal making a basic distinction between two kinds of disbelief. Those whose disbelief is conditioned by the possibility of making them wish that Christianity were not just an illusion (i.e., the "bons") are fundamentally different from those whose hatred of Christianity proceeds from their unconscious fear that it is true.

In fragment 12, Pascal's fundamental distinction between hardened and alterable disbelief enters into one of his key statements of his plan for structuring the Apology. Other fragments (156, 160, 162) in the *liasses* of 1658 take this fundamental dichotomy into account. Yet, . . . nowhere in those dossiers does Pascal ever anchor these hypothetical categories in fully human portraits. It is this paucity of concrete description in the *liasses* of 1658 which renders fragments 427-429 so valuable. Without the conflicting portraits of the hardened skeptic and the seeking agnostic in fragments 427 and 429, Pascal's theories of conversion and catechesis remain extremely theoretical. However, these fragments—so crucial to the larger meaning of the **Pensées**—themselves pose a critical problem related to the history of the composition of the Apology. Why is it that these crucial portraits of disbelief, if we can believe those who have studied these texts most carefully, were composed so late in the course of the writing of the Apology? Has Pascal had these portraits in mind all along? Or does he only finally realize to whom the Apology will be expressly addressed once he is involved in the writing of the Preface?

It can be argued, I believe, that the Preface or *Lettre* (cf. fragment 11) constituted by fragments 427-29 represents Pascal's resolution of a problem which bears directly upon the shape and character of the Apology as a whole. In short, it is in these texts that Pascal finally decides to whom the Apology will be addressed. In fragment 427, we find Pascal deciding that the Apology cannot be primarily addressed to those hardened disbelievers whose hearts have been sealed in disbelief by God himself. This is not to say that the apologist is not obligated to invite the hardened skeptics to read the Apology. Not to do so would be to fail to take into account the inscrutability of Grace. "Quelque aversion qu'ils y apportent, peutêtre rencontreront-ils quelque chose" ("However reluctantly they may approach the task they will perhaps hit upon something"). However, the real audience of the Apology will be those unhappy unbelievers who will bring to their reading of Pascal's arguments and proofs "une sincérité parfaite et un véritable désir de rencontrer la vérité" ("absolute sincerity and a real desire to find the truth"). They are those, exemplified by the potential *chercheur* of fragment 429, who seek God with all their hearts because they have yet to find Him.

Pascal seems to have long harbored the hope that even the hardened skeptics might be shaken from their indifference by turning skepticism itself to the uses of Christian apologetics. During the first half of the Apology anticipated by the *liasses* of 1658, his principal strategy seems to be to question the ultimate authority of human reason and thus to deprive "les impies qui font profession de suivre la raison" ("the ungodly who propose to follow reason") (150) of any logical basis for their disbelief. By the time he comes to write fragment 427, however, Pascal seems to have reached the conclusion that hardened disbelief cannot be modified because it has supernatural origins. Pascal's portrait of the hardened skeptic horrifies its creator: "C'est un monstre pour moi" ("It seems quite monstrous to me") (427). The inability of the *braves* even to act in their own self-interest with regard to the possibility of a life beyond this one convinces Pascal that any effort by him will be futile: "Il n'y a rien à leur dire . . . il faut que Dieu les touche" ("There is nothing to be said to them . . . God must touch them") (821/432-[4]). God Himself has blinded the hardened unbelievers. Only He can open their eyes.

Though they are themselves seemingly immune to seeing the truth, the hardened unbelievers paradoxically have a central role to play in the conversion of those who as yet are only feigning *libertinage*. "Même si nous ne pouvons les toucher, ils ne seront pas inutiles" ("But if we cannot touch them, they will not be without their use") (821/432-18). "Ceux-là même qui semblent les plus opposés à la gloire de la religion n'y seront pas inutiles pour les autres" ("The very people who seem most opposed to the glory of religion will not be without their use for others in this respect") (821/432-[19]). In his notes for the writing of fragment 427,[61] Pascal makes his strategy perfectly clear. The fate of the hardened disbelievers and the fatal indifference into which they have sunk will serve as a warning to those toying with libertine ideas. Hardened disbelief will be shown to be tantamount to insanity. In the most essential of all matters, that is, the question of a life beyond this one, the hardened skeptics can be shown to act directly contrary to their most basic self-interest. They thus demonstrate the supernatural origin of their blindness and paradoxically serve as the means by which their potential disciples (the pseudo-*libertins*) are to be saved from perdition:

> Nous en ferons le premier argument qu'il y a quelque chose de surnaturel car un aveuglement de cette sorte n'est pas une chose naturelle. Et si leur folie les rend si contraires à leur propre bien, elle servira

à en garantir les autres par l'horreur d'un exemple si déplorable, et d'une folie si digne de compassion.

We shall base our first argument on the fact that there is something supernatural about this, for such blindness is not natural. And if their folly makes them run so counter to their own good, the horror of such a deplorable example and so pitiful a folly will help to keep others from it.

(821/432-[20])

This important and long-ignored fragment, another of those found among Pascal's preliminary notes for fragment 427, clearly demonstrates the use to which Pascal intended to put his portraits of the hardened skeptics. The evident insanity ("folie") of the hardened skeptics *servira à en garantir* les autres par l'horreur d'un exemple si déplorable* ("*will serve to keep others from it* by the horror of such a deplorable example") (824/432-20, italics mine). In other words, the hardened skeptics, far from being granted the status of interlocutors in the Apology, will be made to serve the purposes of apologetic discourse by being reduced to a negative, indeed pitiable, example of the tragedy to which toying with disbelief inevitably leads.

Pascal's rethinking of the nature and apologetic uses of disbelief in fragments 427-29 in a sense reorients his entire apologetic project. Henceforth, his demonstration of the credibility of Christianity will be addressed only to those who possess the innate capacity to recognize the truth when it is presented to them. The hardened skeptics will figure in the Apology less as philosophical opponents than as negative examples of the dangers to which an unbridled and invasive skepticism can lead. Now, this is not to say that Pascal's potential *chercheurs* will appear, at the beginning of the Apology, superficially much different from those whose hearts have been eaten away by disbelief. Indeed, these potential future *chercheurs* may consider themselves thoroughly convinced that Christianity is the greatest of all fables. Their true status as *chercheurs* will emerge only as a result of their participation in Pascal's radical analysis of the vanity of human illusions.

This purificatory rite, which corresponds more or less to the first half of the Apology anticipated by the *liasses* of 1658, will serve to separate the potential *chercheurs* from the ranks of those who are truly beyond human help. Having experienced Pascal's vision of the "misère de l'homme sans Dieu" ("wretchedness of man without God") (6), they will come at least to wish that the Christian version of reality were true. It is only at this point, or so thinks Pascal, that they can legitimately claim the status of *chercheurs*. The *réprouvés*, on the other hand, can never be made to see the truth. No matter how hard they are forced to look at human suffering, they are simply unable even to *wish* that Christianity were true. Their inherent inability to make this leap of volition stands, for Pascal, as the chief sign of their irremediable blindness. Far from being a virtue, the stoic indifference they cultivate is a mortal poison. "Est-ce qu'ils sont si fermes qu'ils soient insensibles à tout ce qui les touche? Eprouvons-les dans la perte des biens ou de l'honneur[63] Quoi? C'est un enchantement"[64] ("Are they so firm as to be insensitive to everything that affects them? Try them with the loss of their wealth or honor. What? It is a magic spell") (821/432-[21]).

If Pascal is pessimistic concerning the utility of apologetic discourse in the face of hardened disbelief, he is adamant with regard to the apologist's obligation to rescue those for whom there may be hope. The Second Vatican Council's "Statement on Religious Freedom" speaks of an inherent right to the freedom from "psychological" coercion in religious matters, "an immunity which continues to exist even in those who do not live up to their obligation of seeking the truth and adhering to it."[65] Philippe Sellier, invoking fragment 172, points out that Pascal is "un des rares penseurs" ("one of the very few thinkers") in the entire seventeenth century who completely excludes the use of force in religious conversion[66]:

> La conduite de Dieu, qui dispose toutes choses avec douceur, est de mettre la religion dans l'esprit par les raisons et dans le coeur par la grâce, mais de vouloir mettre dans l'esprit et dans le coeur par la force et par les menaces, ce n'est pas y mettre la religion mais la terreur. *Terrorem potius quam religionem.*
>
> The way of God, who disposes all things with gentleness, is to instill religion into our minds with reasoned arguments and into our hearts with grace, but attempting to instill it into hearts and minds with force and threats is to instill not religion but terror. *Terror rather than religion.*(172)

Though Pascal excludes "la force" and "les menaces" from any role in religious conversion, it could not be said that he shares the modern notion, enunciated in the Second Vatican Council's "Statement on Religious Freedom," that the inherent right to freedom from psychological coercion in religious matters "continues to exist even in those who do not live up to their obligation of seeking the truth."[67] Indeed, his entire apologetic strategy is predicated upon the notion that those capable of grasping the truth must be forced to seek it in every way possible. The kind of psychological coercion implicit in the first half of the Apology, he seems to think, is the only possible antidote to that indifference spawned by doubt. Were he himself in the position of losing his immortal soul, Pascal notes, he would be grateful to be made to see the truth. "Que je serais heureux si j'étais en cet état qu'on eût la bonté de m'en tirer *malgré moi*" ("How happy I should be if I were in such a state and someone took pity on my

foolishness, and was kind enough to save me from it *in spite of myself*") (821/432-[16], italics mine).

The compassion which Pascal professes to feel for "ceux qui cherchent en gémissant" ("those who seek with groans") (405) ultimately proceeds from a somewhat different source than that pity which Christian charity complies him to feel for the hardened atheists unable even to act in their own self-interest. "On doit avoir pitié des uns et des autres, mais on doit avoir pour les uns une pitié qui naît de tendresse, et pour les autres une pitié qui naît de mépris. Il faut être dans la religion qu'ils méprisent pour ne les pas mépriser" ("We should feel sorry for both, but we should feel sorry for the former out of affection and the latter out of contempt. One must belong to the religion they despise in order not to despise them"). In Pascal's view, the act of seeking the truth is laudable and profitable only insofar as it remains oriented toward the ultimate goal of discovering the Christian Revelation. The apologist stands under the strictest of obligations to hold the *chercheur* to this fixed and unalterable course.

Notes

[54] See Chapter I, Two Cautious Skeptics: La Mothe le Vayer and Gabriel Naudé. The ultimate source of this argument is of course Montaigne. See *Oeuvres complètes, Essais*, 2, 12, pp. 238-39. Cf. fragment 149: "Ceux qui nous ont égalé aux bêtes et les mahométans qui nous ont donné les plaisirs de la terre, même dans l'éternité . . .

[55] This line recalls fragment 427: "L'immortalité de l'âme est une chose qui nous importe si fort, qui nous touche si profondément, qu'il faut avoir perdu tout sentiment pour être dans l'indifférence de savoir ce qui en est" ("The immortality of the soul is something of such vital importance to us, affecting us so deeply, that one must have lost all feeling not to care about knowing the facts of the matter"). . . .

[57] *Blaise Pascal: L'Homme et l'oeuvre,* Cahiers de Royaumont (Paris: Editions de Minuit, 1956) pp. 155-56.

[58] R. E. Lacombe, *L'Apologétique de Pascal* (Paris: P.U.F., 1958), p. 306.

[59] Ibid., p. 312. . . .

[61] See Chapter IV, Fragments 418 and 427: The State of the Texts. . . .

[63] Pascal seems to have expanded this sentence into the section of fragment 427 which reads as follows: "Et ce même homme qui passe tant de jours et de nuits dans la rage et dans le désespoir pour *la perte* d'une charge

ou pour quelque offense imaginaire à son *honneur,* c'est celui même qui sait qu'il va tout perdre par la mort, sans inquiétude et sans émotion. C'est une chose monstreuse de voir dans un même coeur et en même temps cette sensibilité pour les moindres choses et cette étrange insensibilité pour les plus grandes" ("And the same man who spends so many days and nights in fury and despair at losing some office or at some imaginary affront to his honor is the very one who knows that he is going to lose everything through death but feels neither anxiety nor emotion. It is a monstrous thing to see one and the same heart at once so sensitive to minor things and so strangely insensitive to the greatest"). In fact, Pascal changes his original idea (the indifference of the stoical skeptics to the loss of goods or honor) when he rewrites the passage. In fragment 427, the unbelievers take on a more universal aspect. There are no longer stoics but rather emblems of a more universal human blindness.

[64] These words seem to be the basis for the following section of fragment 427: "C'est un enchantement incompréhensible, et un assoupissement surnaturel, qui marque une force toute-puissante qui le cause. Il faut qu'il y ait un étrange renversement dans la nature de l'homme pour faire gloire d'être dans cet état, dans lequel il semble incroyable qu'une seule personne puisse être" ("It is an incomprehensible spell, a supernatural torpor that points to an omnipotent power as its cause. Man's nature must have undergone a strange reversal for him to glory in being in a state in which it seems incredible that any single person should be").

[65] *Documents of Vatican II,* p. 679.

[66] Philippe Sellier, "Seminar: Pascal's `Trois Orders'" in *Meaning, Structure and History in the "Pensées" of Pascal,* ed. D. Wetsel (Tübingen: Biblio 17, 1990), p. 83.

[67] *Documents of Vatican II,* p. 679.

Donald Adamson (essay date 1995)

SOURCE: "The Provincial Letters," in *Blaise Pascal: Mathematician, Physicist and Thinker about God*, St. Martin's Press, 1995, pp. 85-114.

[*In the following essay, Adamson analyzes the various structural and stylistic methods Pascal used in the* Provincial Letters *to attack the Jesuits' beliefs about casuistry.*]

'If the ***Provincial Letters*** were serious, nobody would read them any more', Gide has written.[1] The ***Letters*** are in fact profoundly—even, at times, desperately—serious, but Pascal does not become pompously solemn or tediously earnest: he is never boring. Yet to many, if not most, people the subjects he is basically canvassing could rapidly induce boredom! In the first three, or even four, out of eighteen letters, he is concerned with the question of divine grace, a very intangible and metaphysical concept. Is God's grace freely given to all, as the Pelagians and those semi-Pelagians, the Jesuits, maintain? or is it restricted to the Elect? To be more theological still, is it *sufficient* or is it *efficious*? Is it sufficient to enable a man to 'work out his salvation with diligence' whilst not ensuring that he will do so? Or does the very bestowal of divine grace ensure that the recipient will live virtuously and attain salvation? To chop logic about niceties which, if knowable at all, can be known only to the mind of God may to the modern reader appear to be verging on the ludicrous. Pascal makes such a potentially sterile discussion intensely fruitful and human.

The bulk of the ***Provincial Letters*** are, however, concerned not with the dogmatic theology of grace but with the moral theology of casuistry.[2] Casuistry, the application of ethical rules to cases of conscience, was another field in which the Jesuits had specialized to the point of making it peculiarly their own. Indeed, we owe it to the Jesuits—or perhaps to Pascal's somewhat one-sided picture of them?—that in certain quarters the word *casuistry* has become a term of abuse. To many, casuistry has come to mean sophisticated hair-splitting, specious special pleading; yet casuistry is in essence a very respectable and necessary department of moral theology, not invented by the Jesuits but with a distinguished ancestry extending back into the Middle Ages: necessary because wherever the confession of sin is made, not directly to God, but indirectly through the intermediation of a priest, some form of guidance must be available to the priest which will enable him to instruct and direct his penitent.

Well before the advent of Protestantism, a voluminous literature had arisen on every aspect of Christian ethics; and this was considerably added to, during the Counter-Reformation period, by Jesuits (mostly Spanish) such as Luis Molina, Gregorio de Valencia, Francisco Suárez, Gabriel Vasquez, Antonio de Escobar and Leonard Lessius. Just as Molina had been the proponent of a modern semi-Pelagianism, so Escobar diluted the rigour and astringency of the Church's moral teaching. Both men, but Escobar in particular, sought to make the Catholic faith more acceptable to those who were in real danger of falling into Protestantism.

It is a commonplace of moral theology that no two cases of conscience are ever exactly alike. Faced with a variety of moral judgments, the confessor may (in ascending order of inflexibility) be a *Probabilist,* a *Probabiliorist* or a *Tutiorist:* he may, in other words, adopt a consistently lenient attitude, or else the attitude which in all the particular circumstances of the case he considers to be the fair and right one, or else he may adopt a consistently hard line. The Probabilist will always seek the most lenient judgment, even when it is less likely to be the safe, or correct, one. The Probabiliorist will seek the most lenient judgment *only when,* in his opinion, it is more likely than the less lenient judgment to be the safe, or correct, one. The Tutiorist will always seek the least lenient judgment, even when it is less likely to be the safe, or correct, one than some more charitable interpretation of the facts. But not even Escobar denied that the Probabilist must have some solid ground for the moral judgment he proposes, even though that judgment is less likely than other types of judgment to be just and correct.

Pascal accepts the necessity of casuistry, but insists that in the hands of the Jesuits it has become a depraved and distorted thing. Of all the Jesuit practices he abhors, Probabilism is the one which incurs his keenest censure in the ***Provincial Letters***. Cutting through the semantic entanglements of Tutiorism, Probabilism and Probabiliorism, he points out again and again that these are mechanical ways of viewing human sin and human destiny, formulæ which permit those who practise them to evade the true duty of the confessional which is to uplift and correct. All this, however, is done in the lightest and most fanciful way: by revealing and emphasizing the human aspect of every issue, by stressing that behind the theological subtleties lie carefully calculated, even devious ulterior motives, and by hinting—even in most jocular vein—that the Jesuits, far from 'simplifying', 'rationalizing' and 'modernizing' Christian theology, have in fact degraded and debased the Church's view of humanity. From this it is only a step to proving that they will in fact also, in the long run, debase the public's view of the Church.

How then are the distinctly human aspects of these two problems (grace and casuistry) brought into prominence? The first device is Pascal's invention of the Provincial Friend. His attack on the Jesuits is couched in the form of letters supposedly written by an intelligent gentleman—an *honnête homme*—to his friend in the country: the friend, too, is an intelligent man, but both are unversed in theology. The writer of the letters endeavours to explain to his country friend, in layman's language, what all the impassioned controversy is about. This approach enables Pascal to show up the fundamental unreality of the doctrinal dispute and, worse still, the immorality masked by an appearance of sweet reasonableness and forgiving leniency which lies at the heart of the Jesuits' ethical system. The endless charge and counter-charge of the debate about grace emerges, therefore, as shadow-boxing. The dispute about casuistry is proved to be no empty academic disputation about 'isms': for the very integrity of man both as moral agent and worshipping being is shown to be endangered by the Jesuits' debasement of

the language in which the Church speaks to the world—their attempt to present God's yoke as easy and His burden light, even at the expense of encouraging man's hypocrisy and callousness. Pascal, by addressing his readers in the language of an intelligent layman, and by showing them the practical consequences in human terms of the Jesuits' new-fangled approach to moral theology (all this through the device of letters to an intelligent but mystified *provincial* reader), did more than anyone in his century—and perhaps since—to undermine the Jesuits' growing ascendancy.

Strange to say, no one before Pascal's time had thought of satirizing an opponent through the device of intelligent letters written by an apparently unbiased observer to dispel a friend's naive bewilderment. It was a method which was to have its imitators: Montesquieu, in his *Persian Letters,* a satire of French life, religious thought and ways of government supposedly written by two Persian visitors to Paris; and Voltaire's *Philosophical Letters,* exposing the weaknesses of French society by praising the virtues of the English. Voltaire indeed realized that the essence of Pascal's genius, in this respect, was not so much to have used the epistolary form, until then very largely confined to the novel, as to have perfected the use of naive irony. The device of the naive observer was to be used by him, with a success equal to Pascal's if not greater, in such short stories as *Zadig, Micromégas* and *Candide*. The very name 'Candide' epitomizes the apparently frank, impartial, sincere outlook on the world pioneered (as a device of exquisite irony) in the ***Provincial Letters***.

The second device employed by Pascal in the ***Provincial Letters*** is that of the enemy (in this case, a Jesuit priest) damaging himself by the absurdity of his own remarks. Pascal's supreme skill is to present this Jesuit priest as 'a man more sinn'd against than sinning': a basically kind and well-intentioned man, friendly and likable, but unintelligent, simplistic and wholly misguided in his intellectual outlook. As a target for ridicule, and an example of the Jesuits' wicked folly, it would have been totally unconvincing for Pascal to have presented him, in lurid Mephistophelean terms, as an astute Satanic figure. As he is, we love him rather than hate him, pity him rather than scorn him, and look on him as a poor misguided fool unworthy, in his simplicity, of the devious double-dealing Jesuits but of whom, in its calculating heartlessness, the Society of Jesus is equally unworthy. His simplicity is such that he is invariably admitting what ought to be concealed, and not only making the admission but glorying in it—much as a commercial representative might sing the praises of his firm's latest invention: for to the Jesuits (Pascal insinuates it again and again) everything has become mechanical.

A fine example of his ingenuousness occurs in the discussion of Probabilism, in Letter VI, where Pascal is in the process of demonstrating that the Jesuits' new moral theology will permit or condone any crime or sin, however heinous. The priest artlessly observes that, according to the decisions of three successive Popes,[3] bishops who also happen to be regulars are not exempted by their worldly status as bishops from their monastic vow of abstinence from meat throughout their lives. Nevertheless, he continues, Antonino Diana (a Theatine father so renowned as a casuist that he was appointed to be the examiner of bishops) maintains that they are exempted from that vow.

'And how does he reconcile that?' I asked him.

'By the subtlest of all the new methods', replied the Father, 'and by the utmost refinement of probability. I will explain. As you saw the other day, the fact is that both the affirmative and the negative of most opinions have some probability, in the view of our doctors, and enough to be followed with a clear conscience. This does not mean that the pro and the con are both right in the same sense—that would be impossible—but just that both are probable and consequently safe.

'On this principle our good friend Diana speaks thus in Part V, treatise xiii, resolution 39: *I reply to the decision of these three Popes, which runs counter to my own opinion, that they have spoken in that way by adhering to the affirmative, which is indeed probable, even in my own view; but it does not follow from this that the negative does not also have some degree of probability.* And in the same treatise, resolution 65, on another subject where he also disagrees with a pope,[4] he speaks as follows: *That the Pope said this as head of the Church, I freely admit. But he did so only within the extent of the sphere of probability of his own opinion.* So you can see now that this is not offensive to the Popes' feelings; that would never be tolerated in Rome, where Diana is held in such high esteem. For he does not say that what the Popes have decided is not probable, but, whilst leaving their opinion within its full sphere of probability, he nevertheless says that the contrary is probable also.'

'How very respectful of him', I said.

'And it is subtler', he added, 'than what Father Bauny[5] replied when his books had been censured in Rome. For, writing against Monsieur Hallier,[6] who at that time was furiously persecuting him, he let slip the phrase: *What has the censure meted out by Rome got to do with that imposed in France?* You can see clearly enough from this that, whether by interpreting terms or, detecting favourable circumstances or, last but not least, by means of the double probability of pro and con, these alleged contradictions which previously astounded you can always be reconciled without ever offending the decisions of Scripture, Councils or Popes—as you can see!'

'O reverend Father', I replied, 'how lucky the world is to be governed by you! How useful these probabilities are! I did not know why you had gone to such lengths to establish the fact that one doctor, *if he is a serious doctor,* can make an opinion probable;[7] that the contrary may also be probable; and that people can then choose between pro and con just as the spirit moves them, even if they do not believe it to be true, and with such a clear conscience that any confessor refusing to grant absolution on the strength of these casuists would be in a state of damnation. From which I now realize that a single casuist can lay down new moral rules as he pleases, and decide in any way he thinks fit any matter of moral behaviour.'

In these words Pascal shatters the theological, and philosophical, basis of Jesuit casuistry. He mocks, first of all, the semantic haze with which the Jesuits had managed to surround the word 'probable', the lay meaning of which is: 'to be expected.' In the language of mathematics, if a bag contains x green balls and y white ones, and if except for the numerical difference between x and y we are as likely to draw green as we are to draw white, then the probability of drawing green is 7/10 whilst that of drawing white is 3/10. Turning from the language of mathematics to that of every day, we should say that out of a bag of seven green and three white balls *it is probable that* a green one will be drawn: it is merely *possible* (in ordinary parlance) that white will be drawn, whereas the same outcome in mathematical terms is *probable* to the extent that there is a 3/10 probability—although it is, of course, *more probable* that the colour of the ball produced will be green!

As applied by the Jesuits to the moral teaching of the Church, such a quasi-mathematical use of the language of probability was bound to have far-reaching and, in Pascal's view, disastrous consequences. The foundation of the new casuistry was that, although a course of action recommended by the Scriptures, Councils and Popes was admittedly more *probable,* even the opposite course—if backed up by the authority of at least one recognized doctor of the Church—was also probable. By asserting that any course of action, even if condemned by a hundred ecclesiastical authorities, was still morally permissible if supported by one, the Jesuits had opened the way for a drastic easing of moral standards. They, after all, could supply on any issue the one minority opinion which made all things probable.

This general moral free-for-all, so vehemently denounced by Pascal in most of the **Provincial Letters,** has been considered by many commentators (not least by the Jesuits themselves!) to be a travesty of the truth. The **Provincial Letters,** writes Edwyn Bevan,[8] 'were a witty caricature which has had enormous influence in creating the popular idea of the Jesuits.' A caricature is a distortion of the truth in order to reinforce some salient aspect of it. Pascal's attack on the Jesuits' moral theology is not a caricature in the sense that it is either untrue or unfair. He is much too reasonable a logician to have it supposed that, because the *possibility* of an abuse of authority exists, that abuse will necessarily occur. The salient aspect of the truth about their position, in his judgment, is that the mere *ipse dixit* of one of their own number—however comparatively obscure—can of itself destroy the whole traditional teaching of the Bible and the Church throughout the ages. What he denounces is not so much the actual doings of the Jesuits taken as a whole as their *potentially* pernicious influence and, above all, the incoherence of their logical position. 'Behold him who taketh away the sins of the world',[9] François Hallier is supposed to have said of Étienne Bauny; and Pascal, in his Fourth Letter, makes use of this elegant witticism in devastating mockery of his opponents.

Essentially, therefore, it is the unscrupulousness of the Jesuits which irks Pascal, an unscrupulousness which he exposes through the Jesuit father's naivety. Whenever he engages in conversation with the *honnête homme,* the priest finds himself impaled on the horns of a dilemma, or embroiled in a *reductio ad absurdum.* For it is plainly absurd that 'the double probability of pro and con' can exist on any moral issue. Not only is the priest hopelessly incapable of dealing with his interlocutor's irony, he is himself imprisoned within his creator's. Throughout his remarks runs a pathetic strain of complacent modernism, the belief that newer is better and that, in a never-ending march of progress, notable improvements are afoot within the Church. Hence Bauny's reference to 'the censure meted out by Rome.' It had seemed sufficient, and clever enough, to the Jesuits in 1641 or thereabouts to shrug off Papal condemnation with the Gallican remark that what really mattered was the approval of Paris. By 1656, however, a new refinement had been introduced into the system! Fifteen years after Bauny's slighting comment, it is now claimed that the opinions of Rome and Paris matter equally but that equally the teaching of one 'serious doctor' of theology in Paris is just as authoritative as the Pope's!

This unholy chaos in which anything seems ultimately permissible and all views equally probable is further exposed in a subsequent discussion between the *honnête homme* and the Jesuit father. In this conversation the artless priest is extolling the virtues of the newfound Jesuit doctrine of direction of intention. This doctrine is, of course, virtuous because it is so eminently useful.

'Well then, you should know that this marvellous principle is our great method of *directing the intention,* which is of such importance in our moral system that I might almost venture to compare it to the doctrine of probability. You have seen some of its features in passing, in certain maxims I have outlined. For when I explained to you how footmen can run certain tricky errands with a clear conscience did you not notice that that was only by deflecting their intention from the evil they are procuring and applying it to the profit which it brings them? That is what *directing the intention* means. Likewise, you saw that those who give money for benefices would be downright simoniacs if they did not also deflect their intention in that way. But I now want to show you this great method in all its glory, in the matter of homicide, which it justifies in innumerable circumstances, so that you may judge from this all the results it is capable of producing.'

'I can already see', I said, 'that this will make everything permissible; nothing will escape.'

'You are always going from one extreme to the other', the Father replied. 'You must stop doing that. As evidence that we do not permit everything, note, for instance, that we never allow anyone to have the formal intention of sinning just for sinning's sake; and that if anyone insists on having no other end in evil-doing than evil-doing itself, we will have nothing more to do with him; that is diabolical; and to that we make no exception, whether of age, sex or rank. But whenever people are not in that unfortunate frame of mind, then we try to put into practice our method of *directing the intention,* which consists of setting up some lawful objective as the purpose of their actions. Not that we refrain from deterring men from forbidden things as far as is within our power; but whenever we cannot prevent the action, at least we purify the intention; and thus we correct the viciousness of the means by the purity of the end.

This is how our Fathers have found a way of permitting the acts of violence involved in defending one's honour. For all you have to do is to deflect your intention from the desire for revenge, which is criminal, and apply it instead to the desire to defend your honour, which is permissible according to our Fathers. And that is how they fulfil all their duties towards both God and man. For they please the world by permitting such actions; and they satisfy the Gospel by purifying intentions. This is something the Ancients knew nothing about; this is something you must thank our Fathers for. Now do you understand?'

'Very well', I said. 'You allow men to operate in the external and physical realm of action, and you assign to God the internal, spiritual impulse of intention; and by means of this equitable allocation you unite human and divine laws . . .'

Once again Pascal does not castigate the moral attitudes of all Jesuits at all times; he exposes the potential perniciousness of their ethical system. This is shown in its unmistakable colours as a system of expediency, ruthless opportunism and cynical disregard for others. It includes the doctrine that the end justifies the means; and the Jesuit father, in his stupid candour, actually goes so far as to use the words 'end' and 'means' in this extract. In Letter VI Pascal had already applied the same argument to the purchase of benefices, thus (in the Jesuits' view) exonerating such purchasers from the charge of simony. He had gone on, in the same Letter, to show how the Jesuits' doctrine taken to its logical conclusion will permit servants to obey the orders of their dissolute employers, carrying letters and presents, opening doors and windows, helping their masters to climb up to windows,[10] all with a clear conscience. The ultimate conclusion of their doctrine, however, is—as will be shown virtually throughout Letter VII—that not even human life is sacred. Homicide is justifiable 'in innumerable circumstances', and one of the most serviceable of their ethical discoveries is that all, even the taking of life, is permissible in the defence of one's personal reputation and integrity. No moral problem, says the Father, can arise provided one only 'sins' with a laudable purpose in view. Then sin is not sin; yet (in a touch of supreme irony) not even the Society of Jesus can condone sinning for sinning's sake. Even the Jesuits consider it 'diabolical' that anyone should actually insist on having 'no other end in evil-doing than evil-doing itself'! It is all the more diabolical that anyone should be so insistent when so many convenient alibis now exist for painlessly taking away the sins of the world. The extract concludes with a crucial distinction to which Pascal returns many times, as 'external and physical' things are contrasted with the 'internal, spiritual impulse of intention.' The intention may, after all, be so immaculately resplendent that even to an honest man it may seem to justify the rough-hewn methods of its fulfilment. 'The Society of Jesus', writes Edwyn Bevan,[11] 'intent to dominate men for their own good, has been the Church's most effective agent.' In the salvation of a soul, what method is taboo? and from the salvation of a soul it is but a short step to the defence of one's honour.

This distinction between matter and spirit, violence and truth, *might and right,* reaches the height of impassioned eloquence in the twelfth ***Provincial Letter***. Here Pascal begins by discussing the somewhat involved question of the attitude of Lessius, a Jesuit professor at Louvain, towards bankruptcy. The whole passage may be cited as an example of the range of Pascal's eloquence and invective, from the close infighting of a particular dispute about one scholar's quotation of another to the majestic utterance of a thinker who views all things from the standpoint of eternity. Just as remarkable as the range of Pascal's eloquence is the rapidity of his transition from small issues to great. But to him, fundamentally, there are no small issues, for—as his opponents, the Jesuits, know only too well—through the apparently small things of the world great ends may be achieved. 'I', he writes,

shall waste no time in showing you that Lessius . . . takes undue advantage of the law which allows bankrupts merely a bare livelihood but not a decent standard of living: it is enough that I have justified Escobar against such an accusation. That is more than I had to do. But you, Fathers, are not doing what you ought to be doing: for it is up to you to reply to the passage from Escobar, whose decisions are convenient in that, being independent of what precedes and follows, and in so far as they entirely consist of short articles, they are not subject to your distinctions. I quoted the whole of his passage, which allows *people who make a composition with their creditors to retain enough of their admittedly ill-gotten gains to provide their families with a decent standard of living.* At which I exclaimed in my Letters: *Fathers, how can that be? By what strange charity would you rather that these assets should belong to those who have wrongfully acquired them than to their lawful creditors?*

That is the question which must be answered: but it puts you in an awkward position, from which you make pointless attempts to escape by turning the question on its head and quoting other passages from Lessius, ones which are totally irrelevant. So I ask you whether this maxim of Escobar can be followed in all conscience by those who go bankrupt. And mind how you reply. For if you answer no, what will become of your doctor and your doctrine of probability? And if you say yes, I shall report you to the High Court.

I leave you, Fathers, in this awkward dilemma, for I have no more space here to deal with the next imposture concerning Lessius's passage on homicide; that will be for next time, and the rest later on.

Meanwhile I shall say nothing about the Notices, full of scandalous falsehoods, with which you conclude each imposture: I shall reply to all that in the Letter [XIII] in which I hope to reveal the source of your slanders. I pity you, Fathers, for resorting to such remedies. Your insults will not resolve our differences; your various threats will not prevent me from defending myself. You believe that you have might and impunity on your side, but I believe that I have truth and innocence on mine. It is a long and strange war when violence tries to suppress truth. All the efforts resorted to by violence cannot undermine truth: they merely serve to reinforce it. All the enlightenment which truth can bring can do nothing to halt violence and only exasperates it all the more. When might combats might, the greater destroys the less; when words are pitched against words, those that are true and convincing confound and scatter those that are only vanity and lies; however, violence and truth have no power over each other. But let no one claim that they are equal because of this. For there is this huge difference between them, that violence is limited in its course by God's decree as He applies its effects to the glory of the truth it is attacking, whereas truth exists from eternity and will eventually prevail over its enemies, because it is eternal and mighty as God Himself.

The first point at issue in this lofty invective—the apparently, though not really, trivial one—is whether Lessius actually said that bankrupts could keep back enough money in order to maintain a dignified standard of living, or whether he did not. Jacques Nouet, in his *Third Imposture of the Replies to the Provincial Letters Published by the Secretary of Port-Royal against the Fathers of the Society of Jesus,* had tended to give the impression that Lessius never maintained that opinion. With delightful self-confidence Pascal points out, however, that in referring in Letter VIII to Lessius's remark on bankrupts he had merely quoted the arch-priest of casuistry, Escobar, who himself purported to be quoting from Lessius's *Concerning Justice, Law and the Other Cardinal Virtues.* Did he, Pascal, have to verify Escobar's own quotations? Thus he imprisons not only Lessius and Escobar but all Jesuits in an inextricable dilemma. For either Lessius did say this about bankrupts, or he did not. If he said it, then the Jesuits are guilty of imposture for denying that he did. If he did not say this, then Escobar is guilty of imposture for quoting Lessius as having said so. In point of fact, Lessius did argue that bankrupts should be allowed to withhold enough from their creditors for themselves and their families to maintain a dignified standard of living: a point Pascal has lost no time in scoring against the Jesuits, even before this extract begins.

Hence the peremptory manner in which Pascal can dismiss the Jesuits and all their tricks in the brief middle paragraph. With matchless self-assurance he has confronted them with a dilemma from which not even they can extricate themselves. Yet, twisting the rapier within the wound, he does not fail to give them a foretaste of the next 'imposture' he will accuse them of. And that will be merely one of a whole series that can be laid to their account: *that will be for next time, and the rest later on.*

The temporal vista, with its obscure and infinitely receding backcloth of deceit and intrigue, is rapidly followed by the timeless one—the paragraph, fittingly, with which Letter XII ends. This is the vista of the world viewed *sub specie æternitatis,* the cosmic onslaught of the 'principalities [and] powers'[12] on the divine Truth: a Truth which is presented as being so wonderful that it is almost co-equal with God Himself, eternal and all-powerful like its Creator. Again, Pascal seems to have been the first writer to have conceived of levelling such a superb accusation against his opponents (though the echoes of Platonic thought are obvious). This counter-attack on the Jesuits is, in fact, made on two levels; and Pascal very skilfully blends and intermingles the two. The first of these is empirical, as objective as any scientific statement; the second, a fig-

ure of rhetoric. In the first place, he makes the obvious point that the battle which he and his opponents are fighting is an unreal one, this side of the grave, since neither side can hope to convince or confound the other. Their standpoints are alien; between them there is no common ground; philosophically speaking, it is the juxtaposition of orders which are discontinuous. When brute force encounters brute force, there is at least a recognizable outcome: might is right in such circumstances. When thought clashes with thought, truth will come out in the forum of argument and debate; *magna est veritas et prævalebit:* right is mighty then. But when brute force and thought clash, there can be no convincing victory—might belonging to the temporal world, and *right* to the eternal. Arrayed against him and his friends the Jansenists is all the panoply of political power and clandestine intrigue. He accuses the Jesuits elsewhere of what nowadays would be tantamount to brain-washing, or frighteningly close to the strategy of the big lie endlessly repeated: 'It is time for me to put an end once and for all to your audacity in calling me a heretic, an audacity that grows day by day', he writes in Letter XVII to François Annat, the foremost of all French Jesuits and confessor to Louis XIV.

> You do this to such an extent in this book which you have just published[13] that it has become intolerable, and I should eventually incur suspicion if I did not answer as a charge of this kind deserves. I had despised such an insult when it occurred in your colleagues' writings . . . My Fifteenth Letter was a sufficient reply; but you now speak about it differently, making it in all earnestness the crux of your defence; it is virtually the only argument you use. For you say *that to answer my fifteen letters it is only necessary to say fifteen times over that I am a heretic; and that, once having been said to be such, I do not deserve to be believed by anyone.* In a word, you treat my apostasy as if it were beyond question: you take it to be a firm premise upon which you boldly build.

As a scientist and a logician, Pascal objects with all the vehemence at his command to any method of discussion where there is no meaningful meeting of minds. In terms of propaganda and psychological warfare, he and his friends are in any case hopelessly outmatched by the Jesuits. His **Letters** have to be issued clandestinely; Annat's book is published with the King's approval! But it does not follow from this that Annat's book is right, and his own views wrong. Towards the end of the **Letters** it is clear that Jansenism cannot (in the short run, at any rate) hope for any worldly triumph in its clash with the Jesuits. By the end of the controversy, as the last part of the extract from Letter XII shows, Pascal echoes the attitude of Jesus towards Pilate: *My kingdom is not of this world*[14]—for the world may despise the truth, but nevertheless the truth is eternal and God-given. This is the second aspect of the self-vindication to François Annat, the figure of rhet-

oric stemming no doubt from his own unshakable belief in the rightness of his opinions, but certainly not
demonstrable by any objective criteria. Granted that
might and thought can never meaningfully collide, it
does not automatically follow that thought is right. Yet
Pascal boldly arrogates to himself and his Jansenist
friends the certainty that, however much they may be
crushed and downtrodden in the arena of religious
politics, they and they alone represent the Truth which
is eternal and divine. Nor, in this meeting of disparates, is it simply a case of honours even. The Jesuits'
might may triumph in one sphere, the Jansenists' right
in another. But right is as overwhelmingly superior to
might as the eternal is to the temporal. What is more,
God will only countenance might's triumph for a little
day; and ultimately will turn even that short-run triumph of temporal violence to the greater glory of the
eternal Truth. As an arraignment of the Jesuit standpoint, Pascal's invective is notable both for its unself-
questioning self-assurance and for the dignified and
restrained nobility of its language. The case he presents for Jansenism in the Twelfth and Seventeenth
Letters would not of itself stand up to a rigorous examination by either scientists or lawyers. Yet as a figure of majestic rhetoric, Pascal's apologia remains: a
matter not of the mind alone but of the heart, not of
logic but of charity; the embodiment of a poetic truth
higher than any truth of law or physics. No one before
Pascal's time had ever assumed the mantle of eternal
Truth with so much eloquence and passion.

On the level of the Church militant, for the greater
glory of the Church within the world, he accuses the
Jesuits of various devious opportunist tactics—the end
justifying the means. But on the level of the divine
Truth, which he claims to represent, can he likewise be
accused of various devious artifices of argument? Can
he be called unscrupulous at times in the weapons he
employs against his enemies, albeit for the sake of
Christ risen, ascended and glorified? Foremost amongst
the charges of unscrupulousness levelled against Pascal is that, also in Letter XVII, he carefully dissociates
himself from Port-Royal when, defending himself against
Annat's accusation of heresy, he demands the tangible
proof. 'When have I been seen at Charenton?'[15] he
asks.

> When have I been absent from mass, when have I
> failed in my Christian duty towards my parish?
> When have I done anything to act in concert with
> heretics, when have I been in schism with the
> Church? What Council have I contradicted? What
> Papal constitution have I violated? You must reply,
> Father, or . . . you know exactly what I mean. And
> what is your reply? I ask everyone to take note.
> First of all you assume *that the writer of the Letters
> is from Port-Royal.* You then say *that Port-Royal
> has been declared heretical;* from which you
> conclude *that the writer of the Letters has been
> declared heretical.* So it is not on me, Father, that

the onus of this charge falls but on Port-Royal; and
you lay it against me only because you assume that
I am one of them. Thus I shall not find it very hard
to defend myself, as I have only to tell you that I
am not one of them and refer you to my Letters, in
which I have said *that I am alone* and, quite
explicitly, *that I am not from Port-Royal,* as I did
in the Sixteenth Letter which came out before your
book.

Yet it is strictly true to say that Pascal did not belong
to Port-Royal. Indeed, as has been noted, he may only
ever have paid two visits to Port-Royal des Champs,
whilst a total of five visits during his lifetime—when
sometimes he may have stayed at Vaumurier—would
seem to be the absolute maximum. Although he sympathized with the Jansenists as devout holy men and
his personal friends, he may never have fully subscribed
to Jansenism in the theological sense. It was for this
reason that he could preserve his anonymity as the
writer of the *Letters,* an anonymity not officially broken until after his death. The opening of Letter VIII
pokes fun at the difficulty his opponents were having
in piercing the mystery of his identity:

> Some think I am a doctor of the Sorbonne: others
> ascribe my letters to four or five people who, like
> me, are neither priests nor churchmen. All these
> false suspicions bring home to me the fact that I
> have been quite successful in my plan of being
> known only to you, and to the good Father who
> still puts up with my visits and whose conversation
> I still put up with, albeit with great difficulty.

The success of his incognito stemmed from the fact
that he was seldom, if ever, seen at Port-Royal des
Champs, not known as a writer, and not closely associated with Jansenism in the public mind. His visits to
Port-Royal de Paris were, of course, much more frequent; but that, the Jesuits must have assumed, was
more to see his sister than to consort with heretics. . . .

Wherever Pascal could not be directly controverted—
his facts and quotations disproved, his honour im-
pugned—it was, of course, always possible to accuse
him of disrespect for the Church and sacred things;
and this, in fact, was one of the Jesuits' most frequent
lines of attack. 'If you spoke like that in places where
you were not known', the priest cautions the narrator,
'there might be people who would take your remarks
amiss and accuse you of ridiculing religious things.'
Ridicule was Pascal's deadliest weapon, though it is
still untrue for Gide to claim that nobody would read
the ***Provincial Letters*** any more *if* they were serious.
For behind all the fantasy and wit there lies a deadly
seriousness, the seriousness that can be engendered only
when issues of life and death are at stake. Nowhere,
perhaps, is this unique distillation of reportage and
fancifulness more cunningly blended than in the pas-

sage discussing whether priests and monks may commit murder, which is whimsical satire in all earnestness.

'Indeed, according to our celebrated Fr L'Amy,[31] priests and monks are even allowed to strike first against people who are wanting to besmirch and defame them, by killing them so as to prevent that.[32] But only if the intention is properly directed. Here are his words, volume V, disputation 36, number 118: *'It is permissible for a priest or monk to kill any slanderer who threatens to publicize scandalous crimes concerning either his Community or himself if that is the only means of preventing him, granted that he is about to give circulation to his calumnies unless he is promptly killed. For, in this case, just as it would be permissible for such a monk to kill anyone wishing to deprive him of his life, so likewise it is permissible for him to kill anyone wishing to deprive either him or his Community of their honourable name, in the same way as in the secular world.'*[33]

'That's news to me', I replied. 'I believed the exact opposite, without giving the matter any thought, because I had heard that the Church feels such abhorrence for bloodshed that she does not even permit ecclesiastical judges to be present at criminal trials.' 'Don't be put off by that', he said. 'Our Fr L'Amy is very good at proving this doctrine although, in a gesture of humility entirely befitting this great man, he submits it to his readers' discretion. And Caramuel, our illustrious defender, quoting it in his *Fundamental Theology*, page 543,[34] believes it to be so certain that he argues *that the contrary is not probable;* and from this he draws admirable conclusions, such as this, which he calls *the conclusion to end all conclusions, 'conclusionum conclusio':* That not only may a priest kill a slanderer under certain circumstances, but even that there are certain circumstances where there is a duty upon him to do so: *etiam aliquando debet occidere.*[35] He examines several new questions on the basis of this principle, including the following one, for example: MAY THE JESUITS KILL THE JANSENISTS?'

'Oh Father!' I exclaimed, 'that is a very surprising point of theology! I reckon the Jansenists are already as good as dead on the basis of Fr L'Amy's doctrine.'

'That is just where you are wrong', replied the Father. 'Caramuel concludes the opposite from the same principles.'

'Well, Father, how does he manage that?'

'Because', said he, 'they do our reputation no harm. Here are his words, numbers 1146 and 1147, pages 547 and 548: *The Jansenists call the Jesuits Pelagians; can one kill them for that? No, inasmuch as the Jansenists no more dim the splendour of the Society than an owl dims the splendour of the sun.'*

Against such brilliantly lavish scorn there was indeed no other possible line of defence for the Jesuits than to say that Pascal 'ridiculed sacred things.'

What in reality Pascal was doing, though his opponents could not or would not realize it, was to ridicule their travesty of the Church by reference to things that were truly sacred. Sometimes he did this by direct quotation from their writings, sometimes by a flight of imaginative fancy: but always by juxtaposition. 'I can quite see', the narrator admits,

'that anything is acceptable to you except for the ancient Fathers, and that you are masters of the field. You have only to keep pressing on.'

'But I foresee three or four great inconveniences, and powerful obstacles standing in your way.'

'What?' asked the Father, quite astonished.

'There are', I answered, 'Holy Scripture, the Popes and the Councils, which you cannot disown, and which all follow the path of the Gospel.'

'Oh, is that all?' came his reply. 'You did give me a fright . . .'

And: 'Look all through the ancient Fathers to see for what sum of money it is lawful to kill a man. What will they tell you but: *Non occides;* Thou shalt not kill.' 'The Fathers were all right by the moral standards of their times; but they are too remote from ours.' *'It is permissible to kill someone for the value of a crown, according to Molina'*[36]. In countries where the mystery of the Incarnate God crucified, dead and buried would not be reverently accepted, missionary Jesuits 'suppress the scandal of the Cross.' As for praying for *the instant death of people who are preparing to persecute us,* an accurate quotation from Pedro Hurtado de Mendoza,[37] the Church has not (yet!) included in the prayer book 'everything that can be asked of God. Besides, that was not possible; for that opinion is newer than the breviary: you are no good at chronology.' Both the rich man's desire to give alms and his desire to avoid doing so 'are safe according to the same Gospel; one, according to the Gospel in the most literal and straightforward sense;[38] the other, according to that same Gospel as interpreted by Vasquez.'[39] 'When I tell you that our Fathers have reconciled these things [the Gospel law and the world's laws], all you can say is that you are astounded.'

Such fanciful play with a soberly documented historical and theological situation is sustained throughout by an irresistible verve of wit, farce, punning, paradox, antithesis and hyperbole: the joke about Aristotle, the bravura passage on Arnauld whose single but insuperable fault is to be himself, the farcical remission from fasting, the pun about proximate powers and one's neighbour (*prochain* in both cases), the parable of the doctors advising the traveller attacked by robbers, the hyperbolical tirade on the Dominicans' failure to defend Efficacious Grace, the cool irony of 'people seldom think of murdering anyone except their enemies' the neat antithesis that 'it is much eaiser for them to find monks than arguments', and the paradoxical 'I am not even sure whether a man would not feel less resentment at being brutally killed by hotheads than at feeling he was being stabbed to death by devout people for conscientious reasons.' There is the ambling mumbo-jumbo of *'probabiliter obligatus, et probabiliter deobligatus',* and the darting ferocity of 'I believed you could only take away sins; I did not think you could introduce them too.'

It is this stark contrast between the sobriety and rapier-like incisiveness of Pascal's diction and the lush turgescence of his opponents' which explains his method: the contrast between Classicism and the Baroque. Their inflated periods conceal an intellectual void, which his terse precision detects. He has only to let them talk on, in their own (more or less) faithfully transcribed words, for them to talk themselves out of favour.

> *He has no eyes for the beauties of art and nature. He would believe he had taken on an awkward burden if he found pleasure in anything. On feast days he withdraws to the graveyard. He would rather be in a tree-trunk or a cave than in a palace or on a throne. As for insults and injuries, he is as insensitive to these as if he had the eyes and ears of a statue. Honour and glory are things unknown to him, idols to which he has no incense to offer up. To him a beautiful woman is as a phantom. And those haughty and regal faces, those charming tyrants who everywhere make willing conquests, slaves without chains, have the same power over his eyes as the sun has over an owl's:*

these words from the Jesuit Fr Pierre Le Moyne's *Moral Portraits*[40] describe—and denigrate—the 'savage', or uncouth man 'incapable of feeling natural and decent affections';[41] the savage displays in his life an excess, indeed a perversion, of the virtue of temperance. This cento of quotations is the acme of religious worldliness. For, implicitly at least, Le Moyne appears to be denigrating the austere religious life by putting it on a level with that of the savage. Religious self-abnegation is, it seems, more the result of a person's natural disposition or temperament than of any strenuous effort to practise piety. With reproachful impatience Le Moyne condemns the savage for offering up no incense to the idols of honour and glory. Putting words into his own Jesuit father's mouth, Pascal ironically dismisses the savage's (or the saint's?) way of life as 'the ridiculous and brutish ways of a melancholic madman. To Le Moyne's bombast and insipid preciosity his terse astringency is an effective rejoinder: 'if this is the picture of a man

totally detached from the feelings which the Gospel bids us renounce, I confess I can make no sense of it.'

The preciosity and flowery rhetoric of Pierre Le Moyne do not exclude prurience. 'It may be permissible to dress up at an age which is the flower and prime of life', he writes in his *Easy Piety,*[42] in a cento also gathered together by Pascal in Letter IX. 'But that must be as far as we go: it would be strangely inappropriate to look for roses in the snow. It is only for the stars to be always dancing,[43] because they have the gift of eternal youth. The best thing, as far as this is concerned, would therefore be to consult reason and a good mirror, to yield to propriety and necessity, and to withdraw as night approaches.' This is a worldliness which, even when thinking of the stars, cannot resist the metaphor of the ballroom. Not even the Virgin Mary could escape from the cloying fulsomeness and unwholesome attentions of Jesuit writers. Paul de Barry, in his *Paradise Opened to Philagie by Means of a Hundred Easily Performed Devotions to the Mother of God,* writes of her in terms more appropriate to Mary Magadalene than to a 'Virgin undefiled.' All hundred devotions are easy, the Jesuit father explains in another of Pascal's centos, this time a confection from Barry:[44]

> 'Salute the Holy Virgin when you come across images of her; recite the little rosary of the ten pleasures of the Virgin; frequently utter the name of Mary; charge the Angels with paying her our respects; desire to build more churches to her name than all the monarchs in the world have done; wish her 'good day' every morning and 'good evening' as night draws on; and say the Ave Maria every day in honour of the heart of Mary. With such devotions, he says, you can be sure of winning the Virgin's heart.'

> 'But, Father', I interjected, 'only if you give her yours too?'

> 'That is not necessary', he replied, 'when you are too closely attached to the world.'

Mary is presented by Barry as an earthly virgin to be wooed and, worse still, deceived by trinkets, baubles and sham displays of affection: naive, credulous, an *earthly* virgin easily conquerable by a *worldly* man. *'And now say that I do not supply you with easy devotions for winning the favours of Mary',* Pascal quotes Barry as saying (again, with perfect accuracy), to which he replies, with sexual innuendo: 'That is facility itself.' The seven words 'only if you give her yours too' epitomize his rooted objections to the Jesuits: that, far from himself ridiculing sacred things, they are degrading them—defiling even the Virgin by glossing her love for mankind with sexual overtones and, above all, making her love mechanical: a sort of magic superstitious idolatry conveniently dispensing salvation at the turn of a well-worn formula. Exactly the same objection applies to their view of the sacraments, their doctrines of mitigation of confession and automatic absolution, and their trivialization of the Eucharist:

> 'But there is another useful thing in our learned Turrianus, *Selections,* part II, disputation xvi, doubt 7: *That one can hear half of one priest's mass, and then the other half of another's, and even that one can first of all hear the end of one and after that the beginning of another.*[45] And I will tell you something else as well: it has also been declared permissible *to hear two halves of mass at the same time said by two different priests, one of them beginning the mass when the other has reached the Elevation; because it is possible to pay attention to both sides at the same time, and two halves of a mass make up one whole: Duæ medietates unam missam constituunt.*[46] This is what has been decided by our Fathers Bauny, treatise VI, question 9, page 312[47]; Hurtado, *On Sacraments,* volume II, *On the Mass,* disputation v, difficulty 4; Azorius, part I, book VII, chapter iii, question 3;[48] Escobar, treatise I, examination ii, number 73, in the chapter on 'The Practice of Hearing Mass According to our Society.' And you will see, in this same book, in the editions published at Lyons in 1644 and 1646, what consequences he derives from all this when he writes as follows: *I conclude from this that you can hear mass in a very short time: if, for example, you come across four masses being said simultaneously, and so arranged that just as one is beginning, another has reached the Gospel stage, whilst a third has got as far as the Consecration and the fourth has reached the point of Communion.*'[49]

> 'To be sure, Father, mass at Notre-Dame will be over in a minute by this method.'

In Pascal's view, mechanical observance is not enough; what counts, and what is to be hoped for and encouraged in man, is a sincere heartfelt turning to God, a love of Him Who 'so loved the world, that He gave His only begotten Son.' Quoting these words from John III 16 in his final scornful dismissal of the Jesuit priest at the end of the Tenth Letter, he underlines the cheap shallowness of their view that 'the world, redeemed by Him, shall be exempted from loving Him!' Even more than their teaching on probability and sufficient grace, their doctrine of attrition merits his deepest contempt. He cannot accept that a man need only be motivated by the fear of hell-fire in order to win his salvation, rather than come humbly to God out of a contrite heart, longing for the salvation that will eternally unite his love for his Maker with God's love for him. When 'the human mind makes such insolent sport of the love of God', it can stoop no further. 'Our Fathers', inanely boasts the Jesuit priest, 'have released men from the *tiresome* obligation of actually loving God.[50] And there are so many advantages to this doctrine that our Fathers Annat, Pinthereau, Le Moyne and A. Sirmond himself have vigorously defended it against attempts

to attack it.' 'Thus', and the last word is Pascal's, 'people who have never loved God in all their lives are made worthy by you of enjoying God in all eternity.'

From a strictly political and opportunist standpoint the Jesuits were, of course, substantially on the right tack. To lighten God's yoke is the surest means of making, and keeping, the largest number of nominal Christian worshippers. And this Pascal realized, when he made his Jesuit priest say: 'Men are so corrupt nowadays that, since we cannot make them come to us, we really have to go to them.' But he, unlike them, failed to detect any value in a mere religion of formalism and social propriety, the shadow and not the substance of religious worship, devoid of any sense of the supernatural. 'As their morality is wholly pagan', says the narrator's Jansenist friend in Letter V, 'natural powers suffice for its observance.' Hence Pascal's belief in the need for divine support of the fallible human will, hence too the acrimonious controversy about grace. Nevertheless, the doctrine of efficacious grace and the Elect was not too likely to commend itself to that vast majority of human beings whose will, by definition, was weak, whose judgment was fallible, and whose unredeemed nature was corrupt. Pascal was defending a lost cause. Not even his brilliance and tenacity could turn the tables on opponents who were so completely the masters of the tactical opportunity. Intellectually the victory was his; politically he had encountered failure. Arnauld, condemned both in *fact* and in *right,* had for the second, and not the last, time in his life gone into deepest hiding; there was no need for a Nineteenth Letter.

Pascal's personal (though anonymous) condemnation was quick to follow. On 6 September 1657, five months after the publication of the Eighteenth, the ***Provincial Letters*** were placed on the *Index Librorum Prohibitorum* by Pope Alexander VII. For Pascal, as an Ultramontanist at heart rather than a Gallican, a man believing in the supremacy of the Pope over the Church rather than in the semiautonomy of the Church in France, this was a bitter blow. In the first of his two letters to Annat, after declaring that he did not belong to Port-Royal, he had made a clear affirmation of religious loyalty: 'my only allegiance on earth is to the Roman Catholic and Apostolic Church, within which I wish to live and die in communion with the Pope, its sovereign head, and outside which I am fully convinced that there is no salvation.' Although he had not been excommunicated, his first writings on a religious subject had been declared heretical. For all the work's inherent brilliance and public acclaim, such was the bitter-sweet taste of failure. Even today Molinism, the doctrine of sufficient grace, and Probabilism are the approved doctrines of the Roman Catholic Church.

In an eternal perspective, however, Pascal believed that his was the just—and would be the winning—cause.

He is even the winner of the temporal argument in the longer run, at any rate so far as intellectual consistency and moral credibility are concerned, though perhaps a reading of the *Provincial Letters* in 1995 will secure few converts. And all this is chiefly due to his skill and brilliance as a polemist, the inward strength of conviction inspiring the outward eloquence. As an essay in polemical satire, the *Provincial Letters* were a unique phenomenon. Never before had a satirist had so specific a target in view, ridiculing it by so dexterous a combination of realism and fantasy. The reading of the *Provincial Letters,* if not an uplifting religious experience, is certainly a reminder of the versatility of human genius.

The *Letters* are an unfinished and episodic achievement, impossible to discuss from the conventional critical standpoint of a generalized structure. The irony, indeed, of Pascal's literary career is that his two major works, both masterpieces of unusual distinction, are both of them unfinished and in a sense fragmentary. But if the *Provincial Letters* are a reminder of human genius, it is the combined genius of many minds: the genius for folly of Escobar, Molina, Le Moyne, Barry, Diana, Filliucci and numerous other casuists; the scatological genius of Arnauld and Nicole collecting their scabrous specimens in many dark corners, but notably in Escobar; and the arranging and conflating genius of Pascal himself, coupled with his irony, his gift for the terse phrase, the judicious quip, the incisive stab, and the decisive rejoinder.

Sometimes the casuists speak for themselves, always lamentably then. Sometimes—more often indeed—a puppet Jesuit speaks with the idiocy of Pascal's own imaginative verve. Sometimes, but only in the very earliest Letters, the narrator's Jansenist friend contributes a piece of wisdom. Monsieur N, a sympathizer with the Jesuits, defends his friends but never very successfully. With a skill in reportage well ahead of his times, Pascal, journalist-like, rushes from place to place trying to establish the reasons for all this much ado about nothing. He sets down his findings in plain unvarnished French for the cool appraisal of his unbiased correspondent. The turgid rhetoric of his opponents is laughable beside his own sobriety of word and judgment. As a method of denigration, this is essentially truthful. Underlying all the farce, facetiousness and levity is a deep and fundamental seriousness, such as any reading of d'Alba's story would induce.

It is the seriousness of those who fight not only for their lives, reputation and integrity but in defence of a passionately upheld belief. And it is as present in the earlier Letters, beneath all the comedy of the bumbling casuist, as it is in the collective appeals to the Society of Jesus and in the final, despairingly indignant letters to François Annat. Using the world's weapons to condemn worldliness, the *Provincial Letters* are infinitely

more serious than their mordant wit and flippant irony would suggest. Yet to the worldly Jesuits Pascal's layman's gift for unmasking imposture, making the abstruse interesting and appealing beyond the theological faculty to the widest public made him not serious enough!

Hilaire Belloc, noting that the '*Provincial Letters* have been in the past unceasingly used, and are even still used, as a weapon against the Catholic Church', has been the fiercest critic of their treatment of the Jesuits. In what is, he admits, 'a cold way of meeting such excellent writing',[51] he regrets that 'of the thousands of Casuist decisions arrived at by a vast number of professors, regular and secular, Pascal chooses to speak only of the Jesuit decisions' and from the latter 'selects what are in appearance . . . only 132,[52] and in real numbers—if we exclude repetitions—only 89.'[53] A 'just analysis' of these 89 seems to him to leave fourteen in contention, 'of which eight [From Letter VII] were, at one time or another, finally condemned at Rome'[55] whilst another three[56 & 57] are said to be 'capable of confusion with condemned propositions.'[58] Those dealing with financial inducements to judges[59], the Mohatra contract (previously discussed) and Adam Tanner's[60] and Gregorio de Valencia's instructions on simony are, in Belloc's view, 'doubtful'[61] cases. Concerning the Mohatra contract, even he is ready to acknowledge that 'Pascal was probably right, and Escobar was probably wrong.'[62]

The fact is, however, that many more than eight points of Jesuit casuistry have, since 1657, been 'condemned at Rome.' Abuses to which Pascal drew attention, and which were subsequently condemned, include double payment for masses, the murder of slanderers, gluttony, desiring a father's death and theft: all these casuistical interpretations of moral conduct were to be proscribed, either in 1665 or 1679, in Papal decrees.[63] Furthermore, Pascal is surely to be congratulated—rather than, by Belloc, condemned—for the fact that the eight (in reality, more than eight!) casuistical teachings which later were censured by popes cannot now 'be brought up in accusation against the moral system of the Catholic Church.[64] In some things, however, he is undoubtedly inaccurate (in quotations from Valencia[65] and Lessius,[66] for instance) but these, within the total situation he is describing, are of small account. Contrary to Belloc, any 'just analysis' of the *Provincial Letters* would suggest that its quotations, translations and digests are in the main exceedingly reliable.[67]

It is also true, in Kenneth Kirk's words, that 'Vasquez, the first systematic probabilist, . . . [insisted] upon the safer course being taken where there is danger of a breach of the natural law or of charity, or in the case of the sacraments' and that 'even the notorious Escobar had limited the use of probable opinions to cases in which no danger threatens which prudence, justice or charity bids us avoid.'[68] This was the theoretical position. But in every department of life, and not least perhaps in moral theology, theory and practice can be far apart. As had been recognised well before the decade in which the *Provincial Letters* were written,[69] Escobar's Twenty-Four Seniors had indeed opened up the way to moral permissiveness.

With 'so much wit and fervour' (in Belloc's words)[70] Pascal stresses what *might* be perpetrated by casuists, Jesuits or otherwise, under the ægis of the doctrine of probabilism; and furthermore that this, unless eradicated, might *increasingly* be perpetrated in the future. At a literary and philosophical level his device of the Jesuit Father compensates for any shortcomings in generalization. Historically speaking, the fact that so many of the matters censured in the *Provincial Letters* were later to be censured in Papal decrees serves to remind us that Pascal's uneasiness concerning the laxities of probabilism was well founded.

Notes

[1] Gide, A. (1951), 991; 23 June 1930.

[2] On Pascal's attitude towards casuistry see Eliot, T.S. (1931). Perhaps because he felt such a close affinity with Pascal, this essay is one of Eliot's finest achievements.

[3] Popes Paul V, Gregory XV and Urban VIII.

[4] Pope Urban VIII.

[5] Étienne Bauny (1564-1649) was a Jesuit professor of moral theology whose *Compendium of Sins* (1634) was condemned at Rome in September 1640 and in Paris in April 1642.

[6] François Hallier (1595-1659), Bishop of Toul (1643-56) and of Cavaillon (1656-9), secured the condemnation of Bauny's book by the French bishops. He later sympathized with the Jesuits.

[7] This is corroborated in Sánchez, T. (1615), I, 30-38 [1613]. The point is developed in Arnauld, A. (1775-83), XXIX, 74 [1643].

[8] Bevan, E.R. (1932), 192.

[9] John I, 29.

[10] Instructions condemned on 4 March 1679 by Pope Innocent XI (Denzinger, H. J. D. (1957), 1201).

[11] Bevan, E. R. (1932), 193.

[12] Ephesians VI 12.

[13] I.e., Annat, F. (1656).

[14] John XVIII 36.

[15] The church, or *temple,* of Charenton-le-Pont, five miles south-east of Paris, which Henri IV had allowed the Protestants to build and which was destroyed in 1685 at the time of the Revocation of the Edict of Nantes. . . .

[31] Francesco Amico (1578-1651), an Italian Jesuit, Chancellor of the University of Graz.

[32] This instruction was condemned on 24 September 1665 by Pope Alexander VII (Denzinger, H.J.D. (1957), 1117).

[33] Accurately quoted from Amico, F. (1642), V xxxvi (118).

[34] Caramuel de Lobkowitz, J. (1652-3), 543.

[35] 'Sometimes he even has to kill'.

[36] Cognet, L. (1965), 128, n. 4. Escobar y Mendoza, A. (1659), 119 [1644], citing Lessius, L. (1606), 88 [1605]; the reference to Molina, L. (1588) has not been established. The instruction that 'I can properly kill a thief to save a single gold piece' was condemned on 4 March 1679 by Pope Innocent XI (Denzinger, H. J. D. (1957), 1181).

[37] Hurtado de Mendoza, P. (1631), II, xv (iii) 4 (48).

[38] E.g., Matthew XIX 24, Matthew VI, 19-21 and the parables of the widow's mite (Mark XII 41-4) and of Dives and Lazarus (Luke XVI, 19-31).

[39] E.g., Vasquez, G. (1618), 18-21.

[40] Le Moyne, P. (1645), 621-5 [1640-3].

[41] Le Moyne, P. (1645), 621 [1640-3].

[42] Le Moyne, P. (1652), 149, 129, 127, 157, 163.

[43] *Etre toujours au bal* is the phrase used in the original.

[44] de Barry, P. (1655), 33, 143, 172, 420, 261-2, 59-60, 156.

[45] de Escobar y Mendoza, A. (1659), 183 [1644].

[46] 'Two halves constitute one mass'.

[47] Bauny, É. (1646), 312 [1634]. This instruction was condemned on 4 March 1679 by Pope Innocent XI (Denzinger, H. J. D. (1957), 1203).

[48] Azor, J. (1610-16), I, 631.

[49] Cognet, L. (1965), 169, n. 3.

[50] This allegation from Sirmond, A. (1641) was the deepest wound inflicted by Pascal upon the Jesuits. It was, for example, the subject of the fierce argument between Boileau and the Jesuit companion of Bourdaloue which took place on 5 January 1690 (de Sévigné, M. (1963-78), III, 811-12; Marie de Sévigné to Françoise-Marguerite de Grignan, 15 January 1690). The so-called doctrine of *attrition* was condemned on 24 September 1665 and 4 March 1679 by Popes Alexander VII and Innocent XI (Denzinger, H. J. D. (1957), 1101, 1155, 1156, 1157).

[51] Belloc, H.J.P.R. (1920), 355.

[52]. There are reckoned to be 7 in Letter V, 16 in Letter VI, 19 in Letter VII, 28 in Letter VIII, 26 in Letter IX and 35 in Letter X (Belloc, H. J. P. R. (1920), 357 n. 1) although these numbers do not add up to 132.

[53] Belloc, H. J. P. R. (1920), 372-3. . . .

[55] These instructions were condemned on 24 September 1665 by Pope Alexander VII and on 10 November 1752 by Pope Benedict XIV (Denzinger, H. J. D. (1957), 1102, 1491).

[56] Sánchez, T. (1615), II iii 6 (13) [1613]

[57] Filliucci, V. (1633-4), XXV, xi (331).

[58] Belloc, H. J. P. R. (1920), 373.

[59] Cognet, L. (1965), 136 n. 2. A similar instruction was condemned on 24 September 1665 by Pope Alexander VII (Denzinger, H. J. D. (1957), 1126).

[60] Tanner, A. (1621-7), III 1519.

[61] Belloc, H. J. P. R. (1920), 373.

[62] Belloc, H. J. P. R. (1920), 371.

[63] Decrees of Popes Alexander VII and Innocent XI (Denzinger, H. J. D. (1957), 1108, 1117-18/1180, 1158, 1164, 1186).

[64] Belloc, H. J. P. R. (1920), 373.

[65]. de Valencia, G. (1591), III 1042.

[66] Lessius, L. (1606), II, xxi, 16 [1605].

[67] This is borne out by a careful study of the footnotes to Cognet, L. (1965).

[68] Kirk, K. E. (1927), 394.

[69] Cognet, L. (1965), 103 n. 2.

[70] Belloc, H. J. P. R. (1920), 355.

Leszek Kolakowski (essay date 1995)

SOURCE: "Good Reason, Bad Reason, Heart," in *God Owes Us Nothing: A Brief Remark on Pascal's Religion and on the Spirit of Jansenism*, The University of Chicago Press, 1995, pp. 145-60.

[*In the following excerpt, Kolakowski examines several key aspects of Pascal's theology, including his concepts of heart, free will, truth, faith, knowledge, and reason.*]

[The] heart, at least in its primary sense, that related to the acquisition of religious truths, is not a sentimental attitude or an emotion. It is a faculty of *intellectual* intuition whereby we accept truths unattainable either by mathematical reasoning or by the testimony of sense experience. In the essay *De l'Esprit géométrique* the word "heart" does not appear, but fragment 110 of the *Pensées* clearly confirms that the notion is applicable even in the context of geometrical investigation. This essay is immensely rich, and only one crucial point needs to be recalled here. In geometry, "almost the only human science that produces infallible [demonstrations]," it is impossible to define primitive concepts and to prove initial principles; the infinite regress which ensues is out of our grasp. Geometry "defines none of these things, such as space, time, movement, number, equality, or the like, of which there are very many, because these terms designate the things they signify so naturally to people who understand the language that any clarification one could make would bring more obscurity than instruction."[38] This applies to other common notions like "man" or "being" (to try to define the latter would result in an absurd circularity because one would have to say "being *is*" . . .).

The objects and the axioms of geometry are of "extreme natural clarity." We can even prove statements which we are not really capable of understanding, like the infinite divisibility of space and time, or, for that matter, anything that involves the idea of infinity, and we do this by reflecting on the statement that denies the one under scrutiny and perceiving its absurdity (like the finitude of space or the concept of its indivisible units; this is a Cartesian remark, except that, to Descartes, while we are unable to "understand" infinity, we can "conceive" it).

All these undemonstrable truths are, however, according to fragment 110, known by the faculty of the "heart." The heart or the instinct infallibly knows the "first principles"—space, time, movement, number—without the help of reasoning. The heart knows that there are three dimensions of space and that the numbers are infinitely many. And there are other, non-mathematical certainties: "we know that we do not dream" (so much for Descartes). Our impotence to prove such principles "can only humiliate reason."

How does this apply to religious truths? The fragment explains: "therefore those to whom God gave religion by the feeling of their hearts are blessed and legitimately convinced, but to those who do not have it we can give it only by reasoning and wait until God gives it to them by the feeling of their hearts, without which faith is only human and useless for salvation."

There is a perplexing ambiguity in this distinction. It appears that to know God by "feeling in one's heart" is the same as having faith in the proper sense, that is, receiving the supernatural gift of grace. On the other hand the "heart" is an intuition whereby obvious and nonreligious mathematical axioms are absorbed, for the understanding and acceptance of which no grace is required.

Since it is hard to imagine that Pascal, even in the notes he wrote for himself for further elaboration, could be sloppy about or forget the fundamental distinction between genuine faith and natural knowledge, we must suppose that the word "heart," thus used for two disconnected purposes, is implicitly defined only by negation: it is an intuition by which even things that cannot be proved either by infallible mathematical deduction or by the testimony of the senses are nevertheless *known*, either with unshakeable certitude (like the truths of faith for the God-enlightened) or, to use Descartes' idiom, with a "moral assurance"; the latter category would embrace both the proposition that "we do not dream" and unprovable but self-evident axioms of the kind, "if A = B and B = C, then A = C."

There is nothing logically unsound in such a negatively defined notion. And it might include even the knowledge of God by natural light to the extent that such knowledge, albeit "useless for salvation," is nonetheless accessible. When Pascal insists that "it is the heart that feels God, not reason. That is what faith is. God is sensible to the heart, not to reason" (fr. 424), he has real faith in mind; but this is less obvious when he says, "the heart loves the universal being naturally and it loves itself naturally, whichever it devotes itself to, and it hardens against the one or the other according to its choice" (fr. 423). It appears that we believe in God and love him (ultimately, that is the same) naturally. But then the very presence of atheists would be incomprehensible. There is a Pascalian answer to this objection, always the same. Whether we love God or ourselves (mutually exclusive options) is a matter of will, not of reason. "The will is one of the main organs of belief, not because it produces belief but because things are true or false according to the angle from

which one looks at them" (fr. 539). It is our will that directs our mind towards this or that, depending on the pleasure we find in either. Therefore conversion is a matter of healing the will, not of mending the intellect. Atheists, who have no faith, do not lack this "natural feeling," but they do not want to discover it in their hearts because their will and the attraction of temporal pleasures conceal it from them. Probably they are guilty for their incredulity and can never seek an intellectualist refuge: "if only I had proofs. . . ."

Nevertheless it is true that this "natural feeling," whether related to geometrical axioms, to commonsense belief, or to religious matters, is never absolutely reliable, a fact the skeptics do not fail to exploit; the "force of Pyrrhonism" consists in the fact that "we have no certainty of the truth of those principles, apart from faith and revelation, except that we feel them naturally in ourselves. Now, this natural feeling is not a convincing proof of their truth, because, having no certainty, apart from faith, about whether man was created by a good God, by a wicked demon, or by chance, it is doubtful whether those principles given to us are true or false or dubious, according to our origin" (fr. 131).

This remark, obviously inspired by a reading of the *Meditations,* not of Montaigne (and references to Descartes are much more numerous in the **Pensées** than the three cases where his name actually appears, somewhat enigmatically), seems to confirm the incurable uncertainty of *all* natural knowledge unless it is supported by certainty about God. It suggests that as long as the Cartesian hypothesis of the "malicious genius" has not been illuminated—and only faith can disprove it absolutely—even geometrical axioms, not to speak of the belief that we are not dreaming in our waking state, are in the shadow of legitimate doubt. Descartes was perhaps not quite consistent about mathematical truths; we are not ultimately sure whether we can have "metaphysical certitude" without relying on God's veracity; the cogito is beyond the reach of the possible mischievous demon, to be sure, but this is not Pascal's theme. Otherwise everything seems precarious in our knowledge; but Pascal does not say that once God's existence is known to us, those "secular" certainties are thereby established. He admits that the Pyrrhonists have good arguments but he does not believe that they can ever be perfectly consistent. In fact, one need not necessarily to appeal to God to confound their extravagances: "Nature" does this, and lets us rely on the soundness of "bon sens." He says once that man owes to God the acceptance of the religion he gave him, and what God owes to man is not to lead him into error (fr. 840). This seems to contradict the implicit principle of Jansenism that God owes us nothing. The context—miracles—may dispel this contradiction. God would indeed deceive us if he gave us no means to distinguish between true and false miracles: the "error" in question concerns religious truths, not any kind of knowledge. Otherwise we would never err, or at least we would have at our disposal criteria by which in all matters truth could be infallibly distinguished from falsity; that we have no such criteria is self-evident to Pascal. We can commit errors in religious matters as well, of course, and even in understanding the revealed Word we can easily be mistaken. Of such mistakes we are guilty. Since it is always a valid principle that only the faithful have a proper understanding of faith and revelation, and that gratuitously given faith enables them to perceive miracles as miracles and to understand a prophecy as a prophecy, Pascal's claim that God "owes" it to us not to lead us into error can refer only to the elect; in other words, God does not deceive the faithful about the content of faith. In the realm of natural knowledge the light is dimmed and there is no certainty; God is hidden.[39]

While the expression "Deus absconditus" comes from revelation, its Pascalian use displays, . . . a sad resignation in the face of the post-Cartesian universe: birds or sky no longer give testimony of God's omnipresence. Pascal's almost obsessive preoccupation with God's absence is well understandable; that is what religion is ultimately about, apart from the infusion of grace. This alarming "fact" urgently needed an explanation and it was provided by the Augustinian concept of original sin. Since we deserve nothing but God's wrath, it is natural that we do not deserve to see his face clearly. Given human corruption it would be *unjust* if he manifested himself unveiled before our eyes as he will on the day of reckoning; but it would also be unjust if he were so hidden that even those who seek him sincerely and to whom his mercy was offered could not recognize him (fr. 149). Perfect clarity would help the mind and harm the will (fr. 234). We must not complain; if you claim that you are worthy of God's manifest revelation, you prove that you are unworthy, for you are presumptuous; if you say you are unworthy, you confirm the truth: you are unworthy (fr. XIV). You cannot win.

Thus the salutary remedy for the horror of the "mute universe" has been found. God's concealment confirms the truth of Christianity, because no other religion says that God is hidden. To be sure, to complete the picture of the degraded human condition, it was not enough to read the Book of Genesis; a peculiar Augustinian interpretation of hereditary guilt was also necessary. But it fitted perfectly in the Pascalian explanation. This was how Descartes and Augustine were blended into a coherent alloy.

To "seek God sincerely" is to find him. But we know that faith precedes understanding, therefore even to seek God sincerely would seem to require irresistible grace. No good exit from the tormenting circle.

And faith, it appears, does not produce an *intellectual* understanding of God or of any other religious truth. The elect trust God, and indeed, feel his presence, but they do not master divine things in intellectual terms; otherwise they would be capable of convincing the unbelievers by natural light. "It is incomprehensible that God should exist and incomprehensible that he should not, that the soul should be with the body, and that we should not have a soul, that the world should have been created and that it should not, etc., that there should be original sin and that there should not" (fr. 809).

That is a philosopher who speaks, and speaks with a note of despair. The explanation of the mind-body union, either in Thomist categories (rational soul as the form of the body) or in Cartesian manner (the impossibility of causal contact between the two substances) does not help. And God is incomprehensible by definition.

Pascal's "christocentric" religiosity is a part of his radical separation of faith from knowledge. This is what links his fragments on Jesus with his consistent emphasis on the impossibility of converting Christianity into a philosophy. "We do not know God except through Jesus Christ. Without this mediator all communication with God is taken from us. It is through Jesus Christ that we know God. All those who have claimed to know God and to prove his existence without Jesus Christ had nothing but ineffective proofs. . . . Through Jesus Christ and in him one can prove God's existence and teach both morality and doctrine. Jesus Christ is thus the true God of men" (fr. 189). "It is not only impossible, but useless, to know God without Jesus Christ . . ." (fr. 191). "To know God without knowing our own misery produces pride. To know one's own misery without God produces despair. The knowledge of Jesus Christ is in the middle because we find in it both God and our misery" (fr. 192). In other words, the faith of philosophers is not faith at all; their proofs of God's existence are futile. Pascal speaks of historical proofs concerning Jesus; but did he believe that not only his life, deeds, and words were historically proven but the dogma of the Incarnation as well? And would this imply that "normal" historical knowledge can lead to genuine faith? Certainly not, since in the act of faith, knowledge and charity are one, and no knowledge, however extensive and however theological in content, can produce faith. Only faith can "give" us Jesus in the Christian sense, not philosophical or theological inquiry. "God of Abraham, God of Isaac, God of Jacob, not of philosophers and scholars"—as we read in the "classic" formula of the *Mémorial* (fr. 913). It is futile to try to transmute Paul's Epistle to the Romans into a philosophical treatise. Besides, as we know, proofs based on miracles and prophecies are good enough but only the elect can perceive their truth. This is important, otherwise we would think that the godless and the unfaithful can have the same knowledge of God and Jesus as true Christians. Christianity is about salvation and the healing of our corruption; the only Christian knowledge worthy of the name is a knowledge that saves, therefore it cannot be a purely intellectual act of assertion, whether in metaphysical or historical matters.

In what sense, then, is human reason "autonomous" (a word often used in the description of the **Pensées**)? This word requires some *distinguos*.

We find a lucid and precise concept of scientific reason in Pascal's polemics of 1647 with Father Noël about **Expériences nouvelles touchant le vide;** the latter tried to question the results of Pascal's experiments that disproved the traditional belief in the *horror vacui*.[40] Before refuting the peripatetic philosopher's argument against the void, Pascal states the general rules for affirming or denying a proposition. We must not, he says, make a peremptory judgment unless the proposition under scrutiny "appears so clearly and distinctly by itself to our senses or reason . . . that the mind has no means of doubting its certainty"—in which case we are dealing with principles or axioms—or is inferred infallibly from such principles. Other propositions are left undecided (the mysteries of faith are excluded from this consideration). If a hypothesis is such that its negation results in a patent absurdity, it is thereby recognized as true; if its affirmation leads to a patent absurdity, it is thereby refuted; if neither occurs, the hypothesis is doubtful. But the main point of the letter is that, while in order to ascertain the truth of a hypothesis, it is not enough that known phenomena are consistent with or deducible from it, whereas it is disproved if it yields a conclusion that is contrary to even a single phenomenon.

This is a modern scientist speaking; one might say, anachronistically, that he suggests a Popperian rule of empiricism: we cannot be satisfied with an explanation that can give an account of new experiences because the explanation may still be empirically empty and fit into the experimental data only because of its emptiness, because there is no way of falsifying it (as was the case, in Popper's view, with psychoanalysis or historical materialism and, according to Pascal, with the theory which rejects the void; on this point the target of his strictures is both Cartesian and Aristotelian physics). This applies to invisible matter, which has no empirical properties and is supposed, according to the adversary, to fill the universe. Since its existence cannot be proved, there is reason to deny it, whereas it is illicit to believe in it for no better reason than that one cannot prove that it does not exist. An example of the emptiness of Aristotelian categories is given in the (almost untranslatable) definition of light provided by the Jesuit polemicist: "la lumière est un mouvement luminaire de rayons composés de corps lucides, c'est à dire

lumineux." This sounds most distinctly like a learned explanation by a physician from Molière or a scientist's self-parody.

The Pascalian rules of scientific procedure are obviously relevant to his theology, indeed they provide us with a clue to the relationship between a scientist and a believer, and they explain why he was not and could not consistently be a Thomist, but rather was an Augustinian.

Indeed, the fact that empirical phenomena are consistent with a hypothesis does not make this hypothesis credible or even meaningful. The presence of God and his all-encompassing providence is this kind of hypothesis; whatever happens can be "explained" by divine orders and plans, but this is why God's existence is empirically empty (no "birds and sky") and explains nothing in terms of scientific rules. Briefly, God is not an empirical hypothesis, and Pascal knew that.

This then is the first rule: whatever is not scientifically testable (or rationally self-evident, like axioms) is scientifically empty. And the second rule is: whatever is testable is to be accepted or rejected according to the results of the test, and not on any other grounds. Conformably to the first rule, religious truths, in particular the very existence of God, are empirically empty and cannot be ascertained on the basis of empirical evidence. Conformably to the second rule, no scientific truth can be put in doubt by the verdict of a religious dogma; only scientifically valid tests can disprove it.

Both rules are confirmed by the often quoted fragments of the eighteenth **Provincial Letter:** our eyes are the proper judges of facts, our reason of natural things, faith of revealed supernatural matters; these three principles of our knowledge have, each of them, separate objects. "We have to believe the senses in factual matters, our reason when a nonrevealed truth is at stake, the Scriptures and the decisions of the Church in the realm of the supernatural."[41] Whenever the Scriptures seem to assert something that is demonstrably false, we have to look for another interpretation, considering the revealed word to be true as a matter of faith. This is consistent, Pascal says, with the teaching of Aquinas, who tries to explain why the Book of Genesis seems to claim that the moon is greater than all the stars: we should not cling to the literal sense of the biblical context but find another one.

Scripture, of course, is safe: it can never say something that is false according to the natural light, and in case of an apparent conflict it is Scripture's ostensible meaning that has to be differently explained (for instance, the dimension of lunar light in our sight, not the actual size of the moon, etc.). Reason and the senses are safe, too; no ecclesiastical decrees can invalidate their testimony. The monks of Ratisbone, Pascal says, obtained a decree from Leo IX to the effect that the body of St. Dionysius had been taken to their monastery; but this is plainly false and no pope can alter the fact, nor did the verdict of the pope Zacharius annihilate the antipodes.

The real problem of Pascal's time was not, of course, the antipodes or the location of Saint Dionysius' relics but the Galileo affair. And on this point his famous remark is, or seems to be, unambiguous: "in vain did you [the Jesuits] obtain Rome's decree against Galileo condemning his view on the movement of the earth. This will not prove that the earth rests; and, if one had persistent observations proving that it is the earth that revolves, all men together would not hinder it from revolving and themselves from revolving with it."[42]

The rule that human reason, properly working and observing its own code, cannot clash with the content of revelation was stated by Aquinas; he was by no means an advocate of the extravagant "double truths" theory held by some Averroists. And Pascal, like other Jansenists, could cite him when it was suitable. But Aquinas's philosophy did not imply that the reason why revelation and natural light (or faith and intellect) cannot conflict was that they simply had separate objects. On two points Pascal differed from him. The first is less important. According to Thomas, if an apparent contradiction appears between the divine word and the result of intellectual investigations, it is the former that gets the upper hand, and one must assume that the intellect committed errors in terms of its own regulations. Certainly, with his general rationalist preferences, Aquinas did on various occasions explain the meaning of Scripture in a way that would remove noticeable collisions, but his main prescription was that one must keep the revelation intact and discover how reason went wrong. Pascal, on the other hand, thought that in such cases we should manipulate the sense of the revelation to make it agree with the verdict of natural light, provided that the latter has operated properly.

But the major line of difference was this. In Thomist terms revelation and reason have no quite separate areas, they overlap. Along with items that obviously can be known from revelation only (in particular, the Incarnation and the Trinity), there are crucially important truths which God wanted to reveal to us but which can be known with certainty by natural light alone; among them are not only the very existence of God and eternal life but a great number of specific elements of natural theology, in fact most (albeit not everything) of what we are taught in the 453 chapters of *Contra Gentiles*.[43] A separation in the sense that natural knowledge is impotent in proving fundamental tenets of faith is entirely alien to Thomas. His is a philosophy of a cosy world in which all things coexist in a perfect harmony: heaven and earth, faith and knowledge, soul and body, temporal and eternal goods, church and state, holy history and secular history. There is, of course, a clear hierarchy of values and it is assumed that all temporal goods ultimately have to serve God and salvation; but our earthly life, our body, our social bonds, while not creating absolute values, do not deserve scorn, let alone condemnation.

If divine approval of everything created is taken literally, there is no dramatic split between the two worlds of which we are necessarily denizens. But in Pascal's world we are painfully torn asunder between them; call this attitude "baroque" or "gnostic temptation" or "vision tragique." None of the Jansenists, not even Barcos, expressed this incurable discord in similar terms.[44] This is the most general reason why the comforting philosophy of Aquinas was so incompatible with the way Pascal saw and experienced the world.

This might seem out of keeping with the specific case of the faith-versus-reason debate: truths acquired by faith and by natural reason do not clash with each other, and this is now commonly admitted by commentators. But this is not the end of the story. Faith and reason do not contradict each other *in content,* to be sure, and on this point the *Pensées* do not depart from the letter to Noël or from the *Provincial Letters.* Section XIII of the *Pensées* says virtually everything on the subject: "One ought to doubt when it is right to do so, to assert when it is right, and to submit when it is right. Whoever fails to do this does not understand the force of reason. There are people who do not observe these three principles, either asserting everything as proved, since they are ignorant of proof, or doubting everything, since they do not know when they should submit, or submitting in all matters, since they do not know where to judge. Pyrrhonist, mathematician, Christian: doubt, affirmation, submission" (fr. 170). "Nothing is so consistent with reason as this disavowal of reason" (fr. 182). "The last step of reason is to admit that there are infinitely many things which are above it" (fr. 188). But reason has an imperative power (fr. 768).

On the compelling force of "geometrical" reason and its limits there is nothing in the *Pensées* to contradict earlier writings: while "first principles" cannot be proved and must be accepted by the "heart" as self-evident, they are good enough to be thus accepted; the impossibility of proving them humilitates reason and reveals its limits, but this does not imply that within those limits reason cannot arrive at humanly accessible certainty or that we are entitled to doubt everything, let alone admit that any proposition is as good as its negation. While it is true that our reasoning yields to "sentiment," that reason is pliable in all directions (fr. 530), and that it is a sure loser in a conflict with passions and amour-propre, this does not mean that there are no rules at all; if two people disagree about the lapse of time since something happened and I have a watch, I don't care what they say; I am not making a judgment according to my whims precisely because I have a watch (fr. 534).

In other words: we have instruments with which to pass judgment in matters pertaining to the competence of reason. Scholastic reason is unworthy of trust because it tries to go beyond its capacities. As a man whose mind was trained in mathematics and physics, Pascal simply could not believe the Thomists' arguments because they were obviously defective in terms of the procedures that science employed. Their dismissal does not in itself logically imply that no other arguments are possible but this conclusion was at least very strongly suggested if additional considerations are taken into account. Scholastic and Cartesian arguments for God's existence, God's attributes, and the immortality of the soul were all that was available; none were compelling, convincing, or even plausible according to standards stated by Pascal; and if one looked more closely at those standards, it became clear that it was hopeless to search for other arguments that would meet the requirements of scientific reason (the ontological proof is not mentioned but one may safely assume that it would appear dubious to the mind of a mathematician, not to speak of its futility in terms of religious benefits).

Scientific reason is considerably limited even in natural matters, and in matters pertaining to our salvation it is totally fruitless apart from its possible negative capacity: the ability to see its own limitations. Within its legitimate scope of activity it needs to obey its own precepts and nothing else, especially not papal pronouncements when they clearly go beyond the authority of the Church in matters of Christian doctrine and morality.

Recognizing how little value rational arguments have in religious issues does not lead directly to being an Augustinian; one could simply stop bothering about these issues and become a libertine in a stronger or weaker sense of the word. But for a scientist who cannot swallow scholastic rationality and is a Christian who takes his Christianity very seriously (unlike those scientists who kept their watered-down Christianity only in the form of a few nonconfessional tenets—the existence of God, divine providence, immortality) there was, apart from the Augustinian tradition, hardly any option available in terms of a consistent, all-embracing interpretation of the entire body of Christianity. Deism, virtually (or totally) noncommittal, was not such an option, of course. Pascal's option resulted naturally from biographical accidents—his milieu, his father's influence, the meeting with Saint-Cyranian preachers, etc.—but it converged, and was perfectly consistent, with the mental disposition of a scientist to whom religious matters lay "on the other side" of the mind and the heart. He did not actually say, like Jansenius, that for knowledge of

God memory, not intellect, is the proper organ, but he certainly would have approved this assessment. Christianity is not metaphysics. We are initiated into it by studying history—sacred history, to be sure—and not by exercising our logical skills. In the preface to the *Traité du vide,* authority, sense experience, and reason are distinguished in the same way as in the *Pensées.* Continuous and collectively achieved progress in science is stressed (the remark about antiquity being the childhood of mankind rather than its old age, a source of special wisdom, is well in the spirit of both Bacon and Descartes) but this is not denied in the *Apology* ("all the sciences are infinite in the scope of their research; for who would doubt that geometry, for instance, has an infinity of infinities of propositions to set forth?" [fr. 199]).

In terms of the separation of faith from natural light there is thus no break between the *Pensées* and Pascal's earlier writings.

What is characteristic of the period of the *Pensées* is not a denial of the legitimate authority of scientific reason within its limits, but rather a repeatedly stated mistrust of science in moral terms: confronted with what really matters in life, our salvation, science simply brings little profit. The most concise description of the human condition is, after all: "between us and hell or heaven there is only life between the two, and this is the most fragile thing in the world" (fr. 152). In this short journey towards an eternity of beatitude or of agony, curiosity directed to nature and mathematical objects is at best indifferent. "The vanity of science. Knowledge of external things will not console me, in times of affliction, for ignorance of morals, but knowledge of morals will always console me for ignorance of natural science" (fr. 23). "Once I started studying man, I saw that these abstract sciences are not proper to man and that by plunging into them I went further astray from my destiny than did others by being ignorant of them" (fr. 687). Or, as Pascal put it in his famous letter to Fermat of 10 August 1660: "To speak frankly, I consider mathematics the highest employment of the mind; at the same time I know that it is so useless that there is, in my view, little difference between a mathematician and a skilful artisan. I call it the most beautiful craft [métier] in the world but it is, after all, no more than a craft."[45]

If there is anything surprising in such a remark coming from the pen of an Augustinian, it is only that it was not phrased more strongly: the study of nature from disinterested curiosity has always been sinful in the Augustinian tradition. This is, no doubt, an incontestable consequence of the general rule which opposes "the world" and the Church to each other as implacable foes; whatever we do that is not for God is captured by Satan, and there is nothing in between. But then Pascal was not converted to Augustinian piety in the process of writing the *Pensées,* as his earlier texts testify. In his short essay known under the title *A Comparison of Early Christians with Those of Today,*[46] the hostile separation of Christianity from mundane life is stated unambiguously: "one saw then [in early Christianity] the world and the Church as two opposites, two irreconcilable enemies one of which uninterruptedly persecutes the other, and of which the seemingly weaker would one day triumph over the stronger, so that people deserted one of these opposite parties to join the other. They renounced the precepts of the one to espouse the precepts of the other; they rejected the opinions [sentiments] of the one to adopt the opinions of the other." And that was the perfect Christianity, which one could join only after arduous preparation, instead of being baptized just after birth (even though there are "very important reasons" why babies are baptized). To be a Christian, one had to forsake the world and be totally devoted to the Church, whereas today the Church is polluted by people who carry the spirit of ambition, revenge, impurity, and concupiscence. "All virtues, martyrdom, austerities, and good works are useless [when practiced] beyond the Church and without communion with the head of the Church, who is the pope," we read in a letter to Roannez of November 1656.[47]

Pascal never condemned outright the practice of science; he degraded it—against his inclination, no doubt—to a worldly amusement. And he never surrendered it to papal decrees ("the pope hates and fears scholars who are not bound to him by vows," [fr. 677]). Gilberte's claim that her brother abandoned scientific work entirely after his first conversion, and composed his major treatise on cycloids (of 1658) only by accident, when he was tormented by a great pain which prevented him from sleeping, did not withstand examination by Pascal scholars.[48] There might have been a tension between his disparaging remarks and the continuing, if enfeebled, interest of a genius in scientific matters, but this does not make his opinion any less credible and genuine. In accordance with Jansenist piety he wanted to be a Christian and nothing else, and logically this entailed not being a scientist (the exercise of science being, after all, a part of "the world"), not even being an "hônnete homme," that is, a polished, polite member of the educated upper classes, pleasantly conversing with his peers, moderate in his opinions, avoiding obduracy and strong partisan spirit.[49] And yet Pascal was both a scientist—somewhat vain and eager to assert his claims to priority—and an "hônnete homme," apart from being a Christian. If he experienced discomfort as a result of combining these roles—Jesus Christ was not a scientist or an hônnete homme, nor was St. Paul—this was not only a personal psychological problem. This discomfort is an aspect of the *Pensées.* But it is only one aspect, and not a major one, considering the main purpose of the Apology.

And the main purpose, needless to say, was not to show that Christianity is not "contrary to reason," but only "above" it; and also to show that it is because Christianity goes against our instincts that people tend to reject it. In this respect Pascal was obviously much more skeptical than the men of the schools, and he knew perfectly well that attempts to "rationalize" Christianity, to make it, at least to a large extent, a product of the unprejudiced secular intellect, were not only hopeless in terms of the capacities of this intellect, but in a sense sacrilegious, as they would deprive religion of its mystery and make void the gift of faith; such an endeavor, even if successful, would be worthless, because faith, which is necessarily coupled with love, can never spring from reason, however powerful. Pascal believed that Christianity, being contrary to human nature, is not unreasonable, but this belief boils down to two points. In the negative, defensive sense, it means that we can always, by skilful exegesis, remove the seeming contradiction between the text of revelation and natural reason by making clear that the former, being infallible by definition, has a meaning different from its ostensible one. In the positive and intellectually more fragile sense we can show that once we know from the divine word the crucial facts of man's destiny—the history of the Fall and of redemption—we can understand all the things that would otherwise seem depressingly unintelligible and revoltingly absurd: all forms of human misery, suffering, the very frailty of reason, the futility of our aspirations, struggles, persecutions, and poverty. No application of reason can make Christianity "rational"; indeed, to go beyond this would amount to an attempt to convert Christianity into a philosophy, that is, to build a new tower of Babel.

Notes

[38] *OCL,* p. 350.

[39] In the context, this remark on God's "duty" not to deceive us may well hint at what is known as "the miracle of the holy thorn," of which Pascal's family were beneficiaries. Marguerite Périer, the ten-year-old niece of Blaise and a boarder at the Port-Royal school, had suffered for three years from a very painful disease of the eye, which disfigured her face, produced a constant outflow of putrefactive matter, and caused her bones to rot. The disease was considered incurable by physicians. On 24 March 1656, during a religious celebration in the chapel, a sister from the convent touched her with a reliquary which enclosed the thorn of the Holy Crown, and the child was instantaneously cured, with no traces of the terrible affliction left. Many people witnessed the extraordinary event, which immediately became famous in Paris. Considering the location of the divine intervention, the Jansenists, who were then victims of various chicaneries, threats, and persecutions, saw in it, not surprisingly, a sign of a special

providential favor granted not only to the girl but to the convent and, by extension, to the holy cause they themselves defended. The Jesuits, without necessarily denying the miracle, denied, not surprisingly, its meaning as interpreted by their enemies. Ample documentation of the event, including testimonies of witnesses and of the little heroine, the statements of several surgeons, various letters, etc., is to be found in *OCM,* vol. 3. This is perhaps one of the best-documented of reputedly miraculous phenomena (it was soon approved as such by the archbishop of Paris after the interrogation of witnesses). And what could be more natural, in Pascal's view, than to think that God would have deceived us if he had performed a miracle in such circumstances without having a specific edifying purpose in mind, to wit, the affirmation of the Augustinian truth? The *Apology,* according to Brunschvicg, was conceived as an act of gratitude for the miracle. In 922 we read: "Sur le miracle. Comme Dieu n'a pas rendu de famille plus heureuse, qu'il fasse aussi qu'il n'en trouve point de plus reconnaissante."

[40] *OCL,* pp. 199-215.

[41] *OCL,* p. 466.

[42] *OCL,* p. 467.

[43] The most concise exposition of Aquinas's rules concerning the relationship between faith and natural knowledge and their respective areas of competence is to be found in *Contra Gentiles,* I, 2-8.

[44] Mesnard, while accepting the concept of the "vision tragique" for reading Pascal, argues that it does not apply to Barcos; cf. *La culture du XVII siècle,* pp. 287-88.

[45] *OCL,* p. 282.

[46] Ibid., pp. 360-62.

[47] *OCL,* p. 268.

[48] Cf. Mesnard's commentary on Gilberte's *Vie,* in *OCM,* vol. 1, pp. 566-67.

[49] On the concept of the "honnête homme," cf. Mesnard, *Les Pensées de Pascal,* part I, chap. 2, and *La culture du XVIIe siècle,* pp. 142ff., and Edouard Giscard d'Estaign, "Pascal et le bon usage de la raison," in *Chroniques de Port-Royal,* Textes du Tricentenaire, 1965.

FURTHER READING

Biography

Cole, John R. *Pascal: The Man and His Two Loves.* New York: New York University Press, 1995, 349 p.

Seeks to revise Gilberte Périer's (Pascal's sister's) portrayal of Pascal's life in he Vie de Monsieur Pascal. Unlike Périer, Cole presents a "darker conception" of Pascal's life.

Mortimer, Ernest. *Blaise Pascal: The Life and Work of a Realist.* London: Methuen & Co., 1959, 240 p.

A study of Pascal's life that emphasizes his modernity while differentiating Pascal as a man and as a writer.

Criticism

Bloom, Harold, ed. *Blaise Pascal: Modern Critical Views.* New York: Chelsea House Publishers, 1989, 200 p.

A collection of thirteen essays that "brings together a representative selection of the most illuminating modern criticism of Blaise Pascal."

Davidson, Hugh M. "The Unity of Pascal's Thought." In *Blaise Pascal,* edited by Maxwell A. Smith, pp. 96-108. Boston: Twayne Publishers, 1983.

Discusses several aspects of Pascal's writings and argumentation, focusing on the philosopher's various modes of thought.

Hammond, Nicholas. *Playing with Truth: Language and the Human Condition in Pascal's "Pensées."* Oxford, England: Clarendon Press, 1994, 249 p.

Analyzes Pascal's persuasive manipulation of language in the *Pensées.* Hammond focuses of Pascal's use of six key terms to describe the human condition—*inconstance, ennui, inquétude, repos, bonheur / felicité,* and *justice.*

Jordan, Jeff, ed. *Gambling on God: Essays on Pascal's Wager.* Lanham, Md.: Rowan & Littlefield Publishers, 1994, 188 p.

Ten essays on Pascal's wager, addressing such topics as the context of Pascal's argument, decision theory, and the notion of an infinite utility. Also contains the most prominent objections to the wager.

Krailsheimer, A. J. "Ethics and Causistry." In *Pascal,* pp. 27-40. New York: Hill and Wang, 1980.

Analyzes Pascal's ideas on religion and ethics, focusing on his thoughts concerning the relationship between the material and spiritual worlds. The critic also comments on Pascal's political views.

Mariner, Frank. "The Order of Disorder: The Problem of the Fragment in Pascal's *Pensées.*" *Papers on French Seventeenth-Century Literature* XX, No. 38 (1993): 171-82.

Examines the main issues in the critical debate between the traditionalist and modernist readers of the *Pensées* over the correct ordering of the fragments which comprise the work.

Schlesinger, George. "A Central Theistic Argument." In *Gambling on God: Essays on Pascal's Wager*, edited by Jeff Jordan, pp. 83-99. Rowman & Littlefield Publishers, 1994.

>Responds to the most common objections to Pascal's wager—his argument that belief in God is the only rational response when faced with the question of God's existence.

Wetsel, David, ed. *Meaning, Structure and History in the "Pensées" of Pascal.* Papers on French Seventeenth-Century Literature, Biblio 17-56. Seattle: Portland State University, 1990, 111 p.

>A volume of essays on the *Pensées* that discusses their historical context, order and signification, and the nature of the proofs for Christianity.

Literature
Criticism from
1400 to 1800

Cumulative Indexes

How to Use This Index

The main references

list all author entries in the following Gale Literary Criticism series:

BLC = *Black Literature Criticism*
CLC = *Contemporary Literary Criticism*
CLR = *Children's Literature Review*
CMLC = *Classical and Medieval Literature Criticism*
DA = *DISCovering Authors*
DC = *Drama Criticism*
HLC = *Hispanic Literature Criticism*
LC = *Literature Criticism from 1400 to 1800*
NCLC = *Nineteenth-Century Literature Criticism*
PC = *Poetry Criticism*
SSC = *Short Story Criticism*
TCLC = *Twentieth-Century Literary Criticism*
WLC = *World Literature Criticism, 1500 to the Present*

The cross-references

list all author entries in the following Gale biographical and literary sources:

AAYA = *Authors & Artists for Young Adults*
AITN = *Authors in the News*
BEST = *Bestsellers*
BW = *Black Writers*
CA = *Contemporary Authors*
CAAS = *Contemporary Authors Autobiography Series*
CABS = *Contemporary Authors Bibliographical Series*
CANR = *Contemporary Authors New Revision Series*
CAP = *Contemporary Authors Permanent Series*
CDALB = *Concise Dictionary of American Literary Biography*
CDBLB = *Concise Dictionary of British Literary Biography*
DLB = *Dictionary of Literary Biography*
DLBD = *Dictionary of Literary Biography Documentary Series*
DLBY = *Dictionary of Literary Biography Yearbook*
HW = *Hispanic Writers*
JRDA = *Junior DISCovering Authors*
MAICYA = *Major Authors and Illustrators for Children and Young Adults*
MTCW = *Major 20th-Century Writers*
NNAL = *Native North American Literature*
SAAS = *Something about the Author Autobiography Series*
SATA = *Something about the Author*
YABC = *Yesterday's Authors of Books for Children*

Literary Criticism Series
Cumulative Author Index

A. E. . . . . TCLC 3, 10
See also Russell, George William

Abasiyanik, Sait Faik   1906-1954
See Sait Faik
See also CA 123

Abbey, Edward   1927-1989 . . . . . . CLC 36, 59
See also CA 45-48; 128; CANR 2, 41

Abbott, Lee K(ittredge)   1947- . . . . . . CLC 48
See also CA 124; CANR 51; DLB 130

Abe, Kobo
1924-1993 . . . . CLC 8, 22, 53, 81;
DAM NOV
See also CA 65-68; 140; CANR 24; MTCW

Abelard, Peter   c. 1079-c. 1142 . . . CMLC 11
See also DLB 115

Abell, Kjeld   1901-1961. . . . . CLC 15
See also CA 111

Abish, Walter   1931- . . . . CLC 22
See also CA 101; CANR 37; DLB 130

Abrahams, Peter (Henry)   1919- . . . . . CLC 4
See also BW 1; CA 57-60; CANR 26;
DLB 117; MTCW

Abrams, M(eyer) H(oward)   1912-. . . CLC 24
See also CA 57-60; CANR 13, 33; DLB 67

Abse, Dannie
1923- . . . CLC 7, 29; DAB; DAM POET
See also CA 53-56; CAAS 1; CANR 4, 46;
DLB 27

Achebe, (Albert) Chinua(lumogu)
1930- . . . . . CLC 1, 3, 5, 7, 11, 26, 51, 75;
BLC; DA; DAB; DAC; DAM MST,
MULT, NOV; WLC
See also AAYA 15; BW 2; CA 1-4R;
CANR 6, 26, 47; CLR 20; DLB 117;
MAICYA; MTCW; SATA 40;
SATA-Brief 38

Acker, Kathy   1948- . . . . CLC 45
See also CA 117; 122

Ackroyd, Peter   1949- . . . . CLC 34, 52
See also CA 123; 127; CANR 51; DLB 155;
INT 127

Acorn, Milton   1923- . . . . CLC 15; DAC
See also CA 103; DLB 53; INT 103

Adamov, Arthur
1908-1970 . . . . CLC 4, 25; DAM DRAM
See also CA 17-18; 25-28R; CAP 2; MTCW

Adams, Alice (Boyd)   1926- . . . CLC 6, 13, 46
See also CA 81-84; CANR 26, 53;
DLBY 86; INT CANR-26; MTCW

Adams, Andy   1859-1935. . . . . TCLC 56
See also YABC 1

Adams, Douglas (Noel)
1952- . . . . CLC 27, 60; DAM POP
See also AAYA 4; BEST 89:3; CA 106;
CANR 34; DLBY 83; JRDA

Adams, Francis   1862-1893 . . . . NCLC 33

Adams, Henry (Brooks)
1838-1918 . . . . . . TCLC 4, 52; DA; DAB;
DAC; DAM MST
See also CA 104; 133; DLB 12, 47

Adams, Richard (George)
1920- . . . . CLC 4, 5, 18; DAM NOV
See also AAYA 16; AITN 1, 2; CA 49-52;
CANR 3, 35; CLR 20; JRDA; MAICYA;
MTCW; SATA 7, 69

Adamson, Joy(-Friederike Victoria)
1910-1980 . . . . CLC 17
See also CA 69-72; 93-96; CANR 22;
MTCW; SATA 11; SATA-Obit 22

Adcock, Fleur   1934- . . . . CLC 41
See also CA 25-28R; CAAS 23; CANR 11,
34; DLB 40

Addams, Charles (Samuel)
1912-1988 . . . . CLC 30
See also CA 61-64; 126; CANR 12

Addison, Joseph   1672-1719 . . . . LC 18
See also CDBLB 1660-1789; DLB 101

Adler, Alfred (F.)   1870-1937 . . . . . . TCLC 61
See also CA 119

Adler, C(arole) S(chwerdtfeger)
1932- . . . . CLC 35
See also AAYA 4; CA 89-92; CANR 19,
40; JRDA; MAICYA; SAAS 15;
SATA 26, 63

Adler, Renata   1938- . . . . CLC 8, 31
See also CA 49-52; CANR 5, 22, 52;
MTCW

Ady, Endre   1877-1919 . . . . TCLC 11
See also CA 107

Aeschylus
525B.C.-456B.C. . . . . CMLC 11; DA;
DAB; DAC; DAM DRAM, MST

Afton, Effie
See Harper, Frances Ellen Watkins

Agapida, Fray Antonio
See Irving, Washington

Agee, James (Rufus)
1909-1955 . . . . TCLC 1, 19; DAM NOV
See also AITN 1; CA 108; 148;
CDALB 1941-1968; DLB 2, 26, 152

Aghill, Gordon
See Silverberg, Robert

Agnon, S(hmuel) Y(osef Halevi)
1888-1970 . . . . CLC 4, 8, 14
See also CA 17-18; 25-28R; CAP 2; MTCW

Agrippa von Nettesheim, Henry Cornelius
1486-1535 . . . . LC 27

Aherne, Owen
See Cassill, R(onald) V(erlin)

Ai   1947- . . . . CLC 4, 14, 69
See also CA 85-88; CAAS 13; DLB 120

Aickman, Robert (Fordyce)
1914-1981 . . . . CLC 57
See also CA 5-8R; CANR 3

Aiken, Conrad (Potter)
1889-1973 . . . . CLC 1, 3, 5, 10, 52;
DAM NOV, POET; SSC 9
See also CA 5-8R; 45-48; CANR 4;
CDALB 1929-1941; DLB 9, 45, 102;
MTCW; SATA 3, 30

Aiken, Joan (Delano)   1924- . . . . CLC 35
See also AAYA 1; CA 9-12R; CANR 4, 23,
34; CLR 1, 19; DLB 161; JRDA;
MAICYA; MTCW; SAAS 1; SATA 2,
30, 73

Ainsworth, William Harrison
1805-1882 . . . . NCLC 13
See also DLB 21; SATA 24

Aitmatov, Chingiz (Torekulovich)
1928- . . . . CLC 71
See also CA 103; CANR 38; MTCW;
SATA 56

Akers, Floyd
See Baum, L(yman) Frank

Akhmadulina, Bella Akhatovna
1937- . . . . CLC 53; DAM POET
See also CA 65-68

Akhmatova, Anna
1888-1966 . . . . CLC 11, 25, 64;
DAM POET; PC 2
See also CA 19-20; 25-28R; CANR 35;
CAP 1; MTCW

Aksakov, Sergei Timofeyvich
1791-1859 . . . . NCLC 2

Aksenov, Vassily
See Aksyonov, Vassily (Pavlovich)

Aksyonov, Vassily (Pavlovich)
1932- . . . . CLC 22, 37
See also CA 53-56; CANR 12, 48

Akutagawa Ryunosuke
1892-1927 . . . . TCLC 16
See also CA 117

Alain   1868-1951 . . . . TCLC 41

Alain-Fournier. . . . . TCLC 6
See also Fournier, Henri Alban
See also DLB 65

Alarcon, Pedro Antonio de
1833-1891 . . . . NCLC 1

Alas (y Urena), Leopoldo (Enrique Garcia)
1852-1901 . . . . TCLC 29
See also CA 113; 131; HW

Albee, Edward (Franklin III)
1928- . . . . . . CLC 1, 2, 3, 5, 9, 11, 13, 25,
53, 86; DA; DAB; DAC; DAM DRAM,
MST; WLC
See also AITN 1; CA 5-8R; CABS 3;
CANR 8; CDALB 1941-1968; DLB 7;
INT CANR-8; MTCW

Alberti, Rafael   1902- . . . . CLC 7
See also CA 85-88; DLB 108

Albert the Great   1200(?)-1280. . . . CMLC 16
See also DLB 115

Alcala-Galiano, Juan Valera y
See Valera y Alcala-Galiano, Juan

Alcott, Amos Bronson 1799-1888 . . **NCLC 1**
See also DLB 1

Alcott, Louisa May
1832-1888 . . . . **NCLC 6; DA; DAB;**
DAC; DAM MST, NOV; WLC
See also CDALB 1865-1917; CLR 1, 38;
DLB 1, 42, 79; DLBD 14; JRDA;
MAICYA; YABC 1

Aldanov, M. A.
See Aldanov, Mark (Alexandrovich)

Aldanov, Mark (Alexandrovich)
1886(?)-1957 . . . . **TCLC 23**
See also CA 118

Aldington, Richard 1892-1962 . . . . . . **CLC 49**
See also CA 85-88; CANR 45; DLB 20, 36,
100, 149

Aldiss, Brian W(ilson)
1925- . . . . **CLC 5, 14, 40; DAM NOV**
See also CA 5-8R; CAAS 2; CANR 5, 28;
DLB 14; MTCW; SATA 34

Alegria, Claribel
1924- . . . . **CLC 75; DAM MULT**
See also CA 131; CAAS 15; DLB 145; HW

Alegria, Fernando 1918- . . . . **CLC 57**
See also CA 9-12R; CANR 5, 32; HW

Aleichem, Sholom . . . . **TCLC 1, 35**
See also Rabinovitch, Sholem

Aleixandre, Vicente
1898-1984 . . . . **CLC 9, 36; DAM POET;**
PC 15
See also CA 85-88; 114; CANR 26;
DLB 108; HW; MTCW

Alepoudelis, Odysseus
See Elytis, Odysseus

Aleshkovsky, Joseph 1929-
See Aleshkovsky, Yuz
See also CA 121; 128

Aleshkovsky, Yuz . . . . **CLC 44**
See also Aleshkovsky, Joseph

Alexander, Lloyd (Chudley) 1924- . . **CLC 35**
See also AAYA 1; CA 1-4R; CANR 1, 24,
38; CLR 1, 5; DLB 52; JRDA; MAICYA;
MTCW; SAAS 19; SATA 3, 49, 81

Alexie, Sherman (Joseph, Jr.)
1966- . . . . **CLC 96; DAM MULT**
See also CA 138; NNAL

Alfau, Felipe 1902- . . . . **CLC 66**
See also CA 137

Alger, Horatio, Jr. 1832-1899 . . . . . **NCLC 8**
See also DLB 42; SATA 16

Algren, Nelson 1909-1981 . . . . **CLC 4, 10, 33**
See also CA 13-16R; 103; CANR 20;
CDALB 1941-1968; DLB 9; DLBY 81,
82; MTCW

Ali, Ahmed 1910- . . . . **CLC 69**
See also CA 25-28R; CANR 15, 34

Alighieri, Dante 1265-1321 . . . . **CMLC 3, 18**

Allan, John B.
See Westlake, Donald E(dwin)

Allen, Edward 1948- . . . . **CLC 59**

Allen, Paula Gunn
1939- . . . . **CLC 84; DAM MULT**
See also CA 112; 143; NNAL

Allen, Roland
See Ayckbourn, Alan

Allen, Sarah A.
See Hopkins, Pauline Elizabeth

Allen, Woody
1935- . . . . **CLC 16, 52; DAM POP**
See also AAYA 10; CA 33-36R; CANR 27,
38; DLB 44; MTCW

Allende, Isabel
1942- . . . . **CLC 39, 57; DAM MULT,**
NOV; HLC
See also AAYA 18; CA 125; 130;
CANR 51; DLB 145; HW; INT 130;
MTCW

Alleyn, Ellen
See Rossetti, Christina (Georgina)

Allingham, Margery (Louise)
1904-1966 . . . . **CLC 19**
See also CA 5-8R; 25-28R; CANR 4;
DLB 77; MTCW

Allingham, William 1824-1889 . . . **NCLC 25**
See also DLB 35

Allison, Dorothy E. 1949- . . . . **CLC 78**
See also CA 140

Allston, Washington 1779-1843 . . . . **NCLC 2**
See also DLB 1

Almedingen, E. M. . . . . **CLC 12**
See also Almedingen, Martha Edith von
See also SATA 3

Almedingen, Martha Edith von 1898-1971
See Almedingen, E. M.
See also CA 1-4R; CANR 1

Almqvist, Carl Jonas Love
1793-1866 . . . . **NCLC 42**

Alonso, Damaso 1898-1990 . . . . **CLC 14**
See also CA 110; 131; 130; DLB 108; HW

Alov
See Gogol, Nikolai (Vasilyevich)

Alta 1942- . . . . **CLC 19**
See also CA 57-60

Alter, Robert B(ernard) 1935- . . . . . . **CLC 34**
See also CA 49-52; CANR 1, 47

Alther, Lisa 1944- . . . . **CLC 7, 41**
See also CA 65-68; CANR 12, 30, 51;
MTCW

Altman, Robert 1925- . . . . **CLC 16**
See also CA 73-76; CANR 43

Alvarez, A(lfred) 1929- . . . . **CLC 5, 13**
See also CA 1-4R; CANR 3, 33; DLB 14,
40

Alvarez, Alejandro Rodriguez 1903-1965
See Casona, Alejandro
See also CA 131; 93-96; HW

Alvarez, Julia 1950- . . . . **CLC 93**
See also CA 147

Alvaro, Corrado 1896-1956 . . . . **TCLC 60**

Amado, Jorge
1912- . . . . **CLC 13, 40; DAM MULT,**
NOV; HLC
See also CA 77-80; CANR 35; DLB 113;
MTCW

Ambler, Eric 1909- . . . . **CLC 4, 6, 9**
See also CA 9-12R; CANR 7, 38; DLB 77;
MTCW

Amichai, Yehuda 1924- . . . . . . **CLC 9, 22, 57**
See also CA 85-88; CANR 46; MTCW

Amiel, Henri Frederic 1821-1881 . . **NCLC 4**

Amis, Kingsley (William)
1922-1995 . . . . . **CLC 1, 2, 3, 5, 8, 13, 40,**
44; DA; DAB; DAC; DAM MST, NOV
See also AITN 2; CA 9-12R; 150; CANR 8,
28; CDBLB 1945-1960; DLB 15, 27, 100,
139; INT CANR-8; MTCW

Amis, Martin (Louis)
1949- . . . . **CLC 4, 9, 38, 62**
See also BEST 90:3; CA 65-68; CANR 8,
27; DLB 14; INT CANR-27

Ammons, A(rchie) R(andolph)
1926- . . . . **CLC 2, 3, 5, 8, 9, 25, 57;**
DAM POET; PC 16
See also AITN 1; CA 9-12R; CANR 6, 36,
51; DLB 5, 165; MTCW

Amo, Tauraatua i
See Adams, Henry (Brooks)

Anand, Mulk Raj
1905- . . . . **CLC 23, 93; DAM NOV**
See also CA 65-68; CANR 32; MTCW

Anatol
See Schnitzler, Arthur

Anaya, Rudolfo A(lfonso)
1937- . . . . **CLC 23; DAM MULT, NOV;**
HLC
See also CA 45-48; CAAS 4; CANR 1, 32,
51; DLB 82; HW 1; MTCW

Andersen, Hans Christian
1805-1875 . . . . **NCLC 7; DA; DAB;**
DAC; DAM MST, POP; SSC 6; WLC
See also CLR 6; MAICYA; YABC 1

Anderson, C. Farley
See Mencken, H(enry) L(ouis); Nathan,
George Jean

Anderson, Jessica (Margaret) Queale
. . . . **CLC 37**
See also CA 9-12R; CANR 4

Anderson, Jon (Victor)
1940- . . . . **CLC 9; DAM POET**
See also CA 25-28R; CANR 20

Anderson, Lindsay (Gordon)
1923-1994 . . . . **CLC 20**
See also CA 125; 128; 146

Anderson, Maxwell
1888-1959 . . . . . . **TCLC 2; DAM DRAM**
See also CA 105; 152; DLB 7

Anderson, Poul (William) 1926- . . . . **CLC 15**
See also AAYA 5; CA 1-4R; CAAS 2;
CANR 2, 15, 34; DLB 8; INT CANR-15;
MTCW; SATA-Brief 39

Anderson, Robert (Woodruff)
1917- . . . . **CLC 23; DAM DRAM**
See also AITN 1; CA 21-24R; CANR 32;
DLB 7

Anderson, Sherwood
1876-1941 . . . . **TCLC 1, 10, 24; DA;**
DAB; DAC; DAM MST, NOV; SSC 1;
WLC
See also CA 104; 121; CDALB 1917-1929;
DLB 4, 9, 86; DLBD 1; MTCW

Andier, Pierre
See Desnos, Robert

Andouard
See Giraudoux, (Hippolyte) Jean

Andrade, Carlos Drummond de . . . . . . **CLC 18**
See also Drummond de Andrade, Carlos

Andrade, Mario de   1893-1945 . . . . . **TCLC 43**

Andreae, Johann V(alentin)
1586-1654 . . . . **LC 32**
See also DLB 164

Andreas-Salome, Lou   1861-1937 . . . **TCLC 56**
See also DLB 66

Andrewes, Lancelot   1555-1626 . . . . **LC 5**
See also DLB 151

Andrews, Cicily Fairfield
See West, Rebecca

Andrews, Elton V.
See Pohl, Frederik

Andreyev, Leonid (Nikolaevich)
1871-1919 . . . . **TCLC 3**
See also CA 104

Andric, Ivo   1892-1975 . . . . **CLC 8**
See also CA 81-84; 57-60; CANR 43;
DLB 147; MTCW

Angelique, Pierre
See Bataille, Georges

Angell, Roger   1920- . . . . **CLC 26**
See also CA 57-60; CANR 13, 44

Angelou, Maya
1928- . . . . **CLC 12, 35, 64, 77; BLC; DA;**
DAB; DAC; DAM MST, MULT, POET,
POP
See also AAYA 7; BW 2; CA 65-68;
CANR 19, 42; DLB 38; MTCW;
SATA 49

Annensky, Innokenty Fyodorovich
1856-1909 . . . . **TCLC 14**
See also CA 110

Anon, Charles Robert
See Pessoa, Fernando (Antonio Nogueira)

Anouilh, Jean (Marie Lucien Pierre)
1910-1987 . . . . . . **CLC 1, 3, 8, 13, 40, 50;**
DAM DRAM
See also CA 17-20R; 123; CANR 32;
MTCW

Anthony, Florence
See Ai

Anthony, John
See Ciardi, John (Anthony)

Anthony, Peter
See Shaffer, Anthony (Joshua); Shaffer,
Peter (Levin)

Anthony, Piers   1934- . . **CLC 35; DAM POP**
See also AAYA 11; CA 21-24R; CANR 28;
DLB 8; MTCW; SAAS 22; SATA 84

Antoine, Marc
See Proust, (Valentin-Louis-George-Eugene-)
Marcel

Antoninus, Brother
See Everson, William (Oliver)

Antonioni, Michelangelo   1912- . . . . . **CLC 20**
See also CA 73-76; CANR 45

Antschel, Paul   1920-1970
See Celan, Paul
See also CA 85-88; CANR 33; MTCW

Anwar, Chairil   1922-1949 . . . . **TCLC 22**
See also CA 121

Apollinaire, Guillaume
1880-1918 . . . . **TCLC 3, 8, 51;**
DAM POET; PC 7
See also Kostrowitzki, Wilhelm Apollinaris
de
See also CA 152

Appelfeld, Aharon   1932- . . . . **CLC 23, 47**
See also CA 112; 133

Apple, Max (Isaac)   1941- . . . . **CLC 9, 33**
See also CA 81-84; CANR 19; DLB 130

Appleman, Philip (Dean)   1926- . . . . . **CLC 51**
See also CA 13-16R; CAAS 18; CANR 6,
29

Appleton, Lawrence
See Lovecraft, H(oward) P(hillips)

Apteryx
See Eliot, T(homas) S(tearns)

Apuleius, (Lucius Madaurensis)
125(?)-175(?) . . . . **CMLC 1**

Aquin, Hubert   1929-1977 . . . . **CLC 15**
See also CA 105; DLB 53

Aragon, Louis
1897-1982 . . . . . **CLC 3, 22; DAM NOV,**
POET
See also CA 69-72; 108; CANR 28;
DLB 72; MTCW

Arany, Janos   1817-1882 . . . . **NCLC 34**

Arbuthnot, John   1667-1735 . . . . **LC 1**
See also DLB 101

Archer, Herbert Winslow
See Mencken, H(enry) L(ouis)

Archer, Jeffrey (Howard)
1940- . . . . **CLC 28; DAM POP**
See also AAYA 16; BEST 89:3; CA 77-80;
CANR 22, 52; INT CANR-22

Archer, Jules   1915- . . . . **CLC 12**
See also CA 9-12R; CANR 6; SAAS 5;
SATA 4, 85

Archer, Lee
See Ellison, Harlan (Jay)

Arden, John
1930- . . . . . **CLC 6, 13, 15; DAM DRAM**
See also CA 13-16R; CAAS 4; CANR 31;
DLB 13; MTCW

Arenas, Reinaldo
1943-1990 . . . . . . **CLC 41; DAM MULT;**
HLC
See also CA 124; 128; 133; DLB 145; HW

Arendt, Hannah   1906-1975 . . . . **CLC 66**
See also CA 17-20R; 61-64; CANR 26;
MTCW

Aretino, Pietro   1492-1556 . . . . **LC 12**

Arghezi, Tudor . . . . **CLC 80**
See also Theodorescu, Ion N.

Arguedas, Jose Maria
1911-1969 . . . . **CLC 10, 18**
See also CA 89-92; DLB 113; HW

Argueta, Manlio   1936- . . . . **CLC 31**
See also CA 131; DLB 145; HW

Ariosto, Ludovico   1474-1533 . . . . **LC 6**

Aristides
See Epstein, Joseph

Aristophanes
450B.C.-385B.C. . . . . **CMLC 4; DA;**
DAB; DAC; DAM DRAM, MST; DC 2

Arlt, Roberto (Godofredo Christophersen)
1900-1942 . . . . . **TCLC 29; DAM MULT;**
HLC
See also CA 123; 131; HW

Armah, Ayi Kwei
1939- . . . . **CLC 5, 33; BLC;**
DAM MULT, POET
See also BW 1; CA 61-64; CANR 21;
DLB 117; MTCW

Armatrading, Joan   1950- . . . . **CLC 17**
See also CA 114

Arnette, Robert
See Silverberg, Robert

Arnim, Achim von (Ludwig Joachim von
Arnim)   1781-1831 . . . . **NCLC 5**
See also DLB 90

Arnim, Bettina von   1785-1859 . . . . **NCLC 38**
See also DLB 90

Arnold, Matthew
1822-1888 . . . . . **NCLC 6, 29; DA; DAB;**
DAC; DAM MST, POET; PC 5; WLC
See also CDBLB 1832-1890; DLB 32, 57

Arnold, Thomas   1795-1842 . . . . . . **NCLC 18**
See also DLB 55

Arnow, Harriette (Louisa) Simpson
1908-1986 . . . . **CLC 2, 7, 18**
See also CA 9-12R; 118; CANR 14; DLB 6;
MTCW; SATA 42; SATA-Obit 47

Arp, Hans
See Arp, Jean

Arp, Jean   1887-1966 . . . . **CLC 5**
See also CA 81-84; 25-28R; CANR 42

Arrabal
See Arrabal, Fernando

Arrabal, Fernando   1932- . . . **CLC 2, 9, 18, 58**
See also CA 9-12R; CANR 15

Arrick, Fran . . . . **CLC 30**
See also Gaberman, Judie Angell

Artaud, Antonin (Marie Joseph)
1896-1948 . . . **TCLC 3, 36; DAM DRAM**
See also CA 104; 149

Arthur, Ruth M(abel)   1905-1979 . . . . **CLC 12**
See also CA 9-12R; 85-88; CANR 4;
SATA 7, 26

Artsybashev, Mikhail (Petrovich)
1878-1927 . . . . **TCLC 31**

Arundel, Honor (Morfydd)
1919-1973 . . . . **CLC 17**
See also CA 21-22; 41-44R; CAP 2;
CLR 35; SATA 4; SATA-Obit 24

Asch, Sholem   1880-1957 . . . . **TCLC 3**
See also CA 105

Ash, Shalom
See Asch, Sholem

Ashbery, John (Lawrence)
1927- . . . . . . **CLC 2, 3, 4, 6, 9, 13, 15, 25,**
41, 77; DAM POET
See also CA 5-8R; CANR 9, 37; DLB 5,
165; DLBY 81; INT CANR-9; MTCW

Ashdown, Clifford
See Freeman, R(ichard) Austin

Ashe, Gordon
See Creasey, John

Ashton-Warner, Sylvia (Constance)
1908-1984 .... CLC 19
See also CA 69-72; 112; CANR 29; MTCW

Asimov, Isaac
1920-1992 ...... CLC 1, 3, 9, 19, 26, 76,
92; DAM POP
See also AAYA 13; BEST 90:2; CA 1-4R;
137; CANR 2, 19, 36; CLR 12; DLB 8;
DLBY 92; INT CANR-19; JRDA;
MAICYA; MTCW; SATA 1, 26, 74

Astley, Thea (Beatrice May)
1925- .... CLC 41
See also CA 65-68; CANR 11, 43

Aston, James
See White, T(erence) H(anbury)

Asturias, Miguel Angel
1899-1974 .... CLC 3, 8, 13;
DAM MULT, NOV; HLC
See also CA 25-28; 49-52; CANR 32;
CAP 2; DLB 113; HW; MTCW

Atares, Carlos Saura
See Saura (Atares), Carlos

Atheling, William
See Pound, Ezra (Weston Loomis)

Atheling, William, Jr.
See Blish, James (Benjamin)

Atherton, Gertrude (Franklin Horn)
1857-1948 .... TCLC 2
See also CA 104; DLB 9, 78

Atherton, Lucius
See Masters, Edgar Lee

Atkins, Jack
See Harris, Mark

Attaway, William (Alexander)
1911-1986 .... CLC 92; BLC;
DAM MULT
See also BW 2; CA 143; DLB 76

Atticus
See Fleming, Ian (Lancaster)

Atwood, Margaret (Eleanor)
1939- ..... CLC 2, 3, 4, 8, 13, 15, 25, 44,
84; DA; DAB; DAC; DAM MST, NOV,
POET; PC 8; SSC 2; WLC
See also AAYA 12; BEST 89:2; CA 49-52;
CANR 3, 24, 33; DLB 53;
INT CANR-24; MTCW; SATA 50

Aubigny, Pierre d'
See Mencken, H(enry) L(ouis)

Aubin, Penelope 1685-1731(?) .... LC 9
See also DLB 39

Auchincloss, Louis (Stanton)
1917- .... CLC 4, 6, 9, 18, 45;
DAM NOV; SSC 22
See also CA 1-4R; CANR 6, 29; DLB 2;
DLBY 80; INT CANR-29; MTCW

Auden, W(ystan) H(ugh)
1907-1973 ...... CLC 1, 2, 3, 4, 6, 9, 11,
14, 43; DA; DAB; DAC; DAM DRAM,
MST, POET; PC 1; WLC
See also AAYA 18; CA 9-12R; 45-48;
CANR 5; CDBLB 1914-1945; DLB 10,
20; MTCW

Audiberti, Jacques
1900-1965 ...... CLC 38; DAM DRAM
See also CA 25-28R

Audubon, John James
1785-1851 .... NCLC 47

Auel, Jean M(arie)
1936- .... CLC 31; DAM POP
See also AAYA 7; BEST 90:4; CA 103;
CANR 21; INT CANR-21

Auerbach, Erich 1892-1957 .... TCLC 43
See also CA 118

Augier, Emile 1820-1889 .... NCLC 31

August, John
See De Voto, Bernard (Augustine)

Augustine, St. 354-430 ...... CMLC 6; DAB

Aurelius
See Bourne, Randolph S(illiman)

Aurobindo, Sri 1872-1950 .... TCLC 63

Austen, Jane
1775-1817 ..... NCLC 1, 13, 19, 33, 51;
DA; DAB; DAC; DAM MST, NOV;
WLC
See also CDBLB 1789-1832; DLB 116

Auster, Paul 1947- .... CLC 47
See also CA 69-72; CANR 23, 52

Austin, Frank
See Faust, Frederick (Schiller)

Austin, Mary (Hunter)
1868-1934 .... TCLC 25
See also CA 109; DLB 9, 78

Autran Dourado, Waldomiro
See Dourado, (Waldomiro Freitas) Autran

Averroes 1126-1198 .... CMLC 7
See also DLB 115

Avicenna 980-1037 .... CMLC 16
See also DLB 115

Avison, Margaret
1918- .... CLC 2, 4; DAC; DAM POET
See also CA 17-20R; DLB 53; MTCW

Axton, David
See Koontz, Dean R(ay)

Ayckbourn, Alan
1939- ...... CLC 5, 8, 18, 33, 74; DAB;
DAM DRAM
See also CA 21-24R; CANR 31; DLB 13;
MTCW

Aydy, Catherine
See Tennant, Emma (Christina)

Ayme, Marcel (Andre) 1902-1967... CLC 11
See also CA 89-92; CLR 25; DLB 72

Ayrton, Michael 1921-1975 .... CLC 7
See also CA 5-8R; 61-64; CANR 9, 21

Azorin .... CLC 11
See also Martinez Ruiz, Jose

Azuela, Mariano
1873-1952 ..... TCLC 3; DAM MULT;
HLC
See also CA 104; 131; HW; MTCW

Baastad, Babbis Friis
See Friis-Baastad, Babbis Ellinor

Bab
See Gilbert, W(illiam) S(chwenck)

Babbis, Eleanor
See Friis-Baastad, Babbis Ellinor

Babel, Isaak (Emmanuilovich)
1894-1941(?) ...... TCLC 2, 13; SSC 16
See also CA 104

Babits, Mihaly 1883-1941 .... TCLC 14
See also CA 114

Babur 1483-1530 .... LC 18

Bacchelli, Riccardo 1891-1985 ..... CLC 19
See also CA 29-32R; 117

Bach, Richard (David)
1936- ...... CLC 14; DAM NOV, POP
See also AITN 1; BEST 89:2; CA 9-12R;
CANR 18; MTCW; SATA 13

Bachman, Richard
See King, Stephen (Edwin)

Bachmann, Ingeborg 1926-1973 ..... CLC 69
See also CA 93-96; 45-48; DLB 85

Bacon, Francis 1561-1626 .... LC 18, 32
See also CDBLB Before 1660; DLB 151

Bacon, Roger 1214(?)-1292 ...... CMLC 14
See also DLB 115

Bacovia, George .... TCLC 24
See also Vasiliu, Gheorghe

Badanes, Jerome 1937- .... CLC 59

Bagehot, Walter 1826-1877 ...... NCLC 10
See also DLB 55

Bagnold, Enid
1889-1981 ...... CLC 25; DAM DRAM
See also CA 5-8R; 103; CANR 5, 40;
DLB 13, 160; MAICYA; SATA 1, 25

Bagritsky, Eduard 1895-1934 ..... TCLC 60

Bagrjana, Elisaveta
See Belcheva, Elisaveta

Bagryana, Elisaveta .... CLC 10
See also Belcheva, Elisaveta
See also DLB 147

Bailey, Paul 1937- .... CLC 45
See also CA 21-24R; CANR 16; DLB 14

Baillie, Joanna 1762-1851 .... NCLC 2
See also DLB 93

Bainbridge, Beryl (Margaret)
1933- .... CLC 4, 5, 8, 10, 14, 18, 22, 62;
DAM NOV
See also CA 21-24R; CANR 24; DLB 14;
MTCW

Baker, Elliott 1922- .... CLC 8
See also CA 45-48; CANR 2

Baker, Nicholson
1957- .... CLC 61; DAM POP
See also CA 135

Baker, Ray Stannard 1870-1946 ... TCLC 47
See also CA 118

Baker, Russell (Wayne) 1925- ...... CLC 31
See also BEST 89:4; CA 57-60; CANR 11,
41; MTCW

Bakhtin, M.
See Bakhtin, Mikhail Mikhailovich

Bakhtin, M. M.
See Bakhtin, Mikhail Mikhailovich

Bakhtin, Mikhail
See Bakhtin, Mikhail Mikhailovich

Bakhtin, Mikhail Mikhailovich
1895-1975 .... CLC 83
See also CA 128; 113

Bakshi, Ralph 1938(?)-............ **CLC 26**
See also CA 112; 138

Bakunin, Mikhail (Alexandrovich)
1814-1876 .... **NCLC 25**

Baldwin, James (Arthur)
1924-1987 ..... **CLC 1, 2, 3, 4, 5, 8, 13,**
15, 17, 42, 50, 67, 90; BLC; DA; DAB;
DAC; DAM MST, MULT, NOV, POP;
DC 1; SSC 10; WLC
See also AAYA 4; BW 1; CA 1-4R; 124;
CABS 1; CANR 3, 24;
CDALB 1941-1968; DLB 2, 7, 33;
DLBY 87; MTCW; SATA 9;
SATA-Obit 54

Ballard, J(ames) G(raham)
1930- .... **CLC 3, 6, 14, 36; DAM NOV,**
POP; SSC 1
See also AAYA 3; CA 5-8R; CANR 15, 39;
DLB 14; MTCW

Balmont, Konstantin (Dmitriyevich)
1867-1943 .... **TCLC 11**
See also CA 109

Balzac, Honore de
1799-1850 .... **NCLC 5, 35, 53; DA;**
DAB; DAC; DAM MST, NOV; SSC 5;
WLC
See also DLB 119

Bambara, Toni Cade
1939-1995 ...... **CLC 19, 88; BLC; DA;**
DAC; DAM MST, MULT
See also AAYA 5; BW 2; CA 29-32R; 150;
CANR 24, 49; DLB 38; MTCW

Bamdad, A.
See Shamlu, Ahmad

Banat, D. R.
See Bradbury, Ray (Douglas)

Bancroft, Laura
See Baum, L(yman) Frank

Banim, John 1798-1842 .... **NCLC 13**
See also DLB 116, 158, 159

Banim, Michael 1796-1874 ...... **NCLC 13**
See also DLB 158, 159

Banks, Iain
See Banks, Iain M(enzies)

Banks, Iain M(enzies) 1954- .... **CLC 34**
See also CA 123; 128; INT 128

Banks, Lynne Reid .... **CLC 23**
See also Reid Banks, Lynne
See also AAYA 6

Banks, Russell 1940- .... **CLC 37, 72**
See also CA 65-68; CAAS 15; CANR 19,
52; DLB 130

Banville, John 1945-................ **CLC 46**
See also CA 117; 128; DLB 14; INT 128

Banville, Theodore (Faullain) de
1832-1891 .... **NCLC 9**

Baraka, Amiri
1934-........ **CLC 1, 2, 3, 5, 10, 14, 33;**
BLC; DA; DAC; DAM MST, MULT,
POET, POP; DC 6; PC 4
See also Jones, LeRoi
See also BW 2; CA 21-24R; CABS 3;
CANR 27, 38; CDALB 1941-1968;
DLB 5, 7, 16, 38; DLBD 8; MTCW

Barbauld, Anna Laetitia
1743-1825 .... **NCLC 50**
See also DLB 107, 109, 142, 158

Barbellion, W. N. P............... **TCLC 24**
See also Cummings, Bruce F(rederick)

Barbera, Jack (Vincent) 1945-...... **CLC 44**
See also CA 110; CANR 45

Barbey d'Aurevilly, Jules Amedee
1808-1889 .... **NCLC 1; SSC 17**
See also DLB 119

Barbusse, Henri 1873-1935 .... **TCLC 5**
See also CA 105; DLB 65

Barclay, Bill
See Moorcock, Michael (John)

Barclay, William Ewert
See Moorcock, Michael (John)

Barea, Arturo 1897-1957 .... **TCLC 14**
See also CA 111

Barfoot, Joan 1946- .... **CLC 18**
See also CA 105

Baring, Maurice 1874-1945 .... **TCLC 8**
See also CA 105; DLB 34

Barker, Clive 1952- ... **CLC 52; DAM POP**
See also AAYA 10; BEST 90:3; CA 121;
129; INT 129; MTCW

Barker, George Granville
1913-1991 ..... **CLC 8, 48; DAM POET**
See also CA 9-12R; 135; CANR 7, 38;
DLB 20; MTCW

Barker, Harley Granville
See Granville-Barker, Harley
See also DLB 10

Barker, Howard 1946-............ **CLC 37**
See also CA 102; DLB 13

Barker, Pat(ricia) 1943-........ **CLC 32, 94**
See also CA 117; 122; CANR 50; INT 122

Barlow, Joel 1754-1812 .... **NCLC 23**
See also DLB 37

Barnard, Mary (Ethel) 1909-....... **CLC 48**
See also CA 21-22; CAP 2

Barnes, Djuna
1892-1982 ... **CLC 3, 4, 8, 11, 29; SSC 3**
See also CA 9-12R; 107; CANR 16; DLB 4,
9, 45; MTCW

Barnes, Julian 1946-........ **CLC 42; DAB**
See also CA 102; CANR 19; DLBY 93

Barnes, Peter 1931- .... **CLC 5, 56**
See also CA 65-68; CAAS 12; CANR 33,
34; DLB 13; MTCW

Baroja (y Nessi), Pio
1872-1956 .... **TCLC 8; HLC**
See also CA 104

Baron, David
See Pinter, Harold

Baron Corvo
See Rolfe, Frederick (William Serafino
Austin Lewis Mary)

Barondess, Sue K(aufman)
1926-1977 .... **CLC 8**
See also Kaufman, Sue
See also CA 1-4R; 69-72; CANR 1

Baron de Teive
See Pessoa, Fernando (Antonio Nogueira)

Barres, Maurice 1862-1923 .... **TCLC 47**
See also DLB 123

Barreto, Afonso Henrique de Lima
See Lima Barreto, Afonso Henrique de

Barrett, (Roger) Syd 1946- .... **CLC 35**

Barrett, William (Christopher)
1913-1992 .... **CLC 27**
See also CA 13-16R; 139; CANR 11;
INT CANR-11

Barrie, J(ames) M(atthew)
1860-1937 .... **TCLC 2; DAB;**
DAM DRAM
See also CA 104; 136; CDBLB 1890-1914;
CLR 16; DLB 10, 141, 156; MAICYA;
YABC 1

Barrington, Michael
See Moorcock, Michael (John)

Barrol, Grady
See Bograd, Larry

Barry, Mike
See Malzberg, Barry N(athaniel)

Barry, Philip 1896-1949.......... **TCLC 11**
See also CA 109; DLB 7

Bart, Andre Schwarz
See Schwarz-Bart, Andre

Barth, John (Simmons)
1930-...... **CLC 1, 2, 3, 5, 7, 9, 10, 14,**
27, 51, 89; DAM NOV; SSC 10
See also AITN 1, 2; CA 1-4R; CABS 1;
CANR 5, 23, 49; DLB 2; MTCW

Barthelme, Donald
1931-1989 ...... **CLC 1, 2, 3, 5, 6, 8, 13,**
23, 46, 59; DAM NOV; SSC 2
See also CA 21-24R; 129; CANR 20;
DLB 2; DLBY 80, 89; MTCW; SATA 7;
SATA-Obit 62

Barthelme, Frederick 1943-........ **CLC 36**
See also CA 114; 122; DLBY 85; INT 122

Barthes, Roland (Gerard)
1915-1980 .... **CLC 24, 83**
See also CA 130; 97-100; MTCW

Barzun, Jacques (Martin) 1907- .... **CLC 51**
See also CA 61-64; CANR 22

Bashevis, Isaac
See Singer, Isaac Bashevis

Bashkirtseff, Marie 1859-1884 ... **NCLC 27**

Basho
See Matsuo Basho

Bass, Kingsley B., Jr.
See Bullins, Ed

Bass, Rick 1958-................. **CLC 79**
See also CA 126; CANR 53

Bassani, Giorgio 1916-............. **CLC 9**
See also CA 65-68; CANR 33; DLB 128;
MTCW

Bastos, Augusto (Antonio) Roa
See Roa Bastos, Augusto (Antonio)

Bataille, Georges 1897-1962 .... **CLC 29**
See also CA 101; 89-92

Bates, H(erbert) E(rnest)
1905-1974 .... **CLC 46; DAB;**
DAM POP; SSC 10
See also CA 93-96; 45-48; CANR 34;
DLB 162; MTCW

Benedikt, Michael 1935- .... **CLC 4, 14**
See also CA 13-16R; CANR 7; DLB 5

Benet, Juan 1927-................. **CLC 28**
See also CA 143

Benet, Stephen Vincent
1898-1943 ...... **TCLC 7; DAM POET;**
SSC 10
See also CA 104; 152; DLB 4, 48, 102;
YABC 1

Benet, William Rose
1886-1950 ...... **TCLC 28; DAM POET**
See also CA 118; 152; DLB 45

Benford, Gregory (Albert) 1941-.... **CLC 52**
See also CA 69-72; CANR 12, 24, 49;
DLBY 82

Bengtsson, Frans (Gunnar)
1894-1954 .... **TCLC 48**

Benjamin, David
See Slavitt, David R(ytman)

Benjamin, Lois
See Gould, Lois

Benjamin, Walter 1892-1940...... **TCLC 39**

Benn, Gottfried 1886-1956........ **TCLC 3**
See also CA 106; DLB 56

Bennett, Alan
1934- ... **CLC 45, 77; DAB; DAM MST**
See also CA 103; CANR 35; MTCW

Bennett, (Enoch) Arnold
1867-1931 .... **TCLC 5, 20**
See also CA 106; CDBLB 1890-1914;
DLB 10, 34, 98, 135

Bennett, Elizabeth
See Mitchell, Margaret (Munnerlyn)

Bennett, George Harold 1930-
See Bennett, Hal
See also BW 1; CA 97-100

Bennett, Hal .... **CLC 5**
See also Bennett, George Harold
See also DLB 33

Bennett, Jay 1912-................. **CLC 35**
See also AAYA 10; CA 69-72; CANR 11,
42; JRDA; SAAS 4; SATA 41, 87;
SATA-Brief 27

Bennett, Louise (Simone)
1919- ..... **CLC 28; BLC; DAM MULT**
See also BW 2; CA 151; DLB 117

Benson, E(dward) F(rederic)
1867-1940 .... **TCLC 27**
See also CA 114; DLB 135, 153

Benson, Jackson J. 1930-.......... **CLC 34**
See also CA 25-28R; DLB 111

Benson, Sally 1900-1972 .... **CLC 17**
See also CA 19-20; 37-40R; CAP 1;
SATA 1, 35; SATA-Obit 27

Benson, Stella 1892-1933........ **TCLC 17**
See also CA 117; DLB 36, 162

Bentham, Jeremy 1748-1832 ..... **NCLC 38**
See also DLB 107, 158

Bentley, E(dmund) C(lerihew)
1875-1956 .... **TCLC 12**
See also CA 108; DLB 70

Bentley, Eric (Russell) 1916-....... **CLC 24**
See also CA 5-8R; CANR 6; INT CANR-6

Beranger, Pierre Jean de
1780-1857 .... **NCLC 34**

Berendt, John (Lawrence) 1939-.... **CLC 86**
See also CA 146

Berger, Colonel
See Malraux, (Georges-)Andre

Berger, John (Peter) 1926- ...... **CLC 2, 19**
See also CA 81-84; CANR 51; DLB 14

Berger, Melvin H. 1927-.......... **CLC 12**
See also CA 5-8R; CANR 4; CLR 32;
SAAS 2; SATA 5, 88

Berger, Thomas (Louis)
1924- .... **CLC 3, 5, 8, 11, 18, 38;**
DAM NOV
See also CA 1-4R; CANR 5, 28, 51; DLB 2;
DLBY 80; INT CANR-28; MTCW

Bergman, (Ernst) Ingmar
1918- .... **CLC 16, 72**
See also CA 81-84; CANR 33

Bergson, Henri 1859-1941 .... **TCLC 32**

Bergstein, Eleanor 1938-.......... **CLC 4**
See also CA 53-56; CANR 5

Berkoff, Steven 1937-............ **CLC 56**
See also CA 104

Bermant, Chaim (Icyk) 1929- ...... **CLC 40**
See also CA 57-60; CANR 6, 31

Bern, Victoria
See Fisher, M(ary) F(rances) K(ennedy)

Bernanos, (Paul Louis) Georges
1888-1948 .... **TCLC 3**
See also CA 104; 130; DLB 72

Bernard, April 1956- .... **CLC 59**
See also CA 131

Berne, Victoria
See Fisher, M(ary) F(rances) K(ennedy)

Bernhard, Thomas
1931-1989 .... **CLC 3, 32, 61**
See also CA 85-88; 127; CANR 32;
DLB 85, 124; MTCW

Berriault, Gina 1926-............ **CLC 54**
See also CA 116; 129; DLB 130

Berrigan, Daniel 1921-............. **CLC 4**
See also CA 33-36R; CAAS 1; CANR 11,
43; DLB 5

Berrigan, Edmund Joseph Michael, Jr.
1934-1983
See Berrigan, Ted
See also CA 61-64; 110; CANR 14

Berrigan, Ted.................... **CLC 37**
See also Berrigan, Edmund Joseph Michael,
Jr.
See also DLB 5

Berry, Charles Edward Anderson 1931-
See Berry, Chuck
See also CA 115

Berry, Chuck.................... **CLC 17**
See also Berry, Charles Edward Anderson

Berry, Jonas
See Ashbery, John (Lawrence)

Berry, Wendell (Erdman)
1934-............. **CLC 4, 6, 8, 27, 46;**
DAM POET
See also AITN 1; CA 73-76; CANR 50;
DLB 5, 6

Berryman, John
1914-1972 ...... **CLC 1, 2, 3, 4, 6, 8, 10,**
13, 25, 62; DAM POET
See also CA 13-16; 33-36R; CABS 2;
CANR 35; CAP 1; CDALB 1941-1968;
DLB 48; MTCW

Bertolucci, Bernardo 1940- .... **CLC 16**
See also CA 106

Bertrand, Aloysius 1807-1841 .... **NCLC 31**

Bertran de Born c. 1140-1215..... **CMLC 5**

Besant, Annie (Wood) 1847-1933 ... **TCLC 9**
See also CA 105

Bessie, Alvah 1904-1985........... **CLC 23**
See also CA 5-8R; 116; CANR 2; DLB 26

Bethlen, T. D.
See Silverberg, Robert

Beti, Mongo.... **CLC 27; BLC; DAM MULT**
See also Biyidi, Alexandre

Betjeman, John
1906-1984 .... **CLC 2, 6, 10, 34, 43;**
DAB; DAM MST, POET
See also CA 9-12R; 112; CANR 33;
CDBLB 1945-1960; DLB 20; DLBY 84;
MTCW

Bettelheim, Bruno 1903-1990 ...... **CLC 79**
See also CA 81-84; 131; CANR 23; MTCW

Betti, Ugo 1892-1953 .... **TCLC 5**
See also CA 104

Betts, Doris (Waugh) 1932-.... **CLC 3, 6, 28**
See also CA 13-16R; CANR 9; DLBY 82;
INT CANR-9

Bevan, Alistair
See Roberts, Keith (John Kingston)

Bialik, Chaim Nachman
1873-1934 .... **TCLC 25**

Bickerstaff, Isaac
See Swift, Jonathan

Bidart, Frank 1939-.............. **CLC 33**
See also CA 140

Bienek, Horst 1930-............ **CLC 7, 11**
See also CA 73-76; DLB 75

Bierce, Ambrose (Gwinett)
1842-1914(?) .... **TCLC 1, 7, 44; DA;**
DAC; DAM MST; SSC 9; WLC
See also CA 104; 139; CDALB 1865-1917;
DLB 11, 12, 23, 71, 74

Biggers, Earl Derr 1884-1933 ..... **TCLC 65**
See also CA 108

Billings, Josh
See Shaw, Henry Wheeler

Billington, (Lady) Rachel (Mary)
1942-...................... **CLC 43**
See also AITN 2; CA 33-36R; CANR 44

Binyon, T(imothy) J(ohn) 1936- .... **CLC 34**
See also CA 111; CANR 28

Bioy Casares, Adolfo
1914-............... **CLC 4, 8, 13, 88;**
DAM MULT; HLC; SSC 17
See also CA 29-32R; CANR 19, 43;
DLB 113; HW; MTCW

Bird, Cordwainer
See Ellison, Harlan (Jay)

Bird, Robert Montgomery
1806-1854 .... **NCLC 1**

Bonnefoy, Yves
1923- . . . . . . **CLC 9, 15, 58; DAM MST,**
POET
See also CA 85-88; CANR 33; MTCW

Bontemps, Arna(ud Wendell)
1902-1973 . . . . **CLC 1, 18; BLC;**
DAM MULT, NOV, POET
See also BW 1; CA 1-4R; 41-44R; CANR 4,
35; CLR 6; DLB 48, 51; JRDA;
MAICYA; MTCW; SATA 2, 44;
SATA-Obit 24

Booth, Martin 1944- . . . . **CLC 13**
See also CA 93-96; CAAS 2

Booth, Philip 1925- . . . . **CLC 23**
See also CA 5-8R; CANR 5; DLBY 82

Booth, Wayne C(layson) 1921- . . . . . **CLC 24**
See also CA 1-4R; CAAS 5; CANR 3, 43;
DLB 67

Borchert, Wolfgang 1921-1947 . . . . . **TCLC 5**
See also CA 104; DLB 69, 124

Borel, Petrus 1809-1859 . . . . **NCLC 41**

Borges, Jorge Luis
1899-1986 . . . **CLC 1, 2, 3, 4, 6, 8, 9, 10,**
13, 19, 44, 48, 83; DA; DAB; DAC;
DAM MST, MULT; HLC; SSC 4; WLC
See also CA 21-24R; CANR 19, 33;
DLB 113; DLBY 86; HW; MTCW

Borowski, Tadeusz 1922-1951 . . . . . . **TCLC 9**
See also CA 106

Borrow, George (Henry)
1803-1881 . . . . **NCLC 9**
See also DLB 21, 55, 166

Bosman, Herman Charles
1905-1951 . . . . **TCLC 49**

Bosschere, Jean de 1878(?)-1953 . . . **TCLC 19**
See also CA 115

Boswell, James
1740-1795 . . . . . . **LC 4; DA; DAB; DAC;**
DAM MST; WLC
See also CDBLB 1660-1789; DLB 104, 142

Bottoms, David 1949- . . . . **CLC 53**
See also CA 105; CANR 22; DLB 120;
DLBY 83

Boucicault, Dion 1820-1890 . . . . . . **NCLC 41**

Boucolon, Maryse 1937(?)-
See Conde, Maryse
See also CA 110; CANR 30, 53

Bourget, Paul (Charles Joseph)
1852-1935 . . . . **TCLC 12**
See also CA 107; DLB 123

Bourjaily, Vance (Nye) 1922- . . . . **CLC 8, 62**
See also CA 1-4R; CAAS 1; CANR 2;
DLB 2, 143

Bourne, Randolph S(illiman)
1886-1918 . . . . **TCLC 16**
See also CA 117; DLB 63

Bova, Ben(jamin William) 1932- . . . . **CLC 45**
See also AAYA 16; CA 5-8R; CAAS 18;
CANR 11; CLR 3; DLBY 81;
INT CANR-11; MAICYA; MTCW;
SATA 6, 68

Bowen, Elizabeth (Dorothea Cole)
1899-1973 . . . . . **CLC 1, 3, 6, 11, 15, 22;**
DAM NOV; SSC 3
See also CA 17-18; 41-44R; CANR 35;
CAP 2; CDBLB 1945-1960; DLB 15, 162;
MTCW

Bowering, George 1935- . . . . **CLC 15, 47**
See also CA 21-24R; CAAS 16; CANR 10;
DLB 53

Bowering, Marilyn R(uthe) 1949- . . . **CLC 32**
See also CA 101; CANR 49

Bowers, Edgar 1924- . . . . **CLC 9**
See also CA 5-8R; CANR 24; DLB 5

Bowie, David . . . . **CLC 17**
See also Jones, David Robert

Bowles, Jane (Sydney)
1917-1973 . . . . **CLC 3, 68**
See also CA 19-20; 41-44R; CAP 2

Bowles, Paul (Frederick)
1910- . . . . **CLC 1, 2, 19, 53; SSC 3**
See also CA 1-4R; CAAS 1; CANR 1, 19,
50; DLB 5, 6; MTCW

Box, Edgar
See Vidal, Gore

Boyd, Nancy
See Millay, Edna St. Vincent

Boyd, William 1952- . . . . **CLC 28, 53, 70**
See also CA 114; 120; CANR 51

Boyle, Kay
1902-1992 . . . . . **CLC 1, 5, 19, 58; SSC 5**
See also CA 13-16R; 140; CAAS 1;
CANR 29; DLB 4, 9, 48, 86; DLBY 93;
MTCW

Boyle, Mark
See Kienzle, William X(avier)

Boyle, Patrick 1905-1982 . . . . **CLC 19**
See also CA 127

Boyle, T. C. 1948-
See Boyle, T(homas) Coraghessan

Boyle, T(homas) Coraghessan
1948- . . . . . **CLC 36, 55, 90; DAM POP;**
SSC 16
See also BEST 90:4; CA 120; CANR 44;
DLBY 86

Boz
See Dickens, Charles (John Huffam)

Brackenridge, Hugh Henry
1748-1816 . . . . **NCLC 7**
See also DLB 11, 37

Bradbury, Edward P.
See Moorcock, Michael (John)

Bradbury, Malcolm (Stanley)
1932- . . . . **CLC 32, 61; DAM NOV**
See also CA 1-4R; CANR 1, 33; DLB 14;
MTCW

Bradbury, Ray (Douglas)
1920- . . . . **CLC 1, 3, 10, 15, 42; DA;**
DAB; DAC; DAM MST, NOV, POP;
WLC
See also AAYA 15; AITN 1, 2; CA 1-4R;
CANR 2, 30; CDALB 1968-1988; DLB 2,
8; INT CANR-30; MTCW; SATA 11, 64

Bradford, Gamaliel 1863-1932 . . . . . **TCLC 36**
See also DLB 17

Bradley, David (Henry, Jr.)
1950- . . . . . **CLC 23; BLC; DAM MULT**
See also BW 1; CA 104; CANR 26; DLB 33

Bradley, John Ed(mund, Jr.)
1958- . . . . **CLC 55**
See also CA 139

Bradley, Marion Zimmer
1930- . . . . **CLC 30; DAM POP**
See also AAYA 9; CA 57-60; CAAS 10;
CANR 7, 31, 51; DLB 8; MTCW

Bradstreet, Anne
1612(?)-1672 . . . . . . **LC 4, 30; DA; DAC;**
DAM MST, POET; PC 10
See also CDALB 1640-1865; DLB 24

Brady, Joan 1939- . . . . **CLC 86**
See also CA 141

Bragg, Melvyn 1939- . . . . **CLC 10**
See also BEST 89:3; CA 57-60; CANR 10,
48; DLB 14

Braine, John (Gerard)
1922-1986 . . . . **CLC 1, 3, 41**
See also CA 1-4R; 120; CANR 1, 33;
CDBLB 1945-1960; DLB 15; DLBY 86;
MTCW

Brammer, William 1930(?)-1978 . . . . **CLC 31**
See also CA 77-80

Brancati, Vitaliano 1907-1954 . . . . . **TCLC 12**
See also CA 109

Brancato, Robin F(idler) 1936- . . . . . **CLC 35**
See also AAYA 9; CA 69-72; CANR 11,
45; CLR 32; JRDA; SAAS 9; SATA 23

Brand, Max
See Faust, Frederick (Schiller)

Brand, Millen 1906-1980 . . . . **CLC 7**
See also CA 21-24R; 97-100

Branden, Barbara . . . . **CLC 44**
See also CA 148

Brandes, Georg (Morris Cohen)
1842-1927 . . . . **TCLC 10**
See also CA 105

Brandys, Kazimierz 1916- . . . . **CLC 62**

Branley, Franklyn M(ansfield)
1915- . . . . **CLC 21**
See also CA 33-36R; CANR 14, 39;
CLR 13; MAICYA; SAAS 16; SATA 4,
68

Brathwaite, Edward Kamau
1930- . . . . **CLC 11; DAM POET**
See also BW 2; CA 25-28R; CANR 11, 26,
47; DLB 125

Brautigan, Richard (Gary)
1935-1984 . . . . **CLC 1, 3, 5, 9, 12, 34, 42;**
DAM NOV
See also CA 53-56; 113; CANR 34; DLB 2,
5; DLBY 80, 84; MTCW; SATA 56

Brave Bird, Mary 1953-
See Crow Dog, Mary
See also NNAL

Braverman, Kate 1950- . . . . **CLC 67**
See also CA 89-92

Brecht, Bertolt
1898-1956 . . . . . . **TCLC 1, 6, 13, 35; DA;**
DAB; DAC; DAM DRAM, MST; DC 3;
WLC
See also CA 104; 133; DLB 56, 124; MTCW

Brown, William Wells
1813-1884 . . . . NCLC 2; BLC;
DAM MULT; DC 1
See also DLB 3, 50

Browne, (Clyde) Jackson 1948(?)-. . . CLC 21
See also CA 120

Browning, Elizabeth Barrett
1806-1861 . . . . . NCLC 1, 16; DA; DAB;
DAC; DAM MST, POET; PC 6; WLC
See also CDBLB 1832-1890; DLB 32

Browning, Robert
1812-1889 . . . . NCLC 19; DA; DAB;
DAC; DAM MST, POET; PC 2
See also CDBLB 1832-1890; DLB 32, 163;
YABC 1

Browning, Tod 1882-1962 . . . . CLC 16
See also CA 141; 117

Brownson, Orestes (Augustus)
1803-1876 . . . . NCLC 50

Bruccoli, Matthew J(oseph) 1931- . . CLC 34
See also CA 9-12R; CANR 7; DLB 103

Bruce, Lenny . . . . CLC 21
See also Schneider, Leonard Alfred

Bruin, John
See Brutus, Dennis

Brulard, Henri
See Stendhal

Brulls, Christian
See Simenon, Georges (Jacques Christian)

Brunner, John (Kilian Houston)
1934-1995 . . . . . . CLC 8, 10; DAM POP
See also CA 1-4R; 149; CAAS 8; CANR 2,
37; MTCW

Bruno, Giordano 1548-1600 . . . . LC 27

Brutus, Dennis
1924- . . . . . CLC 43; BLC; DAM MULT,
POET
See also BW 2; CA 49-52; CAAS 14;
CANR 2, 27, 42; DLB 117

Bryan, C(ourtlandt) D(ixon) B(arnes)
1936- . . . . CLC 29
See also CA 73-76; CANR 13;
INT CANR-13

Bryan, Michael
See Moore, Brian

Bryant, William Cullen
1794-1878 . . . . . NCLC 6, 46; DA; DAB;
DAC; DAM MST, POET
See also CDALB 1640-1865; DLB 3, 43, 59

Bryusov, Valery Yakovlevich
1873-1924 . . . . TCLC 10
See also CA 107

Buchan, John
1875-1940 . . . . TCLC 41; DAB;
DAM POP
See also CA 108; 145; DLB 34, 70, 156;
YABC 2

Buchanan, George 1506-1582 . . . . LC 4

Buchheim, Lothar-Guenther 1918- . . . CLC 6
See also CA 85-88

Buchner, (Karl) Georg
1813-1837 . . . . NCLC 26

Buchwald, Art(hur) 1925-. . . . . CLC 33
See also AITN 1; CA 5-8R; CANR 21;
MTCW; SATA 10

Buck, Pearl S(ydenstricker)
1892-1973 . . . . CLC 7, 11, 18; DA; DAB;
DAC; DAM MST, NOV
See also AITN 1; CA 1-4R; 41-44R;
CANR 1, 34; DLB 9, 102; MTCW;
SATA 1, 25

Buckler, Ernest
1908-1984 . . CLC 13; DAC; DAM MST
See also CA 11-12; 114; CAP 1; DLB 68;
SATA 47

Buckley, Vincent (Thomas)
1925-1988 . . . . CLC 57
See also CA 101

Buckley, William F(rank), Jr.
1925- . . . . CLC 7, 18, 37; DAM POP
See also AITN 1; CA 1-4R; CANR 1, 24,
53; DLB 137; DLBY 80; INT CANR-24;
MTCW

Buechner, (Carl) Frederick
1926- . . . . . . CLC 2, 4, 6, 9; DAM NOV
See also CA 13-16R; CANR 11, 39;
DLBY 80; INT CANR-11; MTCW

Buell, John (Edward) 1927-. . . . . CLC 10
See also CA 1-4R; DLB 53

Buero Vallejo, Antonio 1916- . . . CLC 15, 46
See also CA 106; CANR 24, 49; HW;
MTCW

Bufalino, Gesualdo 1920(?)-. . . . . CLC 74

Bugayev, Boris Nikolayevich 1880-1934
See Bely, Andrey
See also CA 104

Bukowski, Charles
1920-1994 . . . . CLC 2, 5, 9, 41, 82;
DAM NOV, POET
See also CA 17-20R; 144; CANR 40;
DLB 5, 130; MTCW

Bulgakov, Mikhail (Afanas'evich)
1891-1940 . . . . TCLC 2, 16;
DAM DRAM, NOV; SSC 18
See also CA 105; 152

Bulgya, Alexander Alexandrovich
1901-1956 . . . . TCLC 53
See also Fadeyev, Alexander
See also CA 117

Bullins, Ed
1935- . . . . CLC 1, 5, 7; BLC;
DAM DRAM, MULT; DC 6
See also BW 2; CA 49-52; CAAS 16;
CANR 24, 46; DLB 7, 38; MTCW

Bulwer-Lytton, Edward (George Earle Lytton)
1803-1873 . . . . NCLC 1, 45
See also DLB 21

Bunin, Ivan Alexeyevich
1870-1953 . . . . TCLC 6; SSC 5
See also CA 104

Bunting, Basil
1900-1985 . . . . CLC 10, 39, 47;
DAM POET
See also CA 53-56; 115; CANR 7; DLB 20

Bunuel, Luis
1900-1983 . . . . CLC 16, 80;
DAM MULT; HLC
See also CA 101; 110; CANR 32; HW

Bunyan, John
1628-1688 . . . . . . LC 4; DA; DAB; DAC;
DAM MST; WLC
See also CDBLB 1660-1789; DLB 39

Burckhardt, Jacob (Christoph)
1818-1897 . . . . NCLC 49

Burford, Eleanor
See Hibbert, Eleanor Alice Burford

Burgess, Anthony
CLC 1, 2, 4, 5, 8, 10, 13, 15, 22, 40, 62,
81, 94; DAB
See also Wilson, John (Anthony) Burgess
See also AITN 1; CDBLB 1960 to Present;
DLB 14

Burke, Edmund
1729(?)-1797 . . . . LC 7; DA; DAB; DAC;
DAM MST; WLC
See also DLB 104

Burke, Kenneth (Duva)
1897-1993 . . . . CLC 2, 24
See also CA 5-8R; 143; CANR 39; DLB 45,
63; MTCW

Burke, Leda
See Garnett, David

Burke, Ralph
See Silverberg, Robert

Burke, Thomas 1886-1945 . . . . TCLC 63
See also CA 113

Burney, Fanny 1752-1840 . . . . NCLC 12, 54
See also DLB 39

Burns, Robert 1759-1796. . . . . PC 6
See also CDBLB 1789-1832; DA; DAB;
DAC; DAM MST, POET; DLB 109;
WLC

Burns, Tex
See L'Amour, Louis (Dearborn)

Burnshaw, Stanley 1906-. . . . . CLC 3, 13, 44
See also CA 9-12R; DLB 48

Burr, Anne 1937-. . . . . CLC 6
See also CA 25-28R

Burroughs, Edgar Rice
1875-1950 . . . . TCLC 2, 32; DAM NOV
See also AAYA 11; CA 104; 132; DLB 8;
MTCW; SATA 41

Burroughs, William S(eward)
1914- . . . . CLC 1, 2, 5, 15, 22, 42, 75;
DA; DAB; DAC; DAM MST, NOV,
POP; WLC
See also AITN 2; CA 9-12R; CANR 20, 52;
DLB 2, 8, 16, 152; DLBY 81; MTCW

Burton, Richard F. 1821-1890. . . . NCLC 42
See also DLB 55

Busch, Frederick 1941- . . . CLC 7, 10, 18, 47
See also CA 33-36R; CAAS 1; CANR 45;
DLB 6

Bush, Ronald 1946- . . . . CLC 34
See also CA 136

Bustos, F(rancisco)
See Borges, Jorge Luis

Bustos Domecq, H(onorio)
See Bioy Casares, Adolfo; Borges, Jorge
Luis

Butler, Octavia E(stelle)
1947- . . . . . CLC 38; DAM MULT, POP
See also AAYA 18; BW 2; CA 73-76;
CANR 12, 24, 38; DLB 33; MTCW;
SATA 84

Butler, Robert Olen (Jr.)
1945- .... **CLC 81; DAM POP**
See also CA 112; INT 112

Butler, Samuel 1612-1680 .... **LC 16**
See also DLB 101, 126

Butler, Samuel
1835-1902 ...... **TCLC 1, 33; DA; DAB;**
DAC; DAM MST, NOV; WLC
See also CA 143; CDBLB 1890-1914;
DLB 18, 57

Butler, Walter C.
See Faust, Frederick (Schiller)

Butor, Michel (Marie Francois)
1926- .... **CLC 1, 3, 8, 11, 15**
See also CA 9-12R; CANR 33; DLB 83;
MTCW

Buzo, Alexander (John) 1944-...... **CLC 61**
See also CA 97-100; CANR 17, 39

Buzzati, Dino 1906-1972 .... **CLC 36**
See also CA 33-36R

Byars, Betsy (Cromer) 1928-....... **CLC 35**
See also CA 33-36R; CANR 18, 36; CLR 1,
16; DLB 52; INT CANR-18; JRDA;
MAICYA; MTCW; SAAS 1; SATA 4,
46, 80

Byatt, A(ntonia) S(usan Drabble)
1936- ... **CLC 19, 65; DAM NOV, POP**
See also CA 13-16R; CANR 13, 33, 50;
DLB 14; MTCW

Byrne, David 1952-............... **CLC 26**
See also CA 127

Byrne, John Keyes 1926-
See Leonard, Hugh
See also CA 102; INT 102

Byron, George Gordon (Noel)
1788-1824 ..... **NCLC 2, 12; DA; DAB;**
DAC; DAM MST, POET; PC 16; WLC
See also CDBLB 1789-1832; DLB 96, 110

C. 3. 3.
See Wilde, Oscar (Fingal O'Flahertie Wills)

Caballero, Fernan 1796-1877..... **NCLC 10**

Cabell, Branch
See Cabell, James Branch

Cabell, James Branch 1879-1958 ... **TCLC 6**
See also CA 105; 152; DLB 9, 78

Cable, George Washington
1844-1925 .... **TCLC 4; SSC 4**
See also CA 104; DLB 12, 74; DLBD 13

Cabral de Melo Neto, Joao
1920- .... **CLC 76; DAM MULT**
See also CA 151

Cabrera Infante, G(uillermo)
1929- ..... **CLC 5, 25, 45; DAM MULT;**
HLC
See also CA 85-88; CANR 29; DLB 113;
HW; MTCW

Cade, Toni
See Bambara, Toni Cade

Cadmus and Harmonia
See Buchan, John

Caedmon fl. 658-680............. **CMLC 7**
See also DLB 146

Caeiro, Alberto
See Pessoa, Fernando (Antonio Nogueira)

Cage, John (Milton, Jr.) 1912- ..... **CLC 41**
See also CA 13-16R; CANR 9;
INT CANR-9

Cain, G.
See Cabrera Infante, G(uillermo)

Cain, Guillermo
See Cabrera Infante, G(uillermo)

Cain, James M(allahan)
1892-1977 .... **CLC 3, 11, 28**
See also AITN 1; CA 17-20R; 73-76;
CANR 8, 34; MTCW

Caine, Mark
See Raphael, Frederic (Michael)

Calasso, Roberto 1941- .... **CLC 81**
See also CA 143

Calderon de la Barca, Pedro
1600-1681 .... **LC 23; DC 3**

Caldwell, Erskine (Preston)
1903-1987 .... **CLC 1, 8, 14, 50, 60;**
DAM NOV; SSC 19
See also AITN 1; CA 1-4R; 121; CAAS 1;
CANR 2, 33; DLB 9, 86; MTCW

Caldwell, (Janet Miriam) Taylor (Holland)
1900-1985 .... **CLC 2, 28, 39;**
DAM NOV, POP
See also CA 5-8R; 116; CANR 5

Calhoun, John Caldwell
1782-1850 .... **NCLC 15**
See also DLB 3

Calisher, Hortense
1911- ..... **CLC 2, 4, 8, 38; DAM NOV;**
SSC 15
See also CA 1-4R; CANR 1, 22; DLB 2;
INT CANR-22; MTCW

Callaghan, Morley Edward
1903-1990 ..... **CLC 3, 14, 41, 65; DAC;**
DAM MST
See also CA 9-12R; 132; CANR 33;
DLB 68; MTCW

Callimachus
c. 305B.C.-c. 240B.C......... **CMLC 18**

Calvino, Italo
1923-1985 ..... **CLC 5, 8, 11, 22, 33, 39,**
73; DAM NOV; SSC 3
See also CA 85-88; 116; CANR 23; MTCW

Cameron, Carey 1952-............ **CLC 59**
See also CA 135

Cameron, Peter 1959-............. **CLC 44**
See also CA 125; CANR 50

Campana, Dino 1885-1932........ **TCLC 20**
See also CA 117; DLB 114

Campanella, Tommaso 1568-1639 .... **LC 32**

Campbell, John W(ood, Jr.)
1910-1971 .... **CLC 32**
See also CA 21-22; 29-32R; CANR 34;
CAP 2; DLB 8; MTCW

Campbell, Joseph 1904-1987 .... **CLC 69**
See also AAYA 3; BEST 89:2; CA 1-4R;
124; CANR 3, 28; MTCW

Campbell, Maria 1940-....... **CLC 85; DAC**
See also CA 102; NNAL

Campbell, (John) Ramsey
1946- .... **CLC 42; SSC 19**
See also CA 57-60; CANR 7; INT CANR-7

Campbell, (Ignatius) Roy (Dunnachie)
1901-1957 ....**TCLC 5**
See also CA 104; DLB 20

Campbell, Thomas 1777-1844 .... **NCLC 19**
See also DLB 93; 144

Campbell, Wilfred................ **TCLC 9**
See also Campbell, William

Campbell, William 1858(?)-1918
See Campbell, Wilfred
See also CA 106; DLB 92

Campion, Jane................... **CLC 95**
See also CA 138

Campos, Alvaro de
See Pessoa, Fernando (Antonio Nogueira)

Camus, Albert
1913-1960 .... **CLC 1, 2, 4, 9, 11, 14, 32,**
63, 69; DA; DAB; DAC; DAM DRAM,
MST, NOV; DC 2; SSC 9; WLC
See also CA 89-92; DLB 72; MTCW

Canby, Vincent 1924-............. **CLC 13**
See also CA 81-84

Cancale
See Desnos, Robert

Canetti, Elias
1905-1994 .... **CLC 3, 14, 25, 75, 86**
See also CA 21-24R; 146; CANR 23;
DLB 85, 124; MTCW

Canin, Ethan 1960-............... **CLC 55**
See also CA 131; 135

Cannon, Curt
See Hunter, Evan

Cape, Judith
See Page, P(atricia) K(athleen)

Capek, Karel
1890-1938 ...... **TCLC 6, 37; DA; DAB;**
DAC; DAM DRAM, MST, NOV; DC 1;
WLC
See also CA 104; 140

Capote, Truman
1924-1984 ...... **CLC 1, 3, 8, 13, 19, 34,**
38, 58; DA; DAB; DAC; DAM MST,
NOV, POP; SSC 2; WLC
See also CA 5-8R; 113; CANR 18;
CDALB 1941-1968; DLB 2; DLBY 80,
84; MTCW

Capra, Frank 1897-1991.......... **CLC 16**
See also CA 61-64; 135

Caputo, Philip 1941-............. **CLC 32**
See also CA 73-76; CANR 40

Card, Orson Scott
1951- ...... **CLC 44, 47, 50; DAM POP**
See also AAYA 11; CA 102; CANR 27, 47;
INT CANR-27; MTCW; SATA 83

Cardenal, Ernesto
1925- .... **CLC 31; DAM MULT,**
POET; HLC
See also CA 49-52; CANR 2, 32; HW;
MTCW

Cardozo, Benjamin N(athan)
1870-1938 .... **TCLC 65**
See also CA 117

Carducci, Giosue 1835-1907....... **TCLC 32**

Carew, Thomas 1595(?)-1640........ **LC 13**
See also DLB 126

Carey, Ernestine Gilbreth 1908-.... **CLC 17**
See also CA 5-8R; SATA 2

Carey, Peter 1943-......... **CLC 40, 55, 96**
See also CA 123; 127; CANR 53; INT 127;
MTCW

Carleton, William 1794-1869..... **NCLC 3**
See also DLB 159

Carlisle, Henry (Coffin) 1926-..... **CLC 33**
See also CA 13-16R; CANR 15

Carlsen, Chris
See Holdstock, Robert P.

Carlson, Ron(ald F.) 1947-......... **CLC 54**
See also CA 105; CANR 27

Carlyle, Thomas
1795-1881 .... **NCLC 22; DA; DAB;
DAC; DAM MST**
See also CDBLB 1789-1832; DLB 55; 144

Carman, (William) Bliss
1861-1929 .... **TCLC 7; DAC**
See also CA 104; 152; DLB 92

Carnegie, Dale 1888-1955 .... **TCLC 53**

Carossa, Hans 1878-1956........ **TCLC 48**
See also DLB 66

Carpenter, Don(ald Richard)
1931-1995 .... **CLC 41**
See also CA 45-48; 149; CANR 1

Carpentier (y Valmont), Alejo
1904-1980 .... **CLC 8, 11, 38;
DAM MULT; HLC**
See also CA 65-68; 97-100; CANR 11;
DLB 113; HW

Carr, Caleb 1955(?)-.............. **CLC 86**
See also CA 147

Carr, Emily 1871-1945........... **TCLC 32**
See also DLB 68

Carr, John Dickson 1906-1977 ...... **CLC 3**
See also CA 49-52; 69-72; CANR 3, 33;
MTCW

Carr, Philippa
See Hibbert, Eleanor Alice Burford

Carr, Virginia Spencer 1929-....... **CLC 34**
See also CA 61-64; DLB 111

Carrere, Emmanuel 1957- .... **CLC 89**

Carrier, Roch
1937- ... **CLC 13, 78; DAC; DAM MST**
See also CA 130; DLB 53

Carroll, James P. 1943(?)-......... **CLC 38**
See also CA 81-84

Carroll, Jim 1951- .... **CLC 35**
See also AAYA 17; CA 45-48; CANR 42

Carroll, Lewis .... **NCLC 2, 53; WLC**
See also Dodgson, Charles Lutwidge
See also CDBLB 1832-1890; CLR 2, 18;
DLB 18, 163; JRDA

Carroll, Paul Vincent 1900-1968.... **CLC 10**
See also CA 9-12R; 25-28R; DLB 10

Carruth, Hayden
1921- ...... **CLC 4, 7, 10, 18, 84; PC 10**
See also CA 9-12R; CANR 4, 38; DLB 5,
165; INT CANR-4; MTCW; SATA 47

Carson, Rachel Louise
1907-1964 .... **CLC 71; DAM POP**
See also CA 77-80; CANR 35; MTCW;
SATA 23

Carter, Angela (Olive)
1940-1992 ...... **CLC 5, 41, 76; SSC 13**
See also CA 53-56; 136; CANR 12, 36;
DLB 14; MTCW; SATA 66;
SATA-Obit 70

Carter, Nick
See Smith, Martin Cruz

Carver, Raymond
1938-1988 .... **CLC 22, 36, 53, 55;
DAM NOV; SSC 8**
See also CA 33-36R; 126; CANR 17, 34;
DLB 130; DLBY 84, 88; MTCW

Cary, Elizabeth, Lady Falkland
1585-1639 .... **LC 30**

Cary, (Arthur) Joyce (Lunel)
1888-1957 .... **TCLC 1, 29**
See also CA 104; CDBLB 1914-1945;
DLB 15, 100

Casanova de Seingalt, Giovanni Jacopo
1725-1798 .... **LC 13**

Casares, Adolfo Bioy
See Bioy Casares, Adolfo

Casely-Hayford, J(oseph) E(phraim)
1866-1930 .... **TCLC 24; BLC;
DAM MULT**
See also BW 2; CA 123; 152

Casey, John (Dudley) 1939-........ **CLC 59**
See also BEST 90:2; CA 69-72; CANR 23

Casey, Michael 1947-.............. **CLC 2**
See also CA 65-68; DLB 5

Casey, Patrick
See Thurman, Wallace (Henry)

Casey, Warren (Peter) 1935-1988... **CLC 12**
See also CA 101; 127; INT 101

Casona, Alejandro................. **CLC 49**
See also Alvarez, Alejandro Rodriguez

Cassavetes, John 1929-1989........ **CLC 20**
See also CA 85-88; 127

Cassill, R(onald) V(erlin) 1919-... **CLC 4, 23**
See also CA 9-12R; CAAS 1; CANR 7, 45;
DLB 6

Cassirer, Ernst 1874-1945 .... **TCLC 61**

Cassity, (Allen) Turner 1929- .... **CLC 6, 42**
See also CA 17-20R; CAAS 8; CANR 11;
DLB 105

Castaneda, Carlos 1931(?)-........ **CLC 12**
See also CA 25-28R; CANR 32; HW;
MTCW

Castedo, Elena 1937- .... **CLC 65**
See also CA 132

Castedo-Ellerman, Elena
See Castedo, Elena

Castellanos, Rosario
1925-1974 ...... **CLC 66; DAM MULT;
HLC**
See also CA 131; 53-56; DLB 113; HW

Castelvetro, Lodovico 1505-1571..... **LC 12**

Castiglione, Baldassare 1478-1529 ... **LC 12**

Castle, Robert
See Hamilton, Edmond

Castro, Guillen de 1569-1631........ **LC 19**

Castro, Rosalia de
1837-1885 ...... **NCLC 3; DAM MULT**

Cather, Willa
See Cather, Willa Sibert

Cather, Willa Sibert
1873-1947 .... **TCLC 1, 11, 31; DA;
DAB; DAC; DAM MST, NOV; SSC 2;
WLC**
See also CA 104; 128; CDALB 1865-1917;
DLB 9, 54, 78; DLBD 1; MTCW;
SATA 30

Catton, (Charles) Bruce
1899-1978 .... **CLC 35**
See also AITN 1; CA 5-8R; 81-84;
CANR 7; DLB 17; SATA 2;
SATA-Obit 24

Catullus c. 84B.C.-c. 54B.C. ..... **CMLC 18**

Cauldwell, Frank
See King, Francis (Henry)

Caunitz, William J. 1933-1996 ..... **CLC 34**
See also BEST 89:3; CA 125; 130; 152;
INT 130

Causley, Charles (Stanley) 1917-..... **CLC 7**
See also CA 9-12R; CANR 5, 35; CLR 30;
DLB 27; MTCW; SATA 3, 66

Caute, David 1936-.... **CLC 29; DAM NOV**
See also CA 1-4R; CAAS 4; CANR 1, 33;
DLB 14

Cavafy, C(onstantine) P(eter)
1863-1933 .... **TCLC 2, 7; DAM POET**
See also Kavafis, Konstantinos Petrou
See also CA 148

Cavallo, Evelyn
See Spark, Muriel (Sarah)

Cavanna, Betty .... **CLC 12**
See also Harrison, Elizabeth Cavanna
See also JRDA; MAICYA; SAAS 4;
SATA 1, 30

Cavendish, Margaret Lucas
1623-1673 .... **LC 30**
See also DLB 131

Caxton, William 1421(?)-1491(?)..... **LC 17**

Cayrol, Jean 1911-................ **CLC 11**
See also CA 89-92; DLB 83

Cela, Camilo Jose
1916- ..... **CLC 4, 13, 59; DAM MULT;
HLC**
See also BEST 90:2; CA 21-24R; CAAS 10;
CANR 21, 32; DLBY 89; HW; MTCW

Celan, Paul ...... **CLC 10, 19, 53, 82; PC 10**
See also Antschel, Paul
See also DLB 69

Celine, Louis-Ferdinand
.... **CLC 1, 3, 4, 7, 9, 15, 47**
See also Destouches, Louis-Ferdinand
See also DLB 72

Cellini, Benvenuto 1500-1571 .... **LC 7**

Cendrars, Blaise .... **CLC 18**
See also Sauser-Hall, Frederic

Cernuda (y Bidon), Luis
1902-1963 .... **CLC 54; DAM POET**
See also CA 131; 89-92; DLB 134; HW

Cervantes (Saavedra), Miguel de
1547-1616 .... **LC 6, 23; DA; DAB;
DAC; DAM MST, NOV; SSC 12; WLC**

Christie
See Ichikawa, Kon

Christie, Agatha (Mary Clarissa)
1890-1976 ...... **CLC 1, 6, 8, 12, 39, 48;**
DAB; DAC; DAM NOV
See also AAYA 9; AITN 1, 2; CA 17-20R;
61-64; CANR 10, 37; CDBLB 1914-1945;
DLB 13, 77; MTCW; SATA 36

Christie, (Ann) Philippa
See Pearce, Philippa
See also CA 5-8R; CANR 4

Christine de Pizan 1365(?)-1431(?) .... **LC 9**

Chubb, Elmer
See Masters, Edgar Lee

Chulkov, Mikhail Dmitrievich
1743-1792 .... **LC 2**
See also DLB 150

Churchill, Caryl 1938- ... **CLC 31, 55; DC 5**
See also CA 102; CANR 22, 46; DLB 13;
MTCW

Churchill, Charles 1731-1764........ **LC 3**
See also DLB 109

Chute, Carolyn 1947- .... **CLC 39**
See also CA 123

Ciardi, John (Anthony)
1916-1986 .... **CLC 10, 40, 44;**
DAM POET
See also CA 5-8R; 118; CAAS 2; CANR 5,
33; CLR 19; DLB 5; DLBY 86;
INT CANR-5; MAICYA; MTCW;
SATA 1, 65; SATA-Obit 46

Cicero, Marcus Tullius
106B.C.-43B.C.............. **CMLC 3**

Cimino, Michael 1943-............. **CLC 16**
See also CA 105

Cioran, E(mil) M. 1911-1995....... **CLC 64**
See also CA 25-28R; 149

Cisneros, Sandra
1954- ..... **CLC 69; DAM MULT; HLC**
See also AAYA 9; CA 131; DLB 122, 152;
HW

Cixous, Helene 1937-............. **CLC 92**
See also CA 126; DLB 83; MTCW

Clair, Rene..................... **CLC 20**
See also Chomette, Rene Lucien

Clampitt, Amy 1920-1994 .... **CLC 32**
See also CA 110; 146; CANR 29; DLB 105

Clancy, Thomas L., Jr. 1947-
See Clancy, Tom
See also CA 125; 131; INT 131; MTCW

Clancy, Tom..... **CLC 45; DAM NOV, POP**
See also Clancy, Thomas L., Jr.
See also AAYA 9; BEST 89:1, 90:1

Clare, John
1793-1864 .... **NCLC 9; DAB;**
DAM POET
See also DLB 55, 96

Clarin
See Alas (y Urena), Leopoldo (Enrique
Garcia)

Clark, Al C.
See Goines, Donald

Clark, (Robert) Brian 1932-........ **CLC 29**
See also CA 41-44R

Clark, Curt
See Westlake, Donald E(dwin)

Clark, Eleanor 1913-1996 ...... **CLC 5, 19**
See also CA 9-12R; 151; CANR 41; DLB 6

Clark, J. P.
See Clark, John Pepper
See also DLB 117

Clark, John Pepper
1935- .... **CLC 38; BLC; DAM DRAM,**
MULT; DC 5
See also Clark, J. P.
See also BW 1; CA 65-68; CANR 16

Clark, M. R.
See Clark, Mavis Thorpe

Clark, Mavis Thorpe 1909-........ **CLC 12**
See also CA 57-60; CANR 8, 37; CLR 30;
MAICYA; SAAS 5; SATA 8, 74

Clark, Walter Van Tilburg
1909-1971 .... **CLC 28**
See also CA 9-12R; 33-36R; DLB 9;
SATA 8

Clarke, Arthur C(harles)
1917- .... **CLC 1, 4, 13, 18, 35;**
DAM POP; SSC 3
See also AAYA 4; CA 1-4R; CANR 2, 28;
JRDA; MAICYA; MTCW; SATA 13, 70

Clarke, Austin
1896-1974 ...... **CLC 6, 9; DAM POET**
See also CA 29-32; 49-52; CAP 2; DLB 10,
20

Clarke, Austin C(hesterfield)
1934- .... **CLC 8, 53; BLC; DAC;**
DAM MULT
See also BW 1; CA 25-28R; CAAS 16;
CANR 14, 32; DLB 53, 125

Clarke, Gillian 1937-............. **CLC 61**
See also CA 106; DLB 40

Clarke, Marcus (Andrew Hislop)
1846-1881 .... **NCLC 19**

Clarke, Shirley 1925-............. **CLC 16**

Clash, The
See Headon, (Nicky) Topper; Jones, Mick;
Simonon, Paul; Strummer, Joe

Claudel, Paul (Louis Charles Marie)
1868-1955 .... **TCLC 2, 10**
See also CA 104

Clavell, James (duMaresq)
1925-1994 .... **CLC 6, 25, 87;**
DAM NOV, POP
See also CA 25-28R; 146; CANR 26, 48;
MTCW

Cleaver, (Leroy) Eldridge
1935- ..... **CLC 30; BLC; DAM MULT**
See also BW 1; CA 21-24R; CANR 16

Cleese, John (Marwood) 1939- ..... **CLC 21**
See also Monty Python
See also CA 112; 116; CANR 35; MTCW

Cleishbotham, Jebediah
See Scott, Walter

Cleland, John 1710-1789 .... **LC 2**
See also DLB 39

Clemens, Samuel Langhorne 1835-1910
See Twain, Mark
See also CA 104; 135; CDALB 1865-1917;
DA; DAB; DAC; DAM MST, NOV;
DLB 11, 12, 23, 64, 74; JRDA;
MAICYA; YABC 2

Cleophil
See Congreve, William

Clerihew, E.
See Bentley, E(dmund) C(lerihew)

Clerk, N. W.
See Lewis, C(live) S(taples)

Cliff, Jimmy..................... **CLC 21**
See also Chambers, James

Clifton, (Thelma) Lucille
1936-.............. **CLC 19, 66; BLC;**
DAM MULT, POET
See also BW 2; CA 49-52; CANR 2, 24, 42;
CLR 5; DLB 5, 41; MAICYA; MTCW;
SATA 20, 69

Clinton, Dirk
See Silverberg, Robert

Clough, Arthur Hugh 1819-1861.. **NCLC 27**
See also DLB 32

Clutha, Janet Paterson Frame 1924-
See Frame, Janet
See also CA 1-4R; CANR 2, 36; MTCW

Clyne, Terence
See Blatty, William Peter

Cobalt, Martin
See Mayne, William (James Carter)

Cobbett, William 1763-1835 ..... **NCLC 49**
See also DLB 43, 107, 158

Coburn, D(onald) L(ee) 1938- ...... **CLC 10**
See also CA 89-92

Cocteau, Jean (Maurice Eugene Clement)
1889-1963 .... **CLC 1, 8, 15, 16, 43; DA;**
DAB; DAC; DAM DRAM, MST, NOV;
WLC
See also CA 25-28; CANR 40; CAP 2;
DLB 65; MTCW

Codrescu, Andrei
1946- .... **CLC 46; DAM POET**
See also CA 33-36R; CAAS 19; CANR 13,
34, 53

Coe, Max
See Bourne, Randolph S(illiman)

Coe, Tucker
See Westlake, Donald E(dwin)

Coetzee, J(ohn) M(ichael)
1940- ...... **CLC 23, 33, 66; DAM NOV**
See also CA 77-80; CANR 41; MTCW

Coffey, Brian
See Koontz, Dean R(ay)

Cohan, George M. 1878-1942 ..... **TCLC 60**

Cohen, Arthur A(llen)
1928-1986 .... **CLC 7, 31**
See also CA 1-4R; 120; CANR 1, 17, 42;
DLB 28

Cohen, Leonard (Norman)
1934- .... **CLC 3, 38; DAC; DAM MST**
See also CA 21-24R; CANR 14; DLB 53;
MTCW

Crumb, R(obert) 1943-........... CLC 17
See also CA 106

Crumbum
See Crumb, R(obert)

Crumski
See Crumb, R(obert)

Crum the Bum
See Crumb, R(obert)

Crunk
See Crumb, R(obert)

Crustt
See Crumb, R(obert)

Cryer, Gretchen (Kiger) 1935-...... CLC 21
See also CA 114; 123

Csath, Geza 1887-1919.......... TCLC 13
See also CA 111

Cudlip, David 1933-.............. CLC 34

Cullen, Countee
1903-1946 ...... TCLC 4, 37; BLC; DA;
DAC; DAM MST, MULT, POET
See also BW 1; CA 108; 124;
CDALB 1917-1929; DLB 4, 48, 51;
MTCW; SATA 18

Cum, R.
See Crumb, R(obert)

Cummings, Bruce F(rederick) 1889-1919
See Barbellion, W. N. P.
See also CA 123

Cummings, E(dward) E(stlin)
1894-1962 ...... CLC 1, 3, 8, 12, 15, 68;
DA; DAB; DAC; DAM MST, POET;
PC 5; WLC 2
See also CA 73-76; CANR 31;
CDALB 1929-1941; DLB 4, 48; MTCW

Cunha, Euclides (Rodrigues Pimenta) da
1866-1909 .... TCLC 24
See also CA 123

Cunningham, E. V.
See Fast, Howard (Melvin)

Cunningham, J(ames) V(incent)
1911-1985 .... CLC 3, 31
See also CA 1-4R; 115; CANR 1; DLB 5

Cunningham, Julia (Woolfolk)
1916-....................... CLC 12
See also CA 9-12R; CANR 4, 19, 36;
JRDA; MAICYA; SAAS 2; SATA 1, 26

Cunningham, Michael 1952-....... CLC 34
See also CA 136

Cunninghame Graham, R(obert) B(ontine)
1852-1936 .... TCLC 19
See also Graham, R(obert) B(ontine)
Cunninghame
See also CA 119; DLB 98

Currie, Ellen 19(?)-.............. CLC 44

Curtin, Philip
See Lowndes, Marie Adelaide (Belloc)

Curtis, Price
See Ellison, Harlan (Jay)

Cutrate, Joe
See Spiegelman, Art

Czaczkes, Shmuel Yosef
See Agnon, S(hmuel) Y(osef Halevi)

Dabrowska, Maria (Szumska)
1889-1965 .... CLC 15
See also CA 106

Dabydeen, David 1955-........... CLC 34
See also BW 1; CA 125

Dacey, Philip 1939-.............. CLC 51
See also CA 37-40R; CAAS 17; CANR 14,
32; DLB 105

Dagerman, Stig (Halvard)
1923-1954 .... TCLC 17
See also CA 117

Dahl, Roald
1916-1990 ...... CLC 1, 6, 18, 79; DAB;
DAC; DAM MST, NOV, POP
See also AAYA 15; CA 1-4R; 133;
CANR 6, 32, 37; CLR 1, 7, 41; DLB 139;
JRDA; MAICYA; MTCW; SATA 1, 26,
73; SATA-Obit 65

Dahlberg, Edward 1900-1977... CLC 1, 7, 14
See also CA 9-12R; 69-72; CANR 31;
DLB 48; MTCW

Dale, Colin...................... TCLC 18
See also Lawrence, T(homas) E(dward)

Dale, George E.
See Asimov, Isaac

Daly, Elizabeth 1878-1967........ CLC 52
See also CA 23-24; 25-28R; CAP 2

Daly, Maureen 1921-............. CLC 17
See also AAYA 5; CANR 37; JRDA;
MAICYA; SAAS 1; SATA 2

Damas, Leon-Gontran 1912-1978 ... CLC 84
See also BW 1; CA 125; 73-76

Dana, Richard Henry Sr.
1787-1879 .... NCLC 53

Daniel, Samuel 1562(?)-1619....... LC 24
See also DLB 62

Daniels, Brett
See Adler, Renata

Dannay, Frederic
1905-1982 .... CLC 11; DAM POP
See also Queen, Ellery
See also CA 1-4R; 107; CANR 1, 39;
DLB 137; MTCW

D'Annunzio, Gabriele
1863-1938 .... TCLC 6, 40
See also CA 104

Danois, N. le
See Gourmont, Remy (-Marie-Charles) de

d'Antibes, Germain
See Simenon, Georges (Jacques Christian)

Danticat, Edwidge 1969-.......... CLC 94
See also CA 152

Danvers, Dennis 1947-........... CLC 70

Danziger, Paula 1944-............ CLC 21
See also AAYA 4; CA 112; 115; CANR 37;
CLR 20; JRDA; MAICYA; SATA 36,
63; SATA-Brief 30

Da Ponte, Lorenzo 1749-1838.... NCLC 50

Dario, Ruben
1867-1916 ..... TCLC 4; DAM MULT;
HLC; PC 15
See also CA 131; HW; MTCW

Darley, George 1795-1846........ NCLC 2
See also DLB 96

Darwin, Charles 1809-1882 ...... NCLC 57
See also DLB 57, 166

Daryush, Elizabeth 1887-1977.... CLC 6, 19
See also CA 49-52; CANR 3; DLB 20

Dashwood, Edmee Elizabeth Monica de la
Pasture 1890-1943
See Delafield, E. M.
See also CA 119

Daudet, (Louis Marie) Alphonse
1840-1897 .... NCLC 1
See also DLB 123

Daumal, Rene 1908-1944........ TCLC 14
See also CA 114

Davenport, Guy (Mattison, Jr.)
1927-.......... CLC 6, 14, 38; SSC 16
See also CA 33-36R; CANR 23; DLB 130

Davidson, Avram 1923-
See Queen, Ellery
See also CA 101; CANR 26; DLB 8

Davidson, Donald (Grady)
1893-1968 .... CLC 2, 13, 19
See also CA 5-8R; 25-28R; CANR 4;
DLB 45

Davidson, Hugh
See Hamilton, Edmond

Davidson, John 1857-1909....... TCLC 24
See also CA 118; DLB 19

Davidson, Sara 1943-............. CLC 9
See also CA 81-84; CANR 44

Davie, Donald (Alfred)
1922-1995 .... CLC 5, 8, 10, 31
See also CA 1-4R; 149; CAAS 3; CANR 1,
44; DLB 27; MTCW

Davies, Ray(mond Douglas) 1944- .. CLC 21
See also CA 116; 146

Davies, Rhys 1903-1978........... CLC 23
See also CA 9-12R; 81-84; CANR 4;
DLB 139

Davies, (William) Robertson
1913-1995 ..... CLC 2, 7, 13, 25, 42, 75,
91; DA; DAB; DAC; DAM MST, NOV,
POP; WLC
See also BEST 89:2; CA 33-36R; 150;
CANR 17, 42; DLB 68; INT CANR-17;
MTCW

Davies, W(illiam) H(enry)
1871-1940 .... TCLC 5
See also CA 104; DLB 19

Davies, Walter C.
See Kornbluth, C(yril) M.

Davis, Angela (Yvonne)
1944-.......... CLC 77; DAM MULT
See also BW 2; CA 57-60; CANR 10

Davis, B. Lynch
See Bioy Casares, Adolfo; Borges, Jorge
Luis

Davis, Gordon
See Hunt, E(verette) Howard, (Jr.)

Davis, Harold Lenoir 1896-1960.... CLC 49
See also CA 89-92; DLB 9

Davis, Rebecca (Blaine) Harding
1831-1910 .... TCLC 6
See also CA 104; DLB 74

Davis, Richard Harding
1864-1916 . . . . **TCLC 24**
See also CA 114; DLB 12, 23, 78, 79;
DLBD 13

Davison, Frank Dalby 1893-1970 . . . **CLC 15**
See also CA 116

Davison, Lawrence H.
See Lawrence, D(avid) H(erbert Richards)

Davison, Peter (Hubert) 1928- . . . . . **CLC 28**
See also CA 9-12R; CAAS 4; CANR 3, 43;
DLB 5

Davys, Mary 1674-1732 . . . . **LC 1**
See also DLB 39

Dawson, Fielding 1930- . . . . **CLC 6**
See also CA 85-88; DLB 130

Dawson, Peter
See Faust, Frederick (Schiller)

Day, Clarence (Shepard, Jr.)
1874-1935 . . . . **TCLC 25**
See also CA 108; DLB 11

Day, Thomas 1748-1789 . . . . **LC 1**
See also DLB 39; YABC 1

Day Lewis, C(ecil)
1904-1972 . . . . **CLC 1, 6, 10;**
DAM POET; PC 11
See also Blake, Nicholas
See also CA 13-16; 33-36R; CANR 34;
CAP 1; DLB 15, 20; MTCW

Dazai, Osamu . . . . **TCLC 11**
See also Tsushima, Shuji

de Andrade, Carlos Drummond
See Drummond de Andrade, Carlos

Deane, Norman
See Creasey, John

de Beauvoir, Simone (Lucie Ernestine Marie Bertrand)
See Beauvoir, Simone (Lucie Ernestine
Marie Bertrand) de

de Brissac, Malcolm
See Dickinson, Peter (Malcolm)

de Chardin, Pierre Teilhard
See Teilhard de Chardin, (Marie Joseph)
Pierre

Dee, John 1527-1608 . . . . **LC 20**

Deer, Sandra 1940- . . . . **CLC 45**

De Ferrari, Gabriella 1941- . . . . **CLC 65**
See also CA 146

Defoe, Daniel
1660(?)-1731 . . . . **LC 1; DA; DAB; DAC;**
DAM MST, NOV; WLC
See also CDBLB 1660-1789; DLB 39, 95,
101; JRDA; MAICYA; SATA 22

de Gourmont, Remy(-Marie-Charles)
See Gourmont, Remy (-Marie-Charles) de

de Hartog, Jan 1914- . . . . **CLC 19**
See also CA 1-4R; CANR 1

de Hostos, E. M.
See Hostos (y Bonilla), Eugenio Maria de

de Hostos, Eugenio M.
See Hostos (y Bonilla), Eugenio Maria de

Deighton, Len . . . . **CLC 4, 7, 22, 46**
See also Deighton, Leonard Cyril
See also AAYA 6; BEST 89:2;
CDBLB 1960 to Present; DLB 87

Deighton, Leonard Cyril 1929-
See Deighton, Len
See also CA 9-12R; CANR 19, 33;
DAM NOV, POP; MTCW

Dekker, Thomas
1572(?)-1632 . . . . . **LC 22; DAM DRAM**
See also CDBLB Before 1660; DLB 62

Delafield, E. M. 1890-1943 . . . . **TCLC 61**
See also Dashwood, Edmee Elizabeth
Monica de la Pasture
See also DLB 34

de la Mare, Walter (John)
1873-1956 . . . . **TCLC 4, 53; DAB; DAC;**
DAM MST, POET; SSC 14; WLC
See also CDBLB 1914-1945; CLR 23;
DLB 162; SATA 16

Delaney, Franey
See O'Hara, John (Henry)

Delaney, Shelagh
1939- . . . . **CLC 29; DAM DRAM**
See also CA 17-20R; CANR 30;
CDBLB 1960 to Present; DLB 13;
MTCW

Delany, Mary (Granville Pendarves)
1700-1788 . . . . **LC 12**

Delany, Samuel R(ay, Jr.)
1942- . . . . **CLC 8, 14, 38; BLC;**
DAM MULT
See also BW 2; CA 81-84; CANR 27, 43;
DLB 8, 33; MTCW

De La Ramee, (Marie) Louise 1839-1908
See Ouida
See also SATA 20

de la Roche, Mazo 1879-1961 . . . . . . **CLC 14**
See also CA 85-88; CANR 30; DLB 68;
SATA 64

Delbanco, Nicholas (Franklin)
1942- . . . . **CLC 6, 13**
See also CA 17-20R; CAAS 2; CANR 29;
DLB 6

del Castillo, Michel 1933- . . . . **CLC 38**
See also CA 109

Deledda, Grazia (Cosima)
1875(?)-1936 . . . . **TCLC 23**
See also CA 123

Delibes, Miguel . . . . **CLC 8, 18**
See also Delibes Setien, Miguel

Delibes Setien, Miguel 1920-
See Delibes, Miguel
See also CA 45-48; CANR 1, 32; HW;
MTCW

DeLillo, Don
1936- . . . . . **CLC 8, 10, 13, 27, 39, 54, 76;**
DAM NOV, POP
See also BEST 89:1; CA 81-84; CANR 21;
DLB 6; MTCW

de Lisser, H. G.
See De Lisser, Herbert George
See also DLB 117

De Lisser, Herbert George
1878-1944 . . . . **TCLC 12**
See also de Lisser, H. G.
See also BW 2; CA 109; 152

Deloria, Vine (Victor), Jr.
1933- . . . . **CLC 21; DAM MULT**
See also CA 53-56; CANR 5, 20, 48;
MTCW; NNAL; SATA 21

Del Vecchio, John M(ichael)
1947- . . . . **CLC 29**
See also CA 110; DLBD 9

de Man, Paul (Adolph Michel)
1919-1983 . . . . **CLC 55**
See also CA 128; 111; DLB 67; MTCW

De Marinis, Rick 1934- . . . . **CLC 54**
See also CA 57-60; CAAS 24; CANR 9, 25,
50

Dembry, R. Emmet
See Murfree, Mary Noailles

Demby, William
1922- . . . . . . **CLC 53; BLC; DAM MULT**
See also BW 1; CA 81-84; DLB 33

Demijohn, Thom
See Disch, Thomas M(ichael)

de Montherlant, Henry (Milon)
See Montherlant, Henry (Milon) de

Demosthenes 384B.C.-322B.C. . . . . **CMLC 13**

de Natale, Francine
See Malzberg, Barry N(athaniel)

Denby, Edwin (Orr) 1903-1983 . . . . . **CLC 48**
See also CA 138; 110

Denis, Julio
See Cortazar, Julio

Denmark, Harrison
See Zelazny, Roger (Joseph)

Dennis, John 1658-1734 . . . . **LC 11**
See also DLB 101

Dennis, Nigel (Forbes) 1912-1989 . . . . **CLC 8**
See also CA 25-28R; 129; DLB 13, 15;
MTCW

De Palma, Brian (Russell) 1940- . . . . **CLC 20**
See also CA 109

De Quincey, Thomas 1785-1859 . . . **NCLC 4**
See also CDBLB 1789-1832; DLB 110; 144

Deren, Eleanora 1908(?)-1961
See Deren, Maya
See also CA 111

Deren, Maya . . . . **CLC 16**
See also Deren, Eleanora

Derleth, August (William)
1909-1971 . . . . **CLC 31**
See also CA 1-4R; 29-32R; CANR 4;
DLB 9; SATA 5

Der Nister 1884-1950 . . . . **TCLC 56**

de Routisie, Albert
See Aragon, Louis

Derrida, Jacques 1930- . . . . **CLC 24, 87**
See also CA 124; 127

Derry Down Derry
See Lear, Edward

Dersonnes, Jacques
See Simenon, Georges (Jacques Christian)

Desai, Anita
1937- . . . **CLC 19, 37; DAB; DAM NOV**
See also CA 81-84; CANR 33, 53; MTCW;
SATA 63

de Saint-Luc, Jean
See Glassco, John

de Saint Roman, Arnaud
See Aragon, Louis

Descartes, Rene 1596-1650 . . . . . . LC 20, 35

De Sica, Vittorio 1901(?)-1974 . . . . . CLC 20
See also CA 117

Desnos, Robert 1900-1945 . . . . TCLC 22
See also CA 121; 151

Destouches, Louis-Ferdinand
1894-1961 . . . . CLC 9, 15
See also Celine, Louis-Ferdinand
See also CA 85-88; CANR 28; MTCW

Deutsch, Babette 1895-1982 . . . . CLC 18
See also CA 1-4R; 108; CANR 4; DLB 45;
SATA 1; SATA-Obit 33

Devenant, William 1606-1649 . . . . LC 13

Devkota, Laxmiprasad
1909-1959 . . . . TCLC 23
See also CA 123

De Voto, Bernard (Augustine)
1897-1955 . . . . TCLC 29
See also CA 113; DLB 9

De Vries, Peter
1910-1993 . . . . CLC 1, 2, 3, 7, 10, 28, 46;
DAM NOV
See also CA 17-20R; 142; CANR 41;
DLB 6; DLBY 82; MTCW

Dexter, John
See Bradley, Marion Zimmer

Dexter, Martin
See Faust, Frederick (Schiller)

Dexter, Pete
1943- . . . . CLC 34, 55; DAM POP
See also BEST 89:2; CA 127; 131; INT 131;
MTCW

Diamano, Silmang
See Senghor, Leopold Sedar

Diamond, Neil 1941- . . . . CLC 30
See also CA 108

Diaz del Castillo, Bernal 1496-1584 . . LC 31

di Bassetto, Corno
See Shaw, George Bernard

Dick, Philip K(indred)
1928-1982 . . . . CLC 10, 30, 72;
DAM NOV, POP
See also CA 49-52; 106; CANR 2, 16;
DLB 8; MTCW

Dickens, Charles (John Huffam)
1812-1870 . . . . . . NCLC 3, 8, 18, 26, 37,
50; DA; DAB; DAC; DAM MST, NOV;
SSC 17; WLC
See also CDBLB 1832-1890; DLB 21, 55,
70, 159, 166; JRDA; MAICYA; SATA 15

Dickey, James (Lafayette)
1923- . . . . CLC 1, 2, 4, 7, 10, 15, 47;
DAM NOV, POET, POP
See also AITN 1, 2; CA 9-12R; CABS 2;
CANR 10, 48; CDALB 1968-1988;
DLB 5; DLBD 7; DLBY 82, 93;
INT CANR-10; MTCW

Dickey, William 1928-1994 . . . . . . CLC 3, 28
See also CA 9-12R; 145; CANR 24; DLB 5

Dickinson, Charles 1951- . . . . CLC 49
See also CA 128

Dickinson, Emily (Elizabeth)
1830-1886 . . . . NCLC 21; DA; DAB;
DAC; DAM MST, POET; PC 1; WLC
See also CDALB 1865-1917; DLB 1;
SATA 29

Dickinson, Peter (Malcolm)
1927- . . . . CLC 12, 35
See also AAYA 9; CA 41-44R; CANR 31;
CLR 29; DLB 87, 161; JRDA; MAICYA;
SATA 5, 62

Dickson, Carr
See Carr, John Dickson

Dickson, Carter
See Carr, John Dickson

Diderot, Denis 1713-1784 . . . . LC 26

Didion, Joan
1934- . . CLC 1, 3, 8, 14, 32; DAM NOV
See also AITN 1; CA 5-8R; CANR 14, 52;
CDALB 1968-1988; DLB 2; DLBY 81,
86; MTCW

Dietrich, Robert
See Hunt, E(verette) Howard, (Jr.)

Dillard, Annie
1945- . . . . CLC 9, 60; DAM NOV
See also AAYA 6; CA 49-52; CANR 3, 43;
DLBY 80; MTCW; SATA 10

Dillard, R(ichard) H(enry) W(ilde)
1937- . . . . CLC 5
See also CA 21-24R; CAAS 7; CANR 10;
DLB 5

Dillon, Eilis 1920-1994 . . . . CLC 17
See also CA 9-12R; 147; CAAS 3; CANR 4,
38; CLR 26; MAICYA; SATA 2, 74;
SATA-Obit 83

Dimont, Penelope
See Mortimer, Penelope (Ruth)

Dinesen, Isak . . . . CLC 10, 29, 95; SSC 7
See also Blixen, Karen (Christentze
Dinesen)

Ding Ling . . . . CLC 68
See also Chiang Pin-chin

Disch, Thomas M(ichael) 1940- . . . CLC 7, 36
See also AAYA 17; CA 21-24R; CAAS 4;
CANR 17, 36; CLR 18; DLB 8;
MAICYA; MTCW; SAAS 15; SATA 54

Disch, Tom
See Disch, Thomas M(ichael)

d'Isly, Georges
See Simenon, Georges (Jacques Christian)

Disraeli, Benjamin 1804-1881 . . NCLC 2, 39
See also DLB 21, 55

Ditcum, Steve
See Crumb, R(obert)

Dixon, Paige
See Corcoran, Barbara

Dixon, Stephen 1936- . . . . . CLC 52; SSC 16
See also CA 89-92; CANR 17, 40; DLB 130

Dobell, Sydney Thompson
1824-1874 . . . . NCLC 43
See also DLB 32

Doblin, Alfred . . . . TCLC 13
See also Doeblin, Alfred

Dobrolyubov, Nikolai Alexandrovich
1836-1861 . . . . NCLC 5

Dobyns, Stephen 1941- . . . . CLC 37
See also CA 45-48; CANR 2, 18

Doctorow, E(dgar) L(aurence)
1931- . . . . . CLC 6, 11, 15, 18, 37, 44, 65;
DAM NOV, POP
See also AITN 2; BEST 89:3; CA 45-48;
CANR 2, 33, 51; CDALB 1968-1988;
DLB 2, 28; DLBY 80; MTCW

Dodgson, Charles Lutwidge 1832-1898
See Carroll, Lewis
See also CLR 2; DA; DAB; DAC;
DAM MST, NOV, POET; MAICYA;
YABC 2

Dodson, Owen (Vincent)
1914-1983 . . . . CLC 79; BLC;
DAM MULT
See also BW 1; CA 65-68; 110; CANR 24;
DLB 76

Doeblin, Alfred 1878-1957 . . . . TCLC 13
See also Doblin, Alfred
See also CA 110; 141; DLB 66

Doerr, Harriet 1910- . . . . CLC 34
See also CA 117; 122; CANR 47; INT 122

Domecq, H(onorio) Bustos
See Bioy Casares, Adolfo; Borges, Jorge
Luis

Domini, Rey
See Lorde, Audre (Geraldine)

Dominique
See Proust, (Valentin-Louis-George-Eugene-)
Marcel

Don, A
See Stephen, Leslie

Donaldson, Stephen R.
1947- . . . . CLC 46; DAM POP
See also CA 89-92; CANR 13;
INT CANR-13

Donleavy, J(ames) P(atrick)
1926- . . . . CLC 1, 4, 6, 10, 45
See also AITN 2; CA 9-12R; CANR 24, 49;
DLB 6; INT CANR-24; MTCW

Donne, John
1572-1631 . . . . LC 10, 24; DA; DAB;
DAC; DAM MST, POET; PC 1
See also CDBLB Before 1660; DLB 121,
151

Donnell, David 1939(?)- . . . . CLC 34

Donoghue, P. S.
See Hunt, E(verette) Howard, (Jr.)

Donoso (Yanez), Jose
1924- . . . . CLC 4, 8, 11, 32;
DAM MULT; HLC
See also CA 81-84; CANR 32; DLB 113;
HW; MTCW

Donovan, John 1928-1992 . . . . CLC 35
See also CA 97-100; 137; CLR 3;
MAICYA; SATA 72; SATA-Brief 29

Don Roberto
See Cunninghame Graham, R(obert)
B(ontine)

Doolittle, Hilda
1886-1961 ..... **CLC 3, 8, 14, 31, 34, 73; DA; DAC; DAM MST, POET; PC 5; WLC**
See also H. D.
See also CA 97-100; CANR 35; DLB 4, 45; MTCW

Dorfman, Ariel
1942- .... **CLC 48, 77; DAM MULT; HLC**
See also CA 124; 130; HW; INT 130

Dorn, Edward (Merton) 1929-... **CLC 10, 18**
See also CA 93-96; CANR 42; DLB 5; INT 93-96

Dorsan, Luc
See Simenon, Georges (Jacques Christian)

Dorsange, Jean
See Simenon, Georges (Jacques Christian)

Dos Passos, John (Roderigo)
1896-1970 ..... **CLC 1, 4, 8, 11, 15, 25, 34, 82; DA; DAB; DAC; DAM MST, NOV; WLC**
See also CA 1-4R; 29-32R; CANR 3; CDALB 1929-1941; DLB 4, 9; DLBD 1; MTCW

Dossage, Jean
See Simenon, Georges (Jacques Christian)

Dostoevsky, Fedor Mikhailovich
1821-1881 ..... **NCLC 2, 7, 21, 33, 43; DA; DAB; DAC; DAM MST, NOV; SSC 2; WLC**

Doughty, Charles M(ontagu)
1843-1926 .... **TCLC 27**
See also CA 115; DLB 19, 57

Douglas, Ellen .... **CLC 73**
See also Haxton, Josephine Ayres; Williamson, Ellen Douglas

Douglas, Gavin 1475(?)-1522 .... **LC 20**

Douglas, Keith 1920-1944 .... **TCLC 40**
See also DLB 27

Douglas, Leonard
See Bradbury, Ray (Douglas)

Douglas, Michael
See Crichton, (John) Michael

Douglass, Frederick
1817(?)-1895 .... **NCLC 7, 55; BLC; DA; DAC; DAM MST, MULT; WLC**
See also CDALB 1640-1865; DLB 1, 43, 50, 79; SATA 29

Dourado, (Waldomiro Freitas) Autran
1926- .... **CLC 23, 60**
See also CA 25-28R; CANR 34

Dourado, Waldomiro Autran
See Dourado, (Waldomiro Freitas) Autran

Dove, Rita (Frances)
1952- .... **CLC 50, 81; DAM MULT, POET; PC 6**
See also BW 2; CA 109; CAAS 19; CANR 27, 42; DLB 120

Dowell, Coleman 1925-1985 .... **CLC 60**
See also CA 25-28R; 117; CANR 10; DLB 130

Dowson, Ernest (Christopher)
1867-1900 .... **TCLC 4**
See also CA 105; 150; DLB 19, 135

Doyle, A. Conan
See Doyle, Arthur Conan

Doyle, Arthur Conan
1859-1930 .... **TCLC 7; DA; DAB; DAC; DAM MST, NOV; SSC 12; WLC**
See also AAYA 14; CA 104; 122; CDBLB 1890-1914; DLB 18, 70, 156; MTCW; SATA 24

Doyle, Conan
See Doyle, Arthur Conan

Doyle, John
See Graves, Robert (von Ranke)

Doyle, Roddy 1958(?)- .... **CLC 81**
See also AAYA 14; CA 143

Doyle, Sir A. Conan
See Doyle, Arthur Conan

Doyle, Sir Arthur Conan
See Doyle, Arthur Conan

Dr. A
See Asimov, Isaac; Silverstein, Alvin

Drabble, Margaret
1939- .... **CLC 2, 3, 5, 8, 10, 22, 53; DAB; DAC; DAM MST, NOV, POP**
See also CA 13-16R; CANR 18, 35; CDBLB 1960 to Present; DLB 14, 155; MTCW; SATA 48

Drapier, M. B.
See Swift, Jonathan

Drayham, James
See Mencken, H(enry) L(ouis)

Drayton, Michael 1563-1631 .... **LC 8**

Dreadstone, Carl
See Campbell, (John) Ramsey

Dreiser, Theodore (Herman Albert)
1871-1945 .... **TCLC 10, 18, 35; DA; DAC; DAM MST, NOV; WLC**
See also CA 106; 132; CDALB 1865-1917; DLB 9, 12, 102, 137; DLBD 1; MTCW

Drexler, Rosalyn 1926- .... **CLC 2, 6**
See also CA 81-84

Dreyer, Carl Theodor 1889-1968 .... **CLC 16**
See also CA 116

Drieu la Rochelle, Pierre(-Eugene)
1893-1945 .... **TCLC 21**
See also CA 117; DLB 72

Drinkwater, John 1882-1937 ...... **TCLC 57**
See also CA 109; 149; DLB 10, 19, 149

Drop Shot
See Cable, George Washington

Droste-Hulshoff, Annette Freiin von
1797-1848 .... **NCLC 3**
See also DLB 133

Drummond, Walter
See Silverberg, Robert

Drummond, William Henry
1854-1907 .... **TCLC 25**
See also DLB 92

Drummond de Andrade, Carlos
1902-1987 .... **CLC 18**
See also Andrade, Carlos Drummond de
See also CA 132; 123

Drury, Allen (Stuart) 1918- .... **CLC 37**
See also CA 57-60; CANR 18, 52; INT CANR-18

Dryden, John
1631-1700 .... **LC 3, 21; DA; DAB; DAC; DAM DRAM, MST, POET; DC 3; WLC**
See also CDBLB 1660-1789; DLB 80, 101, 131

Duberman, Martin 1930- .... **CLC 8**
See also CA 1-4R; CANR 2

Dubie, Norman (Evans) 1945- ...... **CLC 36**
See also CA 69-72; CANR 12; DLB 120

Du Bois, W(illiam) E(dward) B(urghardt)
1868-1963 .... **CLC 1, 2, 13, 64, 96; BLC; DA; DAC; DAM MST, MULT, NOV; WLC**
See also BW 1; CA 85-88; CANR 34; CDALB 1865-1917; DLB 47, 50, 91; MTCW; SATA 42

Dubus, Andre 1936-... **CLC 13, 36; SSC 15**
See also CA 21-24R; CANR 17; DLB 130; INT CANR-17

Duca Minimo
See D'Annunzio, Gabriele

Ducharme, Rejean 1941- .... **CLC 74**
See also DLB 60

Duclos, Charles Pinot 1704-1772 ..... **LC 1**

Dudek, Louis 1918- .... **CLC 11, 19**
See also CA 45-48; CAAS 14; CANR 1; DLB 88

Duerrenmatt, Friedrich
1921-1990 ...... **CLC 1, 4, 8, 11, 15, 43; DAM DRAM**
See also CA 17-20R; CANR 33; DLB 69, 124; MTCW

Duffy, Bruce (?)- .... **CLC 50**

Duffy, Maureen 1933- .... **CLC 37**
See also CA 25-28R; CANR 33; DLB 14; MTCW

Dugan, Alan 1923- .... **CLC 2, 6**
See also CA 81-84; DLB 5

du Gard, Roger Martin
See Martin du Gard, Roger

Duhamel, Georges 1884-1966 .... **CLC 8**
See also CA 81-84; 25-28R; CANR 35; DLB 65; MTCW

Dujardin, Edouard (Emile Louis)
1861-1949 .... **TCLC 13**
See also CA 109; DLB 123

Dumas, Alexandre (Davy de la Pailleterie)
1802-1870 .... **NCLC 11; DA; DAB; DAC; DAM MST, NOV; WLC**
See also DLB 119; SATA 18

Dumas, Alexandre
1824-1895 .... **NCLC 9; DC 1**

Dumas, Claudine
See Malzberg, Barry N(athaniel)

Dumas, Henry L. 1934-1968 ..... **CLC 6, 62**
See also BW 1; CA 85-88; DLB 41

du Maurier, Daphne
1907-1989 .... **CLC 6, 11, 59; DAB; DAC; DAM MST, POP; SSC 18**
See also CA 5-8R; 128; CANR 6; MTCW; SATA 27; SATA-Obit 60

Dunbar, Paul Laurence
1872-1906 . . . . . . **TCLC 2, 12; BLC; DA;**
DAC; DAM MST, MULT, POET; PC 5;
SSC 8; WLC
See also BW 1; CA 104; 124;
CDALB 1865-1917; DLB 50, 54, 78;
SATA 34

Dunbar, William 1460(?)-1530(?) . . . . **LC 20**
See also DLB 132, 146

Duncan, Lois 1934- . . . . **CLC 26**
See also AAYA 4; CA 1-4R; CANR 2, 23,
36; CLR 29; JRDA; MAICYA; SAAS 2;
SATA 1, 36, 75

Duncan, Robert (Edward)
1919-1988 . . . . **CLC 1, 2, 4, 7, 15, 41, 55;**
DAM POET; PC 2
See also CA 9-12R; 124; CANR 28; DLB 5,
16; MTCW

Duncan, Sara Jeannette
1861-1922 . . . . **TCLC 60**
See also DLB 92

Dunlap, William 1766-1839 . . . . **NCLC 2**
See also DLB 30, 37, 59

Dunn, Douglas (Eaglesham)
1942- . . . . **CLC 6, 40**
See also CA 45-48; CANR 2, 33; DLB 40;
MTCW

Dunn, Katherine (Karen) 1945- . . . . . **CLC 71**
See also CA 33-36R

Dunn, Stephen 1939- . . . . **CLC 36**
See also CA 33-36R; CANR 12, 48, 53;
DLB 105

Dunne, Finley Peter 1867-1936 . . . . **TCLC 28**
See also CA 108; DLB 11, 23

Dunne, John Gregory 1932- . . . . **CLC 28**
See also CA 25-28R; CANR 14, 50;
DLBY 80

Dunsany, Edward John Moreton Drax
Plunkett 1878-1957
See Dunsany, Lord
See also CA 104; 148; DLB 10

Dunsany, Lord . . . . **TCLC 2, 59**
See also Dunsany, Edward John Moreton
Drax Plunkett
See also DLB 77, 153, 156

du Perry, Jean
See Simenon, Georges (Jacques Christian)

Durang, Christopher (Ferdinand)
1949- . . . . **CLC 27, 38**
See also CA 105; CANR 50

Duras, Marguerite
1914-1996 . . **CLC 3, 6, 11, 20, 34, 40, 68**
See also CA 25-28R; 151; CANR 50;
DLB 83; MTCW

Durban, (Rosa) Pam 1947- . . . . **CLC 39**
See also CA 123

Durcan, Paul
1944- . . . . **CLC 43, 70; DAM POET**
See also CA 134

Durkheim, Emile 1858-1917 . . . . . . **TCLC 55**

Durrell, Lawrence (George)
1912-1990 . . . . **CLC 1, 4, 6, 8, 13, 27, 41;**
DAM NOV
See also CA 9-12R; 132; CANR 40;
CDBLB 1945-1960; DLB 15, 27;
DLBY 90; MTCW

Durrenmatt, Friedrich
See Duerrenmatt, Friedrich

Dutt, Toru 1856-1877 . . . . **NCLC 29**

Dwight, Timothy 1752-1817 . . . . . . **NCLC 13**
See also DLB 37

Dworkin, Andrea 1946- . . . . **CLC 43**
See also CA 77-80; CAAS 21; CANR 16,
39; INT CANR-16; MTCW

Dwyer, Deanna
See Koontz, Dean R(ay)

Dwyer, K. R.
See Koontz, Dean R(ay)

Dylan, Bob 1941- . . . . . . **CLC 3, 4, 6, 12, 77**
See also CA 41-44R; DLB 16

Eagleton, Terence (Francis) 1943-
See Eagleton, Terry
See also CA 57-60; CANR 7, 23; MTCW

Eagleton, Terry . . . . **CLC 63**
See also Eagleton, Terence (Francis)

Early, Jack
See Scoppettone, Sandra

East, Michael
See West, Morris L(anglo)

Eastaway, Edward
See Thomas, (Philip) Edward

Eastlake, William (Derry) 1917- . . . . . **CLC 8**
See also CA 5-8R; CAAS 1; CANR 5;
DLB 6; INT CANR-5

Eastman, Charles A(lexander)
1858-1939 . . . . . **TCLC 55; DAM MULT**
See also NNAL; YABC 1

Eberhart, Richard (Ghormley)
1904- . . **CLC 3, 11, 19, 56; DAM POET**
See also CA 1-4R; CANR 2;
CDALB 1941-1968; DLB 48; MTCW

Eberstadt, Fernanda 1960- . . . . **CLC 39**
See also CA 136

Echegaray (y Eizaguirre), Jose (Maria Waldo)
1832-1916 . . . . **TCLC 4**
See also CA 104; CANR 32; HW; MTCW

Echeverria, (Jose) Esteban (Antonino)
1805-1851 . . . . **NCLC 18**

Echo
See Proust, (Valentin-Louis-George-Eugene-)
Marcel

Eckert, Allan W. 1931- . . . . **CLC 17**
See also AAYA 18; CA 13-16R; CANR 14,
45; INT CANR-14; SAAS 21; SATA 29;
SATA-Brief 27

Eckhart, Meister 1260(?)-1328(?) . . **CMLC 9**
See also DLB 115

Eckmar, F. R.
See de Hartog, Jan

Eco, Umberto
1932- . . . **CLC 28, 60; DAM NOV, POP**
See also BEST 90:1; CA 77-80; CANR 12,
33; MTCW

Eddison, E(ric) R(ucker)
1882-1945 . . . . **TCLC 15**
See also CA 109

Edel, (Joseph) Leon 1907- . . . . . . **CLC 29, 34**
See also CA 1-4R; CANR 1, 22; DLB 103;
INT CANR-22

Eden, Emily 1797-1869 . . . . **NCLC 10**

Edgar, David
1948- . . . . **CLC 42; DAM DRAM**
See also CA 57-60; CANR 12; DLB 13;
MTCW

Edgerton, Clyde (Carlyle) 1944- . . . . **CLC 39**
See also AAYA 17; CA 118; 134; INT 134

Edgeworth, Maria 1768-1849 . . . **NCLC 1, 51**
See also DLB 116, 159, 163; SATA 21

Edmonds, Paul
See Kuttner, Henry

Edmonds, Walter D(umaux) 1903- . . **CLC 35**
See also CA 5-8R; CANR 2; DLB 9;
MAICYA; SAAS 4; SATA 1, 27

Edmondson, Wallace
See Ellison, Harlan (Jay)

Edson, Russell . . . . **CLC 13**
See also CA 33-36R

Edwards, Bronwen Elizabeth
See Rose, Wendy

Edwards, G(erald) B(asil)
1899-1976 . . . . **CLC 25**
See also CA 110

Edwards, Gus 1939- . . . . **CLC 43**
See also CA 108; INT 108

Edwards, Jonathan
1703-1758 . . . . **LC 7; DA; DAC;**
DAM MST
See also DLB 24

Efron, Marina Ivanovna Tsvetaeva
See Tsvetaeva (Efron), Marina (Ivanovna)

Ehle, John (Marsden, Jr.) 1925- . . . . **CLC 27**
See also CA 9-12R

Ehrenbourg, Ilya (Grigoryevich)
See Ehrenburg, Ilya (Grigoryevich)

Ehrenburg, Ilya (Grigoryevich)
1891-1967 . . . . **CLC 18, 34, 62**
See also CA 102; 25-28R

Ehrenburg, Ilyo (Grigoryevich)
See Ehrenburg, Ilya (Grigoryevich)

Eich, Guenter 1907-1972 . . . . **CLC 15**
See also CA 111; 93-96; DLB 69, 124

Eichendorff, Joseph Freiherr von
1788-1857 . . . . **NCLC 8**
See also DLB 90

Eigner, Larry . . . . **CLC 9**
See also Eigner, Laurence (Joel)
See also CAAS 23; DLB 5

Eigner, Laurence (Joel) 1927-1996
See Eigner, Larry
See also CA 9-12R; 151; CANR 6

Einstein, Albert 1879-1955 . . . . **TCLC 65**
See also CA 121; 133; MTCW

Eiseley, Loren Corey 1907-1977 . . . . . **CLC 7**
See also AAYA 5; CA 1-4R; 73-76;
CANR 6

Eisenstadt, Jill 1963- . . . . **CLC 50**
See also CA 140

Eisenstein, Sergei (Mikhailovich)
1898-1948 . . . . **TCLC 57**
See also CA 114; 149

Eisner, Simon
See Kornbluth, C(yril) M.

Ekeloef, (Bengt) Gunnar
  1907-1968 . . . . **CLC 27; DAM POET**
  See also CA 123; 25-28R

Ekelof, (Bengt) Gunnar
  See Ekeloef, (Bengt) Gunnar

Ekwensi, C. O. D.
  See Ekwensi, Cyprian (Odiatu Duaka)

Ekwensi, Cyprian (Odiatu Duaka)
  1921- . . . . . . **CLC 4; BLC; DAM MULT**
  See also BW 2; CA 29-32R; CANR 18, 42;
  DLB 117; MTCW; SATA 66

Elaine . . . . **TCLC 18**
  See also Leverson, Ada

El Crummo
  See Crumb, R(obert)

Elia
  See Lamb, Charles

Eliade, Mircea 1907-1986 . . . . **CLC 19**
  See also CA 65-68; 119; CANR 30; MTCW

Eliot, A. D.
  See Jewett, (Theodora) Sarah Orne

Eliot, Alice
  See Jewett, (Theodora) Sarah Orne

Eliot, Dan
  See Silverberg, Robert

Eliot, George
  1819-1880 . . . . . **NCLC 4, 13, 23, 41, 49;
  DA; DAB; DAC; DAM MST, NOV;
  WLC**
  See also CDBLB 1832-1890; DLB 21, 35, 55

Eliot, John 1604-1690 . . . . **LC 5**
  See also DLB 24

Eliot, T(homas) S(tearns)
  1888-1965 . . . . . **CLC 1, 2, 3, 6, 9, 10, 13,
  15, 24, 34, 41, 55, 57; DA; DAB; DAC;
  DAM DRAM, MST, POET; PC 5;
  WLC 2**
  See also CA 5-8R; 25-28R; CANR 41;
  CDALB 1929-1941; DLB 7, 10, 45, 63;
  DLBY 88; MTCW

Elizabeth 1866-1941 . . . . **TCLC 41**

Elkin, Stanley L(awrence)
  1930-1995 . . . . . . **CLC 4, 6, 9, 14, 27, 51,
  91; DAM NOV, POP; SSC 12**
  See also CA 9-12R; 148; CANR 8, 46;
  DLB 2, 28; DLBY 80; INT CANR-8;
  MTCW

Elledge, Scott . . . . **CLC 34**

Elliott, Don
  See Silverberg, Robert

Elliott, George P(aul) 1918-1980 . . . . . **CLC 2**
  See also CA 1-4R; 97-100; CANR 2

Elliott, Janice 1931- . . . . **CLC 47**
  See also CA 13-16R; CANR 8, 29; DLB 14

Elliott, Sumner Locke 1917-1991 . . . **CLC 38**
  See also CA 5-8R; 134; CANR 2, 21

Elliott, William
  See Bradbury, Ray (Douglas)

Ellis, A. E. . . . . **CLC 7**

Ellis, Alice Thomas . . . . **CLC 40**
  See also Haycraft, Anna

Ellis, Bret Easton
  1964- . . . . **CLC 39, 71; DAM POP**
  See also AAYA 2; CA 118; 123; CANR 51;
  INT 123

Ellis, (Henry) Havelock
  1859-1939 . . . . **TCLC 14**
  See also CA 109

Ellis, Landon
  See Ellison, Harlan (Jay)

Ellis, Trey 1962- . . . . **CLC 55**
  See also CA 146

Ellison, Harlan (Jay)
  1934- . . . . . . **CLC 1, 13, 42; DAM POP;
  SSC 14**
  See also CA 5-8R; CANR 5, 46; DLB 8;
  INT CANR-5; MTCW

Ellison, Ralph (Waldo)
  1914-1994 . . . . **CLC 1, 3, 11, 54, 86;
  BLC; DA; DAB; DAC; DAM MST,
  MULT, NOV; WLC**
  See also BW 1; CA 9-12R; 145; CANR 24,
  53; CDALB 1941-1968; DLB 2, 76;
  DLBY 94; MTCW

Ellmann, Lucy (Elizabeth) 1956- . . . . **CLC 61**
  See also CA 128

Ellmann, Richard (David)
  1918-1987 . . . . **CLC 50**
  See also BEST 89:2; CA 1-4R; 122;
  CANR 2, 28; DLB 103; DLBY 87;
  MTCW

Elman, Richard 1934- . . . . **CLC 19**
  See also CA 17-20R; CAAS 3; CANR 47

Elron
  See Hubbard, L(afayette) Ron(ald)

Eluard, Paul . . . . **TCLC 7, 41**
  See also Grindel, Eugene

Elyot, Sir Thomas 1490(?)-1546 . . . . . **LC 11**

Elytis, Odysseus
  1911-1996 . . . . **CLC 15, 49; DAM POET**
  See also CA 102; 151; MTCW

Emecheta, (Florence Onye) Buchi
  1944- . . **CLC 14, 48; BLC; DAM MULT**
  See also BW 2; CA 81-84; CANR 27;
  DLB 117; MTCW; SATA 66

Emerson, Ralph Waldo
  1803-1882 . . . . . **NCLC 1, 38; DA; DAB;
  DAC; DAM MST, POET; WLC**
  See also CDALB 1640-1865; DLB 1, 59, 73

Eminescu, Mihail 1850-1889 . . . . . **NCLC 33**

Empson, William
  1906-1984 . . . . **CLC 3, 8, 19, 33, 34**
  See also CA 17-20R; 112; CANR 31;
  DLB 20; MTCW

Enchi Fumiko (Ueda) 1905-1986 . . . . **CLC 31**
  See also CA 129; 121

Ende, Michael (Andreas Helmuth)
  1929-1995 . . . . **CLC 31**
  See also CA 118; 124; 149; CANR 36;
  CLR 14; DLB 75; MAICYA; SATA 61;
  SATA-Brief 42; SATA-Obit 86

Endo, Shusaku
  1923- . . . **CLC 7, 14, 19, 54; DAM NOV**
  See also CA 29-32R; CANR 21; MTCW

Engel, Marian 1933-1985 . . . . **CLC 36**
  See also CA 25-28R; CANR 12; DLB 53;
  INT CANR-12

Engelhardt, Frederick
  See Hubbard, L(afayette) Ron(ald)

Enright, D(ennis) J(oseph)
  1920- . . . . **CLC 4, 8, 31**
  See also CA 1-4R; CANR 1, 42; DLB 27;
  SATA 25

Enzensberger, Hans Magnus
  1929- . . . . **CLC 43**
  See also CA 116; 119

Ephron, Nora 1941- . . . . **CLC 17, 31**
  See also AITN 2; CA 65-68; CANR 12, 39

Epsilon
  See Betjeman, John

Epstein, Daniel Mark 1948- . . . . **CLC 7**
  See also CA 49-52; CANR 2, 53

Epstein, Jacob 1956- . . . . **CLC 19**
  See also CA 114

Epstein, Joseph 1937- . . . . **CLC 39**
  See also CA 112; 119; CANR 50

Epstein, Leslie 1938- . . . . **CLC 27**
  See also CA 73-76; CAAS 12; CANR 23

Equiano, Olaudah
  1745(?)-1797 . . . . **LC 16; BLC;
  DAM MULT**
  See also DLB 37, 50

Erasmus, Desiderius 1469(?)-1536 . . . . **LC 16**

Erdman, Paul E(mil) 1932- . . . . **CLC 25**
  See also AITN 1; CA 61-64; CANR 13, 43

Erdrich, Louise
  1954- . . . . **CLC 39, 54; DAM MULT,
  NOV, POP**
  See also AAYA 10; BEST 89:1; CA 114;
  CANR 41; DLB 152; MTCW; NNAL

Erenburg, Ilya (Grigoryevich)
  See Ehrenburg, Ilya (Grigoryevich)

Erickson, Stephen Michael 1950-
  See Erickson, Steve
  See also CA 129

Erickson, Steve . . . . **CLC 64**
  See also Erickson, Stephen Michael

Ericson, Walter
  See Fast, Howard (Melvin)

Eriksson, Buntel
  See Bergman, (Ernst) Ingmar

Ernaux, Annie 1940- . . . . **CLC 88**
  See also CA 147

Eschenbach, Wolfram von
  See Wolfram von Eschenbach

Eseki, Bruno
  See Mphahlele, Ezekiel

Esenin, Sergei (Alexandrovich)
  1895-1925 . . . . **TCLC 4**
  See also CA 104

Eshleman, Clayton 1935- . . . . **CLC 7**
  See also CA 33-36R; CAAS 6; DLB 5

Espriella, Don Manuel Alvarez
  See Southey, Robert

Espriu, Salvador 1913-1985 . . . . **CLC 9**
  See also CA 115; DLB 134

Espronceda, Jose de 1808-1842 . . . **NCLC 39**

Esse, James
  See Stephens, James

Esterbrook, Tom
See Hubbard, L(afayette) Ron(ald)

Estleman, Loren D.
1952- ...... **CLC 48; DAM NOV, POP**
See also CA 85-88; CANR 27;
INT CANR-27; MTCW

Eugenides, Jeffrey 1960(?)- .... **CLC 81**
See also CA 144

Euripides c. 485B.C.-406B.C. .... **DC 4**
See also DA; DAB; DAC; DAM DRAM,
MST

Evan, Evin
See Faust, Frederick (Schiller)

Evans, Evan
See Faust, Frederick (Schiller)

Evans, Marian
See Eliot, George

Evans, Mary Ann
See Eliot, George

Evarts, Esther
See Benson, Sally

Everett, Percival L. 1956- .... **CLC 57**
See also BW 2; CA 129

Everson, R(onald) G(ilmour)
1903- .... **CLC 27**
See also CA 17-20R; DLB 88

Everson, William (Oliver)
1912-1994 .... **CLC 1, 5, 14**
See also CA 9-12R; 145; CANR 20; DLB 5,
16; MTCW

Evtushenko, Evgenii Aleksandrovich
See Yevtushenko, Yevgeny (Alexandrovich)

Ewart, Gavin (Buchanan)
1916-1995 .... **CLC 13, 46**
See also CA 89-92; 150; CANR 17, 46;
DLB 40; MTCW

Ewers, Hanns Heinz 1871-1943 ... **TCLC 12**
See also CA 109; 149

Ewing, Frederick R.
See Sturgeon, Theodore (Hamilton)

Exley, Frederick (Earl)
1929-1992 .... **CLC 6, 11**
See also AITN 2; CA 81-84; 138; DLB 143;
DLBY 81

Eynhardt, Guillermo
See Quiroga, Horacio (Sylvestre)

Ezekiel, Nissim 1924- .... **CLC 61**
See also CA 61-64

Ezekiel, Tish O'Dowd 1943- .... **CLC 34**
See also CA 129

Fadeyev, A.
See Bulgya, Alexander Alexandrovich

Fadeyev, Alexander .... **TCLC 53**
See also Bulgya, Alexander Alexandrovich

Fagen, Donald 1948- .... **CLC 26**

Fainzilberg, Ilya Arnoldovich 1897-1937
See Ilf, Ilya
See also CA 120

Fair, Ronald L. 1932- .... **CLC 18**
See also BW 1; CA 69-72; CANR 25;
DLB 33

Fairbairns, Zoe (Ann) 1948- .... **CLC 32**
See also CA 103; CANR 21

Falco, Gian
See Papini, Giovanni

Falconer, James
See Kirkup, James

Falconer, Kenneth
See Kornbluth, C(yril) M.

Falkland, Samuel
See Heijermans, Herman

Fallaci, Oriana 1930- .... **CLC 11**
See also CA 77-80; CANR 15; MTCW

Faludy, George 1913- .... **CLC 42**
See also CA 21-24R

Faludy, Gyoergy
See Faludy, George

Fanon, Frantz
1925-1961 .... **CLC 74; BLC;**
                                DAM MULT
See also BW 1; CA 116; 89-92

Fanshawe, Ann 1625-1680 .... **LC 11**

Fante, John (Thomas) 1911-1983 ... **CLC 60**
See also CA 69-72; 109; CANR 23;
DLB 130; DLBY 83

Farah, Nuruddin
1945- ..... **CLC 53; BLC; DAM MULT**
See also BW 2; CA 106; DLB 125

Fargue, Leon-Paul 1876(?)-1947 ... **TCLC 11**
See also CA 109

Farigoule, Louis
See Romains, Jules

Farina, Richard 1936(?)-1966 .... **CLC 9**
See also CA 81-84; 25-28R

Farley, Walter (Lorimer)
1915-1989 .... **CLC 17**
See also CA 17-20R; CANR 8, 29; DLB 22;
JRDA; MAICYA; SATA 2, 43

Farmer, Philip Jose 1918- .... **CLC 1, 19**
See also CA 1-4R; CANR 4, 35; DLB 8;
MTCW

Farquhar, George
1677-1707 .... **LC 21; DAM DRAM**
See also DLB 84

Farrell, J(ames) G(ordon)
1935-1979 .... **CLC 6**
See also CA 73-76; 89-92; CANR 36;
DLB 14; MTCW

Farrell, James T(homas)
1904-1979 .... **CLC 1, 4, 8, 11, 66**
See also CA 5-8R; 89-92; CANR 9; DLB 4,
9, 86; DLBD 2; MTCW

Farren, Richard J.
See Betjeman, John

Farren, Richard M.
See Betjeman, John

Fassbinder, Rainer Werner
1946-1982 .... **CLC 20**
See also CA 93-96; 106; CANR 31

Fast, Howard (Melvin)
1914- .... **CLC 23; DAM NOV**
See also AAYA 16; CA 1-4R; CAAS 18;
CANR 1, 33; DLB 9; INT CANR-33;
SATA 7

Faulcon, Robert
See Holdstock, Robert P.

Faulkner, William (Cuthbert)
1897-1962 ..... **CLC 1, 3, 6, 8, 9, 11, 14,**
                18, 28, 52, 68; DA; DAB; DAC;
                DAM MST, NOV; SSC 1; WLC
See also AAYA 7; CA 81-84; CANR 33;
CDALB 1929-1941; DLB 9, 11, 44, 102;
DLBD 2; DLBY 86; MTCW

Fauset, Jessie Redmon
1884(?)-1961 .... **CLC 19, 54; BLC;**
                              DAM MULT
See also BW 1; CA 109; DLB 51

Faust, Frederick (Schiller)
1892-1944(?) ..... **TCLC 49; DAM POP**
See also CA 108; 152

Faust, Irvin 1924- .... **CLC 8**
See also CA 33-36R; CANR 28; DLB 2, 28;
DLBY 80

Fawkes, Guy
See Benchley, Robert (Charles)

Fearing, Kenneth (Flexner)
1902-1961 .... **CLC 51**
See also CA 93-96; DLB 9

Fecamps, Elise
See Creasey, John

Federman, Raymond 1928- ...... **CLC 6, 47**
See also CA 17-20R; CAAS 8; CANR 10,
43; DLBY 80

Federspiel, J(uerg) F. 1931- .... **CLC 42**
See also CA 146

Feiffer, Jules (Ralph)
1929- ...... **CLC 2, 8, 64; DAM DRAM**
See also AAYA 3; CA 17-20R; CANR 30;
DLB 7, 44; INT CANR-30; MTCW;
SATA 8, 61

Feige, Hermann Albert Otto Maximilian
See Traven, B.

Feinberg, David B. 1956-1994 ...... **CLC 59**
See also CA 135; 147

Feinstein, Elaine 1930- .... **CLC 36**
See also CA 69-72; CAAS 1; CANR 31;
DLB 14, 40; MTCW

Feldman, Irving (Mordecai) 1928- .... **CLC 7**
See also CA 1-4R; CANR 1

Fellini, Federico 1920-1993 ..... **CLC 16, 85**
See also CA 65-68; 143; CANR 33

Felsen, Henry Gregor 1916- .... **CLC 17**
See also CA 1-4R; CANR 1; SAAS 2;
SATA 1

Fenton, James Martin 1949- .... **CLC 32**
See also CA 102; DLB 40

Ferber, Edna 1887-1968 .... **CLC 18, 93**
See also AITN 1; CA 5-8R; 25-28R; DLB 9,
28, 86; MTCW; SATA 7

Ferguson, Helen
See Kavan, Anna

Ferguson, Samuel 1810-1886 ..... **NCLC 33**
See also DLB 32

Fergusson, Robert 1750-1774 .... **LC 29**
See also DLB 109

Ferling, Lawrence
See Ferlinghetti, Lawrence (Monsanto)

Ferlinghetti, Lawrence (Monsanto)
    1919(?)-............ CLC 2, 6, 10, 27;
                        DAM POET; PC 1
    See also CA 5-8R; CANR 3, 41;
    CDALB 1941-1968; DLB 5, 16; MTCW

Fernandez, Vicente Garcia Huidobro
    See Huidobro Fernandez, Vicente Garcia

Ferrer, Gabriel (Francisco Victor) Miro
    See Miro (Ferrer), Gabriel (Francisco
    Victor)

Ferrier, Susan (Edmonstone)
    1782-1854 .... NCLC 8
    See also DLB 116

Ferrigno, Robert 1948(?)-.......... CLC 65
    See also CA 140

Ferron, Jacques 1921-1985 ... CLC 94; DAC
    See also CA 117; 129; DLB 60

Feuchtwanger, Lion 1884-1958 ..... TCLC 3
    See also CA 104; DLB 66

Feuillet, Octave 1821-1890 ...... NCLC 45

Feydeau, Georges (Leon Jules Marie)
    1862-1921 ..... TCLC 22; DAM DRAM
    See also CA 113; 152

Ficino, Marsilio 1433-1499 .... LC 12

Fiedeler, Hans
    See Doeblin, Alfred

Fiedler, Leslie A(aron)
    1917- .... CLC 4, 13, 24
    See also CA 9-12R; CANR 7; DLB 28, 67;
    MTCW

Field, Andrew 1938-.............. CLC 44
    See also CA 97-100; CANR 25

Field, Eugene 1850-1895 .... NCLC 3
    See also DLB 23, 42, 140; DLBD 13;
    MAICYA; SATA 16

Field, Gans T.
    See Wellman, Manly Wade

Field, Michael .... TCLC 43

Field, Peter
    See Hobson, Laura Z(ametkin)

Fielding, Henry
    1707-1754 ...... LC 1; DA; DAB; DAC;
                    DAM DRAM, MST, NOV; WLC
    See also CDBLB 1660-1789; DLB 39, 84,
    101

Fielding, Sarah 1710-1768.......... LC 1
    See also DLB 39

Fierstein, Harvey (Forbes)
    1954- ..... CLC 33; DAM DRAM, POP
    See also CA 123; 129

Figes, Eva 1932-................. CLC 31
    See also CA 53-56; CANR 4, 44; DLB 14

Finch, Robert (Duer Claydon)
    1900- .... CLC 18
    See also CA 57-60; CANR 9, 24, 49;
    DLB 88

Findley, Timothy
    1930- ...... CLC 27; DAC; DAM MST
    See also CA 25-28R; CANR 12, 42;
    DLB 53

Fink, William
    See Mencken, H(enry) L(ouis)

Firbank, Louis 1942-
    See Reed, Lou
    See also CA 117

Firbank, (Arthur Annesley) Ronald
    1886-1926 .... TCLC 1
    See also CA 104; DLB 36

Fisher, M(ary) F(rances) K(ennedy)
    1908-1992 .... CLC 76, 87
    See also CA 77-80; 138; CANR 44

Fisher, Roy 1930-................ CLC 25
    See also CA 81-84; CAAS 10; CANR 16;
    DLB 40

Fisher, Rudolph
    1897-1934 .... TCLC 11; BLC;
                          DAM MULT
    See also BW 1; CA 107; 124; DLB 51, 102

Fisher, Vardis (Alvero) 1895-1968.... CLC 7
    See also CA 5-8R; 25-28R; DLB 9

Fiske, Tarleton
    See Bloch, Robert (Albert)

Fitch, Clarke
    See Sinclair, Upton (Beall)

Fitch, John IV
    See Cormier, Robert (Edmund)

Fitzgerald, Captain Hugh
    See Baum, L(yman) Frank

FitzGerald, Edward 1809-1883 .... NCLC 9
    See also DLB 32

Fitzgerald, F(rancis) Scott (Key)
    1896-1940 ...... TCLC 1, 6, 14, 28, 55;
                    DA; DAB; DAC; DAM MST, NOV;
                    SSC 6; WLC
    See also AITN 1; CA 110; 123;
    CDALB 1917-1929; DLB 4, 9, 86;
    DLBD 1; DLBY 81; MTCW

Fitzgerald, Penelope 1916-... CLC 19, 51, 61
    See also CA 85-88; CAAS 10; DLB 14

Fitzgerald, Robert (Stuart)
    1910-1985 .... CLC 39
    See also CA 1-4R; 114; CANR 1; DLBY 80

FitzGerald, Robert D(avid)
    1902-1987 .... CLC 19
    See also CA 17-20R

Fitzgerald, Zelda (Sayre)
    1900-1948 .... TCLC 52
    See also CA 117; 126; DLBY 84

Flanagan, Thomas (James Bonner)
    1923- .... CLC 25, 52
    See also CA 108; DLBY 80; INT 108;
    MTCW

Flaubert, Gustave
    1821-1880 .... NCLC 2, 10, 19; DA;
    DAB; DAC; DAM MST, NOV; SSC 11;
                                WLC
    See also DLB 119

Flecker, Herman Elroy
    See Flecker, (Herman) James Elroy

Flecker, (Herman) James Elroy
    1884-1915 .... TCLC 43
    See also CA 109; 150; DLB 10, 19

Fleming, Ian (Lancaster)
    1908-1964 ..... CLC 3, 30; DAM POP
    See also CA 5-8R; CDBLB 1945-1960;
    DLB 87; MTCW; SATA 9

Fleming, Thomas (James) 1927- .... CLC 37
    See also CA 5-8R; CANR 10;
    INT CANR-10; SATA 8

Fletcher, John 1579-1625..... LC 33; DC 6
    See also CDBLB Before 1660; DLB 58

Fletcher, John Gould 1886-1950 ... TCLC 35
    See also CA 107; DLB 4, 45

Fleur, Paul
    See Pohl, Frederik

Flooglebuckle, Al
    See Spiegelman, Art

Flying Officer X
    See Bates, H(erbert) E(rnest)

Fo, Dario 1926-..... CLC 32; DAM DRAM
    See also CA 116; 128; MTCW

Fogarty, Jonathan Titulescu Esq.
    See Farrell, James T(homas)

Folke, Will
    See Bloch, Robert (Albert)

Follett, Ken(neth Martin)
    1949- ...... CLC 18; DAM NOV, POP
    See also AAYA 6; BEST 89:4; CA 81-84;
    CANR 13, 33; DLB 87; DLBY 81;
    INT CANR-33; MTCW

Fontane, Theodor 1819-1898 ..... NCLC 26
    See also DLB 129

Foote, Horton
    1916- .... CLC 51, 91; DAM DRAM
    See also CA 73-76; CANR 34, 51; DLB 26;
    INT CANR-34

Foote, Shelby
    1916- ...... CLC 75; DAM NOV, POP
    See also CA 5-8R; CANR 3, 45; DLB 2, 17

Forbes, Esther 1891-1967.......... CLC 12
    See also AAYA 17; CA 13-14; 25-28R;
    CAP 1; CLR 27; DLB 22; JRDA;
    MAICYA; SATA 2

Forche, Carolyn (Louise)
    1950- .... CLC 25, 83, 86; DAM POET;
                                PC 10
    See also CA 109; 117; CANR 50; DLB 5;
    INT 117

Ford, Elbur
    See Hibbert, Eleanor Alice Burford

Ford, Ford Madox
    1873-1939 .... TCLC 1, 15, 39, 57;
                        DAM NOV
    See also CA 104; 132; CDBLB 1914-1945;
    DLB 162; MTCW

Ford, John 1895-1973............. CLC 16
    See also CA 45-48

Ford, Richard 1944-.............. CLC 46
    See also CA 69-72; CANR 11, 47

Ford, Webster
    See Masters, Edgar Lee

Foreman, Richard 1937-.......... CLC 50
    See also CA 65-68; CANR 32

Forester, C(ecil) S(cott)
    1899-1966 .... CLC 35
    See also CA 73-76; 25-28R; SATA 13

Forez
    See Mauriac, Francois (Charles)

Forman, James Douglas 1932-...... CLC 21
    See also AAYA 17; CA 9-12R; CANR 4,
    19, 42; JRDA; MAICYA; SATA 8, 70

Fornes, Maria Irene 1930-...... CLC 39, 61
See also CA 25-28R; CANR 28; DLB 7;
HW; INT CANR-28; MTCW

Forrest, Leon 1937-.............. CLC 4
See also BW 2; CA 89-92; CAAS 7;
CANR 25, 52; DLB 33

Forster, E(dward) M(organ)
1879-1970 ..... CLC 1, 2, 3, 4, 9, 10, 13,
15, 22, 45, 77; DA; DAB; DAC;
DAM MST, NOV; WLC
See also AAYA 2; CA 13-14; 25-28R;
CANR 45; CAP 1; CDBLB 1914-1945;
DLB 34, 98, 162; DLBD 10; MTCW;
SATA 57

Forster, John 1812-1876 .... NCLC 11
See also DLB 144

Forsyth, Frederick
1938- .. CLC 2, 5, 36; DAM NOV, POP
See also BEST 89:4; CA 85-88; CANR 38;
DLB 87; MTCW

Forten, Charlotte L. .... TCLC 16; BLC
See also Grimke, Charlotte L(ottie) Forten
See also DLB 50

Foscolo, Ugo 1778-1827......... NCLC 8

Fosse, Bob .... CLC 20
See also Fosse, Robert Louis

Fosse, Robert Louis 1927-1987
See Fosse, Bob
See also CA 110; 123

Foster, Stephen Collins
1826-1864 .... NCLC 26

Foucault, Michel
1926-1984 .... CLC 31, 34, 69
See also CA 105; 113; CANR 34; MTCW

Fouque, Friedrich (Heinrich Karl) de la Motte
1777-1843 .... NCLC 2
See also DLB 90

Fourier, Charles 1772-1837...... NCLC 51

Fournier, Henri Alban 1886-1914
See Alain-Fournier
See also CA 104

Fournier, Pierre 1916-........... CLC 11
See also Gascar, Pierre
See also CA 89-92; CANR 16, 40

Fowles, John
1926-...... CLC 1, 2, 3, 4, 6, 9, 10, 15,
33, 87; DAB; DAC; DAM MST
See also CA 5-8R; CANR 25; CDBLB 1960
to Present; DLB 14, 139; MTCW;
SATA 22

Fox, Paula 1923-................. CLC 2, 8
See also AAYA 3; CA 73-76; CANR 20,
36; CLR 1; DLB 52; JRDA; MAICYA;
MTCW; SATA 17, 60

Fox, William Price (Jr.) 1926- ..... CLC 22
See also CA 17-20R; CAAS 19; CANR 11;
DLB 2; DLBY 81

Foxe, John 1516(?)-1587 .... LC 14

Frame, Janet
1924-......... CLC 2, 3, 6, 22, 66, 96
See also Clutha, Janet Paterson Frame

France, Anatole.................. TCLC 9
See also Thibault, Jacques Anatole Francois
See also DLB 123

Francis, Claude 19(?)- .... CLC 50

Francis, Dick
1920- .... CLC 2, 22, 42; DAM POP
See also AAYA 5; BEST 89:3; CA 5-8R;
CANR 9, 42; CDBLB 1960 to Present;
DLB 87; INT CANR-9; MTCW

Francis, Robert (Churchill)
1901-1987 .... CLC 15
See also CA 1-4R; 123; CANR 1

Frank, Anne(lies Marie)
1929-1945 .... TCLC 17; DA; DAB;
DAC; DAM MST; WLC
See also AAYA 12; CA 113; 133; MTCW;
SATA 87; SATA-Brief 42

Frank, Elizabeth 1945-........... CLC 39
See also CA 121; 126; INT 126

Frankl, Viktor E(mil) 1905-........ CLC 93
See also CA 65-68

Franklin, Benjamin
See Hasek, Jaroslav (Matej Frantisek)

Franklin, Benjamin
1706-1790 ..... LC 25; DA; DAB; DAC;
DAM MST
See also CDALB 1640-1865; DLB 24, 43,
73

Franklin, (Stella Maraia Sarah) Miles
1879-1954 .... TCLC 7
See also CA 104

Fraser, (Lady) Antonia (Pakenham)
1932-....................... CLC 32
See also CA 85-88; CANR 44; MTCW;
SATA-Brief 32

Fraser, George MacDonald 1925-.... CLC 7
See also CA 45-48; CANR 2, 48

Fraser, Sylvia 1935-.............. CLC 64
See also CA 45-48; CANR 1, 16

Frayn, Michael
1933-............... CLC 3, 7, 31, 47;
DAM DRAM, NOV
See also CA 5-8R; CANR 30; DLB 13, 14;
MTCW

Fraze, Candida (Merrill) 1945-..... CLC 50
See also CA 126

Frazer, J(ames) G(eorge)
1854-1941 .... TCLC 32
See also CA 118

Frazer, Robert Caine
See Creasey, John

Frazer, Sir James George
See Frazer, J(ames) G(eorge)

Frazier, Ian 1951-................ CLC 46
See also CA 130

Fredric, Harold 1856-1898...... NCLC 10
See also DLB 12, 23; DLBD 13

Frederick, John
See Faust, Frederick (Schiller)

Frederick the Great 1712-1786...... LC 14

Fredro, Aleksander 1793-1876..... NCLC 8

Freeling, Nicolas 1927- .... CLC 38
See also CA 49-52; CAAS 12; CANR 1, 17,
50; DLB 87

Freeman, Douglas Southall
1886-1953 .... TCLC 11
See also CA 109; DLB 17

Freeman, Judith 1946-........... CLC 55
See also CA 148

Freeman, Mary Eleanor Wilkins
1852-1930 .... TCLC 9; SSC 1
See also CA 106; DLB 12, 78

Freeman, R(ichard) Austin
1862-1943 .... TCLC 21
See also CA 113; DLB 70

French, Albert 1943- .... CLC 86

French, Marilyn
1929-................ CLC 10, 18, 60;
DAM DRAM, NOV, POP
See also CA 69-72; CANR 3, 31;
INT CANR-31; MTCW

French, Paul
See Asimov, Isaac

Freneau, Philip Morin 1752-1832.. NCLC 1
See also DLB 37, 43

Freud, Sigmund 1856-1939 .... TCLC 52
See also CA 115; 133; MTCW

Friedan, Betty (Naomi) 1921-...... CLC 74
See also CA 65-68; CANR 18, 45; MTCW

Friedlander, Saul 1932-........... CLC 90
See also CA 117; 130

Friedman, B(ernard) H(arper)
1926-......................... CLC 7
See also CA 1-4R; CANR 3, 48

Friedman, Bruce Jay 1930-.... CLC 3, 5, 56
See also CA 9-12R; CANR 25, 52; DLB 2,
28; INT CANR-25

Friel, Brian 1929-........... CLC 5, 42, 59
See also CA 21-24R; CANR 33; DLB 13;
MTCW

Friis-Baastad, Babbis Ellinor
1921-1970 .... CLC 12
See also CA 17-20R; 134; SATA 7

Frisch, Max (Rudolf)
1911-1991 ..... CLC 3, 9, 14, 18, 32, 44;
DAM DRAM, NOV
See also CA 85-88; 134; CANR 32;
DLB 69, 124; MTCW

Fromentin, Eugene (Samuel Auguste)
1820-1876 .... NCLC 10
See also DLB 123

Frost, Frederick
See Faust, Frederick (Schiller)

Frost, Robert (Lee)
1874-1963 .... CLC 1, 3, 4, 9, 10, 13, 15,
26, 34, 44; DA; DAB; DAC; DAM MST,
POET; PC 1; WLC
See also CA 89-92; CANR 33;
CDALB 1917-1929; DLB 54; DLBD 7;
MTCW; SATA 14

Froude, James Anthony
1818-1894 .... NCLC 43
See also DLB 18, 57, 144

Froy, Herald
See Waterhouse, Keith (Spencer)

Fry, Christopher
1907-..... CLC 2, 10, 14; DAM DRAM
See also CA 17-20R; CAAS 23; CANR 9,
30; DLB 13; MTCW; SATA 66

Frye, (Herman) Northrop
1912-1991 .... CLC 24, 70
See also CA 5-8R; 133; CANR 8, 37;
DLB 67, 68; MTCW

Fuchs, Daniel 1909-1993 . . . . **CLC 8, 22**
  See also CA 81-84; 142; CAAS 5;
  CANR 40; DLB 9, 26, 28; DLBY 93

Fuchs, Daniel 1934- . . . . **CLC 34**
  See also CA 37-40R; CANR 14, 48

Fuentes, Carlos
  1928- . . . . . . **CLC 3, 8, 10, 13, 22, 41, 60;**
            DA; DAB; DAC; DAM MST, MULT,
                   NOV; HLC; WLC
  See also AAYA 4; AITN 2; CA 69-72;
  CANR 10, 32; DLB 113; HW; MTCW

Fuentes, Gregorio Lopez y
  See Lopez y Fuentes, Gregorio

Fugard, (Harold) Athol
  1932- . . . . **CLC 5, 9, 14, 25, 40, 80;**
                     DAM DRAM; DC 3
  See also AAYA 17; CA 85-88; CANR 32;
  MTCW

Fugard, Sheila 1932- . . . . **CLC 48**
  See also CA 125

Fuller, Charles (H., Jr.)
  1939- . . . . **CLC 25; BLC; DAM DRAM,**
                    MULT; DC 1
  See also BW 2; CA 108; 112; DLB 38;
  INT 112; MTCW

Fuller, John (Leopold) 1937- . . . . **CLC 62**
  See also CA 21-24R; CANR 9, 44; DLB 40

Fuller, Margaret . . . . **NCLC 5, 50**
  See also Ossoli, Sarah Margaret (Fuller
  marchesa d')

Fuller, Roy (Broadbent)
  1912-1991 . . . . **CLC 4, 28**
  See also CA 5-8R; 135; CAAS 10;
  CANR 53; DLB 15, 20; SATA 87

Fulton, Alice 1952- . . . . **CLC 52**
  See also CA 116

Furphy, Joseph 1843-1912 . . . . **TCLC 25**

Fussell, Paul 1924- . . . . **CLC 74**
  See also BEST 90:1; CA 17-20R; CANR 8,
  21, 35; INT CANR-21; MTCW

Futabatei, Shimei 1864-1909 . . . . . . **TCLC 44**

Futrelle, Jacques 1875-1912 . . . . . . **TCLC 19**
  See also CA 113

Gaboriau, Emile 1835-1873 . . . . . . **NCLC 14**

Gadda, Carlo Emilio 1893-1973 . . . . **CLC 11**
  See also CA 89-92

Gaddis, William
  1922- . . **CLC 1, 3, 6, 8, 10, 19, 43, 86**
  See also CA 17-20R; CANR 21, 48; DLB 2;
  MTCW

Gaines, Ernest J(ames)
  1933- . . . . **CLC 3, 11, 18, 86; BLC;**
                      DAM MULT
  See also AAYA 18; AITN 1; BW 2;
  CA 9-12R; CANR 6, 24, 42;
  CDALB 1968-1988; DLB 2, 33, 152;
  DLBY 80; MTCW; SATA 86

Gaitskill, Mary 1954- . . . . **CLC 69**
  See also CA 128

Galdos, Benito Perez
  See Perez Galdos, Benito

Gale, Zona
  1874-1938 . . . . . . **TCLC 7; DAM DRAM**
  See also CA 105; DLB 9, 78

Galeano, Eduardo (Hughes) 1940-. . . **CLC 72**
  See also CA 29-32R; CANR 13, 32; HW

Galiano, Juan Valera y Alcala
  See Valera y Alcala-Galiano, Juan

Gallagher, Tess
  1943- . . **CLC 18, 63; DAM POET; PC 9**
  See also CA 106; DLB 120

Gallant, Mavis
  1922- . . . . **CLC 7, 18, 38; DAC;**
                         DAM MST; SSC 5
  See also CA 69-72; CANR 29; DLB 53;
  MTCW

Gallant, Roy A(rthur) 1924- . . . . **CLC 17**
  See also CA 5-8R; CANR 4, 29; CLR 30;
  MAICYA; SATA 4, 68

Gallico, Paul (William) 1897-1976 . . . **CLC 2**
  See also AITN 1; CA 5-8R; 69-72;
  CANR 23; DLB 9; MAICYA; SATA 13

Gallo, Max Louis 1932- . . . . **CLC 95**
  See also CA 85-88

Gallois, Lucien
  See Desnos, Robert

Gallup, Ralph
  See Whitemore, Hugh (John)

Galsworthy, John
  1867-1933 . . . . . . **TCLC 1, 45; DA; DAB;**
               DAC; DAM DRAM, MST, NOV;
                        SSC 22; WLC 2
  See also CA 104; 141; CDBLB 1890-1914;
  DLB 10, 34, 98, 162

Galt, John 1779-1839 . . . . **NCLC 1**
  See also DLB 99, 116, 159

Galvin, James 1951- . . . . **CLC 38**
  See also CA 108; CANR 26

Gamboa, Federico 1864-1939 . . . . . . **TCLC 36**

Gandhi, M. K.
  See Gandhi, Mohandas Karamchand

Gandhi, Mahatma
  See Gandhi, Mohandas Karamchand

Gandhi, Mohandas Karamchand
  1869-1948 . . . . . **TCLC 59; DAM MULT**
  See also CA 121; 132; MTCW

Gann, Ernest Kellogg 1910-1991 . . . . **CLC 23**
  See also AITN 1; CA 1-4R; 136; CANR 1

Garcia, Cristina 1958- . . . . **CLC 76**
  See also CA 141

Garcia Lorca, Federico
  1898-1936 . . . **TCLC 1, 7, 49; DA; DAB;**
            DAC; DAM DRAM, MST, MULT,
                   POET; DC 2; HLC; PC 3; WLC
  See also CA 104; 131; DLB 108; HW;
  MTCW

Garcia Marquez, Gabriel (Jose)
  1928- . . . . **CLC 2, 3, 8, 10, 15, 27, 47, 55,**
            68; DA; DAB; DAC; DAM MST,
            MULT, NOV, POP; HLC; SSC 8; WLC
  See also AAYA 3; BEST 89:1, 90:4;
  CA 33-36R; CANR 10, 28, 50; DLB 113;
  HW; MTCW

Gard, Janice
  See Latham, Jean Lee

Gard, Roger Martin du
  See Martin du Gard, Roger

Gardam, Jane 1928- . . . . **CLC 43**
  See also CA 49-52; CANR 2, 18, 33;
  CLR 12; DLB 14, 161; MAICYA;
  MTCW; SAAS 9; SATA 39, 76;
  SATA-Brief 28

Gardner, Herb(ert) 1934- . . . . **CLC 44**
  See also CA 149

Gardner, John (Champlin), Jr.
  1933-1982 . . . . . **CLC 2, 3, 5, 7, 8, 10, 18,**
            28, 34; DAM NOV, POP; SSC 7
  See also AITN 1; CA 65-68; 107;
  CANR 33; DLB 2; DLBY 82; MTCW;
  SATA 40; SATA-Obit 31

Gardner, John (Edmund)
  1926- . . . . **CLC 30; DAM POP**
  See also CA 103; CANR 15; MTCW

Gardner, Miriam
  See Bradley, Marion Zimmer

Gardner, Noel
  See Kuttner, Henry

Gardons, S. S.
  See Snodgrass, W(illiam) D(e Witt)

Garfield, Leon 1921-1996 . . . . **CLC 12**
  See also AAYA 8; CA 17-20R; 152;
  CANR 38, 41; CLR 21; DLB 161; JRDA;
  MAICYA; SATA 1, 32, 76

Garland, (Hannibal) Hamlin
  1860-1940 . . . . **TCLC 3; SSC 18**
  See also CA 104; DLB 12, 71, 78

Garneau, (Hector de) Saint-Denys
  1912-1943 . . . . **TCLC 13**
  See also CA 111; DLB 88

Garner, Alan
  1934- . . . . **CLC 17; DAB; DAM POP**
  See also AAYA 18; CA 73-76; CANR 15;
  CLR 20; DLB 161; MAICYA; MTCW;
  SATA 18, 69

Garner, Hugh 1913-1979 . . . . **CLC 13**
  See also CA 69-72; CANR 31; DLB 68

Garnett, David 1892-1981 . . . . **CLC 3**
  See also CA 5-8R; 103; CANR 17; DLB 34

Garos, Stephanie
  See Katz, Steve

Garrett, George (Palmer)
  1929- . . . . **CLC 3, 11, 51**
  See also CA 1-4R; CAAS 5; CANR 1, 42;
  DLB 2, 5, 130, 152; DLBY 83

Garrick, David
  1717-1779 . . . . **LC 15; DAM DRAM**
  See also DLB 84

Garrigue, Jean 1914-1972 . . . . **CLC 2, 8**
  See also CA 5-8R; 37-40R; CANR 20

Garrison, Frederick
  See Sinclair, Upton (Beall)

Garth, Will
  See Hamilton, Edmond; Kuttner, Henry

Garvey, Marcus (Moziah, Jr.)
  1887-1940 . . . . **TCLC 41; BLC;**
                              DAM MULT
  See also BW 1; CA 120; 124

Gary, Romain . . . . **CLC 25**
  See also Kacew, Romain
  See also DLB 83

Gascar, Pierre . . . . **CLC 11**
  See also Fournier, Pierre

Gascoyne, David (Emery) 1916- .... **CLC 45**
See also CA 65-68; CANR 10, 28; DLB 20;
MTCW

Gaskell, Elizabeth Cleghorn
1810-1865 .. **NCLC 5; DAB; DAM MST**
See also CDBLB 1832-1890; DLB 21, 144,
159

Gass, William H(oward)
1924- . . . **CLC 1, 2, 8, 11, 15, 39; SSC 12**
See also CA 17-20R; CANR 30; DLB 2;
MTCW

Gasset, Jose Ortega y
See Ortega y Gasset, Jose

Gates, Henry Louis, Jr.
1950- . . . . **CLC 65; DAM MULT**
See also BW 2; CA 109; CANR 25, 53;
DLB 67

Gautier, Theophile
1811-1872 . . . . . . **NCLC 1; DAM POET;**
SSC 20
See also DLB 119

Gawsworth, John
See Bates, H(erbert) E(rnest)

Gay, Oliver
See Gogarty, Oliver St. John

Gaye, Marvin (Penze) 1939-1984 . . . **CLC 26**
See also CA 112

Gebler, Carlo (Ernest) 1954- . . . . **CLC 39**
See also CA 119; 133

Gee, Maggie (Mary) 1948- . . . . **CLC 57**
See also CA 130

Gee, Maurice (Gough) 1931- . . . . **CLC 29**
See also CA 97-100; SATA 46

Gelbart, Larry (Simon) 1923- . . . **CLC 21, 61**
See also CA 73-76; CANR 45

Gelber, Jack 1932- . . . . **CLC 1, 6, 14, 79**
See also CA 1-4R; CANR 2; DLB 7

Gellhorn, Martha (Ellis) 1908- . . **CLC 14, 60**
See also CA 77-80; CANR 44; DLBY 82

Genet, Jean
1910-1986 . . . . . . **CLC 1, 2, 5, 10, 14, 44,**
46; DAM DRAM
See also CA 13-16R; CANR 18; DLB 72;
DLBY 86; MTCW

Gent, Peter 1942- . . . . **CLC 29**
See also AITN 1; CA 89-92; DLBY 82

Gentlewoman in New England, A
See Bradstreet, Anne

Gentlewoman in Those Parts, A
See Bradstreet, Anne

George, Jean Craighead 1919- . . . . . . **CLC 35**
See also AAYA 8; CA 5-8R; CANR 25;
CLR 1; DLB 52; JRDA; MAICYA;
SATA 2, 68

George, Stefan (Anton)
1868-1933 . . . . **TCLC 2, 14**
See also CA 104

Georges, Georges Martin
See Simenon, Georges (Jacques Christian)

Gerhardi, William Alexander
See Gerhardie, William Alexander

Gerhardie, William Alexander
1895-1977 . . . . **CLC 5**
See also CA 25-28R; 73-76; CANR 18;
DLB 36

Gerstler, Amy 1956- . . . . **CLC 70**
See also CA 146

Gertler, T. . . . . **CLC 34**
See also CA 116; 121; INT 121

gfgg . . . . **CLC XvXzc**

Ghalib . . . . **NCLC 39**
See also Ghalib, Hsadullah Khan

Ghalib, Hsadullah Khan 1797-1869
See Ghalib
See also DAM POET

Ghelderode, Michel de
1898-1962 . . . . **CLC 6, 11; DAM DRAM**
See also CA 85-88; CANR 40

Ghiselin, Brewster 1903- . . . . **CLC 23**
See also CA 13-16R; CAAS 10; CANR 13

Ghose, Zulfikar 1935- . . . . **CLC 42**
See also CA 65-68

Ghosh, Amitav 1956- . . . . **CLC 44**
See also CA 147

Giacosa, Giuseppe 1847-1906 . . . . . . **TCLC 7**
See also CA 104

Gibb, Lee
See Waterhouse, Keith (Spencer)

Gibbon, Lewis Grassic . . . . **TCLC 4**
See also Mitchell, James Leslie

Gibbons, Kaye
1960- . . . . **CLC 50, 88; DAM POP**
See also CA 151

Gibran, Kahlil
1883-1931 . . . . **TCLC 1, 9; DAM POET,**
POP; PC 9
See also CA 104; 150

Gibran, Khalil
See Gibran, Kahlil

Gibson, William
1914- . . . . **CLC 23; DA; DAB; DAC;**
DAM DRAM, MST
See also CA 9-12R; CANR 9, 42; DLB 7;
SATA 66

Gibson, William (Ford)
1948- . . . . **CLC 39, 63; DAM POP**
See also AAYA 12; CA 126; 133; CANR 52

Gide, Andre (Paul Guillaume)
1869-1951 . . . . **TCLC 5, 12, 36; DA;**
DAB; DAC; DAM MST, NOV; SSC 13;
WLC
See also CA 104; 124; DLB 65; MTCW

Gifford, Barry (Colby) 1946- . . . . **CLC 34**
See also CA 65-68; CANR 9, 30, 40

Gilbert, W(illiam) S(chwenck)
1836-1911 . . . . . **TCLC 3; DAM DRAM,**
POET
See also CA 104; SATA 36

Gilbreth, Frank B., Jr. 1911- . . . . **CLC 17**
See also CA 9-12R; SATA 2

Gilchrist, Ellen
1935- . . . . **CLC 34, 48; DAM POP;**
SSC 14
See also CA 113; 116; CANR 41; DLB 130;
MTCW

Giles, Molly 1942- . . . . **CLC 39**
See also CA 126

Gill, Patrick
See Creasey, John

Gilliam, Terry (Vance) 1940- . . . . **CLC 21**
See also Monty Python
See also CA 108; 113; CANR 35; INT 113

Gillian, Jerry
See Gilliam, Terry (Vance)

Gilliatt, Penelope (Ann Douglass)
1932-1993 . . . . **CLC 2, 10, 13, 53**
See also AITN 2; CA 13-16R; 141;
CANR 49; DLB 14

Gilman, Charlotte (Anna) Perkins (Stetson)
1860-1935 . . . . **TCLC 9, 37; SSC 13**
See also CA 106; 150

Gilmour, David 1949- . . . . **CLC 35**
See also CA 138, 147

Gilpin, William 1724-1804 . . . . . . **NCLC 30**

Gilray, J. D.
See Mencken, H(enry) L(ouis)

Gilroy, Frank D(aniel) 1925- . . . . **CLC 2**
See also CA 81-84; CANR 32; DLB 7

Ginsberg, Allen
1926- . . . . . . **CLC 1, 2, 3, 4, 6, 13, 36, 69;**
DA; DAB; DAC; DAM MST, POET;
PC 4; WLC 3
See also AITN 1; CA 1-4R; CANR 2, 41;
CDALB 1941-1968; DLB 5, 16; MTCW

Ginzburg, Natalia
1916-1991 . . . . **CLC 5, 11, 54, 70**
See also CA 85-88; 135; CANR 33; MTCW

Giono, Jean 1895-1970 . . . . **CLC 4, 11**
See also CA 45-48; 29-32R; CANR 2, 35;
DLB 72; MTCW

Giovanni, Nikki
1943- . . . . . . **CLC 2, 4, 19, 64; BLC; DA;**
DAB; DAC; DAM MST, MULT, POET
See also AITN 1; BW 2; CA 29-32R;
CAAS 6; CANR 18, 41; CLR 6; DLB 5,
41; INT CANR-18; MAICYA; MTCW;
SATA 24

Giovene, Andrea 1904- . . . . **CLC 7**
See also CA 85-88

Gippius, Zinaida (Nikolayevna) 1869-1945
See Hippius, Zinaida
See also CA 106

Giraudoux, (Hippolyte) Jean
1882-1944 . . . . **TCLC 2, 7; DAM DRAM**
See also CA 104; DLB 65

Gironella, Jose Maria 1917- . . . . **CLC 11**
See also CA 101

Gissing, George (Robert)
1857-1903 . . . . **TCLC 3, 24, 47**
See also CA 105; DLB 18, 135

Giurlani, Aldo
See Palazzeschi, Aldo

Gladkov, Fyodor (Vasilyevich)
1883-1958 . . . . **TCLC 27**

Glanville, Brian (Lester) 1931- . . . . . . **CLC 6**
See also CA 5-8R; CAAS 9; CANR 3;
DLB 15, 139; SATA 42

Glasgow, Ellen (Anderson Gholson)
1873(?)-1945 . . . . **TCLC 2, 7**
See also CA 104; DLB 9, 12

Glaspell, Susan (Keating)
1882(?)-1948 . . . . **TCLC 55**
See also CA 110; DLB 7, 9, 78; YABC 2

Glassco, John 1909-1981 . . . . **CLC 9**
See also CA 13-16R; 102; CANR 15;
DLB 68

Glasscock, Amnesia
See Steinbeck, John (Ernst)

Glasser, Ronald J. 1940(?)- . . . . **CLC 37**

Glassman, Joyce
See Johnson, Joyce

Glendinning, Victoria 1937- . . . . **CLC 50**
See also CA 120; 127; DLB 155

Glissant, Edouard
1928- . . . . **CLC 10, 68; DAM MULT**

Gloag, Julian 1930- . . . . **CLC 40**
See also AITN 1; CA 65-68; CANR 10

Glowacki, Aleksander
See Prus, Boleslaw

Gluck, Louise (Elisabeth)
1943- . . . . **CLC 7, 22, 44, 81;**
DAM POET; PC 16
See also CA 33-36R; CANR 40; DLB 5

Gobineau, Joseph Arthur (Comte) de
1816-1882 . . . . **NCLC 17**
See also DLB 123

Godard, Jean-Luc 1930- . . . . **CLC 20**
See also CA 93-96

Godden, (Margaret) Rumer 1907- . . . **CLC 53**
See also AAYA 6; CA 5-8R; CANR 4, 27,
36; CLR 20; DLB 161; MAICYA;
SAAS 12; SATA 3, 36

Godoy Alcayaga, Lucila 1889-1957
See Mistral, Gabriela
See also BW 2; CA 104; 131; DAM MULT;
HW; MTCW

Godwin, Gail (Kathleen)
1937- . . . . **CLC 5, 8, 22, 31, 69;**
DAM POP
See also CA 29-32R; CANR 15, 43; DLB 6;
INT CANR-15; MTCW

Godwin, William 1756-1836 . . . . . **NCLC 14**
See also CDBLB 1789-1832; DLB 39, 104,
142, 158, 163

Goethe, Johann Wolfgang von
1749-1832 . . . . **NCLC 4, 22, 34; DA;**
DAB; DAC; DAM DRAM, MST,
POET; PC 5; WLC 3
See also DLB 94

Gogarty, Oliver St. John
1878-1957 . . . . **TCLC 15**
See also CA 109; 150; DLB 15, 19

Gogol, Nikolai (Vasilyevich)
1809-1852 . . . . **NCLC 5, 15, 31; DA;**
DAB; DAC; DAM DRAM, MST; DC 1;
SSC 4; WLC

Goines, Donald
1937(?)-1974 . . . . **CLC 80; BLC;**
DAM MULT, POP
See also AITN 1; BW 1; CA 124; 114;
DLB 33

Gold, Herbert 1924- . . . . **CLC 4, 7, 14, 42**
See also CA 9-12R; CANR 17, 45; DLB 2;
DLBY 81

Goldbarth, Albert 1948- . . . . **CLC 5, 38**
See also CA 53-56; CANR 6, 40; DLB 120

Goldberg, Anatol 1910-1982 . . . . **CLC 34**
See also CA 131; 117

Goldemberg, Isaac 1945- . . . . **CLC 52**
See also CA 69-72; CAAS 12; CANR 11,
32; HW

Golding, William (Gerald)
1911-1993 . . . . **CLC 1, 2, 3, 8, 10, 17, 27,**
58, 81; DA; DAB; DAC; DAM MST,
NOV; WLC
See also AAYA 5; CA 5-8R; 141;
CANR 13, 33; CDBLB 1945-1960;
DLB 15, 100; MTCW

Goldman, Emma 1869-1940 . . . . . . **TCLC 13**
See also CA 110; 150

Goldman, Francisco 1955- . . . . **CLC 76**

Goldman, William (W.) 1931- . . . . **CLC 1, 48**
See also CA 9-12R; CANR 29; DLB 44

Goldmann, Lucien 1913-1970 . . . . . . **CLC 24**
See also CA 25-28; CAP 2

Goldoni, Carlo
1707-1793 . . . . **LC 4; DAM DRAM**

Goldsberry, Steven 1949- . . . . **CLC 34**
See also CA 131

Goldsmith, Oliver
1728-1774 . . . . . . **LC 2; DA; DAB; DAC;**
DAM DRAM, MST, NOV, POET;
WLC
See also CDBLB 1660-1789; DLB 39, 89,
104, 109, 142; SATA 26

Goldsmith, Peter
See Priestley, J(ohn) B(oynton)

Gombrowicz, Witold
1904-1969 . . . . **CLC 4, 7, 11, 49;**
DAM DRAM
See also CA 19-20; 25-28R; CAP 2

Gomez de la Serna, Ramon
1888-1963 . . . . **CLC 9**
See also CA 116; HW

Goncharov, Ivan Alexandrovich
1812-1891 . . . . **NCLC 1**

Goncourt, Edmond (Louis Antoine Huot) de
1822-1896 . . . . **NCLC 7**
See also DLB 123

Goncourt, Jules (Alfred Huot) de
1830-1870 . . . . **NCLC 7**
See also DLB 123

Gontier, Fernande 19(?)- . . . . **CLC 50**

Goodman, Paul 1911-1972 . . . . **CLC 1, 2, 4, 7**
See also CA 19-20; 37-40R; CANR 34;
CAP 2; DLB 130; MTCW

Gordimer, Nadine
1923- . . . . **CLC 3, 5, 7, 10, 18, 33, 51, 70;**
DA; DAB; DAC; DAM MST, NOV;
SSC 17
See also CA 5-8R; CANR 3, 28;
INT CANR-28; MTCW

Gordon, Adam Lindsay
1833-1870 . . . . **NCLC 21**

Gordon, Caroline
1895-1981 . . . **CLC 6, 13, 29, 83; SSC 15**
See also CA 11-12; 103; CANR 36; CAP 1;
DLB 4, 9, 102; DLBY 81; MTCW

Gordon, Charles William 1860-1937
See Connor, Ralph
See also CA 109

Gordon, Mary (Catherine)
1949- . . . . **CLC 13, 22**
See also CA 102; CANR 44; DLB 6;
DLBY 81; INT 102; MTCW

Gordon, Sol 1923- . . . . **CLC 26**
See also CA 53-56; CANR 4; SATA 11

Gordone, Charles
1925-1995 . . . . . **CLC 1, 4; DAM DRAM**
See also BW 1; CA 93-96; 150; DLB 7;
INT 93-96; MTCW

Gorenko, Anna Andreevna
See Akhmatova, Anna

Gorky, Maxim . . . . **TCLC 8; DAB; WLC**
See also Peshkov, Alexei Maximovich

Goryan, Sirak
See Saroyan, William

Gosse, Edmund (William)
1849-1928 . . . . **TCLC 28**
See also CA 117; DLB 57, 144

Gotlieb, Phyllis Fay (Bloom)
1926- . . . . **CLC 18**
See also CA 13-16R; CANR 7; DLB 88

Gottesman, S. D.
See Kornbluth, C(yril) M.; Pohl, Frederik

Gottfried von Strassburg
fl. c. 1210- . . . . **CMLC 10**
See also DLB 138

Gould, Lois . . . . **CLC 4, 10**
See also CA 77-80; CANR 29; MTCW

Gourmont, Remy (-Marie-Charles) de
1858-1915 . . . . **TCLC 17**
See also CA 109; 150

Govier, Katherine 1948- . . . . **CLC 51**
See also CA 101; CANR 18, 40

Goyen, (Charles) William
1915-1983 . . . . **CLC 5, 8, 14, 40**
See also AITN 2; CA 5-8R; 110; CANR 6;
DLB 2; DLBY 83; INT CANR-6

Goytisolo, Juan
1931- . . . . . **CLC 5, 10, 23; DAM MULT;**
HLC
See also CA 85-88; CANR 32; HW; MTCW

Gozzano, Guido 1883-1916 . . . . **PC 10**
See also DLB 114

Gozzi, (Conte) Carlo 1720-1806 . . **NCLC 23**

Grabbe, Christian Dietrich
1801-1836 . . . . **NCLC 2**
See also DLB 133

Grace, Patricia 1937- . . . . **CLC 56**

Gracian y Morales, Baltasar
1601-1658 . . . . **LC 15**

Gracq, Julien . . . . **CLC 11, 48**
See also Poirier, Louis
See also DLB 83

Grade, Chaim 1910-1982 . . . . **CLC 10**
See also CA 93-96; 107

Graduate of Oxford, A
See Ruskin, John

Graham, John
See Phillips, David Graham

Graham, Jorie 1951- . . . . **CLC 48**
See also CA 111; DLB 120

Grossman, David 1954- . . . . CLC 67
See also CA 138

Grossman, Vasily (Semenovich)
1905-1964 . . . . CLC 41
See also CA 124; 130; MTCW

Grove, Frederick Philip . . . . TCLC 4
See also Greve, Felix Paul (Berthold
Friedrich)
See also DLB 92

Grubb
See Crumb, R(obert)

Grumbach, Doris (Isaac)
1918- . . . . CLC 13, 22, 64
See also CA 5-8R; CAAS 2; CANR 9, 42;
INT CANR-9

Grundtvig, Nicolai Frederik Severin
1783-1872 . . . . NCLC 1

Grunge
See Crumb, R(obert)

Grunwald, Lisa 1959- . . . . CLC 44
See also CA 120

Guare, John
1938- . . . . CLC 8, 14, 29, 67;
DAM DRAM
See also CA 73-76; CANR 21; DLB 7;
MTCW

Gudjonsson, Halldor Kiljan 1902-
See Laxness, Halldor
See also CA 103

Guenter, Erich
See Eich, Guenter

Guest, Barbara 1920- . . . . CLC 34
See also CA 25-28R; CANR 11, 44; DLB 5

Guest, Judith (Ann)
1936- . . . . CLC 8, 30; DAM NOV, POP
See also AAYA 7; CA 77-80; CANR 15;
INT CANR-15; MTCW

Guevara, Che . . . . CLC 87; HLC
See also Guevara (Serna), Ernesto

Guevara (Serna), Ernesto 1928-1967
See Guevara, Che
See also CA 127; 111; DAM MULT; HW

Guild, Nicholas M. 1944- . . . . CLC 33
See also CA 93-96

Guillemin, Jacques
See Sartre, Jean-Paul

Guillen, Jorge
1893-1984 . . . . . . CLC 11; DAM MULT,
POET
See also CA 89-92; 112; DLB 108; HW

Guillen, Nicolas (Cristobal)
1902-1989 . . . . CLC 48, 79; BLC;
DAM MST, MULT, POET; HLC
See also BW 2; CA 116; 125; 129; HW

Guillevic, (Eugene) 1907- . . . . CLC 33
See also CA 93-96

Guillois
See Desnos, Robert

Guillois, Valentin
See Desnos, Robert

Guiney, Louise Imogen
1861-1920 . . . . TCLC 41
See also DLB 54

Guiraldes, Ricardo (Guillermo)
1886-1927 . . . . TCLC 39
See also CA 131; HW; MTCW

Gumilev, Nikolai Stephanovich
1886-1921 . . . . TCLC 60

Gunesekera, Romesh . . . . CLC 91

Gunn, Bill . . . . CLC 5
See also Gunn, William Harrison
See also DLB 38

Gunn, Thom(son William)
1929- . . . . CLC 3, 6, 18, 32, 81;
DAM POET
See also CA 17-20R; CANR 9, 33;
CDBLB 1960 to Present; DLB 27;
INT CANR-33; MTCW

Gunn, William Harrison 1934(?)-1989
See Gunn, Bill
See also AITN 1; BW 1; CA 13-16R; 128;
CANR 12, 25

Gunnars, Kristjana 1948- . . . . CLC 69
See also CA 113; DLB 60

Gurganus, Allan
1947- . . . . CLC 70; DAM POP
See also BEST 90:1; CA 135

Gurney, A(lbert) R(amsdell), Jr.
1930- . . . . CLC 32, 50, 54; DAM DRAM
See also CA 77-80; CANR 32

Gurney, Ivor (Bertie) 1890-1937 . . . TCLC 33

Gurney, Peter
See Gurney, A(lbert) R(amsdell), Jr.

Guro, Elena 1877-1913 . . . . TCLC 56

Gustafson, Ralph (Barker) 1909- . . . . CLC 36
See also CA 21-24R; CANR 8, 45; DLB 88

Gut, Gom
See Simenon, Georges (Jacques Christian)

Guterson, David 1956- . . . . CLC 91
See also CA 132

Guthrie, A(lfred) B(ertram), Jr.
1901-1991 . . . . CLC 23
See also CA 57-60; 134; CANR 24; DLB 6;
SATA 62; SATA-Obit 67

Guthrie, Isobel
See Grieve, C(hristopher) M(urray)

Guthrie, Woodrow Wilson 1912-1967
See Guthrie, Woody
See also CA 113; 93-96

Guthrie, Woody . . . . CLC 35
See also Guthrie, Woodrow Wilson

Guy, Rosa (Cuthbert) 1928- . . . . CLC 26
See also AAYA 4; BW 2; CA 17-20R;
CANR 14, 34; CLR 13; DLB 33; JRDA;
MAICYA; SATA 14, 62

Gwendolyn
See Bennett, (Enoch) Arnold

H. D. . . . . CLC 3, 8, 14, 31, 34, 73; PC 5
See also Doolittle, Hilda

H. de V.
See Buchan, John

Haavikko, Paavo Juhani
1931- . . . . CLC 18, 34
See also CA 106

Habbema, Koos
See Heijermans, Herman

Hacker, Marilyn
1942- . . . . CLC 5, 9, 23, 72, 91;
DAM POET
See also CA 77-80; DLB 120

Haggard, H(enry) Rider
1856-1925 . . . . TCLC 11
See also CA 108; 148; DLB 70, 156;
SATA 16

Hagiosy, L.
See Larbaud, Valery (Nicolas)

Hagiwara Sakutaro 1886-1942 . . . . TCLC 60

Haig, Fenil
See Ford, Ford Madox

Haig-Brown, Roderick (Langmere)
1908-1976 . . . . CLC 21
See also CA 5-8R; 69-72; CANR 4, 38;
CLR 31; DLB 88; MAICYA; SATA 12

Hailey, Arthur
1920- . . . . CLC 5; DAM NOV, POP
See also AITN 2; BEST 90:3; CA 1-4R;
CANR 2, 36; DLB 88; DLBY 82; MTCW

Hailey, Elizabeth Forsythe 1938- . . . CLC 40
See also CA 93-96; CAAS 1; CANR 15, 48;
INT CANR-15

Haines, John (Meade) 1924- . . . . CLC 58
See also CA 17-20R; CANR 13, 34; DLB 5

Hakluyt, Richard 1552-1616 . . . . LC 31

Haldeman, Joe (William) 1943- . . . . . CLC 61
See also CA 53-56; CANR 6; DLB 8;
INT CANR-6

Haley, Alex(ander Murray Palmer)
1921-1992 . . . . CLC 8, 12, 76; BLC; DA;
DAB; DAC; DAM MST, MULT, POP
See also BW 2; CA 77-80; 136; DLB 38;
MTCW

Haliburton, Thomas Chandler
1796-1865 . . . . NCLC 15
See also DLB 11, 99

Hall, Donald (Andrew, Jr.)
1928- . . CLC 1, 13, 37, 59; DAM POET
See also CA 5-8R; CAAS 7; CANR 2, 44;
DLB 5; SATA 23

Hall, Frederic Sauser
See Sauser-Hall, Frederic

Hall, James
See Kuttner, Henry

Hall, James Norman 1887-1951 . . . TCLC 23
See also CA 123; SATA 21

Hall, (Marguerite) Radclyffe
1886-1943 . . . . TCLC 12
See also CA 110; 150

Hall, Rodney 1935- . . . . CLC 51
See also CA 109

Halleck, Fitz-Greene 1790-1867 . . NCLC 47
See also DLB 3

Halliday, Michael
See Creasey, John

Halpern, Daniel 1945- . . . . CLC 14
See also CA 33-36R

Hamburger, Michael (Peter Leopold)
1924- . . . . CLC 5, 14
See also CA 5-8R; CAAS 4; CANR 2, 47;
DLB 27

Hamill, Pete 1935- . . . . CLC 10
See also CA 25-28R; CANR 18

Hamilton, Alexander
1755(?)-1804 . . . . NCLC 49
See also DLB 37

Hamilton, Clive
See Lewis, C(live) S(taples)

Hamilton, Edmond 1904-1977 . . . . . . CLC 1
See also CA 1-4R; CANR 3; DLB 8

Hamilton, Eugene (Jacob) Lee
See Lee-Hamilton, Eugene (Jacob)

Hamilton, Franklin
See Silverberg, Robert

Hamilton, Gail
See Corcoran, Barbara

Hamilton, Mollie
See Kaye, M(ary) M(argaret)

Hamilton, (Anthony Walter) Patrick
1904-1962 . . . . CLC 51
See also CA 113; DLB 10

Hamilton, Virginia
1936- . . . . CLC 26; DAM MULT
See also AAYA 2; BW 2; CA 25-28R;
CANR 20, 37; CLR 1, 11, 40; DLB 33,
52; INT CANR-20; JRDA; MAICYA;
MTCW; SATA 4, 56, 79

Hammett, (Samuel) Dashiell
1894-1961 . . . . CLC 3, 5, 10, 19, 47;
SSC 17
See also AITN 1; CA 81-84; CANR 42;
CDALB 1929-1941; DLBD 6; MTCW

Hammon, Jupiter
1711(?)-1800(?) . . . . NCLC 5; BLC;
DAM MULT, POET; PC 16
See also DLB 31, 50

Hammond, Keith
See Kuttner, Henry

Hamner, Earl (Henry), Jr. 1923- . . . CLC 12
See also AITN 2; CA 73-76; DLB 6

Hampton, Christopher (James)
1946- . . . . CLC 4
See also CA 25-28R; DLB 13; MTCW

Hamsun, Knut . . . . TCLC 2, 14, 49
See also Pedersen, Knut

Handke, Peter
1942- . . . . CLC 5, 8, 10, 15, 38;
DAM DRAM, NOV
See also CA 77-80; CANR 33; DLB 85,
124; MTCW

Hanley, James 1901-1985 . . . CLC 3, 5, 8, 13
See also CA 73-76; 117; CANR 36; MTCW

Hannah, Barry 1942- . . . . . . CLC 23, 38, 90
See also CA 108; 110; CANR 43; DLB 6;
INT 110; MTCW

Hannon, Ezra
See Hunter, Evan

Hansberry, Lorraine (Vivian)
1930-1965 . . . . . . CLC 17, 62; BLC; DA;
DAB; DAC; DAM DRAM, MST,
MULT; DC 2
See also BW 1; CA 109; 25-28R; CABS 3;
CDALB 1941-1968; DLB 7, 38; MTCW

Hansen, Joseph 1923- . . . . CLC 38
See also CA 29-32R; CAAS 17; CANR 16,
44; INT CANR-16

Hansen, Martin A. 1909-1955 . . . . . TCLC 32

Hanson, Kenneth O(stlin) 1922- . . . . CLC 13
See also CA 53-56; CANR 7

Hardwick, Elizabeth
1916- . . . . CLC 13; DAM NOV
See also CA 5-8R; CANR 3, 32; DLB 6;
MTCW

Hardy, Thomas
1840-1928 . . . . . . TCLC 4, 10, 18, 32, 48,
53; DA; DAB; DAC; DAM MST, NOV,
POET; PC 8; SSC 2; WLC
See also CA 104; 123; CDBLB 1890-1914;
DLB 18, 19, 135; MTCW

Hare, David 1947- . . . . CLC 29, 58
See also CA 97-100; CANR 39; DLB 13;
MTCW

Harford, Henry
See Hudson, W(illiam) H(enry)

Hargrave, Leonie
See Disch, Thomas M(ichael)

Harjo, Joy 1951- . . . CLC 83; DAM MULT
See also CA 114; CANR 35; DLB 120;
NNAL

Harlan, Louis R(udolph) 1922- . . . . . CLC 34
See also CA 21-24R; CANR 25

Harling, Robert 1951(?)- . . . . CLC 53
See also CA 147

Harmon, William (Ruth) 1938- . . . . . CLC 38
See also CA 33-36R; CANR 14, 32, 35;
SATA 65

Harper, F. E. W.
See Harper, Frances Ellen Watkins

Harper, Frances E. W.
See Harper, Frances Ellen Watkins

Harper, Frances E. Watkins
See Harper, Frances Ellen Watkins

Harper, Frances Ellen
See Harper, Frances Ellen Watkins

Harper, Frances Ellen Watkins
1825-1911 . . . . TCLC 14; BLC;
DAM MULT, POET
See also BW 1; CA 111; 125; DLB 50

Harper, Michael S(teven) 1938- . . CLC 7, 22
See also BW 1; CA 33-36R; CANR 24;
DLB 41

Harper, Mrs. F. E. W.
See Harper, Frances Ellen Watkins

Harris, Christie (Lucy) Irwin
1907- . . . . CLC 12
See also CA 5-8R; CANR 6; DLB 88;
JRDA; MAICYA; SAAS 10; SATA 6, 74

Harris, Frank 1856-1931 . . . . TCLC 24
See also CA 109; 150; DLB 156

Harris, George Washington
1814-1869 . . . . NCLC 23
See also DLB 3, 11

Harris, Joel Chandler
1848-1908 . . . . TCLC 2; SSC 19
See also CA 104; 137; DLB 11, 23, 42, 78,
91; MAICYA; YABC 1

Harris, John (Wyndham Parkes Lucas)
Beynon 1903-1969
See Wyndham, John
See also CA 102; 89-92

Harris, MacDonald . . . . CLC 9
See also Heiney, Donald (William)

Harris, Mark 1922- . . . . CLC 19
See also CA 5-8R; CAAS 3; CANR 2;
DLB 2; DLBY 80

Harris, (Theodore) Wilson 1921- . . . . CLC 25
See also BW 2; CA 65-68; CAAS 16;
CANR 11, 27; DLB 117; MTCW

Harrison, Elizabeth Cavanna 1909-
See Cavanna, Betty
See also CA 9-12R; CANR 6, 27

Harrison, Harry (Max) 1925- . . . . . . CLC 42
See also CA 1-4R; CANR 5, 21; DLB 8;
SATA 4

Harrison, James (Thomas)
1937- . . . . . . CLC 6, 14, 33, 66; SSC 19
See also CA 13-16R; CANR 8, 51;
DLBY 82; INT CANR-8

Harrison, Jim
See Harrison, James (Thomas)

Harrison, Kathryn 1961- . . . . CLC 70
See also CA 144

Harrison, Tony 1937- . . . . CLC 43
See also CA 65-68; CANR 44; DLB 40;
MTCW

Harriss, Will(ard Irvin) 1922- . . . . . . CLC 34
See also CA 111

Harson, Sley
See Ellison, Harlan (Jay)

Hart, Ellis
See Ellison, Harlan (Jay)

Hart, Josephine
1942(?)- . . . . CLC 70; DAM POP
See also CA 138

Hart, Moss
1904-1961 . . . . . . CLC 66; DAM DRAM
See also CA 109; 89-92; DLB 7

Harte, (Francis) Bret(t)
1836(?)-1902 . . . . . . TCLC 1, 25; DA; DAC;
DAM MST; SSC 8; WLC
See also CA 104; 140; CDALB 1865-1917;
DLB 12, 64, 74, 79; SATA 26

Hartley, L(eslie) P(oles)
1895-1972 . . . . CLC 2, 22
See also CA 45-48; 37-40R; CANR 33;
DLB 15, 139; MTCW

Hartman, Geoffrey H. 1929- . . . . CLC 27
See also CA 117; 125; DLB 67

Hartmann von Aue
c. 1160-c. 1205 . . . . CMLC 15
See also DLB 138

Hartmann von Aue 1170-1210 . . . . CMLC 15

Haruf, Kent 1943- . . . . CLC 34
See also CA 149

Harwood, Ronald
1934- . . . . CLC 32; DAM DRAM, MST
See also CA 1-4R; CANR 4; DLB 13

Hasek, Jaroslav (Matej Frantisek)
1883-1923 . . . . TCLC 4
See also CA 104; 129; MTCW

Hass, Robert 1941- . . . . . CLC 18, 39; PC 16
See also CA 111; CANR 30, 50; DLB 105

Hastings, Hudson
See Kuttner, Henry

Hastings, Selina . . . . CLC 44

Hatteras, Amelia
See Mencken, H(enry) L(ouis)

Hatteras, Owen . . . . **TCLC 18**
See also Mencken, H(enry) L(ouis); Nathan, George Jean

Hauptmann, Gerhart (Johann Robert)
1862-1946 . . . . . . **TCLC 4; DAM DRAM**
See also CA 104; DLB 66, 118

Havel, Vaclav
1936- . . . . **CLC 25, 58, 65;**
DAM DRAM; DC 6
See also CA 104; CANR 36; MTCW

Haviaras, Stratis . . . . **CLC 33**
See also Chaviaras, Strates

Hawes, Stephen 1475(?)-1523(?) . . . . . **LC 17**

Hawkes, John (Clendennin Burne, Jr.)
1925- . . . . . . **CLC 1, 2, 3, 4, 7, 9, 14, 15,**
27, 49
See also CA 1-4R; CANR 2, 47; DLB 2, 7;
DLBY 80; MTCW

Hawking, S. W.
See Hawking, Stephen W(illiam)

Hawking, Stephen W(illiam)
1942- . . . . **CLC 63**
See also AAYA 13; BEST 89:1; CA 126;
129; CANR 48

Hawthorne, Julian 1846-1934 . . . . . **TCLC 25**

Hawthorne, Nathaniel
1804-1864 . . . . **NCLC 39; DA; DAB;**
DAC; DAM MST, NOV; SSC 3; WLC
See also AAYA 18; CDALB 1640-1865;
DLB 1, 74; YABC 2

Haxton, Josephine Ayres 1921-
See Douglas, Ellen
See also CA 115; CANR 41

Hayaseca y Eizaguirre, Jorge
See Echegaray (y Eizaguirre), Jose (Maria Waldo)

Hayashi Fumiko 1904-1951 . . . . **TCLC 27**

Haycraft, Anna
See Ellis, Alice Thomas
See also CA 122

Hayden, Robert E(arl)
1913-1980 . . . . . . **CLC 5, 9, 14, 37; BLC;**
DA; DAC; DAM MST, MULT, POET;
PC 6
See also BW 1; CA 69-72; 97-100; CABS 2;
CANR 24; CDALB 1941-1968; DLB 5,
76; MTCW; SATA 19; SATA-Obit 26

Hayford, J(oseph) E(phraim) Casely
See Casely-Hayford, J(oseph) E(phraim)

Hayman, Ronald 1932- . . . . **CLC 44**
See also CA 25-28R; CANR 18, 50;
DLB 155

Haywood, Eliza (Fowler)
1693(?)-1756 . . . . **LC 1**

Hazlitt, William 1778-1830 . . . . . . **NCLC 29**
See also DLB 110, 158

Hazzard, Shirley 1931- . . . . **CLC 18**
See also CA 9-12R; CANR 4; DLBY 82;
MTCW

Head, Bessie
1937-1986 . . . . **CLC 25, 67; BLC;**
DAM MULT
See also BW 2; CA 29-32R; 119; CANR 25;
DLB 117; MTCW

Headon, (Nicky) Topper 1956(?)- . . . **CLC 30**

Heaney, Seamus (Justin)
1939- . . . . . . **CLC 5, 7, 14, 25, 37, 74, 91;**
DAB; DAM POET
See also CA 85-88; CANR 25, 48;
CDBLB 1960 to Present; DLB 40;
DLBY 95; MTCW

Hearn, (Patricio) Lafcadio (Tessima Carlos)
1850-1904 . . . . **TCLC 9**
See also CA 105; DLB 12, 78

Hearne, Vicki 1946- . . . . **CLC 56**
See also CA 139

Hearon, Shelby 1931- . . . . **CLC 63**
See also AITN 2; CA 25-28R; CANR 18,
48

Heat-Moon, William Least . . . . **CLC 29**
See also Trogdon, William (Lewis)
See also AAYA 9

Hebbel, Friedrich
1813-1863 . . . . **NCLC 43; DAM DRAM**
See also DLB 129

Hebert, Anne
1916- . . . . **CLC 4, 13, 29; DAC;**
DAM MST, POET
See also CA 85-88; DLB 68; MTCW

Hecht, Anthony (Evan)
1923- . . . . . . **CLC 8, 13, 19; DAM POET**
See also CA 9-12R; CANR 6; DLB 5

Hecht, Ben 1894-1964 . . . . **CLC 8**
See also CA 85-88; DLB 7, 9, 25, 26, 28, 86

Hedayat, Sadeq 1903-1951 . . . . **TCLC 21**
See also CA 120

Hegel, Georg Wilhelm Friedrich
1770-1831 . . . . **NCLC 46**
See also DLB 90

Heidegger, Martin 1889-1976 . . . . . . **CLC 24**
See also CA 81-84; 65-68; CANR 34;
MTCW

Heidenstam, (Carl Gustaf) Verner von
1859-1940 . . . . **TCLC 5**
See also CA 104

Heifner, Jack 1946- . . . . **CLC 11**
See also CA 105; CANR 47

Heijermans, Herman 1864-1924 . . . **TCLC 24**
See also CA 123

Heilbrun, Carolyn G(old) 1926- . . . . . **CLC 25**
See also CA 45-48; CANR 1, 28

Heine, Heinrich 1797-1856 . . . . **NCLC 4, 54**
See also DLB 90

Heinemann, Larry (Curtiss) 1944- . . **CLC 50**
See also CA 110; CAAS 21; CANR 31;
DLBD 9; INT CANR-31

Heiney, Donald (William) 1921-1993
See Harris, MacDonald
See also CA 1-4R; 142; CANR 3

Heinlein, Robert A(nson)
1907-1988 . . . . . . **CLC 1, 3, 8, 14, 26, 55;**
DAM POP
See also AAYA 17; CA 1-4R; 125;
CANR 1, 20, 53; DLB 8; JRDA;
MAICYA; MTCW; SATA 9, 69;
SATA-Obit 56

Helforth, John
See Doolittle, Hilda

Hellenhofferu, Vojtech Kapristian z
See Hasek, Jaroslav (Matej Frantisek)

Heller, Joseph
1923- . . . . **CLC 1, 3, 5, 8, 11, 36, 63; DA;**
DAB; DAC; DAM MST, NOV, POP;
WLC
See also AITN 1; CA 5-8R; CABS 1;
CANR 8, 42; DLB 2, 28; DLBY 80;
INT CANR-8; MTCW

Hellman, Lillian (Florence)
1906-1984 . . . . . . **CLC 2, 4, 8, 14, 18, 34,**
44, 52; DAM DRAM; DC 1
See also AITN 1, 2; CA 13-16R; 112;
CANR 33; DLB 7; DLBY 84; MTCW

Helprin, Mark
1947- . . . . **CLC 7, 10, 22, 32;**
DAM NOV, POP
See also CA 81-84; CANR 47; DLBY 85;
MTCW

Helvetius, Claude-Adrien
1715-1771 . . . . **LC 26**

Helyar, Jane Penelope Josephine 1933-
See Poole, Josephine
See also CA 21-24R; CANR 10, 26;
SATA 82

Hemans, Felicia 1793-1835 . . . . . . **NCLC 29**
See also DLB 96

Hemingway, Ernest (Miller)
1899-1961 . . . . **CLC 1, 3, 6, 8, 10, 13, 19,**
30, 34, 39, 41, 44, 50, 61, 80; DA; DAB;
DAC; DAM MST, NOV; SSC 1; WLC
See also CA 77-80; CANR 34;
CDALB 1917-1929; DLB 4, 9, 102;
DLBD 1; DLBY 81, 87; MTCW

Hempel, Amy 1951- . . . . **CLC 39**
See also CA 118; 137

Henderson, F. C.
See Mencken, H(enry) L(ouis)

Henderson, Sylvia
See Ashton-Warner, Sylvia (Constance)

Henley, Beth . . . . **CLC 23; DC 6**
See also Henley, Elizabeth Becker
See also CABS 3; DLBY 86

Henley, Elizabeth Becker 1952-
See Henley, Beth
See also CA 107; CANR 32; DAM DRAM,
MST; MTCW

Henley, William Ernest
1849-1903 . . . . **TCLC 8**
See also CA 105; DLB 19

Hennissart, Martha
See Lathen, Emma
See also CA 85-88

Henry, O. . . . . **TCLC 1, 19; SSC 5; WLC**
See also Porter, William Sydney

Henry, Patrick 1736-1799 . . . . **LC 25**

Henryson, Robert   1430(?)-1506(?).... **LC 20**
See also DLB 146

Henry VIII   1491-1547............. **LC 10**

Henschke, Alfred
See Klabund

Hentoff, Nat(han Irving)   1925-..... **CLC 26**
See also AAYA 4; CA 1-4R; CAAS 6;
CANR 5, 25; CLR 1; INT CANR-25;
JRDA; MAICYA; SATA 42, 69;
SATA-Brief 27

Heppenstall, (John) Rayner
1911-1981 .... **CLC 10**
See also CA 1-4R; 103; CANR 29

Herbert, Frank (Patrick)
1920-1986 ...... **CLC 12, 23, 35, 44, 85;**
DAM POP
See also CA 53-56; 118; CANR 5, 43;
DLB 8; INT CANR-5; MTCW; SATA 9,
37; SATA-Obit 47

Herbert, George
1593-1633 .... **LC 24; DAB;**
DAM POET; PC 4
See also CDBLB Before 1660; DLB 126

Herbert, Zbigniew
1924- .... **CLC 9, 43; DAM POET**
See also CA 89-92; CANR 36; MTCW

Herbst, Josephine (Frey)
1897-1969 .... **CLC 34**
See also CA 5-8R; 25-28R; DLB 9

Hergesheimer, Joseph
1880-1954 .... **TCLC 11**
See also CA 109; DLB 102, 9

Herlihy, James Leo   1927-1993 ...... **CLC 6**
See also CA 1-4R; 143; CANR 2

Hermogenes   fl. c. 175-........... **CMLC 6**

Hernandez, Jose   1834-1886...... **NCLC 17**

Herodotus   c. 484B.C.-429B.C..... **CMLC 17**

Herrick, Robert
1591-1674 ..... **LC 13; DA; DAB; DAC;**
DAM MST, POP; PC 9
See also DLB 126

Herring, Guilles
See Somerville, Edith

Herriot, James
1916-1995 .... **CLC 12; DAM POP**
See also Wight, James Alfred
See also AAYA 1; CA 148; CANR 40;
SATA 86

Herrmann, Dorothy   1941-......... **CLC 44**
See also CA 107

Herrmann, Taffy
See Herrmann, Dorothy

Hersey, John (Richard)
1914-1993 .... **CLC 1, 2, 7, 9, 40, 81;**
DAM POP
See also CA 17-20R; 140; CANR 33;
DLB 6; MTCW; SATA 25;
SATA-Obit 76

Herzen, Aleksandr Ivanovich
1812-1870 .... **NCLC 10**

Herzl, Theodor   1860-1904....... **TCLC 36**

Herzog, Werner   1942-............ **CLC 16**
See also CA 89-92

Hesiod   c. 8th cent. B.C.-......... **CMLC 5**

Hesse, Hermann
1877-1962 .... **CLC 1, 2, 3, 6, 11, 17, 25,**
69; DA; DAB; DAC; DAM MST, NOV;
SSC 9; WLC
See also CA 17-18; CAP 2; DLB 66;
MTCW; SATA 50

Hewes, Cady
See De Voto, Bernard (Augustine)

Heyen, William   1940-......... **CLC 13, 18**
See also CA 33-36R; CAAS 9; DLB 5

Heyerdahl, Thor   1914-............ **CLC 26**
See also CA 5-8R; CANR 5, 22; MTCW;
SATA 2, 52

Heym, Georg (Theodor Franz Arthur)
1887-1912 .... **TCLC 9**
See also CA 106

Heym, Stefan   1913-.............. **CLC 41**
See also CA 9-12R; CANR 4; DLB 69

Heyse, Paul (Johann Ludwig von)
1830-1914 .... **TCLC 8**
See also CA 104; DLB 129

Heyward, (Edwin) DuBose
1885-1940 .... **TCLC 59**
See also CA 108; DLB 7, 9, 45; SATA 21

Hibbert, Eleanor Alice Burford
1906-1993 .... **CLC 7; DAM POP**
See also BEST 90:4; CA 17-20R; 140;
CANR 9, 28; SATA 2; SATA-Obit 74

Hichens, Robert S.   1864-1950..... **TCLC 64**
See also DLB 153

Higgins, George V(incent)
1939- .... **CLC 4, 7, 10, 18**
See also CA 77-80; CAAS 5; CANR 17, 51;
DLB 2; DLBY 81; INT CANR-17;
MTCW

Higginson, Thomas Wentworth
1823-1911 .... **TCLC 36**
See also DLB 1, 64

Highet, Helen
See MacInnes, Helen (Clark)

Highsmith, (Mary) Patricia
1921-1995 .... **CLC 2, 4, 14, 42;**
DAM NOV, POP
See also CA 1-4R; 147; CANR 1, 20, 48;
MTCW

Highwater, Jamake (Mamake)
1942(?)- .... **CLC 12**
See also AAYA 7; CA 65-68; CAAS 7;
CANR 10, 34; CLR 17; DLB 52;
DLBY 85; JRDA; MAICYA; SATA 32,
69; SATA-Brief 30

Highway, Tomson
1951- ..... **CLC 92; DAC; DAM MULT**
See also CA 151; NNAL

Higuchi, Ichiyo   1872-1896....... **NCLC 49**

Hijuelos, Oscar
1951- .... **CLC 65; DAM MULT, POP;**
HLC
See also BEST 90:1; CA 123; CANR 50;
DLB 145; HW

Hikmet, Nazim   1902(?)-1963....... **CLC 40**
See also CA 141; 93-96

Hildesheimer, Wolfgang
1916-1991 .... **CLC 49**
See also CA 101; 135; DLB 69, 124

Hill, Geoffrey (William)
1932- ... **CLC 5, 8, 18, 45; DAM POET**
See also CA 81-84; CANR 21;
CDBLB 1960 to Present; DLB 40;
MTCW

Hill, George Roy   1921-........... **CLC 26**
See also CA 110; 122

Hill, John
See Koontz, Dean R(ay)

Hill, Susan (Elizabeth)
1942- .. **CLC 4; DAB; DAM MST, NOV**
See also CA 33-36R; CANR 29; DLB 14,
139; MTCW

Hillerman, Tony
1925- .... **CLC 62; DAM POP**
See also AAYA 6; BEST 89:1; CA 29-32R;
CANR 21, 42; SATA 6

Hillesum, Etty   1914-1943 .... **TCLC 49**
See also CA 137

Hilliard, Noel (Harvey)   1929-...... **CLC 15**
See also CA 9-12R; CANR 7

Hillis, Rick   1956-................ **CLC 66**
See also CA 134

Hilton, James   1900-1954........ **TCLC 21**
See also CA 108; DLB 34, 77; SATA 34

Himes, Chester (Bomar)
1909-1984 .... **CLC 2, 4, 7, 18, 58; BLC;**
DAM MULT
See also BW 2; CA 25-28R; 114; CANR 22;
DLB 2, 76, 143; MTCW

Hinde, Thomas .... **CLC 6, 11**
See also Chitty, Thomas Willes

Hindin, Nathan
See Bloch, Robert (Albert)

Hine, (William) Daryl   1936-....... **CLC 15**
See also CA 1-4R; CAAS 15; CANR 1, 20;
DLB 60

Hinkson, Katharine Tynan
See Tynan, Katharine

Hinton, S(usan) E(loise)
1950- .... **CLC 30; DA; DAB; DAC;**
DAM MST, NOV
See also AAYA 2; CA 81-84; CANR 32;
CLR 3, 23; JRDA; MAICYA; MTCW;
SATA 19, 58

Hippius, Zinaida .... **TCLC 9**
See also Gippius, Zinaida (Nikolayevna)

Hiraoka, Kimitake   1925-1970
See Mishima, Yukio
See also CA 97-100; 29-32R; DAM DRAM;
MTCW

Hirsch, E(ric) D(onald), Jr.   1928-... **CLC 79**
See also CA 25-28R; CANR 27, 51;
DLB 67; INT CANR-27; MTCW

Hirsch, Edward   1950- .... **CLC 31, 50**
See also CA 104; CANR 20, 42; DLB 120

Hitchcock, Alfred (Joseph)
1899-1980 .... **CLC 16**
See also CA 97-100; SATA 27;
SATA-Obit 24

Hitler, Adolf   1889-1945......... **TCLC 53**
See also CA 117; 147

Hoagland, Edward   1932-......... **CLC 28**
See also CA 1-4R; CANR 2, 31; DLB 6;
SATA 51

Hoban, Russell (Conwell)
1925- .... **CLC 7, 25; DAM NOV**
See also CA 5-8R; CANR 23, 37; CLR 3;
DLB 52; MAICYA; MTCW; SATA 1,
40, 78

Hobbs, Perry
See Blackmur, R(ichard) P(almer)

Hobson, Laura Z(ametkin)
1900-1986 .... **CLC 7, 25**
See also CA 17-20R; 118; DLB 28;
SATA 52

Hochhuth, Rolf
1931- ..... **CLC 4, 11, 18; DAM DRAM**
See also CA 5-8R; CANR 33; DLB 124;
MTCW

Hochman, Sandra 1936- .... **CLC 3, 8**
See also CA 5-8R; DLB 5

Hochwaelder, Fritz
1911-1986 ...... **CLC 36; DAM DRAM**
See also CA 29-32R; 120; CANR 42;
MTCW

Hochwalder, Fritz
See Hochwaelder, Fritz

Hocking, Mary (Eunice) 1921- ..... **CLC 13**
See also CA 101; CANR 18, 40

Hodgins, Jack 1938- .... **CLC 23**
See also CA 93-96; DLB 60

Hodgson, William Hope
1877(?)-1918 .... **TCLC 13**
See also CA 111; DLB 70, 153, 156

Hoeg, Peter 1957- .... **CLC 95**
See also CA 151

Hoffman, Alice
1952- .... **CLC 51; DAM NOV**
See also CA 77-80; CANR 34; MTCW

Hoffman, Daniel (Gerard)
1923- .... **CLC 6, 13, 23**
See also CA 1-4R; CANR 4; DLB 5

Hoffman, Stanley 1944- .... **CLC 5**
See also CA 77-80

Hoffman, William M(oses) 1939- ... **CLC 40**
See also CA 57-60; CANR 11

Hoffmann, E(rnst) T(heodor) A(madeus)
1776-1822 ...... **NCLC 2; SSC 13**
See also DLB 90; SATA 27

Hofmann, Gert 1931- .... **CLC 54**
See also CA 128

Hofmannsthal, Hugo von
1874-1929 .... **TCLC 11; DAM DRAM;
DC 4**
See also CA 106; DLB 81, 118

Hogan, Linda
1947- .... **CLC 73; DAM MULT**
See also CA 120; CANR 45; NNAL

Hogarth, Charles
See Creasey, John

Hogarth, Emmett
See Polonsky, Abraham (Lincoln)

Hogg, James 1770-1835.......... **NCLC 4**
See also DLB 93, 116, 159

Holbach, Paul Henri Thiry Baron
1723-1789 .... **LC 14**

Holberg, Ludvig 1684-1754 .... **LC 6**

Holden, Ursula 1921-............. **CLC 18**
See also CA 101; CAAS 8; CANR 22

Holderlin, (Johann Christian) Friedrich
1770-1843 .... **NCLC 16; PC 4**

Holdstock, Robert
See Holdstock, Robert P.

Holdstock, Robert P. 1948-........ **CLC 39**
See also CA 131

Holland, Isabelle 1920- .... **CLC 21**
See also AAYA 11; CA 21-24R; CANR 10,
25, 47; JRDA; MAICYA; SATA 8, 70

Holland, Marcus
See Caldwell, (Janet Miriam) Taylor
(Holland)

Hollander, John 1929-...... **CLC 2, 5, 8, 14**
See also CA 1-4R; CANR 1, 52; DLB 5;
SATA 13

Hollander, Paul
See Silverberg, Robert

Holleran, Andrew 1943(?)-......... **CLC 38**
See also CA 144

Hollinghurst, Alan 1954-....... **CLC 55, 91**
See also CA 114

Hollis, Jim
See Summers, Hollis (Spurgeon, Jr.)

Holly, Buddy 1936-1959 .... **TCLC 65**

Holmes, John
See Souster, (Holmes) Raymond

Holmes, John Clellon 1926-1988.... **CLC 56**
See also CA 9-12R; 125; CANR 4; DLB 16

Holmes, Oliver Wendell
1809-1894 .... **NCLC 14**
See also CDALB 1640-1865; DLB 1;
SATA 34

Holmes, Raymond
See Souster, (Holmes) Raymond

Holt, Victoria
See Hibbert, Eleanor Alice Burford

Holub, Miroslav 1923-............. **CLC 4**
See also CA 21-24R; CANR 10

Homer
c. 8th cent. B.C.-..... **CMLC 1, 16; DA;
DAB; DAC; DAM MST, POET**

Honig, Edwin 1919- .... **CLC 33**
See also CA 5-8R; CAAS 8; CANR 4, 45;
DLB 5

Hood, Hugh (John Blagdon)
1928- .... **CLC 15, 28**
See also CA 49-52; CAAS 17; CANR 1, 33;
DLB 53

Hood, Thomas 1799-1845....... **NCLC 16**
See also DLB 96

Hooker, (Peter) Jeremy 1941-...... **CLC 43**
See also CA 77-80; CANR 22; DLB 40

hooks, bell .... **CLC 94**
See also Watkins, Gloria

Hope, A(lec) D(erwent) 1907- .... **CLC 3, 51**
See also CA 21-24R; CANR 33; MTCW

Hope, Brian
See Creasey, John

Hope, Christopher (David Tully)
1944- .... **CLC 52**
See also CA 106; CANR 47; SATA 62

Hopkins, Gerard Manley
1844-1889 .... **NCLC 17; DA; DAB;
DAC; DAM MST, POET; PC 15; WLC**
See also CDBLB 1890-1914; DLB 35, 57

Hopkins, John (Richard) 1931-...... **CLC 4**
See also CA 85-88

Hopkins, Pauline Elizabeth
1859-1930 .... **TCLC 28; BLC;
DAM MULT**
See also BW 2; CA 141; DLB 50

Hopkinson, Francis 1737-1791 ...... **LC 25**
See also DLB 31

Hopley-Woolrich, Cornell George 1903-1968
See Woolrich, Cornell
See also CA 13-14; CAP 1

Horatio
See Proust, (Valentin-Louis-George-Eugene-)
Marcel

Horgan, Paul (George Vincent O'Shaughnessy)
1903-1995 ...... **CLC 9, 53; DAM NOV**
See also CA 13-16R; 147; CANR 9, 35;
DLB 102; DLBY 85; INT CANR-9;
MTCW; SATA 13; SATA-Obit 84

Horn, Peter
See Kuttner, Henry

Hornem, Horace Esq.
See Byron, George Gordon (Noel)

Hornung, E(rnest) W(illiam)
1866-1921 .... **TCLC 59**
See also CA 108; DLB 70

Horovitz, Israel (Arthur)
1939- .... **CLC 56; DAM DRAM**
See also CA 33-36R; CANR 46; DLB 7

Horvath, Odon von
See Horvath, Oedoen von
See also DLB 85, 124

Horvath, Oedoen von 1901-1938... **TCLC 45**
See also Horvath, Odon von
See also CA 118

Horwitz, Julius 1920-1986......... **CLC 14**
See also CA 9-12R; 119; CANR 12

Hospital, Janette Turner 1942-..... **CLC 42**
See also CA 108; CANR 48

Hostos, E. M. de
See Hostos (y Bonilla), Eugenio Maria de

Hostos, Eugenio M. de
See Hostos (y Bonilla), Eugenio Maria de

Hostos, Eugenio Maria
See Hostos (y Bonilla), Eugenio Maria de

Hostos (y Bonilla), Eugenio Maria de
1839-1903 .... **TCLC 24**
See also CA 123; 131; HW

Houdini
See Lovecraft, H(oward) P(hillips)

Hougan, Carolyn 1943- .... **CLC 34**
See also CA 139

Household, Geoffrey (Edward West)
1900-1988 .... **CLC 11**
See also CA 77-80; 126; DLB 87; SATA 14;
SATA-Obit 59

Housman, A(lfred) E(dward)
1859-1936 ...... **TCLC 1, 10; DA; DAB;
DAC; DAM MST, POET; PC 2**
See also CA 104; 125; DLB 19; MTCW

Ibuse Masuji 1898-1993 . . . . **CLC 22**
See also CA 127; 141

Ichikawa, Kon 1915- . . . . **CLC 20**
See also CA 121

Idle, Eric 1943- . . . . **CLC 21**
See also Monty Python
See also CA 116; CANR 35

Ignatow, David 1914- . . . . . . **CLC 4, 7, 14, 40**
See also CA 9-12R; CAAS 3; CANR 31;
DLB 5

Ihimaera, Witi 1944- . . . . **CLC 46**
See also CA 77-80

Ilf, Ilya . . . . **TCLC 21**
See also Fainzilberg, Ilya Arnoldovich

Illyes, Gyula 1902-1983 . . . . **PC 16**
See also CA 114; 109

Immermann, Karl (Lebrecht)
1796-1840 . . . . **NCLC 4, 49**
See also DLB 133

Inclan, Ramon (Maria) del Valle
See Valle-Inclan, Ramon (Maria) del

Infante, G(uillermo) Cabrera
See Cabrera Infante, G(uillermo)

Ingalls, Rachel (Holmes) 1940- . . . . . **CLC 42**
See also CA 123; 127

Ingamells, Rex 1913-1955 . . . . **TCLC 35**

Inge, William Motter
1913-1973 . . **CLC 1, 8, 19; DAM DRAM**
See also CA 9-12R; CDALB 1941-1968;
DLB 7; MTCW

Ingelow, Jean 1820-1897 . . . . **NCLC 39**
See also DLB 35, 163; SATA 33

Ingram, Willis J.
See Harris, Mark

Innaurato, Albert (F.) 1948(?)- . . **CLC 21, 60**
See also CA 115; 122; INT 122

Innes, Michael
See Stewart, J(ohn) I(nnes) M(ackintosh)

Ionesco, Eugene
1909-1994 . . . . **CLC 1, 4, 6, 9, 11, 15, 41,
86; DA; DAB; DAC; DAM DRAM,
MST; WLC**
See also CA 9-12R; 144; MTCW; SATA 7;
SATA-Obit 79

Iqbal, Muhammad 1873-1938 . . . . . **TCLC 28**

Ireland, Patrick
See O'Doherty, Brian

Iron, Ralph
See Schreiner, Olive (Emilie Albertina)

Irving, John (Winslow)
1942- . . . . . **CLC 13, 23, 38; DAM NOV,
POP**
See also AAYA 8; BEST 89:3; CA 25-28R;
CANR 28; DLB 6; DLBY 82; MTCW

Irving, Washington
1783-1859 . . . . . **NCLC 2, 19; DA; DAB;
DAM MST; SSC 2; WLC**
See also CDALB 1640-1865; DLB 3, 11, 30,
59, 73, 74; YABC 2

Irwin, P. K.
See Page, P(atricia) K(athleen)

Isaacs, Susan 1943- . . . **CLC 32; DAM POP**
See also BEST 89:1; CA 89-92; CANR 20,
41; INT CANR-20; MTCW

Isherwood, Christopher (William Bradshaw)
1904-1986 . . . . **CLC 1, 9, 11, 14, 44;
DAM DRAM, NOV**
See also CA 13-16R; 117; CANR 35;
DLB 15; DLBY 86; MTCW

Ishiguro, Kazuo
1954- . . . . . . **CLC 27, 56, 59; DAM NOV**
See also BEST 90:2; CA 120; CANR 49;
MTCW

Ishikawa, Takuboku
1886(?)-1912 . . . . **TCLC 15;
DAM POET; PC 10**
See also CA 113

Iskander, Fazil 1929- . . . . **CLC 47**
See also CA 102

Isler, Alan . . . . **CLC 91**

Ivan IV 1530-1584 . . . . **LC 17**

Ivanov, Vyacheslav Ivanovich
1866-1949 . . . . **TCLC 33**
See also CA 122

Ivask, Ivar Vidrik 1927-1992 . . . . . . **CLC 14**
See also CA 37-40R; 139; CANR 24

Ives, Morgan
See Bradley, Marion Zimmer

J. R. S.
See Gogarty, Oliver St. John

Jabran, Kahlil
See Gibran, Kahlil

Jabran, Khalil
See Gibran, Kahlil

Jackson, Daniel
See Wingrove, David (John)

Jackson, Jesse 1908-1983 . . . . **CLC 12**
See also BW 1; CA 25-28R; 109; CANR 27;
CLR 28; MAICYA; SATA 2, 29;
SATA-Obit 48

Jackson, Laura (Riding) 1901-1991
See Riding, Laura
See also CA 65-68; 135; CANR 28; DLB 48

Jackson, Sam
See Trumbo, Dalton

Jackson, Sara
See Wingrove, David (John)

Jackson, Shirley
1919-1965 . . . . **CLC 11, 60, 87; DA;
DAC; DAM MST; SSC 9; WLC**
See also AAYA 9; CA 1-4R; 25-28R;
CANR 4, 52; CDALB 1941-1968; DLB 6;
SATA 2

Jacob, (Cyprien-)Max 1876-1944 . . . **TCLC 6**
See also CA 104

Jacobs, Jim 1942- . . . . **CLC 12**
See also CA 97-100; INT 97-100

Jacobs, W(illiam) W(ymark)
1863-1943 . . . . **TCLC 22**
See also CA 121; DLB 135

Jacobsen, Jens Peter 1847-1885 . . **NCLC 34**

Jacobsen, Josephine 1908- . . . . **CLC 48**
See also CA 33-36R; CAAS 18; CANR 23,
48

Jacobson, Dan 1929- . . . . **CLC 4, 14**
See also CA 1-4R; CANR 2, 25; DLB 14;
MTCW

Jacqueline
See Carpentier (y Valmont), Alejo

Jagger, Mick 1944- . . . . **CLC 17**

Jakes, John (William)
1932- . . . . . . **CLC 29; DAM NOV, POP**
See also BEST 89:4; CA 57-60; CANR 10,
43; DLBY 83; INT CANR-10; MTCW;
SATA 62

James, Andrew
See Kirkup, James

James, C(yril) L(ionel) R(obert)
1901-1989 . . . . **CLC 33**
See also BW 2; CA 117; 125; 128; DLB 125;
MTCW

James, Daniel (Lewis) 1911-1988
See Santiago, Danny
See also CA 125

James, Dynely
See Mayne, William (James Carter)

James, Henry Sr. 1811-1882 . . . . . **NCLC 53**

James, Henry
1843-1916 . . . . . . **TCLC 2, 11, 24, 40, 47,
64; DA; DAB; DAC; DAM MST, NOV;
SSC 8; WLC**
See also CA 104; 132; CDALB 1865-1917;
DLB 12, 71, 74; DLBD 13; MTCW

James, M. R.
See James, Montague (Rhodes)
See also DLB 156

James, Montague (Rhodes)
1862-1936 . . . . **TCLC 6; SSC 16**
See also CA 104

James, P. D. . . . . **CLC 18, 46**
See also White, Phyllis Dorothy James
See also BEST 90:2; CDBLB 1960 to
Present; DLB 87

James, Philip
See Moorcock, Michael (John)

James, William 1842-1910 . . . . . **TCLC 15, 32**
See also CA 109

James I 1394-1437 . . . . **LC 20**

Jameson, Anna 1794-1860 . . . . **NCLC 43**
See also DLB 99, 166

Jami, Nur al-Din 'Abd al-Rahman
1414-1492 . . . . **LC 9**

Jandl, Ernst 1925- . . . . **CLC 34**

Janowitz, Tama
1957- . . . . **CLC 43; DAM POP**
See also CA 106; CANR 52

Japrisot, Sebastien 1931- . . . . **CLC 90**

Jarrell, Randall
1914-1965 . . . . **CLC 1, 2, 6, 9, 13, 49;
DAM POET**
See also CA 5-8R; 25-28R; CABS 2;
CANR 6, 34; CDALB 1941-1968; CLR 6;
DLB 48, 52; MAICYA; MTCW; SATA 7

Jarry, Alfred
1873-1907 . . . . **TCLC 2, 14;
DAM DRAM; SSC 20**
See also CA 104

Jarvis, E. K.
See Bloch, Robert (Albert); Ellison, Harlan
(Jay); Silverberg, Robert

Jeake, Samuel, Jr.
See Aiken, Conrad (Potter)

Jonson, Ben(jamin)
　　1572(?)-1637 . . . . . . **LC 6, 33; DA; DAB;**
　　　　DAC; DAM DRAM, MST, POET;
　　　　　　　　　　　　　　DC 4; WLC
　　See also CDBLB Before 1660; DLB 62, 121

Jordan, June
　　1936- . . . . . **CLC 5, 11, 23; DAM MULT,**
　　　　　　　　　　　　　　　　　POET
　　See also AAYA 2; BW 2; CA 33-36R;
　　　　CANR 25; CLR 10; DLB 38; MAICYA;
　　　　MTCW; SATA 4

Jordan, Pat(rick M.)　1941- . . . . **CLC 37**
　　See also CA 33-36R

Jorgensen, Ivar
　　See Ellison, Harlan (Jay)

Jorgenson, Ivar
　　See Silverberg, Robert

Josephus, Flavius　c. 37-100 . . . . . . **CMLC 13**

Josipovici, Gabriel　1940- . . . . **CLC 6, 43**
　　See also CA 37-40R; CAAS 8; CANR 47;
　　　　DLB 14

Joubert, Joseph　1754-1824 . . . . **NCLC 9**

Jouve, Pierre Jean　1887-1976 . . . . . . **CLC 47**
　　See also CA 65-68

Joyce, James (Augustine Aloysius)
　　1882-1941 . . . . **TCLC 3, 8, 16, 35, 52;**
　　　　DA; DAB; DAC; DAM MST, NOV,
　　　　　　　　　　POET; SSC 3; WLC**
　　See also CA 104; 126; CDBLB 1914-1945;
　　　　DLB 10, 19, 36, 162; MTCW

Jozsef, Attila　1905-1937. . . . . **TCLC 22**
　　See also CA 116

Juana Ines de la Cruz　1651(?)-1695 . . . **LC 5**

Judd, Cyril
　　See Kornbluth, C(yril) M.; Pohl, Frederik

Julian of Norwich　1342(?)-1416(?) . . . . **LC 6**
　　See also DLB 146

Juniper, Alex
　　See Hospital, Janette Turner

Junius
　　See Luxemburg, Rosa

Just, Ward (Swift)　1935- . . . . **CLC 4, 27**
　　See also CA 25-28R; CANR 32;
　　　　INT CANR-32

Justice, Donald (Rodney)
　　1925- . . . . **CLC 6, 19; DAM POET**
　　See also CA 5-8R; CANR 26; DLBY 83;
　　　　INT CANR-26

Juvenal　c. 55-c. 127 . . . . **CMLC 8**

Juvenis
　　See Bourne, Randolph S(illiman)

Kacew, Romain　1914-1980
　　See Gary, Romain
　　See also CA 108; 102

Kadare, Ismail　1936- . . . . **CLC 52**

Kadohata, Cynthia. . . . . **CLC 59**
　　See also CA 140

Kafka, Franz
　　1883-1924 . . . . **TCLC 2, 6, 13, 29, 47, 53;**
　　　　DA; DAB; DAC; DAM MST, NOV;
　　　　　　　　　　　　　SSC 5; WLC**
　　See also CA 105; 126; DLB 81; MTCW

Kahanovitsch, Pinkhes
　　See Der Nister

Kahn, Roger　1927- . . . . **CLC 30**
　　See also CA 25-28R; CANR 44; SATA 37

Kain, Saul
　　See Sassoon, Siegfried (Lorraine)

Kaiser, Georg　1878-1945 . . . . **TCLC 9**
　　See also CA 106; DLB 124

Kaletski, Alexander　1946- . . . . **CLC 39**
　　See also CA 118; 143

Kalidasa　fl. c. 400- . . . . **CMLC 9**

Kallman, Chester (Simon)
　　1921-1975 . . . . **CLC 2**
　　See also CA 45-48; 53-56; CANR 3

Kaminsky, Melvin　1926-
　　See Brooks, Mel
　　See also CA 65-68; CANR 16

Kaminsky, Stuart M(elvin)　1934- . . . **CLC 59**
　　See also CA 73-76; CANR 29, 53

Kane, Paul
　　See Simon, Paul

Kane, Wilson
　　See Bloch, Robert (Albert)

Kanin, Garson　1912- . . . . **CLC 22**
　　See also AITN 1; CA 5-8R; CANR 7;
　　　　DLB 7

Kaniuk, Yoram　1930- . . . . **CLC 19**
　　See also CA 134

Kant, Immanuel　1724-1804 . . . . . . **NCLC 27**
　　See also DLB 94

Kantor, MacKinlay　1904-1977 . . . . . . **CLC 7**
　　See also CA 61-64; 73-76; DLB 9, 102

Kaplan, David Michael　1946- . . . . . . **CLC 50**

Kaplan, James　1951- . . . . **CLC 59**
　　See also CA 135

Karageorge, Michael
　　See Anderson, Poul (William)

Karamzin, Nikolai Mikhailovich
　　1766-1826 . . . . **NCLC 3**
　　See also DLB 150

Karapanou, Margarita　1946- . . . . **CLC 13**
　　See also CA 101

Karinthy, Frigyes　1887-1938 . . . . . . **TCLC 47**

Karl, Frederick R(obert)　1927- . . . . . **CLC 34**
　　See also CA 5-8R; CANR 3, 44

Kastel, Warren
　　See Silverberg, Robert

Kataev, Evgeny Petrovich　1903-1942
　　See Petrov, Evgeny
　　See also CA 120

Kataphusin
　　See Ruskin, John

Katz, Steve　1935- . . . . **CLC 47**
　　See also CA 25-28R; CAAS 14; CANR 12;
　　　　DLBY 83

Kauffman, Janet　1945- . . . . **CLC 42**
　　See also CA 117; CANR 43; DLBY 86

Kaufman, Bob (Garnell)
　　1925-1986 . . . . **CLC 49**
　　See also BW 1; CA 41-44R; 118; CANR 22;
　　　　DLB 16, 41

Kaufman, George S.
　　1889-1961 . . . . . . **CLC 38; DAM DRAM**
　　See also CA 108; 93-96; DLB 7; INT 108

Kaufman, Sue . . . . **CLC 3, 8**
　　See also Barondess, Sue K(aufman)

Kavafis, Konstantinos Petrou　1863-1933
　　See Cavafy, C(onstantine) P(eter)
　　See also CA 104

Kavan, Anna　1901-1968 . . . . . . **CLC 5, 13, 82**
　　See also CA 5-8R; CANR 6; MTCW

Kavanagh, Dan
　　See Barnes, Julian

Kavanagh, Patrick (Joseph)
　　1904-1967 . . . . **CLC 22**
　　See also CA 123; 25-28R; DLB 15, 20;
　　　　MTCW

Kawabata, Yasunari
　　1899-1972 . . . . **CLC 2, 5, 9, 18;**
　　　　　　　　　　DAM MULT; SSC 17**
　　See also CA 93-96; 33-36R

Kaye, M(ary) M(argaret)　1909- . . . . . **CLC 28**
　　See also CA 89-92; CANR 24; MTCW;
　　　　SATA 62

Kaye, Mollie
　　See Kaye, M(ary) M(argaret)

Kaye-Smith, Sheila　1887-1956 . . . . . **TCLC 20**
　　See also CA 118; DLB 36

Kaymor, Patrice Maguilene
　　See Senghor, Leopold Sedar

Kazan, Elia　1909- . . . . **CLC 6, 16, 63**
　　See also CA 21-24R; CANR 32

Kazantzakis, Nikos
　　1883(?)-1957 . . . . **TCLC 2, 5, 33**
　　See also CA 105; 132; MTCW

Kazin, Alfred　1915- . . . . **CLC 34, 38**
　　See also CA 1-4R; CAAS 7; CANR 1, 45;
　　　　DLB 67

Keane, Mary Nesta (Skrine)　1904-1996
　　See Keane, Molly
　　See also CA 108; 114; 151

Keane, Molly. **CLC 31**
　　See also Keane, Mary Nesta (Skrine)
　　See also INT 114

Keates, Jonathan　19(?)- . . . . **CLC 34**

Keaton, Buster　1895-1966 . . . . **CLC 20**

Keats, John
　　1795-1821 . . . . **NCLC 8; DA; DAB;**
　　　　DAC; DAM MST, POET; PC 1; WLC**
　　See also CDBLB 1789-1832; DLB 96, 110

Keene, Donald　1922- . . . . **CLC 34**
　　See also CA 1-4R; CANR 5

Keillor, Garrison . . . . **CLC 40**
　　See also Keillor, Gary (Edward)
　　See also AAYA 2; BEST 89:3; DLBY 87;
　　　　SATA 58

Keillor, Gary (Edward)　1942-
　　See Keillor, Garrison
　　See also CA 111; 117; CANR 36;
　　　　DAM POP; MTCW

Keith, Michael
　　See Hubbard, L(afayette) Ron(ald)

Keller, Gottfried　1819-1890 . . . . **NCLC 2**
　　See also DLB 129

Kellerman, Jonathan
　　1949- . . . . **CLC 44; DAM POP**
　　See also BEST 90:1; CA 106; CANR 29, 51;
　　　　INT CANR-29

Kipling, (Joseph) Rudyard
1865-1936 ...... **TCLC 8, 17; DA; DAB;**
DAC; DAM MST, POET; PC 3; SSC 5;
WLC
See also CA 105; 120; CANR 33;
CDBLB 1890-1914; CLR 39; DLB 19, 34,
141, 156; MAICYA; MTCW; YABC 2

Kirkup, James 1918- .... **CLC 1**
See also CA 1-4R; CANR 4; CANR 2;
DLB 27; SATA 12

Kirkwood, James 1930(?)-1989 ...... **CLC 9**
See also AITN 2; CA 1-4R; 128; CANR 6,
40

Kirshner, Sidney
See Kingsley, Sidney

Kis, Danilo 1935-1989 .... **CLC 57**
See also CA 109; 118; 129; MTCW

Kivi, Aleksis 1834-1872 .... **NCLC 30**

Kizer, Carolyn (Ashley)
1925- ..... **CLC 15, 39, 80; DAM POET**
See also CA 65-68; CAAS 5; CANR 24;
DLB 5

Klabund 1890-1928.............. **TCLC 44**
See also DLB 66

Klappert, Peter 1942- .... **CLC 57**
See also CA 33-36R; DLB 5

Klein, A(braham) M(oses)
1909-1972 .... **CLC 19; DAB; DAC;**
DAM MST
See also CA 101; 37-40R; DLB 68

Klein, Norma 1938-1989 .... **CLC 30**
See also AAYA 2; CA 41-44R; 128;
CANR 15, 37; CLR 2, 19;
INT CANR-15; JRDA; MAICYA;
SAAS 1; SATA 7, 57

Klein, T(heodore) E(ibon) D(onald)
1947- .... **CLC 34**
See also CA 119; CANR 44

Kleist, Heinrich von
1777-1811 .... **NCLC 2, 37;**
DAM DRAM; SSC 22
See also DLB 90

Klima, Ivan 1931-..... **CLC 56; DAM NOV**
See also CA 25-28R; CANR 17, 50

Klimentov, Andrei Platonovich 1899-1951
See Platonov, Andrei
See also CA 108

Klinger, Friedrich Maximilian von
1752-1831 .... **NCLC 1**
See also DLB 94

Klopstock, Friedrich Gottlieb
1724-1803 .... **NCLC 11**
See also DLB 97

Knebel, Fletcher 1911-1993 .... **CLC 14**
See also AITN 1; CA 1-4R; 140; CAAS 3;
CANR 1, 36; SATA 36; SATA-Obit 75

Knickerbocker, Diedrich
See Irving, Washington

Knight, Etheridge
1931-1991 .... **CLC 40; BLC;**
DAM POET; PC 14
See also BW 1; CA 21-24R; 133; CANR 23;
DLB 41

Knight, Sarah Kemble 1666-1727 ..... **LC 7**
See also DLB 24

Knister, Raymond 1899-1932..... **TCLC 56**
See also DLB 68

Knowles, John
1926- ...... **CLC 1, 4, 10, 26; DA; DAC;**
DAM MST, NOV
See also AAYA 10; CA 17-20R; CANR 40;
CDALB 1968-1988; DLB 6; MTCW;
SATA 8, 89

Knox, Calvin M.
See Silverberg, Robert

Knye, Cassandra
See Disch, Thomas M(ichael)

Koch, C(hristopher) J(ohn) 1932- ... **CLC 42**
See also CA 127

Koch, Christopher
See Koch, C(hristopher) J(ohn)

Koch, Kenneth
1925- .... **CLC 5, 8, 44; DAM POET**
See also CA 1-4R; CANR 6, 36; DLB 5;
INT CANR-36; SATA 65

Kochanowski, Jan 1530-1584....... **LC 10**

Kock, Charles Paul de
1794-1871 .... **NCLC 16**

Koda Shigeyuki 1867-1947
See Rohan, Koda
See also CA 121

Koestler, Arthur
1905-1983 .... **CLC 1, 3, 6, 8, 15, 33**
See also CA 1-4R; 109; CANR 1, 33;
CDBLB 1945-1960; DLBY 83; MTCW

Kogawa, Joy Nozomi
1935- ...... **CLC 78; DAC; DAM MST,**
MULT
See also CA 101; CANR 19

Kohout, Pavel 1928-.............. **CLC 13**
See also CA 45-48; CANR 3

Koizumi, Yakumo
See Hearn, (Patricio) Lafcadio (Tessima
Carlos)

Kolmar, Gertrud 1894-1943 ...... **TCLC 40**

Komunyakaa, Yusef 1947-...... **CLC 86, 94**
See also CA 147; DLB 120

Konrad, George
See Konrad, Gyoergy

Konrad, Gyoergy 1933- ...... **CLC 4, 10, 73**
See also CA 85-88

Konwicki, Tadeusz 1926-..... **CLC 8, 28, 54**
See also CA 101; CAAS 9; CANR 39;
MTCW

Koontz, Dean R(ay)
1945- ...... **CLC 78; DAM NOV, POP**
See also AAYA 9; BEST 89:3, 90:2;
CA 108; CANR 19, 36, 52; MTCW

Kopit, Arthur (Lee)
1937- ..... **CLC 1, 18, 33; DAM DRAM**
See also AITN 1; CA 81-84; CABS 3;
DLB 7; MTCW

Kops, Bernard 1926-.............. **CLC 4**
See also CA 5-8R; DLB 13

Kornbluth, C(yril) M. 1923-1958.... **TCLC 8**
See also CA 105; DLB 8

Korolenko, V. G.
See Korolenko, Vladimir Galaktionovich

Korolenko, Vladimir
See Korolenko, Vladimir Galaktionovich

Korolenko, Vladimir G.
See Korolenko, Vladimir Galaktionovich

Korolenko, Vladimir Galaktionovich
1853-1921 .... **TCLC 22**
See also CA 121

Korzybski, Alfred (Habdank Skarbek)
1879-1950 .... **TCLC 61**
See also CA 123

Kosinski, Jerzy (Nikodem)
1933-1991 .... **CLC 1, 2, 3, 6, 10, 15, 53,**
70; DAM NOV
See also CA 17-20R; 134; CANR 9, 46;
DLB 2; DLBY 82; MTCW

Kostelanetz, Richard (Cory) 1940- .. **CLC 28**
See also CA 13-16R; CAAS 8; CANR 38

Kostrowitzki, Wilhelm Apollinaris de
1880-1918
See Apollinaire, Guillaume
See also CA 104

Kotlowitz, Robert 1924-............ **CLC 4**
See also CA 33-36R; CANR 36

Kotzebue, August (Friedrich Ferdinand) von
1761-1819 .... **NCLC 25**
See also DLB 94

Kotzwinkle, William 1938- ... **CLC 5, 14, 35**
See also CA 45-48; CANR 3, 44; CLR 6;
MAICYA; SATA 24, 70

Kozol, Jonathan 1936-............ **CLC 17**
See also CA 61-64; CANR 16, 45

Kozoll, Michael 1940(?)- .... **CLC 35**

Kramer, Kathryn 19(?)- .... **CLC 34**

Kramer, Larry 1935- .. **CLC 42; DAM POP**
See also CA 124; 126

Krasicki, Ignacy 1735-1801 .... **NCLC 8**

Krasinski, Zygmunt 1812-1859 .... **NCLC 4**

Kraus, Karl 1874-1936............ **TCLC 5**
See also CA 104; DLB 118

Kreve (Mickevicius), Vincas
1882-1954 .... **TCLC 27**

Kristeva, Julia 1941- .... **CLC 77**

Kristofferson, Kris 1936-.......... **CLC 26**
See also CA 104

Krizanc, John 1956-.............. **CLC 57**

Krleza, Miroslav 1893-1981........ **CLC 8**
See also CA 97-100; 105; CANR 50;
DLB 147

Kroetsch, Robert
1927-............ **CLC 5, 23, 57; DAC;**
DAM POET
See also CA 17-20R; CANR 8, 38; DLB 53;
MTCW

Kroetz, Franz
See Kroetz, Franz Xaver

Kroetz, Franz Xaver 1946- .... **CLC 41**
See also CA 130

Kroker, Arthur 1945-............. **CLC 77**

Kropotkin, Peter (Alekseievich)
1842-1921 .... **TCLC 36**
See also CA 119

Krotkov, Yuri 1917-.............. **CLC 19**
See also CA 102

Lardner, Ring(gold) W(ilmer)
1885-1933 . . . . **TCLC 2, 14**
See also CA 104; 131; CDALB 1917-1929;
DLB 11, 25, 86; MTCW

Laredo, Betty
See Codrescu, Andrei

Larkin, Maia
See Wojciechowska, Maia (Teresa)

Larkin, Philip (Arthur)
1922-1985 . . . . **CLC 3, 5, 8, 9, 13, 18, 33,**
39, 64; DAB; DAM MST, POET
See also CA 5-8R; 117; CANR 24;
CDBLB 1960 to Present; DLB 27;
MTCW

Larra (y Sanchez de Castro), Mariano Jose de
1809-1837 . . . . **NCLC 17**

Larsen, Eric 1941- . . . . **CLC 55**
See also CA 132

Larsen, Nella
1891-1964 . . . . **CLC 37; BLC;**
DAM MULT
See also BW 1; CA 125; DLB 51

Larson, Charles R(aymond) 1938- . . . **CLC 31**
See also CA 53-56; CANR 4

Las Casas, Bartolome de 1474-1566 . . **LC 31**

Lasker-Schueler, Else 1869-1945 . . **TCLC 57**
See also DLB 66, 124

Latham, Jean Lee 1902- . . . . **CLC 12**
See also AITN 1; CA 5-8R; CANR 7;
MAICYA; SATA 2, 68

Latham, Mavis
See Clark, Mavis Thorpe

Lathen, Emma . . . . **CLC 2**
See also Hennissart, Martha; Latsis, Mary
J(ane)

Lathrop, Francis
See Leiber, Fritz (Reuter, Jr.)

Latsis, Mary J(ane)
See Lathen, Emma
See also CA 85-88

Lattimore, Richmond (Alexander)
1906-1984 . . . . **CLC 3**
See also CA 1-4R; 112; CANR 1

Laughlin, James 1914- . . . . **CLC 49**
See also CA 21-24R; CAAS 22; CANR 9,
47; DLB 48

Laurence, (Jean) Margaret (Wemyss)
1926-1987 . . . . **CLC 3, 6, 13, 50, 62;**
DAC; DAM MST; SSC 7
See also CA 5-8R; 121; CANR 33; DLB 53;
MTCW; SATA-Obit 50

Laurent, Antoine 1952- . . . . **CLC 50**

Lauscher, Hermann
See Hesse, Hermann

Lautreamont, Comte de
1846-1870 . . . . **NCLC 12; SSC 14**

Laverty, Donald
See Blish, James (Benjamin)

Lavin, Mary 1912-1996 . . **CLC 4, 18; SSC 4**
See also CA 9-12R; 151; CANR 33;
DLB 15; MTCW

Lavond, Paul Dennis
See Kornbluth, C(yril) M.; Pohl, Frederik

Lawler, Raymond Evenor 1922- . . . . **CLC 58**
See also CA 103

Lawrence, D(avid) H(erbert Richards)
1885-1930 . . . . **TCLC 2, 9, 16, 33, 48, 61;**
DA; DAB; DAC; DAM MST, NOV,
POET; SSC 4, 19; WLC
See also CA 104; 121; CDBLB 1914-1945;
DLB 10, 19, 36, 98, 162; MTCW

Lawrence, T(homas) E(dward)
1888-1935 . . . . **TCLC 18**
See also Dale, Colin
See also CA 115

Lawrence of Arabia
See Lawrence, T(homas) E(dward)

Lawson, Henry (Archibald Hertzberg)
1867-1922 . . . . **TCLC 27; SSC 18**
See also CA 120

Lawton, Dennis
See Faust, Frederick (Schiller)

Laxness, Halldor . . . . **CLC 25**
See also Gudjonsson, Halldor Kiljan

Layamon fl. c. 1200- . . . . **CMLC 10**
See also DLB 146

Laye, Camara
1928-1980 . . . . **CLC 4, 38; BLC;**
DAM MULT
See also BW 1; CA 85-88; 97-100;
CANR 25; MTCW

Layton, Irving (Peter)
1912- . . . . **CLC 2, 15; DAC; DAM MST,**
POET
See also CA 1-4R; CANR 2, 33, 43;
DLB 88; MTCW

Lazarus, Emma 1849-1887 . . . . **NCLC 8**

Lazarus, Felix
See Cable, George Washington

Lazarus, Henry
See Slavitt, David R(ytman)

Lea, Joan
See Neufeld, John (Arthur)

Leacock, Stephen (Butler)
1869-1944 . . **TCLC 2; DAC; DAM MST**
See also CA 104; 141; DLB 92

Lear, Edward 1812-1888 . . . . **NCLC 3**
See also CLR 1; DLB 32, 163, 166;
MAICYA; SATA 18

Lear, Norman (Milton) 1922- . . . . . . **CLC 12**
See also CA 73-76

Leavis, F(rank) R(aymond)
1895-1978 . . . . **CLC 24**
See also CA 21-24R; 77-80; CANR 44;
MTCW

Leavitt, David 1961- . . . **CLC 34; DAM POP**
See also CA 116; 122; CANR 50; DLB 130;
INT 122

Leblanc, Maurice (Marie Emile)
1864-1941 . . . . **TCLC 49**
See also CA 110

Lebowitz, Fran(ces Ann)
1951(?)- . . . . **CLC 11, 36**
See also CA 81-84; CANR 14;
INT CANR-14; MTCW

Lebrecht, Peter
See Tieck, (Johann) Ludwig

le Carre, John . . . . **CLC 3, 5, 9, 15, 28**
See also Cornwell, David (John Moore)
See also BEST 89:4; CDBLB 1960 to
Present; DLB 87

Le Clezio, J(ean) M(arie) G(ustave)
1940- . . . . **CLC 31**
See also CA 116; 128; DLB 83

Leconte de Lisle, Charles-Marie-Rene
1818-1894 . . . . **NCLC 29**

Le Coq, Monsieur
See Simenon, Georges (Jacques Christian)

Leduc, Violette 1907-1972 . . . . **CLC 22**
See also CA 13-14; 33-36R; CAP 1

Ledwidge, Francis 1887(?)-1917 . . . **TCLC 23**
See also CA 123; DLB 20

Lee, Andrea
1953- . . . . . **CLC 36; BLC; DAM MULT**
See also BW 1; CA 125

Lee, Andrew
See Auchincloss, Louis (Stanton)

Lee, Chang-rae 1965- . . . . **CLC 91**
See also CA 148

Lee, Don L. . . . . **CLC 2**
See also Madhubuti, Haki R.

Lee, George W(ashington)
1894-1976 . . . . **CLC 52; BLC;**
DAM MULT
See also BW 1; CA 125; DLB 51

Lee, (Nelle) Harper
1926- . . . . **CLC 12, 60; DA; DAB; DAC;**
DAM MST, NOV; WLC
See also AAYA 13; CA 13-16R; CANR 51;
CDALB 1941-1968; DLB 6; MTCW;
SATA 11

Lee, Helen Elaine 1959(?)- . . . . **CLC 86**
See also CA 148

Lee, Julian
See Latham, Jean Lee

Lee, Larry
See Lee, Lawrence

Lee, Laurie
1914- . . . . **CLC 90; DAB; DAM POP**
See also CA 77-80; CANR 33; DLB 27;
MTCW

Lee, Lawrence 1941-1990 . . . . **CLC 34**
See also CA 131; CANR 43

Lee, Manfred B(ennington)
1905-1971 . . . . **CLC 11**
See also Queen, Ellery
See also CA 1-4R; 29-32R; CANR 2;
DLB 137

Lee, Stan 1922- . . . . **CLC 17**
See also AAYA 5; CA 108; 111; INT 111

Lee, Tanith 1947- . . . . **CLC 46**
See also AAYA 15; CA 37-40R; CANR 53;
SATA 8, 88

Lee, Vernon . . . . **TCLC 5**
See also Paget, Violet
See also DLB 57, 153, 156

Lee, William
See Burroughs, William S(eward)

Lee, Willy
See Burroughs, William S(eward)

Lewis, (Percy) Wyndham
1884(?)-1957 . . . . **TCLC 2, 9**
See also CA 104; DLB 15

Lewisohn, Ludwig 1883-1955 . . . . . . **TCLC 19**
See also CA 107; DLB 4, 9, 28, 102

Leyner, Mark 1956- . . . . **CLC 92**
See also CA 110; CANR 28, 53

Lezama Lima, Jose
1910-1976 . . . . **CLC 4, 10; DAM MULT**
See also CA 77-80; DLB 113; HW

L'Heureux, John (Clarke) 1934- . . . . **CLC 52**
See also CA 13-16R; CANR 23, 45

Liddell, C. H.
See Kuttner, Henry

Lie, Jonas (Lauritz Idemil)
1833-1908(?) . . . . **TCLC 5**
See also CA 115

Lieber, Joel 1937-1971 . . . . **CLC 6**
See also CA 73-76; 29-32R

Lieber, Stanley Martin
See Lee, Stan

Lieberman, Laurence (James)
1935- . . . . **CLC 4, 36**
See also CA 17-20R; CANR 8, 36

Lieksman, Anders
See Haavikko, Paavo Juhani

Li Fei-kan 1904-
See Pa Chin
See also CA 105

Lifton, Robert Jay 1926- . . . . **CLC 67**
See also CA 17-20R; CANR 27;
INT CANR-27; SATA 66

Lightfoot, Gordon 1938- . . . . **CLC 26**
See also CA 109

Lightman, Alan P. 1948- . . . . **CLC 81**
See also CA 141

Ligotti, Thomas (Robert)
1953- . . . . **CLC 44; SSC 16**
See also CA 123; CANR 49

Li Ho 791-817 . . . . **PC 13**

Liliencron, (Friedrich Adolf Axel) Detlev von
1844-1909 . . . . **TCLC 18**
See also CA 117

Lilly, William 1602-1681 . . . . **LC 27**

Lima, Jose Lezama
See Lezama Lima, Jose

Lima Barreto, Afonso Henrique de
1881-1922 . . . . **TCLC 23**
See also CA 117

Limonov, Edward 1944- . . . . **CLC 67**
See also CA 137

Lin, Frank
See Atherton, Gertrude (Franklin Horn)

Lincoln, Abraham 1809-1865 . . . . . **NCLC 18**

Lind, Jakov . . . . **CLC 1, 2, 4, 27, 82**
See also Landwirth, Heinz
See also CAAS 4

Lindbergh, Anne (Spencer) Morrow
1906- . . . . **CLC 82; DAM NOV**
See also CA 17-20R; CANR 16; MTCW;
SATA 33

Lindsay, David 1878-1945 . . . . **TCLC 15**
See also CA 113

Lindsay, (Nicholas) Vachel
1879-1931 . . . . **TCLC 17; DA; DAC;
DAM MST, POET; WLC**
See also CA 114; 135; CDALB 1865-1917;
DLB 54; SATA 40

Linke-Poot
See Doeblin, Alfred

Linney, Romulus 1930- . . . . **CLC 51**
See also CA 1-4R; CANR 40, 44

Linton, Eliza Lynn 1822-1898 . . . . **NCLC 41**
See also DLB 18

Li Po 701-763 . . . . **CMLC 2**

Lipsius, Justus 1547-1606 . . . . **LC 16**

Lipsyte, Robert (Michael)
1938- . . . . **CLC 21; DA; DAC;
DAM MST, NOV**
See also AAYA 7; CA 17-20R; CANR 8;
CLR 23; JRDA; MAICYA; SATA 5, 68

Lish, Gordon (Jay) 1934- . . **CLC 45; SSC 18**
See also CA 113; 117; DLB 130; INT 117

Lispector, Clarice 1925-1977 . . . . **CLC 43**
See also CA 139; 116; DLB 113

Littell, Robert 1935(?)- . . . . **CLC 42**
See also CA 109; 112

Little, Malcolm 1925-1965
See Malcolm X
See also BW 1; CA 125; 111; DA; DAB;
DAC; DAM MST, MULT; MTCW

Littlewit, Humphrey Gent.
See Lovecraft, H(oward) P(hillips)

Litwos
See Sienkiewicz, Henryk (Adam Alexander
Pius)

Liu E 1857-1909 . . . . **TCLC 15**
See also CA 115

Lively, Penelope (Margaret)
1933- . . . . **CLC 32, 50; DAM NOV**
See also CA 41-44R; CANR 29; CLR 7;
DLB 14, 161; JRDA; MAICYA; MTCW;
SATA 7, 60

Livesay, Dorothy (Kathleen)
1909- . . . . **CLC 4, 15, 79; DAC;
DAM MST, POET**
See also AITN 2; CA 25-28R; CAAS 8;
CANR 36; DLB 68; MTCW

Livy c. 59B.C.-c. 17 . . . . **CMLC 11**

Lizardi, Jose Joaquin Fernandez de
1776-1827 . . . . **NCLC 30**

Llewellyn, Richard
See Llewellyn Lloyd, Richard Dafydd
Vivian
See also DLB 15

Llewellyn Lloyd, Richard Dafydd Vivian
1906-1983 . . . . **CLC 7, 80**
See also Llewellyn, Richard
See also CA 53-56; 111; CANR 7;
SATA 11; SATA-Obit 37

Llosa, (Jorge) Mario (Pedro) Vargas
See Vargas Llosa, (Jorge) Mario (Pedro)

Lloyd Webber, Andrew 1948-
See Webber, Andrew Lloyd
See also AAYA 1; CA 116; 149;
DAM DRAM; SATA 56

Llull, Ramon c. 1235-c. 1316 . . . . . **CMLC 12**

Locke, Alain (Le Roy)
1886-1954 . . . . **TCLC 43**
See also BW 1; CA 106; 124; DLB 51

Locke, John 1632-1704 . . . . **LC 7, 35**
See also DLB 101

Locke-Elliott, Sumner
See Elliott, Sumner Locke

Lockhart, John Gibson
1794-1854 . . . . **NCLC 6**
See also DLB 110, 116, 144

Lodge, David (John)
1935- . . . . **CLC 36; DAM POP**
See also BEST 90:1; CA 17-20R; CANR 19,
53; DLB 14; INT CANR-19; MTCW

Loennbohm, Armas Eino Leopold 1878-1926
See Leino, Eino
See also CA 123

Loewinsohn, Ron(ald William)
1937- . . . . **CLC 52**
See also CA 25-28R

Logan, Jake
See Smith, Martin Cruz

Logan, John (Burton) 1923-1987 . . . . . **CLC 5**
See also CA 77-80; 124; CANR 45; DLB 5

Lo Kuan-chung 1330(?)-1400(?) . . . . . . **LC 12**

Lombard, Nap
See Johnson, Pamela Hansford

London, Jack . . **TCLC 9, 15, 39; SSC 4; WLC**
See also London, John Griffith
See also AAYA 13; AITN 2;
CDALB 1865-1917; DLB 8, 12, 78;
SATA 18

London, John Griffith 1876-1916
See London, Jack
See also CA 110; 119; DA; DAB; DAC;
DAM MST, NOV; JRDA; MAICYA;
MTCW

Long, Emmett
See Leonard, Elmore (John, Jr.)

Longbaugh, Harry
See Goldman, William (W.)

Longfellow, Henry Wadsworth
1807-1882 . . . . . **NCLC 2, 45; DA; DAB;
DAC; DAM MST, POET**
See also CDALB 1640-1865; DLB 1, 59;
SATA 19

Longley, Michael 1939- . . . . **CLC 29**
See also CA 102; DLB 40

Longus fl. c. 2nd cent. - . . . . **CMLC 7**

Longway, A. Hugh
See Lang, Andrew

Lonnrot, Elias 1802-1884 . . . . **NCLC 53**

Lopate, Phillip 1943- . . . . **CLC 29**
See also CA 97-100; DLBY 80; INT 97-100

Lopez Portillo (y Pacheco), Jose
1920- . . . . **CLC 46**
See also CA 129; HW

Lopez y Fuentes, Gregorio
1897(?)-1966 . . . . **CLC 32**
See also CA 131; HW

Lorca, Federico Garcia
See Garcia Lorca, Federico

Lord, Bette Bao 1938- . . . . CLC 23
See also BEST 90:3; CA 107; CANR 41;
INT 107; SATA 58

Lord Auch
See Bataille, Georges

Lord Byron
See Byron, George Gordon (Noel)

Lorde, Audre (Geraldine)
1934-1992 . . . . CLC 18, 71; BLC;
DAM MULT, POET; PC 12
See also BW 1; CA 25-28R; 142; CANR 16,
26, 46; DLB 41; MTCW

Lord Jeffrey
See Jeffrey, Francis

Lorenzini, Carlo 1826-1890
See Collodi, Carlo
See also MAICYA; SATA 29

Lorenzo, Heberto Padilla
See Padilla (Lorenzo), Heberto

Loris
See Hofmannsthal, Hugo von

Loti, Pierre . . . . TCLC 11
See also Viaud, (Louis Marie) Julien
See also DLB 123

Louie, David Wong 1954- . . . . CLC 70
See also CA 139

Louis, Father M.
See Merton, Thomas

Lovecraft, H(oward) P(hillips)
1890-1937 . . . . TCLC 4, 22; DAM POP;
SSC 3
See also AAYA 14; CA 104; 133; MTCW

Lovelace, Earl 1935- . . . . CLC 51
See also BW 2; CA 77-80; CANR 41;
DLB 125; MTCW

Lovelace, Richard 1618-1657 . . . . LC 24
See also DLB 131

Lowell, Amy
1874-1925 . . . . TCLC 1, 8; DAM POET;
PC 13
See also CA 104; 151; DLB 54, 140

Lowell, James Russell 1819-1891 . . NCLC 2
See also CDALB 1640-1865; DLB 1, 11, 64,
79

Lowell, Robert (Traill Spence, Jr.)
1917-1977 . . . CLC 1, 2, 3, 4, 5, 8, 9, 11,
15, 37; DA; DAB; DAC; DAM MST,
NOV; PC 3; WLC
See also CA 9-12R; 73-76; CABS 2;
CANR 26; DLB 5; MTCW

Lowndes, Marie Adelaide (Belloc)
1868-1947 . . . . TCLC 12
See also CA 107; DLB 70

Lowry, (Clarence) Malcolm
1909-1957 . . . . TCLC 6, 40
See also CA 105; 131; CDBLB 1945-1960;
DLB 15; MTCW

Lowry, Mina Gertrude 1882-1966
See Loy, Mina
See also CA 113

Loxsmith, John
See Brunner, John (Kilian Houston)

Loy, Mina . . . . CLC 28; DAM POET; PC 16
See also Lowry, Mina Gertrude
See also DLB 4, 54

Loyson-Bridet
See Schwob, (Mayer Andre) Marcel

Lucas, Craig 1951- . . . . CLC 64
See also CA 137

Lucas, George 1944- . . . . CLC 16
See also AAYA 1; CA 77-80; CANR 30;
SATA 56

Lucas, Hans
See Godard, Jean-Luc

Lucas, Victoria
See Plath, Sylvia

Ludlam, Charles 1943-1987 . . . . . CLC 46, 50
See also CA 85-88; 122

Ludlum, Robert
1927- . . . CLC 22, 43; DAM NOV, POP
See also AAYA 10; BEST 89:1, 90:3;
CA 33-36R; CANR 25, 41; DLBY 82;
MTCW

Ludwig, Ken . . . . CLC 60

Ludwig, Otto 1813-1865 . . . . NCLC 4
See also DLB 129

Lugones, Leopoldo 1874-1938 . . . . . TCLC 15
See also CA 116; 131; HW

Lu Hsun 1881-1936 . . . . . . TCLC 3; SSC 20
See also Shu-Jen, Chou

Lukacs, George . . . . CLC 24
See also Lukacs, Gyorgy (Szegeny von)

Lukacs, Gyorgy (Szegeny von) 1885-1971
See Lukacs, George
See also CA 101; 29-32R

Luke, Peter (Ambrose Cyprian)
1919-1995 . . . . CLC 38
See also CA 81-84; 147; DLB 13

Lunar, Dennis
See Mungo, Raymond

Lurie, Alison 1926- . . . . CLC 4, 5, 18, 39
See also CA 1-4R; CANR 2, 17, 50; DLB 2;
MTCW; SATA 46

Lustig, Arnost 1926- . . . . CLC 56
See also AAYA 3; CA 69-72; CANR 47;
SATA 56

Luther, Martin 1483-1546 . . . . LC 9

Luxemburg, Rosa 1870(?)-1919 . . . . TCLC 63
See also CA 118

Luzi, Mario 1914- . . . . CLC 13
See also CA 61-64; CANR 9; DLB 128

L'Ymagier
See Gourmont, Remy (-Marie-Charles) de

Lynch, B. Suarez
See Bioy Casares, Adolfo; Borges, Jorge
Luis

Lynch, David (K.) 1946- . . . . CLC 66
See also CA 124; 129

Lynch, James
See Andreyev, Leonid (Nikolaevich)

Lynch Davis, B.
See Bioy Casares, Adolfo; Borges, Jorge
Luis

Lyndsay, Sir David 1490-1555 . . . . . . LC 20

Lynn, Kenneth S(chuyler) 1923- . . . . CLC 50
See also CA 1-4R; CANR 3, 27

Lynx
See West, Rebecca

Lyons, Marcus
See Blish, James (Benjamin)

Lyre, Pinchbeck
See Sassoon, Siegfried (Lorraine)

Lytle, Andrew (Nelson) 1902-1995 . . CLC 22
See also CA 9-12R; 150; DLB 6; DLBY 95

Lyttelton, George 1709-1773 . . . . LC 10

Maas, Peter 1929- . . . . CLC 29
See also CA 93-96; INT 93-96

Macaulay, Rose 1881-1958 . . . . . TCLC 7, 44
See also CA 104; DLB 36

Macaulay, Thomas Babington
1800-1859 . . . . NCLC 42
See also CDBLB 1832-1890; DLB 32, 55

MacBeth, George (Mann)
1932-1992 . . . . CLC 2, 5, 9
See also CA 25-28R; 136; DLB 40; MTCW;
SATA 4; SATA-Obit 70

MacCaig, Norman (Alexander)
1910- . . . . . CLC 36; DAB; DAM POET
See also CA 9-12R; CANR 3, 34; DLB 27

MacCarthy, (Sir Charles Otto) Desmond
1877-1952 . . . . TCLC 36

MacDiarmid, Hugh
. . . . CLC 2, 4, 11, 19, 63; PC 9
See also Grieve, C(hristopher) M(urray)
See also CDBLB 1945-1960; DLB 20

MacDonald, Anson
See Heinlein, Robert A(nson)

Macdonald, Cynthia 1928- . . . . . . CLC 13, 19
See also CA 49-52; CANR 4, 44; DLB 105

MacDonald, George 1824-1905 . . . . . TCLC 9
See also CA 106; 137; DLB 18, 163;
MAICYA; SATA 33

Macdonald, John
See Millar, Kenneth

MacDonald, John D(ann)
1916-1986 . . . . CLC 3, 27, 44;
DAM NOV, POP
See also CA 1-4R; 121; CANR 1, 19;
DLB 8; DLBY 86; MTCW

Macdonald, John Ross
See Millar, Kenneth

Macdonald, Ross . . . . . CLC 1, 2, 3, 14, 34, 41
See also Millar, Kenneth
See also DLBD 6

MacDougal, John
See Blish, James (Benjamin)

MacEwen, Gwendolyn (Margaret)
1941-1987 . . . . CLC 13, 55
See also CA 9-12R; 124; CANR 7, 22;
DLB 53; SATA 50; SATA-Obit 55

Macha, Karel Hynek 1810-1846 . . NCLC 46

Machado (y Ruiz), Antonio
1875-1939 . . . . TCLC 3
See also CA 104; DLB 108

Machado de Assis, Joaquim Maria
1839-1908 . . . . TCLC 10; BLC
See also CA 107

Machen, Arthur . . . . TCLC 4; SSC 20
See also Jones, Arthur Llewellyn
See also DLB 36, 156

Machiavelli, Niccolo
1469-1527 . . . . . LC 8; DA; DAB; DAC;
DAM MST

MacInnes, Colin   1914-1976 . . . . . . CLC 4, 23
See also CA 69-72; 65-68; CANR 21;
DLB 14; MTCW

MacInnes, Helen (Clark)
1907-1985 . . . . . CLC 27, 39; DAM POP
See also CA 1-4R; 117; CANR 1, 28;
DLB 87; MTCW; SATA 22;
SATA-Obit 44

Mackay, Mary   1855-1924
See Corelli, Marie
See also CA 118

Mackenzie, Compton (Edward Montague)
1883-1972 . . . . CLC 18
See also CA 21-22; 37-40R; CAP 2;
DLB 34, 100

Mackenzie, Henry   1745-1831 . . . . NCLC 41
See also DLB 39

Mackintosh, Elizabeth   1896(?)-1952
See Tey, Josephine
See also CA 110

MacLaren, James
See Grieve, C(hristopher) M(urray)

Mac Laverty, Bernard   1942- . . . . CLC 31
See also CA 116; 118; CANR 43; INT 118

MacLean, Alistair (Stuart)
1922-1987 . . . . CLC 3, 13, 50, 63;
DAM POP
See also CA 57-60; 121; CANR 28; MTCW;
SATA 23; SATA-Obit 50

Maclean, Norman (Fitzroy)
1902-1990 . . . . CLC 78; DAM POP;
SSC 13
See also CA 102; 132; CANR 49

MacLeish, Archibald
1892-1982 . . . . CLC 3, 8, 14, 68;
DAM POET
See also CA 9-12R; 106; CANR 33; DLB 4,
7, 45; DLBY 82; MTCW

MacLennan, (John) Hugh
1907-1990 . . . . CLC 2, 14, 92; DAC;
DAM MST
See also CA 5-8R; 142; CANR 33; DLB 68;
MTCW

MacLeod, Alistair
1936- . . . . . . CLC 56; DAC; DAM MST
See also CA 123; DLB 60

MacNeice, (Frederick) Louis
1907-1963 . . . . . . CLC 1, 4, 10, 53; DAB;
DAM POET
See also CA 85-88; DLB 10, 20; MTCW

MacNeill, Dand
See Fraser, George MacDonald

Macpherson, James   1736-1796 . . . . . . LC 29
See also DLB 109

Macpherson, (Jean) Jay   1931- . . . . . . CLC 14
See also CA 5-8R; DLB 53

MacShane, Frank   1927- . . . . CLC 39
See also CA 9-12R; CANR 3, 33; DLB 111

Macumber, Mari
See Sandoz, Mari(e Susette)

Madach, Imre   1823-1864 . . . . NCLC 19

Madden, (Jerry) David   1933- . . . . CLC 5, 15
See also CA 1-4R; CAAS 3; CANR 4, 45;
DLB 6; MTCW

Maddern, Al(an)
See Ellison, Harlan (Jay)

Madhubuti, Haki R.
1942- . . . . CLC 6, 73; BLC;
DAM MULT, POET; PC 5
See also Lee, Don L.
See also BW 2; CA 73-76; CANR 24, 51;
DLB 5, 41; DLBD 8

Maepenn, Hugh
See Kuttner, Henry

Maepenn, K. H.
See Kuttner, Henry

Maeterlinck, Maurice
1862-1949 . . . . . . TCLC 3; DAM DRAM
See also CA 104; 136; SATA 66

Maginn, William   1794-1842 . . . . . . NCLC 8
See also DLB 110, 159

Mahapatra, Jayanta
1928- . . . . CLC 33; DAM MULT
See also CA 73-76; CAAS 9; CANR 15, 33

Mahfouz, Naguib (Abdel Aziz Al-Sabilgi)
1911(?)-
See Mahfuz, Najib
See also BEST 89:2; CA 128; DAM NOV;
MTCW

Mahfuz, Najib . . . . CLC 52, 55
See also Mahfouz, Naguib (Abdel Aziz
Al-Sabilgi)
See also DLBY 88

Mahon, Derek   1941- . . . . CLC 27
See also CA 113; 128; DLB 40

Mailer, Norman
1923- . . . . . . CLC 1, 2, 3, 4, 5, 8, 11, 14,
28, 39, 74; DA; DAB; DAC; DAM MST,
NOV, POP
See also AITN 2; CA 9-12R; CABS 1;
CANR 28; CDALB 1968-1988; DLB 2,
16, 28; DLBD 3; DLBY 80, 83; MTCW

Maillet, Antonine   1929- . . . . . . CLC 54; DAC
See also CA 115; 120; CANR 46; DLB 60;
INT 120

Mais, Roger   1905-1955 . . . . TCLC 8
See also BW 1; CA 105; 124; DLB 125;
MTCW

Maistre, Joseph de   1753-1821 . . . . NCLC 37

Maitland, Frederic   1850-1906 . . . . . TCLC 65

Maitland, Sara (Louise)   1950- . . . . . . CLC 49
See also CA 69-72; CANR 13

Major, Clarence
1936- . . . . CLC 3, 19, 48; BLC;
DAM MULT
See also BW 2; CA 21-24R; CAAS 6;
CANR 13, 25, 53; DLB 33

Major, Kevin (Gerald)
1949- . . . . CLC 26; DAC
See also AAYA 16; CA 97-100; CANR 21,
38; CLR 11; DLB 60; INT CANR-21;
JRDA; MAICYA; SATA 32, 82

Maki, James
See Ozu, Yasujiro

Malabaila, Damiano
See Levi, Primo

Malamud, Bernard
1914-1986 . . . . . . CLC 1, 2, 3, 5, 8, 9, 11,
18, 27, 44, 78, 85; DA; DAB; DAC;
DAM MST, NOV, POP; SSC 15; WLC
See also AAYA 16; CA 5-8R; 118; CABS 1;
CANR 28; CDALB 1941-1968; DLB 2,
28, 152; DLBY 80, 86; MTCW

Malaparte, Curzio   1898-1957 . . . . . TCLC 52

Malcolm, Dan
See Silverberg, Robert

Malcolm X . . . . CLC 82; BLC
See also Little, Malcolm

Malherbe, Francois de   1555-1628 . . . . . LC 5

Mallarme, Stephane
1842-1898 . . . . NCLC 4, 41;
DAM POET; PC 4

Mallet-Joris, Francoise   1930- . . . . . . CLC 11
See also CA 65-68; CANR 17; DLB 83

Malley, Ern
See McAuley, James Phillip

Mallowan, Agatha Christie
See Christie, Agatha (Mary Clarissa)

Maloff, Saul   1922- . . . . CLC 5
See also CA 33-36R

Malone, Louis
See MacNeice, (Frederick) Louis

Malone, Michael (Christopher)
1942- . . . . CLC 43
See also CA 77-80; CANR 14, 32

Malory, (Sir) Thomas
1410(?)-1471(?) . . . . . . LC 11; DA; DAB;
DAC; DAM MST
See also CDBLB Before 1660; DLB 146;
SATA 59; SATA-Brief 33

Malouf, (George Joseph) David
1934- . . . . CLC 28, 86
See also CA 124; CANR 50

Malraux, (Georges-)Andre
1901-1976 . . . . . . CLC 1, 4, 9, 13, 15, 57;
DAM NOV
See also CA 21-22; 69-72; CANR 34;
CAP 2; DLB 72; MTCW

Malzberg, Barry N(athaniel)   1939- . . . CLC 7
See also CA 61-64; CAAS 4; CANR 16;
DLB 8

Mamet, David (Alan)
1947- . . . . CLC 9, 15, 34, 46, 91;
DAM DRAM; DC 4
See also AAYA 3; CA 81-84; CABS 3;
CANR 15, 41; DLB 7; MTCW

Mamoulian, Rouben (Zachary)
1897-1987 . . . . CLC 16
See also CA 25-28R; 124

Mandelstam, Osip (Emilievich)
1891(?)-1938(?) . . . . . . TCLC 2, 6; PC 14
See also CA 104; 150

Mander, (Mary) Jane   1877-1949 . . . TCLC 31

Mandiargues, Andre Pieyre de . . . . . . CLC 41
See also Pieyre de Mandiargues, Andre
See also DLB 83

Mandrake, Ethel Belle
See Thurman, Wallace (Henry)

Mangan, James Clarence
1803-1849 . . . . NCLC 27

Mason, Nick 1945-............... **CLC 35**

Mason, Tally
See Derleth, August (William)

Mass, William
See Gibson, William

Masters, Edgar Lee
1868-1950 ...... **TCLC 2, 25; DA; DAC; DAM MST, POET; PC 1**
See also CA 104; 133; CDALB 1865-1917; DLB 54; MTCW

Masters, Hilary 1928-............ **CLC 48**
See also CA 25-28R; CANR 13, 47

Mastrosimone, William 19(?)-...... **CLC 36**

Mathe, Albert
See Camus, Albert

Matheson, Richard Burton 1926-... **CLC 37**
See also CA 97-100; DLB 8, 44; INT 97-100

Mathews, Harry 1930-......... **CLC 6, 52**
See also CA 21-24R; CAAS 6; CANR 18, 40

Mathews, John Joseph
1894-1979 ...... **CLC 84; DAM MULT**
See also CA 19-20; 142; CANR 45; CAP 2; NNAL

Mathias, Roland (Glyn) 1915-...... **CLC 45**
See also CA 97-100; CANR 19, 41; DLB 27

Matsuo Basho 1644-1694............ **PC 3**
See also DAM POET

Mattheson, Rodney
See Creasey, John

Matthews, Greg 1949-............ **CLC 45**
See also CA 135

Matthews, William 1942-.......... **CLC 40**
See also CA 29-32R; CAAS 18; CANR 12; DLB 5

Matthias, John (Edward) 1941-...... **CLC 9**
See also CA 33-36R

Matthiessen, Peter
1927-............ **CLC 5, 7, 11, 32, 64; DAM NOV**
See also AAYA 6; BEST 90:4; CA 9-12R; CANR 21, 50; DLB 6; MTCW; SATA 27

Maturin, Charles Robert
1780(?)-1824 .... **NCLC 6**

Matute (Ausejo), Ana Maria
1925-....................... **CLC 11**
See also CA 89-92; MTCW

Maugham, W. S.
See Maugham, W(illiam) Somerset

Maugham, W(illiam) Somerset
1874-1965 ...... **CLC 1, 11, 15, 67, 93; DA; DAB; DAC; DAM DRAM, MST, NOV; SSC 8; WLC**
See also CA 5-8R; 25-28R; CANR 40; CDBLB 1914-1945; DLB 10, 36, 77, 100, 162; MTCW; SATA 54

Maugham, William Somerset
See Maugham, W(illiam) Somerset

Maupassant, (Henri Rene Albert) Guy de
1850-1893 ..... **NCLC 1, 42; DA; DAB; DAC; DAM MST; SSC 1; WLC**
See also DLB 123

Maupin, Armistead
1944-............ **CLC 95; DAM POP**
See also CA 125; 130; INT 130

Maurhut, Richard
See Traven, B.

Mauriac, Claude 1914-1996........ **CLC 9**
See also CA 89-92; 152; DLB 83

Mauriac, Francois (Charles)
1885-1970 .... **CLC 4, 9, 56**
See also CA 25-28; CAP 2; DLB 65; MTCW

Mavor, Osborne Henry 1888-1951
See Bridie, James
See also CA 104

Maxwell, William (Keepers, Jr.)
1908-....................... **CLC 19**
See also CA 93-96; DLBY 80; INT 93-96

May, Elaine 1932-............... **CLC 16**
See also CA 124; 142; DLB 44

Mayakovski, Vladimir (Vladimirovich)
1893-1930 .... **TCLC 4, 18**
See also CA 104

Mayhew, Henry 1812-1887 ...... **NCLC 31**
See also DLB 18, 55

Mayle, Peter 1939(?)-............. **CLC 89**
See also CA 139

Maynard, Joyce 1953-............ **CLC 23**
See also CA 111; 129

Mayne, William (James Carter)
1928-...................... **CLC 12**
See also CA 9-12R; CANR 37; CLR 25; JRDA; MAICYA; SAAS 11; SATA 6, 68

Mayo, Jim
See L'Amour, Louis (Dearborn)

Maysles, Albert 1926-............ **CLC 16**
See also CA 29-32R

Maysles, David 1932-............ **CLC 16**

Mazer, Norma Fox 1931- .... **CLC 26**
See also AAYA 5; CA 69-72; CANR 12, 32; CLR 23; JRDA; MAICYA; SAAS 1; SATA 24, 67

Mazzini, Guiseppe 1805-1872 .... **NCLC 34**

McAuley, James Phillip
1917-1976 .... **CLC 45**
See also CA 97-100

McBain, Ed
See Hunter, Evan

McBrien, William Augustine
1930-..................... **CLC 44**
See also CA 107

McCaffrey, Anne (Inez)
1926- ...... **CLC 17; DAM NOV, POP**
See also AAYA 6; AITN 2; BEST 89:2; CA 25-28R; CANR 15, 35; DLB 8; JRDA; MAICYA; MTCW; SAAS 11; SATA 8, 70

McCall, Nathan 1955(?)-.......... **CLC 86**
See also CA 146

McCann, Arthur
See Campbell, John W(ood, Jr.)

McCann, Edson
See Pohl, Frederik

McCarthy, Charles, Jr. 1933-
See McCarthy, Cormac
See also CANR 42; DAM POP

McCarthy, Cormac 1933-..... **CLC 4, 57, 59**
See also McCarthy, Charles, Jr.
See also DLB 6, 143

McCarthy, Mary (Therese)
1912-1989 ... **CLC 1, 3, 5, 14, 24, 39, 59**
See also CA 5-8R; 129; CANR 16, 50; DLB 2; DLBY 81; INT CANR-16; MTCW

McCartney, (James) Paul
1942-.................... **CLC 12, 35**
See also CA 146

McCauley, Stephen (D.) 1955- ..... **CLC 50**
See also CA 141

McClure, Michael (Thomas)
1932-.................... **CLC 6, 10**
See also CA 21-24R; CANR 17, 46; DLB 16

McCorkle, Jill (Collins) 1958-...... **CLC 51**
See also CA 121; DLBY 87

McCourt, James 1941-............. **CLC 5**
See also CA 57-60

McCoy, Horace (Stanley)
1897-1955 .... **TCLC 28**
See also CA 108; DLB 9

McCrae, John 1872-1918........ **TCLC 12**
See also CA 109; DLB 92

McCreigh, James
See Pohl, Frederik

McCullers, (Lula) Carson (Smith)
1917-1967 .... **CLC 1, 4, 10, 12, 48; DA; DAB; DAC; DAM MST, NOV; SSC 9; WLC**
See also CA 5-8R; 25-28R; CABS 1, 3; CANR 18; CDALB 1941-1968; DLB 2, 7; MTCW; SATA 27

McCulloch, John Tyler
See Burroughs, Edgar Rice

McCullough, Colleen
1938(?)- .... **CLC 27; DAM NOV, POP**
See also CA 81-84; CANR 17, 46; MTCW

McDermott, Alice 1953- .... **CLC 90**
See also CA 109; CANR 40

McElroy, Joseph 1930- .... **CLC 5, 47**
See also CA 17-20R

McEwan, Ian (Russell)
1948-......... **CLC 13, 66; DAM NOV**
See also BEST 90:4; CA 61-64; CANR 14, 41; DLB 14; MTCW

McFadden, David 1940-........... **CLC 48**
See also CA 104; DLB 60; INT 104

McFarland, Dennis 1950- .... **CLC 65**

McGahern, John
1934-........... **CLC 5, 9, 48; SSC 17**
See also CA 17-20R; CANR 29; DLB 14; MTCW

McGinley, Patrick (Anthony)
1937-...................... **CLC 41**
See also CA 120; 127; INT 127

McGinley, Phyllis 1905-1978 ...... **CLC 14**
See also CA 9-12R; 77-80; CANR 19; DLB 11, 48; SATA 2, 44; SATA-Obit 24

McGinniss, Joe 1942-............. **CLC 32**
See also AITN 2; BEST 89:2; CA 25-28R; CANR 26; INT CANR-26

Michaux, Henri 1899-1984 ..... **CLC 8, 19**
See also CA 85-88; 114

Michelangelo 1475-1564........... **LC 12**

Michelet, Jules 1798-1874...... **NCLC 31**

Michener, James A(lbert)
1907(?)-.......... **CLC 1, 5, 11, 29, 60;
DAM NOV, POP**
See also AITN 1; BEST 90:1; CA 5-8R;
CANR 21, 45; DLB 6; MTCW

Mickiewicz, Adam 1798-1855 ..... **NCLC 3**

Middleton, Christopher 1926-...... **CLC 13**
See also CA 13-16R; CANR 29; DLB 40

Middleton, Richard (Barham)
1882-1911 .... **TCLC 56**
See also DLB 156

Middleton, Stanley 1919-........ **CLC 7, 38**
See also CA 25-28R; CAAS 23; CANR 21,
46; DLB 14

Middleton, Thomas
1580-1627 .... **LC 33; DAM DRAM,
MST; DC 5**
See also DLB 58

Migueis, Jose Rodrigues 1901-..... **CLC 10**

Mikszath, Kalman 1847-1910 ..... **TCLC 31**

Miles, Josephine
1911-1985 .... **CLC 1, 2, 14, 34, 39;
DAM POET**
See also CA 1-4R; 116; CANR 2; DLB 48

Militant
See Sandburg, Carl (August)

Mill, John Stuart 1806-1873..... **NCLC 11**
See also CDBLB 1832-1890; DLB 55

Millar, Kenneth
1915-1983 .... **CLC 14; DAM POP**
See also Macdonald, Ross
See also CA 9-12R; 110; CANR 16; DLB 2;
DLBD 6; DLBY 83; MTCW

Millay, E. Vincent
See Millay, Edna St. Vincent

Millay, Edna St. Vincent
1892-1950 ...... **TCLC 4, 49; DA; DAB;
DAC; DAM MST, POET; PC 6**
See also CA 104; 130; CDALB 1917-1929;
DLB 45; MTCW

Miller, Arthur
1915- .... **CLC 1, 2, 6, 10, 15, 26, 47, 78;
DA; DAB; DAC; DAM DRAM, MST;
DC 1; WLC**
See also AAYA 15; AITN 1; CA 1-4R;
CABS 3; CANR 2, 30;
CDALB 1941-1968; DLB 7; MTCW

Miller, Henry (Valentine)
1891-1980 .... **CLC 1, 2, 4, 9, 14, 43, 84;
DA; DAB; DAC; DAM MST, NOV;
WLC**
See also CA 9-12R; 97-100; CANR 33;
CDALB 1929-1941; DLB 4, 9; DLBY 80;
MTCW

Miller, Jason 1939(?)-............. **CLC 2**
See also AITN 1; CA 73-76; DLB 7

Miller, Sue 1943-..... **CLC 44; DAM POP**
See also BEST 90:3; CA 139; DLB 143

Miller, Walter M(ichael, Jr.)
1923-..................... **CLC 4, 30**
See also CA 85-88; DLB 8

Millett, Kate 1934-............... **CLC 67**
See also AITN 1; CA 73-76; CANR 32, 53;
MTCW

Millhauser, Steven 1943-....... **CLC 21, 54**
See also CA 110; 111; DLB 2; INT 111

Millin, Sarah Gertrude 1889-1968 .. **CLC 49**
See also CA 102; 93-96

Milne, A(lan) A(lexander)
1882-1956 .... **TCLC 6; DAB; DAC;
DAM MST**
See also CA 104; 133; CLR 1, 26; DLB 10,
77, 100, 160; MAICYA; MTCW;
YABC 1

Milner, Ron(ald)
1938- ..... **CLC 56; BLC; DAM MULT**
See also AITN 1; BW 1; CA 73-76;
CANR 24; DLB 38; MTCW

Milosz, Czeslaw
1911- .... **CLC 5, 11, 22, 31, 56, 82;
DAM MST, POET; PC 8**
See also CA 81-84; CANR 23, 51; MTCW

Milton, John
1608-1674 ...... **LC 9; DA; DAB; DAC;
DAM MST, POET; WLC**
See also CDBLB 1660-1789; DLB 131, 151

Min, Anchee 1957-............... **CLC 86**
See also CA 146

Minehaha, Cornelius
See Wedekind, (Benjamin) Frank(lin)

Miner, Valerie 1947- .... **CLC 40**
See also CA 97-100

Minimo, Duca
See D'Annunzio, Gabriele

Minot, Susan 1956- .... **CLC 44**
See also CA 134

Minus, Ed 1938-.................. **CLC 39**

Miranda, Javier
See Bioy Casares, Adolfo

Mirbeau, Octave 1848-1917...... **TCLC 55**
See also DLB 123

Miro (Ferrer), Gabriel (Francisco Victor)
1879-1930 .... **TCLC 5**
See also CA 104

Mishima, Yukio
.... **CLC 2, 4, 6, 9, 27; DC 1; SSC 4**
See also Hiraoka, Kimitake

Mistral, Frederic 1830-1914 ...... **TCLC 51**
See also CA 122

Mistral, Gabriela............. **TCLC 2; HLC**
See also Godoy Alcayaga, Lucila

Mistry, Rohinton 1952-...... **CLC 71; DAC**
See also CA 141

Mitchell, Clyde
See Ellison, Harlan (Jay); Silverberg, Robert

Mitchell, James Leslie 1901-1935
See Gibbon, Lewis Grassic
See also CA 104; DLB 15

Mitchell, Joni 1943-.............. **CLC 12**
See also CA 112

Mitchell, Margaret (Munnerlyn)
1900-1949 ...... **TCLC 11; DAM NOV,
POP**
See also CA 109; 125; DLB 9; MTCW

Mitchell, Peggy
See Mitchell, Margaret (Munnerlyn)

Mitchell, S(ilas) Weir 1829-1914 .. **TCLC 36**

Mitchell, W(illiam) O(rmond)
1914-...... **CLC 25; DAC; DAM MST**
See also CA 77-80; CANR 15, 43; DLB 88

Mitford, Mary Russell 1787-1855.. **NCLC 4**
See also DLB 110, 116

Mitford, Nancy 1904-1973........ **CLC 44**
See also CA 9-12R

Miyamoto, Yuriko 1899-1951 ..... **TCLC 37**

Mo, Timothy (Peter) 1950(?)-...... **CLC 46**
See also CA 117; MTCW

Modarressi, Taghi (M.) 1931-...... **CLC 44**
See also CA 121; 134; INT 134

Modiano, Patrick (Jean) 1945-..... **CLC 18**
See also CA 85-88; CANR 17, 40; DLB 83

Moerck, Paal
See Roelvaag, O(le) E(dvart)

Mofolo, Thomas (Mokopu)
1875(?)-1948 .... **TCLC 22; BLC;
DAM MULT**
See also CA 121

Mohr, Nicholasa
1935- ..... **CLC 12; DAM MULT; HLC**
See also AAYA 8; CA 49-52; CANR 1, 32;
CLR 22; DLB 145; HW; JRDA; SAAS 8;
SATA 8

Mojtabai, A(nn) G(race)
1938-................ **CLC 5, 9, 15, 29**
See also CA 85-88

Moliere
1622-1673 ..... **LC 28; DA; DAB; DAC;
DAM DRAM, MST; WLC**

Molin, Charles
See Mayne, William (James Carter)

Molnar, Ferenc
1878-1952 ..... **TCLC 20; DAM DRAM**
See also CA 109

Momaday, N(avarre) Scott
1934- ..... **CLC 2, 19, 85, 95; DA; DAB;
DAC; DAM MST, MULT, NOV, POP**
See also AAYA 11; CA 25-28R; CANR 14,
34; DLB 143; INT CANR-14; MTCW;
NNAL; SATA 48; SATA-Brief 30

Monette, Paul 1945-1995.......... **CLC 82**
See also CA 139; 147

Monroe, Harriet 1860-1936....... **TCLC 12**
See also CA 109; DLB 54, 91

Monroe, Lyle
See Heinlein, Robert A(nson)

Montagu, Elizabeth 1917-........ **NCLC 7**
See also CA 9-12R

Montagu, Mary (Pierrepont) Wortley
1689-1762 .... **LC 9; PC 16**
See also DLB 95, 101

Montagu, W. H.
See Coleridge, Samuel Taylor

Montague, John (Patrick)
1929-.................... **CLC 13, 46**
See also CA 9-12R; CANR 9; DLB 40;
MTCW

Montaigne, Michel (Eyquem) de
1533-1592 ..... **LC 8; DA; DAB; DAC;
DAM MST; WLC**

Montale, Eugenio
1896-1981 .... **CLC 7, 9, 18; PC 13**
See also CA 17-20R; 104; CANR 30;
DLB 114; MTCW

Montesquieu, Charles-Louis de Secondat
1689-1755 .... **LC 7**

Montgomery, (Robert) Bruce   1921-1978
See Crispin, Edmund
See also CA 104

Montgomery, L(ucy) M(aud)
1874-1942 .... **TCLC 51; DAC;
DAM MST**
See also AAYA 12; CA 108; 137; CLR 8;
DLB 92; DLBD 14; JRDA; MAICYA;
YABC 1

Montgomery, Marion H., Jr.   1925- .. **CLC 7**
See also AITN 1; CA 1-4R; CANR 3, 48;
DLB 6

Montgomery, Max
See Davenport, Guy (Mattison, Jr.)

Montherlant, Henry (Milon) de
1896-1972 .... **CLC 8, 19; DAM DRAM**
See also CA 85-88; 37-40R; DLB 72;
MTCW

Monty Python
See Chapman, Graham; Cleese, John
(Marwood); Gilliam, Terry (Vance); Idle,
Eric; Jones, Terence Graham Parry; Palin,
Michael (Edward)
See also AAYA 7

Moodie, Susanna (Strickland)
1803-1885 .... **NCLC 14**
See also DLB 99

Mooney, Edward   1951-
See Mooney, Ted
See also CA 130

Mooney, Ted .... **CLC 25**
See also Mooney, Edward

Moorcock, Michael (John)
1939- .... **CLC 5, 27, 58**
See also CA 45-48; CAAS 5; CANR 2, 17,
38; DLB 14; MTCW

Moore, Brian
1921- ...... **CLC 1, 3, 5, 7, 8, 19, 32, 90;
DAB; DAC; DAM MST**
See also CA 1-4R; CANR 1, 25, 42; MTCW

Moore, Edward
See Muir, Edwin

Moore, George Augustus
1852-1933 .... **TCLC 7; SSC 19**
See also CA 104; DLB 10, 18, 57, 135

Moore, Lorrie .... **CLC 39, 45, 68**
See also Moore, Marie Lorena

Moore, Marianne (Craig)
1887-1972 .... **CLC 1, 2, 4, 8, 10, 13, 19,
47; DA; DAB; DAC; DAM MST, POET;
PC 4**
See also CA 1-4R; 33-36R; CANR 3;
CDALB 1929-1941; DLB 45; DLBD 7;
MTCW; SATA 20

Moore, Marie Lorena   1957-
See Moore, Lorrie
See also CA 116; CANR 39

Moore, Thomas   1779-1852 .... **NCLC 6**
See also DLB 96, 144

Morand, Paul   1888-1976 .. **CLC 41; SSC 22**
See also CA 69-72; DLB 65

Morante, Elsa   1918-1985 .... **CLC 8, 47**
See also CA 85-88; 117; CANR 35; MTCW

Moravia, Alberto .... **CLC 2, 7, 11, 27, 46**
See also Pincherle, Alberto

More, Hannah   1745-1833 .... **NCLC 27**
See also DLB 107, 109, 116, 158

More, Henry   1614-1687 .... **LC 9**
See also DLB 126

More, Sir Thomas   1478-1535 .... **LC 10, 32**

Moreas, Jean .... **TCLC 18**
See also Papadiamantopoulos, Johannes

Morgan, Berry   1919- .... **CLC 6**
See also CA 49-52; DLB 6

Morgan, Claire
See Highsmith, (Mary) Patricia

Morgan, Edwin (George)   1920- ..... **CLC 31**
See also CA 5-8R; CANR 3, 43; DLB 27

Morgan, (George) Frederick
1922- .... **CLC 23**
See also CA 17-20R; CANR 21

Morgan, Harriet
See Mencken, H(enry) L(ouis)

Morgan, Jane
See Cooper, James Fenimore

Morgan, Janet   1945- .... **CLC 39**
See also CA 65-68

Morgan, Lady   1776(?)-1859 ...... **NCLC 29**
See also DLB 116, 158

Morgan, Robin   1941- .... **CLC 2**
See also CA 69-72; CANR 29; MTCW;
SATA 80

Morgan, Scott
See Kuttner, Henry

Morgan, Seth   1949(?)-1990 .... **CLC 65**
See also CA 132

Morgenstern, Christian
1871-1914 .... **TCLC 8**
See also CA 105

Morgenstern, S.
See Goldman, William (W.)

Moricz, Zsigmond   1879-1942 ..... **TCLC 33**

Morike, Eduard (Friedrich)
1804-1875 .... **NCLC 10**
See also DLB 133

Mori Ogai .... **TCLC 14**
See also Mori Rintaro

Mori Rintaro   1862-1922
See Mori Ogai
See also CA 110

Moritz, Karl Philipp   1756-1793 ...... **LC 2**
See also DLB 94

Morland, Peter Henry
See Faust, Frederick (Schiller)

Morren, Theophil
See Hofmannsthal, Hugo von

Morris, Bill   1952- .... **CLC 76**

Morris, Julian
See West, Morris L(anglo)

Morris, Steveland Judkins   1950(?)-
See Wonder, Stevie
See also CA 111

Morris, William   1834-1896 .... **NCLC 4**
See also CDBLB 1832-1890; DLB 18, 35,
57, 156

Morris, Wright   1910- ... **CLC 1, 3, 7, 18, 37**
See also CA 9-12R; CANR 21; DLB 2;
DLBY 81; MTCW

Morrison, Chloe Anthony Wofford
See Morrison, Toni

Morrison, James Douglas   1943-1971
See Morrison, Jim
See also CA 73-76; CANR 40

Morrison, Jim .... **CLC 17**
See also Morrison, James Douglas

Morrison, Toni
1931- .... **CLC 4, 10, 22, 55, 81, 87;
BLC; DA; DAB; DAC; DAM MST,
MULT, NOV, POP**
See also AAYA 1; BW 2; CA 29-32R;
CANR 27, 42; CDALB 1968-1988;
DLB 6, 33, 143; DLBY 81; MTCW;
SATA 57

Morrison, Van   1945- .... **CLC 21**
See also CA 116

Mortimer, John (Clifford)
1923- ...... **CLC 28, 43; DAM DRAM,
POP**
See also CA 13-16R; CANR 21;
CDBLB 1960 to Present; DLB 13;
INT CANR-21; MTCW

Mortimer, Penelope (Ruth)   1918- .... **CLC 5**
See also CA 57-60; CANR 45

Morton, Anthony
See Creasey, John

Mosher, Howard Frank   1943- ...... **CLC 62**
See also CA 139

Mosley, Nicholas   1923- .... **CLC 43, 70**
See also CA 69-72; CANR 41; DLB 14

Moss, Howard
1922-1987 .... **CLC 7, 14, 45, 50;
DAM POET**
See also CA 1-4R; 123; CANR 1, 44;
DLB 5

Mossgiel, Rab
See Burns, Robert

Motion, Andrew (Peter)   1952- ...... **CLC 47**
See also CA 146; DLB 40

Motley, Willard (Francis)
1909-1965 .... **CLC 18**
See also BW 1; CA 117; 106; DLB 76, 143

Motoori, Norinaga   1730-1801 .... **NCLC 45**

Mott, Michael (Charles Alston)
1930- .... **CLC 15, 34**
See also CA 5-8R; CAAS 7; CANR 7, 29

Mountain Wolf Woman
1884-1960 .... **CLC 92**
See also CA 144; NNAL

Moure, Erin   1955- .... **CLC 88**
See also CA 113; DLB 60

Mowat, Farley (McGill)
1921- ..... **CLC 26; DAC; DAM MST**
See also AAYA 1; CA 1-4R; CANR 4, 24,
42; CLR 20; DLB 68; INT CANAR-24;
JRDA; MAICYA; MTCW; SATA 3, 55

Moyers, Bill 1934- .... **CLC 74**
See also AITN 2; CA 61-64; CANR 31, 52

Mphahlele, Es'kia
See Mphahlele, Ezekiel
See also DLB 125

Mphahlele, Ezekiel
1919- ..... **CLC 25; BLC; DAM MULT**
See also Mphahlele, Es'kia
See also BW 2; CA 81-84; CANR 26

Mqhayi, S(amuel) E(dward) K(rune Loliwe)
1875-1945 .... **TCLC 25; BLC;**
DAM MULT

Mrozek, Slawomir 1930- .... **CLC 3, 13**
See also CA 13-16R; CAAS 10; CANR 29;
MTCW

Mrs. Belloc-Lowndes
See Lowndes, Marie Adelaide (Belloc)

Mtwa, Percy (?)- .... **CLC 47**

Mueller, Lisel 1924- .... **CLC 13, 51**
See also CA 93-96; DLB 105

Muir, Edwin 1887-1959 .... **TCLC 2**
See also CA 104; DLB 20, 100

Muir, John 1838-1914 .... **TCLC 28**

Mujica Lainez, Manuel
1910-1984 .... **CLC 31**
See also Lainez, Manuel Mujica
See also CA 81-84; 112; CANR 32; HW

Mukherjee, Bharati
1940- .... **CLC 53; DAM NOV**
See also BEST 89:2; CA 107; CANR 45;
DLB 60; MTCW

Muldoon, Paul
1951- .... **CLC 32, 72; DAM POET**
See also CA 113; 129; CANR 52; DLB 40;
INT 129

Mulisch, Harry 1927- .... **CLC 42**
See also CA 9-12R; CANR 6, 26

Mull, Martin 1943- .... **CLC 17**
See also CA 105

Mulock, Dinah Maria
See Craik, Dinah Maria (Mulock)

Munford, Robert 1737(?)-1783 .... **LC 5**
See also DLB 31

Mungo, Raymond 1946- .... **CLC 72**
See also CA 49-52; CANR 2

Munro, Alice
1931- ...... **CLC 6, 10, 19, 50, 95; DAC;**
DAM MST, NOV; SSC 3
See also AITN 2; CA 33-36R; CANR 33,
53; DLB 53; MTCW; SATA 29

Munro, H(ector) H(ugh) 1870-1916
See Saki
See also CA 104; 130; CDBLB 1890-1914;
DA; DAB; DAC; DAM MST, NOV;
DLB 34, 162; MTCW; WLC

Murasaki, Lady .... **CMLC 1**

Murdoch, (Jean) Iris
1919- ...... **CLC 1, 2, 3, 4, 6, 8, 11, 15,**
22, 31, 51; DAB; DAC; DAM MST,
NOV
See also CA 13-16R; CANR 8, 43;
CDBLB 1960 to Present; DLB 14;
INT CANR-8; MTCW

Murfree, Mary Noailles
1850-1922 .... **SSC 22**
See also CA 122; DLB 12, 74

Murnau, Friedrich Wilhelm
See Plumpe, Friedrich Wilhelm

Murphy, Richard 1927- .... **CLC 41**
See also CA 29-32R; DLB 40

Murphy, Sylvia 1937- .... **CLC 34**
See also CA 121

Murphy, Thomas (Bernard) 1935-... **CLC 51**
See also CA 101

Murray, Albert L. 1916- .... **CLC 73**
See also BW 2; CA 49-52; CANR 26, 52;
DLB 38

Murray, Les(lie) A(llan)
1938- .... **CLC 40; DAM POET**
See also CA 21-24R; CANR 11, 27

Murry, J. Middleton
See Murry, John Middleton

Murry, John Middleton
1889-1957 .... **TCLC 16**
See also CA 118; DLB 149

Musgrave, Susan 1951- .... **CLC 13, 54**
See also CA 69-72; CANR 45

Musil, Robert (Edler von)
1880-1942 .... **TCLC 12; SSC 18**
See also CA 109; DLB 81, 124

Muske, Carol 1945- .... **CLC 90**
See also Muske-Dukes, Carol (Anne)

Muske-Dukes, Carol (Anne) 1945-
See Muske, Carol
See also CA 65-68; CANR 32

Musset, (Louis Charles) Alfred de
1810-1857 .... **NCLC 7**

My Brother's Brother
See Chekhov, Anton (Pavlovich)

Myers, L. H. 1881-1944 .... **TCLC 59**
See also DLB 15

Myers, Walter Dean
1937- ..... **CLC 35; BLC; DAM MULT,**
NOV
See also AAYA 4; BW 2; CA 33-36R;
CANR 20, 42; CLR 4, 16, 35; DLB 33;
INT CANR-20; JRDA; MAICYA;
SAAS 2; SATA 41, 71; SATA-Brief 27

Myers, Walter M.
See Myers, Walter Dean

Myles, Symon
See Follett, Ken(neth Martin)

Nabokov, Vladimir (Vladimirovich)
1899-1977 ..... **CLC 1, 2, 3, 6, 8, 11, 15,**
23, 44, 46, 64; DA; DAB; DAC;
DAM MST, NOV; SSC 11; WLC
See also CA 5-8R; 69-72; CANR 20;
CDALB 1941-1968; DLB 2; DLBD 3;
DLBY 80, 91; MTCW

Nagai Kafu .... **TCLC 51**
See also Nagai Sokichi

Nagai Sokichi 1879-1959
See Nagai Kafu
See also CA 117

Nagy, Laszlo 1925-1978 .... **CLC 7**
See also CA 129; 112

Naipaul, Shiva(dhar Srinivasa)
1945-1985 ..... **CLC 32, 39; DAM NOV**
See also CA 110; 112; 116; CANR 33;
DLB 157; DLBY 85; MTCW

Naipaul, V(idiadhar) S(urajprasad)
1932- .... **CLC 4, 7, 9, 13, 18, 37; DAB;**
DAC; DAM MST, NOV
See also CA 1-4R; CANR 1, 33, 51;
CDBLB 1960 to Present; DLB 125;
DLBY 85; MTCW

Nakos, Lilika 1899(?)- .... **CLC 29**

Narayan, R(asipuram) K(rishnaswami)
1906- .... **CLC 7, 28, 47; DAM NOV**
See also CA 81-84; CANR 33; MTCW;
SATA 62

Nash, (Frediric) Ogden
1902-1971 .... **CLC 23; DAM POET**
See also CA 13-14; 29-32R; CANR 34;
CAP 1; DLB 11; MAICYA; MTCW;
SATA 2, 46

Nathan, Daniel
See Dannay, Frederic

Nathan, George Jean 1882-1958 ... **TCLC 18**
See also Hatteras, Owen
See also CA 114; DLB 137

Natsume, Kinnosuke 1867-1916
See Natsume, Soseki
See also CA 104

Natsume, Soseki .... **TCLC 2, 10**
See also Natsume, Kinnosuke

Natti, (Mary) Lee 1919-
See Kingman, Lee
See also CA 5-8R; CANR 2

Naylor, Gloria
1950- ..... **CLC 28, 52; BLC; DA; DAC;**
DAM MST, MULT, NOV, POP
See also AAYA 6; BW 2; CA 107;
CANR 27, 51; MTCW

Neihardt, John Gneisenau
1881-1973 .... **CLC 32**
See also CA 13-14; CAP 1; DLB 9, 54

Nekrasov, Nikolai Alekseevich
1821-1878 .... **NCLC 11**

Nelligan, Emile 1879-1941 .... **TCLC 14**
See also CA 114; DLB 92

Nelson, Willie 1933- .... **CLC 17**
See also CA 107

Nemerov, Howard (Stanley)
1920-1991 .... **CLC 2, 6, 9, 36;**
DAM POET
See also CA 1-4R; 134; CABS 2; CANR 1,
27, 53; DLB 5, 6; DLBY 83;
INT CANR-27; MTCW

Neruda, Pablo
1904-1973 ..... **CLC 1, 2, 5, 7, 9, 28, 62;**
DA; DAB; DAC; DAM MST, MULT,
POET; HLC; PC 4; WLC
See also CA 19-20; 45-48; CAP 2; HW;
MTCW

Nerval, Gerard de
1808-1855 ..... **NCLC 1; PC 13; SSC 18**

Nervo, (Jose) Amado (Ruiz de)
1870-1919 . . . . **TCLC 11**
See also CA 109; 131; HW

Nessi, Pio Baroja y
See Baroja (y Nessi), Pio

Nestroy, Johann 1801-1862 . . . . . **NCLC 42**
See also DLB 133

Neufeld, John (Arthur) 1938- . . . . . . **CLC 17**
See also AAYA 11; CA 25-28R; CANR 11,
37; MAICYA; SAAS 3; SATA 6, 81

Neville, Emily Cheney 1919- . . . . **CLC 12**
See also CA 5-8R; CANR 3, 37; JRDA;
MAICYA; SAAS 2; SATA 1

Newbound, Bernard Slade 1930-
See Slade, Bernard
See also CA 81-84; CANR 49;
DAM DRAM

Newby, P(ercy) H(oward)
1918- . . . . **CLC 2, 13; DAM NOV**
See also CA 5-8R; CANR 32; DLB 15;
MTCW

Newlove, Donald 1928- . . . . **CLC 6**
See also CA 29-32R; CANR 25

Newlove, John (Herbert) 1938- . . . . . **CLC 14**
See also CA 21-24R; CANR 9, 25

Newman, Charles 1938- . . . . **CLC 2, 8**
See also CA 21-24R

Newman, Edwin (Harold) 1919- . . . . **CLC 14**
See also AITN 1; CA 69-72; CANR 5

Newman, John Henry
1801-1890 . . . . **NCLC 38**
See also DLB 18, 32, 55

Newton, Suzanne 1936- . . . . **CLC 35**
See also CA 41-44R; CANR 14; JRDA;
SATA 5, 77

Nexo, Martin Andersen
1869-1954 . . . . **TCLC 43**

Nezval, Vitezslav 1900-1958 . . . . . . **TCLC 44**
See also CA 123

Ng, Fae Myenne 1957(?)- . . . . **CLC 81**
See also CA 146

Ngema, Mbongeni 1955- . . . . **CLC 57**
See also BW 2; CA 143

Ngugi, James T(hiong'o) . . . . **CLC 3, 7, 13**
See also Ngugi wa Thiong'o

Ngugi wa Thiong'o
1938- . . . . . **CLC 36; BLC; DAM MULT,
NOV**
See also Ngugi, James T(hiong'o)
See also BW 2; CA 81-84; CANR 27;
DLB 125; MTCW

Nichol, B(arrie) P(hillip)
1944-1988 . . . . **CLC 18**
See also CA 53-56; DLB 53; SATA 66

Nichols, John (Treadwell) 1940- . . . . **CLC 38**
See also CA 9-12R; CAAS 2; CANR 6;
DLBY 82

Nichols, Leigh
See Koontz, Dean R(ay)

Nichols, Peter (Richard)
1927- . . . . **CLC 5, 36, 65**
See also CA 104; CANR 33; DLB 13;
MTCW

Nicolas, F. R. E.
See Freeling, Nicolas

Niedecker, Lorine
1903-1970 . . . . **CLC 10, 42; DAM POET**
See also CA 25-28; CAP 2; DLB 48

Nietzsche, Friedrich (Wilhelm)
1844-1900 . . . . **TCLC 10, 18, 55**
See also CA 107; 121; DLB 129

Nievo, Ippolito 1831-1861 . . . . **NCLC 22**

Nightingale, Anne Redmon 1943-
See Redmon, Anne
See also CA 103

Nik. T. O.
See Annensky, Innokenty Fyodorovich

Nin, Anais
1903-1977 . . . . . . **CLC 1, 4, 8, 11, 14, 60;
DAM NOV, POP; SSC 10**
See also AITN 2; CA 13-16R; 69-72;
CANR 22, 53; DLB 2, 4, 152; MTCW

Nishiwaki, Junzaburo 1894-1982 . . . . **PC 15**
See also CA 107

Nissenson, Hugh 1933- . . . . **CLC 4, 9**
See also CA 17-20R; CANR 27; DLB 28

Niven, Larry . . . . **CLC 8**
See also Niven, Laurence Van Cott
See also DLB 8

Niven, Laurence Van Cott 1938-
See Niven, Larry
See also CA 21-24R; CAAS 12; CANR 14,
44; DAM POP; MTCW

Nixon, Agnes Eckhardt 1927- . . . . . . **CLC 21**
See also CA 110

Nizan, Paul 1905-1940 . . . . **TCLC 40**
See also DLB 72

Nkosi, Lewis
1936- . . . . . **CLC 45; BLC; DAM MULT**
See also BW 1; CA 65-68; CANR 27;
DLB 157

Nodier, (Jean) Charles (Emmanuel)
1780-1844 . . . . **NCLC 19**
See also DLB 119

Nolan, Christopher 1965- . . . . **CLC 58**
See also CA 111

Noon, Jeff 1957- . . . . **CLC 91**
See also CA 148

Norden, Charles
See Durrell, Lawrence (George)

Nordhoff, Charles (Bernard)
1887-1947 . . . . **TCLC 23**
See also CA 108; DLB 9; SATA 23

Norfolk, Lawrence 1963- . . . . **CLC 76**
See also CA 144

Norman, Marsha
1947- . . . . **CLC 28; DAM DRAM**
See also CA 105; CABS 3; CANR 41;
DLBY 84

Norris, Benjamin Franklin, Jr.
1870-1902 . . . . **TCLC 24**
See also Norris, Frank
See also CA 110

Norris, Frank
See Norris, Benjamin Franklin, Jr.
See also CDALB 1865-1917; DLB 12, 71

Norris, Leslie 1921- . . . . **CLC 14**
See also CA 11-12; CANR 14; CAP 1;
DLB 27

North, Andrew
See Norton, Andre

North, Anthony
See Koontz, Dean R(ay)

North, Captain George
See Stevenson, Robert Louis (Balfour)

North, Milou
See Erdrich, Louise

Northrup, B. A.
See Hubbard, L(afayette) Ron(ald)

North Staffs
See Hulme, T(homas) E(rnest)

Norton, Alice Mary
See Norton, Andre
See also MAICYA; SATA 1, 43

Norton, Andre 1912- . . . . **CLC 12**
See also Norton, Alice Mary
See also AAYA 14; CA 1-4R; CANR 2, 31;
DLB 8, 52; JRDA; MTCW

Norton, Caroline 1808-1877 . . . . . . **NCLC 47**
See also DLB 21, 159

Norway, Nevil Shute 1899-1960
See Shute, Nevil
See also CA 102; 93-96

Norwid, Cyprian Kamil
1821-1883 . . . . **NCLC 17**

Nosille, Nabrah
See Ellison, Harlan (Jay)

Nossack, Hans Erich 1901-1978 . . . . . **CLC 6**
See also CA 93-96; 85-88; DLB 69

Nostradamus 1503-1566 . . . . **LC 27**

Nosu, Chuji
See Ozu, Yasujiro

Notenburg, Eleanora (Genrikhovna) von
See Guro, Elena

Nova, Craig 1945- . . . . **CLC 7, 31**
See also CA 45-48; CANR 2, 53

Novak, Joseph
See Kosinski, Jerzy (Nikodem)

Novalis 1772-1801 . . . . **NCLC 13**
See also DLB 90

Nowlan, Alden (Albert)
1933-1983 . . **CLC 15; DAC; DAM MST**
See also CA 9-12R; CANR 5; DLB 53

Noyes, Alfred 1880-1958 . . . . **TCLC 7**
See also CA 104; DLB 20

Nunn, Kem 19(?)- . . . . **CLC 34**

Nye, Robert
1939- . . . . **CLC 13, 42; DAM NOV**
See also CA 33-36R; CANR 29; DLB 14;
MTCW; SATA 6

Nyro, Laura 1947- . . . . **CLC 17**

Oates, Joyce Carol
1938- . . . . . . **CLC 1, 2, 3, 6, 9, 11, 15, 19,
33, 52; DA; DAB; DAC; DAM MST,
NOV, POP; SSC 6; WLC**
See also AAYA 15; AITN 1; BEST 89:2;
CA 5-8R; CANR 25, 45;
CDALB 1968-1988; DLB 2, 5, 130;
DLBY 81; INT CANR-25; MTCW

O'Brien, Darcy 1939- . . . . **CLC 11**
See also CA 21-24R; CANR 8

O'Brien, E. G.
See Clarke, Arthur C(harles)

O'Brien, Edna
    1936- . . . . CLC **3, 5, 8, 13, 36, 65;**
                                DAM NOV; SSC 10
    See also CA 1-4R; CANR 6, 41;
        CDBLB 1960 to Present; DLB 14;
        MTCW

O'Brien, Fitz-James 1828-1862. . . NCLC **21**
    See also DLB 74

O'Brien, Flann. . . . . . . CLC **1, 4, 5, 7, 10, 47**
    See also O Nuallain, Brian

O'Brien, Richard 1942- . . . . CLC **17**
    See also CA 124

O'Brien, Tim
    1946- . . . . . . CLC **7, 19, 40; DAM POP**
    See also AAYA 16; CA 85-88; CANR 40;
        DLB 152; DLBD 9; DLBY 80

Obstfelder, Sigbjoern 1866-1900. . . TCLC **23**
    See also CA 123

O'Casey, Sean
    1880-1964 . . . . . . CLC **1, 5, 9, 11, 15, 88;**
            DAB; DAC; DAM DRAM, MST
    See also CA 89-92; CDBLB 1914-1945;
        DLB 10; MTCW

O'Cathasaigh, Sean
    See O'Casey, Sean

Ochs, Phil 1940-1976. . . . . CLC **17**
    See also CA 65-68

O'Connor, Edwin (Greene)
    1918-1968 . . . . CLC **14**
    See also CA 93-96; 25-28R

O'Connor, (Mary) Flannery
    1925-1964 . . . . CLC **1, 2, 3, 6, 10, 13, 15,**
        21, 66; DA; DAB; DAC; DAM MST,
            NOV; SSC 1, 23; WLC
    See also AAYA 7; CA 1-4R; CANR 3, 41;
        CDALB 1941-1968; DLB 2, 152;
        DLBD 12; DLBY 80; MTCW

O'Connor, Frank. . . . . CLC **23; SSC 5**
    See also O'Donovan, Michael John
    See also DLB 162

O'Dell, Scott 1898-1989. . . . . CLC **30**
    See also AAYA 3; CA 61-64; 129;
        CANR 12, 30; CLR 1, 16; DLB 52;
        JRDA; MAICYA; SATA 12, 60

Odets, Clifford
    1906-1963 . . . CLC **2, 28; DAM DRAM;**
                                            DC 6
    See also CA 85-88; DLB 7, 26; MTCW

O'Doherty, Brian 1934- . . . . CLC **76**
    See also CA 105

O'Donnell, K. M.
    See Malzberg, Barry N(athaniel)

O'Donnell, Lawrence
    See Kuttner, Henry

O'Donovan, Michael John
    1903-1966 . . . . CLC **14**
    See also O'Connor, Frank
    See also CA 93-96

Oe, Kenzaburo
    1935- . . . . . CLC **10, 36, 86; DAM NOV;**
                                            SSC 20
    See also CA 97-100; CANR 36, 50;
        DLBY 94; MTCW

O'Faolain, Julia 1932- . . . . CLC **6, 19, 47**
    See also CA 81-84; CAAS 2; CANR 12;
        DLB 14; MTCW

O'Faolain, Sean
    1900-1991 . . . . CLC **1, 7, 14, 32, 70;**
                                            SSC 13
    See also CA 61-64; 134; CANR 12;
        DLB 15, 162; MTCW

O'Flaherty, Liam
    1896-1984 . . . . CLC **5, 34; SSC 6**
    See also CA 101; 113; CANR 35; DLB 36,
        162; DLBY 84; MTCW

Ogilvy, Gavin
    See Barrie, J(ames) M(atthew)

O'Grady, Standish James
    1846-1928 . . . . TCLC **5**
    See also CA 104

O'Grady, Timothy 1951- . . . . CLC **59**
    See also CA 138

O'Hara, Frank
    1926-1966 . . . . CLC **2, 5, 13, 78;**
                                            DAM POET
    See also CA 9-12R; 25-28R; CANR 33;
        DLB 5, 16; MTCW

O'Hara, John (Henry)
    1905-1970 . . . . CLC **1, 2, 3, 6, 11, 42;**
                                            DAM NOV; SSC 15
    See also CA 5-8R; 25-28R; CANR 31;
        CDALB 1929-1941; DLB 9, 86; DLBD 2;
        MTCW

O Hehir, Diana 1922- . . . . CLC **41**
    See also CA 93-96

Okigbo, Christopher (Ifenayichukwu)
    1932-1967 . . . . CLC **25, 84; BLC;**
            DAM MULT, POET; PC 7
    See also BW 1; CA 77-80; DLB 125;
        MTCW

Okri, Ben 1959- . . . . CLC **87**
    See also BW 2; CA 130; 138; DLB 157;
        INT 138

Olds, Sharon
    1942- . . . . . CLC **32, 39, 85; DAM POET**
    See also CA 101; CANR 18, 41; DLB 120

Oldstyle, Jonathan
    See Irving, Washington

Olesha, Yuri (Karlovich)
    1899-1960 . . . . CLC **8**
    See also CA 85-88

Oliphant, Laurence
    1829(?)-1888 . . . . NCLC **47**
    See also DLB 18, 166

Oliphant, Margaret (Oliphant Wilson)
    1828-1897 . . . . NCLC **11**
    See also DLB 18, 159

Oliver, Mary 1935- . . . . CLC **19, 34**
    See also CA 21-24R; CANR 9, 43; DLB 5

Olivier, Laurence (Kerr)
    1907-1989 . . . . CLC **20**
    See also CA 111; 150; 129

Olsen, Tillie
    1913- . . . . . CLC **4, 13; DA; DAB; DAC;**
                            DAM MST; SSC 11
    See also CA 1-4R; CANR 1, 43; DLB 28;
        DLBY 80; MTCW

Olson, Charles (John)
    1910-1970 . . . . . CLC **1, 2, 5, 6, 9, 11, 29;**
                                            DAM POET
    See also CA 13-16; 25-28R; CABS 2;
        CANR 35; CAP 1; DLB 5, 16; MTCW

Olson, Toby 1937- . . . . CLC **28**
    See also CA 65-68; CANR 9, 31

Olyesha, Yuri
    See Olesha, Yuri (Karlovich)

Ondaatje, (Philip) Michael
    1943- . . . . CLC **14, 29, 51, 76; DAB;**
                            DAC; DAM MST
    See also CA 77-80; CANR 42; DLB 60

Oneal, Elizabeth 1934-
    See Oneal, Zibby
    See also CA 106; CANR 28; MAICYA;
        SATA 30, 82

Oneal, Zibby. . . . . CLC **30**
    See also Oneal, Elizabeth
    See also AAYA 5; CLR 13; JRDA

O'Neill, Eugene (Gladstone)
    1888-1953 . . . . . . TCLC **1, 6, 27, 49; DA;**
        DAB; DAC; DAM DRAM, MST; WLC
    See also AITN 1; CA 110; 132;
        CDALB 1929-1941; DLB 7; MTCW

Onetti, Juan Carlos
    1909-1994 . . . . CLC **7, 10; DAM MULT,**
                                            NOV; SSC 23
    See also CA 85-88; 145; CANR 32;
        DLB 113; HW; MTCW

O Nuallain, Brian 1911-1966
    See O'Brien, Flann
    See also CA 21-22; 25-28R; CAP 2

Oppen, George 1908-1984 . . . . CLC **7, 13, 34**
    See also CA 13-16R; 113; CANR 8; DLB 5,
        165

Oppenheim, E(dward) Phillips
    1866-1946 . . . . TCLC **45**
    See also CA 111; DLB 70

Orlovitz, Gil 1918-1973. . . . . CLC **22**
    See also CA 77-80; 45-48; DLB 2, 5

Orris
    See Ingelow, Jean

Ortega y Gasset, Jose
    1883-1955 . . . . . TCLC **9; DAM MULT;**
                                            HLC
    See also CA 106; 130; HW; MTCW

Ortese, Anna Maria 1914- . . . . CLC **89**

Ortiz, Simon J(oseph)
    1941- . . . . CLC **45; DAM MULT, POET**
    See also CA 134; DLB 120; NNAL

Orton, Joe. . . . . CLC **4, 13, 43; DC 3**
    See also Orton, John Kingsley
    See also CDBLB 1960 to Present; DLB 13

Orton, John Kingsley 1933-1967
    See Orton, Joe
    See also CA 85-88; CANR 35;
        DAM DRAM; MTCW

Orwell, George
    . . . . . TCLC **2, 6, 15, 31, 51; DAB; WLC**
    See also Blair, Eric (Arthur)
    See also CDBLB 1945-1960; DLB 15, 98

Osborne, David
    See Silverberg, Robert

Osborne, George
    See Silverberg, Robert

Osborne, John (James)
    1929-1994 . . . . . CLC **1, 2, 5, 11, 45; DA;**
        DAB; DAC; DAM DRAM, MST; WLC
    See also CA 13-16R; 147; CANR 21;
        CDBLB 1945-1960; DLB 13; MTCW

Osborne, Lawrence 1958- .... CLC 50

Oshima, Nagisa 1932- .... CLC 20
See also CA 116; 121

Oskison, John Milton
1874-1947 ..... TCLC 35; DAM MULT
See also CA 144; NNAL

Ossoli, Sarah Margaret (Fuller marchesa d')
1810-1850
See Fuller, Margaret
See also SATA 25

Ostrovsky, Alexander
1823-1886 .... NCLC 30, 57

Otero, Blas de 1916-1979......... CLC 11
See also CA 89-92; DLB 134

Otto, Whitney 1955-............. CLC 70
See also CA 140

Ouida .... TCLC 43
See also De La Ramee, (Marie) Louise
See also DLB 18, 156

Ousmane, Sembene 1923- .... CLC 66; BLC
1; CA 117; 125; MTCW
See also BW 1; CA 117; 125; MTCW

Ovid
43B.C.-18(?) ... CMLC 7; DAM POET;
PC 2

Owen, Hugh
See Faust, Frederick (Schiller)

Owen, Wilfred (Edward Salter)
1893-1918 ...... TCLC 5, 27; DA; DAB;
DAC; DAM MST, POET; WLC
See also CA 104; 141; CDBLB 1914-1945;
DLB 20

Owens, Rochelle 1936-............. CLC 8
See also CA 17-20R; CAAS 2; CANR 39

Oz, Amos
1939- .... CLC 5, 8, 11, 27, 33, 54;
DAM NOV
See also CA 53-56; CANR 27, 47; MTCW

Ozick, Cynthia
1928- .... CLC 3, 7, 28, 62; DAM NOV,
POP; SSC 15
See also BEST 90:1; CA 17-20R; CANR 23;
DLB 28, 152; DLBY 82; INT CANR-23;
MTCW

Ozu, Yasujiro 1903-1963 .... CLC 16
See also CA 112

Pacheco, C.
See Pessoa, Fernando (Antonio Nogueira)

Pa Chin .... CLC 18
See also Li Fei-kan

Pack, Robert 1929-............. CLC 13
See also CA 1-4R; CANR 3, 44; DLB 5

Padgett, Lewis
See Kuttner, Henry

Padilla (Lorenzo), Heberto 1932-... CLC 38
See also AITN 1; CA 123; 131; HW

Page, Jimmy 1944-............... CLC 12

Page, Louise 1955-............. CLC 40
See also CA 140

Page, P(atricia) K(athleen)
1916- .... CLC 7, 18; DAC; DAM MST;
PC 12
See also CA 53-56; CANR 4, 22; DLB 68;
MTCW

Page, Thomas Nelson 1853-1922.... SSC 23
See also CA 118; DLB 12, 78; DLBD 13

Paget, Violet 1856-1935
See Lee, Vernon
See also CA 104

Paget-Lowe, Henry
See Lovecraft, H(oward) P(hillips)

Paglia, Camille (Anna) 1947-...... CLC 68
See also CA 140

Paige, Richard
See Koontz, Dean R(ay)

Pakenham, Antonia
See Fraser, (Lady) Antonia (Pakenham)

Palamas, Kostes 1859-1943 .... TCLC 5
See also CA 105

Palazzeschi, Aldo 1885-1974...... CLC 11
See also CA 89-92; 53-56; DLB 114

Paley, Grace
1922- .... CLC 4, 6, 37; DAM POP;
SSC 8
See also CA 25-28R; CANR 13, 46;
DLB 28; INT CANR-13; MTCW

Palin, Michael (Edward) 1943-..... CLC 21
See also Monty Python
See also CA 107; CANR 35; SATA 67

Palliser, Charles 1947-............ CLC 65
See also CA 136

Palma, Ricardo 1833-1919........ TCLC 29

Pancake, Breece Dexter 1952-1979
See Pancake, Breece D'J
See also CA 123; 109

Pancake, Breece D'J.............. CLC 29
See also Pancake, Breece Dexter
See also DLB 130

Panko, Rudy
See Gogol, Nikolai (Vasilyevich)

Papadiamantis, Alexandros
1851-1911 .... TCLC 29

Papadiamantopoulos, Johannes 1856-1910
See Moreas, Jean
See also CA 117

Papini, Giovanni 1881-1956....... TCLC 22
See also CA 121

Paracelsus 1493-1541.............. LC 14

Parasol, Peter
See Stevens, Wallace

Parfenie, Maria
See Codrescu, Andrei

Parini, Jay (Lee) 1948- .... CLC 54
See also CA 97-100; CAAS 16; CANR 32

Park, Jordan
See Kornbluth, C(yril) M.; Pohl, Frederik

Parker, Bert
See Ellison, Harlan (Jay)

Parker, Dorothy (Rothschild)
1893-1967 .... CLC 15, 68;
DAM POET; SSC 2
See also CA 19-20; 25-28R; CAP 2;
DLB 11, 45, 86; MTCW

Parker, Robert B(rown)
1932- ...... CLC 27; DAM NOV, POP
See also BEST 89:4; CA 49-52; CANR 1,
26, 52; INT CANR-26; MTCW

Parkin, Frank 1940-.............. CLC 43
See also CA 147

Parkman, Francis, Jr.
1823-1893 .... NCLC 12
See also DLB 1, 30

Parks, Gordon (Alexander Buchanan)
1912- ... CLC 1, 16; BLC; DAM MULT
See also AITN 2; BW 2; CA 41-44R;
CANR 26; DLB 33; SATA 8

Parnell, Thomas 1679-1718 .... LC 3
See also DLB 94

Parra, Nicanor
1914- ...... CLC 2; DAM MULT; HLC
See also CA 85-88; CANR 32; HW; MTCW

Parrish, Mary Frances
See Fisher, M(ary) F(rances) K(ennedy)

Parson
See Coleridge, Samuel Taylor

Parson Lot
See Kingsley, Charles

Partridge, Anthony
See Oppenheim, E(dward) Phillips

Pascal, Blaise 1623-1662 .... LC 35

Pascoli, Giovanni 1855-1912 ...... TCLC 45

Pasolini, Pier Paolo
1922-1975 .... CLC 20, 37
See also CA 93-96; 61-64; DLB 128;
MTCW

Pasquini
See Silone, Ignazio

Pastan, Linda (Olenik)
1932- .... CLC 27; DAM POET
See also CA 61-64; CANR 18, 40; DLB 5

Pasternak, Boris (Leonidovich)
1890-1960 ...... CLC 7, 10, 18, 63; DA;
DAB; DAC; DAM MST, NOV, POET;
PC 6; WLC
See also CA 127; 116; MTCW

Patchen, Kenneth
1911-1972 ... CLC 1, 2, 18; DAM POET
See also CA 1-4R; 33-36R; CANR 3, 35;
DLB 16, 48; MTCW

Pater, Walter (Horatio)
1839-1894 .... NCLC 7
See also CDBLB 1832-1890; DLB 57, 156

Paterson, A(ndrew) B(arton)
1864-1941 .... TCLC 32

Paterson, Katherine (Womeldorf)
1932- .... CLC 12, 30
See also AAYA 1; CA 21-24R; CANR 28;
CLR 7; DLB 52; JRDA; MAICYA;
MTCW; SATA 13, 53

Patmore, Coventry Kersey Dighton
1823-1896 .... NCLC 9
See also DLB 35, 98

Paton, Alan (Stewart)
1903-1988 ...... CLC 4, 10, 25, 55; DA;
DAB; DAC; DAM MST, NOV; WLC
See also CA 13-16; 125; CANR 22; CAP 1;
MTCW; SATA 11; SATA-Obit 56

Paton Walsh, Gillian 1937-
See Walsh, Jill Paton
See also CANR 38; JRDA; MAICYA;
SAAS 3; SATA 4, 72

Pincherle, Alberto
1907-1990 ..... **CLC 11, 18; DAM NOV**
See also Moravia, Alberto
See also CA 25-28R; 132; CANR 33;
MTCW

Pinckney, Darryl 1953- .... **CLC 76**
See also BW 2; CA 143

Pindar 518B.C.-446B.C. .... **CMLC 12**

Pineda, Cecile 1942- .... **CLC 39**
See also CA 118

Pinero, Arthur Wing
1855-1934 ..... **TCLC 32; DAM DRAM**
See also CA 110; DLB 10

Pinero, Miguel (Antonio Gomez)
1946-1988 .... **CLC 4, 55**
See also CA 61-64; 125; CANR 29; HW

Pinget, Robert 1919- .... **CLC 7, 13, 37**
See also CA 85-88; DLB 83

Pink Floyd
See Barrett, (Roger) Syd; Gilmour, David;
Mason, Nick; Waters, Roger; Wright,
Rick

Pinkney, Edward 1802-1828 ..... **NCLC 31**

Pinkwater, Daniel Manus 1941- .... **CLC 35**
See also Pinkwater, Manus
See also AAYA 1; CA 29-32R; CANR 12,
38; CLR 4; JRDA; MAICYA; SAAS 3;
SATA 46, 76

Pinkwater, Manus
See Pinkwater, Daniel Manus
See also SATA 8

Pinsky, Robert
1940- .. **CLC 9, 19, 38, 94; DAM POET**
See also CA 29-32R; CAAS 4; DLBY 82

Pinta, Harold
See Pinter, Harold

Pinter, Harold
1930- ..... **CLC 1, 3, 6, 9, 11, 15, 27, 58,
73; DA; DAB; DAC; DAM DRAM,
MST; WLC**
See also CA 5-8R; CANR 33; CDBLB 1960
to Present; DLB 13; MTCW

Piozzi, Hester Lynch (Thrale)
1741-1821 .... **NCLC 57**
See also DLB 104, 142

Pirandello, Luigi
1867-1936 ...... **TCLC 4, 29; DA; DAB;
DAC; DAM DRAM, MST; DC 5;
SSC 22; WLC**
See also CA 104

Pirsig, Robert M(aynard)
1928- .... **CLC 4, 6, 73; DAM POP**
See also CA 53-56; CANR 42; MTCW;
SATA 39

Pisarev, Dmitry Ivanovich
1840-1868 .... **NCLC 25**

Pix, Mary (Griffith) 1666-1709 .... **LC 8**
See also DLB 80

Pixerecourt, Guilbert de
1773-1844 .... **NCLC 39**

Plaidy, Jean
See Hibbert, Eleanor Alice Burford

Planche, James Robinson
1796-1880 .... **NCLC 42**

Plant, Robert 1948- .... **CLC 12**

Plante, David (Robert)
1940- .... **CLC 7, 23, 38; DAM NOV**
See also CA 37-40R; CANR 12, 36;
DLBY 83; INT CANR-12; MTCW

Plath, Sylvia
1932-1963 ..... **CLC 1, 2, 3, 5, 9, 11, 14,
17, 50, 51, 62; DA; DAB; DAC;
DAM MST, POET; PC 1; WLC**
See also AAYA 13; CA 19-20; CANR 34;
CAP 2; CDALB 1941-1968; DLB 5, 6,
152; MTCW

Plato
428(?)B.C.-348(?)B.C. ..... **CMLC 8; DA;
DAB; DAC; DAM MST**

Platonov, Andrei .... **TCLC 14**
See also Klimentov, Andrei Platonovich

Platt, Kin 1911- .... **CLC 26**
See also AAYA 11; CA 17-20R; CANR 11;
JRDA; SAAS 17; SATA 21, 86

Plautus c. 251B.C.-184B.C. .... **DC 6**

Plick et Plock
See Simenon, Georges (Jacques Christian)

Plimpton, George (Ames) 1927- ..... **CLC 36**
See also AITN 1; CA 21-24R; CANR 32;
MTCW; SATA 10

Plomer, William Charles Franklin
1903-1973 .... **CLC 4, 8**
See also CA 21-22; CANR 34; CAP 2;
DLB 20, 162; MTCW; SATA 24

Plowman, Piers
See Kavanagh, Patrick (Joseph)

Plum, J.
See Wodehouse, P(elham) G(renville)

Plumly, Stanley (Ross) 1939- ...... **CLC 33**
See also CA 108; 110; DLB 5; INT 110

Plumpe, Friedrich Wilhelm
1888-1931 .... **TCLC 53**
See also CA 112

Poe, Edgar Allan
1809-1849 .... **NCLC 1, 16, 55; DA;
DAB; DAC; DAM MST, POET; PC 1;
SSC 1, 22; WLC**
See also AAYA 14; CDALB 1640-1865;
DLB 3, 59, 73, 74; SATA 23

Poet of Titchfield Street, The
See Pound, Ezra (Weston Loomis)

Pohl, Frederik 1919- .... **CLC 18**
See also CA 61-64; CAAS 1; CANR 11, 37;
DLB 8; INT CANR-11; MTCW;
SATA 24

Poirier, Louis 1910-
See Gracq, Julien
See also CA 122; 126

Poitier, Sidney 1927- .... **CLC 26**
See also BW 1; CA 117

Polanski, Roman 1933- .... **CLC 16**
See also CA 77-80

Poliakoff, Stephen 1952- .... **CLC 38**
See also CA 106; DLB 13

Police, The
See Copeland, Stewart (Armstrong);
Summers, Andrew James; Sumner,
Gordon Matthew

Polidori, John William
1795-1821 .... **NCLC 51**
See also DLB 116

Pollitt, Katha 1949- .... **CLC 28**
See also CA 120; 122; MTCW

Pollock, (Mary) Sharon
1936- .... **CLC 50; DAC; DAM DRAM,
MST**
See also CA 141; DLB 60

Polo, Marco 1254-1324 .... **CMLC 15**

Polonsky, Abraham (Lincoln)
1910- .... **CLC 92**
See also CA 104; DLB 26; INT 104

Polybius c. 200B.C.-c. 118B.C. .... **CMLC 17**

Pomerance, Bernard
1940- .... **CLC 13; DAM DRAM**
See also CA 101; CANR 49

Ponge, Francis (Jean Gaston Alfred)
1899-1988 ..... **CLC 6, 18; DAM POET**
See also CA 85-88; 126; CANR 40

Pontoppidan, Henrik 1857-1943 ... **TCLC 29**

Poole, Josephine .... **CLC 17**
See also Helyar, Jane Penelope Josephine
See also SAAS 2; SATA 5

Popa, Vasko 1922-1991 .... **CLC 19**
See also CA 112; 148

Pope, Alexander
1688-1744 ...... **LC 3; DA; DAB; DAC;
DAM MST, POET; WLC**
See also CDBLB 1660-1789; DLB 95, 101

Porter, Connie (Rose) 1959(?)- ..... **CLC 70**
See also BW 2; CA 142; SATA 81

Porter, Gene(va Grace) Stratton
1863(?)-1924 .... **TCLC 21**
See also CA 112

Porter, Katherine Anne
1890-1980 ...... **CLC 1, 3, 7, 10, 13, 15,
27; DA; DAB; DAC; DAM MST, NOV;
SSC 4**
See also AITN 2; CA 1-4R; 101; CANR 1;
DLB 4, 9, 102; DLBD 12; DLBY 80;
MTCW; SATA 39; SATA-Obit 23

Porter, Peter (Neville Frederick)
1929- .... **CLC 5, 13, 33**
See also CA 85-88; DLB 40

Porter, William Sydney 1862-1910
See Henry, O.
See also CA 104; 131; CDALB 1865-1917;
DA; DAB; DAC; DAM MST; DLB 12,
78, 79; MTCW; YABC 2

Portillo (y Pacheco), Jose Lopez
See Lopez Portillo (y Pacheco), Jose

Post, Melville Davisson
1869-1930 .... **TCLC 39**
See also CA 110

Potok, Chaim
1929- .... **CLC 2, 7, 14, 26; DAM NOV**
See also AAYA 15; AITN 1, 2; CA 17-20R;
CANR 19, 35; DLB 28, 152;
INT CANR-19; MTCW; SATA 33

Potter, Beatrice
See Webb, (Martha) Beatrice (Potter)
See also MAICYA

Potter, Dennis (Christopher George)
1935-1994 . . . . CLC **58, 86**
See also CA 107; 145; CANR 33; MTCW

Pound, Ezra (Weston Loomis)
1885-1972 . . . . . . CLC **1, 2, 3, 4, 5, 7, 10,**
13, 18, 34, 48, 50; DA; DAB; DAC;
DAM MST, POET; PC 4; WLC
See also CA 5-8R; 37-40R; CANR 40;
CDALB 1917-1929; DLB 4, 45, 63;
MTCW

Povod, Reinaldo 1959-1994 . . . . CLC **44**
See also CA 136; 146

Powell, Adam Clayton, Jr.
1908-1972 . . . . CLC **89; BLC;**
DAM MULT
See also BW 1; CA 102; 33-36R

Powell, Anthony (Dymoke)
1905- . . . . CLC **1, 3, 7, 9, 10, 31**
See also CA 1-4R; CANR 1, 32;
CDBLB 1945-1960; DLB 15; MTCW

Powell, Dawn 1897-1965 . . . . CLC **66**
See also CA 5-8R

Powell, Padgett 1952- . . . . CLC **34**
See also CA 126

Power, Susan . . . . CLC **91**

Powers, J(ames) F(arl)
1917- . . . . CLC **1, 4, 8, 57; SSC 4**
See also CA 1-4R; CANR 2; DLB 130;
MTCW

Powers, John J(ames) 1945-
See Powers, John R.
See also CA 69-72

Powers, John R. . . . . CLC **66**
See also Powers, John J(ames)

Powers, Richard (S.) 1957- . . . . CLC **93**
See also CA 148

Pownall, David 1938- . . . . CLC **10**
See also CA 89-92; CAAS 18; CANR 49;
DLB 14

Powys, John Cowper
1872-1963 . . . . CLC **7, 9, 15, 46**
See also CA 85-88; DLB 15; MTCW

Powys, T(heodore) F(rancis)
1875-1953 . . . . TCLC **9**
See also CA 106; DLB 36, 162

Prager, Emily 1952- . . . . CLC **56**

Pratt, E(dwin) J(ohn)
1883(?)-1964 . . . . CLC **19; DAC;**
DAM POET
See also CA 141; 93-96; DLB 92

Premchand . . . . TCLC **21**
See also Srivastava, Dhanpat Rai

Preussler, Otfried 1923- . . . . CLC **17**
See also CA 77-80; SATA 24

Prevert, Jacques (Henri Marie)
1900-1977 . . . . CLC **15**
See also CA 77-80; 69-72; CANR 29;
MTCW; SATA-Obit 30

Prevost, Abbe (Antoine Francois)
1697-1763 . . . . LC **1**

Price, (Edward) Reynolds
1933- . . . . CLC **3, 6, 13, 43, 50, 63;**
DAM NOV; SSC 22
See also CA 1-4R; CANR 1, 37; DLB 2;
INT CANR-37

Price, Richard 1949- . . . . CLC **6, 12**
See also CA 49-52; CANR 3; DLBY 81

Prichard, Katharine Susannah
1883-1969 . . . . CLC **46**
See also CA 11-12; CANR 33; CAP 1;
MTCW; SATA 66

Priestley, J(ohn) B(oynton)
1894-1984 . . . . CLC **2, 5, 9, 34;**
DAM DRAM, NOV
See also CA 9-12R; 113; CANR 33;
CDBLB 1914-1945; DLB 10, 34, 77, 100,
139; DLBY 84; MTCW

Prince 1958(?)- . . . . CLC **35**

Prince, F(rank) T(empleton) 1912- . . CLC **22**
See also CA 101; CANR 43; DLB 20

Prince Kropotkin
See Kropotkin, Peter (Aleksieevich)

Prior, Matthew 1664-1721 . . . . LC **4**
See also DLB 95

Pritchard, William H(arrison)
1932- . . . . CLC **34**
See also CA 65-68; CANR 23; DLB 111

Pritchett, V(ictor) S(awdon)
1900- . . . . CLC **5, 13, 15, 41;**
DAM NOV; SSC 14
See also CA 61-64; CANR 31; DLB 15,
139; MTCW

Private 19022
See Manning, Frederic

Probst, Mark 1925- . . . . CLC **59**
See also CA 130

Prokosch, Frederic 1908-1989 . . . . CLC **4, 48**
See also CA 73-76; 128; DLB 48

Prophet, The
See Dreiser, Theodore (Herman Albert)

Prose, Francine 1947- . . . . CLC **45**
See also CA 109; 112; CANR 46

Proudhon
See Cunha, Euclides (Rodrigues Pimenta) da

Proulx, E. Annie 1935- . . . . CLC **81**

**Proust, (Valentin-Louis-George-Eugene-)
Marcel**
1871-1922 . . . . TCLC **7, 13, 33; DA;**
DAB; DAC; DAM MST, NOV; WLC
See also CA 104; 120; DLB 65; MTCW

Prowler, Harley
See Masters, Edgar Lee

Prus, Boleslaw 1845-1912 . . . . TCLC **48**

Pryor, Richard (Franklin Lenox Thomas)
1940- . . . . CLC **26**
See also CA 122

Przybyszewski, Stanislaw
1868-1927 . . . . TCLC **36**
See also DLB 66

Pteleon
See Grieve, C(hristopher) M(urray)
See also DAM POET

Puckett, Lute
See Masters, Edgar Lee

Puig, Manuel
1932-1990 . . . . CLC **3, 5, 10, 28, 65;**
DAM MULT; HLC
See also CA 45-48; CANR 2, 32; DLB 113;
HW; MTCW

Purdy, Al(fred Wellington)
1918- . . . . CLC **3, 6, 14, 50; DAC;**
DAM MST, POET
See also CA 81-84; CAAS 17; CANR 42;
DLB 88

Purdy, James (Amos)
1923- . . . . CLC **2, 4, 10, 28, 52**
See also CA 33-36R; CAAS 1; CANR 19,
51; DLB 2; INT CANR-19; MTCW

Pure, Simon
See Swinnerton, Frank Arthur

Pushkin, Alexander (Sergeyevich)
1799-1837 . . . . . NCLC **3, 27; DA; DAB;**
DAC; DAM DRAM, MST, POET;
PC 10; WLC
See also SATA 61

P'u Sung-ling 1640-1715 . . . . LC **3**

Putnam, Arthur Lee
See Alger, Horatio, Jr.

Puzo, Mario
1920- . . . . . CLC **1, 2, 6, 36; DAM NOV,**
POP
See also CA 65-68; CANR 4, 42; DLB 6;
MTCW

Pym, Barbara (Mary Crampton)
1913-1980 . . . . CLC **13, 19, 37**
See also CA 13-14; 97-100; CANR 13, 34;
CAP 1; DLB 14; DLBY 87; MTCW

Pynchon, Thomas (Ruggles, Jr.)
1937- . . . . . CLC **2, 3, 6, 9, 11, 18, 33, 62,**
72; DA; DAB; DAC; DAM MST, NOV,
POP; SSC 14; WLC
See also BEST 90:2; CA 17-20R; CANR 22,
46; DLB 2; MTCW

Qian Zhongshu
See Ch'ien Chung-shu

Qroll
See Dagerman, Stig (Halvard)

Quarrington, Paul (Lewis) 1953- . . . . CLC **65**
See also CA 129

Quasimodo, Salvatore 1901-1968 . . . CLC **10**
See also CA 13-16; 25-28R; CAP 1;
DLB 114; MTCW

Quay, Stephen 1947- . . . . CLC **95**

Quay, The Brothers
See Quay, Stephen; Quay, Timothy

Quay, Timothy 1947- . . . . CLC **95**

Queen, Ellery . . . . CLC **3, 11**
See also Dannay, Frederic; Davidson,
Avram; Lee, Manfred B(ennington);
Sturgeon, Theodore (Hamilton); Vance,
John Holbrook

Queen, Ellery, Jr.
See Dannay, Frederic; Lee, Manfred
B(ennington)

Queneau, Raymond
1903-1976 . . . . CLC **2, 5, 10, 42**
See also CA 77-80; 69-72; CANR 32;
DLB 72; MTCW

Quevedo, Francisco de 1580-1645 . . . . LC **23**

Quiller-Couch, Arthur Thomas
1863-1944 . . . . TCLC **53**
See also CA 118; DLB 135, 153

Quin, Ann (Marie) 1936-1973 . . . . CLC **6**
See also CA 9-12R; 45-48; DLB 14

Author Index

Roberts, Charles G(eorge) D(ouglas)
1860-1943 .... **TCLC 8**
See also CA 105; CLR 33; DLB 92;
SATA 88; SATA-Brief 29

Roberts, Kate 1891-1985 .... **CLC 15**
See also CA 107; 116

Roberts, Keith (John Kingston)
1935- .... **CLC 14**
See also CA 25-28R; CANR 46

Roberts, Kenneth (Lewis)
1885-1957 .... **TCLC 23**
See also CA 109; DLB 9

Roberts, Michele (B.) 1949-........ **CLC 48**
See also CA 115

Robertson, Ellis
See Ellison, Harlan (Jay); Silverberg, Robert

Robertson, Thomas William
1829-1871 .... **NCLC 35; DAM DRAM**

Robinson, Edwin Arlington
1869-1935 .... **TCLC 5; DA; DAC;**
DAM MST, POET; PC 1
See also CA 104; 133; CDALB 1865-1917;
DLB 54; MTCW

Robinson, Henry Crabb
1775-1867 .... **NCLC 15**
See also DLB 107

Robinson, Jill 1936-.............. **CLC 10**
See also CA 102; INT 102

Robinson, Kim Stanley 1952- ...... **CLC 34**
See also CA 126

Robinson, Lloyd
See Silverberg, Robert

Robinson, Marilynne 1944-........ **CLC 25**
See also CA 116

Robinson, Smokey................. **CLC 21**
See also Robinson, William, Jr.

Robinson, William, Jr. 1940-
See Robinson, Smokey
See also CA 116

Robison, Mary 1949-............. **CLC 42**
See also CA 113; 116; DLB 130; INT 116

Rod, Edouard 1857-1910 .... **TCLC 52**

Roddenberry, Eugene Wesley 1921-1991
See Roddenberry, Gene
See also CA 110; 135; CANR 37; SATA 45;
SATA-Obit 69

Roddenberry, Gene................ **CLC 17**
See also Roddenberry, Eugene Wesley
See also AAYA 5; SATA-Obit 69

Rodgers, Mary 1931-.............. **CLC 12**
See also CA 49-52; CANR 8; CLR 20;
INT CANR-8; JRDA; MAICYA;
SATA 8

Rodgers, W(illiam) R(obert)
1909-1969 .... **CLC 7**
See also CA 85-88; DLB 20

Rodman, Eric
See Silverberg, Robert

Rodman, Howard 1920(?)-1985 ..... **CLC 65**
See also CA 118

Rodman, Maia
See Wojciechowska, Maia (Teresa)

Rodriguez, Claudio 1934-.......... **CLC 10**
See also DLB 134

Roelvaag, O(le) E(dvart)
1876-1931 .... **TCLC 17**
See also CA 117; DLB 9

Roethke, Theodore (Huebner)
1908-1963 ..... **CLC 1, 3, 8, 11, 19, 46;**
DAM POET; PC 15
See also CA 81-84; CABS 2;
CDALB 1941-1968; DLB 5; MTCW

Rogers, Thomas Hunton 1927- ..... **CLC 57**
See also CA 89-92; INT 89-92

Rogers, Will(iam Penn Adair)
1879-1935 ...... **TCLC 8; DAM MULT**
See also CA 105; 144; DLB 11; NNAL

Rogin, Gilbert 1929-.............. **CLC 18**
See also CA 65-68; CANR 15

Rohan, Koda .... **TCLC 22**
See also Koda Shigeyuki

Rohmer, Eric.................... **CLC 16**
See also Scherer, Jean-Marie Maurice

Rohmer, Sax .... **TCLC 28**
See also Ward, Arthur Henry Sarsfield
See also DLB 70

Roiphe, Anne (Richardson)
1935- .... **CLC 3, 9**
See also CA 89-92; CANR 45; DLBY 80;
INT 89-92

Rojas, Fernando de 1465-1541 ...... **LC 23**

Rolfe, Frederick (William Serafino Austin
Lewis Mary) 1860-1913...... **TCLC 12**
See also CA 107; DLB 34, 156

Rolland, Romain 1866-1944....... **TCLC 23**
See also CA 118; DLB 65

Rolvaag, O(le) E(dvart)
See Roelvaag, O(le) E(dvart)

Romain Arnaud, Saint
See Aragon, Louis

Romains, Jules 1885-1972 .... **CLC 7**
See also CA 85-88; CANR 34; DLB 65;
MTCW

Romero, Jose Ruben 1890-1952 ... **TCLC 14**
See also CA 114; 131; HW

Ronsard, Pierre de
1524-1585 .... **LC 6; PC 11**

Rooke, Leon
1934- .... **CLC 25, 34; DAM POP**
See also CA 25-28R; CANR 23, 53

Roper, William 1498-1578 .... **LC 10**

Roquelaure, A. N.
See Rice, Anne

Rosa, Joao Guimaraes 1908-1967 ... **CLC 23**
See also CA 89-92; DLB 113

Rose, Wendy
1948- .... **CLC 85; DAM MULT; PC 13**
See also CA 53-56; CANR 5, 51; NNAL;
SATA 12

Rosen, Richard (Dean) 1949-....... **CLC 39**
See also CA 77-80; INT CANR-30

Rosenberg, Isaac 1890-1918....... **TCLC 12**
See also CA 107; DLB 20

Rosenblatt, Joe .... **CLC 15**
See also Rosenblatt, Joseph

Rosenblatt, Joseph 1933-
See Rosenblatt, Joe
See also CA 89-92; INT 89-92

Rosenfeld, Samuel 1896-1963
See Tzara, Tristan
See also CA 89-92

Rosenthal, M(acha) L(ouis)
1917-1996 .... **CLC 28**
See also CA 1-4R; 152; CAAS 6; CANR 4,
51; DLB 5; SATA 59

Ross, Barnaby
See Dannay, Frederic

Ross, Bernard L.
See Follett, Ken(neth Martin)

Ross, J. H.
See Lawrence, T(homas) E(dward)

Ross, Martin
See Martin, Violet Florence
See also DLB 135

Ross, (James) Sinclair
1908- ...... **CLC 13; DAC; DAM MST**
See also CA 73-76; DLB 88

Rossetti, Christina (Georgina)
1830-1894 ..... **NCLC 2, 50; DA; DAB;**
DAC; DAM MST, POET; PC 7; WLC
See also DLB 35, 163; MAICYA; SATA 20

Rossetti, Dante Gabriel
1828-1882 .... **NCLC 4; DA; DAB;**
DAC; DAM MST, POET; WLC
See also CDBLB 1832-1890; DLB 35

Rossner, Judith (Perelman)
1935- .... **CLC 6, 9, 29**
See also AITN 2; BEST 90:3; CA 17-20R;
CANR 18, 51; DLB 6; INT CANR-18;
MTCW

Rostand, Edmond (Eugene Alexis)
1868-1918 ...... **TCLC 6, 37; DA; DAB;**
DAC; DAM DRAM, MST
See also CA 104; 126; MTCW

Roth, Henry 1906-1995 .... **CLC 2, 6, 11**
See also CA 11-12; 149; CANR 38; CAP 1;
DLB 28; MTCW

Roth, Joseph 1894-1939.......... **TCLC 33**
See also DLB 85

Roth, Philip (Milton)
1933- ...... **CLC 1, 2, 3, 4, 6, 9, 15, 22,**
31, 47, 66, 86; DA; DAB; DAC;
DAM MST, NOV, POP; WLC
See also BEST 90:3; CA 1-4R; CANR 1, 22,
36; CDALB 1968-1988; DLB 2, 28;
DLBY 82; MTCW

Rothenberg, Jerome 1931-........ **CLC 6, 57**
See also CA 45-48; CANR 1; DLB 5

Roumain, Jacques (Jean Baptiste)
1907-1944 .... **TCLC 19; BLC;**
DAM MULT
See also BW 1; CA 117; 125

Rourke, Constance (Mayfield)
1885-1941 .... **TCLC 12**
See also CA 107; YABC 1

Rousseau, Jean-Baptiste 1671-1741 ... **LC 9**

Rousseau, Jean-Jacques
1712-1778 ..... **LC 14; DA; DAB; DAC;**
DAM MST; WLC

Roussel, Raymond 1877-1933 ..... **TCLC 20**
See also CA 117

Rovit, Earl (Herbert) 1927-........ **CLC 7**
See also CA 5-8R; CANR 12

Rowe, Nicholas 1674-1718.......... **LC 8**
See also DLB 84

Rowley, Ames Dorrance
See Lovecraft, H(oward) P(hillips)

Rowson, Susanna Haswell
1762(?)-1824 .... **NCLC 5**
See also DLB 37

Roy, Gabrielle
1909-1983 .... **CLC 10, 14; DAB; DAC; DAM MST**
See also CA 53-56; 110; CANR 5; DLB 68; MTCW

Rozewicz, Tadeusz
1921-......... **CLC 9, 23; DAM POET**
See also CA 108; CANR 36; MTCW

Ruark, Gibbons 1941- .... **CLC 3**
See also CA 33-36R; CAAS 23; CANR 14, 31; DLB 120

Rubens, Bernice (Ruth) 1923-... **CLC 19, 31**
See also CA 25-28R; CANR 33; DLB 14; MTCW

Rudkin, (James) David 1936- ...... **CLC 14**
See also CA 89-92; DLB 13

Rudnik, Raphael 1933-............. **CLC 7**
See also CA 29-32R

Ruffian, M.
See Hasek, Jaroslav (Matej Frantisek)

Ruiz, Jose Martinez .... **CLC 11**
See also Martinez Ruiz, Jose

Rukeyser, Muriel
1913-1980 .... **CLC 6, 10, 15, 27; DAM POET; PC 12**
See also CA 5-8R; 93-96; CANR 26; DLB 48; MTCW; SATA-Obit 22

Rule, Jane (Vance) 1931-......... **CLC 27**
See also CA 25-28R; CAAS 18; CANR 12; DLB 60

Rulfo, Juan
1918-1986 .... **CLC 8, 80; DAM MULT; HLC**
See also CA 85-88; 118; CANR 26; DLB 113; HW; MTCW

Runeberg, Johan 1804-1877...... **NCLC 41**

Runyon, (Alfred) Damon
1884(?)-1946 .... **TCLC 10**
See also CA 107; DLB 11, 86

Rush, Norman 1933-............. **CLC 44**
See also CA 121; 126; INT 126

Rushdie, (Ahmed) Salman
1947- ..... **CLC 23, 31, 55; DAB; DAC; DAM MST, NOV, POP**
See also BEST 89:3; CA 108; 111; CANR 33; INT 111; MTCW

Rushforth, Peter (Scott) 1945- ..... **CLC 19**
See also CA 101

Ruskin, John 1819-1900......... **TCLC 63**
See also CA 114; 129; CDBLB 1832-1890; DLB 55, 163; SATA 24

Russ, Joanna 1937-.............. **CLC 15**
See also CA 25-28R; CANR 11, 31; DLB 8; MTCW

Russell, George William 1867-1935
See A. E.
See also CA 104; CDBLB 1890-1914; DAM POET

Russell, (Henry) Ken(neth Alfred)
1927-....................... **CLC 16**
See also CA 105

Russell, Willy 1947-.............. **CLC 60**

Rutherford, Mark .... **TCLC 25**
See also White, William Hale
See also DLB 18

Ruyslinck, Ward 1929-............. **CLC 14**
See also Belser, Reimond Karel Maria de

Ryan, Cornelius (John) 1920-1974 ... **CLC 7**
See also CA 69-72; 53-56; CANR 38

Ryan, Michael 1946- .... **CLC 65**
See also CA 49-52; DLBY 82

Rybakov, Anatoli (Naumovich)
1911-.................... **CLC 23, 53**
See also CA 126; 135; SATA 79

Ryder, Jonathan
See Ludlum, Robert

Ryga, George
1932-1987 .. **CLC 14; DAC; DAM MST**
See also CA 101; 124; CANR 43; DLB 60

S. S.
See Sassoon, Siegfried (Lorraine)

Saba, Umberto 1883-1957 .... **TCLC 33**
See also CA 144; DLB 114

Sabatini, Rafael 1875-1950 .... **TCLC 47**

Sabato, Ernesto (R.)
1911- .... **CLC 10, 23; DAM MULT; HLC**
See also CA 97-100; CANR 32; DLB 145; HW; MTCW

Sacastru, Martin
See Bioy Casares, Adolfo

Sacher-Masoch, Leopold von
1836(?)-1895 .... **NCLC 31**

Sachs, Marilyn (Stickle) 1927- ..... **CLC 35**
See also AAYA 2; CA 17-20R; CANR 13, 47; CLR 2; JRDA; MAICYA; SAAS 2; SATA 3, 68

Sachs, Nelly 1891-1970 .... **CLC 14**
See also CA 17-18; 25-28R; CAP 2

Sackler, Howard (Oliver)
1929-1982 .... **CLC 14**
See also CA 61-64; 108; CANR 30; DLB 7

Sacks, Oliver (Wolf) 1933- .... **CLC 67**
See also CA 53-56; CANR 28, 50; INT CANR-28; MTCW

Sade, Donatien Alphonse Francois Comte
1740-1814 .... **NCLC 47**

Sadoff, Ira 1945-.................. **CLC 9**
See also CA 53-56; CANR 5, 21; DLB 120

Saetone
See Camus, Albert

Safire, William 1929-.............. **CLC 10**
See also CA 17-20R; CANR 31

Sagan, Carl (Edward) 1934-........ **CLC 30**
See also AAYA 2; CA 25-28R; CANR 11, 36; MTCW; SATA 58

Sagan, Francoise .... **CLC 3, 6, 9, 17, 36**
See also Quoirez, Francoise
See also DLB 83

Sahgal, Nayantara (Pandit) 1927-... **CLC 41**
See also CA 9-12R; CANR 11

Saint, H(arry) F. 1941- .... **CLC 50**
See also CA 127

St. Aubin de Teran, Lisa 1953-
See Teran, Lisa St. Aubin de
See also CA 118; 126; INT 126

Sainte-Beuve, Charles Augustin
1804-1869 .... **NCLC 5**

Saint-Exupery, Antoine (Jean Baptiste Marie Roger) de
1900-1944 .... **TCLC 2, 56; DAM NOV; WLC**
See also CA 108; 132; CLR 10; DLB 72; MAICYA; MTCW; SATA 20

St. John, David
See Hunt, E(verette) Howard, (Jr.)

Saint-John Perse
See Leger, (Marie-Rene Auguste) Alexis Saint-Leger

Saintsbury, George (Edward Bateman)
1845-1933 .... **TCLC 31**
See also DLB 57, 149

Sait Faik .... **TCLC 23**
See also Abasiyanik, Sait Faik

Saki .... **TCLC 3; SSC 12**
See also Munro, H(ector) H(ugh)

Sala, George Augustus .... **NCLC 46**

Salama, Hannu 1936-.............. **CLC 18**

Salamanca, J(ack) R(ichard)
1922-.................... **CLC 4, 15**
See also CA 25-28R

Sale, J. Kirkpatrick
See Sale, Kirkpatrick

Sale, Kirkpatrick 1937-........... **CLC 68**
See also CA 13-16R; CANR 10

Salinas, Luis Omar
1937- ..... **CLC 90; DAM MULT; HLC**
See also CA 131; DLB 82; HW

Salinas (y Serrano), Pedro
1891(?)-1951 .... **TCLC 17**
See also CA 117; DLB 134

Salinger, J(erome) D(avid)
1919- ...... **CLC 1, 3, 8, 12, 55, 56; DA; DAB; DAC; DAM MST, NOV, POP; SSC 2; WLC**
See also AAYA 2; CA 5-8R; CANR 39; CDALB 1941-1968; CLR 18; DLB 2, 102; MAICYA; MTCW; SATA 67

Salisbury, John
See Caute, David

Salter, James 1925- .... **CLC 7, 52, 59**
See also CA 73-76; DLB 130

Saltus, Edgar (Everton)
1855-1921 .... **TCLC 8**
See also CA 105

Saltykov, Mikhail Evgrafovich
1826-1889 .... **NCLC 16**

Samarakis, Antonis 1919- .... **CLC 5**
See also CA 25-28R; CAAS 16; CANR 36

Sanchez, Florencio 1875-1910..... **TCLC 37**
See also HW

Sanchez, Luis Rafael 1936-........ **CLC 23**
See also CA 128; DLB 145; HW

Shacochis, Robert G. 1951-
See Shacochis, Bob
See also CA 119; 124; INT 124

Shaffer, Anthony (Joshua)
1926- .... **CLC 19; DAM DRAM**
See also CA 110; 116; DLB 13

Shaffer, Peter (Levin)
1926- ...... **CLC 5, 14, 18, 37, 60; DAB;**
DAM DRAM, MST
See also CA 25-28R; CANR 25, 47;
CDBLB 1960 to Present; DLB 13;
MTCW

Shakey, Bernard
See Young, Neil

Shalamov, Varlam (Tikhonovich)
1907(?)-1982 .... **CLC 18**
See also CA 129; 105

Shamlu, Ahmad 1925- .... **CLC 10**

Shammas, Anton 1951-........... **CLC 55**

Shange, Ntozake
1948- .... **CLC 8, 25, 38, 74; BLC;**
DAM DRAM, MULT; DC 3
See also AAYA 9; BW 2; CA 85-88;
CABS 3; CANR 27, 48; DLB 38; MTCW

Shanley, John Patrick 1950-....... **CLC 75**
See also CA 128; 133

Shapcott, Thomas W(illiam) 1935- .. **CLC 38**
See also CA 69-72; CANR 49

Shapiro, Jane .... **CLC 76**

Shapiro, Karl (Jay) 1913- .. **CLC 4, 8, 15, 53**
See also CA 1-4R; CAAS 6; CANR 1, 36;
DLB 48; MTCW

Sharp, William 1855-1905 .... **TCLC 39**
See also DLB 156

Sharpe, Thomas Ridley 1928-
See Sharpe, Tom
See also CA 114; 122; INT 122

Sharpe, Tom .... **CLC 36**
See Sharpe, Thomas Ridley
See also DLB 14

Shaw, Bernard .... **TCLC 45**
See also Shaw, George Bernard
See also BW 1

Shaw, G. Bernard
See Shaw, George Bernard

Shaw, George Bernard
1856-1950 ... **TCLC 3, 9, 21; DA; DAB;**
DAC; DAM DRAM, MST; WLC
See also Shaw, Bernard
See also CA 104; 128; CDBLB 1914-1945;
DLB 10, 57; MTCW

Shaw, Henry Wheeler
1818-1885 .... **NCLC 15**
See also DLB 11

Shaw, Irwin
1913-1984 .... **CLC 7, 23, 34;**
DAM DRAM, POP
See also AITN 1; CA 13-16R; 112;
CANR 21; CDALB 1941-1968; DLB 6,
102; DLBY 84; MTCW

Shaw, Robert 1927-1978 .... **CLC 5**
See also AITN 1; CA 1-4R; 81-84;
CANR 4; DLB 13, 14

Shaw, T. E.
See Lawrence, T(homas) E(dward)

Shawn, Wallace 1943- .... **CLC 41**
See also CA 112

Shea, Lisa 1953-................. **CLC 86**
See also CA 147

Sheed, Wilfrid (John Joseph)
1930- .... **CLC 2, 4, 10, 53**
See also CA 65-68; CANR 30; DLB 6;
MTCW

Sheldon, Alice Hastings Bradley
1915(?)-1987
See Tiptree, James, Jr.
See also CA 108; 122; CANR 34; INT 108;
MTCW

Sheldon, John
See Bloch, Robert (Albert)

Shelley, Mary Wollstonecraft (Godwin)
1797-1851 .... **NCLC 14; DA; DAB;**
DAC; DAM MST, NOV; WLC
See also CDBLB 1789-1832; DLB 110, 116,
159; SATA 29

Shelley, Percy Bysshe
1792-1822 .... **NCLC 18; DA; DAB;**
DAC; DAM MST, POET; PC 14; WLC
See also CDBLB 1789-1832; DLB 96, 110,
158

Shepard, Jim 1956-............... **CLC 36**
See also CA 137

Shepard, Lucius 1947- .... **CLC 34**
See also CA 128; 141

Shepard, Sam
1943- .... **CLC 4, 6, 17, 34, 41, 44;**
DAM DRAM; DC 5
See also AAYA 1; CA 69-72; CABS 3;
CANR 22; DLB 7; MTCW

Shepherd, Michael
See Ludlum, Robert

Sherburne, Zoa (Morin) 1912-...... **CLC 30**
See also AAYA 13; CA 1-4R; CANR 3, 37;
MAICYA; SAAS 18; SATA 3

Sheridan, Frances 1724-1766........ **LC 7**
See also DLB 39, 84

Sheridan, Richard Brinsley
1751-1816 .... **NCLC 5; DA; DAB;**
DAC; DAM DRAM, MST; DC 1; WLC
See also CDBLB 1660-1789; DLB 89

Sherman, Jonathan Marc .... **CLC 55**

Sherman, Martin 1941(?)-......... **CLC 19**
See also CA 116; 123

Sherwin, Judith Johnson 1936-... **CLC 7, 15**
See also CA 25-28R; CANR 34

Sherwood, Frances 1940-.......... **CLC 81**
See also CA 146

Sherwood, Robert E(mmet)
1896-1955 ...... **TCLC 3; DAM DRAM**
See also CA 104; DLB 7, 26

Shestov, Lev 1866-1938 .... **TCLC 56**

Shevchenko, Taras 1814-1861 .... **NCLC 54**

Shiel, M(atthew) P(hipps)
1865-1947 .... **TCLC 8**
See also CA 106; DLB 153

Shields, Carol 1935-......... **CLC 91; DAC**
See also CA 81-84; CANR 51

Shiga, Naoya 1883-1971... **CLC 33; SSC 23**
See also CA 101; 33-36R

Shilts, Randy 1951-1994 .... **CLC 85**
See also CA 115; 127; 144; CANR 45;
INT 127

Shimazaki, Haruki 1872-1943
See Shimazaki Toson
See also CA 105; 134

Shimazaki Toson .... **TCLC 5**
See also Shimazaki, Haruki

Sholokhov, Mikhail (Aleksandrovich)
1905-1984 .... **CLC 7, 15**
See also CA 101; 112; MTCW;
SATA-Obit 36

Shone, Patric
See Hanley, James

Shreve, Susan Richards 1939-...... **CLC 23**
See also CA 49-52; CAAS 5; CANR 5, 38;
MAICYA; SATA 46; SATA-Brief 41

Shue, Larry
1946-1985 ...... **CLC 52; DAM DRAM**
See also CA 145; 117

Shu-Jen, Chou 1881-1936
See Lu Hsun
See also CA 104

Shulman, Alix Kates 1932- ...... **CLC 2, 10**
See also CA 29-32R; CANR 43; SATA 7

Shuster, Joe 1914- .... **CLC 21**

Shute, Nevil .... **CLC 30**
See also Norway, Nevil Shute

Shuttle, Penelope (Diane) 1947- ..... **CLC 7**
See also CA 93-96; CANR 39; DLB 14, 40

Sidney, Mary 1561-1621 .... **LC 19**

Sidney, Sir Philip
1554-1586 ..... **LC 19; DA; DAB; DAC;**
DAM MST, POET
See also CDBLB Before 1660; DLB 167

Siegel, Jerome 1914-1996 .... **CLC 21**
See also CA 116; 151

Siegel, Jerry
See Siegel, Jerome

Sienkiewicz, Henryk (Adam Alexander Pius)
1846-1916 .... **TCLC 3**
See also CA 104; 134

Sierra, Gregorio Martinez
See Martinez Sierra, Gregorio

Sierra, Maria (de la O'LeJarraga) Martinez
See Martinez Sierra, Maria (de la
O'LeJarraga)

Sigal, Clancy 1926-................ **CLC 7**
See also CA 1-4R

Sigourney, Lydia Howard (Huntley)
1791-1865 .... **NCLC 21**
See also DLB 1, 42, 73

Siguenza y Gongora, Carlos de
1645-1700 .... **LC 8**

Sigurjonsson, Johann 1880-1919... **TCLC 27**

Sikelianos, Angelos 1884-1951 .... **TCLC 39**

Silkin, Jon 1930-............. **CLC 2, 6, 43**
See also CA 5-8R; CAAS 5; DLB 27

Silko, Leslie (Marmon)
1948- .... **CLC 23, 74; DA; DAC;**
DAM MST, MULT, POP
See also AAYA 14; CA 115; 122;
CANR 45; DLB 143; NNAL

Sillanpaa, Frans Eemil 1888-1964... **CLC 19**
See also CA 129; 93-96; MTCW

Sillitoe, Alan
1928- .... **CLC 1, 3, 6, 10, 19, 57**
See also AITN 1; CA 9-12R; CAAS 2;
CANR 8, 26; CDBLB 1960 to Present;
DLB 14, 139; MTCW; SATA 61

Silone, Ignazio 1900-1978 .... **CLC 4**
See also CA 25-28; 81-84; CANR 34;
CAP 2; MTCW

Silver, Joan Micklin 1935- .... **CLC 20**
See also CA 114; 121; INT 121

Silver, Nicholas
See Faust, Frederick (Schiller)

Silverberg, Robert
1935- .... **CLC 7; DAM POP**
See also CA 1-4R; CAAS 3; CANR 1, 20,
36; DLB 8; INT CANR-20; MAICYA;
MTCW; SATA 13

Silverstein, Alvin 1933- .... **CLC 17**
See also CA 49-52; CANR 2; CLR 25;
JRDA; MAICYA; SATA 8, 69

Silverstein, Virginia B(arbara Opshelor)
1937- .... **CLC 17**
See also CA 49-52; CANR 2; CLR 25;
JRDA; MAICYA; SATA 8, 69

Sim, Georges
See Simenon, Georges (Jacques Christian)

Simak, Clifford D(onald)
1904-1988 .... **CLC 1, 55**
See also CA 1-4R; 125; CANR 1, 35;
DLB 8; MTCW; SATA-Obit 56

Simenon, Georges (Jacques Christian)
1903-1989 .... **CLC 1, 2, 3, 8, 18, 47;**
DAM POP
See also CA 85-88; 129; CANR 35;
DLB 72; DLBY 89; MTCW

Simic, Charles
1938- .... **CLC 6, 9, 22, 49, 68;**
DAM POET
See also CA 29-32R; CAAS 4; CANR 12,
33, 52; DLB 105

Simmel, Georg 1858-1918 .... **TCLC 64**

Simmons, Charles (Paul) 1924- ..... **CLC 57**
See also CA 89-92; INT 89-92

Simmons, Dan 1948-... **CLC 44; DAM POP**
See also AAYA 16; CA 138; CANR 53

Simmons, James (Stewart Alexander)
1933- .... **CLC 43**
See also CA 105; CAAS 21; DLB 40

Simms, William Gilmore
1806-1870 .... **NCLC 3**
See also DLB 3, 30, 59, 73

Simon, Carly 1945-................ **CLC 26**
See also CA 105

Simon, Claude
1913- .... **CLC 4, 9, 15, 39; DAM NOV**
See also CA 89-92; CANR 33; DLB 83;
MTCW

Simon, (Marvin) Neil
1927- .... **CLC 6, 11, 31, 39, 70;**
DAM DRAM
See also AITN 1; CA 21-24R; CANR 26;
DLB 7; MTCW

Simon, Paul 1942(?)- .... **CLC 17**
See also CA 116

Simonon, Paul 1956(?)- .... **CLC 30**

Simpson, Harriette
See Arnow, Harriette (Louisa) Simpson

Simpson, Louis (Aston Marantz)
1923- .... **CLC 4, 7, 9, 32; DAM POET**
See also CA 1-4R; CAAS 4; CANR 1;
DLB 5; MTCW

Simpson, Mona (Elizabeth) 1957-... **CLC 44**
See also CA 122; 135

Simpson, N(orman) F(rederick)
1919- .... **CLC 29**
See also CA 13-16R; DLB 13

Sinclair, Andrew (Annandale)
1935- .... **CLC 2, 14**
See also CA 9-12R; CAAS 5; CANR 14, 38;
DLB 14; MTCW

Sinclair, Emil
See Hesse, Hermann

Sinclair, Iain 1943-............... **CLC 76**
See also CA 132

Sinclair, Iain MacGregor
See Sinclair, Iain

Sinclair, Mary Amelia St. Clair 1865(?)-1946
See Sinclair, May
See also CA 104

Sinclair, May................. **TCLC 3, 11**
See also Sinclair, Mary Amelia St. Clair
See also DLB 36, 135

Sinclair, Upton (Beall)
1878-1968 ...... **CLC 1, 11, 15, 63; DA;**
DAB; DAC; DAM MST, NOV; WLC
See also CA 5-8R; 25-28R; CANR 7;
CDALB 1929-1941; DLB 9;
INT CANR-7; MTCW; SATA 9

Singer, Isaac
See Singer, Isaac Bashevis

Singer, Isaac Bashevis
1904-1991 .... **CLC 1, 3, 6, 9, 11, 15, 23,**
38, 69; DA; DAB; DAC; DAM MST,
NOV; SSC 3; WLC
See also AITN 1, 2; CA 1-4R; 134;
CANR 1, 39; CDALB 1941-1968; CLR 1;
DLB 6, 28, 52; DLBY 91; JRDA;
MAICYA; MTCW; SATA 3, 27;
SATA-Obit 68

Singer, Israel Joshua 1893-1944... **TCLC 33**

Singh, Khushwant 1915-.......... **CLC 11**
See also CA 9-12R; CAAS 9; CANR 6

Sinjohn, John
See Galsworthy, John

Sinyavsky, Andrei (Donatevich)
1925- .... **CLC 8**
See also CA 85-88

Sirin, V.
See Nabokov, Vladimir (Vladimirovich)

Sissman, L(ouis) E(dward)
1928-1976 .... **CLC 9, 18**
See also CA 21-24R; 65-68; CANR 13;
DLB 5

Sisson, C(harles) H(ubert) 1914-..... **CLC 8**
See also CA 1-4R; CAAS 3; CANR 3, 48;
DLB 27

Sitwell, Dame Edith
1887-1964 .... **CLC 2, 9, 67;**
DAM POET; PC 3
See also CA 9-12R; CANR 35;
CDBLB 1945-1960; DLB 20; MTCW

Sjoewall, Maj 1935-............... **CLC 7**
See also CA 65-68

Sjowall, Maj
See Sjoewall, Maj

Skelton, Robin 1925- .... **CLC 13**
See also AITN 2; CA 5-8R; CAAS 5;
CANR 28; DLB 27, 53

Skolimowski, Jerzy 1938- .... **CLC 20**
See also CA 128

Skram, Amalie (Bertha)
1847-1905 .... **TCLC 25**

Skvorecky, Josef (Vaclav)
1924- .... **CLC 15, 39, 69; DAC;**
DAM NOV
See also CA 61-64; CAAS 1; CANR 10, 34;
MTCW

Slade, Bernard................. **CLC 11, 46**
See also Newbound, Bernard Slade
See also CAAS 9; DLB 53

Slaughter, Carolyn 1946-.......... **CLC 56**
See also CA 85-88

Slaughter, Frank G(ill) 1908- ...... **CLC 29**
See also AITN 2; CA 5-8R; CANR 5;
INT CANR-5

Slavitt, David R(ytman) 1935-.... **CLC 5, 14**
See also CA 21-24R; CAAS 3; CANR 41;
DLB 5, 6

Slesinger, Tess 1905-1945 .... **TCLC 10**
See also CA 107; DLB 102

Slessor, Kenneth 1901-1971........ **CLC 14**
See also CA 102; 89-92

Slowacki, Juliusz 1809-1849 ..... **NCLC 15**

Smart, Christopher
1722-1771 ... **LC 3; DAM POET; PC 13**
See also DLB 109

Smart, Elizabeth 1913-1986........ **CLC 54**
See also CA 81-84; 118; DLB 88

Smiley, Jane (Graves)
1949- .... **CLC 53, 76; DAM POP**
See also CA 104; CANR 30, 50;
INT CANR-30

Smith, A(rthur) J(ames) M(arshall)
1902-1980.............. **CLC 15; DAC**
See also CA 1-4R; 102; CANR 4; DLB 88

Smith, Anna Deavere 1950-........ **CLC 86**
See also CA 133

Smith, Betty (Wehner) 1896-1972... **CLC 19**
See also CA 5-8R; 33-36R; DLBY 82;
SATA 6

Smith, Charlotte (Turner)
1749-1806 .... **NCLC 23**
See also DLB 39, 109

Smith, Clark Ashton 1893-1961 .... **CLC 43**
See also CA 143

Smith, Dave.................. **CLC 22, 42**
See also Smith, David (Jeddie)
See also CAAS 7; DLB 5

Smith, David (Jeddie) 1942-
See Smith, Dave
See also CA 49-52; CANR 1; DAM POET

Smith, Florence Margaret   1902-1971
See Smith, Stevie
See also CA 17-18; 29-32R; CANR 35;
CAP 2; DAM POET; MTCW

Smith, Iain Crichton   1928- . . . . CLC 64
See also CA 21-24R; DLB 40, 139

Smith, John   1580(?)-1631 . . . . LC 9

Smith, Johnston
See Crane, Stephen (Townley)

Smith, Joseph, Jr.   1805-1844 . . . . NCLC 53

Smith, Lee   1944- . . . . CLC 25, 73
See also CA 114; 119; CANR 46; DLB 143;
DLBY 83; INT 119

Smith, Martin
See Smith, Martin Cruz

Smith, Martin Cruz
1942- . . . . . CLC 25; DAM MULT, POP
See also BEST 89:4; CA 85-88; CANR 6,
23, 43; INT CANR-23; NNAL

Smith, Mary-Ann Tirone   1944- . . . . . CLC 39
See also CA 118; 136

Smith, Patti   1946- . . . . CLC 12
See also CA 93-96

Smith, Pauline (Urmson)
1882-1959 . . . . TCLC 25

Smith, Rosamond
See Oates, Joyce Carol

Smith, Sheila Kaye
See Kaye-Smith, Sheila

Smith, Stevie . . . . . . CLC 3, 8, 25, 44; PC 12
See also Smith, Florence Margaret
See also DLB 20

Smith, Wilbur (Addison)   1933- . . . . . CLC 33
See also CA 13-16R; CANR 7, 46; MTCW

Smith, William Jay   1918- . . . . CLC 6
See also CA 5-8R; CANR 44; DLB 5;
MAICYA; SAAS 22; SATA 2, 68

Smith, Woodrow Wilson
See Kuttner, Henry

Smolenskin, Peretz   1842-1885 . . . . NCLC 30

Smollett, Tobias (George)   1721-1771 . . LC 2
See also CDBLB 1660-1789; DLB 39, 104

Snodgrass, W(illiam) D(e Witt)
1926- . . . . CLC 2, 6, 10, 18, 68;
DAM POET
See also CA 1-4R; CANR 6, 36; DLB 5;
MTCW

Snow, C(harles) P(ercy)
1905-1980 . . . . CLC 1, 4, 6, 9, 13, 19;
DAM NOV
See also CA 5-8R; 101; CANR 28;
CDBLB 1945-1960; DLB 15, 77; MTCW

Snow, Frances Compton
See Adams, Henry (Brooks)

Snyder, Gary (Sherman)
1930- . . CLC 1, 2, 5, 9, 32; DAM POET
See also CA 17-20R; CANR 30; DLB 5, 16,
165

Snyder, Zilpha Keatley   1927- . . . . . . CLC 17
See also AAYA 15; CA 9-12R; CANR 38;
CLR 31; JRDA; MAICYA; SAAS 2;
SATA 1, 28, 75

Soares, Bernardo
See Pessoa, Fernando (Antonio Nogueira)

Sobh, A.
See Shamlu, Ahmad

Sobol, Joshua . . . . CLC 60

Soderberg, Hjalmar   1869-1941 . . . . TCLC 39

Sodergran, Edith (Irene)
See Soedergran, Edith (Irene)

Soedergran, Edith (Irene)
1892-1923 . . . . TCLC 31

Softly, Edgar
See Lovecraft, H(oward) P(hillips)

Softly, Edward
See Lovecraft, H(oward) P(hillips)

Sokolov, Raymond   1941- . . . . CLC 7
See also CA 85-88

Solo, Jay
See Ellison, Harlan (Jay)

Sologub, Fyodor . . . . TCLC 9
See also Teternikov, Fyodor Kuzmich

Solomons, Ikey Esquir
See Thackeray, William Makepeace

Solomos, Dionysios   1798-1857 . . . NCLC 15

Solwoska, Mara
See French, Marilyn

Solzhenitsyn, Aleksandr I(sayevich)
1918- . . . . . . CLC 1, 2, 4, 7, 9, 10, 18, 26,
34, 78; DA; DAB; DAC; DAM MST,
NOV; WLC
See also AITN 1; CA 69-72; CANR 40;
MTCW

Somers, Jane
See Lessing, Doris (May)

Somerville, Edith   1858-1949 . . . . . . TCLC 51
See also DLB 135

Somerville & Ross
See Martin, Violet Florence; Somerville,
Edith

Sommer, Scott   1951- . . . . CLC 25
See also CA 106

Sondheim, Stephen (Joshua)
1930- . . . . CLC 30, 39; DAM DRAM
See also AAYA 11; CA 103; CANR 47

Sontag, Susan
1933- . . . . CLC 1, 2, 10, 13, 31;
DAM POP
See also CA 17-20R; CANR 25, 51; DLB 2,
67; MTCW

Sophocles
496(?)B.C.-406(?)B.C. . . . . CMLC 2; DA;
DAB; DAC; DAM DRAM, MST; DC 1

Sordello   1189-1269 . . . . CMLC 15

Sorel, Julia
See Drexler, Rosalyn

Sorrentino, Gilbert
1929- . . . . CLC 3, 7, 14, 22, 40
See also CA 77-80; CANR 14, 33; DLB 5;
DLBY 80; INT CANR-14

Soto, Gary
1952- . . . . CLC 32, 80; DAM MULT;
HLC
See also AAYA 10; CA 119; 125;
CANR 50; CLR 38; DLB 82; HW;
INT 125; JRDA; SATA 80

Soupault, Philippe   1897-1990 . . . . . . CLC 68
See also CA 116; 147; 131

Souster, (Holmes) Raymond
1921- . . . . CLC 5, 14; DAC; DAM POET
See also CA 13-16R; CAAS 14; CANR 13,
29, 53; DLB 88; SATA 63

Southern, Terry   1924(?)-1995 . . . . CLC 7
See also CA 1-4R; 150; CANR 1; DLB 2

Southey, Robert   1774-1843 . . . . NCLC 8
See also DLB 93, 107, 142; SATA 54

Southworth, Emma Dorothy Eliza Nevitte
1819-1899 . . . . NCLC 26

Souza, Ernest
See Scott, Evelyn

Soyinka, Wole
1934- . . . . CLC 3, 5, 14, 36, 44; BLC;
DA; DAB; DAC; DAM DRAM, MST,
MULT; DC 2; WLC
See also BW 2; CA 13-16R; CANR 27, 39;
DLB 125; MTCW

Spackman, W(illiam) M(ode)
1905-1990 . . . . CLC 46
See also CA 81-84; 132

Spacks, Barry   1931- . . . . CLC 14
See also CA 29-32R; CANR 33; DLB 105

Spanidou, Irini   1946- . . . . CLC 44

Spark, Muriel (Sarah)
1918- . . . . . CLC 2, 3, 5, 8, 13, 18, 40, 94;
DAB; DAC; DAM MST, NOV; SSC 10
See also CA 5-8R; CANR 12, 36;
CDBLB 1945-1960; DLB 15, 139;
INT CANR-12; MTCW

Spaulding, Douglas
See Bradbury, Ray (Douglas)

Spaulding, Leonard
See Bradbury, Ray (Douglas)

Spence, J. A. D.
See Eliot, T(homas) S(tearns)

Spencer, Elizabeth   1921- . . . . CLC 22
See also CA 13-16R; CANR 32; DLB 6;
MTCW; SATA 14

Spencer, Leonard G.
See Silverberg, Robert

Spencer, Scott   1945- . . . . CLC 30
See also CA 113; CANR 51; DLBY 86

Spender, Stephen (Harold)
1909-1995 . . . . . . CLC 1, 2, 5, 10, 41, 91;
DAM POET
See also CA 9-12R; 149; CANR 31;
CDBLB 1945-1960; DLB 20; MTCW

Spengler, Oswald (Arnold Gottfried)
1880-1936 . . . . TCLC 25
See also CA 118

Spenser, Edmund
1552(?)-1599 . . . . LC 5; DA; DAB; DAC;
DAM MST, POET; PC 8; WLC
See also CDBLB Before 1660; DLB 167

Spicer, Jack
1925-1965 . . . . CLC 8, 18, 72;
DAM POET
See also CA 85-88; DLB 5, 16

Spiegelman, Art   1948- . . . . CLC 76
See also AAYA 10; CA 125; CANR 41

Spielberg, Peter   1929- . . . . CLC 6
See also CA 5-8R; CANR 4, 48; DLBY 81

Spielberg, Steven 1947- . . . . CLC 20
See also AAYA 8; CA 77-80; CANR 32;
SATA 32

Spillane, Frank Morrison 1918-
See Spillane, Mickey
See also CA 25-28R; CANR 28; MTCW;
SATA 66

Spillane, Mickey . . . . CLC 3, 13
See also Spillane, Frank Morrison

Spinoza, Benedictus de 1632-1677 . . . . LC 9

Spinrad, Norman (Richard) 1940- . . . CLC 46
See also CA 37-40R; CAAS 19; CANR 20;
DLB 8; INT CANR-20

Spitteler, Carl (Friedrich Georg)
1845-1924 . . . . TCLC 12
See also CA 109; DLB 129

Spivack, Kathleen (Romola Drucker)
1938- . . . . CLC 6
See also CA 49-52

Spoto, Donald 1941- . . . . CLC 39
See also CA 65-68; CANR 11

Springsteen, Bruce (F.) 1949- . . . . . . CLC 17
See also CA 111

Spurling, Hilary 1940- . . . . CLC 34
See also CA 104; CANR 25, 52

Spyker, John Howland
See Elman, Richard

Squires, (James) Radcliffe
1917-1993 . . . . CLC 51
See also CA 1-4R; 140; CANR 6, 21

Srivastava, Dhanpat Rai 1880(?)-1936
See Premchand
See also CA 118

Stacy, Donald
See Pohl, Frederik

Stael, Germaine de
See Stael-Holstein, Anne Louise Germaine
Necker Baronn
See also DLB 119

Stael-Holstein, Anne Louise Germaine Necker
Baronn 1766-1817 . . . . NCLC 3
See also Stael, Germaine de

Stafford, Jean 1915-1979 . . . CLC 4, 7, 19, 68
See also CA 1-4R; 85-88; CANR 3; DLB 2;
MTCW; SATA-Obit 22

Stafford, William (Edgar)
1914-1993 . . . CLC 4, 7, 29; DAM POET
See also CA 5-8R; 142; CAAS 3; CANR 5,
22; DLB 5; INT CANR-22

Staines, Trevor
See Brunner, John (Kilian Houston)

Stairs, Gordon
See Austin, Mary (Hunter)

Stannard, Martin 1947- . . . . CLC 44
See also CA 142; DLB 155

Stanton, Maura 1946- . . . . CLC 9
See also CA 89-92; CANR 15; DLB 120

Stanton, Schuyler
See Baum, L(yman) Frank

Stapledon, (William) Olaf
1886-1950 . . . . TCLC 22
See also CA 111; DLB 15

Starbuck, George (Edwin)
1931- . . . . CLC 53; DAM POET
See also CA 21-24R; CANR 23

Stark, Richard
See Westlake, Donald E(dwin)

Staunton, Schuyler
See Baum, L(yman) Frank

Stead, Christina (Ellen)
1902-1983 . . . . CLC 2, 5, 8, 32, 80
See also CA 13-16R; 109; CANR 33, 40;
MTCW

Stead, William Thomas
1849-1912 . . . . TCLC 48

Steele, Richard 1672-1729 . . . . LC 18
See also CDBLB 1660-1789; DLB 84, 101

Steele, Timothy (Reid) 1948- . . . . . . CLC 45
See also CA 93-96; CANR 16, 50; DLB 120

Steffens, (Joseph) Lincoln
1866-1936 . . . . TCLC 20
See also CA 117

Stegner, Wallace (Earle)
1909-1993 . . . CLC 9, 49, 81; DAM NOV
See also AITN 1; BEST 90:3; CA 1-4R;
141; CAAS 9; CANR 1, 21, 46; DLB 9;
DLBY 93; MTCW

Stein, Gertrude
1874-1946 . . . . . . TCLC 1, 6, 28, 48; DA;
DAB; DAC; DAM MST, NOV, POET;
WLC
See also CA 104; 132; CDALB 1917-1929;
DLB 4, 54, 86; MTCW

Steinbeck, John (Ernst)
1902-1968 . . . . . . CLC 1, 5, 9, 13, 21, 34,
45, 75; DA; DAB; DAC; DAM DRAM,
MST, NOV; SSC 11; WLC
See also AAYA 12; CA 1-4R; 25-28R;
CANR 1, 35; CDALB 1929-1941; DLB 7,
9; DLBD 2; MTCW; SATA 9

Steinem, Gloria 1934- . . . . CLC 63
See also CA 53-56; CANR 28, 51; MTCW

Steiner, George
1929- . . . . CLC 24; DAM NOV
See also CA 73-76; CANR 31; DLB 67;
MTCW; SATA 62

Steiner, K. Leslie
See Delany, Samuel R(ay, Jr.)

Steiner, Rudolf 1861-1925 . . . . TCLC 13
See also CA 107

Stendhal
1783-1842 . . . . NCLC 23, 46; DA; DAB;
DAC; DAM MST, NOV; WLC
See also DLB 119

Stephen, Leslie 1832-1904 . . . . TCLC 23
See also CA 123; DLB 57, 144

Stephen, Sir Leslie
See Stephen, Leslie

Stephen, Virginia
See Woolf, (Adeline) Virginia

Stephens, James 1882(?)-1950 . . . . . . TCLC 4
See also CA 104; DLB 19, 153, 162

Stephens, Reed
See Donaldson, Stephen R.

Steptoe, Lydia
See Barnes, Djuna

Sterchi, Beat 1949- . . . . CLC 65

Sterling, Brett
See Bradbury, Ray (Douglas); Hamilton,
Edmond

Sterling, Bruce 1954- . . . . CLC 72
See also CA 119; CANR 44

Sterling, George 1869-1926 . . . . TCLC 20
See also CA 117; DLB 54

Stern, Gerald 1925- . . . . CLC 40
See also CA 81-84; CANR 28; DLB 105

Stern, Richard (Gustave) 1928- . . . CLC 4, 39
See also CA 1-4R; CANR 1, 25, 52;
DLBY 87; INT CANR-25

Sternberg, Josef von 1894-1969 . . . . . CLC 20
See also CA 81-84

Sterne, Laurence
1713-1768 . . . . . . LC 2; DA; DAB; DAC;
DAM MST, NOV; WLC
See also CDBLB 1660-1789; DLB 39

Sternheim, (William Adolf) Carl
1878-1942 . . . . TCLC 8
See also CA 105; DLB 56, 118

Stevens, Mark 1951- . . . . CLC 34
See also CA 122

Stevens, Wallace
1879-1955 . . . . TCLC 3, 12, 45; DA;
DAB; DAC; DAM MST, POET; PC 6;
WLC
See also CA 104; 124; CDALB 1929-1941;
DLB 54; MTCW

Stevenson, Anne (Katharine)
1933- . . . . CLC 7, 33
See also CA 17-20R; CAAS 9; CANR 9, 33;
DLB 40; MTCW

Stevenson, Robert Louis (Balfour)
1850-1894 . . . . . NCLC 5, 14; DA; DAB;
DAC; DAM MST, NOV; SSC 11; WLC
See also CDBLB 1890-1914; CLR 10, 11;
DLB 18, 57, 141, 156; DLBD 13; JRDA;
MAICYA; YABC 2

Stewart, J(ohn) I(nnes) M(ackintosh)
1906-1994 . . . . CLC 7, 14, 32
See also CA 85-88; 147; CAAS 3;
CANR 47; MTCW

Stewart, Mary (Florence Elinor)
1916- . . . . CLC 7, 35; DAB
See also CA 1-4R; CANR 1; SATA 12

Stewart, Mary Rainbow
See Stewart, Mary (Florence Elinor)

Stifle, June
See Campbell, Maria

Stifter, Adalbert 1805-1868 . . . . . . NCLC 41
See also DLB 133

Still, James 1906- . . . . CLC 49
See also CA 65-68; CAAS 17; CANR 10,
26; DLB 9; SATA 29

Sting
See Sumner, Gordon Matthew

Stirling, Arthur
See Sinclair, Upton (Beall)

Stitt, Milan 1941- . . . . CLC 29
See also CA 69-72

Stockton, Francis Richard 1834-1902
See Stockton, Frank R.
See also CA 108; 137; MAICYA; SATA 44

Swenson, May
1919-1989 .... **CLC 4, 14, 61; DA; DAB;**
DAC; DAM MST, POET; PC 14
See also CA 5-8R; 130; CANR 36; DLB 5;
MTCW; SATA 15

Swift, Augustus
See Lovecraft, H(oward) P(hillips)

Swift, Graham (Colin) 1949- .... **CLC 41, 88**
See also CA 117; 122; CANR 46

Swift, Jonathan
1667-1745 ...... **LC 1; DA; DAB; DAC;**
DAM MST, NOV, POET; PC 9; WLC
See also CDBLB 1660-1789; DLB 39, 95,
101; SATA 19

Swinburne, Algernon Charles
1837-1909 ...... **TCLC 8, 36; DA; DAB;**
DAC; DAM MST, POET; WLC
See also CA 105; 140; CDBLB 1832-1890;
DLB 35, 57

Swinfen, Ann .... **CLC 34**

Swinnerton, Frank Arthur
1884-1982 .... **CLC 31**
See also CA 108; DLB 34

Swithen, John
See King, Stephen (Edwin)

Sylvia
See Ashton-Warner, Sylvia (Constance)

Symmes, Robert Edward
See Duncan, Robert (Edward)

Symonds, John Addington
1840-1893 .... **NCLC 34**
See also DLB 57, 144

Symons, Arthur 1865-1945 .... **TCLC 11**
See also CA 107; DLB 19, 57, 149

Symons, Julian (Gustave)
1912-1994 .... **CLC 2, 14, 32**
See also CA 49-52; 147; CAAS 3; CANR 3,
33; DLB 87, 155; DLBY 92; MTCW

Synge, (Edmund) J(ohn) M(illington)
1871-1909 .... **TCLC 6, 37;**
DAM DRAM; DC 2
See also CA 104; 141; CDBLB 1890-1914;
DLB 10, 19

Syruc, J.
See Milosz, Czeslaw

Szirtes, George 1948- .... **CLC 46**
See also CA 109; CANR 27

Tabori, George 1914- .... **CLC 19**
See also CA 49-52; CANR 4

Tagore, Rabindranath
1861-1941 .... **TCLC 3, 53;**
DAM DRAM, POET; PC 8
See also CA 104; 120; MTCW

Taine, Hippolyte Adolphe
1828-1893 .... **NCLC 15**

Talese, Gay 1932- .... **CLC 37**
See also AITN 1; CA 1-4R; CANR 9;
INT CANR-9; MTCW

Tallent, Elizabeth (Ann) 1954- ..... **CLC 45**
See also CA 117; DLB 130

Tally, Ted 1952- .... **CLC 42**
See also CA 120; 124; INT 124

Tamayo y Baus, Manuel
1829-1898 .... **NCLC 1**

Tammsaare, A(nton) H(ansen)
1878-1940 .... **TCLC 27**

Tan, Amy
1952- .... **CLC 59; DAM MULT, NOV,**
POP
See also AAYA 9; BEST 89:3; CA 136;
SATA 75

Tandem, Felix
See Spitteler, Carl (Friedrich Georg)

Tanizaki, Jun'ichiro
1886-1965 ...... **CLC 8, 14, 28; SSC 21**
See also CA 93-96; 25-28R

Tanner, William
See Amis, Kingsley (William)

Tao Lao
See Storni, Alfonsina

Tarassoff, Lev
See Troyat, Henri

Tarbell, Ida M(inerva)
1857-1944 .... **TCLC 40**
See also CA 122; DLB 47

Tarkington, (Newton) Booth
1869-1946 .... **TCLC 9**
See also CA 110; 143; DLB 9, 102;
SATA 17

Tarkovsky, Andrei (Arsenyevich)
1932-1986 .... **CLC 75**
See also CA 127

Tartt, Donna 1964(?)- .... **CLC 76**
See also CA 142

Tasso, Torquato 1544-1595 .... **LC 5**

Tate, (John Orley) Allen
1899-1979 .... **CLC 2, 4, 6, 9, 11, 14, 24**
See also CA 5-8R; 85-88; CANR 32;
DLB 4, 45, 63; MTCW

Tate, Ellalice
See Hibbert, Eleanor Alice Burford

Tate, James (Vincent) 1943- ... **CLC 2, 6, 25**
See also CA 21-24R; CANR 29; DLB 5

Tavel, Ronald 1940- .... **CLC 6**
See also CA 21-24R; CANR 33

Taylor, C(ecil) P(hilip) 1929-1981... **CLC 27**
See also CA 25-28R; 105; CANR 47

Taylor, Edward
1642(?)-1729 .... **LC 11; DA; DAB;**
DAC; DAM MST, POET
See also DLB 24

Taylor, Eleanor Ross 1920- .... **CLC 5**
See also CA 81-84

Taylor, Elizabeth 1912-1975 ... **CLC 2, 4, 29**
See also CA 13-16R; CANR 9; DLB 139;
MTCW; SATA 13

Taylor, Henry (Splawn) 1942- ...... **CLC 44**
See also CA 33-36R; CAAS 7; CANR 31;
DLB 5

Taylor, Kamala (Purnaiya) 1924-
See Markandaya, Kamala
See also CA 77-80

Taylor, Mildred D. .... **CLC 21**
See also AAYA 10; BW 1; CA 85-88;
CANR 25; CLR 9; DLB 52; JRDA;
MAICYA; SAAS 5; SATA 15, 70

Taylor, Peter (Hillsman)
1917-1994 ..... **CLC 1, 4, 18, 37, 44, 50,**
71; SSC 10
See also CA 13-16R; 147; CANR 9, 50;
DLBY 81, 94; INT CANR-9; MTCW

Taylor, Robert Lewis 1912- .... **CLC 14**
See also CA 1-4R; CANR 3; SATA 10

Tchekhov, Anton
See Chekhov, Anton (Pavlovich)

Teasdale, Sara 1884-1933 .... **TCLC 4**
See also CA 104; DLB 45; SATA 32

Tegner, Esaias 1782-1846 .... **NCLC 2**

Teilhard de Chardin, (Marie Joseph) Pierre
1881-1955 .... **TCLC 9**
See also CA 105

Temple, Ann
See Mortimer, Penelope (Ruth)

Tennant, Emma (Christina)
1937- .... **CLC 13, 52**
See also CA 65-68; CAAS 9; CANR 10, 38;
DLB 14

Tenneshaw, S. M.
See Silverberg, Robert

Tennyson, Alfred
1809-1892 .... **NCLC 30; DA; DAB;**
DAC; DAM MST, POET; PC 6; WLC
See also CDBLB 1832-1890; DLB 32

Teran, Lisa St. Aubin de .... **CLC 36**
See also St. Aubin de Teran, Lisa

Terence 195(?)B.C.-159B.C. .... **CMLC 14**

Teresa de Jesus, St. 1515-1582 ...... **LC 18**

Terkel, Louis 1912-
See Terkel, Studs
See also CA 57-60; CANR 18, 45; MTCW

Terkel, Studs .... **CLC 38**
See also Terkel, Louis
See also AITN 1

Terry, C. V.
See Slaughter, Frank G(ill)

Terry, Megan 1932- .... **CLC 19**
See also CA 77-80; CABS 3; CANR 43;
DLB 7

Tertz, Abram
See Sinyavsky, Andrei (Donatevich)

Tesich, Steve 1943(?)-1996 ...... **CLC 40, 69**
See also CA 105; 152; DLBY 83

Teternikov, Fyodor Kuzmich 1863-1927
See Sologub, Fyodor
See also CA 104

Tevis, Walter 1928-1984 .... **CLC 42**
See also CA 113

Tey, Josephine .... **TCLC 14**
See also Mackintosh, Elizabeth
See also DLB 77

Thackeray, William Makepeace
1811-1863 .... **NCLC 5, 14, 22, 43; DA;**
DAB; DAC; DAM MST, NOV; WLC
See also CDBLB 1832-1890; DLB 21, 55,
159, 163; SATA 23

Thakura, Ravindranatha
See Tagore, Rabindranath

Tharoor, Shashi 1956- .... **CLC 70**
See also CA 141

Thelwell, Michael Miles 1939- . . . . . **CLC 22**
See also BW 2; CA 101

Theobald, Lewis, Jr.
See Lovecraft, H(oward) P(hillips)

Theodorescu, Ion N. 1880-1967
See Arghezi, Tudor
See also CA 116

Theriault, Yves
1915-1983 . . **CLC 79; DAC; DAM MST**
See also CA 102; DLB 88

Theroux, Alexander (Louis)
1939- . . . . **CLC 2, 25**
See also CA 85-88; CANR 20

Theroux, Paul (Edward)
1941- . . . . **CLC 5, 8, 11, 15, 28, 46;**
DAM POP
See also BEST 89:4; CA 33-36R; CANR 20,
45; DLB 2; MTCW; SATA 44

Thesen, Sharon 1946- . . . . **CLC 56**

Thevenin, Denis
See Duhamel, Georges

Thibault, Jacques Anatole Francois
1844-1924
See France, Anatole
See also CA 106; 127; DAM NOV; MTCW

Thiele, Colin (Milton) 1920- . . . . **CLC 17**
See also CA 29-32R; CANR 12, 28, 53;
CLR 27; MAICYA; SAAS 2; SATA 14,
72

Thomas, Audrey (Callahan)
1935- . . . . **CLC 7, 13, 37; SSC 20**
See also AITN 2; CA 21-24R; CAAS 19;
CANR 36; DLB 60; MTCW

Thomas, D(onald) M(ichael)
1935- . . . . **CLC 13, 22, 31**
See also CA 61-64; CAAS 11; CANR 17,
45; CDBLB 1960 to Present; DLB 40;
INT CANR-17; MTCW

Thomas, Dylan (Marlais)
1914-1953 . . . **TCLC 1, 8, 45; DA; DAB;**
DAC; DAM DRAM, MST, POET;
PC 2; SSC 3; WLC
See also CA 104; 120; CDBLB 1945-1960;
DLB 13, 20, 139; MTCW; SATA 60

Thomas, (Philip) Edward
1878-1917 . . . . . . **TCLC 10; DAM POET**
See also CA 106; DLB 19

Thomas, Joyce Carol 1938- . . . . **CLC 35**
See also AAYA 12; BW 2; CA 113; 116;
CANR 48; CLR 19; DLB 33; INT 116;
JRDA; MAICYA; MTCW; SAAS 7;
SATA 40, 78

Thomas, Lewis 1913-1993 . . . . **CLC 35**
See also CA 85-88; 143; CANR 38; MTCW

Thomas, Paul
See Mann, (Paul) Thomas

Thomas, Piri 1928- . . . . **CLC 17**
See also CA 73-76; HW

Thomas, R(onald) S(tuart)
1913- . . . . **CLC 6, 13, 48; DAB;**
DAM POET
See also CA 89-92; CAAS 4; CANR 30;
CDBLB 1960 to Present; DLB 27;
MTCW

Thomas, Ross (Elmore) 1926-1995 . . **CLC 39**
See also CA 33-36R; 150; CANR 22

Thompson, Francis Clegg
See Mencken, H(enry) L(ouis)

Thompson, Francis Joseph
1859-1907 . . . . **TCLC 4**
See also CA 104; CDBLB 1890-1914;
DLB 19

Thompson, Hunter S(tockton)
1939- . . . . **CLC 9, 17, 40; DAM POP**
See also BEST 89:1; CA 17-20R; CANR 23,
46; MTCW

Thompson, James Myers
See Thompson, Jim (Myers)

Thompson, Jim (Myers)
1906-1977(?) . . . . **CLC 69**
See also CA 140

Thompson, Judith . . . . **CLC 39**

Thomson, James
1700-1748 . . . . . **LC 16, 29; DAM POET**
See also DLB 95

Thomson, James
1834-1882 . . . . . **NCLC 18; DAM POET**
See also DLB 35

Thoreau, Henry David
1817-1862 . . . . . **NCLC 7, 21; DA; DAB;**
DAC; DAM MST; WLC
See also CDALB 1640-1865; DLB 1

Thornton, Hall
See Silverberg, Robert

Thucydides c. 455B.C.-399B.C. . . . . **CMLC 17**

Thurber, James (Grover)
1894-1961 . . . . **CLC 5, 11, 25; DA; DAB;**
DAC; DAM DRAM, MST, NOV; SSC 1
See also CA 73-76; CANR 17, 39;
CDALB 1929-1941; DLB 4, 11, 22, 102;
MAICYA; MTCW; SATA 13

Thurman, Wallace (Henry)
1902-1934 . . . . **TCLC 6; BLC;**
DAM MULT
See also BW 1; CA 104; 124; DLB 51

Ticheburn, Cheviot
See Ainsworth, William Harrison

Tieck, (Johann) Ludwig
1773-1853 . . . . **NCLC 5, 46**
See also DLB 90

Tiger, Derry
See Ellison, Harlan (Jay)

Tilghman, Christopher 1948(?)- . . . . . **CLC 65**

Tillinghast, Richard (Williford)
1940- . . . . **CLC 29**
See also CA 29-32R; CAAS 23; CANR 26,
51

Timrod, Henry 1828-1867 . . . . **NCLC 25**
See also DLB 3

Tindall, Gillian 1938- . . . . **CLC 7**
See also CA 21-24R; CANR 11

Tiptree, James, Jr. . . . . **CLC 48, 50**
See also Sheldon, Alice Hastings Bradley
See also DLB 8

Titmarsh, Michael Angelo
See Thackeray, William Makepeace

Tocqueville, Alexis (Charles Henri Maurice
Clerel Comte) 1805-1859 . . . . . **NCLC 7**

Tolkien, J(ohn) R(onald) R(euel)
1892-1973 . . . . **CLC 1, 2, 3, 8, 12, 38;**
DA; DAB; DAC; DAM MST, NOV,
POP; WLC
See also AAYA 10; AITN 1; CA 17-18;
45-48; CANR 36; CAP 2;
CDBLB 1914-1945; DLB 15, 160; JRDA;
MAICYA; MTCW; SATA 2, 32;
SATA-Obit 24

Toller, Ernst 1893-1939 . . . . **TCLC 10**
See also CA 107; DLB 124

Tolson, M. B.
See Tolson, Melvin B(eaunorus)

Tolson, Melvin B(eaunorus)
1898(?)-1966 . . . . **CLC 36; BLC;**
DAM MULT, POET
See also BW 1; CA 124; 89-92; DLB 48, 76

Tolstoi, Aleksei Nikolaevich
See Tolstoy, Alexey Nikolaevich

Tolstoy, Alexey Nikolaevich
1882-1945 . . . . **TCLC 18**
See also CA 107

Tolstoy, Count Leo
See Tolstoy, Leo (Nikolaevich)

Tolstoy, Leo (Nikolaevich)
1828-1910 . . . . . . **TCLC 4, 11, 17, 28, 44;**
DA; DAB; DAC; DAM MST, NOV;
SSC 9; WLC
See also CA 104; 123; SATA 26

Tomasi di Lampedusa, Giuseppe 1896-1957
See Lampedusa, Giuseppe (Tomasi) di
See also CA 111

Tomlin, Lily . . . . **CLC 17**
See also Tomlin, Mary Jean

Tomlin, Mary Jean 1939(?)-
See Tomlin, Lily
See also CA 117

Tomlinson, (Alfred) Charles
1927- . . . . **CLC 2, 4, 6, 13, 45;**
DAM POET
See also CA 5-8R; CANR 33; DLB 40

Tonson, Jacob
See Bennett, (Enoch) Arnold

Toole, John Kennedy
1937-1969 . . . . **CLC 19, 64**
See also CA 104; DLBY 81

Toomer, Jean
1894-1967 . . . . . . **CLC 1, 4, 13, 22; BLC;**
DAM MULT; PC 7; SSC 1
See also BW 1; CA 85-88;
CDALB 1917-1929; DLB 45, 51; MTCW

Torley, Luke
See Blish, James (Benjamin)

Tornimparte, Alessandra
See Ginzburg, Natalia

Torre, Raoul della
See Mencken, H(enry) L(ouis)

Torrey, E(dwin) Fuller 1937- . . . . **CLC 34**
See also CA 119

Torsvan, Ben Traven
See Traven, B.

Torsvan, Benno Traven
See Traven, B.

Torsvan, Berick Traven
See Traven, B.

Torsvan, Berwick Traven
See Traven, B.

Torsvan, Bruno Traven
See Traven, B.

Torsvan, Traven
See Traven, B.

Tournier, Michel (Edouard)
1924- . . . . CLC 6, 23, 36, 95
See also CA 49-52; CANR 3, 36; DLB 83;
MTCW; SATA 23

Tournimparte, Alessandra
See Ginzburg, Natalia

Towers, Ivar
See Kornbluth, C(yril) M.

Towne, Robert (Burton) 1936(?)- . . . . CLC 87
See also CA 108; DLB 44

Townsend, Sue 1946- . . CLC 61; DAB; DAC
See also CA 119; 127; INT 127; MTCW;
SATA 55; SATA-Brief 48

Townshend, Peter (Dennis Blandford)
1945- . . . . CLC 17, 42
See also CA 107

Tozzi, Federigo 1883-1920 . . . . TCLC 31

Traill, Catharine Parr
1802-1899 . . . . NCLC 31
See also DLB 99

Trakl, Georg 1887-1914 . . . . TCLC 5
See also CA 104

Transtroemer, Tomas (Goesta)
1931- . . . . CLC 52, 65; DAM POET
See also CA 117; 129; CAAS 17

Transtromer, Tomas Gosta
See Transtroemer, Tomas (Goesta)

Traven, B. (?)-1969 . . . . CLC 8, 11
See also CA 19-20; 25-28R; CAP 2; DLB 9,
56; MTCW

Treitel, Jonathan 1959- . . . . CLC 70

Tremain, Rose 1943- . . . . CLC 42
See also CA 97-100; CANR 44; DLB 14

Tremblay, Michel
1942- . . . . . . CLC 29; DAC; DAM MST
See also CA 116; 128; DLB 60; MTCW

Trevanian . . . . CLC 29
See also Whitaker, Rod(ney)

Trevor, Glen
See Hilton, James

Trevor, William
1928- . . . . . CLC 7, 9, 14, 25, 71; SSC 21
See also Cox, William Trevor
See also DLB 14, 139

Trifonov, Yuri (Valentinovich)
1925-1981 . . . . CLC 45
See also CA 126; 103; MTCW

Trilling, Lionel 1905-1975 . . . . CLC 9, 11, 24
See also CA 9-12R; 61-64; CANR 10;
DLB 28, 63; INT CANR-10; MTCW

Trimball, W. H.
See Mencken, H(enry) L(ouis)

Tristan
See Gomez de la Serna, Ramon

Tristram
See Housman, A(lfred) E(dward)

Trogdon, William (Lewis) 1939-
See Heat-Moon, William Least
See also CA 115; 119; CANR 47; INT 119

Trollope, Anthony
1815-1882 . . . . . NCLC 6, 33; DA; DAB;
DAC; DAM MST, NOV; WLC
See also CDBLB 1832-1890; DLB 21, 57,
159; SATA 22

Trollope, Frances 1779-1863 . . . . . NCLC 30
See also DLB 21, 166

Trotsky, Leon 1879-1940 . . . . TCLC 22
See also CA 118

Trotter (Cockburn), Catharine
1679-1749 . . . . LC 8
See also DLB 84

Trout, Kilgore
See Farmer, Philip Jose

Trow, George W. S. 1943- . . . . CLC 52
See also CA 126

Troyat, Henri 1911- . . . . CLC 23
See also CA 45-48; CANR 2, 33; MTCW

Trudeau, G(arretson) B(eekman) 1948-
See Trudeau, Garry B.
See also CA 81-84; CANR 31; SATA 35

Trudeau, Garry B. . . . . CLC 12
See also Trudeau, G(arretson) B(eekman)
See also AAYA 10; AITN 2

Truffaut, Francois 1932-1984 . . . . . . CLC 20
See also CA 81-84; 113; CANR 34

Trumbo, Dalton 1905-1976 . . . . CLC 19
See also CA 21-24R; 69-72; CANR 10;
DLB 26

Trumbull, John 1750-1831 . . . . . . NCLC 30
See also DLB 31

Trundlett, Helen B.
See Eliot, T(homas) S(tearns)

Tryon, Thomas
1926-1991 . . . . . CLC 3, 11; DAM POP
See also AITN 1; CA 29-32R; 135;
CANR 32; MTCW

Tryon, Tom
See Tryon, Thomas

Ts'ao Hsueh-ch'in 1715(?)-1763 . . . . . . LC 1

Tsushima, Shuji 1909-1948
See Dazai, Osamu
See also CA 107

Tsvetaeva (Efron), Marina (Ivanovna)
1892-1941 . . . . TCLC 7, 35; PC 14
See also CA 104; 128; MTCW

Tuck, Lily 1938- . . . . CLC 70
See also CA 139

Tu Fu 712-770 . . . . PC 9
See also DAM MULT

Tunis, John R(oberts) 1889-1975 . . . CLC 12
See also CA 61-64; DLB 22; JRDA;
MAICYA; SATA 37; SATA-Brief 30

Tuohy, Frank . . . . CLC 37
See also Tuohy, John Francis
See also DLB 14, 139

Tuohy, John Francis 1925-
See Tuohy, Frank
See also CA 5-8R; CANR 3, 47

Turco, Lewis (Putnam) 1934- . . . CLC 11, 63
See also CA 13-16R; CAAS 22; CANR 24,
51; DLBY 84

Turgenev, Ivan
1818-1883 . . . . NCLC 21; DA; DAB;
DAC; DAM MST, NOV; SSC 7; WLC

Turgot, Anne-Robert-Jacques
1727-1781 . . . . LC 26

Turner, Frederick 1943- . . . . CLC 48
See also CA 73-76; CAAS 10; CANR 12,
30; DLB 40

Tutu, Desmond M(pilo)
1931- . . . . . CLC 80; BLC; DAM MULT
See also BW 1; CA 125

Tutuola, Amos
1920- . . . . CLC 5, 14, 29; BLC;
DAM MULT
See also BW 2; CA 9-12R; CANR 27;
DLB 125; MTCW

Twain, Mark
. . . . . TCLC 6, 12, 19, 36, 48, 59; SSC 6;
WLC
See also Clemens, Samuel Langhorne
See also DLB 11, 12, 23, 64, 74

Tyler, Anne
1941- . . . . CLC 7, 11, 18, 28, 44, 59;
DAM NOV, POP
See also AAYA 18; BEST 89:1; CA 9-12R;
CANR 11, 33, 53; DLB 6, 143; DLBY 82;
MTCW; SATA 7

Tyler, Royall 1757-1826 . . . . NCLC 3
See also DLB 37

Tynan, Katharine 1861-1931 . . . . TCLC 3
See also CA 104; DLB 153

Tyutchev, Fyodor 1803-1873 . . . . . NCLC 34

Tzara, Tristan . . . . CLC 47; DAM POET
See also Rosenfeld, Samuel

Uhry, Alfred
1936- . . . . . CLC 55; DAM DRAM, POP
See also CA 127; 133; INT 133

Ulf, Haerved
See Strindberg, (Johan) August

Ulf, Harved
See Strindberg, (Johan) August

Ulibarri, Sabine R(eyes)
1919- . . . . CLC 83; DAM MULT
See also CA 131; DLB 82; HW

Unamuno (y Jugo), Miguel de
1864-1936 . . . TCLC 2, 9; DAM MULT,
NOV; HLC; SSC 11
See also CA 104; 131; DLB 108; HW;
MTCW

Undercliffe, Errol
See Campbell, (John) Ramsey

Underwood, Miles
See Glassco, John

Undset, Sigrid
1882-1949 . . . . TCLC 3; DA; DAB;
DAC; DAM MST, NOV; WLC
See also CA 104; 129; MTCW

Ungaretti, Giuseppe
1888-1970 . . . . CLC 7, 11, 15
See also CA 19-20; 25-28R; CAP 2;
DLB 114

Unger, Douglas 1952-............. **CLC 34**
See also CA 130

Unsworth, Barry (Forster) 1930-.... **CLC 76**
See also CA 25-28R; CANR 30

Updike, John (Hoyer)
1932-...... **CLC 1, 2, 3, 5, 7, 9, 13, 15,**
23, 34, 43, 70; DA; DAB; DAC;
DAM MST, NOV, POET, POP;
SSC 13; WLC
See also CA 1-4R; CABS 1; CANR 4, 33,
51; CDALB 1968-1988; DLB 2, 5, 143;
DLBD 3; DLBY 80, 82; MTCW

Upshaw, Margaret Mitchell
See Mitchell, Margaret (Munnerlyn)

Upton, Mark
See Sanders, Lawrence

Urdang, Constance (Henriette)
1922-...................... **CLC 47**
See also CA 21-24R; CANR 9, 24

Uriel, Henry
See Faust, Frederick (Schiller)

Uris, Leon (Marcus)
1924-.... **CLC 7, 32; DAM NOV, POP**
See also AITN 1, 2; BEST 89:2; CA 1-4R;
CANR 1, 40; MTCW; SATA 49

Urmuz
See Codrescu, Andrei

Urquhart, Jane 1949-........ **CLC 90; DAC**
See also CA 113; CANR 32

Ustinov, Peter (Alexander) 1921-.... **CLC 1**
See also AITN 1; CA 13-16R; CANR 25,
51; DLB 13

Vaculik, Ludvik 1926-............. **CLC 7**
See also CA 53-56

Valdez, Luis (Miguel)
1940-..... **CLC 84; DAM MULT; HLC**
See also CA 101; CANR 32; DLB 122; HW

Valenzuela, Luisa
1938-... **CLC 31; DAM MULT; SSC 14**
See also CA 101; CANR 32; DLB 113; HW

Valera y Alcala-Galiano, Juan
1824-1905 .... **TCLC 10**
See also CA 106

Valery, (Ambroise) Paul (Toussaint Jules)
1871-1945 .... **TCLC 4, 15;**
DAM POET; PC 9
See also CA 104; 122; MTCW

Valle-Inclan, Ramon (Maria) del
1866-1936 ..... **TCLC 5; DAM MULT;**
HLC
See also CA 106; DLB 134

Vallejo, Antonio Buero
See Buero Vallejo, Antonio

Vallejo, Cesar (Abraham)
1892-1938 .... **TCLC 3, 56;**
DAM MULT; HLC
See also CA 105; HW

Valle Y Pena, Ramon del
See Valle-Inclan, Ramon (Maria) del

Van Ash, Cay 1918-............. **CLC 34**

Vanbrugh, Sir John
1664-1726 .... **LC 21; DAM DRAM**
See also DLB 80

Van Campen, Karl
See Campbell, John W(ood, Jr.)

Vance, Gerald
See Silverberg, Robert

Vance, Jack .... **CLC 35**
See also Vance, John Holbrook
See also DLB 8

Vance, John Holbrook 1916-
See Queen, Ellery; Vance, Jack
See also CA 29-32R; CANR 17; MTCW

Van Den Bogarde, Derek Jules Gaspard Ulric
Niven 1921-
See Bogarde, Dirk
See also CA 77-80

Vandenburgh, Jane .... **CLC 59**

Vanderhaeghe, Guy 1951- .... **CLC 41**
See also CA 113

van der Post, Laurens (Jan) 1906- ... **CLC 5**
See also CA 5-8R; CANR 35

van de Wetering, Janwillem 1931- .. **CLC 47**
See also CA 49-52; CANR 4

Van Dine, S. S. .... **TCLC 23**
See also Wright, Willard Huntington

Van Doren, Carl (Clinton)
1885-1950 .... **TCLC 18**
See also CA 111

Van Doren, Mark 1894-1972..... **CLC 6, 10**
See also CA 1-4R; 37-40R; CANR 3;
DLB 45; MTCW

Van Druten, John (William)
1901-1957 .... **TCLC 2**
See also CA 104; DLB 10

Van Duyn, Mona (Jane)
1921-....... **CLC 3, 7, 63; DAM POET**
See also CA 9-12R; CANR 7, 38; DLB 5

Van Dyne, Edith
See Baum, L(yman) Frank

van Itallie, Jean-Claude 1936-....... **CLC 3**
See also CA 45-48; CAAS 2; CANR 1, 48;
DLB 7

van Ostaijen, Paul 1896-1928 ..... **TCLC 33**

Van Peebles, Melvin
1932-........ **CLC 2, 20; DAM MULT**
See also BW 2; CA 85-88; CANR 27

Vansittart, Peter 1920-............. **CLC 42**
See also CA 1-4R; CANR 3, 49

Van Vechten, Carl 1880-1964 ...... **CLC 33**
See also CA 89-92; DLB 4, 9, 51

Van Vogt, A(lfred) E(lton) 1912-..... **CLC 1**
See also CA 21-24R; CANR 28; DLB 8;
SATA 14

Varda, Agnes 1928-............. **CLC 16**
See also CA 116; 122

Vargas Llosa, (Jorge) Mario (Pedro)
1936-.... **CLC 3, 6, 9, 10, 15, 31, 42, 85;**
DA; DAB; DAC; DAM MST, MULT,
NOV; HLC
See also CA 73-76; CANR 18, 32, 42;
DLB 145; HW; MTCW

Vasiliu, Gheorghe 1881-1957
See Bacovia, George
See also CA 123

Vassa, Gustavus
See Equiano, Olaudah

Vassilikos, Vassilis 1933-......... **CLC 4, 8**
See also CA 81-84

Vaughan, Henry 1621-1695........ **LC 27**
See also DLB 131

Vaughn, Stephanie................. **CLC 62**

Vazov, Ivan (Minchov)
1850-1921 .... **TCLC 25**
See also CA 121; DLB 147

Veblen, Thorstein (Bunde)
1857-1929 .... **TCLC 31**
See also CA 115

Vega, Lope de 1562-1635........... **LC 23**

Venison, Alfred
See Pound, Ezra (Weston Loomis)

Verdi, Marie de
See Mencken, H(enry) L(ouis)

Verdu, Matilde
See Cela, Camilo Jose

Verga, Giovanni (Carmelo)
1840-1922 .... **TCLC 3; SSC 21**
See also CA 104; 123

Vergil
70B.C.-19B.C...... **CMLC 9; DA; DAB;**
DAC; DAM MST, POET; PC 12

Verhaeren, Emile (Adolphe Gustave)
1855-1916 .... **TCLC 12**
See also CA 109

Verlaine, Paul (Marie)
1844-1896 .... **NCLC 2, 51;**
DAM POET; PC 2

Verne, Jules (Gabriel)
1828-1905 .... **TCLC 6, 52**
See also AAYA 16; CA 110; 131; DLB 123;
JRDA; MAICYA; SATA 21

Very, Jones 1813-1880........... **NCLC 9**
See also DLB 1

Vesaas, Tarjei 1897-1970.......... **CLC 48**
See also CA 29-32R

Vialis, Gaston
See Simenon, Georges (Jacques Christian)

Vian, Boris 1920-1959 .... **TCLC 9**
See also CA 106; DLB 72

Viaud, (Louis Marie) Julien 1850-1923
See Loti, Pierre
See also CA 107

Vicar, Henry
See Felsen, Henry Gregor

Vicker, Angus
See Felsen, Henry Gregor

Vidal, Gore
1925- ..... **CLC 2, 4, 6, 8, 10, 22, 33, 72;**
DAM NOV, POP
See also AITN 1; BEST 90:2; CA 5-8R;
CANR 13, 45; DLB 6, 152;
INT CANR-13; MTCW

Viereck, Peter (Robert Edwin)
1916-...................... **CLC 4**
See also CA 1-4R; CANR 1, 47; DLB 5

Vigny, Alfred (Victor) de
1797-1863 ...... **NCLC 7; DAM POET**
See also DLB 119

Vilakazi, Benedict Wallet
1906-1947 .... **TCLC 37**

Walter, Villiam Christian
See Andersen, Hans Christian

Wambaugh, Joseph (Aloysius, Jr.)
1937- .... **CLC 3, 18; DAM NOV, POP**
See also AITN 1; BEST 89:3; CA 33-36R;
CANR 42; DLB 6; DLBY 83; MTCW

Ward, Arthur Henry Sarsfield 1883-1959
See Rohmer, Sax
See also CA 108

Ward, Douglas Turner 1930-....... **CLC 19**
See also BW 1; CA 81-84; CANR 27;
DLB 7, 38

Ward, Mary Augusta
See Ward, Mrs. Humphry

Ward, Mrs. Humphry
1851-1920 .... **TCLC 55**
See also DLB 18

Ward, Peter
See Faust, Frederick (Schiller)

Warhol, Andy 1928(?)-1987........ **CLC 20**
See also AAYA 12; BEST 89:4; CA 89-92;
121; CANR 34

Warner, Francis (Robert le Plastrier)
1937- .... **CLC 14**
See also CA 53-56; CANR 11

Warner, Marina 1946-............ **CLC 59**
See also CA 65-68; CANR 21

Warner, Rex (Ernest) 1905-1986.... **CLC 45**
See also CA 89-92; 119; DLB 15

Warner, Susan (Bogert)
1819-1885 .... **NCLC 31**
See also DLB 3, 42

Warner, Sylvia (Constance) Ashton
See Ashton-Warner, Sylvia (Constance)

Warner, Sylvia Townsend
1893-1978 .... **CLC 7, 19; SSC 23**
See also CA 61-64; 77-80; CANR 16;
DLB 34, 139; MTCW

Warren, Mercy Otis 1728-1814... **NCLC 13**
See also DLB 31

Warren, Robert Penn
1905-1989 .... **CLC 1, 4, 6, 8, 10, 13, 18,
39, 53, 59; DA; DAB; DAC; DAM MST,
NOV, POET; SSC 4; WLC**
See also AITN 1; CA 13-16R; 129;
CANR 10, 47; CDALB 1968-1988;
DLB 2, 48, 152; DLBY 80, 89;
INT CANR-10; MTCW; SATA 46;
SATA-Obit 63

Warshofsky, Isaac
See Singer, Isaac Bashevis

Warton, Thomas
1728-1790 .... **LC 15; DAM POET**
See also DLB 104, 109

Waruk, Kona
See Harris, (Theodore) Wilson

Warung, Price 1855-1911........ **TCLC 45**

Warwick, Jarvis
See Garner, Hugh

Washington, Alex
See Harris, Mark

Washington, Booker T(aliaferro)
1856-1915 .... **TCLC 10; BLC;
DAM MULT**
See also BW 1; CA 114; 125; SATA 28

Washington, George 1732-1799...... **LC 25**
See also DLB 31

Wassermann, (Karl) Jakob
1873-1934 .... **TCLC 6**
See also CA 104; DLB 66

Wasserstein, Wendy
1950- .... **CLC 32, 59, 90;
DAM DRAM; DC 4**
See also CA 121; 129; CABS 3; CANR 53;
INT 129

Waterhouse, Keith (Spencer)
1929- .... **CLC 47**
See also CA 5-8R; CANR 38; DLB 13, 15;
MTCW

Waters, Frank (Joseph)
1902-1995 .... **CLC 88**
See also CA 5-8R; 149; CAAS 13; CANR 3,
18; DLBY 86

Waters, Roger 1944-.............. **CLC 35**

Watkins, Frances Ellen
See Harper, Frances Ellen Watkins

Watkins, Gerrold
See Malzberg, Barry N(athaniel)

Watkins, Gloria 1955(?)-
See hooks, bell
See also BW 2; CA 143

Watkins, Paul 1964-.............. **CLC 55**
See also CA 132

Watkins, Vernon Phillips
1906-1967 .... **CLC 43**
See also CA 9-10; 25-28R; CAP 1; DLB 20

Watson, Irving S.
See Mencken, H(enry) L(ouis)

Watson, John H.
See Farmer, Philip Jose

Watson, Richard F.
See Silverberg, Robert

Waugh, Auberon (Alexander) 1939-.. **CLC 7**
See also CA 45-48; CANR 6, 22; DLB 14

Waugh, Evelyn (Arthur St. John)
1903-1966 ...... **CLC 1, 3, 8, 13, 19, 27,
44; DA; DAB; DAC; DAM MST, NOV,
POP; WLC**
See also CA 85-88; 25-28R; CANR 22;
CDBLB 1914-1945; DLB 15, 162; MTCW

Waugh, Harriet 1944- .... **CLC 6**
See also CA 85-88; CANR 22

Ways, C. R.
See Blount, Roy (Alton), Jr.

Waystaff, Simon
See Swift, Jonathan

Webb, (Martha) Beatrice (Potter)
1858-1943 .... **TCLC 22**
See also Potter, Beatrice
See also CA 117

Webb, Charles (Richard) 1939-...... **CLC 7**
See also CA 25-28R

Webb, James H(enry), Jr. 1946-.... **CLC 22**
See also CA 81-84

Webb, Mary (Gladys Meredith)
1881-1927 .... **TCLC 24**
See also CA 123; DLB 34

Webb, Mrs. Sidney
See Webb, (Martha) Beatrice (Potter)

Webb, Phyllis 1927-.............. **CLC 18**
See also CA 104; CANR 23; DLB 53

Webb, Sidney (James)
1859-1947 .... **TCLC 22**
See also CA 117

Webber, Andrew Lloyd............. **CLC 21**
See also Lloyd Webber, Andrew

Weber, Lenora Mattingly
1895-1971 .... **CLC 12**
See also CA 19-20; 29-32R; CAP 1;
SATA 2; SATA-Obit 26

Webster, John
1579(?)-1634(?) ...... **LC 33; DA; DAB;
DAC; DAM DRAM, MST; DC 2; WLC**
See also CDBLB Before 1660; DLB 58

Webster, Noah 1758-1843 .... **NCLC 30**

Wedekind, (Benjamin) Frank(lin)
1864-1918 ...... **TCLC 7; DAM DRAM**
See also CA 104; DLB 118

Weidman, Jerome 1913-............ **CLC 7**
See also AITN 2; CA 1-4R; CANR 1;
DLB 28

Weil, Simone (Adolphine)
1909-1943 .... **TCLC 23**
See also CA 117

Weinstein, Nathan
See West, Nathanael

Weinstein, Nathan von Wallenstein
See West, Nathanael

Weir, Peter (Lindsay) 1944- .... **CLC 20**
See also CA 113; 123

Weiss, Peter (Ulrich)
1916-1982 .... **CLC 3, 15, 51;
DAM DRAM**
See also CA 45-48; 106; CANR 3; DLB 69,
124

Weiss, Theodore (Russell)
1916- .... **CLC 3, 8, 14**
See also CA 9-12R; CAAS 2; CANR 46;
DLB 5

Welch, (Maurice) Denton
1915-1948 .... **TCLC 22**
See also CA 121; 148

Welch, James
1940- ..... **CLC 6, 14, 52; DAM MULT,
POP**
See also CA 85-88; CANR 42; NNAL

Weldon, Fay
1933- .... **CLC 6, 9, 11, 19, 36, 59;
DAM POP**
See also CA 21-24R; CANR 16, 46;
CDBLB 1960 to Present; DLB 14;
INT CANR-16; MTCW

Wellek, Rene 1903-1995.......... **CLC 28**
See also CA 5-8R; 150; CAAS 7; CANR 8;
DLB 63; INT CANR-8

Weller, Michael 1942-......... **CLC 10, 53**
See also CA 85-88

Weller, Paul 1958-.............. **CLC 26**

Wellershoff, Dieter 1925-.......... **CLC 46**
See also CA 89-92; CANR 16, 37

Welles, (George) Orson
1915-1985 .... **CLC 20, 80**
See also CA 93-96; 117

Wellman, Mac 1945- .... **CLC 65**

Wellman, Manly Wade 1903-1986 .. **CLC 49**
See also CA 1-4R; 118; CANR 6, 16, 44;
SATA 6; SATA-Obit 47

Wells, Carolyn 1869(?)-1942 ...... **TCLC 35**
See also CA 113; DLB 11

Wells, H(erbert) G(eorge)
1866-1946 .... **TCLC 6, 12, 19; DA;**
DAB; DAC; DAM MST, NOV; SSC 6;
WLC
See also AAYA 18; CA 110; 121;
CDBLB 1914-1945; DLB 34, 70, 156;
MTCW; SATA 20

Wells, Rosemary 1943- .... **CLC 12**
See also AAYA 13; CA 85-88; CANR 48;
CLR 16; MAICYA; SAAS 1; SATA 18,
69

Welty, Eudora
1909- ...... **CLC 1, 2, 5, 14, 22, 33; DA;**
DAB; DAC; DAM MST, NOV; SSC 1;
WLC
See also CA 9-12R; CABS 1; CANR 32;
CDALB 1941-1968; DLB 2, 102, 143;
DLBD 12; DLBY 87; MTCW

Wen I-to 1899-1946 .... **TCLC 28**

Wentworth, Robert
See Hamilton, Edmond

Werfel, Franz (V.) 1890-1945 ...... **TCLC 8**
See also CA 104; DLB 81, 124

Wergeland, Henrik Arnold
1808-1845 .... **NCLC 5**

Wersba, Barbara 1932- .... **CLC 30**
See also AAYA 2; CA 29-32R; CANR 16,
38; CLR 3; DLB 52; JRDA; MAICYA;
SAAS 2; SATA 1, 58

Wertmueller, Lina 1928- .... **CLC 16**
See also CA 97-100; CANR 39

Wescott, Glenway 1901-1987 ...... **CLC 13**
See also CA 13-16R; 121; CANR 23;
DLB 4, 9, 102

Wesker, Arnold
1932- .... **CLC 3, 5, 42; DAB;**
DAM DRAM
See also CA 1-4R; CAAS 7; CANR 1, 33;
CDBLB 1960 to Present; DLB 13;
MTCW

Wesley, Richard (Errol) 1945- .... **CLC 7**
See also BW 1; CA 57-60; CANR 27;
DLB 38

Wessel, Johan Herman 1742-1785 .... **LC 7**

West, Anthony (Panther)
1914-1987 .... **CLC 50**
See also CA 45-48; 124; CANR 3, 19;
DLB 15

West, C. P.
See Wodehouse, P(elham) G(renville)

West, (Mary) Jessamyn
1902-1984 .... **CLC 7, 17**
See also CA 9-12R; 112; CANR 27; DLB 6;
DLBY 84; MTCW; SATA-Obit 37

West, Morris L(anglo) 1916- ..... **CLC 6, 33**
See also CA 5-8R; CANR 24, 49; MTCW

West, Nathanael
1903-1940 ..... **TCLC 1, 14, 44; SSC 16**
See also CA 104; 125; CDALB 1929-1941;
DLB 4, 9, 28; MTCW

West, Owen
See Koontz, Dean R(ay)

West, Paul 1930- .... **CLC 7, 14, 96**
See also CA 13-16R; CAAS 7; CANR 22,
53; DLB 14; INT CANR-22

West, Rebecca 1892-1983 .. **CLC 7, 9, 31, 50**
See also CA 5-8R; 109; CANR 19; DLB 36;
DLBY 83; MTCW

Westall, Robert (Atkinson)
1929-1993 .... **CLC 17**
See also AAYA 12; CA 69-72; 141;
CANR 18; CLR 13; JRDA; MAICYA;
SAAS 2; SATA 23, 69; SATA-Obit 75

Westlake, Donald E(dwin)
1933- .... **CLC 7, 33; DAM POP**
See also CA 17-20R; CAAS 13; CANR 16,
44; INT CANR-16

Westmacott, Mary
See Christie, Agatha (Mary Clarissa)

Weston, Allen
See Norton, Andre

Wetcheek, J. L.
See Feuchtwanger, Lion

Wetering, Janwillem van de
See van de Wetering, Janwillem

Wetherell, Elizabeth
See Warner, Susan (Bogert)

Whale, James 1889-1957 .... **TCLC 63**

Whalen, Philip 1923- .... **CLC 6, 29**
See also CA 9-12R; CANR 5, 39; DLB 16

Wharton, Edith (Newbold Jones)
1862-1937 ...... **TCLC 3, 9, 27, 53; DA;**
DAB; DAC; DAM MST, NOV; SSC 6;
WLC
See also CA 104; 132; CDALB 1865-1917;
DLB 4, 9, 12, 78; DLBD 13; MTCW

Wharton, James
See Mencken, H(enry) L(ouis)

Wharton, William (a pseudonym)
.... **CLC 18, 37**
See also CA 93-96; DLBY 80; INT 93-96

Wheatley (Peters), Phillis
1754(?)-1784 .... **LC 3; BLC; DA; DAC;**
DAM MST, MULT, POET; PC 3; WLC
See also CDALB 1640-1865; DLB 31, 50

Wheelock, John Hall 1886-1978 .... **CLC 14**
See also CA 13-16R; 77-80; CANR 14;
DLB 45

White, E(lwyn) B(rooks)
1899-1985 .. **CLC 10, 34, 39; DAM POP**
See also AITN 2; CA 13-16R; 116;
CANR 16, 37; CLR 1, 21; DLB 11, 22;
MAICYA; MTCW; SATA 2, 29;
SATA-Obit 44

White, Edmund (Valentine III)
1940- .... **CLC 27; DAM POP**
See also AAYA 7; CA 45-48; CANR 3, 19,
36; MTCW

White, Patrick (Victor Martindale)
1912-1990 .. **CLC 3, 4, 5, 7, 9, 18, 65, 69**
See also CA 81-84; 132; CANR 43; MTCW

White, Phyllis Dorothy James 1920-
See James, P. D.
See also CA 21-24R; CANR 17, 43;
DAM POP; MTCW

White, T(erence) H(anbury)
1906-1964 .... **CLC 30**
See also CA 73-76; CANR 37; DLB 160;
JRDA; MAICYA; SATA 12

White, Terence de Vere
1912-1994 .... **CLC 49**
See also CA 49-52; 145; CANR 3

White, Walter F(rancis)
1893-1955 .... **TCLC 15**
See also White, Walter
See also BW 1; CA 115; 124; DLB 51

White, William Hale 1831-1913
See Rutherford, Mark
See also CA 121

Whitehead, E(dward) A(nthony)
1933- .... **CLC 5**
See also CA 65-68

Whitemore, Hugh (John) 1936- ..... **CLC 37**
See also CA 132; INT 132

Whitman, Sarah Helen (Power)
1803-1878 .... **NCLC 19**
See also DLB 1

Whitman, Walt(er)
1819-1892 ..... **NCLC 4, 31; DA; DAB;**
DAC; DAM MST, POET; PC 3; WLC
See also CDALB 1640-1865; DLB 3, 64;
SATA 20

Whitney, Phyllis A(yame)
1903- .... **CLC 42; DAM POP**
See also AITN 2; BEST 90:3; CA 1-4R;
CANR 3, 25, 38; JRDA; MAICYA;
SATA 1, 30

Whittemore, (Edward) Reed (Jr.)
1919- .... **CLC 4**
See also CA 9-12R; CAAS 8; CANR 4;
DLB 5

Whittier, John Greenleaf
1807-1892 .... **NCLC 8**
See also DLB 1

Whittlebot, Hernia
See Coward, Noel (Peirce)

Wicker, Thomas Grey 1926-
See Wicker, Tom
See also CA 65-68; CANR 21, 46

Wicker, Tom .... **CLC 7**
See also Wicker, Thomas Grey

Wideman, John Edgar
1941- .... **CLC 5, 34, 36, 67; BLC;**
DAM MULT
See also BW 2; CA 85-88; CANR 14, 42;
DLB 33, 143

Wiebe, Rudy (Henry)
1934- .... **CLC 6, 11, 14; DAC;**
DAM MST
See also CA 37-40R; CANR 42; DLB 60

Wieland, Christoph Martin
1733-1813 .... **NCLC 17**
See also DLB 97

Wiene, Robert 1881-1938 .... **TCLC 56**

Wieners, John 1934- .... **CLC 7**
See also CA 13-16R; DLB 16

Wister, Owen 1860-1938 . . . . TCLC **21**
See also CA 108; DLB 9, 78; SATA 62

Witkacy
See Witkiewicz, Stanislaw Ignacy

Witkiewicz, Stanislaw Ignacy
1885-1939 . . . . TCLC **8**
See also CA 105

Wittgenstein, Ludwig (Josef Johann)
1889-1951 . . . . TCLC **59**
See also CA 113

Wittig, Monique 1935(?)- . . . . CLC **22**
See also CA 116; 135; DLB 83

Wittlin, Jozef 1896-1976 . . . . CLC **25**
See also CA 49-52; 65-68; CANR 3

Wodehouse, P(elham) G(renville)
1881-1975 . . . CLC **1, 2, 5, 10, 22; DAB;
DAC; DAM NOV; SSC 2**
See also AITN 2; CA 45-48; 57-60;
CANR 3, 33; CDBLB 1914-1945;
DLB 34, 162; MTCW; SATA 22

Woiwode, L.
See Woiwode, Larry (Alfred)

Woiwode, Larry (Alfred) 1941- . . . CLC **6, 10**
See also CA 73-76; CANR 16; DLB 6;
INT CANR-16

Wojciechowska, Maia (Teresa)
1927- . . . . CLC **26**
See also AAYA 8; CA 9-12R; CANR 4, 41;
CLR 1; JRDA; MAICYA; SAAS 1;
SATA 1, 28, 83

Wolf, Christa 1929- . . . . CLC **14, 29, 58**
See also CA 85-88; CANR 45; DLB 75;
MTCW

Wolfe, Gene (Rodman)
1931- . . . . CLC **25; DAM POP**
See also CA 57-60; CAAS 9; CANR 6, 32;
DLB 8

Wolfe, George C. 1954- . . . . CLC **49**
See also CA 149

Wolfe, Thomas (Clayton)
1900-1938 . . . . . TCLC **4, 13, 29, 61; DA;
DAB; DAC; DAM MST, NOV; WLC**
See also CA 104; 132; CDALB 1929-1941;
DLB 9, 102; DLBD 2; DLBY 85; MTCW

Wolfe, Thomas Kennerly, Jr. 1931-
See Wolfe, Tom
See also CA 13-16R; CANR 9, 33;
DAM POP; INT CANR-9; MTCW

Wolfe, Tom . . . . CLC **1, 2, 9, 15, 35, 51**
See also Wolfe, Thomas Kennerly, Jr.
See also AAYA 8; AITN 2; BEST 89:1;
DLB 152

Wolff, Geoffrey (Ansell) 1937- . . . . . CLC **41**
See also CA 29-32R; CANR 29, 43

Wolff, Sonia
See Levitin, Sonia (Wolff)

Wolff, Tobias (Jonathan Ansell)
1945- . . . . CLC **39, 64**
See also AAYA 16; BEST 90:2; CA 114;
117; CAAS 22; DLB 130; INT 117

Wolfram von Eschenbach
c. 1170-c. 1220 . . . . CMLC **5**
See also DLB 138

Wolitzer, Hilma 1930- . . . . CLC **17**
See also CA 65-68; CANR 18, 40;
INT CANR-18; SATA 31

Wollstonecraft, Mary 1759-1797 . . . . . . LC **5**
See also CDBLB 1789-1832; DLB 39, 104,
158

Wonder, Stevie . . . . CLC **12**
See also Morris, Steveland Judkins

Wong, Jade Snow 1922- . . . . CLC **17**
See also CA 109

Woodcott, Keith
See Brunner, John (Kilian Houston)

Woodruff, Robert W.
See Mencken, H(enry) L(ouis)

Woolf, (Adeline) Virginia
1882-1941 . . . . . . TCLC **1, 5, 20, 43, 56;
DA; DAB; DAC; DAM MST, NOV;
SSC 7; WLC**
See also CA 104; 130; CDBLB 1914-1945;
DLB 36, 100, 162; DLBD 10; MTCW

Woollcott, Alexander (Humphreys)
1887-1943 . . . . TCLC **5**
See also CA 105; DLB 29

Woolrich, Cornell 1903-1968 . . . . CLC **77**
See also Hopley-Woolrich, Cornell George

Wordsworth, Dorothy
1771-1855 . . . . NCLC **25**
See also DLB 107

Wordsworth, William
1770-1850 . . . . NCLC **12, 38; DA; DAB;
DAC; DAM MST, POET; PC 4; WLC**
See also CDBLB 1789-1832; DLB 93, 107

Wouk, Herman
1915- . . CLC **1, 9, 38; DAM NOV, POP**
See also CA 5-8R; CANR 6, 33; DLBY 82;
INT CANR-6; MTCW

Wright, Charles (Penzel, Jr.)
1935- . . . . CLC **6, 13, 28**
See also CA 29-32R; CAAS 7; CANR 23,
36; DLB 165; DLBY 82; MTCW

Wright, Charles Stevenson
1932- . . . . CLC **49; BLC 3;
DAM MULT, POET**
See also BW 1; CA 9-12R; CANR 26;
DLB 33

Wright, Jack R.
See Harris, Mark

Wright, James (Arlington)
1927-1980 . . . . CLC **3, 5, 10, 28;
DAM POET**
See also AITN 2; CA 49-52; 97-100;
CANR 4, 34; DLB 5; MTCW

Wright, Judith (Arundell)
1915- . . . . CLC **11, 53; PC 14**
See also CA 13-16R; CANR 31; MTCW;
SATA 14

Wright, L(aurali) R. 1939- . . . . CLC **44**
See also CA 138

Wright, Richard (Nathaniel)
1908-1960 . . . . CLC **1, 3, 4, 9, 14, 21, 48,
74; BLC; DA; DAB; DAC; DAM MST,
MULT, NOV; SSC 2; WLC**
See also AAYA 5; BW 1; CA 108;
CDALB 1929-1941; DLB 76, 102;
DLBD 2; MTCW

Wright, Richard B(ruce) 1937- . . . . . . CLC **6**
See also CA 85-88; DLB 53

Wright, Rick 1945- . . . . CLC **35**

Wright, Rowland
See Wells, Carolyn

Wright, Stephen Caldwell 1946- . . . . CLC **33**
See also BW 2

Wright, Willard Huntington 1888-1939
See Van Dine, S. S.
See also CA 115

Wright, William 1930- . . . . CLC **44**
See also CA 53-56; CANR 7, 23

Wroth, LadyMary 1587-1653(?) . . . . . LC **30**
See also DLB 121

Wu Ch'eng-en 1500(?)-1582(?) . . . . LC **7**

Wu Ching-tzu 1701-1754 . . . . LC **2**

Wurlitzer, Rudolph 1938(?)- . . . CLC **2, 4, 15**
See also CA 85-88

Wycherley, William
1641-1715 . . . . . LC **8, 21; DAM DRAM**
See also CDBLB 1660-1789; DLB 80

Wylie, Elinor (Morton Hoyt)
1885-1928 . . . . TCLC **8**
See also CA 105; DLB 9, 45

Wylie, Philip (Gordon) 1902-1971 . . . CLC **43**
See also CA 21-22; 33-36R; CAP 2; DLB 9

Wyndham, John . . . . CLC **19**
See also Harris, John (Wyndham Parkes
Lucas) Beynon

Wyss, Johann David Von
1743-1818 . . . . NCLC **10**
See also JRDA; MAICYA; SATA 29;
SATA-Brief 27

Xenophon
c. 430B.C.-c. 354B.C. . . . . CMLC **17**

Yakumo Koizumi
See Hearn, (Patricio) Lafcadio (Tessima
Carlos)

Yanez, Jose Donoso
See Donoso (Yanez), Jose

Yanovsky, Basile S.
See Yanovsky, V(assily) S(emenovich)

Yanovsky, V(assily) S(emenovich)
1906-1989 . . . . CLC **2, 18**
See also CA 97-100; 129

Yates, Richard 1926-1992 . . . . . CLC **7, 8, 23**
See also CA 5-8R; 139; CANR 10, 43;
DLB 2; DLBY 81, 92; INT CANR-10

Yeats, W. B.
See Yeats, William Butler

Yeats, William Butler
1865-1939 . . . . . TCLC **1, 11, 18, 31; DA;
DAB; DAC; DAM DRAM, MST,
POET; WLC**
See also CA 104; 127; CANR 45;
CDBLB 1890-1914; DLB 10, 19, 98, 156;
MTCW

Yehoshua, A(braham) B.
1936- . . . . CLC **13, 31**
See also CA 33-36R; CANR 43

Yep, Laurence Michael 1948- . . . . . . CLC **35**
See also AAYA 5; CA 49-52; CANR 1, 46;
CLR 3, 17; DLB 52; JRDA; MAICYA;
SATA 7, 69

Yerby, Frank G(arvin)
        1916-1991 . . . . CLC 1, 7, 22; BLC;
                                                                DAM MULT
        See also BW 1; CA 9-12R; 136; CANR 16,
        52; DLB 76; INT CANR-16; MTCW

Yesenin, Sergei Alexandrovich
        See Esenin, Sergei (Alexandrovich)

Yevtushenko, Yevgeny (Alexandrovich)
        1933- . . . . CLC 1, 3, 13, 26, 51;
                                                                DAM POET
        See also CA 81-84; CANR 33; MTCW

Yezierska, Anzia   1885(?)-1970 . . . . . CLC 46
        See also CA 126; 89-92; DLB 28; MTCW

Yglesias, Helen   1915- . . . . CLC 7, 22
        See also CA 37-40R; CAAS 20; CANR 15;
        INT CANR-15; MTCW

Yokomitsu Riichi   1898-1947 . . . . . . TCLC 47

Yonge, Charlotte (Mary)
        1823-1901 . . . . TCLC 48
        See also CA 109; DLB 18, 163; SATA 17

York, Jeremy
        See Creasey, John

York, Simon
        See Heinlein, Robert A(nson)

Yorke, Henry Vincent   1905-1974 . . . CLC 13
        See also Green, Henry
        See also CA 85-88; 49-52

Yosano Akiko   1878-1942 . . TCLC 59; PC 11

Yoshimoto, Banana . . . . CLC 84
        See also Yoshimoto, Mahoko

Yoshimoto, Mahoko   1964-
        See Yoshimoto, Banana
        See also CA 144

Young, Al(bert James)
        1939- . . . . . . CLC 19; BLC; DAM MULT
        See also BW 2; CA 29-32R; CANR 26;
        DLB 33

Young, Andrew (John)   1885-1971 . . . . CLC 5
        See also CA 5-8R; CANR 7, 29

Young, Collier
        See Bloch, Robert (Albert)

Young, Edward   1683-1765 . . . . LC 3
        See also DLB 95

Young, Marguerite (Vivian)
        1909-1995 . . . . CLC 82
        See also CA 13-16; 150; CAP 1

Young, Neil   1945- . . . . CLC 17
        See also CA 110

Young Bear, Ray A.
        1950- . . . . CLC 94; DAM MULT
        See also CA 146; NNAL

Yourcenar, Marguerite
        1903-1987 . . . . CLC 19, 38, 50, 87;
                                                                DAM NOV
        See also CA 69-72; CANR 23; DLB 72;
        DLBY 88; MTCW

Yurick, Sol   1925- . . . . CLC 6
        See also CA 13-16R; CANR 25

Zabolotskii, Nikolai Alekseevich
        1903-1958 . . . . TCLC 52
        See also CA 116

Zamiatin, Yevgenii
        See Zamyatin, Evgeny Ivanovich

Zamora, Bernice (B. Ortiz)
        1938- . . . . . CLC 89; DAM MULT; HLC
        See also CA 151; DLB 82; HW

Zamyatin, Evgeny Ivanovich
        1884-1937 . . . . TCLC 8, 37
        See also CA 105

Zangwill, Israel   1864-1926 . . . . TCLC 16
        See also CA 109; DLB 10, 135

Zappa, Francis Vincent, Jr.   1940-1993
        See Zappa, Frank
        See also CA 108; 143

Zappa, Frank . . . . CLC 17
        See also Zappa, Francis Vincent, Jr.

Zaturenska, Marya   1902-1982 . . . . CLC 6, 11
        See also CA 13-16R; 105; CANR 22

Zelazny, Roger (Joseph)
        1937-1995 . . . . CLC 21
        See also AAYA 7; CA 21-24R; 148;
        CANR 26; DLB 8; MTCW; SATA 57;
        SATA-Brief 39

Zhdanov, Andrei A(lexandrovich)
        1896-1948 . . . . TCLC 18
        See also CA 117

Zhukovsky, Vasily   1783-1852 . . . . NCLC 35

Ziegenhagen, Eric . . . . CLC 55

Zimmer, Jill Schary
        See Robinson, Jill

Zimmerman, Robert
        See Dylan, Bob

Zindel, Paul
        1936- . . . . . CLC 6, 26; DA; DAB; DAC;
                                    DAM DRAM, MST, NOV; DC 5
        See also AAYA 2; CA 73-76; CANR 31;
        CLR 3; DLB 7, 52; JRDA; MAICYA;
        MTCW; SATA 16, 58

Zinov'Ev, A. A.
        See Zinoviev, Alexander (Aleksandrovich)

Zinoviev, Alexander (Aleksandrovich)
        1922- . . . . CLC 19
        See also CA 116; 133; CAAS 10

Zoilus
        See Lovecraft, H(oward) P(hillips)

Zola, Emile (Edouard Charles Antoine)
        1840-1902 . . . . . . TCLC 1, 6, 21, 41; DA;
                                    DAB; DAC; DAM MST, NOV; WLC
        See also CA 104; 138; DLB 123

Zoline, Pamela   1941- . . . . CLC 62

Zorrilla y Moral, Jose   1817-1893 . . NCLC 6

Zoshchenko, Mikhail (Mikhailovich)
        1895-1958 . . . . TCLC 15; SSC 15
        See also CA 115

Zuckmayer, Carl   1896-1977 . . . . CLC 18
        See also CA 69-72; DLB 56, 124

Zuk, Georges
        See Skelton, Robin

Zukofsky, Louis
        1904-1978 . . . . CLC 1, 2, 4, 7, 11, 18;
                                                        DAM POET; PC 11
        See also CA 9-12R; 77-80; CANR 39;
        DLB 5, 165; MTCW

Zweig, Paul   1935-1984 . . . . CLC 34, 42
        See also CA 85-88; 113

Zweig, Stefan   1881-1942 . . . . TCLC 17
        See also CA 112; DLB 81, 118

Literary Criticism Series
Cumulative Topic Index

This index lists all topic entries in Gale's *Classical and Medieval Literature Criticism, Contemporary Literary Criticism, Literature Criticism from 1400 to 1800, Nineteenth-Century Literature Criticism,* and *Twentieth-Century Literary Criticism.*

Topic Index

Topic Index

Topic Index

LC Cumulative Nationality Index

LC Cumulative Title Index

Title Index

Title Index

Title Index

Title Index

Title Index

Title Index

Title Index

Title Index

Title Index

Title Index

Title Index

Title Index

ISBN 0-8103-9977-6